Advanced Accounting
Second Edition

Paul M. Fischer, PhD, CPA
Professor of Accounting

William James Taylor, PhD, CPA
Assistant Professor of Accounting

J. Arthur Leer, MBA, CPA
Professor of Accounting

All of the
University of Wisconsin - Milwaukee

Published by

A26 **SOUTH-WESTERN PUBLISHING CO.**

CINCINNATI   WEST CHICAGO, ILL.   DALLAS   PELHAM MANOR, N.Y.   PALO ALTO, CALIF.

PREFACE

A second edition of a successful book permits the authors to update material which has been altered by pronouncements of authoritative bodies and to offer expanded discussion and illustrations on complex topics. Updating is most pronounced in the areas of accounting for governmental units and nonprofit organizations, estates and trusts, insolvency, and foreign operations. There is continued emphasis on the relationship between theory and practice.

One of the new features of the revised edition is a student study guide, which is designed to reinforce understanding by highlighting essentials and providing immediate feedback for self-evaluation of mastery of a subject area. Available for consolidation problems is a set of preprinted work sheets, which substantially lessen the time necessary to solve a problem without sacrificing the application of consolidation principles.

The second edition retains a design that permits flexibility in its use. There is ample material for a program that devotes two quarters or semesters to advanced accounting topics. From the following independent modules, schools that desire less exposure may select the areas that are most important for their objectives:

Accounting Theory
Real Estate and Franchise Accounting
Income Presentation, including earnings per share, interim and
    segmental reporting
Business Combinations:
    Chapters 5 through 9 provide basic coverage.
    Chapters 10 through 12 present specialized topics.
Foreign Operations
Partnerships
Governmental Accounting
Accounting for Nonprofit Organizations:
    Chapter 18 Accounting for Nonprofit Universities and Hospitals
    Chapter 19 Accounting for Voluntary Health and Welfare
                    Organizations
Estates and Trusts
Insolvency

ACCOUNTING THEORY (CHAPTER 1)

The introductory chapter provides a broad, theoretical framework that establishes a foundation for the student before the practical applications are explored. The recent "Statements of Financial Accounting Concepts" are discussed as they relate to information standards, accounting measurement, and income determination.

REAL ESTATE AND FRANCHISE ACCOUNTING (CHAPTER 2)

The topics of real estate and franchise accounting provide practical applications of revenue recognition concepts reflected in accrual and installment accounting, cost recovery methods, and long-term construction contract accounting. The chapter has been completely revised to identify more clearly the revenue and expense elements of real estate transactions and their respective accounting treatment. Franchise accounting is discussed in conformity with the recent Statement of Financial Accounting Standards dealing with the area.

INCOME PRESENTATION (CHAPTERS 3 AND 4)

The concepts of income presentation are discussed as an introduction to these chapters. Discontinued operations are considered, and case illustrations are used to analyze the accounting and statement presentation of such operations. Actual excerpts from published financial statements are provided to illustrate the disclosure associated with discontinued operations. Interim and segmental reporting are discussed. The calculation of earnings per share is presented using an easy-to-follow format. The procedures used provide for determination of the dilutive nature of a security prior to its inclusion in the EPS calculation.

BUSINESS COMBINATIONS (CHAPTERS 5-12)

The topic of intercompany bonds is included in a new chapter that also provides more complete coverage of intercompany leasing. To improve students' understanding of intercompany bond holdings, concepts are developed first using straight-line amortization before proceeding to amortization under the effective interest method. More detail has also been provided on the preparation of a consolidated statement of changes in financial position. Flexibility has been increased by including complete procedures for investments maintained under the simple equity method, the sophisticated equity method, and the cost method.

The following unique features were retained to assist the students' learning process:

Chapter 5 is a complete discussion of purchase versus pooling theory, which serves as a foundation for the chapters that follow. No consolidation methods are discussed until later chapters.

Work sheets are presented in an easy-to-follow horizontal format, which includes columns for consolidated income, minority interest, controlling retained earnings, and the balance sheet. Procedures for balance sheet work sheets only, which are commonly found on the CPA examination, are contained in an appendix to Chapter 10.

Innovative scheduling is used to accomplish the usually difficult tasks of transferring equities in a pooling, distributing the disparity between cost and book value in a purchase, and distributing income to minority and controlling interests.

FOREIGN OPERATIONS (CHAPTER 13)

The recently issued FASB Statement No. 52 is given complete coverage, including a comprehensive illustration of the translation of financial statements denominated in a foreign functional currency. The accounting for foreign currency transactions and hedging transactions are thoroughly discussed, along with the potential effect on income of such transactions. Special implications regarding highly inflationary economies, intercompany profits, income tax allocation, and financial statement disclosure are presented.

PARTNERSHIPS (CHAPTERS 14 AND 15)

Major tax and nontax differences between partnerships and corporations are explained in order to identify the appropriateness of these competing business forms. Equity theories previously discussed are employed to help the student understand the logic behind partnership accounting. The traditional topics of dissolution and liquidation are clearly and amply illustrated. Reference is made to the Uniform Partnership Act throughout the chapters in order to emphasize the influence of legal provisions on accounting for partnerships.

GOVERNMENTAL ACCOUNTING (CHAPTERS 16 AND 17)

The portion of the book devoted to governmental accounting has been completely revised to be in conformity with the Municipal Finance Officers Association 1980 edition of *Governmental Accounting, Auditing, and Financial Reporting*, as well as with its *Statement 1*. The major changes reflected in the revision are:

(1) General purpose financial statements with columns for each fund type and account group constitute the basic financial statements necessary for presentation in conformity with generally accepted accounting principles.

(2) Funds are categorized as either governmental, proprietary, or fiduciary.

(3) Recording procedures have been altered for some items, such as budgetary entries, interfund transfers, and bond proceeds.

Each fund and account group is discussed and illustrated separately to simplify understanding and to improve teaching effectiveness.

ACCOUNTING FOR NONPROFIT ORGANIZATIONS (CHAPTERS 18 AND 19)

At the request of users of the first edition, the chapter on nonprofit organizations has been expanded into two chapters. Chapter 18 covers nonprofit universities and hospitals, while Chapter 19 deals with the growing field of voluntary health and welfare organizations. The segregation permits expanded discussion with more detailed illustrations that improve understanding.

ESTATES AND TRUSTS (CHAPTER 20)

The topic of estates and trusts has been revised to incorporate changes resulting from the Revenue Act of 1978 and the Economic Recovery Tax Act of 1981. The chapter dwells on the necessity of planning for death, if maximum retention of assets is to be accomplished.

INSOLVENCY (CHAPTER 21)

The chapter on insolvency has been revised to incorporate the provisions of the Bankruptcy Reform Act of 1978. Various relief procedures for individuals and companies that are in financial difficulty are presented.

The text includes 268 questions, 200 exercises, and 229 problems. All relevant CPA problems and theory questions from past examinations have been adapted for use in the text. The questions are designed to help the student review the important points of each chapter. Exercises are an efficient means of focusing on specific applications of the chapter without the time commitment necessary for problems. Problems integrate several procedures and calculations into broader application of the chapter's contents. Problems range in difficulty from those requiring procedural applications to those requiring reasonably complex analytical skill. The authors have found it helpful to assign selected questions and exercises prior to class discussion to provide reinforcement to the students' reading. Problems may then be used after class presentation to integrate and solidify knowledge.

We are indebted to the American Institute of Certified Public Accountants and the Financial Accounting Standards Board for their permission to quote material and to use relevant CPA examination questions and problems. We are grateful to the Municipal Finance Officers Association, and in particular to Richard J. Haas, who permitted us to review the manuscript of *Governmental Accounting, Auditing, and Financial Reporting*. For their creative contributions, we thank Mary Paxton and Maureen Rupple. We appreciate the care in preparation and proofing by G. R. Gehrig and David Carter.

Comments of users were extremely helpful in preparation of the second edition, especially those of Professors Roy Tuttle, Ray Weatherwax, and Carol Walkowiak. We welcome reactions of readers.

Paul M. Fischer
William J. Taylor
J. Arthur Leer

C O N T E N T S

CHAPTER 1

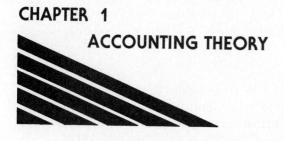

ACCOUNTING THEORY

Contemporary accounting is a service-oriented discipline concerned with measuring and communicating economic or financial data which relate to the activities of economic entities. Accounting is a dynamic discipline which is influenced by numerous environmental factors and by an underlying theoretical structure. In general, accounting can be divided into the following functional areas: managerial, financial, tax, and governmental or not-for-profit accounting. A major emphasis of this text is on financial accounting, which is concerned with measuring enterprise resources and obligations and subsequent changes in these items due to activities which affect the entity. Considerable attention is given to contemporary problems of income determination, accounting for special business entities, and accounting for financially-troubled entities. Another area of emphasis is accounting for nonprofit organizations, including governmental entities. The discussion focuses on the unique accounting methods used to secure the control of activities of such entities. Before attention is focused on these basic areas of concern, however, a brief discussion of accounting and its supportive theory is in order. This discussion is not designed to be all-inclusive, but rather to present aspects of accounting theory which relate to the topics contained in this text.

THE PURPOSE OF ACCOUNTING

The basic purpose of accounting is to measure and communicate relevant financial data for making economic decisions. The specialized data needed for each type of decision require that the various users of financial information be identified. For example, management may need information in a different form or degree of detail than the information needed by other parties. These other parties could include existing or potential creditors and shareholders, as well as those who have a less direct financial interest in the entity, such as employees, unions, financial analysts, and governmental agencies.

As a result of the diversity of specific users of financial accounting data, and the diversity of their specific economic needs, the decision processes of these users have not been adequately described. However, an economic framework which is fundamental to all users has been identified. This framework involves the efficient allocation of scarce resources among competing entities, and is designed to maximize individual and enterprise wealth, as well as to achieve broad social goals.

Informational Needs of Users

Financial accounting data should be the basis for determining whether resources should be allocated to an entity, and how the resources should be allocated. Such information may be provided through a system of reporting which includes financial statements and other supplementary means of communicating an entity's wealth at a point in time and the measurement of changes in wealth over a period of time.

The following basic assumption is useful in identifying the informational needs of users, and in specifying the objectives of financial reporting through which such information is communicated:

> Potential users of financial information most directly concerned with a particular business enterprise are generally interested in its ability to generate favorable cash flows because their decisions relate to amounts, timing, and uncertainties of expected cash flows . . . . Thus, investors, creditors, employees, customers, and managers significantly share a common interest in an enterprise's ability to generate favorable cash flows. Other potential users of financial information share the same interest, derived from investors, creditors, employees, customers, or managers whom they advise or represent or derived from an interest in how those groups (and especially stockholders) are faring.[1]

An analysis of this assumption suggests that the benefits of decisions with respect to the allocation of resources are reflected in the amount of cash which is distributed to those who provided the resources. Thus, the primary goals of an economic entity can be measured in terms of the cash which will ultimately be returned on invested capital.

Information Standards

For a financial reporting system to have maximum utility, given cost/benefit considerations and the needs of users, it should satisfy certain standards or qualitative criteria. These criteria, which provide a basis for evaluating alternative accounting and reporting methods, are concerned with the relevance, reliability, neutrality, and comparability of accounting information.[2]

---

[1] *Statement of Financial Accounting Concepts, No. 1,* "Objectives of Financial Reporting by Business Enterprises" (Stamford: Financial Accounting Standards Board, 1978), par. 25.

[2] *Statement of Financial Accounting Concepts, No. 2,* "Qualitative Characteristics of Accounting Information" (Stamford: Financial Accounting Standards Board, 1980).

Relevance. Accounting information is relevant if it pertains to the economic decisions or actions considered by users. Relevant data should influence or be capable of making a difference in the probabilities of occurrence surrounding an action or decision by the user, such as a decision to buy a security. The relevance or predictive value of data will be enhanced if the data are provided on a timely basis and in an understandable form. Of the various information standards, relevance is of extreme importance, in that data which satisfy all other standards will be marginally useful if they are not relevant to the needs of users.

Reliability. The overall utility of information is also seriously influenced by the reliability or ability of the information to represent or measure the attributes (conditions or events) of interest. Reliability is affected by the verifiability and representational faithfulness of the accounting measurement. Verifiability refers to the bias or judgment required of the one measuring an attribute. Completely verifiable information means that given identical measurement processes or models, independent measures would reach the same conclusion regarding the attribute of interest. In statistical terms, verifiability is measured by the dispersion of independent measurements about the mean of the measurements, which are derived from a common measurement model. For example, the closing price of a security is much more verifiable than the expected value of the security six months hence, as evidenced by comparing the dispersion of the two sets of values which result from independent measurements. Representational faithfulness refers not to the bias or judgment required of the measurer but rather the ability of the measurement model to portray what it purports to portray. Accuracy may be determined by measuring the difference between the mean value produced by the measurement model and the true (although perhaps unknown) value of the attribute. For example, the historical cost of an asset, even though more verifiable, may not be as representationally faithful with respect to measuring the asset's value as the net present value of cash flows traceable to the asset.

Neutrality. Neutrality suggests that financial reporting should not favor one or more user groups or be designed to induce a particular behavior by biasing the selection of what is to be disclosed. Certainly financial reporting should be expected to influence behavior and have a purpose but it should not bias the output in order to achieve some predetermined political or nonpolitical goal.

Comparability. The comparability of financial data is a function of the differences between accounting methods used by various entities to record similar events. Such *interfirm comparability* suggests that the utility of financial data will be enhanced if the similarities and differences between entities are reflected over time. Comparability is also influenced by a single entity's changes in accounting methods used to measure similar events. This *intrafirm comparability*, which involves the consistent application of accounting methods within an entity over time, is an important criterion against which the utility of financial data should be assessed.

THE ACCOUNTING ENTITY

The concept of an entity is indispensable to accounting because it defines the boundaries of accounting activity; therefore, the economic entity must be defined. An entity may be viewed as a unit that controls economic resources which are employed to produce a good or service. Although divisions, profit centers, and branches may be viewed as accounting entities in their own right, they also become a part of a larger entity. The boundaries of an entity are not confined to legal creations but many encompass several entities. For example, even though a parent corporation and its subsidiaries are separate and distinct legal entities, they may be viewed as one reporting entity for accounting purposes.

Equity Theory

When the entity has been defined, a decision must be made as to how it should be viewed theoretically, since the viewpoint adopted could affect the determination of net income, the valuation of assets, the definition of equity, and disclosure requirements. This need to define a viewpoint is not unique to the accounting profession. In the visual arts, for example, given a distinct object, such as a tree, an artist develops an interpretation of the object. A realistic view would suggest different techniques and produce a different result than would a surrealistic or cubist viewpoint.

The theoretical framework of accounting consists, in part, of theories which explain the nature of the equities comprising a business unit, and which also support the accounting principles applicable to that particular entity. This body of theory, often referred to as equity theory, consists of several mutually exclusive concepts. The difference between these concepts is in the manner in which a particular entity is viewed. For example, should the entity be viewed with regard to owners, or creditors, or management, or all providers of capital, or some legal concept? Certainly a choice of one of these viewpoints would influence the accounting principles used and the nature of the resulting financial statements.

It is rare that accounting for an entity can be traced entirely to one equity theory. In fact, there are aspects of accounting within a particular organization which are traceable to more than one theory. Therefore, to understand the basis for applying specific accounting principles to a given entity, the student of accounting must understand the various equity theories. Of these theories, the proprietary, entity, and fund theories have had the most significant impact on the development of modern accounting thought.

Proprietary Theory. The proprietary theory elects to focus on the owners or proprietors of a business unit rather than viewing the unit as a distinct business entity in its own right. As one author stated:

> According to the proprietary viewpoint, the standing and operations of a business firm are interpreted according to the manner in which they affect the proprietors or owners of the business. Whether the business be conducted in the form of an individual proprietorship, a partnership, or a corporation, the proprietary viewpoint looks at the business through the eyes of the owners. Thus, despite the fact that the corporation has a distinct legal identity, the proprietary viewpoint looks upon it essentially as a means whereby several individual enterprenuers can conveniently carry on business together. At most, the corporation is regarded as an agent, representative, or arrangement through which the individual entrepreneurs or shareholders operate.[3]

According to proprietary theory, the wealth and activity of the business unit are analyzed in terms of how they relate to the owners of the business. Assets are viewed as belonging to (or as the property of) the owners, and liabilities are viewed as obligations of the owners, or "negative assets." This emphasis suggests the balance sheet equation of assets minus liabilities equals proprietorship $(A - L = P)$. Income under the proprietary theory is an increase in the owner's wealth, versus the entity's wealth, in that revenues are viewed as increases in proprietorship, and expenses as decreases in proprietorship. Thus, the major objective of a business is that of increasing the proprietor's wealth, and therefore primary emphasis is placed on asset and liability measurement as a means of accurately measuring changes in the proprietary interest or wealth.

The proprietary theory is one of the oldest equity theories supporting the development of accounting. It was frequently discussed in accounting textbooks of the nineteenth century and was extremely relevant to the predominant business forms of that time, i.e., proprietorships and partnerships. The proprietary theory is still relevant, even though the corporate form of organization has become widespread. For example, the corporate concept of net income, which views interest and income taxes as expenses, represents the increase in wealth of the owners rather than that of all providers of capital. The inclusion in net income of the parent corporation's share of subsidiary net income also suggests a proprietary viewpoint which emphasizes the wealth of the owners. The treatment of a sole proprietor's salary as a distribution of income, rather than as an expense, provides an example of how the proprietary theory influences accounting for other forms of organizations.

---

[3] John W. Coughlan, *Guide to Contemporary Theory of Accounts* (Englewood Cliffs: Prentice-Hall, Inc., 1965), p. 155.

Entity Theory. In direct contrast to the proprietary theory is the entity theory, which views the business unit as a separate and distinct entity, possessing its own existence apart from the owners. The capital structure of the firm is made up of creditors and stockholders (owners), both of whom are investors concerned with the success of the entity, thus suggesting a balance sheet equation of assets equal equities. The assets are viewed as rights which accrue to the entity, not the owners, while the equities are viewed as a common group of investors, often divided formally into the liabilities (the creditors' equity) and the stockholders' equity. The liabilities of the entity can normally be valued more objectively and independently than stockholders' equity and, therefore, are viewed as the specific obligations of the entity. The creditors and stockholders have different rights with respect to income, risk, control, and liquidation; nevertheless, they are viewed as being, in substance, members of a common equity element. According to the entity theory, the major objective of the business is generating income, and therefore primary emphasis is placed on the determination of income available to all investors and the importance of the income statement.

A strict interpretation of the entity theory would view income, excluding any charges representing cost of capital, as accruing to the entity, not the equities (owners). Paton and Littleton state that:

> If the corporation were viewed as merely an aggregation of individual investors, it would be consistent to hold that the earnings of the enterprise belonged to the investors from the moment of original realization. Emphasis on the entity point of view, on the other hand, requires the treatment of business earnings as the income of the enterprise itself until such time as transfer to the individual participants has been effected by dividend declaration.[4]

The entity theory is most applicable to the corporate form of organization, which is characterized as a legal unit separate from its owners. This distinct identity is illustrated by the fact that unsatisfied creditors cannot seek recovery from the personal assets of the owners of the corporation, and that changes in the ownership structure of the corporation do not dissolve the entity. The classification of corporate owners' equity and the expensing of salaries paid to employee-shareholders are further evidence of the entity theory.

Fund Theory. The fund theory views the entity as consisting of economic resources (funds) and various restrictions or claims against the use of these resources, thus suggesting an accounting equation of assets equaling restrictions against the use of these assets. Liabilities and owners' equity may be viewed as restrictions on the use of specific assets or assets in general. The theory is asset centered, and places primary emphasis on the administration and appropriate use of these funds versus

---

[4] W. A. Paton and A. C. Littleton, *An Introduction to Corporate Accounting Standards* (Iowa City: American Accounting Association, 1965), p. 8.

the equity or proprietary interests of a particular group. Therefore, a statement of sources and uses of funds is one of the primary statements under this theory, and the income statement is viewed as merely a statement which describes a particular source of funds (i.e., operations).

Fund theory is most applicable to governmental and other not-for-profit organizations, where the profit motive is replaced by social goals which are achieved by the proper management of resources. The fund theory is also emphasized in accounting for bankruptcies and estates and trusts, where attention is placed on funds available for liquidation and the restrictions on those funds.

Accounting Measurement

When the economic entity has been defined, its activity must also be measured. However, before measurement of the economic activities can proceed, three fundamental issues must be resolved. First, the relevant activities and attributes of the entity must be defined. Second, the unit of measure must be defined, and finally, a measurement base must be selected.

The Subject Matter of Measurement. As discussed earlier, a measurement process must measure those activities of an entity which are relevant to the needs of the intended recipients or users. Thus, the general purpose of financial statements is to provide data for determining the allocation of scarce resources among competing entities. Such a focus suggests that accounting should be concerned with providing information which measures an entity's economic wealth and its ability to produce more wealth.

Economic wealth can be determined by measuring an entity's economic resources and obligations at a point in time. However, information concerning changes in resources and obligations over time is also of major importance, as reflected in statements dealing with the objectives of accounting.

The Unit of Measure. The diversity of economic resources and obligations suggests the need for some common unit of measure which can be used to relate these items to one another. In nonbarter economies, the unit of measure for accounting purposes is money. The use of money provides a common denominator for measuring certain attributes of economic resources and obligations and for evaluating activities which influence entity wealth.

Although money serves as a unit of account or common denominator, serious concern has been expressed as to whether money can continue to serve in this role without some adjustment. This concern focuses on the fact that the significant characteristic of money is its purchasing power, or the quantity of goods and services which money can acquire. It is an observable fact that the purchasing power of money has changed over time.

As a common denominator, money provides the means by which the attributes of economic resources and obligations can be measured. The measured amounts are then combined or aggregated. However, if the purchasing power of money has changed over time, the significance of combined monetary amounts may be questionable. For example, if an economic resource measured in 1940 dollars is added to an identical resource measured in 1980 dollars, what meaning can be given to the combined total of the resources? Traditional accounting theory has dealt with the problem by establishing the "stable monetary" assumption, which states that the monetary unit is characterized by a stable purchasing power over time. This assumption is still observed in current financial statements, and is defended on the grounds that financial statements based on this assumption are well understood, compared to alternatives, and that such statements still have utility. However, due to the high inflationary rates in recent years, the accounting profession recognized that the changing purchasing power of the dollar could no longer be ignored by financial reporting. In 1979 the Financial Accounting Standards Board issued a statement requiring supplementary disclosures by certain large firms of certain nonmonetary assets and income statement elements expressed in terms of a constant purchasing power of the dollar (constant dollars) rather than the number of dollars.[5]

The conversion of nonmonetary items into constant dollars is accomplished by multiplying the historical cost basis by a conversion factor, defined as the current price index divided by the historical price index which existed when the nonmonetary item was acquired. To illustrate, assume that land costing $40,000 was acquired when the Consumer Price Index (CPI) was 100 and that the purchasing power of the dollar has decreased as evidenced by a current CPI of 120. In terms of the number of dollars, the land is measured at its original acquisition cost of $40,000, but in terms of the current purchasing power of the dollar (not to be confused with current replacement value), the land is measured at $48,000 ($40,000 × 120/100).

Monetary items (monetary assets and liabilities) represent sums of money which are fixed in amount or determinable without reference to changes in the purchasing power of the dollar. By definition, due to their fixed nature, monetary items are already expressed in terms of the current purchasing power, given changes in the purchasing power of the dollar. To illustrate, assume that at the beginning of the year a company held cash of $10,000 and incurred a long-term debt of $20,000 when the CPI was 100. At year-end, when the CPI is 120, the cash and long-term debt would still be measured at $10,000 and $20,000 respectively. However, the company has experienced a purchasing power loss of $2,000 due to holding monetary assets in the form of cash. This loss results

---

[5] *Statement of Financial Accounting Standards, No. 33*, "Financial Reporting and Changing Prices" (Stamford: Financial Accounting Standards Board, 1979).

from cash which should have been worth $12,000 ($10,000 × 120/100) of current purchasing power, but which is only worth the fixed amount of $10,000 of purchasing power. The company has also experienced a purchasing power gain of $4,000 due to holding a monetary liability in the form of long-term debt. If the debt were not fixed in amount, it would take $24,000 of current purchasing power ($20,000 × 120/100) to repay the loan.

Even though the FASB's constant dollar disclosure requirements are experimental in nature, the following benefits may accrue to users of such data:

1. Comparisons over time will be more meaningful because data for different time periods will be expressed in terms of a uniform constant dollar.
2. The gain or loss arising from holding monetary items may serve as a partial measure of management's ability to manage assets and debts during inflationary times.
3. Accounting income will be a better measure of changes in wealth over time because certain expenses will be expressed in constant dollars, and will be a better measure of a company's ability to achieve real growth and maintain its operating capital.
4. When the changes in the purchasing power of the dollar approximate the changes in prices of the specific goods being restated, nonmonetary items expressed in constant dollars may be a better measure of wealth because their current economic values are approximated.

The Selection of a Measurement Base. As discussed in the previous section, two possible units of measure are currently being used: the number of dollars as employed by the historical cost model and the purchasing power of the dollar as employed by the constant dollar model. Another major decision involves the concept of value to which the unit of measure should be applied. Alternative concepts of value or measurement bases represent differing views on how the wealth or value suggested by financial resources and obligations should be measured. Several measurement bases are used in accounting to various degrees. They are:

Historical cost: The most frequently employed base is historical cost, which measures wealth and changes in wealth in terms of original or allocated acquisition (exchange) prices actually incurred. Changes in value subsequent to acquisition and prior to sale are not recognized, except in certain cases where there has been a permanent downward move in value.

Current cost: In contrast, current cost measures wealth in terms of current (present) money prices. For example, an economic resource is measured in terms of the current cost which would be incurred to acquire or replace the same service potential represented by the resource. Measures of changes in wealth would include increases or decreases in the current replacement value of economic resources and obligations. This measurement base is currently used to a limited extent, as evidenced by the accounting for certain current assets according to the valuation principle of lower of cost or market. However, current applications do not recognize movements in the current prices of items above the originally recorded cost.

Exit values: This measurement base expresses economic resources in terms of the current selling price which would be received if an exchange took place. Economic obligations are measured in terms of the current prices which would be paid to satisfy the obligations. Emphasis is placed on a selling market versus a buying (or replacement) market, as is the case with current cost. Changes in wealth would recognize the changing exit values of the various components of wealth. The base has rarely been used in current practice, except for instances involving the valuation of precious metals and agricultural commodities.

Discounted cash flow: Of increasing interest is discounted cash flow, a base which views the value of economic resources and obligations as being equal to the present value of expected future cash flows associated with the items. The interest factor used for discounting is periodically revised to reflect the timing of cash flows and the associated risks. The base has been applied on a limited basis in current practice. One example of a current application is the valuation of certain receivables and payables (see Accounting Principles Board Opinion No. 21). The capitalization of certain lease payments also employs this measurement base.

The proper selection of a measurement base is dependent upon the information needs of the identified users. Since it is unlikely that all users will have identical information needs, the bases will vary among users. For example, a short-term creditor may be concerned with exit values, while an equity investor may be interested in current costs. Not only should different measurement bases be available to different users, but given a user, different bases should be available to measure various economic resources and obligations. For example, a given user might prefer to have current assets measured in terms of current costs and noncurrent assets measured in terms of past exchange prices. Therefore, the selection of a measurement base should consider the objectives of the financial report as suggested by the intended user.

Accounting has traditionally accepted historical cost as the primary measurement base. A major defense of historical cost is that it represents prima facie evidence of the objectively determined value of a resource or obligation. At the time of acquisition, historical cost is the same as current market value, and therefore measures value at a point in time as suggested by an arm's-length exchange transaction. Because the measure of value is determined by an exchange transaction, it can be measured independently (i.e., it is verifiable), and provides a degree of objectivity often lacking in other measurement bases. The emphasis on objectively determined values supports the historical cost concept of income determination, which generally recognizes changes in value only if they are evidenced by an exchange transaction (i.e., a new historical cost or acquisition price is established).

Historical cost is also supported on the ground that it has a utility for predictive purposes. The relevance of historical costs to certain types of future economic decisions, including those which involve future predictions, is established in the literature.[6] Historical cost is also supported as a satisfactory measure of management's stewardship function.

Although historical cost is the primary measurement base for financial reporting as well as price-level-adjusted (constant dollar) disclosures, the FASB requires the supplemental disclosure of current cost data for certain assets and expenses of large public enterprises.[7] For example, the current cost of year-end inventory and property, plant, and equipment, as well as the increase in specific prices (current cost) of these items held during the year, net of general price-level changes, must be presented as a supplement to the historical cost data. Cost of goods sold and depreciation/amortization expense must also be presented in terms of current costs stated in constant dollars. Supplemental current cost disclosures are part of the FASB's plan to experiment with alternative units of measure and measurement bases.

Current cost disclosures should benefit users of financial reporting in the following ways:

1. As compared to historical cost, measuring assets at current cost should present a more relevant measure of economic wealth at a point in time.
2. Including expenses measured at current cost in the determination of income should produce an income measure which more accurately measures changes in real wealth over time and a firm's ability to maintain operating capital.
3. Comparability between entities will be enhanced by expressing assets and expenses of firms at current cost dollars rather than dated historical costs.
4. Current cost measures of assets and income should provide users with an improved basis for predicting associated cash flows.
5. Income based on current cost measures of expense will provide insight into a firm's ability to maintain operating capital and may serve as a basis for negotiating price increases and for tax rate reductions in order to allow firms to better maintain capital for expanded production and investment.
6. The standard of neutrality may be better satisfied by current cost data in that disclosure of such data may provide certain users with information that had previously been available only to more sophisticated users. Therefore, investment decisions and security valuation may become more efficient and equitable.

[6] Yuji Ijiri, *Theory of Accounting Measurement* (Sarasota: American Accounting Association, 1975), pp. 88-90.
[7] *Statement of Financial Accounting Standards, No. 33, op. cit.*

INCOME DETERMINATION

An important objective of accounting is to provide users with information regarding the economic entity's goal of maximizing the return of net economic resources employed. The ability of an entity to employ resources to generate additional resources is referred to as *enterprise earning power*. The essence of earning power is to generate cash, which represents a return on invested capital. Over the life of an entity, the entity's earning power will equal its cash generating ability. Over shorter periods of time, earnings will not equal cash generated because of lags between resource consumption and subsequent cash returns. However, earnings for these shorter time periods will provide a basis for predicting the ultimate cash generating ability of the entity. The periodic measurement of entity progress toward generating earnings or income represents a major factor which influences the allocation of scarce resources among economic entities, and is of primary concern to accounting.

Income Concepts

The measurement of earning power or income is influenced by a concept of income and certain modifying conventions which are required to make a particular income concept operational. A discussion of various income concepts follows.

Psychic Income. Every individual is motivated by wants and, to varying degrees, every individual attempts to satisfy these wants. The extent to which wants are satisfied represents a measure of psychic income. This concept of income recognizes that human wants may be satisfied by economic resources in the form of goods and services as well as noneconomic gratification. Measurement of psychic income is hindered by the dual forms of satisfaction, economic and noneconomic, and by the fact that the proportion of these satisfactions is constantly changing. To the extent that economic satisfaction can be identified as the dominant element of psychic income, measurements of such income become more objective. However, overemphasis of this element and a failure to consider the noneconomic elements of psychic income may result in socially undesirable economic activities.

Economic Income. To the extent that the subjective, noneconomic elements of income are not definable or measurable, other concepts of income which focus on economic aspects can be defined. These concepts deal with the measurement of increases in economic wealth, as evidenced by the money value of goods and services.

Using the concept of economic income, only an increase in wealth beyond a beginning level of real capital represents income. Therefore, economic income represents the amount of consumption an individual can experience over time and be as well off at the end of the time period as at the beginning.[8] To be as "well off" means that the beginning level of real capital or wealth must be maintained. Income is therefore measured in real terms and is influenced by the changing purchasing power of the monetary unit and changes in the current cost (specific prices) of resources employed. The supplemental disclosure of constant dollar and current cost data is designed to provide users with a more direct measure of economic income than is achieved by traditional historical cost reporting. A simple example may serve to illustrate this point.

Facts:

At the beginning of the year a company has four units of inventory costing $100 each. The general purchasing power of the dollar is evidenced by a Consumer Price Index of 100 at the beginning of the year and an index of 120 at year end. The specific cost to replace a unit of inventory at year end is $140. At year end all four units of inventory were sold for $175 each.

Income Statement:

	Historical Cost	Constant Dollar	Current Cost
Revenue	$700 [1]	$700	$700
Cost of goods sold	400 [2]	480[3]	560[4]
Gross profit	$300	$220	$140

[1] 4 units @ $175
[2] 4 units @ $100
[3] 4 units @ ($100 × 120/100)
[4] 4 units @ $140

Analysis:

If the company is to maintain its beginning level of real capital represented by four units of inventory, it must replace the units at a current cost of $140 per unit, or $560. The historical cost gross profit of $300, if distributed to investors, would leave the entity with only $400 of capital, which would not be adequate to maintain the initial level of operating capital. The constant dollar gross profit, if distributed, would leave the entity with $480 of capital, which would have been adequate if the price of inventory only changed to the extent of the change in the purchasing power of the dollar as evidenced by the CPI. However, the specific price change of inventory suggests that $560 of capital would be required to maintain the beginning level of operating capital. Therefore, if the current cost gross profit of $140 were distributed, the firm would have the necessary $560 of remaining capital with which to maintain its beginning level of operating capital.

An alternative analysis would indicate that the firm had a beginning-of-the-year command over goods equal to four units of inventory. At year end the current command over inventory is equal to five units, or $700 of capital divided by the $140 current cost of inventory. Therefore, the firm's command over inventory has increased from four to five units, or an increase of one unit with a current value of $140. The gross profit per the current cost model best measures the firm's increase in real wealth.

Accounting Income. Accounting income has been defined as:

> . . . the amount of the increase in the owners' equity, assuming no changes in the amount of invested capital during the period either from price-level

---

[8] J. R. Hicks, *Value and Capital* (Oxford: Clarendon Press, 1946), p. 172.

changes or from additional investments and no distributions of any sort to the owners.[9]

Although this definition emphasizes the determination of changes in wealth, as does an economic concept of income, operational constraints require a transactional approach to the determination of accounting income. Such an approach focuses on an entity's activities or transactions which produce changes in asset and liability values and, ultimately, in owners' equity. These basic income transactions are classified as revenue and expense transactions. Thus, definitions of accounting income stress the measurement of income (revenue minus expenses) rather than the nature of income.

Revenue Recognition

Revenue is a primary element in the determination of accounting income, and may be viewed as the "product" of an economic entity as represented by the creation of salable goods and services. However, revenue has frequently been defined from an inflow viewpoint:

> Revenue—gross increases in assets or gross decreases in liabilities recognized and measured in conformity with generally accepted accounting principles that result from those types of profit-directed activities of an enterprise that can change owners' equity.[10]

Other definitions of revenue place emphasis on the transfer of goods or services to parties outside of the entity.

Although definitions of revenue vary, all definitions trace revenue only to the profit-directed activities of the enterprise. These activities generally take the form of providing goods and services to other entities. Therefore, changes in owners' equity, resulting from the investment or withdrawal of assets by owners and the distribution of profits to owners, are excluded from the definition of revenue. A narrow definition of revenue also excludes gains from the sale of assets other than goods held for resale, and gains arising from the favorable settlement of enterprise obligations; however, these elements are typically viewed as separate components of net income.

Revenue is measured by the exchange value of goods and services as represented by their cash equivalent value. In those cases where cash equivalents are not involved, the fair market value of consideration to be received or given, whichever is more clearly evident, is normally viewed as the relevant measure of revenue.

Revenue is produced as a result of the production and/or marketing processes of an entity. The production process refers to the transformation of resources into products (goods) or services, and the marketing process involves the transfer of these goods and services to consumers.

---

[9] *Accounting Research Study, No. 3*, "A Tentative Set of Broad Accounting Principles for Business Enterprises" (New York: American Institute of Certified Public Accountants, 1962), p. 45.

[10] *Statement of the Accounting Principles Board, No. 4*, "Basic Concepts and Accounting Principles Underlying Financial Statements of Business Enterprises" (New York: American Institute of Certified Public Accountants, 1970), par. 134.

In addition to the measurement of revenue, a determination must be made as to when revenue produced by these processes should be recognized. Generally, revenue is not recognized unless the following conditions are satisfied:

1. The earning process is complete or virtually complete.
2. An exchange (arm's-length transaction) has taken place.
3. The revenue-producing event or transaction must possess a high degree of permanence.

The first condition suggests the basic nature of revenue, i.e., increases in entity wealth arising from the profit-directed activities of the entity. Theoretically, these activities must be complete or virtually complete before the related wealth accrues to the entity. The second condition indicates that even if the earning process is complete, the goods and services must be transferred (sold) to a separate, distinct entity. This condition emphasizes that wealth or value traceable to profit-directed activities is most accurately measured by an exchange transaction. Also, the information standards of verifiability and representational faithfulness are inherent in the second condition. The condition of permanence requires that revenues traceable to the entity will not be reversed or reduced by subsequent conditions. For example, if it becomes apparent after an exchange transaction (sale), that the purchaser of goods is unable to pay, serious consideration should be given as to whether revenue from the sale should be recognized, and if so, to what extent. Permanence also influences the extent to which revenue measurement is considered verifiable.

A comprehensive current cost model would set aside at least the first two conditions for revenue recognition. Such a model would recognize as revenue changes in current cost which have accrued to date, even if the earning process is not complete and an exchange has not taken place. For example, if the current cost of undeveloped land has increased, the increase in value would be recognized as income because it represents a change in wealth or "well offness" over time.

The conditions discussed are collectively viewed as the revenue realization principle. This principle is applicable to the profit-directed activities of most entities. However, exceptions exist in those cases where an earlier recognition of revenue is warranted, or where recognition should be delayed. These exceptions are typically found in the area of long-term construction contracts, precious metals, agricultural commodities, and sales made on an installment basis. In these cases, revenue is either recognized prior to sale, or is deferred beyond the point of sale.

Long-Term Construction Contracts. As previously discussed, revenue may theoretically be earned throughout the production process. The correlation between earnings and production might suggest a preference for a production or activity basis of recognizing revenue, as opposed to a sales basis. Emphasis is placed on the production effort rather than the marketing effort as the major factor responsible for the creation of revenues and profits.

The production basis of revenue recognition assumes that as production costs are incurred, a proportionate amount of revenue is earned for every dollar of cost incurred. For example, assume that the cost of constructing an oil tanker is estimated to be $16 million and its selling price is $20 million. For every dollar of cost incurred, $1.25 of revenue (20/16) will be recognized. In some cases, costs incurred to date may not accurately indicate the stage of completion, in which case engineering studies may be employed to serve as a basis for recognizing revenue.

This method of revenue recognition is appropriate in those cases where all of the following conditions are satisfied:

1. The profit-directed activity (production) is expected to take place over several years.
2. The marketing or sales effort takes place prior to construction and is minor when compared to the production process.
3. Costs of construction, along with the degree of completion, can be reasonably estimated.

If estimated total costs exceed the selling price of the constructed item, conservatism would require that the indicated total loss be recognized currently, rather than being deferred.

Precious Metals and Agricultural Commodities. In the case of precious metals and certain agricultural commodities, revenue may be recognized upon completion of the production process, but prior to sale, based on the following facts:

1. The production of these commodities, rather than their sale, is the primary determinant of revenue.
2. There is an established (assured) market price for these commodities. Therefore, the sales effort is insignificant.
3. The inventoriable costs associated with these goods cannot be easily determined.

Typically those goods which have not yet been sold are inventoried at their net realizable value (estimated selling price less estimated costs to complete and market). The effect of this treatment is to carry inventory at a value greater than cost, and to increase the gross profit by the difference between the net realizable value and the cost of the goods not sold.

Installment Sales. In those instances where the collectibility of credit sales is less than certain, an allowance for collection losses is typically established, and estimated collection losses are deducted from sales for the period. However, in certain extreme cases, collection of the sales price may be so uncertain that the condition of permanence and the standard of verifiability may not be satisfied. Therefore, the recognition of revenue is deferred beyond the point of sale. These cases frequently involve sales where a major portion of the sales price is payable in installments over an extended period of time. However, if the cost of goods sold on an installment basis exceeds the selling price, the indicated loss should be recognized in the period of sale, and not deferred to future periods.

Two methods are available for deferring revenue recognition. In the most extreme cases, the *cost recovery method* may be employed. This method initially treats all receipts of the sales price as a recoupment of the product costs. When the product costs have been recovered through collections of the sales price, all additional receipts are treated as gross profits. For example, if a major appliance costing $300 were sold for $500, with a $100 down payment and the balance payable over 24 months, the first $300 collected would be construed as a return of cost, with the balance being recognized as gross profit when collected.

In less extreme cases, the *installment method* may be appropriate. The installment method treats each receipt as a combination of cost recovery and realized gross profit, emphasizing the deferral of gross profit until collections are received. Theoretically, conditions for revenue recognition are met in most cases, and the postponement of gross profit recognition is not justifiable. However, this method has received official sanction in:

> . . . exceptional cases where receivables are collectible over an extended period of time and, because of the terms of the transactions or other conditions, there is no reasonable basis for estimating the degree of collectibility. When such circumstances exist, and as long as they exist, either the installment method or the cost recovery method of accounting may be used.[11]

To illustrate, if an appliance costing $400 were sold for $600, with a $120 down payment and the balance to be paid in eight installments, each dollar of the selling price would be allocated as follows:

Recovery of cost .... 400/600 or 2/3
Receipt of gross profit .... 200/600 or 1/3

The profit to be recognized would be $40 ($120 × 1/3) upon receipt of the down payment and $20 ($60 × 1/3) upon receipt of the first installment.

Expense Recognition

Expenses represent the expiration of service potentials of resources which are traceable to revenue-producing or profit-directed activities of the entity, either currently or in the future. A narrow interpretation of expenses would only include the productive (revenue-producing) expirations of resources, and would exclude unproductive expirations, or losses. However, losses do reduce owners' equity and are typically viewed as expenses from a practical standpoint.

---

[11] *Opinions of the Accounting Principles Board, No. 10*, "Omnibus Opinion—1966" (New York: American Institute of Certified Public Accountants, 1967), footnote to par. 12.

The expiration of service potentials theoretically occurs as the revenue-producing activities of the entity take place. For example, the service potential of fuel inventory is consumed in producing energy to operate a plant. The process of expiration of service potential is not always so direct, however. In the case of raw material consumed in the productive process, expense recognition is typically deferred until the resulting revenues are recognized. By this treatment, the transformation of service potentials into other forms (e.g., raw materials transformed into finished goods) does not represent the final expiration of service potentials because the transformed items still have utility or service potential to the firm. However, when service potentials are sold (an exchange transaction), they are viewed as expired and are therefore recognized as expenses. Thus, the recognition of expenses is a function of the recognition of revenues. This relationship is the basis for the matching principle, which requires that revenues and the related expenses be recognized in the same accounting period.

Theoretically, the matching of revenues and expenses is based on the assumption that there is a correlation between the incurrence of expenses and the production of revenue. Thus, a cause (incurrence of expense) and effect (production of revenue) relationship is suggested. There are many instances where this relationship is present, as in the case of the consumption of labor and raw materials and the resulting revenue from sales of manufactured goods. However, there are instances where a strong correlation between revenues and expenses does not exist. For example, the salaries paid to general administrative personnel are not related to specified revenues but, nevertheless, contribute to the overall revenue-production ability of the entity.

Because of the nature of expenses, several principles of expense recognition influence the determination of entity net income. These principles provide a basic framework for the recognition of expenses and acknowledge the practical difficulties associated with the theoretical matching of expenses and revenues. These principles can be summarized as follows:

> *Associating cause and effect.* Some costs are recognized as expenses on the basis of a presumed direct association with specific revenue.
> *Systematic and rational allocation.* In the absence of a direct means of associating cause and effect, some costs are associated with specific accounting periods as expenses on the basis of an attempt to allocate costs in a systematic and rational manner among the periods in which benefits are provided.
> *Immediate recognition.* Some costs are associated with the current accounting period as expenses because (1) costs incurred during the period provide no discernible future benefits, (2) costs recorded as assets in prior periods no longer provide discernible benefits or (3) allocating costs either on the basis of association with revenue or among several accounting periods is considered to serve no useful purpose.[12]

---

[12] *Statement of the Accounting Principles Board, No. 4, op. cit.,* pars. 157, 159, and 160.

QUESTIONS

1. What is the basic purpose of financial accounting and financial statements?
2. Events or transactions affecting an economic entity are analyzed or screened to determine whether they will be measured by or comprehended in an accounting information model. By what criteria should the output of such a model be evaluated?
3. To measure a particular attribute, two measurement procedures are employed. Measurement procedure A produces a mean value of $70 and a standard deviation of $3. Measurement procedure B produces a mean value of $90 and a standard deviation of $7. The true value of the attribute being measured is $100. Indicate which measurement procedure has the greatest degree of verifiability, and which is most representationally faithful.
4. How is "consistency" defined in accounting and what purpose does it serve?
5. Given an asset which is not held for resale, why would one expect that the "entry value" (historical cost) is less than or equal to the "value in use," which is greater than or equal to the "exit value"?
6. When does an actual exchange between a buyer and seller provide a suitable basis for measuring an asset's value? When might the resulting value not be appropriate?
7. Given established information standards, how would you evaluate (a) measures of income based on the periodic change in the discounted value of future net cash receipts, and (b) measures of income based on changes in value as evidenced by exchange transactions.
8. Business income may be viewed as the amount of assets a firm could distribute to its owners (dividends) and be as well off at the end of the period as it was at the beginning. Is it possible for a firm to have income even though it does not engage in any exchange transactions or production?
9. What criteria must be satisfied before an element of revenue can be recognized?
10. What are the two basic methods of accounting for long-term construction contracts? Under what conditions should one or the other of these methods be used?
11. Under what circumstances would the installment method be an acceptable method of revenue recognition?
12. Critics of financial accounting have referred to the balance sheet as a compilation of meaningless residuals. Discuss the increased emphasis on the determination of income and its effect on the utility of the balance sheet.

EXERCISES

Exercise 1. How would the following items be viewed under the proprietary theory? the entity theory?

(a) Interest on long-term debt	(d) Net income
(b) Cash dividends	(e) Partners' salaries
(c) Stock dividends	(f) Long-term debt

Exercise 2. Birchwood Corporation is preparing financial statements on a constant dollar basis and a current cost basis for the year ending December 31, 19X7. Inflation has been rising at a rate of 10% per year and there has been a 16% rise in replacement costs each year. The base for both indexes on January 1, 19X6, was 100. An analysis of Birchwood's equipment account is as follows:

Date	Acquisition (Retirement)	Estimated Life
January 1, 19X6	$276,000	10 years
January 1, 19X7	240,000	15 years
December 31, 19X7	(102,000)	—

Depreciation is computed on a straight-line basis with no residual values anticipated. The retirement represents assets from the January 1, 19X6 purchase.
(1) Prepare a schedule showing the balance in the equipment account (including accumulated depreciation) as of year-end 19X7 under the historical cost, constant dollar, and current cost bases.
(2) Assuming that $100,000 of the January 1, 19X7 equipment purchase was financed with a long-term note due in five years, explain how the note payable would be valued and how it would affect income for 19X7 under the constant dollar and current cost bases.

Exercise 3. The financial statements of a business entity could be prepared by using historical cost or current cost as a basis. In addition, the basis could be stated in terms of unadjusted dollars or dollars restated for changes in purchasing power. The various permutations of these two separate and distinct areas are shown in the following matrix:

	Unadjusted Dollars	Dollars Restated for Changes in Purchasing Power
Historical cost	1	2
Current cost	3	4

Block 1 of the matrix represents the traditional method of accounting for transactions, wherein the unadjusted amount of dollars given up is recorded for the asset obtained (relationship of resources) and no effect is given to any change in the value of the unit of measure (standard of comparison).

For each of the remaining matrix blocks (2, 3, and 4), describe how this method will affect the relationship between resources and standard of comparison. Limit your discussion to nonmonetary assets only.   (AICPA adapted)

Exercise 4. Revenue is usually recognized at the point of sale. Under special circumstances, however, bases other than the point of sale are used for the timing of revenue recognition.

Disregarding the special circumstances when bases other than the point of sale are used, discuss the merits of each of the following objections to the sales basis of revenue recognition:
(1) It is too conservative because revenue is earned throughout the entire process of production.
(2) It is not conservative enough because accounts receivable do not represent disposable funds; sales returns and allowances may be made; and collection and doubtful account expenses may be incurred in a later period.
                                                                    (AICPA adapted)

Exercise 5. After the independent auditors' report on the examination of the financial statements is presented to the board of directors of the Savage Publishing Company, one of the new directors is surprised that the income statement assumes that an equal proportion of the revenue is earned with the publication of every issue of the company's magazine. The director feels that the "crucial event," i.e., the most difficult task, in the process of earning revenue in the magazine business is the cash sale of the subscription and does not understand why, other than for the smoothing of income, most of the revenue cannot be "realized" in the period of the sale.

Discuss the propriety of timing the recognition of revenue in the Savage Publishing Company's accounts with:

(1) The cash sale of the magazine subscription.
(2) The publication of the magazine every month.
(3) Both events, by recognizing a portion of the revenue with the cash sale of the magazine subscription and a portion of the revenue with the publication of the magazine every month. (AICPA adapted)

Exercise 6. On January 1, 19X4, the Crook Construction Company entered into a contract to build an amusement park. The total cost of the facility has been estimated to be $2,500,000 and will take four years to complete. The selling price to the purchasing company is $3,500,000. The following data pertain to the construction period:

	19X4	19X5	19X6	19X7
Costs to date	$ 500,000	$1,200,000	$1,900,000	$2,500,000
Estimated cost to complete	2,000,000	1,300,000	600,000	—
Progress billings to date	400,000	1,500,000	2,400,000	3,500,000
Cash collections to date	350,000	1,200,000	2,250,000	3,500,000

(1) Using the percentage-of-completion method, compute the estimated income that would be recognized during each year of the construction period.
(2) Under the completed-contract method, when would the income on the project be recognized?

PROBLEMS

Problem 1-1. The concept of the accounting entity, often considered to be the most fundamental of accounting concepts, pervades all of accounting.

Required:

(1) (a) What is an accounting entity? Explain.
    (b) Explain why the accounting entity concept is so fundamental that it pervades all of accounting.
(2) For each of the following, indicate whether the accounting concept of entity is applicable; discuss and give illustrations.
    (a) A unit created by or under law.
    (b) The product-line segment of an enterprise.
    (c) A combination of legal units and/or product-line segments.

(continued)

(d) All of the activities of an owner or a group of owners.
(e) An industry.
(f) The economy of the United States   (AICPA adapted)

Problem 1-2. The Adler Company is preparing supplemental constant dollar and current cost income statements for 19X5, all expressed in year-end dollars. Selected data are as follows:
  (a) The changing purchasing power of the dollar is evidenced by the following consumer price indexes: beginning of 19X5, 100; midyear 19X5, 108; and year-end 19X5, 120.
  (b) At the beginning of the year, Adler purchased 400 units of inventory at a per unit cost of $90.
  (c) At midyear, Adler sold 250 units of inventory for $105 each. At this time, the inventory had a replacement value of $100 per unit. The replacement value of inventory at year end is $120 per unit. Ending inventory at year end consists of 150 units.

Required:

  (1) Calculate the 19X5 gross profit for Adler Company under the historical cost, constant dollar, and current cost methods. Note that the constant dollar and current cost data should be expressed in the year-end purchasing power of the dollar.
  (2) Calculate the monetary gain or loss that has resulted from Adler's activities.
  (3) Calculate the current cost of Adler's year-end inventory and indicate how much of this increase over historical cost is due to general price-level changes.

Problem 1-3. Valuation of assets is an important topic in accounting theory. Suggested valuation methods include the following:
  Historical cost (past purchase prices)
  Historical cost adjusted to reflect general price-level changes
  Discounted cash flow (future exchange prices)
  Market price (current selling prices)
  Current cost (current purchase prices)

Required:

  (1) Why is the valuation of assets a significant issue?
  (2) Explain the basic theory underlying each of the valuation methods cited.
                                        (AICPA adapted)

Problem 1-4. The earning of revenue by a business enterprise is recognized for accounting purposes when the transaction is recorded. In some situations, revenue is recognized approximately as it is earned in the economic sense. In most situations, however, accountants have developed guidelines for recognizing revenue by other criteria, such as the point of sale.

Required:

  (1) Explain and justify why revenue is often recognized as earned at the time of sale.
  (2) Explain in what situations it would be appropriate to apply the accretion

concept (recognizing revenue as the productive activity takes place or as values increase).

(3) At what times, other than those included in (1) and (2), may it be appropriate to recognize revenue? Explain. (AICPA adapted)

Problem 1-5. Flanders Company had the following historical cost financial statements on December 31, 19X7:

Flanders Company
Income Statement
For Year Ended December 31, 19X7

Service revenue		$137,600
Expenses:		
Depreciation	$17,000	
Salaries	78,000	
Other.......................................	23,000	118,000
Net income		$ 19,600

Flanders Company
Balance Sheet
December 31, 19X7

Cash	$ 36,000	Accounts payable	$ 8,500	
Accounts receivable	29,300	Long-term notes payable	19,500	
Equipment	102,000	Owner's equity	71,300	
Accumulated depreciation ...	(68,000)			
	$ 99,300		$99,300	

Additional data:

(a) The equipment consists of delivery trucks purchased on June 1, 19X4. Depreciation is computed on a straight-line basis with a full year's depreciation taken in the year of acquisition.

(b) Revenues and expenses occur uniformly throughout the year.

(c) The December 31, 19X6 values for cash, accounts receivable, accounts payable, and long-term notes payable were $18,000, $13,000, $10,800, and $19,500, respectively.

(d) Price-level index data:

	Index
June 1, 19X4	120
December 31, 19X4	124
December 31, 19X6	150
Average for 19X7	155
December 31, 19X7	162

Required:

Calculate the general purchasing power gain or loss on monetary items during 19X7 and restate Flanders' financial statements on a constant dollar basis, expressed in terms of the year-end 19X7 purchasing power of the dollar.

Problem 1-6. On May 5, 19X1, Sterling Corporation signed a contract with Stony Associates under which Stony agreed (a) to construct an office building on land owned by Sterling, (b) to accept responsibility for procuring financing for the project and finding tenants, and (c) to manage the property for 50 years. The annual profit from the project, after debt service, was to be divided equally between Sterling Corporation and Stony Associates. Stony was to accept its share of future profits as full payment for its services in construction, obtaining finances and tenants, and management of the project.

By April 30, 19X2, the project was nearly completed and tenants had signed leases to occupy 90% of the available space at annual rentals aggregating $2,600,000. It is estimated that, after operating expenses and debt service, the annual profit will amount to $850,000. The management of Stony Associates believed that the economic benefit derived from the contract with Sterling should be reflected on its financial statements for the fiscal year ended April 30, 19X2, and directed that revenue be accrued in an amount equal to the commercial value of the services Stony had rendered during the year, that this amount be carried in contracts receivable, and that all related expenditures be charged against the revenue.

Required:

(1) Explain the main difference between the economic concept of business income as reflected by Stony's management, and the measurement of income under generally accepted accounting principles.

(2) Discuss the factors to be considered in determining when revenue is realized for the purpose of accounting measurement of periodic income.

(3) Is the belief of Stony's management in accord with generally accepted accounting principles for the measurement of revenue and expense for the year ended April 30, 19X2? Support your opinion by discussing the application of the factors to be considered for asset measurement and revenue and expense recognition.   (AICPA adapted)

Problem 1-7. Craig Construction Company was awarded a contract to construct a new sidewalk system in Anytown for a price of $4,330,000. The original estimate by Craig of the cost to complete the contract was $3,750,000. The contract provides for periodic progress billings. A final billing equal to 20% of the selling price is to be made upon final inspection and acceptance by the Anytown Public Improvements Commission.

The construction record for the system was as follows:

Date	Costs to Date	Estimated Cost to Complete
December 31, 19X2	$1,270,000	$2,480,000
December 31, 19X3	3,450,000	920,000
August 20, 19X4	4,440,000	—

Progress billings equal to 20% of the selling price were made every five months during the construction period, following a satisfactory inspection. The sidewalk system was completed, and final inspection and acceptance took place on August 20, 19X4.

Required:

(1) Using the percentage-of-completion method, compute the estimated income (loss) that would be recognized during each year of the construction period.

(2) Using the completed-contract method, when would the income or loss on the project be recognized?   (AICPA adapted)

Problem 1-8. The Tomasco Furniture Company sells merchandise for cash and also on an installment plan. Presented below is summarized information on Tomasco's installment sales for the past three years:

	19X7	19X8	19X9
Installment sales.................	$300,000	$412,000	$465,000
Cost of goods sold	219,000	309,000	297,600
	$ 81,000	$103,000	$167,400
Collections from customers on:			
19X7 installment sales	$112,000	$157,000	$ 31,000
19X8 installment sales		105,500	197,000
19X9 installment sales			126,000

Required:

(1) Compute the gross profit percentages for each year.
(2) Compute the realized gross profit for each of the three years, assuming that:
  (a) Tomasco uses the installment method of accounting.
  (b) Tomasco uses the cost recovery method of accounting.

Problem 1-9. An accountant must be familiar with the concepts involved in determining earnings of a business entity. The amount of earnings reported for a business entity is dependent on the proper recognition, in general, of revenue and expense for a given time period. In some situations, costs are recognized as expenses at the time of product sale; in other situations, guidelines have been developed for recognizing costs as expenses or losses by other criteria.

Required:

(1) Explain the rationale for recognizing costs as expenses at the time of product sale.
(2) What is the rationale underlying the appropriateness of treating costs as expenses of a period, instead of assigning the costs to an asset? Explain.
(3) In what general circumstances would it be appropriate to treat a cost as an asset instead of as an expense? Explain.
(4) Some expenses are assigned to specific accounting periods on the basis of systematic and rational allocation of asset cost. Explain the underlying rationale for this procedure.
(5) Identify the necessary conditions in which it would be appropriate to treat a cost as a loss.   (AICPA adapted)

CHAPTER 2

REAL ESTATE AND FRANCHISE ACCOUNTING

The measurement of business income is one of the most crucial and significant objectives of contemporary accounting. A basic element of business income is revenue from operations, which is recognized according to established principles. In the past, these principles have been interpreted rather liberally for real estate and franchising businesses. In this chapter, the principles of revenue recognition are briefly reviewed and are then applied to real estate and franchise activities.

Revenue may be viewed as an enterprise's product or productive accomplishment, which is generated through the process of operations, whereby goods or services are ultimately transferred to parties external to the entity in return for some form of consideration. Theoretically, revenue is being generated during the entire process of operations as various factors of production are combined. However, to evaluate operations from an applied standpoint, decisions must be made regarding (1) when revenue from operations should be recognized, and (2) how these revenues should be valued or measured.

Basic principles suggest that revenue should be recognized when the earning process is complete and when the value of the revenue can be objectively measured, i.e., when revenue is realized. Various criteria have been established to determine when the earning process is complete. The sale criterion, which is the most common, holds that the sale of goods or services to consumers marks the completion of the earning process. However, other criteria propose variations in the timing of revenue recognition. For example, under the critical event criterion, the completion of the event most critical to the production of revenue marks the completion of the earning process.

The value of revenue is frequently measured by applying the realization criterion, which requires participation in a market or exchange transaction, whereby goods or services are exchanged for liquid assets. Using this criterion, the value of revenue is the value of consideration received in exchange for the entity's goods or services. These values theoretically represent the discounted present value of money claims to be received in the exchange transaction. Significant emphasis is placed on a determination of the collectibility of these values; however, if ultimate collectibility, i.e., realizable value, cannot be determined with reasonable accuracy, the related revenue may be deferred.

ACCOUNTING FOR RETAIL LAND SALES

In the early 1960's, the retail land sales industry catered mainly to localized individuals and groups by providing land for residential or industrial construction. However, in the late 1960's, large land sales corporations became widespread. These corporations acquired huge parcels of land which were marketed as primary or secondary homesites or as recreational property for the placement of recreational vehicles. The dominant activity of these corporations was the development and marketing of lots. The corporations usually assumed responsibility for initial improvements, such as grading, roads, and utilities. In many cases, amenities such as club houses, golf courses, and other recreational facilities were also included.

Normally, retail land sales involve a small down payment, with the seller financing the balance by accepting a receivable. The receivable typically takes the form of a land sales contract, but occasionally a purchase money mortgage is employed. These receivables usually are not based on a credit investigation or personal credit obligation on the part of the buyer. Therefore, the buyer can cancel the contract by discontinuing payment, and the seller has no recourse other than the repossession of the property and possible retention of payments previously made by the buyer.

The rapid growth of the retail land sales industry and the complexity of the development activities in which it became involved resulted in serious accounting problems. For example, the pressing need for additional capital resulted in the use of accounting methods which failed to apply properly principles of revenue realization. Revenue was recognized prematurely by a procedure referred to as "front-end loading."

The resulting balance sheets and income statements were of questionable substance but were nevertheless effective in securing needed capital for real estate companies.

Such methods of revenue recognition produced a major criticism of accounting in the real estate industry and created an uneasiness on the part of investors and accountants alike. In 1970 and 1971, in response to these criticisms, the AICPA created the Committee on Land Development Companies and the Committee on Accounting for Real Estate Transactions. The efforts of these committees resulted in two industry accounting guides, in which significant criteria were established for the proper recognition of revenue from real estate transactions.

To apply principles of revenue recognition properly, the substance of a transaction, rather than its form, should be emphasized. As previously discussed, revenue is normally recognized when the earning process is complete and when an exchange has taken place. Proper application of these criteria is based on an objective measurement of the consideration received in the exchange. The Committee on Land Development Companies (hereafter referred to as the Committee) believed that the recognition of a sale should be deferred until (1) it is apparent that the buyer intends to complete the contract, and (2) that the seller is capable of fulfilling obligations under the contract so that the buyer will not have to proceed against the seller for lack of performance.[1] These conditions served as the basis for the development of the following specific criteria, all of which must be satisfied for a contract to be recorded as a sale:

a. The customer has made the down payment and each regularly required subsequent payment until the period of cancellation with refund has expired. That period should be the longest of the period required by local law, established by company policy, or specified in the contract, regardless of whether refunds are available through simple notification, site visitation, or otherwise.
b. The aggregate payments (including interest) equal or exceed 10 percent of the contract sales price.
c. The selling company is clearly capable of providing both land improvements and offsite facilities promised in the contract and of meeting all other representations it has made. Its current and prospective financial capabilities are sufficient to provide reasonable assurance that it will be able to fund or bond the planned improvements in the project when required. That ability may be demonstrated by the company's adequate equity capitalization, or its borrowing or bonding capacity, or a continuing positive cash flow from operations.[2]

The evaluation of a transaction to determine whether it qualifies as a sale is an important first step when considering real estate transactions. If the transaction does not qualify as a sale, the deposit method of accounting is appropriate. However, if a sale is indicated, either the

---

[1] Committee on Land Development Companies, *Accounting for Retail Land Sales* (New York: American Institute of Certified Public Accountants, 1973), p. 5.
[2] *Ibid.*, pp. 5-6.

accrual method or the installment method of accounting would be appropriate, depending on specific circumstances. These alternative accounting methods are discussed in the following sections.

Deposit Method of Accounting

If all of the criteria for a sale are not satisfied, the deposit method of accounting should be employed until such time that the transaction qualifies as a sale. This method requires that all collections, including interest, should be accounted for as deposits which do not affect income. Furthermore, all costs directly associated with the sale (e.g., selling costs, land cost, and commissions) should be deferred until the time the transaction qualifies and is recorded as a sale. When a sales contract is canceled, deferred costs should be charged against income and forfeited deposits should be credited to income.

Accrual Method of Accounting

Once a contract qualifies as a sale, a decision must be made as to how the sale should be recorded. A primary factor is the expected collectibility of the receivable arising from the sale. If collectibility is reasonably assured, based on the seller's own experience with similar projects, the accrual method should be employed, provided all of the following criteria are met:

   a. The properties clearly will be useful for residential or recreational purposes at the end of the normal payment period. There must be a reasonable expectation that the land can be developed for the purposes represented. For example, it should be expected that local ordinances and other legal restrictions, such as those arising from ecological considerations, will not seriously hamper development and that improvements such as access roads, water supply, and sewage treatment or removal are feasible within a reasonable time. (If ultimate utility seems doubtful, contracts entered into for speculative purposes are unlikely to be completed.)
   b. The project's improvements have progressed beyond preliminary stages, and there is evidence that the work will be completed according to plan. Ordinarily, the work should have begun, although the existence of engineering plans and work commitments relating to lots sold will demonstrate progress. In the absence of efforts directly related to lots already sold, completion of access roads and amenities such as golf courses, clubs, and swimming pools furnishes evidence of progress. The best evidence of progress and commitment by the company is the expenditure of funds on the proposed improvements. Conversely, there should be no evidence of significant delaying factors such as the inability to obtain permits, obtain contractors, or hire personnel and equipment.
   c. The receivable is not subject to subordination to new loans on the property, except that subordination for home construction purposes is permissible provided that collection experience on those contracts is the same as on contracts not subordinated.

    d. Collection experience for the project indicates that collectibility of receivable balances is reasonably predictable and that 90 percent of the contracts in force six months *after sales are recorded* . . . will be collected in full. The greater the customer's investment at risk of forfeiture, the more likely he will honor his commitment; accordingly, a down payment sufficient to record the sale if it were a casual sale (say, 20-25 percent) is an acceptable substitute for this test of collection experience. [3]

These criteria recognize the importance of performance by the seller as a factor which will influence collectibility. Certainly, if performance by the seller is questionable, a possible breach of contract could prevent the collection of the receivable.

The expected collectibility of the receivable is emphasized by the fourth criterion. To satisfy this criterion, the seller must be able to predict the collection experience of current sales. Such a prediction must be based on well-established experience with previous projects of a similar nature. This experience must be based on past contracts which employed similar marketing strategies and which have been collected over a sufficiently long period of time to support a prediction regarding payment to maturity. A sales contract which does not meet these criteria should be accounted for under the installment method until the criteria are satisfied. Proper application of the accrual method involves several procedural considerations which are discussed in the following paragraphs.

Valuation of Seller's Receivable. The exchange price used to value long-term receivables, such as those arising from retail land sales contracts, should be the discounted value of the receivables. APB Opinion No. 21, "Interest on Receivables and Payables," provides guidelines for calculating the discounted value of a contract receivable. This opinion suggests that the discounted value should be based on the current market value of the receivable or the market value of the asset given in exchange, and if those values are not available, an imputed interest rate should be employed for discounting purposes.

The market value of a contract receivable resulting from a retail land sale is not readily ascertainable because of an absence of an opportunity for nonrecourse discounting of such receivables. If the value of the land is also not available, other factors, such as prevailing interest rates, collateral, and credit standing, must therefore be considered in determining the discounted value of contract receivables. The Committee concluded that:

    . . . generally the credit ratings of retail land purchasers approximate those of users of retail consumer installment credit provided by commercial banks and established retail organizations. Accordingly, . . . the effective annual yield on the receivable (without a reduction for deferred

---

[3] *Ibid.*, pp. 7-8.

> revenue or deferred income tax) should not be *less* than the minimum
> annual rate charged locally by commercial banks and established retail
> organizations to borrowers financing purchases of consumer personal
> property with installment credit. In the absence of more definitive criteria,
> the objective of evaluating the gross receivable less contract cancellation
> allowance should be to record the net receivable at the value at which it
> could be sold on a volume basis at the time of the initial transaction
> without recourse to the seller.[4]

Therefore, in the absence of determinable market values for such receivables or land, an imputed interest rate should be employed. This rate should be at least equal to the interest rate charged on installment loans for consumer personal property. However, a lower imputed interest rate could be used if it approximates discounting on a nonrecourse basis. In many cases, the interest rate stated in the seller's receivable will be less than the imputed rate because the seller wants to encourage sales by offering financing at less than market rates.

The valuation discount which results from discounting the receivable at an imputed rate should be amortized to income over the life of the contract, using the "interest method" called for in APB Opinion No. 21. This amortization method requires the use of a constant rate of interest to be applied to the net carrying value of the receivable at the beginning of each period.

Allowance for Cancellation Losses. The Committee established guidelines for determining when contract receivables should be viewed as delinquent and therefore canceled. Sales canceled in the same period in which they were recorded should be included in gross sales and then separately deducted from gross sales. As an alternative, such canceled sales may be omitted from current sales and described in an accompanying footnote.

Losses on sales contracts expected to be canceled in periods subsequent to the period of sale should be accrued through a charge to gross sales and a credit to an allowance account. Estimates of cancellation losses should be based on past experience and should be updated frequently to determine the adequacy of the allowance account. The estimated cancellation loss should equal the unpaid receivable balance less any related valuation discount, deferred revenue, and the expected value of repossessed land. If cash refunds to the buyer are called for upon cancellation of the contract, they should also be considered in estimating the net cancellation loss. When a contract is canceled, the actual net cancellation loss would be charged to the allowance account.

Revenue Associated with Future Performance. A seller of real estate may be obligated for future performance in the form of improvements to lots sold and/or other facilities applicable to those lots (e.g., completion of a swim club to be used by buyers of lots). If significant services of the seller remain to be performed, the total earning process is not complete.

---

[4] *Ibid.*, p. 12.

Therefore, of the total revenue from the sale, a portion representing revenue associated with future performance should be deferred and excluded from gross sales.

The methodology used to account for revenue associated with future performance is similar to that employed for long-term construction contracts accounted for by the percentage-of-completion method. Because it would be difficult to allocate directly the total contract price between performed and unperformed services, the allocation is based on the stage of completion (performance) as suggested by the relationship of costs already incurred to total estimated costs to be incurred. Total estimated costs should include the direct cost of land and improvements, and selling and promotional costs directly associated with the project. The estimated cost of sales should be related to net sales, defined as gross sales minus the estimated contract cancellation losses and minus the discount on contracts receivable. The portion of revenue related to estimated costs yet to be incurred should be deferred and subsequently recognized when such costs are incurred.

Estimated costs to complete the project virtually always change over time due to cost overruns, inflationary forces, and basic changes in project design and utilization. Such changes should not result in an adjustment of previously recognized revenue, but should affect the amount of revenue to be recognized in future periods. However, if estimated remaining costs exceed the amount of deferred revenue, the indicated loss should be charged to the current period's income.

Income Determination—Accrual Method. The procedural considerations discussed in the previous paragraphs all influence how income is determined under the accrual method and when such income is recognized. The various elements influencing the recognition of income are summarized as follows:

Element	How Calculated	When Recognized
Gross sales	Total sales price for all contracts	At point of sale
Net cancellation losses	Value of contracts estimated to be uncollectible less nonrefundable payments	At point of sale
Valuation discount	The difference between the net present value of installment payments discounted at the stated rate (i.e., net contracts receivable) and their net present value when discounted at the imputed interest rate	Immediately as a reduction of sales and then as additional interest income over the payment period of the contract

Net revenue	Gross sales less net cancellation losses and valuation discount	Currently except for revenue traceable to future performance
Land costs	Includes only that portion of costs traceable to uncanceled contracts	At point of sale
Selling expenses	Includes all marketing costs incurred regardless of whether contracts are expected to be canceled	At point of sale
Future improvement costs	Includes only that portion of costs traceable to uncanceled contracts	Deferred to period in which future improvements take place
Gross profit	Net revenue less allocated land costs, marketing costs, and future improvement costs	
Interest income	The accrued interest at the imputed rate on the outstanding balance of the contract receivable less the valuation discount	Over payment period of contract receivable
Net income	Gross profit plus interest income	

The elements of income determination for retail land sales under the accrual method are demonstrated in Illustration I.

Illustration I—Information Used for Retail Land Sales Illustration: Accrual Method

Facts:

Initial gross sales contracts on all lots total $2,000 with payment terms as follows:

(a) A down payment of 10% is due upon signing of the contract.
(b) The balance of the contract price is to be paid in five annual installments payable at year end. The stated interest rate on the installment receivable is 6%.
(c) The down payment portion of the contract price will not be refunded upon cancellation of a contract.

The interest rate charged on retail consumer installment credit is 12%.

Allocated costs associated with the $2,000 of sales contracts are as follows:

Land costs	$235
Initial selling expenses	150
Future improvement costs	235
Total cost of sales	$620

The future improvement costs are expected to be incurred as follows: ¾ in the third year and the balance in the fourth year subsequent to sale.

Of the sales contracts, 15% are expected to be canceled prior to receipt of the first annual installment payment. As previously stated, 10% (the down payment) of the value of contracts canceled will not be refunded.

Analysis:

1. Calculation of net contracts receivable:

Gross sales contracts	$2,000
Less canceled contracts (15%)	300
Uncanceled sales contracts	$1,700
Less down payment on uncanceled sales (10%)	170
Net contracts receivable	$1,530

2. Calculation of the valuation discount:

Annual payment due on net contracts receivable, including interest—($1,530 ÷ 4.2124 present value of an annuity factor for 5 years at 6%)	$ 363
Net contracts receivable—present value of payments at:	
Stated interest rate of 6%	$1,530
Imputed interest rate of 12% ($363 × 3.6048)	1,309
Valuation discount	$ 221

3. Calculation of income for the five-year period:

Gross profit from sales:		
Gross sales		$2,000
Less: Net estimated cancellation losses:		
Cancellation of $300 less 10% down payment		(270)
Valuation discount		(221)
Cost of sales on uncanceled contracts:[1]		
Land (85% of $235)	$ 200	
Selling expenses	150	
Future improvements (85% of $235)	200	(550)
Gross profit		$ 959 [2]
Interest income:		
Total collections ($363 × 5)	$1,815	
Less present value of collections at 12%	(1,309)	
Interest income		506
Net income (gross profit and interest)		$1,465

4. Calculation of deferred revenue:

Future improvement costs (85% × $235)		$ 200
Total cost of sales on uncanceled contracts		$ 550
Percentage of costs traceable to future performance ($200 ÷ $550)		36%
Net revenue on uncanceled contracts:		
Uncanceled sales contracts	$1,700	
Less valuation discount	(221)	
Net revenue	$1,479	
Deferred revenue traceable to future performance ($1,479 × 36%)		$ 532

[1] Because 15% of the contracts are expected to be canceled, only 85% of the land and improvement costs are recognized. However, all selling expenses are to be recognized, because they are incurred regardless of whether contracts are canceled.

[2] This amount includes the nonrefundable down payment on the contracts expected to be canceled.

Income Statement:

	Year					
	1	*2*	*3*	*4*	*5*	Total
Revenue:						
Gross sales	$2,000					$2,000
Less: Net cancellation losses ...	(270)					(270)
Deferred revenue	(532)					(532)
Valuation discount	(221)					(221)
Net sales	$ 977					$ 977
Interest income (Sch. A.)	157	$132	$105	$ 74	$ 38	506
Revenue from improvements[3] ..		—	399	133	—	532
Total revenue	$1,134	$132	$504	$207	$ 38	$2,015
Expenses:						
Cost of land	$ 200					$ 200
Selling expenses	150					150
Improvement costs	—		$150	$ 50		200
Total expenses	$ 350		$150	$ 50		$ 550
Net income.....................	$ 784	$132	$354	$157	$ 38	$1,465

Schedule A

End of Year	Amount Collected	Principal	(a) Interest at 6%	(b) Receivable Balance	(c) Unamortized Discount	(d) Interest Income at 12%	(e) Discount Amortization (d) — (a)
0				$1,530	$221		
1	$ 363	$ 271	$ 92 [4]	1,259	156	$157 [5]	$ 65
2	363	287	76	972	100	132	56
3	363	305	58	667	53	105	47
4	363	323	40	344	19	74	34
5	363	344	19 [6]	-0-	-0-	38 [6]	19
	$1,815	$1,530	$285			$506	$221

[3] The future improvement costs of $200 were incurred in years 3 and 4 in the amount of $150 and $50 respectively. Therefore, $399 of the deferred revenue is to be recognized in year 3 with the balance being recognized in year 4.
[4] 6% × $1,530.
[5] 12% × ($1,530 − $221).
[6] Adjusted for rounding error.

Illustrative Journal Entries:

    Prior to date of sale:

Land Inventory	235	
Deferred Marketing Costs	150	
Cash		385

        To record payment for land and marketing costs.

    Date of sale:

Cash (10% down payment)	200	
Contracts Receivable	1,800	
Sales...		2,000

        To record gross sales contracts.

Cancellation Losses ($300 − $30 nonrefundable deposit) ...	270	
Sales..	221	
Allowance for Canceled Contracts		270
Valuation Discount......................................		221

        To record expected net cancellation losses and
        the valuation discount on net sales.

Allowance for Canceled Contracts	270	
Contracts Receivable		270

        To write off canceled contracts.

Cost of Sales 550
   Land Inventory 200
   Deferred Marketing Costs 150
   Future Improvements Payable 200
     To record cost of sales.
Sales... 1,779
   Cost of Sales 550
   Cancellation Losses 270
   Gross Profit 627
   Deferred Profit on Future Improvements ($532 − $200) .. 332
     To close to gross profit and recognize deferred gross
     profit on future improvements.

End of year one:
   Cash 363
   Valuation Discount....................................... 65
     Interest Income... 157
     Contracts Receivable 271
     To record receipt of first installment allocated
     between interest and principal.

Year three—improvement costs:
   Future Improvements Payable 150
   Deferred Profit on Future Improvements 249
     Cash 150
     Profit on Future Improvements ($332 × 150/200) 249
     To record performance of future improvements
     and recognize related deferred gross profit.

Installment Method of Accounting

As mentioned earlier, retail land sales which do not meet the specific criteria of the accrual method should be accounted for by the installment method. According to this method, profit is recognized as collections are received, using the following procedures:

1. The entire amount of gross sales, not reduced by cancellation losses or valuation discounts, should be recognized as installment sales revenue in the period of sale.
2. The cost of sales (including costs associated with future performance) and selling costs directly associated with the project should be charged against installment sales revenue in the period of sale.
3. The difference between the amounts calculated in (1) and (2) represents the profit on sales contracts which should be deferred and recognized as cash collections are received.

The installment method does not involve special procedures in those cases where revenue is traceable to future performance. Also, the installment method does not involve the computation of a valuation discount traceable to the imputed interest on the contract receivable, although such a computation is relevant in theory. The Committee determined that this computation would increase the complexity of accounting without significantly improving the utility of related financial statements. Therefore, when the installment method is used, interest income will be recognized at the stated rate rather than the imputed rate.

Accounting for Cancellation Losses. With respect to cancellation losses, the Committee stated that:

> Cancellation of sales contracts being accounted for on the installment method should be recorded by removing the unpaid receivables from the accounts, restoring recoverable costs to land and improvements, reducing the liability for future improvements applicable to the cancelled contract, and reducing the applicable unamortized deferred profit. An excess of cancelled receivables over recovered costs and applicable unamortized deferred profit (which will represent unrecovered selling costs) should be recognized as a loss in the period of cancellation.[5]

To illustrate the cancellation of a contract accounted for by the installment method, assume that $600 has been collected on a $2,000 sales contract. Costs associated with this contract consist of initial costs of $300 and future improvement costs of $500, of which $400 has not yet been incurred. The following entries reflect the activity on this contract.

Contracts Receivable	2,000	
Installment Sales Revenue		2,000
To record initial sale.		
Cost of Sales	800	
Cash		300
Future Improvement Costs Payable		500
To record costs associated with contract.		
Installment Sales Revenue	2,000	
Deferred Gross Profit		1,200
Cost of Sales		800
To record initial deferral of gross profit on contract.		
Cash	600	
Contracts Receivable		600
To record cash collections on contract.		
Deferred Gross Profit	360	
Realized Gross Profit		360
To recognize gross profit traceable to actual collections.		

$$\left(\frac{\$\ 600}{\$2,000} \times \$1,200 \text{ deferred gross profit} \right)$$

Future Improvement Costs Payable	100	
Cash		100
To record payment of future improvement costs incurred.		

If the contract is canceled, the following entry is made, assuming that the recoverable cost of the land is $150:

Future Improvement Costs Payable ($500 − $100)	400	
Land	150	
Deferred Gross Profit ($1,200 − $360)	840	
Loss on Contract Cancellation	10	
Contracts Receivable ($2,000 − $600)		1,400
To record contract cancellation.		

---

[5] *Ibid.*, p. 16.

The basic procedures required by the installment method are demonstrated in Illustration II, which presents income statements based on the installment method. It should be noted that both Illustrations I and II are based on the same facts. Both the accrual method and the installment method reflect the same total profit over the life of the contract, as demonstrated in the respective illustrations, but there are significant differences with respect to the periodic recognition of gross profit and interest income.

Changing from Installment Method to Accrual Method. If the criteria established for the accrual method of accounting for retail land sales are subsequently met, a change from the installment method to the accrual method should take place. The change is accounted for as a change in estimate, and therefore does not involve retroactive adjustment of previous financial statements. The effect on income will be equal to the difference between (1) the balance of deferred profit computed by the installment method and (2) the remaining valuation discount on contract receivables plus any deferred profit related to future performance.

Illustration II—Information Used for Retail Land Sales Illustration: Installment Method

Facts:

Initial gross sales contracts (stated interest rate of 6% on receivables)		$2,000
Collected down payments (10% of gross sales)		200
Sales contracts receivable traceable to: Noncanceled sales		1,530
Canceled sales (net)		270
Contracts canceled (all in first year)		300

Cost of sales:

	Traceable to		
	Noncanceled Contracts	*Canceled Contracts*	*Total*
Land	$200	$35	$235
Selling expenses	127	23	150
Future improvements	200	35	235
	$527	$93	$620

Analysis:

1. Calculation of deferred profit:

Total gross sales		$2,000
Total associated costs		(620)
Deferred gross profit (69% of sales)		$1,380

2. Calculation of cancellation loss:

Canceled contracts		$ 300
Less down payment of 10% (nonrefundable)		(30)
Unpaid balance		$ 270
Recoverable costs: Land	$35	
Future improvements	35	(70)
Deferred gross profit (69% × $270)		(186)
Cancellation loss		$ 14

For example, given the basic factual situation in Illustration II, assume that the sale qualifies for the accrual method at the beginning of the third year, when the balance in the deferred profit account is $671 ($210 + $223 + $238). Assuming that the improvement costs of $200 are incurred in years 3 and 4 in the amount of $150 and $50 respectively, the deferred profit associated with these expenditures is $332, which represents the revenue traceable to future improvements of $532 (Illustration I) less the future improvement costs of $200. The unamortized valuation discount traceable to the contract receivable, which is discounted at 12%, is $100 (Schedule A of Illustration I). Therefore, the change from the installment method to the accrual method at the beginning of year 3 would be recorded as follows:

Deferred Gross Profit	671	
Gross Profit on Real Estate Sale		239
Valuation Discount		100
Deferred Profit on Future Improvements		332
To record the change from the installment method to accrual method of accounting for real estate sale.		

Illustration II (continued)

Income Statement:

	Date of Sale	Year 1	2	3	4	5	Total
Gross sales	$2,000						$2,000
Less cost of goods sold:							
Cost of land $235							
Selling expenses 150							
Improvement costs [1] 235	620						620
Deferred gross profit...............	$1,380						$1,380
Realized gross profit (Schedule A) ...	-0-	$325	$198	$210	$223	$238	$1,194 [2]
Less cancellation loss	-0-	14	—	—	—	—	14
	-0-	$311	$198	$210	$223	$238	$1,180
Interest income (Schedule A of Illustration I)	-0-	92	76	58	40	19	285
Net income........................	-0-	$403	$274	$268	$263	$257	$1,465

Schedule A

	Year 1	2	3	4	5
Cash collections:					
Down payment	$200	—	—	—	—
Principal payment (Schedule A of Illustration I)	271	$287	$305	$323	$344
Total	$471	$287	$305	$323	$344
Profit recognized on collections (69% of total)	$325	$198	$210	$223	$238 [3]

[1] Although improvement costs have not yet been incurred, they are included to determine the deferred gross profit. These estimated costs will also be included in the balance sheet as a liability for future improvements.
[2] Notice that the realized gross profit is only $1,194, which is the original deferred gross profit of $1,380 reduced by the $186 of deferred gross profit traceable to the canceled sales.
[3] Adjusted for rounding error.

The $239 adjustment resulting from the change represents the difference between the $677 net income for years 1 and 2 per the installment method in Illustration II ($403 + $274) and the $916 net income for that period per the accrual method in Illustration I ($784 + $132).

The installment method is viewed by some as the most relevant and reliable method of accounting for retail land sales, because cash collections legitimize the realization of revenue. The Securities and Exchange Commission (SEC) supports the installment method because it represents good accrual accounting and avoids many of the practical difficulties associated with the accrual method, such as estimating cancellations and valuation discounts. These estimates and procedural aspects required by the accrual method are viewed by some as opportunities to manipulate income.

Others feel that the accrual method is based on sound criteria which adequately recognize the importance of collection experience and the completion of the earning process. Although estimates are involved, the use of such estimates is a basic element of today's financial reporting environment. Therefore, the accounting profession should play an important role in developing more specific criteria for use of the accrual method and thereby reduce the possibility of income manipulation.

Capitalizable Costs

Although considerable emphasis is placed on recognition of revenue from retail land sales, the capitalization and subsequent allocation of costs is also of major concern. In general, costs directly associated with inventories of unimproved land and/or construction activities required to bring land and improvements to a salable condition are capitalizable until a sale occurs. The total capitalizable costs should not exceed the net realizable value of the properties involved. Interest incurred in order to finance acquisition, development, and improvement costs is a capitalizable cost if it results from:

> . . . (a) loans for which unimproved land or construction in progress is pledged as collateral or (b) other loans if the proceeds are used for improvements or for acquiring unimproved land.[6]

Marketing-related costs incurred should normally be deferred until a sale occurs if they relate to assets to be used during the sales period and such costs are expected to be recovered from the project sales. Examples of such costs would be marketing displays, brochures, signs, sales facilities, and legal fees for the preparation of contracts. Costs whose benefit is limited to the period in which they are incurred, such as advertising, sales salaries, and overhead and grand openings, should be expensed currently.

---

[6] *Ibid.*, p. 19.

Amenities. Many retail land complexes contain amenities, such as lakes, tennis courts, and marinas. When these amenities are not expected to provide a return sufficient to cover the costs of constructing and operating them, their unrecoverable development costs should be matched pro rata against revenues from sales of sites. However, if the amenities are effective selling aids and do provide for the recovery of costs, the costs incurred to develop the amenities should be amortized over the shorter of (1) the period during which homesites are expected to be sold or (2) the estimated useful life of the amenities.

Allocation of Capitalizable Costs. When costs have been capitalized, a reasonable method of allocating these costs to sales must be selected. The industry guide on retail land sales acknowledges the following methods:

  a. Area methods, using square footage, acres, frontage, or other measures based either on simple averaging methods or on some measure of yield differentials (e.g., equivalent lot yield, or geologically influenced factors such as slope and known soil problems).
  b. Value methods (gross or net after estimated future improvement costs), using mortgage release prices, estimated selling prices, or appraisals.
  c. Specific identification method, if possible and appropriate.
  d. Hybrid methods involving elements of two or more of the other methods.[7]

The value method is preferred when the more valuable properties sell first. In this situation, a larger portion of the capitalizable costs will be allocated to the sale of more valuable properties, leaving a smaller portion of capitalizable costs to be recovered through the sale of less valuable properties. Thus, the possibility of deferring losses is reduced.

Disclosure Requirements

The industry guide on retail land sales has identified specific disclosure requirements with respect to such sales. Some of the more significant requirements are that:

1. The statement of changes in financial position should be restricted to sources and uses of cash.
2. Methods of income recognition should be fully disclosed, as well as the amount of sales and receivables traceable to the method.
3. Inventories of land and improvements, as well as the estimated liability for improvements, should be disclosed.
4. Information necessary in determining valuation discounts and cancellation losses should be disclosed.
5. Major categories of sales and related cost of such sales should be disclosed.

---

[7] *Ibid.*, p. 20.

6. Information should be disclosed concerning the future maturities of receivables, value of delinquent accounts, and amounts of contracts not yet recorded as sales.

Although not required by the guide, some individuals feel that disclosure should be made concerning the progress and state of development of projects.

ACCOUNTING FOR OTHER REAL ESTATE SALES

Various other forms of real estate sales are the subject of an industry accounting guide prepared by the AICPA Committee on Accounting for Real Estate Transactions. These transactions do not include retail land sales, but they do include all other real estate sales transactions, such as sales of condominiums, apartment complexes, and industrial sites, and sales of land to builders. Although the form of these transactions may indicate a sale, they should be evaluated to determine whether they are in substance sales. For example, if the risks and rewards of ownership transfer to the buyer, and the seller, at most, only assumes the risks of a secured creditor, a sale is indicated.

Revenue from sales should be recognized if the earning process is complete and if an exchange has taken place. Except in those cases where the seller is committed to some form of future involvement with the project, the sale is considered to be consummated at the date of closing. Typically, all material conditions which relate to the sale have been substantially performed as of the closing date.

In many real estate sales, a major portion of the consideration is represented by the buyer's receivable which is not supported by the full faith and credit of the buyer. If the buyer defaults, the seller's only recourse is to retain the buyer's payments and repossess the property. Therefore, a major factor in the recognition of revenue is contract collectibility. The Committee on Accounting for Real Estate Transactions recognized that both the initial down payment and the continuing investment in the property must be "adequate" to assure collectibility and thus justify the use of the accrual method.

Buyer's Initial Investment

If the payments made by the buyer are substantial, the buyer has a strong motivation to honor the sales contract, rather than lose such payments upon default. Therefore, the amount of down payment relative to the sales value is an indication of future collectibility of sales price. If the down payment is small, so that amounts loaned to the buyer exceed the amounts which would be loaned on such sales by established lending institutions, then the risk of default increases.

A down payment will be deemed adequate if it is 25% or more of the sales value or if it is at least equal to the *greater* of:

1. The down payment required under usual loan agreements; or,
2. The amount by which the sales value exceeds 115% of the loan (or commitment) by the primary lender.[8]

These guidelines must be amended, however, if property improvements are sold to the buyer subject to a lease of the underlying land.[9]

In addition to the amount of the down payment, its composition must also be evaluated to determine if such payments have equivalent cash value and are therefore collectible. Acceptable forms of down payments include:

1. Cash.
2. Irrevocable letters of credit from established lending institutions.
3. Other notes of the buyer when they are converted into cash without recourse to the seller.
4. Verified payments to third parties which will reduce previous indebtedness on the property.
5. Certain payments which represent additional sales proceeds or prepayments of interest and fees which are maintained in an advanced status and later applied against the principal amount due.

Funds which have been or will be loaned to the buyer by the seller, either directly or indirectly, cannot be included as part of the buyer's down payment in determining its adequacy.

Buyer's Continuing Investment

Even if the size and the composition of the down payment are adequate, the collectibility of the receivable may not be reasonably assured if the buyer's continued investment in the property is not adequate. The Committee on Accounting for Real Estate Transactions felt that if the buyer's debt was not paid within the customary term of a first mortgage (or 20 years for a loan on land), the collectibility of the receivable would be questioned. Therefore, the buyer's annual payments must, by contract, be equal to or greater than the annual payment (including principal and interest) required by an independent lending institution. The annual payments must be in cash or other forms similar to those qualifying as acceptable down payments. As in the case of the down payment, funds which have been or will be loaned to the buyer by the seller cannot be included as part of the buyer's continuing investment.

The objective of evaluating the adequacy of the down payment and continuing investment is to determine the buyer's intent or commitment to the purchase. The more the buyer invests in the property, the greater the commitment to pay for the purchase. The adequacy tests are to be made cumulatively by comparing the total of the buyer's investment

---

[8] Committee on Accounting for Real Estate Transactions, *Accounting for Profit Recognition on Sales of Real Estate* (New York: American Institute of Certified Public Accountants, 1973), p.6.

[9] *Ibid.*, pp. 10-11.

required by the contract against that required by the guide. It is possible that a transaction may not be recognized initially as a sale because of an inadequate down payment, but in a subsequent period the totals of the down payment and continuing investment are adequate because of a greater-than-required continuing investment. Once the adequacy tests are satisfied on a cumulative basis and the buyer's commitment results in classification of the transaction as a sale, such adequacy tests need not be employed subsequently. However, as long as a seller holds a receivable from the buyer, collectibility of the receivable should be continually evaluated.

If the indebtedness payments by the buyer do not qualify as an acceptable continuing investment but the buyer's down payment is adequate, profit recognition may be allowed to a limited extent at the date of sale. This exception relates to instances when the aggregate actual indebtedness of the buyer exceeds the maximum first-lien indebtedness that could be obtained.[10]

Accounting Methods

Several accounting methods are available for recording other real estate transactions, although each method is acceptable only for a particular set of circumstances. If the buyer's initial and continuing investment are both adequate, the sale should be recorded by the accrual method at the time of sale. If it appears a sale has not taken place, the deposit method may be appropriate. Under the deposit method, the seller will show the property and related debt in financial statements but will not record the receivable held from the buyer. The cash received from the buyer is recorded as a deposit (liability), except that cash received which represents contractual interest and which is not subject to refund may be recorded as a reduction against carrying costs (insurance, taxes) on the property. If the transaction is a sale, but the collectibility of the sales price is questionable, either the installment method or the cost recovery method of accounting would be required, depending on the circumstances. Given the recourse available to the seller upon default of a sales contract, the installment method of accounting would appear acceptable except in those rare instances where recovery of cost is questionable. If the sale would otherwise qualify for the accrual method but the earning process is not complete, the percentage-of-completion method of accounting should be employed.

It is not uncommon for a party to sell a partial interest in real estate. The profit on partial sales should be recognized, provided (1) the sale is to an independent party, (2) collection of the sales price is reasonably assured, and (3) it is reasonably certain that the seller will not have to support the property, its operations, or related obligations to an extent greater than the seller's ownership interest. If these conditions are not

---

[10] *Ibid.*, pp. 8-9.

satisfied, special methods of recognizing profit must be used, so that the substance of the transaction will be reflected.

Seller's Continued Involvement

A seller of real estate may be obligated to continue to be involved in the property sold. For example, the seller may manage or further develop the property or guarantee the return on investment to the buyer. Generally the seller's continued involvement takes two basic forms:

1. An obligation to perform specific significant parts of the contract (e.g., construct facilities, support operations for some period of time, provide or arrange for financing).
2. An involvement which results in the seller assuming basic risks (and rights) of ownership (e.g., guarantee cash flows, obligation to repurchase property, guarantee of buyer's indebtedness on the property).

This involvement may suggest that the earning process is not yet complete and may, therefore, complicate the recognition of profit. A careful analysis of such situations is required in order to determine if a sale has taken place, and if so, how revenue should be recognized. To aid in the analysis, the Committee on Accounting for Real Estate Transactions discussed several types of continuing involvement, which are summarized as follows: [11]

1. The seller participates solely in future profits. In this case, all income may be recognized, provided the seller participates solely in profits but does not bear any of the losses.
2. The seller is obligated to secure permanent financing for the buyer. In this case, the recognition of profit on the sale should be deferred until such financing is acquired.
3. The seller provides services without compensation or at less than prevailing levels of compensation. All income on the sale can be recognized, except an amount equal to the imputed value of the services to be rendered. Income traceable to such services will be recognized as the services are performed.
4. The seller assumes responsibility for the development and construction of the real estate. Assuming the costs associated with this activity can be reasonably estimated, the percentage-of-completion method should be used to recognize income. The income should be deferred until final completion, if costs cannot be reasonably estimated.
5. The seller is responsible for initiating and supporting operations of the property, such as maintaining minimum rent levels on a rental property. If this responsibility is such that the risks and rights of ownership have not theoretically passed to the buyer, a sale should not be recorded, but payments from the buyer should be viewed as loans, rental payments, or a division of profits, depending on the

---

[11] *Ibid.*, pp. 14-19.

substance of the transaction. This type of treatment would be appropriate if the seller (1) has an obligation to purchase the property, (2) can be compelled to repurchase the property, or (3) guarantees the buyer's return on investment. However, if the seller's responsibility to initiate and support operations suggests that a sale has taken place, profits should be recognized, except that some profits should be deferred to cover the risks and potential costs which may be associated with such involvement.

When the seller is responsible for initiating and supporting operations, the unique aspects of the arrangement must be analyzed, so that the substance of the transaction is properly treated for accounting purposes. In many cases, the seller assumes responsibility for the buyer's operating expenses and debt service until some level of operations has been attained. In other situations, one of the following activities may indicate the seller's obligation to support the buyer's operations:

> A seller obtains an interest as general partner in a limited partnership that acquires an interest in the property sold.
>
> A seller retains an equity interest in the property, such as an undivided interest or an equity interest in a joint venture that holds an interest in the property.
>
> A seller holds a receivable from a buyer for a significant part of the sales price and collection of the receivable is dependent upon the operation of the property.
>
> A seller enters into a management contract with the buyer that provides for compensation on terms not usual for the services to be rendered and that is not terminable by either seller or buyer.[12]

To demonstrate the accounting for a seller's obligation to initiate and support operations, assume that the Vrana Corporation is a developer of large apartment complexes and is currently involved in a complex of 200 units which it expects to complete next year (19X2). On December 31, 19X1, the corporation sold the complex to an investment firm for a total sales price of $2,200,000, including a $600,000 down payment, with the balance represented by an 8% first mortgage. The sales contract called for the seller to support operations of the complex for the first three years of operation (19X3, 19X4, and 19X5). Additional information is provided in items (A), (B), and (C) as follows:

(A) Projected costs associated with construction of complex:

Item	19X1	19X2	Total Costs
Land and improvements...................	$200,000	$ 20,000	$ 220,000
Zoning and architectural	80,000	—	80,000
Financing and other	40,000	20,000	60,000
Building construction	200,000	1,240,000	1,440,000
Total	$520,000	$1,280,000	$1,800,000

(B) Projected revenue and expenses associated with operations of complex:

---

[12] *Ibid.*, p. 16.

Item	19X3	19X4	19X5
Rental revenue	$180,000	$400,000	$500,000
Expense: Rental expense	$120,000	$200,000	$200,000
Debt service on mortgage	150,000	150,000	150,000
Total expenses	$270,000	$350,000	$350,000
Anticipated net income (net loss)	$ (90,000)	$ 50,000	$150,000
Less safety factor (⅓ of revenue *)	60,000	133,000	167,000
Adjusted anticipated net income (net loss) .	$(150,000)	$ (83,000)	$ (17,000)

*The safety factor equal to ⅓ of estimated revenues is recommended by the Committee on Accounting for Real Estate Transactions. This factor will result in a conservative measure of rental revenues and the anticipated net income or loss.

(C) Actual revenues and expenses:

	19X1	19X2	19X3	19X4	19X5
Construction costs	$520,000	$1,300,000	—	—	—
Rental revenue	—	—	$170,000	$345,000	$480,000
Rental expense and debt service	—	—	280,000	355,000	370,000

Illustration III demonstrates how the profit on this project is recognized. In this illustration, projected revenues and expenses are shown in

Illustration III—Profit Recognition

	Construction Period		Support Period		
	19X1	19X2	19X3	19X4	19X5
Revenue:					
Contract price	$2,200,000	$2,200,000	$2,200,000	$2,200,000	$2,200,000
Rental revenue:					
19X3	**120,000**	**120,000**	170,000	170,000	170,000
19X4	**267,000**	**267,000**	**267,000**	345,000	345,000
19X5	**333,000**	**333,000**	**333,000**	**345,000**[1]	370,000[2]
Total revenue	$2,920,000	$2,920,000	$2,970,000	$3,060,000	$3,085,000
Expenses:					
Construction costs:					
19X1	$ 520,000	$ 520,000	$ 520,000	$ 520,000	$ 520,000
19X2	**1,280,000**	1,300,000	1,300,000	1,300,000	1,300,000
Rental expenses and debt service:					
19X3	**270,000**	**270,000**	280,000	280,000	280,000
19X4	**350,000**	**350,000**	**350,000**	355,000	355,000
19X5	**350,000**	**350,000**	**350,000**	**350,000**	370,000
Total expenses	$2,770,000	$2,790,000	$2,800,000	$2,805,000	$2,825,000
Net profit	$ 150,000	$ 130,000	$ 170,000	$ 255,000	$ 260,000
Total profit to be recognized $\left(\frac{\text{Costs to date}}{\text{Total costs}} \times \text{Net profit}\right)$	$ 28,159[3]	$ 84,803	$ 127,500	$ 223,182	$ 260,000
Total profit recognized in prior periods	—	28,159	84,803	127,500	223,182
Profit recognized this period	$ 28,159	$ 56,644	$ 42,697	$ 95,682	$ 36,818

[1] Because rental revenues in 19X4 exceed the adjusted rental revenue projected for 19X5, the 19X5 projection can be based on 19X4 actual results attained, unless there is evidence which suggests that current occupancy rates cannot be sustained.

[2] Rental revenues which exceed "support costs" do not accrue to the seller; therefore, only $370,000 of rental revenue may be recognized.

[3] $\frac{\$ 520,000}{\$2,770,000} \times \$150,000 = \$28,159$

bold type, and the projected revenues reflect the adjustment for the safety factor. The recognized profit consists of the following:

1. Revenues:
   (a) the contract price plus
   (b) the rental revenues (item (B)).
2. Less expenses:
   (a) construction costs (item (A)) plus
   (b) rental expense (item (B)) plus
   (c) debt service (item (B)).
3. The profit represented by the difference between the revenues in (1) and the expenses in (2) is recognized on the basis of actual costs incurred to date compared to total costs (i.e., on a percentage-of-completion basis).

ACCOUNTING FOR FRANCHISE OPERATIONS

Franchising is an established means of distributing goods or services, as evidenced by the traditional automobile, beverage, and gasoline franchises. The 1960's were the start of a "franchise boom," in which franchising experienced tremendous growth. Today, franchising is associated with many types of businesses, including tax services, restaurants, book stores, tobacco stores, convenience grocery stores, computer programming schools, and dance studios. Franchising operations account for over 30% of retail sales and thus make an important contribution to the gross national product.

The Nature of Franchising

A workable definition of franchising is difficult to achieve due to the complexity and diversity of this activity. However, the Federal Trade Commission's ad hoc Committee on Franchising defines franchising as follows:

> At one extreme it is a simple grant from one party to another to sell the granting party's goods. At the other extreme, a franchise relationship is a comprehensive business arrangement in which the franchisor licenses his trade name and trademark; imparts, in confidence, his know-how; and on a continuing basis, provides guidance and details concerning the precise manner in which the franchisee must operate his establishment.

The following major features have been identified as being descriptive of a franchise:

1. The relation between the two parties is contractual, and an instrument of agreement, confirming the rights and responsibilities of each party, is in force for a specified period of time.
2. The continuing relation has as its purpose the efficient distribution of a product or service — or an entire business concept within a particular market area.

3. Both parties contribute resources towards the establishment and maintenance of the franchise. In the case of the franchisor, its contribution may be a trademark, a company reputation, products, procedures, manpower, equipment, a process, etc. The franchisee usually contributes operating capital, as well as the managerial and operational resources required for the initiation and continuation of the local franchised business.
4. The contract between the parties outlines and describes the specific marketing practices to be followed and details the contribution of each party to the operation of the business. It also sets forth certain standards of operating procedure to which both parties agree to conform.
5. The establishment of the franchised business creates a business entity which will, in most cases, require and support the full-time business activity of the franchisee. (There are numerous other contractual distribution arrangements in which a local businessman becomes the "authorized distributor" or "representative" for the sale of a particular good or service, along with many others. But such sale usually represents only a portion of the businessman's total business.)
6. Both the franchisee and the franchisor participate in a common public identity. This identity is achieved most often through the use of common trade names or trademarks and is frequently reinforced through advertising programs designed to promote the recognition and acceptance of these within the franchisee's market area.[13]

A franchising arrangement offers the franchisor an opportunity to distribute a product and/or service and, at the same time, minimize investment in franchised outlets. The franchisor capitalizes on the desire of individuals to own their own businesses, and thus gains the financial rewards which result from providing the franchisee with intangible rights (processes and trade names), services (advertising, site location, training, and accounting), equipment, inventories, capital, and leased facilities. The franchisor's rewards are (1) an initial franchise fee, (2) proceeds from the sale of equipment and inventory, and (3) a continuing fee based on future operations of the franchisee.

Franchisees also benefit in a number of ways: assistance in financing, training, volume purchases of inventory, and guidance from the franchisor. The franchisee, however, must pay for these services, and must be willing to accept the franchisor's control over operations.

Income Recognition and Determination

In the late 1960's, the business press began to express concern over the accounting practices of franchisors. In the summer of 1969, the SEC indicated that revenue reported by franchisors might not be valid. It had become apparent that questionable accounting for initial franchise fees had exaggerated the "true" profitability of franchisors, and thereby supported overstated market values of franchisor's corporate stock. In addition to questionable accounting methods, the courts and legislators

---

[13] "Franchised Distribution," Report No. 253 (New York: The Conference Board, Inc., 1971), p. 3.

were attempting to identify and correct the evils of a business form which often made franchisees the victims of unscrupulous franchisors.

The questionable accounting practices primarily involved recognizing initial franchise fees as revenue at the time an agreement was signed, even if the franchisor was committed to provide substantial future services to the franchisee. In addition to this "front-end loading" of income, franchisors often failed to reflect the collectibility of receivables from franchisees and to properly impute interest on such receivables. In "Accounting for Initial Franchise Fee Revenue," which appeared in the January, 1970, issue of *The Journal of Accountancy*, Archibald E. MacKay identified two separate problems:

> (1) When should the initial franchisee fee be included in revenue? (a timing problem); (2) What is the collectibility of the receivable representing the franchisee's unpaid portion of the initial fee? (a valuation problem)

In 1973, in response to criticisms of franchise accounting, the AICPA's Committee on Franchise Accounting and Auditing issued an accounting industry guide, *Accounting for Franchise Fee Revenue*. The specialized principles and practices contained in this guide have subsequently been extracted by the Financial Accounting Standards Board and presented in a separate statement of financial accounting standards. The major conclusions of this statement are discussed in the following paragraphs.

Initial Franchise Fee. The initial franchise fee represents compensation for establishing the franchise agreement, and for providing certain initial services associated with the agreement (e.g., site selection, training, financing). However, if the initial fee includes payment for the use of intangible rights over the life of the franchise agreement, an appropriate portion of the initial fee should be allocated over the term for which intangible rights are to be provided. The Committee on Franchise Accounting and Auditing considered the nature of the initial franchise fee, and concluded that:

> Perhaps the most important consideration is whether the initial fee is earned by the franchisor without reference to the life of the agreement. In most cases, after the franchisor has performed the initial responsibilities assumed in the agreement, amounts received as an initial fee are irrevocably his regardless of whether the franchisee actually begins operation or operations are successful.
>
> . . . where there is no direct relationship between the initial fee and the life of the agreement and the fee is irrevocably the property of the franchisor, there is no reason to require recognition of the fee over the life of the agreement.[14]

The concept of substantial performance is really the key to recognition of the initial franchise fee. Therefore, when all material services or conditions relating to the sale have been substantially performed by the

---

[14] Committee on Franchise Accounting and Auditing, *Accounting for Franchise Fee Revenue* (New York: American Institute of Certified Public Accountants, 1973), p. 7.

franchisor, revenue from the initial franchise fee should be recognized. Substantial performance by the franchisor represents the consummation of the transaction and is evidenced when:

> (a) the franchisor has no remaining obligation or intent—by agreement, trade practice, or law— to refund any cash received or forgive any unpaid notes or receivables; (b) substantially all of the initial services of the franchisor required by the franchise agreement have been performed; and (c) no other material conditions or obligations related to the determination of substantial performance exist.[15]

The commencement of operations by the franchisee has become recognized as the earliest point at which substantial performance is indicated. Certainly, conditions which suggest a later recognition of the franchise fee should be evaluated. For example, a franchisor's commitment to manage an outlet for several months after operations begin would indicate that revenue should be deferred until substantial performance has occurred.

Although the basis for recognition of the initial fee should be the criterion of substantial performance, there are circumstances when the nature of the initial fee may indicate a different treatment. For example, if the franchisor has an option to acquire the franchisee's business, and there is little evidence to suggest that the option will not be exercised, the initial franchise fee should not be recognized as revenue. Instead, the fee should be deferred until the option is exercised, at which time the fee will be used to reduce the franchisor's basis (investment) in the acquired franchise business. In some instances, the initial franchise fee will also represent compensation for items other than basic franchise rights and initial services. For example, the initial fee may also include the selling price of equipment or inventory transferred to the franchise. Therefore, a relevant portion of the initial fee, representing the fair market value of such other items, may be recognized when the title to property is transferred.

Determining substantial performance with respect to area franchises requires special attention. An area franchise transfers rights for a particular geographical area in which a number of actual franchise outlets may be established. These outlets will either be operated by the purchaser of the area franchise, or by individuals who acquire rights from the initial purchaser. If the franchisor is required to provide initial services regardless of the number of individual franchise outlets within the area, the concept of substantial performance should be applied to the area as a whole. However, if the franchisor's responsibility extends to individual franchise outlets, it may be necessary to view the franchise agreement as being divisible among the estimated number of outlets. Revenue from the initial fee would then be recognized in proportion to

---

[15] *Statement of Financial Accounting Standards, No. 45,* "Accounting for Franchise Fee Revenue" (Stamford: Financial Accounting Standards Board, 1981), par. 5.

the number of outlets for which substantial performance has taken place.

Continuing Fees. Continuing fees are designed to compensate the franchisor for providing specific future services, such as advertising, and for the continued use of intangible rights by the franchisee. These fees should be accounted for on the accrual basis, as they are earned. Expenses relating to these fees should be matched against the revenues when recognized. If the continuing fees are not adequate to cover continuing costs plus a reasonable profit, a portion of the initial franchise fee should be deferred and should be recognized when such continuing costs are incurred.

Certain franchise agreements allow the franchisee to purchase from the franchisor some or all of the equipment or services necessary for operations. If the purchase price for such items is less than the selling price charged other customers or does not provide the franchisor with a reasonable profit, a portion of the initial franchise fee should be deferred and accounted for as an adjustment to the selling price of the items when the sale occurs.

Collectibility of Fees. In many cases, a portion of the initial franchise fee will be represented by a receivable from the franchisee. An evaluation of the collectibility of such receivables should be made, and allowance for collection losses should be established if appropriate. In certain extreme cases, uncertainty regarding the collectibility of the franchise fee may require the use of either the installment method or the cost recovery method of accounting for revenue.

Accounting for Franchising Costs. In principle, costs directly associated with franchises should be deferred until the related revenue is recognized, although the amount of such deferred costs should not exceed the anticipated revenue less estimated additional related costs. In addition, there are often franchise costs which cannot be directly associated with specific franchises, or which are reusable by successive franchisees (e.g., architectural fees for store design). Deferral of these costs is arbitrary; therefore, indirect costs which are of a regular and recurring nature should be expensed as incurred if they are incurred irrespective of the level of franchise sales (e.g., general and administrative expenses).

Some of the various aspects of accounting for franchising transactions are demonstrated in Illustration IV.

Illustration IV—Accounting for Franchising Transactions

Facts:

The franchise agreement calls for an initial and irrevocable fee of $50,000 to be paid as follows:

$10,000 at signing of agreement (July 1, 19X1)
$ 5,000 upon commencement of operations (November 1, 19X1)
$35,000 covered by a non-interest-bearing note calling for 7 annual payments of $5,000 beginning on July 1, 19X2.

Direct costs associated with the initial fee are as follows:

$ 8,000 incurred for equipment, title to which passed upon signing of agreement. Fair market value of the equipment is $12,000.
$14,000 incurred for initial services; $6,000 incurred prior to signing, the balance to be incurred through November 1, 19X1.

The agreement also calls for a continuing fee of 10% of gross sales, estimated to be $9,000 per month the first three years and $15,000 a month thereafter. Continuing costs incurred by the franchisor are expected to be $1,000 per month. These costs have a fair market value of $1,100.

The life of the agreement is 10 years.

Analysis:

Computation of franchisor's net income:

	July, 19X1	November, 19X1	For the Year Ending June 30, 19X2
Revenues:			
Initial fee		$21,832[2]	
Continuing fee			$ 8,800[3]
Interest income			2,083[4]
Other	$12,000[1]		
Total revenues	$12,000	$21,832	$10,883
Expenses:			
Cost of equipment	$ 8,000		
Initial services		$14,000	
Continuing expenses			$ 8,000
Total expenses	$ 8,000	$14,000	$ 8,000
Net income	$ 4,000	$ 7,832	$ 2,883

[1] The fair market value of the equipment transferred is $12,000.
[2] Assume that interest on the note should be imputed at 8%. Therefore, the net present value of the note is $26,032 ($5,000 × 5.20637), and total interest is $8,968 ($35,000 − $26,032). The initial fee is calculated as follows:

Total initial fee	$50,000
Less imputed interest	8,968
	$41,032
Value of equipment	12,000
Value of other initial services before adjustment for inadequate continuing fees	$29,032

The continuing fees are not adequate to cover continuing costs and a reasonable profit. Assuming that the continuing services have a fair market value of $1,100 per month, the continuing fee will only cover $900 (10% × $9,000) of this. Therefore, the deficiency of $200 per month for the first three years of the agreement must be covered by a portion of the initial fee as follows:

Initial fee before adjustment (above)	$29,032
Deficiency ($200 × 36 months)	7,200
Adjusted initial fee	$21,832

[3] This represents $7,200 (10% × $9,000 × 8 months) of continuing fees as stated, plus $200 per month for 8 months ($1,600), which represents the deficiency discussed in Note 2.
[4] Interest on principal (8% × $26,032).

Disclosure Requirements

Before the industry guide on franchising was issued, disclosure of franchise operations left much to be desired. For example, franchisors rarely disclosed the number of franchises yet to be sold or the number of franchises acquired by the franchisor. In the absence of such disclosure, investors were unable to assess properly the future growth of franchisors. In response, the following specific disclosure requirements were established:[16]

1. The basis of accounting for all important aspects of the franchise transaction, such as initial fees, deferred costs, future commitments, and continuing fees.
2. Those sales accounted for by either the installment or cost recovery methods, the sales price of such franchises, the revenue and related deferred costs, and the periods in which such fees become payable. Amounts originally deferred but later recognized because uncertainties have been resolved should also be disclosed.
3. Segregation of initial franchise fees from other franchise revenues. If it is probable that initial franchise fee revenue will decline because sales are predictably reaching a saturation point, disclosure of this fact should be made.
4. Segregation of revenues and costs associated with franchisor operated outlets.
5. When significant changes take place during the period, a footnote should disclose the number of (a) franchises sold, (b) franchises repurchased during the period, (c) outlets in operation, and (d) franchisor-owned outlets in operation.

Although the franchise boom of the 1960's has tapered off drastically, franchising is an important business with which accountants should be familiar. Accounting for franchises has gained a new respectability as a result of reporting in accordance with generally accepted accounting principles.

QUESTIONS

1. For retail land sales, what three conditions must be fulfilled before a sale can be recognized under either the accrual method or the installment method?
2. Describe the deposit method of accounting and indicate when it is used.
3. Briefly summarize the criteria which must be met before the accrual method of accounting for retail land sales can be used. Indicate what types of estimates are involved when a retail land sale is recorded under the accrual method.
4. What relevant criteria are utilized in determining the valuation discount to be applied to a seller's contracts receivable from retail land sales?

---

[16] *Ibid.*, pars. 20-23.

5. How should a retail land seller account for revenues associated with future performance relating to improvements?

6. How is the gain or loss determined on default of an installment contract receivable from a retail land sale?

7. If a change is made from the installment method to the accrual method of accounting for retail land sales, how is it accounted for, and what determines its effect upon income?

8. For real estate sales other than retail land sales, identify the conditions which must be present if the seller's use of the accrual method of accounting is justified.

9. Explain why the amount of the down payment is emphasized in accounting for real estate sales. When is a down payment considered sufficient to permit the use of accrual accounting by the seller in real estate sales other than retail land?

10. What is the underlying importance of a buyer's continuing investment in a property? How is a buyer's continuing investment indicated?

11. What are the advantages of franchising to the franchisor? To the franchisee?

12. What purpose is served by imputing interest on the installment portions of the initial franchise fee? How might the proper annual interest rate be determined?

13. What criteria are employed for determining when revenues from the initial franchise fee should be recognized?

14. What determines substantial performance for purposes of recognizing the initial franchise fee?

15. How is the recognition of the initial franchise fee affected if continuing franchise fees are less than continuing costs?

16. How should doubts concerning the collectibility of future payments from the franchisee be dealt with by the franchisor?

EXERCISES

Present value tables are on pages 942-943.

Exercise 1. Joint-Venture, Inc., was formed in January, 19X3, by a group of seven Wisconsin business people for the purpose of acquiring and developing secondary homesite projects. The firm's initial capitalization was $1,000,000.

In March, 19X3, Joint-Venture acquired a large, partially developed lake development in northwestern Wisconsin. The property, which contained 500 two-acre lots, was purchased from a Chicago bank that had obtained the property through default on a first mortgage by an Illinois developer. The price of the project was $1,000,000, of which Joint-Venture paid $250,000 down and financed the balance with a first mortgage note to First Bank and Trust of Wisconsin. Most of the development work which had been done on the project by the previous owner related to the lake, which was nearly complete. Joint-Venture immediately began making improvements necessary to make the lots salable, such as access roads, finishing of beach frontage, and providing for utilities. The cost of these improvements totaled $600,000. As a part of the proposed sales contracts for the lots, a clubhouse, tennis courts, and a nine-hole golf course were eventually to be provided by Joint-Venture. The estimated cost of these improvements was $1,250,000.

In August, 19X3, Joint-Venture began selling the lots at prices ranging from $6,000 to $8,000. The terms of sale required a 10% down payment, with the balance to be paid within 6 months. Refunds were allowable only if the sales contract was canceled within 2 months of initiation. For the year 19X3, 110 contracts had been initiated, 50 of which had been paid in full, 30 of which were still in force as of December 31, 19X3, and the remaining 30 canceled.

In view of recommended accounting practice, how should Joint-Venture, Inc., account for its revenues? When should revenue and profit be recognized? Discuss fully.

Exercise 2. Describe the basic differences between the deposit, accrual, and installment methods for accounting for retail land sales with respect to:

(1) when it is appropriate to use the method,
(2) valuation of the buyer's receivable,
(3) cancellation losses on sales, and
(4) recognition of interest income.

Exercise 3. Country Club Living, Inc., uses the accrual method to account for its retail land sales. For the year 19X6, Country Club recorded $300,000 in sales of improved lots under contracts which required a 15% nonrefundable down payment, with the balance of the contract to be paid in equal installments due at the end of each of the next four years, with 8% interest on the unpaid balance of the receivable. Country Club estimated that 5% of the contracts would be canceled.

The minimum annual interest rate charged by local commercial banks and retail organizations for consumer personal property installment credit is 12%.

Determine what amounts Country Club should recognize as interest on 19X6 sales for the years 19X6 and 19X8.

Exercise 4. Easyliving Estates, a limited partnership involved in retail land sales, uses the installment method to account for its sales. The following information relates to 19X1, Easyliving's first year of operations.

Sales of lots totaled $975,000.

Direct costs related to gross sales were $390,000, which consisted of $300,000 for land previously purchased and developed, $32,000 for direct selling expenses, and $58,000 for future improvement costs.

Collections on installment contracts totaled $345,000, including $65,000 for interest.

Sales of $48,750 were canceled during 19X1. No installment payments were received on these sales. Original cost values should be assigned to repossessed land and improvements.

Prepare all of the journal entries to record Easyliving Estates' transactions for 19X1.

Exercise 5. Wilderness, Ltd., a 2-year-old land development operation, has been accounting for its land sales under the installment method. The firm's recently hired controller has determined that the firm's collection experience permits it to utilize the accrual method. The controller consults with Wilderness' auditors, Lewis and Clark, who indicate that they would concur with the change, which is to be effective as of December 31, 19X2. The following information relates to 19X1 and 19X2 land sales:

Installment contracts receivable balance as of December 31, 19X2:

19X1 sales	$450,000
19X2 sales	$600,000

The 19X1 gross profit percentage on real estate sales is 50%.

The 19X2 gross profit percentage on real estate sales is 55%.

Minimum annual interest rate charged by local banks and retail stores for installment credit for consumer personal property loans in 19X1 and 19X2 is 12%.

There were no future improvements to be made related to the 19X1 and 19X2 sales.

All sales contracts receivable are originally payable in 5 equal installments to be paid at the end of each year.

Compute the effect on 19X2 income of the change from the installment to the accrual method. Prepare the journal entries to record the change.

Exercise 6. Drayco Development Company has sold various properties in the Johnson, Iowa area. The transactions represent different types of continuing involvement by the seller, and Drayco has asked your assistance in selecting the proper method of accounting for each sale. Analyze independently each of the following situations to determine if a sale has taken place, and describe how any revenue should be recognized.

(1) Drayco has sold Sherwood Mall, Johnson's newest shopping center, to Pilot Promotions, Inc. Drayco will continue to operate the property at its own risk until a sufficient number of tenants are obtained to produce the level of rentals specified. If the number of rentals has not reached the specified level within one year from the date of sale, Drayco will repurchase the property.

(2) Star Attractions has purchased the Johnson Cinema from Drayco. Drayco will obtain permanent financing for Star.

(3) Drayco has sold 35% of the single-family units in a condominium project; the units have been sold to individual purchasers. Construction on the entire project is well beyond preliminary stages and there is no chance that the project will revert to rentals versus condominium sales.

(4) Drayco has sold the Barnes Building and is managing it for the new owners. For a fee of $2,500 per month, Drayco provides management services relating to this executive office site. The prevailing rate for such services is $4,000 per month.

(5) The city of Johnson purchased land from Drayco for a municipal golf course. Drayco has agreed to construct certain facilities on the land and to provide offsite improvements.

(6) Drayco is constructing the Larabee Arms Hotel on Main Street. Under the terms of the agreement, Dave Larabee has the right to defer payment until the work is completed in 19X2.

Exercise 7. Rocky Top Homesites, Inc., began operations in 19X4 by purchasing underdeveloped land for eventual resale. In mid-19X5, the firm began selling partially improved primary homesites. Due to the uncertainty regarding Rocky Top's ability to finance required future improvements, the deposit method of accounting was initially utilized to record sales. In 19X5, Rocky Top recorded the following sales and collection activities:

> 120 lots sold at $5,000 each; total, $600,000
> $120,000 cash collected, of which $20,000 related to 20
> contracts which were canceled

The total costs directly associated with the lots sold (selling, commissions, and land costs) totaled $300,000. The cost of the land which was retained by Rocky Top upon cancellation of the contracts was $40,000.

At the end of 19X5, it is determined that Rocky Top will be able to use the accrual method of accounting, since it has secured additional financing to complete improvments.

Prepare the journal entries to record the transactions.

Exercise 8. Liberty, Inc., a land development company, has completed negotiations for the sale of a large industrial site to Westby Company. The total sales price of the site was $6,350,000, which Westby financed with a down payment of $60,000 in cash, a $575,000 7-year note which Liberty discounted at its bank without recourse for $534,000, and a 90%, $5,715,000 first mortgage note to Cleveland State Bank. The terms and amount of the loan from Cleveland State were considered customary for the property being financed.

Evaluate the adequacy of Westby's down payment and continuing investment in the property to determine if Liberty may recognize this transaction as a sale.

Exercise 9. Hot Oven Bakeries is considering the possibility of selling franchises to smaller outlets in various cities in the Midwest. The corporate officers are concerned with the method of revenue recognition for such contracts.

Provide an explanation of the method of recognizing the revenues from the initial payment. Be sure to discuss factors which would delay such recognition. Do not discuss the subject of continuing fees or continuing costs.

Exercise 10. Lane Daley is about to purchase a franchise from RPM Motors, Inc. The contract provides for a 10-year term and an initial fee of $45,000, payable as follows: $15,000 at the date of signing, $20,000 three months after signing, and the balance one year after signing. The expected date of signing is January 1, 19X6. A continuing fee of 2% of gross sales is also to be paid to the franchisor. Monthly gross sales are expected to be $20,000 for the first four years and $37,500 for the remainder of the contract.

Costs associated with the initial fee are as follows:

(a) Title to a garage, with a cost of $15,000, is to be transferred to the franchisee on the day the agreement is signed. The fair market value of the garage is $18,000.

(b) An additional $5,000 for initial services are incurred on January 17, 19X6.

There are no associated continuing costs. The contract contains a provision which states that if the garage is damaged in any way prior to the opening of business (expected to be one month after signing of the agreement), the contract is voidable.

(1) Assuming that the garage is not damaged prior to opening, and that RPM Motors has a fiscal year ending December 31, prepare schedules in good form to determine the amount of income recognized at January 1, February 1, and December 31, 19X6.

(2) Prepare all journal entries on the books of the franchisor to record the transactions for the first year of the contract.

Exercise 11. Tacos Unlimited sells franchises for fast food outlets in different parts of the country. One such contract is signed on January 15, 19X6. The agreement calls for an initial payment of $22,000 by the franchisee upon the signing of the agreement, with subsequent annual payments of $10,000 each for four years. The installments carry no interest, although similar installment loans would be made at a 10% interest rate. The franchisor's initial costs are $22,500, to be incurred uniformly over the six-month period prior to the scheduled opening date of July 15, 19X6. No future payments are to be made by the franchisee, although there will be continuing costs of $1,800 per year for services rendered during the ten-year term of the contract. The normal return for the franchisor on continuing operations involving other such franchise outlets is 10%.

(1) Prepare schedules showing how much income would be recognized by the franchisor at the time of signing and at opening.

(2) Prepare journal entries on the books of the franchisor to record all activity through January 15, 19X7.

PROBLEMS

Present value tables are on pages 942-943.

Problem 2-1. Following is the December 31, 19X6 trial balance of Mo-Jo Land Sales, Inc.

Cash	28,092	
Contracts Receivable	94,541	
Land and Improvements Inventory	120,000	
Repossessed Land Inventory	19,567	
Prepaid Expenses	4,000	
Accounts Payable		5,000
Real Estate Taxes Payable		4,700
Accrued Expenses...........................		2,500
Note Payable		140,000
Deferred Revenue		50,000
Common Stock		20,000
Paid-In Capital in Excess of Par		40,000
Sales		100,000
Cost of Sales..............................	60,000	
Wages Expense	21,300	
Selling Expenses	7,500	
Miscellaneous Expenses	2,500	
Real Estate Taxes Expense	4,700	
	362,200	362,200

Mo-Jo's first year of operations was 19X6, when it began selling low-priced lots in its development, Oakwood Acres. The company had no prior collection experience and was not able to predict its collection experience on current sales. The terms of the sales contract called for a 10% initial down payment, with the balance to be paid over 4 years and interest at 8% on the unpaid balance. The following information relates to the firm's 19X6 operations:

(a) Total costs traceable to the land sales amount to $100,000, allocated as follows:

Land...	$60,000
Future improvements	35,000
Selling expenses	5,000

(b) Deferred revenue relates to improvements yet to be made at Oakwood Acres on lots sold.

(c) Collections for 19X6 were as follows:

Contract	Down Payment	Principal	Interest	Uncollected
Continuing	$12,250	$11,500	$4,209	—
Canceled	2,750	3,250	1,933	$19,567

(d) Repossessed land from canceled sales contracts was recorded by debiting Repossessed Land Inventory and crediting Contracts Receivable for the unpaid balance of the contract. Mo-Jo's management felt that the best approximation of the value of repossessed land was the original cost actually incurred by the firm, excluding direct selling costs.

(e) Interest income was erroneously credited to the land contracts receivable account.

Required:

Revise the December 31, 19X6, trial balance to arrive at an adjusted trial balance. Use the following format:

12/31/X6 Trial Balance		Adjustments		Adjusted 12/31/X6 Trial Balance	
Dr.	Cr.	Dr.	Cr.	Dr.	Cr.

Note: Formal journal entries are not required. However, computations supporting your adjustments should be in good form.

Problem 2-2. The Property Development Division of Gulf and Eastern Corporation, a large conglomerate firm, sold all of the lots in its Sleepy Hollow project in Pocatello, Idaho, in January, 19X1. The following information relates to sales in Sleepy Hollow:

(a) Two hundred thirty-five (235) lots were sold at a total price of $6,500,000. The terms of the sales contracts called for a nonrefundable down payment of 10% of the sales price, with the balance to be paid in equal yearly installments due at the end of each of 5 years, and interest at 4% per year.

(b) The cost of land related to uncanceled sales for the Sleepy Hollow project totaled $3,000,000. Direct selling costs related to the entire project were $400,000. In addition, future improvement costs traceable to uncanceled sales were $500,000, one half of which were to be paid in 19X2 and the balance in 19X4.

(c) Estimated and actual cancellation losses were 6% of gross sales. All cancellations occurred after the down payment but prior to the due date of the first installment.

(d) The interest rate charged by local banks and retail establishments for consumer personal property credit was 10% per year.

Assume that Gulf and Eastern meets all of the criteria for use of the accrual method to account for the 19X1 Sleepy Hollow land sales.

Required:

(1) Prepare the schedules to compute net income from Sleepy Hollow's 19X1 sales for the years 19X1 through 19X5.

(2) Prepare the necessary journal entries to record the 19X1 Sleepy Hollow transactions.

Problem 2-3. South Lansing Recreational Developments, Inc., completed Northern Aire, a large secondary homesite project, in June of 19X4, the last month of its fiscal year. In July, 19X4, South Lansing began selling lots in Northern Aire. The development was well received, and all of the 200 lots were sold in the first month. All of the 1.5-acre lots were priced at $4,500. The sales contracts for the lots called for a nonrefundable down payment of 10%, with the balance to be paid in five equal installments due each June 30, with interest at 6% per year on the unpaid balance.

The following additional information relates to the 200-lot Northern Aire development project:

(a) Estimated cancellation losses from uncollectible contracts are 5% of gross sales, less the initial down payments received.

(b) The cost of land and improvements totaled $300,000; direct selling expenses were $50,000; and future improvement costs are estimated at $100,000. One half of the future improvement costs were to be paid in the fiscal year ending June 30, 19X7, and the balance in the fiscal year ending June 30, 19X9.

(c) Sales of $45,000 were canceled in the 19X4-X5 fiscal year. No installment payments were received on these sales. Management believes that the most appropriate value to assign to repossessed land and the improvements is their original cost, excluding direct selling expenses.

(d) The prevailing interest rate for installment loans for consumer personal property was 12% at the time of the initial sales.

Required:

(1) Prepare schedules to compute South Lansing's net income from the Northern Aire project for the fiscal years ending June 30, 19X5, through June 30, 19X9, using the installment method to account for land sales.

(2) Prepare schedules to compute South Lansing's net income from the Northern Aire project for the fiscal years ending June 30, 19X5, through June 30, 19X9, using the accrual method.

Problem 2-4. Referring to Problem 2-3, assume that as of July 1, 19X6, South Lansing Recreational Developments, Inc., meets the qualifications for the use of the accrual method to account for the revenues received from its Northern Aire development. The following additional information relates to the Northern Aire development as of July 1, 19X6:

(a) All future improvement costs relating to uncanceled contracts were unpaid.

(b) No additional cancellation losses on Northern Aire's contracts receivable were anticipated.

Required:

(1) Prepare all journal entries to record South Lansing's transactions related to the Northern Aire development for the fiscal years ending June 30, 19X5, and June 30, 19X6, under the installment method.

(2) Prepare journal entries to record the transactions related to the Northern Aire development for the fiscal year ended June 30, 19X7.

Problem 2-5. Pleasant Valley Developers have just opened their newest retirement development, which consists of 100 lots overlooking Stark Lake. Eventually a clubhouse and tennis courts will be constructed. Sales and cost data on a per lot basis are as follows:

Selling price		$20,000
Costs:		
Land	$5,000	
Existing improvements	5,000	
Planned improvements (to be incurred in 19X2)	4,000	
Marketing	2,000	16,000
Gross profit		$ 4,000

The sales contract calls for a 10% down payment upon the signing of the contract, with the balance of the purchase price to be paid in six semiannual payments beginning six months after signing. These installment payments carry a stated interest rate of 6%, even though the interest rate charged on consumer installment credit is 12%.

It is expected that 10% of the contracts will be canceled prior to the first installment due date and that another 5% of the *original* contracts will be canceled immediately after payment of the first installment. Repossessed lots are recorded at their original book value of recoverable costs. All *principal* payments (i.e., payments excluding interest) will be refunded upon cancellation of a contract except for $1,500 of the down payment.

All 100 lots are sold on January 1, 19X1.

Required:

  (1) Calculate the following values, assuming that the installment method is used:

    (a) Interest income for 19X1.

    (b) Deferred gross profit balance at December 31, 19X2.

    (c) Loss (gain) on cancellations recognized in 19X1.

  (2) Calculate the following values, assuming that the accrual method is used:

    (a) Interest income for 19X1.

    (b) Deferred revenue on future improvements as of January 1, 19X1.

    (c) Valuation discount balance at December 31, 19X1.

Problem 2-6. Haven Hill Properties, Inc., commenced operations in 19X1 by purchasing two large tracts of undeveloped land (Heavenly Pleasures and Slumber City). Development work was undertaken immediately.

In June, 19X1, Haven began selling the 200 lots in its exclusive Heavenly Pleasures development. Due to uncertainties surrounding Haven Hill's ability to provide future improvements required by the sales contracts for Heavenly Pleasures, the deposit method of accounting was used during 19X1 to record sales.

As of December 31, 19X1, Haven Hill's balance sheet appeared as follows:

Cash	$463,406	Accounts payable	$ 2,000
Land and improvements		Customer deposits	181,906
inventory[1]	300,000	Common stock, $2 par	40,000
Miscellaneous prepaid		Paid-in capital in excess of	
expenses	1,500	par	760,000
Deferred charges[2]	200,000	Retained earnings	(10,000)
Equipment (net)	9,000		
	$973,906		$973,906

[1] Costs related to unsold Heavenly Pleasures lots (2/3) and the Slumber City Development (1/3).
[2] Land and improvement costs associated with 19X1 Heavenly Pleasures sales.

The sales contracts for all lots in Heavenly Pleasures call for a sales price of $5,000. A 20% nonrefundable down payment is required at the time the contract is signed, with the balance to be paid in equal installments which are due at the end of each quarter for the next two years, and interest at 8% per year on the unpaid balance. During 19X1, 50 sales contracts were initiated during the third quarter. Installment payments were received on each of these sales at the end of the third and fourth quarters. Fifty (50) sales were also made in the fourth quarter of 19X1, and one installment payment was received by Haven Hill on each sale. Because of the high initial down payment and the nature of the Heavenly Pleasures development, no cancellations on lots were experienced in 19X1, and Haven Hill's management expected none in association with the project.

The interest rate charged by local banks and retail organizations for consumer installment credit in 19X1 and 19X2 was 12%. With this information, Haven Hill's accountant prepared the following payment and amortization schedules for the 50 lots sold in Heavenly Pleasures during the third quarter of 19X1.

Payment Number	Amount Collected	Principal	Interest at 2%	Receivable Balance	Unamortized Discount	Interest Income at 3%	Discount Amortization
0				$200,000[3]	$8,348		
1	$27,302[4]	$23,302	$4,000	176,698	6,598	$5,750	$1,750
2	27,302	23,768	3,534	152,930	5,029	5,103	1,569
3	27,302	24,243	3,059	128,687	3,651	4,437	1,378
4	27,302	24,728	2,574	103,959	2,474	3,751	1,177
5	27,302	25,223	2,079	78,736	1,508	3,045	966
6	27,302	25,727	1,575	53,009	766	2,317	742
7	27,302	26,242	1,060	26,767	259	1,567	502
8	27,302	26,767	535	-0-	-0-	794	259

[3] Sales ($5,000 × 50) $250,000
Less 20% down payments 50,000
Unpaid balance $200,000
[4] 200,000 ÷ 7.32548 (2%, 8-period present value of an ordinary annuity factor) = $27,302

In 19X2, Haven Hill completed the development of Slumber City, a 400-lot, low cost project. The sales contracts for Slumber called for an initial down payment of 10% of the sales price of $1,000, with the balance to be paid in monthly install-ments over 5 years, and interest at 1% per month on the unpaid balance, the rate charged locally for installment consumer credit. In view of the small initial down payment and the high expected rate of cancellations, Haven Hill's management determined that the installment method of accounting was appropriate to account for Slumber City's sales.

The following information relates to Haven Hill's 19X2 activities:

(a) Of the remaining lots in the Heavenly Pleasures development, 50 lots were sold in each of the first two quarters of 19X2. Collections (excluding down payments) during 19X2 were as follows:

	1st Qtr.	2d Qtr.	3d Qtr.	4th Qtr.	Total
19X1 sales	$54,604	$ 54,604	$ 54,604	$ 54,604	$218,416
1st qtr. 19X2 sales.........	27,302	27,302	27,302	27,302	109,208
2d qtr. 19X2 sales	—	27,302	27,302	27,302	81,906
	$81,906	$109,208	$109,208	$109,208	$409,530

(b) $50,000 of future improvement costs, relating to 19X1 Heavenly Pleasures sales, were paid. Future improvement costs of $50,000, related to 19X2 Heavenly sales, were unpaid as of December 31, 19X2.

(c) 200 sales contracts for the Slumber City project were initiated. As of De-cember 31, 19X2, 150 of the Slumber City contracts were still in force. Collections in addition to down payments were:

	Principal	Interest	Unpaid Principal
Contracts in force	$10,500	$39,500	—
Canceled contracts	6,000	3,100	$39,000

The fair market value of land repossessed in connection with cancellations of Slumber City contracts was $10,000.

(d) Haven Hill's general and administrative expenses for 19X2 totaled $25,000, of which $1,000 was depreciation.

In mid-19X2, Haven Hill secured additional financing for future improvements. In view of this fact, management decided to use the accrual method to account for

Heavenly Pleasures sales, with the change in accounting procedure to be effective as of January 1, 19X2.

Required:

Prepare all journal entries, in good form, to record Haven Hill's 19X2 transactions, and prepare any schedules necessary to support your entries.

Problem 2-7. At a cost of $800,000, Mitchell Investments, Inc., recently completed construction of a 40,000-square-foot warehouse approximately two miles from a major airport. Mitchell has agreed to sell the warehouse to Mosner Industries with the following terms and conditions:

(a) The selling price of the property is $1,200,000 and the buyer will make a down payment upon closing as follows:
   1. A cash payment of $74,000,
   2. An $80,000 payment to the First Southern Bank of Atlanta, which represents the principal on a construction loan held by Mitchell from First Southern, and
   3. An irrevocable letter of credit from First Southern in the amount of $100,000.

(b) The balance of the purchase price will be financed by the buyer over the next 20 years at a stated interest rate of 10%. If financing were secured from an established lending institution, Mosner could have financed 80% of the purchase price over 25 years at a 10% interest rate. (Assume all loans would have required level annual payments of principal and interest).

(c) For the first 16 months, Mitchell will assume responsibility for managing the warehouse operations for Mosner in return for a management fee of $4,000 per month. Similar services would normally have a monthly value of $5,000.

Required:

(1) If the purchaser's down payment and/or continuing investment in the property are not adequate, how should the sale be accounted for and at what point may the accrual method be used?

(2) Calculate the amount of income to be recognized by Mitchell upon closing of the sale, assuming that a down payment equal to 20% of the sales value is the minimum required for this type of property.

Problem 2-8. Deacon Development and Management Corporation began work on a 200-unit apartment complex in early 19X4. On November 30, 19X4, Deacon completed contract arrangements to sell the complex to a large real estate investment syndicate. The sales contract called for Deacon to:

(a) Deliver to the buyer a legal title to the completed project, including all existing and subsequent improvements called for in the architect's plans, at a total contract price of $3,200,000.

(b) Deliver to the buyer a firm commitment from an outside lender for permanent financing of 75% of the total purchase price.

(c) Support operations of the complex for the first three years of its operation (19X6, 19X7, and 19X8).

(d) Perform property management services for five years subsequent to the end of the support period.

The following additional information relates to the apartment complex and its operations:

(a) The investment syndicate made a down payment of $800,000 cash to Deacon at the closing date.

(b) Deacon arranged a 20-year, 8% first mortgage for the balance of the purchase price in January, 19X5.

(c) The fair market value of Deacon's property management services was established at $20,000 per year.

(d) Costs incurred by Deacon and total costs estimated to complete the project as of December 31, 19X4, were:

	Costs to Date	Estimated Costs To Complete	Total Estimated Costs
Land	$400,000	-0-	$ 400,000
Feasibility, zoning, and architectural	75,000	-0-	75,000
Finance and other	125,000	$ 50,000	175,000
Site improvements	-0-	500,000	500,000
Building construction	-0-	1,250,000	1,250,000
	$600,000	$1,800,000	$2,400,000

On similar past projects, Deacon's actual costs have varied from estimates by less than one half of one percent.

(e) Deacon completed an extensive market research and feasibility study to analyze its cost estimates, the rent-up incubation period, and subsequent rent levels. The initial rent-up will commence in early 19X6. Based on its market analysis, the projected results are as follows:

	19X6	19X7	19X8
Rental expense	$ 175,000	$ 188,000	$ 221,000
Debt service*	245,000	245,000	245,000
Total	$ 420,000	$ 433,000	$ 466,000
Rental revenue	(540,000)	(600,000)	(720,000)
Anticipated net deficit (surplus) in cash flow	$(120,000)	$(167,000)	$(254,000)

*Level annual debt service payments = $2,400,000 ÷ 9.8181 (8%, 20-year PV of an ordinary annuity factor) = approximately $245,000 annual payment

Required:

Prepare a schedule to compute the projected net income for Deacon Development and Management Corporation from the sale of the apartment complex for the years 19X4-19X8. A safety factor of ⅓ should be used.

Problem 2-9. Corner Coops, Inc., is in the business of selling small retail grocery outlets on a franchise basis. Mitchell Christianson signed an agreement for such a franchise on January 12, 19X7, for a term of twenty years. The contract has the following provisions, which were negotiated between the two parties:

(a) An initial payment of $80,000 is to be paid in the following manner: $20,000 in cash at the opening of the franchise and the balance as a non-interest-bearing note for $60,000. The note is to be paid in five equal installments, each payable on the anniversary date of the opening.

(b) Of the initial payment, a portion is for equipment and fixtures, to which title is transferred at signing of the agreement, and a portion is for inventory to be supplied one month before the opening date of July 1, 19X7. The cost of the equipment and fixtures is $6,000, and they could be sold on the open market to yield a 20% gross profit. The retail value of the inventory is $8,000, which includes a 10% gross profit.

(c) Continuing fees are to be three fourths of one percent of monthly revenues. Monthly revenues are expected to be $30,000 for the first four years,

$40,000 for the next 12 years, and $50,000 for the last four years. This pattern has been established by experience, and was based on the demographic trends for the area in which the franchise is to be operated.

(d) Continuing costs for this establishment will be $350 per month for the entire contract period. This amount represents the cost of advertisements, supervision, and special bonuses to management. The market value for these services is $400.

(e) Other initial costs will total $7,000, and will be incurred prior to the opening.

(f) The franchisor has the option to discount the non-interest-bearing note at any time during the payment period. Normally notes are discounted at a rate of 10%.

Required:

Assuming that the opening occurs as scheduled, and that the note is immediately discounted, prepare the appropriate schedules to determine the amounts of income to be recognized by Corner Coops on January 12, June 1, and July 1, 19X7, and on June 30, 19X8.

Problem 2-10. Chicago Style Pizza, Inc., is selling pizza restaurant franchises to qualified franchisees under the following contractual agreement:

(a) An initial franchise fee of $40,000 is required of the franchisee, with $10,000 being paid upon the signing of the agreement and the balance due upon opening of the franchise. Initial costs incurred by the franchisor are estimated to be $7,000.

(b) An additional $10,000 is to be paid upon the delivery of special equipment which has a fair market value of $15,000. Delivery is to be made prior to opening. The payment represents only a recovery of costs.

(c) The contract states that the franchisor will guarantee operations of the franchise to the following extent for the first 18 months following opening:

     1. Guarantee the payment of franchisee's operating costs not covered by operating receipts. Operating costs are estimated to be $10,000 per month for the first twelve months and $9,500 per month for the next six months.

     2. If actual monthly receipts exceed the monthly operating costs, such excess will not accrue to the franchisor.

(d) Continuing fees are to be 2% of gross receipts per year, while estimated continuing costs are $160 per month for the first three years and $100 per month for the remaining seven years of the contract. The yearly receipts are estimated to be $110,000 for the first five years, $75,000 for the next three years, and $45,000 for the remaining two years. Generally the company's experience indicates that the continuing costs represent 80% of their fair market value.

(e) The contract states that the franchisor will provide personnel for the opening of the franchise and for a period of three months thereafter, during which time they agree to train local personnel for takeover at the end of the period. The cost of this program to the franchisor is estimated to be $1,500 per month.

(f) The franchisor will supply the franchisee with all necessary food inventory. During the first six months after opening, the franchisee may purchase inventory at cost (estimated to be $3,000 per month), even though the inventory would normally be sold to the franchisee for $3,300. After the first six months, the franchisee will pay for inventory at its normal selling price.

Required:

Prepare in good form a schedule which presents the amount of net income which should be recognized by the franchisor at the following points in time: prior to opening, opening, 3 months after opening, the next nine months, and the next six months.

Problem 2-11. Barbara Mittelstaedt has purchased an area franchise from Beta Company. Mittelstaedt paid for this purchase with a $90,000 note, payable in ten equal installments of $9,500 each, due on the anniversary date of the signing. The normal interest rate on similar notes is 8% per annum. The franchise is for ice cream shops which will be sold on a franchise basis to other individuals. Mittelstaedt has determined that three franchises would be ideal in this area, and has identified prospective buyers. The initial fees for the three establishments will be $50,000 each, but the individuals who purchase the franchise have the option of selecting one of three alternative payment plans. The plans are as follows:

(a) To sign serial notes, payable at the end of each year in the amount of $10,000 each until the entire $50,000 is paid. These notes are non-interest-bearing.

(b) To arrange bank financing for the entire amount prior to signing the agreement. The bank would presently charge 12% on such small business loans and would discount the amount to yield $50,000.

(c) Individually pay the $50,000 out of personal funds at the date of signing.

The three parties who are interested are X, Y, and Z. Associated with each of these agreements are some continuing costs in the amount of $1,800 per year, which represents 80% of their fair market value. As with the initial fee, there are three alternatives for payment of the continuing fees. The alternatives are:

(a) Payment of a fixed amount of $3,000 per year.

(b) Payment of 2% of the monthly gross revenues.

(c) Payment of a lump sum in the amount of $20,000 at the beginning of the ten-year contract.

The gross revenues are expected to be $15,000 per month over the life of the contract. The three area franchisees have selected the following payment alternatives:

Franchisee	Alternatives	
	Initial Fee	Continuing Fees
X	a	b
Y	c	c
Z	b	a

Required:

(1) Compute the amount of revenue to be recognized by Beta Company from the initial fee, assuming that no continuing costs are to be incurred.

(2) Analyze each alternative for both the initial fee and the continuing fees.

(3) Present the appropriate computations and schedules that will indicate the timing and amounts of revenue to be recognized by Mittelstaedt on each of the three franchise contracts for the first year after the opening of each franchise.

Problem 2-12. Gulf Fried Shrimp sells franchises to independent operators throughout the Southeastern part of the United States. The contract with the franchisee includes the following provisions:

(a) The franchisee is charged an initial fee of $25,000. Of this amount, $5,000 is payable when the agreement is signed, and a $4,000 non-interest-bearing note is payable at the end of each of the five subsequent years.

(b) All of the initial franchise fee collected by Gulf Fried Shrimp is to be refunded and the remaining obligation canceled if, for any reason, the franchisee fails to open the franchise.

(c) In return for the initial franchise fee, Gulf Fried Shrimp agrees to (1) assist the franchisee in selecting the location for the business, (2) negotiate the lease for the land, (3) obtain financing and assist with building design, (4) supervise construction, (5) establish accounting and tax records, and (6) provide expert advice, over a five-year period, relating to such matters as employee and management training, quality control, and promotion.

(d) In addition to the initial franchise fee, the franchisee is required to pay to Gulf Fried Shrimp a monthly fee of 2% of sales. This fee is a payment for menu planning, recipe innovations, and the privilege of purchasing ingredients from Gulf Fried Shrimp at or below prevailing market prices.

Management of Gulf Fried Shrimp estimates that the value of the services rendered to the franchisee at the time the contract is signed amounts to at least $5,000. All franchisees to date have opened their locations at the scheduled time, and none has defaulted on any of the notes receivable.

The credit ratings of all franchisees would entitle them to borrow at the current interest rate of 10%. The present value of an ordinary annuity of five annual receipts of $4,000 each, discounted at 10%, is $15,163.

Required:

(1) Discuss the alternatives that Gulf Fried Shrimp might use to account for the initial franchise fee, evaluate each by applying generally accepted accounting principles to this situation, and give illustrative entries for each alternative.

(2) Given the nature of Gulf Fried Shrimp's agreement with its franchisees, when should revenues be recognized? Discuss the question of revenue recognition for both the initial franchise fee and the additional monthly fee of 2% of sales, and give illustrative entries for both types of revenue.

(AICPA adapted)

CHAPTER 3

INCOME PRESENTATION
AND INTERIM REPORTING

The goals and objectives of accounting discussed in Chapter 1 suggest the need for full and fair disclosure of information relevant to the needs of the various users of accounting data. The adequacy of disclosure is evaluated by the information standards of relevance, reliability, neutrality, and comparability. Like other forms of communication, accounting disclosures should report on various entity attributes which are definable and which are evaluated by authoritative criteria. The consistent application of understandable definitions and criteria will improve the utility and the comparability of the data reported by different entities.

Given established definitions and criteria, questions develop as to who should aggregate and classify data according to these definitions and criteria—management, independent auditors, or perhaps the intended user. Some have suggested that the utility of accounting data would be enhanced if it were presented in an unclassified form. Therefore, rather than management presenting earnings per share (EPS), for example, investors could be provided with the unclassified data with which to develop their own EPS statistic.

This chapter focuses on specific areas of disclosure relating to income statement format and to interim financial statements. The following chapter discusses the presentation of earnings per share and the disclosure of financial information by segments of a business.

INCOME PRESENTATION

Early in the twentieth century, the balance sheet or statement of financial position was viewed as the primary financial statement. In the 1930's, a gradual de-emphasis of the balance sheet began to occur. Currently the income statement or statement of results of operations is viewed as the primary financial statement due to the importance of such information to security valuation theory and resource allocation decisions. This emphasis on the income statement has significantly influenced the development of accounting principles to the extent that the propriety of accounting principles is often evaluated in terms of their potential effect on the determination of income. It is important to note that increased attention is also being focused on the importance of cash flows and working capital flows.

Concepts of Income Presentation

The income statement presents for a period of time the revenues, expenses, gains, losses, and resulting net income or net loss, recognized in accordance with generally accepted accounting principles. This statement emphasizes the calculation of periodic net income and the communication of relevant factors which influence income. Income statement presentation has been influenced by two competing concepts: the current operating concept and the all-inclusive concept. These concepts have been primarily concerned with the proper classification and disclosure of unusual or nonrecurring events which affect the determination of entity wealth.

Current Operating Concept. The current operating concept is based on the premise that the most relevant measure of net income is that which is attributable to normal operations. Therefore, only those revenues and expenses which are considered to be recurring in nature and are normal or dependable with respect to their incidence over time should be included in net income. Unusual or nonrecurrent items and corrections traceable to previously reported income should be excluded from the calculation of income, and they should be treated as direct charges or credits to retained earnings.

Proponents of the current operating concept argue that external users of income data are most concerned with events which are directly related to the normal business purpose or normal operations because such events reflect future earning power. If unusual and/or nonrecurrent revenues and expenses are included, the predictive ability of income statistics could be significantly distorted. Thus, to determine the more useful measure of "operating net income," users of the income statement would be required to separate this data.

All-Inclusive Concept. The proponents of the all-inclusive concept argue that the summation of a series of income statements should reflect the change in entity wealth over time (excluding capital transactions and dividends), as measured by generally accepted accounting principles. Therefore, this concept focuses on the long-range operating performance of the entity and includes in net income the effects of unusual and/or nonrecurring revenues and expenses.

Supporting this viewpoint is the argument that the current operating concept revolves around a distinction between normal operational items and unusual, extraordinary items. These items may therefore be subject to definitional interpretations, which may provide a basis for the manipulation or smoothing of income and may also reduce the comparability between firms. Proponents of the all-inclusive concept suggest that unusual, extraordinary data are relevant to the evaluation of earning power and managerial efficiency, especially over a long-run period. Furthermore, the disclosure of unusual, extraordinary items is more visible in the income statement than in a retained earnings statement to which little attention is given by many external users.

Position of the AICPA Prior to Opinion No. 30. In 1947, the American Institute of Accountants (later to become the American Institute of Certified Public Accountants) issued Accounting Research Bulletin (ARB) No. 32, which basically supported the current operating concept and identified five broad classifications of "material" items which should be excluded in the determination of income. At that time, the American Accounting Association and the Securities and Exchange Commission (SEC) had strongly supported the all-inclusive concept. In 1966, in response to the varied interpretations given ARB No. 32, the AICPA issued Accounting Principles Board (APB) Opinion No. 9, "Reporting the Results of Operations." This Opinion resulted in the development of a concept which possessed characteristics of both the current operating and all-inclusive concepts of income presentation.

The major conclusion of APB Opinion No. 9 was that:

> ... net income should reflect all items of profit and loss recognized during the period with the sole exception of the prior period adjustments. ... *Extraordinary items* should, however, be segregated from the results of ordinary operations and shown separately in the income statement, with disclosure of the nature and amounts thereof.[1]

The prior period adjustments, which were expected to be rare, were defined as those material items which:

> ... (a) can be specifically identified with and directly related to the business activities of particular prior periods, and (b) are not attributable to economic events occurring subsequent to the date of the financial statements for the prior period, and (c) depend primarily on determinations by persons other than management and (d) were not susceptible of reasonable estimation prior to such determination.[2]

Prior period adjustments should not include normal recurring adjustments which result from the use of estimates, such as estimates of useful

---

[1] *Opinions of the Accounting Principles Board, No. 9.* "Reporting the Results of Operations" (New York: American Institute of Certified Public Accountants, 1966), par. 17.

[2] *Ibid.,* par. 23.

life and residual value for depreciable assets. However, according to APB Opinion No. 9, examples of prior period adjustments would include adjustments on settlements of taxes, renegotiation proceedings, and litigation.

In single period financial statements, prior period adjustments should be shown in the retained earnings statement as adjustments to the beginning balance of retained earnings. However, if comparative statements are prepared, adjustments should be made to the previous period income statements and retained earnings balances which are presented.

APB Opinion No. 9 viewed extraordinary items as material gains or losses resulting from events which were not expected to recur frequently. These items would be shown on the income statement but would not be considered in the evaluation of operating performance.

APB Opinion No. 30—"Reporting the Results of Operations"

In 1973, the Accounting Principles Board issued Opinion No. 30, "Reporting the Results of Operations." This Opinion acknowledges the difficulties associated with the interpretation of extraordinary items as described in APB Opinion No. 9 and evaluates the merits of the current operating and all-inclusive concepts of income presentation. The majority of the APB concluded that an income statement should present elements of income in an all-inclusive sense, and should provide adequate disclosure, so that users can assess individual income components. Thus, the Opinion proposes an income classification or presentation scheme which includes several nonrecurring items as a component of normal operating results. As a part of this scheme, the Opinion expands the definition of extraordinary items by specifying that such items must be both unusual in nature and occurring infrequently (nonrecurring).

APB Opinion No. 30 observed the definition for prior period adjustments as established in APB Opinion No. 9 and continued to view these items as adjustments to beginning retained earnings balances. In 1977, however, in FASB Statement No. 16, "Prior Period Adjustments," the Financial Accounting Standards Board (FASB) redefined prior period adjustments to include only the following two items:

(a) Correction of an error in the financial statements of a prior period, and

(b) Adjustments that result from realization of income tax benefits of preacquisition operating loss carryforwards of purchased subsidiaries.[3]

An analysis of APB Opinion No. 30 suggests the following income statement format:

---

[3] *Statement of Financial Accounting Standards, No. 16,* "Prior Period Adjustments" (Stamford: Financial Accounting Standards Board, 1977), par. 11.

Income from continuing operations before income taxes, extraordinary items, and the cumulative effect of changes in accounting principles	$xxxx	
Provision for income taxes	xxxx	
Income from continuing operations before extraordinary items and the cumulative effect of changes in accounting principles		$xxxx
Discontinued operations (Note ____):		
Income (loss) from operations of discontinued segment (less applicable income taxes of $___)	$xxxx	
Loss on disposal of segment, including provision of $___ for operating losses during phase-out period (less applicable income taxes of $___)	xxxx	xxxx
Extraordinary items (less applicable income taxes of $___) (Note ___)		xxxx
Cumulative effect on prior years of changes in accounting principles (less applicable income taxes of $___) (Note ____)		xxxx
Net income		$xxxx

Income from Continuing Operations

Income from continuing operations before taxes and extraordinary items includes:

1. All items of revenue and expense which are traceable to the normal operations of continuing business segments. These items are considered to be of a usual and recurring nature.
2. Items which are unusual in nature *or* which occur infrequently, but not both. These items are not extraordinary items, but should be disclosed in the body of the income statement as a separate component of income from continuing operations.

The taxes traceable to income from continuing operations should be shown as a single deduction from such income. Therefore, individual components of income from continuing operations are not shown net of tax. However, several critics of this presentation of taxes have expressed the opinion that the utility of the income statement would be enhanced if certain items were shown net of tax, especially those items which are unusual *or* nonrecurring in nature, such as relocation expenses. Net-of-tax treatment would allow users to adjust reported income for these items, thereby making the income statement more useful for predictive and other purposes.

Discontinued Operations

A separate component of net income is the income and losses traceable to a discontinued segment of a business. A segment of a business is defined as:

. . . a component of an entity whose activities represent a separate major line of business or class of customer. A segment may be in the form of a subsidiary, a division, or a department, and in some cases a joint venture or other nonsubsidiary investee, provided that its assets, results of operations, and activities can be clearly distinguished, physically and operationally and for financial reporting purposes, from the other assets, results of operations, and activities of the entity. . . . The fact that the results of operations of the segment being sold or abandoned cannot be separately identified strongly suggests that the transaction should not be classified as the disposal of a segment of the business. The disposal of a segment of a business should be distinguished from other disposals of assets incident to the evolution of the entity's business, such as the disposal of part of a line of business, the shifting of production or marketing activities for a particular line of business from one location to another, the phasing out of a product line or class of service, and other changes occasioned by technological improvements.[4]

A segment which is discontinued is one which has been sold, disposed of, spun off, or abandoned. A segment which is still operating, but is the subject of a formal plan calling for its discontinuance, should also be viewed as a discontinued segment for reporting purposes. The following examples of disposals which are considered to be discontinued operations, as well as disposals which are not viewed as discontinuances, were identified by the APB.[5]

Disposals Qualifying As Discontinued Operations

A sale by a diversified company of a major division which represents the company's only activities in the electronics industry. The assets and results of operations of the division are clearly segregated for internal financial reporting purposes from the other assets and results of operations of the company.

A sale by a meat packing company of a 25% interest in a professional football team which has been accounted for under the equity method. All other activities of the company are in the meat packing business.

A sale by a communications company of all its radio stations, which represent 30% of gross revenues. The company's remaining activities are three television stations and a publishing company. The assets and results of operations of the radio stations are clearly distinguishable physically, operationally and for financial reporting purposes.

A food distributor disposes of one of its two divisions. One division sells food wholesale primarily to supermarket chains and the other division sells food through its chain of fast food restaurants, some of which are franchised and some of which are company-owned. Both divisions are in the business of distribution of food. However, the nature of selling food through fast food outlets is vastly different than that of wholesaling food to supermarket chains. Thus, by having two major classes of customers, the company has two segments of its business.

Disposals Not Qualifying As Discontinued Operations

The sale of a major foreign subsidiary engaged in silver mining by a mining company which represents all of the company's activities in that particular country. Even though the subsidiary being sold may account for a significant percentage of gross revenue of the consolidated group and all of its revenues in the particular country, the fact that the company continues to engage in silver mining activities in other countries would indicate that there was a sale of a part of a line of business.

---

[4] *Opinions of the Accounting Principles Board, No. 30,* "Reporting the Results of Operations" (New York: American Institute of Certified Public Accountants, 1973), par. 13.

[5] *Accounting Interpretations,* "Reporting the Results of Operations: Accounting Interpretations of APB Opinion No. 30" (New York: American Institute of Certified Public Accountants, 1973), pp. 9753-9754.

The sale by a petrochemical company of a 25% interest in a petro-chemical plant which is accounted for as an investment in a corporate joint venture under the equity method. Since the remaining activities of the company are in the same line of business as the 25% interest which has been sold, there has not been a sale of a major line of business but rather a sale of part of a line of business.

A manufacturer of children's wear discontinues all of its operations in Italy which were composed of designing and selling children's wear for the Italian market. In the context of determining a segment of a business by class of customer, the nationality of customers or slight variations in product lines in order to appeal to particular groups are not determining factors.

A diversified company sells a subsidiary which manufactures furniture. The company has retained its other furniture manufacturing subsidiary. The disposal of the subsidiary, therefore, is not a disposal of a segment of the business but rather a disposal of part of a line of business.

The sale of all the assets (including the plant) related to the manufacture of men's woolen suits by an apparel manufacturer in order to concentrate activities in the manufacture of men's suits from synthetic products. This would represent a disposal of a product line as distinguished from the disposal of a major line of business.

Key Terms. The following terms and definitions are essential to the analysis of the presentation of discontinued operations:

1. Measurement date—the date on which management, given proper authority, commits itself to a formal plan of disposal, whether by sale or abandonment.
2. Disposal date—the date of closing if the segment is sold, or the date on which operations cease if the segment is abandoned.
3. Plan of disposal—a plan which includes, as a minimum, the following items: identification of assets to be disposed of, the method of disposal (sale or abandonment), the time required to dispose of the segment, the means by which potential buyers of disposed assets will be identified, estimated results of operations of the segment for the period from the measurement date to the disposal date, and estimated proceeds to be realized from disposal.

Reporting Discontinued Operations. In the current period, financial information pertaining to discontinued operations must be classified as to: (1) that which is traceable to the period prior to the measurement date, and (2) that which is traceable to the period beginning with the measurement date. As shown previously, the activity relating to discontinued operations is divided into two line items. The income or loss from operations of the discontinued segment prior to the measurement date is shown as the first line item, "Income (loss) from operations of discontinued segment (less applicable income taxes of $—)". This amount would include only realized elements of income which currently accrue to the segment and gains and losses resulting from the disposition of segment assets prior to the measurement date. When comparative financial data are presented, the net income for prior periods must be restated to reflect that portion of income which was traceable to the operations currently discontinued.

Activity of the discontinued segment between the measurement date and the disposal date must be separately disclosed in the income statement as part of the line item entitled "Loss (gain) on disposal of segment, including provision for operating losses (gains) during the phase-out period (less applicable income taxes of $—)." Assuming that the measurement date and disposal date occur within the same accounting period, the segment's activity traceable to this time span would, as of year end, consist of realized elements of income or loss from operations and realized gains or losses from the disposition of segment assets. If the measurement date and the disposal date do not occur within the same accounting period, the gain or loss to be reported as of the fiscal year end prior to the year of disposal should include:

A. Net realized items for the period from the measurement date to the end of the fiscal period, consisting of:
  1. The *realized* income (loss) from operations of the segment, net of taxes (part of Item A on the following diagram), and
  2. The *realized* gain or loss from the disposal or abandonment of segment assets, net of taxes (part of Item A on the following diagram), and

B. Net expected items for the period from the beginning of the new fiscal period to the disposal date, consisting of:
  1. The *expected* income (loss) from operations of the segment, net of taxes (part of Item B on the diagram), and
  2. The *expected* gain or loss from the disposal or abandonment of segment assets, net of taxes (part of Item B on the diagram).

		A		B	
Beginning of Fiscal Period	Measurement Date		End of Fiscal Period		Disposal Date

As of the end of the fiscal period, the reported gain or loss on disposal of the discontinued segment should consist of the net realized items (A.1 and A.2) plus the net expected items (B.1 and B.2), except that the final result may not be an overall net *expected* gain. This rule is summarized as follows:

Given a net realized gain (A.1 plus A.2),
(a) a net expected gain is not recognized because revenues should not be anticipated;
(b) a net expected loss is recognized in total.

Given a net realized loss (A.1 plus A.2),
(a) a net expected gain can be recognized only to the extent of the net realized loss;
(b) a net expected loss is recognized in total.

Financial information regarding a discontinued segment is dependent upon estimates which may be revised in subsequent periods. According to APB Opinion No. 20, "Accounting Changes," subsequent adjustments of these estimates should be disclosed in the period of adjustment in the same manner as the original item.

Illustrations of Accounting for Discontinued Operations. The principles of accounting for discontinued operations are illustrated in Cases A, B, C, and D of Illustration I.

Illustration I

Case A

1. The fiscal year end is April 30.
2. No extraordinary items or accounting changes occurred during the year ended April 30, 19X8.
3. On December 1, 19X7, management decided to dispose of a processing operation. This operation qualifies as a segment, and the disposition is expected to take place over the next 12 months.
4. The following information relates to the discontinued segment:

Income from operations of discontinued segment from May 1, 19X7, to measurement date, December 1, 19X7 (less applicable income taxes of $350,000)			$ 380,000
Loss on disposal of segment:			
Realized loss from operations from measurement date to April 30, 19X8 (less applicable income tax benefits of $137,000) ..	$(152,000)		
Realized loss from asset disposals from measurement date to April 30, 19X8 (less applicable income tax benefits of $30,000)	(40,000)	$(192,000)	
Expected loss from operations subsequent to April 30, 19X8 (less applicable income tax benefits of $130,000)	$(139,000)		
Expected loss on disposal of segment assets subsequent to April 30, 19X8 (less applicable income tax benefits of $128,000) ..	(137,000)	(276,000)	(468,000)
Net loss from discontinued operations			$ (88,000)

Given a net realized loss of $192,000, the net expected loss of $276,000 is recognized in total, resulting in a total loss on disposal of $468,000. In the income statement for the year ended April 30, 19X8, the $380,000 income and the $468,000 loss would be reported as the two line items. Other information required by APB Opinion No. 30 would be disclosed in a footnote.

Case B

Assume the same facts as in Case A, except that the results of operations from December 1, 19X7, to April 30, 19X8 (less applicable income taxes of $325,000) were $356,000. The results of the disposal of the discontinued segment are combined as follows:

Income from operations of discontinued segment from May 1, 19X7, to measurement date, December 1, 19X7 (less applicable income taxes of $350,000)			$380,000
Gain on disposal of segment:			
Realized income from operations from measurement date to April 30, 19X8 (less applicable income taxes of $325,000)	$356,000		
Realized loss from asset disposals from measurement date to April 30, 19X8 (less applicable income tax benefits of $30,000)	(40,000)	$316,000	
Expected loss from operations subsequent to April 30, 19X8 (less applicable income tax benefits of $130,000)	$(139,000)		
Expected loss on disposal of segment assets subsequent to April 30, 19X8 (less applicable income tax benefits of $128,000) ..	(137,000)	(276,000)	40,000
Net income from discontinued operations			$420,000

Given a net realized gain of $316,000, the net expected loss of $276,000 is recognized in its entirety.

Case C

Assume the same facts as in Case A, except that the expected income from operations from May 1, 19X8, to the disposal date (less applicable income taxes of $327,000) is $350,000. The results of the disposal of the discontinued segment are combined as follows:

Income from operations of discontinued segment from May 1, 19X7, to measurement date, December 1, 19X7 (less applicable income taxes of $350,000)			$380,000
Loss on disposal of segment:			
Realized loss from operations from measurement date to April 30, 19X8 (less applicable income tax benefits of $137,000) ..	$(152,000)		
Realized loss from asset disposals from measurement date to April 30, 19X8 (less applicable income tax benefits of $30,000)	(40,000)	$(192,000)	
Expected income from operations subsequent to April 30, 19X8 (less applicable income taxes of $327,000)	$ 350,000		
Expected loss on disposal of segment assets subsequent to April 30, 19X8 (less applicable income tax benefits of $128,000) ..	(137,000)	213,000	-0-
Net income from discontinued operations			$380,000

Given a net realized loss of $192,000, a net expected gain can only be recognized to the extent of the realized loss. Therefore, $192,000 of the net expected gain is offset against the net realized loss of $192,000, resulting in no reported loss on disposal. The remainder of the after-tax net expected gain ($21,000) will be recognized when it becomes realized.

Case D

Assume the same facts as in Case A, except that the realized gain on the sale of segment assets from December 1, 19X7, to April 30, 19X8 (less applicable income taxes of $340,000), is $400,000, and the expected gain on disposal of segment assets (less applicable income taxes of $90,000) is $360,000. The results of the disposal of the discontinued segment are combined as follows:

Income from operations of discontinued segment from May 1, 19X7, to measurement date, December 1, 19X7 (less applicable income taxes of $350,000)			$380,000
Loss on disposal of segment:			
Realized loss from operations from measurement date to April 30, 19X8 (less applicable income tax benefits of $137,000) ..	$(152,000)		
Realized gain from asset disposals from measurement date to April 30, 19X8 (less applicable income taxes of $340,000) ...	400,000	$248,000	
Expected loss from operations subsequent to April 30, 19X8 (less applicable income tax benefits of $130,000)	$(139,000)		
Expected gain on disposal of segment assets subsequent to April 30, 19X8 (less applicable income taxes of $135,000)	360,000	221,000	248,000
Net income from discontinued operations			$628,000

Given a realized gain of $248,000, the net expected gain of $221,000 is not recognized. The expected gain will be recognized when it becomes realized.

Illustration II contains excerpts from published financial statements of GAF Corp. which demonstrate the disclosure of a discontinued operation.

Illustration II

Year Ended December 31	1980	1979	1978
Income from Continuing Operations before Income Taxes (Benefits)	$ 9,077,000	$40,586,000	$53,397,000
Income Taxes (Benefits) (Note 9)	(1,246,000)	14,758,000	25,341,000
Income from Continuing Operations ...	$ 10,323,000	$25,828,000	$28,056,000
Discontinued Segments (Notes 1 & 9)			
Operating income, net of income taxes (benefits) of $(466,000) in 1980, $(5,287,000) in 1979, and $750,000 in 1978	$ 441,000	$ 2,355,000	$ 6,108,000
Estimated loss from disposition, net of income tax benefit of $10,460,000	(244,240,000)	—	—
Income (Loss) from Discontinued Segments	$(233,476,000)	$ 2,355,000	$ 6,108,000

Notes to Consolidated Financial Statements

1 Discontinued Segments

The company announced on December 30, 1980 its decision to classify as discontinued a number of businesses including its reprographics, photographic graphic arts products, pictorial products, resilient flooring and certain other smaller businesses. Also included in the discontinuance program is a latex plant, sold in December, 1980, and the company's x-ray film and related chemical businesses that were terminated on March 21, 1980. To provide for its working capital needs during the period of this program, the company is negotiating a three-year, $225 million revolving line of credit with a group of banks. See Note 13 for further discussion.

Operating income of the discontinued segments reflects income earned prior to the effec-

tive date of the discontinuance. All anticipated losses subsequent to the effective date of discontinuance have been provided in the Estimated loss from disposition.

As of December 31, 1980, a provision of $254.7 million ($244.2 million after tax benefits of $10.5 million) was recorded and consists of a reserve for the loss on disposition of assets and a liability for anticipated phase-out costs. An analysis of these accounts follows:

	Reserve For Loss On Disposition of Assets	Liability For Phase-Out Costs	Total
	Dollars in Millions		
Total Provision	$127.0	$127.7	$254.7
Activity during 1980:			
X-ray phase-out costs		(6.0)	(6.0)
Sale of latex business	(1.0)		(1.0)
Balance, December 31, 1980	$126.0	$121.7	$247.7

Future adjustments to this provision may occur for tax benefits of up to $65.0 million, which will not be reflected in the financial statements until realization is assured.

The current portion of the liability for phase-out costs is estimated at $68.1 million and is included in accrued liabilities; the non current portion of $53.6 million is included in other liabilities. In addition, $29.9 million of long-

term debt has been reclassified to the current portion of long-term debt.

For 1980, the assets of discontinued segments have been reclassified to remove them from their historic classifications and to separately identify them at their estimated net realizable value. The 1979 Consolidated Balance Sheet has not been similarly reclassified; however, amounts for both years are presented below.

	Dollars in Millions	
December 31	**1980**	1979
Accounts Receivable—Net	**$ 80.2**	$ 85.6
Inventories—Net	**148.5**	171.5
Property, Plant and Equipment—Net	**135.0**	135.5
Other	**28.0**	22.9
Total Assets	**$391.7**	$415.5
Less reserve for loss on disposition of assets	**126.0**	
Total Assets at Estimated Net Realizable Value	**$265.7**	

The Consolidated Statements of Income for the years ended December 31, 1979 and 1978 have been restated to exclude the sales, costs and expenses of the discontinued segments from the captions applicable to the continuing operations, and the net income from the discontinued segments has been reported separately.

Sales applicable to the discontinued segments, prior to the dates at which they have been accounted for as discontinued, were $553.4 million for 1980, $529.5 million for 1979, and $454.3 million for 1978.

Extraordinary Items

In describing extraordinary items, APB Opinion No. 30 recognizes the attributes of unusual nature and infrequency of occurrence as the sole criteria for classifying such items. These attributes are defined as follows:

(a) *Unusual nature*—the underlying event or transaction should possess a high degree of abnormality and be of a type clearly unrelated to, or only incidentally related to, the ordinary and typical activities of the entity, taking into account the environment in which the entity operates.

(b) *Infrequency of occurrence*—the underlying event or transaction should be of a type that would not reasonably be expected to recur in the foreseeable future, taking into account the environment in which the entity operates.[6]

An extraordinary item must possess *both* of these attributes. If one but not both of the attributes is present, the item in question should be included as a separate component of net income from continuing operations and should:

1. Not be disclosed net of taxes;
2. Not be disclosed in any manner which suggests that it is an extraordinary item; and
3. Not be listed as a separate component or determinant of earnings per share (EPS).

The criteria established in APB Opinion No. 30 are more restrictive and definitive than those established in APB Opinion No. 9, so that certain items formerly viewed as extraordinary no longer qualify. The following events, by themselves, should not be viewed as extraordinary items:

(a) Write-down or write-off of receivables, inventories, equipment leased to others, deferred research and development costs, or other intangible assets.

(b) Gains or losses from exchange or translation of foreign currencies, including those relating to major devaluations and revaluations.

(c) Gains or losses on disposal of a segment of a business.

(d) Other gains or losses from sale or abandonment of property, plant, or equipment used in the business.

(e) Effects of a strike, including those against competitors and major suppliers.

(f) Adjustments of accruals on long-term contracts.[7]

It is possible, however, for items (a) and (d) to be included as extraordinary items if they are the direct result of an event which otherwise qualifies as extraordinary, e.g., write-down of inventory destroyed by natural disaster which is unusual in nature and infrequent in occurrence.

Another possibly extraordinary event is the subject of FASB Statement No. 4, "Reporting Gains and Losses from Extinguishment of

---

[6] *Opinions of the Accounting Principles Board, No. 30, op. cit.,* par. 20.
[7] *Ibid.,* par. 23.

Debt." This Statement, which was issued in 1975 by the Financial
Accounting Standards Board, concluded that:

> Gains and losses from extinguishment of debt that are included in the
> determination of net income shall be aggregated and, if material,
> classified as an extraordinary item, net of related income tax effect. That
> conclusion shall apply whether an extinguishment is early or at scheduled
> maturity date or later. The conclusion does not apply, however, to gains or
> losses from cash purchases of debt made to satisfy current or future
> sinking-fund requirements. Those gains and losses shall be aggregated
> and the amount shall be identified as a separate item.[8]

APB Opinion No. 30 emphasizes that only extraordinary items
which are material "in relation to income before extraordinary items or
to the trend of annual earnings before extraordinary items, or . . . by
other appropriate criteria"[9] should be separately disclosed. To assess
materiality, items should be considered individually and not in the
aggregate. Therefore, it is possible that a series of unrelated immaterial
extraordinary items would not be disclosed, even though they may be
material in the aggregate. However, a series of events or transactions
which are related because they arise from a single specific and identifiable extraordinary event should be aggregated to determine materiality.

The treatment of events or transactions which are unusual or nonrecurring, but not both, has been criticized on the basis that these events
may be perceived as extraordinary. Furthermore, several members of
the APB found the established criteria for an extraordinary event to be
subjective, unworkable, and/or too narrow. Questions have also been
raised as to whether the term "extraordinary" truly conveys the nature
of items currently included in this category. Since the criteria for an
extraordinary item have been changed from those established in APB
Opinion No. 9, a new descriptive phrase might be appropriate.

Changes in Accounting Principles

A change in accounting principle is defined as a change from one
generally accepted accounting principle to another generally accepted
accounting principle, or a change in the method of applying a given
principle, with the change justified on the basis that the newly adopted
principle or method of application is preferable. Most changes in accounting principle should be separately disclosed in financial statements
for the year of change by showing the change's cumulative effect on
income of prior periods, as well as certain other information.[10] APB
Opinion No. 20 states that:

---

[8] *Statement of Financial Accounting Standards, No. 4,* "Reporting Gains and Losses from Extinguishment
of Debt" (Stamford: Financial Accounting Standards Board, 1975), par. 8.

[9] *Opinions of the Accounting Principles Board, No. 30, op. cit.,* par. 24.

[10] Certain changes in accounting principles are not accounted for by showing cumulative effect, but require the
restatement of all prior periods presented. Changes accorded this treatment are: (a) a change from lifo to some
other method, (b) a change in the method of accounting for long-term construction contracts, and (c) a change to
or from the "full cost" method of accounting used in the extractive industries.

The amount shown in the income statement for the cumulative effect of changing to a new accounting principle is the difference between (a) the amount of retained earnings at the beginning of the period of a change and (b) the amount of retained earnings that would have been reported at that date if the new accounting principle had been applied retroactively for all prior periods which would have been affected and by recognizing only the direct effects of the change and related income tax effect. The amount of the cumulative effect should be shown in the income statement between the captions "extraordinary items" and "net income." The cumulative effect is not an extraordinary item but should be reported in a manner similar to an extraordinary item. The per share information shown on the face of the income statement should include the per share amount of the cumulative effect of the accounting change.[11]

If financial statements for those periods prior to the period of change are presented, such statements and the related earnings per share (EPS) statistics should not be restated to reflect the adoption of the new principle. However, pro forma income and EPS amounts are required. These pro forma amounts indicate what the income and EPS would have been in previous periods and the current period if the newly adopted principle had been in use for all these periods.

To illustrate the disclosure of a change in principle, assume that a company employed the straight-line method of depreciation for the years 19X1 through 19X2 and changes to the sum-of-the-years-digits method beginning in 19X3. The effect of changing to the new method must be computed for the years 19X1 through 19X2, and this amount, net of tax, is then included in the 19X3 income statement as a separate item. The complete treatment of the change is shown in Illustration III.

Illustration III—A CHANGE IN ACCOUNTING PRINCIPLE

Facts:

1. The company acquired a plant asset on January 1, 19X1, at a cost of $15,000. The asset is estimated to have a useful life of 5 years and no residual value.
2. For the years 19X1 through 19X2, the asset was depreciated by the straight-line (SL) method. However, beginning in 19X3, the sum-of-the-years-digits (SYD) method is employed.
3. The effective tax rate for all years is 40%. The change in depreciation methods is for financial reporting purposes only.
4. Income statistics for years prior to the change in principle are as follows:

	19X1	19X2
Income from continuing operations before extraordinary items	$10,000	$17,500
Extraordinary items (less taxes)	—	(2,500)
Earnings per share (EPS)	$1.00	$1.50
Number of shares used to calculate EPS	10,000	10,000

5. 19X3 income from normal operations, based on the use of the new depreciation method, is $21,000. There are no extraordinary items in 19X3.

---

[11] *Opinions of the Accounting Principles Board, No. 20,* "Accounting Changes" (New York: American Institute of Certified Public Accountants, 1971), par. 20.

Analysis of Depreciation:

	19X1	19X2	Total
Old method—SL	$3,000	$3,000	$6,000
New method—SYD	5,000	4,000	9,000
Cumulative effect	$2,000	$1,000	$3,000

The following entry records the change in principle:

Deferred Income Tax	1,200	
Cumulative Effect of Change in Principle.....................	1,800[1]	
·Accumulated Depreciation		3,000

[1] The cumulative effect of $3,000 less the tax effect of $1,200 (40% × $3,000).

Income Statement Presentation:

Comparative income statements and EPS data for 19X2 and 19X3 appear as follows:

	19X2 Amounts	19X2 EPS	19X3 Amounts	19X3 EPS
Income from continuing operations before extraordinary items	$17,500	$1.75	$21,000	$2.10
Extraordinary items (less taxes)	(2,500)	(0.25)	—	—
Cumulative effect of change in principle (less taxes)	—	—	(1,800)	(0.18)
Net income..............................	$15,000	$1.50	$19,200	$1.92

Pro Forma Data:

Pro forma amounts and EPS data are also shown on the income statements. The pro forma amounts, based on the assumption that the new depreciation method had always been employed, appear as follows:

	19X2 Amounts	19X2 Pro Forma EPS	19X3 Amounts	19X3 Pro Forma EPS
Income from continuing operations before extraordinary items....................	$16,900[2]	$1.69	$21,000	$2.10
Extraordinary items (less taxes)	(2,500)	(0.25)	—	—
Net income	$14,400	$1.44	$21,000[3]	$2.10

[2] Based on SYD depreciation of $4,000, versus SL depreciation of $3,000, less the tax effect.
[3] Net income does not include the cumulative effect, because it is assumed that the new principle had always been employed.

INTERIM REPORTING

The timely reporting of financial information is recognized as an important feature of an information system if information is to be considered relevant to the needs of decision makers. To satisfy the need for timely financial information, many business entities have developed interim reporting models which provide financial information on a monthly or quarterly basis or at other defined intervals. This interim data may consist of statements of financial position, income statements, and statements of changes in financial position. However, primary emphasis is placed on the public disclosure of interim income data.

A substantial amount of empirical research has been devoted to an examination of the utility of publicly disclosed interim financial reports. This research has identified significant stock market reaction to the issuance of interim reports, and the influence of interim reports in actual investment decisions. Interim reports also provide an important basis for the prediction of annual income, so that the demand for these reports nearly parallels the demand for annual reports.

The established utility of interim data emphasizes the importance of applying generally accepted accounting principles to interim reports, including the principle of adequate disclosure. Therefore, the National Association of Accountants, the Financial Executives Institute, the Financial Analysts Federation, the Securities and Exchange Commission, principal stock exchanges, and the AICPA have directed efforts toward the development and improvement of interim financial reporting.

Approaches to Reporting Interim Data

Earlier forms of interim reporting provided the user of such data with various disclosures other than the computation of net income. However, as the importance of interim income statements became more apparent, various views of the interim period developed. One view of the interim period is that it represents a distinct, independent accounting period, separate from the annual accounting period. Therefore, interim net income should be determined by employing the same principles and estimations as would be employed if the interim period were an annual accounting period. For example, advertising expenditures incurred during the interim period should be expensed in that period, rather than deferred to future interim periods.

Another view of the interim period is that it is an integral part of the annual period and, therefore, does not stand as a distinct, independent period. Thus, deferrals, accruals, and estimations at the end of the interim period should depend upon estimates of annual revenue and expense relationships. For example, a portion of advertising expenditures made during the interim period may be deferred, based on the relationship between anticipated annual advertising expenditures and anticipated annual revenues. Although this viewpoint requires estimates not required by the independent period viewpoint, it may result in interim data which are more indicative of annual values, and which are more useful for predictive and comparative purposes.

APB Opinion No. 28

In 1973, the Accounting Principles Board issued Opinion No. 28, "Interim Financial Reporting," which applies to both internally and externally issued reports. This Opinion was in response to the growing interest in the credibility of interim data, and to the apparent need for an authoritative statement from the accounting profession regarding generally accepted accounting principles for such data. The Opinion may also have been influenced by the interim reporting requirements of the SEC.

APB Opinion No. 28 is based on the conclusion that an interim period should be viewed as an integral part of the annual period, not as a distinct, independent period. The Opinion reflects the APB's concern for the consistent application of principles by stating that financial statements for each interim period should be based on the same accounting principles and practices which are used for the preparation of annual financial statements. However, certain modifications of these principles and practices which relate to costs and expenses may be necessary, so that the reported results of an interim period more closely relate to the annual income statement.

Modifications for Costs and Expenses. Those costs which are directly related or allocated to products sold or to services rendered for annual reporting purposes should be given similar treatment for interim reporting purposes. However, the following modifications are acceptable in the area of inventory costing: [12]

1. The gross profit method or other methods which are not employed for annual purposes may be used for interim purposes in those instances where taking an interim physical inventory would be too costly or where perpetual inventory records are lacking and/or unreliable. The inventory method used for interim purposes should be disclosed. Significant differences between estimates of the inventory and the annual physical inventory should also be disclosed.
2. Use of the lifo inventory method for interim purposes may result in inventory liquidations which will be replaced by year end. To compensate for these interim liquidations, the interim cost of goods sold should include the replacement cost of liquidated inventory.
3. The use of lower of cost or market may suggest inventory losses for the interim period. Recoveries of these losses in subsequent periods should be recognized as gains to the extent of the losses previously recognized in interim periods within the same fiscal year. An exception to this rule is that temporary market declines need not be recognized for the interim period.
4. The use of standard costs for determining inventory should be applied on the same basis as is required for annual purposes. Material price variances and volume variances that are planned and expected to be absorbed by year end should ordinarily be deferred until year end.

In reporting costs and expenses which are not allocated to products sold or to services rendered, but which are charged against income in the interim period, the following standards apply:

---

[12] *Opinions of the Accounting Principles Board, No. 28,* "Interim Financial Reporting" (New York: American Institute of Certified Public Accountants, 1973), par. 14.

(a) Costs and expenses other than product costs should be charged to income in interim periods as incurred, or be allocated among interim periods based on an estimate of time expired, benefit received or activity associated with the periods. Procedures adopted for assigning specific cost and expense items to an interim period should be consistent with the bases followed by the company in reporting results of operations at annual reporting dates. However, when a specific cost or expense item charged to expense for annual reporting purposes benefits more than one interim period, the cost or expense item may be allocated to those interim periods.

(b) Some costs and expenses incurred in an interim period, however, cannot be readily identified with the activities or benefits of other interim periods and should be charged to the interim period in which incurred. Disclosure should be made as to the nature and amount of such costs unless items of a comparable nature are included in both the current interim period and in the corresponding interim period of the preceding year.

(c) Arbitrary assignment of the amount of such costs to an interim period should not be made.

(d) Gains and losses that arise in any interim period similar to those that would not be deferred at year end should not be deferred to later interim periods within the same fiscal year.[13]

Certain costs and expenses of an entity are subject to year-end adjustments, such as inventory shrinkage, allowance for uncollectible accounts, and year-end bonuses. These adjustments should not be recognized totally in the final interim period if they relate to activities of other interim periods. Therefore, to generate interim financial reports which contain a reasonable portion of annual expenses, a portion of estimated year-end adjustments should be allocated to each interim period on the basis of a revenue or cost relationship.

The costs and expenses as well as revenues of some businesses are subject to seasonal variations. Since interim reports for such businesses must be considered as representative of the annual period, APB Opinion No. 28 states that:

> ... such businesses should disclose the seasonal nature of their activities, and consider supplementing their interim reports with information for twelve-month periods ended at the interim date for the current and preceding years.[14]

Adjustments Related to Prior Interim Periods. By the definitions set forth in FASB Statement No. 16, "Prior Period Adjustments," many items which were previously viewed as prior period adjustments became elements of current operating income. However, certain items are given special treatment in interim reports. For example, an adjustment or settlement of litigation or of income taxes should not affect current interim income, provided all of the following criteria are met:

(a) The effect of the adjustment or settlement is material in relation to income from continuing operations of the current fiscal year or in

---

[13] *Ibid.*, par. 15.
[14] *Ibid.*, par. 18.

relation to the trend of income from continuing operations or is material by other appropriate criteria, and

(b) All or part of the adjustment or settlement can be specifically identified with and is directly related to business activities of specific prior
interim periods of the current fiscal year, and

(c) The amount of the adjustment or settlement could not be reasonably
estimated prior to the current interim period but becomes reasonably estimable in the current interim period.[15]

If such an item occurs in other than the first interim period of the
current fiscal year, and all or part of the item is an adjustment related to
prior interim periods of the current fiscal year, it should be reported as
follows:

(a) The portion of the item that is directly related to business activities of
the enterprise during the current interim period, if any, shall be included in the determination of net income for that period.

(b) Prior interim periods of the current fiscal year shall be restated to
include the portion of the item that is directly related to business
activities of the enterprise during each prior interim period in the
determination of net income for that period.

(c) The portion of the item that is directly related to business activities of
the enterprise during prior fiscal years, if any, shall be included in the
determination of net income of the first interim period of the current
fiscal year.[16]

Accounting for Income Taxes in Interim Statements

Accounting for income taxes in interim financial statements is based
on the application of principles established in APB Opinion Nos. 11, 23,
and 24, and in FASB Interpretation No. 18. In addition, the following
guidelines are applicable: [17]

1. The effective tax rate for the entire current fiscal period must be
estimated at the end of each interim period and applied to interim
income. The interim tax expense (or benefit) should be the difference between (a) the year-to-date tax expense or benefit and (b) the
amounts of tax reported in previous interim periods.

2. The estimated effective tax rate should reflect tax planning alternatives, such as capital gains rates and tax credits. The tax effect of
operating loss carryforwards, however, should not be recognized
unless such losses can be offset, beyond any reasonable doubt,
against the income of subsequent interim periods.

3. Nonordinary items of income or loss (unusual *or* infrequently occurring items, extraordinary items, discontinued operations, and the
cumulative effect of changes in accounting principles) are not included in the computation of the estimated effective tax rate, nor are
these items prorated over the balance of the fiscal period.

4. Changes in tax legislation are to be accounted for in interim periods
subsequent to the effective date of the legislation.

---

[15] *Statement of Financial Accounting Standards, No. 16, op. cit.,* par. 13.
[16] *Ibid.,* par. 14.
[17] *Opinions of the Accounting Principles Board, No. 28, op. cit.,* pars. 19-20.

The first guideline is designed to insure that the interim income tax rate is representative of the tax rate applicable to the entire fiscal period. For example, if income from continuing operations during the first interim period is $25,000, the effective tax rate would be 17%. However, if the annual "ordinary income" is expected to be $200,000, the effective annual tax rate might be 36%. Therefore, this rate should be used as the interim tax rate.

As stated in the second guideline, the estimated effective tax rate should also reflect tax planning alternatives. The rate should be revised, if necessary, each interim period in order to reflect changed expectations.

The computation of the estimated effective tax rate is illustrated in Cases A and B of Illustration IV. Case C demonstrates the determination of the tax expense traceable to interim income and the handling of a change in the estimated effective tax rate.

Illustration IV

Case A

Annual operating income is expected to be $250,000, of which $220,000 is ordinary income to be taxed at 40%; the balance represents capital gains to be taxed at 28%. It is anticipated that an investment tax credit of $14,000 will be available. The effective tax rate is computed as follows:

Item	Amount	Tax Rate	Tax Expense
Ordinary income	$220,000	40%	$88,000
Capital gains	30,000	28%	8,400
Tax credit			(14,000)
	$250,000		$82,400

Effective tax rate = $82,400 ÷ $250,000 = 33%

Case B

An expected annual operating loss of $180,000 can be used to offset $140,000 of income which was previously taxed at 30%. Therefore, a tax benefit of $42,000 ($140,000 × 30%), representing the tax previously paid, is traceable to the expected operating loss of $180,000.

Effective tax rate = $42,000 ÷ $180,000 = 23%

Case C
Income in All Interim Periods—Change in Estimated Tax Rate

Interim Period (Quarter)	Ordinary Income		Estimated Tax Rate	Tax Expense (Benefit)		
	Current Period	Year-to-Date		Year-to-Date	Previously Reported	Current Period
First	$30,000	$ 30,000	40%	$12,000	—	$12,000
Second	40,000	70,000	40	28,000	$12,000	16,000
Third	20,000	90,000	45	40,500	28,000	12,500
Fourth	50,000	140,000	45	63,000	40,500	22,500

Operating Loss Carryforwards. The criteria for the recognition of the tax effects of operating loss carryforwards which develop in an interim period are specified in APB Opinion No. 28, which states that:

> An established seasonal pattern of loss in early interim periods offset by income in later interim periods should constitute evidence that realization is assured beyond reasonable doubt, unless other evidence indicates the established seasonal pattern will not prevail. The tax effects of losses incurred in early interim periods may be recognized in a later interim period of a fiscal year if their realization, although initially uncertain, later becomes assured beyond reasonable doubt. When the tax effects of losses that arise in the early portions of a fiscal year are not recognized in that interim period, no tax provision should be made for income that arises in later interim periods until the tax effects of the previous interim losses are utilized.[18]

When the tax effects of an interim period loss are recognized in a later interim period, the tax benefit which offsets the tax provision is not reported as an extraordinary item. However, the tax benefit of a prior year operating loss carryforward which is recognized in a current interim period should be viewed as an extraordinary item in that period. This procedure parallels the reporting of operating loss carryforward benefits in a subsequent annual period.

The tax effects of operating loss carryforwards which develop in an interim period are demonstrated in Cases A, B, and C of Illustration V.

Illustration V

Case A
Loss in Period (Carryback to Prior Years Not Possible)
Tax Benefit of Loss Assured

Interim Period (Quarter)	Ordinary Income Current Period	Ordinary Income Year-to-Date	Estimated Tax Rate	Tax Expense (Benefit) Year-to-Date	Tax Expense (Benefit) Previously Reported	Tax Expense (Benefit) Current Period
First	$(30,000)	$(30,000)	40%	$(12,000)	—	$(12,000)
Second	20,000	(10,000)	40	(4,000)	$(12,000)	8,000
Third	40,000	30,000	40	12,000	(4,000)	16,000
Fourth	40,000	70,000	40	28,000	12,000	16,000

Case B
Loss in Period (Carryback to Prior Years Not Possible)
Tax Benefit of Loss Not Assured

Interim Period (Quarter)	Ordinary Income Current Period	Ordinary Income Year-to-Date	Estimated Tax Rate	Tax Expense (Benefit) Year-to-Date	Tax Expense (Benefit) Previously Reported	Tax Expense (Benefit) Current Period
First	$(30,000)	$(30,000)	40%	—	—	—
Second	20,000	(10,000)	40	—	—	—
Third	40,000	30,000	40	$ 12,000	—	$ 12,000
Fourth	40,000	70,000	40	28,000	$ 12,000	16,000

---

[18] *Ibid.*, par. 20.

Case C
Loss of $80,000 Anticipated for Year
Carryback to Prior Years Possible to the Extent of a $32,000 Tax Benefit

Interim Period (Quarter)	Ordinary Income		Estimated Tax Rate	Tax Expense (Benefit)		
	Current Period	Year-to-Date		Year-to-Date	Previously Reported	Current Period
First	$ 10,000	$ 10,000	40%	$ 4,000	—	$ 4,000
Second	(30,000)	(20,000)	40	(8,000)	$ 4,000	(12,000)
Third	(70,000)	(90,000)	40	(32,000)*	(8,000)	(24,000)
Fourth	10,000	(80,000)	40	(32,000)	(32,000)	—

* The year-to-date tax benefit is limited to the total tax benefit which is assured beyond a reasonable doubt (i.e., $80,000 × 40% = $32,000). Therefore, of the suggested third quarter year-to-date tax benefit of $36,000, only $32,000 is assured beyond a reasonable doubt.

Nonordinary Items of Income or Loss. Although the influence of non-ordinary items should be excluded in the determination of the estimated effective tax rate for the fiscal year, the tax expense or benefit relating to unusual or infrequent items should be included in the total tax expense or benefit relating to continuing operations. The tax effects of other nonordinary items (extraordinary items, discontinued operations, or cumulative effect of changes in accounting principles) must be presented with their respective item as a separate component of net income. However, if a nonordinary item is a loss or charge against income, the tax benefit of the loss or charge should not be recognized unless there is assurance beyond a reasonable doubt that it will be realized.

The tax effect of nonordinary items is demonstrated in Cases A, B, and C of Illustration VI.

As discussed on pages 75-77, the accounting effects of a discontinued segment should be reflected in an income statement as two distinct components: (1) income or loss from operations of the discontinued segment prior to the measurement date and (2) income or loss on disposal of the discontinued segment. Both of these items should be

Illustration VI

Case A
Extraordinary Gain

Interim Period (Quarter)	Ordinary Income		Extra-ordinary Item	Estimated Tax Rate	Current Period Tax Expense (Benefit)	
	Current Period	Year-to-Date			Ordinary Income	Extraordinary Income
First	$20,000	$ 20,000	—	40%	$ 8,000	—
Second	40,000	60,000	—	40	16,000	—
Third	40,000	100,000	$ 30,000	40	16,000	$ 12,000
Fourth	40,000	140,000	—	40	16,000	—

(continued)

Case B
Extraordinary Loss (Carryback to Prior Years Not Possible)
Tax Benefit of Loss Assured

Interim Period (Quarter)	Ordinary Income		Extra-ordinary Item	Estimated Tax Rate	Current Period Tax Expense (Benefit)	
	Current Period	Year-to-Date			Ordinary Income	Extraordinary Income
First	$20,000	$ 20,000	—	40%	$ 8,000	—
Second	10,000	30,000	$(40,000)	40	4,000	$(16,000)
Third	20,000	50,000	—	40	8,000	—
Fourth	40,000	90,000	—	40	16,000	—

Case C
Extraordinary Loss (Carryback to Prior Years Not Possible)
Tax Benefit of Loss Not Assured

Interim Period (Quarter)	Ordinary Income		Extra-ordinary Item	Estimated Tax Rate	Current Period Tax Expense (Benefit)	
	Current Period	Year-to-Date			Ordinary Income	Extraordinary Income
First	$20,000	$ 20,000	—	40%	$ 8,000	—
Second	10,000	30,000	$(40,000)	40	4,000	$(12,000)*
Third	20,000	50,000	—	40	8,000	(4,000)
Fourth	40,000	90,000	—	40	16,000	—

* The tax benefit of the extraordinary loss is limited to the extent that it offsets ordinary income already recognized.

presented net of tax. When interim statements are prepared, a problem arises in that income or loss from operations of the discontinued segment, recognized in an interim period prior to the measurement date, will have been included in ordinary income of the prior period(s) and in the determination of the effective tax rate of the prior period(s). Once the measurement date has been established, total taxes of the prior periods must be reallocated between ordinary income (loss) traceable to continuing operations and ordinary income (loss) traceable to the discontinued operations, as demonstrated in Illustration VII.

Illustration VII

Facts:

After issuing first quarter interim data, the company adopted in the second quarter a formal plan calling for the disposal of one of its segments. Ordinary income reported in the first quarter included a $10,000 loss traceable to the segment being discontinued. It is assumed that any loss traceable to the discontinued segment will have tax benefits and that the estimated effective tax rate of 40% on income from continuing operations, employed in the first quarter, is to be revised to 45% applicable to the remaining continuing segments.

Analysis:

The following schedule illustrates the retroactive restatement of previously issued interim data in order to separately disclose both continuing and discontinued operations.

Interim Period (Quarter)	Ordinary Income		Discontinued Segment		Estimated Tax Rate	Current Period Tax Expense (Benefit) Applicable to		
	Current Period	Year-to-Date	Operating Income	Estimated Loss on Disposal		Continuing Segments	Discontinued Segment	
							Operations	Loss on Disposal
First	$40,000	$ 40,000	—	—	40%	$16,000	—	—
First—								
Restated	50,000	50,000	$(10,000)	—	45	22,500	$(6,500)[1]	—
Second	30,000	80,000	5,000	$(60,000)	45	13,500	4,250 [2]	$(27,000)
Third	50,000	130,000	—	—	45	22,500	—	—
Fourth	60,000	190,000	—	—	45	27,000	—	—

[1] The $6,500 tax benefit traceable to the operations of the discontinued segment is the result of comparing the tax of $22,500 traceable to continuing operations with the $16,000 of tax previously recognized as being traceable to continuing operations, which at that time included the results of the discontinued segment. Therefore, the difference between the two tax amounts relates to the exclusion and inclusion respectively of the results traceable to the discontinued segment. Notice that the total tax expense presented for the first period, restated, totals $16,000, which is the tax on final income at a 40% rate.

[2] The $4,250 represents the difference between (1) the tax benefit on the loss to date traceable to the discontinued segment (45% × $5,000) and (2) the tax benefit of $6,500 traceable to the discontinued segment loss recognized in prior periods.

APB Opinion No. 28 indicates that, in general, a change in accounting principle during an interim period should be accounted for in accordance with APB Opinion No. 20, "Accounting Changes." To simplify the accounting for such changes, the APB encouraged management to adopt accounting changes in the first interim period of the current fiscal year. Nevertheless, the APB recognized that changes would continue to be made in other than the first interim period and, therefore, prescribed special procedures. However, these procedures were amended in 1974 by FASB Statement No. 3, "Reporting Accounting Changes in Interim Financial Statements."

When interim reports are prepared, the proper accounting for changes in accounting principles depends on (a) whether the change requires the determination of a cumulative effect and (b) whether the change takes place in the first interim period of the fiscal year. Changes requiring retroactive restatement of previously issued financial statements, rather than the determination of the cumulative effect, will require the restatement of previously issued interim financial information. If such a change occurs in other than the first interim period, such restatement will also involve the restatement of taxes to reflect the estimated effective tax rate, which is based on annual ordinary income (or loss) as determined in accordance with the newly adopted accounting principle.

If a cumulative effect type change takes place in the first interim period of the fiscal year, the cumulative effect of the change on retained earnings as of the beginning of the year should be included in net income of the first interim period. However, if the cumulative effect type change is made in other than the first interim period, it is assumed for accounting purposes that it took place in the first interim period. Therefore, the change should be accounted for as follows: [19]

1. Financial statements for all interim periods in the current fiscal year should be restated to reflect the adoption of the new principle, and
2. The cumulative effect of the change on retained earnings as of the beginning of the current fiscal year should be included in the restated net income of the first interim period rather than in the interim period in which the change was adopted.

A cumulative effect type change in principle also requires the following disclosures:

(a) In financial reports for the interim period in which the new accounting principle is adopted, disclosure shall be made of the nature of and justification for the change.
(b) In financial reports for the interim period in which the new accounting principle is adopted, disclosure shall be made of the effect of the change on income from continuing operations, net income, and related per share amounts for the interim period in which the change is made. In addition, when the change is made in other than the first interim period of a fiscal year, financial reports for the period of change shall also disclose (i) the effect of the change on income from continuing operations, net income, and related per share amounts for each pre-change interim period of that fiscal year and (ii) income from continuing operations, net income, and related per share amounts for each pre-change interim period restated. . . .
(c) In financial reports for the interim period in which the new accounting principle is adopted, disclosure shall be made of income from continuing operations, net income, and related per share amounts computed on a pro forma basis for (i) the interim period in which the change is made and (ii) any interim periods of prior fiscal years for which financial information is being presented. If no financial information for interim periods of prior fiscal years is being presented, disclosure shall be made, in the period of change, of the actual and pro forma amounts of income from continuing operations, net income, and related per share amounts for the interim period of the immediately preceding fiscal year that corresponds to the interim period in which the change is made.
(d) In year-to-date and last-twelve-months-to-date financial reports that include the interim period in which the new accounting principle is adopted, the disclosures specified in the first sentence of subparagraph (b) above and in subparagraph (c) above shall be made.
(e) In financial reports for a subsequent (post-change) interim period of the fiscal year in which the new accounting principle is adopted, disclosure shall be made of the effect of the change on income from continuing operations, net income, and related per share amounts for that post-change interim period.[20]

---

[19] *Statement of Financial Accounting Standards, No. 3,* "Reporting Accounting Changes in Interim Financial Statements" (Stamford: Financial Accounting Standards Board, 1974), par. 10.
[20] *Ibid.,* par. 11.

In a change to the lifo inventory method, the disclosures for a cumulative effect type change are required, except that the cumulative effect of the change on retained earnings and pro forma amounts should not be determined. If the change is made in other than the first interim period, all pre-change interim statements must be restated to reflect the adoption of the new accounting principle. The beginning inventory computed by the previous inventory method is assumed to be the beginning measure of base stock for purposes of applying lifo.

Disclosure of Summarized Interim Data. To maintain the timeliness of interim data, companies frequently report summarized interim data rather than complete financial statements. When publicly traded companies report summarized interim data, the following disclosure is required at a minimum:

    (a) Sales or gross revenues, provision for income taxes, extraordinary items (including related income tax effects), cumulative effect of a change in accounting principles or practices, and net income.

    (b) Primary and fully diluted earnings per share data for each period presented, determined in accordance with the provisions of APB Opinion No. 15, "Earnings per Share."

    (c) Seasonal revenue, costs or expenses.

    (d) Significant changes in estimates or provisions for income taxes.

    (e) Disposal of a segment of a business and extraordinary, unusual or infrequently occurring items.

    (f) Contingent items.

    (g) Changes in accounting principles or estimates.

    (h) Significant changes in financial position.[21]

In addition to providing the above data for the current quarter, such data should also be provided for the current year to date or the last twelve months to date, plus comparable data for the preceding year.

Frequently, companies do not issue separate fourth quarter reports or provide fourth quarter disclosure of summarized data because annual audited statements will be forthcoming. In such cases, a note to the annual financial statements should disclose the effect of the following items for the fourth quarter: disposals of a segment, extraordinary items, unusual or infrequently occurring items, and changes in accounting principles. Disclosure in the annual financial statements should also include the aggregate effect of year-end adjustments which are material to the fourth quarter results.

QUESTIONS

    1. Identify those items that qualify as prior period adjustments.

---

[21] *Opinions of the Accounting Principles Board, No. 28, op.cit.,* par. 30.

2. Define a segment. What criteria are necessary for the sale of assets to qualify as a discontinuance of a segment?

3. Define the following terms as they apply to the accounting for a discontinued segment: measurement date, date of disposition.

4. How do the results of a segment which has been discontinued in the current year affect the presentation of comparative financial data from prior years?

5. If the disposition of a segment results in a gain, under what circumstances may the gain be recognized before it is realized?

6. Discuss the two key determinants for classifying a gain or loss as an extraordinary item. How could flood damage be classified as both an ordinary and an extraordinary item?

7. Define the account, "Allowance for Lifo Replacement Cost." Where would such an account appear on the financial statements and under what conditions?

8. For purposes of presentation in interim financial statements, discuss the procedures for reporting costs which are not directly related to the products sold or services rendered.

9. Describe the variations in the normal yearly computation and the interim computation of provision for income taxes on ordinary operating income.

10. How are extraordinary items treated on interim financial statements?

11. If a change in accounting principle occurs in the third quarter, how should it be disclosed in the interim statement?

EXERCISES

Exercise 1. Kemar Corporation operates numerous divisions, one of which produces appliances for the home. The division consists of four plants in various areas of the country. At a meeting on May 1, 19X8, the board of directors adopted a plan for the disposition of this division. The following data related to the operations of the division for the fiscal year ended July 31, 19X8:

	1st Quarter	2d Quarter	3d Quarter	4th Quarter
Sales...................	$1,275,000	$1,350,000	$949,000	$1,042,000
Cost of goods sold	1,046,000	1,107,000	778,000	820,000
Gross profit	$ 229,000	$ 243,000	$171,000	$ 222,000
Expenses...............	310,000	322,000	249,000	278,000
Income before taxes	$ (81,000)	$ (79,000)	$ (78,000)	$ (56,000)

The proposed date of disposal is January 31, 19X9, at which time a firm contract price of $62,000,000 will be received for the entire division. The book value of the assets at the time of disposition will be $73,500,000. The future performance of the segment is expected to repeat that of the first two quarters of the current year. The income tax rate is 55%.

Present that portion of the income statement, for the year ended July 31, 19X8, to show the results of this decision by the board of Kemar Corporation.

Exercise 2. On August 1, 19X4, Bates Manufacturing, Inc., decided to dispose of its metal casting operation, which is viewed as a distinct segment of the company. Although Bates's year end is December 31, management does not expect final disposal of the segment to take place prior to May 1, 19X5. During the first seven months of 19X4, the segment had pretax operating losses of $1,420,000, not including a pretax gain from the sale of segment assets amounting to $530,000. The segment experienced a pretax operating loss of $1,280,000 during the balance of 19X4, not including a pretax gain of $2,030,000 resulting from the sale of certain segment assets. Remaining segmental assets with a basis of $14,200,000 are expected to be disposed of during 19X5 at a gain of $1,800,000. Limited operations of the segment during 19X5 will result in pretax operating losses of $550,000. Assume an effective tax rate of 40%.

Prepare that portion of the 19X4 income statement which would reflect management's decision to discontinue the segment.

Exercise 3.   After serious consideration, the Board of Directors of Modern Electronics, Inc., adopted on May 1, 19X4, a plan calling for:
1. The discontinuation of their satellite guidance operation.
2. The disposal of their transistor radio production operation.

Although the satellite guidance operation will be phased out, the company will still be actively involved in the development and manufacturing of other guidance systems, similar to satellite systems, to be used in missile and aircraft applications. Virtually all past and present activity in guidance systems has been undertaken on a government contract basis. The decision to dispose of the transistor radio operation is in response to increasing foreign competition and marks the end of Modern's involvement in any form of consumer-oriented communication devices.

Relevant pretax data relating to the satellite and radio operations for calendar years 19X4 and 19X5 are as follows:

	Satellite Guidance	Radio Production
Operating income (loss):		
1/1/X4 to 4/30/X4	$(1,480,000)	$ (810,000)
5/1/X4 to 12/31/X4	(2,360,000)	(1,410,000)
Anticipated 19X5 as of 12/31/X4	(3,700,000)	(270,000)
Actual 19X5	(3,330,000)	(360,000)
Gain (loss) on disposal of assets:		
1/1/X4 to 4/30/X4	0	230,000
5/1/X4 to 12/31/X4	1,440,000	290,000
Anticipated 19X5 as of 12/31/X4	(1,260,000)	580,000
Actual 19X5	(835,000)	360,000

Assuming that the board of directors' plans are carried out completely by the end of April, 19X5, prepare that portion of the 19X4 and 19X5 income statement dealing with discontinued operations. An effective tax rate of 40% existed during 19X4 and 19X5.

Exercise 4.   Stien, Inc., had two incidents occur during its last fiscal year which ended on November 30, 19X2.

First, on May 17 of the current fiscal year, a flash flood inundated their Texas facilities. The destruction was only partial, but as a result the corporation suffered a loss of $235,300. These flash floods occur every few years, but this flood is the first to cause any damage at Stien's plant.

Second, Stien disposed of securities which it had held for twenty-seven years as an investment. The securities were corporate bonds and the only investment the company has made in all of its ninety-four years of existence. The board of directors of Stien has indicated that it has no intention of ever purchasing any more securities. The gain on the sale of the securities was $96,200.

Excluding these items, earnings from continuing operations before taxes for the year were $1,789,000 and the provision for taxes was $858,720. There were no deferred items.

(1) Discuss the criteria for evaluating an item as extraordinary as it applies to the two situations which Stien has encountered.

(2) Prepare in good form a partial income statement for the current year.

Exercise 5. Brett Corporation has decided that in the preparation of its 19X3 financial statements, two changes will be made from the methods used in prior years:

1. *Depreciation.* Brett has always used the declining-balance method for tax and financial reporting purposes, but has decided to change during 19X3 to the straight-line method for financial reporting only. The effect of this change is as follows:

	Excess of Accelerated Depreciation Over Straight-Line Depreciation
Prior to 19X2	$1,300,000
19X2	101,000
19X3	99,000
	$1,500,000

Depreciation is charged to cost of goods sold and to selling, general, and administrative expenses on the basis of 75% and 25%, respectively.

2. *Uncollectible accounts expense.* In the past, Brett has recognized uncollectible accounts expense equal to 1.5% of net sales. After careful review, a rate of 2% is determined to be more appropriate for 19X3. Uncollectible accounts expense is charged to selling, general, and administrative expenses.

The following information is taken from financial statements which were prepared before giving effect to the two changes.

Brett Corporation
Condensed Balance Sheet
December 31, 19X2 and 19X3

	19X3	19X2
Assets		
Current assets	$43,561,000	$43,900,000
Property, plant, and equipment (at cost)	45,792,000	43,974,000
Less accumulated depreciation	(23,761,000)	(22,946,000)
	$65,592,000	$64,928,000
Equities		
Current liabilities	$21,124,000	$23,650,000
Long-term debt	15,154,000	14,097,000
Capital stock	11,620,000	11,620,000
Retained earnings	17,694,000	15,561,000
	$65,592,000	$64,928,000

Brett Corporation
Income Statement
For Year Ended December 31, 19X2 and 19X3

	19X3	19X2
Net sales	$80,520,000	$78,920,000
Cost of goods sold	54,847,000	53,074,000
	$25,673,000	$25,846,000
Selling, general, and administrative expenses	19,540,000	18,411,000
	$ 6,133,000	$ 7,435,000
Other income (expense)	(1,198,000)	(1,079,000)
Income before federal income tax	$ 4,935,000	$ 6,356,000
Federal income tax	2,368,800	3,050,880
Net income	$ 2,566,200	$ 3,305,120

There have been no timing differences between any book and tax items prior to the above changes. The effective tax rate is 48%.

Based on APB Opinion No. 20, "Accounting Changes," compute for the following items the amounts which would appear on the comparative (19X3 and 19X2) financial statements of Brett Corporation after adjustment for the two accounting changes. Show amounts for both 19X3 and 19X2 and prepare supporting schedules as necessary.

(1) Accumulated depreciation
(2) Selling, general, and administrative expenses
(3) Retained earnings
(4) Deferred income tax expense at year end
(5) Pro forma net income   (AICPA adapted)

Exercise 6.   The following is a list of account titles found on the books of Seymour Corporation:

(a) Advertising
(b) Research and Development Costs
(c) Inventory
(d) Prepaid Expenses
(e) Accounts Payable

Discuss the methods for evaluating each account for presentation in interim financial statements of the corporation. Indicate any deviation from normal accounting procedures that are required for presentation. If there are alternatives, discuss each separately.

Exercise 7.   In the third year of operations, MJS Company has decided to report its results of operations on a quarterly basis. Some questions developed regarding the allocation of taxes for these interim periods. Pretax information related to the MJS Company for 19X6 is as follows:

Quarter	Ordinary Income (Loss)	Extraordinary Item
First	$ 10,500	
Second	(82,000)	
Third	44,500	$(45,000)
Fourth	97,000	

All income is taxable in one jurisdiction at a 50% rate. Anticipated tax credits for 19X6 total $9,800. No permanent differences are anticipated. No changes in estimated ordinary income, tax rates, or tax credits occur during the year.
(1) Calculate MJS Company's estimated annual effective tax rate for 19X6.
(2) Assuming that the tax benefits of all net operating losses are assured because of carryback provisions, calculate the tax expense (benefit) for each quarter. Show all computations in good form.
(3) Assume that the company anticipates an annual operating loss of $15,000 up until year end, and that the tax benefit of the anticipated ordinary loss is assured beyond any reasonable doubt only to the extent of $15,000 of prior income available to be offset by carryback. The statutory tax rate remains at 50%, but anticipated tax credits are only $1,500. Calculate the tax expense (benefit) for each quarter, assuming that the company realizes the same ordinary income and extraordinary items as originally presented in the problem.

Exercise 8. Wert Company has sought assistance in preparing its second quarter, 19X2, income statement. Figures for sales revenue, selling expenses, and general and administrative expenses are $860,000, $68,000, and $117,000 respectively.

For each of the following situations, determine the cost of goods sold and prepare an interim income statement in good form for the three months ended June 30, 19X2.
(1) Wert uses a standard cost accounting system for inventory and product costs. Net unfavorable cost variances for the second quarter total $2,600 and represent the difference between actual and standard production costs. Management considers such variances a manufacturing cost and includes them in the income statement above the gross profit line. It is expected that an unfavorable purchase price variance of $900 will be absorbed by December 31, 19X2.

   Production for the second quarter at standard cost was $600,000. Beginning and ending finished goods inventories (standard cost) were $71,000 and $98,000 respectively.
(2) The lifo cost of goods sold was $596,000 and includes sales of 15,000 units costed out at their 19X1 base layer cost of $7 per unit. The current replacement cost of these units is $11 per unit. It is expected that the 19X2 year-end inventory will be 2,000 units less than the 19X1 year-end inventory.
(3) Beginning inventory of $52,000 reflects a first quarter write-down of $2,200 due to the application of the lower of cost or market rule. Through a market price recovery in the second quarter, inventory increased in value by $3,750. Wert purchased 18,000 units of inventory ($28 per unit) in the second quarter. Ending inventory (fifo basis) was $60,500.

Exercise 9. Huntly Company, a highly diversified company, reports the results of operations on a quarterly basis. At the beginning of the third quarter, management decided to discontinue its recreational division. At this time, a formal plan was authorized, calling for disposal by year end. Results for the current year, excluding taxes, are as follows:

Quarter	Continuing Operations	Discontinued Segment
First	$33,000	
Second	40,200	
Third	62,000	$(6,500)
Fourth	71,500	1,200

The following information was also provided:
(a) The first two quarters include results of operations of the discontinued segment. The segment reported first and second quarter pretax losses of $8,000 and $12,000 respectively.
(b) The annual income tax rate in the first and second quarters was 35%. Due to the decision to discontinue, the revised annual effective tax rate was determined to be 40%.

For each quarter, present the results of operations and the tax expense or tax benefit as they would appear on the interim period financial statements of Huntly Company. Where applicable, include the original and restated amounts in the presentation.

PROBLEMS

Problem 3-1. Metro, Inc., is composed of four separate manufacturing divisions: electronics, industrial pumps, commercial aircraft, and woolen mills. The president of Metro provides you with the following account balances for the two years ending June 30, 19X3, and June 30, 19X2.

	Net Sales		Cost of Goods Sold		Operating Expenses	
	19X3	19X2	19X3	19X2	19X3	19X2
Electronics	$2,650,000	$2,010,000	$1,590,000	$1,307,000	$ 397,000	$ 241,000
Industrial pumps..	1,800,000	1,456,000	1,002,000	885,000	288,000	215,000
Commercial aircraft	4,300,000	3,780,000	3,010,000	2,848,000	650,000	566,000
Woolen mills	990,000	1,427,000	841,000	1,070,000	698,000	863,000
	$9,740,000	$8,673,000	$6,443,000	$6,110,000	$2,033,000	$1,885,000

In September, 19X2, the electronics division was unable to obtain certain inventory due to a strike at the plant of its major supplier. The resulting loss of $583,000 is not considered in the above financial data.

On October 1, 19X2, Metro received an offer from Fleece Corporation regarding purchase of the assets and product line of the woolen mills division. At this time, a plan was authorized for disposal of the division and on February 1, 19X3, the assets and product line were sold for a pretax gain of $705,000 (exclusive of operations during the phase-out period). Of the 19X3 fiscal-year data, 30% relate to the time period prior to October 1, 19X2.

During the 19X2 fiscal year, Metro discontinued its production of fiberglass pumps at its main plant in order to concentrate on the manufacture of stainless steel pumps. The sale of all assets related to the fiberglass pumps resulted in a $347,000 gain.

Income from rental of a vacant plant site was $336,000 and $196,000, respectively, for the two years ended June 30, 19X3, and June 30, 19X2.

Metro's net income for the two years ended June 30, 19X3, and June 30, 19X2, was $947,100 and $671,550 respectively.

The applicable income tax rate for each of the two years is 45%.

Required:

Prepare in proper form a comparative statement of income of Metro, Inc., for the two years ended June 30, 19X3, and June 30, 19X2. Footnotes are not required.　　　　　　　　　　　　　　　　　　　　　　　　　　(AICPA adapted)

Problem 3-2. On July 31, 19X3, Dayton Corporation implemented a schedule to discontinue operations of one of its subsidiaries. The results of the subsidiary's operations for the fiscal year ended April 30, 19X4, by quarter are:

Quarter	Income (Loss)
First	$720,000
Second	405,000
Third	(193,700)
Fourth	(516,000)
Total	$415,300

The disposal date is to be June 30, 19X4, and operations during May and June of 19X4 are expected to result in a loss of $485,000. The sales price of the subsidiary is $30,007,000, and the net book value of the assets remaining at the date of disposition will be $29,285,000.

After the measurement date but prior to year end, assets with a book value of $9,873,000 were disposed of for $10,610,000 according to the authorized plan. The results of this transaction are not included in the results of operations by quarter. Dayton Corporation is subject to a 38% tax rate.

The income from continuing operations is $7,324,000 after taxes.

Required:

Assume that Dayton's disposal plan meets the criteria for discontinued operations. Present the necessary information in a partial income statement for Dayton Corporation as of April 30, 19X4. Show all supporting schedules and computations in good form.

Problem 3-3. XYZ Company decided in 19X9 to adopt the straight-line method of depreciation for equipment. The straight-line method will be used for new acquisitions as well as for previously acquired equipment for which an accelerated method had been used. The effect of this change on manufacturing overhead is not material. Data concerning this change are presented in the following table.

Years	Accelerated Depreciation	Straight-Line
Prior to 19X5	$67,290,000	$67,270,000
19X5	257,600	177,600
19X6	275,400	205,400
19X7	309,000	259,000
19X8	289,000	259,000
19X9	332,000	322,000

The depreciation for 19X9 was recorded properly. The applicable income tax rate for the XYZ Company is 48%. Income for years 19X8 and 19X9 was as follows:

	19X8	19X9
Income before extraordinary item and cumulative effect of change in accounting principle....................	$970,000	$1,106,000
Extraordinary item	65,000	

Required:

(1) Present computations, in good form, to compute the effect of the change in accounting principle.
(2) Present the method of reporting this change in the financial statements of XYZ Company.   *(continued)*

(3) Write a footnote to disclose the change in principle in accordance with the requirements of APB Opinion No. 30.

Problem 3-4. The condensed income and retained earnings statement of Shiloh Company for the years ended December 31, 19X4, and December 31, 19X3, is as follows:

Shiloh Company
Condensed Income and Retained Earnings Statement
For Year Ended December 31

	19X4	19X3
Sales	$3,000,000	$2,400,000
Cost of goods sold	1,300,000	1,150,000
Gross profit	$1,700,000	$1,250,000
Selling, general, and administrative expenses	1,200,000	950,000
Income before extraordinary item	$ 500,000	$ 300,000
Extraordinary item	(400,000)	—
Net income	$ 100,000	$ 300,000
Retained earnings, January 1	750,000	450,000
Retained earnings, December 31	$ 850,000	$ 750,000

The following are four unrelated situations involving accounting changes and classification of certain items as ordinary or extraordinary. Each situation is based upon the 19X4 and 19X3 condensed income and retained earnings statements of Shiloh Company and requires revisions of these statements.

Situation A

On January 1, 19X2, Shiloh acquired machinery at a cost of $150,000. The company adopted the double-declining-balance method of depreciation for this machinery, and has been recording depreciation over an estimated life of ten years, with no residual value. At the beginning of 19X4, a decision was made to adopt the straight-line method of depreciation for this machinery. Due to an oversight, however, the double-declining-balance method was used for 19X4. For financial reporting purposes, depreciation is included in selling, general, and administrative expenses.

The extraordinary item in the condensed income and retained earnings statement for 19X4 relates to shutdown expenses incurred by the company during a major strike by its operating employees during 19X4.

Situation B

At the end of 19X4, Shiloh's management decided that the estimated loss rate on uncollectible accounts receivable was too low. The loss rate used for the years 19X3 and 19X4 was 1% of total sales, and due to an increase in the write-off of uncollectible accounts, the rate has been raised to 3% of total sales. The amount recorded in uncollectible accounts expense under the heading of selling, general, and administrative expenses for 19X4 was $30,000 and for 19X3 was $24,000.

The extraordinary item in the condensed income and retained earnings statement for 19X4 relates to a loss incurred in the abandonment of outmoded equipment formerly used in the business.

Situation C

The extraordinary item in the condensed income and retained earnings statement for 19X4 relates to a settlement agreement between Shiloh and the Internal Revenue Service in which Shiloh was assessed and agreed to pay additional income taxes of $60,000 for 19X3 and $340,000 for the four prior years.

Situation D

Late in 19X4, it was discovered that 19X2 administrative expenses did not include $90,000 of compensation expense associated with certain stock option plans. The extraordinary item in the condensed income and retained earnings statement for 19X4 relates to a loss incurred as the result of a flood. No floods had previously occurred in the area.

Required:

For each of the four unrelated situations, prepare revised condensed income and retained earnings statements of the Shiloh Company on a work sheet for the years ended December 31, 19X4, and December 31, 19X3. Each answer should recognize the appropriate accounting changes and other items outlined in the situation. Ignore all earnings per share computations and all pro forma computations.

Problem 3-5. The Freedom Company is preparing its year-end financial statements. The auditor has been asked to examine the statements and to properly classify the operations for income statement purposes. The following information is available:

(a) Income after taxes from all activity during the period is $1,500,000.

(b) On March 1, 19X7, a decision was made to sell the fertilizer segment of the business to a competitor. The segment results for the year were sales of $300,000; cost of goods sold of $270,000; and other expenses of $60,000. Two thirds of these revenues and costs of goods sold accumulated after the measurement date, but only one half of the other expenses were incurred during that period of time. The book value of the discontinued segment was $4,250,000, and the disposal price of $4,325,000 is contained in a firm sales contract. The disposal date is to be March 1, 19X8, and projected data indicate the same future revenues and expenses as have been incurred in this fiscal year up to March 1.

(c) During this fiscal year, the company changed from the sum-of-the-years-digits method to the straight-line method of computing depreciation for all segments except the fertilizer segment. The depreciable property subject to this change is as follows:

Year of Acquisition	Cost	Useful Life
19X4	$1,050,000	20 years
19X5	4,200,000	20 years
19X6	550,000	10 years
19X7	1,515,000	5 years

A full year of depreciation is taken in the year of acquisition. It has been determined that there is no salvage value for any of these assets and that the depreciation expense for the current year was erroneously recorded under the sum-of-the-years-digits method.

(d) The company moved its main cattle feed operation from a plant in Ohio to other plants already producing these goods. The plant was disposed of at a loss of $250,000.

(e) A flood destroyed a warehouse and its contents, the total book value of which is $2,300,000. The insurance proceeds of $480,000 were only for the contents of the warehouse. A flood has never before been experienced in this area.

(f) The applicable tax rate is 40%.

Required:

(1) Present the necessary supporting schedules for all net income adjustments resulting from any reclassification of the additional data.
(2) Present the portion of the income statement for Freedom Company starting with income from continuing operations for the fiscal year ending December 31, 19X7.

Problem 3-6. The Paxton Company has sought assistance in preparing its third quarter, 19X8, income statement. Pertinent data for the third quarter are as follows:

(a) The estimated effective tax rate has been revised in the third quarter to 40% as compared to management's earlier estimate of 30%.
(b) Income before taxes from all operations was $1,420,000.
(c) The cost of goods sold from *all* operations was determined by the lifo inventory method as follows:

	Total	Average Cost Per Unit
Beginning inventory...........	$ 500,000	$50
Purchases....................	1,800,000	60
Goods available..............	$2,300,000	
Ending inventory..............	100,000	
	$2,200,000	

It is expected that the annual 19X8 ending inventory will be $400,000 and that the expected replacement cost of inventory will be $65 per unit during the fourth quarter of 19X8.

(d) Included in the revenues is a rather unusual, first-time sale of marketable securities which were acquired in an earlier year as part of an investment portfolio. The securities sold during the third quarter had a basis of $210,000 and were sold for $185,000.

(e) During the third quarter, management adopted a plan calling for the discontinuation of its engineering consulting segment. The performance of this segment, excluding disposals of assets, is as follows:

	Quarter			
	1	*2*	*3*	*4 (Expected)*
Revenue	$ 800,000	$ 400,000	$ 200,000	$ 300,000
Depreciation...............	(25,000)	(20,000)	(18,000)	(18,000)
Other operating expenses ..	(700,000)	(1,100,000)	(622,000)	(632,000)
Income before taxes	$ 75,000	$ (720,000)	$(440,000)	$(350,000)

Approximately 90% of all third-quarter revenue and expenses relate to the period prior to the measurement date. It is expected that operations of the segment during 19X9 prior to final disposal will result in a pretax loss of $100,000.

Some of the assets of the discontinued segment were sold prior to the measurement date for a loss of $50,000. The balance of the segment's assets will be disposed of in 19X9 for an estimated gain of $500,000.

(f) Revenue for the third quarter also includes $160,000 of revenue resulting from the settlement of a rate dispute traceable to the first quarter of 19X8. The amount of the settlement was previously not capable of estimation.

Previously issued interim income statements reported pretax net losses of $950,000 for the first two quarters of 19X8 respectively. At that time only $400,000 of the losses were carried back to prior years, with no assurance that the balance of the loss had tax benefits (i.e., could be carried forward).

Required:

Prepare in good form the income statement for the third quarter of 19X8 and all necessary supporting schedules.

Problem 3-7. The Mikelson Company, a California corporation listed on the Pacific Coast Stock Exchange, budgeted activities for 19X5 as follows:

	Amount	Units
Net sales	$6,000,000	1,000,000
Cost of goods sold	3,600,000	1,000,000
Gross profit	$2,400,000	
Selling, general, and administrative expenses	1,400,000	
Operating income	$1,000,000	
Nonoperating revenue and expenses	-0-	
Income before income taxes	$1,000,000	
Estimated income taxes (current and deferred)	550,000	
Net income	$ 450,000	
Earnings per share of common stock	$4.50	

Mikelson has operated profitably for many years and has experienced a seasonal pattern of sales volume and production. For 19X5, sales volume is expected to follow a quarterly pattern of 10%, 20%, 35%, and 35%, respectively, because of the seasonality of the industry. Also, due to production and storage capacity limitations, it is expected that production will follow a pattern of 20%, 25%, 30%, and 25% per quarter, respectively.

At the end of the first quarter of 19X5, the controller of Mikelson prepared and issued the following interim report for public release:

	Amount	Units
Net sales	$ 600,000	100,000
Cost of goods sold	360,000	100,000
Gross profit	$ 240,000	
Selling, general, and administrative expenses	275,000	
Operating loss	$ (35,000)	
Loss from warehouse fire	(175,000)	
Loss before income taxes	$(210,000)	
Estimated income taxes	-0-	
Net loss	$(210,000)	
Loss per share of common stock	$(2.10)	

The following additional information is available for the first quarter, but was not included in the public information released:

(a) The company uses a standard cost system in which standards are set at currently attainable levels on an annual basis. At the end of the first quarter, there was underapplied fixed factory overhead (volume variance) of $50,000 that was treated as an asset at the end of the quarter. Production during the quarter was 200,000 units, of which 100,000 were sold.

(b) The selling, general, and administrative expenses were budgeted on a basis of $900,000 fixed expenses for the year plus 50 cents variable expenses per unit of sales.

(c) Assume that the warehouse fire loss met the conditions of an extraordinary loss. The warehouse had an undepreciated cost of $320,000; $145,000 was recovered from insurance on the warehouse. No other gains or losses are anticipated this year from similar events or transactions, nor has Mikelson had ,any similar losses in preceding years; thus, the full loss will be deductible as an ordinary loss for income tax purposes.

(d) The effective income tax rate, for federal and state taxes combined, is expected to average 55% of income before income taxes during 19X5. There are no permanent differences between pretax accounting income and taxable income.

Required:

(1) Without reference to the specific situations described above, what are the standards of disclosure for interim financial data (published interim financial reports) for publicly traded companies? Explain.

(2) Identify the weaknesses in form and content of Mikelson's interim report without reference to the additional information.

(3) For each of the four items of additional information, indicate the preferable treatment for each item for interim reporting purposes and explain why that treatment is preferable.   (AICPA adapted)

Problem 3-8.   Reese, Inc., reports the results of operations on a quarterly basis. The management of Reese has asked you to examine the following data so that you may assist in preparing the quarterly financial reports.

(a) For the full fiscal year, Reese anticipates ordinary income of $55,000. All income is taxable at a 45% rate. Anticipated tax credits for the fiscal year are $2,750. No permanent differences between accounting and taxable income are anticipated. No changes in estimated ordinary income, tax rates, or tax credits occur during the year.

(b) Only $30,000 of a prior year's income is available for possible operating loss carrybacks that may arise in the current period. The tax effects of losses incurred are not assured until income is earned in later interim periods.

(c) Results for the current year are as follows:

Quarter	Continuing Operations	Extraordinary Item
First	$(46,000)	
Second	18,200	
Third	15,800	$(105,000)
Fourth	35,000	

(d) In the fourth quarter, the board of directors of Reese, Inc., voted to sell a segment of the operations which represents all of the company's dealings in the publishing field. The disposition was completed by year end. The first three quarters include results of operations of the discontinued segment, while the fourth quarter does not. The segment reported net losses for the first three quarters of $10,000, $7,000 and $15,000 respectively. The fourth quarter showed the following:

Operating income	$ 4,000
Gain on sale	23,000

Required:

(1) Calculate the estimated annual effective tax rate for Reese, Inc., for the current fiscal year.
(2) For each quarter, present the amount of tax expense or tax benefit that would appear on the published quarterly financial statements of Reese, Inc. For comparative purposes, Reese presents the results of operations of all previous quarters with each new quarter. Show all computations in good form. If restatement of a quarter is necessary, show data for both the original presentation and the restatement.

Problem 3-9. The Spandel Corporation began operations early in January of 19X5. At the beginning of the current year, 19X7, management projected a loss of $20,000 for the fiscal year. A breakdown of this figure by quarters reveals the following pretax amounts:

Quarter	Income (Loss)
First	$(240,000)
Second	325,000
Third	200,000
Fourth	(305,000)
	$ (20,000)

The actual quarterly pretax results were as follows:

Quarter	Income (Loss)
First	$(180,000)
Second	200,000
Third	210,000
Fourth	440,000
	$ 670,000

In addition to the above results from normal operations, the following other transactions affected the net earnings:

(a) A change in accounting principle occurred in the second quarter. A cumulative gain of $40,000 resulted as of the beginning of that quarter, but a gain of only $30,000 would have resulted if the change had been made at the beginning of the year.
(b) There was a nonrecurring and unusual loss of $120,000 in the third quarter.
(c) The tax rates changed in midyear due to a revision of anticipated tax credits. Estimates of the quarterly tax rates were as follows:

Quarters	Tax Rate
First and second	40%
Third and fourth	45%

Required:

Compute the amount of tax expense for presentation on the interim financial statements of the company.

Present your solution based on the information that would have been available at the end of each quarter. If any restatement is necessary, present the tax expense computations before and after restatement of income. Your solution should employ the following columnar headings:

(1) Quarter
(2) Ordinary Income (Loss)
(3) Cumulative Effect of Change in Principle
(4) Extraordinary Items
(5) Cumulative Total
(6) Tax Rate

Tax Expense (Benefit)
   (7) Total Year-to-Date
   (8) Prior Periods
   (9) Current Ordinary
  (10) Extraordinary
  (11) Change in Principle

CHAPTER 4

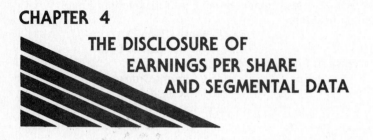

THE DISCLOSURE OF
EARNINGS PER SHARE
AND SEGMENTAL DATA

The income statement is designed to provide the user with a measure of an entity's current economic performance and also provide data which may be useful for predicting future performance. Therefore, in addition to disclosing the various components of income on an aggregate basis, as discussed in Chapter 3, each component must also be disclosed on a per share of common stock basis.

The first section of the chapter sets forth the basic principles governing the calculation of earnings per share (EPS). Although the determination of EPS is extremely complex, the resulting information represents an important measure of an economic entity's performance.

The second topic in this chapter deals with special disclosure requirements for companies with diversified business operations. Many modern businesses operate within several industries or product areas and, in the past, have presented income and other data on a total enterprise basis. However, financial information is more useful if it is also presented for the various operating components or segments within the enterprise.

EARNINGS PER SHARE

The determination of earnings per share (EPS) of common stock has received considerable attention by both accounting and financial communities because EPS is significant with respect to the evaluation of an entity's past and future operations. The importance of EPS has also been demonstrated by both theoretical analysis and empirical research dealing with security valuation and dividend policy.

Although some may feel that the calculation of EPS is an area best left to the various users of financial data, the AICPA has committed substantial effort to the establishment of principles to govern the calculation and disclosure of EPS data. For example, the calculation of EPS was the topic of Accounting Research Bulletin No. 49, issued in 1958, and Accounting Principles Board (APB) Opinion No. 9, "Reporting the Results of Operations," issued in 1966. However, the validity of the principles established in APB Opinion No. 9 was questioned to the extent that the APB issued Opinion No. 15, "Earnings per Share," in 1969. This Opinion attempts to establish principles which will be consistently applied among various entities. To provide a more complete discussion of these principles, an interpretation of APB Opinion No. 15 was issued in 1970.

The Substance of APB Opinion No. 15

APB Opinion No. 15 requires the disclosure, on the face of the income statement, of EPS data for each of the following levels of income: income from continuing operations, discontinued operations, extraordinary items, the cumulative effect of changes in principles, and net income.[1] The purpose of this per share disclosure is to show the potential or prospective effect which certain securities will have on EPS. These securities include common and preferred stocks, bonds, warrants, stock options, stock purchase contracts, stock subscriptions, and other agreements to issue stock.

Rather than focusing on earnings per share of outstanding stock, the per share calculation emphasizes a statistic which will have maximum predictive value. Therefore, attention is placed on determining what EPS would be if certain securities were converted into common stock, and if the conversion effect would be dilutive (i.e., cause a decrease in EPS). This approach is conservative, since, in most cases, the disclosure of antidilutive effects on EPS (i.e., potential increases in EPS) is not permitted.

The extent of the EPS disclosure is also dependent upon whether the capital structure of the entity is viewed as simple or complex. A *simple* capital structure has no securities outstanding (or agreements to issue such securities) that, in the aggregate, could dilute earnings per outstanding common share. If there are securities outstanding which, in the aggregate, could dilute earnings per outstanding common share, but such dilution is less than 3%, this capital structure is also considered to be simple. A capital structure is *complex* if various securities outstanding could have a dilutive effect of at least 3%.

For simple capital structures, per share data should be labeled as "earnings per common share." Corporations whose capital structures are complex are required to present two measures of EPS (dual presentation): primary earnings per share and fully diluted earnings per share.

Primary earnings per share (PEPS) is the amount of net income attributable to each share of common stock plus other securities which are in substance common stock and are technically referred to as common stock equivalents. The PEPS disclosure reflects the prospective

---

[1] Mutual companies, registered investment companies, government-owned corporations, and nonprofit corporations are not subject to this requirement. Per share data also need not be prepared for parent company statements accompanying consolidated statements, for statements of wholly-owned subsidiaries, and for special purpose statements. *Statement of Financial Accounting Standards, No. 21,* has amended APB Opinion No. 15 to the extent that earnings per share disclosure for nonpublic enterprises is no longer required.

viewpoint of APB Opinion No. 15. For example, a user of financial statements may be concerned with the following question: Given a constant level of income, if changes occur in the entity's capital structure, what would future EPS be? Such a question is particularly significant when agreements which could increase outstanding shares already exist. If EPS data are to serve predictive purposes, then the possible effect of common stock equivalents, which may or may not eventually increase the number of outstanding shares of common stock, must be disclosed. If EPS data were to serve only as an indicator of past operations, however, then the effect of common stock equivalents would be of little value.

Fully diluted earnings per share (FDEPS) is the amount of net income attributable to each share of common stock, common stock equivalent, and other dilutive securities. For the most part, the other dilutive securities influencing FDEPS will consist of securities which failed to meet the conditions established for common stock equivalents, and of common stock equivalents whose effect on FDEPS and PEPS is computed differently. The intent of disclosing FDEPS is to provide per share data which reflect the maximum potential dilution arising from securities which, upon conversion or exercise, would increase the number of common shares outstanding. PEPS may be described as a conservative measure, while FDEPS is an ultraconservative measure.

The basic starting point for the calculation of PEPS and FDEPS is earnings per common share. This latter per share statistic is computed as follows:

$$\text{Earnings per Common Share} = \frac{\text{Adjusted Net Income (ANI)}}{\substack{\text{Weighted Average Number of}\\ \text{Shares Outstanding During}\\ \text{the Period (S)}}}$$

The adjusted net income (ANI) represents reported net income, reduced by the amount of preferred dividends paid or declared this period or the current period dividends in arrears on cumulative preferred stock. In those capital structures where two or more classes of common stock exist, per share data are computed for the "ordinary" class of common stock. Therefore, net income must also be adjusted for the dividends paid (declared) or currently in arrears on other classes of common stock.

The computation of PEPS and FDEPS is an iterative process for assessing the prospective effect of potentially dilutive securities on per share data. Each potentially dilutive security will have an assumed effect on the number of shares used to compute EPS, and may have an assumed effect on the net income used in the computation. As each security is considered, a "Share Adjustment" (SA), representing the change in shares traceable to the security, and an "Income Adjustment" (IA), representing the change in income traceable to the security, must be determined. For example, if a convertible preferred stock were considered the equivalent of common stock, the number of shares used to compute EPS would be increaséd by a share adjustment equal to the number of common shares which would have been issued upon conversion of the preferred stock. The earnings used to compute EPS would also be increased by an income adjustment equal to the current dividends on preferred stock which would not have been declared if the preferred stock had been converted into common stock.

The basic methodology for computing EPS is demonstrated in Illustration I, and involves the following steps:

1. For each security, calculate

$$EPS_i = \frac{ANI_{i-1} + IA_i}{S_{i-1} + SA_i} = \frac{ANI_i}{S_i}$$

where: ANI_{i-1} = the adjusted net income before considering security i.

IA_i = the income adjustment traceable to security i.

S_{i-1} = the shares assumed to be outstanding before considering security i.

SA_i = the share adjustment traceable to security i.

ANI_i = the adjusted net income considering security i.

S_i = the shares assumed outstanding considering security i.

2. Determine the change in EPS, as follows:

$$\Delta EPS_i = EPS_i - EPS_{i-1}$$

where: ΔEPS_i = the change in EPS resulting from the evaluation of security i.

3. Consider whether security i is dilutive, as follows:

If ΔEPS_i is negative, then security i has a dilutive effect and should be considered.

If ΔEPS_i is positive, then security i has an antidilutive effect and should usually be ignored.

Although the sign of ΔEPS will indicate whether a security is dilutive, other procedures can be used to identify antidilutive securities before the change in EPS is actually measured. These procedures are discussed in later sections of the chapter.

Illustration I—BASIC METHODOLOGY FOR COMPUTING EPS

Assume that earnings per share of common stock is $2 $\left(\frac{ANI}{S} = \frac{\$200,000}{100,000}\right)$.

Assume that there are two common stock equivalents (i = 1, 2) with income adjustments (IA) and share adjustments (SA) as indicated in the following analysis:

	ANI_{i-1}	IA_i	ANI_i	S_{i-1}	SA_i	S_i	EPS_i
Earnings per common share	$200,000	—	$200,000	100,000	—	100,000	$2.00
i = 1	200,000	$20,000	220,000	100,000	20,000	120,000	1.83
i = 2	220,000	—	220,000	120,000	10,000	130,000	1.69*

*This amount will be reported as the EPS.

The earnings per common share, $\dfrac{ANI}{S}$, is the basis upon which the potential dilutive effect of the first security is determined. It may also be necessary to compare EPS_{i-1} with the earnings per share for another level of income because a security may have a dilutive effect on one level of income (e.g., income from continuing operations), and an antidilutive effect on another level of income (e.g., an extraordinary loss). Since a security which has a dilutive effect on any level of income should be included in the computation of per share data for all other levels, the base EPS against which the dilutive effects of other securities is assessed should be the highest income figure (e.g., income from continuing operations or perhaps income after extraordinary gains).

To demonstrate this concept of assessing the dilutive effect of a common stock equivalent, assume the following:

Income from continuing operations	$100,000
Extraordinary loss	(20,000)
Net income	$ 80,000
Weighted average number of common shares outstanding	40,000

The earnings per common share is as follows:

Income from continuing operations per common share	$2.50
Extraordinary loss per common share	(.50)
Net income per common share	$2.00

Assuming that a common stock equivalent will result in a share adjustment of 10,000 shares and an income adjustment of $22,500 on income from continuing operations, the EPS considering the common stock equivalent is as follows:

Income from continuing operations per share	
[($100,000 + $22,500) ÷ (40,000 + 10,000)]	$2.45
Extraordinary loss per share [$20,000 ÷ (40,000 + 10,000)]	(.40)
Net income per share	$2.05

If the base against which potential dilution is evaluated is final net income, the common stock equivalent would be ignored because it is antidilutive ($2.05 versus $2.00). However, if the base against which dilution is evaluated is the highest income figure, or income from continuing operations in this example, the common stock equivalent would be considered as dilutive ($2.45 versus $2.50). Therefore, in order to assess properly the dilutive nature of a common stock equivalent, its effect on the highest level of income should be the determining factor.

Primary Earnings per Share

As mentioned previously, primary earnings per share represents the earnings per share of common stock and common stock equivalents. The initial problem in calculating PEPS is to determine which securities are common stock equivalents. As defined in APB Opinion No. 15, a common stock equivalent is:

. . . a security which is not, in form, a common stock but which usually contains provisions to enable its holder to become a common stockholder and which, because of its terms and the circumstances under which it was issued, is in substance equivalent to a common stock.[2]

The designation of a security as a common stock equivalent is based on an evaluation of the security's substance rather than its form. Changes in the economic value of a common stock equivalent are to a large extent a function of changing values resulting from earnings and earnings potential of the common stock to which they are equivalent. This functional relationship exists even if the common stock equivalent is not converted into the common stock or such conversion is not imminent. The various types of common stock equivalents are discussed in the following paragraphs.

Options and Warrants. Options and warrants represent rights to acquire shares of common stock in exchange for cash (exercise price) in accordance with underlying agreements. The following securities are also considered to be the equivalent of options and warrants: stock purchase contracts, stock subscriptions not yet fully paid, deferred compensation plans requiring the issuance of common stock, and convertible securities allowing or requiring the payment of cash at conversion (regardless of yield).[3] These securities derive their entire value from the right to acquire common stock and, therefore, are automatically viewed as common stock equivalents at all times. However, according to APB Opinion No. 15, a security will not be recognized as a common stock equivalent and will not be included in the calculation of PEPS unless the following criteria are satisfied:

1. The security must be exercisable within five years from the end of the current period.
2. The market price of the common stock obtainable upon exercise must be greater than the exercise price for substantially all of three consecutive months ending with the last month of any past or present period for which per share data are being presented. Once the three-month test is satisfied in any period, past or present, the security will be considered a common stock equivalent from that period on (assuming that the first criterion is also satisfied).

The second criterion is established as a practical matter rather than as an absolute necessity. It prevents securities from being in and out of the EPS computation because of market price fluctuations above and below the exercise price.

Assuming that the two criteria have been met, the option or warrant will not enter into the calculation of PEPS unless the effect is dilutive. Such an effect will be experienced if, during the reporting period, the

---

[2] *Opinions of the Accounting Principles Board, No. 15,* "Earnings per Share" (New York: American Institute of Certified Public Accountants, 1969), par. 25.

[3] For a detailed discussion of the treatment of stock compensation plans in earnings per share computations, see *FASB Interpretation No. 31,* "Treatment of Stock Compensation Plans in EPS Computations" (Stamford: Financial Accounting Standards Board, 1980).

average market price of the common stock obtainable upon exercise is greater than the exercise price. The reporting period is typically three months; however, if a longer period is involved, a quarterly averaging technique is employed.

Outstanding options or warrants that qualify as common stock equivalents are assumed to be exercised at the beginning of the period or at the issuance date, if later. The assumed exercise of these securities would result in the generation of funds in an amount equal to the earliest effective exercise price during the five-year period multiplied by the assumed number of shares to be obtained. These hypothetical funds could be employed in a variety of ways. For example, the funds could be used to reduce debt and thereby reduce interest expense, to purchase short-term government securities as an investment, or to expand the business and thereby earn the corporation's normal return on invested capital.

The APB recognized that some use of the funds had to be assumed, even though there was no certainty that the assumed use would even approach the actual use of funds received when options or warrants were actually exercised. Therefore, to achieve consistency, the Board recommended the use of the *treasury stock method*, which assumes that the generated funds are used to acquire common stock at the average market price for the period. This assumption is advantageous because the purchase of common stock does not result in an income adjustment. However, if a warrant allows or requires the tendering or retirement of debt, or if a convertible security requires the payment of cash upon conversion, an income adjustment is necessary. This adjustment is equal to the net-of-tax interest on debt, or the dividend on convertible preferred stock.

For each option or warrant, the share adjustment under the treasury stock method is determined by using the following formula:

$$\text{Share Adjustment (SA)} = \frac{\text{Total Shares Obtainable}}{\text{Upon Exercise of Security}} - \frac{\text{Exercise Proceeds}}{\text{Average Market Price of Shares}}$$

The share adjustment will always be a positive number because options or warrants cannot influence PEPS unless the effect is dilutive, i.e., unless the average market price is greater than the exercise price. The share adjustment must be converted into a weighted average in those instances where the security was not outstanding during the entire period. If a security is exercised during the period, the number of treasury shares assumed to be acquired is also based on the average market price of the shares prior to exercise.

To demonstrate the treasury stock method, assume that options to acquire 4,000 shares of common stock were granted on January 1, 19X2, and are still outstanding as of December 31, 19X2. The options expire two years from the date of grant, and can be exercised at a price of $12 per share. EPS prior to considering the options is $2, based on 25,000 shares. Assuming an average market price of $13.25, EPS would be computed as follows:

Income adjustment (IA): Not applicable
Share adjustment (SA):

$$SA = \frac{\text{Total Shares Obtainable}}{\text{Upon Exercise of Security}} - \frac{\text{Exercise Proceeds}}{\text{Average Market Price of Shares}}$$

$$= 4{,}000 - \frac{\$48{,}000}{\$13.25}$$

$$= 4{,}000 - 3{,}623$$

$$= 377 \text{ shares}$$

EPS considering option (EPS$_i$):

$$EPS_i = \frac{ANI_{i-1} + IA_i}{S_{i-1} + SA_i}$$

$$= \frac{\$50{,}000 + 0}{25{,}000 + 377}$$

$$= \$1.97$$

When the reporting period is longer than three months and there are significant flucutations in market values during the year, a *quarterly averaging technique* is used in applying the treasury stock method. However, if market prices are relatively stable during the year, the treasury stock method may be applied on an annual basis using the annual average market price, as was done in the previous example. The quarterly averaging technique, as well as the concepts affecting the application of the treasury stock method for options and warrants to be considered in the computation of PEPS, are demonstrated in Illustration II.

Illustration II—PRIMARY EPS COMPUTATIONS: OPTIONS AND WARRANTS

1. At the beginning of 19X6, 250,000 shares of common stock were outstanding. The net income for 19X6 was $400,000.
2. During 19X6, the following stock warrants existed:
   Warrant X—10,000 warrants issued in 19X2, giving the holder of each warrant the right to purchase one share of common stock for $40. One thousand warrants were exercised on June 30, 19X6.
   Warrant Y—5,000 warrants issued in 19X4, giving the holder of each warrant the right to purchase one share of common stock for $50 anytime after December 31, 19Y2.
3. Both warrants X and Y had previously met the three-month test.
4. Relevant market price information for 19X6 was as follows:

Quarter	Average Market Price
1	$41
2	43
3	49
4	53

(continued)

Calculation of Income and Share Adjustments for PEPS

Stock Warrant X

This warrant is considered in the calculation of PEPS because it meets both the five-year and three-month tests.

9,000 Warrants Not Exercised

Income adjustment: Not applicable
Share adjustment:

Using the Quarterly Averaging Technique

Quarter	Shares Obtainable	Treasury Shares Acquired	SA
1	9,000	$\dfrac{\$360,000}{\$41} = 8,780$	220
2	9,000	$\dfrac{\$360,000}{\$43} = 8,372$	628
3	9,000	$\dfrac{\$360,000}{\$49} = 7,347$	1,653
4	9,000	$\dfrac{\$360,000}{\$53} = 6,792$	2,208
			4,709

Weighted average SA = 4,709 ÷ 4 = 1,177 shares

1,000 Warrants Exercised

Income adjustment: Not applicable
Share adjustment:

Using the Quarterly Averaging Technique

Quarter	Shares Obtainable	Treasury Shares Acquired	SA
1	1,000	$\dfrac{\$40,000}{\$41^*} = 976$	24
2	1,000	$\dfrac{\$40,000}{\$43^*} = 930$	70
3	Not applicable		-0-
4	Not applicable		-0-
			94

Weighted average SA = 94 ÷ 4 = 24 shares

* Average market price during period prior to exercise

Stock Warrant Y

This warrant is not considered in the calculation of PEPS because it fails to meet the five-year test.

Calculation of PEPS

	ANI_{i-1}	IA_i	ANI_i	S_{i-1}	SA_i	S_i	EPS_i
Earnings per common share	$400,000	—	$400,000	250,500*	—	250,500	$1.5968
X (not exercised)	400,000	—	400,000	250,500	1,177	251,677	1.5893
X (exercised)	400,000	—	400,000	251,677	24	251,701	1.5892
Y	Not a common stock equivalent—fails 5-year test						

*Weighted average of shares outstanding during the year: 250,000 shares + ½ of 1,000 shares issued on June 30 = 250,500

The Special "20%" Rule. The treasury stock method is further complicated when the potential exercise of all options and warrants, whether dilutive or not, would result in the actual issuance of additional shares which, in the aggregate, exceed 20% of the outstanding shares of common stock at the end of the period. In this case, all options and warrants which meet the five-year and three-month criteria are assumed to be exercised, whether dilutive or not, and the aggregate exercise proceeds are applied as follows:

   a. As if the funds obtained were first applied to the repurchase of outstanding common shares at the average market price during the period (treasury stock method) but not to exceed 20% of the outstanding shares; and then
   b. As if the balance of funds were applied first to reduce any short-term or long-term borrowings and any remaining funds were invested in U.S. government securities or commercial paper, with appropriate recognition of any income tax effect.[4]

The results of these two steps are aggregated for all options and warrants, and if the net effect is dilutive, all options and warrants should enter into the determination of PEPS. With the "20%" rule in effect, an income adjustment may result, as well as a share adjustment.

To demonstrate the "20%" rule, assume that options to acquire 15,000 shares of common stock were granted on November 1, 19X0, and are outstanding at the end of 19X2. The options expire on December 31, 19X4, and may be exercised at $20 per share. In addition, on April 30, 19X1, warrants to acquire 10,000 shares of common stock were issued. These warrants are outstanding as of December 31, 19X2, expire on December 31, 19X6, and may be exercised at $25 per share. For the year 19X2, 100,000 shares of common stock were outstanding, net income was $450,000 and the only outstanding debt of the company was $200,000 in 5% bonds. The tax rate is 40% and the average market price of common stock in all quarters was $22 per share. Because the total number of shares (15,000 + 10,000, or 25,000) obtainable by the options is greater than 20% of the outstanding common stock (20% of 100,000, or 20,000 shares), the special 20% rule is applicable and would be applied to 19X2 as follows:

Total proceeds [15,000 ($20) + 10,000 ($25)]	$550,000
Less proceeds used to purchase up to 20,000 shares at $22 each ..	440,000
Proceeds available to retire debt and interest	$110,000

Share adjustment:
   SA = 25,000 shares − 20,000 shares = 5,000 shares
Income adjustment:
   IA = $110,000 × 5% interest rate × (1 - 40% tax rate) = $3,300

The PEPS is calculated as follows:

$$EPS_i = \frac{\$450,000 \;+\; \$3,300}{100,000 \;+\; 5,000} = \$4.32$$

[4] *Ibid.*, par. 38.

If the market value had been high enough, it is possible that it would not be feasible to acquire 20,000 shares of treasury stock. For example, using the same assumptions, except that the average market price was $30 per share, the share and income adjustments would be as follows:

Share adjustment:

SA = 25,000 shares − 18,333 shares ($550,000 ÷ $30) = 6,667 shares

Income adjustment:

Not applicable because all available proceeds were used to acquire treasury stock in an amount not exceeding 20% of the outstanding common stock.

Contingent Shares. Contingent shares are shares which are issuable in the future, based upon the passage of time or upon the attainment of certain conditions which typically relate to the level of future income or future stock market values. For shares issuable upon the passage of time, there is no income adjustment, and the share adjustment should be based on the assumption that the shares involved have always been outstanding since the inception of the contingent share agreement. For purposes of computing PEPS, contingent shares which are issuable upon the attainment of specified conditions should only be considered outstanding if the specified conditions are currently being met.

To illustrate, assume that Musketeer, Inc., has 500,000 common shares outstanding for 19X9 and income of $750,000. In addition, Musketeer has an agreement to issue 75,000 shares to management if income is at least $700,000 per year in 19X9, and an additional 15,000 shares if income is in excess of $800,000. Calculation of PEPS would be as follows:

$$\text{EPS}_i = \frac{\$750,000 + 0}{500,000 + 75,000} = \$1.30$$

There is no income adjustment for a contingent agreement based on the passage of time or for one in which the attainment of a goal is currently being met. The 15,000 additional shares cannot be included in PEPS because the desired income level of more than $800,000 is not currently being met.

Convertible Securities. A convertible security is one which can be converted into common stock at the option of the holder. Therefore, a portion of the security's value may be traceable to the value of the related common stock. At the time of original issuance, if a significant portion of the convertible security's value is traceable to this conversion feature, the security should be considered a common stock equivalent.

Cash Yield Test. Primarily for practical reasons, the APB adopted the cash yield test for determining whether a convertible security is a common stock equivalent. According to this test, if the convertible security's cash yield, based on the market price at time of issuance, is less than two thirds of the then current bank prime interest rate, the security should be considered a common stock equivalent. If the yield test is satisfied, it would suggest that the holder of convertible securities is willing to accept less than the current rate of return (as indicated by the prime interest rate) because of the intrinsic value associated with the convertible securities being equivalent to common stock.

In applying the cash yield test, it should be noted that:

1. It is a one-time test, applied at issuance, and the security either is or is not classified as a common stock equivalent at that time. However, if another convertible security, with the same terms as the security failing the yield test, exists or is later issued and is considered a common stock equivalent, the security initially failing the test should be reclassified as a common stock equivalent.
2. The current bank prime interest rate is a short-term borrowing rate which has been volatile in recent years. Therefore, to apply the yield test to securities issued after February 28, 1982, the FASB requires that the average Aa corporate bond yield be used.

Other Criteria and Guidelines. In addition to meeting the cash yield test, a convertible security must be convertible within five years from the end of the current reporting period, if the security is to be considered a common stock equivalent. If various conversion rates exist over the five-year period, the conversion rate in effect during the current period (or if not immediately convertible, the earliest effective conversion rate) should be employed. If the dividend or interest rate on the convertible security is scheduled to change over the five-year period, the lowest scheduled rate during the five-year period should be used for the yield test.

The "If Converted" Method. For each outstanding convertible security which is determined to be a common stock equivalent, it is assumed that the security was converted into common stock as of the beginning of the period or the issuance date, if later.[5] Therefore, a share adjustment and an income adjustment are necessary. The share adjustment is determined by calculating the weighted average number of common shares which would have been outstanding if conversion had taken place. The income adjustment is equal to the net-of-tax interest expense or the preferred stock dividend which would not have been paid or accumulated if the assumed conversion had taken place. Furthermore, the after-tax effect of a premium or discount amortization must be eliminated from income. In the case of convertible bonds, the income adjustment should also include "nondiscretionary" adjustments which were based on some measure of net income, e.g., bonus expense or royalty expense.

To illustrate, assume that $100,000, 4%, 20-year bonds were issued on July 1, 19X2, at a price of 98. Each $1,000 bond is convertible into 10 shares of common stock, beginning July 1, 19X3. Assuming that the cash yield test is satisfied and that the effective tax rate is 40%, the

---

[5] When a common stock equivalent convertible security has actually been converted during a period, the "if converted" method is applied for the period prior to actual conversion. However, the results of applying this method are only included in EPS calculations if the effect is dilutive.

income adjustment and share adjustment would be computed as follows
for 19X2:

Income adjustment:
  Interest = [(4% × $100,000) + ($2,000 discount ÷ 20 years)] × ½ year = $2,050
  Interest after tax = $2,050 × (1 - 40% tax rate) = $1,230
Share adjustment:
  Number of shares = 100 bonds × 10 shares = 1,000 shares
  Weighted average shares = 1,000 × ½ year = 500 shares

When a convertible security is considered a common stock equivalent, it will be included in the PEPS calculation only if its effect is
dilutive. To determine whether a convertible security is dilutive, an
"incremental impact per share" test can be applied as follows:

1. Divide the income adjustment traceable to the convertible security
   by the share adjustment traceable to the convertible security. This
   amount is the "incremental impact per share."
2. If the "incremental impact per share" is greater than EPS_{i-1}, then
   the new EPS_i will be greater than EPS_{i-1}. Therefore, if the "incremental impact per share" is greater than EPS_{i-1}, ignore the security
   because it is antidilutive.
3. If the "incremental impact per share" is less than EPS_{i-1}, the new
   EPS_i will be lower than EPS_{i-1}. Therefore, if the "incremental
   impact per share" is less than EPS_{i-1}, include the security because
   it is dilutive.

To insure that only the dilutive securities enter the per share computations, the following guidelines should be followed:[6]

1. All other primary EPS dilution adjustments must first be deducted,
   i.e., consider convertibles *last*.
2. Each convertible security must be considered individually in the
   order of increasing incremental impacts per share, starting with the
   lowest. (This insures that no security is initially considered dilutive
   only to find that, due to the presence of more dilutive securities, it
   has a greater incremental impact than the final adjusted primary
   EPS.)

To demonstrate these guidelines for determining whether securities
are dilutive, assume the following information regarding convertible securities A and B:

1.

	Yield	Income Adjustment	Share Adjustment	Incremental Impact per Share
Security A	8%	$9,700	1,000	$9.70
Security B	4	4,000	1,500	2.67

2. EPS before considering the convertible securities is $10, based on
   10,000 shares.

---

[6] Paul M. Fischer and Martin J. Gregorcich, "Calculating Earnings per Share," *The Journal of Accountancy* (May, 1973), p. 64.

If the convertible securities are considered in the order presented, EPS would be as follows:

	ANI_i	S_i	EPS_i
EPS before convertibles	$100,000	10,000	$10.00
Security A	109,700	11,000	9.97
Security B	113,700	12,500	9.10

However, if the convertible securities are considered individually in the order of increasing incremental impacts, as suggested by the guideline, EPS would be as follows:

	ANI_i	S_i	EPS_i
EPS before convertibles	$100,000	10,000	$10.00
Security B	104,000	11,500	9.04
Security A	113,700	12,500	9.10

In this case, security A is antidilutive. Therefore, the EPS should be reported as $9.04, rather than the $9.10 from the previous analysis.

Fully Diluted Earnings per Share

The actual calculation of fully diluted earnings per share (FDEPS) is generally based on the weighted average of shares used to calculate PEPS, adjusted in certain instances, plus the effect of other dilutive securities.[7] FDEPS reflects the maximum dilution of EPS which would have resulted if all conversions, exercises of options and warrants, and issuances of contingent shares had taken place at the beginning of the period (or issuance date, if later). However, FDEPS may sometimes include the antidilutive effects of actual conversions and/or exercises.

Options and Warrants. The impact that options and warrants may have on FDEPS is determined by: (1) reconsidering options and warrants which were viewed as common stock equivalents for purposes of calculating PEPS and (2) considering for the first time options and warrants which did not qualify for purposes of calculating PEPS. The three-month test and the 20% test, which were discussed previously, are applicable to the calculation of FDEPS.

The reconsideration of options and warrants which were viewed as common stock equivalents for PEPS is necessary because of certain modifications governing the calculation of FDEPS. For options and warrants which have not been exercised, the share adjustment is based on the use of the market price at the end of the period or the average market price, whichever is greater. Therefore, the share adjustment is determined as follows:

---

[7] Generally a security which affects the calculation of PEPS will also influence the calculation of FDEPS. However, it is possible that a security will be dilutive for PEPS purposes but antidilutive, and thereby excluded, for FDEPS purposes.

$$\text{Share Adjustment (SA)} = \frac{\text{Total Shares Obtainable}}{\text{Upon Exercise of Security}} - \frac{\text{Exercise Proceeds}}{\text{Ending Market Price of Shares or}}$$
Average Market Price, Whichever
Is Greater

If options and/or warrants have been exercised during the period, the share adjustment for the time prior to exercise is always based on the market price at the date of exercise.

Certain options and warrants which did not qualify for purposes of calculating PEPS must be considered for purposes of calculating FDEPS. These options and warrants include those which:

1. Were not exercisable within five years from the end of the current period, or
2. Met the five-year and three-month tests but would have had an antidilutive effect on PEPS.

Options and warrants which fail the five-year criterion for common stock equivalency will enter the calculation of FDEPS if the security is exercisable within ten years from the end of the period, and the higher of the average market price or the ending market price exceeds the lowest exercise price during the ten-year period. This rule will produce the maximum dilutive effect possible.

Another unique aspect of the fully diluted computation involves those securities which are omitted from the calculation of PEPS only because the average market price is less than the exercise price. If the ending market price is higher than the exercise price, even though the average market price is not, the security is included in the computation of FDEPS.

Although financially unattractive and antidilutive, options and/or warrants which are exercised when the market price is less than the exercise price are included in the computation of FDEPS for the period prior to exercise. For this calculation, it is assumed that the securities are exercised at the beginning of the period or at the date of issuance, if later, and the market price at exercise is used in the calculation of the share adjustment.

When there are significant variations between quarterly ending market prices and the annual ending market price, a quarterly averaging technique may be used when the share adjustment is computed for FDEPS. After each quarter is considered in the weighted average, using the higher of the quarter's average or the ending market price, the weighted average share adjustment is compared to the share adjustment calculated by using the actual market price at year end or at the date of exercise, if earlier. The share adjustment used for FDEPS will be the larger of (1) the share adjustment derived by the quarterly averaging technique or (2) the share adjustment derived by use of the year-end market price.

The quarterly averaging technique, as well as the concepts affecting the application of the treasury stock method for options and warrants to be considered in the computation of FDEPS, are demonstrated in Illustration III. This illustration is based on the same facts as in Illustration II, which was concerned with options and warrants in the calculation of PEPS. Illustrations II and III should be compared in order to note the differing treatment given options and warrants in the PEPS and FDEPS computations.

Illustration III—FULLY DILUTED EPS COMPUTATIONS: OPTIONS AND WARRANTS

In addition to the facts given in Illustration II, relevant market price information for 19X6 was as follows:

Quarter	Market Price Average	Market Price Ending
1	$41	$42
2	43	44
3	49	52
4	53	51

Calculation of Income and Share Adjustments for FDEPS

Stock Warrant X

This warrant was considered in the calculation of PEPS because it met both the five-year and three-month tests. However, 9,000 shares must be reconsidered for purposes of calculating FDEPS, using the market prices at the end of the period. The adjustments for the 1,000 shares exercised must be recalculated, using the market price on the exercise date.

9,000 Warrants Not Exercised

Income adjustment: Not applicable
Share adjustment: The greater number of shares according to the following calculations:

Using the Quarterly Averaging Technique

Quarter	Shares Obtainable	Treasury Shares Acquired	SA
1	9,000	$\frac{\$360,000}{\$42} = 8,571$	429
2	9,000	$\frac{\$360,000}{\$44} = 8,182$	818
3	9,000	$\frac{\$360,000}{\$52} = 6,923$	2,077
4	9,000	$\frac{\$360,000}{\$53} = 6,792$	2,208
			5,532

Weighted average SA = 5,532 ÷ 4 = 1,383 shares

Using the Year-End Market Price

Shares Obtainable	Treasury Shares Acquired	SA
9,000	$\frac{\$360,000}{\$51} = 7,059$	1,941 shares

(continued)

<u>1,000 Warrants Exercised</u>

Income adjustment: Not applicable

Share adjustment:

Quarter	Shares Obtainable	Treasury Shares Acquired	SA
1	1,000	$\dfrac{\$40,000}{\$44^*} = 909$	91
2	1,000	$\dfrac{\$40,000}{\$44} = 909$	91
3	Not applicable		-0-
4	Not applicable		-0-
			182

Weighted average SA: 182 ÷ 4 = 46 shares

*Market price at date exercised

Stock Warrant Y

This warrant was excluded from the calculation of PEPS because it failed the five-year test; however, it is considered for FDEPS because it satisfies the ten-year test.

Income adjustment: Not applicable

Share adjustment: The greater number of shares according to the following calculations.

Using the Quarterly Averaging Technique

Quarter	Shares Obtainable	Treasury Shares Acquired	SA
1	Not applicable—antidilutive		-0-
2	Not applicable—antidilutive		-0-
3	5,000	$\dfrac{\$250,000}{\$52} = 4,808$	192
4	5,000	$\dfrac{\$250,000}{\$53} = 4,717$	283
			475

Weighted average SA: 475 ÷ 4 = 119 shares

Using the Year-End Market Price

Shares Obtainable	Treasury Shares Acquired	SA
5,000	$\dfrac{\$250,000}{\$51} = 4,902$	98 shares

Calculation of FDEPS:

	ANI_{i-1}	IA_i	ANI_i	S_{i-1}	SA_i	S_i	EPS_i
Earnings per common share	$400,000	—	$400,000	250,500*	—	250,500	$1.5968
X (not exercised)	400,000	—	400,000	250,500	1941	252,441	1.5845
X (exercised)	400,000	—	400,000	252,441	46	252,487	1.5842
Y			400,000	252,487	119	252,606	1.5835

*Weighted average of shares outstanding during the year: 250,000 shares + ½ of 1,000 shares issued on June 30 = 250,500

Contingent Shares. As in the case of PEPS, contingent shares which are issuable upon the passage of time are included in FDEPS. For PEPS purposes, contingent shares which are issuable upon the attainment of certain conditions are not considered common stock equivalents prior to the current attainment of the conditions. However, these securities are included in the fully diluted computation if the effect is dilutive, even though the specified conditions have not yet been attained. In this case, it is assumed that the specified conditions were satisfied at the beginning of the period (or at the time the contingency arose, if later). As a result, the following adjustments are necessary: [8]

1. If applicable, an income adjustment equal to the net-of-tax difference between reported income and the level of income stated as a specific condition, and
2. A share adjustment equal to the number of common shares needed to satisfy the contingency.

Contingent shares which are issuable upon the attainment of certain conditions will be dilutive only if their incremental impact, as measured by the income adjustment divided by the share adjustment, is less than EPS prior to this calculation.

Shares may also be issuable contingent upon the level of future market prices per share of common stock. These contingent arrangements will not require an income adjustment, but a share adjustment will be required, based on the number of shares which would be issuable using the actual end-of-period market price. Contrary to the general prohibition against restatement, EPS which included the effect of contingent shares may be restated if: [9]

1. The terms of a contingent issuance have not been satisfied as of expiration date and therefore all previous adjustments for the contingency must be removed, or
2. Information available in the current period suggests that the number of contingently issuable shares included in previous period calculations of EPS should be revised.

To demonstrate contingent share agreements, assume that Schrubbe, Inc., had the following contingent agreements outstanding in 19X5:

Agreement A—To issue 5,000 shares to management if after-tax income reaches $1,000,000 by 19X8.

Agreement B—Former shareholders of another company were issued 20,000 shares of Schrubbe common stock as part of a business combination. If the actual total market value of the stock issued is less than $1,000,000 ($50 per share) on June 30, 19X6, the shareholders will be issued additional shares so that their total investment is then equal to $1,000,000.

---

[8] *Opinions of the Accounting Principles Board, No. 15, op.cit.,* par. 62.
[9] *Ibid.,* pars. 62-64.

During 19X5, net income was $950,000 and there were 50,000 common shares outstanding. The market price of common stock was $48 per share on December 31, 19X5.

The calculations for PEPS are as follows:

	ANI_{i-1}	IA_i	ANI_i	S_{i-1}	SA_i	S_i	EPS_i
Earnings per common share	$950,000	—	$950,000	50,000	—	50,000	$19.00
Agreement A	Not a common stock equivalent—specified conditions not attained						
Agreement B	950,000	—[1]	950,000	50,000	833[2]	50,833	18.69

[1] Income adjustment: Not applicable
[2] Share adjustment:

$$SA = \frac{20{,}000\ (\$50) - 20{,}000\ (\$48)}{\$48} = 833 \text{ shares}$$

If the $50 per share market price is attained by June 30, 19X6, no additional shares would be issued, and past EPS, which included the share adjustment, would be restated.

The calculations for FDEPS are as follows:

	ANI_{i-1}	IA_i	ANI_i	S_{i-1}	SA_i	S_i	EPS_i
Earnings per common share	$ 950,000	—	$ 950,000	50,000	—	50,000	$19.00
Agreement A	950,000	$50,000*	1,000,000	50,000	5,000	55,000	18.18
Agreement B	1,000,000	—	1,000,000	55,000	833	55,833	17.91

* Income adjustment:
  IA = $1,000,000 − $950,000 = $50,000

Convertible Securities. Convertible securities which satisfied the cash yield test for common stock equivalency will be considered in FDEPS. In addition, convertible securities which failed this test and/or the five-year test may be included in the calculation of FDEPS if both of the following conditions are satisfied:

1. The security must be convertible within ten years from the end of the current period. If the conversion rate varies during this time, the conversion rate most favorable to the holder of the security (i.e., the rate giving the holder the greatest number of common shares per convertible security) should be employed.
2. The effect of the convertible security must be dilutive, as determined in calculating PEPS.

The "if converted" method is also employed in the calculation of FDEPS. Therefore, the income adjustment and share adjustment are determined in the same manner as for PEPS. However, if a security was converted during the period, conversion is assumed at the beginning of the period, and the "if converted" method is employed, using the conversion rate which existed at the date of actual conversion regardless of whether the effect is dilutive or antidilutive.

To illustrate the proper treatment of a conversion during the period, assume that on July 1, 19X2, $1,000,000 of 6% bonds were converted into 5,000 shares of common stock. The bonds were originally issued at par and the effective tax rate is 40%. The FDEPS prior to considering this security is $6.50.

The income and share adjustments for this security are as follows:
Income adjustment:

IA = 6% × $1,000,000 × (1 - 40% tax rate) × ½ year = $18,000

Share adjustment:

SA = 5,000 shares × ½ year = 2,500 shares

The effect of the income and share adjustments is antidilutive ($18,000 ÷ 2,500 shares = $7.20 per share) when compared to the pre-conversion FDEPS of $6.50. However, both the income and share adjustments would be included in the calculation of FDEPS, because the security was actually converted during the period.

Disclosure Requirements

In addition to presenting both primary and fully diluted earnings per share on the face of the income statement, entities with complex capital structures are required to provide the following disclosures:

> . . . a description, in summary form, sufficient to explain the pertinent rights and privileges of the various securities outstanding. Examples of information which should be disclosed are dividend and liquidation preferences, participation rights, call prices and dates, conversion or exercise prices or rates and pertinent dates, sinking fund requirements, usual voting rights, etc.
>
> A schedule or note relating to the earnings per share data should explain the bases upon which both primary and fully diluted earnings per share are calculated. This information should include identification of any issues regarded as common stock equivalents in the computation of primary earnings per share and the securities included in the computation of fully diluted earnings per share. It should describe all assumptions and any resulting adjustments used in deriving the earnings per share data. There should also be disclosed the number of shares issued upon conversion, exercise or satisfaction of required conditions, etc., during at least the most recent annual fiscal period and any subsequent interim period presented.[10]

In addition to this disclosure, it may be desirable to provide computations which indicate how the various EPS amounts were determined.

The Opinion also requires disclosure of the following supplementary EPS data:[11]

1. EPS data based on the assumption that all significant conversions which occurred during the period took place at the beginning of the period. This disclosure would be provided regardless of whether the effect was dilutive.
2. EPS data reflecting subsequent period conversions which took place prior to completion of the financial report.
3. EPS data reflecting the assumption that preferred stock or debt is retired at the beginning of the period (or date of issuance, if later) when the proceeds from an actual sale of common stock or equivalent occurring during the current period or shortly thereafter are used, or are intended to be used, to retire preferred stock or debt.

---

[10] *Ibid.*, pars. 19-20.
[11] *Ibid.*, pars. 22-23.

It is important to note that the supplementary disclosures are in addition to the normal disclosures required by APB Opinion No. 15, and that the supplementary disclosures are not to appear on the face of the income statement, but rather in related notes.

General Guidelines

The following general guidelines summarize the basic aspects of computing and disclosing PEPS and FDEPS. Many of these aspects are demonstrated in Illustration IV, which is a comprehensive problem demonstrating both the PEPS and FDEPS computations.

1. Per share data should only reflect the potential dilution of EPS. Normally, securities whose conversion or exercise would increase EPS are not included in the computation of per share data unless the securities have actually been converted or exercised during the current period.
2. Securities whose conversion or exercise would decrease a reported loss per share are not included in the computation of per share data if all levels of the income statement (e.g., net loss from continuing operations, extraordinary items) are losses. However, if at least one level of the income statement is not a loss, dilutive securities must be included in the computation of per share data for all levels of the income statement.
3. Except in certain instances involving contingent issuances, previously reported EPS are not to be retroactively restated when estimates which influence the calculation of per share data are subsequently revised. However, EPS data are retroactively restated for stock dividends, stock splits, and pooling agreements. When stock dividends and/or splits have taken place after the end of the period but before completion of the financial statements, EPS data for the period should give effect to the stock dividend and/or split.
4. The computation of the number of shares to be used as the denominator in the EPS statistic is based on a weighted average of shares rather than the number of shares outstanding at the end of the period. This refinement gives recognition to the fact that capital provided by equity investors may have been available for only a portion of the period. The weighted average number of shares is also considered to be representative of the future number of shares to which earnings are traceable; therefore, the prospective nature of the per share calculation is emphasized. It is important to note that when a security is converted into common shares, it is automatically included in the weighted average number of outstanding common shares. For example, if a bond were converted at midyear into 1,000 shares of common stock, the shares of common stock would not be considered as outstanding in the first six months, but would be included as outstanding common stock for the last six months of the year. Therefore, the 1,000 shares traceable to the convertible bond should not be added to outstanding shares in the last six months because the 1,000 shares are already included.

5. If PEPS and FDEPS represent dilution which is less than three percent of simple earnings per common share, disclosure of PEPS and FDEPS is not required. In this case, only earnings per common share would be disclosed. However, if the current period is to be included in comparative financial statements, the disclosure of PEPS and FDEPS is recommended. Therefore, the cumulative change in PEPS and FDEPS can be traced to specific years, even if the yearly change is less than three percent.

6. It is not common to consider options and warrants in either the PEPS or FDEPS computations until they meet the three-month test, although it is permissible to do so. All options and warrants in the illustrations, exercises, and problems in this text are assumed to have satisfied the test, unless data with which to make the test are given.

Illustration IV—DEMONSTRATION OF PRIMARY AND FULLY DILUTED PER SHARE COMPUTATIONS

1. The Manchester Corporation's 19X2 income statement reflects the following:

Income from continuing operations before cumulative effect of changes in accounting principles	$88,100
Cumulative effect on prior years of changes in accounting principles	(7,300)
Net income	$80,800

2. As of January 1, 19X2, 20,000 shares of common stock were issued and outstanding. On May 1, 19X2, 10,000 shares of common stock were sold for $15 per share.

3. An analysis of securities relevant to the computation of earnings per share is as follows:

Security A—consisting of 2,000 stock options granted in 19X1. Each option is exchangeable for one share of common stock at an option price of $13 per share up to October 1, 19X2, and $14 per share thereafter. The options expire on October 1, 19X6. One half of the options were exercised on July 1, 19X2. The market price exceeded the exercise price for substantially all of the last three months in 19X1.

Security B—consisting of 1,000 warrants, each exchangeable for one share of common stock at a price of $13 beginning after December 31, 19X9.

Security C—consisting of a contingent share agreement (adopted on June 30, 19X2) whereby 4,000 shares of common stock will be issued to key personnel if pretax income increases by $3,000 in 19X3 and again in 19X4.

Security D—consisting of 5%, $100,000 convertible bonds, issued on April 1, 19X2, at a price of 100. The prime interest rate was 9% on April 1, 19X2. Each $1,000 bond is convertible into 20 shares of common stock beginning April 1, 19X4.

Security E—consisting of 2,000 shares of 6% cumulative, convertible preferred stock, which was issued in 19X1 at par when the prime interest rate was 8%. Each share of preferred stock (par value,

(continued)

$10) is convertible into one share of common stock until the end of 19X5, after which time two shares of common stock will be received. All of the preferred stock was converted on August 30, 19X2. During 19X2, dividends were paid on the convertible preferred stock up to the date of conversion.

4. The corporate tax rate is 40%.

5. Daily market prices per share of common stock were as follows:

Date	Price	Date	Price
1/1/X2	$11.00	6/30/X2	$14.00
3/31/X2	14.00	7/1/X2	14.50
5/1/X2	15.00	9/30/X2	14.00
		12/31/X2	16.00

6. Average market prices per share of common stock during 19X2 were as follows:

First quarter	$12.00
Second quarter	15.00
Third quarter	14.50
Fourth quarter	15.50

Calculation of Earnings per Common Share[1]

An analysis of the common stock account reveals the following changes in the number of shares outstanding:

[1] Since the illustration involves a complex capital structure, earnings per common share would not be presented in the financial statements; however, it must be computed as the basis for the computations of PEPS and FDEPS.

Date	Item	No. of Shares
1/1/X2	Beginning balance	20,000
5/1/X2	Additional sale	10,000
7/1/X2	Exercise of Security A	1,000
8/30/X2	Conversion of Security E	2,000

The weighted average of shares outstanding is as follows:

Time Span	No. of Shares	Weight (in Months)	Share-Months
1/1/X2—4/30/X2	20,000	4	80,000
5/1/X2—6/30/X2	30,000	2	60,000
7/1/X2—8/29/X2	31,000	2	62,000
8/30/X2—12/31/X2	33,000	4	132,000
Total		12	334,000

Weighted average: 334,000 ÷ 12 = 27,833 shares

Earnings per common share would be as follows:

Income from continuing operations before cumulative effect of changes in accounting principles	$3.14 [2]
Cumulative effect on prior years of changes in accounting principles	(0.26)
Net income	$2.88

[2] Before computing EPS, the reported income has been appropriately reduced by the 19X2 preferred stock dividend of $800 (6% × $20,000 × 2/3 year). Therefore, the EPS before the cumulative effect of changes in principles is based on income of $87,300.

Calculation of Primary Earnings per Share

The basic methodology presented in Illustration I is used to compute the PEPS as follows:

	ANI_{i-1}	IA_i	ANI_i	S_{i-1}	SA_i	S_i	EPS_i
Earnings per common share	$87,300	—	$87,300	27,833	—	27,833	$3.14[3]
Security A	87,300	—	87,300	27,833	117[4]	27,950	3.12
Security B	Not a common stock equivalent—fails 5-year test						
Security C	Not a common stock equivalent—specified conditions not attained						
Security D	87,300	$2,250[5]	89,550	27,950	1,500[6]	29,450	3.04
Security E	Not a common stock equivalent—fails cash yield test						

[3] To insure that antidilutive securities would be properly identified, notice that earnings per common share of $3.14 was used instead of the final per-share figure of $2.88.

[4] Weighted average of quarters for Security A:

Quarter	Dilutive*	Shares Obtainable	Treasury Shares Acquired		SA
1	No	—	—		-0-
2	Yes	2,000	$\dfrac{\$26,000}{\$15}$ =	1,733	267
3	Yes	1,000	$\dfrac{\$13,000}{\$14.50}$ =	897	103
4	Yes	1,000	$\dfrac{\$14,000}{\$15.50}$ =	903	97
					467

Weighted average: $467 \div 4 = 117$ shares

*Dilutive if average market price is greater than exercise price.

[5] $5\% \times \$100,000 \times 9/12$ year = $3,750. After-tax effect = $60\% \times \$3,750 = \$2,250$.
[6] 100 bonds × 20 shares = 2,000 assumed outstanding as of April 1, 19X2. Therefore, weighted average = $2,000 \times 3/4$ year = 1,500 shares.

Primary earnings per share would be presented as follows:

Earnings per common share and common equivalent share:
Income from continuing operations before cumulative effect of changes
in accounting principles $3.04
Cumulative effect on prior years of changes in accounting principles... (0.25) *
Net income $2.79

* The $7,300 cumulative effect divided by the final S_i of 29,450.

Calculation of Fully Diluted Earnings per Share

The method shown in Illustration III is used to compute the FDEPS:

	ANI_{i-1}	IA_i	ANI_i	S_{i-1}	SA_i	S_i	EPS_i
Earnings per common share	$87,300	—	$87,300	27,833	—	27,833	$3.14
Security A (not exercised)	87,300	—	87,300	27,833	125[7]	27,958	3.12
Security A (exercised)	87,300	—	87,300	27,958	52[8]	28,010	3.12
Security B	87,300	—	87,300	28,010	187[9]	28,197	3.10
Security C	87,300	$3,600[10]	90,900	28,197	2,000[10]	30,197	3.01
Security D	90,900	2,250[11]	93,150	30,197	1,500[11]	31,697	2.94
Security E	93,150	800[12]	93,950	31,697	1,333[13]	33,030	2.84

(continued)

[7] The year-end market price is used for the entire period when it produces greater dilution than the quarterly average. Thus, the share adjustment is the 125 incremental shares resulting from use of the year-end market price, rather than the quarterly average of 108 shares. These amounts are computed as follows:

Quarter	Dilutive*	Shares Obtainable	Treasury Shares Acquired		SA
1	Yes	1,000	$\dfrac{\$13,000}{\$14}$	= 929	71
2	Yes	1,000	$\dfrac{\$13,000}{\$15}$	= 867	133
3	Yes	1,000	$\dfrac{\$13,000}{\$14.50}$	= 897	103
4	Yes	1,000	$\dfrac{\$14,000}{\$16}$	= 875	**125**
					432

Weighted average: 432 ÷ 4 = 108 shares

  * Dilutive if ending market price is greater than exercise price. If ending market price is less than average market price, use the latter.

[8] Weighted average of quarters for Security A—Exercised:

Quarter	Dilutive*	Shares Obtainable	Treasury Shares Acquired		SA
1	Yes	1,000	$\dfrac{\$13,000}{\$14.50}$	= 897	103
2	Yes	1,000	$\dfrac{\$13,000}{\$14.50}$	= 897	103
3	Not applicable				-0-
4	Not applicable				-0-
					206

Weighted average: 206 ÷ 4 = 52 shares

  *Dilutive if market price at date of exercise is greater than exercise price. The share adjustment for the time prior to exercise is always based on the market price at date of exercise, regardless of whether the result is dilutive. Note that securities exercised when the market price is less than the exercise price are always included in FDEPS, even if the effect is antidilutive.

[9] The year-end market price is used for the entire period when it produces greater dilution than the quarterly average. Thus, the share adjustment is the 187 incremental shares resulting from use of the year-end market price, rather than the quarterly average of 124 shares. These amounts are computed as follows:

Quarter	Dilutive*	Shares Obtainable	Treasury Shares Acquired		SA
1	Yes	1,000	$\dfrac{\$13,000}{\$14}$	= 929	71
2	Yes	1,000	$\dfrac{\$13,000}{\$15}$	= 867	133
3	Yes	1,000	$\dfrac{\$13,000}{\$14.50}$	= 897	103
4	Yes	1,000	$\dfrac{\$13,000}{\$16}$	= 813	**187**
					494

Weighted average: 494 ÷ 4 = 124 shares

  *Dilutive if the higher of the average or ending market price exceeds the exercise price.

[10] For purposes of computing FDEPS, it is assumed that the net-of-tax increases in 19X3 and 19X4 income [($3,000 + $3,000) × 60% = $3,600] have been realized. The weighted average number of shares would be 2,000 (4,000 × ½ year).

[11] The income and share adjustments for the convertible bonds are the same as they were in the PEPS computation.

[12] The preferred stock dividend is $800, computed as follows:

Dividend = 6% × $20,000 × 2/3 year = $800

[13] When actual conversion of a security takes place during the period, conversion is assumed at the beginning of the period or at issuance, if later, for purposes of calculating FDEPS. Since the shares issued upon conversion have already been considered as outstanding, the SA is based on the period prior to conversion (2,000 × 8/12 = 1,333).

Fully diluted earnings per share would be presented as follows:

Earnings per common share—assuming full dilution:

Income from continuing operations before cumulative effect of changes in accounting principles	$2.84
Cumulative effect on prior years of changes in accounting principles	(0.22*)
Net income	$2.62

*The $7,300 cumulative effect divided by the final S_i of 33,030.

REPORTING FOR BUSINESS SEGMENTS OF AN ENTERPRISE

As discussed in Chapter 1, the concept of an accounting entity is indispensable because it defines the boundaries of the activity which is the subject matter of accounting. Typically, the accounting entity is defined for external reporting purposes as the entire enterprise. However, many modern enterprises are so diversified that disclosure of the financial activity of various components or segments of the enterprise is most useful in some instances.

Importance of Segmental Reporting

The significance of reporting for segments is closely related to the corporate merger activity which took place during the 1960's. Prior to this time, merger activity could be characterized as either horizontal or vertical integration. Horizontal integration refers to the acquisition of companies in similar or closely related businesses, while vertical integration refers to acquisitions which would improve the production and/or marketing efforts of the acquiring company. However, due to increased legal and governmental pressure, the merger activity of the 1960's departed from earlier patterns, and was characterized by the acquisition of companies with activities which were primarily unrelated to the activities of the acquiring company. These mergers resulted in what are generally referred to as conglomerates or diversified companies. To adapt to the competitive pressures of these companies, many other firms began to diversify internally, rather than through business acquisitions.

It soon became apparent that disclosure of the aggregate activities of diversified companies in the form of consolidated financial statements would no longer singularly satisfy the informational needs of various parties. In the mid 1960's, professional business groups, governmental agencies, and investors began to emphasize the importance of disclosing the business activities of the unrelated segments which composed a diversified company. While differing on the means and extent of implementing the desire for additional information, the concept of segmental reporting has been endorsed by the American Institute of Certified Public Accountants, the Financial Executives Institute, the Financial Analysts Federation, the National Association of Accountants, the Securities and Exchange Commission, and the Federal Trade Commission.

Although total enterprise financial statements provide users with a basis for evaluating the performance of an enterprise as a whole, total performance is a function of the performance of the various segments which constitute the enterprise. Therefore, an analysis of the investment opportunities, the risks indicated by a segment's profitability, the growth potential, and the production and marketing processes provide interested parties with an excellent basis for evaluating present and future performance of the segment and the enterprise as a whole. Segmental information may also provide users with an improved basis for making interenterprise comparisons between companies which have a single industry or product affiliation and segments of a similar nature within diversified companies.

There is a strong body of empirical research which supports the position that segmental data have utility. This research, and the prominence of diversified companies, have effectively established the importance of segmental data for maintaining an efficient capital market. For example, studies have suggested that segmental data can lead to more accurate predictions of enterprise earnings and changes in earning levels. Surveys have also shown that sophisticated users, such as financial analysts, find the use of segmental data to be a significant factor in the area of security valuation.

FASB Statement No. 14

Prior to 1976, diversified companies were free to determine the extent of segmental information to be disclosed in their financial reports to the public. These disclosures frequently concentrated on information concerning segmental revenues and profit contributions. In 1976, the Financial Accounting Standards Board issued Statement No. 14, "Financial Reporting for Segments of a Business Enterprise," which deals with the following topics:

1. The qualifications of a reportable segment.
2. The specific segmental data which must be disclosed and how such data should be disclosed.
3. The additional data which must be disclosed concerning foreign operations, export sales, and sales to major customers.

The Statement sets forth minimum disclosure requirements for all companies which are composed of reportable segments. Reporting companies are also encouraged to provide additional disclosures when relevant. However, the minimum disclosure requirements need only be presented when a public enterprise issues a complete set of annual financial statements which present financial position, results of operations, and changes in financial position in conformity with generally accepted accounting principles.[12]

Defining a Segment. A major issue involved in segmental reporting is the determination of a business segment. Theoretically, a segment should be defined in reponse to the informational needs of user groups. For example, an equity investor may find the definition of segments in terms of product lines to be most useful, while the needs of another user may suggest that segments be defined in terms of broad geographical areas served by the company. Approaches to the definition of a segment have focused on such variables as geographical markets, product lines, broad industry groups, and/or "profit centers" employed for internal planning and control. Established classification systems for segmental reporting, such as the Standard Industrial Classification and the Enterprise Standard Industrial Classification, have been used in certain instances; however, research has suggested that such systems may not be the most appropriate means of defining business segments.

The FASB elected to define a segment as:

> A component of an enterprise engaged in providing a product or service or a group of related products and services primarily to unaffiliated customers (i.e., customers outside the enterprise) for a profit.[13]

Although more decisive guidelines for the definition of a segment could have been established, the FASB recognized that no single set of segment criteria would be universally applicable to all companies. Therefore, the FASB concluded that the definition of a segment should be left to the discretion of management. However, the following factors should be considered when determining segments:

(a) *The nature of the product.* Related products or services have similar purposes or end uses. Thus, they may be expected to have similar rates of profitability, similar degrees of risk, and similar opportunities for growth.

(b) *The nature of the production process.* Sharing of common or interchangeable production or sales facilities, equipment, labor force, or service group or use of the same or similar basic raw materials may suggest that products or services are related. Likewise, similar degrees of labor intensiveness or similar degrees of capital intensiveness may indicate a relationship among products or services.

(c) *Markets and marketing methods.* Similarity of geographic marketing areas, types of customers, or marketing methods may indicate a relationship among products or services. . . . The sensitivity of the market to price changes and to changes in general economic conditions may also indicate whether products or services are related or unrelated.[14]

---

[12] FASB Statement No. 18, "Financial Reporting for Segments of a Business Enterprise—Interim Financial Statements," removed the former requirement that interim financial statements include segmental information.

[13] *Statement of Financial Accounting Standards, No. 14,* "Financial Reporting for Segments of a Business Enterprise" (Stamford: Financial Accounting Standards Board, 1976), par. 10.

[14] *Ibid.,* par. 100.

If practicable, these factors should be applied on a worldwide basis. However, if it is not practicable, foreign operations may be viewed as a single segment.

Given a defined industry segment, segmental data need not be disclosed unless the segment qualifies as a reportable segment by satisfying one or more of the following criteria:

(a) Its revenue (including both sales to unaffiliated customers and intersegment sales or transfers) is 10 percent or more of the combined revenue (sales to unaffiliated customers and intersegment sales or transfers) of all of the enterprise's industry segments.

(b) The absolute amount of its operating profit or operating loss is 10 percent or more of the greater, in absolute amount, of:
  (i) The combined operating profit of all industry segments that did not incur an operating loss, or
  (ii) The combined operating loss of all industry segments that did incur an operating loss.

(c) Its identifiable assets are 10 percent or more of the combined identifiable assets of all industry segments.[15]

Certain exceptions to these criteria are permitted. For example, if a segment currently fails to satisfy the above criteria, but has satisfied the criteria in the past or is expected to satisfy them in the future, segmental disclosures should be presented so that the comparability of past and future reporting periods is preserved. Alternatively, if a segment currently happens to satisfy the criteria, but normally does not, it may be best to view the segment as nonreportable. However, in this situation, appropriate reasons for not reporting segmental activities should be disclosed. Illustration V demonstrates the application of the criteria for determining whether a segment is reportable.

Illustration V

Facts:

The Whalen Corporation has classified its operations into industry segments and provided the following data for each segment:

	Revenues				
Segment	Unaffiliated Customers	Intersegment Sales	Total	Operating Profit (Loss)	Identifiable Assets
A	$100,000	$15,000	$115,000	$ 45,000	$ 280,000
B	20,000	-0-	20,000	(10,000)	80,000
C	230,000	40,000	270,000	130,000	1,100,000
D	45,000	5,000	50,000	(60,000)	320,000
E	37,000	8,000	45,000	25,000	295,000
F	140,000	14,000	154,000	85,000	760,000
	$572,000	$82,000	$654,000	$215,000	$2,835,000
Corporate level	60,000	-0-	60,000	20,000	705,000
Total	$632,000	$82,000	$714,000	$235,000	$3,540,000

---

[15] *Ibid.*, par. 15.

Analysis:

The determination of which segments are reportable requires the following evaluation, in which only combined data relating to the *segments* (not the total entity) are employed:

1. Sales to unaffiliated customers $572,000
   Intersegment sales 82,000
   Combined revenue $654,000
   Segment revenue required to satisfy criterion (a):
   $$\$654,000 \times 10\% = \$65,400$$

2.
Segment	Operating Profit	Operating Loss
A	$ 45,000	
B		$10,000
C	130,000	
D		60,000
E	25,000	
F	85,000	
Total	$285,000	$70,000

Portion of absolute amount of the greater of the operating profit or the operating loss to satisfy criterion (b):
$$\$285,000 \times 10\% = \$28,500$$

3. Segment identifiable assets required to satisfy criterion (c):
$$\$2,835,000 \times 10\% = \$283,500$$

Whether the criteria are satisfied is summarized as follows:

Segment	Revenue	Criterion Satisfied Operating Profit (Loss)	Identifiable Assets	Segment Reportable
A	Yes ($115,000 > $65,400)	Yes ($ 45,000 > $28,500)	No ($ 280,000 < $283,500)	Yes
B	No ($ 20,000 < $65,400)	No ($ 10,000 < $28,500)	No ($ 80,000 < $283,500)	No
C	Yes ($270,000 > $65,400)	Yes ($130,000 > $28,500)	Yes ($1,100,000 > $283,500)	Yes
D	No ($ 50,000 < $65,400)	Yes ($ 60,000 > $28,500)	Yes ($ 320,000 > $283,500)	Yes
E	No ($ 45,000 < $65,400)	No ($ 25,000 < $28,500)	Yes ($ 295,000 > $283,500)	Yes
F	Yes ($154,000 > $65,400)	Yes ($ 85,000 > $28,500)	Yes ($ 760,000 > $283,500)	Yes

All of the segments are reportable except for Segment B.

Other practical limitations concerning the number of reportable segments are identified as follows:

1. As the number of reportable segments increases above 10, serious consideration should be given as to whether the volume of segmental data begins to diminish the utility of segmental reporting.
2. The reportable segments should, in the aggregate, represent a substantial portion of the total enterprise's activities. The substantial portion test is satisfied if the combined revenue from *sales to unaffiliated customers* of all *reportable* segments is at least 75 percent of the combined revenue from *sales to unaffiliated customers* of all *industry* segments. If this test is not satisfied, additional segments should be classified as reportable until the test is satisfied, subject to the practical limitation discussed in item (1).

3. If a single reportable segment accounts for a "dominant" portion of the total enterprise's activities, segmental reporting is not required, although the nature of this dominant segment should be disclosed. A "dominant" segment is one whose "revenue, operating profit or loss, and identifiable assets each constitute more than 90 percent of related combined totals for all industry segments, and no other industry segment meets any of the 10-percent tests. . ."[16]

Using the basic facts presented in Illustration V as an example, the practical limitations regarding the number of reportable segments have been satisfied. There are no more than ten reportable segments; no segment is dominant; and the reportable segments represent a substantial portion of the enterprise's activities, determined as follows:

Sales to unaffiliated customers of all reportable segments (all segments except Segment B):
$572,000 − $20,000 = $552,000
Minimum level of sales to unaffiliated customers of all industry segments:
$572,000 × 75% = $429,000
The sales to unaffiliated customers of the reportable segments exceed the minimum level needed to satisfy the substantial portion limitation.

Content of Segment Disclosure. For all segments which have been determined to be reportable, as well as the aggregate of all segments not deemed to be reportable, the nature of the segment's products and services and their respective revenue, operating profit or loss, and identifiable assets must be disclosed. In addition, certain other disclosures are required.

The revenue to be disclosed by each of the reporting segments should include sales to unaffiliated customers and separate disclosure of sales to other segments (intersegment sales). With respect to intersegment sales, the method of pricing sales between segments (transfer pricing) should be disclosed, and any change in methods should be fully discussed in terms of the nature and effect of the change.

Although a specific transfer pricing method is not required by FASB Statement No. 14, several methods are available. Alternative methods range from pricing based on incremental cost incurred to pricing based on negotiations which are intended to simulate actual market conditions. In the opinion of the authors, the objectives and utility of segmental reporting are best served by a transfer pricing method which, when possible, approximates the actual selling prices which would have been experienced if the sale had involved an unaffiliated customer.

Reported revenues of the segments should also include interest earned from outside sources and interest earned on intersegment trade receivables. However, interest earned on advances or loans to other segments should not be included in revenues unless the lending segment's principal operations are of a financial nature.

---

[16] *Ibid.*, par. 20.

Since operating profit is of primary interest to users of segmental data, each reportable segment must also disclose its operating profit or loss, which represents the revenues discussed previously, including intersegment sales, less the operating expenses traceable to the revenues. Operating expenses which are not directly traceable to one segment but are common or traceable to several segments should be allocated among the benefiting segments on a reasonable basis. The allocation method selected should be disclosed as well as the nature and effect of any changes in methods.

A variety of expense allocation methods have been used, ranging from sophisticated modeling techniques to arbitrary methods which have not captured the true relationship between cost incurrence and segment performance. Theoretically, the allocation of common costs should be based on a cause and effect approach, since the costs would not be incurred if they did not ultimately benefit the segments. However, a controversy has focused on whether allocation is practical and whether it produces comparability among companies. As a result, an acceptable alternative approach avoids allocation altogether by disclosing only directly traceable costs. This alternative, however, presents the problem of having to distinguish clearly between "directly traceable" costs and "allocable" costs.

Operating profit or loss by segments should not include the effects of any of the following: general corporate expenses, interest expense on nontrade advances or loans from other segments (except in the case of a segment which has borrowed from another segment whose operations are financial), domestic and foreign income taxes, equity in the profits or losses of unconsolidated subsidiaries and investees, gains or losses on discontinued operations, extraordinary items (not including items which are unusual or infrequently occurring), the cumulative effect of changes in accounting principles, and minority interests. The nature of the items excluded from operating profit or loss should be disclosed, as well as an analysis of how items relate to each segment. In addition to the disclosure of operating profit or loss, management may also disclose other measures of segmental profit, such as profit contribution (segment revenue less directly traceable costs), if the nature of the profit measure is adequately disclosed.

To evaluate more fully segmental profitability, FASB Statement No. 14 requires disclosure of each reportable segment's identifiable assets which were employed to generate the revenue and operating profit or loss of that segment. Therefore, the tangible and intangible assets used exclusively by the segment and the allocated portion of jointly employed assets are presented net of their related valuation allowances such as accumulated depreciation and allowances for uncollectible accounts. Excluded from the measure of identifiable assets are those assets not used in the operations of a segment, such as corporate-level assets. Advances or loans to other segments should also be excluded unless the lending segment's operations are primarily financial in nature.

The information required to be disclosed by reportable segments must also be presented in the aggregate for the remainder of the segments which do not qualify as reportable segments. Revenues, profits, and identifiable assets presented for all reportable segments and the aggregate of nonreportable segments must be reconciled to the related amounts appearing in the financial statements for the enterprise as a whole. To accomplish this reconciliation, certain adjustments and eliminations for intersegment transactions must be presented and explained in the accompanying footnotes. For example, sales between segments are included in segmental revenues but must be eliminated from the financial statements for the whole enterprise in order to agree with the consolidated total revenues.

In addition to the above disclosures, the following related disclosures are required:

(a) Disclosure shall be made of the aggregate amount of depreciation, depletion, and amortization expense for each reportable segment.
(b) Disclosure shall be made of the amount of each reportable segment's capital expenditures, i.e., additions to its property, plant, and equipment.
(c) For each reportable segment disclosure shall be made of the enterprise's equity in the net income from and investment in the net assets of unconsolidated subsidiaries and other equity method investees whose operations are vertically integrated with the operations of that segment. Disclosure shall also be made of the geographic areas in which those vertically integrated equity method investees operate.
(d) Paragraph 17 of APB Opinion No. 20 requires that the effect on income of a change in accounting principle be disclosed in the financial statements of an enterprise in the period in which the change is made. Disclosure shall also be made of the effect of the change on the operating profit of reportable segments in the period in which the change is made.[17]

The segmental disclosures required by FASB Statement No. 14 must be presented within the body of the financial statements, entirely in the footnotes to the financial statements, or in separate schedules which are included as an integral part of the financial statements. An example of the disclosure format appears in Illustration VI.

Disclosing Foreign Operations. To this point, the reporting requirements associated with segments have been defined primarily around product or service lines. In addition to this disclosure, enterprises are also required to disclose key financial data for each significant foreign geographical area, which is an area whose revenue from sales to unaffiliated customers or whose identifiable assets account for 10 percent or more of the respective consolidated amounts. An enterprise's foreign operations are defined as:

. . . those revenue-producing operations (except for unconsolidated subsidiaries and other unconsolidated investees) that (a) are located outside

---

[17]*Ibid.*, par. 27.

Illustration VI

Segmental Reports

For Year Ended December 31, 19X8

	Reportable Segments		Other Segments	Adjustments and Eliminations*	Consoli-dated
	A	B			
Revenues:					
From unaffiliated customers	$10,000	$12,000	$5,000	——	$27,000
From intersegment sales	3,000	——	2,000	$(5,000)	——
Total	$13,000	$12,000	$7,000	$(5,000)	$27,000
Operating profit	$ 3,000	$ 1,000	$ 500	$ (400)	$ 4,100
Equity in income of X Co.					300
General corporate expenses					(600)
Interest expense.........................					(200)
Income from continuing operations before income taxes					$ 3,600
Identifiable assets at 12/31/X8	$20,000	$17,000	$8,000	$ (350)	$44,650
Investment in net assets of X Co.					6,350
Corporate assets.........................					5,000
Total assets at 12/31/X8					$56,000

*The nature of these adjustments and eliminations would be discussed in the notes accompanying this segmental report.

of the enterprise's home country and (b) are generating revenue either from sales to unaffiliated customers or from intraenterprise sales or transfers between geographic areas.[18]

If either of the following criteria which relate to revenues and assets is satisfied, an enterprise must disclose separately the results of its domestic operations, significant foreign operations by geographic area, and the aggregate of foreign operations not qualifying as significant:

(a) Revenue generated by the enterprise's foreign operations from sales to unaffiliated customers is 10 percent or more of consolidated revenue as reported in the enterprise's income statement.

(b) Identifiable assets of the enterprise's foreign operations are 10 percent or more of consolidated total assets as reported in the enterprise's balance sheet.[19]

The following information should be disclosed:

1. Revenue as defined for segment disclosure, including sales between geographic areas,
2. Operating profit or loss as defined for segment disclosure, or net income or some other measure of profitability, and
3. Identifiable assets as defined for segment disclosure.

This information should be reconciled to the respective consolidated totals in a manner similar to that demonstrated in Illustration VI.

---
[18]*Ibid.*, par. 31.
[19]*Ibid.*, par. 32.

An example of the financial reporting for foreign and domestic segments of General Electric and consolidated affiliates for the years 1978 to 1980 is presented in Illustration VII.

Illustration VII

Industry segment information

Revenues
(In millions) For the years ended December 31

	Total revenues			Intersegment sales			External sales and other income		
	1980	1979	1978	1980	1979	1978	1980	1979	1978
Consumer products and services	$ 5,599	$ 5,358	$ 4,788	$ 201	$ 199	$ 188	$ 5,398	$ 5,159	$ 4,600
Net earnings of GE Credit Corp.	115	90	77	—	—	—	115	90	77
Total consumer products and services	5,714	5,448	4,865	201	199	188	5,513	5,249	4,677
Industrial products and components	5,157	4,803	4,124	565	508	468	4,592	4,295	3,656
Power systems	4,023	3,564	3,486	175	210	174	3,848	3,354	3,312
Technical systems and materials	7,128	6,061	4,745	258	255	190	6,870	5,806	4,555
Natural resources	1,374	1,260	1,032	—	—	—	1,374	1,260	1,032
Foreign multi-industry operations	3,234	2,901	2,767	75	64	55	3,159	2,837	2,712
Corporate items and eliminations	(1,107)	(1,057)	(946)	(1,274)	(1,236)	(1,075)	167	179	129
Total	$25,523	$22,980	$20,073	$ —	$ —	$ —	$25,523	$22,980	$20,073

Operating profit / Net earnings
For the years ended December 31

	Operating profit			Net earnings		
	1980	1979	1978	1980	1979	1978
Consumer products and services	$ 558	$ 568	$ 574	$ 292	$ 311	$ 300
Net earnings of GE Credit Corp.	115	90	77	115	90	77
Total consumer products and services	673	658	651	407	401	377
Industrial products and components	568	485	426	315	272	223
Power systems	194	174	196	141	114	93
Technical systems and materials	774	672	545	373	356	278
Natural resources	404	431	372	224	208	180
Foreign multi-industry operations	285	241	245	68	65	76
Total segment operating profit	2,898	2,661	2,435			
Interest and other financial charges	(314)	(258)	(224)			
Corporate items and eliminations	(91)	(12)	(58)	(14)	(7)	3
Total	$ 2,493	$ 2,391	$ 2,153	$ 1,514	$ 1,409	$ 1,230

Assets / Property, plant and equipment

	Assets			Property, plant and equipment					
	At December 31			Additions			Depreciation, depletion and amortization		
	1980	1979	1978	1980	1979	1978	1980	1979	1978
Consumer products and services	$ 2,325	$ 2,157	$ 2,018	$ 238	$ 208	$ 169	$ 133	$ 115	$ 104
Investment in GE Credit Corp.	931	817	677	—	—	—	—	—	—
Total consumer products and services	3,256	2,974	2,695	238	208	169	133	115	104
Industrial products and components	2,595	2,329	2,125	224	176	166	109	106	91
Power systems	2,289	2,135	2,105	129	101	84	91	84	79
Technical systems and materials	4,475	3,422	2,683	693	444	289	200	163	150
Natural resources	2,109	1,679	1,489	446	201	212	94	83	77
Foreign multi-industry operations	2,564	2,259	2,100	161	109	119	66	61	64
Corporate items and eliminations	1,223	1,846	1,839	57	23	16	14	12	11
Total	$18,511	$16,644	$15,036	$ 1,948	$ 1,262	$ 1,055	$ 707	$ 624	$ 576

Consumer Products and Services consists of major appliances, air conditioning equipment, lighting products, housewares and audio products, television receivers, and broadcasting and cablevision services. It also includes service operations for major appliances, air conditioners, TV receivers, and housewares and audio products.

General Electric Credit Corporation, a wholly owned nonconsolidated finance affiliate, engages primarily in consumer, commercial and industrial financing, principally in the U.S. It also participates, to a lesser degree, in life insurance and fire and casualty insurance activities. Products of companies other than GE constitute virtually all products financed by GECC.

Illustration VII (Concluded)

Industrial Products and Components includes components (appliance controls, small motors and electronic components); industrial capital equipment (construction, automation and transportation); maintenance, inspection, repair and rebuilding of electric, electronic and mechanical apparatus; and a network of supply houses offering products of General Electric and other manufacturers.

Power Systems includes steam turbine-generators, gas turbines, nuclear power reactors and nuclear fuel assemblies, transformers, switchgear, meters, and installation and maintenance engineering services.

Technical Systems and Materials consists of jet engines for aircraft, industrial and marine applications; electronic and other high-technology products and services primarily for aerospace applications and defense; materials (engineered plastics, silicones, industrial cutting materials, laminated and insulating materials, and batteries); medical and communications equipment; and time sharing, computing, and remote data processing.

Natural Resources includes the mining of coking coal (principally in Australia), uranium, steam coal, iron and copper. In addition, it includes oil and natural gas production, ocean shipping (primarily in support of mining operations) and land acquisition and development.

Foreign Multi-industry Operations consists principally of foreign affiliates which manufacture products primarily for sale in their respective home markets.

Net earnings for industry segments include allocation of corporate interest income, expense and other financial charges to parent company components based on change in individual component average nonfixed investment. Interest and other financial charges of affiliated companies recognize that such companies generally service their own debt.

General corporate expenses are allocated principally on the basis of cost of operations, with certain exceptions and reductions which recognize the varying degrees to which affiliated companies maintain their own corporate structures.

In addition, provision for income taxes ($958 million in 1980, $953 million in 1979, and $894 million in 1978) is allocated based on the total corporate effective tax rate, except for GECC and Natural Resources, whose income taxes are calculated separately.

Minority interest ($21 million in 1980 and $29 million in both 1979 and 1978) is allocated to operating components having responsibility for investments in consolidated affiliates.

In general, it is GE's policy to price internal sales as nearly as practicable to equivalent commercial selling prices.

Geographic segment information

(In millions)	**Revenues** For the years ended December 31								
	Total revenues			Intersegment sales			External sales and other income		
	1980	1979	1978	1980	1979	1978	1980	1979	1978
United States	$20,750	$18,859	$16,443	$ 484	$ 467	$ 362	$20,266	$18,392	$16,081
Far East including Australia	1,277	1,183	1,109	355	280	242	922	903	867
Other areas of the world	4,459	3,814	3,270	124	129	145	4,335	3,685	3,125
Elimination of intracompany transactions	(963)	(876)	(749)	(963)	(876)	(749)	—	—	—
Total	$25,523	$22,980	$20,073	$ —	$ —	$ —	$25,523	$22,980	$20,073

	Net Earnings For the years ended December 31			**Assets** At December 31		
	1980	1979	1978	1980	1979	1978
United States	$ 1,175	$ 1,120	$ 961	$13,732	$12,693	$11,410
Far East including Australia	169	174	170	1,090	842	889
Other areas of the world	181	120	104	3,808	3,207	2,827
Elimination of intracompany transactions	(11)	(5)	(5)	(119)	(98)	(90)
Total	$ 1,514	$ 1,409	$ 1,230	$18,511	$16,644	$15,036

Geographic segment information (including allocation of income taxes and minority interest in earnings of consolidated affiliates) is based on the location of the operation furnishing goods or services. Included in United States revenues were export sales to unaffiliated customers of $3,781 million in 1980, $2,772 million in 1979, and $2,571 million in 1978. Of such sales, $2,089 million in 1980 ($1,581 million in 1979 and $1,662 million in 1978) were to customers in Europe, Africa and the Middle East; and $926 million in 1980 ($741 million in 1979 and $498 million in 1978) were to customers in the Far East including Australia.

U.S. revenues also include royalty and licensing income from unaffiliated foreign sources.

Revenues, net earnings and assets associated with foreign operations are shown in the tabulations above. At December 31, 1980, foreign operation liabilities, minority interest in equity and GE interest in equity were $2,562 million, $141 million and $2,195 million, respectively. On a comparable basis, the amounts were $2,101 million, $139 million and $1,809 million, respectively, at December 31, 1979; and $1,910 million, $150 million and $1,656 million, respectively, at December 31, 1978.

Export Sales and Sales to Major Customers. If an enterprise's domestic operations contain sales to unaffiliated foreign customers, these export sales must be disclosed if they account for 10% or more of total enterprise revenue from sales to unaffiliated customers. An enterprise may also have sales to major customers or governmental agencies, for which information should be disclosed if:[20]

1. Sales to any single customer account for 10% or more of total enterprise revenue.
2. Sales to an individual domestic or foreign governmental agency account for 10% or more of total enterprise revenue.

When these provisions are satisfied, the nature and amount of the major sales and the identity of the segments making the sales should be disclosed. However, the names of the customers or the agencies need not be disclosed.

QUESTIONS

1. Why do EPS calculations assume conversions of securities which were in fact not converted during the year? Is this valid? Why?
2. Define dual presentation. Is there any situation in which it is not applicable?
3. What assumption is necessary to make the treasury stock method of handling options and warrants viable? How does the 20% factor affect these assumptions?
4. What is the cash yield test? Does its application to different securities vary? If so, how?
5. Describe the treatment of the currently amortized portion of discount or premium on convertible debentures in computing earnings per share.
6. In what order should convertible securities be evaluated for determining their dilutive effect?
7. How are contingent share agreements analyzed for purposes of computing primary EPS? Fully diluted EPS?
8. Indicate the major purpose served by segmental information.
9. What factors should be considered in the determination of what constitutes a segment?
10. What criteria must be satisfied for an identified segment to be considered a "reportable segment"?
11. Assume that a diversified company neither acquires nor disposes of any segments during the current period, but does redefine the segments which compose the enterprise. What accounting treatment would you propose for the change in segment definition?
12. Segmental measures of profit do not include the effects of extraordinary items, changes in accounting principles, and discontinued segments. What justification exists for this position?

---

[20] *Statement of Financial Accounting Standards, No. 30*, "Disclosure of Information about Major Customers" (Stamford: Financial Accounting Standards Board, 1979), par. 6.

EXERCISES

Exercise 1. The fiscal year for D & L Corporation ended on May 31, 19X7. The net income for the year is $350,000 and the following additional information is available:

(a) On August 1, 19X6, 5,000 shares of authorized common stock were acquired for treasury stock.

(b) To facilitate the trading of D & L Corporation stock, the board of directors declared a 2-for-1 stock split which was effective on December 1, 19X6.

(c) The total number of common shares outstanding at year end is 120,000 shares.

(d) The only other securities outstanding are 100, 6%, 5-year, $1,000 convertible bonds which the company issued at par on September 1, 19X6. Interest is paid semiannually on February 28th and August 30th. Each bond is convertible into 10 shares of common stock. (After the stock split, each bond is convertible into 20 shares of common stock.) The bank prime interest rate was 10% on September 1, 19X6.

Present all schedules and computations for the EPS figures required for the year ending May 31, 19X7. Assume a 40% tax rate.

Exercise 2. Oklahoma Crude Oil, Inc., has issued numerous stock options over the past several years. Information regarding the options is summarized in the following table:

Year Granted	Option Price	Year First Exercisable	Number of Options Outstanding
19X2	$33	19X8	1,000
19X3	35	19X9	1,500
19X4	40	19Y0	2,000
19X5	35	19Y0	1,000
19X6	36	19Y0	700

The 19X6 average market price of the common stock was $39 per share, and the year-end closing price was $41 per share. At the beginning of the current fiscal period, which ends on December 31, 19X6, the common stock account showed 25,000 shares outstanding, with a $100 par value. The stock options in 19X6 were all granted on January 1. All of the earlier options have previously qualified as common stock equivalents.

Net income for the year was $125,000 after taxes at the rate of 40%. The balance sheet for Oklahoma Crude shows $4,000,000 of long-term debt outstanding, with an interest rate of 8%.

Compute both primary and fully diluted EPS data for the year 19X6. (Consider the 20% rule.) Include all necessary computations and schedules. Assume that the company has no other outstanding securities.

Exercise 3. Hale Manufacturing, Inc., has the following stock options outstanding for the year 19X7. Each option entitles the holder to acquire one share of common stock.

	Option Price	Year First Exercisable	Number of Options
Option A	$16	19X6	10,000
Option B	19	19X8	15,000
Option C	20	19Y0	5,000

For the year 19X7, the average market price of Hale's common stock was $22 per share and the year-end market price was $25 per share.

During 19X7, net income was $125,000 and there were 80,000 shares of common stock outstanding for the entire year. The only outstanding debts were 6%, $150,000 bonds which were issued at par in 19X5. Assume that the tax rate is 40% and government securities are earning 7½%.

(1) Calculate PEPS and FDEPS.

(2) If the average market price was $35 per share, determine the income adjustment and the share adjustment for the purpose of calculating PEPS.

Exercise 4. Throughout the year, Mayflower Corporation has issued common stock to various individuals. An analysis of the common stock account provides the following information:

Outstanding on February 1, 19X5	1,420,000 shares
Issues:	
April 15, 19X5	18,000 shares
July 1, 19X5	12,000 shares
August 15, 19X5	15,000 shares
October 31, 19X5	6,000 shares

Earnings for the fiscal year ending January 31, 19X6, were $1,650,000. On September 1, 19X5, the company issued options for 12,000 shares of common stock at $26 per share. None of the options were exercised during the year. The options expire in five years. The average market price for the common stock of Mayflower during the last quarter was $30 and the ending market price was $25. The company also has a contingent share agreement with its officers to issue 50,000 shares if the earnings of the company exceed $1,500,000 for two consecutive years. The earnings have not reached this point in previous years.

Present EPS data for both primary and fully diluted EPS. Show all computations and schedules in good form.

Exercise 5. Write a footnote to adequately disclose the factual situation described in Exercise 4.

Exercise 6. Earth Corporation has net income of $900,000 for the fiscal year ending September 30, 19X9. The common stock account on October 1, 19X8, showed 240,000 shares outstanding. The company also issued $2,000,000 of 6%, ten-year convertible bonds on June 1, 19X9, at 98. The bonds were dated June 1, 19X9, with interest payable on June 1 and December 1. The bond discount is amortized semiannually on a straight-line basis. Each $100 bond is convertible into one share of common stock. On August 1, 19X9, $500,000 of these bonds were converted. The remaining bonds should be considered common stock equivalents. The only other securities that the company has outstanding on October 1, 19X8, are 14,000 shares of convertible preferred stock, which returns a yearly dividend of $2.25 per share and is convertible into one share of common stock for each share of preferred. At date of issue, the market price of the preferred stock was $40 and the prime interest rate was 9%. On December 1, 19X8, an additional 6,000 shares of the same convertible preferred stock were issued at a price of $60 per share, when the prime interest rate was 9½%. All shares of preferred stock outstanding during the year received the full cash dividend. The tax rate applicable to Earth Corporation is 48%.

Present all EPS data required for Earth Corporation. Show all schedules and computations in good form.

Exercise 7. Various users of financial data recognize that there are certain factors, such as the availability of alternative accounting principles (e.g., lifo, fifo), which in general reduce intercompany comparability. However, segmental reporting has been suggested as a means of improving comparability between single-industry companies and diversified companies.

Limiting your response to the unique aspects of segmental reporting, identify those factors that would tend to reduce the intercompany comparability of segmental data.

Exercise 8. A diversified company has the following segments:

Segment	Operating Profit (Loss) Year 1	Year 2
A	$400	$350
B	500	200
C	(700)	(500)
D	150	(170)
E	(80)	20
F	70	80
	$340	$ (20)

For each year, indicate which segments qualify as reportable segments.

Exercise 9. Capital Unlimited consists of eight industry segments. Measures of revenues, operating profit, and identifiable assets for each segment are as follows:

Segment	Revenues	Operating Profit (Loss)	Identifiable Assets
A	$ 55,000	$(30,800)	$ 117,000
B	39,000	9,000	72,000
C	98,500*	19,300	96,000
D	51,000	24,000	84,000
E	120,000	32,200	220,000
F	80,500*	(16,500)	128,000
G	46,000*	(21,000)	103,000
H	28,000	6,500	60,000
Corporate level items and items not allocated to the above segments	254,500	47,300	268,000
	$772,500	$ 70,000	$1,148,000
Intercompany adjustments and eliminations	(22,500)	(8,860)	(215,000)
Consolidated total	$750,000	$ 61,140	$ 933,000

*Only 90% of these revenues are to unaffiliated customers.

(1) Identify which segments would qualify as reportable segments.
(2) Determine whether a substantial portion of Capital's total operations is represented by reportable segments.
(3) Identify which locations would qualify as significant geographical areas, assuming that the segments are classified geographically as follows:

Location	Segments
Australia	A, B
Western Europe	C, D, E, F
South America	G, H

Exercise 10.   Badger Industries is a large international company with extremely diversified activities. These activities include:

(a) Food processing operations in Chicago, Tulsa, and Louisville. Processed foods under several labels are sold to independent grocers throughout the Midwest and Southwest. Cans used in the operation are manufactured by the Krystal Can Company, a wholly-owned subsidiary.

(b) Seven citrus groves in central Florida. Approximately 70% of a harvest is trucked to the company's Louisville food processing operation and the balance of the harvest is processed, on location, into frozen juice concentrates.

(c) A Cleveland operation which manufactures packaging for perishable food products, and cardboard packaging for transporting equipment components, such as engines and transmissions.

(d) Four large resort hotels, three of which are located along the eastern seaboard and one of which is located in the Bahamas.

(e) A chain of travel agencies in the New York and Boston areas.

(f) A paper products division which manufactures napkins, paper plates, paper towels, and greeting cards. These products are sold to grocery stores and variety stores.

Determine how the activities of Badger should be classified into segments for external reporting purposes.

PROBLEMS

Problem 4-1.   On January 1, 19X9, Back Rowe, Inc., had 100,000 shares of common stock outstanding along with the following other securities:

Warrant Q—Exercise price of $25 for each share of common stock; 10,000 issued, of which 2,000 were exercised on September 30, 19X9.

8% cumulative preferred stock—Par value $50; 9,000 shares were issued when the bank prime rate was 12%.

8% convertible bonds—100, 10-year, $1,000 bonds were issued on July 1, 19X5, at 103 when the bank prime rate was 11¾%. Each bond is convertible into ten shares of common stock and on April 1, 19X9, 20 bonds were converted.

The effective tax rate is 45% and quarterly stock market prices are as follows:

Quarter	Average	End of Quarter
1	$26	$25
2	25	26
3	28	32
4	30	26

For the year ended December 31, 19X9, the company reported final net income of $4,090,000, including an extraordinary loss of $400,000.

Required:

Prepare all necessary schedules and computations to calculate the primary and fully diluted earnings per share for the year ended December 31, 19X9.

Problem 4-2. Earnings per share (EPS) is the most featured single financial statistic about modern corporations. Daily published quotations of stock prices for many securities have recently been expanded to include a "times earnings" figure which is based on EPS. Often the focus of analysts' discussions will be on the EPS of the corporation receiving their attention.

Required:

(1) Explain how dividends or dividend requirements on any class of preferred stock that may be outstanding affect the computation of EPS.
(2) One of the technical procedures applicable in EPS computations is the "treasury stock method."
   (a) Briefly describe the circumstances under which it might be appropriate to apply the treasury stock method.
   (b) There is a limit to the extent to which the treasury stock method is applicable. Indicate what this limit is, and give a succinct indication of the procedures that should be followed beyond the treasury stock limits.
(3) Under some circumstances, convertible debentures would be considered "common stock equivalents," while under other circumstances they would not.
   (a) When is it proper to treat convertible debentures as common stock equivalents? What is the effect on the computation of EPS in such cases?
   (b) If convertible debentures are not considered as common stock equivalents, explain how they are handled for purposes of EPS computations.

(AICPA adapted)

Problem 4-3. Grace, Inc., reported net income of $8,000,000 for 19X2. Grace's common stock, which is traded over one of the major exchanges, had an average market price of $50 during the last twelve months. On November 30, 19X2, the market price was $80. The following information is obtained from Grace:

Long-term debt:
   6% bonds due in 19X9.
   4% convertible bonds, convertible into 3 shares of common per $100 bond. Bonds were issued at face value of $10,000,000, when the prime interest rate was 7%.

Stockholders' equity:
   $4.50 preferred stock, $100 par, cumulative, callable at $100, and convertible into 2 shares of common stock for each share of preferred. Issued when the prime rate was 7%. 150,000 shares outstanding.
   $2.50 preferred stock, $50 par, cumulative, callable at $60, and convertible into one share of common stock for each share of preferred. Issued when the prime rate was 4%. 400,000 shares outstanding. All preferred stock was issued at par.
   Common stock, $10 par, 1,500,000 shares issued and outstanding.
   Warrants to purchase common:
      100,000 shares at $20.
      200,000 shares at $52.

Assume that all securities were outstanding for the entire year, and that the three-month test for warrants was met in the previous year.

Required:

Present all computations required to determine the earnings per share data for Grace, Inc., for the year ending November 30, 19X2. (Assume an effective income tax rate of 48%.)

Problem 4-4. The Epco Corporation reported a net income for 19X5 as follows:

Income from continuing operations before cumulative effect of change in accounting principle*	$8,070,000
Cumulative effect on prior years of change in accounting principle	390,000
Net income	$8,460,000

*The effective tax rate is 48%.

Average 19X5 market prices of the corporation's stock were:

January	$65	July	$62
February	68	August	68
March	59	September	71
April	58	October	69
May	57	November	64
June	62	December	62

Market prices for certain specific dates in 19X5 were:

March 31	$58
June 30	61
September 30	72
December 31	66

The following equity is shown on the books of Epco:

6% nonconvertible bonds, $200,000 face value, due 19Y5.

4% convertible bonds, convertible into two shares of common stock per $100 bond. The bonds with a face value of $2,000,000 were issued for 97 when the prime interest rate was 7%. The annual amortization of the discount is $3,000 and an unamortized balance of $52,500 remains as of December 31, 19X5. Five thousand (5,000) bonds were converted on September 1, 19X5.

4½% preferred stock, $100 par, issued at par on April 1, 19X5, 1,000 shares issued and outstanding, cumulative and callable at 100. The prime interest rate at issuance was 6½%. The preferred stock is convertible into common stock as follows:

19X5 — one share of preferred for 2 shares of common
19X6 — one share of preferred for 3 shares of common
19X7 — one share of preferred for 3 shares of common
19X8 — one share of preferred for 4 shares of common

5% preferred stock, $10 par, issued in 19X4, 100,000 shares issued and outstanding.

The company paid dividends quarterly on all preferred stock and an additional 10 cents per share per quarter on common shares. The common stock has a $10 par value, and an analysis of the common stock account reveals the following information on the number of shares outstanding:

Period	Shares Outstanding
January-March	170,000
April-May	180,000
June-August	185,000
September-October	190,000
November-December	190,000

In addition, the company data show the following information concerning warrants issued (all warrants expire one year after issuance):

Warrant A, issued November 1, 19X5, for 10,000 shares of common stock at $68 per share. The proceeds are to be used to retire the 6% bonds.

Warrant B, issued March 1, 19X5, for 10,000 shares of common stock at $55 per share during the first and second quarters of 19X5, $58 per share during the third quarter of 19X5, and $60 per share in all later periods. On April 1, 19X5, 5,000 shares of common stock were issued through the exercise of these warrants.

Warrant C, issued July 1, 19X5, for 2,000 of the 4% convertible bonds at $110, which was always above the fair market value of the bond.

On February 1, 19X5, the board of directors agreed to issue 10,000 shares of common stock if the income from operations reached $9,000,000 by January 1, 19X7, and remained at that level at least two years.

Required

Present all necessary schedules and computations to calculate the primary and fully diluted earnings per share for Epco's financial statements for the fiscal year ended December 31, 19X5.

Problem 4-5. Simplex Corporation has a complex capital structure. The controller of Simplex has asked for assistance in computing earnings per share data for the corporation. The market prices of Simplex common stock were as follows:

	19X8	19X7	19X6
Average market price:			
First quarter	$60	$55	$50
Second quarter	70	62	51
Third quarter	80	60	50
Fourth quarter	80	60	55
December 31 closing price......................	82	61	54

After-tax income for the year 19X8 was $16,400,000 (the tax rate is 50%).

Cash dividends of 25 cents per share of common stock were declared and paid for each quarter of 19X6 and 19X7. Cash dividends of 30 cents per share of common stock were paid for each quarter in 19X8.

The company had outstanding $20,000,000 of 4%, 20-year convertible debentures. At the date of issuance, October 1, 19X6, they sold for $100. Each $100 debenture is convertible into 4 shares of common stock. No debentures were converted in 19X6 or 19X7; however, the entire issue was converted at the beginning of the third quarter of 19X8. The bank prime interest rate at the date of issue was 6½%.

Two classes of preferred stock are outstanding:

Class A — 6½% noncumulative, nonparticipating, $50 par, 10,000 shares issued and outstanding for the entire year.

Class B — $.20 convertible preferred, 600,000 shares issued and outstanding at the beginning of the second quarter of 19X7. A quarterly dividend of $.05 per share is paid at the beginning of each quarter on shares outstanding as of the first of the quarter. Immediately after each dividend during 19X8, 62,500 shares of preferred stock were converted into an equal number of common shares. At the time of original issuance, the market price of the convertible stock was $61. The bank prime interest rate was 6% at date of issuance.

During the year, the corporation had warrants outstanding to purchase 250,000 shares of common stock at $70 a share for a period of five years. To date, no warrants have been exercised.

At the beginning of 19X8, an analysis of the common stock account showed 8,300,000 shares outstanding.

Required:

(1) Prepare 19X8 EPS data for the Simplex Corporation.
(2) Prepare the appropriate footnote disclosure for the above situation.

Problem 4-6. The controller of Midar Corporation has requested assistance in determining primary and fully diluted earnings per share figures for the company for the fiscal year just ended on September 30, 19X1.

Working papers disclose the following beginning balances and transactions in the company's capital stock accounts during the current fiscal year:

(a) Common stock (at October 1, 19X0, stated value $10, authorized 300,000 shares; effective December 1, 19X0, stated value $5, authorized 600,000 shares):
   Balance, October 1, 19X0 — 60,000 shares issued and outstanding.
   December 1, 19X0 — 60,000 shares issued in a 2-for-1 stock split.
   December 1, 19X0 — 280,000 shares (stated value $5) issued at $39 per share.

(b) Treasury stock — common:
   March 1, 19X1 — purchased 40,000 shares at $38 per share.
   April 1, 19X1 — sold 40,000 shares at $40 per share.

(c) Stock purchase warrants, Series A (initially, each warrant was exchangeable with $60 for one common share; effective December 1, 19X0, each warrant became exchangeable for two common shares at $30 per share):
   October 1, 19X0 — 25,000 warrants issued at $6 each.

(d) Stock purchase warrants, Series B (each warrant is exchangeable with $40 for one common share):
   April 1, 19X1 — 20,000 warrants authorized and issued at $10 each.

(e) First mortgage bonds, 5½%, due 19Y5 (nonconvertible; priced to yield 5% when issued):
   Balance, October 1, 19X0 — authorized, issued and outstanding — the face value of $1,400,000.

(f) Convertible debentures, 7%, due 19Y9 (initially each $1,000 bond was convertible at any time until maturity into 12½ common shares; effective December 1, 19X0, the conversion rate became 25 shares for each bond):
   October 1, 19X0 — authorized and issued at their face value (no premium or discount) of $2,400,000.

The following table shows market prices for the company's securities and the assumed bank prime interest rate during 19X0-19X1:

| | Price (or Rate) at | | | Average for Year Ended |
	October 1, 19X0	April 1, 19X1	September 30, 19X1	September 30, 19X1
Common stock	66	40	36¼	37½*
First mortgage bonds......	88½	87	86	87
Convertible debentures	100	120	119	115
Series A warrants	6	22	19½	15
Series B warrants	—	10	9	9½
Bank prime interest rate ..	8%	7¾%	7½%	7¾%

*Adjusted for stock split

Required:

Compute the earnings per share data which the controller has requested, assuming that net income for the year is $540,000. Show all supporting schedules in good form. (Because of the relative stability of the market price for its shares of common stock, the annual average market price may be used where appropriate in the calculations. Assume an income tax rate of 48%.)

(AICPA adapted)

Problem 4-7. The following schedule sets forth the short-term debt, long-term debt, and stockholders' equity of the Globig Company as of December 31, 19X4.

Short-term debt:		
Notes payable—banks	$ 4,000,000	
Current portion of long-term debt...	10,000,000	
Total short-term debt	$ 14,000,000	
Long-term debt:		
4% convertible debentures, due April 15, 19Y6	$ 30,000,000	
Other long-term debt, less current portion	20,000,000	
Total long-term debt	$ 50,000,000	
Stockholders' equity:		
Preferred stock: $4 cumulative convertible; $20 par; 2,000,000 shares authorized; 1,200,000 shares issued and outstanding; $30 per share liquidation preference, aggregating $36,000,000	$ 24,000,000	
Common stock: $1 par; 20,000,000 shares authorized; 7,500,000 shares issued, including 600,000 shares held in treasury.......................................	7,500,000	
Additional paid-in capital...	4,200,000	
Retained earnings	76,500,000	
Total	$112,200,000	
Less cost of 600,000 shares of common stock held in treasury (acquired prior to 19X4)..	900,000	
Total stockholders' equity	$111,300,000	
Total long-term debt and stockholders' equity	$161,300,000	

The 4% convertible debentures were issued at face value in 19W6 when the bank prime interest rate was 5%. The debentures are convertible into the common stock of Globig at the rate of 25 shares for each $1,000 debenture.

In 19X3, 1,300,000 shares of $4 cumulative convertible preferred stock were issued. The stock had a market value of $75 at the time of issuance, when the bank prime interest rate was 9%. On July 1, 19X4, and on October 1, 19X4, holders of the preferred stock converted 80,000 and 20,000 preferred shares, respectively, into common stock. Each share of preferred stock is convertible into 1.2 shares of common stock. Appropriate dividends are paid on all preferred stock which is actually converted.

On April 1, 19X4, Globig issued 800,000 shares of common stock.

On October 1, 19X3, the company granted options to its officers and selected employees to purchase 100,000 shares of Globig common stock at a price of $33 per share. The options are not exercisable until 19X6.

During 19X4, the average and ending market prices of Globig common stock were as follows:

	Average Market Price	Ending Market Price
First quarter	$31	$29
Second quarter	35	32
Third quarter	32	34
Fourth quarter................	37	34
Average for the year	34	—

Dividends on the preferred stock have been paid through December 31, 19X4. Dividends paid on the common stock were 50 cents per share for each quarter.

The net income of Globig Company for the year ended December 31, 19X4, is $8,600,000. On January 1, 19X4, 5,980,000 common shares were outstanding. The provision for income taxes is computed at a rate of 48%.

Required:

Prepare a schedule to compute for 19X4:

(1) Primary earnings per share.

(2) Fully diluted earnings per share.   (AICPA adapted)

Problem 4-8. The Luoma Company is a dynamic company which has grown from a manufacturer of plastic automobile parts into a major diversified company serving both domestic and foreign markets. The company's operations are located entirely in the United States and include such diverse activities as offshore drilling, furniture manufacturing, and fast-food chains. The company's management information system is being extensively reviewed. Management is particularly interested in moving to a data base system which will satisfy both internal and external reporting needs. As part of the analysis with respect to external reporting needs, it is important to identify the various disclosure requirements called for by APB Opinions and FASB Statements.

Required:

Identify the various elements which must be disclosed to satisfy the company's responsibilities in the area of segmental reporting.

Problem 4-9. Thel Corporation is a highly diversified company composed of four industry segments. Segment A involves the production of commercial fishing equipment, Segment B manufactures health aids, Segment C consists of several pulp and paper mills, and Segment D produces recreational vehicles. Thel has prepared the following consolidated income statement and has asked for assistance in the preparation of segmental data.

Thel Corporation
Consolidated Income Statement
For Year Ended December 31, 19X3

Sales		$ 240,000
Cost of goods sold	$ 168,250	
General and administrative expenses	22,000	
Selling expenses	14,000	204,250
Operating income		$ 35,750
Other income and expenses:		
Interest income	$ 3,500	
Equity in income of unconsolidated investees	8,750	
Interest expense	(4,500)	7,750
Income from continuing operations before income taxes		$ 43,500
Provision for income taxes		13,050
Income from continuing operations		$ 30,450
Discontinued operations:		
Loss from operations of Florida plant (net of income tax effect)	$ (6,500)	
Gain on disposal of Florida plant (net of income tax effect)	10,300	3,800
Income before extraordinary item		$ 34,250
Extraordinary loss (net of income tax effect)		(2,600)
Net income		$ 31,650

Of the total annual sales, 20% are to foreign customers, most of whom are located in certain Scandinavian countries. The revenues generated by segments during 19X3 were as follows: $125,000 by A, $23,000 by B, $21,000 by C, and $71,000 by D. An additional transaction occurring in 19X3, but not considered in the segment sales figures, was a sale by Segment D to Segment C. Goods costing $7,500 were sold for $10,000, and 30% of these goods remain in C's inventory at year end.

The cost of goods sold by segment is:

Segment A .... $72,000   Segment C $14,000
Segment B 15,500   Segment D 76,000

General and administrative expenses are analyzed as follows:

Directly traceable to the corporate level $7,400
Directly traceable to Segment A 3,700
Directly traceable to Segment B 2,200
Directly traceable to Segment C 1,900
Directly traceable to Segment D 2,800

The balance of these expenses and the selling expenses are allocated to the segments based on sales (including intersegment sales).

The interest income of $3,500 represents the earnings on marketable securities controlled by corporate headquarters. The gain on discontinued operations is traceable to Segment A, while the extraordinary loss is traceable to operations in Segment B.

Consolidated assets (net of appropriate contra assets) total $601,000 and are identifiable as follows:

Corporate level .... $ 89,000
Segment A 251,000
Segment B 37,000
Segment C 43,000
Segment D 158,000
Investment in unconsolidated
   subsidiaries 23,000

Eliminated from total assets is a $9,000 loan receivable held by Segment A against Segment B.

Required:

(1) Develop a schedule which will report the revenues, operating profits, and identifiable assets of the reportable segments and other segments and will reconcile these items with the related consolidated amounts.

(2) Write the footnote that would accompany the reports generated in part (1).

Problem 4-10. A-1 Industries is a multinational manufacturer of photographic equipment and supplies. A consolidated income statement for the year ended December 31, 19X1, is as follows:

Sales		$860,000
Cost of goods sold		570,000
Gross profit		$290,000
General, administrative, and selling expenses		167,500
Operating income		$122,500
Other income and expenses:		
Equity in income of Meadows Company	$14,500	
Interest expense on corporate-level debt	(11,000)	3,500
Income from continuing operations before income taxes		$126,000
Provision for income taxes		50,400
Income from continuing operations		$75,600
Extraordinary loss (net of tax benefit of $17,600)		(26,400)
Cumulative effect of changes in accounting principles (net of income taxes of $30,000)		45,000
Net income		$ 94,200

Consolidated sales of $350,000 are traceable to foreign operations, of which 50% is traceable to geographic area A, 27% to geographic area B, 13% to geographic area C, and the balance to geographic area D. Not included in consolidated amounts are the following intersegment transactions:

(a) Sale of goods from domestic segment J to domestic segment K. The goods were transferred at a price of $8,600, which represents 125% of cost. As of year end, all of these goods were sold by K to unaffiliated customers.

(b) Sale of goods from domestic segment K to foreign segment Y, which is located in geographical area A. The goods were transferred at a price of $12,000, which represents 150% of cost. As of year end, 35% of these goods remain in segment Y's inventory.

(c) At midyear, domestic segment A advanced to foreign segment Y the sum of $9,000, which is to be repaid with interest in one year at an annual interest rate of 8%.

Prior to consolidation, cost of goods sold consisted of the following:

Domestic operations	$323,000
Foreign operations:	
Area A	126,000
Area B	52,000
Area C	41,000
Area D	38,600
Total	$580,600

Corporate expenses account for $45,000 of the general, administrative, and selling expenses, with the balance being allocated as follows:

Domestic operations	$ 60,000
Foreign operations:	
Area A	28,000
Area B	19,000
Area C	8,500
Area D	7,000
Total	$122,500

Included in consolidated sales is interest income of $40,000 earned by domestic Segment A, a financial institution, from loans to unaffiliated customers. Also included in the consolidated cost of goods sold is $25,000 of interest expense traceable to Segment A.

Consolidated assets, less relevant contra accounts, total $1,216,000 which is traceable to the following operations:

Corporate activities	$ 65,000
Domestic operations	421,000
Foreign operations:	
Area A	302,000
Area B	243,000
Area C	99,00(
Area D	86,00(
Total	$1,216,000

Required:

Develop a segmental report for A-1 Industries.

CHAPTER 5

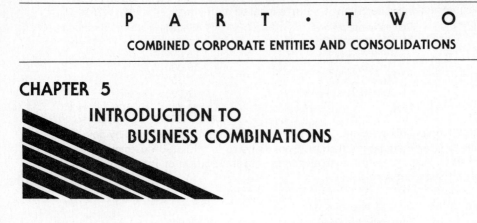

INTRODUCTION TO
BUSINESS COMBINATIONS

The combining of two or more business entities into one larger firm has been a commonplace business practice since the turn of the century. Historically, the popularity of business combinations has been correlated to the general level of business activity. The periods of greatest combination activity were the 1890's, the 1920's, and, most recently, the 1960's. The first two periods were characterized by the formation of large dominant firms within specific industries. Unlike the earlier periods, the business combinations of the 1960's often resulted in diversified firms spreading risk by investing in unrelated industries.

The 1970's were marked by a drastic decline in the number of business combinations. Uncertainties caused by recessions, energy shortages, and inflation appeared to reduce the motivation to grow through business combinations. However, a flurry of combination activity has occurred in the early 1980's. Perhaps increased financial strength and diversification are viewed as partial solutions to the problems which business has faced in recent years.

There are several alternative procedures available for accomplishing business combinations, but all are characterized by one business entity gaining control over the assets and liabilities of another entity or group of entities. Most current combinations are termed consolidations, mergers, or parent company investments in a subsidiary. Technically, a *consolidation* refers to the combining of two or more previously independent entities into one new entity. Each of the previous firms is dissolved and is replaced by a single, continuing firm. By contrast, a *merger* involves the absorption of one or more former entities by another firm which continues as the sole survivor. Another type of combination is characterized by a firm acquiring a controlling interest of usually more than 50% in another company's common stock. The firm making the acquisition is termed the *parent*, and the firm controlled is termed a *subsidiary*. Often the parent and subsidiary will combine their individual financial statements into a single set of statements which are labeled ''Consolidated Statements.'' Thus it occurs in practice that a consolidation may refer to a special type of combination or, more commonly, to the combined statements of a parent and its subsidiary.

The accountant may be involved in various activities pertaining to business combinations. Accountants frequently aid a buyer or seller in arriving at a tentative price and may also advise the firms on how to accomplish the combination in view of tax and financial reporting implications. The accountant must record the combination in a manner that conforms to generally accepted accounting principles. The accountant must present the effects of the combination in the accounting statements of the current and subsequent periods.

MOTIVATIONS TO COMBINE

The most obvious reason to combine is to achieve profitable growth. It is also possible that combinations result from a desire of management to elevate its status or to realize tax advantages.

Accelerated Growth

Acquisition of a going concern may be an accelerated means of achieving growth. Very likely, economies of scale may be enjoyed almost immediately, not only in production, marketing, and administration, but also in financing. All other conditions being equal, larger firms typically may be able to issue both debt and equity on more favorable terms. External growth through the combination of business entities may also offer greater immediate profitability, since the revenue flow already exists and need not be created. Long-run profitability may benefit from the elimination rather than the intensification of potential competition.

Combinations may involve three basic types of growth:

1. Horizontal growth is the result of acquiring a firm that performs similar functions, thereby increasing the acquiring firm's share of the market. Horizontal growth implies a lessening of competition, and therefore may be subject to federal antitrust laws. Section 7 of the Clayton Act of 1914 prohibits combinations which substantially lessen competition or tend to create a monopoly.

2. Vertical growth is the result of acquiring a firm that performs dissimilar but related functions. If a steel manufacturing company acquires a coal mining operation or an iron ore shipping firm, vertical growth has resulted. Such expansion involves combinations with suppliers or customers. Vertical combinations are subject to federal antitrust laws when they eliminate a substantial share of the market.

3. Diversified growth is the result of acquiring a firm that engages in unrelated activities. If a steel manufacturing company acquires a national chain of restaurants, diversified growth results. These combinations of unrelated business units are referred to as conglomerates. Constituent firms are merely parts of a diversified investment structure.

Though not bothered unduly by antitrust legislation, conglomerates may have significant reporting problems. The combined firm is merely a holding company and not an integrated economic entity. Limited information is derived from reading only the financial statements of a conglomerate. The separate statements of the constituent firms should be presented, and disclosure may also include segmental results.

Executive Prestige

Several writers in the area of business combinations point to the psychological desire on the part of a firm's executives to elevate their status by extending their authority over a larger organization. Such motivation alone, without adequate concern for the effects of the action on future profitability, should not lead to a combination.

Tax Advantages

The owners of a closely held corporation may desire to liquidate their interest in a manner that avoids immediate taxation. This result may be accomplished by trading their interests for the marketable securities of a large corporation in a transaction carefully structured as a tax-free exchange, rather than selling their interests for cash.

Further advantages exist when the firm to be absorbed has incurred losses in previous years. Section 172(b) of the Internal Revenue Code provides that operating losses can be carried back three years to obtain a refund of taxes levied in profitable years. Should the loss not be absorbed by income in the three previous years, the loss may be carried forward fifteen years to offset taxable income, thus eliminating or reducing taxes which would otherwise be payable. These tax loss maneuvers are of little value to the firm originating them if the firm has not had sufficient taxable income in past years and does not expect enough future income to offset the loss. Since the tax loss is transferable in a business combination, it may have value for a profitable acquiring firm. Thus, by combining, the unprofitable absorbed firm is able to realize immediate value from its past tax losses by selling them to the acquiring firm. The acquiring firm also benefits in that it seldom pays a price equal to the full tax value of the tax loss. However, the acquiring firm should exercise caution in anticipating the benefits of past tax losses, since the deductions may be disallowed if the primary purpose of acquiring a corporation is to receive tax benefits.

A firm may also obtain a tax advantage by filing a consolidated tax return for all corporations in the affiliated group. The operating losses of one corporation offset immediately the profits of another member of the affiliated group.

OBTAINING CONTROL

Control of another firm's assets may be achieved in one of two ways. One option is to acquire the assets of the firm directly from the owner. Payment might include cash, property, or securities issued by the acquiring firm. The use of debt or equity securities as a means of payment is popular since it avoids depleting assets, particularly cash, that may be needed for future operations. The other method of acquiring control of a corporation's assets is to acquire over 50% of its outstanding common stock. There may be numerous advantages inherent in this type of acquisition. Most obvious is the fact that the total cost is lower, since only a controlling interest in the assets and not the total assets must be acquired. Control through stock ownership may also be simpler to achieve, since no formal negotiations or transactions with the acquired firm's management are necessary. Further advantages may result from maintaining the separate legal identity of the former firm. For example, risk is lowered since the legal liability of any one corporation is limited to its own assets. Separate legal entities may also be desirable when only one of the firms is subject to government control. Lastly, there may be tax advantages resulting from the preservation of the legal entities.

Control through asset acquisition results in the assets of the acquired firm being recorded on the books of the acquiring firm. All future transactions will be recorded in the combined set of accounts. Combined financial statements will automatically result for periods subsequent to the acquisition.

Achieving control of a firm through the acquisition of its stock leads to more involved accounting requirements. Since the firms maintain their individual legal identity, they also maintain separate accounting records and prepare separate financial statements. Despite the existing segregation, accounting views most of these acquisitions as creating only one viable, economic entity. As a result, the financial statements of each firm involved are blended into one set of "consolidated statements."

This chapter will discuss business combinations resulting from the direct acquisition of assets, since the accounting principles involved are more easily understood in this context. Later chapters will treat the topic of accounting for business combinations where control is achieved through stock acquisition. This chapter will proceed to discuss the two basic alternative theories of treating business combinations, *purchase* and *pooling of interests*. The theories and their resulting procedures apply to all combinations, whether achieved through an asset or a stock acquisition.

PURCHASE VS. POOLING

Current accounting practice is based on APB Opinion No. 16, "Business Combinations," which views most business combinations as a purchase of one firm by another for cash or other consideration. Purchase accounting requires that the assets acquired be recorded at their current market value or the value of the consideration given, whichever is more readily determinable. The combination is viewed as a group purchase of assets. The total price paid for the firm must be allocated to the individual assets, using their estimated market values as a guide. Should the price paid exceed the total market values of the identifiable assets, the excess is viewed as a payment for intangible future benefits and is captioned "goodwill" on the balance sheet. Subsequent income statements will include depreciation charges based on the market value of the depreciable assets and amortization deductions for goodwill. Where the acquiring firm issues securities as consideration, debt or equity accounts should reflect the market values of the securities issued.

According to APB Opinion No. 16 (par. 47), the only exception to accounting for a combination as a purchase may apply to situations in which the surviving company issues only common stock for all the assets or substantially all the voting common stock of the acquired firm. The term "pooling of interests" is used to describe this fusion of previously separate stockholder groups. The proper structuring of such a combination supports the argument that no sale has occurred, but rather that the stockholders of the acquired firm are merely exchanging their interest in the former firm for an interest in the combined corporation. The absence of a sale thus makes it unnecessary for the accountant to acknowledge the market values of the assets acquired and the securities issued. The acquiring firm combines the book values of the acquired company's assets and liabilities with its own. The total paid-in capital of the acquired firm is assigned to the securities issued by the surviving corporation. The retained earnings of the acquired firm is, in most cases, added to the retained earnings of the surviving company.

Effect on Future Statements

The consequences of the purchase versus pooling methods may be very pronounced. The following chart compares the impact of the two accounting methods on future balance sheets.

Item	Purchase Method	Pooling Method
1. Recording of assets and liabilities.	At current market values with a possibility of goodwill.	At book value of acquired firm. No additional goodwill acknowledged. (a)
2. Securities issued.	Market value of shares added to paid-in capital.	Paid-in capital of acquired firm assigned as paid-in value of shares issued. (b)
3. Retained earnings of acquired firm.	Not acknowledged.	Added to retained earnings. (b)

(a) Goodwill previously recorded by the acquired firm would be recorded at book value.
(b) The retained earnings of the acquired firm may be reduced to meet the issuer's par or stated value requirement.

Future income statements are also affected by the values assigned to the assets of the acquired firm. Typically, long-lived assets[1] will have market values in excess of their book values. Recording a combination as a purchase will therefore cause higher depreciation and amortization expense in future years. In addition, any goodwill resulting from a purchase must be amortized over a period not to exceed 40 years,[2] thus burdening future income statements with a charge that would not have existed under the pooling method. Income statements for a period following a combination under the purchase and pooling methods would be prepared as follows:

	Purchase	Pooling
Revenue	$250,000	$250,000
Less:		
All expenses except depreciation on acquired firm's assets and amortization of goodwill	(100,000)	(100,000)
Depreciation of building acquired in combination:		
Purchase: 1/10 of $500,000 market value	(50,000)	
Pooling: 1/10 of $200,000 net book value		(20,000)
Goodwill amortization:		
Purchase: 1/40 of $200,000	(5,000)	
Income before tax	$ 95,000	$130,000
Less income tax (.4 × $130,000) *	(52,000)	(52,000)
Net income	$ 43,000	$ 78,000

* Tax computation is based on taxable income, which permits book value depreciation and no deduction for goodwill amortization. Therefore, the tax computation is identical under purchase and pooling.

The only differences in the two income statements involve depreciation and goodwill amortization. The book value of the building acknowl-

[1] The term "long-lived assets" will be used in this text to refer to all identifiable tangible and intangible noncurrent assets.

[2] *Opinions of the Accounting Principles Board, No. 17,* "Intangible Assets" (New York: American Institute of Certified Public Accountants, 1970), par. 29.

edged in a pooling is assumed to be $200,000, while the market value acknowledged in a purchase is $500,000. In both cases, depreciation is calculated on a straight-line basis with a 10-year remaining life. In addition, the price paid for the firm exceeded the market values of the separate identifiable assets by $200,000. Thus the goodwill recorded under the purchase method is $200,000, and it is amortized on a straight-line basis with a maximum 40-year life. The dollar disparity between the incomes does not result in different amounts of income tax because goodwill amortization is not tax deductible. Also, the portion of depreciation based on the excess of the building's market value over book value is commonly disallowed as a tax deduction.[3] The purchase method causes a permanent difference between financial and taxable incomes. Thus, while the effect of all other expenses is mitigated by their tax deductibility, the added expenses caused by the purchase method receive no such offset.

In summary, most firms, if given a choice, would choose to account for combinations under the pooling method. Where assets are undervalued and/or goodwill exists, the pooling method will produce higher incomes in future years. The balance sheet of the continuing firm is also enhanced when the retained earnings of the acquired firm is added to existing retained earnings. The only likely disadvantage of the pooling method is that acquired assets may not be shown on the balance sheet at their full value; thus, the total worth of the combined firms may be considerably less than would have resulted under the purchase method.

Criteria for the Use of the Pooling Method

Prior to the issuance of APB Opinion No. 16 in 1970, many firms tended to ignore the then loosely-defined criteria for the use of the purchase and pooling methods. A choice between the methods was often based on the impact of the methods on future statements. APB Opinion No. 16 states that the purchase and pooling methods are not alternative recording methods available for a given combination. Past abuses of the pooling method led the APB to designate strict criteria that had to be met for a combination to qualify as a pooling of interests. Any combination not meeting all of the criteria is designated as a purchase. The criteria seek to insure that only a true fusion of previous stockholder interests and assets will be accorded the pooling treatment. APB Opinion No. 16 classifies the criteria according to the attributes of the combining firms, the agreement as to how interests are to be combined, and the absence of planned subsequent transactions. The Opinion also introduces special terminology for referring to firms combining under the pooling method. The acquiring firm which will continue in existence is termed the *issuer*, while the acquired firm is termed the *combiner*. These terms will be used in subsequent discussions to avoid any con-

---

[3] Many business combinations are structured as nontaxable exchanges. In such cases, the value assigned to the asset reflects the fact that any assigned value in excess of the existing book value is not deductible.

notation of a purchase-sale having occurred when the pooling method is appropriate.

Attributes of the Combining Firms. APB Opinion No. 16 (par. 46) provides two criteria which establish essential attributes of the combining firms.

> *Criterion 1.* Each of the combining firms may not have been a subsidiary or division of another firm for two years preceding the date on which a plan of combination is initiated. The initiation date is the earliest date at which the stockholders of the combining firms are informed of the terms of the combination (including the stock exchange ratio) either through a public announcement or through written notification.

The intent of this condition is that a company should not be able to fragment a business enterprise and pool only part of it. For new firms created within the two years, this condition is applicable only to the firm's period of existence. For the purposes of this condition, a former subsidiary which was separated from the parent by government order is considered a "new" firm.

> *Criterion 2.* Each of the combining firms must be independent of one another. On the date of initiation of the plan and until its consummation, no firm may own more than 10% of the voting common stock of any other combining firm. Shares acquired as a part of the plan of combination are exempted.

Agreement as to How Interests Are To Be Combined. APB Opinion No. 16 (par. 47) provides six criteria that relate to the manner in which interests are combined.

> *Criterion 1.* The combination must be accomplished in a single transaction or in accordance with a specific plan, in which case the plan must be executed within one year of its initiation. One exception is allowed when there is a delay which is beyond the control of the combining firms. The only delays considered uncontrollable are (1) proceedings and deliberations of a federal or state regulatory agency on whether to approve or disapprove a combination where the combination cannot be effected without approval, and (2) litigation aimed at prohibiting the combination.

The intent of this condition is to prevent a piecemeal, selective displacement of stockholders on possibly different terms.

> *Criterion 2.* Subsequent to the initiation date, the issuer must issue its common stock for either all the assets of the combining firm or at least 90% of the outstanding voting common shares of the combiner in a stock acquisition. The shares issued must have rights identical to those of the majority of the issuer's outstanding voting common shares.

For the purpose of the 90% provision, the computation of the combiner shares received excludes:

(a) Shares held by the issuer or its subsidiaries prior to the initiation date, and

(b) Shares acquired after the initiation date by giving any consideration other than the voting common shares of the issuer. Fractional shares acquired for cash cannot be considered in meeting the 90% provision.

To illustrate, assume that Company C (combiner) has 20,000 shares of voting common stock outstanding, and that Company I (issuer) exchanges 8,500 shares of its voting common stock for 17,000 shares of Company C stock. Assume further that Company I, prior to the date of initiation, acquired 1,000 shares of the Company C stock in exchange for its own shares. In addition, Company I paid cash for 500 shares of the Company C stock as a part of the plan of combination. Even though Company I holds 92.5% (18,500/20,000) of Company C shares at the consummation date, it acquired only 85% (17,000/20,000) of the shares through the exchange of its own voting common shares after the date of initiation. Thus the 90% rule is not met, and the combination is accounted for as a purchase.

The application of the 90% rule becomes more complex when the combiner company holds shares of the issuer. To illustrate, assume that Company I issues 9,250 shares of its stock for 18,500 of the 20,000 shares of outstanding Company C stock subsequent to the initiation date of a plan of combination. In addition, assume that Company C previously acquired 500 shares of Company I stock. The following diagram summarizes the interfirm stock transactions:

	Company I	Company C
Prior to initiation date.........		Owns 500 shares of Company I stock
Subsequent to initiation date ..	Issues 9,250 shares of its stock to Company C ————————————➤ 18,500 shares of ◄———— Company C stock	In exchange for ┐ │

According to the exchange ratio, 1 share of Company I stock is equal in value to 2 shares of Company C stock;[4] thus, 1,000 (500 × 2) shares of the Company C stock represent an equity in Company I. Viewed in another manner, 1,000 shares of Company C stock support the investment in 500 shares of Company I. APB Opinion No. 16 holds that on an equivalent share basis, 1,000 of the 18,500 shares of Company C stock received by Company I are in essence a return of its own shares. The equivalent shares must be subtracted from the total combiner shares held on the consummation date. Thus, only 17,500 shares of Company C stock have been received for purposes of applying the 90% rule. In this illustration, only 17,500 of the total 20,000 shares qualify, and the applicable percentage of shares received is 87.5% (17,500 ÷ 20,000), requiring that the combination be accounted for as a purchase. If the combiner

---

[4] The exchange rate used is the actual resulting ratio at the consummation date. Any cash given for fractional shares will diminish the exchange rate.

acquires shares of the issuer subsequent to the initiation date, these shares are also subtracted, on an equivalent share basis, from the total shares acquired by the issuer in determining compliance with the 90% rule.

Criterion 3. The combining companies may not change their equity interests in contemplation of a combination for the period of time beginning two years before the initiation date and extending through the consummation date.

The intent of this provision is to prevent a combining firm from purchasing and reselling common shares in an attempt to create a group of shareholders who own 90% of the shares and who agree to combine. It is also the intent of the provision that the issuing firm be prevented from realigning its shareholders in an attempt to create a majority group who are willing to combine. Treasury stock purchases must be defended as normal and for other purposes in order not to violate this condition. "Other purposes" would, for example, include acquisition of shares to satisfy employee stock option plans.

Criterion 4. Dividend distributions (other than in common stock) must be no greater than normal for two years before the initiation date through the consummation date.

"Normal" is defined by reference to past dividend policy and earnings of the period. Greater than normal dividends would allow a firm to distribute part of its assets to shareholders and to pool only the residual. Shareholders would then receive part assets and part equity of the pooled firm, which is counter to the concept of pooling as a fusion of existing interests.

Criterion 5. The voting common stockholders of the combiner firm must receive issuer company voting shares proportionate to their holdings in the combining firm.

For example, Mr. X., who owned 30% of the Company Q voting common stock obtained by the issuer corporation, must receive 30% of the issuer corporation's voting common stock given in exchange for the shares of Company Q. In this way, the relative stockholder interests of the combiner firm are preserved.

Criterion 6. There can be no contingent consideration agreements based on events subsequent to the consummation date.

The most common type of contingent consideration involves future payments based on profits in subsequent periods. Another type of contingent consideration involves an agreement which provides that the issuer will compensate the combiner firm's shareholders for a decline in the value of the securities they receive as payment.

Absence of Planned Subsequent Transactions. Stipulations were necessary to prevent planned subsequent transactions that would counteract the conditions of a pooling of interests and allow a purchase to appear in the guise of a pooling. The pooling treatment is denied by APB Opinion No. 16 if any one of the following conditions is included explicitly or by intent in the negotiations and/or terms of the agreement to combine:

1. An agreement by which the issuer will retire or reacquire the common shares issued to effect the combination.
2. An agreement to aid financially a faction of the stockholders of the former combiner firm.
3. A plan to dispose of a significant part of the assets of the combining firms within two years of the consummation of the combination.[5]

ACCOUNTING FOR A PURCHASE

When the acquisition of an existing company is being considered, the current value of the firm's assets and the amount of its liabilities must be carefully appraised. Such an evaluation usually precedes negotiations. Very likely the prospective purchaser will seek permission to conduct a preacquisition audit to determine whether all assets and liabilities are properly recorded. The purchaser knows that while book values may be indicative of the current value of some current assets, these values may not represent a reasonable market value for inventories, plant assets, or intangibles. Inventories priced on a lifo basis will have little relationship to current market value. Inventories priced at fifo or average cost may be closer to market value but may still depart significantly when prices fluctuate quickly. Plant assets and intangibles are presented at historical cost less an arbitrary depreciation or amortization allowance, with no relationship to current market value.

Acknowledging the limitations of book values, the purchaser may engage an independent appraiser to estimate the current market values of the assets to be acquired. Market values are an estimate of the price to which a willing buyer and seller would agree. These estimates provide only a guide to establishing the price to be paid for the entire firm.

Assume that Acquisitions, Inc., is considering the purchase of the Jacobs Company and has secured the following audited condensed balance sheet:

Jacobs Company
Balance Sheet
December 31, 19X3

Accounts receivable	$ 20,000	Current liabilities	$ 20,000
Inventory	40,000	Capital stock	10,000
Land	10,000	Paid-in capital in excess of par	50,000
Buildings (net)	40,000	Retained earnings	50,000
Equipment (net)	20,000		
		Total liabilities and	
Total assets	$130,000	equity	$130,000

---

[5] APB Opinion No. 16 (par. 60) provides that if there is a material gain or loss on a sale of the assets of the previously separate firms within two years of a pooling, the gain or loss is shown as an extraordinary item.

Aware of the deficiencies of book values, management obtains the following appraisal of market values:

Accounts receivable (book value)	$ 20,000
Inventory	45,000
Land	10,000
Buildings	50,000
Equipment	40,000
Total market value of assets	$165,000

If the market values are accurate, Acquisitions will expect to pay at least $165,000 for the assets of the Jacobs Company. The $165,000 asset valuation is unaffected by the existence of $20,000 in liabilities. The purchaser may either assume the liabilities and pay $145,000 in cash, or pay the full $165,000 in cash and assume no liabilities. Perhaps a bargain could be struck for less than $165,000, but very likely more will be paid. Acquisitions may be willing to pay a premium for the Jacobs Company assets, since Jacobs is a functioning firm with an established trade. If the assets were purchased individually from other sources, time would be required to combine them into a viable, profitable firm. The payment for this advantage is considered the purchase of goodwill. The amount of the payment depends on the expected future profitability of the assets to be acquired and the outcome of the bargaining process.

Calculating and Recording Goodwill

In addition to obtaining market values for other assets, the purchaser must try to appraise the value of potential goodwill. Typically the appraisal is based on a comparison of estimated future income with normal income for the type and size of firm involved. Estimates of future income will likely be based on an analysis of the Jacobs Company income in the recent past. Normal income is calculated by applying an appropriate industry rate of return to the market value of the firm's assets (except for previously recorded goodwill). The following calculation of earnings in excess of normal might be made for the Jacobs Company:

Expected average future income		$ 21,000
Less normal return on assets:		
Market value of total assets	$165,000	
Industry normal rate of return	10%	
Normal return on assets		16,500
Expected annual earnings in excess of normal		$ 4,500

There are several methods of using the expected annual earnings in excess of normal to estimate goodwill. A common approach is to pay for a given number of years' excess earnings. For example, Acquisitions, Inc., might offer to pay for four years of excess earnings, which would total $18,000. Alternative methods view the excess earnings as an annuity. The most optimistic purchaser might expect the excess earnings to continue forever. If so, the buyer might capitalize the excess earnings as a perpetuity at the normal industry rate of return according to the following formula:

$$\text{Goodwill} = \frac{\text{Annual excess earnings}}{\text{Industry normal rate of return}}$$
$$= \frac{\$4,500}{.10}$$
$$= \$45,000$$

A less optimistic purchaser might feel that the factors producing excess earnings are of limited duration, such as 10 years, for example. This purchaser would calculate goodwill as follows:

Goodwill = discounted present value of a \$4,500-per-year annuity for 10 years at 10%
= \$4,500 × 10-year, 10% annuity present value factor
= \$4,500 × 6.145
= \$27,652

Other purchasers might feel that the normal industry earning rate is appropriate only for tangible assets and not goodwill. Thus they might capitalize excess earnings at a higher rate of return to reflect the higher risk inherent in goodwill.

All calculations of goodwill are estimates used to assist in the determination of the price to be paid for a firm. For example, Acquisitions might add the \$27,652 estimate of goodwill to the \$165,000 market value of Jacob's other assets to arrive at a tentative maximum price of \$192,652. However, estimates of goodwill may differ from actual bargained goodwill. Suppose that the final bargained price for the Jacobs Company assets was \$180,000. Then actual bargained goodwill would be \$15,000, the price paid less the market value of the other assets acquired.

Recording a Purchase

To continue the previous example, assume that the combining firms agree to a total value of \$180,000 for the Jacobs Company assets, including goodwill. If the transaction is to be a purchase of "gross assets," Acquisitions will pay \$180,000 in cash and will not assume the existing \$20,000 of liabilities. Instead, the Jacobs Company will discharge its debts using the proceeds of the sale. If, however, the transaction is to be a purchase of "net assets," Acquisitions will only pay \$160,000 and will assume the \$20,000 of liabilities. Most transactions are purchases of net assets, and assumed liabilities are paid by the surviving firm when due.

The following entry would be made by Acquisitions to record a net asset purchase, assuming that $1,000 of expenses were specifically incurred in consummating the purchase:

Accounts Receivable (market value)	20,000	
Inventory (market value)	45,000	
Land (market value)	10,000	
Buildings (market value)	50,000	
Equipment (market value)	40,000	
Goodwill (price minus sum of above market values)	16,000	
Current Liabilities (market value)		20,000
Cash (includes acquisition costs)		161,000

The total value assigned to purchased assets includes direct acquisition costs such as finder's fees and legal costs. Thus, in this case, the total consideration given is $181,000, determined as follows:

Cash paid to selling firm	$160,000
Cash paid for direct acquisition costs	1,000
Liabilities assumed	20,000
Total consideration	$181,000

APB Opinion No. 16 (par. 76) requires that expenses indirectly attributable to the purchase, such as secretarial and management time, are to be expensed in the period of the purchase.

Each asset and assumed liability is recorded at its estimated fair market value.[6] Goodwill is recorded at the bargained price, which is always the excess of the total consideration given ($181,000 in the example) over the sum of the values assigned to all other identifiable assets acquired (all assets other than goodwill). If an acquired firm already has goodwill on its books, such goodwill is ignored except as it is confirmed by the purchase price. For example, if the Jacobs Company had recorded goodwill of $25,000, Acquisitions would still assign $165,000 to the identifiable assets and assign the extra $16,000 paid to goodwill. In this case, only $16,000 of the $25,000 recorded former goodwill was confirmed by the current purchase price.

It should be noted that the selling firm's entries do not parallel those of the purchaser. The seller records the removal of assets at their book values. The excess of the price received by the seller ($180,000) over the sum of the asset book values ($130,000) is recorded as a gain on the sale. In this case, the gain is $50,000. The abbreviated entry on Jacob's books would be:

Cash	160,000	
Current Liabilities	20,000	
Itemized Assets (at book value)		130,000
Gain on Sale		50,000

---

[6] A liability may have a market value different from its book value when interest rates have changed since the liability was incurred.

Recording Bargain Purchases

Occasionally a firm will be purchased at a bargain, or at a price below the sum of the estimated market values of its separate identifiable assets. Naturally, when this situation occurs, any goodwill existing or the books of the seller is ignored, since the price paid does not confirm it. The least reliable estimates of market values are assumed to be those applicable to long-lived assets other than investments in marketable securities because a ready market often does not exist for such assets. Consequently, according to APB Opinion No. 16 (par. 87), current assets, assumed liabilities, and long-term investments in marketable securities are recorded at their full market value regardless of the total price paid for the firm. Any excess of the sum of the market values of identifiable assets over the price paid is to be deducted only from long-lived assets other than investments in marketable securities. For example, assume that Acquisitions, Inc., acquired the Jacobs Company by paying $152,000 to the seller ($132,000 cash plus assumption of $20,000 of liabilities), and $1,000 for direct acquisition costs.

The excess of the market value of the assets over cost would be determined as follows:

Total estimated market value of separate assets	$165,000
Less price paid (including direct acquisition costs)	153,000
Excess of market value over cost	$ 12,000

The excess must now be deducted from the total estimated market value of the long-lived assets to arrive at the purchase cost assignable to these assets. The assignable cost is then allocated to the individual long-lived assets in proportion to their fair market values.

The total estimated market value of the long-lived assets is first calculated:

	Estimated Market Value	Percent of Total
Land	$ 10,000	10%
Buildings	50,000	50
Equipment	40,000	40
Total market value	$100,000	100%

The cost assignable to long-lived assets is the $100,000 total market value less the $12,000 excess of market value over cost, or $88,000. This cost is assigned to the individual assets according to their relative market values as follows:

Asset	Percent of Total Market Value		Total Cost Assignable		Assigned Value
Land	10%	×	$88,000	=	$ 8,800
Buildings	50	×	88,000	=	44,000
Equipment	40	×	88,000	=	35,200
	100%				$88,000

The entry to record the purchase is:

Accounts Receivable (market value)	20,000	
Inventory (market value)	45,000	
Land (assigned purchase cost)	8,800	
Buildings (assigned purchase cost)	44,000	
Equipment (assigned purchase cost)	35,200	
Cash (price paid, less liabilities assumed, plus direct acquisition costs)		133,000
Current Liabilities (market value)		20,000

In some cases, long-lived assets are given current asset status and recorded at net realizable value, regardless of the price paid for the firm. This situation occurs only when the purchaser intends to sell some of these assets soon after the date of the combination, as in the case of acquired assets which duplicate those already owned by the purchaser.

Though a rare occurrence, the price paid for a firm could perhaps be less than the market value of the current assets and any long-term investment in marketable securities. Since market values must be recorded for current assets and marketable securities, no value would remain to be assigned to long-lived assets. According to APB Opinion No. 16 (par. 91), the excess of the value assigned to the current assets and marketable securities over the price paid is to be recorded as a deferred credit, Excess of Market Value of Current Assets over Cost. The credit is to be amortized to income over a period not to exceed 40 years.

In summary, when a bargain purchase occurs:

1. Current assets, long-term investments in marketable securities, and liabilities assumed are always recorded at fair market value.
2. Long-lived assets are recorded at fair market value less a reduction for the bargain.
3. A deferred credit is recorded only after all long-lived assets other than marketable securities are reduced to zero. The deferred credit is amortized over a period of 40 years or less.

Special Allocations of Purchase Price

There are several allocations of the purchase price in a business combination that require special analysis. The first complication occurs when assets are acquired in a purchase transaction that meets the criteria of a nontaxable exchange to the seller. In a nontaxable exchange, future depreciation on the assets received by the purchasing firm is limited for tax purposes to the selling firm's tax basis. As a result, depreciation on the excess of an asset's market value over its tax basis is not tax deductible. The value assigned to the asset must give effect to the nondeductible status of the excess. As an example, assume that the tax basis to the seller of a given asset is $50,000, and the fair market value of the asset is $150,000. The asset is worth $150,000 only if the entire value may be depreciated. In this example, $100,000 of the asset's value is not deductible on future tax returns. Therefore, if the purchasing firm is in a 40% tax bracket, it must deduct $40,000 from the

$150,000 market value. The purchasing firm would assign an adjusted market value of $110,000 ($150,000 market less $40,000 nondeductible depreciation) to the acquired asset.

The market value concept must also be applied to liabilities assumed in a purchase. The recorded book values of liabilities may not be indicative of their market values when prevailing interest rates have changed since the incurrence of the liabilities. When the debt instrument, such as bonds of a large corporation, is publicly traded, a quoted market value may be readily available. When such quotations are not available, the market value of a debt obligation must be estimated. The estimate is made by discounting all future cash flows required, using the current interest rate for debt issuances with similar risk and maturity. As an example, assume that the firm being acquired has outstanding $100,000 of 10% bonds which mature in 5 years. Assume further that interest is payable at the end of each of the next 5 years. If the prevailing interest rate for similar issuances is 12%, the market value of the debt would be estimated as follows:

Present value of interest payments at 12% ($10,000 annual interest × 5-year, 12% present value of annuity factor of 3.6048)	$36,048
Present value of principal ($100,000 × 5-year present value factor of .5674)	56,740
Estimated market value of liability	$92,788

The market value of the debt would be acknowledged in the purchase entry by recording a discount of $7,212 ($100,000 face value less $92,788 market value).

Leases. Analysis of the purchase price in a business combination is also necessary when the firm acquired in a purchase transaction is contractually bound by existing leases as either a lessee or lessor. In some cases, the terms of the lease may be modified as a result of the combination. These modifications would require the consent of a third party— either the lessor, when the selling firm is the lessee, or the lessee, when the selling firm is the lessor. When the terms of the lease are modified to the extent that a new lease is created, the new lease is classified and recorded according to the requirements of FASB Statement No. 13.[7] It is more common, however, to find that the contractual terms of a lease are not altered as a result of the purchase. In such cases it is only necessary to record the market value of the seller's existing rights and obligations under the lease.

When the firm acquired is a lessee under an operating lease, it has recorded rent as an expense, but has not recorded any asset or long-term liability. Thus, at the time of purchase there is no existing recorded asset or liability to adjust. If at the time of the purchase the contractual rent under the remaining lease term is materially below fair market

---

[7] *Statement of Financial Accounting Standards, No. 13*, "Accounting for Leases" (Stamford: Financial Accounting Standards Board, 1976), par. 9.

rental value, an asset should be recorded equal to the value of the rent savings. The asset should be amortized over the lease term as an adjustment to rent expense. If the contractual rent exceeds the market rental value, a loss on the commitment should be recorded and a liability should be credited for the excess. The liability should be amortized as a reduction of rent expense in future periods. Under both procedures, future rent expense would reflect market rental value as of the date of the combination.

When the acquired firm is a lessee under a capital lease, it has recorded the asset under the capital lease and has also recorded the liability under the lease. At the time of the purchase, both the asset and the liability should be independently analyzed and recorded at their separate market values.

When the acquired firm is a lessor under an operating lease, it has recorded the cost of the leased asset less accumulated depreciation. In the purchase transaction, the asset should be recorded at its current market value. However, the market value may be based in part on the present value of rents due under existing leases.

When the firm acquired is a lessor under a capital lease, it has recorded only a receivable due for future rents and perhaps an unguaranteed residual value. In the purchase transaction, the receivable should be recorded at its fair market value based on prevailing current interest rates. The unguaranteed residual value should be estimated and discounted to present value, using the same current interest rate.

Contingencies. Special procedures should be followed when a contingent asset, liability, or asset impairment exists on the date of the purchase. FASB Statement No. 5 defines a contingency as "an existing condition, situation, or set of circumstances involving uncertainty as to possible gain or loss to an enterprise that will ultimately be resolved when one or more future events occur or fail to occur."[8] An example would be a lawsuit that existed or was filed shortly after the purchase, but that involved an event which occurred prior to the purchase.

When the existence of the contingent asset, liability, or asset impairment is probable and can be reasonably estimated, it should be recorded at the estimated amount as part of the allocation of the purchase price.[9] It is not necessary that the amount be probable and estimable on the date of the purchase. The assessments may be made subsequent to the purchase date during what is called the "allocation period," which is the time period when noncontingent assets and liabilities acquired in the purchase are quantified and valued. Normally, this period should not exceed one year. Amounts not recorded during the allocation period should be included in income in the period in which they are determined.

---

[8] *Statement of Financial Accounting Standards, No. 5,* "Accounting for Contingencies" (Stamford: Financial Accounting Standards Board, 1975), par. 1.

[9] *Statement of Financial Accounting Standards, No. 38,* "Accounting for Preacquisition Contingencies of Purchased Enterprises" (Stamford: Financial Accounting Standards Board, 1980), par. 5.

Tax Loss Carryforwards

According to APB Opinion No. 11, loss carryforwards, which are permitted under the tax law, are not to be recorded as an asset during the period of the loss unless "in unusual circumstances when realization is *assured beyond any reasonable doubt* at the time the loss carry*forwards* arise"[10] If a firm is purchased, and the firm has recorded a tax loss carryforward as an asset, the purchaser may also consider the carryforward as an asset and record it at its estimated value, which may differ from its recorded amount. When the tax loss carryforward has not been previously recorded by the seller, the purchaser may still estimate the value of the carryforward and record it as an asset, provided that realization is now assured beyond reasonable doubt. This condition may be satisfied, for example, when the carryforward of the acquired firm will be used to offset income of the acquiring firm.

When realization of the tax loss carryforward is not assured beyond reasonable doubt at the time of the purchase, no separate asset is recorded. Any value that might be attributed to the carryforward would be indirectly included in goodwill. Consequently, APB Opinion No. 16 (par. 88) requires that goodwill recorded in a purchase be reduced when the benefits of a previously unrecorded tax loss carryforward of the acquired firm are realized in subsequent periods. As a result of the reduction in goodwill, it is necessary to correct the amortization of goodwill recorded in prior periods. The total correction for previous periods is a prior period adjustment and is treated as a correction of beginning retained earnings.[11] Goodwill amortization for the current and future periods will also be reduced or eliminated. Any excess of realized tax loss carryforward benefits of the acquired firm over the amount recorded as goodwill would be used to reduce identifiable assets and, if large enough, could result in a deferred credit.

Securities Issued as Consideration

As previously mentioned, many major acquisitions involve the issuance of the purchaser's securities as payment. The use of securities preserves cash for future operations and may allow the transaction to qualify as a tax-free exchange to the seller. The principles for recording the purchase are not changed; only the recording of the consideration differs. The market value of the securities issued becomes the total consideration to be assigned to the acquired firm. The purchaser must also add the market value of the securities issued to its debt or paid-in capital. Using the previous acquisition example, which involved a $180,000 acquisition price for the Jacobs Company, assume that

---

[10] *Opinions of the Accounting Principles Board, No. 11*, "Accounting for Income Taxes" (New York: American Institute of Certified Public Accountants, 1967), par. 45.

[11] *Statement of Financial Accounting Standards, No. 16*, "Prior Period Adjustments" (Stamford: Financial Accounting Standards Board, 1977), par. 11.

Acquisitions will issue its $2 par common stock as consideration. The total market value of the shares issued to the Jacobs Company must equal the agreed net price of $160,000 ($180,000 minus $20,000 liabilities assumed). Assuming a $20 market value for its shares, Acquisitions must issue 8,000 shares ($160,000 ÷ $20). The following entry to record the purchase is identical to the entry on page 175, except that the addition to Acquisitions' paid-in capital is substituted for the cash payment.

Accounts Receivable (market value)	20,000	
Inventory (market value)	45,000	
Land (appraised market value)........................	10,000	
Buildings (appraised market value)	50,000	
Equipment (appraised market value)	40,000	
Goodwill ($181,000 price minus sum of above		
market values).......................................	16,000	
Current Liabilities (market value)		20,000
Common Stock (8,000 shares × $2 par)..............		16,000
Paid-In Capital in Excess of Par ($160,000 −		
$16,000 par value)................................		144,000
Cash (for acquisition costs).........................		1,000

Another form of consideration involves the issuance of the purchaser company's bonds for the assets of the acquired firm. Market values are recorded in the same manner as in the preceding entry. However, care must be taken to record properly the market value of the bonds issued. The applicable bond premium or discount must be recorded. For example, assume that Acquisitions plans to issue $1,000, 8% bonds in exchange for the $160,000 net assets of the Jacobs Company. Normally, the purchaser would exchange 160 bonds ($160,000 ÷ $1,000 per bond) for the net assets of the Jacobs Company. Assume, however, that on the settlement date the bonds have a market value of $990 each. A discount of $1,600 ($10 per bond × 160 bonds) should therefore be recorded. Assuming that the discount is settled by cash payment, the purchase would be recorded as follows:

Accounts Receivable	20,000	
Inventory	45,000	
Land	10,000	
Buildings	50,000	
Equipment	40,000	
Goodwill...	16,000	
Discount on Bonds Payable	1,600	
Current Liabilities....................................		20,000
Cash (acquisition cost plus discount on bonds)		2,600
Bonds Payable......................................		160,000

The resulting discount (or premium) must be amortized over the life of the bond issue. As an alternative to the cash payment, additional bonds could have been issued to compensate for the discount.

Any direct costs incurred to register and issue securities are subtracted from the value assigned to securities and are not treated as a direct acquisition cost. For example, had there been a $500 issuance cost in this example, the discount recorded would have been $2,100.

Mix of Securities as Consideration

The purchaser may exchange different types of securities in a single transaction. The differing securities may reflect the nature of the assets acquired. For example, the seller may initially desire debt or preferred equity securities equal to the market value of all assets, excluding goodwill. These securities provide a senior claim on earnings as well as on assets, should foreclosure become necessary. In this way, a preference in dissolution equal to the asset contribution of the purchased firm is provided. Common stock is typically issued as payment for goodwill, reflecting the uncertainty involved in estimating this intangible asset.

Low-risk securities, however, have the disadvantage of lacking a long-run speculative appeal. Very likely, the seller will prefer to become a common stockholder if, at a later date, the acquiring firm prospers. Convertible debt or convertible equity securities may therefore be used to satisfy both the seller's short-run security concern and long-run speculative interest. As an alternative to convertible securities, participating preferred stock is used, since it offers a permanent preference on both assets and income by allowing full or limited participation with common stockholders in dividend distributions.

CONTINGENT CONSIDERATION

A purchase agreement may provide that the purchaser will transfer additional consideration to the seller, contingent upon the occurrence of specified future events or transactions. This consideration could involve the transfer of cash or other assets, or the issuance of additional securities. During the period preceding the date on which the contingency is resolved, the purchaser has a contingent liability that is disclosed in a footnote to the financial statements but is not recorded. On the date that the contingency is resolved, the contingent liability ceases, and the purchaser records any additional consideration as an adjustment to the original purchase transaction. The method used to make the adjustment is dependent upon the nature of the contingency.

Contingent Consideration Based on Earnings

A purchaser may agree to make a final payment contingent upon the earnings of the acquired firm during a specified future time period. If, during this period, the earnings of the acquired firm reach or exceed an agreed amount, further payment will be made at the end of the contingency period. In essence, the value of all or part of the goodwill is to be confirmed before full payment is made. Clearly, when an earnings contingency exists, the total price to be paid for the acquired firm is not known until the end of the contingency period. As is the case for the initial payment, the purchaser must record the fair market value of the consideration given, including the market value of additional securities issued. APB Opinion No. 16 (par. 80) provides that this type of additional consideration results in an increase in the goodwill account.

To illustrate, assume that Company A acquires the assets of Company B on January 1, 19X2, in exchange for Company A common stock under conditions that require the acquisition to be recorded as a purchase. Company A also agrees to issue 10,000 additional common shares to the former stockholders of Company B on January 1, 19X5, if the acquired firm's average annual income before taxes for the three years reaches or exceeds $50,000. During the contingency period, Company A will disclose the contingent liability in the footnotes to its financial statements. If the earnings condition is met, Company A will record the final payment as goodwill on January 1, 19X5. Assuming that the 10,000 shares issued have a par value of $1 and a market value of $8, the following entry would be made:

Goodwill ($8 market value × 10,000 shares)	80,000	
Common Stock ($1 par × 10,000 shares)		10,000
Paid-In Capital in Excess of Par		70,000

Since the payment is, in essence, the final payment of a previous purchase, the full market value of the consideration given must be recorded. As was the case with the original recording of the purchase, the par value of common stock issued must be recorded, and the difference between the par and market values of the shares issued must be added to the purchaser's paid-in capital in excess of par.

Goodwill recorded as a result of a contingency payment must be amortized. Accounting principles require that the payment be added to any existing goodwill and that the adjusted balance be amortized over the remaining life of the goodwill. The period of amortization must end within 40 years of the original date of the combination. No retroactive adjustment may be made for amortization applicable to prior periods.[12]

Contingent Consideration Based on Issuer's Security Prices

A seller may be reluctant to accept the purchaser firm's securities in exchange for its assets. This reluctance is caused by the seller's fear of a possible future decline in the market value of the purchaser's securities. When a stock issuance is involved, the concern may be based, in part, on the dilutive effect of a significant increase in the number of shares outstanding. To combat this apprehension, the purchaser may guarantee

---

[12] When the contingency involves the value of an asset other than goodwill, that asset's value is to be adjusted as a result of the contingent payment. If, for example, the contingency involved the value of a building, the value would be adjusted at the time the contingency was resolved and the added payment made.

the total value of the securities as of a given future date. The purchaser agrees to transfer additional assets or issue additional securities on that date for the amount by which the guaranteed value exceeds the market value on the date selected. For example, on January 1, 19X2, Company C issues 100,000 shares of its common stock, which has a $1 par value and a $12 market value, in exchange for the assets of Company D. The conditions of the exchange require the acquisition to be recorded as a purchase. The following summarized entry would be recorded:

```
Net Assets ($12 market value × 100,000 shares)......  1,200,000
    Common Stock ($1 par × 100,000 shares) ..........             100,000
    Paid-In Capital in Excess of Par .....................           1,100,000
```

Company C guarantees the value of the stock at $12 per share as of January 1, 19X3. If necessary, additional consideration will be paid in cash. During the contingency period, Company C must disclose the contingent liability. Should the market price of the common stock be less than $12 per share on January 1, 19X3, additional consideration will be recorded.

Assume that on January 1, 19X3, the market value is $10 per share. Then $200,000 (100,000 shares × $2 per share deficiency) is the amount by which the guaranteed value exceeds the total value of the shares. Company C will have to pay an additional $200,000 in cash. How should the payment be recorded? The payment is not based on a revaluation of the goodwill, as is the case with an earnings contingency. Instead, the payment reflects the fact that the value assigned to the original security issuance was only an estimate, with the final amount to be determined later. To record the adjustment of the original estimate, the original credit to Paid-In Capital should be decreased as shown by the following entry:

```
Paid-In Capital in Excess of Par ......................  200,000
    Cash ...............................................             200,000
```

In the preceding example, the value guaranteed was satisfied in cash. More often the satisfaction will involve the issuance of additional securities. In that case, for example, Company C would issue 20,000 additional shares ($200,000 market value deficiency ÷ $10 current market value per share). Company C needs 120,000 shares to equate to the $1,200,000 original consideration, rather than the 100,000 shares previously issued. Accordingly, the $1,200,000 originally assigned to the 100,000 shares must be reassigned to 120,000 shares. The following entry will accomplish the reassignment:

```
Paid-In Capital in Excess of Par ......................  20,000
    Common Stock ($1 par × 20,000 shares) ............            20,000
```

Less frequently, price guarantees may apply to debt securities issued in a purchase transaction. Since bond prices react more to general money market conditions than to the operating performance of a particular firm, it is not common to guarantee their value. When a price guarantee is used for bonds issued in a purchase, recording procedures parallel those used for stock. The settlement of a guarantee results in allocating the value assigned to the original bonds to a greater number of bonds. This allocation will decrease or eliminate an original premium and/or will increase or create a discount.

POOLING OF INTERESTS

Asset acquisitions deemed to be a pooling of interests require that all of the assets and liabilities of the combiner be acquired in exchange for the issuer's common stock. Poolings are viewed as a fusion of existing accounting entities, not as an exchange between entities. Assets, liabilities, and equities are combined at their existing book values. Adjustments to the accounts are allowed only to the extent that they would be proper for any firm in the course of normal operations. An example of a proper adjustment would be the write-down of inventory from cost to market value.

Assume that Expansion, Inc., is going to pool with the Jacobs Company by issuing common stock, and that Expansion will be the surviving accounting entity. Expansion is the issuer, not the purchaser, and Jacobs is the combiner, not the seller. These terms emphasize that the firms are joint owners in a pooling and are not parties to an exchange. When the pooling is consummated, the *book values* of the Jacobs Company will be recorded on the books of Expansion, Inc.

The fact that market values are not recorded does not mean that they are ignored during negotiations preceding the combination. Both parties to a pooling must agree on the market values of the items involved in order to arrive at the number of issuer's shares to be exchanged for the combiner's assets.

Assume that the firms agree on the following values for the assets of the Jacobs Company:

	Book Value	Market Value
Accounts receivable	$ 20,000	$ 20,000
Inventory	40,000	45,000
Land	10,000	10,000
Buildings	40,000	50,000
Equipment	20,000	40,000
Total	$130,000	$165,000

Expansion agrees that the value of goodwill is $15,000. To satisfy the total $180,000 price, Expansion will assume the $20,000 in liabilities of the Jacobs Company and issue 8,000 shares of its $20 market value ($2 par) common stock. While negotiations and settlement are based on market values, these values are ignored in recording the combination. If the combiner has previously recorded goodwill and/or tax loss carryforwards on its books, these assets are also recorded by the issuer at their book values. Book values of the Jacobs Company are transferred to Expansion by recording the following entry:

Accounts Receivable	20,000	
Inventory	40,000	
Land	10,000	
Buildings	40,000	
Equipment	20,000	
Current Liabilities		20,000
Common Stock (8,000 shares × $2 par)		16,000
Paid-In Capital in Excess of Par		44,000
Retained Earnings		50,000

One difficult aspect of recording a pooling of interests is the combining of stockholders' equities. The total paid-in capital of the combiner must be carried as a unit to the total paid-in capital of the issuer firm. The composition of the combiner's paid-in capital is ignored and is redistributed between the par or stated value and the additional paid-in capital of the issuer. Normally, the retained earnings of the combiner is added directly to the retained earnings of the issuer firm. In the previous example, $16,000 (8,000 shares × $2 par) of the combiner's $60,000 total paid-in capital was used to meet the issuer's par value requirement, and the $44,000 balance is added to additional paid-in capital. The following chart summarizes the equity transfer of the previous example:

Jacobs Company (combiner) Balances		Increase in Expansion, Inc. (issuer) Balances	
Capital stock, $10 par	$ 10,000	Capital stock, $2 par	$ 16,000
Paid-in capital in excess of par	50,000	Paid-in capital in excess of par	44,000
Total paid-in capital	$ 60,000	→Total paid-in capital	$ 60,000
Retained earnings	50,000	→Retained earnings	50,000
Total equity	$110,000	Total equity	$110,000

Equity transfer rules must accommodate combinations in which the par or stated value of the shares issued exceeds the total paid-in capital of the combiner firm. When this situation occurs, the issuer must first use its own paid-in capital in excess of par to cover the deficiency. Only when such an excess is depleted, or when it does not exist, may retained earnings be reduced. Assume that in the previous example, Expansion was issuing $10 par stock and that all other facts were unchanged. The issuer must add $80,000 (8,000 shares × $10 par) to its par value, while the total paid-in capital of the combining firm is only $60,000. Assuming first that the issuer has sufficient additional paid-in capital upon which to draw, the $20,000 deficiency would be met by reducing the issuer's additional paid-in capital as shown in the following chart:

Jacobs Company (combiner) Balances		Increase (Decrease) in Expansion, Inc. (issuer) Balances	
Capital stock, $10 par	$ 10,000	Capital stock, $10 par	$ 80,000
Paid-in capital in excess of par	50,000	Paid-in capital in excess of par	(20,000)
Total paid-in capital	$ 60,000	→ Total paid-in capital	$ 60,000
Retained earnings	50,000	→Retained earnings	50,000
Total equity	$110,000	Total equity	$110,000

The entry to record the pooling in this case would be:

Accounts Receivable	20,000	
Inventory	40,000	
Land	10,000	
Buildings	40,000	
Equipment	20,000	
Paid-In Capital in Excess of Par	20,000	
Current Liabilities		20,000
Common Stock ($10 par)		80,000
Retained Earnings		50,000

If the issuer has no additional paid-in capital with which to meet the deficiency, the combiner's retained earnings would be used as shown in the following chart:

Jacobs Company (combiner) Balances		Reassignment	Increase in Expansion, Inc. (issuer) Balances	
Capital stock, $10 par	$ 10,000		Capital stock, $10 par	$ 80,000
Paid-in capital in excess of par	50,000			
Total paid-in capital	$ 60,000	+20,000	Total paid-in capital	$ 80,000
Retained earnings	50,000	−20,000	Retained earnings	30,000
Total equity	$110,000		Total equity	$110,000

The entry to record the pooling would then be:

Accounts Receivable	20,000	
Inventory	40,000	
Land	10,000	
Buildings	40,000	
Equipment	20,000	
Current Liabilities		20,000
Common Stock ($10 par)		80,000
Retained Earnings		30,000

In some cases, it may be necessary to consume all of the combiner's retained earnings and draw upon the retained earnings of the issuer.

In a pooling, shareholders of the combiner firm must become shareholders in the continuing issuer firm. To accomplish the continuity of ownership, the combiner firm will usually dissolve itself by distributing the shares it receives from the issuer to its shareholders.

Pooling principles require that the assets of the combiner firm be recorded at book values and that combined assets may not be increased through the combination. Consequently, the direct costs of consummating the combination may not be capitalized as an asset. Similarly, the issuance cost of new securities may not be deducted from the value assigned to the securities. These expenditures, even though benefiting future periods, must be entirely expensed in the period that the acquisition occurs, according to APB Opinion No. 16 (par. 58). Assume that in the previous example, Expansion paid $1,000 in direct acquisition costs. A separate entry would expense the cost as follows:

Professional Services	1,000	
Cash		1,000

Another complication arises when an issuer uses previously issued and reacquired stock (treasury stock) to accomplish a pooling. Pooling principles require that the book value of the combiner's capital be assigned to stock issued in a pooling. Clearly, the issuer would violate these principles if it could reacquire previously issued shares and use their cost as the value assigned to the shares exchanged in the pooling. The problem that arises is: How does the issuer dispose of the difference between the price paid for the treasury shares and the value which must be assigned to them in a pooling of interests? For instance, assume that Company E reacquired 10,000 shares of its common stock for $250,000 and later exchanged these shares for the assets of Company F. The summarized balance sheets of Companies E and F immediately prior to the pooling are as follows:

Issuer Company E

Total assets	$750,000	Liabilities	$200,000
		Common stock (50,000 shares,	
		$2 par)	100,000
		Retained earnings	700,000
		Less treasury stock at cost	(250,000)
		Total liabilities and equity	$750,000

Combiner Company F

Total assets	$150,000	Liabilities	$ 50,000
		Common stock (20,000 shares,	
		$1 par)	20,000
		Paid-in capital in excess of par	40,000
		Retained earnings	40,000
		Total liabilities and equity	$150,000

In this case, the shares to be used in the combination were purchased for $25 each, but must carry a book value of $10 each ($100,000 of combining firm equity ÷ 10,000 shares issued). Since shares issued to accomplish a pooling must be treated as newly issued, APB Opinion No. 16 (par. 54) requires that previously acquired shares be accounted for as if retired. Therefore, Company E would first account for the 10,000 treasury shares as follows:

Common Stock (10,000 shares × $2 par)	20,000	
Retained Earnings	230,000	
Treasury Stock (at cost)		250,000

The shares released to accomplish the pooling are then recorded as newly issued:

Assets	150,000	
Liabilities		50,000
Common Stock (10,000 shares × $2 par)		20,000
Paid-In Capital in Excess of Par ($60,000 total paid-		
in less $20,000 par)		40,000
Retained Earnings		40,000

REPORTING REQUIREMENTS

As is true of all asset acquisitions, the purchase of another firm affects the financial statements of the purchaser only for periods following the purchase date. Therefore, no adjustments are made that would affect statements of prior periods. Unfortunately, the purchase of another firm partially destroys the comparability of the purchaser's current statements with those of prior periods. To aid in solving this dilemma, APB Opinion No. 16 requires that if comparative statements are used, footnotes must disclose the estimated results of operations which would have occurred during the financial period preceding the one in which the purchase was made, as though the purchase had been made (on comparable terms) at the start of that preceding period. Such an estimate requires restatement of depreciation expense for the purchased firm's plant assets and an inclusion of goodwill amortization expense if the purchase included a payment for goodwill. Any intercompany transactions should also be eliminated.

Since operating results are combined only after the purchase date, comparability of the current period's results to those of future periods will also be hindered when an acquisition occurs during the reporting period. Consequently, when an acquisition is made during the period, footnotes must disclose the estimated operating results that would have occurred had the purchase taken place at the start of the period.

When the financial statements of prior periods are compared with the statements prepared subsequent to a pooling of interests, it would be helpful to also pool the statements of the previously separate firms. In essence, the question is: How well did the pooled firms perform this period as compared to previous periods? To answer this question, APB Opinion No. 16 requires that if comparative statements are used, statements of the previous periods must be restated as if the firms were pooled during these prior periods. This restatement is a simple task, since pooling is a mere fusion of previously separate stockholder groups, and book values are combined. Consequently, no restatement of depreciation is necessary, and since no goodwill results in a pooling, no goodwill amortization need be considered. Intercompany transactions, however, must be eliminated. Disclosure must be made in the footnotes, stating that the financial statements of previously separate firms have been combined.

When a pooling occurs during a reporting period, financial statements should be prepared as though the firms were pooled for the entire period. Footnotes must disclose the operating results of the separate firms for the partial period preceding the pooling.

In a purchase or a pooling, the firms involved may have used different accounting principles to account for similar types of transactions. For example, one company might use lifo inventory valuation, while the other uses fifo. To achieve uniformity or to improve future reporting, it may be desirable to change the accounting principles of one or both members of the combination. However, when a change in accounting principle occurs as part of a business combination, APB Opinion No. 20 makes an exception to the usual procedure of including the cumulative effect of the change in accounting principle in the current year's income statement. APB Opinion No. 20 allows financial statements for previous periods to be restated retroactively when the change results from a business combination.[13]

QUESTIONS

1. Discuss the advantages of growth accomplished through business combinations.
2. Distinguish between the types of growth which may be accomplished in business combinations.
3. What are the two basic methods by which control of another firm's assets might be obtained? Which method would most likely involve a lower total cost? Which method will require consolidation procedures to be used in future periods?
4. Compare the balance sheet ramifications of a purchase versus a pooling of interests. Include the effects on assets, liabilities, and equity. Why might a pooling of interests create a balance sheet with a more profitable appearance?
5. Explain why income of future periods will usually be greater in a business combination accomplished using the pooling method as opposed to a combination accomplished under the purchase method.
6. What provisions in the pooling criteria assure that only entire firms combine?
7. How are the voting common stockholders of the combining firm assured "equality of treatment" by the pooling of interests criteria?
8. One of the criteria to be met in order to use the pooling method is the 90% stock acquisition rule. Specifically, how and when must the stock of the combining firm be obtained if it is to be included in the qualifying 90% of the combiner's outstanding stock?
9. Assets with a market value of $150,000 are purchased for a total consideration of $150,000. Liabilities with a market value of $30,000 are assumed, and common stock with a $10 par and a $60 market value is issued for the remaining balance of $120,000. What entry would be needed by the acquiring firm to record this transaction under the purchase method?
10. Under the purchase and pooling methods, what recognition is given to previously recorded goodwill (goodwill already recorded on the books of the acquired firm) by the acquiring firm?
11. Under the purchase method, which accounts are always recorded at full market value by the acquiring firm? Why are only these accounts given this priority? What procedure is used when the price paid for the firm is less than the total market value of these "priority" accounts?
12. A firm is contemplating the purchase of another company in a transaction that qualifies as a nontaxable exchange for tax purposes. How would the value

[13] *Opinions of the Accounting Principles Board, No. 20,* "Accounting Changes" (New York: American Institute of Certified Public Accountants, 1971), pars. 29 and 30.

assigned to depreciable assets acquired as part of the purchase be affected by the tax status of the exchange?

13. What procedures should be followed in recording long-term bonded debt assumed in the purchase of another firm, when interest rates have increased substantially since the bonds were issued?

14. A company which has been acquired is a party to several leases, in the capacity of both a lessee and a lessor. In each of the following situations, indicate which accounts should be used and state how to arrive at an amount:
    (a) The company is a lessee on a 2-year operating lease. The rent is below that which would be paid if currently negotiated.
    (b) The company is a lessee under a capital lease with a 6-year remaining term.
    (c) The company is a lessor under an operating lease with a remaining term of 3 years. The rents are below current rental value.
    (d) The company is a lessor under a direct financing (capital) lease with a 4-year remaining term. Title to the asset passes to the lessee at the end of the term.

15. Differentiate between the types of contingent consideration that may be utilized in a purchase.

16. An acquiring firm guaranteed that if the total market value of the 2,000 shares of $10 par stock issued in an acquisition fell below $120,000 on January 1, 19XX, additional shares would be issued to make up the deficiency. What entry would be made on January 1, 19XX, if the market value of the stock dropped to $40 per share?

17. What uses are made of market values in a business combination accomplished through a pooling of interests versus a business combination accomplished through a purchase?

18. In a pooling of interests, how is the total paid-in capital and retained earnings of the combining firm recorded on the books of the issuing firm? Describe the "basic equity transfer" rule.

19. How are direct acquisition costs, indirect acquisition costs, and issue costs recorded under (a) the purchase method and (b) the pooling method?

EXERCISES

Present value tables are on pages 942-943.

Exercise 1. The Alpha Corporation desires to pool with the Bravo Company. Bravo has a total of 25,000 outstanding shares. Alpha will issue three shares of its stock in exchange for five Bravo shares. On the initiation date, Alpha owns 500 Bravo shares, and a wholly-owned subsidiary of Alpha owns 700 Bravo shares.

One year after the initiation date, Alpha has issued 13,800 shares of its stock in exchange for additional shares of the Bravo Corporation according to the planned exchange rate. Alpha also purchased 800 Bravo shares for cash.

Determine the total number of the Bravo shares that are eligible for meeting the 90% requirement necessary to treat the acquisition as a pooling of interests. Has the 90% requirement been satisfied?

Exercise 2. The Adams Company is contemplating the acquisition of the King Corporation on January 1, 19X1, at which time it is anticipated that the King Corporation will have the following balance sheet:

King Corporation
Pro Forma Balance Sheet
January 1, 19X1

Assets			Liabilities and Equity		
Current assets:			Current liabilities:		
Cash	$ 20,000		Accounts payable	$ 25,000	
Accounts receivable ..	15,000		Accrued liabilities.....	5,000	$ 30,000
Inventory	30,000	$ 65,000	Stockholders' equity:		
Property, plant, and			Common stock,		
equipment:			$10 par	$ 80,000	
Building (net).........	$100,000		Retained earnings	115,000	195,000
Machines (net)	60,000	160,000			
			Total liabilities and		
Total assets		$225,000	equity		$225,000

The market values for King's plant assets are $120,000 for the machines and $250,000 for the building. These values have been adjusted for the nondeductible status of the excess of market over book value. Current assets are stated at amounts approximating market values.

Adams will issue 20,000 shares of its $5 par stock ($22.25 market value) to acquire King in a transaction that would qualify as a nontaxable exchange for tax purposes. It has not been determined whether the transaction meets the criteria for a pooling of interests.

The Adams Company is concerned about the effect of purchase versus pooling on future income statements. An accountant has been asked to compare 19X1 income under the pooling versus purchase methods. The accountant estimated combined revenues of $300,000 for Adams and King in 19X1, and has estimated that combined expenses will be $120,000, excluding depreciation of King assets and amortization of any goodwill resulting from the acquisition of King. Straight-line depreciation will be used for all plant assets. The machines have a 10-year remaining life; the building has a 20-year life. The maximum amortization period would be used for goodwill. The corporate tax rate to be used is 40%.

Compare the net incomes for the combined firm for 19X1 under the purchase and pooling methods. Prepare adequate support for all calculations.

Exercise 3. The Dan Company has made a formal offer to the stockholders of the Boone Company. The Dan Company will exchange two shares of its common stock for each share of the Boone Company. On the initiation date, the Dan Company already held 3,000 shares of Boone. On the initiation date, the Boone Company also owned 5,000 shares of Dan Company's common stock.

In cash transactions subsequent to the initiation date, the Dan Company purchased 2,800 shares of Boone common stock and the Boone Company purchased 2,500 shares of Dan common stock.

During the period subsequent to the initiation date and up to the consummation date, the Dan Company had 1,000,000 common shares outstanding and the Boone Company had 100,000 outstanding shares. On the consummation date, Dan Company owned 96,000 shares of the Boone Company common stock.

Determine the total number of Boone shares acquired by the Dan Company that can be used in applying the 90% requirement necessary to record the transaction as a pooling of interests. Explain the reason for excluding any shares from those considered eligible to meet the 90% requirement.

Exercise 4. Apollo Company is considering the acquisition of Daphne Company. The following balance sheet has been prepared for Daphne Company:

Daphne Company
Balance Sheet
December 31, 19X1

Assets		Liabilities and Equity	
Current assets	$260,000	Total liabilities	$400,000
Property, plant, and equipment		Capital stock, $10 par	160,000
(net)	650,000	Retained earnings	350,000
Total assets	$910,000	Total liabilities and equity	$910,000

An appraisal has indicated that market value of the current assets is approximately equal to their book value. The appraisal provided a market value of $740,000 for the property, plant, and equipment. Apollo Company predicts that Daphne Company will provide an average annual net income of $150,000 in future years. This income is above the 12% per year return on tangible assets considered normal for the industry.

(1) Prepare an estimate of goodwill based on each of the following assumptions:
  (a) The purchaser paid for 5 years' excess earnings.
  (b) Excess earnings will continue for five years and should be capitalized at the normal industry rate of return.
  (c) Excess earnings will occur forever, but they should be capitalized at the higher rate of return of 20% due to the risk involved in such an asset.
(2) Determine the actual goodwill to be recorded if the Apollo Company pays $800,000 cash and assumes the liabilities of the Daphne Company.

Exercise 5. The Bishop Company is willing to pay $650,000 for the entire net assets of the North Company, which has the following balance sheet on the purchase date:

North Company
Balance Sheet
December 31, 19X1

Assets			Liabilities and Equity		
Current assets:			Liabilities		$ 80,000
Accounts			Stockholders' equity:		
receivable	$ 25,000		Common stock,		
Inventory	50,000	$ 75,000	$10 par	$100,000	
Property, plant, and			Paid-in capital in		
equipment:			excess of par	160,000	
Land	$ 40,000		Retained earnings .	245,000	505,000
Building (net)......	260,000				
Equipment (net) ...	210,000	510,000			
Total assets		$585,000	Total liabilities and equity		$585,000

The following market values have been secured for the assets and liabilities of the North Company:

Inventory	$ 60,000
Building and land	320,000
Equipment	150,000
Liabilities (including unrecorded interest)	81,200

To consummate the transaction, Bishop must spend $10,000 to cover direct acquisition costs.

(1) On Bishop's books, record the purchase of the net assets of the North Company for $650,000.

(2) On North's books, record the sale of the net assets for $650,000.

(3) On Bishop's books, record the purchase of all of the common stock of the North Company for $650,000.

(4) Assuming that all of the shares purchased in part (3) were acquired from existing shareholders of the North Company, what entry would be needed on the books of the North Company to record Bishop's purchase?

Exercise 6. The Webb Company was merged into the Martin Corporation on July 1, 19X1. The combination must be treated as a purchase because the pooling criteria were not completely met. Martin exchanged 50,000 shares of its $5 par stock, with a market value of $25 per share, for the net assets of the Webb Company. The Martin Corporation paid cash for the following costs as the result of the transaction:

Direct acquisition costs	$10,000
Indirect acquisition costs	15,000
Costs to register and issue stock	20,000
Total costs	$45,000

Immediately prior to the merger, the Webb Company's balance sheet was as follows:

Webb Company
Balance Sheet
July 1, 19X1

Assets			Liabilities and Equity		
Current assets		$340,000	Current liabilities		$ 70,000
Equipment under capital lease (net)		175,000	Liability under capital lease		100,000
Property, plant, and equipment:			Bonds payable		300,000
Land	$200,000		Stockholders' equity:		
Buildings (net)	150,000	350,000	Common stock,		
			$10 par	$200,000	
			Paid-in capital in		
			excess of par	100,000	
			Retained earnings	95,000	395,000
Total assets		$865,000	Total liabilities and equity		$865,000

The asset and liability under lease, the plant assets, and the bonds payable have market values which differ from book values. The appraised market values are:

Equipment under capital lease	$220,000
Land	150,000
Buildings	300,000
Liability under capital lease	95,000
Bonds payable	285,000

Record the purchase of the net assets of the Webb Company by the Martin Corporation.

Exercise 7. Delta Corporation acquired the net assets of the Litcon Corporation in exchange for $500,000 in cash. Prior to the merger, Litcon Corporation had the following balance sheet:

Litcon Corporation
Balance Sheet
January 1, 19X1

Assets			Liabilities and Equity		
Current assets:			Current liabilities		$ 50,000
Accounts			Stockholders' equity:		
receivable	$120,000		Common stock,		
Inventories	100,000	$220,000	$10 par	$200,000	
Property, plant, and equipment		280,000	Retained earnings .	250,000	450,000
Total assets		$500,000	Total liabilities and equity		$500,000

Market values agree with book values except for inventory and property, plant, and equipment, which have market values of $140,000 and $300,000, respectively. To consummate the transaction, Delta incurred $5,000 in direct acquisition costs.

(1) Record the acquisition on the Delta Corporation books; provide support for your entry as needed.
(2) Record the sale on the books of the Litcon Corporation and the subsequent total liquidation of the corporation.

Exercise 8. Sails Corporation has agreed to purchase the net assets of the Banding Corporation for $120,000 in cash. Just prior to the purchase, Banding's balance sheet was as follows:

Banding Corporation
Balance Sheet
January 1, 19X1

Assets		Liabilities and Equity		
Current assets	$240,000	Current liabilities		$100,000
Equipment (net)	100,000	Stockholders' equity:		
		Common stock,		
		$10 par	$100,000	
		Retained earnings .	140,000	240,000
Total assets	$340,000	Total liabilities and equity		$340,000

The following market values have been obtained:

Current assets	$260,000
Equipment	35,000

The Sails Corporation paid $10,000 in direct acquisition costs and $15,000 in indirect acquisition costs to consummate the transaction.

Record the purchase on the books of the Sails Corporation.

Exercise 9. Alan Company purchased the net assets of Barry Company in a business combination accounted for as a purchase. As a result, goodwill was recorded. For tax purposes, this combination was considered to be a nontaxable exchange.

One of Barry's assets that Alan purchased was a building with an appraised value of $150,000 at the date of the business combination. This asset had a net book value of $90,000, which was net of depreciation based on the sum-of-the-years-digits method used for financial reporting. The building is depreciated straight-line for tax purposes and has a tax basis of $100,000. Assuming a 40% income tax rate, at what amount should Alan record this building on its books as a result of the purchase?   (AICPA adapted)

Exercise 10. The Imperial and Cisco Corporations have agreed to merge in a transaction which will qualify as a pooling of interests. Imperial Corporation will issue the required number of previously unissued shares of $5 par common stock in exchange for all of the net assets of the Cisco Corporation. The number of shares issued will be based on the assumed market value of $48 per share of Imperial common stock and on the fair market value of the Cisco Corporation.

Immediately prior to the pooling, the Cisco Corporation prepared the following summarized balance sheet:

Cisco Corporation
Balance Sheet
December 31, 19X1

Assets		Liabilities and Equity	
Current assets	$ 450,000	Current liabilities	$ 100,000
Property, plant, and equipment	2,000,000	Bonds payable	800,000
Accumulated depreciation	(500,000)	Common stock, $10 par	250,000
Goodwill	150,000	Retained earnings	950,000
Total assets	$2,100,000	Total liabilities and equity	$2,100,000

Current assets and liabilities are recorded at amounts approximating their market values. The following appraisals have been made:

Property, plant, and equipment	$1,550,000
Goodwill	200,000
Bonds payable	780,000

In consummating the transaction, the Imperial Corporation spent $5,000 for direct acquisition costs and $15,000 for registering and issuing the shares of stock used to acquire the Cisco Corporation.

(1) Determine the number of shares of stock the Imperial Corporation will issue.
(2) Record the pooling of interests on the books of the Imperial Corporation.
(3) What entry would the Cisco Corporation make to record the receipt of the shares and their distribution to shareholders in order to liquidate the corporation?

Exercise 11. The Bergman Company will be the issuing company in a pooling of interests with the Young Company. The two firms had the following summarized balance sheets just prior to the pooling:

Assets	Bergman	Young
Current assets	$ 50,000	$ 40,000
Property, plant, and equipment	750,000	312,500
Accumulated depreciation	(250,000)	(62,500)
Other assets	30,000	10,000
Total assets	$580,000	$300,000

Liabilities and Equity		
Accounts payable	$ 40,000	$ 30,000
Accrued liabilities	10,000	—
Common stock .... ($20 par)	200,000 ($10 par)	100,000
Paid-in capital in excess of par	50,000	10,000
Retained earnings	280,000	160,000
Total liabilities and equity	$580,000	$300,000

Record the pooling of interests on the Bergman Company books in each of the following situations:

(1) The pooling agreement requires Bergman to issue 7,500 shares of its $20 par stock for the net assets of the Young Company.

(2) The pooling agreement requires Bergman to issue 12,500 shares of its $20 par stock for the net assets of the Young Company. The Bergman Company will also pay $20,000 for stock registration and issuance costs.

Exercise 12. On December 31, 19X6, Cole Company and Bond Company entered into a business combination appropriately accounted for as a pooling of interests. A new company, Gold Corporation, was formed with 500,000 authorized shares of no-par, $1-stated-value common stock. The management of Gold did not intend to retain either Cole or Bond as subsidiaries.

On December 31, 19X6, Gold issued its common stock in exchange for all of the outstanding common stock of Cole and Bond as follows:

Cole: 300,000 shares of Gold common stock for all 10,000 outstanding shares of Cole's $5 par common stock.

Bond: 200,000 shares of Gold common stock for all 4,000 outstanding shares of Bond's $10 par common stock.

There were no intercompany transactions between these companies.

Following are the condensed financial statements of Cole and Bond for the year ended December 31, 19X6, prior to the pooling of interests.

Balance Sheets Assets	Cole Company	Bond Company
Current assets	$260,000	$235,000
Property, plant, and equipment (net)	410,000	320,000
Other assets	90,000	65,000
Total assets	$760,000	$620,000
Liabilities and Stockholders' Equity		
Current liabilities	$167,000	$124,000
Long-term debt	300,000	—
Common stock	50,000	40,000
Paid-in capital in excess of par	10,000	160,000
Retained earnings	233,000	296,000
Total liabilities and stockholders' equity	$760,000	$620,000

Income and Retained Earnings Statements

	Cole Company	Bond Company
Net sales	$1,600,000	$2,200,000
Costs and expenses:		
Cost of goods sold	$1,120,000	$1,560,000
Operating and other expenses	330,000	480,000
Total costs and expenses................................	$1,450,000	2,040,000
Net income	$ 150,000	$ 160,000
Retained earnings, January 1, 19X6	83,000	136,000
Retained earnings, December 31, 19X6	$ 233,000	$ 296,000

Cole values its inventory using the fifo method; Bond uses the lifo method for its inventory. Bond agreed to change its method of inventory valuation from lifo to fifo prior to the business combination.

Bond began operations on January 1, 19X5, and data relevant to Bond's inventory are as follows:

	Lifo	Fifo
Inventory, December 31, 19X5	$42,000	$62,000
Inventory, December 31, 19X6	$55,000	$85,000

(1) Prepare the adjusting journal entry to be made by Bond Company on December 31, 19X6, to change its inventory from lifo cost to fifo cost. Income taxes should not be considered in the solution.

(2) Prepare a schedule computing pooled retained earnings of Gold Corporation as of December 31, 19X6.

(3) Prepare the December 31, 19X6 journal entry on the books of Gold Corporation to record the business combination as a pooling of interests.

(AICPA adapted)

Exercise 13. The Palto Corporation has agreed to exchange 10,000 shares currently held as treasury stock for the net assets of the Salvo Corporation. Just prior to the exchange, the two firms had the following summarized balance sheets:

Assets

	Palto	Salvo
Current assets	$ 450,000	$ 200,000
Property, plant, and equipment (net) ...	1,250,000	800,000
Total assets	$1,700,000	$1,000,000

Liabilities and Equity

		Palto		Salvo
Current liabilities		$ 200,000		$ 90,000
Common stock.........................	($10 par)	1,000,000	($5 par)	150,000
Paid-in capital in excess of par		100,000		120,000
Retained earnings		480,000		640,000
Treasury stock at cost		(80,000)		—
Total liabilities and equity		$1,700,000		$1,000,000

Prepare the journal entries for the Palto Corporation to record the pooling of interests. (Retire the treasury stock prior to recording the pooling.)

Exercise 14. The Norton Corporation acquired the net assets of the Wisling Company on January 1, 19X1, when Wisling Company had the following summarized balance sheet:

Wisling Company
Balance Sheet
January 1, 19X1

Assets		Liabilities and Equity		
Current assets.....................	$ 60,000	Current liabilities		$ 40,000
Property, plant, and equipment (net)	150,000	Stockholders' equity:		
Goodwill...........................	40,000	Common stock,		
		$10 par	$ 10,000	
		Paid-in capital in		
		excess of par	40,000	
		Retained earnings .	160,000	210,000
Total assets	$250,000	Total liabilities and equity		$250,000

Norton arrived at the following market values for the Wisling Company assets and liabilities:

Current assets.......................................	$ 70,000
Property, plant, and equipment.......................	210,000
Current liabilities	43,000

Norton agreed to issue 8%, $1,000 10-year bonds in an amount equal to the market value of Wisling's net assets other than goodwill. The quoted value of 102 will be used in the computation. Any fractional bond equivalent will be paid in cash. Norton also agreed to issue 500 shares of its $10 par common stock as additional consideration. The stock has a market value of $12 per share.

(1) Calculate the total price paid for the Wisling Company.
(2) Record the acquisition on the books of the Norton Company.

PROBLEMS

Present value tables are on pages 942-943.

Problem 5-1. The following summarized balance sheets were prepared for the Wood and Central Corporations on December 31, 19X1:

Assets	Wood	Central
Current assets	$350,000	$185,000
Land	80,000	25,000
Buildings	455,000	337,500
Accumulated depreciation...................................	(130,000)	(87,500)
Goodwill...	120,000	100,000
Total assets	$875,000	$560,000

Liabilities and Equity		
Accounts payable	$115,000	$ 85,000
Bonds payable (6%)	170,000	150,000
Common stock, $10 par	150,000	75,000
Paid-in capital in excess of par	200,000	140,000
Retained earnings	240,000	110,000
Total liabilities and equity	$875,000	$560,000

The appraised values of the Central Corporation land and buildings are $50,000 and $350,000 respectively. Wood will issue 10,000 shares of its common stock with a market value of $40 each for the net assets of Central. Wood will also pay $2,000 in cash for direct acquisition costs.

Additional information:

(a) Wood's buildings have a remaining life of 25 years, and Central's buildings have a remaining life of 20 years. Both firms use straight-line depreciation and no salvage value.

(b) All goodwill will be amortized over a remaining life of 25 years.

(c) During 19X2, it is anticipated that expected revenue will be $500,000 and that out-of-pocket costs (not including depreciation and amortization) will be $400,000.

Required:

(1) Assume that the pooling criteria are met. Record the entry for the acquisition on the books of the Wood Corporation.

(2) Assume that the pooling criteria are not met. Record the acquisition on the books of the Wood Corporation.

(3) Prepare a columnar comparison for the purchase versus pooling recording of pro forma net income for 19X2. Assume that the combination will qualify as a nontaxable exchange and that the market values given for depreciable assets have been adjusted for nondeductible depreciation. The corporate tax rate is 40%.

Problem 5-2. Company CD is being formed to consolidate the former Companies C and D. Prior to the consolidation, Companies C and D have the following balance sheets on December 31, 19X1:

Assets	Company C	Company D
Current assets	$ 120,000	$ 65,000
Long-term investment in marketable securities (at cost)	200,000	40,000
Land	100,000	40,000
Buildings (net)	370,000	210,000
Equipment (net)	430,000	125,000
Total assets	$1,220,000	$480,000

Liabilities and Equity	Company C	Company D
Current liabilities	$ 170,000	$ 55,000
Bonds payable	200,000	100,000
Common stock, $10 par	400,000	180,000
Retained earnings	450,000	145,000
Total liabilities and equity	$1,220,000	$480,000

The following market values are agreed upon by the two firms:

	Company C	Company D
Current assets	$150,000	$ 50,000
Marketable securities	270,000	30,000
Land	100,000	60,000
Buildings	350,000	350,000
Equipment	500,000	250,000
Goodwill	170,000	45,000

Newly formed Company CD will issue a total of 24,000 shares of its $10 par stock to acquire the net assets of the two predecessor firms. Company CD will incur $10,000 of direct acquisition costs and $25,000 of registration and stock issuance costs.

Required:

(1) Record the acquisition on the books of Company CD, using purchase accounting principles.
(2) Calculate the number of Company CD shares that will be received by each predecessor firm.

Problem 5-3. The Fairfax Company is planning to purchase the net assets of Companies X and Y. The following balance sheets were secured for the two firms on January 1, 19X8:

Assets	Company X	Company Y
Current assets	$ 150,000	$ 110,000
Property, plant, and equipment (net)	1,200,000	980,000
Goodwill	100,000	90,000
Total assets	$1,450,000	$1,180,000

Liabilities and Equity		
Current liabilities	$ 140,000	$ 120,000
Bonds payable, 7%	400,000	—
Bonds payable, 9%	—	300,000
Common stock, $10 par	500,000	400,000
Retained earnings	410,000	360,000
Total liabilities and equity	$1,450,000	$1,180,000

The Fairfax Company has agreed that market values equal book values, except for goodwill and bonds payable. For these accounts, the following information was found:

(a) The market rate of interest for bonds similar to those of Companies X and Y is 8% on January 1, 19X8, the date of acquisition. The Company X 7% bonds are 10-year bonds and were first issued January 1, 19X3. The Company Y 9% bonds are 20-year bonds and were first issued on January 1, 19X6. Both bonds pay interest annually on December 31.
(b) The industry average rate of return for firms such as X and Y is 10% on tangible gross assets. In the past, Companies X and Y have had the following net incomes:

Year	Company X	Company Y
19X3	$120,000	$100,000
19X4	160,000	90,000
19X5	115,000	120,000
19X6	150,000	130,000
19X7	165,000	135,000

Fairfax will pay for average earnings in excess of the industry norm. Such excess earnings will be capitalized at 16% on the assumption of a 5-year life.

Required:

(1) Calculate the price paid for Company X and Company Y. Include complete calculations for the present value of the bonds and for the estimate of goodwill.
(2) Using the values calculated in part (1), prepare the journal entries recorded by the Fairfax Company to account for the purchase.

Problem 5-4. The Richard Corporation is planning to acquire the net assets of the Cloud Company in a transaction that will not meet the pooling criteria. The Richard Corporation will issue to Cloud either common stock or bonds for the assets received. The balance sheet for the Cloud Company just prior to the acquisition is as follows:

Cloud Company
Balance Sheet
December 31, 19X1

Assets			Liabilities and Equity		
Current assets:					
Cash	$115,000		Liabilities:		
Marketable securities .	100,000		Accounts payable	$ 40,000	
Accounts receivable ..	130,000		Bonds payable, 8% ...	200,000	$240,000
Inventory	110,000	$455,000	Equity:		
Property, plant, and			Common stock, $10 par	$ 40,000	
equipment:			Paid-in capital in		
Land	$ 25,000		excess of par	110,000	
Building (net)	125,000		Retained earnings	275,000	425,000
Equipment (net)	60,000	210,000			
Total assets.........................		$665,000	Total liabilities and equity		$665,000

The firms agree that the following market values should replace Cloud's book values for the purpose of the purchase:

Marketable securities	$ 85,000
Inventory	75,000
Land	45,000
Buildings	180,000
Equipment	75,000

Required:

(1) Assume that the Richard Corporation will issue 20,000 shares of its common stock with a market value of $20 each ($2 par value) for the net assets, exclusive of cash, of the Cloud Company.
   (a) Prepare the entry to record the purchase on the books of the Richard Corporation.
   (b) Prepare the entry to record the sale on the books of the Cloud Company.

(2) Assume that the Richard Corporation will issue 300, $1,000 bonds, which are currently quoted at 102, for the net assets, exclusive of cash, of the Cloud Company.
   (a) Prepare the entry to record the purchase on the books of the Richard Corporation.
   (b) Prepare the entry to record the sale on the books of the Cloud Company.

Problem 5-5. In a business combination to be accounted for as a pooling of interests, Blazer Corporation will issue 40,000 shares of its common stock which has a $20 market value ($10 par value) in exchange for the net assets of the Clinton Corporation, including cash, on December 31, 19X6. Just prior to the exchange, Blazer and Clinton Corporations had the following balance sheets:

Assets	Blazer	Clinton
Cash	$ 180,000	$ 80,000
Accounts receivable	400,000	200,000
Inventories	475,000	190,000
Property, plant, and equipment (net)	1,100,000	600,000
Total assets	$2,155,000	$1,070,000

Liabilities and Equity		
Current liabilities	$ 300,000	$ 140,000
Bonds payable...........................	—	300,000
Common stock........................... ($10 par)	1,500,000	($5 par) 200,000
Paid-in capital in excess of par	—	150,000
Retained earnings	355,000	280,000
Total liabilities and equity	$2,155,000	$1,070,000

Blazer and Clinton Corporations, both of which were organized on January 1, 19X4, have agreed that Clinton's accounts receivable should be adjusted to give effect to uncollectibles on an aging basis (Clinton previously had used the direct write-off method), and that Clinton should change from the fifo method of valuing inventory to the lifo method. The board of directors of Clinton Corporation agreed that these adjustments will be made on a retroactive basis.

Additional data for Clinton Corporation:

Age of receivables (in months)	0-1	2-3	4-6	Over 6
Amount of receivables	$100,000	$60,000	$30,000	$10,000
Percent deemed uncollectible......	1%	3%	5%	10%

End-of-the-year inventories:

	Fifo	Lifo
19X5................	$180,000	$150,000
19X6................	190,000	146,000

Income statement data before giving effect to this information:

	19X5		19X6	
	Blazer	Clinton	Blazer	Clinton
Sales.........................	$1,000,000	$600,000	$1,200,000	$650,000
Cost of sales	580,000	400,000	696,000	430,000
Operating expenses	150,000	100,000	200,000	110,000

Required:

(1) Prepare a pro forma balance sheet to give effect to the business combination regarded as a pooling of interests.
(2) Prepare a comparative income statement for the years 19X5 and 19X6 for the combined corporation (ignore income taxes).

Problem 5-6. Sensor, Inc., purchased for $1,800,000 cash the net assets of All-Equipment Leasing Company. The purchase was made on December 31, 19X1, at which time All-Equipment had prepared the balance sheet shown on page 202.

The following information is available concerning the assets and liabilities of All-Equipment:

(a) Current assets and liabilities are fairly stated. No payments resulting from leases are included in current accounts since all payments are due each December 31 and payment for 19X1 has been made.
(b) Assets under operating leases have an estimated value of $580,000. This figure includes consideration of remaining rents and the value of the assets at the end of the lease terms.

All-Equipment Leasing Company
Balance Sheet
December 31, 19X1

Assets		Liabilities and Equity	
Current assets......................	$ 100,000	Current liabilities	$ 150,000
Assets under operating leases	520,000	Obligation under capital lease of	
Net investment in direct		equipment	35,000
financing (capital) leases..........	730,000	Common stock, $5 par	100,000
Leased equipment under		Paid-in capital in excess	
capital lease (net)	40,000	of par	400,000
Buildings (net)......................	200,000	Retained earnings	955,000
Land	50,000		
Total assets	$1,640,000	Total liabilities and equity	$1,640,000

(c) The net investment in direct financing leases represents receivables at their discounted present values. All leases are written at the current market interest rate of 12%, except one equipment lease requiring payments of $50,000 per year for 5 remaining years. The $50,000 payments include interest at 8%.

(d) Buildings and land have appraised market values of $400,000 and $100,000 respectively.

(e) The leased equipment under the capital lease pertains to a computer used by All-Equipment. The obligation under the capital lease of equipment includes the present value of 5 remaining payments of $9,233 due at the end of each year and discounted at 10%. The current interest rate for this type of transaction is 12%. The market value of the equipment under the lease is $60,000.

(f) All-Equipment has been named in a $200,000 lawsuit involving an accident by a lessee using its equipment. It is likely that All-Equipment will be found liable in the amount of $50,000.

Required:

Record the purchase of the All-Equipment Leasing Company by Sensor, Inc. Carefully support your entry.

Problem 5-7. Blue Corporation was merged into Ace Corporation on August 31, 19X6, with Blue Corporation going out of existence. Both corporations had fiscal years ending on August 31, and Ace Corporation will retain this fiscal year. Prior to the merger, the balance sheets shown on page 203 were obtained.

The following information was obtained as of the date of the merger:

(a) The fair market values of the assets and liabilities on August 31:

	Ace	Blue
Current assets	$ 4,950,000	$ 3,400,000
Property, plant, and equipment (net)	22,000,000	14,000,000
Patents	570,000	360,000
Market research	150,000	40,000
Total assets	$27,670,000	$17,800,000
Liabilities	(2,650,000)	(2,100,000)
Net assets..	$25,020,000	$15,700,000

(b) Ace Corporation believes that its past market research has a value of $150,000; however, all past expenditures have been expensed as required

Assets	Ace	Blue
Current assets	$ 4,350,000	$ 3,000,000
Property, plant, and equipment (net)	18,500,000	11,300,000
Patents	450,000	200,000
Market research	—	40,000
Total assets	$23,300,000	$14,540,000
Liabilities and Equity		
Current liabilities	$ 2,650,000	$ 2,100,000
Common stock, $10 par	12,000,000	—
Common stock, $5 par	—	3,750,000
Paid-in capital in excess of par	4,200,000	3,200,000
Retained earnings	5,700,000	5,490,000
Treasury stock at cost	(1,250,000)	—
Total liabilities and capital	$23,300,000	$14,540,000

by FASB Statement No. 2. The Blue Corporation spent $50,000 on September 1, 19X5, for research and development. The amount was capitalized and is being amortized over five years.

(c) Internally generated expenses incurred because of the merger were $25,000 and are included in the current assets of Ace Corporation as a prepaid expense.

(d) There were no intercompany transactions during the year.

(e) Before the merger, Ace had 3,000,000 shares of common stock authorized, 1,200,000 shares issued, and 1,100,000 shares outstanding. Blue had 750,000 shares of common stock authorized, issued, and outstanding.

Required:

(1) Ace Corporation exchanged 400,000 shares of previously unissued common stock and 100,000 shares of treasury stock for all the outstanding common stock of Blue Corporation. All of the conditions for a pooling of interests were met. Prepare a pro forma balance sheet to give effect to the merger.

(2) Ace Corporation purchased the assets and assumed the liabilities of Blue Corporation by paying $3,100,000 cash and issuing debentures of $16,900,000 at face value. Prepare a pro forma balance sheet to give effect to the merger. (AICPA adapted)

Problem 5-8. The B & Q Company was organized on July 1, 19X1. Under the partnership agreement $900,000 was provided by Beke and $600,000 by Quinn as initial capital; income and losses were to be shared in the same ratio as the initial capital contributions. No additional capital contributions have been made. The June 30, 19X6 balance sheet is as follows:

Assets		
Cash		$ 500,500
Accounts receivable	$1,250,000	
Allowance for doubtful accounts	(300,000)	950,000
Inventory		1,500,000
Prepaid insurance		18,000
Land		58,000
Machinery and equipment (net)		1,473,500
Total assets		$4,500,000

Liabilities and Equity

Current liabilities	$1,475,000
Beke, capital	1,815,000
Quinn, capital	1,210,000
Total liabilities and capital	$4,500,000

Machinery was purchased in fiscal years 19X2, 19X4, and 19X5 for $500,000, $850,000, and $660,000, respectively. The straight-line method of depreciation and a 10-year estimated life with no salvage value have been used for all machinery, with a half year of depreciation taken in the year of acquisition. The experience of other companies over the last several years indicates that the machinery can be sold at 125% of its book value.

An aging of the accounts receivable disclosed the following:

Fiscal Year	Amount	Allowance for Doubtful Accounts
19X3	$ 40,000	$ 35,000
19X4	125,000	105,000
19X5	160,000	67,500
19X6	925,000	92,500
	$1,250,000	$300,000

A review of past experience shows that all receivables over two years old have been uncollectible; those over one year old have been 50% collectible; and those less than one year old have been 90% collectible.

An independent appraisal made in June, 19X1, valued land at $70,000.

Beke agrees to accept 8,700 shares and Quinn agrees to accept 5,800 shares of Preston Corporation common stock in exchange for all partnership interests. During June, 19X6, the market value of a share of Preston Corporation stock was $265. The stockholders' equity account balances of Preston Corporation as of June 30, 19X6, follow:

Common stock, $100 par	$2,000,000
Additional paid-in capital	580,000
Retained earnings	2,496,400
Total stockholders' equity	$5,076,400

Required:

Assuming that the books of Preston Corporation are to be retained, prepare the necessary journal entry (or entries) to effect the business combination on July 1, 19X6, as:

(1) A pooling of interests.
(2) A purchase.

All supporting schedules should be in good form.   (AICPA adapted)

Problem 5-9. Point Company is offering to purchase the net assets of Grant Company, which has prepared the following summarized balance sheet as of December 31, 19X1:

Assets		Liabilities and Equity	
Current assets	$ 80,000	Current liabilities	$ 75,000
Property, plant, and equipment (net)	170,000	Common stock, $10 par	100,000
Goodwill	80,000	Retained earnings	155,000
Total assets	$330,000	Total liabilities and equity	$330,000

The Point Company has given Grant Company two offers to consider:
(a) Point will purchase the net assets for $400,000 cash. After three years, Point will pay cash for average annual earnings of the former Grant Company which are in excess of the industry average of $60,000 per year. Point will pay an amount equal to four years of average excess earnings.
(b) Point will issue 10,000 shares of its common stock with a $5 stated value and $45 market value (December 31, 19X1) for the net assets of Grant. One year later, Point will issue additional stock to Grant for any amount by which the value of the shares transferred falls below $42 per share. Fractional shares will be rounded to the nearest whole share.

An appraisal has been made and it is felt that the book value of Grant's tangible assets and liabilities approximates their market values.

Required:

(1) Assume that Grant Company chooses Offer (a), and that income of the former company is $65,000, $52,000, and $75,000 for the next three years.
  (a) Prepare the journal entry Point Company would make on December 31, 19X1, to record the purchase.
  (b) Prepare the journal entry (if any) Point Company would make on December 31, 19X4, to record contingent consideration.
(2) Assume that Grant Company chooses Offer (b), and that the market value of the Point Company stock falls to $35 on December 31, 19X2.
  (a) Prepare the journal entry Point Company would make on December 31, 19X1, to record the purchase.
  (b) Prepare the journal entry (if any) that Point Company would make on December 31, 19X2, to record contingent consideration.

Problem 5-10. The Pace Corporation is purchasing the net assets, exclusive of cash, of the Austin Company as of January 1, 19X1, at which time Austin Company's balance sheet was as follows:

Assets			Liabilities and Equity		
Current assets:			Current liabilities:		
Cash	$10,000		Accounts payable ..	$ 150,000	
Accounts receivable	50,000	$ 60,000	Income tax payable	190,000	$ 340,000
Noncurrent assets:			Equity:		
Investment in			Common		
marketable			stock, $5 par	$1,200,000	
securities	$120,000		Retained		
Land	600,000		earnings.........	610,000	1,810,000
Buildings (net).....	450,000				
Equipment (net) ...	800,000				
Patents	20,000				
Goodwill..........	100,000	2,090,000			
Total assets		$2,150,000	Total liabilities and equity		$2,150,000

Pace Corporation feels that the market values shown at the top of page 206 should be substituted for Austin's book values.

Pace will issue 20,000 shares of its common stock with a $2 par and a quoted market value of $65 per share on January 1, 19X1, to Austin Company to acquire

Accounts receivable	$ 60,000
Investment in marketable securities	150,000
Land	300,000
Buildings	450,000
Equipment	600,000
Patents	150,000
Accounts payable	165,000

the net assets, exclusive of cash. Pace also agrees that two years later it will issue additional securities to compensate Austin for any decline in value below that on the date of issue.

Required:

(1) Record the purchase on the books of Pace Corporation on January 1, 19X1. Include support for calculations used to arrive at the values assigned to the assets and liabilities.
(2) Indicate the disclosure which would be necessary in the financial statements of Pace Corporation on December 31, 19X1, assuming that the quoted value of the stock is $67 per share.
(3) Record the payment (if any) of contingent consideration on January 1, 19X3, assuming that the quoted value of the stock is $62.50.

Problem 5-11. Financial statements of Don Corporation and Mariner Corporation appear as follows:

Balance Sheets
June 30, 19X6

Assets	Don Corporation	Mariner Corporation
Cash	$ 25,500	$ 1,500
Receivables (net)	24,500	7,500
Inventories	42,000	8,800
Due from Mariner Corporation	7,600	—
Property, plant, and equipment (net)	59,500	35,800
Other assets...	4,500	200
Total assets	$163,600	$53,800
Liabilities and Equity		
Accounts and notes payable............................	$ 22,600	$35,400
Due to Don Corporation	—	7,600
Accrued expenses	1,500	2,200
Federal income tax payable	9,500	—
Total liabilities.......................................	$ 33,600	$45,200
Capital stock, $10 par	$ 50,000	—
Capital stock, $100 par	—	$25,000
Paid-in capital in excess of par	30,000	32,000
Retained earnings, Dec. 31, 19X5	43,000	(42,300)
Net income (loss) from Jan. 1, 19X6, to June 30, 19X6	9,500	(6,100)
Dividends paid...	(2,500)	—
Total equity	$130,000	$ 8,600
Total liabilities and equity	$163,600	$53,800

Income Statements
For Six Months Ended June 30, 19X6

	Don Corporation	Mariner Corporation
Sales..	$150,000	$60,000
Cost of goods sold	105,000	54,000
Gross profit	$ 45,000	$ 6,000
Operating expenses	31,000	8,200
Operating profit (loss)...................................	$ 14,000	$(2,200)
Other income (deductions)	5,000	(3,900)
Income (loss) before tax.................................	$ 19,000	$ (6,100)
Provisions for income tax................................	9,500	—
Net income..	$ 9,500	$ (6,100)

On July 1, 19X6, Mariner Corporation transferred to Don Corporation all of its assets, subject to all liabilities, in exchange for unissued Don Corporation capital stock. Since their inception in 19X0, both corporations have been owned by the same group of stockholders, although in different proportions as to individuals. The terms of the merger provided that the fair value of the stock in each case is to be its book value, except that an allowance is to be made for the value of any net operating loss carryforwards. Obtaining the benefit of the loss carryforward deduction was not the principal purpose for the merger. Don Corporation is certain that any tax loss carryforward will be realized. (Assume a 50% tax rate.)

The income before income taxes and the losses that are available as tax loss carryforwards are as follows for the two corporations (income per books and taxable income are the same):

	Don Corporation	Mariner Corporation
19X3..........................	$14,900	$(21,000)
19X4..........................	31,200	(7,000)
19X5..........................	28,900	(11,100)

Required:

(1) Compute the number of shares of Don Corporation stock (a) to be distributed to shareholders of Mariner Corporation, and (b) to be exchanged for each share of Mariner stock.

(2) For the books of Don Corporation, prepare the journal entry to record the merger with Mariner as a pooling of interests. The acquisition should be recorded in a manner that will allow the combined income statement prepared for 19X6 to include the nominal accounts of both firms for the entire year.

(3) For the books of Mariner Corporation, prepare the journal entries to record the merger with Don, the distribution of Don Corporation stock to the stockholders of Mariner Corporation, and the dissolution of Mariner Corporation. (AICPA adapted)

Problem 5-12. P Corporation acquired all of the outstanding stock of S Corporation as of June 30, 19X7. As consideration for the acquisition, P Corporation gave the stockholders of S Corporation $550,000 and 500,000 shares of previously unissued common stock in exchange for all the outstanding stock of the S Corporation. The P Corporation stock had a par value of $1 and a quoted market value of $2.50 both before and after this transaction.

The balance sheet of S Corporation as of June 30, 19X7, was as follows:

Assets

Current assets:

Cash	$120,000	
Accounts receivable	240,000	
Inventories	210,000	$ 570,000

Property, plant, and equipment:

	Cost	Accumulated Depreciation	Net	
Property A.................	$ 310,000	$160,000	$150,000	
Property B	370,000	170,000	200,000	
Property C.................	480,000	180,000	300,000	
Property D	250,000	150,000	100,000	
	$1,410,000	$660,000	$750,000	750,000
Total assets				$1,320,000

Liabilities and Stockholders' Equity

Accounts payable		$ 470,000
Stockholders' equity:		
Common stock, 500,000 shares authorized and outstanding, $1 par	$500,000	
Paid-in capital in excess of par	100,000	
Retained earnings	250,000	850,000
Total liabilities and stockholders' equity..................		$1,320,000

All receivables are considered collectible. Inventories are stated at cost, which is also equivalent to replacement cost and is not in excess of market. Properties B, C, and D have been appraised at $600,000, $800,000, and $200,000, respectively. Goodwill is not considered to be a significant factor in this business.

An engineer of the P Corporation estimates that the properties of the S Corporation will have a 10-year useful life from July 1, 19X7, with no salvage value at the end of that period. P Corporation uses the straight-line method of depreciating its assets.

On July 1, 19X7, S Corporation sold Property A for $500,000, and for the six months ended December 31, 19X7, reported a net income of $450,000, which included the gain from the sale of Property A and depreciation expense of $55,000.

The balance sheet of S Corporation at December 31, 19X7, was as shown on page 209.

On January 1,19X8, S Corporation was dissolved and all of its assets were transferred to, and its liabilities assumed by, P Corporation. The transaction is to be accounted for as a purchase and not as a pooling of interests.

Required:

(1) Prepare the journal entry of P Corporation to record its investment in S Corporation as of June 30, 19X7.

(2) Prepare the journal entries to record the accounts of S Corporation on the books of P Corporation upon dissolution of S Corporation, and explain how the amounts were determined. (Disregard income tax implications.)

(AICPA adapted)

Assets

Current assets:

Cash	$390,000	
Accounts receivable	355,000	
Inventories	260,000	$1,005,000

Property, plant, and equipment:

	Cost	Accumulated Depreciation	Net	
Property B	$ 370,000	$188,500	$181,500	
Property C................	480,000	204,000	276,000	
Property D	250,000	162,500	87,500	
	$1,100,000	$555,000	$545,000	545,000
Total assets				$1,550,000

Liabilities and Stockholders' Equity

Accounts payable		$ 250,000
Stockholders' equity:		
Common stock..	$500,000	
Paid-in capital in excess of par	100,000	
Retained earnings	700,000	1,300,000
Total liabilities and stockholders' equity..................		$1,550,000

CHAPTER 6

CONSOLIDATED STATEMENTS AT THE DATE OF ACQUISITION

The preceding chapter has discussed accounting principles applicable to business combinations accomplished by an acquisition of assets. Control over another firm's assets can also be achieved indirectly by purchasing a controlling interest in the firm's voting common stock. Legally the controlling parent firm has only an investment in another firm, the subsidiary. However, the parent is able to control the subsidiary's operations, and often the subsidiary's activities will become integrated with those of the parent. Under these circumstances, consolidated statements are necessary to erase the legal boundaries between the parent and subsidiary, and to present the financial statements of the unified group as those of a single economic entity. This chapter is the first of several which attempt to build a comprehensive set of principles and methods for the preparation of consolidated statements.

CONDITIONS FOR CONSOLIDATED STATEMENTS

Consolidated financial statements are designed to present the results of operations and the financial position of the parent and its subsidiaries as if the affiliated group were one firm. Consolidated statements are more informative to the owners of the parent firm than are statements of the individual entities; but consolidated statements are not sufficient for the stockholders or the creditors of the individual entities. The rights of the minority stockholders extend only to the entity whose shares they hold. Creditors may look only to the legal entity which is indebted to them for satisfaction of their claims. Therefore, to be adequately informed, both minority shareholders and creditors require financial statements of the separate entities.

Two basic conditions must exist in order to permit the consolidation of a subsidiary. First, the parent must have effective operating control over the subsidiary. Second, only those firms whose operations are integrated so as to form a logical economic entity are to be consolidated.

The accountant must apply professional judgment in deciding which subsidiaries are to be consolidated with the parent and which are to be shown as investments. The resulting consolidation policy of the firm must be disclosed on the financial statements.[1]

Effective Operating Control

Ownership of over 50% of a firm's voting shares, directly or indirectly, "is a condition pointing toward consolidation."[2] When over 50% of another firm's stock is owned, control may be assumed to exist unless one of the following impediments to effective control is present, as discussed in ARB No. 51 (par. 2) and Chapter 12 of ARB No. 43 (par. 8):

1. Control is likely to be only temporary.
2. There is legal restriction on control, as in the case of a subsidiary controlled by a court in a bankruptcy proceeding or a legal reorganization. A parent is also preempted from preparing consolidated statements when the shares of the subsidiary are held in a voting trust.
3. A powerful minority stockholder group acts to limit the effectiveness of the parent's control.
4. Restrictions are placed on foreign subsidiaries by the countries in which they operate. Restrictions may affect the subsidiaries' operations or the ability to transfer profits to the parent.

Integrated Operations

In making the decision as to whether or not to consolidate a subsidiary, "the aim should be to make the financial presentation which is most meaningful in the circumstances."[3] A factor pointing to consolidated financial reporting is a homogeneity of operations between the parent and its subsidiaries. For example, ARB No. 51 indicates that it would be inappropriate to consolidate the statements of a manufacturing parent with a banking or an insurance subsidiary. Homogeneity has been interpreted in practice to mean that affiliated firms should be consolidated if their operations are integrated. This interpretation is confirmed by APB Opinion No. 10, which states that all subsidiaries whose principal business activity is leasing property or facilities to their parents or other affiliates should be consolidated.[4]

Major ownership interests which do not meet the conditions for consolidated reporting are shown as long-term investments on the investor's statements. The methods used to account for these investments are discussed in a later chapter.

---

[1] *Accounting Research and Terminology Bulletin, No. 51,* "Consolidated Financial Statements" (New York: American Institute of Certified Public Accountants, 1959), par. 5.

[2] *Ibid.,* par. 2.

[3] *Ibid.,* par. 4.

[4] *Opinions of the Accounting Principles Board, No. 10,* "Omnibus Opinion—1966" (New York: American Institute of Certified Public Accountants, 1966), par. 4.

TECHNIQUE OF CONSOLIDATION

This chapter seeks to build an understanding of the techniques used to consolidate the separate balance sheets of a parent and its subsidiary immediately subsequent to the acquisition. The consolidated balance sheet as of the acquisition date is discussed first to focus on the combining of the balance sheet accounts, without the complication of subsequent operating results.

As discussed in Chapter 5, there are two basic means by which a company may gain control over the assets of another firm. A firm may directly acquire the assets of another firm, or it may purchase a controlling interest in the other firm's common stock. In the asset acquisition, the firm over which control is sought is dissolved. In a stock acquisition, the acquired firm is preserved as a separate legal and accounting entity. While initial accounting for the two types of acquisitions is significantly different, both types have the same practical effect of creating one larger economic entity, and thus both should produce the same balance sheet. In the following discussion, the recording of the two types of acquisitions is compared, and then the balance sheet that results from each type is presented.

Reviewing an Asset Acquisition

Illustration I demonstrates an asset acquisition of Company S by Company P for cash. Part A of the exhibit presents the balance sheets of the two firms just prior to acquisition. Part B shows the entry to record the acquisition of Company S's assets. In the illustration, Company P paid $500,000 cash and assumed the liabilities of Company S. The book value of the assets acquired is assumed to be representative of their market values, and no goodwill is acknowledged. The assets and liabilities of Company S are added to those of Company P to produce the balance sheet for the combined firm shown in Part C. Since balances are combined in recording the acquisition, statements for the single combined entity are "automatically" produced, and no consolidation process is needed.

Consolidating a Stock Acquisition

In a stock acquisition, the acquiring firm deals with existing stockholders only, not the firm itself. Assuming the same facts as those used in Illustration I, except that Company P purchases all of the outstanding stock of Company S for $500,000, Company P would make the following entry:

```
Investment in Subsidiary S .............................    500,000
    Cash ...................................................              500,000
```

Illustration I—Asset Acquisition

A. Balance sheets of Companies P and S prior to acquisition:

Company P Balance Sheet

Assets		Liabilities and Equity	
Cash	$ 600,000	Current liabilities	$ 150,000
Accounts receivable	300,000	Bonds payable	300,000
Inventory	100,000	Paid-in capital	100,000
Equipment (net)	150,000	Retained earnings	600,000
Total	$1,150,000	Total	$1,150,000

Company S Balance Sheet

Assets		Liabilities and Equity	
Accounts receivable	$ 200,000	Current liabilities	$ 100,000
Inventory	100,000	Paid-in capital	200,000
Equipment (net)	300,000	Retained earnings	300,000
Total	$ 600,000	Total	$ 600,000

B. Entry to record acquisition of the net assets of Company S by Company P:

Accounts Receivable	200,000	
Inventory	100,000	
Equipment	300,000	
Current Liabilities		100,000
Cash		500,000

C. Balance sheet of Company P subsequent to asset acquisition:

Company P Balance Sheet

Assets		Liabilities and Equity	
Cash	$ 100,000	Current liabilities	$ 250,000
Accounts receivable	500,000	Bonds payable	300,000
Inventory	200,000	Paid-in capital	100,000
Equipment (net)	450,000	Retained earnings	600,000
Total	$1,250,000	Total	$1,250,000

This entry does not acknowledge the underlying assets over which control is achieved. Instead, the acquisition is recorded as an investment which represents the controlling interest in net assets. If no further action were taken, the investment in Subsidiary S account would appear as a long-term investment on the balance sheet of Company P. This presentation is permitted, however, only if the conditions for consolidated statements are not met.

Assuming that the conditions for consolidated statements are met, the balance sheets of the separate firms must be combined into a consolidated balance sheet for the single resulting economic entity. The consolidation process is a supplement to the existing accounting records of the firms. The process begins with the two firms' individual balance sheets, from which the accounts representing the intercompany investment must be eliminated.

The consolidation process is demonstrated in Illustration II. The stockholders' equity accounts of the subsidiary are eliminated against the investment in Subsidiary S account of the parent. These accounts do not appear on a consolidated balance sheet. The equity accounts of the subsidiary have no economic substance, since the only common stock owned by parties outside the consolidated firm are the shares issued by the parent company. The investment in subsidiary account is not needed since it will be replaced by the specific assets and liabilities of the subsidiary company.

After the intercompany investment accounts are eliminated, the account balances of the two firms are combined. The work sheet of Illus-

Illustration II—100% Ownership
Company P and
Work Sheet for Consolidated
December

	Trial Balance	
	Company P	**Company S**
Debits:		
Cash	100,000	
Accounts Receivable	300,000	200,000
Inventory	100,000	100,000
Investment in Subsidiary S	500,000	
Equipment (net)	150,000	300,000
	1,150,000	600,000
Credits:		
Current Liabilities	150,000	100,000
Bonds Payable	300,000	
Paid-In Capital, Co. P	100,000	
Retained Earnings, Co. P	600,000	
Paid-In Capital, Co. S		200,000
Retained Earnings, Co. S		300,000
	1,150,000	600,000

1 Eliminate investment in subsidiary against subsidiary equity.

tration II leads to the following formal consolidated balance sheet for Companies P and S:

Company P and Subsidiary Company S Consolidated Balance Sheet December 31, 19X1				
Assets			**Liabilities and Equity**	
Current assets:			Current liabilities	$ 250,000
Cash	$100,000		Bonds payable	300,000
Accounts receivable	500,000		Stockholders' equity:	
Inventory	200,000	$ 800,000	Paid-in capital $100,000	
Equipment (net).........		450,000	Retained earnings...... 600,000	700,000
Total assets.......................		$1,250,000	Total liabilities and equity	$1,250,000

The format of Illustration II should be carefully analyzed, since it will be used in subsequent illustrations. It is acceptable to use a single line for like accounts of both firms. However, stockholders' equity accounts are shown on separate lines because the subsidiary equity is partially or entirely eliminated, while the equity of the parent survives as the controlling interest in the consolidated firm. Separation of the

Price Equals Book Value
Subsidiary Company S
Balance Sheet
31, 19X1

Eliminations		Consolidated Balance Sheet	
Dr.	**Cr.**	**Dr.**	**Cr.**
		100,000	
		500,000	
		200,000	
	1 500,000		
		450,000	
			250,000
			300,000
			100,000
			600,000
1 200,000			
1 300,000			
500,000	500,000	1,250,000	1,250,000

equities will thus avoid confusion when the elimination entries are made.

It must again be emphasized that the consolidated financial statements are only a supplement to the statements of the separate firms. Eliminations are made only on the work sheet and are not recorded on either firm's books. Since consolidation eliminations are never recorded, each year the consolidation process starts anew from the statements of the separate firms.

RECORDING STOCK ACQUISITIONS AS A PURCHASE

The acquisition of a controlling interest in another firm must be analyzed before it can be recorded. When 90% or more of another firm's common stock is obtained and all other pooling criteria are met, the transaction must be recorded according to pooling procedures. All stock acquisitions not meeting the pooling criteria must be recorded under purchase procedures. Since most stock acquisitions do not qualify for the pooling treatment, the purchase treatment is discussed first.

When a stock acquisition is recorded as a purchase, the investment in the stock of the subsidiary is recorded at the fair market value of the property received or the securities issued, whichever is more readily determinable. The market value of securities issued must be added to the total paid-in capital of the parent.

To illustrate, assume that Company P has the following balance sheet on December 31, 19X1, just prior to acquiring Company S:

Company P
Balance Sheet
December 31, 19X1

Assets		Liabilities and Equity	
Cash	$ 210,000	Current liabilities	$ 300,000
Accounts receivable	300,000	Bonds payable	500,000
Inventory	500,000	Common stock	500,000
Land	100,000	Paid-in capital in excess	
Buildings (net)	900,000	of par	500,000
Equipment (net)	650,000	Retained earnings	860,000
Total assets	$2,660,000	Total liabilities and equity	$2,660,000

On December 31, 19X1, Company P issues 20,000 shares of its $10 par stock to acquire all the common shares of Company S and pays $10,000 for direct acquisition costs. Assuming that Company P shares have a market value of $50 each, the investment is recorded by the following entry:

Investment in Subsidiary S (20,000 shares × $50		
market value plus $10,000 acquisition costs)	1,010,000	
Common Stock (20,000 shares × $10 par)		200,000
Paid-In Capital in Excess of Par		800,000
Cash (for acquisition costs)		10,000

This entry must acknowledge the market value of the shares exchanged, regardless of the underlying book value of the subsidiary interest acquired. As in the case of an asset acquisition, direct acquisition costs are considered part of the cost of the interest acquired. Thus, in summary:

When deemed to be a purchase, the investment in a subsidiary is always recorded at the fair market value of the property received or the securities issued in exchange, plus the direct acquisition costs.

CONSOLIDATING THE PURCHASE OF A 100% INTEREST

The example in Illustration II portrayed a stock purchase in which the parent's payment for the subsidiary interest was equal to the book value of the equity acquired. The book value of the equity acquired may be expressed as the subsidiary's net assets or the total stockholders' equity. The equality of price paid and equity acquired is rare, since market values and book values are seldom identical. As was true in the case of an asset purchase, the price paid for stock will reflect the market value of the underlying assets and possibly the existence of goodwill.

Investment Equals or Exceeds Market Value of Subsidiary Assets

When the price paid for the stock of the subsidiary equals or exceeds the market value of the net identifiable assets, it is necessary, for consolidated reporting purposes, to increase the carrying value of these net assets to their market value. Any excess of the price paid over the market value of these assets is attributed to goodwill. To provide guidance in making these work sheet adjustments, a supporting schedule is suggested for analyzing the excess of the price paid over the book value acquired. This schedule is termed the "determination and distribution of excess schedule." Its function is (1) to calculate the difference between the price paid for the subsidiary interest and the recorded book value of the subsidiary equity, and (2) to distribute this excess to those assets and liabilities which require revaluation for consolidated reporting purposes. To illustrate the schedule, assume that, at the time of the purchase, Company S has the account balances shown in the Company S column of the trial balance included in Illustration III on pages 220 and 221. The market value of Company S's inventory and equipment is assumed to be $350,000 and $550,000 respectively. The determination and distribution of excess schedule on page 218 compares the price paid for the subsidiary investment with the recorded book value of the interest acquired to arrive at an excess of cost over book value of $310,000.

As was true with an asset purchase, the excess of cost over book value must first be used to adjust current assets, long-term investments

Company P and Subsidiary Company S
Determination and Distribution of Excess Schedule
December 31, 19X1

Price paid for investment in Co. S (including direct acquisition costs)		$1,010,000
Less interest acquired:		
Common stock, $5 par	$ 50,000	
Paid-in capital in excess of par	350,000	
Retained earnings	300,000	
Total stockholders' equity	$700,000	
Interest acquired	100%	700,000
Excess of cost over book value		$ 310,000
Less undervaluation of current assets:		
Inventory		**50,000**
Excess attributable to long-lived assets		$ 260,000
Less undervaluation of identifiable long-lived assets:		
Equipment		**150,000**
Goodwill		**$ 110,000**

in marketable securities, and liabilities. These accounts are to be adjusted to their market values for consolidated reporting regardless of the price paid for the subsidiary interest. In this case, after the $50,000 undervaluation of current assets is deducted, the schedule shows that identifiable long-lived assets are undervalued by a total of $260,000, $150,000 of which is attributed to the equipment, with the $110,000 balance reflecting goodwill.

The information contained in the determination and distribution of excess schedule is used in preparing the work sheet eliminations and adjustments shown in Illustration III. After intercompany accounts are eliminated and the excess of cost is distributed, the account balances are added to arrive at the consolidated balance sheet amounts. If the price paid for a controlling interest equals the market value of the subsidiary's identifiable assets, work sheet procedures would parallel those of Illustration III, except that no goodwill would be recognized.

Investment Is Less Than Market but More Than Recorded Book Values of Subsidiary Assets

Bargain purchases occur when the price paid for an interest in a subsidiary falls below the total market value of the subsidiary's separate, identifiable assets. However, the price paid in a bargain purchase may exceed the recorded book value of the subsidiary's assets. In such a case, the determination and distribution of excess schedule will still show an excess of cost over book value. This situation is discussed next, followed by a discussion of the case in which the bargain purchase price is below the recorded book value of the subsidiary's assets.

Slightly changing the example of Illustration III, assume that Company P issued only 16,000 of its $50 market value ($10 par) stock to acquire its 100% interest in Company S, and paid $10,000 in direct acquisition costs. The entry to record the acquisition would be:

Investment in Subsidiary S (16,000 shares × $50
   market value plus $10,000 acquisition costs)......... 810,000
     Common Stock (16,000 shares × $10 par)   160,000
     Paid-In Capital in Excess of Par   640,000
     Cash (for acquisition costs)........................   10,000

The acquisition would lead to the account balances shown in the first two columns of Illustration IV on pages 222 and 223. Note that both the investment in Subsidiary S and the paid-in equity accounts of Company P reflect the above entry. Again assume that Company S's book values equal market values except for inventory and equipment, which have a market value of $350,000 and $550,000 respectively.

After intercompany accounts are eliminated, and the excess of cost over book value of the subsidiary equity is distributed, the account balances are added to arrive at the consolidated balance sheet amounts. Before work sheet adjustments are made, however, a determination and distribution of excess schedule should be prepared. The schedule below calculates an excess of cost over book value of $110,000. The excess must always be used first to increase current assets, liabilities, and long-term investments in marketable securities to their full market value. In this example, $50,000 is used to increase the value of the current asset, inventory. The remaining $60,000 is used to increase the carrying value of the plant asset, equipment. Since the price paid for the interest in the firm did not fully reflect the market value of the plant asset ($550,000), the equipment may be increased to only a portion of its market value.

Two circumstances would complicate the preparation of the determination and distribution of excess schedule. The first would be a situa-

Company P and Subsidiary Company S
Determination and Distribution of Excess Schedule
December 31, 19X1

Price paid for investment in Co. S (includes direct acquisition costs)		$810,000
Less interest acquired:		
Common stock, $5 par	$ 50,000	
Paid-in capital in excess of par	350,000	
Retained earnings	300,000	
Total stockholders' equity	$700,000	
Interest acquired	100%	700,000
Excess of cost over book value		$110,000
Less undervaluation of current assets:		
Inventory		**50,000**
Excess attributable to long-lived assets:		
Equipment		**$ 60,000**

Illustration III—100% Interest
Company P and
Work Sheet for Consolidated
December

	Trial Balance	
	Company P	Company S
Debits:		
Cash	200,000	150,000
Accounts Receivable	300,000	250,000
Inventory	500,000	300,000
Land	100,000	
Buildings (net)	900,000	
Equipment (net)	650,000	400,000
Investment in Subsidiary S	1,010,000	
Goodwill		
Total	3,660,000	1,100,000
Credits:		
Current Liabilities	300,000	100,000
Bonds Payable	500,000	300,000
Common Stock ($10 par), Co. P	700,000	
Paid-In Capital in Excess of Par, Co. P	1,300,000	
Retained Earnings, Co. P	860,000	
Common Stock ($5 par), Co. S		50,000
Paid-In Capital in Excess of Par, Co. S		350,000
Retained Earnings, Co. S		300,000
Total	3,660,000	1,100,000

1 Eliminate intercompany accounts. The investment in Subsidiary S account includes a 100% interest in the stockholders' equity of Company S. Therefore, the entire stockholders' equity of Company S is eliminated against the investment account. The balance of the investment account, $310,000, has no intercompany counterpart, but rather reflects the total undervaluation of Company S's assets.

---

tion in which the excess of cost is less than the amount required to adjust current assets, long-term investments in marketable securities, and liabilities to market value. It must be remembered that these accounts are always recorded at their market value on the acquisition date for consolidated reporting purposes. Since the excess of cost is insufficient for the write-up, the remainder of the write-up is made by decreasing long-lived assets of the subsidiary below their recorded book values on the consolidated work sheet. For example, assume that the price paid in the immediately preceding example was $725,000. Even though the excess of cost over book value would be only $25,000, inventory would have to be increased by $50,000, which would require a deduction of $25,000 from the book value of the equipment.

A second complication occurs when there is more than one subsidiary long-lived asset. The excess of cost over book value attributable

Price Exceeds Market Value
Subsidiary Company S
Balance Sheet
31, 19X1

Eliminations and Adjustments		Consolidated Balance Sheet	
Dr.	Cr.	Dr.	Cr.
		350,000	
		550,000	
2 50,000		850,000	
		100,000	
		900,000	
2 150,000		1,200,000	
	1 700,000		
	2 310,000		
2 110,000		110,000	
		400,000	
		800,000	
		700,000	
		1,300,000	
			860,000
1 50,000			
1 350,000			
1 300,000			
1,010,000	1,010,000	4,060,000	4,060,000

2 Distribute the total undervaluation of Company S assets, represented by the balance in the investment account, to the proper asset accounts. The information for this distribution is taken from the determination and distribution of excess schedule.

---

to long-lived assets, as produced by the determination and distribution of excess schedule, must then be apportioned to each asset, since the price paid is not sufficient to increase all long-lived assets to their full market value. The following procedure apportions the excess:

1. The total assigned value of the long-lived assets will be the sum of the existing book values plus the remaining excess of cost attributable to long-lived assets.
2. Allocate the total assigned value of the long-lived assets to each asset in proportion to each asset's market value.
3. Apportion to each asset the difference between the allocated assigned value above and the existing book value.

As an example, assume that the excess cost attributable to the long-lived assets of subsidiary Company S, as shown in the determination

Illustration IV—100% Interest, Price
Company P and
Work Sheet for
December

	Trial Balance	
	Company P	**Company S**
Debits:		
Cash	200,000	150,000
Accounts Receivable	300,000	250,000
Inventory	500,000	300,000
Land	100,000	
Buildings (net)	900,000	
Equipment (net)	650,000	400,000
Investment in Subsidiary S	810,000	
Total	3,460,000	1,100,000
Credits:		
Current Liabilities	300,000	100,000
Bonds Payable	500,000	300,000
Common Stock ($10 par), Co. P	660,000	
Paid-In Capital in Excess of Par, Co. P	1,140,000	
Retained Earnings, Co. P	860,000	
Common Stock ($5 par), Co. S		50,000
Paid-In Capital in Excess of Par, Co. S		350,000
Retained Earnings, Co. S		300,000
Total	3,460,000	1,100,000

1 Eliminate intercompany accounts. The investment in Subsidiary S account includes a 100% interest in the stockholders' equity of Company S. Thus, the entire Company S equity is eliminated against the investment account.

---

and distribution of excess schedule on page 219, is $60,000, and that the long-lived assets of Company S have the following values:

	Book Value	Market Value
Land	$125,000	$135,000
Buildings (net)	75,000	180,000
Equipment (net)	50,000	45,000
Total	$250,000	$360,000

The following steps apportion the $60,000 excess cost attributable to long-lived assets:

1. Total assigned value:
   $250,000 book value plus $60,000 excess = $310,000

2. Allocation of total assigned value:

Between Book Value and Market Value
Subsidiary Company S
Consolidated Balance Sheet
31, 19X1

Eliminations and Adjustments		Consolidated Balance Sheet	
Dr.	Cr.	Dr.	Cr.
		350,000	
		550,000	
2 50,000		850,000	
		100,000	
		900,000	
2 60,000		1,110,000	
	1 700,000		
	2 110,000		
			400,000
			800,000
			660,000
			1,140,000
			860,000
1 50,000			
1 350,000			
1 300,000			
810,000	810,000	3,860,000	3,860,000

2 The balance of the investment account represents the total undervaluation of Company S assets. Distribute the total undervaluation of Company S assets to the proper asset accounts as shown in the determination and distribution of excess schedule.

	Market Value	Fraction of Market Value	×	Total Assigned Value	=	Allocated Assigned Value
Land	$135,000	3/8	×	$310,000	=	$116,250
Buildings	180,000	4/8	×	310,000	=	155,000
Equipment	45,000	1/8	×	310,000	=	38,750
Total	$360,000					$310,000

3. Apportionment of the difference between allocated assigned value and book value to each asset:

	Allocated Assigned Value	Book Value	Increase (Decrease)
Land	$116,250	$125,000	$ (8,750)
Buildings	155,000	75,000	80,000
Equipment	38,750	50,000	(11,250)
Total	$310,000	$250,000	$60,000

As a result of the allocation, the determination and distribution of excess schedule would conclude as follows:

Excess attributable to long-lived assets:
Land . . . . $ (8,750)
Buildings   80,000
Equipment . . . .   (11,250) $60,000

The procedures illustrated result in each long-lived asset sharing the assignable value in proportion to its market value. For example, each asset in the preceding illustration received 86.1% of its market value. It may be tempting to short-cut the procedure by allocating the $60,000 excess of cost by relative market values and then adding each asset's allocated portion of the excess to its recorded book value. The shortcut will not, however, result in each asset being recorded at the same percentage of market value unless the original book values of each asset were an equal percentage of market value. It is highly unlikely that book values would be so aligned.

Investment Is Less Than Recorded Book Value of Subsidiary Equity

An investment in a subsidiary amounting to less than the recorded book value of the subsidiary's stockholders' equity indicates that the recorded book value of the subsidiary's assets and equity is overstated. Again changing Illustration III, assume that Company P acquired 100% of the common stock of Company S by issuing 12,000 shares of its $50 market value ($10 par) stock and paying $10,000 in direct acquisition costs. The entry to record the acquisition would be:

Investment in Subsidiary S (12,000 shares × $50 market
value plus $10,000 acquisition costs)   610,000
Common Stock (12,000 shares × $10 par)   120,000
Paid-In Capital in Excess of Par   480,000
Cash (for acquisition costs)   10,000

This investment would lead to the account balances shown in the first two columns of Illustration V on pages 226 and 227. Note again that both the investment in Subsidiary S and paid-in capital accounts of Company P reflect the new lower acquisition cost. Book values of Company S are assumed to equal market values, except for inventory and equipment, which have a market value of $350,000 and $300,000 respectively.

The following determination and distribution of excess schedule calculates a $90,000 excess of book value over the cost of the investment. As in previous schedules, the excess is first modified by the amount necessary to restate to market value the current assets, long-term investments in marketable securities, and liabilities. In this example, the current asset, inventory, is understated by $50,000 and is increased to market value. The excess book value attributable to the equipment is $140,000 ($90,000 excess of book value of all assets over cost plus $50,000 write-up to market value for inventory). Thus, only $260,000

($400,000 book value less $140,000) is assigned to the equipment acquired from Company S. Again, current assets, long-term investments in marketable securities, and liabilities are always adjusted to market value regardless of the price paid for the subsidiary interest.

Company P and Subsidiary Company S
Determination and Distribution of Excess Schedule
December 31, 19X1

Price paid for investment in Co. S (including direct acquisition costs)		$610,000
Less equity acquired:		
Common stock, $5 par	$ 50,000	
Paid-in capital in excess of par	350,000	
Retained earnings	300,000	
Total stockholders' equity	$700,000	
Interest acquired	100%	700,000
Excess of book value over cost		$ 90,000
Add undervaluation of current assets:		
Inventory		**50,000**
Excess of book value attributable to long-lived assets:		
Equipment		**$140,000**

Two added complications may arise in handling an investment at a price below the book value of the subsidiary. First, there may be several subsidiary long-lived assets whose market values differ from their book values. In this case, the excess of book value must be apportioned among all long-lived assets. The procedure for apportionment is as follows:

1. The total assigned value of all long-lived assets will be the sum of the existing long-lived asset book values, reduced by the excess of book value over the cost of the investment attributable to long-lived assets, as computed in the determination and distribution of excess schedule. The excess attributable to long-lived assets is the original excess of book value for the investment plus or minus any market value adjustment made for current assets, long-term investments in marketable securities, and liabilities.
2. Allocate the total assigned value of all long-lived assets to each asset in proportion to its market value.
3. Apportion to each asset the difference between the allocated assigned value and the existing book value.

As an example of this procedure, assume that in Illustration V there were three long-lived assets with book and market values as follows:

	Book Value	Market Value
Land	$100,000	$ 75,000
Buildings (net).................................	250,000	175,000
Equipment (net)	50,000	50,000
Total	$400,000	$300,000

	Trial Balance	
	Company P	Company S
Debits:		
Cash	200,000	150,000
Accounts Receivable	300,000	250,000
Inventory	500,000	300,000
Land	100,000	
Buildings (net)	900,000	
Equipment (net)	650,000	400,000
Investment in Subsidiary S	610,000	
Total	3,260,000	1,100,000
Credits:		
Current Liabilities	300,000	100,000
Bonds Payable	500,000	300,000
Common Stock ($10 par), Co. P	620,000	
Paid-In Capital in Excess of Par, Co. P	980,000	
Retained Earnings, Co. P	860,000	
Common Stock ($5 par), Co. S		50,000
Paid-In Capital in Excess of Par, Co. S		350,000
Retained Earnings, Co. S		300,000
Total	3,260,000	1,100,000

1 Eliminate intercompany accounts. Since the entire stockholders' equity of Company S is owned by Company P, it must be completely eliminated against the investment account. The negative or credit balance of $90,000 which results from elimination represents the net overvaluation of Company S assets.

The following steps apportion the $140,000 excess of book value over cost attributable to long-lived assets:

1. Total assigned value:
   $400,000 book value less $140,000 excess book value = $260,000
2. Allocation of total assigned value:

	Market Value	Fraction of Market Value	×	Total Assigned Value	=	Allocated Assigned Value
Land	$ 75,000	3/12	×	$260,000	=	$ 65,000
Buildings	175,000	7/12	×	260,000	=	151,667
Equipment	50,000	2/12	×	260,000	=	43,333
Total	$300,000					$260,000

3. Apportionment of the difference between allocated assigned value and book value to each asset:

Cost Less Than Book Value
Subsidiary Company S
Balance Sheet
31, 19X1

Eliminations and Adjustments		Consolidated Balance Sheet	
Dr.	Cr.	Dr.	Cr.
		350,000	
		550,000	
2️⃣ 50,000		850,000	
		100,000	
		900,000	
	2️⃣ 140,000	910,000	
2️⃣ 90,000	1️⃣ 700,000		
		400,000	
		800,000	
		620,000	
		980,000	
		860,000	
1️⃣ 50,000			
1️⃣ 350,000			
1️⃣ 300,000			
840,000	840,000	3,660,000	3,660,000

2️⃣ Distribute the credit balance of the investment account to specific subsidiary assets according to the determination and distribution of excess schedule. In this example, the net decrease in asset value is distributed so as to increase Inventory by $50,000 and to decrease Equipment by $140,000.

	Allocated Assigned Value	Book Value	Increase (Decrease)
Land	$ 65,000	$100,000	$ (35,000)
Buildings	151,667	250,000	(98,333)
Equipment	43,333	50,000	(6,667)
Total	$260,000	$400,000	$(140,000)

As a result of these computations, the revised determination and distribution of excess schedule, on page 228 for Illustration V, is based on the presence of the three long-lived assets.

A second complication occurs when the excess of the book value over cost attributable to long-lived assets exceeds the total book value of the subsidiary's long-lived assets. In such a case, the subsidiary long-lived assets are reduced to zero. The remaining excess is carried on the consolidated balance sheet in the account Excess of Market Value of Subsidiary Current Assets over Cost, which is a deferred credit that is amortized to consolidated income over a period of 40 years or less.

Price paid for investment in Company S (including direct acquisition
  costs) $610,000

Less equity acquired:

Common stock, $5 par	$ 50,000	
Paid-in capital in excess of par	350,000	
Retained earnings	300,000	
Total stockholders' equity	$700,000	
Interest acquired	100%	700,000
Excess of book value over cost		$ 90,000
Add undervaluation of current assets:		
Inventory		**50,000**
Excess of book value attributable to long-lived assets:		
Land	$ 35,000	
Buildings	98,333	
Equipment	6,667	**$140,000**

Subsidiary with Previously Recorded Goodwill

It should be recalled from the discussion of direct asset acquisitions that goodwill on the books of an acquired firm is disregarded, unless it is confirmed by the price paid to acquire the firm. Similarly, previously recorded goodwill of a subsidiary is disregarded in the preparation of a consolidated balance sheet, unless it is confirmed by the price paid by the parent to acquire control.

The existence of previously recorded goodwill may require an extra step in the preparation of the determination and distribution of excess schedule. When the excess of cost over book value attributable to iden-tifiable long-lived assets is not sufficient to adjust these assets to their full market value, previously recorded goodwill must be added to the excess. By this procedure, the amount recorded as goodwill is available for distribution to identifiable long-lived assets. For a hypothetical case, the schedule might read as follows:

Price paid for investment $800,000

Less equity acquired:

Common stock, $5 par	$100,000	
Retained earnings	500,000	
Total stockholders' equity	$600,000	
Interest acquired	100%	600,000
Excess of cost over book value		$200,000
Less undervaluation of current assets:		
Inventory		**50,000**
Remaining excess..		$150,000
Add previously recorded goodwill		50,000
Excess attributable to long-lived assets:		
Buildings	$150,000	
Equipment	50,000	**$200,000**

If equipment and buildings require a total write-up to market value of only $160,000, previously recorded goodwill would be reduced only $10,000, and $40,000 of previously recorded goodwill would remain on the consolidated balance sheet.

Recording Plant Assets

Previous examples have used "net" values for depreciable assets to simplify explanations. In reality, the subsidiary will list original cost less accumulated depreciation. According to purchase theory, there is little justification for carrying to the consolidated balance sheet an amount for accumulated depreciation on a subsidiary asset existing prior to the purchase. To do so would imply that the asset was used by the new owner prior to the purchase date. Thus, the preferable practice is to have the consolidated amounts reflect the market value, with no accumulated depreciation.

To illustrate, assume that an acquired firm has a building on its books at an original cost of $600,000 less $400,000 accumulated depreciation. Assume further that the building has a $300,000 market value on the purchase date. The net write-up required is $100,000. The preferable procedure is to produce a net asset value of $300,000, as shown in the following partial work sheet:

	Trial Balance		Eliminations		Consolidated Balance Sheet
	Co. P	Co. S	Debit	Credit	
Building		600,000		**300,000**	300,000
Accumulated depreciation		(400,000)	**400,000**		—
Investment in Subsidiary				**100,000***	—

* The $100,000 is the balance remaining after elimination of the subsidiary equity accounts.

A less acceptable but common practice is not to eliminate all accumulated depreciation, but rather to adjust plant assets by:

1. Increasing net book values through a reduction of the accumulated depreciation, or
2. Decreasing net book values through a reduction of the original cost of the asset.

This practical approach tends to be used when the parent owns less than a 100% interest.

Adjustment of Assumed Liabilities

Liabilities assumed in a purchase may have a market value which is at variance with their recorded book values. This situation could exist as a result of failing to record accrued interest or as the result of a change in interest rates. If interest rates decrease and the market value of the debt increases, the price paid for the firm increases, and the excess of cost available for long-lived assets increases. On the other hand, if interest rates increase and the market value of the debt decreases, the excess available for long-lived assets decreases.

Liabilities are adjusted to reflect their market value regardless of the price paid in a business combination. For example, assume that Company P pays $500,000 for all the outstanding stock of Company S at a time when Company S has the following balance sheet:

Assets		Liabilities and Equity	
Current assets................	$250,000	Bonds payable	$200,000
Long-lived assets	350,000	Common stock	100,000
		Retained earnings	300,000
Total assets	$600,000	Total liabilities and equity......	$600,000

Assume also that current assets have a book value equal to market value; however, certain equipment is undervalued by $40,000. Assume further that, due to a decrease in the interest rates, the bonds payable have a market value of $208,000. A determination and distribution of excess schedule would be prepared as follows:

Price paid for investment		$500,000
Less interest acquired:		
Common stock..	$100,000	
Retained earnings	300,000	
Total	$400,000	
Ownership interest...	100%	400,000
Excess of cost over book value		$100,000
Add undervaluation of bonds payable...........................		**8,000**
Excess of cost available for long-lived assets:		$108,000
Equipment		**40,000**
Goodwill		**$ 68,000**

CONSOLIDATING THE PURCHASE OF A LESS-THAN-100% INTEREST

When control of a firm is achieved through the purchase of common stock and the conditions for the use of consolidated statements are met, consolidation procedures are applied. Control can be secured by purchasing less than 100% but usually over 50% of the subsidiary's voting stock. In those cases in which a less-than-100% interest is purchased, only a portion of the subsidiary stockholders' equity is eliminated against the parent's investment in subsidiary account. The remaining portion of the subsidiary's common stock interest belongs to the minority interest, represented by subsidiary stockholders other than the parent. From a consolidated viewpoint, these shareholders are a special group of owners of the consolidated firm. However, their ownership rights are limited to their interest in the subsidiary as a separate legal entity. For example, minority stockholders receive only those dividends which are paid by the subsidiary. In liquidation, the only assets of the subsidiary available to minority stockholders are the assets remaining after creditor and preferred stockholder claims have been satisfied.

To illustrate, assume that Company P purchased an 80% interest in Company S for $400,000 in cash. The entry to record the purchase would be:

Investment in Subsidiary S 400,000
    Cash   400,000

Immediately following the acquisition, the account balances of Companies P and S would appear as shown in the first two columns of Illustration VI on pages 232 and 233. Prior to preparing the work sheet eliminations and adjustments, the determination and distribution of excess schedule is prepared as shown below. The total subsidiary stockholders' equity is multiplied by the 80% ownership interest in calculating the interest acquired. Intercompany balances are then eliminated in the work sheet of Illustration VI. That portion of the subsidiary stockholders' equity not eliminated as intercompany is extended to the Minority Interest column of the work sheet. Remaining balances are then added to arrive at the amounts for the consolidated balance sheet.

Company P and Subsidiary Company S
Determination and Distribution of Excess Schedule
December 31, 19X1

Price paid for investment in Co. S		$400,000
Less interest acquired:		
Paid-in capital	$200,000	
Retained earnings	300,000	
Total stockholders' equity	$500,000	
Interest acquired	80%	400,000
Excess		-0-

The work sheet would be the source for the formal balance sheet on page 232.

The balance sheet illustrated summarizes the total minority interest and includes it in stockholders' equity. As an alternative, the paid-in and earned elements of the minority interest may be shown. It is not common, however, to specify composition of the ownership by minority groups when the parent controls several subsidiaries.

The published financial statements of many consolidated firms exclude the minority interest from the stockholders' equity section of the balance sheet. These statements list the minority interest under noncurrent liabilities, or place it between liabilities and equity. Though there is no theoretical support for these procedures, the inference that the minority interest is a liability is based on the concept that consolidated statements reflect the position of the parent firm's stockholders. From the viewpoint of these shareholders, the minority interest is a claim against consolidated assets and is thus a "quasi-liability."

	Trial Balance	
	Company P	**Company S**
Debits:		
Cash	200,000	
Accounts Receivable	300,000	200,000
Inventory	100,000	100,000
Investment in Subsidiary S	400,000	
Equipment	150,000	300,000
Total	1,150,000	600,000
Credits:		
Current Liabilities	150,000	100,000
Bonds Payable	300,000	
Paid-In Capital, Co. P	100,000	
Retained Earnings, Co. P	600,000	
Paid-In Capital, Co. S		200,000
Retained Earnings, Co. S		300,000
Minority Interest		
Total	1,150,000	600,000

1 Eliminate 80% of subsidiary equity against investment in subsidiary.

Company P and Subsidiary Company S
Consolidated Balance Sheet
December 31, 19X1

Assets

Current assets:

Cash	$200,000	
Accounts receivable	500,000	
Inventory	200,000	$ 900,000
Equipment		450,000
Total assets		$1,350,000

Liabilities

Current liabilities	$250,000	
Bonds payable	300,000	$ 550,000

Stockholders' Equity

Minority interest		100,000
Controlling interest:		
Paid-in capital	$100,000	
Retained earnings	600,000	700,000
Total liabilities and stockholders' equity		$1,350,000

Price Equals Book Value
Subsidiary Company S
Balance Sheet
31, 19X1

Eliminations and Adjustments		Minority Interest	Consolidated Balance Sheet	
Dr.	Cr.		Dr.	Cr.
			200,000	
			500,000	
			200,000	
	① 400,000			
			450,000	
				250,000
				300,000
				100,000
				600,000
① 160,000		40,000		
① 240,000		60,000		
		100,000		100,000
400,000	400,000		1,350,000	1,350,000

Investment Exceeds Market Value of Controlling Interest

The purchase of a subsidiary interest at a price in excess of the book value of the total assets, multiplied by the parent's ownership interest, suggests that subsidiary assets are undervalued. For consolidated reporting purposes, the carrying value of subsidiary assets must be adjusted to reflect the price paid by the parent to acquire an interest in them. The only change from the previous 100% acquisition illustrations is that assets are adjusted on the work sheet by multiplying the parent's ownership percentage by the difference between book and market values. For example, assume that a parent pays $40,000 above the book value for an 80% interest in a subsidiary's stockholders' equity. Further assume that the subsidiary has one long-lived asset to which the excess is attributable. Logic might dictate that if a $40,000 excess was paid for an 80% interest in the asset, a $50,000 ($40,000 ÷ .8) excess would be paid for a 100% interest. Even though the asset appears to be under-valued by $50,000, only the $40,000 increase is acknowledged. The work sheet write-up is limited to reflect the interest acquired. Recognition of the full increase would, in essence, require the recognition of a gain prior to its realization through a bargained exchange. Since an 80% interest in the asset is conveyed to the parent, only 80% of the difference between the asset's former book value and its current market value is acknowledged.

The purchase shown in Illustration III will be revised in order to apply what might be termed the "pro rata market value" adjustments. Assume that Company P purchases only an 80% interest in Company S and that all other facts, including the market value of the subsidiary's assets, remain the same. Since Company P was willing to issue 20,000 shares of its $50 market value ($10 par) stock for a 100% interest in Company S, assume that it now issues 16,000 shares (80% × 20,000 shares) for the 80% interest and pays $10,000 in direct acquisition costs. The entry to record the acquisition would be:

Investment in Subsidiary S (16,000 shares × $50 market value plus $10,000 acquisition costs)	810,000	
Common Stock (16,000 shares × $10 par)		160,000
Paid-In Capital in Excess of Par		640,000
Cash (for acquisition costs)		10,000

Again assume that the subsidiary's book values equal market values except for inventory and equipment, which have a market value of $350,000 and $550,000 respectively. If trial balances were prepared for each company immediately following the acquisition, balances would appear as shown in the first two columns of the work sheet in Illustration VII on pages 236 and 237. Work sheet adjustments for Illustration VII are made on the basis of the distribution included in the following determination and distribution of excess schedule.

Company P and Subsidiary Company S
Determination and Distribution of Excess Schedule
December 31, 19X1

Price paid for investment in Co. S		$810,000
Less interest acquired:		
Common stock, $5 par	$ 50,000	
Paid-in capital in excess of par	350,000	
Retained earnings	300,000	
Total stockholders' equity	$700,000	
Interest acquired	80%	560,000
Excess of cost over book value		$250,000
Less undervaluation of interest in current assets:		
Inventory ($50,000 total × 80%)		**40,000**
Excess attributable to interest in long-lived assets		$210,000
Less undervaluation of interest in identifiable long-lived assets:		
Equipment ($150,000 total × 80%)		**120,000**
Interest in goodwill		**$ 90,000**

Note the unique features of a schedule for a less-than-100% interest.

1. The excess of cost over book value is based on a comparison of the price paid and a pro rata share of subsidiary stockholders' equity.
2. Current assets, assumed liabilities, and long-lived assets are adjusted by multiplying the ownership interest acquired by the difference between their book and market values.

3. Only the goodwill attributable to the parent's equity is recognized.

The "pro rata market value" method of preparing consolidated work sheets is a feature of the "proprietary theory" of business combinations, which limits adjustments of subsidiary assets to the interest purchased by the controlling firm. Some accounting theorists advocate an alternative "entity theory" of business combinations, which holds that the entire entity over which control is achieved should be revalued. All subsidiary assets, including goodwill, would be restated at market value in preparing consolidated reports, regardless of the percentage of ownership by the parent.

To demonstrate the entity theory approach, return to the determination and distribution of excess schedule of Illustration VII. An entity theorist would argue that if $810,000 was paid for an 80% interest, the entire firm is worth $1,012,500 ($810,000 ÷ 80%). The determination and distribution of excess schedule would revalue the entire firm, not just the interest purchased, as follows:

Implied value of entire firm	$1,012,500
Less book value of subsidiary equity	700,000
Excess of market value over book value	$ 312,500
Less undervaluation of inventory	50,000
Excess attributable to long-lived assets	$ 262,500
Less undervaluation of equipment	150,000
Goodwill applicable to entire firm	$ 112,500

The following entry would replace Step (2) on the work sheet of Illustration VII:

Inventory	50,000	
Equipment (net)	150,000	
Goodwill	112,500	
Investment in Subsidiary S		250,000
Appraisal Capital—Minority Interest		62,500

Appraisal capital would be amortized to the minority retained earnings in future periods. The amortization would equal each period's extra depreciation or amortization charge caused by the write-up of assets applicable to the minority interest.

The entity theory, though supported by some theorists, is not generally accepted since it involves appraisal accounting. However, a compromise method, called the parent company theory, is sometimes used in practice and appears to be generally accepted. This method writes up tangible assets to 100% of market value regardless of the parent ownership percentage, and lets any remaining excess of cost flow to goodwill. Supporters of this method feel that it is more meaningful to the readers of consolidated statements if tangible assets are stated at their full market value regardless of the percentage interest purchased.

The following determination and distribution of excess schedule illustrates the compromise approach for Illustration VII:

	Trial Balance	
	Company P	Company S
Debits:		
Cash	200,000	150,000
Accounts Receivable	300,000	250,000
Inventory	500,000	300,000
Land	100,000	
Buildings (net)	900,000	
Equipment (net)	650,000	400,000
Investment in Subsidiary S	810,000	
Goodwill		
Total	3,460,000	1,100,000
Credits:		
Current Liabilities	300,000	100,000
Bonds Payable	500,000	300,000
Common Stock ($10 par), Co. P	660,000	
Paid-In Capital in Excess of Par, Co. P	1,140,000	
Retained Earnings, Co. P	860,000	
Common Stock ($5 par), Co. S		50,000
Paid-In Capital in Excess of Par, Co. S		350,000
Retained Earnings, Co. S		300,000
Minority Interest		
Total	3,460,000	1,100,000

1 Eliminate 80% of subsidiary equity against investment account.

Price paid for investment in Co. S	$810,000
Less book value of interest acquired	560,000
Excess of cost over book value	$250,000
Less undervaluation of inventory	50,000
Excess attributable to long-lived assets	$200,000
Less undervaluation of equipment	150,000
Remaining excess to goodwill	$ 50,000

The distribution of excess contained in Step (2) of Illustration VII would be replaced by the following entry:

Inventory	50,000	
Equipment (net)	150,000	
Goodwill	50,000	
Investment in Subsidiary S		250,000

Price Exceeds Market Value
Subsidiary Company S
Balance Sheet
31, 19X1

Eliminations and Adjustments		Minority Interest.	Consolidated Balance Sheet	
Dr.	Cr.		Dr.	Cr.
			350,000	
			550,000	
2 40,000			840,000	
			100,000	
			900,000	
2 120,000			1,170,000	
	1 560,000			
	2 250,000			
2 90,000			90,000	
				400,000
				800,000
				660,000
				1,140,000
				860,000
1 40,000		10,000		
1 280,000		70,000		
1 240,000		60,000		
		140,000		140,000
810,000	810,000		4,000,000	4,000,000

2 Distribute excess of cost over book value of subsidiary equity according to the determination and distribution of excess schedule.

This text will use the pro rata market value approach derived from the proprietary theory, since the authors consider it to be consistent with current consolidation theory.

Investment Falls Between Market and Recorded Book Values of Controlling Interest in Subsidiary Assets

A bargain purchase may occur when a fraction of a subsidiary's stock is purchased. For a bargain purchase to occur, the parent's ownership percentage times the total market value of the subsidiary assets must exceed the cost of the investment.

The following determination and distribution of excess schedule uses the same facts as those used in the schedule of Illustration IV, except that an 80% interest is presented.

Price paid for 80% interest in Subsidiary S (including $10,000 direct acquisition costs)		$650,000
Less interest acquired:		
Common stock, $5 par	$ 50,000	
Paid-in capital in excess of par	350,000	
Retained earnings	300,000	
Total stockholders' equity	$700,000	
Interest acquired	80%	560,000
Excess of cost over book value		$ 90,000
Less undervaluation of current assets:		
Inventory (80% × $50,000).................................		**40,000**
Excess attributable to long-lived assets:		
Equipment		**$ 50,000**

Note that current assets, as well as long-term investments in marketable securities and all liabilities, are increased by the amount of their undervaluation multiplied by the parent ownership percentage, regardless of the price paid for the interest.

Goodwill recorded by the subsidiary should be reassigned to long-lived assets. The maximum amount of goodwill available for reassignment is, however, the previously recorded goodwill multiplied by the parent's ownership interest.

In those cases where several long-lived assets exist, the excess of cost attributable to those assets should be apportioned according to the procedure described on page 225. The market values of the separate long-lived assets should still be used as the weights for distributing the total assigned value of the long-lived assets. The difference between the assigned and book values of each long-lived asset should be entered in the determination and distribution of excess schedule. This difference is *not* multiplied by the controlling ownership percentage, since the assignable value includes only the excess applicable to the controlling interest.

Investment Is Less Than Book Value of Controlling Interest in Subsidiary Assets

An investment in a subsidiary at a price below the parent ownership percentage times the subsidiary stockholders' equity necessitates a write-down of total assets to remove the overvaluation. However, as is true with write-ups, only the parent ownership percentage times the total value difference is acknowledged. Also, the values of the subsidiary's current assets, long-term investments in marketable securities, and liabilities must always be adjusted by the full amount of the ownership percentage times the difference between book and market values, regardless of the price paid.

To illustrate the consolidation procedures applicable to acquisitions producing an excess of book value over cost, the determination and distribution of excess schedule of Illustration V is recast as follows to reflect an 80% acquisition.

Price paid for 80% interest in Subsidiary S (including $10,000 direct acquisition costs)		$490,000
Less equity acquired:		
Common stock, $5 par	$ 50,000	
Paid-in capital in excess of par	350,000	
Retained earnings	300,000	
Total stockholders' equity	$700,000	
Interest acquired	80%	560,000
Excess of book value over cost		$ 70,000
Add undervaluation of interest in current assets:		
Inventory (80% × $50,000)...............................		**40,000**
Excess of book value over cost attributable to interest in long-lived assets..		**$110,000**

If several long-lived assets exist, the apportionment procedure described on page 225 would be applied. Also, a special procedure is required if previously recorded goodwill appears on the subsidiary's books. As in the case of a 100% acquisition, previously recorded goodwill may have to be reassigned to identifiable long-lived assets on the determination and distribution of excess schedule. However, only a portion equal to the ownership percentage may be made available for reassignment; the minority portion of goodwill is not available for reassignment.

SUBSIDIARY INVESTMENT RECORDED AS A POOLING OF INTERESTS

When the pooling criteria are met, as discussed in Chapter 5, the acquisition of a controlling interest in the common stock of another firm is recorded as a pooling of interests. Consolidated financial statements will also be required when the operations of the pooled firms are integrated.

Consolidating a 100% Interest Under Pooling

The recording and consolidations of poolings achieved through stock acquisition are better understood by reviewing the recording of a pooling achieved through asset acquisition. Assume that combining Company C had the following abbreviated balance sheet just prior to pooling with Company I:

Company C
Balance Sheet
December 31, 19X1

Current assets	$10,000	Liabilities		$10,000
Property, plant, and equipment (net)	30,000	Stockholders' equity:		
		Common stock, $10 par	$10,000	
		Retained earnings	20,000	30,000
Total assets...........................	$40,000	Total liabilities and equity		$40,000

Assume also that Company I is willing to issue 3,000 shares of its stock for the $30,000 net assets of Company C. Company I stock has a par value of $2 and a market value of $15 per share. Since pooling principles ignore market values and combine book balances, the entry to record the pooling on Company I's books would be:

Current Assets	10,000	
Property, Plant, and Equipment	30,000	
Liabilities		10,000
Common Stock ($2 per share × 3,000 shares)		6,000
Paid-In Capital in Excess of Par		4,000
Retained Earnings		20,000

The original amount of Company C's total paid-in capital is preserved, although it is redistributed between the par value and paid-in capital in excess of par of Company I. The full amount of Company C's retained earnings is transferred to Company I, since a reduction was not necessary to meet a par or stated value requirement of the issuer.

In this example, in which a pooling through asset acquisition is portrayed, the combiner corporation was dissolved and its accounts were merged with those of the issuer. Assume now that Company I exchanges its shares for Company C's shares by dealing with stockholders, and all other pooling criteria are met. Assume further that Company I elects not to dissolve Company C, but to let Company C continue as a separate legal entity with its own accounting records. In effect, a pooling through stock acquisition occurs. Since the assets and liabilities of Company C remain on Company C's books, Company I can record only an investment in Company C. This investment must, however, be recorded at the *book value* of the underlying net assets to comply with pooling principles. The market value of the securities exchanged is ignored. Company I must normally add to its paid-in capital an amount equal to the paid-in capital of Company C, and it must acknowledge its equity in Company C's retained earnings if it is necessary to meet a par or stated value requirement and Company I has no additional paid-in capital available for redistribution. From these principles, the following entry is derived:

Investment in Subsidiary C	30,000	
Common Stock ($2 per share × 3,000 shares)		6,000
Paid-In Capital in Excess of Par		4,000
Retained Earnings		20,000

This entry would lead to the separate trial balances for Companies I and C shown in the first two columns of Illustration VIII on pages 242 and 243, which proceeds to consolidate the balance sheets of the parent and subsidiary as of the date of the pooling. Prior to adding account balances, intercompany balances are eliminated. When properly recorded, the investment in subsidiary account will always be eliminated against the subsidiary's stockholders' equity, with no excess of any type remaining after the elimination. This procedure must be followed, since the recorded value of the investment account equals the parent's ownership percentage (100% in this example) times the subsidiary's stockholders' equity. As a result of this equality, no determination and distribution of excess schedule is needed when pooling.

Consolidating a Less-Than-100% Interest Under Pooling

Often the issuer will not acquire 100% of the combiner's stock, although it must acquire at least 90% to pool. In such a case, the issuer records only the pro rata book value acquired. If Company I of the previous example exchanges only 2,700 shares ($2 par) for 90% of Company C's shares, the entry to record the investment would be:

Investment in Subsidiary C	27,000	
Common Stock ($2 per share × 2,700 shares)		5,400
Paid-In Capital in Excess of Par		3,600
Retained Earnings		18,000

Subsequent work sheet eliminations would cancel Investment in Subsidiary against 90% of Company C's equities, with a 10% minority interest remaining. Procedures for displaying the minority interest parallel those previously discussed.

If the parent firm later acquires all or part of the minority interest, the later acquisition is considered a purchase, since it could not possibly meet the pooling criteria. Such a situation would require a consolidated work sheet in which both pooling and purchase procedures were used.

Improperly Recorded Investment Account

Ordinarily, when a corporation issues stock, it must increase its paid-in capital by the entire amount of consideration received. When it issues stock to acquire noncash assets, including shares of another firm's stock, the consideration received is the market value of the assets received or the shares given, whichever is more readily determinable. The only exception to these principles is an investment in a subsidiary to effect a pooling. In this case, only the net book value of the assets received is recorded, as was previously illustrated. It is common to find a firm which ignores this exception, however. Such a firm will increase both its investment and paid-in capital accounts by an amount equal to the market value of the shares given or received. When this mistake is found, the issuer firm's accounts should be corrected prior to preparing the consolidated work sheet.[5]

To illustrate, assume that Company I made the following incorrect investment entry when it acquired 90% of the stock of Company C, although pooling criteria were met:

---

[5] Some states require the investment to be recorded at market value. Where this is true, the "correction" entries would be made on the work sheet as part of the eliminations.

	Trial Balance	
	Company I	Company C
Debits:		
Current Assets	20,000	10,000
Property, Plant, and Equipment (net)	70,000	30,000
Investment in Subsidiary C	30,000	
Total	120,000	40,000
Credits:		
Liabilities	15,000	10,000
Common Stock, Co. I	56,000	
Paid-In Capital in Excess of Par, Co. I	4,000	
Retained Earnings, Co. I	45,000	
Common Stock, Co. C		10,000
Retained Earnings, Co. C		20,000
Total	120,000	40,000

1 Eliminate subsidiary investment against subsidiary equity.

Investment in Subsidiary C ($15 per share market value × 2,700 shares)	40,500	
Common Stock ($2 per share × 2,700 shares)		5,400
Paid-In Capital in Excess of Par		35,100

Prior to preparing the consolidated work sheet, the issuer firm's books would be corrected by reversing the original incorrect entry and recording the investment as a pooling. The following entries would be made:

Common Stock ($2 per share × 2,700 shares)	5,400	
Paid-In Capital in Excess of Par	35,100	
Investment in Subsidiary C		40,500
Investment in Subsidiary C (90% of company equity)	27,000	
Common Stock ($2 per share × 2,700 shares)		5,400
Paid-In Capital in Excess of Par ($9,000 − $5,400)		3,600
Retained Earnings (90% × $20,000)		18,000

When these corrections have been made, the proper amounts have been recorded by the issuer firm, and subsequent work sheet eliminations would be identical to those for a less-than-100% interest pooling.

Pooling of Interests
Subsidiary Company C
Balance Sheet
31, 19X1

Eliminations		Consolidated Balance Sheet	
Dr.	Cr.	Dr.	Cr.
		30,000	
		100,000	
	1 30,000		
		25,000	
		56,000	
		4,000	
		45,000	
1 10,000			
1 20,000			
30,000	30,000	130,000	130,000

QUESTIONS

1. What two conditions must be met before the consolidation of two firms is permitted? Is a greater-than-50% ownership interest required?
2. A company may gain control over the assets of another firm by acquiring the assets of the firm or by purchasing a controlling interest in stock. Under which method is the acquired firm dissolved? Under which method is the acquired firm preserved as a separate legal and accounting entity?
3. What is the purpose of the consolidation process, and why does it start anew each year?
4. Describe the two ways a stock acquisition may be recorded. At what value is the investment in the stock of the subsidiary recorded under each method?
5. What are the functions of the determination and distribution of excess schedule? Is it used for both a pooling and a purchase?
6. Under the purchase method, several accounts are always adjusted to their market value in consolidating, regardless of the price paid for the subsidiary interest. What are these accounts?
7. What is a "bargain purchase," and what complications does it present to the consolidation process?
8. In a bargain purchase, describe how the value assigned to long-lived assets is determined when more than one long-lived asset exists.

9. Acquisition Company purchased an 80% ownership interest in Controlled Company at a price in excess of market value. A long-lived asset has a book value of $37,500 and a market value of $55,000. For consolidated reporting purposes, at what value is the asset recorded under (a) the proprietary theory of business combinations; (b) the entity theory of business combinations; (c) the parent company theory (compromise method) of business combinations?

10. Under the pooling method, the "Investment in the Stock of Subsidiary" account should be eliminated against the parent's share of the subsidiary's stockholders' equity with no excess. If this result does not occur, what is the likely cause and how is it corrected?

EXERCISES

Exercise 1.   The following balance sheets of the Abbot and Burns Companies were prepared just prior to the purchase of a 100% interest in Burns by Abbot.

Assets	Abbot	Burns	Liabilities and Equity	Abbot	Burns
Cash	$450,000	$ 50,000	Current liabilities	$100,000	$100,000
Accounts receivable	100,000	80,000	Bonds payable	300,000	100,000
Inventory	50,000	100,000	Common stock,		
Property, plant, and			$100 par	200,000	150,000
equipment (net)	200,000	300,000	Retained earnings	200,000	180,000
			Total liabilities and		
Total assets.............	$800,000	$530,000	equity	$800,000	$530,000

Abbot paid $300,000 for a 100% interest in the net assets of Burns. The book values of Burns' assets and liabilities equal market values.
(1) Assuming that the net assets are purchased directly from the Burns Company:
  (a) prepare the entry Abbot would make to record the purchase;
  (b) prepare a balance sheet for the Abbot Company immediately following the purchase.
(2) Assuming that 100% of the outstanding stock of the Burns Company is purchased from the former stockholders for a total of $300,000:
  (a) prepare the entry Abbot would make to record the purchase;
  (b) state how the investment would appear on Abbot's unconsolidated balance sheet prepared immediately subsequent to the purchase;
  (c) indicate how the consolidated balance sheet would appear.

Exercise 2.   Pare Company purchased 100% of the outstanding stock of the Sale Corporation for $300,000 cash on January 1, 19X1. Just prior to the purchase, the Sale Corporation prepared the following balance sheet:

Assets			Liabilities and Equity		
Current assets:			Current liabilities.....................		$ 80,000
Cash	$50,000		Common stock, $5 par	$100,000	
Accounts receivable	60,000		Retained earnings	190,000	290,000
Inventory...............	90,000	$200,000			
Property, plant, and equip-					
ment (net)		170,000			
Total assets........................		$370,000	Total liabilities and equity		$370,000

Pare feels that market values equal book values except for the inventory, which is worth $110,000, and the equipment, which is appraised at $250,000.
(1) Record the acquisition on the books of the Pare Company.
(2) Prepare a determination and distribution of excess schedule.

Exercise 3. The Beebo Company purchased all of the outstanding stock of the Doni Company for $100,000 and paid $2,000 for direct acquisition costs. Just prior to the investment, the two firms had the following balance sheets:

Assets	Beebo	Doni	Liabilities and Equity	Beebo	Doni
Current assets..........	$120,000	$ 40,000	Current liabilities	$ 70,000	$ 35,000
Property, plant, and			Bonds payable..........	60,000	—
equipment (net)	180,000	80,000	Common stock, $10 par .	70,000	30,000
			Retained earnings	100,000	55,000
			Total liabilities and		
Total assets	$300,000	$120,000	equity	$300,000	$120,000

The Beebo Company feels that the Doni current assets and liabilities are correctly valued, but that the property, plant, and equipment has a market value of $90,000.
(1) Prepare the entry to record the purchase.
(2) Prepare a determination and distribution of excess schedule.
(3) Prepare a consolidated balance sheet.

Exercise 4. The Black Company is contemplating the purchase of 8,000 shares of the outstanding stock of the Wight Company, which has the following balance sheet just prior to acquisition:

Assets		Liabilities and Equity	
Cash	$ 20,000	Current liabilities.....................	$250,000
Inventory	280,000	Common stock, $5 par	50,000
Property, plant, and equipment (net) ..	400,000	Paid-in capital in excess of par........	130,000
Goodwill	100,000	Retained earnings	370,000
Total assets.......................	$800,000	Total liabilities and equity	$800,000

The Black Company believes that the inventory has a market value of $400,000, and that the property, plant, and equipment is worth $500,000. For each of the following alternative purchase prices, prepare a determination and distribution of excess schedule and the investment elimination entries that would be made on a work sheet subsequent to the purchase.
(1) The price paid per share acquired was $90.
(2) The price paid per share acquired was $74.
(3) The price paid per share acquired was $42.

Exercise 5. The Vette Company purchased 80% of the common stock of the Bird Company for $200,000 when Bird had the following balance sheet:

Assets		Liabilities and Equity	
Cash	$ 10,000	Liabilities	$100,000
Inventory	40,000	Common stock	50,000
Equipment (net)............	200,000	Retained earnings	100,000
Total assets................	$250,000	Total liabilities and equity ...	$250,000

The inventory has a market value of $40,000, and the equipment has a market value of $250,000. Prepare determination and distribution of excess schedules reflecting each of the following approaches:

(1) The pro rata market value approach of the proprietary theory.
(2) The entity theory.
(3) The parent company (compromise) approach.

Exercise 6. The Tree Company acquired 18,000 of the total 20,000 shares of the Schrub Company for $240,000. Immediately prior to the purchase, the balance sheets of the two firms were as follows:

Assets	Tree	Schrub	Liabilities and Equity	Tree	Schrub
Cash	$ 600,000	$100,000	Current liabilities	$ 120,000	$200,000
Inventory	250,000	250,000	Common stock	400,000	200,000
Property, plant, and			Paid-in capital in		
equipment (net)	450,000	300,000	excess of par	200,000	150,000
			Retained earnings	580,000	100,000
Total assets	$1,300,000	$650,000	Total liabilities and equity	$1,300,000	$650,000

The Tree Company feels that the inventory of the Schrub Company is worth $300,000, and that the property, plant, and equipment is worth $200,000. Based on these values:
(1) Record the investment.
(2) Prepare a determination and distribution of excess schedule.
(3) Prepare a consolidated balance sheet immediately subsequent to the purchase.

Exercise 7. The balance sheet for the Connor Corporation was as follows on January 1, 19X3.

Assets			Liabilities and Equity		
Current assets:			Current liabilities		$ 90,000
Cash	$ 60,000		Long-term liabilites:		
Accounts receivable	280,000		Bonds payable	$300,000	
Prepaid expenses	20,000	$ 360,000	Deferred taxes	50,000	350,000
Property, plant, and			Stockholders' equity:		
equipment:			Common stock, $10		
Land	$600,000		par	$300,000	
Building (net)	150,000	750,000	Retained earnings	370,000	670,000
Total assets		$1,110,000	Total liabilities and equity		$1,110,000

On January 1, 19X3, Belden Company purchased 27,000 shares of Connor common stock on the open market for $750,000. The Belden Company received the following appraisals supplementary to Connor's balance sheet:

Accounts receivable	$260,000
Land	650,000
Bonds payable	280,000
Deferred taxes	40,000

(1) Record the investment.
(2) Prepare a determination and distribution of excess schedule.

Exercise 8. The Afram and Carlos Companies are planning to combine their operations through a pooling of interests. The Afram Company will exchange one share of its common stock for each two shares of Carlos Company common stock. All of the Carlos shares will be exchanged by their owners for Afram shares. Immediately prior to the pooling of interests, the two firms have the following balance sheets:

Assets	Afram	Carlos	Liabilities and Equity	Afram	Carlos
Current assets	$250,000	$100,000	Liabilities	$120,000	$ 80,000
Property, plant, and			Common stock, $10 par ..	200,000	—
equipment (net)........	450,000	160,000	Common stock, $1		
Goodwill	—	40,000	stated value	—	10,000
			Additional paid-in capital .	50,000	90,000
			Retained earnings	330,000	120,000
Total assets..............	$700,000	$300,000	Total liabilities and equity	$700,000	$300,000

(1) Prepare the entry to record the investment as a pooling of interests.
(2) Prepare a consolidated balance sheet immediately subsequent to the investment.

Exercise 9. The Varsity and Top Companies had the following balance sheets immediately prior to a pooling of interests:

Assets	Varsity	Top	Liabilities and Equity	Varsity	Top
Current assets	$ 500,000	$ 300,000	Liabilities	$ 300,000	$ 500,000
Property, plant, and			Common stock, $2 par .	400,000	—
equipment (net)	1,200,000	800,000	Common stock, $1 par .	—	150,000
			Paid-in capital in		
			excess of par	150,000	50,000
			Retained earnings......	850,000	400,000
			Total liabilities and		
Total assets	$1,700,000	$1,100,000	equity	$1,700,000	$1,100,000

Varsity will exchange its stock for all of the outstanding stock of the Top Company. On Varsity's books, record the investment for the following situations:
(1) Varsity issues 80,000 shares. (3) Varsity issues 150,000 shares.
(2) Varsity issues 100,000 shares. (4) Varsity issues 250,000 shares.

Exercise 10. The Desmond and Ruby Companies are the respective issuer and combiner companies in a pooling of interests. Desmond acquired 90% of the Ruby shares by exchanging Desmond shares in a 2-to-1 ratio. The two firms had the following balance sheets just prior to the pooling:

Assets	Desmond	Ruby	Liabilities and Equity	Desmond	Ruby
Current assets	$ 400,000	$300,000	Liabilities	$ 200,000	$100,000
Property, plant, and			Common stock, $10 par ..	300,000	—
equipment (net)........	900,000	500,000	Common stock, $5 par ...	—	150,000
			Paid-in capital in		
			excess of par	300,000	—
			Retained earnings	500,000	550,000
Total assets..............	$1,300,000	$800,000	Total liabilities and equity	$1,300,000	$800,000

(1) Record the investment on the books of the Desmond Company.
(2) Prepare a consolidated balance sheet immediately subsequent to the pooling.

Exercise 11. The Jax Company will issue shares of $5 par stock for all of the outstanding stock of the Thomas Company. Jax Company common stock has a current market value of $20 per share. The Thomas Company prepared the following balance sheet just prior to the acquisition:

Assets		Liabilities and Equity	
Current assets.........................	$ 80,000	Liabilities	$100,000
Property, plant, and equipment (net) ...	220,000	Common stock, $2 par	20,000
		Paid-in capital in excess of par	80,000
		Retained earnings	100,000
Total assets	$300,000	Total liabilities and equity	$300,000

The Jax Company estimated the value of the current assets to be $100,000, and the value of the property, plant, and equipment to be $400,000. Jax agreed that the liabilities were correctly stated. Jax issued sufficient shares of stock so that the market value of the stock equaled the market value of Thomas' net assets.

(1) Calculate the stock exchange ratio.
(2) Assuming that the criteria for a pooling of interests are met, record the investment in the stock of the Thomas Company.
(3) Assuming that the criteria for a pooling of interests are not met, record the investment in the stock of the Thomas Company.

Exercise 12. Wainberg Industries acquired 90% of the outstanding stock of Mitertec Corporation by exchanging 20,000 shares of $40 market value ($5 stated value) stock directly with Mitertec's stockholders on October 1, 19X6. On the exchange date, Mitertec had the following stockholders' equity:

Common stock, $2 par...	$100,000
Paid-in capital in excess of par......................................	150,000
Retained earnings	250,000
Total equity	$500,000

Wainberg had the following balance sheet on December 31, 19X6:

Assets		Liabilities and Equity		
Current assets......................	$ 836,000	Liabilities		$ 900,000
Investment in Mitertec Corporation ..	800,000	Common stock, $5		
Property, plant, and equipment (net) .	2,150,000	stated value	$1,000,000	
		Additional paid-in		
		capital	700,000	
		Retained earnings	1,186,000	2,886,000
		Total liabilities and		
Total assets	$3,786,000	equity		$3,786,000

No entries have been made in the investment account since the inception of the pooling.

Prepare the necessary journal entry to correctly portray the above combination as a pooling of interests.

Exercise 13. On January 1, 19X6, Trio Corporation exchanged 6,600 shares of its $5 par ($12 market value) common stock for 90% of the outstanding shares of the Kling Corporation in a legitimate pooling of interests. Just prior to the combination, the Kling Corporation had the following balance sheet:

Assets		Liabilities and Equity		
Current assets	$ 40,000	Current liabilities		$ 50,000
Property, plant, and equipment (net) ..	360,000	Common stock, $1 par	$ 44,000	
Patents............................	20,000	Paid-in capital in excess of		
		par.....................	66,000	
		Retained earnings	260,000	370,000
Total assets........................	$420,000	Total liabilities and equity		$420,000

On December 31, 19X6, the Trio Corporation purchased 3,000 shares of the Kling Corporation common stock for $11 per share. By December 31, Kling's income for 19X6 was $200,000.

(1) Prepare the journal entry to record the investment acquired on January 1, 19X6, as a pooling of interests.
(2) Prepare the journal entry to record the acquisition of the 3,000 additional shares on December 31, 19X6.

PROBLEMS

Present value tables are on pages 942-943.

Problem 6-1. Rice Company and Quarry Company had the following balance sheets on June 30, 19X1:

Assets	Rice	Quarry
Current assets	$210,000	$ 80,000
Land	100,000	40,000
Building (net)...	240,000	90,000
Equipment (net)	390,000	110,000
Goodwill..	—	30,000
Total assets	$940,000	$350,000

Liabilities and Equity		
Current liabilities	$160,000	$ 40,000
Common stock, $5 par	400,000	200,000
Retained earnings	380,000	110,000
Total liabilities and equity	$940,000	$350,000

On June 30, 19X1, Rice Company exchanged 300, $1,000 bonds for 80% of the outstanding stock of the Quarry Company. On July 1, 19X1, some of the former stockholders of Quarry Company sold the bonds received at the quoted price of 97. Rice Company hired an independent appraiser, who found that the land is undervalued by $50,000 and the equipment is undervalued by $20,000.

Required:

(1) Record the investment in Quarry Company common stock.
(2) Prepare a determination and distribution of excess schedule.
(3) Prepare a consolidated balance sheet for July 1, 19X1, immediately subsequent to the acquisition.

Problem 6-2. Balance sheets for the Algo, Balko, and Cram Companies on December 31, 19X1, are as follows:

	Algo	Balko	Cram
Cash	$ 200,000	$100,000	$ 50,000
Inventory...............................	300,000	150,000	100,000
Property, plant, and equipment (net) ...	500,000	200,000	150,000
Goodwill................................	100,000	50,000	25,000
Total assets	$1,100,000	$500,000	$325,000
Liabilities	$ 300,000	$100,000	$150,000
Common stock, $10 par	200,000	100,000	50,000
Paid-in capital in excess of par	400,000	50,000	75,000
Retained earnings	200,000	250,000	50,000
Total liabilities and equity	$1,100,000	$500,000	$325,000

On this date, Algo purchased all of the common stock of the Balko Company by issuing 500, 8% bonds with a face value of $1,000 each (8% was the prevailing rate for similar bonds on the day of the sale). Algo also exchanged 5,000 shares of its common stock, with a market value of $30 each, for 80% of the common stock of the Cram Company.

Required:

Prepare a determination and distribution of excess schedule and a consolidated balance sheet for December 31, 19X1, under each of the following assumptions:

(1) Balko's inventory has a market value of $175,000, and the property, plant, and equipment is appraised at $250,000. Cram's inventory is understated by $50,000.

(2) Balko's inventory is understated by $100,000, and the market value of the property, plant, and equipment is $500,000. Cram's liabilities are overstated by $10,000. Cram's inventory is grossly understated; its fair market value is $250,000.

Problem 6-3. Balance sheets for the Delta and Essex Companies on December 31, 19X1, are as follows:

Assets	Delta	Essex
Cash	$ 800,000	$100,000
Inventory	600,000	300,000
Property, plant, and equipment (net)	1,200,000	400,000
Total assets..............................	$2,600,000	$800,000

Liabilities and Equity	Delta	Essex
Liabilities	$ 500,000	$100,000
Capital stock, $10 par	200,000	50,000
Paid-in capital in excess of par...........	800,000	350,000
Retained earnings	1,100,000	300,000
Total liabilities and equity	$2,600,000	$800,000

On this date, Delta purchased 80% of the Essex Company common stock.

Required:

Record the investment, prepare a determination and distribution of excess schedule when needed, and prepare a consolidated balance sheet for December 31, 19X1, under each of the following assumptions:

(1) Delta issues 10,000 shares of common stock in exchange for 4,000 Essex shares. The market values of Delta and Essex stock are not known since

neither are traded publicly. Reliable market values are available for Essex's assets: the inventory and property, plant, and equipment are valued at $400,000 and $500,000 respectively. Goodwill does not appear to exist.

(2) Delta issues 10,000 shares of its common stock with a market value of $60 each for 4,000 Essex shares. The Essex assets and liabilities are fairly stated except for property, plant, and equipment, which is undervalued by $100,000.

(3) Delta pays $360,000 cash for the Essex stock. Appraisals indicate that the Essex inventory is worth $400,000 and the property, plant, and equipment is worth approximately $100,000 due to its specialized nature.

Problem 6-4. The Spruce Company has the following balance sheet on December 31, 19X1:

Assets		Liabilities and Equity	
Cash	$ 50,000	Current liabilities	$100,000
Accounts receivable	60,000	Deferred rental income.................	50,000
Inventory.............................	100,000	Bonds payable, 6%	250,000
Property, plant, and equipment (net) ...	300,000	Common stock, $10 par	100,000
Long-term investment in marketable		Paid-in capital in excess of par	200,000
securities	150,000	Retained earnings	100,000
Patents	40,000		
Goodwill.............................	100,000		
Total assets	$800,000	Total liabilities and equity	$800,000

On this date, the Pine Company purchased an 80% interest in the Spruce Company. The Pine Company paid cash for the shares of the Spruce Company. The following market values were secured for the assets and liabilities of the Spruce Company:

Accounts receivable, $50,000 due to substantial number of doubtful accounts.
Inventory, $200,000 due to previous use of lifo.
Property, plant, and equipment, $500,000.
Investment in marketable securities, $170,000.
Patents, $10,000.
Bonds payable have a present value of $240,000 due to the market interest rate having increased.

Required:

Record the investment and prepare a determination and distribution of excess schedule under each of the following assumptions:
(1) The price paid was $600,000.
(2) The price paid was $400,000.

Problem 6-5. Davis Corporation had the following balance sheet on January 1, 19X3, the date that the Spike Company purchased a controlling interest:

Assets		Liabilities and Equity		
Current assets	$ 220,000	Current liabilities		$ 200,000
Land	300,000	Bonds payable		400,000
Buildings (net)	150,000	Common stock, $2 par	$100,000	
Equipment (net)	400,000	Paid-in capital in excess of		
Goodwill	40,000	par......................	50,000	
		Retained earnings	360,000	510,000
Total assets........................	$1,110,000	Total liabilities and equity		$1,110,000

Assets and liabilities which had market values different from cost are as follows:

	Market Value
Current assets	$250,000
Land	490,000
Buildings	160,000
Equipment	350,000
Bonds payable	420,000

Spike purchased 45,000 shares of Davis common stock for $495,000.

Required:

(1) Record the investment.
(2) Prepare a determination and distribution of excess schedule.
(3) Prepare the elimination entries that would be made on the consolidated work sheet.

Problem 6-6. The balance sheets of Manor and Frome Companies are as follows on December 31, 19X1:

Assets	Manor	Frome
Current assets	$ 300,000	$250,000
Property, plant, and equipment	1,000,000	500,000
Accumulated depreciation	(300,000)	(200,000)
Total assets	$1,000,000	$550,000

Liabilities and Equity		
Liabilities	$ 200,000	$150,000
Common stock, $10 par	300,000	—
Common stock, $1 par	—	50,000
Paid-in capital in excess of par	200,000	250,000
Retained earnings	300,000	100,000
Total liabilities and equity	$1,000,000	$550,000

On this date, the Manor Company exchanged one share of newly issued common stock for every two shares of Frome Company common stock. Manor acquired all of the Frome stock outstanding. The market value of a share of Manor common stock is $25. Frome Company assets are stated at values approximating market values, except for the property, plant, and equipment, which has a market value of $400,000.

Required:

(1) Assume that the acquisition does not meet the pooling criteria:
  (a) record the investment in Frome Company stock;
  (b) prepare a determination and distribution of excess schedule;
  (c) prepare a consolidated balance sheet for December 31, 19X1, immediately subsequent to the investment.
(2) Assume that the acquisition does meet the pooling criteria:
  (a) record the investment in Frome Company common stock;
  (b) prepare a consolidated balance sheet for December 31, 19X1, immediately subsequent to the investment.

Problem 6-7. On December 31, 19X1, the Mac Company purchased on the open market 60% of the outstanding shares of the Van Company common stock and

75% of the outstanding shares of the Dorn Company common stock. The following unconsolidated balance sheets were prepared for the companies immediately subsequent to the purchase:

	Mac	Van	Dorn
Cash	$ 50,000	$ 30,000	$ 60,000
Inventory	300,000	170,000	200,000
Property, plant, and equipment (net)	500,000	200,000	340,000
Investment in Van Company	300,000	—	—
Investment in Dorn Company	350,000	—	—
Total assets	$1,500,000	$400,000	$600,000
Current liabilities	$ 150,000	$ 50,000	$ 80,000
Common stock, $10 par	500,000	—	—
Common stock, $5 par	—	100,000	—
Common stock, $1 par	—	—	10,000
Paid-in capital in excess of par	700,000	80,000	290,000
Retained earnings	150,000	170,000	220,000
Total liabilities and equity	$1,500,000	$400,000	$600,000

Mac Company feels that the inventory and property, plant, and equipment accounts of the subsidiaries do not reflect market values. Mac Company has secured the following market values:

	Van	Dorn
Inventory	$220,000	$300,000
Property, plant, and equipment	260,000	400,000

Required:

(1) Prepare a determination and distribution of excess schedule for each investment.
(2) Prepare a work sheet for a consolidated balance sheet for December 31, 19X1.
(3) Prepare the formal consolidated balance sheet for December 31, 19X1.

Problem 6-8. Quail Corporation acquired 80% of the outstanding shares of Plum Corporation on December 31, 1982, the last day of the fiscal year for both firms. Quail paid $11,000 in direct acquisition costs to consummate the purchase. The following balance sheets were prepared for the parent and subsidiary immediately subsequent to the investment:

	Quail	Plum
Cash	$ 190,000	$ 90,000
Accounts receivable	340,000	120,000
Inventory	520,000	—
Land	1,200,000	110,000
Building (net)	700,000	230,000
Equipment (net)..	1,500,000	400,000
Investment in Plum	311,000	—
Total assets	$4,761,000	$950,000
Current liabilities..	$ 500,000	$ 85,000
Bonds payable, 6%, due December 31, 1987	—	400,000
Discount on bonds payable	—	(7,270)
Common stock, $1 par	600,000	50,000
Paid-in capital in excess of par..........................	1,400,000	110,000
Retained earnings..	2,261,000	312,270
Total liabilities and equity	$4,761,000	$950,000

Plum Corporation's 6% bonds were originally issued on January 1, 1978, at a discount of $14,540. The original discount has been amortized on a straight-line basis. Interest on the bonds is paid annually on December 31. Similar bonds are currently yielding 8% per annum.

On the purchase date, some Plum Corporation assets were recorded at book values not consistent with market values. The following market values were obtained:

Land	$186,000
Building	279,000
Equipment	465,000

Required:

(1) Prepare a determination and distribution of excess schedule for the investment in Plum Corporation. The schedule should include revaluation of the bonds based on the present value of the future cash flows at the current rate of interest.

(2) Prepare a work sheet for a consolidated balance sheet on December 31, 1982.

(3) Prepare a formal consolidated balance sheet for December 31, 1982.

Problem 6-9. The balance sheets for Gohlke and Hanson Company as of December 31, 19X6, are as follows:

Gohlke Company

Cash	$ 50,000	Payables	$1,750,000
Receivables (net)	300,000	Accruals	450,000
Inventories	1,600,000	Common stock, $100 par	1,000,000
Prepayments	47,000	Retained earnings	800,000
Property, plant, and equipment (net)	2,003,000		
Total assets	$ 4,000,000	Total liabilities and equity	$ 4,000,000

Hanson Company

Cash	$ 5,200,000	Payables	$ 7,872,000
Receivables (net)	2,400,000	Accruals	1,615,000
Inventories	11,200,000	Common stock, $100 par	10,000,000
Prepayments	422,000	Retained earnings	20,513,000
Property, plant, and equipment (net)	18,978,000		
Investment in Gohlke Company	1,800,000		
Total assets	$40,000,000	Total liabilities and equity	$40,000,000

An appraisal on December 31, 19X6, which was carefully considered and approved by the boards of directors of both firms, placed a total replacement value, less depreciation, of $3,203,000 on the property, plant, and equipment of the Gohlke Company.

The Hanson Company offered to purchase all the assets of the Gohlke Company, subject to its liabilities, as of December 31, 19X6, for $3,000,000. However, 40% of the stockholders of the Gohlke Company objected to the price because it did not include any consideration for goodwill, which they believed to be worth at least $500,000. A counterproposal was made and final agreement was reached on the basis that Hanson acquired 60% of the common stock of the Gohlke Company at a price of $300 per share.

Required:

Prepare a consolidated work sheet and a consolidated balance sheet as of December 31, 19X6.   (AICPA adapted)

Problem 6-10. Balance sheets for the Hellon and Vermat Companies on December 31, 19X1, are as follows:

	Hellon	Vermat
Current assets	$ 800,000	$ 300,000
Property, plant, and equipment	2,700,000	1,700,000
Accumulated depreciation	(750,000)	(600,000)
Investment in Vermat Company	1,200,000	—
Total assets	$3,950,000	$1,400,000
Current liabilities	$ 600,000	$ 200,000
Common stock, $10 par	1,400,000	—
Common stock, $2 par	—	300,000
Paid-in capital in excess of par	800,000	400,000
Retained earnings	1,150,000	500,000
Total liabilities and equity	$3,950,000	$1,400,000

Just prior to the preparation of these balance sheets, Hellon and Vermat combined in a pooling of interests. Hellon issued 20,000 shares of its common stock for all the outstanding stock of the Vermat Company. The investment was properly recorded.

Required:

(1) Prepare a work sheet for a consolidated balance sheet on December 31, 19X1.
(2) Prepare a formal consolidated balance sheet on December 31, 19X1.

Problem 6-11. Knox Company acquired 90% of the outstanding stock of Arlan Corporation on April 15, 19X1, by exchanging three shares of its common stock for every five shares of Arlan Corporation common stock. At this time, Knox's stock had a market value of $15 per share.

Immediately following this transaction, the two companies had the following balance sheets:

	Knox	Arlan
Current assets	$ 650,000	$ 300,000
Property, plant, and equipment	3,000,000	1,650,000
Accumulated depreciation	(900,000)	(500,000)
Investment in Arlan Corporation	1,620,000	—
Total assets	$4,370,000	$1,450,000
Liabilities	$ 520,000	$ 440,000
Common stock, $5 par	2,040,000	—
Common stock, $1 stated value	—	200,000
Additional paid-in capital	1,180,000	150,000
Retained earnings	630,000	660,000
Total liabilities and equity	$4,370,000	$1,450,000

Knox's investment account reflects the market value of the shares issued.

Required:

Prepare a consolidated work sheet and a consolidated balance sheet under each of the following assumptions:

(1) The combination is considered to be a purchase.
(2) The combination is considered to be a pooling of interests. (If necessary, correct the investment account prior to consolidating.)

Problem 6-12. On April 30, 19X1, Petrofab Corporation acquired 95% of the outstanding stock of AMCO Industries in exchange for 20,000 shares of its previously unissued stock. Petrofab's shares have a market value of $32. Out-of-pocket costs of the business combination, paid by Petrofab Corporation on April 30, 19X1, were as follows:

Direct acquisition costs (legal fees and finder's fees) $18,500
Security and stock issuance costs   22,250

There were no intercompany transactions prior to the business combination. AMCO Industries will become a subsidiary of Petrofab Corporation.

Comparative balance sheets of the two companies just prior to the combination are as follows:

	Petrofab Corporation	AMCO Industries
Cash	$ 300,000	$ 100,000
Marketable securities	80,000	40,000
Other current assets	650,000	160,000
Property, plant, and equipment (net)	2,500,000	850,000
Patents	40,000	60,000
Total assets	$3,570,000	$1,210,000
Current liabilities	$ 410,000	$ 340,000
Bonds payable	1,000,000	300,000
Common stock, $1 par	300,000	—
Common stock, $25 par	—	25,000
Paid-in capital in excess of par	1,200,000	275,000
Retained earnings	660,000	270,000
Total liabilities and equity	$3,570,000	$1,210,000

On April 30, 19X1, AMCO's book values approximated market values, except for the following:

Marketable securities .... $ 60,000
Property, plant, and equipment   910,000
Patents   80,000
Bonds payable   280,000

Required:

(1) Record the entry Petrofab would make on April 30, 19X1, to record the investment in the stock of AMCO Industries as: (a) a purchase, (b) a pooling of interests.
(2) Prepare a consolidated balance sheet for April 30, 19X1, immediately subsequent to the acquisition: (a) assuming that the acquisition is regarded as a purchase, (b) assuming that the acquisition qualifies as a pooling of interests.
(3) Compare the differences that would result on the 19X1 fiscal year income statement as a result of the purchase versus pooling treatment.

Problem 6-13. Comparative balance sheets of Edmond Corporation and its subsidiary Held Corporation on June 30, 19X7, are as follows:

	Edmond Corporation	Held Corporation
Cash	$ 161,250	$ 40,000
Accounts receivable	416,100	110,000
Prepayments	48,000	5,500
Land	750,000	160,000
Buildings	690,000	147,000
Accumulated depreciation	(50,000)	(12,000)
Delivery trucks	515,500	190,000
Accumulated depreciation	(35,000)	(10,000)
Investment in Held Corporation	572,000	—
Total assets	$3,067,850	$ 630,500
Accounts payable	$ 152,210	$ 80,500
Accrued expenses	16,100	3,600
Bonds payable	400,000	—
Common stock, $2 par	412,000	—
Common stock, $10 par	—	400,000
Paid-in capital in excess of par	755,000	—
Retained earnings	1,332,540	146,400
Total liabilities and equity	$3,067,850	$ 630,500

On July 1, 19X6, Edmond Corporation exchanged on a one-for-one basis enough of its shares of common stock to acquire a 90% interest in Held Corporation. Edmond Corporation shares had a market value at that time of $14 each. The balance in the investment account at that time reflected the market value of the shares exchanged. In issuing the stock, Edmond Corporation incurred $10,000 of SEC and issuance costs. These costs were considered a reduction in the proceeds received in issuing the common stock.

Edmond Corporation acquired the remaining shares of Held Corporation stock on June 30, 19X7, at a price of $17 per share. The cost of these shares was added to the investment account.

Edmond and Held Corporations have fiscal years ending June 30.

Held Corporation had no income and paid no dividends during its fiscal year ending June 30, 19X7.

Required:

Prepare the correcting entries to be made on Edmond's books and a consolidated work sheet for a consolidated balance sheet, assuming that the pooling of interests criteria were met at the time of the original acquisition.

CHAPTER 7
CONSOLIDATED STATEMENTS SUBSEQUENT TO ACQUISITION

The consolidation procedures required in periods subsequent to a parent's investment in a subsidiary depend on the method the parent uses to account for its investment. This chapter discusses the alternative recording methods and the influence of each on consolidation procedures, without consideration of income taxes.[1]

In the preceding chapter, work sheet procedures for a combination deemed to be a purchase included asset and liability adjustments to reflect market values on the date of the purchase. This chapter discusses the subsequent depreciation and amortization of these asset and liability revaluations. Also, work sheet procedures are developed that will allow consolidation of income statements, retained earnings statements, and balance sheets.

RECORDING THE INVESTMENT IN A SUBSIDIARY

Two basic methods may be used by a parent to account for its investment in a subsidiary: the *equity method* or the *cost method*. The equity method records as income an ownership percentage of subsidiary reported income, whether or not it was received by the parent. The cost method treats the investment in the subsidiary as a normal stock investment by recording income only when dividends are declared by the subsidiary.

Equity Method

In its simplest form, the *equity method* records as income the parent ownership interest multiplied by subsidiary reported income each period. The pro rata share of income is added to the investment account balance, the pro rata share of a loss is subtracted, and any dividends received on the investment are viewed as a partial liquidation of the

---

[1] The impact of income taxes on consolidated statements is discussed in Chapter 12.

investment. Consequently, dividends reduce the investment balance. The investment account at any point in time can be summarized as follows:

Investment in Subsidiary (equity method)	
Original cost plus: Ownership interest × reported income of subsidiary since acquisition	less: Ownership interest × reported losses of subsidiary since acquisition. less: Ownership interest × dividends declared by subsidiary since acquisition
equals: Equity-adjusted balance	

The "simple" equity method makes no adjustment to subsidiary income for amortization resulting from differences between the book and market values of the investment on the date of acquisition. There is no danger in omitting these amortizations in the investment account when consolidated statements are to be prepared, since the investment account is always entirely eliminated. The real advantage of using the simple equity method when consolidating is that every dollar of change in the subsidiary's stockholders' equity is recorded on a pro rata basis in the investment account. This method will thus expedite elimination of the investment account in the consolidated work sheets in future periods, and is favored in this text because of its simplicity.

For unconsolidated investments, a more sophisticated equity method is required by APB Opinion No. 18, "The Equity Method of Accounting for Investments in Common Stock." According to this Opinion, the parent's investment should be adjusted for amortizations when the parent has an "influential" investment of 20% or more of the voting stock of another firm. Thus, the parent must use the sophisticated equity method to account for investments in unconsolidated subsidiaries which are reported in parent-company financial statements or unconsolidated financial statements. The procedures for eliminating an investment recorded under the sophisticated equity method are more cumbersome than those of the simple equity method.

Cost Method

When the *cost method* is used, the investment in the subsidiary is retained at the original amount assigned to the acquisition. No adjustments are made for income as it is earned by the subsidiary; income on the investment is limited to dividends received from the subsidiary. An exception is made for subsidiary dividends which are based on income earned prior to the acquisition date. Such dividends are viewed as a partial liquidation and are deducted from the original investment. The cost method is acceptable for subsidiaries which are to be consolidated, since the investment account is entirely eliminated in the consolidation process.

Example of the Equity and Cost Methods

The simple equity, sophisticated equity, and cost methods will be illustrated by an example covering two years. This example, which will become the foundation for several consolidated work sheets in this chapter, is based on the following facts:

1. The following determination and distribution of excess schedule was prepared on the date of purchase. This schedule, which states how the resulting adjustments are to be amortized in future years, will be used in preparing all future work sheets.

Price paid, January 1, 19X1........................		$145,000
Interest acquired:		
Common stock, $10 par	$100,000	
Retained earnings.............................	50,000	
Total equity..................................	$150,000	
Ownership interest	90%	135,000
Excess of cost over book value attributed to goodwill (10-year amortization)		**$ 10,000**

2. Income during 19X1 was $30,000 for Company S; dividends declared during 19X1 were $10,000.
3. During 19X2, Company S had a loss of $10,000 and declared dividends of $5,000.

The journal entries shown below and on page 261 record this information on the books of Company P, using the simple equity, sophisticated equity, and cost methods. The investment account balances resulting from the three methods are also shown.

The balance in the simple-equity-adjusted investment account of a parent can easily be tested for its correctness. Under the simple equity

	Event	Simple Equity Method		
19X1		Investment in Company S.............	145,000	
Jan. 1	Purchase of stock	Cash..............................		145,000
Dec. 31	Subsidiary income of $30,000 reported to parent	Investment in Company S.............	27,000	
		Subsidiary Income..................		27,000
31	Dividends of $10,000 declared by subsidiary	Dividends Receivable	9,000	
		Investment in Company S		9,000
		Investment balance, Dec. 31, 19X1..........		**$163,000**
19X2		Loss on Subsidiary Operations	9,000	
Dec. 31	Subsidiary loss of $10,000 reported to parent	Investment in Company S		9,000
31	Dividends of $5,000 declared by subsidiary	Dividends Receivable	4,500	
		Investment in Company S		4,500
		Investment balance, Dec. 31, 19X2..........		**$149,500**

method, every change in the retained earnings of the subsidiary leads to an equity adjustment in the investment account for an amount equal to the change multiplied by the ownership interest. At any time, the balance in a simple-equity-adjusted investment account can be stated as follows:

Cost + [(Ownership interest) × (Change in subsidiary Retained Earnings since acquisition)]

In the preceding example, the December 31, 19X2 balance in the simple-equity-adjusted Investment in Company S would be verified as follows:

$$
\begin{aligned}
\text{Balance} &= \text{Cost} + .90 \text{ (Change in Company S Retained Earnings since acquisition)} \\
&= \$145{,}000 + .90 \text{ ($55{,}000$ December 31, 19X2, balance} - \$50{,}000 \\
&\qquad\qquad\qquad\text{January 1, 19X1, balance)} \\
&= \$145{,}000 + .90 \text{ ($\$5{,}000$)} \\
&= \underline{\underline{\$149{,}500}}
\end{aligned}
$$

This procedure will be valuable in checking the balance in an investment account prior to consolidating. Later in the chapter, this technique becomes the basis for converting investments recorded under the cost method to the simple equity method. If it is desired, the sophisticated equity balance can be obtained by subtracting the cumulative amortizations of excess from the simple equity balance.

Presentations of work sheet elimination procedures in subsequent chapters are based on the use of the simple equity method. Rather than mastering a separate set of procedures for investments carried at cost, such investments will be converted to the simple equity method prior to the application of elimination procedures.

Sophisticated Equity Method			Cost Method		
Investment in Company S	145,000		Investment in Company S	145,000	
Cash		145,000	Cash		145,000
Investment in Company S	26,000[1]		No entry.		
Subsidiary Income		26,000			
Dividends Receivable	9,000		Dividends Receivable	9,000	
Investment in Company S		9,000	Subsidiary (Dividend) Income		9,000
Investment balance, Dec. 31, 19X1	**$162,000**		**Investment balance, Dec. 31, 19X1**	**$145,000**	
Loss on Subsidiary Operations	10,000[2]		No entry.		
Investment in Company S		10,000			
Dividends Receivable	4,500		Dividends Receivable	4,500	
Investment in Company S		4,500	Subsidiary (Dividend) Income		4,500
Investment balance, Dec. 31, 19X2	**$147,500**		**Investment balance, Dec. 31, 19X2**	**$145,000**	

[1] Parent's share of subsidiary income, less amortization of excess of $1,000 per year.
[2] Parent's share of subsidiary loss, plus amortization of excess of $1,000 per year.

ELIMINATION PROCEDURES: EQUITY-ADJUSTED INVESTMENTS

Work sheet procedures necessary to prepare consolidated income statements, retained earnings statements, and balance sheets are examined in the following section. It must be recalled that the consolidation procedure is used each year as it is applied to each period's separate parent and subsidiary accounts. Each year the consolidation process is performed independently, since the work sheet eliminations of previous years are never recorded by the parent or subsidiary.

The illustrations which follow are based on the facts concerning the investment in Company S, as detailed in the previous example. The procedures for consolidating an investment maintained under the simple equity method will be discussed first, followed by an explanation of how procedures would differ under the sophisticated equity method.

Effect of Simple Equity Method on Consolidation

The trial balances of Company P and Company S at the end of 19X1 appear in the first two columns of Illustration I on pages 264 and 265. The balances reflect the simple equity adjustments for 19X1, which were illustrated on page 260. A Consolidated Income Statement column follows the Eliminations columns. The nominal accounts of the constituent firms, as adjusted by eliminations, are combined to calculate the consolidated entity's net income, which in this case is $69,000. The consolidated income is distributed to the controlling and minority interests. Note that the minority receives 10% of the $30,000 subsidiary reported net income, or $3,000. The goodwill amortization is borne entirely by the controlling interest, since only the goodwill applicable to the purchaser's interest is originally acknowledged. The controlling interest receives the balance of the consolidated net income, or $66,000. The correctness of this balance may be verified as follows:

Company P internally generated income (exclusive of subsidiary income) ..	$40,000
90% of Company S reported income of $30,000	27,000
Less amortization of goodwill	(1,000)
Total controlling interest in consolidated income	$66,000

The Minority Interest column of the work sheet summarizes the total ownership interest of the minority stockholders at the close of the period. The column includes the minority's interest in each of the following: subsidiary paid-in capital, subsidiary retained earnings at the beginning of the period, consolidated net income, and dividends declared during the period.

The Controlling Retained Earnings column produces the controlling retained earnings at the close of the period. The column includes the parent firm's retained earnings at the beginning of the period, plus the controlling interest's share of consolidated net income. If the parent had declared dividends, the dividends would be shown as a deduction in this column.

The Consolidated Balance Sheet column includes the combined asset and liability balances. The paid-in equity balances of the parent firm are extended as the consolidated paid-in capital. The net minority interest is usually extended to the balance sheet without enumeration of its components. The total of the Controlling Retained Earnings column is also extended to the balance sheet.

Dual columns may be used for the consolidated balance sheet. This arrangement may minimize errors and aid analysis. Single columns are not advocated, but are used to facilitate the inclusion of lengthy work sheets in a summarized fashion.

The information for the formal statements which follow is taken directly from the work sheet of Illustration I.

Company P and Subsidiary Company S
Consolidated Income Statement
For Year Ended December 31, 19X1

Revenue	$180,000
Less expenses	111,000
Consolidated net income	$ 69,000
Distribution of consolidated net income:	
To controlling interest	$ 66,000
To minority interest	3,000
Total	$ 69,000

Company P and Subsidiary Company S
Consolidated Retained Earnings Statement
For Year Ended December 31, 19X1

	Minority	Controlling
Retained earnings, January 1, 19X1	$ 5,000	$123,000
Add distribution of consolidated net income	3,000	66,000
Less dividends declared	(1,000)	—
Balance, December 31, 19X1	$ 7,000	$189,000

Company P and Subsidiary Company S
Consolidated Balance Sheet
December 31, 19X1

Assets		Stockholders' Equity		
Net tangible assets	$397,000	Minority interest		$17,000
Goodwill	9,000	Controlling interest:		
		Common stock	$200,000	
		Retained earnings	189,000	389,000
Total assets	$406,000	Total stockholders' equity		$406,000

There are two features of these statements which deserve attention. First, the income statement should emphasize that consolidated net

Illustration I
Company P and
Work Sheet for Consolidated
For Year Ended

(Credit balance amounts
are in parentheses)

	Trial Balance	
	Company P	**Company S**
Net Assets	227,000	170,000
Investment in Co. S	163,000	
Goodwill		
Common Stock ($10 par), Co. P	(200,000)	
Retained Earnings, Jan. 1, 19X1, Co. P	(123,000)	
Common Stock ($10 par), Co. S		(100,000)
Retained Earnings, Jan. 1, 19X1, Co. S		(50,000)
Revenue	(100,000)	(80,000)
Expenses	60,000	50,000
Subsidiary Income	(27,000)	
Dividends Declared		10,000
	0	0
Net Income, Consolidated		
To Minority Interest (10% × $30,000 Co. S Net Income)		
Balance to Controlling Interest		
Minority Interest, Dec. 31, 19X1		
Retained Earnings, Controlling Interest, Dec. 31, 19X1		

Eliminations **(Key numbers for steps being emphasized are shaded.)**:
1 Eliminate the current-year entries made in the investment account and in the subsidiary income account. It
should be noted that when this step is completed, the balance in the investment account is the balance at
the beginning of the year. At this point the investment account and the Company S equity accounts are
adjusted to a common point in time and are ready for elimination. Only dividends paid to outside minority
stockholders remain on the work sheet.

income is $69,000, which includes the minority share of income. The
income statement should not imply that the controlling share of income
is synonymous with consolidated net income, unless there is no minority interest. Published financial statements do, however, often show the
minority share of income as an expense. This presentation reflects the
position that the consolidated statements are oriented to the controlling
firm's shareholders who view the minority share of income as a quasi-
expense, since it is not available to them. Second, the balance sheet
should include the minority stockholders' equity as a part of total stockholders' equity. Some firms treat the minority interest as a liability or
place it in a separate category, but neither treatment is defensible in
theory.

Simple Equity Method
Subsidiary Company S
Financial Statements
December 31, 19X1

Eliminations		Consolidated Income Statement	Minority Interest	Controlling Retained Earnings	Consolidated Balance Sheet
Dr.	Cr.				
					397,000
(1) 9,000	(1) 27,000				
	(2) 135,000				
	(3) 10,000				
(3) 10,000	(4) 1,000				9,000
					(200,000)
				(123,000)	
(2) 90,000			(10,000)		
(2) 45,000			(5,000)		
		(180,000)			
(4) 1,000		111,000			
(1) 27,000					
	(1) 9,000		1,000		
182,000	182,000				
		(69,000)			
		3,000	(3,000)		
		66,000		(66,000)	
			(17,000)		(17,000)
				(189,000)	(189,000)
					0

(2) Eliminate the pro rata share of Company S equity balances at the beginning of the year against the investment account. The elimination of the parent's share of subsidiary stockholders' equity leaves only the minority interest in each element of subsidiary equity.

(3) Distribute the $10,000 excess cost as required by the determination and distribution of excess schedule.

(4) Amortize the resulting goodwill over the ten-year period.

The consolidation procedures for 19X2, as they would apply to Companies P and S under the simple equity method, are now examined to provide added practice in preparing work sheets, and to emphasize that each year consolidation procedures are applied to the separate statements of the constituent firms. In essence, *each year's consolidation procedures begin as if there never had been a previous consolidation*. However, reference to past work sheets is commonly used to save time.

The separate trial balances of Companies P and S are displayed in the first two columns of the work sheet in Illustration II. The investment in the subsidiary account includes the simple-equity-adjusted investment balance as calculated on page 260. Note that the balances in Retained Earnings of Companies P and S are calculated as follows:

Illustration II
Company P and
Work Sheet for Consolidated
For Year Ended

(Credit balance amounts
are in parentheses)

	Trial Balance	
	Company P	Company S
Net Assets	251,500	155,000
Investment in Co. S	149,500	
Goodwill		
Common Stock ($10 par), Co. P	(200,000)	
Retained Earnings, Jan. 1, 19X2, Co. P	(190,000)	
Common Stock ($10 par), Co. S		(100,000)
Retained Earnings, Jan. 1, 19X2, Co. S		(70,000)
Revenue	(100,000)	(50,000)
Expenses	80,000	60,000
Subsidiary Loss	9,000	
Dividends Declared		5,000
	0	0
Net Income, Consolidated		
To Minority Interest (10% × $10,000 Co. S Net Loss)		
Balance to Controlling Interest		
Minority Interest, Dec. 31, 19X2		
Retained Earnings, Controlling Interest, Dec. 31, 19X2		

Eliminations:
1 Eliminate the current-year entries made in the investment account and in the subsidiary loss account. This step returns the investment in Company S account to its January 1, 19X2, balance. The investment account and the subsidiary equity accounts are stated at a common point in time which will facilitate their elimination.
(2) Using balances at the beginning of the year, eliminate 90% of Company S equity balances against the remaining investment account.
(3) Distribute the $10,000 excess cost as indicated by the determination and distribution of excess schedule which was prepared on the date of acquisition. In this example, goodwill is recorded for $10,000.

Company P: January 1, 19X1, balance ....,........ $123,000
           Net income, 19X1 (including subsidiary income)........   67,000
           Balance, January 1, 19X2 .... $190,000

Company S: January 1, 19X1, balance .... $ 50,000
           Net income, 19X1   30,000
           Dividends declared ....   (10,000)
           Balance, January 1, 19X2 .... $ 70,000

It should now be clear that the original determination and distribution of excess schedule prepared on the date of acquisition becomes the foundation for all subsequent work sheets. Once prepared, the schedule is used without modification.

Simple Equity Method, Second Year
Subsidiary Company S
Financial Statements
December 31, 19X2

Eliminations		Consolidated Income Statement	Minority Interest	Controlling Retained Earnings	Consolidated Balance Sheet
Dr.	Cr.				
					406,500
1 9,000	(2) 153,000				
1 4,500	(3) 10,000				
(3) 10,000	**4** 2,000				8,000
					(200,000)
4 1,000				(189,000)	
(2) 90,000			(10,000)		
(2) 63,000			(7,000)		
		(150,000)			
4 1,000		141,000			
	1 9,000				
	1 4,500		500		
178,500	178,500				
		(9,000)			
		(1,000)	1,000		
		10,000		(10,000)	
			(15,500)		(15,500)
				(199,000)	(199,000)
					0

4 Amortize goodwill over the selected 10-year period. It is necessary to record goodwill amortization for current and past periods, because asset adjustments resulting from the consolidation process do not appear on the separate statements of the constituent firms. Thus, Step 4 reduces goodwill by $2,000 for the 19X1 and 19X2 amortization. The amount for the current year is expensed, while the cumulative amortization for prior years is deducted from the beginning controlling Retained Earnings. The minority interest does not share in the adjustments, since the only goodwill originally acknowledged is that which is applicable to the controlling interest.

Effect of Sophisticated Equity Method on Consolidation

A parent preparing consolidated statements may desire to prepare separate parent company statements as a supplement to consolidated statements. In this situation, the investment in the subsidiary must be shown on the parent's statements at the sophisticated equity balance. This requirement may lead the parent to maintain its subsidiary investment account under the sophisticated equity method. Two ramifications occur when such an investment is consolidated. First, the current year's equity adjustment is net of excess amortizations; and second, the investment account contains only the remaining unamortized excess applicable to the investment.

The use of the sophisticated equity method complicates the elimination of the investment account in that the distribution and amortization of the excess is altered. However, there is no impact on the other consolidation procedures. To illustrate, the information given in Illustration II will be used. The trial balance of Company P will show the following changes as a result of using the sophisticated equity method:

1. The Investment in Company S will be carried at $147,500 ($149,500 simple equity balance, less 2 years' amortization of excess at $1,000 per year).
2. The January 1, 19X2 balance for Company P Retained Earnings will be $189,000 ($190,000 under simple equity, less 1 year's amortization of excess of $1,000).
3. The subsidiary loss account will have a balance of $10,000 ($9,000 share of subsidiary loss, plus $1,000 amortization of excess).

Based on these changes, a partial work sheet under the sophisticated equity method follows:

	Trial Balance		Eliminations	
	Company P	Company S	Dr.	Cr.
Investment in Co. S	147,500		(1) 10,000	(2) 153,000
			(1) 4,500	(3) 9,000
Goodwill			(3) 9,000	(4) 1,000
Retained Earnings, Jan. 1, 19X2, Co. P	(189,000)			
Common Stock ($10 par), Co. S		(100,000)	(2) 90,000	
Retained Earnings, Jan 1, 19X2, Co. S		(70,000)	(2) 63,000	
Revenue	(100,000)	(50,000)		
Expenses	80,000	60,000	(4) 1,000	
Subsidiary Loss	10,000			(1) 10,000
Dividends Declared		5,000		(1) 4,500

Eliminations:

(1) Eliminate the current-year entries made in the investment account and the subsidiary loss account. The loss account now includes the $1,000 excess amortization.
(2) Using the balances at the beginning of the year, eliminate 90% of the Company S equity balances against the remaining investment account.
(3) Distribute the remaining unamortized excess ($10,000 on purchase date, less $1,000 19X1 amortization) to goodwill.
(4) Amortize goodwill for the current year.

The sophisticated equity method is essentially a modification of simple equity procedures. The major difference in the consolidation procedures under the two methods is that, subsequent to the acquisition, the original excess calculated on the determination and distribution of excess schedule does not appear when the sophisticated equity method is used. Only the remaining unamortized excess appears. Since the investment account is eliminated in the consolidation process, the added complexities of the sophisticated method are not justified for most firms.

ELIMINATION PROCEDURES: COST METHOD INVESTMENTS

It will be recalled that a parent may choose to record its investment in a subsidiary under the cost method, whereby the investment is maintained at its original cost, with income from the investment recorded when dividends are declared by the subsidiary. The use of the cost method means that the investment account does not reflect changes in the subsidiary equity. Rather than develop a new set of procedures for elimination of investments under the cost method, cost method investments will be converted to the simple equity balance at the beginning of the period. The elimination procedures developed earlier may then be applied.

Illustration III on pages 270-271 is a consolidated financial statements work sheet for Companies P and S for the first year of combined operations, based upon the entries under the cost method, as shown on page 261. Reference to the Company P Trial Balance column in Illustration III reveals that the investment in subsidiary account at year end is still stated at the original $145,000 cost, and that the income recorded by the parent as a result of subsidiary ownership is limited to $9,000, or 90% of the subsidiary's declared dividends. When the cost method is used, the account title "Dividend Income" may be used in place of Subsidiary Income.

At the end of the first year of operations, it is not necessary to convert to the simple equity method before eliminating. The investment account and the equity of Company S are already stated as of a common point in time, January 1, 19X1. For Step 1, it is only necessary to eliminate the intercompany dividends. The remaining eliminations, Steps 2-4 in Illustration III, are identical to their corresponding entries in Illustration I. The last four columns of the work sheet in Illustration III are identical to their counterparts in Illustration I.

For periods subsequent to the first year of combined operations, an entry converting to the simple equity method will be needed on the consolidated work sheets. To illustrate, the work sheet on pages 272-273 (Illustration IV) covers the second year of operations for Companies P and S. Illustration IV is identical to Illustration II except for the use of the cost method for the investment in Company S. The balance in the investment account is still the original $145,000 cost. However, the Retained Earnings of Company S carries the January 1, 19X2 balance. Thus, these accounts do not share a common point in time, and elimination cannot proceed. It should be noted that the parent's balance in Retained Earnings is $18,000 less, since it does not include the undistributed income of the subsidiary. The conversion step, labeled "C" in Illustration IV, converts the investment account to its balance on January 1, 19X2, so that the account shares a common point in

Illustration III
Company P and
Work Sheet for Consolidated
For the Year Ended

(Credit balance amounts
are in parentheses)

	Trial Balance	
	Company P	**Company S**
Net Assets	227,000	170,000
Investment in Co. S	145,000	
Goodwill		
Common Stock ($10 par), Co. P	(200,000)	
Retained Earnings, Jan. 1, 19X1, Co. P	(123,000)	
Common Stock ($10 par), Co. S		(100,000)
Retained Earnings, Jan. 1, 19X1, Co. S		(50,000)
Revenue	(100,000)	(80,000)
Expenses	60,000	50,000
Subsidiary (Dividend) Income	(9,000)	
Dividends Declared		10,000
	0	0
Consolidated Income		
To Minority Interest (10% × $30,000 Co. S Net Income)		
Balance to Controlling Interest		
Minority Interest, Dec. 31, 19X1		
Retained Earnings, Controlling Interest, Dec. 31, 19X1		

Eliminations:
(1) Eliminate intercompany dividends.
(2) Eliminate 90% of Company S equity balances at the beginning of the year against the investment account.

---

time with the subsidiary equity balances against which it is to be eliminated. The conversion entry retroactively updates the investment in Company S and the Company P retained earnings to the simple equity method as of January 1, 19X2. Such a conversion is made by multiplying the ownership interest by the change in Retained Earnings between the date of acquisition and the beginning of the current year. In this case, the adjustment is made as follows:

Conversion = .90 (Company S Retained Earnings, January 1, 19X2 − Company S
                 Retained Earnings, January 1, 19X1)
      = .90 ($70,000 − $50,000) = .90 × $20,000
      = $18,000

The simplicity of this technique of converting from the cost to the simple equity method should be appreciated. It is only necessary at any future date to compare the subsidiary balance in Retained Earnings on the work sheet with the balance on the original date of acquisition (included in the determination and distribution of excess schedule) in order to convert to the simple equity method. Specific reference to

Cost Method
Subsidiary Company S
Financial Statements
December 31, 19X1

Eliminations		Consolidated Income Statement	Minority Interest	Controlling Retained Earnings	Consolidated Balance Sheet
Dr.	Cr.				
					397,000
	(2) 135,000				
	(3) 10,000				
(3) 10,000	(4) 1,000				9,000
					(200,000)
				(123,000)	
(2) 90,000			(10,000)		
(2) 45,000			(5,000)		
		(180,000)			
(4) 1,000		111,000			
① 9,000					
	① 9,000		1,000		
155,000	155,000				
		(69,000)			
		3,000	(3,000)		
		66,000		(66,000)	
			(17,000)		(17,000)
				(189,000)	(189,000)
					0

(3) Distribute the $10,000 excess cost as indicated by the determination and distribution of excess schedule on page 260.
(4) Amortize goodwill for the current year.

income earned and dividends paid by the subsidiary in each intervening year is unnecessary. The only complications occur when stock dividends have been issued by the subsidiary, or when the subsidiary has issued or retired stock. These complications are examined in Chapter 11.

After the conversion, eliminations may proceed. Since the cost method is being used, the first elimination is confined to intercompany dividends. Steps 2-4 are identical to the corresponding steps in Illustration II. Note that Step 2 is possible only after the conversion step brings the account balances to a common point in time.

COMPLICATED PURCHASE, SEVERAL CAUSES OF EXCESS

The examples in Illustrations I through IV assumed that the entire excess of cost over book value was attributable to goodwill. In reality, this assumption will seldom be true. The following example illustrates a more complicated purchase.

Illustration IV
Company P and
Work Sheet for Consolidated
For Year Ended

(Credit balance amounts
are in parentheses)

	Trial Balance	
	Company P	Company S
Net Assets	251,500	155,000
Investment in Co. S	145,000	
Goodwill		
Common Stock ($10 par), Co. P	(200,000)	
Retained Earnings, Jan. 1, 19X2, Co. P	(172,000)	
Common Stock ($10 par), Co. S		(100,000)
Retained Earnings, Jan. 1, 19X2, Co. S		(70,000)
Revenue	(100,000)	(50,000)
Expenses	80,000	60,000
Subsidiary (Dividend) Income	(4,500)	
Dividends Declared		5,000
	0	0
Consolidated Income		
To Minority Interest (10% × Co. S Net Loss of $10,000)		
Balance to Controlling Interest		
Minority Interest, Dec. 31, 19X2		
Retained Earnings, Controlling Interest, Dec. 31, 19X2		

Eliminations:
C Convert to simple equity method as of January 1, 19X2.
1 Eliminate the current-year intercompany dividends.
(2) Eliminate 90% of Company S equity balances at the beginning of the year against the investment account.

The Paulos Company paid $790,000 to obtain 8,000 shares (80% interest) of the Carlos Company on January 1, 19X1. In addition, $10,000 of direct acquisition costs were paid by the Paulos Company. At the time of the purchase, Carlos Company had the following summarized balance sheet:

Carlos Company
Balance Sheet
January 1, 19X1

Assets			Liabilities and Equity	
Inventory		$ 75,000	Current liabilities	$ 50,000
Land		150,000	Bonds payable, 6%, due	
Building	$600,000		Dec. 31, 19X4	200,000
Less accumulated depreciation	300,000	300,000	Capital stock, $10 par	100,000
Equipment	$150,000		Paid-in capital in excess of par	150,000
Less accumulated depreciation	50,000	100,000	Retained earnings	250,000
Goodwill		125,000		
Total assets		$750,000	Total liabilities and equity	$750,000

Cost Method, Second Year
Subsidiary Company S
Financial Statements
December 31, 19X2

Eliminations		Consolidated Income Statement	Minority Interest	Controlling Retained Earnings	Consolidated Balance Sheet
Dr.	Cr.				
					406,500
C 18,000	(2) 153,000				
	(3) 10,000				
(3) 10,000	(4) 2,000				8,000
					(200,000)
(4) 1,000	**C** 18,000			(189,000)	
(2) 90,000			(10,000)		
(2) 63,000			(7,000)		
		(150,000)			
(4) 1,000		141,000			
1 4,500					
	1 4,500		500		
187,500	187,500				
		(9,000)			
		(1,000)	1,000		
		10,000		(10,000)	
		(15,500)			(15,500)
				(199,000)	(199,000)
					0

(3) Distribute the $10,000 excess cost as indicated by the determination and distribution of excess schedule on page 260.
(4) Amortize goodwill for the current year and one previous year.

The following market values were secured:

Inventory	$ 80,000
Land	200,000
Building (20-year remaining life)	500,000
Equipment (5-year remaining life)..............................	80,000
Bonds payable based on current 8% market interest rate as follows:	
Present value of interest payment at 8% = $12,000 annual interest	
× 4-year, 8% present value of annuity factor of 3.31213 .... $ 39,746	
Present value of principal = $200,000 × 4-year, 8% present value	
factor of .73503 147,006	186,752

Based on these market values, the following determination and distribution of excess schedule would be prepared. This schedule calculates an excess of cost of $400,000 on the interest acquired; $14,598 of this excess is consumed revaluing current assets and liabilities. Previously recorded goodwill was not added to the excess available for long-lived assets, since only $184,000 was needed to adjust these assets to market value. The balance of the excess, $201,402, was allocated to additional goodwill.

Price paid (including $10,000 direct acquisition costs)		$800,000
Less interest acquired:		
Capital stock, $10 par	$100,000	
Paid-in capital in excess of par	150,000	
Retained earnings	250,000	
Total equity	$500,000	
Ownership interest...	80%	400,000
Excess of cost over book value of subsidiary interest		$400,000
Less adjustments to current assets and debt:		
Inventory undervalued $5,000; 80% × $5,000	**$ 4,000**	
Bonds payable overstated by $13,248; record discount of 80% × $13,248 (4-year life)	**10,598**	**14,598**
Excess available to adjust long-lived assets		$385,402
Land understated $50,000; increase land 80% × $50,000	**$ 40,000**	
Building (20-year life) understated $200,000; decrease accumulated depreciation 80% × $200,000	**160,000**	
Equipment (5-year life) overstated $20,000; reduce equipment 80% × $20,000	**(16,000)**	**184,000**
Balance of excess reflecting additional goodwill (10-year life)		**$201,402**

Theoretically, the plant asset adjustments required by the determination and distribution of excess schedule should be made in a manner that would not include any accumulated depreciation applicable to the controlling interest as of the purchase date. This procedure would unduly complicate future work sheets. As a practical alternative when possible, the plant asset adjustments should be made in such a way as to reduce accumulated depreciation, and in no event should adjustments increase accumulated depreciation. Therefore, the increase in the net value of the building was accomplished by decreasing accumulated depreciation, not by increasing the asset account. The reduction in the equipment was accomplished by decreasing the asset account rather than increasing accumulated depreciation.

Illustration V, on pages 276-277, shows a consolidated financial statements work sheet for the Paulos and Carlos Companies one year after acquisition. During the year, Carlos had a net income of $60,000 and paid $20,000 in dividends. Paulos company shows the following simple-equity-adjusted balance for its investment in Carlos:

Original cost	$800,000
Add 80% of 19X1 income of $60,000	48,000
Deduct 80% of $20,000 dividends paid by Carlos	(16,000)
Investment balance, December 31, 19X1.........................	$832,000

The work sheet is completed by allocating the consolidated income of $108,708 to the minority and controlling interests, with the minority interest receiving 20% of the subsidiary's reported $60,000 net income. None of the amortizations resulting from revaluations affect the minority interest, because only the adjustments relating to the 80% controlling interest in assets and liabilities are recorded initially. Therefore, all amortizations pertain only to the controlling interest.

At this point it should be understood that the amortizations of excess cost applicable to long-lived assets could become more complex than they are in Illustration V. The amortization adjustments found in Steps 4c and 4d divide the applicable excess by the assets' remaining lives as shown in the determination and distribution of excess schedule. It was implicitly assumed that the amortization period was the asset's remaining life used by the subsidiary and that the subsidiary used straight-line depreciation. If the subsidiary had used an alternative depreciation method, that method would have been applied to the excess. It may occur that the parent company does not wish to use the subsidiary's depreciation method and/or remaining life. In this case, the parent recomputes depreciation, based on its ownership interest in the asset. The recomputed amount would be compared to the parent's ownership interest in the subsidiary's recorded depreciation expense and the difference would become the amortization adjustment for the period.

Illustration VI, on pages 280-283, shows the work sheet for the second year of combined operations for the purchase which was analyzed in Illustration V. The second year is included to emphasize that *each year the consolidation starts anew from the separate trial balances of the two firms.* None of the eliminations made on the previous period's work sheet are reflected in the 19X2 separate trial balances of the Paulos and Carlos Companies.

The following information may be inferred from the trial balance figures in Illustration VI:

Carlos reported a net income of $100,000 for 19X2 and paid $20,000 in dividends. This income is based on the asset values maintained on Carlos' books, and does not reflect revaluations caused by the 80% purchase by Paulos.

The investment in Carlos account reflects:

Balance, December 31, 19X1	$832,000
Add 80% of Carlos net income of $100,000	80,000
Deduct 80% of Carlos dividends declared of $20,000 ...	(16,000)
Balance, December 31, 19X2	$896,000

Subsidiary income of $80,000 was recorded by Paulos, which is 80% of Carlos' reported net income.

The January 1, 19X2, balance in Paulos' retained earnings is derived as follows:

Balance, January 1, 19X1	$700,000
Add: 19X1 income generated by the Paulos Company ..	80,000
Subsidiary income under the equity method	48,000
Balance, January 1, 19X2	$828,000

This balance reflects 80% of the subsidiary's reported net income, and does not include adjustments resulting from the amortizations of the excess of the price paid for the 80% interest. These amortizations appear only on the consolidated work sheet.

(Credit balance amounts
are in parentheses)

	Trial Balance	
	Paulos	**Carlos**
Cash	100,000	50,000
Inventory	226,000	62,500
Land	200,000	150,000
Building	800,000	600,000
Accumulated Depreciation—Building	(80,000)	(315,000)
Equipment	400,000	150,000
Accumulated Depreciation—Equipment	(50,000)	(70,000)
Investment in Carlos	832,000	
Goodwill		112,500
Current Liabilities	(100,000)	
Bonds Payable		(200,000)
Discount on Bonds		
Capital Stock, Paulos	(1,500,000)	
Retained Earnings, Jan. 1, 19X1, Paulos	(700,000)	
Capital Stock ($10 par), Carlos		(100,000)
Paid-In Capital in Excess of Par, Carlos		(150,000)
Retained Earnings, Jan. 1, 19X1, Carlos		(250,000)
Sales	(350,000)	(200,000)
Cost of Goods Sold	150,000	80,000
Expenses	120,000	60,000
Subsidiary Income	(48,000)	
Dividends Declared		20,000
	0	0

Consolidated Net Income
To Minority Interest (20% × $60,000 Carlos Income)
Balance to Controlling Interest
Total Minority Interest, Dec. 31, 19X1
Retained Earnings, Controlling Interest, Dec. 31, 19X1

Eliminations:
(1) Eliminate the current-year entries made in the investment account and in the subsidiary income account. The investment in Carlos account is now adjusted to its January 1, 19X1, balance so that it may be eliminated.
(2) Eliminate the 80% ownership portion of the subsidiary equity accounts against the investment. A $400,000 excess cost remains.
3 Distribute the $400,000 excess cost as follows, in accordance with the determination and distribution of excess schedule:
  a. Increase the beginning inventory $4,000. However, the beginning inventory has been closed to the cost of goods sold; thus, the cost of goods sold is increased by $4,000. If the inventory had not been sold, the

Simple Equity Method, First Year
Subsidiary Carlos Company
Financial Statements
December 31, 19X1

Eliminations Dr.	Eliminations Cr.	Consolidated Income Statement	Minority Interest	Controlling Retained Earnings	Consolidated Balance Sheet
					150,000
					288,500
3e 40,000					390,000
					1,400,000
3d 160,000	4d 8,000				(243,000)
	3c 16,000				534,000
4c 3,200					(116,800)
(1) 16,000	(1) 48,000				
	(2) 400,000				
	3 400,000				
3f 201,402	4f 20,140				293,762
					(100,000)
					(200,000)
3b 10,598	4b 2,352				8,246
					(1,500,000)
				(700,000)	
(2) 80,000			(20,000)		
(2) 120,000			(30,000)		
(2) 200,000			(50,000)		
		(550,000)			
3a 4,000		234,000			
4b 2,352	4c 3,200	207,292			
4d 8,000					
4f 20,140					
(1) 48,000					
	(1) 16,000		4,000		
913,692	913,692				
		(108,708)			
		12,000	(12,000)		
		96,708		(96,708)	
			(108,000)		(108,000)
				(796,708)	(796,708)
					0

      inventory account would be adjusted. The cost of goods sold in the later period of sale would then be adjusted on a subsequent work sheet.

   b. Record discount of $10,598 on the bonds payable.

   c. Reduce the equipment $16,000 by reducing the equipment account directly.

   d. Increase the building $160,000 by decreasing accumulated depreciation.

   e. Increase land $40,000.

   f. Increase goodwill $201,402.

4 Record amortizations resulting from the asset and liability revaluations of Step 3. The adjustments are lettered (a) through (f) to correspond with the revaluations in Step 3:

(continued)

a. No amortization required; adjustment already charged to cost of goods sold.

b. Amortize discount as follows:

Net present value of controlling interest in Carlos bonds, January 1, 19X1:

Face, 80% × $200,000	$160,000	
Discount	10,598	$149,402
Multiply by 8% effective interest rate		.08
Effective interest expense		$ 11,952
Nominal interest, 6% × $160,000		9,600
Discount amortization		$ 2,352

c. Record annual decrease in equipment depreciation expense; $16,000 net decrease in equipment divided by 5-year life equals $3,200.

d. Record annual increase in building depreciation expense; $160,000 net increase in building divided by 20-year life equals $8,000.

e. No amortization results from adjustment of land.

f. Record additional annual amortization of goodwill; $201,402 net increase in goodwill divided by 10-year life equals $20,140. It is assumed that the previously recorded goodwill of $125,000 on January 1, 19X1, is also being amortized over 10 years.

Intraperiod Purchase Under the Simple Equity Method

The accountant will be required to apply specialized procedures when consolidating a controlling investment in common stock which is acquired on a date other than the balance sheet date of the subsidiary. When the acquisition is deemed to be a purchase, the determination and distribution of excess schedule must be based on the subsidiary's stockholders' equity on the interim purchase date, including the subsidiary's retained earnings balance on that date. A further complication under purchase accounting is that the consolidated net income of the combined firm, as derived on the work sheet, is to include only subsidiary income earned subsequent to the purchase date.

There are two options available for consolidating an intraperiod purchase. The first option is to require the subsidiary to close its books as of the purchase date. This procedure would make retained earnings on the acquisition date available for use in the determination and distribution of excess schedule, and would mean that consolidated work sheets would include only subsidiary operations subsequent to the purchase date. The second and more realistic option is to modify the determination and distribution of excess schedule to include the purchased share of undistributed income for the portion of the year prior to the purchase. It is then possible to include the subsidiary's operations for the entire fiscal year in the consolidated work sheet.

Option 1: Close Subsidiary Books. Company S has the following trial balance on July 1, 19X1, the date of an 80% purchase by Company P:

Current Assets...	68,000	
Equipment	80,000	
Accumulated Depreciation		30,000
Liabilities		10,000
Capital Stock ($10 par)		50,000
Retained Earnings, January 1, 19X1		40,000
Sales..		90,000
Cost of Goods Sold	60,000	
Expenses...	12,000	
Total	220,000	220,000

If Company P requires Company S to close its nominal accounts as of July 1, Company S would increase its retained earnings by $18,000 with the following entry:

Sales...	90,000	
Cost of Goods Sold		60,000
Expenses...		12,000
Retained Earnings		18,000

Assume that Company P pays $106,400 for its 80% interest in Company S. Assume also that equipment is undervalued by $40,000 and has a 10-year remaining life. The determination and distribution of excess schedule would be as follows:

Price paid		$106,400
Interest acquired:		
Common stock ($10 par)	$ 50,000	
Retained earnings, July 1, 19X1	58,000	
Total	$108,000	
Interest acquired	80%	86,400
Excess of cost over book value attributed to equipment, 10-year life		
(maximum asset increase would be 80% × $40,000, or $32,000)		**$ 20,000**

Proceeding to the end of the year, assume that Company S operations for the last six months result in a net income of $20,000, and that $5,000 of dividends are paid by Company S on December 31. The consolidated work sheet (Illustration VII on pages 282 and 283) would include Company S nominal accounts only for the second six-month period, since nominal accounts were closed on July 1. Company S retained earnings shows the July 1, 19X1, balance. The trial balance for the parent Company P would include operations for the entire year. The subsidiary income listed by Company P would include 80% of the subsidiary's $20,000 second six-months' income. The investment account balance shows:

Original cost	$106,400
80% of subsidiary's second six-months' income of $20,000	16,000
Less 80% of $5,000 dividends paid by subsidiary	(4,000)
Total, December 31, 19X1	$118,400

The Consolidated Income Statement column of Illustration VII includes subsidiary income earned only after the acquisition date, which

(Credit balance amounts
are in parentheses)

	Trial Balance	
	Paulos	**Carlos**
Cash	322,000	160,000
Inventory	210,000	120,000
Land	200,000	150,000
Building	800,000	600,000
Accumulated Depreciation—Building	(120,000)	(330,000)
Equipment	400,000	150,000
Accumulated Depreciation—Equipment	(100,000)	(90,000)
Investment in Carlos	896,000	
Goodwill		100,000
Current Liabilities	(150,000)	(40,000)
Bonds Payable		(200,000)
Discount on Bonds		
Capital Stock, Paulos	(1,500,000)	
Retained Earnings, Jan. 1, 19X2, Paulos	(828,000)	
Capital Stock, Carlos		(100,000)
Paid-In Capital in Excess of Par, Carlos		(150,000)
Retained Earnings, Jan. 1, 19X2, Carlos		(290,000)
Sales	(400,000)	(300,000)
Cost of Goods Sold	200,000	120,000
Expenses	150,000	80,000
Subsidiary Income	(80,000)	
Dividends Declared		20,000
	0	0
Consolidated Net Income		
To Minority Interest (20% × $100,000 Carlos Income)		
Balance to Controlling Interest		
Total Minority Interest, Dec. 31, 19X2		
Retained Earnings, Controlling Interest, Dec. 31, 19X2		

Eliminations (the steps are keyed to correspond with those in Illustration V):
(1) Eliminate the current-year entries made in the investment account and in the subsidiary income account. The investment in Carlos account is now adjusted back to its January 1, 19X2, balance so that it may be eliminated against the January 1, 19X2, Carlos stockholders' equity.
(2) Eliminate the 80% ownership portion of the January 1, 19X2, subsidiary equity accounts against the investment. A $400,000 excess cost remains.
3 Distribute the $400,000 excess cost as required by the determination and distribution of excess schedule. The distribution is identical to that shown in Illustration V, except for the January 1, 19X1, inventory

Equity Method, Second Year
Subsidiary Carlos Company
Financial Statements
December 31, 19X2

| Eliminations | | Consolidated Income Statement | Minority Interest | Controlling Retained Earnings | Consolidated Balance Sheet |
Dr.	Cr.				
					482,000
					330,000
3e 40,000					390,000
					1,400,000
3d 160,000	4d 16,000				(306,000)
	3c 16,000				534,000
4c 6,400					(183,600)
(1) 16,000	(1) 80,000				
	(2) 432,000				
	3 400,000				
3f 201,402	4f 40,280				261,122
					(190,000)
					(200,000)
3b 10,598	4b 4,892				5,706
					(1,500,000)
3a 4,000	4c 3,200			(796,708)	
4b 2,352					
4d 8,000					
4f 20,140					
(2) 80,000			(20,000)		
(2) 120,000			(30,000)		
(2) 232,000			(58,000)		
		(700,000)			
		320,000			
4b 2,540	4c 3,200	257,480			
4d 8,000					
4f 20,140					
(1) 80,000					
	(1) 16,000		4,000		
1,011,572	1,011,572				
		(122,520)			
		20,000	(20,000)		
		102,520		(102,520)	
			(124,000)		(124,000)
				(899,228)	(899,228)
					0

adjustment of $4,000. This adjustment is now carried to the purchaser's January 1, 19X2, retained earnings balance, since it is an adjustment to 19X1 income.

4 Record amortizations resulting from the asset and liability revaluations of Step 3. The amortizations include those for the current and previous periods because the trial balances of the separate firms do not reflect the amortizations on the December 31, 19X1, consolidated work sheet. The adjustments are lettered (a) through (f) to correspond with the revaluations in Step 3 of Illustration V:

a. No amortization required; adjustment already charged to January 1, 19X2, controlling Retained Earnings.

(continued)

b. Amortize discount as follows:

Face, 80% × $200,000	$160,000	
Discount, December 31, 19X1 (see Illustration V)	(8,246)	$151,754
Multiply by 8% effective interest rate		.08
Effective interest expense..		$ 12,140
Nominal interest, 6% × $160,000		9,600
19X2 discount amortization		$ 2,540
Add 19X1 discount amortization (from page 278)..........................		2,352
Total amortization to date		$ 4,892

Illustration VII—Intraperiod Purchase
Company P and
Work Sheet for Consolidated
For Year Ended

(Credit balance amounts
are in parentheses)

	Trial Balance	
	Company P	**Company S**
Current Assets	187,600	87,500
Investment in Co. S	118,400	
Equipment	400,000	80,000
Accumulated Depreciation	(200,000)	(32,500)
Liabilities	(60,000)	(12,000)
Common Stock, Co. P	(250,000)	
Retained Earnings, Jan. 1, 19X1, Co. P	(100,000)	
Common Stock, Co. S		(50,000)
Retained Earnings, July 1, 19X1, Co. S		(58,000)
Sales	(500,000)	(92,000)
Cost of Goods Sold	350,000	60,000
Expenses	70,000	12,000
Subsidiary Income	(16,000)	
Dividends Declared		5,000
	0	0

Consolidated Net Income

To Minority Interest (20% × Subsidiary Income of $20,000 for Second Half of Year)

To Controlling Interest ($80,000 Co. P Operating Income Plus 80% × Subsidiary Income of $20,000 for Second Half of Year, Less $1,000 Depreciation Adjustment)

Total Minority Interest, Dec. 31, 19X1

Retained Earnings, Controlling Interest, Dec. 31, 19X1

Eliminations:

(1) Eliminate the entries made in the investment account and in the subsidiary income account to record the parent's 80% controlling interest in the subsidiary's second six-months' income and the subsidiary dividends, restoring the investment account to its balance as of the July 1, 19X1, investment date.

(2) Eliminate 80% of the subsidiary's July 1, 19X1, equity balances against the balance of the investment in Company S account.

The current year's amortization is charged to expense, while the 19X1 amortization is charged to January 1, 19X2, controlling Retained Earnings.

c. Record $3,200 annual decrease in equipment depreciation for 19X1 and 19X2. The 19X1 portion is carried to January 1, 19X2, controlling Retained Earnings, while the 19X2 adjustment is reflected in current expense.

d. Record $8,000 annual increase in 19X1 and 19X2 building depreciation; 19X1 adjustment reduces January 1, 19X2, controlling Retained Earnings; 19X2 adjustment increases current expense.

e. No amortization results from adjustment of land.

f. Amortize goodwill for the current year by increasing expenses, and for the past year by reducing controlling Retained Earnings on January 1, 19X2.

Subsidiary Books Closed on Purchase Date

Subsidiary Company S
Financial Statements
December 31, 19X1

Eliminations				Consolidated Income Statement	Minority Interest	Controlling Retained Earnings	Consolidated Balance Sheet
Dr.		Cr.					
							275,100
1	4,000	(1)	16,000				
		(2)	86,400				
		(3)	20,000				
							480,000
(3)	20,000	**4**	1,000				(213,500)
							(72,000)
							(250,000)
						(100,000)	
(2)	40,000				(10,000)		
(2)	46,400				(11,600)		
				(592,000)			
				410,000			
4	1,000			83,000			
(1)	16,000						
		1	4,000		1,000		
	127,400		127,400				
				(99,000)			
				4,000	(4,000)		
				95,000		(95,000)	
					(24,600)		(24,600)
						(195,000)	(195,000)
							0

(3) Distribute the excess of cost over book value of $20,000 to the accumulated depreciation account in accordance with the determination and distribution of excess schedule.

4 Amortize for one-half year the excess attributable to the equipment.

is in conformance with purchase theory. Likewise, only subsidiary income earned after the purchase date is distributed to the minority and controlling interests. Income earned prior to the purchase date is a part of the July 1, 19X1, Company S retained earnings balance, of which the minority is granted its share.

Option 2: Subsidiary Books Not Closed. Usually, a subsidiary does not close its books as a result of the parent company securing a controlling interest in its stock. Normally the parent company is able to ascertain the income earned by the subsidiary between the beginning of the year and the date control is achieved. If the subsidiary has already paid dividends as of the time of the acquisition, these dividends would be deducted in arriving at the total subsidiary equity interest as of that date.

Assume that the parent had access to the Company S trial balance shown on page 279, but Company S did not close its books as of July 1, 19X1. Company P would then prepare its determination and distribution of excess schedule as follows:

Price paid		$106,400
Interest acquired:		
Common stock ($10 par)	$ 50,000	
Retained earnings, January 1, 19X1	40,000	
Income of Company S, January 1-July 1	18,000	
Total interest, July 1, 19X1	$108,000	
Interest acquired	80%	86,400
Excess of cost over book value attributed to equipment, 10-year life:		
(maximum asset increase would be 80% × $40,000, or $32,000)		**$ 20,000**

Since the subsidiary has not closed its books as of July 1, 19X1, the consolidated work sheet of Illustration VIII, on pages 286 and 287, will include the Company S trial balance reflecting the entire year's operations. Company S Retained Earnings is dated January 1, 19X1. The Company P investment and subsidiary income accounts are identical to those of Illustration VII.

In Illustration VIII, "Purchased Income" is deducted in arriving at consolidated net income because the nominal accounts of the subsidiary for the entire year are included in the consolidated income column. However, 80% of the income for the first half of the year was earned by outside interests (shareholders that are no longer members of the affiliated group). This income must be deleted to arrive at consolidated net income which belongs to current members of the affiliated group. The minority interest existed for the entire year and thus is permitted a 20% share of subsidiary income for the full year. The work sheet of Illustration VIII leads to the unique income statement on page 285.

The format of this income statement has the advantage of disclosing the combined income of the two firms for the year and consolidated net income. The combined income figure becomes the basis for a pro forma

Company P and Subsidiary Company S
Consolidated Income Statement
For Year Ended December 31, 19X1

Sales..	$682,000
Less cost of goods sold	470,000
Gross profit	$212,000
Less other expenses	95,000
Net income of Company P and Company S combined	$117,000
Less income earned by outside interests existing prior to Company P purchase	14,400
Consolidated net income	$102,600
Distributed:	
To minority interest .... $ 7,600	
To controlling interest.................................... 95,000	$102,600

statement of what income would have been if the combination had occurred at the beginning of the year. This figure would only need to be supplemented by a disclosure that there would have been an additional $1,000 of equipment depreciation for the first six months of the year. The disclosure is required by APB Opinion No. 16 (par. 96) for intra-period purchases.

Special care must be taken in consolidating an intraperiod purchase in subsequent periods. It is a common error to find that a firm has taken a full year's share of equity income in the period of acquisition rather than including only income after the date of acquisition. When this error is found, a correcting entry should be recorded by the parent.

Intraperiod Purchase Under the Cost Method

There are only two variations of the procedures discussed in the preceding section if the cost method is used by the parent firm to record its investment in the subsidiary:

1. During the year of acquisition, the parent would record as income only its share of subsidiary dividends declared. Thus, eliminating entries would be confined to the intercompany dividends.
2. In subsequent years, the cost-to-equity conversion adjustment would be based on the change in retained earnings from the intraperiod purchase date to the beginning of the year for which the work sheet is being prepared.

POOLING OF INTERESTS: SUBSEQUENT TO ACQUISITION

In a pooling of interests, work sheet procedures in subsequent periods are simple if the original acquisition is recorded properly, since there is no excess of cost over book value. Thus, the cumbersome amortizations of the excess are not present. For example, using information based on Illustration VIII of Chapter 6 on page 242, Company I

Illustration VIII—Intraperiod Purchase
Company P and
(Credit balance amounts   Work Sheet for Consolidated
are in parentheses)   For Year Ended

	Trial Balance	
	Company P	Company S
Current Assets	187,600	87,500
Investment in Co. S	118,400	
Equipment	400,000	80,000
Accumulated Depreciation	(200,000)	(32,500)
Liabilities	(60,000)	(12,000)
Common Stock, Co. P	(250,000)	
Retained Earnings, Jan. 1, 19X1, Co. P	(100,000)	
Common Stock, Co. S		(50,000)
Retained Earnings, Jan. 1, 19X1, Co. S		(40,000)
Sales	(500,000)	(182,000)
Cost of Goods Sold	350,000	120,000
Expenses	70,000	24,000
Subsidiary Income	(16,000)	
Dividends Declared		5,000
Purchased Income		
	0	0

Consolidated Net Income

To Minority Interest (20% × Subsidiary Income of $38,000 for Entire Year)

To Controlling Interest ($80,000 Co. P Operating Income Plus 80% × Subsidiary Income of $20,000 for Second Half of Year, Less $1,000 Depreciation Adjustment)

Total Minority Interest

Retained Earnings, Controlling Interest, Dec. 31, 19X1

Eliminations:
(1) Eliminate the entries made in the investment account and in the subsidiary income account (same as Illustration VII).
2 Eliminate 80% of subsidiary equity balances at the beginning of the year, plus 80% of the undistributed subsidiary income as of July 1, 19X1, against the investment account. The share of undistributed income is entered as "Purchased Income" to emphasize that this income was earned prior to date of purchase by

---

issued 2,700 shares of its $2 par stock ($15 market value) for a 90% interest in Company C on January 1, 19X1, when Company C had the following condensed balance sheet:

Assets		Liabilities and Equity	
Current assets	$10,000	Liabilities	$10,000
Property, plant, and equipment		Common stock ($10 par)	10,000
(net)	30,000	Retained earnings	20,000
Total assets	$40,000	Total liabilities and equity	$40,000

Subsidiary Books Not Closed on Purchase Date
Subsidiary Company S
Financial Statements
December 31, 19X1

Eliminations Dr.	Eliminations Cr.	Consolidated Income Statement	Minority Interest	Controlling Retained Earnings	Consolidated Balance Sheet
					275,100
(1) 4,000	(1) 16,000				
	(2) 86,400				
	(3) 20,000				
					480,000
(3) 20,000	(4) 1,000				(213,500)
					(72,000)
					(250,000)
				(100,000)	
(2) 40,000			(10,000)		
(2) 32,000			(8,000)		
		(682,000)			
		470,000			
(4) 1,000		95,000			
(1) 16,000					
	(1) 4,000		1,000		
(2) 14,400		14,400			
127,400	127,400				
		(102,600)			
		7,600	(7,600)		
		95,000		(95,000)	
			(24,600)		(24,600)
				(195,000)	(195,000)
					0

Company P. For elimination purposes, this account can be viewed as a supplement to retained earnings. If the subsidiary paid dividends prior to July 1, 19X1, the controlling percentage of the dividends would also be eliminated in this entry.
(3) Distribute the $20,000 excess of cost over book value (same as Illustration VII).
(4) Amortize for one-half year the excess attributable to equipment (same as Illustration VII).

The following net income figures were reported by Company C subsequent to the acquisition date:

19X1	$20,000
19X2	15,000
19X3 (current year)..............................	25,000

Pooling rules require the issuing firm to record the investment at the book value of the underlying equity. Thus, Company I would have recorded the original acquisition as follows:

Investment in Company C (90% × $30,000 total Company C equity)	27,000	
Common Stock (2,700 shares × $2 par).................		5,400
Paid-In Capital in Excess of Par (90% Company C paid-in capital, $9,000, less $5,400 assigned to par)...........		3,600
Retained Earnings (90% × $20,000 Company C January 1, 19X1, Retained Earnings)		18,000

A consolidated financial statements work sheet for Companies I and C on December 31, 19X3, is found in Illustration IX. The balance in the investment in Company C account is the result of Company I's use of the equity method, as follows:

Illustration IX—Pooling of Interests
Company I and
Work Sheet for Consolidated
For Year Ended

(Credit balance amounts
are in parentheses)

	Trial Balance	
	Company I	**Company C**
Current Assets	46,000	35,000
Property, Plant, and Equipment (net)	64,500	60,000
Investment in Co. C	81,000	
Liabilities		(5,000)
Common Stock ($2 par), Co. I	(55,400)	
Paid-In Capital in Excess of Par, Co. I	(3,600)	
Retained Earnings, Jan. 1, 19X3, Co. I	(60,000)	
Common Stock ($10 par), Co. C		(10,000)
Retained Earnings, Jan. 1, 19X3, Co. C		(55,000)
Sales	(150,000)	(100,000)
Cost of Goods Sold	70,000	50,000
Expenses	30,000	25,000
Subsidiary Income	(22,500)	
	0	0
Consolidated Net Income		
To Minority Interest (10% × Co. C Net Income of $25,000)		
Balance to Controlling Interest		
Total Minority Interest, Dec. 31, 19X3		
Retained Earnings, Controlling Interest, Dec. 31, 19X3		

Eliminations:
(1) Eliminate the current-year entries in the investment account and in the subsidiary income account, restoring the investment account to its January 1, 19X3, balance so that it may be eliminated against the January 1, 19X3, Company C equity.

Original recorded value on January 1, 19X1	$27,000
90% × 19X1 Company C income of $20,000	18,000
90% × 19X2 Company C income of $15,000	13,500
90% × 19X3 Company C income of $25,000	22,500
Total equity balance, December 31, 19X3	$81,000

An investment might be properly recorded as a pooling initially, and not be equity-adjusted in subsequent periods. When an investment deemed to be a pooling is maintained at cost, a simple equity conversion entry may be made to update the investment account to its beginning-of-the-period balance. After the conversion, eliminations

Pooling Correctly Recorded
Subsidiary Company C
Financial Statements
December 31, 19X3

Eliminations		Consolidated Income Statement	Minority Interest	Controlling Retained Earnings	Consolidated Balance Sheet
Dr.	**Cr.**				
					81,000
					124,500
	(1) 22,500				
	2 58,500				
					(5,000)
					(55,400)
					(3,600)
				(60,000)	
2 9,000			(1,000)		
2 49,500			(5,500)		
		(250,000)			
		120,000			
		55,000			
(1) 22,500					
81,000	81,000				
		(75,000)			
		2,500	(2,500)		
		72,500		(72,500)	
			(9,000)		(9,000)
				(132,500)	(132,500)
					0

2 Eliminate 90% of the balances of the stockholders' equity accounts of Company C against the investment account. No excess results.

proceed as under the simple equity method, except that the elimination entry is limited to the intercompany dividends. The conversion procedures follow those used in Illustrations III and IV of this chapter for an investment recorded at cost.

It may also occur that the investment was originally recorded incorrectly at market value. This complication was discussed in Chapter 6. If this situation is encountered, it is suggested that the investment account be corrected to reflect the book value of the investment prior to proceeding to the consolidated work sheet. The investment account should be adjusted to the correct balance under either the cost or equity method, depending on the parent company's desires.

Intraperiod Pooling

It should be recalled that under pooling theory, income of the parent and subsidiary are to be consolidated at the beginning of the year, regardless of when control is achieved during the year. Thus, there is no reason to close the subsidiary books on the date control is achieved. Closing the books would, in fact, hinder the preparation of consolidated statements. Consolidated financial statements work sheets must begin with a subsidiary trial balance which includes the entire year's operations and the beginning-of-the-year balance for subsidiary retained earnings. Since consolidation procedures are applied retroactively to the beginning of the year, the entire incomes of the parent and subsidiary are distributed to the controlling and minority interests. No income is regarded as earned by outside interests. In summary, the consolidation procedures are identical to those used if the controlling investment had been made at the beginning of the year.

_____

QUESTIONS _____

1. Discuss the difference between the simple equity method and the cost method of recording an investment in a subsidiary.
2. Why doesn't it really matter whether the cost or equity method is used to account for an investment when the consolidation process is required?
3. The Subsidiary Company paid dividends of $10,000 from income earned prior to the firm's acquisition by the Parent Company. The Parent acquired an 85% interest in Subsidiary at a cost of $178,000. Under the cost method, at what dollar value is the investment recorded after receipt of the dividend by the Parent?
4. Describe the eliminations to be made on the work sheet when the investment in a subsidiary is accounted for under the equity method.

5. What is the minority interest comprised of? How is the minority interest presented on the consolidated balance sheet?

6. Describe the eliminations to be made on the work sheet when the investment in a subsidiary is carried by the cost method.

7. In a purchase, the parent's share of subsidiary liabilities is adjusted to reflect current market values at the time of acquisition. How are an undervalued and an overvalued subsidiary liability treated on the determination and distribution of excess schedule?

8. Why is the minority share of subsidiary income unaffected by amortizations which result from the revaluation of subsidiary assets and liabilities?

9. What effect does an intraperiod purchase have on the determination and distribution of excess schedule and on work sheets covering the period of acquisition? What special disclosure is required on the consolidated income statement due to the intraperiod purchase?

10. In an intraperiod purchase, subsidiary income is allocated to three different interest groups in the year of acquisition. What are these groups?

11. How do the problems created by an intraperiod pooling differ from an intraperiod purchase?

EXERCISES

Exercise 1. On January 1, 19X6, Bydlon Corporation purchased 80% of the outstanding stock of Upton Company for $268,000 in cash. Immediately prior to the purchase, Upton Company had the following balance sheet:

Assets		Liabilities and Equity	
Current assets	$ 90,000	Liabilities	$100,000
Land	80,000	Common stock, $5 par	100,000
Building and equipment (net) ...	170,000	Paid-in capital in excess of par..	20,000
		Retained earnings	120,000
Total assets	$340,000	Total liabilities and equity	$340,000

Book values approximated market values except for the land, which is worth $100,000. Any goodwill resulting from the purchase will be amortized over 40 years. Prepare a determination and distribution of excess schedule for this investment, and record the investment by Bydlon Corporation.

Exercise 2. Assume that Upton Company of Exercise 1 reports the following changes in retained earnings during 19X6 and 19X7.

Retained earnings, January 1, 19X6		$120,000
Add 19X6 net income	$ 40,000	
Less 19X6 dividends	24,000	16,000
Balance, December 31, 19X6........................		$136,000
Add 19X7 net income	$ 45,000	
Less 19X7 dividends	21,600	23,400
Balance, December 31, 19X7........................		$159,400

Prepare the journal entries that Bydlon Corporation would make to record this information relative to its 80% investment during 19X6 and 19X7 under (a) the simple equity method, (b) the sophisticated equity method, and (c) the cost method.

Exercise 3. Aron Company purchased an 80% interest in Brewer Company on January 1, 19X1, for $230,000 cash when Brewer Company had the following balance sheet:

Assets		Liabilities and Equity	
Current assets	$100,000	Current liabilities	$ 50,000
Property, plant, and equipment		Common stock, $10 par	100,000
(net)	200,000	Retained earnings	150,000
Total assets	$300,000	Total liabilities and equity	$300,000

Any excess of price paid over book value is attributable only to the plant assets, which have a 10-year remaining life. Aron Company uses the equity method to record its investment in Brewer Company.

The following trial balances were prepared by the two companies on December 31, 19X1:

	Aron	Brewer
Current Assets	80,000	130,000
Property, Plant, and Equipment	400,000	200,000
Accumulated Depreciation	(106,000)	(20,000)
Investment in Brewer Company	246,000	—
Current Liabilities	(60,000)	(40,000)
Common Stock ($10 par)	(300,000)	(100,000)
Retained Earnings, January 1, 19X1	(200,000)	(150,000)
Sales	(150,000)	(100,000)
Expenses	110,000	75,000
Subsidiary Income	(20,000)	—
Dividends Declared	—	5,000
Total	0	0

(1) Prepare a determination and distribution of excess schedule.
(2) Prepare all eliminations that would be made on a consolidated work sheet.
(3) Prepare a consolidated income statement which includes the distribution of consolidated income.
(4) Prepare a consolidated balance sheet.

Exercise 4. A trial balance for Aron and Brewer Companies of Exercise 3 for December 31, 19X2, is presented as follows:

	Aron	Brewer
Current Assets	172,000	105,000
Property, Plant, and Equipment	400,000	200,000
Accumulated Depreciation	(130,000)	(40,000)
Investment in Brewer Company	242,000	—
Current Liabilities	(80,000)	—
Common Stock, ($10 par)	(300,000)	(100,000)
Retained Earnings, January 1, 19X2	(260,000)	(170,000)
Sales	(200,000)	(100,000)
Expenses	160,000	95,000
Subsidiary Income	(4,000)	—
Dividends Declared	—	10,000
Total	0	0

(1) Prepare all the eliminations that would be made on a consolidated work sheet.

(2) Prepare a consolidated income statement which includes the distribution of consolidated income.

Exercise 5. Pepper Company purchased a 90% interest in Salt Company on January 1, 19X1, when Salt Company had the following balance sheet:

Assets		Liabilities and Equity	
Current assets	$200,000	Current liabilities..................	$100,000
Property, plant, and equipment		Common stock, $10 par	150,000
(net)...........................	300,000	Retained earnings	250,000
Total assets.....................	$500,000	Total liabilities and equity	$500,000

Pepper Company paid $300,000 for a 90% interest and paid $10,000 in direct acquisition costs. Any excess which results is attributable to the plant assets, which have a 10-year remaining life. The investment is maintained under the cost method.

The following trial balances were prepared by the two companies on December 31, 19X1:

	Pepper	Salt
Current Assets..	149,000	240,000
Property, Plant, and Equipment	800,000	300,000
Accumulated Depreciation	(100,000)	(30,000)
Investment in Salt Company	310,000	—
Current Liabilities....................................	(150,000)	(80,000)
Common Stock ($10 par)	(400,000)	(150,000)
Retained Earnings, January 1, 19X1	(500,000)	(250,000)
Sales...	(300,000)	(120,000)
Expenses...	200,000	80,000
Dividend Income (from Salt Co.)	(9,000)	—
Dividends Declared	—	10,000
Total	0	0

(1) Prepare a determination and distribution of excess schedule for the investment in Salt Company.
(2) Prepare all the eliminations that would be made on a consolidated work sheet.
(3) Prepare a consolidated income statement, including distribution of the consolidated net income.

Exercise 6. Pepper and Salt Companies of Exercise 5 prepared the following trial balances on December 31, 19X2.

	Pepper	Salt
Current Assets..	278,000	320,000
Property, Plant, and Equipment	800,000	300,000
Accumulated Depreciation	(150,000)	(60,000)
Investment in Salt Company	310,000	—
Current Liabilities....................................	(140,000)	(90,000)
Common Stock ($10 par)	(400,000)	(150,000)
Retained Earnings, January 1, 19X2	(609,000)	(280,000)
Sales...	(200,000)	(150,000)
Expenses...	120,000	100,000
Dividend Income (from Salt Co.)	(9,000)	—
Dividends Declared	—	10,000
Total	0	0

Prepare all eliminations that would be made on the consolidated work sheet prepared on December 31, 19X2.

Exercise 7. Martin Company paid $300,000 for a 90% interest in Senior Company on January 1, 19X1, at which time Senior Company had the following balance sheet:

Assets		Liabilities and Equity	
Accounts receivable	$ 70,000	Current liabilities	$ 70,000
Inventory	80,000	Common stock, $5 par	100,000
Land	20,000	Paid-in capital in excess of par	130,000
Building (net)	150,000	Retained earnings	20,000
Total assets	$320,000	Total liabilities and equity	$320,000

It was believed that the inventory and building were undervalued by $20,000 and $50,000, respectively, and that land is overvalued by $10,000. The building has a 10-year remaining life; the inventory on hand January 1, 19X1, was sold during the year. Goodwill, if any, would be amortized over the maximum 40 years.

The following separate income statements were prepared by the two companies for 19X1:

	Martin	Senior
Sales	$400,000	$150,000
Less cost of goods sold	(200,000)	(90,000)
Gross profit	$200,000	$ 60,000
Less: General expenses	(50,000)	(25,000)
Depreciation expense	(60,000)	(15,000)
Operating income	$ 90,000	$ 20,000
Subsidiary income	18,000	—
Net income	$108,000	$ 20,000

(1) Prepare a determination and distribution of excess schedule for the investment in Senior Company.
(2) Prepare a consolidated income statement for 19X1, including distribution of the consolidated net income.

Exercise 8. Carns Company had the following balance sheet on January 1, 19X1:

Assets		Liabilities and Equity	
Current assets	$150,000	Current liabilities	$ 50,000
Equipment (net)	300,000	Common stock, $10 par	100,000
		Retained earnings	300,000
Total assets	$450,000	Total liabilities and equity	$450,000

Between January 1 and July 1, 19X1, Carns Company estimated its net income to be $25,000. On July 1, 19X1, Abrams Company purchased 80% of the outstanding common stock of Carns Company for $300,000. Any excess of cost or book value is attributable to equipment with a 5-year life. Carns Company did not close its books on July 1.

On December 31, 19X1, Abrams and Carns Companies prepared the trial balances shown at the top of page 295.

(1) Prepare a determination and distribution of excess schedule for the investment in Carns.

	Abrams	Carns
Current Assets...	150,000	250,000
Equipment	500,000	300,000
Accumulated Depreciation	(140,000)	(20,000)
Investment in Carns Company	300,000	—
Current Liabilities....................................	(150,000)	(70,000)
Common Stock ($10 par).............................	(200,000)	(100,000)
Retained Earnings, January 1, 19X1	(400,000)	(300,000)
Sales..	(300,000)	(200,000)
Cost of Goods Sold	180,000	90,000
General Expenses.....................................	60,000	50,000
Total	0	0

(2) Prepare all eliminations that would be made on the December 31, 19X1, consolidated work sheet.

(3) Prepare a consolidated income statement, including distribution of the consolidated net income.

Exercise 9.   Baker Company had the following balance sheet on January 1, 19X1:

Assets		Liabilities and Equity	
Current assets................	$ 60,000	Common stock, $5 par	$ 50,000
Property, plant, and equipment	210,000	Paid-in capital in excess of par	60,000
Accumulated depreciation.....	(40,000)	Retained earnings	140,000
Goodwill......................	20,000		
Total assets	$250,000	Total liabilities and equity	$250,000

On July 1, 19X1, Dressel Company acquired 100% of the outstanding stock of Baker Company in a transaction that met the criteria for a pooling of interests. Dressel issued 8,000 shares of $10 par common stock, with a market value of $50 each. Baker Company estimated its first six months' income to be $200,000; the books were not closed. Dressel and Baker Companies prepared the following trial balances on December 31, 19X1:

	Dressel	Baker
Current Assets..	200,000	112,000
Property, Plant, and Equipment	1,950,000	210,000
Accumulated Depreciation	(350,000)	(50,000)
Investment in Baker Company	400,000	—
Goodwill..	—	18,000
Common Stock ($10 par).............................	(580,000)	—
Common Stock ($5 par)	—	(50,000)
Paid-In Capital in Excess of Par	(720,000)	(60,000)
Retained Earnings, January 1, 19X1	(860,000)	(140,000)
Sales...	(100,000)	(80,000)
Expenses...	60,000	40,000
Total	0	0

Prepare a consolidated income statement and balance sheet for December 31, 19X1.

Exercise 10.   On January 1, 19X6, Pluto, Inc., issued 200,000 additional shares of its voting common stock in exchange for 100,000 shares of Sherry Company's outstanding voting common stock in a business combination appropriately accounted for by the pooling-of-interests method. The market value of Pluto's voting common stock was $40 per share on the date of the business combination. The balance sheets of Pluto and Sherry immediately before the business combination contained the following information:

Pluto, Inc.

Common stock, $5 par; authorized 1,000,000 shares; issued and outstanding 600,000 shares	$ 3,000,000
Additional paid-in capital	6,000,000
Retained earnings	11,000,000
Total stockholders' equity	$20,000,000

Sherry Company

Common stock, $10 par; authorized 250,000 shares; issued and outstanding 100,000 shares	$ 1,000,000
Additional paid-in capital	2,000,000
Retained earnings	4,000,000
Total stockholders' equity	$ 7,000,000

Additional information is as follows:
(a) Net income for the year ended December 31, 19X6, was $1,150,000 for Pluto and $350,000 for Sherry.
(b) During 19X6, Pluto paid $900,000 in dividends to its stockholders and Sherry paid $210,000 in dividends to Pluto.

Prepare the consolidated stockholders' equity section of the balance sheet of Pluto, Inc., and its subsidiary, Sherry Company, at December 31, 19X6.

(AICPA adapted)

PROBLEMS

Problem 7-1. Ace, Barns, and Charms Companies had the following balance sheets on January 1, 19X1:

Assets	Ace	Barns	Charms
Current assets	$1,500,000	$100,000	$200,000
Property, plant, and equipment (net)	4,500,000	300,000	400,000
Total assets	$6,000,000	$400,000	$600,000

Equity			
Common stock, $10 par	$2,000,000	$100,000	$200,000
Paid-in capital in excess of par	3,000,000	100,000	300,000
Retained earnings	1,000,000	200,000	100,000
Total equity	$6,000,000	$400,000	$600,000

Subsequent to the preparation of these balance sheets. Ace acquires 80% of the outstanding stock of Barns Company in exchange for 12,000 newly issued shares. Ace also acquires 90% of Charms Company stock in exchange for 16,000 newly issued shares. Both acquisitions are deemed to be a purchase. The market value of the newly issued Ace Company shares is $30 each.

All assets of Barns and Charms Companies are recorded at values approximating market value. All plant assets have a 10-year remaining life. Any resulting goodwill is to be amortized over the maximum allowable life.

During 19X1 and 19X2, the three companies report the following:

	Ace Company		Barns Company		Charms Company	
	Income	Dividends	Income	Dividends	Income	Dividends
19X1	$200,000	$50,000	$50,000	$10,000	$10,000	$20,000
19X2	300,000	50,000	5,000	10,000	30,000	0

Required:

(1) Prepare determination and distribution of excess schedules for the invest-ments.
(2) Record all entries pertaining to the investments for 19X1 and 19X2:
   (a) under the simple equity method,
   (b) under the cost method.
(3) Assuming the use of the cost method, prepare the cost-to-equity conver-sion entries that would be made on the December 31, 19X2, consolidated work sheet.
(4) As of December 31, 19X2, calculate the minority and controlling interests in consolidated Retained Earnings.

Problem 7-2. The trial balances of Carswold Corporation and Davidson Corpora-tion as of December 31, 19X1, are as follows:

	Carswold Corporation	Davidson Corporation
Current Assets.................................	200,000	100,000
Land...	400,000	100,000
Building and Equipment (net)	900,000	240,000
Investment in Davidson Corporation	249,000	—
Current Liabilities.............................	(150,000)	(120,000)
Common Stock ($5 par)	(500,000)	—
Common Stock ($50 par)	—	(200,000)
Paid-In Capital in Excess of Par	(550,000)	—
Retained Earnings, January 1, 19X1	(485,000)	(100,000)
Sales...	(309,000)	(150,000)
Subsidiary Income	(14,000)	—
Cost of Goods Sold	170,000	80,000
Expenses......................................	89,000	50,000
Total	0	0

On January 1, 19X1, Carswold purchased 70% of the outstanding stock of Davidson Corporation for $235,000. Direct acquisition costs amounted to $5,000, which was subsequently expensed by Carswold Corporation. At the purchase date, Davidson's land had a market value of $140,000. All other assets had a book value that approximated market value. Any resulting goodwill is to be amortized over 20 years.

Required:

(1) Prepare a determination and distribution of excess schedule.
(2) Prepare consolidated statements for 19X1, including the income state-ment, retained earnings statement, and a balance sheet (a work sheet is not required).

Problem 7-3. On January 1, 19X4, Tucker, Inc., acquired 80% of the outstanding stock of Call Enterprises for $135,000. Tucker, Inc., also paid $5,000 for direct acquisition costs which were added to the investment account. At the time of the acquisition, Call Enterprises had the following stockholders' equity:

Common stock, $10 par	$100,000
Paid-in capital in excess of par	30,000
Retained earnings	70,000
Total stockholders' equity	$200,000

Any discrepancy between the price paid and the underlying book value is attributable to equipment, which had a 10-year remaining life on January 1, 19X4.

Tucker, Inc., uses the simple equity method to account for its investment in Call Enterprises. The two companies have prepared the following trial balances for the year ending December 31, 19X7:

	Tucker, Inc.	Call Enterprises
Current Assets.....................................	297,000	113,000
Equipment	1,200,000	400,000
Accumulated Depreciation	(310,000)	(174,000)
Investment in Call Enterprises	208,000	—
Liabilities	(507,000)	(54,000)
Common Stock ($10 par)	(400,000)	(100,000)
Paid-In Capital in Excess of Par	(20,000)	(30,000)
Retained Earnings, January 1, 19X7	(404,400)	(120,000)
Sales..	(291,000)	(105,000)
Subsidiary Income	(33,600)	—
Cost of Goods Sold	145,000	38,000
Expenses..	100,000	25,000
Dividends Declared	16,000	7,000
Total	0	0

Required:

(1) Prepare the determination and distribution of excess schedule.
(2) Prepare consolidated statements for 19X7, including the income statement, retained earnings statement, and balance sheet (a work sheet is not required).

Problem 7-4. Stone Company had the following balance sheet on January 1, 19X1:

Assets		Liabilities and Equity	
Current assets	$ 50,000	Liabilities	$140,000
Land	75,000	Common stock, $10 par	100,000
Buildings	350,000	Paid-in capital in excess of	
Accumulated depreciation		par	120,000
—buildings	(140,000)	Retained earnings (deficit) ...	(25,000)
Total assets................	$335,000	Total liabilities and equity ...	$335,000

On this date, Rock Company purchased 8,000 shares of Stone Company stock for a total price of $170,000. Any discrepancy between this price and book value was attributed to the buildings, which have been overdepreciated in past years. It is felt that the buildings have a 10-year remaining life. Rock Company uses the cost method to record the investment and related income.

Rock and Stone Companies prepared the following separate trial balances on December 31, 19X1:

	Rock	Stone
Current Assets...............................	80,000	110,000
Land	150,000	75,000
Buildings	540,000	350,000
Accumulated Depreciation—Buildings	(215,000)	(161,000)
Investment in Stone Company	170,000	—
Liabilities	(150,000)	(169,000)
Common Stock ($10 par)	(200,000)	(100,000)
Paid-In Capital in Excess of Par	—	(120,000)
Retained Earnings, January 1, 19X1	(315,000)	25,000
Sales..	(320,000)	(90,000)
Cost of Goods Sold	150,000	40,000
Expenses.....................................	100,000	40,000
Dividends Declared	10,000	—
Total	0	0

Required:

(1) Prepare a determination and distribution of excess schedule for the investment.

(2) Prepare consolidated statements for 19X1, including the income statement, retained earnings statement, and balance sheet (a work sheet is not required).

Problem 7-5.   Rock and Stone Companies of Problem 7-4 have prepared the following separate trial balances for 19X2.

	Rock	Stone
Current Assets..............................	160,000	115,000
Land	150,000	75,000
Buildings	590,000	350,000
Accumulated Depreciation—Buildings	(265,000)	(182,000)
Investment in Stone Company	170,000	—
Liabilities	(175,000)	(133,000)
Common Stock ($10 par)	(200,000)	(100,000)
Paid-In Capital in Excess of Par	—	(120,000)
Retained Earnings, January 1, 19X2	(375,000)	15,000
Sales..	(360,000)	(120,000)
Dividend Income	(4,000)	—
Cost of Goods Sold	179,000	50,000
Expenses.....................................	120,000	45,000
Dividends Declared	10,000	5,000
Total	0	0

Required:

Assuming the same facts applicable to the acquisition as used in Problem 7-4, prepare consolidated statements for 19X2, including the income statement, retained earnings statement, and balance sheet (a work sheet is not required).

Problem 7-6.   On January 1, 19X1, Zelton Corporation exchanged 50,000 newly issued shares for all of the outstanding stock of Ash, Inc. The combination meets the criteria for a pooling of interests. Zelton Corporation maintains its investment in the subsidiary under the equity method. Trial balances for the two companies were as follows on December 31, 19X1:

	Zelton Corporation	Ash, Inc.
Current Assets.....................................	425,000	340,000
Property, Plant, and Equipment	2,155,000	830,000
Accumulated Depreciation	(355,000)	(90,000)
Investment in Ash, Inc.	620,000	—
Liabilities	(740,000)	(460,000)
Common Stock ($5 par)	(1,000,000)	—
Common Stock ($10 par)	—	(300,000)
Paid-In Capital in Excess of Par	(560,000)	—
Retained Earnings, January 1, 19X1	(490,000)	(280,000)
Revenues	(440,000)	(210,000)
Subsidiary Income	(70,000)	—
Expenses..	415,000	140,000
Dividends Declared	40,000	30,000
Total	0	0

Required:

Prepare consolidated statements for 19X1, including an income statement, retained earnings statement, and a balance sheet (a work sheet is not required).

Problem 7-7. The following trial balances were prepared on December 31, 19X1, for Erin Company and its subsidiary, Crystal, Inc.

	Erin Company	Crystal, Inc.
Current Assets.....................................	570,000	130,000
Property, Plant, and Equipment	1,805,000	440,000
Accumulated Depreciation	(405,000)	(70,000)
Investment in Crystal, Inc.	340,000	—
Liabilities	(900,000)	(225,000)
Common Stock ($1 par)	(220,000)	—
Common Stock ($5 par)	—	(50,000)
Paid-In Capital in Excess of Par	(880,000)	(15,000)
Retained Earnings, January 1, 19X1	(270,000)	(170,000)
Revenues	(460,000)	(210,000)
Subsidiary Income	(40,000)	—
Expenses..	450,000	170,000
Dividends Declared	10,000	—
Total	0	0

On July 5, 19X1, Erin Company exchanged 20,000 shares with a market value of $15 each for all of the outstanding stock of Crystal, Inc., in a transaction meeting the criteria for a pooling of interests.

Required:

Prepare consolidated statements for 19X1, including an income statement, retained earnings statement, and a balance sheet (a work sheet is not required).

Problem 7-8. On January 1, 19X1, Fields Corporation exchanged 100,000 shares of its $5 par stock, with a market value of $12 per share, for 90% of the outstanding common stock of Reed Corporation in a transaction qualifying as a pooling of interests. The account Investment in Reed Corporation reflects the market value of the shares exchanged and the issuance cost related to the Fields Corporation common stock.

Immediately prior to the exchange, Reed Corporation had the following owners' equity accounts:

Common Stock, $2 par	$200,000
Paid-In Capital in Excess of Par	400,000
Retained Earnings (deficit)	(50,000)
Total equity	$550,000

Since the exchange, Fields Corporation has used the cost method to account for its investment in Reed.

No intercompany transactions have ever occurred.

On December 31, 19X3, Fields Corporation and Reed Corporation had the following trial balances:

	Fields Corporation	Reed Corporation
Current Assets	840,000	360,000
Property, Plant, and Equipment	4,800,000	1,570,000
Accumulated Depreciation	(1,600,000)	(520,000)
Investment in Reed Corp.	1,250,000	—
Liabilities	(1,830,000)	(790,000)
Common Stock ($5 par)	(1,000,000)	—
Common Stock ($2 par)	—	(200,000)
Paid-In Capital in Excess of Par	(1,500,000)	(400,000)
Retained Earnings	(900,000)	10,000
Sales	(1,050,000)	(440,000)
Cost of Goods Sold	600,000	250,000
Expenses	350,000	160,000
Dividends Paid	40,000	—
Total	0	0

Required:

(1) Prepare the journal entries that should be made to properly reflect this investment on the books of the parent company.

(2) Prepare a consolidated work sheet for 19X3. Include a column for consolidated income, the minority stockholders' interest, the controlling retained earnings, and a balance sheet.

Problem 7-9. Stiles Corporation purchased the outstanding stock of Maybee Corporation for $50,000 cash on January 1, 19X7. On the purchase date, Maybee Corporation had the following condensed balance sheet:

Assets		Liabilities and Equity	
Cash and receivables	$ 40,000	Liabilities	$ 80,000
Inventory	20,000	Stockholders' equity	100,000
Land	120,000		
Total assets	$180,000	Total liabilities and equity	$180,000

Maybee's land has lost significant value. The inventory is judged to have a market value of $10,000 at the time of the acquisition. During 19X7, half of the land and all of the inventory were sold by Maybee Corporation. None of Maybee's assets were sold to Stiles, and there were no other intercompany transactions during 19X7. Trial balances for the two firms on December 31, 19X7, appeared as follows:

	Stiles Corporation	Maybee Corporation
Cash and Receivables	150,000	20,000
Inventory	60,000	10,000
Land	120,000	60,000
Buildings (net)..................................	600,000	—
Investment in Maybee Corporation	50,000	—
Liabilities	(405,000)	(20,000)
Common Stock ($3 par)	(300,000)	—
Common Stock ($.50 par)	—	(20,000)
Paid-In Capital in Excess of Par	(100,000)	(90,000)
Retained Earnings, January 1, 19X7	(135,000)	10,000
Sales..	(210,000)	(40,000)
Cost of Goods Sold	120,000	35,000
Expenses......................................	45,000	10,000
Loss on Sale of Land...........................	—	25,000
Dividends Declared	5,000	—
Total	0	0

Required:

(1) Prepare a determination and distribution of excess schedule for the investment.
(2) Prepare a consolidated work sheet for 19X7, including columns for consolidated income, controlling interest in retained earnings, and balance sheet.
(3) Prepare consolidated statements for 19X7, including an income statement, retained earnings statement, and balance sheet.

Problem 7-10. Gray Steel Corporation purchased 80% of the outstanding stock of Pig Iron Company for $200,000 on January 1, 19X1, at which time Pig Iron Company had the following stockholders' equity:

Common stock, $5 par	$150,000
Retained earnings	50,000
Total equity	$200,000

The market value of Pig Iron's assets and liabilities agreed with the book values, except for the equipment, which was overdepreciated by $10,000 and was thought to have a 5-year remaining life. Any goodwill that results is to be amortized over 20 years. Gray Steel uses the sophisticated equity method to record its investment.

Since the purchase date, both firms have operated separately and no intercompany transactions have occurred.

The separate trial balances of the firms on December 31, 19X2, are shown at the top of page 303.

Required:

(1) Prepare a determination and distribution of excess schedule for the investment in Pig Iron Company.
(2) Prepare a consolidated work sheet for December 31, 19X2, including columns for consolidated income, minority stockholders' interest, controlling interest in retained earnings, and balance sheet.
(3) Prepare consolidated statements for December 31, 19X2, including an income statement, retained earnings statement, and balance sheet.

	Gray Steel	Pig Iron
Current Assets	380,000	90,000
Investment in Pig Iron Company	213,600	—
Land	160,000	90,000
Building	225,000	135,000
Accumulated Depreciation—Building	(100,000)	(50,000)
Equipment	450,000	150,000
Accumulated Depreciation—Equipment	(115,000)	(60,000)
Liabilities	(500,000)	(130,000)
Common Stock ($100 par)	(400,000)	—
Common Stock ($5 par)	—	(150,000)
Paid-In Capital in Excess of Par	(40,000)	—
Retained Earnings, January 1, 19X2	(248,800)	(65,000)
Sales	(460,000)	(120,000)
Subsidiary Income	(4,800)	—
Cost of Goods Sold	220,000	60,000
Expenses	210,000	50,000
Dividends Declared	10,000	—
Total	0	0

Problem 7-11. Test Electronics purchased 100% of the outstanding stock of Electron Beam, Inc., for $1,850,000 on January 1, 19X4. At the purchase date, Electron Beam's book values approximated market values, except for the equipment and the patents, which had fair market values of $44,000 and $50,000, respectively, in excess of their book values. The two companies agreed that the equipment had a remaining life of 8 years and the patents, 10 years. On the purchase date, Electron Beam's owners' equity section was as follows:

Common stock, $10 stated value	$1,000,000
Additional paid-in capital	300,000
Retained earnings	390,000
Total equity	$1,690,000

During the next two years, Electron Beam, Inc., had income and paid dividends as follows:

	Income	Dividends
19X4	$ 90,000	$30,000
19X5	120,000	30,000

The trial balances of the two corporations as of December 31, 19X6, are shown at the top of page 304.

Required:

Assuming that any goodwill which results is to be amortized over 20 years, and that no intercompany transactions occurred:
(1) Prepare the original determination and distribution of excess schedule.
(2) Prepare a consolidated work sheet for December 31, 19X6, including columns for consolidated income, controlling interest in retained earnings, and balance sheet.

	Test Electronics	Electron Beam
Current Assets..................................	910,000	430,000
Equipment (net)	1,290,000	940,000
Patents	100,000	35,000
Other Assets	1,620,000	730,000
Investment in Electron Beam....................	1,850,000	—
Liabilities	(1,150,000)	(205,000)
Common Stock ($5 par)	(2,000,000)	—
Common Stock ($10 stated value)	—	(1,000,000)
Additional Paid-In Capital	(1,200,000)	(300,000)
Retained Earnings	(1,255,000)	(540,000)
Sales..	(905,000)	(400,000)
Subsidiary Dividend Income	(30,000)	—
Cost of Goods Sold	470,000	170,000
Expenses....................................	250,000	110,000
Dividends Declared	50,000	30,000
Total	0	0

Problem 7-12. Pearl Corporation acquired 80% of the outstanding common stock of Satern Corporation on April 1, 19X4, for $300,000. Satern Corporation did not close its books on April 1, 19X4. The following trial balance for Satern Corporation was secured as of April 1, 19X4.

Current Assets.....................................	250,000	—
Marketable Securities	50,000	—
Land	100,000	—
Building	350,000	—
Accumulated Depreciation—Building	—	150,000
Equipment	300,000	—
Accumulated Depreciation—Equipment	—	200,000
Current Liabilities.................................	—	150,000
Bonds Payable (8%)	—	200,000
Common Stock ($10 par)	—	100,000
Paid-In Capital in Excess of Par	—	50,000
Retained Earnings, January 1, 19X4	—	180,000
Sales..	—	60,000
Cost of Goods Sold	20,000	—
Expenses..	20,000	—
Total	1,090,000	1,090,000

Depreciation for the first three months of the year is included in the contra asset and expenses accounts.

As of April 1, 19X4, the following book values differed materially from market:

	Book Value	Market Value
Marketable securities..........................	$ 50,000	$ 55,375
Land	100,000	160,000
Building (net)	200,000	150,000
Bonds payable	200,000	203,375

The bonds payable were issued on January 1, 19X1, to mature in 10 years and pay 8% interest annually. For the purpose of this problem, any discount or premium resulting from the purchase may be amortized by the straight-line method.

As of the purchase date, the buildings have an estimated future life of 10 years. Any goodwill that results from the purchase will be amortized over 20 years.

Trial balances of Pearl Corporation and Satern Corporation on December 31, 19X4, are as follows:

	Pearl	Satern
Current Assets..................................	600,000	235,000
Marketable Securities	—	100,000
Land	400,000	150,000
Building	900,000	350,000
Accumulated Depreciation—Building	(425,000)	(165,000)
Equipment	1,100,000	300,000
Accumulated Depreciation—Equipment	(600,000)	(220,000)
Investment in Satern Corporation	336,000	—
Current Liabilities..............................	(340,000)	(155,000)
Bonds Payable.................................	(300,000)	(200,000)
Common Stock ($5 par)	(500,000)	—
Common Stock ($10 par)	—	(100,000)
Paid-In Capital in Excess of Par	(300,000)	(50,000)
Retained Earnings, January 1, 19X4	(750,000)	(180,000)
Sales...	(490,000)	(220,000)
Cost of Goods Sold	245,000	74,000
Expenses.....................................	144,000	76,000
Subsidiary Income	(40,000)	—
Dividends Declared	20,000	5,000
Total	0	0

Required:

(1) Prepare a determination and distribution of excess schedule for the investment in the Satern Corporation.
(2) Prepare a consolidated work sheet for December 31, 19X4.
(3) Prepare consolidated statements for 19X4, including an income statement, retained earnings statement, and a balance sheet.

Problem 7-13.   On January 1, 19X1, Green Corporation purchased 80% of the outstanding common stock of Ivan, Inc., for $6,000,000 cash. The book and market values for Ivan, Inc., were as follows:

	Recorded Book Value	Market Value
Cash and Receivables	$1,305,000	$1,305,000
Inventory	790,000	823,345
Land	2,500,000	3,900,000
Building	2,400,000	1,200,000
Accumulated Depreciation—Building	(1,600,000)	—
Equipment	2,750,000	1,700,000
Accumulated Depreciation—Equipment	(1,850,000)	—
Goodwill	120,000	200,000*
Current Liabilities..............................	(580,000)	(580,000)
Bonds Payable, 6%	(2,000,000)	(1,730,845)
Common Stock ($5 par)	(3,000,000)	—
Retained Earnings	(835,000)	—
Total	0	

* Estimate, final value dependent on total purchase price.

By the end of 19X1, the January 1, 19X1, inventory of Ivan, Inc., had been sold. As of the purchase date, the building and equipment are judged to have remaining lives of 10 years and 6 years respectively. The goodwill is to be amortized over a 10-year remaining life. As of January 1, 19X1, the 6% bonds had six years remaining to maturity. The fair market value of the bonds was based on the 9% prevailing interest rate on January 1, 19X1.

The following trial balances were prepared for Green and Ivan on December 31, 19X1:

	Green	Ivan
Cash and Receivables	2,400,000	1,581,800
Inventory	1,600,000	800,000
Land	4,000,000	2,500,000
Buildings	6,900,000	2,400,000
Accumulated Depreciation—Buildings	(3,400,000)	(1,680,000)
Equipment	10,000,000	2,750,000
Accumulated Depreciation—Equipment	(5,000,000)	(2,000,000)
Goodwill	200,000	108,000
Investment in Ivan, Inc.	6,011,840	—
Current Liabilities	(2,000,000)	(610,000)
Bonds Payable	(6,000,000)	(2,000,000)
Common Stock ($5 par)	(13,000,000)	(3,000,000)
Retained Earnings, January 1, 19X1	(1,550,000)	(835,000)
Sales	(3,000,000)	(1,490,000)
Cost of Goods Sold	1,900,000	968,500
Expenses	900,000	476,700
Subsidiary Income	(35,840)	—
Dividends Declared	74,000	30,000
Total	0	0

Required:

(1) Prepare a determination and distribution of excess schedule for the investment in Ivan, Inc.
(2) Prepare a consolidated work sheet for December 31, 19X1, including columns for consolidated income, minority stockholders' interest, controlling interest in retained earnings, and balance sheet.   (AICPA adapted)

Problem 7-14. On April 1, 19X1, Jansen, Inc., purchased 100% of the common stock of Murdock Company for $5,850,000. At the date of purchase, the book values and market values of Murdock's assets and liabilities were shown at the top of page 307.

By the year-end, December 31, 19X1, the following transactions had occurred:
(a) The balance of Murdock's net accounts receivable at April 1, 19X1, had been collected.
(b) The inventory on hand at April 1, 19X1, had been charged to cost of goods sold. Murdock used a perpetual inventory system in accounting for inventories.
(c) Included in Jansen's investment account is $1,500,000 of Daley Corporation, 7% subordinated debentures. These debentures mature on October 31, 19X7, with interest payable annually on October 31.
(d) As of April 1, 19X1, Jansen viewed the machinery and equipment as having an estimated remaining life of six years. Murdock used the straight-line

	Book Value	Market Value
Cash	$ 200,000	$ 200,000
Notes Receivable (net)	85,000	85,000
Accounts Receivable (net)	980,000	980,000
Inventories	828,000	700,000
Land	1,560,000	2,100,000
Machinery and Equipment	7,850,000	10,600,000
Accumulated Depreciation	(3,250,000)	(4,000,000)
Other Assets	140,000	50,000
Total assets	$8,393,000	$10,715,000
Notes Payable	$ 115,000	$ 115,000
Accounts Payable..............................	1,150,000	1,150,000
Subordinated Debentures (7%)	5,000,000	5,000,000
Common Stock ($10 par)	1,000,000	
Paid-In Capital in Excess of Par	122,000	
Retained Earnings	1,006,000	
Total liabilities...............................	$8,393,000	

method of depreciation and a different remaining life. Murdock's depreciation expense calculation for the nine months ended December 31, 19X1,
was based upon the old depreciation rates.

(e) The other assets consist entirely of long-term investments made by Murdock and do not include any investment in Jansen.

(f) Accrued interest on debt is recorded by both companies in their respective
accounts receivable and accounts payable accounts.

(g) Jansen's policy is to amortize intangible assets over a 20-year period.

(h) Murdock Company closed its books on April 1, 19X1. Therefore, the trial
balances shown on page 308 provide revenue and expense figures for 12
months for Jansen and 9 months for Murdock.

Required:

(1) Prepare a determination and distribution of excess schedule for the
investment in Murdock Company common stock. Jansen, Inc., desires that
the consolidated statements reflect the replacement cost and related
depreciation as shown in the market value information.

(2) Prepare a consolidated work sheet which converts the separate trial balances into a consolidated trial balance. This work sheet should have the
following columns:

Trial Balance		Eliminations		Consolidated Trial Balance
Jansen, Inc.	Murdock Co.	Debit	Credit	

(AICPA adapted)

	Jansen, Inc.	Murdock Co.
Cash	972,000	530,000
Notes Receivable	—	85,000
Accounts Receivable (net)	2,758,000	1,368,400
Inventories	3,204,000	1,182,000
Land	4,000,000	1,560,000
Buildings	1,286,000	—
Accumulated Depreciation—Buildings	(372,000)	—
Machinery and Equipment	15,875,000	7,850,000
Accumulated Depreciation—Machinery and		
Equipment	(6,301,000)	(3,838,750)
Investments	7,350,000	—
Other Assets	263,000	140,000
Notes Payable	—	(115,000)
Accounts Payable	(1,364,000)	(954,000)
Long-Term Debt	(10,000,000)	—
Subordinated Debentures, 7%	—	(5,000,000)
Common Stock	(2,400,000)	(1,000,000)
Paid-In Capital in Excess of Par	(240,000)	(122,000)
Retained Earnings	(12,683,500)	(1,006,000)
Sales..	(18,200,000)	(5,760,000)
Cost of Goods Sold	10,600,000	3,160,000
Selling, General, and Administrative Expenses.	3,448,500	1,063,900
Depreciation Expense—Buildings	127,000	—
Depreciation Expense—Equipment	976,000	588,750
Interest Revenue	(105,000)	(1,700)
Interest Expense...........................	806,000	269,400
Total	0	0

CHAPTER 8
INTERCOMPANY TRANSACTIONS: MERCHANDISE, PLANT ASSETS, AND NOTES

Consolidated financial reporting for members of an affiliated group requires that the parent firm must have effective operating control over its subsidiaries and that the operations of the member firms be integrated. When these conditions exist, it is very likely that there will be continuing business transactions between the affiliates. The most common types of such transactions are intercompany sales of merchandise, services, and plant assets. It will also be common to find intercompany loan transactions which may result from or be independent of intercompany sales.

For each type of intercompany transaction, the applicable theory is mastered by answering the question: "From the viewpoint of a single, consolidated entity, what evidence of the transaction should remain on the consolidated statements?" To answer that question, attention is focused on the mechanics of the elimination procedures to be used on the consolidated work sheet.

INTERCOMPANY MERCHANDISE SALES

It is very common to find that the goods sold by one member of an affiliated group have been purchased from another member of the group. Frequently one firm may produce component parts which are assembled by another affiliate which sells the final product. In other cases, the product may be entirely produced by one member firm and sold on a wholesale basis to another member firm, which is responsible for selling and servicing the product to the final users. Merchandise sales are the most common type of intercompany transaction, and thus must be understood as a basic feature of consolidated reporting.

Sales between affiliated firms will be recorded in the normal manner on the books of the separate firms. The financial statements of the separate firms will include the purchase and sale transactions. However, when the statements of the affiliates are consolidated, such sales become transfers of goods within the consolidated entity. These sales cannot be acknowledged in consolidated statements, since they do not involve transactions with parties outside the consolidated group.

Following are the procedures for consolidating affiliated firms engaged in intercompany merchandise sales:

1. The intercompany sale must be eliminated to avoid double counting. To understand this requirement, assume that Company P sells merchandise, which cost $1,000, to a subsidiary, Company S, for $1,200. Company S sells the merchandise to an outside party for $1,500. If no elimination is made, the consolidated income statement would show the following with respect to the transaction:

Sales	$2,700 ($1,500 outside sale plus $1,200 internal sale)
Less cost of goods sold........	2,200 ($1,000 cost to Company P plus $1,200 internal purchase)
Gross profit	$ 500 (18.5 % gross profit rate)

While the gross profit is correct, sales and the cost of goods sold are inflated. As a result, the gross profit percentage is understated, since the $500 gross profit appears to relate to $2,700 of sales. The intercompany sale must be eliminated from the consolidated statements. All that should remain on the consolidated income statement with respect to this transaction is:

Sales	$1,500 (only the final sale to outside parties)
Less cost of goods sold.......	1,000 (only the purchase from outside parties)
Gross profit	$ 500 (33⅓% gross profit rate)

When the goods sold internally are manufactured by the selling affiliate, the consolidated cost of goods sold includes only those costs which can normally be inventoried, such as labor, materials, and overhead.

The intercompany sale, though eliminated, does have an effect on the distribution of consolidated income to the controlling and minority interests. The reported net income of the subsidiary reflects the intercompany sales price. The subsidiary's separate income statement becomes the base from which the minority share of income is calculated. In effect, the intercompany transfer price becomes an agreement as to how a portion of consolidated income will be divided. For example, if Company S is an 80%-owned subsidiary, the minority interest will receive 20% of the $300 profit made on the final sale by Company S, or $60. If the intercompany transfer price is increased from $1,200 to $1,300 and the final sale price remains at $1,500, Company S would earn only $200, and the minority interest would receive 20% of $200, or $40.

2. Intercompany sales will often be made on credit, so that intercompany trade balances will appear in the separate accounts of the affiliated firms. From a consolidated viewpoint, intercompany receivables and payables are an internal transfer of funds. Internal debt has no effect on consolidated statements and must be eliminated. Only debt transactions with entities outside the consolidated firms should appear on the consolidated balance sheet.

3. No profit on intercompany sales may be recognized until the profit is realized by a sale to an outside party. Any profit contained in the ending inventory of intercompany goods must be eliminated and its recognition deferred until the period in which the goods are sold to outsiders. Recall the example of Companies P and S, involving the $1,200 intercompany merchandise sale. Assume that the sale by Company P to Company S was made on December 30, 19X1, and that Company S did not sell the goods until March of 19X2. From a consolidated viewpoint, there can be no profit recognized until the outside sale occurs in March of 19X2. At that time, consolidation theory will acknowledge a $500 profit, of which $200 will be distributed to Company P and $300 to Company S as part of the 19X2 consolidated income. However, until that time, the $200 profit on the intercompany sale, recorded by Company P, must be deferred. Not only must the $1,200 intercompany sale be eliminated, but the inventory on December 31, 19X1, must be reduced by $200 to its $1,000 cost to the consolidated firms.

The work sheet procedures to eliminate the effects of intercompany sales are discussed in the following section. In the first illustration, no intercompany goods remain in the ending inventory. In the second illustration, which is the more common situation, some portion of the intercompany goods is still on hand at the end of the period.

No Intercompany Goods in the Ending Inventory

In the simplest case, which is demonstrated in Illustration I on pages 312 and 313, all goods sold between the affiliates have, in turn, been sold to outside parties by the end of the accounting period. The work sheet for this situation is based on the following assumptions:

Company S is an 80%-owned subsidiary of Company P. Company P purchased its interest in Company S at a price equal to its pro rata share of Company S's book value. Company P uses the simple equity method to record the investment.

Companies P and S had the following separate income statements for 19X1:

	Company P		Company S	
Sales......................		$700,000		$500,000
Less cost of goods sold:				
Beginning inventory......	$ 60,000		$ 50,000	
Purchases...............	520,000		340,000	
Ending inventory........	(70,000)	510,000	(40,000)	350,000
Gross profit		$190,000		$150,000
Subsidiary income		60,000		
Other expenses............		(90,000)		(75,000)
Net income...............		$160,000		$ 75,000

Note that under the simple equity method, Company P's income includes 80% of the reported income of Company S.

Illustration I—Intercompany Sales
Company P and
Work Sheet for Consolidated
For Year Ended

(Credit balance amounts
are in parentheses)

	Trial Balance	
	Company P	Company S
Accounts Receivable	110,000	150,000
Inventory, Dec. 31, 19X1	70,000	40,000
Investment in Co. S	196,000	
Other Assets	314,000	155,000
Accounts Payable	(80,000)	(100,000)
Common Stock ($10 par), Co. P	(200,000)	
Retained Earnings, Jan. 1, 19X1, Co. P	(250,000)	
Common Stock ($10 par), Co. S		(100,000)
Retained Earnings, Jan. 1, 19X1, Co. S		(70,000)
Sales	(700,000)	(500,000)
Cost of Goods Sold	510,000	350,000
Expenses	90,000	75,000
Subsidiary Income	(60,000)	
	0	0
Consolidated Net Income		
To Minority Interest (20% × $75,000 Net Income of Co. S)		
To Controlling Interest		
Total Minority Interest, Dec. 31, 19X1		
Retained Earnings, Controlling Interest, Dec. 31, 19X1		

Eliminations:
(1) Eliminate the entry recording parent's share of subsidiary net income.
(2) Eliminate the investment in Company S account. To simplify the example, there is no discrepancy between the cost and book values of the investment. The work sheet process is expedited by always eliminating the intercompany investment first.

Company S sold goods to Company P for $100,000. Company S recorded a 20% gross profit on the sales price. Company P has sold all of the goods by the end of 19X1. Company P has not yet paid for $25,000 of these purchases. This amount is included in the payables of Company P and the receivables of Company S.

The consolidated net income of $175,000 is distributed to the minority and controlling interests. The profit on intercompany sales, which is included in the subsidiary income of $75,000, is recognized, since the goods have been resold to outside interests. No work sheet adjustment is required for the ending inventory, since it does not include any goods resulting from intercompany sales. These procedures would be identical if Company P were the seller of the intercompany goods.

No Intercompany Goods in Ending Inventory
Subsidiary Company S
Financial Statements
December 31, 19X1

Eliminations		Consolidated Income Statement	Minority Interest	Controlling Retained Earnings	Consolidated Balance Sheet
Dr.	Cr.				
	(4) 25,000				235,000
					110,000
	(1) 60,000				
	(2) 136,000				
					469,000
(4) 25,000					(155,000)
					(200,000)
				(250,000)	
(2) 80,000			(20,000)		
(2) 56,000			(14,000)		
(3) 100,000		(1,100,000)			
	(3) 100,000	760,000			
		165,000			
(1) 60,000					
321,000	321,000				
		(175,000)			
		15,000	(15,000)		
		160,000		(160,000)	
			(49,000)		(49,000)
				(410,000)	(410,000)
					0

(3) Eliminate the intercompany sales to avoid double counting, with only the original purchase by Company S and the final sale by Company P remaining in the consolidated statement.

(4) Eliminate the $25,000 intercompany trade balances resulting from intercompany sales.

Intercompany Goods in the Purchasing Firm's Ending Inventory

Now assume that $20,000 of the goods purchased from Company S, in Illustration I, are still unsold and are included in Company P's ending inventory of $70,000. In Illustration II below, elimination Steps 1

Illustration II—Intercompany
Company P and
Work Sheet for Consolidated
For Year Ended

(Credit balance amounts
are in parentheses)

| | Trial Balance ||
	Company P	Company S
Accounts Receivable	110,000	150,000
Inventory, Dec. 31, 19X1	70,000	40,000
Investment in Co. S	196,000	
Other Assets	314,000	155,000
Accounts Payable	(80,000)	(100,000)
Common Stock ($10 par), Co. P	(200,000)	
Retained Earnings, Jan. 1, 19X1, Co. P	(250,000)	
Common Stock ($10 par), Co. S		(100,000)
Retained Earnings, Jan. 1, 19X1, Co. S		(70,000)
Sales	(700,000)	(500,000)
Cost of Goods Sold	510,000	350,000
Expenses	90,000	75,000
Subsidiary Income	(60,000)	
	0	0
Consolidated Net Income		
To Minority Interest (see distribution schedule)		
To Controlling Interest (see distribution schedule)		
Total Minority Interest, Dec. 31, 19X1		
Retained Earnings, Controlling Interest, Dec. 31, 19X1		

Eliminations:
(1) Eliminate the entry recording the parent's share of subsidiary net income.
(2) Eliminate the investment in Company S account.
(3) Eliminate the intercompany sales.

Income Distribution Schedules

Subsidiary Company S income distribution

Unrealized profit in ending inventory **5** $4,000	Internally generated net income . $75,000
	Adjusted income................ $71,000
	Minority share 20%
	Minority interest $14,200

through 4 are exactly the same as in the previous illustration. Step 5 must be added. The ending inventory of Company P now includes inter-company goods which must be inventoried at their *cost to the consolidated entity*, not at their cost to Company P. The $4,000

Goods in Ending Inventory
Subsidiary Company S
Financial Statements
December 31, 19X1

Eliminations		Consolidated Income Statement	Minority Interest	Controlling Retained Earnings	Consolidated Balance Sheet
Dr.	Cr.				
	(4) 25,000				235,000
	5 4,000				106,000
	(1) 60,000				
	(2) 136,000				
					469,000
(4) 25,000					(155,000)
					(200,000)
				(250,000)	
(2) 80,000			(20,000)		
(2) 56,000			(14,000)		
(3) 100,000		(1,100,000)			
5 4,000	(3) 100,000	764,000			
		165,000			
(1) 60,000					
325,000	325,000				
		(171,000)			
		14,200	(14,200)		
		156,800		(156,800)	
			(48,200)		(48,200)
				(406,800)	(406,800)
					0

(4) Eliminate the intercompany trade balances.
5 Eliminate the profit in the ending inventory.

Parent Company P income distribution

Internally generated net income	$100,000
80% × Company S adjusted income of $71,000	56,800
Controlling interest	$156,800

(20% × $20,000) profit recorded by Company S cannot be recognized until it is realized by a sale of the goods to an outside party. In arriving at the cost of goods sold for the firm purchasing intercompany goods, the ending inventory of intercompany goods was deducted in determining the cost of goods sold at the intercompany price of $20,000. The consolidated view requires that only the original cost of $16,000 be deducted. The additional Step 5 thus reduces the ending inventory and restores $4,000 to the cost of goods sold. As a result, a lower consolidated net income is reported.

An additional complexity is encountered in distributing the consolidated net income to the controlling and minority interests. To aid in this process, a new set of schedules, called "Income Distribution Schedules," is introduced. These schedules will become a routine part of future work sheets. Each schedule begins with the reported internally generated net income of each affiliate. Internally generated net income of the parent *excludes* subsidiary income. All unrealized profits originating from intercompany transactions are deducted from the firm that made the intercompany sale, and the *adjusted* income is then distributed to the minority and controlling interests.

In Illustration II, the unrealized profit of $4,000 is deducted from the subsidiary's internally generated net income of $75,000. The adjusted net income of $71,000 is apportioned, with $14,200 (20%) distributed to the minority interest and $56,800 (80%) distributed to the controlling interest.

There is no change in work sheet elimination procedures if the parent is the seller and the subsidiary has intercompany goods in its ending inventory. Only the distribution of consolidated income changes. To illustrate, assume that the parent, Company P, is the seller of the intercompany goods. The income distribution schedules would then be prepared as follows:

Subsidiary Company S income distribution

	Internally generated net income	$75,000
	Adjusted income	$75,000
	Minority share	20%
	Minority interest	$15,000

Parent Company P income distribution

Unrealized profit in ending inventory .... $ 4,000	Internally generated net income	$100,000
	80% × Company S adjusted income of $75,000	60,000
	Controlling interest	$156,000

Intercompany Goods in the Purchasing Firm's Beginning Inventory

When intercompany goods are included in the purchaser's beginning inventory, the amount of that inventory includes the profit made by the seller. The intercompany seller of the goods has, in the prior period, included such sales in its separate income statement as though the transactions were consummated. Thus, the beginning retained earnings balance of the seller also includes the profit on these goods. While this profit should be reflected on the separate books of the affiliates, it should not be recognized when taking a consolidated view. In the consolidating process, the beginning inventory of intercompany goods must be reduced to its cost to the consolidated firm. Likewise, the retained earnings of the consolidated firm must be reduced by deleting the profit which was recorded in prior periods on intercompany goods contained in the buyer's previous year's ending inventory. Profit must not be recognized until it is realized in the subsequent period through the sale of the goods to an outside party.

Consider the following example of Company P and Company S of Illustration II for 19X2. Company P and Company S have the following individual income data for 19X2:

	Company P		Company S	
Sales.........................		$800,000		$600,000
Less cost of goods sold:				
Beginning inventory.........	$ 70,000		$ 40,000	
Purchases	600,000		450,000	
Ending inventory...........	(60,000)	610,000	(50,000)	440,000
Gross profit		$190,000		$160,000
Subsidiary income		48,000		
Other expenses		(120,000)		(100,000)
Net income..................		$118,000		$ 60,000

Assume the following additional facts:

Company P's beginning inventory includes $20,000 of goods purchased from Company S. The gross profit rate on the sale was 20%.

Company S sold $120,000 of goods to Company P during 19X2.

Company S recorded a 20% gross profit on these sales.

Company P still owed $60,000 to Company S for purchases at the end of 19X2. Company P had $30,000 of the intercompany purchases in its ending inventory on December 31, 19X2.

Illustration III on pages 318 and 319 contains the 19X2 year-end trial balances of Company P and Company S. After the eliminations are made, the resulting consolidated net income of $128,000 is distributed as shown in the income distribution schedules. The adjustments for intercompany inventory profits are reflected in the selling company's schedule. It might appear that the example assumes that intercompany goods in the beginning inventory are sold in the current period, since the deferred profit of the previous period is realized during the current

Illustration III—Intercompany Goods in
Company P and
Work Sheet for Consolidated
For Year Ended

(Credit balance amounts
are in parentheses)

	Trial Balance	
	Company P	Company S
Accounts Receivable	160,000	170,000
Inventory, Dec. 31, 19X2	60,000	50,000
Investment in Co. S	244,000	
Other Assets	354,000	165,000
Accounts Payable	(90,000)	(80,000)
Common Stock ($10 par), Co. P	(200,000)	
Retained Earnings, Jan. 1, 19X2, Co. P	(410,000)	
Common Stock ($10 par), Co. S		(100,000)
Retained Earnings, Jan. 1, 19X2, Co. S		(145,000)
Sales	(800,000)	(600,000)
Cost of Goods Sold	610,000	440,000
Expenses	120,000	100,000
Subsidiary Income	(48,000)	
	0	0
Consolidated Net Income		
To Minority Interest (see distribution schedule)		
To Controlling Interest (see distribution schedule)		
Total Minority Interest, Dec. 31, 19X2		
Retained Earnings, Controlling Interest, Dec. 31, 19X2		

Eliminations:
(1) Eliminate the entry recording parent's share of subsidiary net income.
(2) Eliminate the pro rata portion of subsidiary equity balances owned by the parent (80%) against the investment account. Again, there is no excess of cost or book value.
3 Eliminate the intercompany profit of $4,000 (20% × $20,000) in the beginning inventory by reducing the cost of goods sold and the beginning retained earnings. The decrease is shared 20% by the minority interest, since, in this case, the selling firm was the subsidiary. If the parent had been the seller, only the controlling interest in retained earnings would be decreased. It should be noted that the $4,000 profit is shifted from

Income Distribution Schedules

Subsidiary Company S income distribution

Less unrealized profit in ending inventory, 20% × $30,000... **6** $6,000	Internally generated net income . $60,000
	Add realized profit in beginning inventory, 20% × $20,000 .. **3** 4,000
	Adjusted income................ $58,000
	Minority share 20%
	Minority interest $11,600

Beginning and Ending Inventories
Subsidiary Company S
Financial Statements
December 31, 19X2

Eliminations Dr.	Eliminations Cr.	Consolidated Income Statement	Minority Interest	Controlling Retained Earnings	Consolidated Balance Sheet
	(5) 60,000				270,000
	(6) 6,000				104,000
	(1) 48,000				
	(2) 196,000				
					519,000
(5) 60,000					(110,000)
					(200,000)
(3) 3,200				(406,800)	
(2) 80,000			(20,000)		
(2) 116,000					
(3) 800			(28,200)		
(4) 120,000		(1,280,000)			
(6) 6,000	(3) 4,000				
	(4) 120,000	932,000			
		220,000			
(1) 48,000					
434,000	434,000				
		(128,000)			
		11,600	(11,600)		
		116,400		(116,400)	
			(59,800)		(59,800)
				(523,200)	(523,200)
					0

19X1 to 19X2, since, as a result of the entry, 19X2 consolidated cost of goods sold is reduced $4,000. This procedure emphasizes the concept that intercompany inventory profit is not eliminated but only deferred until inventory is sold to an outsider.

(4) Eliminate the intercompany sale to eliminate double counting.
(5) Eliminate the intercompany trade balances.
(6) Eliminate the 20% intercompany profit of $6,000 recorded by Company S for the $30,000 of intercompany goods contained in Company P's ending inventory, and increase cost of goods sold.

Parent Company P income distribution

Internally generated net income	$ 70,000
80% × Company S adjusted income of $58,000	46,400
Controlling interest	$116,400

period in the seller's income distribution schedule. That assumption need not be made, however. If the $20,000 beginning inventory is still unsold at year end, it would again be a part of the ending $30,000 inventory on which $6,000 of profit is deferred. The $4,000 profit would be shown in the schedule as both realized beginning inventory profit and as unrealized ending inventory profit. The use of the lifo method for inventories could cause a given period's inventory profit to be deferred indefinitely. Unless otherwise stated, the examples and problems of the text will assume a fifo flow assumption.

The Effect of the "Lower of Cost or Market" Method on Inventory Profit

Intercompany inventory in the hands of the purchaser may have been written down by the purchaser to a market value below its inter-company transfer cost. Assume that Subsidiary S purchased, for $50,000, goods that cost the parent $40,000. Assume further that Company S has all the goods in its ending inventory but has written them down to $42,000, the lower market value at the end of the period. As a result of the markdown already made, the inventory need only be reduced by another $2,000 to reflect its cost to the consolidated firm ($40,000). The only remaining issue is how to defer the $2,000 profit in the income distribution schedules. As before, the profit is deferred by removing it from the seller's schedule. In the subsequent period, the profit will be realized by the seller.

It may seem strange that the $8,000 of profit written off is, in effect, realized by the seller, since it is not deducted in the seller's distribution schedule. This procedure is proper, however, since a loss has been recognized by the buyer. There is no need to defer the offsetting profit.

Losses on Intercompany Sales

Assume that a parent sells goods to a subsidiary for $5,000, and that the goods cost the parent $6,000. If the market value of the goods is $5,000 or less, the loss may be recognized on the consolidated statement even if the goods are still in the subsidiary's ending inventory. Such a loss can be recognized under the lower of cost or market principle which applies to inventory. If, however, the intercompany sales price is below market value, that part of the loss which results from the price being below market value is not recognized until the goods are sold to an outside party by the subsidiary. Elimination procedures would parallel those used for unrealized gains.

INTERCOMPANY PLANT ASSET SALES

Plant assets may be sold between members of an affiliated group, and these sales may result in a gain to the seller. The buyer will record the asset at a price which includes the gain, and when the sale involves a depreciable asset, the buyer will base future depreciation charges on the price paid. While these recordings are proper for the firms as separate entities, the transaction is an internal transfer for which there is no basis for recognizing a gain, according to consolidation theory. Unlike the case of merchandise sales, however, recognition of the gain does not have to await sale of the asset to an outside party. Rather, the gain may be periodically recognized during the asset's life in an amount equal to the difference between the depreciation based on the intercompany sales price and the depreciation based on the book value of the asset on the sale date. This procedure allows the gain to be realized as the asset is used rather than postponing the gain until the asset is sold.

Intercompany Sale of a Nondepreciable Asset

One member of the affiliated group may sell land to another affiliate and record a gain. For consolidated purposes, there has been no sale, and thus there is no cause to recognize a gain. Since the asset is not depreciable, the entire gain must be deferred until the land is sold to an outside party. This deferment may be permanent if there is no intent to sell at a later date. For example, assume that in 19X1, Company S (80% owned) sells land to the parent, Company P. The sales price is $30,000, and Company S's original cost of the land was $20,000. Consolidation theory would rule that until Company P sells the land to an outside party, recognition of profit must be deferred. The following work sheet elimination is made in the year of sale:

	Partial Trial Balance		Eliminations	
	Company P	Company S	Dr.	Cr.
Land	30,000			10,000
Gain on Sale of Land		(10,000)	10,000	

The selling firm's income distribution schedule would also reflect the deferment of the gain.

In subsequent years, assuming that the land is not sold by Company P, the gain must be removed from consolidated retained earnings. Since the sale was made by Company S, which is 80% owned by Company P, the controlling interest absorbs 80% of the deferment while the minority interest absorbs 20%. For example, the elimination in 19X2 would be:

	Partial Trial Balance		Eliminations	
	Company P	Company S	Dr.	Cr.
Land	30,000			10,000
Retained Earnings, Jan. 1, 19X2, Company P .	(100,000)*		8,000	
Retained Earnings, Jan. 1, 19X2, Company S .		(20,000)*	2,000	
*arbitrary balance				

Now assume that in 19X3, Company P sells the land to an outside party for $45,000, recording a gain of $15,000. When this sale occurs, the $10,000 intercompany gain is realized. The following elimination would remove the previously unrealized gain from consolidated retained earnings and would add it to the gain already recorded by Company P. The retained earnings adjustment is allocated 80% to the controlling interest and 20% to the minority interest, since the original sale was made by the subsidiary.

	Partial Trial Balance		Eliminations	
	Company P	Company S	Dr.	Cr.
Gain on Sale of Land	(15,000)			10,000
Retained Earnings, Jan. 1, 19X3, Company P .	(120,000)*		8,000	
Retained Earnings, Jan. 1, 19X3, Company S.		(15,000)*	2,000	
*arbitrary balance				

The income distribution schedule would add the $10,000 gain to the 19X3 internally generated net income of Company S. It should now be obvious that the gain was not eliminated, but was deferred. The original gain of $10,000 on the intercompany sale is eventually credited to the subsidiary, and thus does affect the minority share of consolidated income at a future date. Such sales should be viewed as an agreement between the controlling and minority interests regarding future distributions of consolidated net income.

When a parent sells a nondepreciable asset to a subsidiary, the work sheet is the same, except:

1. In the years subsequent to the sale, the related adjustment is made exclusively through controlling retained earnings.
2. The deferment of the gain in the year of the intercompany sale and the recognition of the gain in the year of the sale of the asset to an outside party flow through the parent company income distribution schedule.

Intercompany Sale of a Depreciable Asset

Work sheet procedures must be developed which will recognize a gain on an intercompany sale of a depreciable asset over its useful life. To illustrate these procedures, assume that the parent, Company P, sells a machine to a subsidiary, Company S, for $30,000 on January 1, 19X1. The machine originally cost $32,000. Accumulated depreciation is $12,000. Thus, the book value is $20,000, and the gain on the sale is $10,000. Further assume that the asset has a 5-year remaining life, and that straight-line depreciation of $6,000 is recorded annually by Company S.

The eliminations must allocate the gain over the 5-year life of the asset and must reduce depreciation charges, basing them on the asset's $20,000 book value to the consolidated firm. Illustration IV on pages 326 and 327 is based on the following additional facts:

Company P owns an 80% investment in Company S. The amount paid for the investment was equal to the book value of Company S's underlying equity. The simple equity method is used by Company P to record the investment.

There were no beginning or ending inventories, and the firms had the following separate income statements for 19X1:

	Company P	Company S
Sales......................................	$200,000	$100,000
Less cost of goods sold	(150,000)	(59,000)
Gross profit	$ 50,000	$ 41,000
Depreciation expense	(30,000)	(16,000)
Gain on sale of machine.....................	10,000	
Subsidiary income (80%)....................	20,000	
Net income................................	$ 50,000	$25,000

The allocation of consolidated net income of $47,000 is shown in the income distribution schedules. Note that Company S must absorb depreciation based on the agreed sales price. The controlling interest realizes the gain, but only as the asset is used. It will be noticed that the realizable profit for the seller in any year is the depreciation absorbed by the buyer minus depreciation for consolidated purposes. If the sale had been made by Company S, the profit deferment and recognition entries would flow through its income distribution schedule.

Work sheets for periods subsequent to the sale of the equipment must correct the current-year nominal accounts and must remove unrealized profit in the beginning consolidated retained earnings. Illustration V on pages 328 and 329 portrays a consolidated work sheet for 19X2, based on the following separate income statements for Company P and Company S:

	Company P	Company S
Sales..	$250,000	$120,000
Less cost of goods sold	(180,000)	(80,000)
Gross profit	$ 70,000	$ 40,000
Depreciation expense	(20,000)	(16,000)
Subsidiary income (80%)...........................	19,200	
Net income..	$ 69,200	$ 24,000

The resulting consolidated net income of $76,000 is distributed as shown in the income distribution schedules which follow the work sheet. During each year, Company S must absorb the larger depreciation expense which resulted from its purchase of the asset. Company P has the right to realize $2,000 more of the original deferred profit.

It may occur that an asset purchased from an affiliate may be sold before it is fully depreciated. To illustrate this possibility, assume that Company S sells the asset in Illustration V for $14,000 at the end of the second year. Since Company S's cost is $30,000, with $12,000 of accumulated depreciation, the loss recorded by Company S is $4,000. However, on a consolidated basis, the $4,000 loss ($14,000 less $18,000 net book value) becomes a $2,000 gain, determined as follows:

	On Books of Company S	For Consolidated Entity
Cost of machine	$30,000	$32,000
Accumulated depreciation....................	12,000	20,000
Book value at end of second year following sale	$18,000	$12,000
Sale price	14,000	14,000
Gain or (loss)	$(4,000)	$ 2,000

Illustration VI on pages 330 and 331 is a worksheet for Companies P and S for the second year, revised to include the subsequent sale of the asset by Company S.

A loss on an intercompany plant asset sale may be recorded at the time of the sale if the fair market value is approximated by the sale price. This procedure is allowable because a plant asset may be written down to a market value below the asset's book value in the absence of a sale. However, when a sale results in a loss because the price is below fair market value, that part of the loss which results from the price being below market value is not recognized for consolidated reporting purposes, but rather must be deferred until the asset is used or the asset is sold to an outside party. The elimination procedures parallel those used for gains.

Intercompany Long-Term Construction Contracts

One member of an affiliated firm may construct a plant asset for another affiliate over an extended period of time. The firm constructing the asset will record progress under the completed-contract method or the percentage-of-completion method. During construction, special adjustments may be necessary when consolidating, since from a consolidated viewpoint such activity amounts to the self-construction of an asset to be used by the consolidated entity. Once the asset has been sold to an affiliate, consolidation procedures are similar to those used for normal intercompany plant asset sales. It is only during the construction period that additional analysis is required, depending on the method used to record the contract by the constructing affiliate.

Completed-Contract Method. The constructing affiliate using the completed-contract method records no profit on the asset until it is completed and transferred to the purchasing affiliate. However, costs incurred to date on the contract are capitalized in an account such as "Cost of Construction in Progress." This account will then appear on the trial balance of the constructing affiliate. Since there is no intercompany profit included, the account requires no adjustment and is carried to the consolidated balance sheet.

The constructing affiliate may bill the affiliate for whom the asset is being constructed for work done prior to completion of the asset. When this occurs, the constructing affiliate will record billed amounts by debiting Contracts Receivable and crediting Billings on Long-Term

Contracts. The billings account acts as a contra account to Cost of Construction in Progress. The purchasing affiliate would debit Asset Under Construction and credit Contracts Payable for billings received. Consolidation procedures require that the constructing affiliate's account Billings on Long-Term Contracts be eliminated against the purchaser's account Asset Under Construction, since only the costs incurred to date by the constructing affiliate should appear on the consolidated balance sheet. It is also necessary to eliminate any remaining intercompany contracts receivable/payable recorded on the long-term contracts.

Percentage-of-Completion Method. This method allows the constructing firm to recognize a portion of the total estimated profit on the contract as construction progresses. During the construction period, the contracting firm debits an account usually titled Construction in Progress for costs that are incurred. The contractor also debits Construction in Progress and credits Earned Income on Long-Term Contracts for estimated profit earned during each accounting period. Thus, the construction in progress account includes *accumulated costs* and *estimated earnings*. When the purchaser is billed, the amount billed is debited to Contracts Receivable and credited to Billings on Construction in Progress.

To illustrate the elimination procedures when the percentage-of-completion method is used, assume that a subsidiary, Company S, enters into a contract to construct a building for the parent, Company P, for $500,000, and that Company S estimates the cost of the building to be $400,000. During 19X1, the building is 50% completed, and $200,000 of cost has been incurred as of December 31, 19X1, but only $150,000 has been billed. The contract is completed in 19X2 at an additional cost of $200,000. The entries on the books of the separate affiliates for December, 19X1, are as follows:

Company P

Asset Under Construction	150,000	
Contracts Payable		150,000
To record billing from subsidiary for amount due.		

Company S

Construction in Progress	200,000	
Payables (to outsiders)		200,000
To record costs incurred for long-term contracts under the percentage-of-completion method.		
Construction in Progress	50,000	
Earned Income on Long-Term Contracts		50,000
To record pro rata share of estimated profit [50% × ($500,000 − $400,000)].		
Contracts Receivable	150,000	
Billings on Construction in Progress		150,000
To record billing to parent for portion of amount due under contracts.		

Illustration IV—Intercompany
Company P and
Work Sheet for Consolidated
For Year Ended

(Credit balance amounts
are in parentheses)

	Trial Balance	
	Company P	**Company S**
Current Assets	15,000	20,000
Machinery	50,000	(a) 230,000
Accumulated Depreciation—Machinery	(25,000)	(b) (100,000)
Investment in Co. S	120,000	
Common Stock ($10 par), Co. P	(100,000)	
Retained Earnings, Jan. 1, 19X1, Co. P	(10,000)	
Common Stock ($10 par), Co. S		(50,000)
Retained Earnings, Jan. 1, 19X1, Co. S		(75,000)
Sales	(200,000)	(100,000)
Cost of Goods Sold	150,000	59,000
Depreciation Expense	30,000	(b) 16,000
Gain on Sale of Machine	(10,000)	
Subsidiary Income	(20,000)	
	0	0

Consolidated Net Income

   To Minority Interest (see distribution schedule)

   To Controlling Interest (see distribution schedule)

Total Minority Interest, Dec. 31, 19X1

Retained Earnings, Controlling Interest, Dec. 31, 19X1

Notes to Trial Balance:
(a) Includes machine purchased for $30,000 from Company P on January 1, 19X1.
(b) Includes $6,000 depreciation on machine purchased from Company P on January 1, 19X1.

Eliminations:
(1) Eliminate the entry recording parent's share of subsidiary net income for the current year.
(2) Eliminate 80% of subsidiary equity balances against the investment account. There is no excess to be distributed.

Income Distribution Schedules

Subsidiary Company S income distribution

	Internally generated net income . $25,000
Adjusted income	$25,000
Minority share	20%
Minority interest	$ 5,000

Sale of Depreciable Asset
Subsidiary Company S
Financial Statements
December 31, 19X1

Eliminations		Consolidated Income Statement	Minority Interest	Controlling Retained Earnings	Consolidated Balance Sheet
Dr.	Cr.				
					35,000
3 2,000					282,000
4 2,000	**3** 12,000				(135,000)
	(1) 20,000				
	(2) 100,000				
					(100,000)
				(10,000)	
(2) 40,000			(10,000)		
(2) 60,000			(15,000)		
		(300,000)			
		209,000			
	4 2,000	44,000			
3 10,000					
(1) 20,000					
134,000	134,000				
		(47,000)			
		5,000	(5,000)		
		42,000		(42,000)	
			(30,000)		(30,000)
				(52,000)	(52,000)
					0

3 Eliminate the $10,000 gain on the sale of the machine, and adjust the machine to $32,000 and related accumulated depreciation to $12,000 to reflect the book value of the asset to the consolidated firm on January 1, 19X1.

4 Reduce depreciation expense and accumulated depreciation to reflect depreciation ($4,000 per year) based on the consolidated book value of the machine rather than depreciation ($6,000 per year) based on the sales price.

Parent Company P income distribution

Unrealized gain on sale of equipment............... **3** $10,000	Internally generated net income (including sale of machine) ...	$30,000
	Share of subsidiary income (80% × $25,000).............	20,000
	Gain realized through use of equipment sold to subsidiary **4**	2,000
	Controlling interest	$42,000

(Credit balance amounts
are in parentheses)

	Trial Balance	
	Company P	**Company S**
Current Assets	85,000	60,000
Machinery	50,000	(a) 230,000
Accumulated Depreciation—Machinery	(45,000)	(b) (116,000)
Investment in Co. S	139,200	
Common Stock ($10 par), Co. P	(100,000)	
Retained Earnings, Jan. 1, 19X2, Co. P	(60,000)	
Common Stock ($10 par), Co. S		(50,000)
Retained Earnings, Jan. 1, 19X2, Co. S		(100,000)
Sales	(250,000)	(120,000)
Cost of Goods Sold	180,000	80,000
Depreciation Expense	20,000	(c) 16,000
Subsidiary Income	(19,200)	
	0	0
Consolidated Net Income		
To Minority Interest (see distribution schedule)		
To Controlling Interest (see distribution schedule)		
Total Minority Interest, Dec. 31, 19X2		
Retained Earnings, Controlling Interest, Dec. 31, 19X2		

Notes to Trial Balance:
(a) Includes machine purchased for $30,000 from Company P on January 1, 19X1.
(b) Includes $12,000 accumulated depreciation ($6,000 per year) on machine purchased from Company P on January 1, 19X1.
(c) Includes $6,000 depreciation on machine purchased from Company P on January 1, 19X1.

Eliminations:
(1) Eliminate the entry recording parent's share of subsidiary net income for the current year.
(2) Eliminate 80% of subsidiary equity balances against the investment account. There is no excess to be distributed.
3 Eliminate the gain on the intercompany sale as it is reflected in beginning retained earnings on the parent's

Income Distribution Schedules

Subsidiary Company S income distribution

Internally generated net income .	$24,000
Adjusted income	$24,000
Minority share	20%
Minority interest	$ 4,800

Sale of Depreciable Asset
Subsidiary Company S
Financial Statements
December 31, 19X2

Eliminations Dr.		Eliminations Cr.		Consolidated Income Statement	Minority Interest	Controlling Retained Earnings	Consolidated Balance Sheet
							145,000
3	2,000						282,000
3	2,000	**3**	12,000				
4	2,000						(169,000)
		(1)	19,200				
		(2)	120,000				
							(100,000)
3	8,000					(52,000)	
(2)	40,000				(10,000)		
(2)	80,000				(20,000)		
				(370,000)			
				260,000			
		4	2,000	34,000			
(1)	19,200						
	153,200		153,200				
				(76,000)			
				4,800	(4,800)		
				71,200		(71,200)	
					(34,800)		(34,800)
						(123,200)	(123,200)
							0

trial balance. This entry also adjusts the machine account to $32,000 and restates accumulated depreciation as of the beginning of the year. The adjustment to accumulated depreciation includes a $12,000 increase to acknowledge the $12,000 balance on the sale date less a $2,000 reduction for the profit element of 19X1 depreciation. Since the sale was made by the parent, Company P, the entire unrealized gain at the beginning of the year (now $8,000) is removed from controlling retained earnings. If the sale had been made by the subsidiary to the parent, the adjustment of retained earnings would be split 80% to the controlling interest and 20% to the minority interest.

4 Reduce current depreciation expense and accumulated depreciation to reflect depreciation based on the consolidated book value of the asset. This entry will bring the accumulated depreciation account to its correct consolidated end-of-the-year balance.

Parent Company P income distribution

Internally generated net income .	$50,000
Share of subsidiary income (80% × $24,000)	19,200
Gain realized through use of equipment sold to subsidiary **4**	2,000
Controlling interest	$71,200

Illustration VI—Intercompany Sale of Depreciable Asset
Company P and
Work Sheet for Consolidated

(Credit balance amounts
are in parentheses)

For Year Ended

	Trial Balance	
	Company P	Company S
Current Assets	85,000	74,000
Machinery	50,000	200,000
Accumulated Depreciation—Machinery	(45,000)	(104,000)
Investment in Co. S	136,000	
Common Stock ($10 par), Co. P	(100,000)	
Retained Earnings, Jan. 1, 19X2, Co. P	(60,000)	
Common Stock ($10 par), Co. S		(50,000)
Retained Earnings, Jan. 1, 19X2, Co. S		(100,000)
Sales	(250,000)	(120,000)
Cost of Goods Sold	180,000	80,000
Depreciation Expense	20,000	16,000
Loss on Sale of Equipment		4,000
Subsidiary Income	(16,000)	
Gain on Sale of Equipment		
	0	0
Consolidated Net Income		
To Minority Interest (see distribution schedule)		
To Controlling Interest (see distribution schedule)		
Total Minority Interest, Dec. 31, 19X2		
Retained Earnings, Controlling Interest, Dec. 31, 19X2		

Eliminations:
(1) Eliminate the entry recording the parent's share of subsidiary net income for the current year.
(2) Eliminate 80% of subsidiary equity balances against the investment account. There is no excess to be distributed.

Income Distribution Schedules

Subsidiary Company S income distribution

Internally generated net income .	$20,000
Adjusted income	$20,000
Minority share	20%
Minority interest	$ 4,000

Followed by Subsequent Sale to an Outside Party
Subsidiary Company S
Financial Statements
December 31, 19X2

Eliminations		Consolidated Income Statement	Minority Interest	Controlling Retained Earnings	Consolidated Balance Sheet
Dr.	Cr.				
					159,000
					250,000
					(149,000)
	(1) 16,000				
	(2) 120,000				
					(100,000)
3 8,000				(52,000)	
(2) 40,000			(10,000)		
(2) 80,000			(20,000)		
		(370,000)			
		260,000			
	3 2,000	34,000			
	3 4,000				
(1) 16,000					
	3 2,000	(2,000)			
144,000	144,000				
		(78,000)			
		4,000	(4,000)		
		74,000		(74,000)	
			(34,000)		(34,000)
				(126,000)	(126,000)
					0

3 Eliminate the gain on the intercompany sale as it is reflected in the parent's beginning retained earnings, adjust the current year's depreciation expense, and revise the recording of the sale of the equipment to an outside party to reflect the net book value of the asset to the consolidated firm.

Parent Company P income distribution

Internally generated net income .	$50,000
Share of subsidiary income	
(80% × $20,000)	16,000
Gain realized on sale of	
machine **3**	8,000*
Controlling interest	**$74,000**

*$10,000 original gain less $2,000 realized in 19X1.

The subsidiary balance sheet prepared at the end of 19X1 would list a net current asset of $100,000. The $150,000 in Billings on Construction in Progress would be offset against the $250,000 in Construction in Progress. If billings exceed the amount recorded for construction in progress, a net current liability would be shown on the balance sheet.

Illustration VII shows the relevant accounts and the eliminations that would appear in a consolidated work sheet. The elimination procedures are complex and involve answering the question: What should remain on the consolidated statements? From a consolidated viewpoint, a self-constructed asset is in progress and $200,000 has been spent to date. All that should remain on the consolidated statements is a $200,000 asset under construction and $200,000 payable to outside interests. The income distribution schedule which would accompany a complete work sheet would also reflect the profit deferral. The income distribution schedule of the constructing affiliate would be debited for $50,000.

As is true with all intercompany plant asset sales, any intercompany profit is deferred until realized through subsequent sale or use. Thus, the intercompany profit resulting from long-term construction contracts may be realized as the asset is depreciated. The unrealized profit will result in an adjustment to retained earnings in subsequent years.

Illustration VII—Long-Term Contracts, Percentage-of-Completion Method
Company P and Subsidiary Company S
Partial Work Sheet
For Year Ended December 31, 19X1

(Credit balance amounts are in parentheses)

	Trial Balance		Eliminations	
	Company P	Company S	Dr.	Cr.
Assets Under Construction	150,000		(3) 50,000	
Contracts Receivable		150,000		(1) 150,000
Billings on Construction in Progress		(150,000)	(3) 150,000	
Construction in Progress		250,000		(2) 50,000
				(3) 200,000
Earned Income on Long-Term Contracts		(50,000)	(2) 50,000	
Contracts Payable	(150,000)		(1) 150,000	
Payables (to outsiders)		(200,000)		

Eliminations:
(1) Eliminate intercompany debt.
(2) Eliminate the income recorded on long-term contracts and remove profit from Construction in Progress.
(3) Eliminate balances of Construction in Progress and Billings on Construction in Progress, and increase Assets Under Construction for unbilled costs on long-term intercompany contracts.

INTERCOMPANY DEBT

Often a parent firm will advance cash to a subsidiary. A parent may accept a note from the subsidiary as security for a loan, or the parent may discount a note which the subsidiary received from a customer. Typically, the parent is a larger firm which can secure funds under more favorable terms. In most cases, the parent will charge a competitive interest rate for funds advanced to the subsidiary.

The examples which follow assume the more common situation in which the parent is the lender. If the subsidiary were the lender, the theory and practice are identical, with the only differences being the books on which the applicable accounts appear and the distribution of consolidated income.

Intercompany Notes

Assume that on July 1, 19X1, a subsidiary, Company S, borrows $10,000 from the parent, Company P, signing a one-year, 8% note, with interest payable on the due date. This intercompany loan may involve the following accounts of the separate affiliated firms:

Parent Company P	Subsidiary Company S
Notes Receivable	Notes Payable
Interest Income	Interest Expense
Interest Receivable	Interest Payable

While these accounts are required on the books of the separate firms, they should not appear on the consolidated statements. The procedures needed to eliminate intercompany notes and related interest amounts are demonstrated in Illustration VIII (pages 334 and 335), which is based on the intercompany note described.

Illustration VIII assumes an 80% ownership interest for the parent and 19X1 subsidiary net income of $10,000. In this case, the intercompany notes are the only notes recorded, but it may occur that intercompany notes and the related interest expense, revenue, and accruals are commingled with notes to outside parties. Before the trial balances are entered on the work sheet and before consolidation is attempted, intercompany interest expense and revenue must be properly accrued on the parent and subsidiary books.

After all the necessary adjustments have been made on each firm's books, the effect of the note on the distribution of consolidated net income must be determined. There might be a temptation to restate the subsidiary income as $10,400 as a result of eliminating the interest expense on the intercompany note, but this amount is not correct. Even though the interest does not appear on the consolidated statement, it is a legitimate expense for Company S as a separate entity and a legitimate revenue for Company P as a separate entity. In essence, Company S has agreed to transfer $400 to Company P for interest during 19X1, and the minority must respect this agreement when calculating its share of income. Thus, the basis for calculating the minority share is the income of Company S as a separate entity. The minority receives 20% of the $10,000 net income after interest is deducted.

A parent receiving a note from a subsidiary may subsequently discount the note at a nonaffiliated financial institution in order to receive immediate cash, resulting in a note receivable discounted being recorded by the parent. From a consolidated viewpoint, there is now a note payable to outside parties. Consolidation procedures should eliminate the internal note receivable against the notes receivable discounted. This elimination will result in the note, now payable to an outside party, being extended to the consolidated balance sheet. No eliminations are necessary for interest expense and revenue. The interest paid by the subsidiary is now paid to an outside party and need not be eliminated. The net interest expense or revenue on the discounting of the note is a transaction between the parent and an outside interest and thus is not eliminated. When consolidated statements are prepared,

Illustration VIII
Company P and
Work Sheet for Consolidated
For Year Ended

(Credit balance amounts
are in parentheses)

	Trial Balance	
	Company P	**Company S**
Cash	35,000	20,400
Notes Receivable from Co. S	10,000	
Interest Receivable	400	
Property, Plant, and Equipment (net)	140,000	150,000
Investment in Company S (80%)	128,000	
Note Payable to Co. P		(10,000)
Interest Payable		(400)
Common Stock, Co. P	(100,000)	
Retained Earnings, Jan. 1, 19X1, Co. P	(200,000)	
Common Stock, Company S		(50,000)
Retained Earnings, Jan. 1, 19X1, Co. S		(100,000)
Sales	(120,000)	(50,000)
Interest Income	(400)	
Subsidiary Income	(8,000)	
Cost of Goods Sold	75,000	20,000
Other Expense	40,000	19,600
Interest Expense		400
	0	0
Consolidated Net Income		
To Minority Interest (20% × $10,000 Company S Income)		
To Controlling Interest		
Total Minority Interest, Dec. 31, 19X1		
Retained Earnings, Controlling Interest, Dec. 31, 19X1		

Eliminations:
(1) Eliminate the equity adjustment for 80% of Company S's net income.
(2) Eliminate the controlling 80% portion of Company S's January 1, 19X1 stockholders' equity against the investment in Company S. No excess results.

however, it is desirable to net the interest expense on the note by closing the net interest expense or revenue on the discounting against interest recorded by the subsidiary.

Intercompany Discounting of Notes

A note received from a customer of the parent or the subsidiary is a valid asset from a consolidated viewpoint, and no adjustment or elimination is required. However, if a subsidiary discounts a customer's note with the parent, an internal contingent liability and asset are created.

Intercompany Notes
Subsidiary Company S
Financial Statements
December 31, 19X1

Eliminations Dr.	Eliminations Cr.	Consolidated Income Statement	Minority Interest	Controlling Retained Earnings	Consolidated Balance Sheet
					55,400
	3 10,000				
	3 400				
					290,000
	(1) 8,000				
	(2) 120,000				
3 10,000					
3 400					
					(100,000)
				(200,000)	
(2) 40,000			(10,000)		
(2) 80,000			(20,000)		
		(170,000)			
4 400					
(1) 8,000					
		95,000			
		59,600			
	4 400				
138,800	138,800				
		(15,400)			
		2,000	(2,000)		
		13,400		(13,400)	
			(32,000)		(32,000)
				(213,400)	(213,400)
					0

3 Eliminate the intercompany note and accrued interest applicable to the note. This step removes the "internal note" from the consolidated balance sheet.

4 Eliminate intercompany interest expense and revenue. Since an equal amount of expense and revenue is eliminated, there is no change in consolidated net income as a result of the elimination.

This internal transaction has no validity from a consolidated viewpoint and thus is eliminated.

To demonstrate disclosure on the consolidated work sheet, a customer's note is traced through its receipt and the discounting process. Assume that a subsidiary, Company S, receives a one-year, 6%, $20,000 note from a customer on April 1, 19X1, and that on October 1, 19X1, Company S discounts the note to the parent, Company P, at an 8% discount rate. The proceeds are calculated as follows:

Principal of note	$20,000
Interest due at maturity, 6% × $20,000	1,200
Total maturity value	$21,200
Multiply maturity value by 8% discount rate for ½ year[1]	(848)
Net proceeds of note	$20,352

The entries recorded on the separate books of Companies P and S as a result of the note and its discounting are illustrated below. These entries would produce the trial balance figures shown on page 337 in Illustration IX, which is a partial financial statements work sheet containing only the accounts relevant to the note.

	Subsidiary Company S			Parent Company P		
1. Receipt of note on April 1, 19X1	Notes Receivable .	20,000				
	Sales		20,000			
2. Discounting of note on October 1, 19X1, at 8%	Cash	20,352		Notes Receivable .	20,000	
	Notes Receivable Discounted* . .		20,000	Interest Receivable (6% cash interest for 6 months)	600	
	Interest Income .		352	Cash		20,352
				Unearned Interest Income (net gain, interest in excess of 6% face rate)		248
3. Year-end adjusting entry	None			Interest Receivable (6% cash interest for 3 months)	300	
				Unearned Interest Income	124	
				Interest Income (effective, an 8% discount rate, 3 months)		424
	*or Notes Receivable					

The elimination procedures have the effect of canceling the intercompany discounting transaction. The consolidated statements will include only the external note and interest related to it. The discounting

---

[1] The discount rate is a percentage applied to maturity value. This is in contrast to an effective interest rate, which is applied to the original principal. In this case, the effective interest rate is $848 ÷ $20,352, or 4.17% for a half year (8.34% annual).

Illustration IX—Intercompany Notes Receivable Discounted
Company P and Subsidiary Company S
Partial Work Sheet for Consolidated Financial Statements
For Year Ended December 31, 19X1

(Credit balance amounts
are in parentheses)

	Partial Trial Balance		Eliminations		Consolidated Income Statement	Consolidated Balance Sheet
	Company P	Company S	Dr.	Cr.		
Notes Receivable	20,000	20,000		**1** 20,000		20,000
Notes Receivable Discounted		(20,000)	**1** 20,000			
Interest Receivable..........	900					900
Interest Income	(424)	(352)		**2** 124	(900)	
Unearned Interest Income ...	(124)		**2** 124			

Eliminations:

1 Eliminate the intercompany discounted note by removing the receivable on the books of Company P and the contingent liability account on the books of Company S. Only the external notes receivable will be extended to the consolidated balance sheet. If Company S credited Notes Receivable rather than Notes Receivable Discounted, this elimination is not necessary.

2 To record entire parent company gain on interest in excess of 6% face rate in period transaction occurred. Since $124 of the gain has already been amortized, only the unamortized balance of the unearned interest income must be transferred to the current period's interest revenue. The entire $248 gain is realized to offset the $248 loss of revenue recorded by Company S. (Based on the 6% original interest rate, Company S would have earned $600 for the first 6 months; the $352 recorded reflects the $248 discount charged by Company P.)

Income Distribution:

Company P's internally reported net income is increased $124 in 19X1 and reduced $124 in 19X2. This procedure allows Company P to record the $248 net gain on the discounting on the date of the transaction and to earn 6% interest during the term of the note.

---

transaction, however, is considered in the distribution of consolidated net income. The net gain on the discounting is included as an expense of the subsidiary and as revenue of the parent when distributing consolidated net income.

SOPHISTICATED EQUITY METHOD: INTERCOMPANY TRANSACTIONS

A major difference between the simple and sophisticated equity methods, as discussed in Chapter 7, is that the sophisticated method records subsidiary income net of amortizations of excess. The simple equity method ignores amortizations and records as income the subsidiary's reported income multiplied by the parent's percentage of ownership. Another major difference between the two methods is that the simple equity method is based on reported subsidiary income without an adjustment for subsidiary-generated intercompany profits. The sophisticated equity method, however, first adjusts the subsidiary income for deferments of intercompany profits and then applies the parent's ownership percentage.

The added complexity of the sophisticated equity method is unwarranted for consolidation purposes, since the subsidiary income and investment in subsidiary accounts are entirely eliminated. However, this procedure must be used when parent-only statements are prepared as a supplement to the consolidated statements.

Unrealized Profits of the Current Period

The case of intercompany profits generated only during the current period will be considered first. Although the same procedure applies to all types of current period subsidiary-generated unrealized intercompany profits and losses, the impact of the sophisticated equity method will be demonstrated using inventory profits.

Illustration X is a partial work sheet based on the information given in Illustration II. The parent's investment account and its subsidiary income account in the trial balance are $3,200 less than in Illustration II as a result of deducting the parent's share (80%) of the unrealized ending inventory profit. The only elimination that differs from Illustration II is No. 1, which eliminates the entry made by the parent to record its share of the subsidiary's current period income. There is no impact on other work sheet procedures, and the balance of the work sheet included originally in Illustration II is unchanged.

Illustration X—Sophisticated Equity Method: Ending Inventory Profits

(Credit balance amounts
are in parentheses)

Company P and Subsidiary Company S
Partial Work Sheet
For Year Ended December 31, 19X1

	Trial Balance		Eliminations	
	Company P	Company S	Dr.	Cr.
Accounts Receivable.............................	110,000	150,000		(4) 25,000
Inventory, Dec. 31, 19X1......................	70,000	40,000		(5) 4,000
Investment in Co. S............................	(b) 192,800			① 56,800
				(2) 136,000
Other Assets	314,000	155,000		
Accounts Payable	(80,000)	(100,000)	(4) 25,000	
Common Stock ($10 par), Co. P	(200,000)			
Retained Earnings, Jan. 1, 19X1, Co. P	(250,000)			
Common Stock ($10 par), Co. S		(100,000)	(2) 80,000	
Retained Earnings, Jan. 1, 19X1, Co. S		(70,000)	(2) 56,000	
Sales	(700,000)	(500,000)	(3) 100,000	
Cost of Goods Sold	510,000	350,000	(5) 4,000	(3) 100,000
Expenses..	90,000	75,000		
Subsidiary Income	(a) (56,800)		① 56,800	
	0	0	321,800	321,800

Notes to Trial Balance:
(a) .80 × ($75,000 subsidiary reported income − $4,000 unrealized inventory profit)
(b) $136,000 beginning-of-year balance + $56,800 sophisticated equity-method income
Eliminations:
① Eliminate the entry recording the parent's share of subsidiary net income under the sophisticated equity method.
(2-5) Same as Illustration II.

Unrealized Profits of Current and Prior Periods

The effect of the sophisticated equity method when there are intercompany profits from current and prior periods is demonstrated in Illustration XI. The work sheet procedures illustrated are applicable to all types of prior period and current period subsidiary-generated intercompany profits and losses.

The partial work sheet of Illustration XI is based on the information given in Illustration III. The differences in the parent's trial balance are explained in the notes that follow the work sheet. The balance of the parent's subsidiary income account is the pro rata share of subsidiary income adjusted for both *realized prior period inventory profits* and *unrealized current period ending inventory profits*.

When the sophisticated equity method is used, work sheet eliminations are complicated by the inconsistency between the parent and sub-

Illustration XI—Sophisticated Equity Method: Beginning and Ending Inventory Profits

Company P and Subsidiary Company S
(Credit balance amounts
are in parentheses)
Partial Work Sheet
For Year Ended December 31, 19X2

	Trial Balance		Eliminations	
	Company P	Company S	Dr.	Cr.
Accounts Receivable	160,000	170,000		(5) 60,000
Inventory, Dec. 31, 19X2	60,000	50,000		(6) 6,000
Investment in Co. S	(c) 239,200			① 46,400
				(2) 192,800
Other Assets	354,000	165,000		
Accounts Payable	(90,000)	(80,000)	(5) 60,000	
Common Stock ($10 par), Co. P	(200,000)			
Retained Earnings, Jan. 1, 19X2, Co. P	(b)(406,800)			
Common Stock ($10 par), Co. S		(100,000)	(2) 80,000	
Retained Earnings, Jan 1, 19X2, Co. S		(145,000)	**Adj** 4,000	
			(2) 112,800	
Sales	(800,000)	(600,000)	(4) 120,000	
Cost of Goods Sold	610,000	440,000	(6) 6,000	**Adj** 4,000
				(4) 120,000
Expenses	120,000	100,000		
Subsidiary Income	(a) (46,400)		① 46,400	
	0	0	429,200	429,200

Notes to Trial Balance:
(a) .80 × ($60,000 subsidiary reported income + $4,000 realized beginning inventory profit − $6,000 unrealized inventory profit)
(b) $410,000 simple equity balance − 80% of $4,000 subsidiary beginning inventory profit
(c) $136,000 original balance + $56,800 sophisticated equity-method income for 19X1 + $46,400 sophisticated equity-method income for 19X2

Eliminations:
Adj Eliminate $4,000 beginning inventory profit from cost of goods sold and subsidiary Retained Earnings.
① Eliminate the entry recording the parent's share of subsidiary income under the sophisticated equity method.
(2) Eliminate the pro rata portion (80%) of subsidiary equity balances against the investment account. The elimination of Retained Earnings is 80% of the adjusted balance of $141,000 ($145,000 − $4,000).
(4-6) Same as Illustration III.

sidiary trial balances. In Illustration XI, the parent's investment account and retained earnings account do not include the parent's share (80%) of the $4,000 subsidiary beginning inventory profit. The subsidiary's trial balance does, however, include the $4,000 profit in both the beginning inventory and in the January 1, 19X1 Retained Earnings balance. This inconsistency is removed by an adjustment ("Adj") which eliminates the profit from the subsidiary's trial balance. This adjustment replaces Elimination No. 3 from Illustration III.

Elimination No. 1 of Illustration XI removes the subsidiary income as recorded by the parent. Elimination No. 2 reflects the adjustment of the subsidiary's Retained Earnings. The remaining eliminations (Nos. 4-6) and work sheet procedures are identical to those in Illustration III.

SUMMARY—WORK SHEET TECHNIQUE

At this point, it might be wise to review an overall approach to the preparation of more complex work sheets. The following procedures are designed to provide for efficiency and correctness:

1. When recopying the trial balances, always sum them to be sure that no errors have been made.
2. Carefully key all eliminations to aid future reference. It is suggested that a symbol such as an asterisk, a line, or a circle be used to identify those adjustments which affect current consolidated net income. This identification will make it easier to locate the adjustments that must later be posted to the income distribution schedules. Recall that any adjustment to income must be assigned to some firm's income distribution.
3. Sum the eliminations to be sure that they balance.
4. When eliminations are complete, horizontally determine account totals and extend them to the appropriate work sheet columns. Accounts which are to be eliminated should sum to zero.
5. Calculate consolidated net income.
6. Prepare the income distribution schedules. Assign each adjustment in Step 2 that has an impact upon net income to some firm's schedule. Adjustments due to intercompany transactions are assigned to the originating (selling) firm. Amortizations of excess are assigned only to the parent firm, since only the parent's interest is adjusted originally. Notice that adjustments made to the subsidiary's schedule are automatically allocated to the minority and controlling interests because the adjustments are reflected in the final adjusted income which is distributed according to the ownership percentages.

    Verify that the sum of the distributions equals consolidated net income. If equality exists, distribute the consolidated net income on the work sheet to the minority interest and consolidated retained earnings columns.
7. Sum the minority interest and controlling retained earnings columns and extend their balances to the balance sheet columns.
8. Verify that the balance sheet column totals are equal.

QUESTIONS

1. After the elimination of the intercompany investment, additional adjustments are necessary to produce consolidated statements. Indicate several types of intercompany transactions that will require adjustments, and give reasons why the adjustments are needed.

2. A parent company sold to its subsidiary merchandise costing $10,000, at a 25% markup, for cash. The subsidiary company sold ¾ of the goods for $12,000. What adjustments are required in the consolidation process?

3. Explain why the intercompany sale of merchandise has an influence on the distribution of consolidated income, even though the sale is eliminated on the consolidated statements.

4. A parent company sold to its subsidiary merchandise costing $75,000 for $100,000. Half of the goods were unsold at year end and had been written down to $40,000, the lower market value. What adjusting entries are required in the consolidation process?

5. Provide the entries to delete unrealized profit on intercompany sales from beginning and ending inventories for the following situations, assuming that the parent has a 90% ownership interest in the subsidiary:

    (a) Subsidiary's beginning inventory includes $25,000 of goods purchased from the parent company. Parent sells all merchandise at a 25% markup on cost. Subsidiary purchased goods at a price of $100,000 from Parent during the year and had $37,500 of the goods in ending inventory.

    (b) Parent's beginning inventory includes $48,000 of goods purchased from the subsidiary company. Subsidiary sells all merchandise at a 20% markup. Parent purchased goods at a price of $360,000 from Subsidiary during the year and had $24,000 of the goods in ending inventory.

6. How does the treatment of a gain on an intercompany sale of a depreciable plant asset differ from the treatment of a gain on an intercompany sale of a nondepreciable plant asset?

7. What is the general treatment of losses on intercompany merchandise and asset sales?

8. Prepare parent and subsidiary income distribution schedules and enter the following items in the correct column: (a) intercompany profit on unsold ending inventory—parent seller; (b) realized intercompany profit on beginning inventory—subsidiary seller; (c) internally generated net income of parent; (d) internally generated net income of subsidiary; (e) unrealized gain on intercompany sale of depreciable asset—subsidiary seller; (f) gain on intercompany sale of depreciable asset realized through use—subsidiary seller; (g) realized intercompany profit on beginning inventory—parent seller; (h) retirement loss on bonds—bonds issued by subsidiary, purchased by parent.

9. Harvey Construction Company is a 90%-owned subsidiary of Area-Wide Properties, Inc. Harvey is building an office complex for Area-Wide and is accounting for the contract under the percentage-of-completion method. To date, Harvey has billed but not collected $900,000, recorded costs of $850,000, and recorded earned income of $50,000.

    No adjustments or eliminations were made concerning this transaction in the process of preparing the consolidated statements. What misstatements are now found on the consolidated income statement and balance sheet?

10. An accounting theorist once said, "Intercompany gains and losses are never eliminated. They are just postponed." Discuss this statement.
11. Frequently, related firms will have outstanding intercompany loan balances. What effect do intercompany interest revenue and expense have on the consolidation process, including distribution of consolidated net income?

EXERCISES

Exercise 1. The Higgins Company is a wholly-owned subsidiary of the Daley Company. Both firms were newly organized on January 1, 19X1. Daley sells all of its production to its sales subsidiary, which sells no other goods than those purchased from the parent. The following facts apply to 19X1-19X3 operations:

	Daley Sales to Higgins	Daley Gross Profit	Higgins Dec. 31 Inventory	Higgins Sales
19X1	$200,000	25%	$40,000	$300,000
19X2	240,000	25	35,000	350,000
19X3	250,000	30	50,000	370,000

The inventory on hand each December 31 is sold during the following year. Prepare a schedule in columnar form which states for each period:
(1) The gross profit recorded by the Daley Company,
(2) The gross profit recorded by the Higgins Company, and
(3) The gross profit shown on the consolidated income statement.

Exercise 2. The Gale Company, a wholly-owned subsidiary, sold all of its 19X5 output to the parent company for $40,000, which included a 25% markup on cost. Gale had not sold any output to the parent in prior years. The parent company sold 75% of the goods it purchased from Gale at a gross profit of 20%. The balance of the goods purchased from Gale was in the parent's December 31, 19X5 inventory. The value assigned to the goods under the lower of cost or market method was $8,500.
(1) Determine the gross profit on these sales recorded on the separate books of the Gale Company and its parent.
(2) Calculate the gross profit shown as a result of these sales on the 19X5 consolidated income statement. Any write-down of inventory is an adjustment to the cost of goods sold.

Exercise 3. The Champion Company is an 80%-owned subsidiary of Braun, Inc. The separate income statements of the two firms for 19X6 are as follows:

	Braun, Inc.	Champion Co.
Sales	$200,000	$100,000
Cost of goods sold	140,000	75,000
Gross profit	$ 60,000	$ 25,000
Other expenses	(40,000)	(15,000)
Other income	5,000	
Operating income	$ 25,000	$ 10,000
Subsidiary income	8,000	—
Net income	$ 33,000	$ 10,000

The following additional facts apply to 19X6:
(a) Champion sold $50,000 of goods to Braun, Inc. The gross profit on sales to Braun and to unrelated firms is equal and has not changed from previous years.
(b) Braun, Inc., held $20,000 of Champion's goods in its beginning inventory and $30,000 in its ending inventory.
(c) Braun billed Champion $5,000 for consulting services. The charge was expensed by Champion and treated as other income by Braun, Inc.

Prepare a consolidated income statement for 19X6, including the distribution of the consolidated income to the controlling and minority interests. Income distribution schedules should be prepared as supporting schedules.

Exercise 4. On January 1, 19X2, the Furey Company sold a machine to the Bardon Company for $20,000. The machine had an original cost of $24,000 and accumulated depreciation of $9,000 at the time of sale. The machine has a 5-year remaining life and will be depreciated on a straight-line basis with no salvage value. The Bardon Company is an 80%-owned subsidiary of the Furey Company.
(1) Explain the adjustments that would have to be made to arrive at consolidated net income for the years 19X2 through 19X6 as a result of this sale.
(2) Prepare the elimination that would be required on the December 31, 19X3 consolidated work sheet as a result of this sale.
(3) Assuming that Bardon Company was the seller of the machine and that all other facts remained constant, prepare the elimination that would be required on the December 31, 19X3 consolidated work sheet as a result of this sale.

Exercise 5. On July 1, 19X5, the Yonkton Company sold a parcel of land to its 90%-owned subsidiary, the Zarden Company, for $80,000. Yonkton had originally paid $60,000 for the land. On November 30, 19X6, Zarden sold the land to the Externe Corporation for $77,500.
(1) Prepare the eliminations relating to the land sale for the December 31, 19X5 consolidated work sheet.
(2) Prepare the eliminations relating to the sale for the December 31, 19X6 work sheet.

Exercise 6. The Highton Corporation sold a press to its 80%-owned subsidiary, Steel Fab, Inc., for $15,000 on January 1, 19X2. The press was purchased by Highton on January 1, 19X1, for $30,000, and $6,000 of depreciation for 19X1 had been recorded. The fair market value of the press on January 1, 19X2, was $20,000. Steel Fab, Inc., proceeded to depreciate the press on a straight-line basis using a 5-year life and no salvage value. On December 31, 19X3, Steel Fab, Inc., having no further need for the machine, sold it for $5,000 and recorded a loss on the sale.
(1) Explain the adjustments which would have to be made to the income statements of the two firms to arrive at a consolidated income statement for 19X2 and 19X3.
(2) Prepare the eliminations that would have to be made on the December 31, 19X3 consolidated work sheet as a result of the sale.

Exercise 7. The Illings Company contracted with its 80%-owned subsidiary, Worth Equipment Company, for the construction of two stamping machines. The first machine was completed and put into operation on July 1, 19X9. It cost Worth $40,000 and has a 5-year estimated life with no salvage value. The contract price was $50,000. The machine is being depreciated on a straight-line basis. The second machine, with an estimated total cost of $60,000 and contract price of $74,000, was 75% complete at December 31, 19X9. To date, costs on the second contract total $45,000. By the statement date, Illings had completely paid for the first machine and still owed $3,000 of the $40,000 billed to date on the second machine. Worth uses the completed-contract method to account for its long-term construction contracts.

(1) Prepare the necessary eliminations for the consolidated work sheet at December 31, 19X9.

(2) What is the effect of this contract on the income distribution schedules?

Exercise 8. The separate income statements of the Purin Company and its 90%-owned subsidiary, the Jaines Company, for the year ended December 31, 19X3, are as follows:

	Purin Co.	Jaines Co.
Sales..	$600,000	$250,000
Cost of goods sold	400,000	170,000
Gross profit	$200,000	$ 80,000
Expenses....................................	(150,000)	(65,000)
Other income		18,000
Operating income	$ 50,000	$ 33,000
Subsidiary income	29,700	—
Net income..................................	$ 79,700	$ 33,000

The following additional facts apply:

(a) On January 1, 19X2, Jaines purchased a building with a book value of $100,000 and an estimated 25-year life from Purin for $125,000, to be depreciated on a straight-line basis with no salvage value. On December 30, 19X3, Jaines sold the building to the nonaffiliated Fuera Corporation for $123,000.

(b) On January 1, 19X3, Jaines sold a machine with a book value of $50,000 to Purin for $60,000. The machine has an expected life of 4 years and will be depreciated on a straight-line basis with no salvage value.

Prepare the consolidated income statement for 19X3 and the supporting income distribution schedules.

Exercise 9. Dover Contractors, an 80%-owned subsidiary, is constructing a warehouse for its parent, the Aero-Parts Corporation. The following information is available at December 31, 19X5:

Percent of completion	60%
Costs incurred to date	$150,000
Estimated costs to complete	100,000
Contract price	325,000
Amount billed to date (no amounts collected) .	130,000

Dover uses the percentage-of-completion method to account for its long-term contracts.

Prepare a partial trial balance and show the eliminations relating to the contract for the December 31, 19X5 consolidated work sheet.

Exercise 10. The Day Company is a wholly-owned subsidiary of the Crane Company. On April 1, 19X1, Crane loaned Day $30,000 in exchange for a six-month, 8% note payable. Interest will be paid at maturity. Based on the preceding facts:

(1) Prepare the entries Crane and Day would make concerning the note during the fiscal year ending June 30, 19X1 (including adjusting entries).

(2) Prepare the eliminations that would be made on the June 30, 19X1 consolidated work sheet for the Crane and Day Companies.

Exercise 11.   Assume that Crane discounted the note described in Exercise 10 to a bank on June 1, 19X1, and that the bank discounted the note at a 10% annual interest rate.

(1) Prepare the entries Crane and Day would make concerning the note and its discounting during the fiscal year ending June 30, 19X1 (including adjusting entries).

(2) Prepare the eliminations that would be made on the June 30, 19X1 consolidated work sheet for the Crane and Day Companies.

Exercise 12.   The Verso Company is a wholly-owned subsidiary of the Roger Company. On April 1, 19X1, Verso accepted from a customer a $10,000, 6% one-year note with interest due at maturity. Being in need of cash, the Verso Company discounted the note to the parent, Roger Company, on October 1, 19X1. A 9% annual discount rate was used by the parent.

(1) Prepare the entries (including adjusting entries) the Roger and Verso Companies would make to record the note and its discounting during the fiscal year ending December 31, 19X1.

(2) Prepare the eliminations that would be made on the December 31, 19X1 consolidated work sheet for the Roger and Verso Companies.

PROBLEMS

Problem 8-1.   On April 1, 19X1, Air-Jet Corporation purchased 80% of the outstanding stock of Fremling Company for $425,000. A condensed balance sheet of Fremling Company at the purchase date follows:

Assets		Liabilities and Equity	
Current assets	$180,000	Liabilities	$100,000
Long-lived assets (net)......	320,000	Equity.....................	400,000
Total assets	$500,000	Total liabilities and equity ..	$500,000

All book values approximated market values on the purchase date. Air-Jet Corporation amortizes its intangibles over 20 years or their legal life, whichever is shorter.

The following information has been gathered pertaining to the first two years of operation since Air-Jet's purchase of Fremling Company stock.

(a) Intercompany merchandise sales are summarized as follows:

Date	Transaction	Sales	Gross Profit	Merchandise Remaining in Purchaser's Ending Inventory
April 1, 19X1 to	Air-Jet to Fremling	$35,000	20%	$8,000
March 31, 19X2	Fremling to Air-Jet	20,000	25	3,000
April 1, 19X2 to	Air-Jet to Fremling	32,000	20	5,000
March 31, 19X3	Fremling to Air-Jet	30,000	20	2,000

(b) On March 31, 19X3, Air-Jet owed Fremling $5,000 and Fremling owed Air-Jet $10,000 pertaining to intercompany sales.

(c) Air-Jet paid $25,000 in cash dividends on March 20, 19X2 and 19X3. Fremling paid its first cash dividend on March 10, 19X3. Each share of outstanding common stock received a $.15 cash dividend.

Trial balances for the two companies as of March 31, 19X3, follow:

	Air-Jet Corporation	Fremling Company
Cash	216,200	44,300
Accounts Receivable (net)	290,000	97,000
Inventory	310,000	80,000
Investment in Fremling Company	425,000	—
Land	1,081,000	150,000
Building and Equipment	1,850,000	400,000
Accumulated Depreciation	(940,000)	(210,000)
Intangibles (net)	60,000	—
Accounts Payable	(242,200)	(106,300)
Bonds Payable	(400,000)	—
Common Stock ($.50 par)	(250,000)	—
Common Stock ($1 par)	—	(200,000)
Paid-In Capital in Excess of Par	(1,250,000)	(100,000)
Retained Earnings	(1,105,000)	(140,000)
Sales	(880,000)	(630,000)
Dividend Income	(24,000)	—
Cost of Goods Sold	704,000	504,000
Other Expenses	130,000	81,000
Dividends Declared	25,000	30,000
Total	0	0

Required:

(1) Prepare the necessary work sheet for the preparation of consolidated financial statements for Air-Jet Corporation and its subsidiary, Fremling Company, for the year ended March 31, 19X3.

(2) Prepare the formal consolidated income statement for the fiscal year 19X2-19X3.

Problem 8-2. In a transaction on July 1, 19W9, properly recorded as a pooling, the Halonen Record Company exchanged 19,200 shares of its common stock, which had a par value of $5, for 90% of the outstanding stock of Marquis Distributors. Marquis' stockholders' equity at that date was as follows: common stock, $80,000; paid-in capital in excess of par, $20,000; retained earnings, $34,000. Marquis had net income of $6,000 for 19W9. Just prior to the pooling, Halonen's records showed account balances of $105,000 in Common Stock and $75,600 in Retained Earnings. Halonen's net income for 19W9 was $40,000. Neither firm paid dividends in 19W9, and no further stock transactions have occurred.

On November 1, 19W9, Halonen purchased a parcel of land from Marquis for $35,000. Late in 19X0, Halonen sold the land, which had originally cost Marquis $30,000, to the Erikal Company for $42,500.

Since the pooling, Halonen has been selling records to Marquis at 30% above cost. Marquis' merchandise inventory at December 31, 19W9, included $9,100 of records purchased from Halonen. Intercompany sales for 19X0 totaled $30,000, of which $3,000 remained to be paid for at year end. Purchases from Halonen accounted for $7,150 of Marquis' inventory balance at December 31, 19X0.

The following account balances for the two firms were available at December 31, 19X0:

	Halonen	Marquis
Cash	50,500	5,000
Accounts Receivable (net)	91,400	30,000
Merchandise Inventory	60,000	40,000
Property, Plant, and Equipment ..	290,000	85,000
Investment in Marquis	135,000	—
Liabilities	(193,800)	(10,000)
Sales	(970,000)	(200,000)
Gain on Sale of Land	(7,500)	—
Subsidiary Income	(9,000)	—
Cost of Goods Sold	600,000	120,000
Other Expenses	300,000	70,000

Required:

(1) Determine the stockholders' equity balances on the books of both firms at January 1, 19X0.

(2) Prepare the work sheet necessary for the preparation of consolidated statements at December 31, 19X0.

Problem 8-3.   On January 1, 19X3, the Berger Company exchanged its shares on a one-for-one basis with the stockholders of Dell, Inc. A total of 9,000 shares were acquired in a transaction that met the criteria for a pooling of interests. The investment was properly recorded at book value and it has been maintained at cost. The equity balances of Dell, Inc., on the acquisition date were:

Common stock, $10 par	$100,000
Paid-in capital in excess of par	200,000
Retained earnings	300,000

No dividends were paid by either firm during 19X6. The following trial balances were prepared for the Berger Company and its subsidiary, Dell, Inc., on December 31, 19X6:

	Berger Co.	Dell, Inc.
Cash	140,000	62,000
Accounts Receivable	270,000	194,000
Inventory	350,000	176,000
Land	800,000	180,000
Building and Equipment	1,100,000	400,000
Accumulated Depreciation	(180,000)	(120,000)
Investment in Dell, Inc.	540,000	—
Accounts Payable	(110,000)	(50,000)
Common Stock ($10 par)	(800,000)	(100,000)
Paid-In Capital in Excess of Par	(600,000)	(200,000)
Retained Earnings................	(1,340,000)	(450,000)
Sales	(600,000)	(300,000)
Other Income	(40,000)	(12,000)
Cost of Goods Sold	320,000	180,000
Other Expenses	150,000	40,000
Total	0	0

Dell, Inc., sold a machine to the Berger Company for $20,000 on July 1, 19X6. The machine cost Dell $30,000, and $15,000 of accumulated depreciation had been recorded as of the sale date. The machine has a 5-year remaining life and no salvage value. Berger Company is using straight-line depreciation.

Since the pooling date, Berger sells merchandise for resale to Dell, Inc., at cost plus 20%. Sales during 19X6 were $120,000. The inventory of these goods held by Dell was $15,000 on January 1, 19X6, and $8,000 on December 31, 19X6. Dell, Inc., owes Berger for $12,000 of these goods as of December 31, 19X6.

Required:

(1) Prepare the necessary work sheet to arrive at consolidated statements for 19X6.
(2) Prepare formal consolidated statements for 19X6, including the income statement, retained earnings statement, and balance sheet.

Problem 8-4. On January 1, 19X1, Prentice Corporation reached a final agreement with the three major stockholders of the Strong Company to purchase their 90% interest. Terms of the agreement called for the following:

(a) Jones would give up a 30% interest and receive $120,000 in cash.
(b) Doe would give up a 20% interest and receive 8,000 shares of Prentice common stock ($10 market value per share).
(c) Gregg would give up a 40% interest and receive $60,000 in cash and $100,000 of 8% ten-year debentures. These bonds were selling at face value on the agreement date.

A condensed balance sheet as of January 1, 19X1, for Strong Company is as follows:

Assets		Liabilities and Equity	
Current assets	$160,000	Liabilities	$ 80,000
Property, plant, and equipment		Common stock, $5 par	300,000
(net)	300,000	Retained earnings	120,000
Goodwill..................	40,000		
Total assets	$500,000	Total liabilities and equity ..	$500,000

Included in Strong's current assets were items of inventory which were undervalued by $10,000. This inventory was sold during 19X1.

Strong's plant assets approximated market value, except for land, which had a $40,000 book value and was undervalued by $10,000.

Recorded goodwill has a 32-year remaining life.

On July 1, 19X2, Prentice sold to Strong a machine for $12,000. The machine had an original cost of $20,000, accumulated depreciation of $12,000, and a remaining life of four years at the sale date. Both Prentice and Strong use straight-line depreciation.

Strong produces printed circuits that it has been selling to Prentice since July, 19X1, at a price to realize a gross profit of 30% to Strong. During 19X3, Strong's sales to Prentice amounted to $60,000. Prentice still owes Strong $10,000 of this amount on December 31, 19X3.

Prentice had $4,000 of these circuits in its beginning 19X3 inventory, and $2,000 in its December 31, 19X3 inventory.

Trial balances as of December 31, 19X3, are shown at the top of page 349.

Required:

(1) Prepare a work sheet necessary for the preparation of a consolidated balance sheet and consolidated income statement for Prentice Corporation and subsidiary for the year ended December 31, 19X3.
(2) Prepare consolidated statements, including the income statement, retained earnings statement, and balance sheet.

	Prentice Corporation	Strong Company
Cash	160,900	44,250
Receivables (net)	195,000	72,000
Inventory	335,000	88,500
Investment in Strong Company	449,100	—
Land	780,000	80,000
Building and Equipment	1,399,000	490,000
Accumulated Depreciation	(590,000)	(200,000)
Goodwill	—	36,250
Accounts Payable	(250,000)	(92,000)
Bonds Payable, 8%	(500,000)	—
Common Stock ($5 par)	(1,000,000)	(300,000)
Paid-In Capital in Excess of Par	(200,000)	—
Retained Earnings	(585,000)	(175,000)
Sales	(1,210,000)	(510,000)
Subsidiary Income	(45,000)	—
Cost of Goods Sold	786,500	357,000
Other Expenses	224,500	103,000
Dividends Declared	50,000	6,000
Total	0	0

Problem 8-5. On January 1, 19X3, Company X exchanged on a one-for-three basis common stock held in its treasury for 70% of the outstanding stock of Company Z. Company X common stock had a stable market price of $35 per share at the exchange date.

On January 1, 19X3, the stockholders' equity section of Company Z's balance sheet was as follows:

Common stock, $5 par	$ 450,000
Paid-in capital in excess of par	180,000
Retained earnings	370,000
Total	$1,000,000

At this date Company Z's book values approximated market, except for the land, which was undervalued by $30,000.

Any goodwill recognized is to be amortized over 40 years.

Information regarding intercompany transactions for 19X5 follows:

(a) Parent Company X sells merchandise to subsidiary Company Z, realizing a 40% gross profit rate. Sales during 19X5 were $80,000. Company Z had $10,000 of 19X4 purchases in its beginning inventory and $15,000 of 19X5 purchases in its ending inventory.

(b) Company Z signed a 6%, 4-month, $10,000 note to Company X to cover the remaining balance of its payables on November 1, 19X5. No new merchandise was purchased after this date.

(c) Company Z wrote down to $10,000 the merchandise purchased from Company X and remaining in its ending inventory on December 31, 19X5.

Trial balances of Company X and its subsidiary, Company Z, as of December 31, 19X5, are shown at the top of page 350.

Required:

Prepare a work sheet necessary for the preparation of a consolidated balance sheet and income statement for Company X and its subsidiary for the year ending December 31, 19X5.

	Company X	Company Z
Cash	265,000	200,100
Interest Receivable	1,200	—
Notes Receivable	50,000	—
Accounts Receivable	395,000	110,000
Inventory	470,000	160,000
Investment in Company Z	878,500	—
Land	350,000	300,000
Building and Equipment	1,110,000	810,000
Accumulated Depreciation	(500,000)	(200,000)
Intangibles	60,000	—
Liabilities	(611,500)	(175,000)
Interest Payable	—	(100)
Common Stock ($1 par)	(400,000)	—
Common Stock ($5 par)	—	(450,000)
Paid-In Capital in Excess of Par	(1,235,000)	(180,000)
Retained Earnings	(958,500)	(470,000)
Treasury Stock (at cost)	315,000	—
Sales	(1,020,000)	(500,000)
Interest Income	(1,200)	—
Subsidiary Income	(73,500)	—
Cost of Goods Sold	705,000	300,000
Other Expenses	200,000	95,000
Total	0	0

Problem 8-6. On July 1, 19X4, Price Mfg. Co. purchased 80% of the outstanding stock of Snow Industries for $800,000. At the purchase date, Snow's stockholders' equity showed:

Common stock, $2 par	$200,000
Paid-in capital in excess of par	500,000
Retained earnings	200,000
Total	$900,000

All of Snow's book values approximated market values at the purchase date.

On January 1, 19X6, Price sold a machine to Snow for $15,000. The machine had an original cost of $32,000, accumulated depreciation of $22,000, and an estimated life of 5 years at the sale date. Snow sold the machine on December 31, 19X7, for $7,000.

Snow Industries sold Price Mfg. Co. a used punch press for $30,000 on July 1, 19X6. At this time, the punch press had an estimated future life of 10 years. Snow paid $50,000 for the punch press and has recorded accumulated depreciation of $27,500 as of the sale date.

On January 1, 19X1, Snow Industries issued $400,000 of 7%, 10-year bonds. The bonds were sold at face value and pay interest on April 1 and October 1 of each year. On June 30, 19X7, Price Mfg. Co. loaned Snow Industries $200,000 to retire one half of the outstanding bonds. Snow signed a four-year, 8% note, with interest payable each June 30.

On July 1, 19X7, Snow called one half of the bonds at 102 plus accrued interest.

Snow Industries has paid 10% of its net income in dividends since 19X3.

Trial balances of Price Mfg. Co. and Snow Industries as of December 31, 19X7, are as follows:

	Price Mfg. Co.	Snow Industries
Cash	162,040	107,200
Accounts and Notes Receivable	405,000	130,500
Interest Receivable	14,000	2,000
Inventory	420,000	140,000
Investment in Snow Industries	800,000	—
Notes Receivable (long-term)	200,000	—
Property, Plant, and Equipment	3,650,000	1,510,000
Accumulated Depreciation	(1,400,000)	(360,000)
Accounts Payable	—	(94,000)
Interest Payable	(6,000)	(11,500)
Notes Payable (long-term 8%)	(150,000)	(200,000)
Bonds Payable, 7%	—	(200,000)
Common Stock ($2 par)	(600,000)	(200,000)
Paid-In Capital in Excess of Par	(2,400,000)	(500,000)
Retained Earnings	(986,000)	(290,000)
Sales	(1,400,000)	(500,000)
Dividend Income	(3,040)	
Cost of Goods Sold	952,000	325,000
Interest Expense	16,000	25,500
Other Expenses	276,000	105,500
Loss on Machine Sale	—	2,000
Loss on Bond Redemption	—	4,000
Other Income	(10,000)	—
Dividends Declared	60,000	3,800
Total	0	0

Required:

Prepare a work sheet for the preparation of a consolidated balance sheet and consolidated income statement for Price Mfg. Co. and its subsidiary, Snow Industries, for the year ended December 31, 19X7. Any goodwill is to be amortized over 40 years.

Problem 8-7. On January 1, 19X1, the Kertz Corporation acquired 80% of the outstanding common stock of the Decker Company for $680,000. Decker had the following stockholders' equity at that date:

Common stock, $10 par	$450,000
Paid-in capital in excess of par	200,000
Retained earnings	150,000
Total equity	$800,000

Any excess of cost over book value is attributed to goodwill with a life of only 4 years.

Decker had net income of $68,000 for 19X1, but it has paid no dividends in recent years.

On December 31, 19X1, Kertz sold new equipment to Decker which had a cost of $60,000. Decker paid $72,000 for the equipment, which has an estimated four-year life with no salvage value.

Since the acquisition, Kertz has been purchasing all of its raw materials from Decker at a price which yields a 20% gross profit to Decker. Decker's materials sales to Kertz totaled $800,000 during 19X2. Kertz still owes Decker $40,000 on open account. Information pertaining to year-end inventory balances for Kertz Corporation since the acquisition is as follows:

	Materials	Labor and Overhead	Total
Materials, December 31, 19X1..........................	$20,875	—	$20,875
Work in process, December 31, 19X1	7,500	$17,500	25,000
Finished goods, December 31, 19X1	6,000	14,000	20,000
Materials, December 31, 19X2.........................	30,000	—	30,000
Work in process, December 31, 19X2	24,000	56,000	80,000
Finished goods, December 31, 19X2	12,000	28,000	40,000

Trial balances for the two companies at December 31, 19X2, were as follows:

	Kertz Corp.	Decker Co.
Cash	68,000	28,000
Accounts Receivable (net)	204,000	60,000
Finished Goods	40,000	50,000
Work in Process	80,000	90,000
Materials	30,000	25,000
Land	100,000	70,000
Buildings (net)	372,000	200,000
Equipment..	500,000	520,000
Accumulated Depreciation—Equipment	(224,400)	(78,000)
Investment in Decker	798,400	—
Goodwill	—	20,000
Accounts Payable	(134,000)	(37,000)
Common Stock ($10 par)	(750,000)	(450,000)
Paid-In Capital in Excess of Par	(100,000)	(200,000)
Retained Earnings...	(660,000)	(218,000)
Sales	(3,000,000)	(940,000)
Subsidiary Income	(64,000)	—
Cost of Goods Sold	2,100,000	750,000
Other Expenses	640,000	110,000
Total	0	0

Required:

Prepare a work sheet for the preparation of a consolidated income statement and balance sheet for Kertz Corporation and its subsidiary, Decker Company, for the year ended December 31, 19X2.

Problem 8-8.   On January 1, 19X5, Williams Industries acquired an 80% interest in Redline Corporation by exchanging, on a one-for-four basis, previously unissued common stock for outstanding common stock of Redline Corporation. The value per share of Williams Industries common stock immediately after the exchange was $50. At the purchase date, Redline Corporation book values approximated market values, and it had 200,000 shares of common stock outstanding with a total stockholders' equity of $2,225,000.

Most of Redline Corporation's revenue is generated by long-term construction projects. Redline uses the percentage-of-completion method to account for all its long-term construction projects.

Redline constructed for its own use a special machine at a cost of $250,000, which was put into use on January 1, 19X1. The machine was sold to Williams Industries on January 1, 19X5, for $250,000 when it had a remaining life of 15 years and a book value of $190,000. Both the estimated remaining life and straight-line depreciation will continue to be used by Williams Industries.

Redline Corporation started two long-term construction projects for Williams Industries. The first project was started in 19X6 and was completed December 31, 19X6, at a total cost of $250,000. Total sales price to Williams for the completed project was $300,000, of which $60,000 was still unpaid on December 31, 19X6. The second project was started in 19X5 and was not completed as of December 31, 19X6. The following table presents the relevant information regarding this contract as of December 31, 19X6:

	19X5	19X6
Contract price	$1,500,000	$1,500,000
Less costs:		
Actual costs to date	$ 300,000	$ 900,000
Estimated cost to complete	900,000	310,000
Estimated total costs	$1,200,000	$1,210,000
Estimated total income	$ 300,000	$ 290,000
Apportionment of total income:		
19X5 ($300,000/$1,200,000 × $300,000)	$ 75,000	
19X6 ($900,000/$1,210,000 × $290,000)	$ 215,702	
Less income recognized to date	75,000	
Income recognized in 19X6	$ 140,702	

Billings on this contract were $250,000 in 19X5 and $550,000 in 19X6, of which $100,000 was still uncollected as of December 31, 19X6. Amounts paid or owed by the parent are included in its property, plant, and equipment account.

Trial balances of Williams Industries and Redline Corporation as of December 31, 19X6, are as follows:

	Williams Industries	Redline Corporation
Cash	1,140,000	180,000
Accounts Receivable (net)	1,345,000	135,000
Construction Contracts Receivable	—	830,000
Billings on Construction in Progress	—	(1,790,000)
Inventory	1,500,000	215,000
Investment in Redline Corporation	2,236,000	—
Property, Plant, and Equipment	6,800,000	3,800,000
Accumulated Depreciation	(1,900,000)	(1,000,000)
Accounts Payable	(1,200,000)	(750,000)
Bonds Payable	(3,000,000)	(1,300,000)
Common Stock ($10 par)	(5,000,000)	(2,000,000)
Retained Earnings	(1,574,000)	(340,000)
Earned Income on Long-Term Contracts	—	(650,000)
Sales	(3,900,000)	(390,000)
Other Income	(205,000)	(28,000)
Construction in Progress	—	2,200,000
Cost of Goods Sold	2,340,000	210,000
Other Expenses	1,410,000	618,000
Subsidiary Income	(192,000)	—
Dividends Declared	200,000	60,000
Total	0	0

Required:

Prepare a work sheet necessary for the preparation of a consolidated balance sheet and a consolidated income statement for Williams Industries and its subsidiary, Redline Corporation, for the year ended December 31, 19X6. Assume that all necessary adjusting entries have been made unless an obvious discrepancy exists. Any goodwill that could be attributed to the purchase should be amortized over 40 years.

Problem 8-9. Place, Inc., purchased for $141,000 cash, 100% of the common stock of Scandia Corporation on June 30, 19X6. At that date, Scandia's stockholders' equity was as follows:

100,000 shares common stock, $1 par	$100,000
Retained earnings	41,000
Total	$141,000

The fair market values of the assets and liabilities did not differ materially from their book values. Scandia has made no adjustments on its books to reflect the purchase by Place. On December 31, 19X6, Place and Scandia prepared consolidated financial statements.

Transactions between Place and Scandia during the year ended December 31, 19X7, follow:

(a) On January 3, 19X7, land with an $11,000 book value was sold by Place to Scandia for $15,000. Scandia made a $3,000 down payment and signed an 8% mortgage note, payable in 12 equal quarterly payments of $1,135, including interest, beginning March 31, 19X7.

(b) Scandia produced equipment for Place under two separate contracts. The first contract, which was for office equipment, was begun and completed during the year at a cost to Scandia of $17,500. Place paid $22,000 cash for the equipment on April 17, 19X7. The second contract was begun on February 15, 19X7, but will not be completed until May 19X8. Scandia has incurred $45,000 costs as of December 31, 19X7, and anticipates an additional $30,000 cost to complete the $95,000 contract. Scandia accounts for all contracts under the percentage-of-completion method of accounting. Place has made no account on its books for this uncompleted contract as of December 31, 19X7.

(c) Place sells merchandise to Scandia at an average markup of 12% on cost. During the year, Place charged Scandia $238,000 for merchandise purchased, of which Scandia paid $211,000. Scandia has $11,200 of this merchandise on hand on December 31, 19X7.

(d) Place depreciates all of its equipment over a 10-year estimated economic life, with no salvage value. Place takes a half-year's depreciation in the year of purchase.

Both companies have made all of the adjusting entries required for separate financial statements, unless an obvious discrepancy exists.

Trial balances for Place, Inc., and its subsidiary as of December 31, 19X7, are shown at the top of page 355.

Required:

Prepare a work sheet necessary for the preparation of a consolidated balance sheet and income statement for Place, Inc., and Scandia Corporation, for the year ended December 31, 19X7. (AICPA adapted)

	Place, Inc.	Scandia Corp.
Cash	53,000	31,211
Accounts Receivable	119,000	53,000
Billings on Construction in Progress	—	(1,201,900)
Mortgage Receivable	8,311	—
Unsecured Notes Receivable	18,000	—
Inventories	217,000	117,500
Land	34,000	42,000
Building and Equipment (net)	717,000	408,000
Investment in Scandia Corporation	141,000	—
Accounts Payable	(203,000)	(147,000)
Mortgages Payable	(592,000)	(397,311)
Common Stock	(250,000)	(100,000)
Retained Earnings	(139,311)	(49,500)
Sales	(1,800,000)	—
Earned Income on Long-Term Contracts	—	(437,000)
Cost of Goods Sold	1,155,000	—
Construction in Progress	—	1,289,000
Selling, General, and Administrative Expenses	497,000	360,000
Interest Income	(20,000)	—
Interest Expense	49,000	32,000
Gain on Sale of Land	(4,000)	—
Total	0	0

Problem 8-10. The following trial balances were prepared after completion of the examination of the December 31, 19X4 financial statements of Basic Corporation and its subsidiaries, Noah Corporation and Abel Corporation. The subsidiary investments are accounted for by the cost method.

	Basic	Noah	Abel
Cash	82,000	11,000	27,000
Accounts Receivable	104,000	41,000	143,000
Inventories	241,000	70,000	78,000
Investment in Noah Corporation	150,000	—	—
Investment in Abel Corporation	175,000	—	—
Investments (other)	185,000	—	—
Property, Plant, and Equipment	375,000	58,000	99,000
Accumulated Depreciation	(96,000)	(7,000)	(21,000)
Cost of Goods Sold	820,000	300,000	350,000
Operating Expenses	60,000	35,000	40,000
Accounts Payable	(46,000)	(33,000)	(24,000)
Sales	(960,000)	(275,000)	(570,000)
Gain on Sale of Assets	(9,000)	—	—
Dividend Income	(18,000)	—	—
Common Stock ($20 par):			
Basic	(500,000)	—	—
Noah	—	(200,000)	—
Abel	—	—	(100,000)
Retained Earnings:			
Basic	(563,000)	—	—
Abel	—	—	(12,000)
Appropriation for Contingency	—	—	(10,000)
	0	0	0

The audit working papers provide the following additional information:
(a) The Noah Corporation was formed by the Basic Corporation on January 1, 19X4. To secure additional capital, 25% of the capital stock was sold at par value in the securities market. Basic purchased the remaining capital stock at par value for cash.
(b) On July 1, 19X4, Basic acquired from stockholders 4,000 shares of Abel Corporation capital stock for $175,000. Any excess is attributable to goodwill with a 10-year life. A condensed trial balance for Abel Corporation at July 1, 19X4, is as follows:

	Debit	Credit
Current Assets	165,000	—
Property, Plant, and Equipment (net)	60,000	—
Current Liabilities	—	45,000
Capital Stock ($20 par)	—	100,000
Retained Earnings	—	36,000
Sales	—	200,000
Cost of Goods Sold	140,000	—
Operating Expenses	16,000	—
Total	381,000	381,000

(c) The following intercompany product sales were made in 19X4:

	Sales	Gross Profit on Sales	Included in Purchaser's Inventory on December 31, 19X4, at Lower of Cost or Market
Basic to Abel	$ 40,000	20%	$15,000
Noah to Abel	30,000	10	10,000
Abel to Basic	60,000	30	20,000
Total	$130,000		$45,000

In valuing the Basic Corporation inventory at the lower of cost or market, the portion of the inventory purchased from the Abel Corporation was written down by $1,900.
(d) On January 2, 19X4, Basic Corporation sold a punch press to Noah Corporation. The machine was purchased on January 1, 19X2, and was being depreciated by the straight-line method over a 10-year life. Noah Corporation computed depreciation by the same method based on the remaining useful life. Details of the sale are as follows:

Cost of punch press	$25,000
Accumulated depreciation	5,000
Net book value	$20,000
Sales price	24,000
Gain on sale	$ 4,000

(e) Cash dividends were paid on the following dates in 19X4:

	Basic	Abel
June 30	$22,000	$ 6,000
December 31	26,000	14,000
	$48,000	$20,000

(f) Basic Corporation billed $6,000 to each subsidiary at year end for executive services in 19X4. The billing was treated as an operating expense and a reduction of operating expense, respectively. The invoices were paid in January, 19X5.

(g) At year end, Abel Corporation appropriated $10,000 for a contingent loss in connection with a lawsuit that had been pending since 19X2.

Required:

Prepare a work sheet for consolidated statements for Basic Corporation and its subsidiaries for the year ended December 31, 19X4.   (AICPA adapted)

Problem 8-11. Potter Company, a wholesaler, purchased 80% of the issued and outstanding stock of Star, Inc., a retailer, on December 31, 19X3, for $120,000. At that date, Star, Inc., had one class of common stock outstanding at a stated value of $100,000 and retained earnings of $30,000. Potter Company had a $50,000 deficit balance in Retained Earnings.

Potter Company purchased the Star, Inc., stock from Star's major stockholders primarily to acquire control of signboard leases owned by Star. The leases will expire on December 31, 19X8, and Potter Company executives estimate the leases, which cannot be renewed, were worth at least $25,000 more than their book value when the stock was purchased. Any remaining excess is attributable to goodwill with a 40-year life.

The trial balances for both companies for the year ended December 31, 19X7, follow:

	Potter Company	Star, Inc.
Cash	14,200	19,300
Accounts Receivable	80,000	76,000
Inventories	54,800	85,600
Other Current Assets	15,000	18,200
Investment in Star, Inc.	120,000	—
Notes Receivable	8,000	—
Land	25,000	10,500
Building and Equipment	200,000	40,000
Accumulated Depreciation	(102,000)	(7,000)
Signboard Leases	—	42,000
Accumulated Amortization	—	(33,600)
Accounts Payable	(35,500)	(47,000)
Dividends Payable	—	(9,000)
Other Current Liabilities	(24,500)	(12,000)
Notes Payable	—	(8,000)
Common Stock	(300,000)	(100,000)
Retained Earnings	(15,000)	(59,000)
Sales	(420,000)	(300,000)
Cost of Goods Sold	315,000	240,000
Expenses	65,000	35,000
Dividends Declared	—	9,000
	0	0

Potter Company sells merchandise to Star, Inc., at the same price and terms applicable to other customers. During 19X7, Potter's sales to Star totaled $100,000. Star had $30,000 of merchandise purchased from Potter on hand on December 31, 19X7, which was an increase of $10,000 over the previous year. Star had not paid Potter for $21,000 of the merchandise in inventory, and also owed Potter for a $10,000 cash advance which was in Star's cash account on December 31, 19X7.

On July 1, 19X4, Star purchased a parcel of land from Potter for $10,500 cash. A building on the land was also purchased the same date from Potter for $40,000. Star paid $8,000 cash and gave a mortgage which called for four payments of $8,000 each plus interest at six percent, to be paid annually on the anniversary of the sale. Potter credits the interest earned from Star to Interest Expense. The land originally cost Potter $10,500, and Potter's book value of the building was $30,000 at the date of the sale. Star estimated the building had a 20-year life and no salvage value when purchased and has computed depreciation on a monthly basis.

Star declared a 9% cash dividend on December 20, 19X7, payable on January 16, 19X8, to stockholders of record on December 31, 19X7. Potter carries its investment at cost and had not recorded this dividend on December 31, 19X7. Neither company paid a dividend during 19X6.

Required:

Prepare a work sheet for the preparation of consolidated financial statements for the Potter Company and its subsidiary, Star, Inc. as of December 31, 19X7. The work sheet should show adjustments and eliminations, consolidated income statement, and consolidated balance sheet, and should include other accounts affected by the adjustments and eliminations. Assume that both companies made all the adjusting entries required for separate financial statements, unless an obvious discrepancy exists. Income taxes should not be considered in the solution.

(AICPA adapted)

Problem 8-12. On January 1, 19X7, Boras Corporation purchased 80% of the outstanding stock of Elias Company for $450,000. At that time, the stockholders' equity of Elias reflected the following:

Common stock, $10 par	$300,000
Retained earnings	200,000
Total stockholders' equity	$500,000

It was agreed by the two firms that Elias' equipment was undervalued by $100,000. The equipment has a 5-year remaining life and is being depreciated by the straight-line method.

During 19X7, the following intercompany transactions occurred:
(a) On November 1, Elias discounted a $20,000, 6%, 6-month trade note receivable with Boras Corporation. The note had four months left until maturity, and Boras discounted the note at 9%.
(b) Boras' sales included $20,000 of merchandise sold to Elias. The sales price provides a 25% gross profit for Boras. Elias had none of this merchandise in its ending inventory, but still owed Boras $5,000 on account.

At December 31, 19X7, Boras and Elias had the trial balances shown at the top of page 359.

Required:

(1) Prepare a work sheet necessary to produce consolidated statements for the year ended December 31, 19X7. Key and explain all eliminations.
(2) Prepare a consolidated income statement and balance sheet for 19X7.

	Boras Corporation	Elias Company
Cash	109,109	68,591
Notes Receivable	30,000	35,000
Interest Receivable	400	—
Notes Receivable Discounted	—	(20,000)
Accounts Receivable	45,600	71,200
Inventory	130,300	83,100
Investment in Elias Company	489,753	—
Land	350,000	150,000
Building	210,000	170,000
Equipment	175,000	100,000
Accumulated Depreciation	(125,000)	(33,200)
Accounts Payable	(120,000)	(75,000)
Unearned Interest Income	(109)	—
Common Stock ($10 par)	(800,000)	(300,000)
Retained Earnings, January 1, 19X7	(315,200)	(200,000)
Sales	(1,200,000)	(350,000)
Interest Income	(309)	—
Interest Expense	—	18
Cost of Goods Sold	900,000	245,000
Other Expenses	160,209	55,291
Subsidiary Income	(39,753)	—
	0	0

Problem 8-13. Pelican, Inc., purchased an 80% interest in the Stork Company on January 1, 19X1, at which time the following determination and distribution of excess schedule was prepared:

Price paid		$600,000
Interest acquired:		
Common stock, $10 par	$100,000	
Paid-in capital in excess of par	250,000	
Retained earnings	300,000	
Total equity	$650,000	
Interest acquired	80%	520,000
Excess of cost over book value		$ 80,000
Less excess attributable to building (10-year remaining life)		60,000
Goodwill (40-year life)		$ 20,000

The building is depreciated and the goodwill is amortized on a straight-line basis.

The two firms prepared trial balances on December 31, 19X3, which are shown on page 360.

The following additional information is applicable:

(a) Pelican prepares separate "parent only" statements as a supplement to its consolidated statements. To facilitate their preparation, the investment account is maintained under the APB Opinion No. 18 equity method.

(b) Stork sells goods to Pelican at a price to yield a 25% gross profit. There were $50,000 of such sales during 19X3. Pelican had $10,000 of Stork goods in its beginning inventory and $16,000 of Stork goods in its ending inventory.

	Pelican	Stork
Current Assets	480,000	215,000
Property, Plant, and Equipment	1,200,000	900,000
Accumulated Depreciation	(400,000)	(200,000)
Investment in Stork Co.	693,300	
Liabilities	(200,000)	(120,000)
Common Stock ($20 par)—Pelican	(300,000)	
Paid-In Capital in Excess of Par—Pelican	(700,000)	
Retained Earnings—Pelican	(625,000)	
Common Stock ($10)—Stork		(100,000)
Paid-In Capital in Excess of Par—Stork		(250,000)
Retained Earnings—Stork		(380,000)
Sales	(1,000,000)	(600,000)
Cost of Goods Sold	750,000	450,000
Expenses	150,000	80,000
Investment Income	(48,300)	
Dividends Declared		5,000
	0	0

Required:

Prepare a consolidated work sheet for a consolidated income statement and balance sheet for December 31, 19X3.

CHAPTER 9
INTERCOMPANY TRANSACTIONS: BONDS AND LEASES

This chapter continues the analysis of common types of intercompany transactions. The debtor-creditor relationship that is created when one affiliate buys the outstanding bonds of another member of the consolidated firm is analyzed first. Though the purchase of such bonds is recorded as an investment by the purchasing affiliate, the bonds are viewed as retired when consolidated statements are prepared. Following the discussion of intercompany bonds, long-term leasing transactions between affiliates are analyzed. Intercompany leases are essentially a type of hybrid loan. One affiliate, the lessor, provides the funds needed to acquire an asset which is used by and eventually paid for by another affiliate, the lessee.

INTERCOMPANY INVESTMENT IN BONDS

To secure long-term funds, one member of a consolidated group may sell its bonds directly to another member of the group. Clearly, such a transaction results in intercompany debt which must be eliminated from consolidated statements. On the work sheet, the investment in bonds recorded by one firm must be eliminated against the bonds payable of the other. The interest income, expense, and accruals recorded on the books of the separate firms must also be eliminated.

A more complicated situation arises when one affiliate has bonds outstanding in the hands of outside parties that are not members of the affiliated group, and a decision is made to purchase and retire the bonds. The most common way to accomplish the removal of subsidiary bonds from the hands of outsiders is for the parent to advance funds to the subsidiary so that the subsidiary may retire the bonds. From an accounting standpoint, this transaction is easy to record. The former debt is retired and a new, long-term intercompany debt originates. The only procedures required on future consolidated work sheets involve the elimination of the resulting intercompany debt.

A less common method is to have the parent purchase the bonds from the outside parties and to hold them as an investment. This method creates an intercompany investment in bonds which must be eliminated on future consolidated work sheets. While the bonds appear as a liability on one set of books and as an investment on the other set, from a consolidated viewpoint the bonds have been retired, and the debt to outside parties has been liquidated. As a result:

1. Consolidated statements will show a gain or loss on the retirement of the bonds in the period of their purchase by the affiliated firm. A gain or loss will result whenever the price paid by the purchasing firm does not agree with the book value of the bonds on the issuer's records.
2. Consolidated statements must not include the intercompany investment, the bond liability, or interest applicable to the intercompany bonds.

Bonds Originally Issued at Face Value

The complexity of the elimination procedures for intercompany bond investments depends on whether a discount or premium exists as the result of the original issuance to the outside parties. When the bonds were originally sold by a subsidiary to outside parties at face value, contract (nominal) interest agrees with the effective or market interest, and there are no amortizations of issuance premiums or discounts to be recorded. However, the market rate of interest will subsequently deviate from the contract rate. Thus, while there is no original issuance premium or discount, almost certainly there will be what could be termed an "investment premium or discount" resulting from the intercompany purchase of the bonds.

To illustrate the procedures required for the intercompany bonds originally issued at face value, assume that a subsidiary, Company S, issued 8%, 5-year bonds at face value of $100,000 to outside parties on January 1, 19X1. Interest is paid on January 1 for the preceding year. On January 2, 19X4, the parent, Company P, purchased the bonds from the outside parties for $103,600.

The subsidiary, Company S, will continue to list $100,000 bonded debt and to record interest expense of $8,000 during 19X4 and 19X5.

The parent, Company P, however, will record an investment of $103,600 and will amortize $1,800 per year by reducing the investment account and adjusting interest revenue. Though the interest method of amortization is preferable, the straight-line method is permitted if results are not materially different. The initial examples of this chapter will use the straight-line method to simplify analysis. A summary example will be used to demonstrate the interest method of amortization.

Although the investment and liability accounts continue to exist on the books of the separate firms, retirement has occurred from a consolidated viewpoint. Debt with a book value of $100,000 was retired by a payment of $103,600, and there is a $3,600 retirement loss. If a consolidated work sheet is prepared on the day the bonds are purchased, Bonds Payable would be eliminated against Investment in Bonds, and a loss on retirement would be reported on the consolidated income statement. The abbreviated work sheet which follows displays the procedures used to retire the bonds as a part of the elimination process:

| | Trial Balance | | Eliminations | |
	Company P	Company S	Dr.	Cr.
Investment in Company S Bonds	103,600			**103,600**
Bonds Payable		(100,000)	**100,000**	
Loss on Bond Retirement .			**3,600**	

This partial work sheet is only hypothetical, since, in reality, there will be no consolidated work sheet prepared until December 31, 19X4, the end of the period. During 19X4, Companies P and S will record transactions for interest as follows:

Company P			Company S		
Interest Receivable	8,000		Interest Expense....................	8,000	
Investment in Company S Bonds ..		1,800	Interest Payable		8,000
Interest Income		6,200	To record interest expense.		
To record interest revenue net of $1,800 per year premium amortization.					

On the December 31, 19X4 consolidated work sheet, these entries will be reflected in the trial balance as shown in Illustration I on pages 364 and 365. Note that Investment in Company S Bonds reflects the premium amortization, since the balance is $101,800 ($103,600 original cost less $1,800 amortization). Illustration I assumes that Investment in Company S Stock reflects a 90% interest purchased at a price equal to the book value of the underlying equity. The simple equity method is used to record the investment in stock.

As a result of the elimination entries, the consolidated income statement will include the retirement loss but will exclude intercompany interest payments. The consolidated balance sheet will not list the intercompany bonds payable or investment in bonds.

(Credit balance amounts
are in parentheses)

	Trial Balance	
	Company P	Company S
Other Assets	56,400	220,000
Interest Receivable	8,000	
Investment in Company S Stock (90%)	100,800	
Investment in Company S Bonds (100%)	101,800	
Interest Payable		(8,000)
Bonds Payable, 8%		(100,000)
Common Stock ($10 par), Co. P	(100,000)	
Retained Earnings, Jan. 1, 19X4, Co. P	(120,000)	
Common Stock ($10 par), Co. S		(80,000)
Retained Earnings, Jan. 1, 19X4, Co. S		(20,000)
Operating Revenue	(100,000)	(80,000)
Operating Expense	70,000	60,000
Interest Income	(6,200)	
Interest Expense		8,000
Subsidiary Income	(10,800)	
Loss on Bond Retirement		
	0	0
Consolidated Net Income		
To Minority Interest (see distribution schedule)		
To Controlling Interest (see distribution schedule)		
Total Minority Interest, Dec. 31, 19X4		
Retained Earnings, Controlling Interest, Dec. 31, 19X4		

Eliminations:
(1) Eliminate the entry recording parent's share of subsidiary net income for the current year.
(2) Eliminate 90% of the subsidiary equity balances of January 1, 19X4, against the investment in Company S stock account. No excess results.
3 Restore the current year's amortization of the premium on the investment in Company S bonds. This procedure returns the investment in Company S bonds account to its balance on the date the bonds were purchased, so that the original gain or loss may be isolated. This step also converts interest revenue adjusted for amortization to contract interest revenue so that it may be easily eliminated against the interest expense recorded by Company S, as shown in Step 5.

Income Distribution Schedules

Subsidiary Company S income distribution

Retirement loss on bonds **4** $3,600	Internally generated net income, including interest expense	$12,000
	Interest adjustment ($8,000 − $6,200) **3**	1,800
	Adjusted income	$10,200
	Minority share	10%
	Minority interest	$ 1,020

Year of Acquisition; Straight-Line Method of Amortization
Subsidiary Company S
Financial Statements
December 31, 19X4

Eliminations Dr.	Eliminations Cr.	Consolidated Income Statement	Minority Interest	Controlling Retained Earnings	Consolidated Balance Sheet
					276,400
	(6) 8,000				
	(1) 10,800				
	(2) 90,000				
3 1,800	4 103,600				
(6) 8,000					
4 100,000					
					(100,000)
				(120,000)	
(2) 72,000			(8,000)		
(2) 18,000			(2,000)		
		(180,000)			
		130,000			
(5) 8,000	3 1,800				
	(5) 8,000				
(1) 10,800					
4 3,600		3,600			
222,200	222,200				
		(46,400)			
		1,020	(1,020)		
		45,380		(45,380)	
			(11,020)		(11,020)
				(165,380)	(165,380)
					0

4 Retire the bonds by eliminating the original Investment In Bonds (as adjusted by Step 3) against the bond liability. Any difference between the amounts is the retirement gain or loss, which is extended to the consolidated income statement.
(5) Eliminate intercompany interest expense and revenue.
(6) Eliminate intercompany interest payable and receivable.

Parent Company P income distribution

Internally generated net income, including interest revenue	$36,200
Share of subsidiary adjusted income (90% × $10,200)	9,180
Controlling interest	$45,380

The only remaining problem is the distribution of consolidated income to the controlling and minority interests. The income distribution schedule shows Company S absorbing all the retirement loss. Consolidation theory views the purchasing affiliate as a mere agent of the issuing affiliate. Therefore, it is not the purchaser but the issuer that must bear the entire gain or loss on retirement. Even though the debt is retired from a consolidated viewpoint, it does still exist internally. Company P has a right to collect the interest as a part of its share of Company S's operations. Based on the value of the debt on January 2, 19X4, the interest expense/revenue is $6,200. The interest cost of $8,000 recorded by Company S must now be corrected to reflect the revised internal interest expense of $6,200. The income distribution schedule increases the operating income of Company S to reflect the adjustment ($1,800) to interest expense. It should be noted that the retirement loss borne by Company S will entirely offset the adjustments to interest expense by the time the bonds mature. If the parent, Company P, had issued the bonds and if the subsidiary, Company S, had purchased them, the only change would be that the income distribution schedule for Company P would absorb the loss on retirement and the interest adjustment.

The work sheet procedures that would be needed at the end of 19X5 are shown in Illustration II on pages 368 and 369. The interest revenue and expense have been recorded on the books of the separate firms. The investment in Company S bonds on the parent's books reflects its maturity value at the end of 19X5.

As a result of the procedures discussed on pages 362 and 363, the consolidated income statement will not include intercompany interest. The income distribution schedules for Illustration II reflect the fact that the debt still existed internally during the period. However, the interest expense recorded by Company S is reduced to reflect the interest cost based on the January 2, 19X4 purchase price.

In Illustration II, if Company S were the purchaser and Company P the issuer of the bonds, the work sheet would differ as follows:

1. The January 1, 19X5 retained earnings adjustment would be completely absorbed by controlling Retained Earnings, since the parent company would be the issuer absorbing the loss.
2. The income distribution schedule of Company P, the parent, would contain the interest adjustment.

Bonds Not Originally Issued at Face Value

The principles of eliminating intercompany investments in bonds are not altered by the existence of a premium or discount stemming from original issuance. The numerical calculations just become more complex. To illustrate, assume that Subsidiary S issued $100,000 of 5-year, 8% bonds on January 1, 19X1. The market interest rate approximated 9% and, as a result, the bonds sold at a discount of $3,900. Interest is paid each December 31. On each interest payment date, the discount is amortized $780 ($3,900 ÷ 5 years) by decreasing the discount and by increasing interest expense. On December 31, 19X3, the balance of the discount is $1,560 [$3,900 − (3 × $780 annual amortization)].

The parent, Company P, purchased the bonds on December 31, 19X3, after interest had been paid, for $103,600. The parent will amortize $1,800 of the investment each subsequent December 31, reducing the parent's interest income to $6,200 ($8,000 cash − $1,800 amortization) for 19X4 and 19X5.

The abbreviated December 31, 19X3 (date of purchase) work sheet which follows lists the investment in Company S bonds, the bonds payable, and the remaining issuance discount. Eliminating the price paid by Company P, $103,600, against the book value of $98,440 ($100,000 − $1,560) creates a retirement loss of $5,160 which is carried to consolidated net income.

	Trial Balance		Eliminations	
	Company P	Company S	Dr.	Cr.
Investment in Company S Bonds	103,600			103,600
8% Bonds Payable.............		(100,000)	100,000	
Discount on Bonds Payable		1,560		1,560
Loss on Bond Retirement			5,160	
Interest Expense..............		8,780*		

*$8,000 cash + $780 straight-line amortization.

Interest expense on the books of Company S is extended to the consolidated income statement, since this interest was incurred as a result of transactions with outside parties. There would be no interest adjustment for 19X3, since the bonds were not purchased by the parent until December 31, 19X3. The income distribution schedules accompanying the work sheet would assess the loss against the issuer, Company S.

The implications of these intercompany bonds on the 19X4 consolidated work sheet are reflected in Illustration III on pages 370 and 371. Assume that Company P acquired a 90% interest in the common stock of Company S at a price equal to the book value of the underlying equity. The simple equity method is used to record the investment in the stock of Company P. The trial balances include the following items:

The Investment in Company S Bonds at its amortized December 31, 19X4 balance of $101,800 ($103,600 − $1,800 amortization).

Interest revenue (adjusted for amortization) of $6,200 on the books of Company P.

The discount on bonds account at its amortized December 31, 19X4 balance of $780.

Interest expense (adjusted for discount amortization) of $8,780 ($8,000 cash + $780 amortization) on the books of Company S.

Illustration II—Intercompany Investment in Bonds
Company P and
Work Sheet for Consolidated
For Year Ended

(Credit balance amounts
are in parentheses)

	Trial Balance	
	Company P	**Company S**
Other Assets	94,400	242,000
Interest Receivable	8,000	
Investment in Company S Stock (90%)	120,600	
Investment in Company S Bonds (100%)	100,000	
Interest Payable		(8,000)
Bonds Payable, 8%		(100,000)
Common Stock ($10 par), Co. P	(100,000)	
Retained Earnings, Jan. 1, 19X5, Co. P	(167,000)	
Common Stock ($10 par), Co. S		(80,000)
Retained Earnings, Jan. 1, 19X5, Co. S		(32,000)
Operating Revenue	(130,000)	(100,000)
Operating Expense	100,000	70,000
Subsidiary Income	(19,800)	
Interest Expense		8,000
Interest Income	(6,200)	
	0	0
Consolidated Net Income		
To Minority Interest (see distribution schedule)		
To Controlling Interest (see distribution schedule)		
Total Minority Interest, Dec. 31, 19X5		
Retained Earnings, Controlling Interest, Dec. 31, 19X5		

Eliminations:
(1) Eliminate the entry recording parent's share of subsidiary net income for the current year.
(2) Eliminate the pro rata share of subsidiary equity balances against the investment in stock account. There is no excess to be distributed.
3 Restore the current year's amortization of the premium on the investment in Company S bonds. This procedure restores the Investment in Company S Bonds to its January 1, 19X5 balance, so that the remaining unamortized premium may be isolated. In this case, $1,800 of the original premium remains on January 1, 19X5, since $1,800 of the premium was amortized on the separate books of Company P during 19X4. The concern here is with the premium not recognized to date in the retained earnings balances of the separate firms.

Income Distribution Schedules

Subsidiary Company S income distribution

Internally generated net income, including interest expense	$22,000
Interest adjustment ($8,000 − $6,200) **3**	1,800
Adjusted income	$23,800
Minority share	10%
Minority interest	$ 2,380

Year Subsequent to Acquisition; Straight-Line Method of Amortization
Subsidiary Company S
Financial Statements
December 31, 19X5

Eliminations Dr.	Eliminations Cr.	Consolidated Income Statement	Minority Interest	Controlling Retained Earnings	Consolidated Balance Sheet
					336,400
	(6) 8,000				
	(1) 19,800				
	(2) 100,800				
3 1,800	4 101,800				
(6) 8,000					
4 100,000					
					(100,000)
4 1,620				(165,380)	
(2) 72,000			(8,000)		
(2) 28,800			(3,020)		
4 180					
		(230,000)			
		170,000			
(1) 19,800					
	(5) 8,000				
(5) 8,000	3 1,800				
240,200	240,200				
		(60,000)			
		2,380	(2,380)		
		57,620		(57,620)	
			(13,400)		(13,400)
				(223,000)	(223,000)
					0

4 Retire the bonds as of January 1, 19X5. The investment in Company S bonds is eliminated against Bonds Payable. The unrecorded loss remaining on January 1 is isolated and carried to Retained Earnings, since it involves a transaction of a previous year. (The balance of the $1,800 loss is already in January 1 Retained Earnings, since the subsidiary's interest expense is overstated in 19X4 by $1,800 on its separate statements.) It should be noted that only by returning Investment in Bonds to its January 1 balance can the remaining loss needed to correct January 1 Retained Earnings be isolated. Since the retirement loss is to be borne by the issuer, the minority interest's share of Retained Earnings absorbs 10% of the adjustment.

(5) Eliminate intercompany interest expense and revenue.

(6) Eliminate intercompany interest payable and receivable.

Parent Company P income distribution

Internally generated net income, including interest revenue	$36,200
Share of subsidiary adjusted income (90% × $23,800)	21,420
Controlling interest	$57,620

(Credit balance amounts
are in parentheses)

	Trial Balance	
	Company P	Company S
Investment in Company S Stock	143,876	
Investment in Company S Bonds	101,800	
Other Assets	59,400	259,082
Common Stock, Co. P	(100,000)	
Retained Earnings, Jan. 1, 19X4, Co. P	(160,000)	
Common Stock, Co. S		(40,000)
Retained Earnings, Jan. 1, 19X4 Co. S		(110,000)
Bonds Payable		(100,000)
Discount on Bonds		780
Sales	(80,000)	(50,000)
Interest Income	(6,200)	
Cost of Goods Sold	50,000	31,358
Interest Expense		8,780
Subsidiary Income	(8,876)	
	0	0
Consolidated Net Income		
To Minority Interest (see distribution schedule)		
To Controlling Interest (see distribution schedule)		
Total Minority Interest, Dec. 31, 19X5		
Retained Earnings, Controlling Interest, Dec. 31, 19X5		

Eliminations:
(1) Eliminate the entry recording parent's share of subsidiary net income for the current year.
(2) Eliminate 90% of the January 1, 19X4 subsidiary equity balances against the January 1, 19X4 investment in Company S stock balance. No excess results.
3 Restore the current year's premium amortization to Investment in Company S Bonds. This procedure restores the investment account to its January 1, 19X4 balance.
4 Restore the current year's amortization of the bond issuance discount, and thus the net book value of the bonds, to the January 1, 19X4 balance.

Income Distribution Schedules

Subsidiary Company S income distribution

Internally generated net income, including interest expense	$ 9,862
Interest adjustment ($8,780 − $6,200) **3, 4**	2,580
Adjusted income	$12,442
Minority share	10%
Minority interest	$ 1,244

Subsequent Periods; Straight-Line Method of Amortization
Subsidiary Company S
Financial Statements
December 31, 19X4

Eliminations Dr.	Eliminations Cr.	Consolidated Income Statement	Minority Interest	Controlling Retained Earnings	Consolidated Balance Sheet
	(1) 8,876				
	(2) 135,000				
③ 1,800	⑤ 103,600				
					318,482
					(100,000)
⑤ 4,644				(155,356)	
(2) 36,000			(4,000)		
(2) 99,000			(10,484)		
⑤ 516					
⑤ 100,000					
④ 780	⑤ 1,560				
		(130,000)			
(6) 8,000	③ 1,800				
		81,358			
	④ 780				
	(6) 8,000				
(1) 8,876					
259,616	259,616				
		(48,642)			
		1,244	(1,244)		
		47,398		(47,398)	
			(15,728)		(15,728)
				(202,754)	(202,754)
					0

⑤ The balance of the investment in bonds account is closed against Bonds Payable and Discount on Bonds Payable as of January 1, 19X4. The remaining retirement loss (same as the original loss since "retirement" occurred December 31, 19X3) of $5,160 is deducted from January 1, 19X4 Retained Earnings. Since the subsidiary was the issuer of the bonds, the minority interest absorbs 10% of the loss.

(6) Eliminate remaining intercompany interest expense and interest revenue.

Parent Company P income distribution

Internally generated net income, including interest revenue	$36,200
Share of Company S adjusted income (90% × $12,442)	11,198
Controlling interest	$47,398

Again, the consolidated income statement does not include inter-company interest. However, the income distribution schedule does reflect the adjustment of Company S's interest expense. The original $8,780 interest expense has been replaced by a $6,200 expense, based on the purchase price paid by Company P. The smaller interest expense compensates the subsidiary for the retirement loss absorbed in a previous period.

Interest Method of Amortization

The procedures used to eliminate intercompany bonds are not altered by the interest method of amortization; only the dollar values change. To illustrate the calculations, Subsidiary S in the preceding example issued $100,000 of 5-year, 8% bonds on January 1, 19X1. The market interest rate on that date was 9%, so that the bonds sold at a discount of $3,890. Interest on the bonds is paid each December 31. The discount amortization for the term of the bonds follows:

Year	Balance January 1	Effective Interest	Nominal Interest	Discount Amortization
1	$96,110	$8,650 (.09 × $96,110)	$8,000	$ 650
2	96,760 ($96,110 + $650)	8,708 (.09 × $96,760)	8,000	708
3	97,468 ($96,760 + $708)	8,772 (.09 × $97,468)	8,000	772
4	98,240 ($97,468 + $772)	8,842 (.09 × $98,240)	8,000	842
5	99,082 ($98,240 + $842)	8,918* (.09 × $99,082)	8,000	918
	*Includes $1 rounding error.			$3,890

The bonds were purchased by parent Company P on December 31, 19X3, after interest had been paid, at a price to yield 6%. Based on present value computations, $103,667 was paid for the bonds. The premium on the bonds would be amortized as follows by Company P:

Year	Investment Balance, January 1	Effective Interest	Nominal Interest	Premium Amortization
4	$103,667	$6,220 (.06 × $103,667)	$8,000	$1,780
5	101,887 ($103,667 − $1,780)	6,113 (.06 × $101,887)	8,000	1,887
				$3,667

The abbreviated December 31, 19X3 (date of purchase) work sheet which follows lists the investment in Company S bonds, the bonds payable, and the remaining issuance discount. Eliminating the price paid by Company P, $103,667, against the book value of $98,240 ($100,000 − $1,760) creates a retirement loss of $5,427 which is carried to consolidated net income.

	Trial Balance		Eliminations	
	Company P	Company S	Dr.	Cr.
Investment in Company S Bonds	103,667			**103,667**
8% Bonds Payable		(100,000)	**100,000**	
Discount on Bonds Payable		1,760*		**1,760**
Loss on Bond Retirement			**5,427**	
Interest Expense		8,772*		

*See preceding amortization schedule for issuer.

The differences caused by the interest method of amortization are shown in the 19X4 consolidated work sheet in Illustration IV on pages 374 and 375. Note particularly the change in Company S's income distribution schedule. The original 9% interest, totaling $8,842, has been replaced by $6,220 of interest calculated using the 6% rate.

INTERCOMPANY LEASES

Intercompany leases have become one of the most frequently encountered types of transactions between affiliated firms. It is particularly common for parent firms with substantial financial resources to acquire major assets and to lease the assets to their subsidiaries. This action may occur because the financially stronger parent may be able both to purchase and to finance assets on more favorable terms. The parent company may also desire close control over plant assets and may prefer centralized ownership and management of assets. Leasing becomes a mechanism through which the parent may convey the use of centrally-owned assets to subsidiaries. Some firms achieve centralized asset management by forming separate leasing subsidiaries whose major function is to lease assets to affiliated firms. When such subsidiaries exist, their accounts must automatically be consolidated with those of the parent without regard to the normal criteria for consolidation discussed in Chapter 6.[1]

Operating Leases

Consolidation procedures for intercompany leases depend on the original recording of the lease by the separate firms. When an operating lease exists, the lessor has recorded the purchase of the asset and depreciates the asset. The lessor records rent revenue while the lessee records rent expense. In such cases, it is necessary to eliminate the intercompany rent expense/revenue and any related rent receivable/payable in the consolidation process. The lessor's asset and related accumulated depreciation should also be reclassified as a normal productive asset rather than as property under an operating lease. As an

---

[1] *Statement of Financial Accounting Standards, No. 13,* "Accounting for Leases," (Stamford: Financial Accounting Standards Board, 1976), par. 31.

Illustration IV—Intercompany Bonds
Company P and
Work Sheet for Consolidated
For Year Ended

(Credit balance amounts
are in parentheses)

	Trial Balance	
	Company P	Company S
Investment in Company S Stock	144,000	
Investment in Company S Bonds	101,887	
Other Assets	59,333	259,082
Common Stock, Co. P	(100,000)	
Retained Earnings, Jan. 1, 19X4, Co. P	(160,180)	
Common Stock, Co. S		(40,000)
Retained Earnings, Jan. 1, 19X4, Co. S		(110,200)
Bonds Payable		(100,000)
Discount on Bonds		918
Sales	(80,000)	(50,000)
Interest Income	(6,220)	
Cost of Goods Sold	50,000	31,358
Interest Expense		8,842
Subsidiary Income	(8,820)	
	0	0
Consolidated Net Income		
To Minority Interest (see distribution schedule)		
To Controlling Interest (see distribution schedule)		
Total Minority Interest, Dec. 31, 19X5		
Retained Earnings, Controlling Interest, Dec. 31, 19X5		

Eliminations:
(1) Eliminate the entry recording parent's share of subsidiary net income for the current year.
(2) Eliminate 90% of the January 1, 19X4 subsidiary equity balances against the January 1, 19X4 investment in Company S stock balance. No excess results.
3 Restore the current year's premium amortization to Investment in Company S Bonds. This procedure restores the investment account to its January 1, 19X4 balance.
4 Restore the current year's amortization of the bond issuance discount, and thus the net book value of the bonds, to the January 1, 19X4 balance.

Income Distribution Schedules

Subsidiary Company S income distribution

Internally generated net income, including interest expense	$ 9,800
Interest adjustment ($8,842 − $6,220) **3, 4**	2,622
Adjusted income	$12,422
Minority share	10%
Minority interest	$ 1,242

Interest Method of Amortization
Subsidiary Company S
Financial Statements
December 31, 19X4

Eliminations Dr.	Eliminations Cr.	Consolidated Income Statement	Minority Interest	Controlling Retained Earnings	Consolidated Balance Sheet
	(1)　8,820				
	(2)　135,180				
3　1,780	5　103,667				
					318,415
					(100,000)
5　4,884				(155,296)	
(2)　36,000			(4,000)		
(2)　99,180			(10,477)		
5　543					
5　100,000					
4　842	5　1,760				
		(130,000)			
(6)　8,000	3　1,780				
		81,358			
	4　842				
	(6)　8,000				
(1)　8,820					
260,049	260,049				
		(48,642)			
		1,242	(1,242)		
		47,400		(47,400)	
			(15,719)		(15,719)
				(202,696)	(202,696)
					0

5 The balance of the investment in bonds account is closed against Bonds Payable and Discount on Bonds Payable as of January 1, 19X4. The remaining retirement loss (same as the original loss since "retirement" occurred December 31, 19X3) of $5,427 is deducted from January 1, 19X4 Retained Earnings. Since the subsidiary was the issuer of the bonds, the minority interest absorbs 10% of the loss.

(6) Eliminate remaining intercompany interest expense and interest revenue.

Parent Company P income distribution

Internally generated net income, including interest revenue	$36,220
Share of Company S adjusted income (90% × $12,422)	11,180
Controlling interest	$47,400

example, assume that the parent, Company P, has both productive equipment used in its own operations and equipment which is under operating leases to a subsidiary, Company S. The following partial work sheet may be used to analyze required consolidation procedures:

	Trial Balance		Eliminations	
	Company P	Company S	Dr.	Cr.
Equipment	800,000		**3** 100,000	
Accumulated Depreciation—Equipment	(300,000)			**3** 40,000
Equipment Under Operating Lease	100,000			**3** 100,000
Accumulated Depreciation—Equipment				
Under Operating lease	(40,000)		**3** 40,000	
Rent Receivable	1,200			(2) 1,200
Rent Payable		(1,200)	(2) 1,200	
Rental Income	(14,400)		(1) 14,400	
Rent Expense		14,400		(1) 14,400
Depreciation Expense	50,000			

Eliminations:
  (1) Eliminate intercompany rent expense and revenue of $1,200 per month.
  (2) Eliminate one month's accrued rent.
  3 Reclassify asset under the intercompany operating lease and related accumulated depreciation as a normal productive asset.

No adjustments are made in the income distribution schedules as a result of operating leases. The eliminations made on the work sheet do not change the amount of income or the distribution of income between the minority and controlling interests.

Capitalizable Leases

Consolidation procedures become more complicated when the lease is recorded as a capital lease by the lessee and as a direct-financing or sales-type lease by the lessor. The lessee records an asset and recognizes intercompany long-term debt. Generally the criteria for determining when a lease requires such accounting treatment are the same for affiliated firms as for independent firms. However, when the terms of the lease are significantly affected by the fact that the lessee and lessor are affiliates, the usual criteria for classification of leases do not apply. Lease terms could be considered "significantly affected" when they could not be reasonably expected to occur between independent firms.[2] For example, a parent might lease to a subsidiary at a rent far below the market rate, or a parent might rent a highly specialized machine to a subsidiary on a month-to-month basis. Typically, such specialized machinery would only be leased on a long-term lease promising a full recovery of cost to the lessor, since there would be no use for the machine by other lessees if it were returned to the lessor. The month-to-month lease is only possible because the parent's control of the sub-

---

[2] *Ibid.*, par. 29.

sidiary assures a continued flow of rent payments. When, in the accountant's judgment, the terms of the lease are significantly affected by the parent-subsidiary relationship, the normal criteria are not used and the transaction is recorded so as to reflect its true economic substance.[3] In these circumstances, the lessee is usually viewed as having purchased the asset, using funds borrowed from the lessor.

Consolidation Procedures for Direct-Financing Leases. A direct-financing lease is viewed as a unique type of asset transfer by the lessor, who accepts a long-term receivable from the lessee as consideration for the asset received by the lessee. There is no profit or loss to the lessor on the transfer, but only future investment revenue as payments become due.

Prior to studying consolidated work sheet procedures, the entries made by the affiliated lessee and lessor will be analyzed. In its simplest form, a direct-financing lease is recorded by the lessee as an asset, and debt is recorded to recognize the lease obligation. The lessor records the lease as a receivable from the lessee. If all payments to be received by the lessor will come from or are guaranteed by the original lessee, the present value of the net receivable recorded by the lessor will equal the present value of the payable recorded by the lessee, and the interest rates used to amortize the debt will be equal.

To illustrate, assume that Company S in an 80%-owned subsidiary of Company P. On January 1, 19X1, Company P purchased a machine for $5,851 and leased it to Company S. The terms of the direct-financing lease provide for rental payments of $2,000 per year at the beginning of each period and allow the lessee to exercise an option to purchase the machine for $1,000 at the end of 19X3. The $1,000 purchase option is considered a bargain purchase option which will be exercised. The implicit interest rate, which equates all payments including the bargain purchase option to the lessor's purchase cost, is 16%. The lessee will depreciate the capitalized cost of the machine over 5 years, using the straight-line method. The lessee may use a 5-year life despite the 3-year lease term, because it is assumed that the bargain purchase option will be exercised and that the asset will be used for 5 years.

The amortization of the debt at the implicit 16% interest rate is as follows:

Date	Payment	Interest at 16% on Previous Balance	Reduction of Principal	Principal Balance
Jan. 1, 19X1	$2,000	—	$2,000	$3,851*
Jan. 1, 19X2	2,000	$ 616	1,384	2,467
Jan. 1, 19X3	2,000	395	1,605	862
Dec. 31, 19X3	1,000	138	862	—
Total	$7,000	$1,149	$5,851	

*Purchase price of $5,851 less initial $2,000 payment.

---

[3] *Ibid.*

The journal entries for the separate firms would be as follows for the first two years:

Date	Company S (Lessee)			Company P (Lessor)		
19X1						
Jan. 1	Assets Under Capital Lease	5,851		Minimum Lease Payments Receivable	5,000	
	Obligations Under			Cash	2,000	
	Capital Lease		3,851	Unearned Interest Income		1,149
	Cash		2,000	Accounts Payable (for asset)		5,851
Dec. 31	Interest Expense	616		Unearned Interest Income	616	
	Interest Payable		616	Interest Income		616
	Depreciation Expense (1/5 × $5,851)	1,170				
	Accumulated Depreciation—Assets Under Capital Lease		1,170			
19X2						
Jan. 1	Interest Payable	616		Cash	2,000	
	Obligations Under			Minimum Lease Payments		
	Capital Lease	1,384		Receivable		2,000
	Cash		2,000			
Dec. 31	Interest Expense	395		Unearned Interest Income	395	
	Interest Payable		395	Income Income		395
	Depreciation Expense	1,170				
	Accumulated Depreciation—Assets Under Capital Lease		1,170			

At the end of each period, consolidation procedures would be needed to eliminate the intercompany transactions. In substance, there appears on the separate records of the affiliates an intercompany transfer of a plant asset with resulting intercompany debt. The intercompany debt, related interest expense/revenue, and interest accruals must be eliminated. It is also necessary to reclassify the assets under capital leases as productive assets owned by the consolidated group. The adjusted partial work sheets shown on page 379 illustrate elimination procedures at the end of 19X1 and 19X2.

A review of the work sheet eliminations reveals that consolidated net income is not changed, because equal amounts of interest expense and revenue were eliminated. Therefore, no adjustments are required in the income distribution schedules.

Some capital leases will designate a portion of the annual rent as being applicable to executory costs incurred by the lessor, such as property taxes or maintenance. Such payments for executory costs are not included in the obligation of the lessee or the minimum lease payments receivable recorded by the lessor. Instead, such payments are recorded as rent expense and revenue in each period. In the consolidating process, that portion of rent applicable to executory costs is eliminated like any other charge for intercompany services.

Partial Work Sheet
December 31, 19X1

	Trial Balance		Eliminations	
	Company P	Company S	Dr.	Cr.
Assets Under Capital Lease		5,851		(3) 5,851
Accumulated Depreciation—Assets Under Capital Lease		(1,170)	(3) 1,170	
Property, Plant, and Equipment	200,000	120,000	(3) 5,851	
Accumulated Depreciation—Property, Plant, and Equipment...................	(80,000)	(50,000)		(3) 1,170
Obligations Under Capital Lease		(3,851)	**2** 3,851	
Interest Payable		(616)	**2** 616	
Minimum Lease Payments Receivable	5,000			**2** 5,000
Unearned Interest Income	(533)		**2** 533	
Interest Expense		616		(1) 616
Interest Income	(616)		(1) 616	

Eliminations:
(1) Eliminate intercompany interest expense/revenue of $616.
2 Eliminate intercompany debt recorded by lessee (obligation under capital lease plus accrued interest payable) against the net intercompany receivable of lessor (minimum lease payments receivable less unearned interest income).
(3) Reclassify asset under capital lease and related accumulated depreciation as a productive asset owned by the consolidated firm.

Partial Work Sheet
December 31, 19X2

	Trial Balance		Eliminations	
	Company P	Company S	Dr.	Cr.
Assets Under Capital Lease		5,851		(3) 5,851
Accumulated Depreciation—Assets Under Capital Lease		(2,340)	(3) 2,340	
Property, Plant, and Equipment	200,000	120,000	(3) 5,851	
Accumulated Depreciation—Property, Plant, and Equipment....................	(100,000)	(60,000)		(3) 2,340
Obligations Under Capital Lease		(2,467)	**2** 2,467	
Interest Payable		(395)	**2** 395	
Minimum Lease Payments Receivable	3,000			**2** 3,000
Unearned Interest Income...................	(138)		**2** 138	
Interest Expense		395		(1) 395
Interest Income	(395)		(1) 395	

Eliminations:
(1) Eliminate intercompany interest expense/revenue of $395.
2 Eliminate intercompany debt and net receivable.
(3) Reclassify asset under capital lease and related accumulated depreciation as a productive asset owned by the consolidated firm.

The lessor may have an *unguaranteed residual value* in a lease at the end of a lease term. As a result, some of the expected cash flow from a leased asset may come from parties other than the original lessee. The original lessee is, therefore, contractually bound to provide only part of the total cash flow expected by the lessor. The lessee records the asset and the resulting obligation under the capital lease at the present value of the minimum lease payments to be made by the lessee. The present value is computed using the lessee's incremental borrowing rate, unless the lessor's implicit rate in the lease is known or is reasonably estimable and is lower, in which case the lessor's implicit interest rate is used.[4] In most cases, the lessor's implicit rate should be available or estimable, since the lessee and the lessor are members of the same consolidated firm. Therefore, the lessor's implicit rate will be used for leases between affiliates of the consolidated firm. Leases recorded using any other rate would be corrected prior to consolidating.

The lessor records the gross investment in the lease, which is the sum of the minimum lease payments receivable and the unguaranteed residual value. Unearned interest income is recorded as a contra account at an amount that reduces the gross investment to the market value of the asset at the inception of the lease. Unearned interest is amortized using the implicit rate of the lessor. The implicit rate of the lessor thus equates the present value of all payments expected, including the unguaranteed residual value, to the market value of the asset. The lessee will record the asset and debt at the present value of the minimum lease payments using the lessor's implicit rate, which will also be used to amortize the lessee's debt.

The recording methods used by the lessee and lessor for leases with an unguaranteed residual value present a complication to the consolidation process. The amount of the asset under the capital lease recorded by the lessee will be less than the asset's market value, since the present value of the lease payments recorded by the lessee will not include the asset's unguaranteed residual value. To understand this complication, the previous example may be used, with one change. Instead of a $1,000 bargain purchase option which was included in the set of minimum lease payments, assume that there is a $1,000 unguaranteed residual value. Since the residual value is not guaranteed, it is not part of the minimum lease payments. The revised facts are as follows:

Cost of asset to lessor: $5,851

Lease terms: Three annual payments of $2,000 due at the start of each year. Unguaranteed residual value of $1,000 to lessor at the end of 19X3.

Lessor implicit rate: 16% equates above payments plus the unguaranteed residual value to $5,851.

Lessee interest rate: 16% (lessor implicit rate) which, when applied to only the lease payments, results in a present value of $5,210.

Depreciation: Straight-line over 3-year lease term.

---

[4] When the present value of the minimum lease payments using the incremental borrowing rate exceeds the market value of the asset, the asset and the obligation are recorded at the market value of the asset. The interest rate which equates the present value of the payments to the market value of the asset is then used to amortize the debt.

Amortization tables:

Lessor (16%)

Date	Payment	Interest at 16% on Previous Balance	Reduction of Principal	Principal Balance
Jan. 1, 19X1	$2,000	—	$2,000	$3,851[1]
Jan. 1, 19X2	2,000	$ 616	1,384	2,467
Jan. 1, 19X3	2,000	395	1,605	862
Dec. 31, 19X3	1,000	138	862	—
Total	$7,000	$1,149	$5,851	

[1] Purchase price of $5,851 less initial $2,000 payment.

Lessee (16%)

Date	Payment	Interest at 16% on Previous Balance	Reduction of Principal	Principal Balance
Jan. 1, 19X1	$2,000	—	$2,000	$3,210 [2]
Jan. 1, 19X2	2,000	$ 514	1,486	1,724
Jan. 1, 19X3	2,000	276	1,724	
Total	$6,000	$ 790	$5,210	

[2] Present value of $5,210 less initial $2,000 paymen

The journal entries for the separate firms would be as follows for the first two years:

Date	Company S (Lessee)			Company P (Lessor)		
19X1						
Jan. 1	Assets Under Capital Lease	5,210		Minimum Lease Payments Receivable	4,000	
	Cash		2,000	Unguaranteed Residual Value	1,000	
	Obligations Under Capital Lease		3,210	Cash	2,000	
				Unearned Interest Income		1,149
				Accounts Payable (for asset)		5,851
Dec. 31	Interest Expense (at 16%)	514		Unearned Interest Income	616	
	Interest Payable		514	Interest Income (at 16%)		616
	Depreciation Expense (⅓ × $5,210)	1,737				
	Accumulated Depreciation—Assets Under Capital Lease		1,737			
19X2						
Jan. 1	Obligations Under Capital Lease	1,486		Cash	2,000	
	Interest Payable	514		Minimum Lease Payments Receivable		2,000
	Cash		2,000			
Dec. 31	Interest Expense (at 16%)	276		Unearned Interest Income	395	
	Interest Payable		276	Interest Income (at 16%)		395
	Depreciation Expense	1,737				
	Accumulated Depreciation—Assets Under Capital Lease		1,737			

A comparison of the lessor's and lessee's amortization tables shows the following difference between the lessee's interest expense and the lessor's interest income each period:

Year Ending December 31	16% Lessor Implicit Interest	16% Lessee Interest	Difference
19X1	$ 616	$514	$102
19X2	395	276	119
19X3	138	—	138
Total	$1,149	$790	$359

The difference is the interest on the unguaranteed residual value, which is recorded only by the lessor. This can be demonstrated as follows:

Date	16% Implicit Interest	Difference in Principal Balances
January 1, 19X1		$ 641*
December 31, 19X1	$102	743
December 31, 19X2	119	862
December 31, 19X3	138	1,000
Total	$359	

* $5,851 − $5,210.

In the consolidation process, the intercompany debt and interest applicable to the lease should be eliminated. The present value of the unguaranteed residual value and the asset recorded by the lessee are eliminated. The total of these two amounts is recorded as a productive asset owned by the consolidated firm.

Illustration V on pages 384 and 385 contains the detailed steps for the elimination of the intercompany lease at the end of 19X1. In this illustration, it is assumed that the interest in the 80%-owned subsidiary was purchased at its book value. Steps 1 and 2 eliminate the investment. Step 3 eliminates the $514 of intercompany interest expense/revenue. Note that the $102 of interest applicable to the unguaranteed residual value is not eliminated, since it is not an obligation of the lessee. Step 4 eliminates the intercompany debt balances. The $257 disparity in the recorded debt is combined with the unguaranteed residual value, which is eliminated, and a net asset increase of $743 results. The $743 increase is combined in Step 4 with the asset under the capital lease of $5,210 recorded by the lessee, and an owned asset of $5,953 is recorded on the work sheet.[5] Step 5 reclassifies the recorded amount of accumulated depreciation.

Illustration VI on pages 386 and 387 demonstrates consolidation procedures for the second year of the lease term.

Consolidation Procedures for Sales-Type Leases. Under a sales-type lease, a lessor records a sales profit or loss at the inception of the lease.

---

[5] An acceptable alternative is to reduce the asset to its original cost of $5,851 and to eliminate the $102 of interest income on the unguaranteed residual value. Under this approach, all interest income on the unguaranteed residual value is denied the lessor until the asset is sold, at which time a larger gain equal to the unrecognized interest is recorded.

The sales profit or loss is the difference between the fair market value of the asset at the inception of the lease and the cost of the asset to the lessor. Consolidation procedures do not allow recognition of this gain or loss at the inception of the lease. Instead, the gain or loss is deferred and then amortized over the lessee's period of usage. This period will be the lease term, unless there is a bargain purchase or bargain renewal option, in which case the asset's useful life would be used.

To illustrate, assume that in the previous example the asset leased to Company S had a cost to Company P of $4,951. Company P would have recorded the following entry at the inception of the lease:

Minimum Lease Payments Receivable	4,000	
Unguaranteed Residual Value	1,000	
Cash	2,000	
Unearned Interest Income		1,149
Asset (cost of asset leased)		4,951
Sales Profit on Leases		900

This entry differs from that of the previous example only to the extent of recording the gain and transferring an existing asset. None of the lessor's subsequent entries recording the earning of interest and the payment of the receivable would change. The lessee's entries are also unaffected by the existence of the sales profit.

Consolidation procedures for a sales-type lease do, however, require added steps to those already illustrated. The $900 sales profit is similar to a profit on the sale of a plant asset. The profit in this example must be deferred over the lease term. Thus, the asset and related depreciation accounts must be adjusted to reflect the original sales profit.

The following added adjustments on the work sheet would be needed for the original $900 sales profit in Illustration V:

Sales Profit on Leases	900	
Property, Plant, and Equipment		900
To reduce cost of asset for gain on sales-type lease.		
Accumulated Depreciation—Property, Plant, and Equipment	300	
Depreciation Expense		300
To reduce depreciation expense at the rate of $300 per year.		

The income distribution schedule of the parent-lessor would reflect deferral of the original $900 in the year of the sale and would recognize $300 per year during the asset's life.

Illustration VI would require the following added adjustments on the work sheet if a sales-type lease were involved:

Retained Earnings—Controlling Interest	600	
Accumulated Depreciation—Property, Plant, and Equipment	300	
Property, Plant, and Equipment		900
To adjust the remaining sales profit at the beginning of the period.		
Accumulated Depreciation—Property, Plant, and Equipment	300	
Depreciation Expense		300
To reduce depreciation expense at the rate of $300 per year.		

Illustration V
Company P and
Work Sheet for Consolidated
For Year Ended

(Credit balance amounts
are in parentheses)

	Trial Balance	
	Company P	Company S
Accounts Receivable	30,149	44,793
Minimum Lease Payments Receivable	4,000	
Unguaranteed Residual Value	1,000	
Unearned Interest Income	(533)	
Assets Under Capital Lease		5,210
Accumulated Depreciation—Assets Under Capital Lease		(1,737)
Property, Plant, and Equipment	200,000	120,000
Accumulated Depreciation—Property, Plant, and Equipment	(80,000)	(50,000)
Investment in Company S	87,634	
Accounts Payable	(21,000)	(5,000)
Obligations Under Capital Lease		(3,210)
Interest Payable		(514)
Common Stock ($10 par), Co. P	(50,000)	
Retained Earnings, Jan. 1, 19X1, Co. P	(120,000)	
Common Stock ($5 par), Co. S		(40,000)
Retained Earnings, Jan. 1, 19X1, Co. S		(50,000)
Sales	(120,000)	(70,000)
Interest Income	(616)	
Subsidiary Income	(15,634)	
Operating Expense	65,000	38,207
Interest Expense		514
Depreciation Expense	20,000	11,737
	-0-	-0-
Consolidated Net Income		
To Minority Interest (.2 × $19,542)		
To Controlling Interest [$35,616 + (.8 × $19,542)]		
Total Minority Interest, Dec. 31, 19X1		
Retained Earnings, Controlling Interest, Dec. 31, 19X1		

Eliminations:
(1) Eliminate the parent company's entry recording its share of Company S income. This step returns the investment account to its January 1, 19X1 balance to aid the elimination process.
(2) Eliminate 80% of the January 1, 19X1 Company S equity balances against the investment in Company S.
3 Eliminate intercompany interest expense/revenue as recorded by lessee, $514.
4 Eliminate intercompany debt and the unguaranteed residual value; eliminate the asset under capital lease and record the owned asset. The amounts are reconciled as follows:

Intercompany Capital Lease
Subsidiary Company S
Financial Statements
December 31, 19X1

Eliminations Dr.		Eliminations Cr.		Consolidated Income Statement	Minority Interest	Controlling Retained Earnings	Consolidated Balance Sheet
							74,942
		(4)	4,000				
		(4)	1,000				
(4)	533						
		(4)	5,210				
(5)	1,737						
(4)	5,953						325,953
		(5)	1,737				(131,737)
		(1)	15,634				
		(2)	72,000				
							(26,000)
(4)	3,210						
(4)	514						
							(50,000)
						(120,000)	
(2)	32,000				(8,000)		
(2)	40,000				(10,000)		
				(190,000)			
(3)	514			(102)			
(1)	15,634						
				103,207			
		(3)	514				
				31,737			
100,095		100,095					
				(55,158)			
				3,908	(3,908)		
				51,250		(51,250)	
					(21,908)		(21,908)
						171,250	(171,250)
							0

Disparity in recorded debt:
Lessor balance, $4,000 − $533 unearned income $3,467
Lessee balance, $3,210 + $514 accrued interest .... 3,724 $ (257)
Unguaranteed residual value 1,000
Present value of unguaranteed residual value .... $ 743
Asset under capital lease.. 5,210
Owned asset... $5,953

(5) Reclassify accumulated depreciation.

(Credit balance amounts
are in parentheses)

	Trial Balance	
	Company P	Company S
Accounts Receivable	102,149	82,925
Minimum Lease Payments Receivable	2,000	
Unguaranteed Residual Value	1,000	
Unearned Interest Income	(138)	
Assets Under Capital Lease		5,210
Accumulated Depreciation—Assets Under Capital Lease		(3,474)
Property, Plant, and Equipment	200,000	120,000
Accumulated Depreciation—Property, Plant, and Equipment	(100,000)	(60,000)
Investment in Company S	102,129	
Accounts Payable	(41,000)	(15,000)
Obligations Under Capital Lease		(1,724)
Interest Payable		(276)
Common Stock ($10 par), Co. P	(50,000)	
Retained Earnings, Jan. 1, 19X2, Co. P	(171,250)	
Common Stock ($5 par), Co. S		(40,000)
Retained Earnings, Jan. 1, 19X2, Co. S		(69,542)
Sales	(150,000)	(80,000)
Interest Income	(395)	
Subsidiary Income	(14,495)	
Operating Expense	100,000	49,868
Interest Expense		276
Depreciation Expense	20,000	11,737
	0	0

Consolidated Net Income
To Minority Interest (.2 × $18,119)
To Controlling Interest [$30,395 + (.8 × $18,119)]
Total Minority Interest, Dec. 31, 19X2
Retained Earnings, Controlling Interest, Dec. 31, 19X2

Eliminations:
(1) Eliminate the parent company's entry recording its share of Company S income. This step returns the investment account to its January 1, 19X2 balance to aid the elimination process.
(2) Eliminate 80% of the January 1, 19X2 Company S equity balances against the investment in Company S.
3 Eliminate intercompany interest expense/revenue as recorded by lessee, $276.
4 Eliminate intercompany debt and the unguaranteed residual value; eliminate the asset under the capital lease and record the owned asset. The amounts are reconciled as follows:

Capital Lease, Subsequent Period
Subsidiary Company S
Financial Statements
December 31, 19X2

Eliminations Dr.	Eliminations Cr.	Consolidated Income Statement	Minority Interest	Controlling Retained Earnings	Consolidated Balance Sheet
					185,074
	(4) 2,000				
	(4) 1,000				
(4) 138					
	(4) 5,210				
(5) 3,474					
(4) 6,072					326,072
	(5) 3,474				(163,474)
	(1) 14,495				
	(2) 87,634				
					(56,000)
(4) 1,724					
(4) 276					
					(50,000)
				(171,250)	
(2) 32,000			(8,000)		
(2) 55,634			(13,908)		
		(230,000)			
(3) 276		(119)			
(1) 14,495					
		149,868			
	(3) 276				
		31,737			
114,089	114,089				
		(48,514)			
		3,624	(3,624)		
		44,890	(44,890)		
			(25,532)		(25,532)
				(216,140)	(216,140)
					0

Disparity in recorded debt:

Lessor balance, $2,000 − $138 unearned income	$1,862	
Lessee balance, $1,724 + $276 accrued interest	2,000	$ (138)
Unguaranteed residual value		1,000
Present value of unguaranteed residual value		$ 862
Assets under capital lease		5,210
Owned asset		$6,072

The value of the owned asset is verified as follows:

Asset value, December 31, 19X1	$5,953
Interest on unguaranteed residual value for 19X2	119
Asset value, December 31, 19X2	$6,072

(5) Reclassify accumulated depreciation.

INTERCOMPANY TRANSACTIONS PRIOR TO BUSINESS COMBINATION

It is possible that the firms involved in a business combination may have had dealings with each other prior to the consummation of an acquisition. The ramifications of such dealings on the consolidation process depend on whether the combination is a purchase or a pooling of interests.

When the acquisition is a purchase, there is no need to be concerned with intercompany sales occurring prior to the acquisition. It is assumed that the sales were arm's-length transactions between unrelated parties. Even though assets containing the profit are still on the balance sheet on the acquisition date, no adjustments are needed when consolidating. When one affiliate previously purchased the other affiliate's bonds, a complication does arise. The bonds become an intercompany debt as of the purchase date and thus are viewed as retired on the purchase date when consolidating.

Acquisitions deemed to be a pooling of interests create a need for eliminating intercompany transactions occurring prior to the acquisition date. Recall that poolings are retroactive to the entire current period and to earlier periods. This means that all intercompany transactions during the period in which a pooling occurs are eliminated, no matter when the pooling occurs. In essence, consolidated statements for the period during which a pooling occurs are the same as they would appear if the pooling occurred at the beginning of the year. When comparative statements are prepared, pooling is also retroactive for all such statements. This means that transactions between the firms during those previous periods must also be eliminated. In summary, consolidation procedures are applied as they would be if the firms had been pooled from their inception.

QUESTIONS

1. What are the alternative methods of extinguishing debt in the hands of outsiders, and how is the consolidation process affected by each method? When the parent purchases bonds issued by the subsidiary from an outside party, why is the resulting gain or loss borne entirely by the issuer?

2. What is the effect on consolidated income in the year of acquisition and in following periods of the following parent purchases of 8% subsidiary bonds?
   (a) Issued at 9%, purchased to yield 7%
   (b) Issued at 7%, purchased to yield 9%
   (c) Issued at 9%, purchased to yield 10%
   (d) Issued at 10%, purchased to yield 9%

3. What adjustments to the interest revenue and expense accounts are required on a consolidated work sheet when bonds not originally issued at face value by the subsidiary are purchased by the parent?

4. Assume that a subsidiary company's outstanding bonds are purchased at a gain by the parent company.
   (a) Explain why a gain on bond retirement appears on the consolidated statements, even though the subsidiary has not retired the bonded debt.

(b) The income distribution schedule for the subsidiary company shows internally generated net income and adjusted income. Assuming no other intercompany transactions, compare these two income figures:
   (1) In the year of bond acquisition;
   (2) Each succeeding year until maturity;
   (3) In the aggregate for the periods during which the bonds are outstanding.
   Briefly justify each answer.

5. Company P purchased Company S's $50,000, 5-year, 6% bonds three years after issuance. The bonds were originally issued at face value and later purchased by Company P at a market rate of 5% for $50,928. Using the straight-line method of amortization, compute the income distribution schedule interest adjustments over the remaining term of the bonds and explain their relationship to the original consolidated gain or loss on retirement. On whose income distribution schedule do these items appear?

6. What are the benefits of intercompany leasing among affiliated firms?

7. Why are no adjustments made on the income distribution schedules of the controlling and minority interests as a result of operating and direct-financing leases?

8. Distinguish between a direct-financing lease and a sales-type lease from the standpoint of the lessor.

9. Company X is leasing several plant assets from its parent firm, Company T. Which of the following items should Company X include in minimum lease payments if the lease is classified as an operating lease? As a capital lease?
   (a) Annual rental payments
   (b) Amounts reimbursing the lessor for executory costs such as insurance, maintenance, and taxes
   (c) Guaranteed residual value
   (d) Unguaranteed residual value
   (e) Penalties paid for failure to renew
   (f) Bargain purchase option

10. Designate whether the following accounts are normally recorded on the books of the lessor or the lessee. Which are eliminated or reclassified in the consolidation process?
   (a) Equipment Under Operating Lease
   (b) Rent Expense—Executory Costs
   (c) Accounts Payable (for asset)
   (d) Unguaranteed Residual Value
   (e) Depreciation Expense—Operating Lease
   (f) Depreciation Expense—Capital Lease
   (g) Unearned Interest Income
   (h) Assets Under Capital Lease

11. Parent Company purchased an asset for $30,850 and has agreed to lease the asset to its subsidiary over a 5-year period. The fair market value at the inception of the lease term was $32,000. Record the adjustments pertaining to the sales profit on the lease that would be made on the consolidated work sheet for the first and final years of the lease term.

EXERCISES

Exercise 1. The Estran Corporation is an 80%-owned subsidiary of Biza Fittings Company. Estran has $800,000 of 10% bonds outstanding which were originally

sold at face value and mature on June 30, 19X9. Interest is paid semiannually on June 30 and December 31. On January 1, 19X5, the market rate for similar bonds is 10%. Compare the effects on the consolidated statements under the following alternative possibilities:
(1) Biza loans Estran the funds necessary to retire the bonds on January 1, 19X5, at 10% interest.
(2) Biza purchases the bonds in the market on January 1, 19X5.

Exercise 2. Hertel Distributing Company is an 80%-owned subsidiary of Gifford Global Industries. On October 1, 19W5, Hertel issued $200,000 of 10-year, 9% bonds payable at face value. Interest is paid annually on October 1. On July 1, 19X2, Gifford purchased the bonds for $196,100; the resulting discount is being amortized on a straight-line basis. For the years ending (a) December 31, 19X2, and (b) December 31, 19X3, determine the effects of this transaction:
(1) On consolidated net income.
(2) On the distribution of income to parent and subsidiary.

Exercise 3. Conway Concrete is an 80%-owned subsidiary of Patterson Construction Company. Conway issued $100,000 of 10%, 8-year bonds for $101,440 on March 1, 19X1. Annual interest is paid on March 1. Patterson purchased the bonds on March 2, 19X5, for $100,480. Both firms are using the straight-line method to amortize the premium on these bonds.
(1) Prepare the eliminations that would be made on the December 31, 19X5 consolidated work sheet as a result of this purchase.
(2) Prepare the eliminations that would be made on the December 31, 19X6 consolidated work sheet.

Exercise 4. On January 1, 19X4, Spartan Corporation, an 85%-owned subsidiary of Ithaca Industries, received $47,896 for the $50,000 of 5%, five-year bonds it issued when the market rate was 6%. When Ithaca purchased these bonds for $46,133 on January 2, 19X6, the market rate was 8%. Given the following amortization schedules for both firms, calculate the gain or loss on retirement and the interest adjustments to the issuer's income distribution schedules over the remaining term of the bonds.

Spartan (Issuer)

Date	Effective Interest (6%)	Nominal Interest	Discount Amortization	Balance
1/1/X4	—	—	—	$47,896
1/1/X5	$2,874	$2,500	$374	48,270
1/1/X6	2,896	2,500	396	48,666
1/1/X7	2,920	2,500	420	49,086
1/1/X8	2,945	2,500	445	49,531
1/1/X9	2,969*	2,500	469	50,000

*$3 rounding error

Ithaca (purchaser)

Date	Effective Interest (8%)	Nominal Interest	Discount Amortization	Balance
1/1/X6	—	—	—	$46,133
1/1/X7	$3,691	$2,500	$1,191	47,324
1/1/X8	3,786	2,500	1,286	48,610
1/1/X9	3,890*	2,500	1,390	50,000

*$1 rounding error

Exercise 5.   Porter Pork Products is an 80%-owned subsidiary of Vetter Veal Packers, Inc. On January 1, 19W8, Porter sold $100,000 of 10-year, 9% bonds for $94,000. Interest is paid annually on January 1. The discount is amortized using the straight-line method. The market rate for this type of bond was 12% on January 2, 19X0, when Vetter purchased 40% of the Porter bonds for $34,000.
(1) Prepare the eliminations required for this purchase on the December 31, 19X0 consolidated work sheet.
(2) Prepare the eliminations required on the December 31, 19X1 consolidated work sheet.

Exercise 6.   Wavrin Industries, an 85%-owned subsidiary of Cook, Incorporated, issued $150,000 of 12-year, 9% bonds on January 1, 19X5, to yield 8% interest. Interest is paid annually on January 1. The interest method is used to amortize the premium. Cook purchased the bonds for $180,608 on January 2, 19X8, when the market rate of interest was 6%. On the purchase date, the remaining premium on the bonds was $9,367. Wavrin's 19X8 net income was $475,000.
(1) Prepare the eliminations required for this purchase on the December 31, 19X8 consolidated work sheet.
(2) Prepare the 19X8 income distribution schedule for Wavrin Industries.

Exercise 7.   The Wallmark Company is a 90%-owned subsidiary of Kingwill Industries. On January 1, 19X2, Wallmark signed a five-year lease with Kingwill for a small building with a 15-year life and a book value of $105,000. Wallmark's payments under the contract were $1,000 each, payable the first of each month. The separate books of the two firms provide the following information for 19X3:

	Kingwill	Wallmark
Sales...	$600,000	$300,000
Cost of goods sold	360,000	190,000
General expenses	160,000	60,000
Depreciation expense (including leased assets) ...	27,000	9,000

Rental revenue and expense are not included in the above amounts.
Prepare the consolidated income statement for 19X3, including the distribution of income to the controlling and minority interests.

Exercise 8.   On January 1, 19X0, the Adams Company, an 80%-owned subsidiary of Beatrix Electronics, Inc., signed a 4-year direct-financing lease with its parent for the rental of electronic equipment. The terms of the lease require a $6,000 payment on January 1 of each year, and Adams may purchase the equipment under a bargain purchase option for $2,000 on January 1, 19X4. The equipment cost $21,682 and has an estimated life of six years. The lessor's implicit interest rate is 12%. The lessee also uses the 12% rate to record the transaction.
(1) Prepare the eliminations required for this lease on the December 31, 19X0 consolidated work sheet.
(2) Prepare the eliminations for the December 31, 19X1 consolidated work sheet.

Exercise 9.   The Luxor Company leased a production machine to its 80%-owned subsidiary, the Lutze Company. The machine cost $50,098, had a 5-year expected life and no salvage value, and was depreciated on the straight-line basis. The present value of the machine at Luxor's 16% implicit interest rate is $50,098. The lease agreement, dated January 1, 19X1, requires Lutze to pay $18,000 each January 1 for three years. There is an unguaranteed residual value of $5,000.

Lutze also uses the 16% lessor implicit rate to record the lease. Lease payment amortization schedules are as follows:

Luxor (16%)

Date	Payment	Interest at 16% on Previous Balance	Reduction of Principal	Principal Balance
Jan. 1, 19X1	$18,000	—	$18,000	$32,098
Jan. 1, 19X2	18,000	$5,136	12,864	19,234
Jan. 1, 19X3	18,000	3,078	14,922	4,312
Jan. 1, 19X4	5,000	688	4,312	
Total	$59,000	$8,902	$50,098	

Lutze (16%)

Date	Payment	Interest at 16% on Previous Balance	Reduction of Principal	Principal Balance
Jan. 1, 19X1	$18,000	—	$18,000	$28,894
Jan. 1, 19X2	18,000	$4,623	13,377	15,517
Jan. 1, 19X3	18,000	2,483	15,517	—
Total	$54,000	$7,106	$46,894	

(1) Prepare the eliminations required for this lease on the December 31, 19X1 consolidated work sheet.
(2) Prepare eliminations for the December 31, 19X2 consolidated work sheet.

Exercise 10. McGuale Medical Clinic is an 80%-owned subsidiary of Kierek Diagnostic Equipment. On January 1, 19X3, McGuale signed a 3-year lease with Kierek for the rental of diagnostic equipment. Under the terms of the lease, McGuale is to pay $11,500 each January 1, with a bargain renewal option for the following 2 years at $2,500 per year. Each payment includes $1,500 for maintenance to be provided by Kierek. The present value of the minimum payments, net of executory costs, at the 10% lessor implicit rate is $28,789. The equipment cost Kierek $25,000. It is being depreciated on a straight-line basis over its 5-year expected life, with no anticipated salvage value. Prepare the eliminations required for this lease on the December 31, 19X3 consolidated work sheet.

Exercise 11. Fleury Department Stores, Inc., is leasing specialized display fixtures from its 80%-owned subsidiary, Rosen Promotions. Lease payments are $20,000 per year, payable at the beginning of each year. The lessor paid $52,000 for the asset, which has a market value of $57,717. The lessor estimates the fixtures have a residual value (unguaranteed) of $5,500 at the end of the 3-year lease. The lessor's implicit interest rate is 12%. The 12% rate is also used by the lessee to record the lease. Lease amortization schedules are as follows:

Rosen (12%)

Date	Payment	Interest at 12% on Previous Balance	Reduction of Principal	Principal Balance
Jan. 1, 19X5	$20,000	—	$20,000	$37,717
Jan. 1, 19X6	20,000	$4,526	15,474	22,243
Jan. 1, 19X7	20,000	2,669	17,331	4,912
Jan. 1, 19X8	5,500	588	4,912	
Total	$65,500	$7,783	$57,717	

Fleury (12%)

Date	Payment	Interest at 12% on Previous Balance	Reduction of Principal	Principal Balance
Jan. 1, 19X5	$20,000	—	$20,000	$33,802
Jan. 1, 19X6	20,000	$4,056	15,944	17,858
Jan. 1, 19X7	20,000	2,142	17,858	—
Total	$60,000	$6,198	$53,802	

Prepare the eliminations required for this lease on the December 31, 19X5 consolidated work sheet.

PROBLEMS

Problem 9-1. DeWitt Diversified Industries acquired an 80% interest in Janden Corporation on January 1, 19X0, by purchasing 96,000 shares of its $5 par common stock for $970,000. Direct acquisition costs were $5,000. Janden's stockholders' equity accounts at that date showed a balance of $260,000 in Paid-In Capital in Excess of Par and $140,000 in Retained Earnings. At January 1, 19X0, it was determined that Janden's inventory was undervalued by $8,000, land was undervalued by $70,000, and equipment with an 8-year life was undervalued by $80,000. Any goodwill is to be amortized over six years.

On July 1, 19X0, Janden issued $80,000 of 8-year, 11% bonds at face value. Interest payment dates are January 1 and July 1. DeWitt purchased these bonds in the market for $83,087 on July 2, 19X3, when the market rate was 10%. The purchase premium is being amortized on the straight-line basis.

The following trial balances were prepared by the two companies on December 31, 19X3:

	DeWitt Diversified Industries	Janden Corporation
Cash	130,088	80,000
Receivables (net)	190,000	140,000
Inventory	98,000	75,000
Investment in Janden	1,119,000	—
Investment in 11% Bonds	82,778	—
Land	220,000	240,000
Buildings and Equipment	1,350,000	1,060,000
Accumulated Depreciation	(651,000)	(230,000)
Accounts Payable	(210,000)	(105,000)
Bonds Payable, 11%	—	(80,000)
Common Stock ($5 par)	(975,000)	(600,000)
Paid-In Capital in Excess of Par	(724,375)	(260,000)
Retained Earnings	(463,400)	(260,000)
Sales	(1,940,000)	(1,020,000)
Interest Income	(4,091)	—
Subsidiary Income	(76,000)	—
Cost of Goods Sold	1,010,000	610,000
Interest Expense	—	8,800
Other Expenses	769,000	306,200
Dividends Declared	75,000	35,000
Total	0	0

Required:

Prepare a work sheet for the preparation of the consolidated income statement and balance sheet for DeWitt Diversified Industries and its subsidiary at December 31, 19X3.

Problem 9-2. In a transaction properly recorded as a pooling, Hansen Restaurant Supplies issued 28,000 shares of its $5 par common stock on January 1, 19X4, when the market value of the stock was $9, in exchange for 90% of the outstanding stock of KMK Coffee Shops. KMK had the following stockholders' equity on January 1, 19X4:

Common stock, $5 par	$120,000
Paid-in capital in excess of par	90,000
Retained earnings	70,000
Total equity	$280,000

On January 1, 19X3, KMK issued $50,000 of 5-year, 7% bonds for $48,000. Interest is paid annually on January 1. Hansen purchased the bonds for $46,400 on January 2, 19X5, when the market rate was approximately 10%. Both firms are using the straight-line method of discount amortization on these bonds.

The following trial balances were prepared by the separate firms on December 31, 19X5:

	Hansen Restaurant Supplies	KMK Coffee Shops
Cash	9,800	20,200
Accounts Receivable (net)....................	106,000	9,000
Inventory...................................	92,000	25,000
Investment in KMK Coffee Shops.............	310,500	—
Investment in 7% Bonds	47,600	—
Property, Plant, and Equipment	500,000	500,000
Accumulated Depreciation	(115,000)	(128,000)
Accounts Payable...........................	(30,200)	(32,000)
Bonds Payable, 7%	—	(50,000)
Discount on Bonds Payable	—	800
Common Stock ($5 par)	(540,000)	(120,000)
Paid-In Capital in Excess of Par	(89,000)	(90,000)
Retained Earnings	(185,500)	(100,000)
Sales.......................................	(1,150,000)	(429,000)
Interest Income.............................	(4,700)	—
Subsidiary Income	(31,500)	—
Cost of Goods Sold	730,000	164,500
Interest Expense............................	—	3,900
Other Expenses.............................	350,000	225,600
Total	0	0

Required:

Prepare the work sheet for the preparation of consolidated statements for Hansen Restaurant Supplies and its subsidiary, KMK Coffee Shops, for the year ended December 31, 19X5.

Problem 9-3. On January 1, 19X3, Warehouse Outlets had the following balances in its stockholders' equity accounts: common stock—$10 par, $800,000; paid-in capital in excess of par, $625,000; and retained earnings, $450,000. General Appliances purchased 64,000 shares of Warehouse Outlets' common stock for $1,700,000 on that date. Any excess of cost over book value was attributed to goodwill with a 10-year life.

Warehouse Outlets issued $500,000 of 8-year, 11% bonds on December 31, 19X2. The bonds sold for $476,000. General Appliances purchased one half of these bonds in the market on January 1, 19X5, for $259,000. Both firms use the straight-line method of amortization of premiums and discounts.

On July 1, 19X6, General Appliances sold to Warehouse Outlets an old building with a book value of $167,500, remaining life of 10 years, and $30,000 salvage value, for $195,000. The building is being depreciated on a straight-line basis. Warehouse Outlets paid $20,000 cash, and signed a mortgage note with its parent for the balance. Interest, at 11% of the unpaid balance, and principal payments are due annually beginning July 1, 19X7. (For convenience, the mortgage balances are not divided into current and long-term portions.)

The following balances appeared in the separate trial balances of the two firms at December 31, 19X6:

	General Appliances	Warehouse Outlets
Cash	401,986	72,625
Accounts Receivable (net)	752,500	105,000
Interest Receivable	9,625	—
Inventory	1,950,000	900,000
Investment in Warehouse Outlets	1,700,000	—
Investment in 11% Bonds	256,000	—
Investment in Mortgage	175,000	—
Property, Plant, and Equipment	9,000,000	2,950,000
Accumulated Depreciation	(1,695,000)	(940,000)
Accounts Payable	(670,000)	(80,000)
Interest Payable	(18,333)	(9,625)
Bonds Payable, 11%	(2,000,000)	(500,000)
Discount on Bonds Payable	10,470	12,000
Mortgage Payable	—	(175,000)
Common Stock ($5 par)	(3,200,000)	—
Common Stock ($10 par)	—	(800,000)
Paid-In Capital in Excess of Par	(4,550,000)	(625,000)
Retained Earnings	(1,011,123)	(770,000)
Sales	(9,800,000)	(3,000,000)
Gain on Sale of Building	(27,500)	—
Interest Income	(35,625)	—
Dividend Income	(48,000)	—
Cost of Goods Sold	4,940,000	1,700,000
Depreciation Expense	717,000	95,950
Interest Expense	223,000	67,544
Other Expenses	2,600,000	936,506
Dividends Declared	320,000	60,000
	0	0

Required:

Prepare a work sheet for the preparation of consolidated financial statements for General Appliances and its subsidiary, Warehouse Outlets, for the year ended December 31, 19X6.

Problem 9-4. On January 1, 19X2, Lindeman Company purchased 60% of the outstanding stock of Yundem, Inc., for $350,000. Yundem, Inc., had the following stockholders' equity at that time:

Common stock, $.50 par	$ 25,000
Paid-in capital in excess of par	225,000
Retained earnings	300,000
Total equity	$550,000

Yundem's book values approximated market values, except for the patents, which were undervalued by $10,000.

During 19X2, Yundem, Inc., sold merchandise to Lindeman Company at cost plus 40%. These merchandise sales totaled $77,000, of which $25,000 remained unpaid at December 31, 19X1. Lindeman Company had $14,000 worth of this merchandise remaining in its ending inventory.

Lindeman Company purchased $100,000 of Yundem's 7%, 20-year bonds on July 2, 19X2, for $90,668. These bonds were originally issued at face value on January 1, 19X0, and pay interest on January 1 and July 1 of each year. The price paid reflects an 8% annual interest rate. The interest method of amortization is used.

Trial balances of Lindeman Company and its subsidiary, Yundem, Inc., as of December 31, 19X2, are as follows:

	Lindeman Company	Yundem, Inc.
Cash	119,832	69,500
Receivables (net)	80,000	74,000
Inventory	270,000	100,000
Prepaid Expenses	16,000	3,500
Investment in Yundem, Inc.	350,000	—
Investment in 7% Bonds	90,795	—
Land	600,000	193,000
Building and Equipment	1,750,000	850,000
Accumulated Depreciation	(800,000)	(350,000)
Patents and Other Intangibles	60,000	50,000
Accounts Payable	(170,000)	(107,000)
Bonds Payable, 7%	—	(300,000)
Common Stock ($5 stated value)	(500,000)	—
Common Stock ($.50 par)	—	(25,000)
Paid-In Capital in Excess of Par	—	(225,000)
Retained Earnings	(1,830,000)	(300,000)
Sales	(800,000)	(300,000)
Interest Income	(3,627)	—
Dividend Income	(3,000)	—
Cost of Goods Sold	480,000	150,000
Interest Expense	90,000	21,000
Other Expenses	180,000	91,000
Dividends Declared	20,000	5,000
Total	0	0

Required:

(1) Prepare a work sheet for a consolidated balance sheet and a consolidated income statement for Lindeman Company and its subsidiary, Yundem, Inc.,

for the year ending December 31, 19X2. Any intangibles associated with the purchase should be amortized over 10 years.
(2) Prepare consolidated statements, including the income statement, retained earnings statement, and balance sheet.

Problem 9-5. In a transaction meeting the pooling rules, the Hartner Company acquired 90% of the outstanding common stock of the Jordan Company on January 1, 19X0. Jordan's stockholders' equity on January 1, 19X0, consisted of $200,000 in common stock and $120,000 in retained earnings.

Jordan issued $100,000 of 8-year, 10% bonds for $90,066 on January 1, 19W9, when the market rate was 12%. The market rate for this type of bond declined substantially. The discount remaining on January 1, 19X3, was $6,073.

On January 2, 19X2, Hartner purchased 60% of Jordan's bonds for $64,792, to yield 8%. Hartner purchased the remaining bonds for $45,544 on January 2, 19X3, when the market rate was 6%.

Hartner routinely sells merchandise inventory to Jordan at a price to yield a gross profit of 30%. Intercompany merchandise sales in 19X3 were $100,000. Purchases from Hartner accounted for $20,000 of Jordan's beginning inventory and $15,000 of its ending inventory.

Separate trial balances prepared by the two firms at December 31, 19X3, showed the following information:

	Hartner Company	Jordan Company
Cash	25,031	40,000
Accounts Receivable (net)	68,800	58,000
Inventory	70,000	67,000
Investment in Jordan	390,600	—
Investment in 10% Bonds	107,370	—
Property, Plant, and Equipment	700,000	500,000
Accumulated Depreciation	(210,000)	(92,000)
Accounts Payable	(70,000)	(43,802)
Bonds Payable, 10%	—	(100,000)
Discount on Bonds Payable	—	4,802
Common Stock ($10 par)	(300,000)	—
Common Stock ($2 par)	—	(200,000)
Paid-In Capital in Excess of Par	(425,000)	—
Retained Earnings	(265,000)	(202,000)
Sales	(900,000)	(390,000)
Interest Income	(7,851)	—
Cost of Goods Sold	580,000	210,000
Interest Expense	—	11,271
Other Expenses	234,850	136,729
Subsidiary Income	(28,800)	—
Dividends Declared	30,000	—
	0	0

Required:

Prepare a work sheet for the prepration of the consolidated income statement and balance sheet for Hartner Company and its subsidiary, Jordan Company, for the year ended December 31, 19X3.

Problem 9-6. On January 1, 19X4, Kaeppler Corporation purchased 80% of the outstanding stock of Hacker Company for $1,000,000 in cash.

A condensed January 1, 19X4 Hacker Company balance sheet follows:

Assets		Liabilities and Stockholders' Equity	
Current assets...................	$ 450,000	Liabilities, net	$ 760,000
Property, plant, and equipment		Common stock, $8 par	640,000
(net)	1,100,000		
Other assets....................	50,000	Retained earnings	200,000
Total assets	$1,600,000	Total liabilities and equity	$1,600,000

At the purchase date, Hacker Company's inventory and land were understated by $25,000 and $100,000 respectively. Any remaining excess is attributable to goodwill with a 40-year life. The inventory on hand January 1, 19X4, was sold during 19X4.

On January 1, 19X1, Hacker Company issued $500,000 of 8%, 20-year bonds. The bonds, which sold at a price to yield 7%, pay interest on each December 31. The premium on these bonds was $47,233 on January 1, 19X5.

On January 1, 19X5, Kaeppler Corporation purchased $200,000 (face value) of these bonds for $168,705, to yield 10%.

Trial balances of Kaeppler Corporation and Hacker Company as of December 31, 19X5, are as follows:

	Kaeppler Corporation	Hacker Company
Cash	386,024	147,789
Accounts and Notes Receivable (net)	495,000	225,000
Inventory	510,000	235,000
Investment in 8% Bonds	169,576	—
Investment in Hacker Company	1,146,000	—
Land	1,000,000	400,000
Building and Equipment	3,650,000	1,400,000
Accumulated Depreciation	(1,400,000)	(650,000)
Other Assets	—	40,250
Accounts and Notes Payable	(475,000)	(230,000)
Bonds Payable, 7%	(2,000,000)	—
Bonds Payable, 8%	—	(500,000)
Premium on Bonds Payable	—	(45,539)
Common Stock ($5 stated value)	(2,500,000)	—
Common Stock ($8 par)	—	(640,000)
Retained Earnings	(705,000)	(300,000)
Sales...	(2,400,000)	(1,050,000)
Subsidiary Income	(90,000)	—
Other Income..................................	(46,600)	(12,000)
Cost of Goods Sold	1,560,000	693,000
Other Expenses................................	600,000	256,500
Dividends Declared	100,000	30,000
Total	0	0

Interest income and expense related to Hacker Company bonds payable are included in other income and other expense. Amounts included reflect amortization of premiums or discounts, using the interest method of amortization.

Required:

Prepare a work sheet for the preparation of a consolidated balance sheet and income statement for the Kaeppler Corporation and its subsidiary for the year ended December 31, 19X5. Support should be provided for amounts pertaining to interest on the Hacker Company 7% bonds.

Problem 9-7. On January 1, 19X3, Gothic Galleries acquired 80% of the outstanding common stock of Gargoyle Art Supplies for $280,000. Gargoyle's stockholders' equity balances at that date were $250,000 in common stock and $90,000 in retained earnings. An appraisal showed that Gargoyle's inventory was undervalued by $30,000 and its buildings, which have a 20-year life, were overvalued by $20,000. Any remaining excess, attributable to goodwill, is to be amortized over a 5-year period.

Gothic purchased some fixtures from Gargoyle for $20,000 on July 1, 19X3. Book value of the fixtures to Gargoyle was $16,000. They have an estimated life of five years and a salvage value of $2,000. Straight-line depreciation is being used.

Gargoyle sells a variety of merchandise to Gothic at 20% above cost. Intercompany sales in 19X4 amounted to $24,500. Gothic's beginning inventory included $2,640 of merchandise purchased from Gargoyle, and its ending inventory included $2,100.

A $50,000, 10%, 8-year bond issue on January 1, 19X2, provided $55,600 to Gargoyle. The premium is amortized using the straight-line method. Gothic purchased these bonds, net of interest, in the market on December 31, 19X4, when the market rate was 12%.

Trial balances prepared by each firm at December 31, 19X4, showed the following:

	Gothic Galleries	Gargoyle Art Supplies
Cash	24,606	43,000
Accounts Receivable	74,000	56,000
Inventory	130,000	90,000
Investment in Gargoyle	280,000	—
Investment in 10% Bonds	46,394	—
Land	90,000	60,000
Buildings	250,000	190,000
Accumulated Depreciation—Buildings	(80,000)	(28,000)
Fixtures and Equipment	130,000	105,000
Accumulated Depreciation—Fixtures and Equipment	(43,000)	(21,000)
Accounts Payable	(49,000)	(80,500)
Bonds Payable, 10%	(100,000)	(50,000)
Premium on Bonds Payable	—	(3,500)
Common Stock ($5 par)	(450,000)	(250,000)
Retained Earnings	(237,000)	(88,000)
Sales	(950,000)	(400,000)
Dividend Income	(4,000)	—
Cost of Goods Sold	620,000	210,000
Interest Expense	10,000	4,300
Other Expenses	240,000	157,700
Dividends Declared	18,000	5,000
	0	0

Required:

Prepare a work sheet for the preparation of consolidated financial statements for Gothic Galleries and its subsidiary, Gargoyle Art Supplies, for the year ended December 31, 19X4.

Problem 9-8.   On June 30, 19X7, Webster, Inc., purchased 100% of the outstanding common stock of Stanton Corporation for Webster's common stock valued at $4,100,000 and $3,605,000 cash. At the date of purchase, the book and fair values of Stanton's assets and liabilities were as follows:

	Book Value	Fair Value
Cash	$ 160,000	$ 160,000
Accounts receivable (net)	910,000	910,000
Inventory	860,000	1,025,186
Building	9,000,000	7,250,000
Furniture, fixtures, and machinery	3,000,000	2,550,000
Accumulated depreciation	(5,450,000)	—
Intangible assets (net)	150,000	220,000
	$8,630,000	
Accounts payable	$ 580,000	580,000
Notes payable	500,000	500,000
5% Mortgage note payable	4,000,000	3,710,186
Common stock.................................	2,900,000	—
Retained earnings	650,000	—
	$8,630,000	

By the year end, December 31, 19X7, the net balance of Stanton's accounts receivable at June 30, 19X7, had been collected; the inventory on hand at June 30, 19X7, had been charged to cost of goods sold; the accounts payable at June 30, 19X7, had been paid; the $500,000 note had been paid.

As of June 30, 19X7, Stanton's building and furniture, fixtures, and machinery had an estimated remaining life of ten and eight years, respectively. All intangible assets had an estimated remaining life of 20 years. All depreciation and amortization is to be computed using the straight-line method.

As of June 30, 19X7, the 5% mortgage note payable had eight annual payments remaining, with the next payment due June 30, 19X8. The fair value of the note was based on a 7% rate.

Prior to June 30, 19X7, there were no intercompany transactions between Webster and Stanton; however, during the last six months of 19X7, the following intercompany transactions occurred:

(a) Webster sold $400,000 of merchandise to Stanton. The cost of the merchandise to Webster was $360,000. Of this merchandise, $75,000 remained on hand at December 31, 19X7.

(b) On December 29, 19X7, Stanton purchased in the market $300,000 of Webster's 7½% bonds payable for $312,500, including $22,500 interest receivable. Webster had issued $1,000,000 of these 20-year, 7½% bonds payable on January 1, 19X0, for $960,000.

(c) Many of the management functions of the two companies have been consolidated since the merger. Webster charges Stanton a $30,000 per month management fee.

(d) At December 31, 19X7, Stanton owes Webster two months' management fees and $18,000 for merchandise purchased.

Trial balances for Webster and Stanton at December 31, 19X7, are shown on page 401.

Webster's profit and loss figures are for the 12-month period, while Stanton's are for the last six months. Assume that both companies made all the adjusting

	Webster, Inc.	Stanton Corporation
Cash	507,000	200,750
Accounts Receivable (net)	1,890,000	817,125
Inventory	2,031,000	1,009,500
Buildings	17,000,000	9,000,000
Furniture, Fixtures, and Machinery	4,200,000	3,000,000
Accumulated Depreciation	(8,000,000)	(6,050,000)
Intangible Assets (net)	—	146,250
Investment in Subsidiary	7,705,000	—
Investment in Webster's 7½% Bonds (net)	—	290,000
Interest Receivable	—	22,500
Discount on 7½% Bonds........................	24,000	—
Accounts Payable..............................	(1,843,000)	(575,875)
Interest Payable	(200,500)	(100,000)
Mortgage Notes Payable	(6,786,500)	(4,000,000)
7½% Bonds Payable	(1,000,000)	—
8¼% Bonds Payable	(3,900,000)	—
Common Stock	(8,772,500)	(2,900,000)
Retained Earnings	(2,167,500)	(650,000)
Sales...	(26,000,000)	(6,000,000)
Cost of Goods Sold	18,000,000	3,950,000
Selling, General, and Administrative Expenses....	3,130,000	956,000
Management Service Income	(180,000)	—
Management Service Expense	—	180,000
Interest Expense..............................	662,000	100,000
Depreciation Expense	3,701,000	600,000
Amortization Expense	—	3,750
	0	0

entries required for separate financial statements, unless an obvious discrepancy exists.

Required:

Prepare a work sheet necessary for the preparation of a consolidated balance sheet and income statement for Webster, Inc., and its subsidiary Stanton Corporation, for the year ended December 31, 19X7.   (AICPA adapted)

Problem 9-9. On January 1, 19X1, Turner Distributing Company acquired an 80% interest in Wright Warehousing, Inc., for $1,168,000. Wright's Retained Earnings balance at that date was $320,000. Its book values approximated market values, and any excess was attributed to goodwill with a 5-year life.

Turner is leasing a warehouse from Wright which originally cost Wright $825,000. On July 1, 19X1, the date the lease agreement was signed, the warehouse had an estimated remaining life of 20 years, a salvage value of $50,000, and accumulated depreciation of $155,000 under the straight-line method. The terms of the 10-year lease require a $4,300 rental payment on the first of each month, including executory costs of $300 per month.

In conjunction with its warehousing operations, Wright purchases and sells merchandise to distributors. Sales to Turner, at 25% above cost, totaled $240,000 for 19X2. At year end, Turner owed $15,000 on these purchases. Turner's beginning inventory balance included $50,000 in merchandise purchased from Wright, and its ending inventory balance included $45,000.

The following trial balances were prepared by the separate firms on December 31, 19X2:

	Turner Distributing Company	Wright Warehousing, Inc.
Cash	63,000	40,000
Receivables (net)	145,000	85,000
Inventory	180,000	100,000
Investment in Wright	1,272,000	—
Property, Plant, and Equipment	2,580,000	2,000,000
Accumulated Depreciation—Property, Plant, and Equipment	(1,249,000)	(1,550,000)
Assets Under Operating Lease	—	1,975,000
Accumulated Depreciation—Assets Under Operating Lease	—	(990,000)
Accounts Payable	(125,000)	(70,000)
Bonds Payable, 10%	(400,000)	—
Common Stock ($10 par)	(1,000,000)	—
Common Stock ($5 par)	—	(600,000)
Paid-In Capital in Excess of Par	(720,000)	(540,000)
Retained Earnings	(526,000)	(380,000)
Sales	(2,400,000)	(1,000,000)
Rent Income	—	(150,000)
Cost of Goods Sold	1,390,000	600,000
Rent Expense	51,600	—
Interest Expense	40,000	—
Other Expenses	698,400	450,000
Subsidiary Income	(80,000)	—
Dividends Declared	80,000	30,000
	0	0

Required:

Prepare a work sheet for the preparation of consolidated financial statements for Turner Distributing Company and its subsidiary, Wright Warehousing, Inc., for the year ended December 31, 19X2.

Problem 9-10. Plessor Industries acquired 80% of the outstanding common stock of the Slessee Company on January 1, 19X1, for $320,000. On that date, Slessee's book values approximated market values, and the balance of its retained earnings account was $80,000. Any excess was attributed to goodwill with a five-year life. Slessee's net income was $20,000 for 19X1 and $30,000 for 19X2. No dividends were paid in either year.

On January 1, 19X2, Slessee signed a 5-year lease with Plessor for the rental of a small factory building with a 10-year life. Payments of $25,000 are due each January 1, and Slessee is expected to exercise the $5,000 bargain purchase option at the end of the fifth year. The current market value of the factory is $103,770. Plessor's implicit rate on the lease is 12%.

A second lease agreement, for the rental of production equipment with an 8-year life, was signed by Slessee on January 1, 19X3. The terms of this 4-year lease require a payment of $15,000 each January 1. The present value of the lease payments at Plessor's 12% implicit rate is equal to the current market value of the equipment, $52,298. The cost of the equipment to Plessor was $45,000, and there is a $2,000 bargain purchase option. Eight-year, straight-line depreciation is being used, with no salvage value.

The following trial balances were prepared by the separate firms at December 31, 19X3:

	Plessor Industries	Slessee Company
Cash	60,000	40,745
Accounts Receivable	97,778	76,000
Inventory	140,000	120,000
Minimum Lease Payments Receivable	127,000	—
Unearned Interest Income	(14,417)	—
Investment in Slessee	320,000	—
Assets Under Capital Lease	—	156,068
Accumulated Depreciation—Assets Under Capital Lease ...	—	(27,291)
Property, Plant, and Equipment	1,900,000	310,000
Accumulated Depreciation—Property, Plant, and Equipment	(1,077,000)	(72,000)
Accounts Payable	(148,000)	(45,065)
Obligations Under Capital Lease	—	(100,520)
Common Stock ($10 par)	(700,000)	(300,000)
Paid-In Capital in Excess of Par	(325,000)	—
Retained Earnings	(295,000)	(130,000)
Sales...	(1,400,000)	(600,000)
Sales Profit on Leases	(7,298)	—
Interest Income.......................................	(12,063)	—
Cost of Goods Sold	780,000	380,000
Interest Expense......................................	—	12,063
Other Expenses.......................................	510,000	165,000
Dividend Income......................................	(12,000)	—
Dividends Declared	56,000	15,000
	0	0

Required:

Prepare a work sheet for the preparation of the consolidated income statement and balance sheet for Plessor Industries and its subsidiary, the Slessee Company, for the year ended December 31, 19X3.

Problem 9-11. Slawton Truck Company has been an 80%-owned subsidiary of Passaic Heavy Equipment since January 1, 19X3, when Passaic purchased 128,000 shares of Slawton common stock for $832,000, an amount equal to the book value of Slawton's net assets at that date. Slawton's net income and dividends paid since acquisition are as follows:

Year	Net Income	Dividends
19X3	$70,000	$25,000
19X4	75,600	25,000
19X5	81,650	30,000

On January 1, 19X5, Passaic leased a truck with a 5-year life from Slawton. The 3-year financing-type lease provides for payments of $10,000 each January 1. The present value of the truck at Slawton's 8% implicit rate, including the unguaranteed residual value of $6,000 at the end of the third year, was $32,596. Straight-line depreciation is being used. Passaic has also used the 8% implicit rate to record the lease.

On January 1, 19X6, Slawton signed a 4-year financing-type lease with Passaic for the rental of specialized production machinery which has an 8-year life. There is a $7,000 purchase option at the end of the fourth year. The lease agreement requires lease payments of $30,000 each January 1 plus $1,500 for maintenance of the equipment. It also calls for contingent payments equal to 10% of Slawton's cost savings through the use of this equipment, as reflected in any increase in net income (excluding gains or losses on sale of assets) above the previous growth rate of Slawton's net income. The present value of the equipment on January 1, 19X6, at Passaic's 10% implicit rate, was $109,388.

On October 1, 19X6, Slawton sold Passaic a warehouse having a 20-year remaining life, book value of $120,000 and estimated salvage value of $20,000. Passaic paid $160,000 for the building, which is being depreciated on a straight-line basis.

The following trial balances were prepared by the separate firms on December 31, 19X6:

	Passaic Heavy Equipment	Slawton Truck Company
Cash	90,484	80,000
Accounts Receivable (net)	228,000	120,000
Inventory	200,000	140,000
Minimum Lease Payments Receivable	97,000	54,000
Unguaranteed Residual Value	—	14,000
Unearned Interest Income	(9,673)	(9,137)
Assets Under Capital Lease	27,833	109,388
Accumulated Depreciation—Assets Under Capital Lease	(18,555)	(13,674)
Property, Plant, and Equipment	2,075,000	1,125,000
Accumulated Depreciation—Property, Plant, and Equipment	(713,000)	(160,000)
Investment in Slawton Truck Company	1,029,800	—
Accounts Payable	(100,000)	(85,000)
Interest Payable	(740)	(7,939)
Obligations Under Capital Lease	(9,260)	(79,388)
Common Stock ($5 par)	(1,800,000)	(800,000)
Retained Earnings	(864,834)	(387,250)
Sales	(3,200,000)	(1,400,000)
Gain on Sale of Assets	—	(40,000)
Interest Income	(7,939)	(4,939)
Rent Income	(2,182)	—
Cost of Goods Sold	1,882,000	770,000
Interest Expense	740	7,939
Depreciation Expense	135,000	45,000
Other Expenses	924,326	487,000
Subsidiary Income	(108,000)	—
Dividends Declared	144,000	35,000
	0	0

Required:

Prepare a work sheet for consolidated financial statements for Passaic Heavy Equipment and its subsidiary, Slawton Truck Company, for the year ended December 31, 19X6.

Problem 9-12. In a transaction that did not qualify as a pooling, Priceless Computers acquired 90% of the outstanding common stock of Superior Electronics for $990,000 on January 1, 19X0. Superior had the following stockholders' equity balances on that date: common stock, $760,000; retained earnings, $250,000. Book values approximated market values, and any excess was attributed to goodwill with a 10-year life. Superior had net income of $95,000 and $111,000, and paid dividends of $30,000 and $38,000 for 19X0 and 19X1, respectively.

Superior issued $100,000 of 8-year, 8% bonds on January 1, 19W9. Annual interest is paid on January 1, and the bonds were sold for $89,329, to yield 10%. Priceless purchased all of these bonds in the market for $83,551 on January 2, 19X1, when the market rate was 12%.

Superior sells electronic parts to Priceless at 25% above cost. Intercompany sales during 19X2 amounted to $350,000, and Priceless had not paid for 5% of this merchandise at year end. Priceless's beginning inventory included $60,000 of parts bought from Superior, and its ending inventory included $46,000.

On December 31, 19X1, Priceless leased a small computer to Superior. Payments of $30,000 are due in advance each December 31 for 4 years, and Superior will purchase the computer for $7,000 at the end of the fourth year under a bargain purchase option. The present value of the lease payments at Superior's 10% incremental borrowing rate of 10% was $109,388. The computer cost Priceless $85,000, has a six-year expected life, and is being depreciated on a straight-line basis.

The following trial balances were prepared by the separate firms on December 31, 19X2:

	Priceless Computers	Superior Electronics
Cash	130,322	54,648
Accounts Receivable (net)	317,000	140,000
Interest Receivable	28,500	—
Inventory	1,050,000	130,000
Minimum Lease Payments Receivable	204,000	—
Unearned Interest Income	(43,500)	—
Assets Under Capital Lease	—	109,388
Accumulated Depreciation—Assets Under Capital Lease	—	(18,231)
Property, Plant, and Equipment	6,900,000	1,660,000
Accumulated Depreciation—Property, Plant, and Equipment	(4,510,000)	(562,000)
Investment in Superior Electronics	990,000	—
Investment in 8% Bonds	87,846	—
Accounts Payable	(557,000)	(117,000)
Interest Payable	(60,000)	(8,000)
Obligations Under Capital Lease	—	(57,327)
Bonds Payable, 8%	(1,000,000)	(100,000)
Discount on Bonds Payable	18,500	6,341
Common Stock ($10 par)	(2,400,000)	(760,000)
Retained Earnings	(950,000)	(388,000)
Sales	(3,920,000)	(1,500,000)
Sales Profit on Leases	(54,000)	—
Interest Income	(45,468)	—
Cost of Goods Sold	2,400,000	820,000
Interest Expense	84,000	17,181
Depreciation Expense	320,000	120,000
Other Expenses	900,000	415,000
Dividend Income	(34,200)	—
Dividends Declared	144,000	38,000
	0	0

Required:

Prepare the work sheet for consolidated financial statements for Priceless Computers and its subsidiary, Superior Electronics, for the year ended December 31, 19X2.

Problem 9-13. Masters, Inc., purchased an 80% interest in All-Lease Company for $480,000 on January 1, 19X1, when All-Lease had the following stockholders' equity:

Common stock, $10 par..............	$100,000
Additional paid-in capital	300,000
Retained earnings	100,000
Total.............................	$500,000

Any excess is attributable to goodwill with a 40-year life.

The following intercompany leases have been written by All-Lease since the acquisition:

1. On January 1, 19X3, All-Lease purchased for $140,000 land and a building which it leased to Masters, Inc., under a 5-year operating lease. Payments of $11,000 per year are required at the beginning of each year. The $120,000 building cost is being depreciated over 20 years on a straight-line basis.
2. On January 1, 19X4, All-Lease purchased a machine for $15,200 and leased it to Masters, Inc. The 4-year lease qualifies as a capital lease. The rentals are $5,000 per year payable at the beginning of each year. There is a bargain purchase option whereby Masters will purchase the machine at the end of 4 years for $2,000.

   The market value of the machine is $17,335. The lease payments, including the purchase option, yield an implicit rate of 16% to the lessor. Masters will depreciate the machine over 7 years on a straight-line basis with no salvage value.
3. On January 1, 19X5, All-Lease purchased a truck for $23,116 and leased it to Masters, Inc., under a 3-year capital lease. Payments of $8,000 per year are required at the beginning of each year. The market value of the truck was $23,116; there was no dealer's profit for All-Lease. The truck has an estimated unguaranteed residual value of $5,000 at the end of 3 years. Based on the rents and the salvage value, the lease has a lessor implicit rate of 20%. Masters, Inc., has an incremental borrowing rate of 12%, but will record the lease based on the 20% rate.
4. Masters, Inc., has accrued interest on its capital lease obligations. All-Lease has recognized earned interest for the year on its capital leases.

The trial balances on page 407 were prepared for Masters, Inc., and All-Lease on December 31, 19X5.

Required:

Prepare a work sheet for the preparation of consolidated financial statements for Masters, Inc., and its subsidiary, All-Lease Company, for the year ended December 31, 19X5.

	Masters, Inc.	All-Lease
Cash	92,000	115,000
Inventory	70,000	20,000
Property, Plant, and Equipment	320,000	50,000
Accumulated Depreciation—Property, Plant, and Equipment	(70,000)	(20,000)
Assets Under Capital Lease	37,557	
Accumulated Depreciation—Assets Under Capital Lease	(11,693)	
Assets Under Operating Lease		420,000
Accumulated Depreciation—Assets Under Operating Lease		(80,000)
Minimum Lease Payments Receivable		350,000
Unguaranteed Residual Value (leases)		62,000
Unearned Interest Income on Leases		(182,000)
Investment in All-Lease Company	480,000	
Accounts Payable	(130,000)	(80,000)
Obligations Under Capital Lease	(21,531)	
Interest Payable	(3,933)	
Common Stock ($10 par)	(200,000)	(100,000)
Paid-In Capital in Excess of Par	(300,000)	(300,000)
Retained Earnings	(278,333)	(226,610)
Sales	(300,000)	(130,000)
Rent Income		(34,000)
Interest Income—Capital Lease		(15,390)
Depreciation Expense	41,000	23,000
Interest Expense	3,933	
Selling and General Expense	70,000	38,000
Cost of Goods Sold	190,000	90,000
Rent Expense	11,000	
	0	0

CHAPTER 10

SPECIAL ISSUES IN ACCOUNTING FOR AN INVESTMENT IN A SUBSIDIARY

The complete mastery of business combinations requires an understanding of specialized types of investment situations. This chapter will first consider the procedures to be used when a parent acquires its controlling interest in stock directly from the subsidiary. The special procedures needed to consolidate subsidiary investments which have been acquired in a piecemeal manner at different points in time will then be analyzed.

This chapter will also discuss special procedures needed to consolidate subsidiaries which have preferred stock as well as common stock outstanding. Additional consolidation procedures are needed to segregate the preferred stockholders' interest in the subsidiary equity accounts. Further analysis is needed when the parent owns subsidiary preferred stock, since all intercompany investments must be eliminated in the process of consolidating.

The chapter will then present the theory and the recording of a sale of all or a portion of the parent's investment in a subsidiary. The procedures used vary substantially, depending on the relative proportion of the investment sold.

PARENT ACQUIRES STOCK DIRECTLY FROM SUBSIDIARY

A parent firm may organize a new corporation and supply all of the common stock equity funds in exchange for all of the newly organized firm's common stock. Since the newly formed corporation receives the funds directly, there will be no difference between the price paid for the shares and the equity in assets acquired. Thus, the determination and distribution of excess schedule will show no excess of cost or book value.

In other cases, the parent firm will allow the newly organized subsidiary to sell a portion of the shares to persons outside the consolidated group. If the shares are sold to outsiders at a price equal to the price paid by the parent, the cost and book value will again be equal. However, if a price greater or less than the price paid by the parent is charged to outside parties, an excess of cost or book value will result. This excess occurs because the total price paid by the parent will not equal its ownership interest multiplied by the total subsidiary firm's common stockholders' equity. Normally, the excess of cost is recorded as goodwill, and an excess of book value is recorded as a deferred credit, since the only asset held by a newly organized firm is cash, which is not subject to adjustment. If noncash assets are given in exchange for the subsidiary shares, these assets would be adjusted according to the normal distribution of excess procedures.

An existing corporation might also sell a sufficient number of new shares to grant a controlling interest to the buying firm. For example, assume that Company S had the following equity balances prior to a sale of shares to Company P:

Common stock, $10 par, 10,000 shares	$100,000
Paid-in capital in excess of par...........................	150,000
Retained earnings	220,000
Total stockholders' equity	$470,000

Assume that Company S sells 30,000 additional shares directly to Company P for $50 per share, a total of $1,500,000. Subsequent to the sale, the equity balances of Company S appear as follows:

Common stock, $10 par, 40,000 shares	$ 400,000
Paid-in capital in excess of par...........................	1,350,000
Retained earnings	220,000
Total stockholders' equity	$1,970,000

The fact that the payment was made directly to the subsidiary does not alter the relationship between the price paid and the newly acquired controlling interest. The determination and distribution of excess schedule must still compare the price paid with the portion of total subsidiary equity acquired. The excess, as determined in the following schedule, would then be distributed according to purchase rules.

Price paid		$1,500,000
Interest acquired:		
Common stock, $10 par	$ 400,000	
Paid-in capital in excess of par	1,350,000	
Retained earnings	220,000	
Total subsidiary equity	$1,970,000	
Interest acquired	75%	1,477,500
Excess of cost over book value		$ 22,500

PIECEMEAL ACQUISITION OF INTEREST IN SUBSIDIARY

Past combinations have involved an acquisition of a controlling interest in a subsidiary by a single purchase of stock. A parent may also acquire a controlling interest as a result of a series of purchases of subsidiary stock. Very likely there will be a different excess of cost or book value for each block, and the causal factors for the differences may vary at the time of each acquisition. Each block acquired must be accompanied by a separate determination and distribution of excess schedule. The excess of cost or book value must be distributed and amortized separately for each block.

Control Achieved upon Initial Investment

When control is achieved with the initial investment, consolidation procedures are already in effect when subsequent blocks are purchased. Thus, no major change in accounting methods is required. Another determination and distribution of excess schedule must be prepared for the new investment, and the addition to the existing consolidated work sheet procedures must be acknowledged.

Assume that Company P purchases on the open market its original 60% interest in Company S on January 1, 19X1, for $126,000, when Company S has the following balance sheet:

Assets		Liabilities and Equity	
Current assets	$ 50,000	Liabilities	$ 40,000
Equipment (net)	150,000	Common stock ($10 par)	100,000
		Retained earnings	60,000
Total assets	$200,000	Total liabilities and equity	$200,000

Further assume that the current assets require no adjustment, and that the equipment has a net market value of $180,000 and a 5-year remaining life. Goodwill resulting from the purchase of the stock will be amortized over a 10-year period. The following determination and distribution of excess schedule would be prepared on January 1, 19X1, for the first acquisition:

Price paid		$126,000
Interest acquired:		
Common stock...	$100,000	
Retained earnings	60,000	
Total equity	$160,000	
Interest acquired	60%	96,000
Excess of cost over book value		$ 30,000
Attributable to equipment:		
.6 × $30,000 undervaluation (to be amortized over 5 years) ..		**18,000**
Goodwill (10-year amortization)..............................		**$ 12,000**

On January 1, 19X3, Company P purchases on the open market another 20% interest in Company S by paying $50,000. The balance sheet for Company S on January 1, 19X3, reflects two years of continued operations:

Assets		Liabilities and Equity	
Current assets	$ 80,000	Liabilities	$ 50,000
Building (net).................	80,000	Common stock ($10 par)	100,000
Equipment (net)	90,000	Retained earnings	100,000
Total assets	$250,000	Total liabilities and equity	$250,000

Company P's analysis on January 1, 19X3, indicates that the equipment listed on Company S's balance sheet is now undervalued by $24,000, and has a 3-year remaining life. The current assets and the building appear to have market values equal to their book values. Goodwill is assumed to have a 10-year life. Based on this analysis, the following determination and distribution of excess schedule would be prepared for the January 1, 19X3 investment:

Price paid		$50,000
Interest acquired:		
Common stock...	$100,000	
Retained earnings	100,000	
Total	$200,000	
Interest acquired	20%	40,000
Excess of cost over book value		$10,000
Attributable to equipment:		
.2 × $24,000 undervaluation (to be amortized over 3 years) ..		**4,800**
Goodwill (10-year amortization)		**$ 5,200**

Note that the above determination and distribution of excess schedule is "free standing," in that it is completely independent of the appraisals made for the January 1, 19X1 schedule.

The additional work sheet procedures that arise from this piecemeal acquisition are shown in Illustration I on pages 412 and 413. The trial balances for Companies P and S are shown as they would appear on December 31, 19X3. The investment in Company S account is based on the use of the simple equity method during the current and previous years. The December 31, 19X3 balance was determined as follows:

Cost of 60% investment (January 1, 19X1)			$126,000
Add equity share of change in Company S retained earnings as of January 1, 19X3:			
Balance, January 1, 19X3..........................	$100,000		
Balance, January 1, 19X1..........................	60,000		
	$ 40,000	× 60% =	24,000
Cost of 20% investment (January 1, 19X3)			50,000
Equity share of Company S 19X3 income:			
80% × $35,000.......................................			28,000
Investment account balance, December 31, 19X3........			$228,000

The consolidated net income of $78,080 is distributed to the controlling and minority interests as shown in the income distribution schedules

Illustration I—Investment Acquired in Blocks
Company P and
Work Sheet for Consolidated
For Year Ended

(Credit balance amounts
are in parentheses)

	Trial Balance	
	Company P	Company S
Current Assets	60,000	130,000
Investment in Co. S	228,000	
Building	400,000	80,000
Accumulated Depreciation—Building	(100,000)	(5,000)
Equipment		150,000
Accumulated Depreciation—Equipment		(90,000)
Goodwill		
Liabilities	(100,000)	(30,000)
Common Stock, Co. P	(200,000)	
Retained Earnings, Jan. 1, 19X3, Co. P	(210,000)	
Common Stock, Co. S		(100,000)
Retained Earnings, Jan. 1, 19X3, Co. S		(100,000)
Sales	(400,000)	(200,000)
Cost of Goods Sold	300,000	120,000
Expenses	50,000	45,000
Subsidiary Income	(28,000)	
	0	0
Consolidated Net Income		
To Minority Interest (see distribution schedule, page 414)		
To Controlling Interest (see distribution schedule)		
Minority Interest, Dec. 31, 19X3		
Retained Earnings, Controlling Interest, Dec. 31, 19X3		

Eliminations:
(1) Eliminate parent's entry recognizing 80% of the subsidiary's income for the current year. This step restores the investment account to its balance at the beginning of the year, so that it can be eliminated against the Company S beginning-of-the-year equity balances.
(2) Eliminate the 80% controlling interest in beginning-of-the-year subsidiary equity against the investment account. The 60% and 20% investments could be eliminated separately if desired.
3 a. The $30,000 excess of cost on the original 60% investment is distributed to the accumulated depreciation and goodwill accounts according to the determination and distribution of excess schedule prepared on January 1, 19X1.
  b. Since the equipment has a 5-year remaining life on January 1, 19X1, the depreciation should be increased $3,600 per year for 3 years. This entry corrects controlling Retained Earnings for the past 2 years

Immediate Control
Subsidiary Company S
Financial Statements
December 31, 19X3

Eliminations Dr.	Eliminations Cr.	Consolidated Income Statement	Minority Interest	Controlling Retained Earnings	Consolidated Balance Sheet
					190,000
	(1) 28,000				
	(2) 160,000				
	3a 30,000				
	4a 10,000				
					480,000
					(105,000)
					150,000
3a 18,000	3b 10,800				(79,600)
4a 4,800	4b 1,600				
3a 12,000	3c 3,600				13,080
4a 5,200	4c 520				
					(130,000)
					(200,000)
3b 7,200				(200,400)	
3c 2,400					
(2) 80,000			(20,000)		
(2) 80,000			(20,000)		
		(600,000)			
		420,000			
3b 3,600		101,920			
3c 1,200					
4b 1,600					
4c 520					
(1) 28,000					
244,520	244,520				
		(78,080)			
		7,000	(7,000)		
		71,080		(71,080)	
			(47,000)		(47,000)
				(271,480)	(271,480)
					0

by $7,200, and corrects the current depreciation expense by $3,600.

c. The $12,000 original goodwill is to be amortized $1,200 per year for 3 years. Controlling Retained Earnings must be corrected for 2 past years ($2,400), and current year's expenses are increased by $1,200.

4 a. The $10,000 excess of cost on the 20% block is distributed to the accumulated depreciation and goodwill accounts according to the determination and distribution of excess schedule prepared on January 1, 19X3.

b. The $4,800 excess attributable to equipment is to be depreciated over 3 years. Therefore, current expenses are increased by $1,600.

c. The $5,200 increase to Goodwill is to be amortized over 10 years, requiring current expenses to be increased by $520.

Income Distribution Schedules

Subsidiary Company S income distribution

	Internally generated net income .	$35,000
	Adjusted income...............	$35,000
	Minority interest	20%
	To minority	$ 7,000

Parent Company P income distribution

Equipment depreciation:			Internally generated net	
Block 1, 60% **3b**	$3,600		income	$50,000
Block 2, 20% **4b**	1,600		80% × subsidiary income	
Goodwill amortization:			of $35,000..................	28,000
Block 1, 60% **3c**	1,200			
Block 2, 20% **4c**	520			
			Controlling interest	$71,080

of Illustration I. As has always been the case, all amortizations of excess resulting from parent company purchases are deducted only from the controlling interest.

When investment blocks are carried at cost, each block is separately converted to the simple equity method as of the beginning of the year. For each block, the adjustment is based on the change in subsidiary retained earnings between the date of acquisition of the individual block and the beginning of the current year.

Suppose that the subsidiary of the previous example sold merchandise to the parent during 19X2, and that a $2,000 subsidiary profit is included in the parent's ending inventory of merchandise and in subsidiary retained earnings. In theory, the determination and distribution of excess schedule prepared for the 20% investment purchased on January 1, 19X3, should reflect the unrealized gross profit on sales applicable to the 20% interest purchased. Thus, the schedule on page 411 would be revised to distribute the excess as follows:

Excess of cost over book value	$10,000
Deferred gross profit on inventory sale (20%)	400
Attributable to equipment (3-year life)	(4,800)
Goodwill (10-year life)	$ 5,600

The following entry would distribute the excess on the 19X3 work sheet:

Accumulated Depreciation—Equipment	4,800	
Goodwill..	5,600	
Deferred Gross Profit on Inventory Sale		400
Investment in Company S		10,000

The following elimination for the $2,000 profit in the beginning inventory would then be made:

Retained Earnings—Controlling Interest (60% interest at time of original sale)	1,200	
Retained Earnings—Minority Interest (20%)	400	
Deferred Gross Profit on Inventory Sale	400	
Cost of Goods Sold (beginning inventory)		2,000

In practice, the concept of materiality will often prevail, and the above procedure will not be followed. The determination and distribution of excess schedule will not recognize the unrealized profit, which will increase the excess cost available for other assets. Work sheets for periods subsequent to the second purchase will distribute the retained earnings adjustments according to the ownership percentages prevailing at the time the work sheet is prepared. The following elimination would result:

Retained Earnings—Controlling Interest (80%)	1,600	
Retained Earnings—Minority Interest (20%)	400	
Cost of Goods Sold (beginning inventory)		2,000

This practical approach corrects the controlling interest for unrealized profits existing at the time of the second purchase and is consistent with the practice of charging all excess amortizations to the controlling interest. The procedures discussed on page 414 are also applicable to retained earnings adjustments resulting from sales of plant assets and intercompany investments in subsidiary bonds.

Control Not Achieved upon Initial Investment

When an initial investment in the stock of another firm represents less than a 50% interest, it is ordinarily improper to prepare consolidated statements. Such an investment is carried under the cost or the equity method, depending upon the interest acquired. APB Opinion No. 18 generally requires the use of the equity method when the interest equals or exceeds 20% of the outstanding common shares of an investee corporation.[1] If a second block of stock is purchased, resulting in an interest that exceeds 50%, consolidation becomes appropriate. It will be necessary to treat separately each block of stock acquired when the determination and distribution of excess schedule and the work sheet are prepared. Added complications arise because the original investment must be retroactively subjected to the consolidation process. The complexities involved depend on whether the original investment was recorded under the equity or the cost method.

Original Interest Under the Equity Method. The "sophisticated" equity method of APB Opinion No. 18, described in Chapter 7, requires that

---

[1] *Opinions of the Accounting Principles Board. No. 18,* "The Equity Method of Accounting for Investments in Common Stock" (New York: American Institute of Certified Public Accountants, 1971), par. 17.

the original excess of cost over book value be amortized as an adjustment of investment income in subsequent years. The amortization pattern depends on the underlying nature of the excess. The Opinion admits that it may be difficult to ascertain the nature of the excess, and thus goodwill may be assumed to be the "inferred" cause of the entire excess of cost over book value of an investment.

To illustrate the sophisticated equity method, suppose that Company P purchases on the open market a 20% interest in Company S on January 1, 19X1, for $48,000. The balance sheet of Company S on January 1, 19X1, is:

Assets		Liabilities and Equity	
Current assets	$ 50,000	Liabilities	$ 50,000
Building and equipment (net) ..	150,000	Common stock ($10 par)	50,000
		Retained earnings	100,000
Total assets	$200,000	Total liabilities and equity	$200,000

Assuming that the excess of cost is attributable to goodwill, the determination and distribution of excess schedule would be prepared as follows:

Price paid		$ 48,000
Interest acquired:		
Common stock...	$ 50,000	
Retained earnings	100,000	
Total	$150,000	
Ownership interest..	20%	30,000
Excess of cost attributed to goodwill (to be amortized over 20 years).		**$ 18,000**

This schedule requires that the investor reduce the investment account $900 ($18,000 ÷ 20) per year. Since goodwill cannot be recorded in the absence of consolidation and is merely buried in the investment account, the amortization required must be accomplished indirectly *through the investment account.* If Company S reports income of $15,000 for 19X1, for example, Company P would record the following sophisticated equity adjustment to the $48,000 recorded investment cost:

Investment in Company S	2,100	
Subsidiary Income		2,100
To recognize 20% of $15,000 reported income less amortization of goodwill [(20% × $15,000) − $900].		

Note that under the simple equity method used in past examples, $3,000 of investment income would be recorded. The goodwill amortization was not necessary since it was made on the consolidated work sheet.

Continuing this example, assume that on January 1, 19X2, Company P acquires an additional 60% interest on the open market for a price of $130,000. The balance sheet of Company S appears as follows on January 1, 19X2:

Assets			Liabilities and Equity	
Current assets		$ 70,000	Liabilities	$ 40,000
Building and			Common stock, $10 par	50,000
equipment	$150,000		Retained earnings	115,000
Less accumulated				
depreciation	15,000	135,000		
Total assets		$205,000	Total liabilities and equity	$205,000

If it is assumed that the current assets have a book value equal to their market values, and that equipment with a 9-year remaining life is undervalued by $9,000, the determination and distribution of excess schedule for the 60% acquisition on January 1, 19X2, would be prepared as follows:

Price paid		$130,000
Interest acquired:		
Common stock...	$ 50,000	
Retained earnings	115,000	
Total	$165,000	
Ownership interest...	60%	99,000
Excess of cost over book value		$ 31,000
Attributable to equipment: 60% × $9,000 undervaluation (amortized		
over 9 years)		**5,400**
Goodwill (to be amortized over 20 years)		**$ 25,600**

Assuming that Company S reports net income of $20,000 for 19X2, Company P would make the following simple equity adjustment for its entire investment:

Investment in Company S	16,000	
Subsidiary Income		16,000
To adjust for 80% of Company S's reported income of $20,000.		

It is no longer necessary to amortize the excess resulting from the January 1, 19X1 and January 1, 19X2 investments through the investment account, since the amortizations will be recorded on the consolidated work sheet, as shown in Illustration II on pages 418 and 419. The balance in the investment account results from the investments and income adjustments, which are summarized as follows:

Cost of January 1, 19X1 20% investment	$ 48,000
19X1 sophisticated equity adjustment	2,100
Cost of January 1, 19X2 60% investment	130,000
19X2 simple equity adjustment for 80% interest	16,000
Investment balance, December 31, 19X2.........................	$196,100

Original Interest Under the Cost Method. When the investment acquired prior to obtaining control is recorded under the cost method, the easiest procedure is to convert the investment account to the simple equity method, if the later investment in the subsidiary is to be recorded under the simple equity method in future periods. Conversion to the simple

Illustration II—Investment Acquired in Blocks
Company P and

(Credit balance amounts
are in parentheses)

Work Sheet for Consolidated
For Year Ended

	Trial Balance	
	Company P	Company S
Current Assets	69,900	85,000
Investment in Co. S	196,100	
Building and Equipment	300,000	150,000
Accumulated Depreciation—Building and Equipment	(200,000)	(30,000)
Goodwill		
Liabilities		(20,000)
Common Stock, Co. P	(100,000)	
Retained Earnings, Jan. 1, 19X2, Co. P	(200,000)	
Common Stock, Co. S		(50,000)
Retained Earnings, Jan. 1, 19X2, Co. S		(115,000)
Sales	(300,000)	(100,000)
Cost of Goods Sold	200,000	60,000
Expenses	50,000	20,000
Subsidiary Income	(16,000)	
	0	0

Consolidated Net Income
To Minority Interest (see distribution schedule)
To Controlling Interest (see distribution schedule)
Minority Interest, Dec. 31, 19X2
Retained Earnings, Controlling Interest, Dec. 31, 19X2

Eliminations:
(1) Eliminate parent's entry recognizing the 80% interest in subsidiary income under the simple equity method. This step restores the investment account to its balance at the beginning of the year.
(2) The 80% controlling interest in the beginning-of-the-year subsidiary stockholders' equity accounts is eliminated against the investment account. If desired, the two investment blocks may be separately eliminated.
3 a. The remaining excess of cost over book value on the original 20% investment is $17,100 ($18,000 less 1 year of $900 amortization). It must be remembered that under the sophisticated equity method, amortization entries prior to securing control reduce the investment account. Always remember that *only the unamortized original excess remains*. The remaining $17,100 excess is carried to goodwill according to the determination and distribution of excess schedule prepared on January 1, 19X1.
b. Goodwill amortization of $900 is recorded for the current year. Recall that no amortization is needed for

Income Distribution Schedules   Subsidiary Company S income distribution

Internally generated net income .	$20,000
Adjusted income	$20,000
Minority interest	.2
To minority	$ 4,000

Control Achieved with Second Block
Subsidiary Company S
Financial Statements
December 31, 19X2

| Eliminations | | Consolidated Income Statement | Minority Interest | Controlling Retained Earnings | Consolidated Balance Sheet |
Dr.	Cr.				
					154,900
	(1) 16,000				
	(2) 132,000				
	3a 17,100				
	4a 31,000				
					450,000
4a 5,400	4b 600				(225,200)
3a 17,100	3b 900				40,520
4a 25,600	4c 1,280				
					(20,000)
					(100,000)
				(200,000)	
(2) 40,000			(10,000)		
(2) 92,000			(23,000)		
		(400,000)			
		260,000			
3b 900		72,780			
4b 600					
4c 1,280					
(1) 16,000					
198,880	198,880				
		(67,220)			
		4,000	(4,000)		
		63,220		(63,220)	
			(37,000)		(37,000)
				(263,220)	(263,220)
					0

periods prior to achieving control since that amortization was previously recorded through the parent's investment account. Thus, the controlling interest share of retained earnings is already reduced.

4 a. The excess attributable to the January 1, 19X2 60% acquisition is distributed to the accumulated depreciation and goodwill accounts according to the determination and distribution of excess schedule for the second 60% acquisition.

b. Depreciation for the current year is increased $600 according to the determination and distribution of excess schedule prepared on January 1, 19X2.

c. Goodwill amortization of $1,280 increases expenses for the current year as required by the determination and distribution of excess schedule prepared on January 1, 19X2.

Parent Company P income distribution

Equipment depreciation:		Internally generated net income .	$50,000
Block 2, 60% **4b**	$ 600	Share of subsidiary income	
Goodwill amortization:		(.8 × $20,000)	16,000
Block 1, 20% **3b**	900		
Block 2, 60% **4c**	1,280		
		Controlling interest	$63,220

equity method will thus make the prior investment compatible with the later investment made to secure control. The conversion should preferably be made directly on the parent's books.

Assume that Company P in Illustration II used the cost method to record its original 20% interest in Company S. The investment in Company S account would then show $48,000 cost on January 1, 19X2, the date the 60% interest is acquired. Company P would convert the 20% interest to the simple equity method as follows:

Investment in Company S	3,000	
Retained Earnings		3,000
To adjust for change in subsidiary's Retained Earnings during 19X1.		

It would not be necessary to amortize the $900 of goodwill through the investment account, since that amortization can be done in the normal manner on the 19X2 work sheet for consolidated statements. The conversion process simplifies eliminations because the entire original excess of cost of $18,000 will appear on the work sheet.

If the parent does not make the conversion entry on its books, a "cost conversion" entry can be made on the work sheet. Illustration III, on pages 422 and 423, is similar to Illustration II, except that Company P used the cost method on the original 20% investment in Company S and did not convert to the simple equity method on January 1, 19X2. Note that the balance in the investment account would be:

Cost of original 20% investment	$ 48,000
Cost of 60% investment....................................	130,000
Simple equity adjustment for 19X2	16,000
Investment balance, December 31, 19X2....................	$194,000

When control is not achieved on the first purchase, ARB No. 51 permits a parent to use the date control is achieved as the date of acquisition for both blocks.[2] Thus, a parent is excused from analyzing the cause of excess for a "prior to achieving control" investment, and is allowed to use the cost method if the result of doing so is not material. In the case of Companies P and S, the original $48,000 cost could be added to the $130,000 cost of the second investment to produce the following determination and distribution of excess schedule on January 1, 19X2:

Price paid (January 1, 19X1, plus January 1, 19X2 investment) ...		$178,000
Interest acquired:		
Common stock..	$ 50,000	
Retained earnings	115,000	
Total	$165,000	
Ownership interest..	80%	132,000
Excess of cost over book value		$ 46,000
Attributable to equipment:		
80% × $9,000 undervaluation (amortized over 9 years)		7,200
Goodwill (to be amortized over 20 years)		**$ 38,800**

[2] *Accounting Research Bulletin No. 51,* "Consolidated Financial Statements" (New York: American Institute of Certified Public Accountants, 1959), par. 10.

The procedure of lumping investments together cannot be recommended on theoretical grounds, since the facts surrounding the separate investments are ignored. Also, when the original investment meets or exceeds 20% of the shares of the subsidiary, this procedure would be a direct violation of APB Opinion No. 18.

The parent may use the cost method for blocks which are acquired prior to achieving control and continue to use it for blocks acquired after achieving control. In this situation, each block would be independently converted to the equity method as of the beginning of the year.

SUBSIDIARY PREFERRED STOCK

The existence of preferred stock in the capital structure of a subsidiary complicates the calculation of a parent's claim on subsidiary retained earnings, both at the time of acquisition and in the preparation of subsequent consolidated statements. In previous examples, the subsidiary had only common stock outstanding, so that all retained earnings were associated with common stock, and the parent had a claim on subsidiary retained earnings proportionate to its ownership interest. When a subsidiary has preferred stock outstanding, however, the preferred stock may also have a claim on retained earnings. This claim may be caused by a liquidation value in excess of par value and/or by participation and cumulative dividend rights. When these conditions exist, the retained earnings must be divided between the preferred and common stockholder interests. This division is accomplished by employing the procedures used to calculate the book value of preferred and common stock. Although typically covered in intermediate accounting, the topic will be briefly reviewed in this text.

Once retained earnings are allocated between the common and preferred stockholders, the intercompany investments can be eliminated. The investment in subsidiary common stock account will be eliminated against the total equity claim of the common stockholders. If there is an investment in subsidiary preferred stock account, it will be eliminated against the preferred stockholders' total equity.

Determining the Preferred Shareholders' Claim on Retained Earnings

The preferred shareholders' claim on retained earnings equals the claim they would have if the firm were dissolved. In addition to the par value of the preferred shares, there may be a stipulated liquidation value in excess of par and/or dividend preferences. In the rare case of a liquidation value in excess of par, an amount equal to the liquidation bonus (liquidation less par value) must be segregated from retained earnings as a preferred shareholder claim.

In addition to this liquidation bonus, there must be an analysis of preferred shareholder claims resulting from cumulative and/or participation clauses applicable to the preferred stock. These claims reduce

Illustration III—Investment Acquired in Blocks
Company P and
Work Sheet for Consolidated
For Year Ended

(Credit balance amounts
are in parentheses)

	Trial Balance	
	Company P	Company S
Current Assets	69,900	85,000
Investment in Co. S	194,000	
Building and Equipment	300,000	150,000
Accumulated Depreciation—Building and Equipment	(200,000)	(30,000)
Goodwill		
Liabilities		(20,000)
Common Stock, Co. P	(100,000)	
Retained Earnings, Jan. 1, 19X2, Co. P	(197,900)	
Common Stock, Co. S		(50,000)
Retained Earnings, Jan. 1, 19X2, Co. S		(115,000)
Sales	(300,000)	(100,000)
Cost of Goods Sold	200,000	60,000
Expenses	50,000	20,000
Subsidiary Income	(16,000)	
	0	0
Consolidated Net Income		
To Minority Interest (same as Illustration II)		
To Controlling Interest (same as Illustration II)		
Minority Interest, Dec. 31, 19X2		
Retained Earnings, Controlling Interest, Dec. 31, 19X2		

Eliminations:
Conv. Convert original 20% investment to simple equity method. 20% × $15,000 change in Company S
Retained Earnings.
(1) Eliminate parent's entry recognizing the 80% interest in subsidiary income under the simple equity method.
This step restores the investment account to its balance at the beginning of the year.
(2) The 80% controlling interest in the beginning-of-the-year subsidiary stockholders' equity accounts is eliminated against the investment account.
3 a. The original excess of cost on the 20% investment ($18,000) is still contained in the investment account
and can now be recognized as goodwill according to the January 1, 19X1 determination and distribution
of excess schedule.

---

the retained earnings applicable to the common stock. For example, if a
common stock dividend had been recorded and the preferred stock
dividend had not, a liability should be recorded for the preferred
dividend legally due. If, however, the preferred stock is noncumulative

Control Achieved with Second Purchase; Cost Method on First Investment
Subsidiary Company S
Financial Statements
December 31, 19X2

Eliminations		Consolidated Income Statement	Minority Interest	Controlling Retained Earnings	Consolidated Balance Sheet
Dr.	**Cr.**				
					154,900
Conv. 3,000	(1) 16,000				
	(2) 132,000				
	3a 18,000				
	(4a) 31,000				
					450,000
(4a) 5,400	(4b) 600				(225,200)
3a 18,000	3b 1,800				40,520
(4a) 25,600	(4c) 1,280				
					(20,000)
					(100,000)
3b 900	Conv. 3,000			(200,000)	
(2) 40,000			(10,000)		
(2) 92,000			(23,000)		
		(400,000)			
		260,000			
3b 900		72,780			
(4b) 600					
(4c) 1,280					
(1) 16,000					
203,680	203,680				
		(67,220)			
		4,000	(4,000)		
		63,220		(63,220)	
					(37,000)
		(37,000)			(37,000)
				(263,220)	(263,220)
					0

b. Goodwill for the past year and current year is amortized at $900 per year. Note that the Company P beginning-of-the-year Retained Earnings is corrected for the prior years' goodwill amortization. Amortization was not previously recorded, since the cost method was in use.

(4) a. The excess attributable to the January 1, 19X2 60% acquisition is distributed to the accumulated depreciation and goodwill accounts according to the determination and distribution of excess schedule prepared for the 60% block on January 1, 19X2.

   b. Depreciation for the current year is increased $600.

   c. Goodwill of $1,280 is amortized for the current year.

---

and nonparticipating, all the retained earnings attaches to common stock.

If the preferred stock is noncumulative but is fully participating, the retained earnings are allocated pro rata according to the total par or stated values of the preferred and common stock. If the preferred stock is cumulative and nonparticipating and has, for example, two years' dividends in arrears, a claim on retained earnings exists, although there is no liability to pay the preferred dividends until a dividend is declared.

When preferred stock is both cumulative and fully participating, the arrearage for prior periods is met first. The remaining retained earnings are allocated pro rata according to the total par values of preferred and common stock. When preferred stock is cumulative and participating but no dividends are in arrears, the analysis is the same as if the preferred stock were noncumulative and fully participating.

When preferred stock is cumulative and limited in participation to a percentage of par value, the arrearage for prior periods is met first and is excluded from the limited participation. The lesser of a pro rata share of the remaining retained earnings or the limiting percentage of the preferred stock's par value is allocated to the preferred claim. Any retained earnings remaining after this allocation are assigned to the common stock.

Apportionment of Retained Earnings

Additional procedures are required when a subsidiary with preferred stock which has liquidation and/or dividend preferences is consolidated, even though none of the preferred shares are owned by the parent. In this situation, allocation of retained earnings to the preferred and common stock is as follows:

1. The determination and distribution of excess schedule prepared as of the date of the parent's investment in common stock must include only that portion of retained earnings which is allocable to the common stock on the purchase date.
2. Periodic equity adjustments for the parent's investment in common stock are made only for the common shareholders' claim on income. The preferred shareholders' claim on periodic income, including dividends paid and additional participation or arrearage claims, must be deducted to arrive at income available to common shareholders. When the cost method is used, the work sheet simple equity conversion adjustment is made for the parent's share of change in retained earnings applicable to common stock since the date of acquisition.
3. Subsidiary retained earnings must be allocated between preferred and common stockholders on consolidated work sheets. The parent's Investment in Common Stock is then eliminated against the parent's pro rata share of only the equity attaching to common stock.

To illustrate these procedures, assume that Company S had the following stockholders' equity on January 1, 19X3, the date on which Company P purchased an 80% interest in the common stock for $150,000:

Preferred stock, $100 par, 6% cumulative	$100,000
Common stock, $10 par	100,000
Retained earnings	80,000
Total	$280,000

Preferred stock has a liquidation value equal to par value, and dividends are two years in arrears as of January 1, 19X3. Company S assets have a market value equal to book value. Any excess purchase price is attributable to goodwill with a 10-year life. The determination and distribution of excess schedule would be prepared as follows:

Price paid			$150,000
Interest acquired:			
Common stock, $10 par		$100,000	
Retained earnings:			
Balance, Jan. 1, 19X3	$80,000		
Less preferred dividends in			
arrears (2 years × $6,000)	12,000	68,000	
Total equity applicable to common stock .		$168,000	
Ownership interest......................		80%	134,400
Goodwill (10-year amortization)			**$ 15,600**

Assume that income is exactly $25,000 per year in future years and that no dividends are paid. Each year, the following entry would be made by a parent using the simple equity method of accounting for subsidiary investments:

Investment in Subsidiary	15,200	
Subsidiary Income		15,200
To adjust for 80% of subsidiary income applicable to common stock ($25,000 reported income − $6,000 cumulative claim of preferred stock).		

Assuming that the periodic equity adjustments have been made properly, Illustration IV, on pages 426 and 427, shows a consolidated financial statements work sheet for the year ended December 31, 19X5 (3 years subsequent to the purchase). The investment in subsidiary common stock account includes the original cost of the investment plus 3 years (3 × $15,200 = $45,600) of simple equity adjustments for income and dividends. The work sheet is unique in that it contains two retained earnings accounts for the subsidiary, one for the common and one for the preferred portion of retained earnings.

After the eliminations are completed, the resulting consolidated net income of $173,440 is allocated as shown in the income distribution schedules. Since none of the preferred stock is owned by controlling shareholders, the minority interest receives all applicable preferred income plus 20% of the income allocable to common stock. It should be observed that the Minority Interest column, as well as the minority interest shown on a formal balance sheet, includes the minority interest in both preferred and common shares.

The work sheet just analyzed can handle all types of subsidiary preferred stockholder claims. Once the claim is determined, with sup-

(Credit balance amounts
are in parentheses)

	Trial Balance	
	Company P	**Company S**
Current Assets	259,600	150,000
Property, Plant, and Equipment (net)	400,000	250,000
Investment in Common Stock of Co. S	195,600	
Goodwill		
Liabilities	(150,000)	(45,000)
Common Stock, Co. P	(200,000)	
Retained Earnings, Jan. 1, 19X5, Co. P	(340,000)	
Preferred Stock ($100 par), Co. S		(100,000)
Retained Earnings Allocated to Preferred Stock, Jan. 1, 19X5, Co. S		
Common Stock ($10 par), Co. S		(100,000)
Retained Earnings, Jan. 1, 19X5, Co. S		(130,000)
Sales	(450,000)	(200,000)
Cost of Goods Sold	200,000	150,000
Expenses	100,000	25,000
Subsidiary Income	(15,200)	
	0	0
Consolidated Net Income		
To Minority Interest (see distribution schedule)		
To Controlling Interest (see distribution schedule)		
Minority Interest, Dec. 31, 19X5		
Retained Earnings, Controlling Interest, Dec. 31, 19X5		

Eliminations:
1 Distribute beginning-of-the-period retained earnings into the portions allocable to common and preferred stock. The typical procedure would be to consider the stated subsidiary retained earnings as applicable to common and to remove the preferred portion. This distribution reflects 4 years of arrearage (as of January 1, 19X5) at $6,000 per year.
(2) Eliminate parent's entry recording its share of subsidiary's current income.

Income Distribution Schedules   Subsidiary Company S income distribution

Internally generated net income (no adjustments)	$25,000
Less preferred cumulative claim to minority	6,000
Common stock interest	$19,000
Minority share of common income (20%)	$ 3,800
Total minority interest ($6,000 + $3,800)	$ 9,800

None Owned by Parent
Subsidiary Company S
Financial Statements
December 31, 19X5

| Eliminations | | Consolidated Income Statement | Minority Interest | Controlling Retained Earnings | Consolidated Balance Sheet |
Dr.	Cr.				
					409,600
					650,000
	(2) 15,200				
	(3) 164,800				
	(4) 15,600				
(4) 15,600	(5) 4,680				10,920
					(195,000)
					(200,000)
(5) 3,120				(336,880)	
			(100,000)		
	1 24,000		(24,000)		
(3) 80,000			(20,000)		
1 24,000			(21,200)		
(3) 84,800					
		(650,000)			
		350,000			
(5) 1,560		126,560			
(2) 15,200					
224,280	224,280				
		(173,440)			
		9,800	(9,800)		
		163,640		(163,640)	
		(175,000)			(175,000)
				(500,520)	(500,520)
					0

(3) Eliminate the pro rata subsidiary common stockholders' equity at the beginning of the period against the investment account. This step includes elimination of 80% of the subsidiary retained earnings applicable to common stock.
(4) Distribute the excess of cost according to the determination and distribution of excess schedule.
(5) Amortize goodwill for the past two years and the current year.

Parent Company P income distribution

Amortization of goodwill	$ 1,560	Internally generated net income .	$150,000
		80% of Co. S adjusted income on common stock (.8 × $19,000)	15,200
		Controlling interest	$163,640

porting calculations, it is isolated in a separate account, Retained Earnings Allocated to Preferred Stock.

When a parent uses the cost method to record its investment in a subsidiary, slightly different work sheet procedures are used. In Illustration IV, if Company P had used the cost method, the investment account would still be at the $150,000 original cost, there would be no subsidiary income shown, and the January 1, 19X5 Retained Earnings of Company P would not reflect the 19X3 and 19X4 simple equity adjustments. As described earlier, a *conversion to simple equity* adjustment is made on the work sheet. Since the beginning-of-the-period investment balance is needed for elimination, the equity adjustment converts the investment account only to the January 1, 19X5 balance, as follows:

Retained earnings, Company S, January 1, 19X5	$130,000	
Less 4 years' arrearage of preferred dividends..........	24,000	
Retained earnings applicable to common stock, January 1, 19X5		$106,000
Retained earnings, Company S, January 1, 19X3	$ 80,000	
Less 2 years' arrearage of preferred dividends..........	12,000	
Retained earnings applicable to common stock, January 1, 19X3		68,000
Increase in common stock portion of retained earnings .		$ 38,000
Controlling interest (80%)		$ 30,400

The conversion entry for $30,400 would debit the investment account and credit Company P Retained Earnings. The investment account would now be stated at its simple-equity-adjusted, January 1, 19X5 balance. Elimination Steps 1, 3, 4, and 5 would be made just as in Illustration IV. Only Step 2 would be omitted, since it is not applicable to the cost method. The following partial work sheet includes the conversion and subsequent elimination entries under the cost method. All remaining procedures for this example would be identical to those used in Illustration IV.

	Trial Balance		Eliminations			
	Company P	Company S	Dr.		Cr.	
Investment in Common Stock of Co. S.	150,000		Conv. 30,400	(3)	164,800	
				(4)	15,600	
Goodwill.......................................			(4) 15,600	(5)	4,680	
Retained Earnings, Jan. 1, 19X5, Co. P	(309,600)		(5) 3,120	Conv.	30,400	
Preferred Stock ($100 par), Co. S		(100,000)				
Retained Earnings Allocated to Preferred Stock, Jan. 1, 19X5, Co. S......				(1)	24,000	
Common Stock ($10 par), Co. S		(100,000)	(3) 80,000			
Retained Earnings, Jan. 1, 19X5, Co. S		(130,000)	(1) 24,000			
			(3) 84,800			
Expenses......................................	100,000	25,000	(5) 1,560			

Parent Company Investment in Subsidiary Preferred Stock

A parent company may purchase all or a portion of a subsidiary's preferred stock. Such an investment is not considered in determining whether the parent owns a controlling interest. Controlling interest for purposes of consolidated statements applies only to the parent's interest in voting common stock, since preferred stock is generally nonvoting. Thus, a 100% ownership of preferred stock and a 49% interest in common stock would not usually require preparation of consolidated statements.

From a consolidated viewpoint, the parent's purchase of subsidiary preferred stock amounts to retirement of the stock. The amount paid is compared to the sum of the original proceeds resulting from the issuance of the shares, plus any claim the shares have on retained earnings, and a gain or loss on retirement is calculated. A retirement gain is credited to controlling Paid-In Capital, not Retained Earnings, since it results from a transaction with the consolidated firm's shareholders. A loss would be offset against paid-in capital applicable to the preferred stock, or if none exists, the loss would be taken from controlling Retained Earnings and viewed as a retirement dividend. To illustrate this type of investment, assume that Company P, in Illustration IV, purchased 600 (60%) of the Company S preferred shares on January 1, 19X3, for $65,000. The gain or loss on retirement would be calculated as follows:

Price paid		$65,000
Less preferred interest acquired:		
Preferred stock, $100 par	$100,000	
Claim on dividends (2 years in arrears × $6,000 per year)	12,000	
Total preferred interest	$112,000	
Interest acquired	60%	67,200
Gain on retirement (credit Paid-In Capital)		**$ 2,200**

Though viewed as retired, the preferred stock investment account will continue on the books of the parent in subsequent periods. Each period, the investment must be "retired" on the work sheet. The procedures used depend on whether the parent accounts for the investment in preferred stock under the equity method or the cost method. Under the equity method, the parent adjusts Investment in Preferred Stock each period for any additional claim on the subsidiary's retained earnings, including any continued arrearage or participation privilege. In this example, the arrearage of dividends would be recorded each year, 19X3 to 19X5, as follows:

Investment in Company S Preferred Stock	3,600	
Subsidiary Income		3,600
To acknowledge 60% of the annual increase in the Company S preferred stock arrearage.		

Assuming that the equity adjustments are made properly, any original discrepancy between the price paid for the preferred shares and their book value would be maintained. The equity method also acknowledges

077

that even though the shares are viewed as retired in consolidated reports, the controlling interest is entitled to its proportionate share of consolidated income based on both its common and preferred stock holdings.

The work sheet of Illustration V displays the consolidation procedures that would be used for the ownership interest in preferred stock

Illustration V
Company P and
Work Sheet for Consolidated
For Year Ended

(Credit balance amounts
are in parentheses)

	Trial Balance	
	Company P	Company S
Current Assets	194,600	150,000
Property, Plant, and Equipment (net)	400,000	250,000
Investment in Co. S Common Stock	195,600	
Investment in Co. S Preferred Stock	75,800	
Goodwill		
Liabilities	(150,000)	(45,000)
Common Stock, Co. P	(200,000)	
Retained Earnings, Jan. 1, 19X5, Co. P	(347,200)	
Preferred Stock ($100 par), Co. S		(100,000)
Retained Earnings Allocated to Preferred Stock, Jan. 1, 19X5, Co. S		
Common Stock ($10 par), Co. S		(100,000)
Retained Earnings, Jan. 1, 19X5, Co. S		(130,000)
Sales	(450,000)	(200,000)
Cost of Goods Sold	200,000	150,000
Expenses	100,000	25,000
Subsidiary Income—Common	(15,200)	
Subsidiary Income—Preferred	(3,600)	
Paid-In Capital, Co. P		
	0	0
Consolidated Net Income		
To Minority Interest (see distribution schedule, page 432)		
To Controlling Interest (see distribution schedule)		
Minority Interest, Dec. 31, 19X5		
Retained Earnings, Controlling Interest, Dec. 31, 19X5		

Eliminations:
(1-5) Same as Illustration IV; the common stock investment elimination procedures are unaffected by the investment in preferred stock.

6 Eliminate the entry recording parent's share of income allocable to preferred stock. If declared, intercompany preferred dividends would have also been eliminated. This adjustment restores the investment described on page 429. The work sheet parallels Illustration IV, except that the parent owns 60% of the subsidiary preferred stock. The investment is listed at its $65,000 cost plus three years of equity adjustments to reflect the increasing dividend arrearage.

Consolidated net income is distributed as shown in the income distribution schedules on the next page. The distributions respect the

Subsidiary Preferred Stock Owned by Parent
Subsidiary Company S
Financial Statements
December 31, 19X5

Eliminations		Consolidated Income Statement	Minority Interest	Controlling Retained Earnings	Consolidated Balance Sheet
Dr.	Cr.				
					344,600
					650,000
	(2) 15,200				
	(3) 164,800				
	(4) 15,600				
	6 3,600				
	7 72,200				
(4) 15,600	(5) 4,680				10,920
					(195,000)
					(200,000)
(5) 3,120				(344,080)	
7 60,000			(40,000)		
7 14,400	(1) 24,000		(9,600)		
(3) 80,000			(20,000)		
(1) 24,000			(21,200)		
(3) 84,800					
		(650,000)			
		350,000			
(5) 1,560		126,560			
(2) 15,200					
6 3,600					
	7 2,200				(2,200)
302,280	302,280				
		(173,440)			
		6,200	(6,200)		
		167,240		(167,240)	
			(97,000)		(97,000)
				(511,320)	(511,320)
					0

account to its beginning-of-the-period equity balance.

7 The parent ownership portion of the par value and beginning-of-the-period retained earnings applicable to preferred stock is eliminated against the balance in the investment account. The difference in this case was a gain, and it was carried to the controlling Paid-In Capital.

Income Distribution Schedules

Subsidiary Company S income distribution

Internally generated net income (no adjustments)	$25,000
Less preferred cumulative claim:	
to minority, 40% × $6,000 . . .	(2,400)
to controlling, 60% × $6,000 .	(3,600)
Common stock interest	$19,000
Minority share of common income (20%)	3,800
Total minority interest ($2,400 + $3,800)	$ 6,200

Parent Company P income distribution

Amortization of goodwill	$ 1,560	Internally generated net income .	$150,000
		60% of Co. S income attributable to preferred stock	3,600
		80% of Co. S adjusted income on common stock (80% × $19,000)	15,200
		Controlling interest	$167,240

controlling/minority ownership of both common and preferred shares. The common and preferred equity interests of the minority are again summarized both on the work sheet and for presentation on the formal balance sheet.

If a parent uses the cost method for its investment in subsidiary preferred stock, the investment should be converted to the equity method as of the beginning of the period. In this example, if the cost method is used for the investment in preferred stock, the following equity conversion adjustment would be made on the work sheet:

Investment in Company S Preferred Stock	7,200	
Retained Earnings (January 1, 19X5, Co. P)		7,200

Eliminations would then proceed as in Illustration V, except that there would be no need for Step 6.

This example contains only cumulative preferred stock. However, the same principles would apply to participating preferred stock. Only the equity adjustments would differ.

SALE OF A PARENT'S INVESTMENT IN COMMON STOCK

A parent may sell all of its subsidiary interest, or enough shares to fall below the greater-than-50% interest generally required for consolidated reporting. Such an action makes it unnecessary to continue consolidated reporting and requires that a gain or loss on the sale of the investment be recorded. There may be other situations in which a parent sells a part of its shares of subsidiary common stock but still retains a greater-than-50% interest subsequent to the sale. When such an event occurs, subsequent financial reports would still be prepared on a consolidated basis. The consolidated, single-firm viewpoint would also be used to analyze the stock sale. Such a view holds that the consolidated firm has sold shares to the minority interest and that no gain or loss may be reflected on the consolidated income statement as a result of the intercompany transaction.

Sale of Entire Parent Interest

The sale of the entire investment in a subsidiary terminates the need for consolidated financial statements. In fact, when a sale occurs during the parent's fiscal year, the results of the subsidiary operations prior to the sale date are typically not consolidated. Instead, the net results of the subsidiary operations up to the sale date are shown as a separate line item on the parent's statements. In recording the sale of the investment in a subsidiary, the accountant's primary concern is to adjust the carrying value of the investment so that the correct gain or loss on the sale is recorded.

The accountant must also determine if the sale of the investment in a subsidiary constitutes a disposal of a segment of a business as defined by APB Opinion No. 30. The Opinion states: "the term *segment of a business* refers to a component of an entity whose activities represent a separate major line of business or class of customer."[3] The Opinion indicates that a segment may be in the form of a subsidiary. However, an interpretation of the Opinion makes it clear that not all subsidiaries qualify as segments of a business. For example, a parent may own several subsidiaries engaged in mining coal. If one subsidiary is sold, there would not be a sale of a major line of business, since the parent is still involved in coal mining. When the sale of a subsidiary qualifies as a disposal of a business segment, both the gain or loss on the sale and the results of operations for the period are shown net of tax in a separate discontinued-segment section of the income statement (see Chapter 3). When the sale does not qualify as a disposal of a business segment, the gain or loss and the results of operations for the period are usually shown on the income statement as a part of the normal recurring operations.

The complexities of properly recording the sale of an entire subsidiary investment are shown in the following example. Suppose that Company P purchased an 80% interest in Company S on January 1, 19X1, for $250,000, and the following determination and distribution of excess schedule was prepared.

---

[3] *Opinions of the Accounting Principles Board, No. 30,* "Reporting the Results of Operations" (New York: American Institute of Certified Public Accountants, 1973), par 13.

Price paid		$250,000
Interest acquired:		
Common stock ($10 par)	$100,000	
Retained earnings, January 1, 19X1	150,000	
Total equity	$250,000	
Interest acquired	80%	200,000
Excess of cost over book value		$ 50,000
Attributable to equipment (5-year life)		**20,000**
Attributable to goodwill (10-year life)............................		**$ 30,000**

Company S earned $40,000 in 19X1 and $25,000 in 19X2. Company P sells the entire 80% interest on January 1, 19X3, for $320,000. Assuming the use of the simple equity method, Company P's separate statements reflect the following:

Purchase price	$250,000
Share of subsidiary income, 19X1, 80% × $40,000	32,000
Share of subsidiary income, 19X2, 80% × $25,000	20,000
Investment in Co. S, December 31, 19X2	$302,000

The investment account and the parent's January 1, 19X3 Retained Earnings balance reflect a $52,000 increase as a result of subsidiary operations in 19X1 and 19X2. On this basis, it appears that there is an $18,000 gain on the sale of the investment ($320,000 price less $302,000 simple-equity-adjusted cost). This result does not agree, however, with the consolidated financial statements prepared for 19X1 and 19X2, which included, as an expense, the amortizations of excess required by the determination and distribution of excess schedule. The parent's share of subsidiary income appeared as follows in the consolidated statements:

	19X1	19X2	Total
Share of subsidiary income to Company P (80%)	$32,000	$20,000	$52,000
Less amortization of excess of cost of investment over book value:			
Adjustment for depreciation on equipment:			
$20,000 ÷ 5 = $4,000 per year	(4,000)	(4,000)	(8,000)
Adjustment for amortization of goodwill:			
$30,000 ÷ 10 = $3,000 per year	(3,000)	(3,000)	(6,000)
Net increase in Company P income due to ownership of Company S investment	$25,000	$13,000	$38,000

Thus, while Company P's separate books show a $52,000 share of Company S income, the consolidated statements reflect only $38,000, the difference being caused by the $14,000 of amortizations required by the determination and distribution of excess schedule. Clearly, the recording of the sale of the parent's interest must be based on the $38,000 share of income, since this amount of income is shown on the prior income statements of the consolidated firm. Before recording the sale of the investment, Company P must adjust its books to be consistent with prior consolidated statements. The entry needed will adjust the January

1, 19X3 Retained Earnings on the separate books of the parent to the December 31, 19X2 balance shown for the controlling interest in Retained Earnings on the consolidated statements. The adjusting entry on the books of Company P is:

Retained Earnings (January 1, 19X3).....................	14,000	
Investment in Company S		14,000
To adjust investment account and Company P Retained Earnings for amortizations made on past consolidated statements.		

If the sophisticated equity method were used, the amortizations would already be reflected in the investment account and no adjustment would be needed. Under either method, the entry to record the sale would then be:

Cash	320,000	
Investment in Company S ($302,000 less $14,000)		288,000
Gain on Disposal of Subsidiary		32,000
To record the gain on the sale of the 80% interest in Company S.		

Note that the $14,000 adjusting entry for the past years' amortizations of excess would normally have been made on the consolidated work sheet for 19X3. However, since there will be no further consolidations, the adjustment must be made directly on Company P's books. The gain (net of tax) on the disposal of the subsidiary will appear as a separate item on the income statement for 19X3 if the sale of the subsidiary meets the criteria for a disposal of a business segment.

In this example, if Company P had used the cost method, the investment account would still be shown at the original cost of $250,000. It would then be necessary to update the investment account and Retained Earnings on the separate books of Company P to include the $38,000 (net of amortizations) 19X1 and 19X2 Company P share of subsidiary income. This adjustment would allow the accounts of the parent on January 1, 19X3, to conform to past consolidated statements. The following entries on the books of Company P would be made to record the sale of the parent's 80% interest:

Investment in Company S	38,000	
Retained Earnings (January 1, 19X3).................		38,000
To record parent's share of subsidiary income as shown on prior years' consolidated statements.		
Cash	320,000	
Investment in Company S ($250,000 + $38,000)		288,000
Gain on Disposal of Subsidiary		32,000

Assume that the investment in the previous example was sold for $320,000 on July 1, 19X3, and that Company S reported income of $12,000 for the first six months of 19X3. Since Company S will not be a part of the consolidated group at the end of the period, the results of its operations will not be consolidated with those of the parent. The parent must therefore record its share of subsidiary income for the current period to the date of disposal. The parent's net share of subsidiary income would be calculated on a basis consistent with past consolidated statements, as follows:

80% Company P interest		$ 9,600
Less amortizations of excess of cost over book value that would have been made on consolidated statements:		
Equipment depreciation adjustment, $4,000 per year × ½ year		(2,000)
Amortization of goodwill adjustment, $3,000 per year × ½ year		(1,500)
Net share of subsidiary income		$ 6,100

The parent would proceed to record the July 1, 19X3 sale of its subsidiary investment as follows:

1. Assuming the past use of the simple equity method, the parent will adjust its investment account on January 1, 19X3, to reflect the amortizations made on past consolidated statements (as calculated on page 434).

Retained Earnings (January 1, 19X3).............	14,000	
Investment in Company S		14,000

2. Record the parent's net share of subsidiary income for the partial year. This amount is the $6,100 income net of amortizations.

Investment in Company S	6,100	
Operating Income for Subsidiary Disposed of During Year		6,100

3. Record sale of investment for $320,000.

Cash	320,000	
Investment in Company S		294,100
Gain on Disposal of Subsidiary		25,900

The adjusted cost of the investment is determined as follows:

Original cost (January 1, 19X1)	$250,000
Simple equity income adjustments for 19X1 and 19X2	52,000
Amortization of excess (entry 1)	(14,000)
Share of Company S income for six months (entry 2)	6,100
Net cost, July 1, 19X3	$294,100

Sale of Portion of Subsidiary Investment

The sale of a portion of an investment in a subsidiary requires unique treatment, depending on whether effective control is lost as a result of the sale. Special procedures must also be used when a sale of a partial interest occurs during a reporting period.

Loss of Control. Though it is unusual to do so, a parent may sell a portion of its investment in a subsidiary, so that its remaining interest falls below 50%. This situation may occur for foreign subsidiaries when the foreign government passes a law forbidding control of its firms by nonresidents. If an interest is reduced below 50%, consolidation procedures will no longer apply. This situation would require that the parent company books be adjusted to make them consistent with prior consolidated statements. Exactly the same adjusting entries as in the immediately preceding section are needed to adjust the parent's investment account. Note that the adjustments are made for the entire interest previously owned, not just the portion sold. In the preceding example, if Company P sells one half of its 80% interest, the investment account is adjusted for the entire 80% interest in past and current years' subsidiary income, net of amortizations. The 40% interest sold must be adjusted to record the sale properly, but the 40% interest retained must also be adjusted, since it will no longer be consolidated. Past adjustments that would be handled as a part of the annual consolidation process must now be made directly in the investment account, so that the investment remaining conforms with APB Opinion No. 18. The sophisticated equity method described in APB Opinion No. 18 will be applied to remaining interests of 20% or more.

Assume that one half of the Company P investment of the preceding section is sold for $160,000 on July 1, 19X3. The entries would be made as follows:

1. Assuming the past use of the simple equity method, the parent will adjust its investment account on January 1, 19X3, to reflect the amortizations made on past consolidated statements.

Retained Earnings (January 1, 19X3).............	14,000	
Investment in Company S		14,000

2. Record the parent's net share of subsidiary income for the partial year. This amount is the $6,100 income net of amortizations, as calculated on page 436.

Investment in Company S	6,100	
Subsidiary Income		6,100

    Note that this income is no longer from a "disposed-of subsidiary," and is treated as ordinary income. A sale of a partial interest will not qualify as a "discontinued segment."

3. Record the sale of the investment for $160,000. The resulting gain is always ordinary income and never a gain from a "discontinued segment."

Cash	160,000	
Investment in Company S (½ of $294,100 adjusted cost calculated on page 436)		147,050
Gain on Sale of Investment...................		12,950

These entries indicate that although the sale of a portion of an investment in a subsidiary could result in loss of control, it is ordinarily not sufficient to qualify as a discontinued segment. Thus, the operating results on the investment to the sale date and the gain or loss on the sale would be shown as a part of ordinary income from continuing operations.

Control Retained. The parent may sell a portion of its interest in a subsidiary but still have an interest that exceeds 50% after the sale. While it is tempting to view such transactions as resulting in a gain or loss which would be included in net income, it is theoretically unsound to do so. From a consolidated viewpoint, a portion of the combined shares of the subsidiary has been previously purchased from outside parties and is now being sold to the minority shareholders. For example, on January 1, 19X1, a parent might purchase from outside parties 8,000 of the total 10,000 shares of a subsidiary. On January 1, 19X3, the parent might sell 2,000 shares and thereby lower its percentage of ownership to 60%. Since the parent still has control, the 2,000 shares are, in essence, sold to minority shareholders. Such a transaction is strictly one between the consolidated firm and its shareholders and amounts to a treasury stock transaction. The parent must adjust its paid-in capital, rather than its income, for such transactions.

To illustrate the recording of such a partial sale, return to the example for which a determination and distribution of excess schedule was prepared on page 434. Assume that on January 1, 19X3, Company P sells 2,000 shares to lower its total interest to 60%. Only the portion of the investment account sold is to be adjusted to the sophisticated equity method to allow the proper recording of the sale. The 60% retained need not be adjusted on the Company P books, since all amortization adjustments on the 60% interest will be made on future consolidated statements. The adjustment of the 20% interest on the separate books of Company P must agree with the treatment of that interest in prior consolidated statements. Assuming the use of the simple equity method, the portion of the investment sold must be adjusted for its share of the past amortizations made on consolidated statements. Since the 19X1 and 19X2 amortizations on page 436 totaled $14,000 for an 80% interest, the amortizations for the 20% interest sold would be one fourth of $14,000, or $3,500. The parent would make the following entry:

Retained Earnings (January 1, 19X3)..................	3,500	
Investment in Company S		3,500
To adjust for amortizations made on previous con-		
solidated statements for the portion of the subsidiary		
investment sold.		

To record the sale of the investment for $80,000, the parent would next remove one fourth of the simple-equity-adjusted cost of January 1, 19X3 ($302,000 as shown on page 434), as modified by the previous $3,500 adjustment:

Cash	80,000	
Investment in Company S [(¼ × $302,000) − $3,500		
amortization adjustment].......................		72,000
Paid-In Capital from Sale of Subsidiary Stock		8,000

A sale price below $72,000 would decrease previous paid-in capital. If no paid-in capital existed, the parent's Retained Earnings would be decreased. If the parent fails to record the transaction properly, a correcting entry would be needed in future consolidated work sheets. The most common errors would be failing to adjust the investment account for consolidated amortizations, and/or treating the sale as resulting in ordinary gain or loss. In practice, the lack of materiality may permit these errors to be tolerated.

If the parent in the previous example had used the cost method, only the portion of the investment sold would be adjusted to the sophisticated equity method on the parent's books. The analysis on page 434 shows that the parent's 80% share of income for 19X1 and 19X2 was $38,000 on a consolidated basis, net of amortizations. The 20% interest sold must be adjusted by one fourth of $38,000, or $9,500. The remaining 60% will be adjusted in future work sheets. The entry to adjust the 20% interest would be:

```
Investment in Company S .............................     9,500
    Retained Earnings (January 1, 19X3)................              9,500
        To adjust for the parent's share of past consolidated
        income pertaining to the interest sold.
```

The parent would then proceed to record the sale as follows:

```
Cash ................................................    80,000
    Investment in Company S (¼ of original $250,000
        cost + $9,500 equity income) ..................            72,000
    Paid-In Capital from Sale of Subsidiary Stock ......             8,000
```

Intraperiod Sale of a Partial Interest. When a sale of an interest during the reporting period does not result in loss of control, careful analysis is needed to insure that the work sheet closely adheres to consolidation theory. Referring to the situation on pages 433 and 434, assume that Company P sells one fourth of its 80% interest for $80,000 on July 1, 19X3, and that subsidiary income for the first half of the year is $12,000. Assuming the use of the simple equity method, the parent would adjust the investment account and Retained Earnings at the beginning of the year as follows:

```
Retained Earnings (January 1, 19X3)..................     3,500
    Investment in Company S ...........................              3,500
        To record one fourth of the $14,000 amortizations
        shown on page 434 for 19X1 and 19X2.
```

A parent using the cost method would adjust Retained Earnings for the subsidiary income net of amortizations for 19X1 and 19X2 (20% × $38,000 income on a consolidated basis).

The parent would next make a sophisticated equity method adjustment for its share of consolidated income for the first half of 19X3, applicable to the 20% interest sold:

```
Investment in Company S .............................     1,525
    Subsidiary Income .................................              1,525
        To record share of first six months' consolidated in-
        come applicable to the 20% interest sold. Calculated
        as follows:
```

Income on 20% Company S interest sold...........................	$2,400
Less amortizations of excess over cost that would be necessary on consolidated statements:	
Equipment depreciation adjustment, $4,000 per year × ½ year × ¼ interest sold	(500)
Amortization of goodwill adjustment, $3,000 per year × ½ year × ¼ interest sold	(375)
Net share of income on interest sold..............................	$1,525

Finally, the parent would record the sale:

Cash	80,000	
Investment in Company S [(¼ of $302,000) − $3,500 amortizations + $1,525 income]....................		73,525
Paid-In Capital from Sale of Subsidiary Stock		6,475

The sale of a partial interest that does not result in loss of control requires special procedures on the consolidated work sheet for the period in which the sale occurs. Illustration VI on pages 442-443 is a consolidated financial statements work sheet for Companies P and S for the year 19X3. The following should be noted in the illustration:

1. Investment in Company S reflects the simple equity balance on December 31, 19X3, for the remaining 60% interest held.
   The balance is computed as follows:

December 31, 19X2 balance applicable to remaining (60%) interest held at year end, ¾ × $302,000	$226,500
Add 60% of subsidiary reported income of $30,000	18,000
Simple equity balance, December 31, 19X3.............	$244,500

2. Paid-In Capital from Sale of Subsidiary Stock is the additional paid-in capital resulting from the 20% interest sold.
3. Subsidiary Income includes 60% of the subsidiary's $30,000 19X3 income, plus the $1,525 earned on the 20% interest prior to its sale.

Illustration VI concludes by distributing consolidated income according to the ownership interests in effect during the period. Work sheets of later periods would not include any complications resulting from the sale. Only the period of sale requires special analysis. The income distribution schedules are as follows:

Income Distribution Schedules

Subsidiary Company S income distribution

	Internally generated net income	$30,000
Minority interest for full year (40%)	$12,000	
Less income purchased (20% of $12,000, first 6 months)	2,400	
Minority interest	$ 9,600	

Parent Company P income distribution

Depreciation adjustment on 60% interest	$ 3,000	Internally generated net income	$100,000
Goodwill amortization on 60% interest	2,250		
		Adjusted net income	$ 94,750
		60% of subsidiary income of $30,000	18,000
		20% of subsidiary income for first 6 months (net of amortizations)	1,525
		Controlling interest	$114,275

If the parent, Company P, had used the cost method, there would be very few changes in Illustration VI. Step 1 would be unchanged; however, an entry would be needed to convert the remaining 60% interest to the simple equity method at the beginning of the year. Step 2 would not be applicable, since there would be no current-year equity adjustment to reverse. Steps 3 through 6 would remain the same.

Complications Resulting from Intercompany Transactions. When a sale of subsidiary stock results in a loss of control, the parent should adjust its investment account on the date of the sale for its share of unrealized subsidiary gains and losses resulting from intercompany transactions. When control is not lost as the result of a sale of subsidiary shares, the adjustment on the consolidated work sheet for unrealized gains and losses resulting from previous intercompany transactions need be recorded only as it applies to the interest sold. The remaining controlling interest share of these gains and losses can be adjusted on subsequent consolidated work sheets. On these work sheets, retained earnings adjustments for unrealized gains and losses would be distributed according to the relative ownership interests existing on the dates the work sheets are prepared.

APPENDIX: WORK SHEET FOR A CONSOLIDATED BALANCE SHEET

Previous chapters displayed procedures applicable to financial statement work sheets that produced a consolidated income statement, a retained earnings statement, and a balance sheet. However, there may be occasions when only consolidated balance sheets are required, and the separate balance sheets of the affiliates form the starting point for consolidation procedures. Such occasions are rare in practice, but are of concern to students desiring to take the CPA examination. Past examinations have used balance-sheet-only consolidation problems as an expedient method for testing purposes. This type of problem requires

(Credit balance amounts
are in parentheses)

	Trial Balance	
	Company P	Company S
Investment in Co. S (60%)	244,500	
Equipment	600,000	100,000
Accumulated Depreciation—Equipment	(100,000)	(60,000)
Other Assets	581,500	305,000
Goodwill		
Common Stock, Co. P	(500,000)	
Paid-In Capital from Sale of Subsidiary Stock, Co. P	(6,475)	
Retained Earnings, Jan. 1, 19X3, Co. P	(700,000)	
Common Stock, Co. S		(100,000)
Retained Earnings, Jan. 1, 19X3, Co. S		(215,000)
Sales	(500,000)	(200,000)
Cost of Goods Sold	350,000	140,000
Expenses	50,000	30,000
Subsidiary Income	(19,525)	
Income Sold to Minority (second 20% block)		
	0	0
Consolidated Net Income		
To Minority Interest (see distribution schedule)		
To Controlling Interest (see distribution schedule)		
Total Minority Interest, Dec. 31, 19X3		
Retained Earnings, Controlling Interest, Dec. 31, 19X3		

Eliminations:

1. The income earned by the parent on the 20% interest sold on July 1, though earned by the controlling interest, now belongs to the minority interest. The minority interest owns 20% of the reported subsidiary income for the half year ($12,000). The minority is unaffected by amortizations resulting from a previous price paid by the parent. Note that Step 1 credits the account, Income Sold to Minority, to accomplish the transfer of the income to the minority interest. The offsetting debits include the elimination of the subsidiary income recorded by the parent on the 20% interest and the recording of the half-year's amortizations of the excess price paid by the parent for the interest sold. Amortizations based on an 80% interest for the first half of the year are proper, since the consolidation involves an 80% controlling interest for the first half of the year and a 60% controlling interest for the second half of the year.

(2) Eliminate parent's entry recording its 60% share of subsidiary's net income. This step restores the 60% interest to its simple-equity-adjusted cost at the beginning of the year, so that the investment can be eliminated against subsidiary equity balances at the beginning of the year.

Interest During Period—No Loss of Control
Subsidiary Company S
Financial Statements
December 31, 19X3

Eliminations Dr.	Eliminations Cr.	Consolidated Income Statement	Minority Interest	Controlling Retained Earnings	Consolidated Balance Sheet
	(2) 18,000				
	(3) 189,000				
	(4) 37,500				
					700,000
(4) 15,000	(5) 9,000				(154,000)
					886,500
(4) 22,500	(6) 6,750				15,750
					(500,000)
					(6,475)
(5) 6,000				(689,500)	
(6) 4,500					
(3) 60,000			(40,000)		
(3) 129,000			(86,000)		
		(700,000)			
		490,000			
(1) 875		86,125			
(5) 3,000					
(6) 2,250					
(1) 1,525					
(2) 18,000					
	(1) 2,400		(2,400)		
262,650	262,650				
		(123,875)			
		9,600	(9,600)		
		114,275		(114,275)	
			(138,000)		(138,000)
				(803,775)	(803,775)
					0

(3) Eliminate 60% of the subsidiary equity balances at the beginning of the year against the investment account. An excess cost of $37,500 remains. This amount is three fourths (60% ÷ 80%) of the original excess shown on page 434, since only a 60% interest is retained, as compared to an original investment of 80%.

(4) Since only three fourths of the original investment remains, 75% of the excesses shown in the original determination and distribution of excess schedule on page 434 are recorded.

(5) Seventy-five percent of the original $4,000 annual depreciation adjustments is recorded for the past two years and the current year. Note that the remaining depreciation adjustments applicable to the interest sold are already recorded.

(6) Seventy-five percent of the original $3,000 annual goodwill amortization is recorded for the past two years and the current year. Again, amortizations of goodwill applicable to the interest sold have already been recorded.

less time to solve, while still testing the candidates' knowledge of consolidations.

A balance sheet work sheet requires only adjustments to balance sheet accounts. No adjustments for nominal accounts are required. For example, intercompany merchandise sales require no elimination except for the profit contained in the ending inventory. The following sections examine the simplified procedures that are used on a consolidated balance sheet work sheet.

Investment Account

When the investment account is maintained under the simple equity method, it will reflect the same point in time as do the subsidiary equity balances. There is no need to eliminate the parent's entry for its share of subsidiary income. Instead, the pro rata share of subsidiary equity balances may be eliminated directly against the investment account.

Investments maintained at cost should be converted to the simple equity method as of the end of the year to agree in time with the subsidiary equity balances. The entire conversion adjustment is carried to controlling Retained Earnings.

Excesses are distributed according to the determination and distribution of excess schedules. Once distributed, the excesses are amortized to the balance sheet date, and the entire amortization is carried to controlling Retained Earnings.

Merchandise Sales

Only the intercompany profit in the ending inventory needs adjustment. The profit is eliminated from the inventory and from Retained Earnings. The adjustment to Retained Earnings is allocated according to the minority/controlling ownership percentages in effect when the subsidiary made the intercompany sale. If the parent made the sale, the adjustment is made only to controlling Retained Earnings. The intercompany profit in the beginning inventory either has been realized through subsequent sale of the merchandise to an outside party, or if the units in the beginning inventory are still on hand at year end, they would be included in the adjustment for intercompany profit in the ending inventory.

Plant Asset Sales

The only matter for concern in the case of intercompany plant asset sales is adjustment of the asset accounts and Retained Earnings for the undepreciated portion of intercompany gain or loss as of the end of the year. The asset account is adjusted to its cost to the consolidated firm; accumulated depreciation is adjusted for all periods to date; and Retained Earnings is adjusted for the undepreciated profit or loss which is to be deferred to future periods. If the subsidiary sells to the parent, the Retained Earnings adjustment is allocated to the minority and controlling interests that existed when the subsidiary sold the plant asset.

Intercompany Investment in Bonds

The amortized balance in the investment account is simply eliminated against Bonds Payable and any related discount or premium balance. The net disparity in amounts is the remaining net retirement gain or loss at year end, which is carried to Retained Earnings. When the subsidiary is the issuer, the Retained Earnings adjustment is allocated to the minority and controlling interests.

To illustrate the procedures used for balance sheet work sheets, assume that Company P purchased an 80% interest in Company S on January 1, 19X1. The determination and distribution of excess schedule prepared for this purchase is presented below. Company P uses the cost method to record its investment in Company S.

Price paid		$750,000
Interest acquired:		
Common stock, $10 par	$200,000	
Retained earnings, January 1, 19X1	600,000	
Total equity	$800,000	
Ownership interest.................................	80%	640,000
Excess of cost over book value		$110,000
Attributable to building (10-year remaining life)		30,000
Attributable to goodwill (20-year life)...................		$ 80,000

The facts pertaining to intercompany sales by Company S to Company P are as follows:

	19X3	19X4
Intercompany sales	$80,000	$100,000
Gross profit	30%	40%
Intercompany sales in ending inventory	20,000	40,000
Unpaid balance, end of the year	30,000	35,000

On January 1, 19X2, Company P sold a new piece of equipment, which cost $10,000, to Company S for $15,000. Company S is depreciating the equipment over five years on a straight-line basis.

Company S has outstanding $100,000 of 5%, 20-year bonds due January 1, 19X9. Interest is payable January 1 for the previous year. The bonds were originally sold to yield 6%. On January 1, 19X3, Company P purchased the bonds on the open market at a price to yield 8%.

Illustration VII on pages 446-447 contains the balance sheets and eliminations for Companies P and S on December 31, 19X4. After the eliminations are completed, the amounts are combined to produce the consolidated balance sheet. The real time saving of the balance sheet work sheet results from the fact that there is no consolidated income to calculate and to distribute.

Illustration
Company P and
Work Sheet for
December

(Credit balance amounts
are in parentheses)

	Balance Sheet	
	Company P	Company S
Cash	61,936	106,535
Accounts Receivable	80,000	200,000
Inventory, Dec. 31, 19X4	60,000	150,000
Land	300,000	250,000
Building	800,000	600,000
Accumulated Depreciation—Building	(400,000)	(100,000)
Equipment	120,000	95,000
Accumulated Depreciation—Equipment	(70,000)	(30,000)
Investment in Company S Bonds	90,064	
Investment in Company S Stock	750,000	
Goodwill		
Accounts Payable	(92,000)	(75,000)
Bonds Payable		(100,000)
Discount on Bonds Payable		3,465
Common Stock, Company P	(500,000)	
Retained Earnings, Dec. 31, 19X4, Co. P	(1,200,000)	
Common Stock, Company S		(200,000)
Retained Earnings, Dec. 31, 19X4, Co. S		(900,000)
	0	0
Minority Interest		

Eliminations:

Conv. The Investment in Company S Stock is converted to the simple equity method as of December 31, 19X4, as follows: 80% × $300,000 increase in Retained Earnings = $240,000.

(1) Eighty percent of the Company S subsidiary equity balances are eliminated against the investment in stock account.

(2) The $110,000 excess of cost is distributed according to the determination and distribution of excess schedule.

(3) The excess attributable to the building is amortized for four years at $3,000 per year.

(4) The excess attributable to goodwill is amortized for four years at $4,000 per year.

(5) The intercompany trade balance is eliminated.

(6) The gross profit of $16,000 (40% × $40,000) recorded by Company S and applicable to merchandise in Company P's ending inventory is deferred by reducing the inventory and reducing Retained Earnings. Since the sale was made by Company S, the adjustment was allocated to minority and controlling Retained Earnings.

(7) As of December 31, 19X4, $2,000 (2/5) of profit on the equipment sale is still to be deferred. Since the sale was by Company P, the controlling Retained Earnings absorbs this adjustment, and the equipment and accumulated depreciation accounts are adjusted.

(8) The Investment in Company S Bonds is eliminated against the net book value of the bonds. The net gain on the work sheet retirement is allocated to the minority and controlling Retained Earnings, since the subsidiary originally issued the bonds.

VII
Subsidiary Company S
Consolidated Balance Sheet
31, 19X4

| Eliminations | | | | Consolidated |
Dr.		Cr.	Minority Interest	Balance Sheet
				168,471
		(5) 35,000		245,000
		(6) 16,000		194,000
				550,000
				1,400,000
(2) 30,000		(3) 12,000		(482,000)
		(7) 5,000		210,000
(7) 3,000				(97,000)
		(8) 90,064		
Conv. 240,000		(1) 880,000		
		(2) 110,000		
(2) 80,000		(4) 16,000		64,000
(5) 35,000				(132,000)
(8) 100,000				
		(8) 3,465		
				(500,000)
(3) 12,000		Conv. 240,000		(1,402,377)
(4) 16,000				
(6) 12,800		(8) 5,177		
(7) 2,000				
(1) 160,000			(40,000)	
(1) 720,000		(8) 1,294	(178,094)	
(6) 3,200				
1,414,000		1,414,000		
			(218,094)	(218,094)
				0

QUESTIONS

1. Under what circumstances is a determination and distribution of excess schedule needed when a parent acquires its controlling interest in stock directly from the subsidiary?
2. What is a piecemeal purchase? Describe the accounting consequences of such an acquisition as they affect the determination and distribution of excess schedules and work sheet procedures.
3. Is it possible that a piecemeal acquisition could include a transaction which qualifies as a pooling of interests? If so, explain the ramifications.

4. Explain how the equity method investment account balance can generally be recalculated to verify its correctness.
5. What special consolidation procedures are required when a subsidiary has preferred stock outstanding?
6. If a parent company owns 80% of a subsidiary company's preferred stock and 45% of the subsidiary's common stock, would the parent company normally have a controlling interest in the subsidiary company?
7. What factors determine whether the sale of an entire parent interest in a subsidiary qualifies as a disposal of a segment?
8. Parent Company sold its entire 75% interest in the Subsidiary Company for $100,000. May it be said that the parent realized a $20,000 gain on the sale (a) assuming a correct simple equity method investment account balance of $80,000? (b) assuming a correct cost method investment account balance of $80,000?
9. Describe the adjustments required when a parent sells enough of its ownership interest in a subsidiary so as to lose control. How do these adjustments differ when the parent sells part of its ownership interest, but not enough to lose control?

EXERCISES

Exercise 1. On January 1, 19X1, Power Company purchased a 70% interest in Titan Company common stock for $100,000. Power purchased another 20% of Titan's common stock on December 31, 19X2, for $40,000. Immediately prior to the second purchase, Power and Titan Companies had the following balance sheets:

Assets	Power Company	Titan Company
Current assets	$ 250,000	$ 50,000
Investment in Titan Company	121,000	—
Property, plant, and equipment (net)	650,000	150,000
Total assets	$1,021,000	$200,000

Liabilities and Equity				
Liabilities		$ 300,000		$ 50,000
Equity:				
Common stock, $10 par	$600,000		$120,000	
Retained earnings	121,000	721,000	30,000	150,000
Total liabilities and equity		$1,021,000		$200,000

Any excess of cost over book value, on either purchase, is to be attributed to goodwill with a 10-year life. The investment in Titan Company account is correctly adjusted for the simple equity method as of December 31, 19X2.

Prepare a consolidated balance sheet for Power Company and its subsidiary immediately subsequent to the purchase of the additional 20% block by Power.

Exercise 2. The following determination and distribution of excess schedule was prepared by Siedle Company on January 1, 19X4, the date it acquired a 60% interest in Todd Company:

Price paid		$200,000
Interest acquired:		
Common stock, $1 par	$ 20,000	
Paid-in capital in excess of par	220,000	
Retained earnings	60,000	
Total subsidiary equity	$300,000	
Interest acquired	60%	180,000
Excess of cost over book value		$ 20,000
Attributable to machine:		
60% × $20,000 undervaluation (to be amortized over 4 years)		(12,000)
Goodwill (20-year life)		$ 8,000

On January 1, 19X6, Siedle Company purchases another 20% interest in Todd Company for $80,000. Immediately prior to this purchase, Todd Company had the following balance sheet:

Assets			Liabilities and Equity		
Current assets	$100,000		Liabilities		$ 60,000
Land	30,000		Equity:		
Buildings (net)	150,000		Common stock,		
Machinery (net)	120,000		$1 par	$ 20,000	
			Paid-in capital in		
			excess of par	220,000	
			Retained earnings .	100,000	340,000
Total assets	$400,000		Total liabilities and equity		$400,000

Siedle Company's analysis on January 1, 19X6, indicated that the machinery on Todd's balance sheet is now undervalued by $8,000 with a 2-year remaining life, and the land is undervalued by $10,000.

Prepare the determination and distribution of excess schedule for the 20% purchase.

Exercise 3. Garlock Corporation acquired a 10% interest in Tidewater Company for $25,000 on January 1, 19X1. The following determination and distribution of excess schedule was prepared at that time:

Price paid		$25,000
Interest acquired:		
Common stock, $20 par	$250,000	
Retained earnings (deficit)	(50,000)	
Total subsidiary equity	$200,000	
Ownership interest	10%	20,000
Excess of cost over book value		$ 5,000
Attributed to equipment:		
10% × $30,000 undervaluation (to be amortized over 10 years)		3,000
Attributed to goodwill (20-year life)		$ 2,000

From January 1, 19X1, through December 31, 19X5, Tidewater Company paid no dividends on common stock and earned the following annual incomes:

19X1	($10,000)	19X4	$40,000
19X2	5,000	19X5	30,000
19X3	20,000		

On January 1, 19X6, Garlock purchased 6,250 additional shares of Tidewater common stock for $160,000. This purchase increased Garlock's ownership interest in Tidewater to 60%. Tidewater had the following balance sheet immediately prior to Garlock's second purchase:

Assets		Liabilities and Equity		
Current assets	$110,000	Liabilities		$ 65,000
Building (net)	140,000	Equity:		
Equipment (net)...............	100,000	Common stock,		
		$20 par	$250,000	
		Retained earnings .	35,000	285,000
Total assets	$350,000	Total liabilities and equity		$350,000

Garlock has determined that Tidewater's equipment is now undervalued by $20,000 with a 5-year remaining life. All other book values approximate market value.

(1) Prepare a determination and distribution of excess schedule for the second purchase. Any goodwill is assumed to have a 20-year life.
(2) Record the investment made on January 1, 19X6.
(3) Since control has now been achieved, Garlock will use the simple equity method for its investment in Tidewater. Assuming that the cost method was used for the original 10% investment, convert the 10% block to the equity method as of January 1, 19X6.

Exercise 4. James Company purchased a 10% interest in PB Industries on January 1, 19X2, and another 60% interest on January 1, 19X4, for $50,000 and $360,000 respectively. PB had the following stockholders' equity immediately prior to each purchase:

Stockholders' Equity	Jan. 1, 19X2	Jan. 1, 19X4
Common stock, $7 par	$350,000	$350,000
Paid-in capital in excess of par	100,000	100,000
Retained earnings	20,000	100,000
Total equity	$470,000	$550,000

James' analysis on the two purchase dates revealed the following: (1) On January 1, 19X2, PB's equipment was undervalued by $10,000 and had a remaining life of 5 years. (2) On January 1, 19X4, PB's equipment was undervalued by $9,000 with a 3-year remaining life. (3) Any excess attributable to goodwill is to be amortized over 10 years.

Assume that PB had income of $30,000 in 19X4 and $50,000 in 19X5 and paid its first dividend, a $.20 per share dividend to common stock, on December 30, 19X5.

(1) Prepare a determination and distribution of excess schedule for each investment.
(2) Assuming that the cost method is used for both investments, prepare the calculations necessary to convert the investment account to its simple-equity-adjusted balance on December 31, 19X5.

Exercise 5. On January 1, 19X2, Beatley Company purchased 80% of the outstanding common stock of Mullen Corporation for $225,000. On this date, Mullen Corporation's stockholders' equity was as follows:

6% Preferred stock, 1,000 shares, $100 par	$100,000
Common stock, 20,000 shares, $10 par	200,000
Retained earnings	60,000
Total stockholders' equity	$360,000

Prepare a determination and distribution of excess schedule under each of the following situations (any excess of cost over book value is attributable to goodwill with a 40-year life):

(a) The preferred stock is cumulative, two years in arrears at January 1, 19X2, and has a liquidation value equal to par.

(b) The preferred stock is noncumulative, but fully participating.

(c) The preferred stock is cumulative, 3 years in arrears as of January 1, 19X2, and 10% (limited) participating.

Exercise 6. Ace Construction Company had the following stockholders' equity on January 1, 19X1, the date on which Ressel Company purchased a 60% interest in the common stock for $600,000:

8% Cumulative preferred stock, 5,000 shares, $100 par	$ 500,000
Common stock, 40,000 shares, $20 par	800,000
Retained earnings	100,000
Total stockholders' equity	$1,400,000

Ace Construction Company did not pay preferred dividends in 19X0.

(1) Prepare a determination and distribution of excess schedule. Assume that the preferred stock's liquidation value is equal to par and any excess of cost is attributuable to goodwill with a 20-year life.

(2) Assume that Ace Construction has the following net income (loss) for 19X1 and 19X2, and does not pay any dividends:

19X1	$50,000
19X2	(10,000)

Prepare the entries necessary on Ressel's books to adjust its investment account to simple equity at the end of 19X1 and 19X2.

Exercise 7. Limback Corporation purchased 1,000 shares of 8%, $100 par cumulative preferred stock of the Lakeside Corporation on January 1, 19X1, for their par value. Lakeside issued a total of 2,000 preferred shares. Dividends were paid on preferred stock in 19X1, but not in subsequent years. Limback accounts for its investment using the cost method.

On December 31, 19X4, Limback purchased an 80% interest in the common stock of the Lakeside Corporation for $300,000. The stockholders' equity of Lakeside was as follows on December 31, 19X4:

8% Cumulative preferred stock, 2,000 shares, $100 par	$200,000
Common stock, $10 stated value	300,000
Retained earnings	60,000
Total stockholders' equity	$560,000

Any excess of cost over book value is attributable to goodwill with a 20-year life. The investment is accounted for under the cost method.

During 19X5 and 19X6, no dividends were paid. Retained Earnings on December 31, 19X6, was $100,000. Income during 19X7 was $50,000.

(1) Calculate the preferred and common stockholders' equity claim on retained earnings on January 1, 19X7.
(2) Prepare the cost-to-simple-equity conversion that would be made on the December 31, 19X7 consolidated work sheet for the investment in preferred stock. Prepare the work sheet elimination for the investment in preferred stock.
(3) Prepare the cost-to-simple-equity conversion which would be made on the December 31, 19X7 consolidated work sheet elimination for the investment in common stock. Prepare the work sheet elimination for the investment in common stock.

Exercise 8. On January 1, 19X1, the Fritz Fiber Company purchased an 80% interest in Colfax Cotton Company for $300,000. Fritz Fiber Company prepared the following determination and distribution of excess schedule at that time:

Price paid		$300,000
Interest acquired:		
Common stock, $50 par	$250,000	
Retained earnings	40,000	
Total subsidiary equity	$290,000	
Ownership interest	80%	232,000
Excess of cost over book value attributed to goodwill (10-year life)		$ 68,000

Colfax Cotton Company had income of $30,000 for 19X1 and $40,000 for 19X2. No dividends were paid. Fritz sold its entire investment in Colfax Cotton Company on January 1, 19X3, for $325,000.
(1) Assuming that Fritz used the simple equity method to reflect its investment in Colfax, prepare Fritz's entries to record the sale.
(2) Assuming that Fritz used the cost method to reflect its investment in Colfax, prepare the entry to record the sale on Fritz's books.

Exercise 9. The Jose Company has the following balance sheet on December 31, 19X5:

Assets		Liabilities and Equity		
Current assets	$180,000	Liabilities		$100,000
Investment in Bathke Company .	100,000	Equity:		
Property, plant, and equipment		Common stock,		
(net)	420,000	$10 par	$500,000	
		Retained earnings ...	100,000	600,000
Total assets	$700,000	Total liabilities and equity		$700,000

The investment in Bathke Company account reflects the original cost of a 60% investment (30,000 shares) purchased on January 1, 19X2. On the date of the purchase, Bathke's stockholders' equity had a book value of $150,000. Bathke's book values approximated market, except for a machine that was undervalued by $10,000 with a 5-year remaining life. Any additional excess was attributed to goodwill with a 10-year life.
A review of Bathke's past financial statements reveals the following:

	Income	Dividends Paid
19X2	$ 20,000	$ 2,400
19X3	40,000	3,600
19X4	30,000	3,600
19X5	20,000	3,600
	$110,000	$13,200

Jose sold 2,500 shares of Bathke common stock on January 1, 19X6, for $14,500.

Prepare the necessary entries on Jose's books to accurately account for the sale of the 2,500 Bathke shares.

Exercise 10. On July 1, 19X8, Dynamo Company sold 4,500 shares of Stibbins Company stock to reduce its investment from 60% to 45%. Stibbins Company is a foreign firm. The sale was in response to a recent change in law in Stibbins' country which prohibits the ownership of a controlling interest by a nonresident. Dynamo received $150,000 from the sale of Stibbins stock. Dynamo had originally purchased the 60% interest on January 1, 19X5, at which time the following determination and distribution of excess schedule was prepared:

Price paid		$450,000
Interest acquired:		
Common stock, $15 par	$450,000	
Retained earnings	150,000	
Total subsidiary equity	$600,000	
Ownership interest	60%	360,000
Excess of cost over book value		$ 90,000
Attributable to building:		
60% × $50,000 undervaluation (to be amortized over		
15 years)		(30,000)
Goodwill (20-year life)		$ 60,000

Stibbins Company reported net income of $35,000 for the six months ended July 1, 19X8. Dynamo's simple-equity-adjusted investment account was $498,000 as of December 31, 19X7.

Prepare all the entries necessary on Dynamo's books to account for the partial sale of its investment in Stibbins Company. (Control is assumed to be lost with the sale.)

PROBLEMS

Problem 10-1. The following determination and distribution of excess schedule was prepared on January 1, 19X2, the date Ajax Company purchased a 60% interest in Marat Company:

Price paid		$90,000
Interest acquired:		
Common stock, $10 par	$ 75,000	
Retained earnings	50,000	
Total subsidiary equity	$125,000	
Ownership interest	60%	75,000
Excess of cost over book value attributable to goodwill		
(20-year life)		$15,000

On December 31, 19X4, Ajax Company purchased an additional 30% interest in Marat Company for $60,000. Marat's stockholders' equity was determined to be the following at that date:

Common stock	$ 75,000
Retained earnings	85,000
Total stockholders' equity	$160,000

Any excess of cost over book value is attributable to goodwill with a 20-year life. On December 31, 19X5, the following trial balances are available:

	Ajax Company	Marat Company
Current Assets................................	210,000	40,000
Investment in Marat Company	198,450	—
Property, Plant, and Equipment (net)	450,000	170,500
Current Liabilities..............................	(110,000)	(20,000)
Common Stock ($10 par)......................	(500,000)	(75,000)
Retained Earnings	(141,950)	(85,000)
Sales...	(400,000)	(100,000)
Subsidiary Income	(31,500)	—
Cost of Goods Sold	200,000	50,000
Other Expenses................................	100,000	15,000
Dividends Declared	25,000	4,500
	0	0

Required:

(1) Prepare a determination and distribution of excess schedule for the second purchase of Marat stock by Ajax Company.

(2) Prepare a consolidated work sheet necessary for the preparation of consolidated statements for Ajax Company and subsidiary as of December 31, 19X5.

Problem 10-2. The following balance sheets were condensed from past annual reports of the Loeb Corporation:

Assets	Jan. 1, 19X1	Jan. 1, 19X4
Current assets	$ 70,000	$ 80,000
Land	30,000	30,000
Buildings (net)	80,000	65,000
Equipment (net).............................	70,000	105,000
Total assets.................................	$250,000	$280,000

Liabilities and Equity		
Liabilities	$100,000	$ 90,000
Equity:		
Common stock, $2.50 par	$ 25,000	$ 25,000
Paid-in capital in excess of par...............	55,000	55,000
Retained earnings	70,000	110,000
Total equity	$150,000	$190,000
Total liabilities and equity	$250,000	$280,000

Mrazek Company purchased a 70% interest in Loeb Corporation on January 1, 19X1, for $125,000, and an additional 10% interest on January 1, 19X4, for $25,000.

An analysis of Loeb's accounts on the purchase date indicated:

(a) On January 1, 19X1, Loeb's land was undervalued by $10,000.

(b) On January 1, 19X4, Loeb's land was undervalued by $15,000, and the equipment was undervalued by $15,000 and had an estimated remaining life of 5 years.

(c) Any other excess of cost over book value on either investment is attributed to goodwill with an estimated future life of 10 years.

Loeb's income and dividends paid for 19X1-19X5 were as follows:

	Income	Dividends Paid
19X1	$20,000	$10,000
19X2	40,000	20,000
19X3	30,000	20,000
19X4	30,000	20,000
19X5	50,000	20,000

On December 31, 19X5, the following trial balances for Mrazek Company and its subsidiary are secured:

	Mrazek Company	Loeb Corporation
Current Assets	200,000	60,000
Land	100,000	30,000
Buildings	400,000	120,000
Accumulated Depreciation—Buildings	(150,000)	(40,000)
Equipment	500,000	200,000
Accumulated Depreciation—Equipment	(200,000)	(90,000)
Investment in Loeb Corporation	150,000	—
Liabilities	(329,000)	(50,000)
Common Stock ($20 par)	(300,000)	—
Common Stock ($2.50 par)	—	(25,000)
Paid-In Capital in Excess of Par	—	(55,000)
Retained Earnings	(305,000)	(120,000)
Sales	(500,000)	(150,000)
Subsidiary Income (dividend)	(16,000)	—
Cost of Goods Sold	250,000	60,000
Other Expenses	150,000	40,000
Dividends Declared	50,000	20,000
	0	0

Required:

(1) Prepare determination and distribution of excess schedules for each purchase of Loeb stock by Mrazek Company.

(2) Prepare a consolidated work sheet necessary to prepare a consolidated balance sheet and income statement as of December 31, 19X5.

Problem 10-3. On January 1, 19X4, Melchior Company purchased a 15% interest in Claymore Company for $70,000. Two years subsequent to this purchase, Melchior Company acquired an additional 45% interest in Claymore Company for $250,000.

Balance sheets of the Claymore Company immediately prior to the above purchases were as follows:

Assets	Jan. 1, 19X4	Jan. 1, 19X6
Current assets	$150,000	$120,000
Land	150,000	150,000
Equipment (net)	200,000	300,000
Total assets	$500,000	$570,000

Liabilities and Equity	Jan. 1, 19X4	Jan. 1, 19X6
Liabilities	$100,000	$110,000
Equity:		
Common stock, $5 par	$100,000	$100,000
Paid-in capital in excess of par..............	150,000	150,000
Retained earnings	150,000	210,000
Total equity	$400,000	$460,000
Total liabilities and equity	$500,000	$570,000

On January 1, 19X4, and January 1, 19X6, Claymore's book values approximated market values, except for the land, which was undervalued by $50,000. Any resulting goodwill is to be amortized over 20 years.

On December 31, 19X6, Melchior's investment in Claymore Company was determined as follows:

Original cost of 15% investment	$ 70,000
Original cost of 45% investment	250,000
60% of income, January 1, 19X6—December 31, 19X6	24,000
Investment in Claymore Company	$344,000

The following trial balances were prepared on December 31, 19X6:

	Melchior Company	Claymore Company
Current Assets...................................	250,000	225,000
Investment in Claymore Company	344,000	—
Land	240,000	150,000
Building (net)...................................	480,000	—
Equipment (net)	400,000	220,000
Other Assets	20,000	5,000
Liabilities	(340,000)	(100,000)
Common Stock ($10 par)	(1,000,000)	—
Common Stock ($5 par)	—	(100,000)
Paid-In Capital in Excess of Par	—	(150,000)
Retained Earnings	(310,000)	(210,000)
Sales...	(900,000)	(350,000)
Subsidiary Income	(24,000)	—
Cost of Goods Sold	540,000	180,000
Other Expenses.................................	250,000	130,000
Dividends Declared	50,000	—
	0	0

Required:

Prepare a consolidated work sheet for December 31, 19X6, including all columns necessary for a consolidated income statement and balance sheet.

Problem 10-4. The following information is available regarding the investments of Broderick Corporation in Chesewick Company for the years 19X1-19X5.

Date	Transactions	Interest	Price
1/1/X1......................	Purchased common	10%	$ 20,000
1/1/X2......................	Purchased preferred	60	30,000
1/1/X3......................	Purchased common	50	140,000
1/1/X5......................	Purchased common	20	60,000
12/31/X5	Sold common	20	50,000

The stockholders' equity section of Chesewick Company's balance sheet has not changed since the original sale of preferred stock on January 1, 19X0, except for the balance in Retained Earnings. The stockholders' equity of Chesewick Company as of January 1, 19X5, follows:

6% Cumulative preferred stock, $50 par (liquidation value equals par value)	$ 50,000
Common stock, $10 par	100,000
Paid-in capital in excess of par	20,000
Retained earnings	150,000
Total stockholders' equity	$320,000

Other relevant facts are as follows:
(a) On January 1, 19X1, Chesewick had $60,000 of Retained Earnings, and there were no dividends in arrears on the preferred stock.
(b) The excess of cost over book value on each investment in common stock is viewed as goodwill with a 10-year life.
(c) The 20% interest sold on December 31, 19X5, was the interest purchased on January 1, 19X5.
(d) Income and dividends were as follows for 19X1-19X5:

	Net Income	Preferred Dividends	Common Dividends
19X1	$25,000	$3,000	None
19X2	30,000	3,000	$6,000
19X3	30,000	3,000	5,000
19X4	25,000	None	None
19X5	20,000	None	None

Broderick's investment account balances for its interests in the Chesewick Company were calculated as follows on December 31, 19X5:

Investment in preferred stock:

Original cost	$30,000
Plus dividends in arrears for 19X4	1,800
Balance on December 31, 19X5	$31,800

Investment in common stock:

January 1, 19X1 purchase	$ 20,000
January 1, 19X3 purchase	140,000
19X3 Chesewick income, $30,000 × 60%	18,000
19X3 Chesewick dividends, $5,000 × 60%	(3,000)
19X4 Chesewick income, $25,000 × 60%	15,000
January 1, 19X5 purchase	60,000
19X5 Chesewick income, $20,000 × 80%	16,000
December 31, 19X5 sale	(50,000)
Balance, December 31, 19X5	$216,000

Required:

Assume that the investment accounts are to be properly maintained under the simple equity method. Prepare all necessary correcting entries on the books of the Broderick Corporation as of December 31, 19X5. (Assume that nominal accounts are open.)

Problem 10-5. The Blaine Corporation purchased a 60% interest in the common stock of the Tricor Corporation on December 31, 19X3, for $500,000, when Tricor had the following condensed balance sheet:

Assets		Liabilities and Stockholders' Equity	
Current assets	$ 400,000	Liabilities	$ 600,000
Land	200,000	Preferred stock, 8%	
Building (net)	400,000	cumulative, $100 par	100,000
Equipment (net)............	500,000	Common stock, $20 par	750,000
		Retained earnings	50,000
Total assets	$1,500,000	Total liabilities and equity ...	$1,500,000

On December 31, 19X3, the dividends on the preferred stock were three years in arrears. On the purchase date, the book values of the Tricor assets approximated market values, except for the building, which was undervalued by $30,000 and had a 20-year remaining life. Any goodwill which results is to be amortized over a 10-year life.

For 19X4-19X6, earnings and dividends were as follows for the Tricor Corporation:

	Income	Preferred Dividends	Common Dividends
19X4	$40,000	—	—
19X5	50,000	$16,000	—
19X6	90,000	32,000	$18,750

The following trial balances were prepared for the two firms on December 31, 19X6:

	Blaine Corporation	Tricor Corporation
Current Assets....................................	1,020,000	483,250
Investment in Tricor Corporation.................	500,000	—
Land...	400,000	200,000
Building......................................	950,000	500,000
Accumulated Depreciation—Building	(200,000)	(160,000)
Equipment	1,500,000	740,000
Accumulated Depreciation—Equipment	(400,000)	(200,000)
Liabilities	(800,000)	(550,000)
Preferred Stock, 8%	—	(100,000)
Common Stock ($20 par).......................	(2,000,000)	(750,000)
Retained Earnings	(863,750)	(124,000)
Sales...	(2,100,000)	(1,000,000)
Subsidiary Dividend Income	(11,250)	—
Cost of Goods Sold	1,155,000	600,000
Other Expenses...............................	650,000	310,000
Dividends Declared	200,000	50,750
	0	0

Required:

Prepare a consolidated work sheet for all consolidated financial statements for Blaine Corporation and its subsidiary as of December 31, 19X6.

Problem 10-6. On January 1, 19X5, Dalton Corporation purchased 60% of the common stock and all of the preferred stock of Groner International for $425,000 and $110,000 respectively. Dalton Corporation increased its interest in Groner International to 80% by purchasing an additional 20% of Groner Corporation's common stock on January 1, 19X7, for $160,000.

Comparative stockholder equities of Groner International at the purchase dates were as follows:

	Jan. 1, 19X5	Jan. 1, 19X7
Preferred stock, 6% noncumulative, $100 par .	$100,000	$100,000
Common stock, $10 par	400,000	400,000
Retained earnings	300,000	360,000
	$800,000	$860,000

On January 1, 19X5, it was determined that certain equipment of Groner International was undervalued by $16,000 and had an 8-year remaining life. Straight-line depreciation is assumed.

On January 1, 19X7, it was determined that certain equipment of Groner International was undervalued by $12,000 and had a 6-year remaining life. Straight-line depreciation was used. Any additional excesses are considered attributable to goodwill with a 10-year life.

The December 31, 19X7 trial balances of the Dalton Corporation and its subsidiary are as follows:

	Dalton Corporation	Groner International
Cash	240,000	25,000
Accounts Receivable	480,000	95,000
Inventory	800,000	110,000
Investment in Preferred Stock	110,000	—
Investment in Common Stock	693,000	—
Property, Plant, and Equipment	4,800,000	1,125,000
Accumulated Depreciation	(1,200,000)	(357,500)
Accounts Payable	(280,000)	(45,000)
Other Liabilities	(800,000)	(2,500)
Preferred Stock ($100 par)	—	(100,000)
Common Stock ($10 par)	(4,000,000)	(400,000)
Retained Earnings	(671,000)	(360,000)
Sales	(3,400,000)	(900,000)
Subsidiary Income (common)	(72,000)	—
Cost of Goods Sold	2,380,000	540,000
Other Expenses	720,000	270,000
Dividends Declared	200,000	—
	0	0

Additional information follows:
(a) Dalton Corporation's January 1, 19X7 inventory contained $10,400 of merchandise purchased from Groner International. During 19X7, Groner International sold $48,000 of merchandise to Dalton Corporation. Dalton still owes $10,000 for these goods. Dalton Corporation's December 31, 19X7 inventory shows $5,600 of Groner International merchandise. Groner International marks up this type of merchandise 60% on cost.
(b) On July 1, 19X6, Dalton Corporation sold to Groner International, for $30,000, a piece of equipment which had a book value of $20,000. This piece of equipment had an estimated future life of 5 years and is being depreciated on a straight-line basis.

Required:

(1) Prepare a consolidated work sheet for Dalton Corporation and its subsidiary necessary for the preparation of all consolidated financial statements as of December 31, 19X7.

(2) Prepare the formal consolidated income statement, retained earnings statement, and balance sheet for December 31, 19X7.

Problem 10-7. On January 1, 19X3, Holton Corporation purchased 80% of the outstanding common stock of Nof Company for $416,000. Just prior to Holton Corporation's purchase, Nof Company had the following stockholders' equity:

Common stock, $20 par	$400,000
Retained earnings	100,000
Total stockholders' equity	$500,000

At this time, Nof Company's book values approximated market values. Any excess of cost is attributable to goodwill with a 20-year life.

On January 1, 19X7, Nof Company's Retained Earnings amounted to $200,000. No changes had taken place in the common stock account since the original sale on July 10, 19X0.

On July 1, 19X7, Holton Corporation sold one eighth of its interest in Nof Company to Welch Corporation for $50,000. At the time of this sale, Holton Corporation had no intention of selling the balance of its holding in Nof Company. Nof estimated its income for the first half of 19X7 to be $30,000. Nof Company had paid dividends of $.50 per share of common stock during the first half of 19X7.

On December 31, 19X7, Holton Corporation sold its remaining 70% interest in Nof Company to Welch Corporation for $400,000.

Nof Company's reported income and dividends for 19X7 are as follows:

	Income	Dividends
January 1, 19X7—July 1, 19X7	$30,000	$.50/share
July 1, 19X7—December 31, 19X7	35,000	.50/share

Required:

Prepare all the entries on Holton's books to reflect the changes in its investment account from January 1, 19X7, to December 31, 19X7. (Assume that Holton uses the cost method to report its investment in Nof Company.)

Problem 10-8. During 19X7, the Ansul Company acquired a controlling interest in Stephens, Inc. Trial balances of the companies at December 31, 19X7, are shown at the top of page 461.

The following information is available regarding the transactions and accounts of the companies:

(a) An analysis of the companies' retained earnings accounts:

	Ansul Company	Stephens, Inc.
Balance, January 1, 19X7	$1,605,000	$400,000
December 31, 19X7:		
Cash dividend declared (payable January 15, 19X8)	—	(5,000)
90% of Stephens, Inc., income for 19X7	45,000	—
Balance, December 31, 19X7	$1,650,000	$395,000

	Ansul Company	Stephens, Inc.
Cash	100,000	80,000
Notes Receivable..............................	100,000	—
Accounts Receivable	200,000	100,000
Interest Receivable	1,000	—
Inventories....................................	924,000	125,000
Investment in Stephens, Inc.	475,000	—
Property, Plant, and Equipment................	1,250,000	500,000
Accumulated Depreciation	(500,000)	(150,000)
Deferred Charges	25,000	—
Patents and Licenses..........................	—	50,000
Accounts Payable	(425,000)	(80,000)
Notes Payable	—	(75,000)
Dividends Payable............................	—	(5,000)
Capital Stock	(300,000)	(100,000)
Retained Earnings............................	(1,605,000)	(395,000)
Sales and Services	(1,800,000)	(750,000)
Subsidiary Income	(45,000)	—
Interest Income	(1,000)	—
Cost of Goods Sold	1,350,000	525,000
Administrative and Selling Expenses	251,000	174,000
Interest Expense	—	1,000
	0	0

(b) An analysis of the investment in Stephens, Inc., account:

	Description	Amount	Interest Acquired
January 1, 19X7	Investment	$325,000	70%
September 30, 19X7	Investment	105,000	20
Total		$430,000	90%
December 31, 19X7	90% of Stephens' income for 19X7	45,000	
		$475,000	

The net income of Stephens, Inc., for the nine months ended September 30, 19X7, was $25,000.

(c) The price paid by the parent on January 1, 19X7, to achieve control reflects uncertainty as to the future value of the patents. The remaining amortization is 5 years.

(d) On September 30, 19X7, Ansul Company loaned its subsidiary $100,000 on a 4% note. Interest and principal are payable in quarterly installments beginning December 31, 19X7. Ansul Company has no other notes receivable outstanding.

(e) Stephens, Inc., sales are principally engineering services billed at cost plus 50%. During 19X7, $40,000 was billed to Ansul Company, of which $16,500 was treated as a deferred charge at December 31, 19X7.

(f) During the year, parent company sales to the subsidiary aggregated $60,000, of which $10,000 remained in the inventory of Stephens, Inc., at December 31, 19X7.

(g) In 19X7, Ansul constructed certain tools at a cost of $15,000 that were sold to Stephens, Inc., for $25,000. Stephens, Inc., depreciates such tools using the straight-line method over a 5-year life. One-half year's depreciation is provided in the year of acquisition.

Required:

Prepare a work sheet for all consolidated statements for the year ended December 31, 19X7. The work sheet should be accompanied by explanations and computations in support of each adjustment or elimination. Income tax implications are to be disregarded.   (AICPA adapted)

Problem 10-9. The December 31, 19X8 trial balances of the Titan Corporation and its two subsidiaries, Boat Corporation and Motor Corporation, appear as follows:

	Titan Corporation	Boat Corporation	Motor Corporation
Cash	100,000	87,000	95,000
Accounts Receivable	158,200	210,000	105,000
Inventories	290,000	90,000	115,000
Advance to Boat Corporation	17,000	—	—
Dividends Receivable	24,000	—	—
Property, Plant, and Equipment	777,600	325,000	470,000
Accumulated Depreciation	(180,000)	(55,000)	(160,000)
Investment in Boat Corporation:			
6% bonds	23,800	—	—
Common stock	308,600	—	—
Investment in Motor Corporation:			
Preferred stock	7,400	—	—
Common stock	207,200	—	—
Notes Payable	(45,000)	(14,000)	(44,000)
Accounts Payable	(170,000)	(96,000)	(86,000)
Bonds Payable	(285,000)	(150,000)	(125,000)
Discount on Bonds Payable	8,000	—	—
Dividends Payable	(22,000)	(30,000)	—
Preferred Stock ($20 par)	(400,000)	—	(50,000)
Common Stock ($10 par)	(600,000)	(250,000)	(200,000)
Retained Earnings	(154,600)	(107,000)	(100,000)
Sales	(1,050,000)	(500,000)	(650,000)
Other Revenue	(2,100)	—	—
Subsidiary Income:			
Common Stock (Boat)	(32,000)	—	—
Preferred Stock (Motor)	(400)	—	—
Common Stock (Motor)	(11,200)	—	—
Cost of Goods Sold	650,000	300,000	400,000
Other Expenses	358,500	160,000	230,000
Dividends Declared	22,000	30,000	—
	0	0	0

Additional information available includes the following:
(a) The investment in Boat Corporation stock account is composed of the items shown in the schedule at the top of page 463.
(b) Boat Corporation had a Retained Earnings balance of $92,000 at January 1, 19X7, and had income of $15,000 for the first three months of 19X7 and $20,000 for the first six months of 19X8.
(c) Titan Corporation acquired 250 shares of fully participating Motor preferred stock for $7,000, and 14,000 shares of Motor common stock for

Date	Description	Amount
4/1/X7	Cost of 5,000 shares of Boat Corp. stock	$ 71,400
12/31/X7	20% of dividends declared in December, 19X7, by Boat Corp.	(9,000)
12/31/X7	20% of the 19X7 annual net income of the Boat Corp.	12,000
7/1/X8	Cost of 15,000 shares of the Boat Corp.	226,200
12/31/X8	80% of the dividends declared in December, 19X8, by the Boat Corp.	(24,000)
12/31/X8	80% of the 19X8 annual net income of the Boat Corp.	32,000
12/31/X8	Total	$308,600

$196,000 on January 2, 19X8. Motor Corporation had a net income of $20,000 in 19X8 and did not declare any dividends.

(d) Motor Corporation's inventory includes $22,400 of merchandise acquired from Boat Corporation subsequent to July, 19X8, for which no payment has been made. Boat Corporation marked up the merchandise 40% on cost.

(e) Titan Corporation acquired in the open market 25, $1,000, 6% bonds of the Boat Corporation for $21,400 on January 1, 19X5. The Boat Corporation bonds mature December 31, 19Y0. Interest is paid each June 30 and December 31. Straight-line amortization is allowed on the basis of materiality.

(f) The three corporations are all in the same industry and their operations are homogeneous. Titan Corporation exercises control over the boards of directors of both Boat Corporation and Motor Corporation, and has installed new principal officers in both.

Required:

Prepare a work sheet for the preparation of a consolidated balance sheet as of December 31, 19X8, for Titan Corporation and its subsidiaries. Consolidated Retained Earnings should be allocated to Titan Corporation, and the minority interest should be shown separately. The consolidation is to be accounted for as a purchase. All supporting computations should be in good form.   (AICPA adapted)

Problem 10-10.   Blake Company purchased 90% of the stock of Western Industries when the latter company was organized in 19X2. On April 1, 19X8, it acquired the remaining 10% of the stock for $7,000. On October 1, 19X8, Blake Company sold 30% of its interest in Western Industries for $22,000. December 31, 19X8 trial balances of the two companies are as follows:

	Blake Company	Western Industries
Current Assets.....................................	34,400	23,800
Investment in Western Industries (70%)	48,550	—
Property, Plant, and Equipment	85,000	71,200
Accumulated Depreciation	(28,000)	(20,500)
Liabilities	(11,500)	(6,500)
Common Stock ($10 par)..........................	(75,000)	(50,000)
Retained Earnings	(22,600)	(8,000)
Sales..	(280,000)	(190,000)
Subsidiary Income	(9,000)	—
Gain on Sale of Stock	(2,350)	—
Cost of Goods Sold	198,000	120,000
Other Expenses...................................	62,500	60,000
	0	0

Assume that the net income of Western Industries was earned at a uniform rate during 19X8. The parent company made it a practice to record its share of the earnings of its subsidiary quarterly. The following credit entries were made in the subsidiary income account during 19X8:

March 31 (90% of $2,500)	$2,250
June 30 (100% of $2,500)	2,500
September 30 (100% of $2,500)	2,500
December 31 (70% of $2,500)	1,750
	$9,000

Assume that any excess is attributable to goodwill with a 10-year life, and that the sale of 30% of Blake's interest in Western Industries is on a fifo basis.

Required:

Prepare a consolidated work sheet necessary to prepare consolidated statements for Blake Company and its subsidiary as of December 31, 19X8.

Problem 10-11. On January 1, 19X7, Davis Corporation purchased all of the preferred stock and 60% of the common stock of Baldwin Company for $60,000 and $50,000 respectively. Immediately prior to the purchase, Baldwin Company had the following stockholders' equity:

8% Cumulative preferred stock, $100 par (3 years in arrears)......	$ 50,000
Common stock, $10 par	100,000
Paid-in capital in excess of par, common stock	20,000
Retained earnings	(20,000)
Total stockholders' equity	$150,000

Additional information:

(a) On the purchase date, Baldwin Company's only plant asset, equipment, had a book value equal to market value, as did all other assets and liabilities of Baldwin Company. The equipment had an estimated remaining life of seven years and was being depreciated on a straight-line basis.

(b) On December 31, 19X7, and June 30, 19X8, Baldwin Company paid preferred stock dividends of $8 per share.

(c) Baldwin Company had a net income of $15,000 in 19X7 and earnings of $10,000 for the first half of 19X8.

(d) Davis Corporation sold a piece of equipment with a book value of $8,000 to Baldwin Company for $11,000 on January 2, 19X7. The machine had an estimated future life of five years, and straight-line depreciation is being used.

(e) Information regarding intercompany merchandise sales follows:

	Davis Corporation	Baldwin Company
Merchandise in beginning inventory of purchaser, January 1, 19X8.................................	$ 1,200	$2,800
Sales, January 1, 19X8—June 30, 19X8	20,000	8,000
Merchandise in purchaser's inventory, June 30, 19X8	1,600	7,000
Merchandise not paid for as of June 30, 19X8	2,000	6,000
Markup on cost	40%	60%

(f) On July 1, 19X8, Davis Corporation sold its 60% interest in Baldwin Company common stock for $70,000.

June 30, 19X8 trial balances of Davis Corporation and its subsidiary are as follows:

	Davis Corporation	Baldwin Company
Cash	47,400	10,000
Accounts Receivable (net)	120,000	26,000
Inventories	230,000	44,000
Other Current Assets	20,000	8,000
Investment in Baldwin Company:		
Preferred stock	58,000	—
Common stock	61,400	—
Property, Plant, and Equipment	1,450,000	122,000
Accumulated Depreciation	(420,000)	(25,000)
Liabilities	(350,000)	(18,000)
Preferred Stock ($100 par)	—	(50,000)
Common Stock ($10 par)	(1,000,000)	(100,000)
Paid-In Capital in Excess of Par (common stock)	—	(20,000)
Retained Earnings (January 1, 19X8)	(195,000)	9,000
Sales	(420,000)	(96,000)
Subsidiary Income (preferred)	(2,000)	—
Subsidiary Income (common)	(4,800)	—
Cost of Goods Sold	300,000	60,000
Other Expenses	80,000	26,000
Dividends Declared	25,000	4,000
	0	0

Required:

(1) Prepare a consolidated work sheet necessary to prepare consolidated financial statements for Davis Corporation and its subsidiary as of June 30, 19X8.

(2) Prepare the entries on Davis' books to reflect the sale of its investment in Baldwin Company's common stock on July 1, 19X8.

Problem 10-12. Condensed statements of income (unconsolidated) for the year ended December 31, 19X5, retained earnings statements for the year ended December 31, 19X5, and the balance sheets as of December 31, 19X5, for Pace Company and its subsidiary, Smith Company, are as follows:

Condensed Statements of Income	Pace Company	Smith Company
Sales	$ 4,000,000	$ 1,700,000
Cost of goods sold	(2,982,000)	(1,015,000)
Operating expenses	(400,000)	(377,200)
Dividend income	75,000	—
Subsidiary income	232,000	—
Interest expense	—	(7,800)
Net income	$ 925,000	$ 300,000

Retained Earnings Statements	Pace Company	Smith Company
Balance, January 1, 19X5	$(2,100,000)	$ (640,000)
Net income..	(925,000)	(300,000)
Dividends declared	170,000	100,000
Balance, December 31, 19X5......................	$(2,855,000)	$ (840,000)

Balance Sheets

Assets

	Pace Company	Smith Company
Cash	$ 486,000	$ 249,600
Accounts receivable	235,000	185,000
Inventories	475,000	355,000
Machinery and equipment (net)....................	2,231,000	530,000
Investment in stock of Smith Company	954,000	—
Investment in bonds of Smith Company	58,000	—
Total assets	$ 4,439,000	$ 1,319,600

Liabilities and Stockholders' Equity

	Pace Company	Smith Company
Accounts payable	$ (384,000)	$ (62,000)
Bonds payable....................................	—	(120,000)
Unamortized discount on bonds payable	—	2,400
Common stock, Pace Company	(1,200,000)	—
Common stock, Smith Company	—	(250,000)
Paid-in capital in excess of par	—	(50,000)
Retained earnings (brought forward)	(2,855,000)	(840,000)
Total liabilities and stockholders' equity............	$(4,439,000)	$(1,319,600)

Additional information:

(a) On January 3, 19X3, Pace acquired from Fred Biffel, the sole stockholder of Smith Company, for $440,000 cash, a patent valued at $40,000 and 80% of the outstanding stock of Smith. The net book value of Smith's stock on the date of acquisition was $500,000, and the book values of the individual assets and liabilities were equal to their fair market values. Pace charged the entire $440,000 to the account Investment in Stock of Smith Company. The patent, for which no amortization had been charged, had a remaining legal life of four years as of January 3, 19X3.

(b) On July 1, 19X5, Pace reduced its investment in Smith to 75% of Smith's outstanding common stock by selling shares for $70,000 to an unaffiliated company at a profit of $16,000. Pace recorded the proceeds as a credit to its investment account.

(c) For the six months ended June 30, 19X5, Smith had net income of $140,000. Pace recorded 80% of this amount on its books of account prior to the time of sale.

(d) During 19X4, Smith sold merchandise to Pace for $130,000, which was at a markup of 30% over Smith's cost. On January 1, 19X5, $52,000 of this merchandise remained in Pace's inventory. This merchandise was subsequently sold by Pace in February, 19X5, at a profit of $8,000.

(e) In November, 19X5, Pace sold merchandise to Smith for the first time. Pace's cost for this merchandise was $80,000, and the sale was made at 120% of cost. Smith's inventory at December 31, 19X5, contained merchandise that was purchased from Pace for $24,000.

(f) On December 31, 19X5, there was a $45,000 payment in transit from Smith Company to Pace Company. Accounts Receivable and Accounts Payable include intercompany receivables and payables.

(g) In December, 19X5, Smith declared and paid cash dividends of $100,000 to its stockholders.

(h) On December 31, 19X5, Pace purchased, for $58,000, 50% of the outstanding bonds issued by Smith. The bonds mature on December 31, 19X9, and were originally issued at a discount. On December 31, 19X5, the balance in Smith's account, Unamortized Discount on Bonds Payable, was $2,400. It is the intention of the management of Pace to hold these bonds until their maturity.

Required:

Prepare the work sheet necessary to prepare a consolidated retained earnings statement and a consolidated balance sheet of Pace Company and its subsidiary as of December 31, 19X5. Formal statements and journal entries are not required. Ignore income taxes.   (AICPA adapted)

APPENDIX PROBLEMS—BALANCE SHEET ONLY

Problem 10A-1. The December 31, 19X9 balance sheets of Encanto Corporation and its subsidiary, Norris Corporation, are as follows:

Assets	Encanto Corporation	Norris Corporation
Cash	$ 167,250	$101,000
Accounts receivable	178,450	72,000
Notes receivable	87,500	28,000
Dividends receivable	36,000	
Inventories	122,000	68,000
Property, plant, and equipment	487,000	252,000
Accumulated depreciation	(117,000)	(64,000)
Investment in Norris Corporation	240,800	
	$1,202,000	$457,000

Liabilities and Stockholders' Equity		
Accounts payable	$ 222,000	$ 76,000
Notes payable	79,000	89,000
Dividends payable		40,000
Common stock, $10 par:		
Encanto Corporation	400,000	
Norris Corporation		100,000
Retained earnings:		
Encanto Corporation	501,000	
Norris Corporation		152,000
	$1,202,000	$457,000

The following additional information is available:

(a) Encanto initially acquired 60% of the outstanding common stock of Norris in 19X7. There was no difference between cost and book value of net assets acquired. As of December 31, 19X9, the percentage owned is 90%. An analysis of the investment in Norris Corporation account is as follows:

Description	Amount
December 31, 19X7..... Acquired 6,000 shares	$ 70,800
December 31, 19X8..... 60% of 19X8 net income of $78,000	46,800
September 1, 19X9 ..... Acquired 3,000 shares	92,000
December 31, 19X9..... Subsidiary income for 19X9	67,200*
December 31, 19X9..... 90% of dividends declared	(36,000)
	$240,800

*Subsidiary income for 19X9:

60% of $96,000................	$57,600
30% of $96,000 × 33⅓%	9,600
	$67,200

Assume that Norris's net income is earned ratably during the year. Amortization of the excess of cost over the net assets acquired is to be recorded over sixty months.

(b) On December 15, 19X9, Norris declared a cash dividend of $4 per share of common stock, payable to shareholders on January 7, 19Y0.

(c) During 19X9 Encanto sold merchandise to Norris. Encanto's cost for this merchandise was $68,000, and the sale was made at 125% of cost. Norris's inventory at December 31, 19X9, included merchandise purchased from Encanto at a cost to Norris of $35,000.

(d) In December 19X8, Norris sold merchandise to Encanto for $67,000, which was at a markup of 35% over Norris's cost. On January 1, 19X9, $54,000 of this merchandise remained in Encanto's inventory. This merchandise was subsequently sold by Encanto at a profit of $11,000 during 19X9.

(e) On October 1, 19X9, Encanto sold excess equipment to Norris for $42,000. Data relating to this equipment are as follows:

Book value on Encanto's records.....................	$36,000
Method of depreciation.............................	Straight-line
Estimated remaining life on October 1, 19X9	10 years

(f) Near the end of 19X9, Norris reduced the balance of its intercompany account payable to Encanto to zero by transferring $8,000 to Encanto. This payment was still in transit on December 31, 19X9.

Required:

Prepare a consolidated work sheet necessary to prepare a consolidated balance sheet for Encanto Corporation and its subsidiary, Norris Corporation, as of December 31, 19X9. Formal statements and journal entries are not required. Supporting computations should be in good form.   (AICPA adapted)

Problem 10A-2. Prior to January 1, 19X7, the stockholders of East Company and West Company approved the merger of the two companies. On January 1, 19X7, 5,000 shares of East Company common stock were issued to the West Company stockholders in exchange for the 3,000 shares of West Company common stock outstanding.

The following additional information is available:

(a) Net income for 19X7 (disregard income taxes):

East Company	$21,700
West Company	10,200

(b) On December 31, 19X7, West Company owed East Company $16,000 on open account and $8,000 in interest-bearing notes. East Company discounted $3,000 of the notes received from West Company with the First State Bank.

(c) On December 31, 19X7, West Company accrued interest payable of $120 on the notes payable to East Company: $40 on the note of $3,000 discounted with the bank, and $80 on the remaining note of $5,000. East Company did not accrue interest receivable from West Company.

(d) During 19X7, East Company sold merchandise, which cost $30,000, to West Company for $40,000. West Company's December 31 inventory included $10,000 of this merchandise priced at West Company's cost.

(e) On July 1, West Company sold equipment, which had a book value of $15,000, to East Company for $17,000. East Company recorded depreciation on the equipment in the amount of $850 for 19X7. The remaining life of the equipment at the date of sale was 10 years.

(f) West Company shipped merchandise to East Company on December 31, 19X7, and recorded an account receivable of $6,000 for the sale. West Company's cost for the merchandise was $4,800. Because the merchandise was in transit, East Company did not record the transaction. The terms of the sale were F.O.B. shipping point.

(g) West Company declared a dividend of $1.50 per share on December 30, 19X7, payable on January 1, 19X8. East Company made no entry for the declaration.

The December 31, 19X7 post-closing trial balances of the two companies are as follows:

	East Company	West Company
Cash	36,400	28,200
Notes Receivable	22,000	9,000
Accounts Receivable	20,900	21,700
Interest Receivable	13,000	3,300
Inventories	81,200	49,600
Property, Plant, and Equipment	83,200	43,500
Accumulated Depreciation	(12,800)	(9,300)
Investment in West Company	50,000	—
Notes Payable	(4,000)	(12,000)
Accounts Payable	(42,000)	(19,600)
Dividends Payable	—	(4,500)
Interest Payable	(2,600)	(2,100)
Notes Receivable Discounted	(8,100)	—
Common Stock ($10 par)	(120,000)	—
Common Stock ($20 par)	—	(60,000)
Paid-In Capital in Excess of Par	(28,500)	(20,000)
Retained Earnings	(88,700)	(27,800)
	0	0

Required:

Prepare a consolidated work sheet necessary for the preparation of a consolidated balance sheet for East Company and subsidiary as of December 31, 19X7. The consolidation is to be accounted for as a pooling of interests.

Problem 10A-3. Madison, Inc., acquired all of the outstanding $10 par voting common stock of Adams Corporation on December 31, 19X9, in exchange for 90,000 shares of its $10 par voting common stock in a business combination which meets all of the conditions for a pooling of interests. On the acquisition date, Madison's common stock had a closing market price of $26 per share on a national stock exchange. Both corporations continued to operate as separate businesses, maintaining separate accounting records with years ending December 31.

On December 31, 19X9, after the nominal accounts were closed and immediately after the acquisition, the condensed balance sheets for both corporations were as follows:

Assets	Madison	Adams
Cash	$ 750,000	$ 300,000
Accounts receivable (net)	1,950,000	750,000
Inventories	2,100,000	950,000
Land	500,000	200,000
Depreciable assets (net)	4,160,000	1,800,000
Investment in Adams Corporation	2,205,000	—
Long-term investments and other assets	785,000	350,000
Total assets	$12,450,000	$4,350,000

Liabilities and Stockholders' Equity	Madison	Adams
Accounts payable and other current liabilities	$ 1,750,000	$ 945,000
Long-term debt	1,500,000	1,200,000
Common stock, $10 par	3,000,000	900,000
Additional paid-in capital	1,370,000	175,000
Retained earnings	4,830,000	1,130,000
Total liabilities and stockholders' equity	$12,450,000	$4,350,000

Additional information:

(a) Madison recorded its investment in Adams at the underlying equity in the net assets of Adams of $2,205,000.

(b) On December 31, 19X9, Adams' assets and liabilities had fair market values equal to the book balances with the exception of land, which had a fair value of $400,000.

(c) Madison's accounting policy is to amortize any excess of cost over fair market value of net assets acquired over a 40-year period.

(d) On December 15, 19X9, Adams paid a cash dividend of $3 per share on its common stock.

(e) Adams' long-term debt consisted of 9%, ten-year bonds, issued at face value on June 30, 19X5, and due on June 30, 19Y5. Interest is paid semiannually on June 30 and December 31. Madison had purchased Adams' bonds at face value of $250,000. There was no change in Madison's ownership of Adams' bonds through December 31, 19X9.

(f) During the three-month period ended December 31, 19X9, Madison purchased merchandise from Adams at an aggregate invoice price of $600,000. Madison had not paid for the merchandise as of December 31, 19X9. The amount of profit realized by Adams on these transactions was $120,000. At December 31, 19X9, one half of the merchandise remained in Madison's inventory. There were no intercompany merchandise transactions prior to October 1, 19X9.

(g) The 19X9 net income amounts per the separate books of Madison and Adams were $2,100,000 and $1,125,000, respectively.

(h) The balances in Retained Earnings at December 31, 19X8, were $1,600,000 and $275,000 for Madison and Adams, respectively.

Required:

(1) Prepare a consolidated work sheet necessary to prepare a consolidated balance sheet for Madison, Inc., and its subsidiary, Adams Corporation, as of December 31, 19X9. A formal balance sheet is not required.
(2) Prepare a formal consolidated statement of retained earnings for the year ended December 31, 19X9. Show supporting computations in good form.

(AICPA adapted)

Problem 10A-4. Wiley Corporation acquired 10% of the 100,000 shares of the $2.50 par common stock outstanding of Dole Company on December 31, 19X7, for $38,000. An additional 70,000 shares were acquired for $331,600 on June 30, 19X9 (at which time there was no material difference between market values and book values of Dole's assets and liabilities). Wiley uses the equity method of accounting for its investment in Dole.

The post-closing trial balances for both companies on December 31, 19X9, are as follows:

	Wiley	Dole
Cash	130,000	60,000
Marketable Securities	31,240	9,700
Notes Receivable	15,000	12,200
Accounts Receivable	160,000	75,000
Interest Receivable	2,100	1,600
Dividends Receivable	8,800	—
Inventories	180,000	96,000
Advance to Dole Company	32,000	—
Investment in Dole Company Stock	405,600	—
Investment in Dole Company Bonds	30,560	—
Property, Plant, and Equipment	781,500	510,000
Accumulated Depreciation	(87,000)	(85,000)
Unamortized Bond Discount	—	7,500
Notes Payable	(5,500)	(3,800)
Accounts Payable	(34,500)	(16,000)
Dividends Payable	(20,000)	(11,000)
Interest Payable	(18,000)	(13,000)
Accrued Liabilities	(15,000)	(1,200)
Advance from Wiley Corporation	—	(32,000)
Bonds Payable	(400,000)	(150,000)
Capital Stock	(500,000)	(250,000)
Paid-In Capital in Excess of Par	(14,000)	(29,000)
Retained Earnings	(682,800)	(181,000)
	0	0

The following information is also available:
(a) An analysis of Investment in Dole Company Stock:

Date	Description	Amount
December 31, 19X7	Investment	$ 38,000
June 30, 19X9	Investment	331,600
December 31, 19X9	80% of net increase in retained earnings of Dole Corporation during 19X9	36,000
		$405,600

(b) An analysis of the companies' retained earnings accounts:

	Wiley Corporation	Dole Company
Balance, December 31, 19X7	$540,000	$101,000
Net income for 19X8	55,000	40,000
Cash dividends in 19X8	—	(5,000)
Balance, December 31, 19X8	$595,000	$136,000
Net income:		
January 1—June 30, 19X9	31,000	23,000
June 30—December 31, 19X9	40,800	33,000
Dividends declared, December 15, 19X9	(20,000)	(11,000)
80% of net increase in retained earnings of Dole Company during 19X9	36,000	—
Balance, December 31, 19X9	$682,800	$181,000

(c) Dole's other equity accounts have not changed since 19X3.

(d) Data on 19X9 intercompany sales and ending inventories were as follows:

	Wiley Corporation	Dole Company
Intercompany sales:		
January 1—June 30	$39,000	$24,000
July 1—December 31	41,600	41,000
Gross profit on sales	30%	25%
Intercompany payables at year end	12,000	7,000
Year-end inventory of intercompany purchases at fifo cost	26,000	22,000

(e) Wiley Corporation acquired $30,000 of the Dole Company 6% bonds on August 31, 19X9, for $30,588 plus accrued interest. Dole Company issued the 20-year bonds on January 1, 19X0, at 90 and has been paying the interest on each January 1 and July 1 due date. Straight-line amortization has been used on the issuer's bond discount and the premium paid by the investor.

(f) On September 1, 19X9, Wiley Corporation sold equipment with a cost of $40,000 and accumulated depreciation of $9,300 to Dole Company for $20,200. Dole Company recorded the equipment as having a cost of $29,500 with accumulated depreciation of $9,300. At that date, the equipment had a market value of $35,000, an estimated salvage value of $500, and an estimated life of 10 years.

(g) Included in Wiley Corporation's Notes Receivable are $2,000 in non-interest-bearing notes of Dole Company.

Required:

Prepare a consolidated work sheet necessary to prepare a consolidated balance sheet for Wiley Corporation and its subsidiary as of December 31, 19X9. Any amortization required by APB Opinion No. 17, "Intangible Assets," is to be computed by the straight-line method over a 40-year period.   (AICPA adapted)

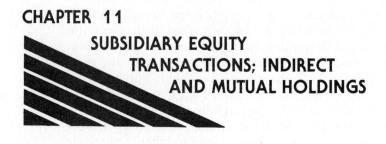

CHAPTER 11
SUBSIDIARY EQUITY
TRANSACTIONS; INDIRECT
AND MUTUAL HOLDINGS

This chapter deals with some additional complications involving the recording and elimination of the parent's account, Investment in Subsidiary. Complications stemming from equity transactions of the subsidiary are considered first. These transactions include the issuance of stock dividends, and subsidiary sales of additional shares and retirements of its common stock. Even though these transactions never produce income or losses for the parent company, they may affect the value of the controlling interest.

This chapter also deals with multilevel affiliate holdings. This topic includes subsidiaries which are, in turn, parent companies with respect to another subsidiary, and subsidiaries which own shares of their parent company.

SUBSIDIARY STOCK DIVIDENDS

A subsidiary may issue stock dividends in order to convert retained earnings into paid-in capital. The minimum amount to be removed from retained earnings is the par value or stated value of the shares distributed. However, according to accounting principles, when the distribution does not exceed 20% to 25% of the previously outstanding shares, an amount equal to the market value of the shares may be removed from retained earnings and transferred to paid-in capital. The recording of stock dividends at market value is defended by the following statement from ARB No. 43:

> . . . a stock dividend does not, in fact, give rise to any change whatsoever in either the corporation's assets or its respective shareholders' proportionate interests therein. However, it cannot fail to be recognized that,

merely as a consequence of the expressed purpose of the transaction and its characterization as a *dividend* in related notices to shareholders and the public at large, many recipients of stock dividends look upon them as distributions of corporate earnings and usually in an amount equivalent to the fair value of the additional shares received.[1]

Unfortunately, accounting theory is not consistent when it comes to recording the receipt of dividends by an investor. Even though the false impression of the "typical" investor is sufficient reason to allow the issuing corporation to record the market value of the shares distributed, the investor is not permitted to do likewise. In fact, the investor must not record income when stock dividends are received, but must acknowledge the true impact of the transaction, which is that nothing of substance has been given or received. Thus, the investor merely makes a memo entry indicating that the cost of the original investment is now allocated to a greater number of shares. The revised number of shares is important in computing cost per share if there is a subsequent partial sale of the investment.

To review the recording of a stock dividend, and to provide a basis for work sheets, assume that Company P acquired an 80% interest in Company S on January 1, 19X1, at which time the following determination and distribution of excess schedule was prepared:

Price paid		$200,000
Interest acquired:		
Common stock, $10 par	$100,000	
Retained earnings	80,000	
Total equity	$180,000	
Interest acquired	80%	144,000
Excess of cost over book value attributed to goodwill (10-year life)		**$ 56,000**

On January 2, 19X3, Company S declared and distributed a 10% stock dividend. Prior to declaration of the dividend, its stockholders' equity appeared as follows:

Common stock, $10 par	$100,000
Retained earnings	120,000
Total stockholders' equity	$220,000

In the following entry to record the stock dividend, Company S acknowledged the $25 market value of the 1,000 shares distributed:

Retained Earnings (or Stock Dividends Declared) ($25 market value × 1,000 shares)	25,000	
Common Stock ($10 par × 1,000 shares)		10,000
Additional Paid-In Capital from Stock Dividend (1,000 shares × $15 excess over par)		15,000

[1] *Accounting Research and Terminology Bulletins, No. 43,* "Restatement and Revision of Accounting Research Bulletins" (New York: American Institute of Certified Public Accountants, 1961), Ch. 7, Sec. B, par. 10.

Parent Using the Simple Equity Method

Continuing the example, on January 1, 19X3, Company P has a simple-equity-adjusted balance of $232,000 in its investment in Company S account, derived as follows:

Original cost		$200,000
Share of undistributed income:		
Company S retained earnings, January 1, 19X3	$120,000	
Company S retained earnings, January 1, 19X1	80,000	
Increase in retained earnings	$ 40,000	
Ownership interest	80%	32,000
Simple-equity-adjusted cost, January 1, 19X3		$232,000

During 19X3, Company S earned $20,000 and made no other dividend declarations. Company P would make the following entries under the simple equity method:

Receipt of stock dividend

Jan. 2, 19X3   Memo: Investment in Company S now includes 800 added shares for a total of 8,800 shares.

Recording of equity income

Dec. 31, 19X3   Investment in Company S 16,000
                Subsidiary Income 16,000
                To record 80% interest in Company
                S's $20,000 reported net income for 19X3.

The following partial work sheet lists the investment in Company S at the December 31, 19X3 simple-equity-adjusted cost of $248,000:

	Trial Balance		Eliminations	
	Company P	Company S	Dr.	Cr.
Investment in Co. S	248,000			(1) 16,000
				❷ 176,000
				(3) 56,000
Goodwill			(3) 56,000	(4) 16,800
Common Stock, Co. P	(500,000)			
Retained Earnings, Co. P	(420,000)		(4) 11,200	
Common Stock ($10 par), Co. S		(110,000)	❷ 88,000	
Additional Paid-In Capital from Stock Dividend, Co. S		(15,000)	❷ 12,000	
Retained Earnings, Co. S		(95,000)	❷ 76,000	
Subsidiary Income	(16,000)		(1) 16,000	
Expenses	30,000	18,000	(4) 5,600	

Eliminations:
(1) Eliminate the parent's entries recording its share of subsidiary earnings for the current year. There is no complication caused by the stock dividend, since it does not constitute income to Company P.
❷ Eliminate 80% of the Company S equity balances as restructured by the stock dividend. If the subsidiary

(continued)

recorded the stock dividend with a debit to Stock Dividends Declared, 80% of that account would be eliminated in this step.
(3) Distribute the excess cost to goodwill as required by the determination and distribution of excess schedule.
(4) Amortize goodwill for three years. The two prior years reduce the controlling interest in retained earnings, while the current-year amortization reduces current consolidated income.

Note that the work sheet includes the redistributed capital structure of Company S, which results from the stock dividend. It should now be clear that the complications arising from stock dividends pertain primarily to their recording by the separate affiliated firms. There is a minimal effect on the consolidated work sheet.

Parent Using the Cost Method

In the preceding example, if the parent, Company P, had used the cost method to record its investment in Company S, no adjustments would have been made to the investment account. The investment in Company S would still be carried at its original cost of $200,000 on the December 31, 19X3 work sheet.

The declaration of a stock dividend by a subsidiary requires a more difficult process for the conversion of the parent's investment account from a cost to a simple equity basis. The conversion must reflect the total changes in subsidiary retained earnings since acquisition, including the retained earnings transferred to paid-in capital as a result of stock dividends. The correct simple equity conversion would be made as follows for the preceding example:

Retained earnings, January 1, 19X3	$95,000
Retained earnings, January 1, 19X1	80,000
Change in retained earnings balance...........................	$15,000
Retained earnings transferred to paid-in capital ($25 × 1,000 shares) as a result of stock dividend	25,000
Total change in retained earnings	$40,000
Multiplied by ownership interest	80%
Simple equity conversion	$32,000

A faster approach to the simple equity conversion is to consider the change in total subsidiary stockholders' equity as follows:

Subsidiary equity, January 1, 19X3	$220,000
Subsidiary equity, January 1, 19X1	180,000
Net change..	$ 40,000
Multiplied by ownership interest	80%
Simple equity conversion......................................	$ 32,000

This faster method will be especially desirable in later years, when the facts surrounding the stock dividend are not readily available. The procedure will work well, provided there have been no other changes in subsidiary paid-in capital in the interim periods, such as a sale or a retirement of subsidiary shares.

The $32,000 simple equity conversion would be the first step on a work sheet when the cost method is used for the subsidiary investment. This step converts the investment in subsidiary account to its simple equity balance at the beginning of 19X3. The entry would be:

Investment in Company S 32,000
　Retained Earnings (January 1, 19X3).................... 　　　 32,000

The remaining work sheet procedures would not include elimination of the current year's subsidiary income, but would otherwise be identical to Steps 2-4 of the preceding work sheet.

SUBSIDIARY SALES AND RETIREMENTS OF COMMON STOCK

A parent's investment in a subsidiary is affected by stock transactions of the subsidiary whether or not the parent participates in the transactions. These transactions include the subsidiary's sale of additional stock to the parent and/or minority shareholders, the retirement of common stock, and treasury stock transactions.

Sale of Subsidiary Stock to Minority Shareholders

A parent may allow a subsidiary to sell additional shares of stock in order to raise additional equity funds. A sale of stock by the subsidiary to its minority shareholders results in an increase in the total stockholders' equity against which the controlling interest has a claim. However, the effect of increasing the number of subsidiary shares in the hands of minority stockholders is to lower the controlling interest ownership percentage. Thus, the controlling interest ownership percentage is reduced to a relatively smaller portion of a larger subsidiary equity. The net effect on the value of the controlling interest depends on the price at which the shares are sold.

A subsidiary stock sale appears to create a gain or loss to the parent, since there is an effect on the value of the controlling interest. However, from a consolidated viewpoint, this gain or loss is a result of transactions between the consolidated firm and its shareholders. On this basis, such gains are treated as additional paid-in capital of the parent. Losses are an offset to paid-in capital, unless none exists, in which case the loss is removed from the parent's retained earnings.

Parent Using the Equity Method. A parent company using either the simple or sophisticated equity method may need to adjust its investment account when its subsidiary sells additional shares of stock to minority shareholders. To illustrate, assume that Company P has a 90% interest in Company S. The interest was purchased on January 1, 19X1, at which time the following determination and distribution of excess schedule was prepared:

Price paid		$140,000
Interest acquired:		
Common stock ($10 par)	$100,000	
Retained earnings, January 1, 19X1	50,000	
Total equity	$150,000	
Interest acquired	90%	135,000
Excess of cost over book value attributed to goodwill (10-year life)		**$ 5,000**

On January 1, 19X4, 2,000 shares of previously unissued stock are sold to the minority interest. As a result, the parent's interest is reduced to 75% (9,000 ÷ 12,000). An analysis of the subsidiary's sale of shares to the minority interest at alternative prices is as follows:

	Change in Controlling Interest		
	Case 1—None	Case 2—Increase	Case 3—Decrease
Sale price per share	$24	$30	$20
Company S shareholders' equity prior to sale	$240,000	$240,000	$240,000
Add to common stock, $10 par	20,000	20,000	20,000
Add to paid-in capital in excess of par	28,000	40,000	20,000
Company S shareholders' equity subsequent to sale	$288,000	$300,000	$280,000
Controlling interest subsequent to sale (75%)	$216,000	$225,000	$210,000
Prior controlling interest (90% × $240,000)......	216,000	216,000	216,000
Net increase (decrease), controlling interest ...	0	$ 9,000	$ (6,000)

The parent would record the effect on the controlling interest in each case as follows:

Case 1:   Memo entry only to record a change from a 90% to a 75% interest.

Case 2:

Investment in Company S...............................	9,000	
Paid-In Capital in Excess of Par		9,000
To record increase in ownership interest.		

Case 3:

Retained Earnings.....................................	6,000	
Investment in Company S..............................		6,000
To record decrease in ownership interest. It is assumed that no parent additional paid-in capital exists to offset the decrease.		

To illustrate the effect of Case 2 on consolidation, assume that subsidiary income for 19X4 was $40,000, and that no dividends were declared. The investment account balance under the simple equity method would be determined as follows:

Original cost	$140,000
Simple equity income adjustments, 19X1 through 19X3, 90% × $90,000 increase in retained earnings	81,000
Increase from stock sale to minority on January 1, 19X4	9,000
Simple equity adjustment for 19X4 subsidiary income, 75% × $40,000 income	30,000
Balance, December 31, 19X4	$260,000

In the following partial work sheet for the year ended December 31, 19X4, the trial balances of Company P and Company S reflect the sale of 2,000 additional shares at $30 per share.

Companies P and S
Partial Work Sheet (Simple Equity Method)
For Year Ended December 31, 19X4

	Trial Balance		Eliminations	
	Company P	Company S	Dr.	Cr.
Investment in Co. S (75%)	260,000			(1) 30,000
				(2) 225,000
				(3) 5,000
Goodwill...................................			(3) 5,000	(4) 2,000
Common Stock, Co. P......................	(400,000)			
Paid-In Capital in Excess of Par, Co. P	(9,000)			
Retained Earnings, Co. P..................	(320,000)		(4) 1,500	
Common Stock, Co. S......................		(120,000)	(2) 90,000	
Paid-In Capital in Excess of Par, Co. S		(40,000)	(2) 30,000	
Retained Earnings, Co. S..................		(140,000)	(2) 105,000	
Subsidiary Income	(30,000)		(1) 30,000	
Expenses.................................	40,000	27,000	(4) 500	

Eliminations:
(1) Eliminate the parent's entries recording subsidiary income for the current year. The parent's share is now 75% of the subsidiary's undistributed net income. If the sale had occurred during the year, the old percentage of ownership would be used prior to the sale date.
(2) Eliminate the current 75% share of subsidiary equity balances at the beginning of the year against the investment in Company S account.
(3) Distribute to goodwill the original excess of cost over book value which has been preserved as required by the original determination and distribution of excess schedule.
(4) Amortize the goodwill for the past three years and the current year.

The consolidated work sheet may require the adjustment of controlling and minority shares of beginning Retained Earnings balances for intercompany transactions originating in previous periods. When such adjustments are to be allocated between the controlling and minority retained earnings, the current, not the original, ownership interest percentages are used.

Parent Using the Cost Method. A parent using the cost method records only dividends received from a subsidiary. No adjustment is made for any other changes in the subsidiary stockholders' equity, including changes caused by sales of subsidiary stock. As a result, the entry to convert from the cost method to the equity method on future work sheets must consider not only the equity adjustments for the subsidiary's undistributed income, but also adjustments caused by subsidiary stock sales. A parent using the cost method would still list the subsidiary investment at the original cost, $140,000. The partial work sheet which follows is the same as the previous work sheet for Case 2, except for the use of the cost method.

Companies P and S
Partial Work Sheet (Cost Method)
For Year Ended December 31, 19X4

	Trial Balance		Eliminations	
	Company P	Company S	Dr.	Cr.
Investment in Co. S (75%)	140,000		**Conv.** 90,000	(1) 225,000
				(2) 5,000
Goodwill......................................			(2) 5,000	(3) 2,000
Common Stock, Co. P......................	(400,000)			
Paid-In Capital in Excess of Par, Co. P				**Conv.** 9,000
Retained Earnings, Co. P..................	(239,000)		(3) 1,500	**Conv.** 81,000
Common Stock, Co. S......................		(120,000)	(1) 90,000	
Paid-In Capital in Excess of Par, Co. S		(40,000)	(1) 30,000	
Retained Earnings, Co. S..................		(140,000)	(1) 105,000	
Expenses...................................	40,000	27,000	(3) 500	

Eliminations:

Conv. The simple equity conversion is recorded:
    Undistributed income:
        90% of change in retained earnings of Company S from January 1,
            19X1, to January 1, 19X4, 90% × $90,000....................... $81,000
    Adjustment to paid-in capital:
        Controlling equity interest subsequent to sale on January 1, 19X4, 75%
            × $300,000 .... $225,000
        Controlling equity interest prior to sale on January 1, 19X4, 90% ×
            $240,000 216,000
            Net increase in paid-in capital   9,000
    Total increase in the investment account $90,000

(1) Eliminate 75% of the subsidiary equity balances at the beginning of the year against the investment account.
(2) Distribute the excess of cost to goodwill as shown by the original determination and distribution of excess schedule.
(3) Amortize goodwill for three past years and the current year.

      To review this process, the cost-to-simple-equity conversion amount
for Case 2 is determined as it would apply to the December 31, 19X5
work sheet:

    Undistributed income:
        90% of change in retained earnings of Company S from
            January 1, 19X1, to January 1, 19X4, 90% × $90,000 . $ 81,000
        75% of change in retained earnings of Company S from
            January 1, 19X4, to January 1, 19X5, 75% × $40,000 .   30,000
        Increase in Company P retained earnings $111,000
    Adjustment to paid-in capital:
        Controlling equity interest subsequent to sale on January
            1, 19X4, 75% × $300,000 .... $225,000
        Controlling equity interest prior to sale on January 1, 19X4,
            90% × $240,000 216,000
            Net increase in paid-in capital   9,000
    Total increase in investment account $120,000

Occasionally a dangerous shortcut is attempted, whereby the net change in the controlling ownership interest is calculated by comparing 90% of the total subsidiary equity on January 1, 19X1, to 75% of the total subsidiary equity on January 1, 19X5. This shortcut will produce the correct adjustment to the investment in subsidiary account, but it will not provide the analysis needed to distribute the adjustment to the parent's paid-in capital and retained earnings.

Parent Purchase of Newly Issued Stock

When a subsidiary issues additional stock, a parent may exercise its preemptive right and purchase additional stock proportionate to its original ownership interest. When this occurs, the investment account is increased by the price paid for the newly purchased stock. For example, Company P of the previous examples would make the following entry if it maintained its 90% interest by purchasing 90% of the 2,000 newly issued Company S shares for $30 each:

Investment in Company S (1,800 shares × $30)	54,000	
Cash		54,000

The subsidiary, Company S, would make the following entry to record the sale of the entire 2,000 shares for $30 each:

Cash	60,000	
Common Stock ($10 × 2,000 shares)		20,000
Paid-In Capital in Excess of Par		40,000

The consolidation process will eliminate 90% of all subsidiary equity, including the above increment. Thus, $54,000 of the $60,000 addition will be eliminated. No new excess is created, and the original disparity between the investment account and the underlying equity is not altered. As a result, no additional equity adjustment is needed when the parent maintains its ownership interest and the same price is paid by all buyers. Future equity adjustments and eliminations continue, based on a 90% interest.

The parent might purchase more than 90% of the newly issued shares. In this situation, an additional excess of cost or book value may be created. The stock purchased in excess of that needed to preserve the original ownership interest must be treated as a new block for which a separate determination and distribution of excess schedule is prepared. For example, if the parent purchased all 2,000 shares at $30 per share, the schedule would be prepared as follows for the 200 shares acquired in excess of those needed to preserve the original 90% interest:

Price paid (200 × $30)		$6,000
Interest acquired:		
Total as shown in Case 2	$300,000	
Incremental interest (200 ÷ 12,000)	1⅔%	5,000
Excess of cost over book value regarded as goodwill to be amortized over 10 years		**$1,000**

Future eliminations would be based on a 91⅔% ownership interest. The $1,000 excess would require separate distribution and amortization on future work sheets.

If the parent buys fewer shares than needed to preserve its original ownership percentage, it must make an equity adjustment for the change in its interest caused by the increased minority ownership. Assume that Company P purchased 1,000 of the 2,000 newly issued shares for $30 per share. The parent would then own 10,000 of the 12,000 total subsidiary shares, or ⁵/₆. Consequently, future eliminations would be based on an 83⅓% (⁵/₆) ownership interest. As a result of the subsidiary stock issuance, the parent would calculate an equity adjustment as follows:

Total shareholder equity subsequent to sale	$300,000	
Controlling interest	83⅓%	$250,000
Prior interest adjusted for purchase of new shares:		
Ownership interest prior to sale, 90% × $240,000	$216,000	
Add cost of new shares, 1,000 × $30	30,000	246,000
Net increase in ownership interest		$ 4,000

The parent would then make the following entry:

Investment in Company S	4,000	
Paid-In Capital in Excess of Par		4,000

Subsidiary Retirement of Common Stock

Rather than purchasing additional shares to increase its relative ownership interest, the parent may direct the subsidiary to retire shares held by minority stockholders. Such transactions may affect the value of the parent's ownership interest, depending on the price paid for the shares. From a consolidated viewpoint, any gain that results must be viewed as a change in paid-in capital, since the gain or loss results from transactions with stockholders.

To illustrate a subsidiary stock retirement, assume that prior to recording the retirement of 2,000 of its 10,000 outstanding shares of common stock, a subsidiary, Company S, had the following stockholders' equity:

Capital stock, $10 par	$100,000
Paid-in capital in excess of par	50,000
Retained earnings	90,000
Total stockholders' equity	$240,000

The following entry was then recorded by Company S as a result of the retirement of 2,000 shares, owned by the minority shareholders, at a cost of $26 each:

Capital Stock ($10 par)	20,000	
Paid-In Capital in Excess of Par (²/₁₀ × $50,000)	10,000	
Retained Earnings	22,000	
Cash		52,000

As a result of the retirement, Company S has the following stockholders' equity:

Capital stock, $10 par	$ 80,000
Paid-in capital in excess of par	40,000
Retained earnings	68,000
Total stockholders' equity	$188,000

Instead of directly retiring the shares, the subsidiary might hold them as treasury shares at cost. In this situation, total stockholders' equity would still be reduced to $188,000. Work sheet procedures would eliminate the controlling percentage of both the subsidiary equity accounts and the treasury stock account carried at cost.

Parent Using the Equity Method. A parent using either the simple or sophisticated equity method would record the change in the amount of its ownership interest in a manner similar to that used for subsidiary sales of stock. A comparison is made of the parent's ownership interest immediately before and after the subsidiary retirement. The resulting adjustment is not treated as income or an operating loss, since it results from transactions with stockholders of the consolidated firm.

The equity adjustment for a parent owning 6,000 shares of Subsidiary S's common stock is determined as follows:

Parent ownership interest prior to retirement, $240,000 subsidiary equity × 6,000/10,000 interest	$144,000
Parent ownership interest subsequent to retirement, $188,000 subsidiary equity × 6,000/8,000 interest	141,000
Decrease in parent ownership interest	$ 3,000

The following entry would be recorded if the parent has prior additional paid-in capital to offset the decrease in its interest. If not, Retained Earnings would be debited.

Paid-In Capital in Excess of Par	3,000	
Investment in Subsidiary		3,000

Subsequent to the retirement, the parent will adjust for 75% of the subsidiary's income under the equity method. Any intercompany profit adjustments resulting from subsidiary operations subsequent to the retirement will be shared on a 75/25 basis.

Parent Using the Cost Method. When the cost method is used, the equity conversion entry required on the work sheet would again be separated into the adjustment for undistributed income and the adjustment for a change in the subsidiary's outstanding stock. This procedure is similar to that used for a sale of subsidiary stock. It will again be necessary to adjust for undistributed income, using the old ownership interest for income earned prior to the retirement and the new ownership interest for income earned subsequent to the retirement.

Subsidiary Treasury Stock Transactions

When a subsidiary purchases its outstanding shares and subsequently resells them to the minority interest, no new analysis is required. The parent's investment account would reflect the purchase as a retirement and the sale as a reissue. However, when the treasury stock is purchased and resold within the consolidated firm's fiscal period, a shortcut is possible if the subsidiary uses the cost method of accounting for treasury stock transactions. Since there would be no change in the parent's percentage of ownership by the end of the period, the parent need only make an adjustment equal to its ownership interest multiplied by the "gain or loss" on the treasury stock transaction. This adjustment is carried to the additional paid-in capital of the parent and is not viewed as an operating gain or loss. A loss reduces parent retained earnings only when no additional paid-in capital is available. This method may also be used for the cost-to-equity conversion entry when the treasury stock transaction is consummated during the periods for which the conversion is made.

INDIRECT HOLDINGS

A parent company may own a controlling interest in a subsidiary, which, in turn, owns a controlling interest in another firm. For example, Company A may own a 75% interest in Company B, which, in turn, owns an 80% interest in Company C. Thus, A has indirect holdings in C. This situation could be diagrammed as follows:

Level 1	Level 2
owns 75%	owns 80%

A ⟶ B ⟶ C

The treatment of the "level one" investment in B and the "level two" investment in C can be mastered with the theory that has been discussed, but the procedures must be carefully applied. The procedures are easily applied to indirect holdings when the level one investment already exists at the time of the level two purchase. Complications arise when the level two investment exists prior to the time that the parent achieves control over the subsidiary (level one investment). These complications result because the level two investment held by the subsidiary represents one of the subsidiary's assets which may require adjustment to market value. The investment of the subsidiary in another firm must be carefully included in the determination and distribution of excess schedule prepared at the time of the parent's level one acquisition.

Level One Holding Acquired First

Suppose that Company A purchased a 75% interest in Company B on January 1, 19X1, at which time the following determination and distribution of excess schedule was prepared:

Price paid		$400,000
Interest acquired in Company B:		
Common stock ($10 par)	$200,000	
Retained earnings, January 1, 19X1	100,000	
Total equity	$300,000	
Interest acquired	75%	225,000
Excess of cost over book value attributed to building and equipment (10-year life)		**$175,000**

On January 1, 19X2, the subsidiary, Company B, purchased an 80% interest in Company C, at which time the following schedule was prepared:

Price paid		$270,000
B's interest acquired in Company C:		
Common stock ($10 par)	$100,000	
Retained earnings	120,000	
Total equity	$220,000	
Interest acquired	80%	176,000
Excess of cost over book value attributed to goodwill (20-year life)		**$ 94,000**

Equity adjustments must now be made very carefully. Company A must be sure that Company B has included its equity income from Company C in its net income before Company A records its percentage share of Company B's income.

Assume the following internally generated net incomes:

	Company A	Company B	Company C
19X1	$100,000	$100,000	$20,000
19X2	70,000	76,000	30,000
19X3	90,000	100,000	30,000

On this basis, the following simple equity adjustments would be required:

	Company B's Books	Company A's Books

19X1
Dec. 31
	None (interest in Company C not yet acquired).	Investment in Company B ... 75,000
		   Subsidiary Income 75,000
		   To adjust for 75% of Company B's reported income.

19X2
Dec. 31
	Investment in Company C.... 24,000
	   Subsidiary Income 24,000
	   To adjust for 80% of Company C's reported income.
		Investment in Company B ... 75,000
		   Subsidiary Income 75,000
		   To adjust for 75% of Company B's total income ($76,000 plus $24,000 subsidiary income).

19X3
Dec. 31
	Investment in Company C.... 24,000
	   Subsidiary Income 24,000
	   To adjust for 80% of Company C's reported income.
		Investment in Company B ... 93,000
		   Subsidiary Income 93,000
		   To adjust for 75% of Company B's total income ($100,000 plus $24,000 subsidiary income).

The work sheet of Illustration I, on pages 488 and 489, is based on the trial balances of the three separate firms on December 31, 19X3. The investment account balances reflect the equity adjustments as previously shown. The following additional information for 19X3 is assumed:

	Intercompany Sales by B to A	Intercompany Sales by C to B
Selling company goods in buyer's January 1, 19X3 inventory	$ 8,000	$ 6,000
Sales during 19X3	50,000	40,000
Selling company goods in buyer's December 31, 19X3 inventory	10,000	10,000
Gross profit on all intercompany sales .	25%	30%

The investment accounts must be handled very carefully when any eliminations are made. It is suggested that the level one investment be eliminated first, thereby reducing the Company B retained earnings to the minority interest. Now it is possible to allocate amortizations of excess resulting from the level two (Company C) holding to the controlling interest (Company A) and the Company B minority interest. Since Company B owns the interest in Company C, its minority interest must share in the amortizations of excess resulting from the investment in Company C.

Illustration I produces a consolidated net income of $196,100, which must be distributed to the two minority interests and to the controlling interest. Distribution must proceed from the lowest level (level two) to assure proper distribution. Company B adjusted income includes 80% of the Company C adjusted income; thus, the Company C income distribution schedule must be completed first. The income distribution schedules for Companies C, B, and A are as follows:

Company C

Ending inventory profit .... (13)	$ 3,000	Internally generated income	$ 30,000
		Beginning inventory profit .... **(12)**	1,800
		Adjusted	$ 28,800
		Company B interest, 80%	23,040
		To Company C minority, 20%	$ 5,760

Company B

Ending inventory profit .... (11)	$ 2,500	Internally generated income	$100,000
Amortization of goodwill resulting		Beginning inventory profit .... (10)	2,000
from purchase of investment in		80% of Company C adjusted income	23,040
Company C **8**	4,700		
		Adjusted	$117,840
		Company A interest, 75%	88,380
		To Company B minority, 25%	$ 29,460

Company A

Building and equipment depreciation resulting from investment in Company B .... (4) $17,500	Internally generated income .... $ 90,000
	75% of Company B adjusted income.... 88,380
	Controlling interest $160,880

When the cost method is used, the investment account balances would still contain the January 1, 19X1 $400,000 cost of the Company B investment and the January 1, 19X2 $270,000 cost of the Company C investment. Conversion entries would be made to update both investment accounts to their January 1, 19X3 simple equity balances on the consolidated work sheet. It is advisable to make equity adjustments at the lowest level of investment first because the retained earnings of the midlevel firm must be adjusted for its share of investment income before the parent can adjust for the change in its subsidiary's retained earnings. If the cost method were used in the previous example, the following simple equity conversion entry would be made first for Company B's investment in Company C:

Investment in Company C 24,000
 Retained Earnings (Company B) 24,000
  80% times $30,000 increase in Company C retained
  earnings between January 1, 19X2, and January 1,
  19X3.

The following conversion entry would then be made for Company A's investment in Company B:

Investment in Company B 150,000
 Retained Earnings (Company A) 150,000
  75% times $200,000 increase in Company B retained
  earnings (including previous equity adjustment for
  Company B) between January 1, 19X1, and January
  1, 19X3.

Elimination entries would be made as on the work sheet in Illustration I, except that there would be no need to eliminate the current year's equity adjustment.

Level Two Holding Exists at the Time of the Parent's Purchase

When a parent acquires a controlling interest in another parent company, the determination and distribution of excess schedule must be based on the acquired firm's *consolidated* balance sheet. For example, suppose that Company Y purchased an 80% interest in Company Z on January 1, 19X1, and that Company X purchased a 70% interest in Company Y on January 1, 19X3. Assume that on January 1, 19X3, Company Y owns equipment that is undervalued by $40,000, and that Company Z (the subsidiary) has equipment which is undervalued by

(Credit balance amounts
are in parentheses)

	Trial Balance		
	Company A	Company B	Company C
Inventory, Dec. 31, 19X3	80,000	20,000	30,000
Other Assets	60,000	146,000	130,000
Building and Equipment	300,000	200,000	150,000
Accumulated Depreciation	(100,000)	(60,000)	(30,000)
Investment in Co. B	643,000		
Investment in Co. C		318,000	
Goodwill			
Common Stock ($10 par), Co. A	(300,000)		
Retained Earnings, Jan. 1, 19X3, Co. A	(500,000)		
Common Stock ($10 par), Co. B		(200,000)	
Retained Earnings, Jan. 1, 19X3, Co. B		(300,000)	
Common Stock ($10 par), Co. C			(100,000)
Retained Earnings, Jan. 1, 19X3, Co. C			(150,000)
Sales	(400,000)	(300,000)	(150,000)
Cost of Goods Sold	250,000	160,000	80,000
Expenses	60,000	40,000	40,000
Subsidiary Income	(93,000)	(24,000)	
	0	0	0

Consolidated Net Income

   To Minority Interest, Company C (see income distribution schedule)

   To Minority Interest, Company B (see income distribution schedule)

   To Controlling Retained Earnings (see income distribution schedule)

Total Minority Interest, Dec. 31, 19X1

Retained Earnings, Controlling Interest, Dec. 31, 19X3

Eliminations:

(1) Eliminate the entry made by Company A to record its share of Company B income. This step returns the investment in Company B account to its January 1, 19X3 balance to aid the elimination process.

Intercompany Sales
Subsidiary Companies B and C
Financial Statements
December 31, 19X3

Eliminations		Consolidated Income Statement	Minority Interest	Controlling Retained Earnings	Consolidated Balance Sheet
Dr.	Cr.				
	(11) 2,500				124,500
	(13) 3,000				
					336,000
(3) 175,000					825,000
	(4) 52,500				(242,500)
	(1) 93,000				
	(2) 375,000				
	(3) 175,000				
	(5) 24,000				
	(6) 200,000				
	(7) 94,000				
(7) 94,000	8 9,400				84,600
					(300,000)
(4) 35,000				(458,895)	
8 3,525					
(10) 1,500					
12 1,080					
(2) 150,000			(50,000)		
(2) 225,000			(72,965)		
8 1,175					
(10) 500					
12 360					
(6) 80,000			(20,000)		
(6) 120,000			(29,640)		
12 360					
(9) 90,000		(760,000)			
(11) 2,500	(9) 90,000	401,700			
(13) 3,000	(10) 2,000				
	12 1,800				
(4) 17,500		162,200			
8 4,700					
(1) 93,000					
(5) 24,000					
1,122,200	1,122,200				
		(196,100)			
		5,760	(5,760)		
		29,460	(29,460)		
		160,880		(160,880)	
			(207,825)		(207,825)
				(619,775)	(619,775)
					0

(2) Eliminate 75% of the January 1, 19X3 Company B equity balances against the investment in company B.

(continued)

(3) Distribute the $175,000 excess of cost to the building and equipment account according to the determination and distribution of excess schedule applicable to the level one investment.

(4) Amortize the excess (added depreciation) according to the determination and distribution of excess schedule. This step requires adjustment of Company A retained earnings for 19X1 and 19X2, plus adjustment of 19X3 expenses.

(5) Eliminate the entry made by Company B to record its share of Company C income. This returns the investment in Company C account to its January 1, 19X3 balance to aid elimination.

(6) Eliminate 80% of the January 1, 19X3 Company C equity balances against the investment in Company C.

(7) Distribute the $94,000 excess of cost to goodwill according to the determination and distribution of excess schedule applicable to the level two investment.

8 Amortize the excess (goodwill amortization) according to the determination and distribution of excess schedule. Since created by actions of subsidiary Company B, 19X2 amortization must be prorated 25% ($1,175) to the Company B minority interest and 75% ($3,525) to the controlling interest. Note that the Company B minority interest appears on the work sheet only after the first level investment has been eliminated, again pointing to the need to eliminate the level one investment first.

(9) Eliminate intercompany sales to prevent double counting in the consolidated sales and cost of goods sold.

(10) Eliminate the Company B profit contained in the beginning inventory. Since Company B generated the sale, the correction of beginning retained earnings is split 75% to the controlling interest and 25% to the minority interest. The cost of goods sold is decreased, since the beginning inventory was overstated.

(11) Cost of goods sold is adjusted, and the ending inventory is reduced by the $2,500 of Company B profit contained in the ending inventory.

12 Eliminate the Company C profit contained in the beginning inventory. Since Company C generated the retained earnings adjustment, it is apportioned as follows:

To minority interest in Company C (20%)...	$ 360
To minority interest in Company B (25% of 80%)...	360
To controlling interest (75% of 80%)	1,080
Total	$1,800

(13) Cost of goods sold is adjusted, and the ending inventory is reduced by the $3,000 of Company C profit contained in the ending inventory.

$100,000. Company X would prepare the following determination and distribution of excess schedule, based on the controlling interest in Company Y:

Price paid		$700,000
Interest acquired:		
Company Y common stock	$400,000	
Company Y controlling interest in consolidated retained		
earnings..	320,000	
Total Company Y equity	$720,000	
Interest acquired	70%	504,000
Excess of cost over book value		$196,000
Attributable to Company Y equipment, 70% × $40,000 under-		
valuation	$ 28,000	
Attributable to Company Z equipment, 70% × 80% × $100,000		
undervaluation	56,000	84,000
Attributable to goodwill (20-year life)........................		**$112,000**

Note the following features of the above schedule:

1. The Company Y *consolidated* equity is multiplied by the parent's ownership interest to arrive at the excess of cost over book value.

2. When a Company Y (level one investment) asset is to be adjusted, it can be adjusted only for the parent ownership (70%) portion of the value discrepancy.
3. When a Company Z (level two investment) asset is to be adjusted, it can be adjusted only for the Company X ownership share of the Company Y share of the value discrepancy (70% × 80%, or 56%).
4. Resulting goodwill is based on consolidated asset values for Companies Y and Z.

When the simple equity method is used for the investments, the procedures of Illustration I apply without modification. When the cost method is used, simple equity conversion adjustments again proceed from the lowest level. Be sure to note, however, that in this example Company X would convert to the equity basis for the change in Company Y retained earnings after January 1, 19X3.

Connecting Affiliates

A business combination involving connecting affiliates exists when a parent firm has a direct (level one) investment in a company and an indirect (level two) investment in the same company sufficient to result in control. For example, the following diagram illustrates a connecting affiliate structure:

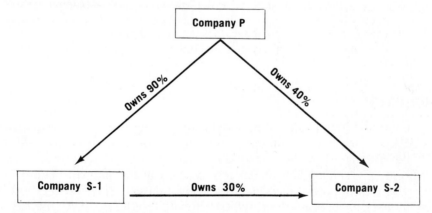

Not only does Company P have a 90% interest in Company S-1, but it also has, effectively, a 67% interest in Company S-2, calculated as follows:

Direct	40%
Indirect (90% × 30%)	27%
Total	67%

This type of structure is more readily consolidated once the determination and distribution of excess schedule has been prepared. Caution must be used in the schedule preparation because of differing dates for each investment. Referring to the diagram, the special concerns in consolidating connecting affiliates are as follows:

1. Company S-2 is not generally included in the consolidation process until the total percentage of shares held by the parent and its subsidiaries (70% in this example) exceeds 50%. Prior to that time, an investment of 20% or more is treated according to APB Opinion No. 18, and a lesser investment is accounted for under the cost method.
2. Any amortizations of excess resulting from the 30% investment of S-1 in S-2 are distributed to controlling and S-1 minority interests in retained earnings on a 90/10 basis.
3. Any corrections to retained earnings caused by Company S-2 generated transactions are distributed 30% to minority S-2, 3% (10% × 30%) to minority S-1, and 67% [40% + (90% × 30%)] to the controlling interest.
4. Income distributions would begin with S-2: 30% of its income would go to minority S-2, 30% would flow to the Company S-1 distribution schedule, and 40% would flow to the Company P schedule. Company P will receive 90% of the Company S-1 adjusted income (including the 30% share of Company S-2).
5. When either equity method is used, each firm must adjust for its interest in Company S-2, even though neither interest by itself would merit consolidation techniques.
6. When the cost method is used, each investment is converted to the simple equity method from the purchase date forward. Again, equity conversions must begin at the lowest level. For example, the Company S-1 investment in Company S-2 must be converted first so that Company S-1 retained earnings is updated before the Company P investment in Company S-1 is converted to the simple equity method.

MUTUAL HOLDINGS

A mutual holding structure exists when the subsidiary owns any percentage of the parent company's common stock. Such an investment must be eliminated in the consolidation process. From a consolidated viewpoint, the shares have been removed from the market. There are two ways that such holdings may be consolidated. The first method is termed the *reciprocal method*, which allocates to the minority interest a percentage of the parent income. This method requires simultaneous equations and becomes very complicated when there are excesses of cost or book value applicable to each set of investments and/or intercompany profit transactions. The method will be explained in its simplest state, but it is considered obsolete and theoretically unsound in that it views parent shares held by the subsidiary as being alive and entitled to a share of consolidated income. The second and more currently popular method is called the *treasury stock* approach. From a consolidated viewpoint, the subsidiary acquisition of parent shares is viewed as a retirement of the shares or as a temporary treasury stock purchase where there is an intent to resell the shares. Under the treasury stock method, the shares are "off the market" and have no claim to income.

Reciprocal Method

To understand the objections to the reciprocal method, it is necessary to understand the procedures required by the method. The example which follows is simplified, since the reciprocal method is not often found in practice. Suppose that Company P acquired an 80% interest in Company S on January 1, 19X1, at which time the following determination and distribution of excess schedule was prepared:

Price paid		$200,000
Interest acquired:		
Common stock ($10 par)	$100,000	
Retained earnings	50,000	
Total equity	$150,000	
Interest acquired	80%	120,000
Excess of cost over book value attributed to equipment (20-year remaining life)		**$ 80,000**

On January 1, 19X3, Company S purchases a 10% interest in the parent, Company P. The determination and distribution of excess schedule for this investment is prepared as follows:

Price paid		$ 80,000
Interest acquired:		
Common stock..	$500,000	
Retained earnings	200,000	
Total equity	$700,000	
Ownership interest.....................................	10%	70,000
Excess of cost over book value attributed to goodwill (10-year life)...		**$ 10,000**

Typically, the determination and distribution of excess schedule will be based only on Company P equity, not the total controlling interest. The excess could be distributed to the separate assets of Company P (including the investment in Company S), but based on materiality, it would usually be distributed only to goodwill. The parent and the subsidiary may use either the cost method or the equity method to account for intercompany investments. In Illustration II, on pages 494-495, both firms are assumed to use the simple equity method. Company P has recorded subsidiary income of $16,000 (80% × Company S reported income of $20,000), and Company S has recorded investment income of $4,000 (10% × Company P internal income of $40,000).

In Illustration II, the consolidated net income is distributed to Company P and Company S by solving simultaneously the equations shown at the top of page 496. These equations are based on each company's adjusted internally generated income.

Illustration II—Mutual Holdings
Company P and
Work Sheet for
For Year Ended

(Credit balance amounts
are in parentheses)

	Trial Balance	
	Company P	Company S
Investment in Company S (80%)	248,000	
Investment in Company P (10%)		84,000
Equipment	608,000	180,000
Accumulated Depreciation	(100,000)	(50,000)
Goodwill		
Common Stock, Co. P	(500,000)	
Retained Earnings, Jan. 1, 19X3, Co. P	(200,000)	
Common Stock, Co. S		(100,000)
Retained Earnings, Jan. 1, 19X3, Co. S		(90,000)
Sales	(300,000)	(200,000)
Cost of Goods Sold	180,000	120,000
Expenses	80,000	60,000
Subsidiary (or Investment) Income	(16,000)	(4,000)
	0	0
Consolidated Net Income		
To Minority Interest (see solution to simultaneous equations, page 496)		
To Controlling Interest (see solution to simultaneous equations)		
Total Minority Interest, Dec. 31, 19X3		
Retained Earnings, Controlling Interest, Dec. 31, 19X3		

Eliminations:
(1) Eliminate the entry made by the parent during the current year to record its share of Company S income. It does not matter which investment account is eliminated first.
(2) Eliminate 80% of the January 1, 19X3 subsidiary equity balances against the investment in Company S account.
(3) Distribute the excess of cost over book value to the equipment account as specified by the determination and distribution of excess schedule.
(4) Amortize the excess of $80,000 for the past two years and the current year.
(5) Eliminate the entry made by Company S to record its share of Company P income.

Income Distribution Schedules

Company S Adjusted Internally Generated Income

Amortization of excess cost— goodwill amortization $1,000	Unadjusted internally generated income $20,000
	Adjusted...................... $19,000

Reciprocal Method
Subsidiary Company S
Consolidated Financial Statements
December 31, 19X3

Eliminations		Consolidated Income Statement	Minority Interest	Controlling Retained Earnings	Consolidated Balance Sheet
Dr.	Cr.				
	(1)　16,000				
	(2)　152,000				
	(3)　80,000				
	(5)　4,000				
	(6)　70,000				
	(7)　10,000				
(3)　80,000					868,000
	(4)　12,000				(162,000)
(7)　10,000	(8)　1,000				9,000
(6)　50,000					(450,000)
(4)　8,000				(172,000)	
(6)　20,000					
(2)　80,000			(20,000)		
(2)　72,000			(18,000)		
		(500,000)			
		300,000			
(4)　4,000		145,000			
(8)　1,000					
(1)　16,000					
(5)　4,000					
345,000	345,000				
		(55,000)			
		4,913	(4,913)		
		50,087		(50,087)	
			(42,913)		(42,913)
				(222,087)	(222,087)
					0

(6) Eliminate 10% of the January 1, 19X3 parent equity balances against the investment in Company P account. Note that 10% of the original January 1, 19X3 Company P retained earnings is eliminated without regard to the $8,000 amortization of excess adjustment, since this adjustment was not included in the original determination and distribution of excess schedule.

(7) Distribute the excess of cost over book value to goodwill as specified by the determination and distribution of excess schedule.

(8) Amortize the excess for the current year.

Company P Adjusted Internally Generated Income

Amortization of excess cost—	Unadjusted internally generated
depreciation $4,000	income $40,000
	Adjusted...................... $36,000

Note: If intercompany profit adjustments existed, they would be entered in the income distribution schedule.

$$P = \$36,000 + .8S$$
$$S = \$19,000 + .1P$$

Solution: $\quad P - .8S = \$36,000$
$\quad\quad\quad -.1P + \quad S = \$19,000$

Multiplying the first equation by .1 and adding equations,

$$.1P - \quad .08S = \$\ 3,600$$
$$-.1P + 1.00S = \$19,000$$
$$\overline{\quad\quad\quad .92S = \$22,600}$$
$$S = \$24,565$$
$$P = \$36,000 + .8\ (\$24,565)$$
$$P = \$55,652$$

To minority interest: $20\% \times$ Company S income of $\$24,565 = \$\ 4,913$

To controlling interest: $90\% \times$ Company P income of $\$55,652 = \$50,087$

Treasury Stock Method

The treasury stock method does not view parent shares held by the subsidiary as outstanding. When it is intended that the shares are to be reissued, they are viewed as treasury shares which are recorded at cost. When resold, an excess received over cost is carried to additional paid-in capital. If cost exceeds proceeds on resale, the difference is offset against existing paid-in capital. If there is no paid-in capital, retained earnings is reduced. When it is not intended that the shares be reissued, the stock is retired on the work sheet, using the original investment cost as the retirement price. Regardless of the method used, the resulting capital account adjustments fall entirely upon the parent. The subsidiary is viewed as an agent accomplishing the transaction. An important requirement of either of the treasury stock approaches is that the subsidiary investment in the parent is *maintained at its original cost*. Since the stock is not to be viewed as outstanding, it has no claim on income. If equity adjustments have been made in error, they must be reversed on the consolidated work sheet.

To illustrate the treasury stock method, return to the example in Illustration II. The determination and distribution of excess schedule for the parent's investment in the subsidiary would be unchanged. There would be no need for a determination and distribution of excess schedule for the subsidiary investment, since the investment will not be eliminated. During 19X3, the parent will make the normal simple equity adjustment to acknowledge its 80% interest in subsidiary income:

Investment in Company S	16,000	
Subsidiary Income		16,000
To record 80% of subsidiary reported income of $20,000.		

There is no equity adjustment for the Company S investment in the parent, since it must remain at cost. The investment in Company S account on the trial balance work sheet of Illustration III, on pages 498-499, is computed as follows:

Original cost..	$200,000
80% × 19X1 and 19X2 undistributed income of $40,000	32,000
19X3 simple equity adjustment	16,000
Balance, December 31, 19X3..................................	$248,000

Examination of the formal statements for the consolidated firm reveals that the treasury shares are held by the consolidated firm, and that no income accrues to them. These statements are as follows:

Company P and Subsidiary Company S
Consolidated Income Statement
For Year Ended December 31, 19X3

Sales	$500,000
Less cost of goods sold	300,000
Gross profit	$200,000
Less expenses	144,000
Consolidated net income	$ 56,000
Distributed to:	
Minority interest of Company S	$ 4,000
Controlling interest of Company P...................................	52,000
Total	$ 56,000

Company P and Subsidiary Company S
Retained Earnings Statement
For Year Ended December 31, 19X3

	Minority Interest	Controlling Interest
Balance, January 1, 19X3...............................	$ 18,000	$192,000
Net income	4,000	52,000
Balance, December 31, 19X3	$ 22,000	$244,000

Company P and Subsidiary Company S
Consolidated Balance Sheet
December 31, 19X3

Assets		Stockholders' Equity		
Equipment	$868,000	Minority interest		$ 42,000
Less accumulated depreciation	162,000	Controlling interest:		
		Common stock ...	$500,000	
		Retained earnings	244,000	744,000
		Total		$786,000
		Less treasury stock at cost		80,000
Total assets	$706,000	Net stockholders' equity		$706,000

(Credit balance amounts
are in parentheses)

	Trial Balance	
	Company P	Company S
Investment in Company S (80%)	248,000	
Investment in Company P (10%), at cost		80,000
Equipment	608,000	180,000
Accumulated Depreciation	(100,000)	(50,000)
Common Stock, Co. P	(500,000)	
Retained Earnings, Jan. 1, 19X3, Co. P	(200,000)	
Common Stock, Co. S		(100,000)
Retained Earnings, Jan. 1, 19X3, Co. S		(90,000)
Sales	(300,000)	(200,000)
Cost of Goods Sold	180,000	120,000
Expenses	80,000	60,000
Subsidiary Income	(16,000)	
Treasury Stock (cost)		
	0	0
Consolidated Net Income		
To Minority Interest (see distribution schedule)		
To Controlling Retained Earnings (see distribution schedule)		
Minority Interest, Dec. 31, 19X3		
Retained Earnings, Controlling Interest, Dec. 31, 19X3		

Eliminations:
(1-4) Same as entries 1-4 of Illustration II.
 5 The Investment in Company P must be at cost. If any equity adjustments have been made, they must be reversed and the investment in the parent returned to cost. If the shares are to be reissued, the investment is then transferred to the treasury stock account, a contra account to total consolidated stockholders' equity.

Income Distribution Schedules

Subsidiary Company S income distribution

Internally generated net income .	$20,000
Minority share	20%
Minority interest	$ 4,000

The treasury stock method is usually more practical to use than the reciprocal method and is supported by ARB 51, which states: "Shares of the parent held by a subsidiary should not be treated as outstanding stock in the consolidated balance sheet."[2] Further support comes from an American Accounting Association publication which states:

[2] *Accounting Research Bulletin No. 51,* "Consolidated Financial Statements" (New York: American Institute of Certified Public Accountants, 1959), par. 13.

Treasury Stock Method
Subsidiary Company S
Financial Statements
December 31, 19X3

Eliminations Dr.	Eliminations Cr.	Consolidated Income Statement	Minority Interest	Controlling Retained Earnings	Consolidated Balance Sheet
	(1) 16,000				
	(2) 152,000				
	(3) 80,000				
	5 80,000				
(3) 80,000					868,000
	(4) 12,000				(162,000)
					(500,000)
(4) 8,000				(192,000)	
(2) 80,000			(20,000)		
(2) 72,000			(18,000)		
		(500,000)			
		300,000			
(4) 4,000		144,000			
(1) 16,000					
5 80,000					80,000
340,000	340,000				
		(56,000)			
		4,000	(4,000)		
		52,000		(52,000)	
			(42,000)		(42,000)
				(244,000)	(244,000)
					0

As an alternative to Step 5, the cost of the treasury shares could be used to retire them on the work sheet as follows:

Common Stock, Company P	50,000	
Retained Earnings, Company P	30,000	
Investment in Company P		80,000

Parent Company P income distribution

Amortization of excess cost—depreciation .... $ 4,000	Internally generated net income . $40,000
	80% × Company S income 16,000
	Controlling interest $52,000

Shares of the controlling company's capital stock owned by a subsidiary before the date of acquisition of control should be treated in consolidation as treasury stock. Any subsequent acquisition or sale by a subsidiary should likewise be treated in the consolidated statements as though it had been the act of the controlling company.[3]

---

[3] *Accounting and Reporting Standards for Corporate Financial Statements and Preceding Statements and Supplements* (Columbus: American Accounting Association, 1957), p. 44.

QUESTIONS

1. What effect does a subsidiary stock dividend have on consolidation procedures (a) when the equity method is used, (b) when the cost method is used?
2. How does a subsidiary's sale of additional shares of stock affect a parent's ownership interest, assuming that the parent did not participate in the sale?
3. When does the value of a parent's ownership interest increase as a result of a sale of subsidiary stock to minority shareholders, and why is this increase not reflected in income?
4. Describe the complications which develop when the parent purchases stock newly issued by the subsidiary, but the parent buys (a) more than its previous ownership percentage, (b) less than its previous ownership percentage of the newly issued shares.
5. What special procedures are necessary when making equity adjustments to record subsidiary income when an indirect holding situation exists?
6. What new procedures are needed on the determination and distribution of excess schedule when a parent acquires a controlling interest in a subsidiary company which, at the time of the acquisition, also owns a controlling interest in another firm?
7. What is a connecting affiliate, and how is income distributed to the parent calculated?
8. Describe a mutual holding and the alternative methods used to consolidate such holdings.
9. Why might the reciprocal method of accounting for mutual holdings be considered theoretically unsound?
10. Under the treasury stock method of accounting for mutual holdings, intent determines the exact treatment of the parent shares owned by the subsidiary. Explain the different treatments available under the treasury stock method.

EXERCISES

Exercise 1. On January 1, 19X7, Pattern Industries purchased 80% of the outstanding stock of Becker Controls for $400,000. At the time of the acquisition, Becker Controls had the following stockholders' equity:

Common stock, $10 par	$300,000
Paid-in capital in excess of par.......................	90,000
Retained earnings....................................	110,000
Total stockholders' equity	$500,000

It was determined that Becker Controls' book values approximated market as of the purchase date.

On July 1, 19X7, Becker Controls distributed a 10% stock dividend when the market value of its common stock was $15 per share. A cash dividend of $.50 per share was distributed on December 31, 19X7. Becker Controls' net income for 19X7 amounted to $40,000 and was earned evenly throughout the year.

(1) Prepare the entry required on Becker Controls' books to reflect the stock dividend distributed on July 1, 19X7. Prepare the stockholders' equity section of Becker Controls' balance sheet as of December 31, 19X7.

(2) Prepare the simple equity method entries that Pattern Industries would make during 19X7 to record its investment in Becker Controls.

(3) Prepare the elimination that would be made on the December 31, 19X7 consolidated work sheet (assume the use of the simple equity method).

Exercise 2. The Beta Corporation had the following stockholders' equity on January 1, 19X8:

Common stock, $10 par	$200,000
Paid-in capital in excess of par.......................	100,000
Retained earnings	100,000
Total stockholders' equity	$400,000

Colfax Company purchased 75% of the outstanding common stock of Beta Corporation for $270,000 on January 1, 19X7, at which time the Beta Corporation had retained earnings of $60,000. At that time, there was no difference between the price paid and the interest acquired in Beta Corporation.

On July 1, 19X8, Beta Corporation sold 5,000 shares of stock to the general public. Beta Corporation had net income of $20,000 for the first half of 19X8 and $30,000 for the second half. No cash dividends have ever been distributed by Beta Corporation.

Prepare the entries on Colfax Company's books, using the simple equity method, to reflect the investment in Beta Corporation. Assume that the stock was sold to the public at (1) $18 per share, (2) $21 per share, and (3) $23 per share.

Exercise 3. Assume the same facts as in Exercise 2, except that Colfax Company accounts for its investment in Beta Corporation by the cost method.

Prepare the entry that would be needed on the 19X9 work sheet to convert the investment account to the simple equity balance as of January 1, 19X9. Prepare the entry based on each of the following prices for the 5,000 shares issued July 1, 19X8: (1) $18 per share, (2) $21 per share, and (3) $23 per share.

Exercise 4. On January 1, 19X8, Toth Company purchased an 80% interest in Casper Company for $300,000. On the purchase date, Casper Company had the following stockholders' equity:

Common stock, $5 par	$150,000
Paid-in capital in excess of par.......................	120,000
Retained earnings	105,000
Total stockholders' equity	$375,000

Casper Company had net income of $25,000 for 19X8. No dividends were paid or declared during 19X8.

On January 1, 19X9, Casper Company sold 10,000 shares of common stock at $15 per share.

Assuming that the parent uses the simple equity method, prepare all parent company entries required for the issuance of the shares. Also prepare a new determination and distribution of excess schedule for the investment if it is needed. Assume the following alternative situations:

(1) Toth Company purchased 5,000 shares

(2) Toth Company purchased 8,000 shares.

(3) Toth Company purchased 9,000 shares.

Exercise 5. The following comparative statements of stockholders' equity were prepared for the Newman Corporation:

	Jan. 1, 19X3	Jan. 1, 19X5	Jan. 1, 19X8
Common stock, $10 par	$250,000	$200,000	$200,000
Paid-in capital in excess of par........	50,000	40,000	40,000
Retained earnings	0	35,000	110,000
Total stockholders' equity	$300,000	$275,000	$350,000

Tessman Corporation purchased 60% of Newman Corporation common stock for $12 per share on January 1, 19X3, when the latter corporation was formed.

On December 31, 19X4, Newman Corporation purchased 5,000 shares of its own common stock from minority interests for $15 per share. These shares were retired on January 1, 19X5.

Newman Corporation had $50,000 of net income in 19X8 and has never declared a cash dividend.

Assuming that Tessman Corporation uses the cost method to record its investment in Newman Corporation, prepare the necessary cost-to-simple-equity conversion and the eliminations required on the consolidated work sheet as of December 31, 19X8.

Exercise 6. You have secured the following information for Companies A, B, and C concerning their internally generated net incomes (excluding subsidiary income) and dividends paid:

	A	B	C
19X5 Internally generated net income...............	$30,000	$20,000	$10,000
Dividends declared and paid	10,000	5,000	—
19X6 Internally generated net income...............	50,000	30,000	25,000
Dividends declared and paid	10,000	5,000	5,000
19X7 Internally generated net income...............	40,000	40,000	30,000
Dividends declared and paid	10,000	5,000	5,000

(1) Assume that Company A purchased an 80% interest in Company B on January 1, 19X5, and Company B purchased a 60% interest in Company C on January 1, 19X6. Prepare the simple equity method adjusting entries made by Companies A and B for subsidiary investments for the years 19X5 through 19X7.

(2) Assume that Company B buys a 70% interest in Company C on January 1, 19X5, and Company A buys a 90% interest in Company B on January 1, 19X7. Prepare the simple equity method adjusting entries made by Companies A and B for subsidiary investments.

Exercise 7. Companies A, B, and C produced the following separate internally generated net incomes during 19X9:

	A	B	C
Sales..	$300,000	$375,000	$100,000
Less cost of goods sold	200,000	300,000	60,000
Gross profit	$100,000	$ 75,000	$ 40,000
Expenses...	50,000	30,000	10,000
Internally generated net income	$ 50,000	$ 45,000	$ 30,000

Company A purchased a 60% interest in Company B on January 1, 19X6, and Company B purchased an 80% interest in Company C on January 1, 19X7. Both investments were purchased at a price equal to the book value of the stock purchased.

Additional information:

(a) Company B sold a machine to Company C on January 1, 19X8, for $15,000, when the machine had a book value of $10,000. The machine is being depreciated on a straight-line basis over five years.

(b) Company A purchased goods billed at $20,000 from Company C during 19X9. The price includes a 66⅔% markup on cost. One half of the goods are still held in Company A's year-end inventory.

(c) Company B purchased goods billed at $25,000 from Company A during 19X9. Company A always bills Company B for cost plus 50%. Company B had $6,000 of Company A goods in its beginning inventory and $1,800 of Company A goods in its ending inventory.

(d) Company C purchased goods billed at $15,000 from Company B during 19X9. Company B bills Company C at cost plus 25%. $7,500 of the goods remain unsold at year end. The goods were inventoried at $5,000 under the lower of cost or market procedure.

Prepare a consolidated income statement for 19X9, including the distribution of consolidated net income supported by income distribution schedules.

Exercise 8. On January 1, 19X6, Hanson Company purchased a 60% interest in Kalko Company for $110,000. The purchase price represented a $10,000 excess of cost over book value, which was attributable to goodwill with a 10-year life. The investment is recorded under the simple equity method.

On January 1, 19X8, Globig Company purchased a 70% interest in Hanson Company for $325,000. The Globig Company believes that the goodwill remaining on the investment by Hanson in Kalko is correctly stated. Comparative equities of Hanson Company and Kalko Company immediately prior to the purchase revealed:

Stockholders' Equity	Hanson Company	Kalko Company
Common stock, $5 par	$150,000	—
Common stock, $10 par	—	$100,000
Paid-in capital in excess of par	90,000	20,000
Retained earnings	165,000	80,000
Total stockholders' equity	$405,000	$200,000

An analysis of the accounts of Hanson Company and Kalko Company on January 1, 19X8, revealed that Kalko's land was undervalued by $10,000, and that Hanson's equipment with a 5-year future life was undervalued by $15,000. All other book values approximated market values for Hanson and Kalko.

Prepare a determination and distribution of excess schedule for Globig's purchase of Hanson Company stock on January 1, 19X8.

Exercise 9. The following diagram depicts the investment affiliations between Companies X, Y, and Z:

The following facts apply to 19X3 operations:

	X	Y	Z
Internally generated net income	$120,000	$80,000	$50,000
Dividends declared and paid	50,000	20,000	10,000

All investments were made at a price equal to book value.

(1) Prepare the simple equity method adjustments that would be made for investments owned by Companies X and Y during the year 19X3.

(2) Assume that Company Z sold a piece of equipment to Company Y on January 1, 19X3, for $32,000. The book value of the machine was $20,000, and it has an 8-year remaining life. Straight-line depreciation is used. Determine the consolidated net income, using the facts given, and indicate the interest of each ownership group. Income distribution schedules may be used for support.

Exercise 10. The Myles Corporation and its subsidiary, Dowling Corporation, had the following trial balances as of December 31, 19X8:

	Myles Corporation	Dowling Corporation
Current Assets..	400,000	182,000
Investment in Dowling Corporation...........................	398,000	—
Investment in Myles Corporation.............................	—	150,000
Property, Plant, and Equipment (net)	850,000	400,000
Liabilities	(200,000)	(100,000)
Common Stock ($10 par)....................................	(1,000,000)	(500,000)
Retained Earnings	(400,000)	(100,000)
Sales...	(800,000)	(350,000)
Dividend Income...	—	(2,000)
Subsidiary Income	(18,000)	—
Cost of Goods Sold	600,000	240,000
Expenses...	150,000	80,000
Dividends Declared	20,000	—
	0	0

Myles Corporation purchased its 60% interest in Dowling Corporation for $350,000 on January 1, 19X6. At that time, Dowling's Retained Earnings balance was $50,000. Any excess of cost over book value was attributable to goodwill with a 20-year life.

Dowling Corporation purchased a 10% interest in Myles Corporation on January 1, 19X8, for $150,000. Myles' book values approximated market values at the time of the purchase. Any resulting goodwill will be amortized over 20 years.

No intercompany transactions occurred during the year.

(1) Prepare determination and distribution of excess schedules for the intercompany investments.

(2) Prepare a consolidated income statement, including the income distribution, using the reciprocal method for mutual holdings.

(3) Prepare a consolidated income statement, including the income distribution, using the treasury stock method for mutual holdings.

(4) State how the investment in Myles stock will appear on the consolidated balance sheet under the two alternative methods of accounting for mutual holdings.

PROBLEMS

Problem 11-1. On January 1, 19X7, Zilke Corporation purchased 8,000 shares of Tempe Company and 18,000 shares of Semple Company for $175,000 and $250,000 respectively.

Tempe Company and Semple Company had the following stockholders' equities immediately prior to Zilke's purchase:

	Tempe Company	Semple Company
Common stock, $5 par	$ 50,000	—
Common stock, $10 par	—	$300,000
Paid-in capital in excess of par	100,000	—
Retained earnings	50,000	100,000
Total stockholders' equity	$200,000	$400,000

Additional information:
(a) Net income for Tempe Company and Semple Company for 19X7 and 19X8 follows (income is assumed to be earned evenly throughout the year):

	19X7	19X8
Tempe Company	$30,000	$40,000
Semple Company	50,000	40,000

(b) No cash dividends were paid or declared by Tempe Company or Semple Company during 19X7 and 19X8.
(c) Tempe Company distributed a 10% stock dividend on December 31, 19X7. Tempe's stock was selling at $20 per share when the stock dividend was declared.
(d) On July 1, 19X8, Tempe Company sold 2,750 shares of stock at $30 per share. Zilke Corporation purchased none of these shares.
(e) Semple Company sold 5,000 shares of stock on July 1, 19X7, at $15 per share. Zilke Corporation purchased 3,000 of these shares.
(f) On January 1, 19X8, Semple Company purchased 5,000 shares of its common stock from minority interests at $12 per share. These shares were subsequently sold on January 5, 19X8, at $15 per share. Zilke Corporation did not purchase any of these shares.

Required:

Assume that the Zilke Corporation uses the simple equity method. Record each of the adjustments required during 19X7 and 19X8.

Problem 11-2. On January 1, 19X6, Bennington Corporation acquired a 60% interest in Keesey Company and an 80% interest in Singstock Company. The purchase prices were $200,000 and $250,000 respectively.

Immediately prior to the purchase, Keesey Company and Singstock Company had the following stockholders' equities:

	Keesey Company	Singstock Company
Common stock, $10 par	$200,000	—
Common stock, $20 par	—	$200,000
Paid-in capital in excess of par	50,000	—
Retained earnings	100,000	100,000
Total stockholders' equity	$350,000	$300,000

Additional information:

(a) Keesey Company and Singstock Company had the following net incomes for 19X6 through 19X8 (incomes were earned evenly throughout the year):

	19X6	19X7	19X8
Keesey Company	$50,000	$60,000	$60,000
Singstock Company	40,000	30,000	55,000

(b) Keesey Company had the following equity-related transactions for the first three years after it became a subsidiary of Bennington Corporation:

July 1, 19X6	Sold 5,000 shares of stock at $20 per share. Bennington purchased 3,000 of these shares.
December 31, 19X7	Paid a cash dividend of $1 per share.
July 1, 19X8	Retired 5,000 shares of minority-owned stock at $25 per share.

(c) Singstock Company had the following equity-related transactions for the first three years after it became a subsidiary of Bennington Corporation:

December 31, 19X6	Issued a 10% stock dividend. Market value of Singstock common stock was $30 per share on the declaration date.
October 1, 19X7	Sold 4,000 shares at $25 per share. Of these shares, 200 were purchased by Bennington Corporation.
December 31, 19X8	Retired 5,000 minority shares at $40 per share.

(d) Bennington Corporation has $200,000 of additional paid-in capital on December 31, 19X8.

Required:

Bennington uses the cost method to account for its investments in subsidiaries. Convert its investments to the simple equity method as of December 31, 19X8, and provide adequate support for the entries. Assume that the 19X8 nominal accounts are closed.

Problem 11-3. On January 1, 19X6, Partyka Company purchased 80% of the outstanding common stock of Scholl Company for $600,000.

On January 1, 19X8, Scholl Company sold 25,000 shares of common stock to the public at $10 per share. Partyka Company did not purchase any of these shares. Scholl Company had the following stockholders' equity at the end of 19X5 and 19X7:

	December 31	
	19X5	19X7
Common stock, $2 par	$200,000	$200,000
Paid-in capital in excess of par	400,000	400,000
Retained earnings	100,000	180,000
Total stockholders' equity	$700,000	$780,000

On the January 1, 19X6 purchase date, Scholl Company's book values approximated market values, except for a building which was undervalued by $30,000. The building had an estimated future life of 20 years. Any additional excess is attributed to goodwill with a 5-year life.

Trial balances for Partyka Company and its subsidiary, Scholl Company, as of December 31, 19X8, are as follows:

	Partyka Company	Scholl Company
Cash	249,040	55,000
Accounts Receivable (net)	310,000	190,000
Inventory	325,000	175,000
Investment in Scholl Company	600,000	—
Property, Plant, and Equipment	2,450,000	1,400,000
Accumulated Depreciation	(1,256,000)	(536,000)
Liabilities	(750,000)	(210,000)
Common Stock ($10 par)	(1,500,000)	—
Common Stock ($2 par)	—	(250,000)
Paid-In Capital in Excess of Par	—	(600,000)
Retained Earnings	(375,000)	(180,000)
Sales..	(1,600,000)	(750,000)
Subsidiary Dividend Income	(23,040)	—
Cost of Goods Sold	1,120,000	450,000
Other Expenses....................................	405,000	220,000
Dividends Declared	45,000	36,000
	0	0

No intercompany transactions have ever taken place between Partyka Company and Scholl Company.

Required:

Prepare a consolidated work sheet necessary for the preparation of a consolidated balance sheet and income statement for Partyka Company and its subsidiary, Scholl Company, as of December 31, 19X8. Ignore income tax considerations.

Problem 11-4. On January 1, 19X7, Welch Corporation purchased a 60% interest in Farmside Company for $150,000. Farmside's stockholders' equity on the purchase date was as follows:

Common stock, $5 par	$100,000
Paid-in capital in excess of par.......................	70,000
Retained earnings	60,000
Total stockholders' equity	$230,000

It was determined that the book values of Farmside's assets and liabilities approximated market values, except for a piece of equipment that was undervalued by $20,000. This particular piece of equipment was being depreciated on a straight-line basis and had an estimated remaining life of 10 years at the date of purchase.

On January 1, 19X8, Farmside Company sold 5,000 shares of common stock, of which 2,000 shares were purchased by Welch Corporation at $12 per share.

The following schedule summarizes the intercompany merchandise sales for 19X8:

	Welch Corporation	Farmside Company
Merchandise in inventory, January 1, 19X8..................	$ 5,000	$ 3,000
Sales for 19X8...	30,000	20,000
Merchandise in inventory, December 31, 19X8	2,000	4,000
Gross profit on sales	40%	30%

No intercompany debt remained as of December 31, 19X8.

Welch's investment in Farmside Company was determined as follows:

Original cost	$150,000
60% of Farmside's 19X7 income ($40,000 × 60%).........................	24,000
	$174,000
Less 60% of Farmside dividends declared in 19X7 (60% × $8,000)	(4,800)
	$169,200
Cost to acquire additional shares (new issue)	24,000
56% of Farmside's 19X8 income ($50,000 × 56%).........................	28,000
	$221,200
Less 56% of Farmside's dividend declared in 19X8 (56% × $10,000)	(5,600)
Investment balance, December 31, 19X8	$215,600

Farmside has paid a quarterly $.10 dividend per outstanding common share since the second quarter of 19X6.

The trial balances of Welch Corporation and its subsidiary as of December 31, 19X8, are as follows:

	Welch	Farmside
Cash	76,000	23,500
Accounts Receivable	205,000	60,000
Inventory	350,000	80,000
Investment in Farmside Company	215,600	—
Property, Plant, and Equipment	1,800,000	360,000
Accumulated Depreciation	(600,000)	(89,500)
Accounts Payable	(180,000)	(64,000)
Other Current Liabilities...................................	(26,000)	(8,000)
Bonds Payable...	(500,000)	—
Common Stock ($10 par)	(1,000,000)	—
Common Stock ($5 par)	—	(125,000)
Paid-In Capital in Excess of Par	—	(105,000)
Retained Earnings	(212,600)	(92,000)
Sales...	(1,950,000)	(600,000)
Subsidiary Income	(28,000)	—
Cost of Goods Sold	1,170,000	420,000
Other Expenses...	630,000	130,000
Dividends Declared	50,000	10,000
	0	0

Required:

Assuming that Farmside earned its income evenly during 19X7 and 19X8, prepare a consolidated work sheet necessary to prepare a consolidated balance sheet and income statement for Welch Company and subsidiary as of December 31, 19X8.

Problem 11-5. The audit of Bell Company and its subsidiaries for the year ended December 31, 19X2, was completed, and the trial balances shown at the top of page 509 were prepared. The working papers contain the following information:

(a) Bell Company acquired 4,000 shares of Ware Company common stock for $320,000 on January 1, 19X1, and an additional 500 shares for $45,000 on January 1, 19X2.

(b) Bell Company acquired all of Eddy Company's 8,000 outstanding shares of stock on January 1, 19X1, for $600,000. On January 1, 19X2, Eddy Company

	Bell	Ware	Eddy
Cash	68,000	41,500	175,200
Accounts Receivable	85,000	97,500	105,000
Inventories	137,500	163,000	150,000
Investment in Ware	365,000	—	—
Investment in Eddy	600,000	—	—
Investment in Eddy Bonds	—	^148,000	—
Property, Plant, and Equipment	700,000	525,000	834,000
Accumulated Depreciation	(402,000)	(325,000)	(240,000)
Accounts Payable	(202,000)	(150,500)	(90,000)
Dividends Payable	(12,000)	(5,000)	—
Bonds Payable	(400,000)	—	(200,000)
Unamortized Bond Discount	—	—	800
Capital Stock ($50 par)	(600,000)	(250,000)	(500,000)
Paid-In Capital in Excess of Par	—	—	(70,000)
Retained Earnings	(278,200)	(170,000)	(115,000)
Gain on Sale of Equipment	(2,000)	—	—
Sales	(2,950,000)	(1,550,000)	(1,750,000)
Interest Income on Bonds	—	(7,000)	—
Dividend Income	(30,500)	—	—
Cost of Goods Sold	2,500,000	1,200,000	1,400,000
Operating Expenses	405,000	280,000	290,500
Interest Expense	16,200	2,500	9,500
	0	0	0

issued 2,000 additional shares to new minority shareholders at $85 per share. Bell has no investments other than the stock of Ware and Eddy.

(c) Eddy Company originally issued $200,000 of 10-year, 4% mortgage bonds at 98, due on January 1, 19X5. On January 1, 19X2, Ware Company purchased $150,000 of these bonds in the open market at 98. Interest is paid on the bonds on June 30 and December 31.

(d) Condensed balance sheets of Ware and Eddy on January 1, 19X1, and January 1, 19X2, are as follows:

	Ware Company		Eddy Company	
	Jan. 1, 19X2	Jan. 1, 19X1	Jan. 1, 19X2	Jan. 1, 19X1
Current assets	$225,000	$195,000	$205,000	$280,400
Property, plant, and equipment	350,000	305,000	623,800	613,000
Unamortized bond discount	—	—	1,200	1,600
Total	$575,000	$500,000	$830,000	$895,000
Current liabilities	$125,000	$100,000	$105,000	$ 95,000
Bonds payable	—	—	200,000	200,000
Capital stock, $50 par	250,000	250,000	400,000	400,000
Retained earnings	200,000	150,000	125,000	200,000
Total	$575,000	$500,000	$830,000	$895,000

(e) Total dividends declared and paid during 19X2 were as follows:

Bell Company	$24,000
Ware Company	25,000
Eddy Company	10,000

In addition to the dividend payments, Bell Company and Ware Company had each declared dividends of $1 per share payable in January, 19X3.

(f) On June 30, 19X2, Bell sold equipment with a book value of $8,000 to Ware for $10,000. Ware depreciates equipment by the straight-line method based on a 10-year life.

(g) Bell Company consistently sells to its subsidiaries at prices which realize a gross profit of 25% on sales. Ware and Eddy Companies sell to each other and to Bell Company at cost. Prior to 19X2, intercompany sales were negligible; but during 19X2, the following sales were made:

	Total Sales	Included in Purchaser's Inventory at December 31, 19X2
Bell Company to Ware Company	$172,000	$20,000
Bell Company to Eddy Company	160,000	40,000
Ware Company to Eddy Company	25,000	5,000
Ware Company to Bell Company	28,000	8,000
	$385,000	$73,000

(h) At December 31, 19X2:

Bell Company owed Ware Company....................	$24,000
Ware Company owed Eddy Company	16,000
Eddy Company owed Bell Company...................	12,000
	$52,000

Required:

Prepare a consolidated work sheet for Bell Company and subsidiaries for the year ended December 31, 19X2. All bond discounts are assumed to be amortized on a straight-line basis.   (AICPA adapted)

Problem 11-6. The following diagram depicts the relationships between Rose Company, Spike Company, and Tallow Company on December 31, 19X8:

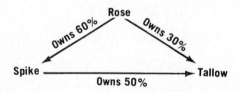

Rose Company purchased its interest in Spike Company on January 1, 19X6, for $200,000. Spike Company purchased its interest in Tallow Company on January 1, 19X7, for $75,000. Rose Company purchased its interest in Tallow Company on January 1, 19X8, for $54,000.

The following stockholders' equities are available:

	Spike Company December 31, 19X5	Tallow Company December 31, 19X6	Tallow Company December 31, 19X7
Common stock, $10 par	$150,000	—	—
Common stock, $20 par		$100,000	$100,000
Paid-in capital in excess of par	75,000	—	—
Retained earnings	75,000	50,000	80,000
Total equity	$300,000	$150,000	$180,000

On January 2, 19X8, Tallow Company sold a machine to Rose Company for $15,000. The machine had a book value of $10,000, an estimated life of five years, and is being depreciated on a straight-line basis.

Spike Company sold $20,000 of merchandise to Tallow Company during 19X8 to realize a gross profit of 30%. Of this merchandise, $5,000 remained in Tallow Company's December 31, 19X8 inventory. Tallow owes Spike $3,000 on December 31, 19X8, for merchandise delivered during 19X8.

Trial balances prepared from general ledger account balances on December 31, 19X8, for Rose Company, Spike Company, and Tallow Company are as follows:

	Rose	Spike	Tallow
Cash	84,000	60,000	25,000
Accounts Receivable	200,000	55,000	30,000
Inventory	360,000	80,000	50,000
Investment in Spike Company	264,500	—	—
Investment in Tallow Company	63,000	105,000	—
Property, Plant, and Equipment	2,250,000	850,000	350,000
Accumulated Depreciation	(938,000)	(377,500)	(121,800)
Intangibles	15,000	—	—
Accounts Payable	(215,500)	(61,000)	(22,000)
Accrued Expenses	(12,000)	(4,000)	(1,200)
Bonds Payable	(500,000)	(300,000)	(100,000)
Common Stock ($5 par)	(500,000)	—	—
Common Stock ($10 par)	—	(150,000)	—
Common Stock ($20 par)	—	—	(100,000)
Paid-In Capital in Excess of Par	(700,000)	(75,000)	—
Retained Earnings	(290,000)	(130,000)	(80,000)
Sales	(1,800,000)	(500,000)	(300,000)
Gain on Sale of Equipment	—	—	(5,000)
Subsidiary Income	(51,000)	(17,500)	—
Cost of Goods Sold	1,170,000	350,000	180,000
Other Expenses	525,000	100,000	90,000
Dividends Declared	75,000	15,000	5,000
	0	0	0

Required:

Prepare a consolidated work sheet necessary to prepare a consolidated balance sheet and income statement for Rose Company and subsidiaries as of December 31, 19X8. (Any excess of cost is assumed to be attributable to goodwill with a 20-year life.)

Problem 11-7. On January 1, 19X6, Irving Company purchased an 80% interest in Jason Company for $500,000. The following determination and distribution of excess schedule was prepared at that time:

Price paid		$500,000
Interest acquired:		
Common stock, $20 par	$500,000	
Retained earnings	100,000	
Total equity	$600,000	
Interest acquired	80%	480,000
Excess of cost over book value		$ 20,000
Attributable to inventory, 80% × $10,000	$ 8,000	
Attributable to equipment, (8-year amortization)		
80% × $15,000	12,000	20,000
		0

All of the undervalued inventory was sold by Jason Company during 19X6.

On January 1, 19X7, Jason Company purchased a 60% interest in Kelsie Company for $100,000. The following determination and distribution of excess schedule was prepared at that time.

Price paid		$100,000
Interest acquired:		
Common stock, $10 par	$100,000	
Retained earnings	50,000	
Total equity	$150,000	
Interest acquired	60%	90,000
Excess of cost over book value		$ 10,000
Attributable to building, 60% × $10,000 (15-year		
amortization)		6,000
Attributable to goodwill (20-year amortization)		$ 4,000

The following intercompany sales transactions occurred during 19X7:

	Irving to Jason	Kelsie to Irving
Seller's goods in buyer's January 1, 19X7 inventory	$ 5,000	—
Sales during 19X7	20,000	$10,000
Seller's goods in buyer's December 31, 19X7 inventory .	4,000	2,000
Gross profit on intercompany sales	25%	30%

On December 31, 19X7, Irving Company owed Kelsie Company $1,000 for merchandise received in 19X7. Jason Company had no outstanding liabilities to Irving Company on December 31, 19X7.

Trial balances for Irving, Jason, and Kelsie Companies as of December 31, 19X7, follow:

	Irving Company	Jason Company	Kelsie Company
Cash	103,000	40,000	15,000
Accounts Receivable	170,000	70,000	35,000
Inventory	250,000	105,000	53,000
Prepaid Expenses	6,000	1,500	—
Investment in Jason Company	500,000	—	—
Investment in Kelsie Company	—	100,000	—
Land	300,000	140,000	25,000
Building	500,000	275,000	140,000
Accumulated Depreciation — Building	(200,000)	(100,000)	(50,000)
Equipment....................................	650,000	380,000	100,000
Accumulated Depreciation — Equipment	(350,000)	(73,500)	(70,000)
Accounts Payable	(150,000)	(70,000)	(70,000)
Other Liabilities	(20,000)	(8,000)	(3,000)
Bonds Payable	(400,000)	(200,000)	—
Common Stock ($20 par)	(1,000,000)	(500,000)	—
Common Stock ($10 par)	—	—	(100,000)
Retained Earnings.............................	(300,000)	(125,000)	(50,000)
Sales	(1,500,000)	(700,000)	(400,000)
Subsidiary Dividend Income	(4,000)	—	—
Cost of Goods Sold	1,125,000	510,000	280,000
Other Expenses	275,000	150,000	95,000
Dividends Declared	45,000	5,000	—
	0	0	0

Required:

Prepare a consolidated work sheet necessary to produce a consolidated balance sheet and income statement for Irving Company and subsidiaries as of December 31, 19X7.

Problem 11-8. The following diagram depicts the relationships between the Ackley Company, Biernat Company, and Cromwell Company on December 31, 19X7:

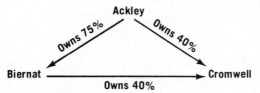

Information regarding the above investments follows:

(a) Ackley Company purchased its 40% interest in Cromwell Company on December 31, 19X3, for $50,000. On that date, Cromwell Company's book values approximated market values. Cromwell Company's plant assets consisted of a number of pieces of equipment that were being depreciated on a straight-line basis with estimated future lives of ten years.

(b) On January 1, 19X6, Ackley Company purchased a 75% interest in Biernat Company for $400,000. The following determination and distribution of excess schedule was subsequently prepared:

Price paid		$400,000
Interest acquired:		
Common stock, $5 par	$300,000	
Paid-in capital in excess of par	100,000	
Retained earnings	30,000	
Total equity	$430,000	
Interest acquired	75%	322,500
Excess of cost over book value		$ 77,500
Attributed to building (to be amortized over 20 years), 75% × $40,000		30,000
Attributable to goodwill (to be amortized over 10 years)		$ 47,500

(c) On January 1, 19X7, Biernat Company acquired a 40% interest in Cromwell Company for $92,000. Cromwell Company's book values approximated market values at this date.

(d) The following stockholders' equities have been made available:

	Cromwell Company December 31, 19X3	Cromwell Company December 31, 19X6	Biernat Co. December 31, 19X5
Noncumulative $6 preferred stock, $100 par and liquidating value	—	—	$ 50,000
Common stock, $5 par	—	—	300,000
Common stock, $10 par	$200,000	$200,000	—
Paid-in capital in excess of par..	—	—	100,000
Retained earnings (deficit)	(50,000)	30,000	30,000
Total equity	$150,000	$230,000	$480,000

(e) The following is information regarding intercompany merchandise sales of 19X7:

	Ackley to Cromwell	Cromwell to Biernat
Seller's merchandise in buyer's December 31, 19X6 inventory	$ 2,000	—
19X7 sales	16,000	$ 5,000
Seller's merchandise in buyer's December 31, 19X7 inventory	1,000	1,000
Intercompany receivable/payable on December 31, 19X7	3,000	500
Gross profit on sales	30%	40%

Trial balances for Ackley Company, Biernat Company, and Cromwell Company as of December 31, 19X7 are as follows:

	Ackley Company	Biernat Company	Cromwell Company
Cash	117,800	49,300	20,000
Accounts Receivable (net)	200,000	100,000	44,000
Inventory	277,000	206,000	58,000
Investment in Cromwell Co.	50,000	92,000	—
Investment in Biernat Co.	400,000	—	—
Property, Plant, and Equipment	2,800,000	1,500,000	220,000
Accumulated Depreciation	(1,120,000)	(593,000)	(90,000)
Accounts Payable	(206,000)	(112,000)	(4,000)
Bonds Payable	(1,000,000)	(700,000)	—
Preferred Stock	—	(50,000)	—
Common Stock ($5 par)	(500,000)	(300,000)	—
Common Stock ($10 par)	—	—	(200,000)
Paid-In Capital in Excess of Par	(700,000)	(100,000)	—
Retained Earnings	(270,000)	(61,000)	(30,000)
Sales	(1,500,000)	(850,000)	(400,000)
Subsidiary Dividend Income	(18,800)	(800)	—
Cost of Goods Sold	1,050,000	552,500	240,000
Other Expenses	350,000	240,000	140,000
Preferred Dividends Declared	—	3,000	—
Common Dividends Declared	70,000	24,000	2,000
	0	0	0

Required:

Prepare a consolidated work sheet for Ackley Company, Biernat Company, and Cromwell Company, as of December 31, 19X7.

Problem 11-9. Paxton Corporation purchased a 70% interest in Sames Company for $485,000 on January 1, 19X7. The following determination and distribution of excess schedule was prepared:

Price paid		$485,000
Interest acquired:		
Common stock, $15 par	$450,000	
Retained earnings	200,000	
Total equity	$650,000	
Interest acquired	70%	455,000
Excess of cost over book value attributable to goodwill (20-year life)		$ 30,000

On January 1, 19X8, Sames Company purchased 10% of Paxton Corporation common stock on the open market for $150,000. After the purchase, the following determination and distribution of excess schedule was prepared:

Price paid		$150,000
Interest acquired:		
Common stock, $5 par	$ 375,000	
Paid-in capital in excess of par	600,000	
Retained earnings	350,000	
Total equity	$1,325,000	
Interest acquired	10%	132,500
Excess of cost over book value attributable to building and equipment, 10% × $175,000 (10-year life)..................		$ 17,500

Paxton Corporation has paid a $.15 per share quarterly dividend since January, 19X3, while Sames Company has paid a $.10 per share quarterly dividend since mid-19X5.

Trial balances for Paxton Corporation and Sames Company as of December 31, 19X8, are as follows:

	Paxton Corporation	Sames Company
Current Assets.....................................	370,000	185,000
Investment in Sames Company	525,600	—
Investment in Paxton Corporation..................	—	150,000
Property, Plant, and Equipment	1,900,000	1,000,000
Accumulated Depreciation	(717,600)	(332,500)
Liabilities	(680,000)	(290,000)
Common Stock ($5 par)	(375,000)	—
Common Stock ($15 par)	—	(450,000)
Paid-In Capital in Excess of Par	(600,000)	—
Retained Earnings	(350,000)	(230,000)
Sales..	(2,200,000)	(900,000)
Investment Income	(28,000)	(4,500)
Cost of Goods Sold	1,540,000	630,000
Other Expenses...................................	570,000	230,000
Dividends Declared	45,000	12,000
	0	0

Required:

(1) Prepare a consolidated work sheet for Paxton Corporation and Sames Company as of December 31, 19X8, using the treasury stock method.

(2) Prepare a formal consolidated balance sheet for December 31, 19X8.

Problem 11-10. Using the data of Problem 11-9, (1) prepare a consolidated work sheet for Paxton Corporation and Sames Company as of December 31, 19X8, using the reciprocal method, and (2) prepare a formal consolidated balance sheet for December 31, 19X8.

Problem 11-11. On January 1, 19X6, Pollack Company purchased a controlling interest in Allen Company. The trial balances for Pollack Company and Allen Company at December 31, 19X6, are shown at the top of page 516.

The following information is also available:

(a) Pollack Company purchased 1,600 shares of Allen Company's outstanding stock on January 1, 19X5, for $48,000, and on January 1, 19X6, purchased an additional 1,400 shares for $52,000.

	Pollack Company	Allen Company
Cash	37,900	29,050
Marketable Securities	33,000	18,000
Trade Accounts Receivable	210,000	88,000
Allowance for Doubtful Accounts	(6,800)	(2,300)
Intercompany Receivables	24,000	—
Inventories	275,000	135,000
Machinery and Equipment	514,000	279,000
Accumulated Depreciation	(298,200)	(196,700)
Investment in Allen Company (at cost)	100,000	—
Patents	35,000	—
Dividends Payable	(7,500)	—
Trade Accounts Payable	(195,500)	(174,050)
Intercompany Payables	(8,000)	—
Common Stock ($10 par)	(150,000)	—
Common Stock ($5 par)	—	(22,000)
Paid-In Capital in Excess of Par	(36,000)	(14,000)
Retained Earnings	(370,500)	(102,000)
Sales and Services	(850,000)	(530,000)
Dividend Income	(3,000)	—
Other Income	(9,000)	(3,700)
Cost of Goods Sold	510,000	374,000
Depreciation Expense	65,600	11,200
Administrative and Selling Expenses	130,000	110,500
	0	0

(b) An analysis of the stockholders' equity accounts at December 31, 19X5, and 19X4, follows:

	Pollack Company December 31, 19X5	Pollack Company December 31, 19X4	Allen Company December 31, 19X5	Allen Company December 31, 19X4
Common stock, $10 par	$150,000	$150,000	—	—
Common stock, $5 par	—	—	$ 20,000	$ 20,000
Paid-in capital in excess of par	36,000	36,000	10,000	10,000
Retained earnings	378,000	285,000	112,000	82,000
Totals	$564,000	$471,000	$142,000	$112,000

(c) Allen Company's marketable securities consist of 1,500 shares of Pollack Company stock purchased on June 15, 19X6, in the open market for $18,000. The securities were purchased as a temporary investment and were sold on January 15, 19X7, for $25,000.

(d) On December 10, 19X6, Pollack Company declared a cash dividend of $.50 per share, payable January 10, 19X7, to stockholders of record on December 20, 19X6. Allen Company paid a cash dividend of $1 per share on June 30, 19X6, and distributed a 10% stock dividend on September 30, 19X6. The stock was selling for $15 per share ex-dividend on September 30, 19X6. Allen Company paid no dividends in 19X5.

(e) Allen Company sold machinery, with a book value of $4,000 and a remaining life of five years, to Pollack Company for $4,800 on December 31, 19X6. The gain on the sale was credited to the other income account.

(f) Allen Company includes all intercompany receivable and payable accounts in its trade accounts receivable and trade accounts payable accounts.

(g) During 19X6, the following intercompany sales were made:

	Net Sales	Included in Purchaser's Inventory at December 31, 19X6
Pollack Company to Allen Company ..	$ 78,000	$24,300
Allen Company to Pollack Company ..	104,000	18,000
	$182,000	$42,300

Pollack Company sells merchandise to Allen Company at cost. Allen Company sells merchandise to Pollack Company at regular selling price to make a normal profit margin of 30%. There were no intercompany sales in prior years.

Required:

Prepare a consolidated work sheet for Pollack Company and its subsidiary, Allen Company, for the year ended December 31, 19X6. (Assume any excess of cost over book value is attributable to goodwill with a 20-year life.) For any mutual holdings, use the treasury stock method.   (AICPA adapted)

CHAPTER 12

SPECIAL APPLICATIONS OF
CONSOLIDATION PROCEDURES

This chapter explores the application of consolidation procedures to additional areas, starting with the preparation of a statement of changes in financial position for a consolidated firm. The special procedures necessary to compute earnings per share for a consolidated firm will then be analyzed. Following these topics, the taxation of a consolidated firm is discussed. Members of a group subject to consolidation procedures may be taxed as separate entities or, in some cases, they may be taxed as a single, consolidated firm.

The application of the sophisticated equity method, which is required by APB Opinion No. 18 for certain unconsolidated investments, is also considered. Basically, the Opinion requires the application of the elimination procedures used in consolidations, so that the net income of the investor using the equity method will be similar to the net income which would result if consolidation procedures were used.

Finally, consolidation procedures are applied to a firm that is a single entity, but has chosen to decentralize its accounting so as to create various separate accounting units. While individual reporting for the created entities meets internal reporting needs, the separate statements must be combined for external reporting purposes.

CONSOLIDATED STATEMENT OF CHANGES IN FINANCIAL POSITION

APB Opinion No. 19 requires that a statement of changes in financial position accompany a firm's published income statement and balance sheet. Although alternative definitions of funds are allowed, the analysis is most commonly based on changes in working capital. The analysis must, however, use the "all financial resources" concept of funds, which requires the inclusion of changes in financial position that do not involve working capital. For example, the net impact on working capital of issuing stock to acquire a plant asset is zero. Under the "all financial resources" concept, the stock issuance must be listed as a source and the asset acquisition as a use of funds.

Effect of the Parent-Subsidiary Relationship

The process of preparing a consolidated statement of changes in financial position is essentially similar to that used for a single firm, a topic covered in depth in intermediate accounting texts. Since the analysis of changes in the working capital of a consolidated entity begins with consolidated statements, intercompany transactions will already have been eliminated and thus will not cause any complications. However, because of the parent-subsidiary relationship, there are some situations that require special consideration. These situations are discussed in the following paragraphs.

Acquisition of Controlling Interest. When an acquisition qualifies as a pooling of interests, all prior statements are retroactively consolidated. This procedure requires that funds flow analyses proceed from a comparison of the consolidated balance sheets of the current and previous periods. Such an acquisition will not normally cause any change in net assets and will only redistribute previous stockholders' equity. There is, therefore, no effect on working capital.

The acquisition of a controlling interest deemed to be a purchase will have an effect on the analysis of working capital. The analysis will be based on a comparison of the current period's consolidated balance sheet with last period's "parent company only" balance sheet, since consolidation procedures are not applied retroactively in a purchase. The increase in long-term assets is a use of funds which would be included in the statement of changes in financial position. The long-term liabilities of the subsidiary will be included as a source of funds in the period of acquisition. When the parent company issues securities as consideration for the purchase, the market value of securities issued would be treated as a source of funds. If the purchase is of less than a 100% interest, the minority interest is also a source of funds to the consolidated firm.

To illustrate, assume that Company S had the following balance sheet on January 1, 19X1, when Company P acquired an 80% interest for $540,000, issuing common stock as payment:

Assets		Liabilities and Equity	
Net current assets	$100,000	Long-term liabilities	$150,000
Equipment (net)................	200,000	Common stock, $10 par	200,000
Building (net)	400,000	Retained earnings	350,000
Total assets...................	$700,000	Total liabilities and equity	$700,000

Assuming that the market value of the net current assets, equipment, and buildings is $100,000, $250,000, and $425,000 respectively, and that any remaining excess of cost is attributed to goodwill with a 20-year life, the following determination and distribution of excess schedule would be prepared:

Price paid for 80% interest......................................		$540,000
Interest acquired:		
Common stock, $10 par......................................	$200,000	
Retained earnings	350,000	
Total	$550,000	
Interest acquired	80%	440,000
Excess of cost over book value		$100,000
Attributable to plant assets:		
Equipment, 80% × $50,000	**$ 40,000**	
Building, 80% × $25,000....................................	**20,000**	**60,000**
Goodwill (20-year amortization)................................		**$ 40,000**

The effect of the purchase on the statement of changes in financial position for 19X1 would be as follows:

Sources:		
Long-term liabilities acquired in business combination	$150,000	
Issuance of common stock in business combination	540,000	
Minority interest of Company S (20% × $550,000)	110,000	
Total sources		$800,000
Applications:		
Long-lived assets acquired in business combination:		
Equipment ($200,000 book value + $40,000 increase)	$240,000	
Building ($400,000 book value + $20,000 increase)	420,000	
Goodwill...	40,000	
Total applications...		700,000
Net increase in working capital (equal to the subsidiary's net current assets acquired)		$100,000

Amortization of Excesses. Income statements prepared for periods including or following a purchase of another firm will include the amortization of the excesses that are shown on the determination and distribution of excess schedule, as well as book value amortizations recorded by both parent and subsidiary. These amortizations, while reflected in consolidated net income, do not require the use of working capital and thus must be included as an adjustment to consolidated net income to arrive at funds provided by operations. For example, if the building and equipment of Company S have useful lives of 20 years and

5 years, respectively, the following adjustments would appear on the statement of changes in financial position for 19X1:

Funds provided by operations:	
Consolidated net income	$XXXX
Add amortizations resulting from business combination:	
Depreciation [(1/5 × $40,000) + (1/20 × $20,000)].............	9,000
Goodwill amortization (1/20 × $40,000)	2,000

In addition, funds provided by operations would be adjusted for depreciation and amortizations of book value recorded by the constituent firms on their separate books.

Purchase of Additional Subsidiary Shares. The purchase of additional shares directly from the subsidiary results in no added funds flowing to the consolidated firm. This transfer of funds within the consolidated firm would not appear in the consolidated statement of changes in financial position.

The purchase of additional shares from the minority does result in an outflow of funds. In essence, it is a treasury stock purchase from a consolidated viewpoint. The acquisition cost of such shares would be an application of funds.

Subsidiary Dividends. Dividends paid by the subsidiary to the parent are a transfer of funds within the consolidated entity. However, dividends paid by the subsidiary to minority shareholders are a flow of funds to persons outside the consolidated group and would appear as an application of funds in the consolidated statement of changes in financial position.

Illustration of the Preparation of a Consolidated Statement of Changes in Financial Position

A complete example of the process of preparing a consolidated statement of changes in financial position is now presented. Assume that Company P originally purchased a 70% interest in Company S on January 1, 19X1, and purchased another 10% interest on January 1, 19X3, the beginning of the current year. In addition, Company P owns a 20% interest in Company E, accounted for under the sophisticated equity method. The following information was taken from the determination and distribution of excess schedules prepared for each investment:

Date	Investment	Distribution of Excess	Amortization Period
January 1, 19X1	70%, Company S	$ 25,000 to equipment	5 years
		$100,000 to goodwill	10 years
January 1, 19X3	10%, Company S	$ 20,000 to goodwill	10 years
January 1, 19X2	20%, Company E	$ 5,000 to goodwill	10 years

The following consolidated statements were prepared for Company P and its subsidiary, Company S, for 19X3:

Company P and Subsidiary Company S
Consolidated Income Statement
For Year Ended December 31, 19X3

Sales...		$900,000
Less cost of goods sold		525,000
Gross profit		$375,000
Less expenses:		
General and administrative	$150,500	
Depreciation...	70,000[1]	
Goodwill amortization	12,000[2]	232,500
Operating income		$142,500
Investment income (equity method)......................		15,500[3]
Net income...		$158,000
Distribution of consolidated net income:		
To controlling interest.................................		$146,800
To minority interest....................................		11,200
Total		$158,000

[1] Includes $5,000 of depreciation resulting from the excess of market value of subsidiary equipment over book value on January 1, 19X1, the date upon which the 70% interest was acquired.
[2] Consists of $10,000 amortization on the 70% interest acquired January 1, 19X1, and $2,000 amortization on the 10% interest acquired January 1, 19X3.
[3] 20% of Company E net income of $80,000 less $500 amortization of goodwill. Dividends received were $2,000.

Company P and Subsidiary Company S
Consolidated Retained Earnings Statement
For Year Ended December 31, 19X3

	Minority	Controlling
Retained earnings, January 1, 19X3	$32,000*	$420,000
Add distribution of consolidated net income..............	11,200	146,800
Less dividends declared.................................	(4,000)	(50,000)
Balance, December 31, 19X3...........................	$39,200	$516,800

* Retained earnings for Company S on January 1, 19X3, were $160,000; $32,000 represents the minority's 20% remaining interest subsequent to Company P's 10% interest acquired on January 1, 19X3.

Company P and Subsidiary Company S
Consolidated Balance Sheet
December 31, 19X2 and 19X3

Assets	19X3	19X2
Current assets	$ 489,000	$ 460,000
Property, plant, and equipment.........................	1,330,000	1,250,000
Accumulated depreciation...............................	(370,000)	(300,000)
Goodwill...	168,000	160,000
Investment in Company E (20%).........................	333,500	320,000
Total assets	$1,950,500	$1,890,000

Liabilities and Stockholders' Equity		
Current liabilities	$ 202,500	$ 210,000
Bonds payable	300,000	300,000
Minority interest	79,200	108,000*
Controlling interest:		
Common stock, par	200,000	200,000
Paid-in capital in excess of par	652,000	652,000
Retained earnings	516,800	420,000
Total liabilities and stockholders' equity..................	$1,950,500	$1,890,000

* Represents 30% interest as of December 31, 19X2; interest was reduced to 20% on January 1, 19X3.

The net change in working capital is computed as follows:

	December 31 19X2	December 31 19X3	Change in Working Capital
Current assets	$460,000	$489,000	$29,000
Current liabilities	210,000	202,500	7,500
Working capital (net)	$250,000	$286,500	$36,500

The following additional facts are available to aid in the preparation of a consolidated statement of changes in financial position:

1. Company P paid $56,000 for an additional 10% interest in Company S on January 1, 19X3. The book value of the 10% interest was $36,000. The $20,000 excess cost was attributed to goodwill with a 10-year life.
2. Company P purchased a new piece of equipment during 19X3 for $80,000.
3. Company P paid $50,000 in dividends, and Company S paid $20,000 in dividends.

The following statement may now be prepared:

Company P and Subsidiary Company S
Consolidated Statement of Changes in Financial Position
For Year Ended December 31, 19X3

Funds provided by operations:		
Consolidated net income	$158,000	
Add: Depreciation	70,000	
Amortization of goodwill	12,000	
Deduct: Equity income from Company E in excess of divi-		
dends received	(13,500)	$226,500
Funds applied:		
Purchase of equipment	$ 80,000	
Acquisition of 10% minority interest	56,000	
Dividends paid:		
By Company P.......................................	50,000	
By Company S to minority shareholders	4,000	190,000
Increase in working capital		$ 36,500

CONSOLIDATED EARNINGS PER SHARE

The computation of consolidated earnings per share (EPS) observes all of the guidelines regarding income and share adjustments discussed in Chapter 4. When these guidelines are used, the calculation of consolidated EPS depends on whether the subsidiary's warrants, options, and convertible securities enable the holders to acquire common stock of the subsidiary or common stock of the parent.

If the subsidiary's dilutive securities enable the holder to acquire common stock of the subsidiary, the computation of the subsidiary's EPS is directly influenced by these securities. The subsidiary's EPS is then included in the consolidated EPS. The amount of subsidiary EPS to be included is based on the parent's holdings (or ownership interest) of each type of the subsidiary's securities which was used to compute subsidiary EPS. For example, if subsidiary EPS includes common stock and warrants in the denominator, the parent's holdings in both types of securities must be determined.

The basic model by which to compute consolidated EPS in this situation is as follows:

$$
\text{Consolidated EPS} = \frac{\text{Parent's internally generated net income} + \text{Parent's EPS income adjustments} + \text{Parent's percentage holdings of subsidiary shares} \left(\begin{array}{c}\text{Number of subsidiary shares} \\ \times \\ \text{Subsidiary EPS}\end{array}\right)}{\text{Parent's common stock outstanding} + \text{Parent's share adjustments}}
$$

This model may be used to compute either primary or fully diluted EPS. The parent's internally generated net income should be adjusted for unrealized profits recorded during the current period and for realization of profits deferred from previous periods. Likewise, the income used to compute the subsidiary EPS must be adjusted for intercompany transactions.

To illustrate, assume that an 80%-owned subsidiary has 5,000 shares of common stock outstanding. The subsidiary also has outstanding 1,000 warrants to acquire 1,000 shares of subsidiary common stock, and debentures which are convertible into 2,000 shares of common stock. The parent holds 500 warrants and 90% of the debentures. The subsidiary reports net income of $22,000 and computes its primary EPS as follows:

$$
\text{Primary EPS} = \frac{\overset{(1)}{\$22,000} - \overset{(2)}{\$2,000} + \$3,000}{\underset{(3)}{5,000} + \underset{(4)}{2,000} + 500} = \$3.07
$$

(1) Dividend on nonconvertible preferred stock, none of which is owned by the parent.
(2) Income adjustment for convertible debentures, which are considered a common stock equivalent.

(3) Share adjustment associated with convertible debentures.

(4) Share adjustment (treasury stock method) associated with the warrants.

Assuming that the parent has internally generated net income of $40,000 and 10,000 shares of common stock outstanding, the consolidated primary EPS would be computed as follows:

$$\text{Consolidated Primary EPS} = \frac{\overset{(1)}{\$40,000} + \overset{(2)}{\$5,000} + \overset{(3)}{\$12,280} + \overset{(4)}{\$5,526} + \$768}{\underset{(5)}{10,000} + 3,000} = \$4.89$$

(1) Income adjustment associated with the parent's common stock equivalent.

(2) Parent's interest in subsidiary earnings associated with common stock, (4,000 ÷ 5,000) × (5,000 shares × $3.07 EPS).

(3) Parent's interest in subsidiary earnings associated with convertible debentures, (1,800 ÷ 2,000) × (2,000 shares × $3.07 EPS).

(4) Parent's interest in subsidiary earnings associated with warrants, (500 ÷ 1,000) × (500 incremental shares × $3.07 EPS).

(5) Parent's share adjustment associated with its common stock equivalent.

If the subsidiary's securities enable the holder to acquire common stock of the parent, these securities are not included in the computation of subsidiary EPS. However, these securities must be included in the *parent's* share adjustment in computing consolidated EPS.

The basic model by which to compute consolidated EPS in this situation is as follows:

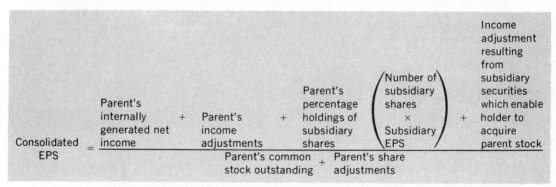

To illustrate, assume that a parent has internally generated net income of $20,000 and 10,000 shares of common stock outstanding. The parent's capital structure includes a convertible security which satisfies the yield test and requires an income adjustment of $1,000 and a share adjustment of 2,000 shares for purposes of computing primary EPS. The subsidiary reports net income of $7,000 and has 4,000 shares of common stock outstanding, of which 90% are held by the parent. The subsidiary also has 1,000 shares of preferred stock outstanding which are convertible into 2,000 shares of the parent's common stock. The preferred stock pays an annual dividend of $1,200 and qualifies as a common stock equivalent for purposes of parent EPS. The subsidiary also has outstanding 100 warrants to acquire 100 shares of the parent's common stock. Under the treasury stock method, these warrants would result in the issuance of 50 incremental shares.

The consolidated primary EPS would be computed as follows:

$$\text{Consolidated Primary EPS} = \frac{\overset{(1)}{\$20,000 + \$1,000} + 90\%\overset{(2)}{\left(4,000 \times \dfrac{\$7,000 - \$1,200}{4,000}\right)} + \overset{(3)}{\$1,200}}{\underset{(4)}{10,000 + (2,000 + 2,000 + 50)}} = \$1.95$$

(1) Income adjustment associated with the parent's convertible security.

(2) The subsidiary's primary EPS reflects the $7,000 net income less the dividends paid on the convertible preferred stock. The preferred stock is not a common stock equivalent for purposes of subsidiary EPS.

(3) Income adjustment representing the dividend on subsidiary preferred stock which would not be paid if the stock were converted into common stock of the parent. Note that 100% of the adjustment is added back, even though the parent's interest in the subsidiary is less than 100%.

(4) The parent's share adjustment consisting of 2,000 shares traceable to the parent's convertible security; 2,000 shares traceable to the subsidiary's preferred stock which is convertible into parent common stock; and 50 incremental shares traceable to the subsidiary's warrants to acquire parent common stock.

Special analysis is required in computing consolidated EPS when an acquisition occurs during a reporting period. When the acquisition is a pooling of interests, the computation of EPS includes subsidiary income and securities for the entire period. However, when the acquisition is a purchase, only subsidiary income since the acquisition date is included. In the latter case, the number of subsidiary shares is weighted for the partial period.

TAXATION OF CONSOLIDATED FIRMS

Consolidated firms that do not meet the requirements to be an "affiliated group," as defined by the tax law, must pay their taxes as separate entities. The tax definition of an affiliated group is less inclusive than that used in accounting theory. Section 1504(a) of the Internal Revenue Code states that an affiliated group exists when:

1. Stock possessing at least 80 percent of the voting power of all classes of stock and at least 80 percent of each class of the nonvoting stock of each of the includible corporations (except the common parent corporation) is owned directly by one or more of the other includible corporations; and

2. The common parent corporation owns directly stock possessing at least 80 percent of the voting power of all classes of stock and at least 80 percent of each class of the nonvoting stock of at least one of the other includible corporations.

Comparison of these criteria with those required for consolidated financial reporting should make it obvious that many consolidated firms have no choice but to submit to separate taxation of the member firms.

Consolidated firms that meet the requirements to be an affiliated group may elect to be taxed as a single entity or as separate entities. Firms that elect to be taxed as a single entity file a consolidated tax return, which may provide several tax advantages. For example, a consolidated return permits the offset of operating profits and losses and of capital gains against capital losses. Also, intercompany profits are not taxed until realized in later periods.

When affiliated firms elect not to file a consolidated return, each legal entity within the group computes and pays its tax independently. These separate returns may provide several tax advantages. For example, affiliated firms that file separate tax returns are not required to use the same tax year and uniform accounting methods. Significant intercompany losses, which would be deferred on a consolidated return, are immediately deductible on separate returns.

Consolidated Tax Return

When an affiliated group, as defined by the tax law, elects to be taxed as a single entity, consolidated income as determined on the work sheet is the basis for the tax calculation. The affiliated firms should not record a provision for income tax based on their own separate incomes. Rather, the income tax expense is calculated as a part of the consolidated work sheet process. Once calculated, the tax provision may be recorded on the books of the separate firms.

As an example of an affiliated group choosing to be taxed as a single entity, assume that Company P purchased an 80% interest in Company S on January 1, 19X1, at which time the following determination and distribution of excess schedule was prepared:

Price paid		$800,000
Interest acquired:		
Common stock.....................................	$500,000	
Retained earnings, January 1, 19X1	400,000	
Total equity	$900,000	
Ownership interest.................................	80%	720,000
Excess of cost over book value attributed to goodwill with a 40-year life		**$ 80,000**

The income statements which follow are for Companies P and S for 19X3. Since the firms desire to file a consolidated tax return, neither firm has recorded a provision for income tax. The corporate tax rate is 40%.

	Company P	Company S
Sales...	$600,000	$400,000
Less cost of goods sold	350,000	200,000
Gross profit	$250,000	$200,000
Less operating expenses	100,000	100,000
Operating income..................................	$150,000	$100,000
Subsidiary income	80,000	—
Income before tax	$230,000	$100,000

On January 1, 19X2, Company P sold a piece of equipment with a net book value of $40,000 to Company S for $60,000. The equipment is depreciated by Company S on a straight-line basis over a 5-year life.

The following applies to intercompany merchandise sales to Company P by Company S:

Intercompany sales in beginning inventory of Company P	$ 50,000
Intercompany sales in ending inventory of Company P	70,000
Sales to Company P during 19X3	100,000
Gross profit rate	50%

Illustration I on pages 530-532 contains the trial balances of Companies P and S on December 31, 19X3. Since the income tax is to be calculated on the work sheet, no provision exists on the separate books. If separate provisions appear in the trial balances, they should be eliminated as an initial procedure in consolidating.

The balance of the account Investment in Company S results from the use of the simple equity method. Steps 1 through 9 are identical to the steps prepared in previous work sheets; Step 10 is the only new procedure. In Step 10, the provision for income tax is calculated by multiplying the consolidated taxable income by the tax rate. The consolidated taxable income is determined by adding the goodwill amortization to the consolidated income before tax. As mentioned in Chapter 5, in most purchase situations the amortizations of excess resulting from the investment are not tax deductible.

The final complexity caused by a consolidated return involves the distribution of consolidated income. In Illustration I, the income distributions start with internally generated income before taxes. All adjustments to the work sheet are also entered before tax effects. This procedure results in an adjusted income for each firm before tax.

The consolidated income tax expense of the member firms is then calculated. The income distribution schedules allocate the income tax expense and proceed to calculate each firm's adjusted net income, which is distributed to the controlling and minority interests according to their ownership percentages.

It will be necessary for each member firm to record its share of the consolidated income tax on its own books. The subsidiary, Company S, would record the following:

Provision for Income Tax	36,000	
Income Tax Payable		36,000
To record allocated portion of consolidated income tax expense.		

The parent, Company P, would record the following:

Subsidiary Income (80% × $36,000 tax provision)	28,800	
Investment in Company S		28,800
To adjust subsidiary income for tax expense recorded by Company S.		

Provision for Income Tax	61,600	
Income Tax Payable.................................		61,600
To record allocated portion of consolidated income		
tax expense.		

In review, consolidated returns are consistent with consolidated reporting procedures and do not in any way alter procedures that have been discussed in previous chapters. It is only necessary to add new procedures to the work sheet to provide for income taxes.

Separate Tax Returns

When separate returns are required or elected to be filed, each member of the consolidated group must base its tax calculation on its separate income. In determining their taxable income, corporations are generally allowed a deduction of 85% of the dividends received from nonaffiliated taxable domestic corporations in order to reduce multiple taxation of the same income. Affiliated firms filing separate returns may deduct 100% of the dividends. In the illustrations that follow, 15% of the dividends received are subject to income taxes. Since each firm calculates its tax separately, the trial balances in the consolidated work sheet should include the provision for income tax and the related liability.

The major complication that arises in the computation of taxes for individual firms is that, since taxation is based on the income of the separate entities, intercompany gains and losses are included. Thus, the majority of intercompany transactions create timing differences which will require an adjustment of the amounts provided for applicable taxes. This complication leads to a need for interperiod tax allocation when companies are consolidated. For example, assume that a parent sells a piece of equipment, with a book value of $20,000, to a subsidiary for $40,000 on January 1, 19X1. The asset has a 5-year life and straight-line depreciation is used. Assuming a 40% tax rate, the parent will record a $20,000 gain and $8,000 in taxes in the period in which the equipment is sold. However, from a consolidated viewpoint, the gain should be pro-rated over the 5-year life, requiring the $8,000 tax provision to be allocated over 5 years at a rate of $1,600 per year. On December 31, 19X1, the following entry would be made on the consolidated work sheet for tax applicable to the sale:

Deferred Tax Expense (4 years × $1,600)	6,400	
Provision for Income Tax		6,400

In subsequent periods, the tax applicable to the period would be recognized on the work sheet and the remaining deferred tax established. The following entry would be made on the December 31, 19X2 consolidated work sheet:

Deferred Tax Expense (3 remaining years × $1,600)	4,800	
Provision for Income Tax (for 19X2)	1,600	
Retained Earnings—Parent Company (adjustment for 4		
years, expensed by the parent in 19X1)		6,400

(Credit balance amounts
are in parentheses)

	Trial Balance	
	Company P	Company S
Cash	200,000	380,000
Inventory, Dec. 31, 19X3	150,000	120,000
Plant and Equipment	900,000	1,100,000
Accumulated Depreciation	(440,000)	(150,000)
Investment in Company S	1,120,000	
Goodwill		
Liabilities		(150,000)
Common Stock, Co. P	(800,000)	
Retained Earnings, Jan. 1, 19X3, Co. P	(900,000)	
Common Stock, Co. S		(500,000)
Retained Earnings, Jan. 1, 19X3, Co. S		(700,000)
Sales	(600,000)	(400,000)
Cost of Goods Sold	350,000	200,000
Expenses	100,000	100,000
Subsidiary Income	(80,000)	
	0	0
Consolidated Income Before Tax		
Provision for Income Tax		
Income Tax Payable		
Consolidated Net Income		
To Minority Interest (see distribution schedule, page 532)		
To Consolidated Interest (see distribution schedule)		
Minority Interest, Dec. 31, 19X3		
Retained Earnings, Controlling Interest, December 31, 19X3		

(1) Eliminate the parent's entry recording its share of the current year's subsidiary income. This step returns the investment account to its balance on January 1, 19X3.

(2) Eliminate 80% of the January 1, 19X3 subsidiary equity balances against the investment in Company S.

(3) Distribute the $80,000 excess of cost to goodwill.

(4) Amortize goodwill at an annual amount of $2,000 for the past two years and for the current year.

(5) Remove the undepreciated gain on the sale of the equipment at the beginning of the year from retained earnings. Since the sale was by the parent, the entire adjustment is removed from the controlling interest in retained earnings.

(6) Adjust accumulated depreciation and the current year's depreciation expense for the $4,000 overstatement of depreciation caused by the original $20,000 intercompany gain.

(7) Eliminate intercompany merchandise sales of $100,000 to avoid double counting.

Consolidated Income Tax Return
Subsidiary Company S
Financial Statements
December 31, 19X3

Eliminations		Consolidated Income Statement	Minority Interest	Controlling Retained Earnings	Consolidated Balance Sheet
Dr.	Cr.				
					580,000
	(9) 35,000				235,000
	(5) 20,000				1,980,000
(5) 4,000					(582,000)
(6) 4,000					
	(1) 80,000				
	(2) 960,000				
	(3) 80,000				
(3) 80,000	(4) 6,000				74,000
					(150,000)
					(800,000)
(4) 4,000					
(5) 16,000					
(8) 20,000				(860,000)	
(2) 400,000			(100,000)		
(2) 560,000					
(8) 5,000			(135,000)		
(7) 100,000		(900,000)			
(9) 35,000	(7) 100,000	460,000			
	(8) 25,000				
(4) 2,000	(6) 4,000	198,000			
(1) 80,000					
		(242,000)			
10 97,600		97,600			
	10 97,600				(97,600)
1,407,600	1,407,600				
		(144,400)			
		10,800	(10,800)		
		133,600		(133,600)	
			(245,800)		(245,800)
				(993,600)	(993,600)
					0

(8) Reduce the cost of goods sold by the $25,000 of intercompany profit included in the beginning inventory. Since the sale was made by the subsidiary, the reduction to retained earnings is borne 80% by the controlling interest and 20% by the minority interest.

(9) Reduce the ending inventory to its cost to the consolidated firm by decreasing it $35,000, and increase the cost of goods sold by $35,000.

10 Record the provision for income tax, calculated as follows:

Consolidated income before tax	$242,000
Add back goodwill deduction not allowed as tax deduction	2,000
Consolidated taxable income	$244,000
Consolidated tax (40% × $244,000)	$ 97,600

Income Distribution Schedules

Subsidiary Company S income distribution

Gross profit on ending inventory (50% × $70,000) .... (9)	$35,000	Internally generated income before tax $100,000
		Gross profit on beginning inventory (50% × $50,000) ... (8) 25,000
		Adjusted income before tax ... $ 90,000
		Company S share of taxes (40% × $90,000) **10** 36,000
		Company S net income........ $ 54,000
		Minority share 20%
		Minority interest .... $ 10,800

Parent Company P income distribution

Amortization of goodwill ... (4)	$2,000	Internally generated income before tax $150,000
		Realized profit on equipment ($20,000 ÷ 5) .... (6) 4,000
		Adjusted income before tax ... $152,000
		Company P share of taxes (40% × $154,000)* **10** 61,600
		Company P net income........ $ 90,400
		Share of subsidiary net income (80% × $54,000) 43,200
		Total controlling interest $133,600

* The parent's share of taxes is based on its share of consolidated income before tax, $152,000, plus the nondeductible goodwill amortization of $2,000.

The use of separate tax returns for a consolidated group leads to a very complicated application of interperiod tax allocation techniques. The calculations may become cumbersome, even when only intercompany sales of plant assets and merchandise are involved. To illustrate, assume that Company P purchased a 70% interest in Company S on January 1, 19X1, at which time the following determination and distribution of excess schedule was prepared:

Price paid		$285,000
Interest acquired:		
Common stock.....................................	$100,000	
Retained earnings, Jan. 1, 19X1	250,000	
Total equity	$350,000	
Ownership interest.................................	70%	245,000
Excess of cost over book value attributed to goodwill with a 20-year life		**$ 40,000**

On January 1, 19X3, Company S sold equipment with a book value of $60,000 to the parent, Company P, for $100,000. Company P is depreciating the asset over 5 years on a straight-line basis.

During 19X4, Companies P and S reported the following operating incomes before tax:

	Company P	Company S
Sales	$430,000	$240,000
Less cost of goods sold	280,000	150,000
Gross profit	$150,000	$ 90,000
Less operating expenses	70,000	30,000
Operating income before tax	$ 80,000	$ 60,000

A 40% corporate tax rate is assumed for both firms. The following data apply to intercompany merchandise sales to Company S by the parent, Company P:

Intercompany sales in the beginning inventory of Company S	$ 60,000
Intercompany sales in the ending inventory of Company S	40,000
Sales to Company S during 19X4	100,000
Gross profit rate	40%

Taxation of the Separate Entities. Before Companies P and S can be consolidated, it is necessary to calculate their separate tax liabilities, since the 80% test of an affiliated group for tax purposes is not met. The tax provision of the subsidiary is $24,000 (40% × $60,000 Company S income before tax). Company S would record its tax provision as follows:

Provision for Income Tax	24,000	
Income Tax Payable		24,000

The tax provision for Company P requires consideration of the tax status of subsidiary income. When the conditions for an affiliated group are not met or the option to submit a consolidated return is not exercised, the parent company includes 15% of the dividends it receives from a subsidiary in its taxable income. According to APB Opinion No. 23, subsidiary income included in the pretax income of a parent leads to a timing difference between the earning of the income and its inclusion in the tax return as dividend income.[1] APB Opinion No. 23 presumes that all subsidiary income will be transferred to the parent unless:

1. There are definite plans on the part of the parent to reinvest the undistributed earnings of the subsidiary, which will allow indefinite postponement of their remittance to the parent; or
2. The earnings will be remitted as a part of a tax-free liquidation.

Assuming that these exceptions do not apply, Company P must provide for tax expense equal to 15% of the subsidiary net income. For 19X4, this tax liability would be calculated as follows:

Subsidiary net income (after tax)	$36,000
Controlling interest, 70% × $36,000	25,200
Provision for tax on subsidiary income, 40% (15% × $25,200)	1,512

---

[1] *Opinions of the Accounting Principles Board, No. 23,* "Accounting for Income Taxes—Special Areas" (New York: American Institute of Certified Public Accountants, 1971), pars. 9-12.

Company P would add this amount to the tax it has provided for its internally generated income to arrive at its total tax provision for the period:

Tax on internally generated income, 40% × $80,000	$32,000
Tax provision for subsidiary income	1,512
Total Company P provision for tax	$33,512

Since Company P has not yet received its share of the income of Company S, the tax is not immediately payable, and a deferred tax liability for $1,512 is recorded. Assuming that the tax on internally generated income is currently payable, Company P would make the following entry to record its 19X4 tax provision:

Provision for Income Tax	33,512	
Income Tax Payable		32,000
Deferred Tax Liability		1,512

If dividends had been paid by the subsidiary, the tax applicable to the dividends received by Company P would be included in the current tax liability.

Work Sheet Procedures. Illustration II, on pages 536-539, includes the trial balances of Companies P and S. Several observations should be made regarding the amounts listed:

The balance in Investment in Company S is computed as follows according to the simple equity method:

Original cost		$285,000
Subsidiary income, 19X1-19X3 (after tax):		
Company S retained earnings, Jan. 1, 19X4	$350,000	
Company S retained earnings, Jan. 1, 19X1	250,000	
Net increase	$100,000	
Ownership interest	70%	70,000
Subsidiary income, 19X4 (70% × $36,000)		25,200
Equity-adjusted balance, Dec. 31, 19X4		$380,200

Since the parent's share of undistributed income has been recorded from the date of acquisition, a deferred tax liability has been recorded by Company P each year. The total provision on December 31, 19X4, is calculated as follows:

Deferred tax liability on 19X1-19X3 income (15% × 40% × $70,000 19X1-19X3 undistributed income)	$4,200
Current year's additional deferment (15% × 40% × $25,200)	1,512
Total deferred tax liability	$5,712

The trial balances of both companies include their separate provisions for income tax and the current tax liabilities.

When the eliminations are completed, Illustration II produces a consolidated net income of $89,886, which is distributed to the controlling and minority interests. The distribution schedules start with internally generated net income after tax, since the tax expense is calculated by each firm separately. Thus, each adjustment must be made to the internally generated net income after tax.

THE EQUITY METHOD FOR UNCONSOLIDATED INVESTMENTS

Prior to the issuance in 1971 of APB Opinion No. 18, "The Equity Method of Accounting for Investments in Common Stock," investors could freely choose between the equity and cost methods to recognize income on their investments. When the equity method was used, it tended to be a simple equity method which recognized only a pro rata share of the investee's income, without any attempt to amortize an excess of cost or book value on the investment, or to defer intercompany gains and losses. The choice between these two divergent methods is not significant when consolidation is required, since the investment and investment income accounts are eliminated in the consolidation process. However, the accounting profession did become concerned with the use of the cost method for major investments not subject to consolidation. The APB reasoned that in such cases, the investor may have significant influence over the investee's dividend policy, and that the payment of dividends would often be unrelated to the investee's income during a given period. For example, dividend payments are often level over a period of years during which income varies significantly. This reasoning led the APB to state:

> The equity method tends to be most appropriate if an investment enables the investor to influence the operating or financial decisions of the investee. The investor then has a degree of responsibility for the return on its investment, and it is appropriate to include in the results of operations of the investor its share of earnings or losses of the investee. Influence tends to be more effective as the investor's percent of ownership in the voting stock of the investee increases. Investments of relatively small percentages of voting stock of an investee tend to be passive in nature and enable the investor to have little or no influence on the operations of the investee.[2]

APB Opinion No. 18 requires the use of the sophisticated equity method for the following types of investments:

Influential investments. The APB defines influence as "representation on the board of directors, participation in policy-making processes, material intercompany transactions, interchange of managerial personnel, or technological dependency."[3] When the investor holds 20% or more of the voting shares of an investee, influence is assumed, and the equity method is required unless the investor assumes the burden of proof to show that influence does not exist, in which case the cost

---

[2] *Opinions of the Accounting Principles Board, No. 18,* "The Equity Method of Accounting for Investments in Common Stock" (New York: American Institute of Certified Public Accountants, 1971), par. 12.
[3] *Ibid.,* p. 17.

(Credit balance amounts
are in parentheses)

	Trial Balance	
	Company P	Company S
Cash	19,200	80,000
Inventory, Dec. 31, 19X4	170,000	150,000
Plant and Equipment	600,000	400,000
Accumulated Depreciation	(410,000)	(120,000)
Investment in Company S	380,200	
Goodwill		
Common Stock, Co. P	(250,000)	
Retained Earnings, Jan. 1, 19X4, Co. P	(400,000)	
Common Stock, Co. S		(100,000)
Retained Earnings, Jan. 1, 19X4, Co. S		(350,000)
Sales	(430,000)	(240,000)
Cost of Goods Sold	280,000	150,000
Expenses	70,000	30,000
Provision for Income Tax	33,512	24,000
Subsidiary Income	(25,200)	
Income Tax Payable	(32,000)	(24,000)
Deferred Tax Liability	(5,712)	
	0	0
Consolidated Net Income		
To Minority Interest (see distribution schedule on page 538)		
To Controlling Interest (see distribution schedule on page 539)		
Minority Interest, Dec. 31, 19X4		
Retained Earnings, Controlling Interest, Dec. 31, 19X4		

Eliminations:
(1) Eliminate the parent's entry to record its share of subsidiary income for the current year. This entry now includes the parent's share of the subsidiary's income after tax, since the firms are taxed as separate entities.
(2) Eliminate 70% of the subsidiary equity balances against the investment in Company S account.
(3) Distribute the $40,000 excess of cost in the investment account to goodwill.
(4) Amortize goodwill for the current year and three previous years at $2,000 per year.
(5) Eliminate the unamortized intercompany profit on the equipment sale by Company S as of January 1, 19X4. This elimination includes a $40,000 reduction in the asset account, an $8,000 decrease in accumulated depreciation, and a $32,000 decrease in beginning retained earnings. Since the sale was by the subsidiary, the retained earnings adjustment is allocated 70% to the controlling interest and 30% to the minority interest.

Group for Tax Purposes
Company S
Financial Statements
December 31, 19X4

Eliminations Dr.	Eliminations Cr.	Consolidated Income Statement	Minority Interest	Controlling Retained Earnings	Consolidated Balance Sheet
					99,200
	(9) 16,000				304,000
	(5) 40,000				960,000
(5) 8,000					(514,000)
(6) 8,000					
	(1) 25,200				
	(2) 315,000				
	(3) 40,000				
(3) 40,000	(4) 8,000				32,000
					(250,000)
(4) 6,000				(366,966)	
(5) 22,400					
(8) 24,000	10 19,366				
(2) 70,000			(30,000)		
(2) 245,000			(99,240)		
(5) 9,600	10 3,840				
(7) 100,000		(570,000)			
	(7) 100,000	322,000			
(9) 16,000	(8) 24,000				
(4) 2,000	(6) 8,000	94,000			
11 6,602		64,114			
(1) 25,200					
					(56,000)
10 23,206	11 6,602				10,892
606,008	606,008				
		(89,886)			
		12,240	(12,240)		
		77,646		(77,646)	
			(141,480)		(141,480)
				(444,612)	(444,612)
					0

(6) Adjust the current year's depreciation expense and accumulated depreciation by the $8,000 current year's portion of intercompany profit on the equipment sale.

(7) Eliminate intercompany sales of $100,000 to avoid double counting.

(8) Remove the gross profit recorded by Company P in 19X3 from its January 1, 19X4 retained earnings. The beginning inventory included $60,000 of goods sold by Company P with a gross profit of 40%, or $24,000. On a consolidated basis, the cost of goods sold is overstated, and Step 8 removes $24,000 from the consolidated cost of goods sold.

(9) Remove the $16,000 gross profit from the ending inventory and increase the cost of goods sold by a corresponding amount. The ending inventory includes $40,000 of goods sold by Company P with a gross profit of 40%.

10 Adjust the beginning retained earnings balances for the tax effects of previous adjustments as follows:

	Total	Retained Earnings Increase	
		30% Minority Interest	70% Controlling Interest
Prepaid tax on $32,000 unamortized intercompany equipment gain of Step 5, paid by Company S (40% × $32,000)	$12,800	$3,840	$ 8,960
Prepaid tax on $32,000 unamortized intercompany equipment gain of Step 5, paid by Company P (40% tax on 15% of 70% share of after-tax gain of $19,200 *)	806	—	806
Prepaid tax relating to Company P goods in Company S beginning inventory, Step 8 (40% × $24,000)	9,600	—	9,600
Total	$23,206	$3,840	$19,366

* 60% × $32,000 = $19,200

Step 10 increases the minority share of January 1, 19X4 retained earnings by $3,840, and increases the controlling share of January 1, 19X4 retained earnings by $19,366. The deferred tax liability is decreased by the total, $23,206.

11 Adjust current-year provision for tax effects of previous adjustments to current year's income as follows:

	Total	Increase in Provision for Income Tax	
		30% Minority Interest	70% Controlling Interest
Expiration of prepaid tax on equipment gain of Step 6, paid by Company S (40% × $8,000)	$ 3,200	$960	$ 2,240
Expiration of prepaid tax on equipment gain of Step 6, paid by Company P (40% tax on 15% of 70% share of after-tax realized gain of $4,800 *)	202	—	202
Expiration of prepaid tax relating to Company P goods in Company S beginning inventory, Step 8 (40% × $24,000)	9,600	—	9,600
Prepaid tax originating on profit on Company P goods in Company S ending inventory, Step 7 (40% × $16,000)	(6,400)	—	(6,400)
Total increase in provision for income tax	$ 6,602	$960	$ 5,642

* 60% × $8,000 = $4,800

No adjustment results from the amortization of goodwill, since it is not tax deductible. As a result of this adjustment and Step 10, the original deferred tax liability of $5,712 becomes a deferred tax expense (asset) of $10,892 on the consolidated balance sheet.

Income Distribution Schedules

Subsidiary Company S income distribution

Internally generated net income after tax (60% × $60,000)....	$36,000
Realized gain on depreciable asset sale ($8,000 − $3,200 tax) .... (6), (11)	4,800
Adjusted net income	$40,800
Minority share	30%
Minority interest	$12,240

Parent Company P income distribution

Ending inventory profit ($16,000 − $6,400 tax) (9), (11) $ 9,600 Goodwill amortization, not tax deductible 2,000	Internally generated net income after tax (60% × $80,000) .... $48,000 Beginning inventory profit ($24,000 − $9,600 tax) . (8),(11) 14,400 70% of subsidiary adjusted income, less tax [(70% × $40,800) − (40% × 15% × $28,560)] 26,846
	Controlling interest $77,646

method would be used.[4] When the investment falls below 20%, the presumption is that influence does not exist, and the cost method is to be used unless the investor can show that influence does exist despite the low percentage of ownership. Since the most common use of the sophisticated equity method is for influential (20% to 50%) investments, such investments are used in subsequent illustrations.

Corporate joint ventures. A corporate joint venture is a separate, specific project organized for the benefit of several corporations. An example would be a research project undertaken jointly by several members of a given industry. The member firms typically participate in the management of the venture and share the gains and losses. Since such an arrangement does not involve passive investors, the equity method is required.

Unconsolidated subsidiaries. A parent may own over 50% of the shares of a subsidiary, but may not meet the requirements for consolidated reporting discussed in Chapter 6. The equity method may be used in the absence of consolidation. It is also possible that an affiliated group will prepare consolidated reports as its primary statements, but will include the statements of the separate member firms as supplemental information. In such cases, the separate (supplemental) statements of the parent firm must use the equity method for investments in unconsolidated subsidiaries.

As defined by APB Opinion No. 18, the use of the equity method requires that the investment in common stock appear as a single, equity-adjusted amount on the balance sheet of the investor. The investor's income statement will include the investor's share of the investee ordinary income as a single amount in the ordinary income section. However, the investor's share of investee discontinued operations, extraordinary items, and cumulative effects of changes in accounting principles will appear as single amounts in the sections of the investor's

---

[4] For examples of situations which may overcome the presumption of influence, see FASB Interpretation No. 35, "Criteria for Applying the Equity Method of Accounting for Investments in Common Stock" (Stamford: Financial Accounting Standards Board, 1981).

statement which correspond to the placement of these items in the investee's income statement.

Calculation of Equity Income

In its simplest form, the equity method requires the investor to recognize its pro rata share of investee reported income. Dividends, when received, do not constitute income, but are instead viewed as a partial liquidation of the investment. In reality, however, the price paid for the investment will not usually agree with the underlying book value of the investee, which requires that any amortization of an excess of cost or book value be treated as an adjustment of the investor's pro rata share of investee income. It is also very likely that the reported income of the investee will include gains and losses on transactions with the investor. As was true in consolidations, these gains and losses cannot be recognized until they are confirmed by a transaction between the affiliated group and unrelated parties. The proper application of the sophisticated equity method will generally mean that the income recognized by the investor will be the same as it would be under consolidation procedures; in fact, the sophisticated equity method is sometimes referred to as "one-line consolidation."

Amortization of Excesses. A determination and distribution of excess schedule is prepared for an equity-method investment just as it would be if the investment were to be consolidated. For example, the following schedule might be prepared by the Excel Corporation for a 30% interest in the Flag Company:

Price paid		$300,000
Interest acquired:		
Common stock, $10 par	$200,000	
Retained earnings, January 1, 19X1	600,000	
Total equity	$800,000	
Ownership interest......................................	30%	240,000
Excess of cost over book value		$ 60,000
Less excess attributable to equipment with a 5-year remaining life		
and undervalued by $80,000, 30% × $80,000		**24,000**
Goodwill (40-year life)		**$ 36,000**

As a practical matter, APB Opinion No. 18 states that it may not be possible to relate the excess to specific assets, in which case the entire excess may be considered goodwill. However, an attempt should be made to allocate the excess in the same manner as would be done for the purchase of a controlling interest in a subsidiary.

The determination and distribution of excess schedule states the pattern of amortization to be followed. The required amortizations must be made directly through the investment account, since the distributions indicated by the schedule are not recorded in the absence of consolidation procedures. Assume that the Flag Company reported net income of

$50,000 for 19X1. The Excel Corporation would make the following entry for 19X1:

Investment in Flag Company	9,300	
Investment Income		9,300

Income is calculated as follows:

30% × Flag reported net income of $50,000		$15,000
Less amortizations of excess cost:		
Equipment, $24,000 ÷ 5	$4,800	
Goodwill, $36,000 ÷ 40	900	5,700
Investment income, net of amortizations ...		$ 9,300

If an investment is acquired for less than book value, the excess of book value over cost would be amortized over a period not to exceed 40 years. This procedure would increase investment income in the years of amortization.

Intercompany Transactions by the Investee. The investee may sell inventory to the investor. As would be true if the investment were consolidated, the share of the investee's profit on goods still held by the investor at the end of a period cannot be included in income of that period. Instead, the profit must be deferred until the goods are sold by the investor. Since the two firms are separate reporting entities, the intercompany sales and related debt cannot be eliminated. Only the investor's share of the investee's profit on unsold goods in the hands of the investor is deferred. In a like manner, the investor may have plant assets that were purchased from the investee. The investor's share of the investee's gains and losses on these sales must also be deferred and allocated over the depreciable life of the asset. Profit deferments should be handled in an income distribution schedule similar to that used for consolidated work sheets. To illustrate, assume the following facts for the example of the 30% investment in Flag by Excel:

Excel had the following merchandise acquired from Flag Company in its ending inventories:

Year	Amount	Gross Profit of Flag Co.
19X1	$30,000	40%
19X2	40,000	45%

Excel purchased a truck from the Flag Company on January 1, 19X1, for $20,000. The truck is being depreciated over a 4-year life on a straight-line basis with no salvage value. The truck had a net book value of $16,000 when it was sold by Flag.

The Flag Company had a net income of $50,000 in 19X1 and $70,000 in 19X2.

Flag paid $10,000 in dividends in 19X2.

Based on these facts, the Excel Corporation would prepare the following income distribution schedules:

19X1 Income Distribution for Flag Co.

Gain on sale of truck, to be amortized over 4 years	$ 4,000	Reported net income of Flag Co.	$50,000
Profit in Excel ending inventory, 40% × $30,000	12,000	Realization of ¼ of profit on sale of truck	1,000
		Adjusted income of Flag Co.	$35,000
		Ownership interest, 30%	$10,500
		Less amortization of excess cost:	
		Equipment $4,800	
		Goodwill................... 900	5,700
		Net income from investment	$4,800

19X2 Income Distribution for Flag Co.

Profit in Excel ending inventory, 45% × $40,000	$18,000	Reported net income of Flag Co.	$70,000
		Profit in Excel beginning inventory, 40% × $30,000	12,000
		Realization of ¼ of profit on sale of truck	1,000
		Adjusted income of Flag Co.	$65,000
		Ownership interest, 30%	$19,500
		Less amortization of excess cost:	
		Equipment $4,800	
		Goodwill................... 900	5,700
		Net income from investment	$13,800

The schedules would lead to the following entries to record investment income:

19X1	Investment in Flag Co............................	4,800	
	Investment Income		4,800
19X2	Investment in Flag Co............................	13,800	
	Investment Income		13,800

In addition, the following entry would be made in 19X2 to record dividends received:

Cash	3,000	
Investment in Flag Co.		3,000

It should be noted that only the investor's share of intercompany gains and losses is deferred. The investee's remaining stockholders are not affected by the Excel Corporation investment.

Tax Effects of Equity Method

The investor not meeting the requirements of affiliation as defined by tax law pays income taxes on dividends received. In the case of a domestic corporation, 15% of the dividends are includable in taxable income. However, according to APB Opinion No. 24, a timing difference is created through the use of the equity method for financial reporting.[5] As a result, the provision for tax must be based on the equity income, and a deferred tax liability must be created for undistributed investment income. The provision may be based on the assumption that investment income will be distributed in dividends, or that it will be realized via the sale of the investment, in which case it would likely be taxed in the form of a capital gain. The assumption used will determine the rate to be applied to the undistributed income. The provision for tax is based on the investor's net investment income after adjustments and amortizations. However, amortizations of excess cost are not deductible and thus must be added back to the net investment income to compute the tax.

The following entries are based on the previous example of the Flag Company and the Excel Corporation, but it is assumed that each firm is subject to a 40% income tax. The Excel Corporation's share of Flag Company net income would now be calculated as follows:

	19X1	19X2
Adjusted income of Flag Co., before tax	$35,000	$65,000
Tax provision (40%)	14,000	26,000
Adjusted net income of Flag Co.	$21,000	$39,000
Ownership interest in adjusted net income (30%)	$ 6,300	$11,700
Less amortizations of excess	5,700	5,700
Net income from investment	$ 600	$ 6,000

The 19X1 and 19X2 entries to record investment income and the applicable tax provision would be:

19X1	Investment in Flag Co.	600	
	Investment Income		600
	Provision for Income Tax [15% × 40% × ($600 net income + $5,700 nondeductible amortizations of excess)]	378	
	Deferred Tax Liability		378
19X2	Investment in Flag Co.	6,000	
	Investment Income		6,000
	Cash	3,000	
	Investment in Flag Co.		3,000
	Provision for Income Tax [15% × 40% × ($6,000 net income + $5,700 nondeductible amortizations of excess)]	702	
	Income Tax Payable (15% × 40% × $3,000 dividends)		180
	Deferred Tax Liability ($702 − $180)		522

---

[5] *Opinions of the Accounting Principles Board, No. 24,* "Accounting for Income Taxes—Investments in Common Stock Accounted for by the Equity Method (Other than Subsidiaries and Corporate Joint Ventures)" (New York: American Institute of Certified Public Accountants, 1972), par. 7.

Unusual Equity Adjustments

There are several unusual situations involving the investee which require special procedures for the proper recording of investment income. These situations are described in the following paragraphs.

Investee with Preferred Stock. In the absence of consolidation, an investment in preferred stock does not require elimination. However, the existence of preferred stock in the capital structure of the investee requires that the investor's equity adjustment be based on only that portion of investee income available for common stockholders. Dividends declared on preferred stock must be subtracted from income of the investee. When the preferred stock has cumulative or participation rights, the claim of preferred stockholders must be subtracted from the investee's income each period to arrive at the income available for common stockholders. This income would be the basis for the equity adjustment.

Investee Stock Transactions. The investee corporation may engage in transactions with its common stockholders, such as issuing additional shares, retiring shares, or engaging in treasury stock transactions. Each of these transactions affects the investor's equity interest. The dollar effect is calculated in the same manner as in subsidiary stock transactions. The equity of the investor is calculated immediately prior to and subsequent to the investee transaction. The net change calculated is treated as investment income (loss) in the case of an investor-investee relationship. A parent corporation would treat such a gain or loss as resulting from stockholder transactions, and would not include it in income when the one-firm view prevails.

Write-Down to Market Value. The investment in another firm is subject to reduction to a lower market value if it appears that a relatively permanent fall in value has occurred. The fact that the current market value of the shares is temporarily less than the equity-adjusted cost of the shares is not sufficient cause for a write-down. When the equity method is used and a permanent decline in value occurs, a reduction would be made to the equity-adjusted cost. The equity method would continue to be applied subsequent to the write-down. There can be no subsequent write-ups, however, other than normal equity adjustments.

Zero Investment Balance. It is possible that an investee will suffer losses to the extent that the continued application of the equity method would produce a negative balance in the investment account. Equity adjustments are to be discontinued when the investment balance becomes zero. Further losses are acknowledged only by memo entries, which are needed to maintain the total unrecorded share of losses. If the investee again becomes profitable, the investor must not record income on the investment until its subsequent share of income equals the previously unrecorded share of losses. To illustrate the above procedures, assume that the Grate Corporation has a 30% investment in the Dittmar Company, with an equity-adjusted cost of $30,000 on January 1, 19X1, and that Dittmar reports the following results:

Period	Income (loss)
19X1	$(80,000)
19X2	(50,000)
19X3	(20,000)
19X4	90,000

The following T account summarizes entries for 19X1 through 19X4 (taxes are ignored):

Investment in Dittmar Company

Equity-adjusted balance, Jan. 1, 19X1 ... $30,000	Equity loss for 19X1, 30% × $80,000 Dittmar loss...........................	$24,000
	Recorded equity loss for 19X2, 30% × $50,000 Dittmar loss = $15,000; loss limited to investment balance..........	6,000
Unrecorded share of 19X4 Dittmar income $15,000	Unrecorded 19X2 loss, $15,000 − $6,000	$9,000
	Unrecorded share of loss for 19X3, 30% × $20,000 Dittmar loss	6,000
Equity income, 19X4, 30% × $90,000 Dittmar income, less amount to cover unrecorded losses ($9,000 + $6,000) $12,000		
Balance, Dec. 31, 19X4 .... $12,000		

An investor sometimes makes cash advances to an investee. If these advances have not been repaid or previously written off, the investor's share of the investee's losses may also be used to reduce the advances to a zero balance.

Intercompany Transactions by the Investor. An investor may sell merchandise and/or plant assets to an investee at a gain or loss. When influence is deemed to exist, it might seem appropriate to defer the entire gain or loss until the asset is resold or depreciated by the investee. An interpretation of APB Opinion No. 18 requires that the entire gain or loss need only be deferred when the transaction is with a controlled (over 50%-owned) investee, and is not at arm's length. In all other cases, it is appropriate to defer only part of the gain or loss proportionate to the investor's ownership interest.[6]

---

[6] *Accounting Interpretations,* "The Equity Method of Accounting for Investments in Common Stock: Accounting Interpretations of APB Opinion No. 18" (New York: American Institute of Certified Public Accountants, 1971), par. 1.

To illustrate, assume that the Grate Corporation, which owns a 30% interest in the Dittmar Company, sold $50,000 of merchandise to Dittmar at a gross profit of 40%. Of this merchandise, $20,000 is still in Dittmar's 19X1 ending inventory. Grate need defer only profit equal to its 30% interest times the $8,000 (40% × $20,000) unrealized gross profit, or $2,400. Grate would make the following entry on December 31, 19X1:

Sales...	2,400	
Deferred Gross Profit on Sales to Investee		2,400

Assuming that the investor recorded the provision for income tax prior to this adjustment, the tax applicable to the unrealized gain would be deferred by the following entry, which is based on a 40% tax rate:

Deferred Tax Expense (40% × $2,400)	960	
Provision for Income Tax		960

The deferred gross profit and the related tax deferment would be realized in the period in which the goods are sold to outside parties. The deferred profit and related tax effects on plant asset sales would be realized proportionate to the depreciation recorded by the investee company.

It may occur that the investor will purchase outstanding bonds of the investee. Unlike consolidation procedures, the bonds are not assumed to be retired, since the investor and investee are separate reporting entities. Similarly, a purchase of investor bonds by the investee is not a retirement of the bonds. Thus, no adjustments to income are necessary as a result of intercompany bondholdings.

Gain or Loss of Influence. An investor may own less than a 20% interest in an investee, in which case the cost method would ordinarily be used to record investment income. If the investor company subsequently buys sufficient additional shares to have its total interest equal or exceed 20%, the investor must retroactively apply the equity method to the total holding period of the investment. APB Opinion No. 18 requires a retroactive correction of retained earnings for the period prior to the time a 20% interest is achieved.

It is also possible that an investor will own 20% or more of the voting shares of the investee, but will sell a portion of the shares so that the ownership interest falls below 20%. In such cases, the equity method is discontinued as of the sale date. However, there is no retroactive adjustment back to the cost method. The balance of the investment account remains at its equity-adjusted cost on the sale date. Should influence again be attained, a retroactive "catch-up" equity adjustment would be made.

When all or part of an investment recorded under the equity method is sold, the gain or loss is based on the equity-adjusted cost as of the sale date. An adjustment would also be necessary for deferred tax balances applicable to the investment.

Disclosure Requirements

Since a significant portion of the investor's income may be derived from investments, added disclosures are required to properly inform readers of the financial statements. For investments of 20% or more, the investor must disclose the name of each investee, the percentage of ownership in each investee, and the disparity between cost and underlying book value for each investment. If the equity method is not being applied, the reasons must be given. When investments are material with respect to the investor's financial position or income, the financial statements of the investees should be included as supplemental information.

When a market value for the investment is available, it should be disclosed. However, if the investor owns a relatively large block of a subsidiary's shares, quoted market values would have little relevance because the sale of an entire controlling interest would involve different motivations and would result in a unique value.

BRANCH ACCOUNTING

Thus far in the text, consolidation procedures have been used to prepare combined statements for affiliates which are separate legal entities. Consolidation procedures may also be used to combine the separate statements of segments of a single firm. A large firm may divide itself into separate reporting units for internal management purposes, using the separate statements of these units to provide the information needed for decentralized decision making. As useful as these statements might be internally, however, they are limited to internal reporting purposes and may not be used for external financial reporting. Therefore, segment statements must be combined into a single set of statements that reflect the economic entity. The following sections discuss the accounting procedures used to prepare separate statements for segments and to combine these statements.

Preparation of Segment Statements

A commonly used type of segment reporting involves a home office with decentralized sales branches. Accounting principles for home office and branch accounting are well defined and are used to illustrate segmental accounting. Typically, the home office will keep a perpetual record of its investment in a branch office. The investment includes the original funds given to a branch to start operations. Subsequent advances are also included, as well as billings for merchandise and other assets provided to the branch. The investment account receives equity-method adjustments to recognize the reported income of the branch, and the account is reduced by payments received from the branch. Payments may include the satisfaction of trade debt or remittance of profits. The home office also uses special procedures to record shipments of merchandise to a branch. Since no actual sale has occurred, shipments are recorded in the account Shipments to Branch at the cost of the goods shipped. When shipments are billed to the branch at a price in excess of the home office cost, it is common to record the markup in an unrealized intercompany inventory profit account which is available for later analysis. Profit on merchandise sold by the branch during the period may be recognized, while profit applicable to unsold goods in the branch ending inventory must be deferred.

The branch usually accounts for its operations as if it were a separate entity. It records its own purchases, sales, asset acquisitions, and expenses. Merchandise acquisitions are separated into purchases from outside firms and shipments from the home office. The branch also maintains an account called Home Office Equity, in which its cumulative liability to the home office for all funds, merchandise, and other assets received is recorded. The account is reduced for remittances to the home office. The income calculated each period is credited to the home office equity account on the branch's books.

When all entries are recorded properly by the home office and branch, the account recorded by the home office, Investment in Branch, and the reciprocal account recorded by the branch, Home Office Equity, should agree. Likewise, the amounts representing intercompany merchandise transfers, recorded as Shipments to Branch, and the reciprocal account, Shipments from Home Office, should agree. These reciprocal accounts may require adjustments on both books to account for merchandise and/or cash in transit to bring them into agreement. Equality of the reciprocal accounts, while not necessary for separate statements, is required for the consolidation process.

The income reported by a branch is typically not its correct operating income. Merchandise may be sold by the home office to the branch at a profit. The profit realized on home office shipments sold by the branch must be added to the branch's income to arrive at the branch's real impact on corporate income. It is also possible that the home office incurred expenses attributable to the branch but not billed to the branch. For example, the building used by the branch may be carried on home office records. Depreciation may not be billed to the branch on the theory that the branch manager has no discretion in the amount of the expense and thus should not be charged with it. Expenses attributable to the branch, but not billed to it, must be subtracted from its reported income. In summary, a T account for Branch Income could be envisioned as follows:

Branch Income

Depreciation on branch office not billed to branch	$6,000	Reported operating income of branch $20,000
		Add profit on merchandise transferred to branch, realized by branch sale 4,000
		Branch income $18,000

Following is a typical set of transactions and entries as they would be recorded on the home office and branch books.

1. The home office sends $100,000 to a newly formed branch so that it may begin operations.

Home Office		Branch	
Investment in Branch. 100,000		Cash 100,000	
Cash	100,000	Home Office Equity.	100,000

2. The branch purchases inventory and equipment from outside firms.

No entry		Equipment 50,000	
		Purchases 40,000	
		Cash	90,000

3. The home office, which is using a periodic inventory system, transfers goods with a cost of $40,000 to the branch for $50,000. The unrealized profit on the sale is isolated by the parent in a separate account.

Investment in Branch. 50,000		Shipments from Home	
Shipments to		Office 50,000	
Branch	40,000	Home Office Equity.	50,000
Unrealized Inter-			
company Inventory			
Profit	10,000		

4. The branch sells goods for $110,000.

No entry		Cash 110,000	
		Sales..............	110,000

5. The home office pays $2,000 for insurance applicable to the branch, and charges the branch.

Investment in Branch. 2,000		Selling and Administra-	
Cash	2,000	tive Expense 2,000	
		Home Office Equity.	2,000

6. The home office records but does not charge the branch for depreciation on branch office.

Depreciation Expense		No entry	
—Branch 10,000			
Accumulated Depre-			
ciation—Buildings .	10,000		

7. The branch records depreciation on equipment it purchased.

No entry		Depreciation Expense	
		—Equipment 5,000	
		Accumulated Depre-	
		ciation—Equipment .	5,000

8. Remaining expenses incurred by the branch are recorded.

No entry		Selling and Adminis-	
		trative Expense 20,000	
		Cash	20,000

9. The branch remits $45,000 to the home office.

Home Office			Branch		
Cash	45,000		Home Office Equity ..	45,000	
Investment in Branch.		45,000	Cash		45,000

10. The branch prepares the following trial balance, which is the basis for the branch's closing entries and which will be used in the preparation of combined home office and branch statements:

Cash	55,000	
Equipment	50,000	
Accumulated Depreciation—Equipment		5,000
Purchases	40,000	
Shipments from Home Office	50,000	
Depreciation Expense—Equipment	5,000	
Selling and Administrative Expense	22,000	
Sales...		110,000
Home Office Equity		107,000
Total	222,000	222,000

Assuming that the branch has $20,000 of goods in its ending inventory, of which $10,000 was acquired from the home office, the branch records the cost of goods sold.

Inventory	20,000	
Cost of Goods Sold ..	70,000	
Purchases		40,000
Shipments From Home Office		50,000

The branch then closes its operating income to the home office equity account and reports its income to the home office.

Investment in Branch .	13,000		Sales................	110,000	
Branch Income		13,000	Cost of Goods Sold		70,000
			Depreciation Expense—Equipment.		5,000
			Selling and Administrative Expense		22,000
			Home Office Equity .		13,000

After the branch closes its nominal accounts, it prepares its separate internal statements based on these entries. The branch's separate income statement and balance sheet follow.

Branch
Income Statement
For Year Ended December 31, 19X1

Sales		$110,000
Less cost of goods sold		70,000
Gross profit		$ 40,000
Less expenses:		
Selling and administrative	$22,000	
Depreciation	5,000	27,000
Branch operating income before taxes		$ 13,000

Branch
Balance Sheet
December 31, 19X1

Assets			Liabilities and Equity	
Cash.......................		$ 55,000	Home office equity	$120,000
Inventory		20,000		
Equipment	$50,000			
Less accumu- lated depre- ciation	5,000	45,000		
Total assets		$120,000	Total liabilities and equity ..	$120,000

11. The home office adjusts the branch's reported income for the gross profit realized on the branch's sale of shipments received from the home office. Of the original shipments, 80% are sold, and thus 80% of the intercompany profit is realized.

Home Office			Branch
Unrealized Intercompany Inventory Profit.	8,000		No entry
Branch Income		8,000	

12. The home office adjusts branch income for depreciation expense incurred for, but not charged to, the branch.

Branch Income	10,000		No entry
Depreciation Expense—Branch ..		10,000	

As a result of these adjustments, the home office will disclose adjusted branch income of $11,000 on its separate internal statements.

Combined Statements

With separate home office and branch statements prepared for internal purposes, a single set of combined statements for the entire firm must be prepared next. The separate trial balances of the home office and its branch become the basis for a combined work sheet. Before the accounts are combined, the reciprocal accounts, Investment in Branch and Home Office Equity, and Shipments to Branch and Shipments from Home Office, must have equal balances. If there is inequality, adjusting entries must be made on the separate records of the home office and its branches.

Illustration III, on pages 552 and 553, is a combined financial statement work sheet for 19X1, based on the preceding home office and branch example. The pre-closing trial balance of the branch, on page 550, is combined with a pre-closing home office trial balance. The home office trial balance is prepared prior to recording the branch income in entries 11 and 12. This work sheet deviates from a consolidated work

(Credit balance amounts
are in parentheses)

Illustration III
Work Sheet for
For Year Ended

	Trial Balance	
	Home	Branch
Cash	41,000	55,000
Inventory, Jan. 1, 19X1	60,000	
Buildings	400,000	
Accumulated Depreciation—Buildings	(120,000)	
Equipment	80,000	50,000
Accumulated Depreciation—Equipment	(10,000)	(5,000)
Investment in Branch	107,000	
Common Stock	(200,000)	
Retained Earnings, Jan. 1, 19X1	(300,000)	
Home Office Equity		(107,000)
Sales	(150,000)	(110,000)
Purchases	90,000	40,000
Shipments to Branch	(40,000)	
Shipments from Home Office		50,000
Unrealized Intercompany Inventory Profit	(10,000)	
Selling and Admin. Expense	25,000	22,000
Depreciation Expense—Buildings	12,000	
Depreciation Expense—Equip.	5,000	5,000
Depreciation Expense—Branch	10,000	
	0	0
Inventory, Dec. 31, 19X1		
Cost of Goods Sold		
Net Income		
Retained Earnings, Dec. 31, 19X1		

Eliminations:
(1) Eliminate the reciprocal accounts, Investment in Branch and Home Office Equity. In essence, these accounts are intercompany receivable/payable accounts.
(2) Eliminate Shipments to Branch plus Unrealized Intercompany Inventory Profit against Shipments from Home Office. This entry eliminates intercompany sales.
(3) Merge the separate branch expense accounts on the home office books with home office expenses.
(4) Enter the ending inventory twice: as a debit which is extended to the Balance Sheet column and as a credit which is extended to the Cost of Goods Sold column. The amount of inventory entered is net of intercompany

---

sheet for a parent and subsidiary as follows:

1. A summarized cost of goods sold account is not used in the trial balances. To avoid any error, the reciprocal merchandise shipment accounts should appear on the work sheet. Thus, the ending inventory of the single firm should be entered as an adjusting entry on the work sheet. As a result, a Cost of Goods Sold column is added to the work sheet.

Home Office and Branch
Combined Financial Statements
December 31, 19X1

Eliminations Dr.	Eliminations Cr.	Cost of Goods Sold	Net Income	Retained Earnings	Balance Sheet
					96,000
		60,000			
					400,000
					(120,000)
					130,000
					(15,000)
	(1) 107,000				
					(200,000)
				(300,000)	
(1) 107,000					
			(260,000)		
		130,000			
(2) 40,000					
	(2) 50,000				
(2) 10,000					
			47,000		
(3) 10,000			22,000		
			10,000		
	(3) 10,000				
4 68,000	4 68,000	(68,000)			68,000
235,000	235,000				
		122,000	122,000		
			(59,000)	(59,000)	
				(359,000)	(359,000)
					0

profit. In this case, the figure is calculated as follows:

Home office inventory (arbitrary)		$50,000
Branch inventory acquired from outside parties		10,000
Branch inventory from home office	$10,000	
Less unrealized home office profit (20%)	2,000	8,000
Combined inventory, December 31, 19X1		$68,000

2. There is never a minority interest and there is no distribution of income and no Minority Interest column.
3. The account Home Office Equity replaces the usual subsidiary company stockholders' equity accounts.

The work sheet of Illustration III is the basis for the following formal combined statements:

Home Office and Branch
Income Statement
For Year Ended December 31, 19X1

Sales..		$260,000
Less cost of goods sold		122,000
Gross profit		$138,000
Less expenses:		
Selling and administrative expense	$47,000	
Depreciation expense—buildings	22,000	
Depreciation expense—equipment	10,000	79,000
Net income..		$ 59,000

Home Office and Branch
Retained Earnings Statement
For Year Ended December 31, 19X1

Balance, January 1, 19X1...	$300,000
Net income for 19X1	59,000
Balance, December 31, 19X1	$359,000

Home Office and Branch
Balance Sheet
December 31, 19X1

Assets			Stockholders' Equity		
Cash	$ 96,000		Common stock................		$200,000
Inventory	68,000	$164,000	Retained earnings		359,000
Buildings	$400,000				
Less accumulated					
depreciation	120,000	280,000			
Equipment.........	$130,000				
Less accumulated					
depreciation	15,000	115,000			
Total assets		$559,000	Total stockholders' equity		$559,000

The only complication in subsequent periods is the unrealized inter-company inventory profit applicable to the branch beginning inventory. The branch beginning inventory includes such profit and thus is over-stated for combined reporting purposes. To illustrate the additional elimination procedures, the previous example is continued into 19X2. The branch has $10,000 of merchandise in its December 31, 19X1 inventory, and the home office has $2,000 of unrealized intercompany inventory profit remaining on December 31, 19X1. Assume that during 19X2, the home office transfers goods with a cost of $60,000 to the branch at a billed price of $75,000 (25% markup on cost). The following entries are made:

Home Office		Branch	
Investment in Branch ... 75,000		Shipments from Home	
Shipments to Branch .	60,000	Office 75,000	
Unrealized		Home Office Equity ...	75,000
Intercompany			
Inventory Profit	15,000		

The following partial work sheet illustrates the eliminations required as a result of intercompany merchandise transactions in 19X2:

Home Office and Branch
Partial Work Sheet
For Year Ended December 31, 19X2

	Trial Balance		Eliminations	
	Home	Branch	Dr.	Cr.
Inventory, Jan. 1, 19X2	50,000	20,000*		(1) 2,000
Shipments to Branch	(60,000)		(2) 60,000	
Shipments from Home Office..............		75,000		(2) 75,000
Unrealized Intercompany Inventory Profit ...	(17,000)		(1) 2,000 (2) 15,000	

* $10,000 was acquired from the home office.

Eliminations:
(1) Reduce the beginning inventory held by the branch to cost by removing the $2,000 of unrealized intercompany inventory profit applicable to it. The unrealized profit of $2,000, plus the unrealized profit on 19X2 shipments, is the balance of the unrealized intercompany inventory profit account.
(2) Eliminate the cost of the shipments to branch and the $15,000 unrealized profit applicable to them against Shipments from Home Office. All remaining eliminations, adjustments, and procedures continue as in Illustration III.

It is possible that other types of transactions, such as sales of plant assets, could occur between the home office and branch. In each case, the usual procedures applicable to consolidations of parent-subsidiary firms are applied. Other than the existence of unique reciprocal accounts, branch accounting is simply the consolidation of a 100%-owned subsidiary acquired at a cost equal to book value.

QUESTIONS

1. Describe the all financial resources concept as used in measuring changes in working capital.
2. Parent Company sells a portion of its investment in Subsidiary Company, but maintains a controlling interest. How would this transaction be treated on the consolidated statement of changes in financial position?
3. Do the following items have an impact upon resources provided, resources applied, or neither?

(a) Amortization of excesses.
(b) Parent company investment in subsidiary bonds purchased directly from the subsidiary.
(c) Parent company acquisition which meets the pooling criteria.
(d) Acquisition of remaining interest in a subsidiary following a pooling of interests.
(e) Minority interest in subsidiary equity in year of acquisition.
(f) Minority interest in subsidiary equity in years following acquisition.

4. Indicate how the computation of consolidated earnings per share is influenced by the minority interest in a subsidiary's equity.

5. In calculating the tax provision for an affiliated group, what adjustments must be made to consolidated income to arrive at consolidated taxable income? Explain why the adjustments are necessary.

6. Discuss the need for interperiod tax allocation as a part of the consolidation process when members of the consolidated group file separate tax returns.

7. The S Company has operating income of $100,000 before tax. The P Company has a 70% ownership interest in S Company. Assuming that P and S Companies are taxed as separate entities, what provision for tax must P make for its share of S income? Assume a 40% tax rate for both companies.

8. Briefly describe when the APB Opinion No. 18 sophisticated equity method must be used in accounting for an investment.

9. Why is the APB Opinion No. 18 sophisticated equity method viewed as requiring a "one-line" consolidation?

10. Is it possible for the investment account to have a negative balance under the sophisticated equity method?

11. The Horvath Corporation owns a 25% interest in the Candle Company. Determine how much profit should be deferred if (a) Horvath sold merchandise to Candle during the year and $1,000 of unrealized profit from the sale remains in Candle's year-end inventory; (b) Candle sold to Horvath merchandise during the year and $1,000 of unrealized profit remains in Horvath's year-end inventory.

12. Discuss the use of lower of cost or market values in regard to investments carried under the APB Opinion No. 18 equity method.

13. Describe the accounting procedures for (a) an investor who owns less than a 20% interest in an investee and subsequently purchases enough stock to exceed 20%, and (b) an investor whose ownership interest exceeds 20%, but who subsequently sells a portion of the investment to cause the interest to fall below 20%.

14. What disclosures concerning material investments must be made on the financial statements?

15. What is the purpose of a branch?

16. Describe the nature of reciprocal accounts as used by the home office and branch. What special accounting procedures might be required with regard to these accounts prior to elimination?

EXERCISES

Exercise 1. Perry Corporation purchased 80% of the Schmidt Corporation's outstanding common stock for $400,000 on January 1, 19X3. Part of the purchase price was provided by Perry's January 1, 19X3 issuance of $200,000 in bonds at face value. Schmidt's balance sheet at that date showed the following balances:

Assets		Liabilities and Stockholders' Equity	
Current assets	$140,000	Current liabilities	$ 90,000
Property, plant, and equipment (net)	550,000	Bonds payable	100,000
		Common stock	350,000
		Retained earnings	150,000
Total assets	$690,000	Total liabilities and equity ..	$690,000

Consolidated net income for 19X3 was $120,000, of which the minority's interest was $8,000. The Perry Corporation paid dividends of $10,000, and Schmidt paid dividends of $5,000.

Using the following balance sheet information as a basis, prepare the consolidated statement of changes in financial position for Perry Corporation and its subsidiary, Schmidt Corporation, for the year ended December 31, 19X3.

	Perry Corp. December 31, 19X2	Consolidated December 31, 19X3
Current assets	$ 320,000	$ 434,000
Property, plant, and equipment (net)	800,000	1,265,000
Current liabilities	(160,000)	(230,000)
Bonds payable	(200,000)	(500,000)
Minority interest	—	(107,000)
Controlling common stock	(500,000)	(500,000)
Controlling retained earnings	(260,000)	(362,000)
	0	0

Exercise 2. When the Krueger Corporation acquired 80% of the outstanding common stock of the Neske Company on January 1, 19X0, an appraisal showed that Neske's assets included equipment that had a 5-year life and was overvalued $25,000, and a building that had a 20-year remaining life and that was undervalued $40,000. In 19X3, Krueger reported income of $100,000 (exclusive of subsidiary income) and Neske reported income of $45,000. Neske's ending inventory included $20,000 of goods purchased in 19X3, the sale of which had yielded a 25% gross profit to Krueger.

Prepare the funds provided by operations section of the consolidated statement of changes in financial position for Krueger and Neske for the year ended December 31, 19X3, based solely on the information given. Ignore tax considerations.

Exercise 3. The Johnstone Company purchased 70% of the 10,000 outstanding shares of Gleason Company common stock on March 1, 19X0, and wants to increase its ownership interest to 80% as of January 1, 19X2. Compare the effect that the following alternatives would have on the 19X2 consolidated statement of changes in financial position:
(1) An additional 1,000 common shares are purchased from the minority stockholders.
(2) Johnstone succeeds in purchasing 9,000 shares of Gleason's new 10,000-share common stock issuance. Assume that there is no excess under either alternative.

Exercise 4. On January 1, 19X8, Rhodan Industries purchased an 80% interest in Colt Supply Company for $450,000. No excess of cost or book value resulted from the purchase. Separate income statements for the two firms for 19X8 are as follows:

	Rhodan Industries	Colt Supply Company
Sales	$1,000,000	$600,000
Less cost of goods sold	700,000	400,000
Gross profit	$ 300,000	$200,000
Less other expenses	200,000	150,000
Operating income	$ 100,000	$ 50,000
Subsidiary dividend income	8,000	—
Income before tax	$ 108,000	$ 50,000

Since the firms desire to file a consolidated tax return, neither firm has recorded a provision for income tax.

Assuming a 40% corporate tax rate, prepare a consolidated income statement with a provision for tax. Include a schedule computing the provision for tax to be allocated to the separate firms. Assume that there were no intercompany transactions.

Exercise 5. On July 1, 19X7, Daly Company purchased a 70% interest in Dole Company for $350,000. The following determination and distribution of excess schedule was prepared:

Price paid		$350,000
Interest acquired:		
Common stock, $10 par	$350,000	
Retained earnings	100,000	
Total equity	$450,000	
Interest acquired	70%	315,000
Excess of cost over book value attributable to goodwill (20-year life)		$ 35,000

The companies had the following income statements for 19X8:

	Daly Company	Dole Company
Sales	$750,000	$500,000
Less cost of goods sold	400,000	300,000
Gross profit	$350,000	$200,000
Less other expenses	200,000	125,000
Operating income	$150,000	$ 75,000
Subsidiary income	52,500	—
Income before tax	$202,500	$ 75,000
Provision for income tax (40%)	81,000	30,000
Net income	$121,500	$ 45,000

Since the firms do not meet the requirements to be taxed as a single entity, each firm pays its taxes separately. It is assumed that all subsidiary income will be eventually distributed as dividends.

Prepare a consolidated income statement for Daly Company and subsidiary for 19X8. Include the distribution of consolidated net income. Assume that there were no intercompany transactions.

Exercise 6. On May 1, 19X6, Karson Company purchased a 70% interest in Boise Company for $300,000. The following determination and distribution of excess schedule was prepared:

Price paid		$300,000
Interest acquired:		
Common stock, $12 par	$300,000	
Retained earnings	100,000	
Total equity	$400,000	
Interest acquired	70%	280,000
Excess of cost over book value attributable to goodwill (20-year life)		$ 20,000

Karson Company and Boise Company had the following separate income statements for the year ended December 31, 19X8:

	Karson Company	Boise Company
Sales	$800,000	$550,000
Less cost of goods sold	480,000	357,500
Gross profit	$320,000	$192,500
Less other expenses	200,000	140,000
Income before dividends	$120,000	$ 52,500
Dividends received	17,500	—
Income before tax	$137,500	$ 52,500

During 19X8, Boise Company paid cash dividends of $1 per share of common stock. Assume a 40% corporate income tax rate.

Prepare the entry to record income tax payable on each firm's books.

Exercise 7. The separate income statements for Conner Company and its 60%-owned subsidiary, Venn Company, for the year ended December 31, 19X7, are as follows:

	Conner Company	Venn Company
Sales	$500,000	$300,000
Less cost of goods sold	350,000	180,000
Gross profit	$150,000	$120,000
Less operating expenses	100,000	90,000
Operating income	$ 50,000	$ 30,000
Subsidiary income	10,800	—
Income before tax	$ 60,800	$ 30,000
Provision for income tax	20,648	12,000
Net income	$ 40,152	$ 18,000

The following additional information is available:

(a) Conner Company purchased its interest in Venn Company on July 1, 19X5. There was no excess of cost or book value associated with the original purchase.

(b) Conner Company sold a piece of equipment to Venn Company on December 31, 19X6, for $10,000. This piece of equipment had a book value of $5,000 and an estimated future life of four years at the purchase date. Straight-line depreciation is assumed.

(c) Venn Company sold $15,000 worth of merchandise to Conner Company during 19X7. Venn sells its merchandise at a price that enables it to realize a gross profit of 30%.

(d) Conner Company had $2,000 worth of this merchandise in its ending inventory.

(e) A corporate income tax rate of 40% is assumed.

Prepare the work sheet adjustments pertaining to intercompany transactions, and the interperiod tax allocations which result from the elimination of intercompany transactions.

Exercise 8. Tailor Corporation purchased a 25% interest in Libby Company for $100,000 on January 1, 19X7. The following determination and distribution of excess schedule was subsequently prepared:

Price paid		$100,000
Interest acquired:		
Common stock, $10 par	$200,000	
Retained earnings	100,000	
Total equity	$300,000	
Interest acquired	25%	75,000
Excess of cost over book value		$ 25,000
Less excess attributable to equipment, 25% × $40,000 (10-year life)		10,000
Goodwill (20-year life)		$ 15,000

Libby Company earned income of $16,000 in 19X7 and $24,000 in 19X8. Libby Company declared a 25-cent per share cash dividend on December 22, 19X8, payable January 12, 19X9, to stockholders of record December 30, 19X8.

Prepare the equity adjustment required by APB Opinion No. 18 on Tailor's books on December 31, 19X7, and December 31, 19X8, to account for its investment in Libby Company. Assume that Tailor Corporation makes no adjustment except at the end of each calendar year. Ignore income tax considerations.

Exercise 9. On January 1, 19X7, Petero Corporation purchased a 30% interest in Yancy Company for $220,000. The following determination and distribution of excess schedule was prepared:

Price paid		$220,000
Interest acquired:		
Common stock, $5 par	$200,000	
Paid-in capital in excess of par	320,000	
Retained earnings	130,000	
Total equity	$650,000	
Interest acquired	30%	195,000
Excess of cost over book value attributable to goodwill (10-year life)		$ 25,000

The following information relates to intercompany merchandise sales:

	Petero to Yancy	Yancy to Petero
Sales for 19X7	$40,000	$20,000
Seller inventory in buyer's December 31, 19X7 inventory	2,000	5,000
Sales for 19X8	35,000	30,000
Seller inventory in buyer's December 31, 19X8 inventory	3,000	2,000
Gross profit on sales	25%	30%

The following schedule summarizes Yancy's income and dividends paid in 19X7 and 19X8.

	19X7	19X8
Income	$40,000	$35,000
Dividends paid	12,000	12,000

Prepare the equity adjusting entries required by APB Opinion No. 18 for Petero Corporation's investment in Yancy Company on December 31, 19X7, and December 31, 19X8. Assume that Petero Corporation adjusts its account only at the end of each calendar year, and income taxes are ignored.

Exercise 10. The following determination and distribution of excess schedule was prepared on January 1, 19X4, when the Ananda Corporation purchased 25% of the outstanding common stock of the Pramila Company:

Price paid		$430,000
Interest acquired:		
Common stock, $10 par	$ 850,000	
Retained earnings	490,000	
Total equity	$1,340,000	
Interest acquired	25%	335,000
Excess of cost over book value		$ 95,000
Less excess attributable to building, 25% × $160,000 (15-year life)		40,000
Goodwill (10-year life)		$ 55,000

On May 1, 19X5, Pramila sold to Ananda for $254,000 a building which had a book value of $200,000 and a 20-year remaining life. Straight-line depreciation is being used.

Pramila purchases merchandise from Ananda on a regular basis. The following information is relevant to these sales:

	19X4	19X5
Intercompany sales of merchandise	$90,000	$110,000
Intercompany goods in ending inventory	10,000	12,000
Gross profit on sales	35%	30%

Pramila earned $90,000 income in 19X4 and $140,000 in 19X5. Dividends of $34,000 were paid in each of those years.

Assume that Ananda adjusts its investment account only at year end. Prepare the equity adjusting entries required by APB Opinion No. 18 for Ananda Corporation's investment in Pramila Company on December 31, 19X4, and December 31, 19X5. Ignore income taxes.

Exercise 11. Hanson Corporation purchased a 10% interest in Novic Company on January 1, 19X6, and an additional 15% interest on January 1, 19X8. These investments cost Hanson Corporation $80,000 and $110,000 respectively.

The following stockholders' equities for Novic Company are available:

	December 31, 19X5	December 31, 19X7
Common stock, $10 par	$500,000	$500,000
Retained earnings	250,000	300,000
Total equity	$750,000	$800,000

Any excess of cost over book value on the original investment was attributable to goodwill with a 5-year life. Any excess on the second purchase is attributable to equipment with a 4-year life.

Novic Company had income of $30,000, $30,000, and $40,000, for 19X6, 19X7, and 19X8 respectively. Novic Company paid dividends of $.20 per share in 19X7 and in 19X8.

Ignore income tax considerations and assume that adjusting entries are made at the end of the calendar year only.

(1) Prepare the equity "catch-up" entry, as required by APB Opinion No. 18, on January 1, 19X8, when Hanson's investment in Novic Company first exceeded 20%.

(2) Prepare the equity adjustment on December 31, 19X8, on Hanson's books.

Exercise 12. On January 1, 19X7, Wiley Corporation purchased a 30% interest in Southern Realty Company for $150,000. Southern Realty Company had the following stockholders' equity at that time:

Common stock, $6 par	$120,000
Paid-in capital in excess of par......................	100,000
Retained earnings	180,000
Total stockholders' equity	$400,000

Any excess of cost over book value in the purchase price is attributable to goodwill with a 10-year life.

The following schedule summarizes Southern Realty's income and dividends paid in 19X7 and 19X8.

	19X7	19X8
Income..........................	$50,000	$65,000
Dividends paid...................	30,000	30,000

On January 1, 19X9, Wiley Corporation sold its interest in Southern Realty Company for $175,000.

Prepare the entry to record the sale of Wiley Corporation's interest in Southern Realty. Assume that all equity adjustments were properly made. (Ignore tax considerations.)

Exercise 13. On January 1, 19X7, Potter Company purchased a 20% interest in Berland Industries for $200,000. Berland Industries had the following stockholders' equity at that time:

Common stock, $1 par	$100,000
Paid-in capital in excess of par......................	500,000
Retained earnings	250,000
Total stockholders' equity	$850,000

On the purchase date, Berland Industries' book value approximated market value. Any excess of cost over book value was attributable to goodwill with a life of five years.

Berland Industries earned $40,000 (net of tax) in 19X7, and paid dividends of $.20 per share.

Prepare the necessary equity adjusting entries on December 31, 19X7, required by APB Opinion No. 18, for Potter Company's investment in Berland Industries. Assume a 50% tax rate, and that all of Berland's income will eventually be distributed as dividends.

Exercise 14. The December 31, 19X8 trial balances of a home office and its branch are as follows:

	Home Office	Branch
Cash	25,000	21,000
Inventory (Jan. 1, 19X8)	80,000	—
Buildings	200,000	—
Accumulated Depreciation—Buildings	(60,000)	—
Equipment.....................................	100,000	20,000
Accumulated Depreciation—Equipment	(20,000)	(2,000)
Investment in Branch	45,000	—
Common Stock ($10 par)	(250,000)	—
Retained Earnings.............................	(74,500)	—
Home Office Equity	—	(45,000)
Sales	(300,000)	(60,000)
Purchases	250,000	30,000
Shipments to Branch	(15,000)	—
Shipments from Home Office	—	20,000
Unrealized Intercompany Inventory Profit.......	(5,000)	—
Selling and Administrative Expense	10,000	14,000
Depreciation Expense	12,000	2,000
Depreciation Expense—Branch	2,500	—
	0	0

On December 31, 19X8, the home office had merchandise of $50,000 on hand, and the branch had merchandise of $10,000, including $5,000 of merchandise received from the home office.

(1) Prepare the eliminations needed on a work sheet for all combined statements.

(2) Prepare the combined income statement for 19X8.

PROBLEMS

Problem 12-1. Redfield Industries purchased an 80% interest in the outstanding common stock of the Alcott Company on January 1, 19X0. The determination and distribution of excess schedule prepared at the date of acquisition was based on a purchase price of $568,000, a total Alcott equity of $650,000, and a $22,500 undervaluation of equipment with a 3-year life. Any remaining excess was attributed to goodwill with a 10-year life.

Comparative consolidated balance sheet data are as follows:

	December 31, 19X0	December 31, 19X1
Current assets	$ 400,000	$ 687,500
Property, plant, and equipment	3,000,000	3,050,000
Accumulated depreciation	(1,080,000)	(1,280,000)
Investment in Chester Corp. (30%) .	—	216,500
Goodwill	27,000	24,000
Current liabilities..................	(117,000)	(200,000)
Bonds payable	(100,000)	(200,000)
Minority interest	(138,000)	(151,000)
Controlling interest:		
Common stock, par..............	(1,000,000)	(1,000,000)
Additional paid-in capital	(650,000)	(650,000)
Retained earnings	(342,000)	(497,000)
	0	0

The following additional information concerning Redfield and Alcott is available for 19X1:

(a) Alcott purchased equipment for $50,000 cash.

(b) On January 1, 19X1, Redfield purchased 30% of the outstanding common stock of the Chester Corporation for $200,000. No excess resulted from this transaction. Chester earned $80,000 net income in 19X1 and paid $25,000 in dividends.

(c) In December, 19X1, Alcott issued $100,000 of bonds payable at face value to help finance a building addition on which construction is slated to begin in January.

(d) Consolidated net income for 19X1 was $271,000, of which $16,000 was attributable to the minority interest. Redfield paid $100,000 in dividends in 19X1, and Alcott paid $15,000.

Required:

Prepare the consolidated statement of changes in financial position to accompany the other financial statements of Redfield Industries and its subsidiary, the Alcott Company, for the year ended December 31, 19X1.

Problem 12-2. The Monberg Corporation purchased an 80% interest in the Slade Corporation on January 1, 19X3, for $170,000. The appraisal showed that some of Slade's equipment, with a 4-year estimated remaining life, was overvalued $20,000. Goodwill is to be amortized over a five-year period. The following is the Slade Corporation balance sheet at December 31, 19X2:

Assets		Liabilities and Equity	
Current assets	$60,000	Current liabilities	$ 30,000
Property, plant, and equipment	300,000	Long-term liabilities	40,000
Accumulated depreciation ..	(90,000)	Common stock, $10 par	150,000
		Retained earnings	50,000
Total assets	$270,000	Total liabilities and equity ..	$270,000

Comparative balance sheet data are as follows:

	December 31, 19X2 (Parent only)	December 31, 19X3 (Consolidated)
Current assets	$ 160,000	$ 236,200
Property, plant, and equipment	950,000	1,310,000
Accumulated depreciation	(360,000)	(566,000)
Goodwill	—	20,800
Current liabilities	(80,000)	(115,000)
Long-term liabilities	(100,000)	(130,000)
Minority interest	—	(43,000)
Controlling interest:		
Common stock, $10 par	(350,000)	(400,000)
Additional paid-in capital	(50,000)	(75,000)
Retained earnings	(170,000)	(238,000)
	0	0

The following information relates to the activities of the two firms for 19X3:

(a) Monberg issued 5,000 shares of common stock for $15 a share.

(b) Slade paid off $10,000 of its long-term debt.

(c) Monberg purchased production equipment for $76,000.

    (d) Consolidated net income was $104,000; the minority interest's share was $6,000. Depreciation expense taken by Monberg and Slade on their separate books was $92,000 and $28,000, respectively.

    (e) Monberg paid $30,000 in dividends; Slade paid $15,000.

Required:

Prepare the consolidated statement of changes in financial position for the year ended December 31, 19X3, for the Monberg Corporation and its subsidiary, the Slade Corporation.

Problem 12-3. The Panther Company acquired 90% of the outstanding stock of the Snowdon Company on January 2, 19X4, in exchange for:

500 shares Panther Co. common stock, par value $50, market value, $200	$100,000
Note payable due July 2, 19X6, 10% annual interest	78,400
	$178,400

The note payable due July 2, 19X6, was paid on December 1, 19X5. Interest for 19X4 was paid on December 31, 19X4. Comparative balance sheets are presented as follows:

	December 31, 19X5			December 31, 19X4		
	Panther Company	*Snowdon Company*	*Combined*	*Panther Company*	*Snowdon Company*	*Combined*
Cash	$ 21,100	$ 34,700	$ 55,800	$ 56,700	$ 25,800	$ 82,500
Accounts receivable	49,700	64,200	113,900	54,200	31,500	85,700
Inventories	46,600	64,400	111,000	49,800	41,400	91,200
Other current receivables	41,300	22,400	63,700	32,300	15,500	47,800
Investment in Snowdon......	178,400	—	178,400	178,400	—	178,400
Other investments	10,800	33,400	44,200	92,800	33,400	126,200
Land	18,200	15,000	33,200	28,700	15,000	43,700
Buildings	135,800	87,000	222,800	106,700	65,000	171,700
Equipment...................	61,000	45,000	106,000	48,000	45,000	93,000
Total debits	$562,900	$366,100	$929,000	$647,600	$272,600	$920,200

	December 31, 19X5			December 31,19X4		
	Panther Company	*Snowdon Company*	*Combined*	*Panther Company*	*Snowdon Company*	*Combined*
Allowance for doubtful accounts	$ 4,500	$ 3,900	$ 8,400	$ 4,100	$ 3,700	$ 7,800
Accumulated depreciation ...	69,500	50,600	120,100	41,300	31,200	72,500
Accounts payable	22,900	45,900	68,800	31,200	36,800	68,000
Notes payable	41,000	25,000	66,000	88,400	—	88,400
Dividends payable	—	14,000	14,000	—	—	—
Other accruals	5,900	20,800	26,700	2,700	2,600	5,300
Income tax payable	19,600	19,400	39,000	46,500	22,300	68,800
Bonds payable	—	—	—	30,000	—	30,000
Common stock	175,000	75,000	250,000	175,000	75,000	250,000
Additional paid-in capital...................	117,000	38,200	155,200	117,000	38,200	155,200
Retained earnings...........	87,400	48,800	136,200	62,300	38,700	101,000
Net income for year	20,100	24,500	44,600	49,100	24,100	73,200
Total credits	$562,900	$366,100	$929,000	$647,600	$272,600	$920,200

The following additional information is available:

(a) In January, 19X5, Panther Company sold some investments that cost $85,400 for $101,300. All investments are considered to be long-term. In March, 19X5, Panther Company sold a parcel of land that cost $10,500 for $18,800.

(b) On June 30, 19X5, Panther Company demolished an unneeded warehouse building that cost $18,900 and had a book value of $5,400 on that date.

(c) During 19X5 Panther Company declared and paid cash dividends totaling $24,000. Snowdon Company declared a cash dividend of $14,000 on December 1, 19X5, payable on January 10, 19X6, to holders of record on December 15, 19X5. The dividend receivable was recorded in Panther Company's other receivables account.

(d) The Panther Company bonds, which had a maturity date of December 1, 19X7, were retired in 19X5 at a total consideration of $32,500, including $600 for accrued interest and $1,900 loss on retirement.

(e) On December 31, 19X5, Snowdon Company borrowed $25,000 from Panther Company, issuing a 6-month, 11% note receivable.

(f) At December 31, 19X5, Snowdon's accounts receivable balance included $18,500 due from Panther for merchandise purchases. Panther's inventory account included intercompany profit of $5,000 arising from purchases from Snowdon.

(g) The amounts for net income for the year are after all deductions; no expenses or income were recorded in the retained earnings accounts.

Required:

1. Prepare a consolidated schedule of changes in working capital for Panther Company and Snowdon Company for the year ended Dexember 31, 19X5. Use parenthetical explanations within the schedule to account for the required eliminations.

2. Prepare the consolidated statement of changes in financial position for Panther Company and Snowdon Company for the year ended December 31, 19X5. Use a footnote schedule to determine consolidated net income. Ignore tax considerations.   (AICPA adapted)

Problem 12-4. On January 1, 19X2, the Holton Corporation acquired an 80% interest in the Myers Corporation. Information regarding the income and equity structure of the two companies as of the year ended December 31, 19X4, is as follows:

	Holton	Myers
Internally generated net income	$42,500	$28,000
Common stock outstanding during the year	20,000 shares	12,000 shares
Warrants to acquire Holton stock, outstanding during the year	2,000	1,000
5% convertible preferred stock outstanding during the year	—	800 shares
Nonconvertible preferred stock outstanding	1,000 shares	—

Additional information is as follows:

(a) The warrants to acquire Holton stock were issued in 19X3. Each warrant can be exchanged for one share of Holton Common stock at an exercise price of $12 per share. The three-month test was met in 19X3.

(b) Each share of convertible preferred stock can be converted into two shares of Myers' common stock. The preferred stock pays an annual dividend totaling $1,600. When issued in 19X2, the prime interest rate was 6%. Holton owns 60% of the convertible preferred stock.

(c) The nonconvertible preferred stock was issued on July 1, 19X4, and paid a six-month dividend totaling $500.

(d) Relevant market prices per share of Holton common stock during 19X4 are as follows:

	Average	Ending
1st Quarter	$10	$11
2d Quarter	12	14
3d Quarter	13	15
4th Quarter	16	15

Required:

Compute the primary and fully diluted consolidated EPS for the year ended December 31, 19X4.

Problem 12-5. On January 1, 19X8, Delos Company exchanged 10,000 shares of its common stock, with a market value of $15 per share (par value, $10), for 80% of the outstanding stock of Morle, Inc. Morle, Inc., had the following stockholders' equity on January 1, 19X8:

Common stock, $2 par	$ 20,000
Paid-in capital in excess of par	50,000
Retained earnings	80,000
Total equity	$150,000

At the time of the purchase, equipment with an 8-year remaining life was undervalued $12,000. Any remaining excess was attributable to goodwill with a 10-year life.

Intercompany merchandise transactions during 19X8 were as follows:

	Delos to Morle	Morle to Delos
Sales	$12,000	$7,000
Markup on cost	25%	40%

Delos had $1,120 of Morle's goods in its ending inventory, and Morle had $1,500 of Delos' goods in its ending inventory.

Morle and Delos qualify as an affiliated group for tax purposes and thus will file a consolidated tax return. A 40% tax rate is assumed.

Delos uses the cost method to record its investment in Morle. Since Morle paid no dividends in 19X8, Delos has recorded no income on its investment in Morle. The two firms prepared the following separate income statements for 19X8:

	Delos	Morle
Sales	$900,000	$600,000
Less cost of goods sold	800,000	375,000
Gross profit	$100,000	$225,000
Less expenses	80,000	185,000
Income before tax	$ 20,000	$ 40,000

Required:

Prepare a consolidated income statement, including distribution of the income to the minority and controlling interests.

Problem 12-6. Trial balances for Panegis Company and its subsidiary, Standard Company, as of December 31, 19X8, are as follows:

	Panegis Company	Standard Company
Cash	159,696	96,000
Accounts Receivable	270,000	130,000
Inventory	350,000	175,000
Investment in Standard Company	550,400	—
Property, Plant, and Equipment	2,600,000	1,500,000
Accumulated Depreciation	(1,440,000)	(535,000)
Liabilities	(1,000,000)	(450,000)
Common Stock ($10 par)	(1,000,000)	(500,000)
Retained Earnings............................	(400,000)	(336,000)
Sales	(2,200,000)	(1,400,000)
Subsidiary Income	(28,800)	—
Gain on Sale of Machine	—	(20,000)
Cost of Goods Sold	1,500,000	950,000
Other Expenses	640,000	390,000
Provision for Income Tax	25,728	32,000
Income Tax Payable	(24,000)	(32,000)
Deferred Tax Liability..........................	(3,024)	—
	0	0

Additional information:
(a) Panegis Company originally purchased its 60% interest in Standard Company for $500,000 on January 1, 19X7. At that time, Standard Company's book values approximated market values and any excess of cost over book value was attributed to goodwill with a 10-year life. Standard's retained earnings was $300,000 at the time of the purchase.
(b) Standard Company sold a machine to Panegis Company on January 2, 19X8, for $50,000. The machine had a book value of $30,000 and an estimated future life of eight years as of the purchase date. Straight-line depreciation is used. For income tax purposes, the $20,000 gain is taxable in the year of sale.
(c) Panegis Company's deferred tax liability was calculated as follows:

15% inclusion × 40% tax rate × $21,600 19X7 subsidiary income	$1,296
15% inclusion × 40% tax rate × $28,800 19X8 subsidiary income	1,728
Total deferred tax liability on undistributed subsidiary income..............	$3,024

(d) A 40% tax rate is assumed for both firms.

Required:

Prepare a consolidated work sheet necessary to prepare consolidated financial statements for Panegis Company and its subsidiary, Standard Company, as of December 31, 19X8.

Problem 12-7. On January 1, 19X7, Pauly Company purchased a 70% interest in Stiles Company for $250,000. Any excess of cost over book value was attributed to goodwill with a 5-year life. At the time of the purchase, Stiles Company's retained earnings was $100,000.

The following additional information is available:

(a) Pauly Company sold a machine to Stiles Company for $15,000 on July 1, 19X7. At the purchase date, the machine had a book value of $9,000, and an estimated future life of ten years. Straight-line depreciation is used by both companies for all their equipment. For income tax purposes, the gain on the sale of the equipment is taxable in the year of the sale.

(b) The following information applies to intercompany merchandise sales from Stiles Company to Pauly Company during 19X8:

19X8 sales	$25,000
Intercompany merchandise in January 1, 19X8 inventory	2,000
Intercompany merchandise in December 31, 19X8 inventory	4,000
Gross profit on sales	30%

(c) Stiles Company paid cash dividends of $.20 per share during 19X8. The 19X8 dividends were the first paid in the company's history.

(d) A 40% tax rate is applicable to both firms. The firms do not qualify as an affiliated group for tax purposes.

(e) Trial balances for Pauly Company and its subsidiary, Stiles Company, as of December 31, 19X8, are as follows:

	Pauly Company	Stiles Company
Cash	119,364	67,000
Accounts Receivable	310,000	95,000
Inventory	340,000	110,000
Investment in Stiles Company	306,000	—
Land	400,000	200,000
Buildings and Equipment	1,750,000	750,000
Accumulated Depreciation	(940,000)	(260,000)
Liabilities	(800,000)	(500,000)
Common Stock ($1 par)	(100,000)	—
Common Stock ($2 par)	—	(100,000)
Paid-In Capital in Excess of Par	(900,000)	(150,000)
Retained Earnings	(380,000)	(142,000)
Sales	(2,000,000)	(700,000)
Subsidiary Income	(33,600)	—
Cost of Goods Sold	1,300,000	400,000
Other Expenses	580,000	220,000
Provision for Income Tax	50,016	32,000
Income Tax Payable	(48,420)	(32,000)
Deferred Tax Liability	(3,360)	—
Dividends Declared	50,000	10,000
	0	0

Required:

Prepare a consolidated work sheet necessary to prepare consolidated financial statements for Pauly Company and its subsidiary, Stiles Company, as of December 31, 19X8.

Problem 12-8. On January 1, 19X6, Miller Company purchased an 80% interest in Braun Company for $400,000. Miller Company prepared the following determination and distribution of excess schedule for its investment:

Price paid		$400,000
Interest acquired:		
Common stock, $10 par	$100,000	
Paid-in capital in excess of par	150,000	
Retained earnings	200,000	
Total equity	$450,000	
Interest acquired	80%	360,000
Excess of cost over book value		$ 40,000
Less excess attributable to building, 80% × $30,000 undervaluation (20-year life)		24,000
Attributable to goodwill (5-year life)		$ 16,000

Additional information:
(a) On July 1, 19X6, Miller Company sold a machine to Braun Company for $30,000. The machine had a book value of $18,000 and an estimated future life of 8 years as of the sale date. Straight-line depreciation is assumed.
(b) Miller Company and Braun Company have had intercompany merchandise sales since January 1, 19X6. A summary of the 19X8 intercompany merchandise sales follows:

	Miller to Braun	Braun to Miller
Seller's merchandise in buyer's January 1, 19X8 inventory	$ 3,000	$ 1,000
19X8 sales	20,000	30,000
Seller's merchandise in buyer's December 31, 19X8 inventory....	2,000	3,000
Outstanding intercompany payables, December 31, 19X8	1,500	2,000
Gross profit on sales	30%	25%

(c) Trial balances for Miller Company and Braun Company as of December 31, 19X8, are as follows:

	Miller Company	Braun Company
Cash	132,600	35,000
Accounts Receivable	180,000	84,000
Inventory	200,000	100,000
Investment in Braun Company	400,000	—
Property, Plant, and Equipment	1,800,000	750,000
Accumulated Depreciation	(1,180,000)	(365,500)
Accounts Payable	(136,000)	(68,000)
Other Liabilities	(46,000)	(6,000)
Common Stock ($10 par)	(1,000,000)	(100,000)
Paid-In Capital in Excess of Par	—	(150,000)
Retained Earnings...........................	(260,000)	(250,000)
Sales	(1,200,000)	(400,000)
Subsidiary Dividend Income	(10,000)	—
Cost of Goods Sold	800,000	250,000
Other Expenses	259,400	108,000
Dividends Declared..........................	60,000	12,500
	0	0

(d) Neither firm has provided for income tax. The firms qualify as an affiliated group and thus will file a consolidated tax return based on a 40% corporate tax rate.

Required:

(1) Prepare a consolidated work sheet based on the trial balances. Include a provision for income tax.
(2) Record the provisions for tax on the books of the separate firms.

Problem 12-9. On January 1, 19X6, Parker Company purchased a 25% interest in Thomas Company for $300,000. Thomas Company's stockholders' equity immediately prior to the purchase was as follows:

Common stock, $10 par	$ 750,000
Retained earnings	250,000
Total stockholders' equity	$1,000,000

Thomas Company's book values approximated market values, except for a building which was undervalued by $40,000. The building had an estimated future life of 20 years. Any additional excess was attributable to goodwill with a 10-year life.

(a) On July 1, 19X6, Thomas Company sold a machine to Parker Company for $24,000. At the sale date, the machine had a book value of $16,000 and an estimated future life of 10 years. Straight-line depreciation is to be used.
(b) Parker Company had provided specialized management services to Thomas Company since January, 19X6. Parker Company charges Thomas Company $15,000 per year for these services. Thomas Company has always paid $7,500 of this fee on July 15, and the remaining $7,500 on January 15 of the following year.
(c) The following chart summarizes intercompany merchandise transactions:

	19X6		19X7		19X8	
	P to T	T to P	P to T	T to P	P to T	T to P
Seller's merchandise in buyer's beginning inventory	—	—	$ 1,000	—	$ 4,000	$ 2,000
Yearly sales	$10,000	—	30,000	$10,000	25,000	25,000
Sellers' merchandise in buyer's ending inventory	1,000	—	4,000	2,000	2,000	3,000
Gross profit on sales	30%	—	30%	25%	30%	25%

(d) Parker Company and Thomas Company's income and dividends paid in 19X6-19X8 were as follows (tax effects are ignored):

	19X6		19X7		19X8	
	Parker	Thomas	Parker	Thomas	Parker	Thomas
Income	$100,000	$48,000	$60,000	$50,000	$75,000	$65,000
Dividends paid	60,000	30,000	50,000	30,000	50,000	35,000

Required:

Prepare all entries necessitated by Parker Company's investment in Thomas Company (as required by APB Opinion No. 18) for 19X6 through 19X8. Ignore income tax.

Problem 12-10.   On January 1, 19X6, Amos Company purchased a 30% interest in Chetek Company for $100,000. Amos Company prepared the following determination and distribution of excess schedule:

Price paid		$100,000
Interest acquired:		
Common stock, $5 par	$100,000	
Paid-in capital in excess of par	100,000	
Retained earnings	100,000	
Total equity	$300,000	
Interest acquired	30%	90,000
Excess of cost over book value		$ 10,000
Less excess attributable to equipment, 30% × $20,000 (10-year		
life)		6,000
Attributable to goodwill (5-year life)		$ 4,000

(a) Amos Company sold a machine to Chetek Company for $20,000 on January 1, 19X7. At this date, the machine had a book value of $10,000 and an estimated future life of ten years. Straight-line depreciation is to be used. For income tax purposes, the gain on the sale is taxable in the year of the sale.

(b) The following applies to Chetek Company merchandise sales to Amos Company for 19X7 and 19X8:

	19X7	19X8
Intercompany merchandise in beginning inventory	—	$ 2,500
Sales for the year	$10,000	15,000
Intercompany merchandise in ending inventory .	2,500	5,000
Gross profit on sales	40%	30%

(c) Internally generated net incomes (after taxes) for Amos Company and Chetek Company are as follows:

	19X6	19X7	19X8
Amos Company	$40,000	$50,000	$55,000
Chetek Company	25,000	30,000	25,000

(d) Chetek paid dividends of $5,000, $10,000, and $10,000, in 19X6, 19X7, and 19X8, respectively.

(e) Assume a corporate income tax rate of 40%.

Required:

Prepare all adjustments to Amos Company's investment in Chetek Company account, as required by APB Opinion No. 18, on December 31, 19X6, 19X7, and 19X8. Consider income tax implications. (Note: only the incremental taxes applicable to the intercompany investment need be considered.)

Problem 12-11.   Bastian, Inc., a domestic corporation having a fiscal year ending June 30, has purchased common stock in several other domestic corporations. As of June 30, 19X8, the balance in Bastian's investment account was $870,600, the total cost of stock purchased less the cost of stock sold. Bastian, Inc., wishes to restate the investment account to reflect the provisions of APB Opinion No. 18.

Data concerning the investment follow:

		Hupp, Inc.	Geer, Inc.	Cargo, Inc.
Shares of common stock outstanding		3,000	32,000	100,000
Shares purchased by Bastian	(a) ..	300	8,000	30,000
	(b) ..	810		
Date of purchase	(a) ..	July 1, 19X5	June 30, 19X6	June 30, 19X7
	(b) ..	July 1, 19X7		
Cost of shares purchased	(a) ..	$ 49,400	$ 46,000	$ 670,000
	(b) ..	142,000		

Balance sheet at date indicated:

Assets	Hupp, Inc. July 1, 19X7	Geer, Inc. June 30, 19X6	Cargo, Inc. June 30, 19X7
Current assets	$ 362,000	$ 39,600	$ 994,500
Property, plant, and equipment, net of depreciation	1,638,000	716,400	3,300,000
Patent, net of amortization	—	—	148,500
	$2,000,000	$756,000	$4,443,000

Liabilities and Equity			
Liabilities	$1,500,000	$572,000	$2,494,500
Common stock	260,000	80,000	1,400,000
Retained earnings	240,000	104,000	548,500
	$2,000,000	$756,000	$4,443,000

Additional information:	Hupp, Inc.	Geer, Inc.	Cargo, Inc.
Changes in common stock since July 1, 19X5	None	None	None
Average remaining life of plant assets at date of balance sheet (above)	12 years	9 years	22 years
Analysis of retained earnings:			
Balance, July 1, 19X5	$ 234,000		
Net income, July 1, 19X5, to June 30, 19X6	53,400		
Dividend paid—April 1, 19X6	(51,000)		
Balance, June 30, 19X6	$ 236,400	$104,000	
Net income (loss), July 1, 19X6, to June 30, 19X7 ..	55,600	(2,000)	
Dividend paid—April 1, 19X7	(52,000)		
Balance, June 30, 19X7	$ 240,000	$102,000	$ 548,500
Net income, July 1, 19X7, to June 30, 19X8	25,000	18,000	330,000
Dividends paid:			
December 31, 19X7	—	—	(150,000)
June 1, 19X8	—	(5,600)	—
Balance, June 30, 19X8	$ 265,000	$114,400	$ 728,500

Bastian's first purchase of Hupp's stock was made because of the high rate of return expected on the investment. All later purchases of stock have been made to gain substantial influence over the operations of the various companies.

In December, 19X7, changing market conditions caused Bastian to reevaluate its relation to Geer. On December 31, 19X7, Bastian sold 6,400 shares of Geer for $54,400.

For Hupp and Geer, the fair values of the net assets did not differ materially from the book values as shown in the balance sheets. For Cargo, fair values exceeded book values only with respect to the patent, which had a fair value of $300,000 and a remaining life of 15 years as of June 30, 19X7.

At June 30, 19X8, Bastian's inventory included $48,600 of items purchased from Cargo during May and June at a 20% markup over Cargo's cost.

Required:

Prepare a work sheet to calculate the balance of Bastian's investment account as of June 30, 19X8, and its investment income by year for the three years then ended. Transactions should be listed in chronological order, and supporting computations should be in good form. Ignore income taxes. Amortization of goodwill, if any, is to be over a 40-year period. Use the following columnar headings for the work sheet:

| Date | Descrip-tion | Investments | | | Investment Income For Year Ended June 30 | | | Other Accounts | |
		Hupp Dr. (Cr.)	Geer Dr. (Cr.)	Cargo Dr. (Cr.)	19X6 Cr. (Dr.)	19X7 Cr. (Dr.)	19X8 Cr. (Dr.)	Name	Amount Dr. (Cr.)

(AICPA adapted)

Problem 12-12. The following series of transactions refer to the first year of operation of a newly formed branch:
  (a) The home office sends $50,000 to a newly formed branch to start operations.
  (b) The home office transfers merchandise, with a cost of $30,000, to the branch for $40,000. The unrealized profit is isolated by the parent in a separate account.
  (c) The branch purchases $40,000 worth of merchandise from outside suppliers.
  (d) The home office transfers machinery, with a book value of $50,000, to the branch for $60,000. Transportation charges of $2,000 are paid by the home office.
  (e) The branch sells $75,000 worth of merchandise.
  (f) The home office pays $2,500 of expenses applicable to the branch but does not charge the branch for them.
  (g) The branch records depreciation of $6,000 on the machinery.
  (h) The branch incurs and records $15,000 of selling and administrative expense.
  (i) The branch remits $35,000 to the home office.

Required:

Journalize the above transactions on the books of the home office and branch.

Problem 12-13. On October 1, 19X7, O'Reilly Company opened a branch office. Transactions affecting the branch office for the fiscal year ending September 30, 19X8, follow:
  (a) The home office sends $50,000 to branch so that operations can begin.
  (b) The home office billed the branch $48,000 for merchandise shipments. The billed amount includes a 20% markup on cost. The home office uses an unrealized intercompany inventory profit account.
  (c) The branch office purchases $20,000 of merchandise from outside suppliers.
  (d) Branch office sales amounted to $75,000, all on credit.
  (e) Branch receivables of $15,000 were outstanding at September 30, 19X8. The branch office deemed $2,000 worth of these receivables uncollectible and set up an allowance account.
  (f) The home office paid $2,000 of branch expenses but did not charge the branch.

(g) The branch office paid $8,000 of expenses during the fiscal year ending September 30, 19X8. Of these expenses, $2,000 related to home office activities and was charged to the home office.

(h) Included in the expenses of the home office are $5,000 of depreciation for the building and equipment and $2,000 of selling and administrative expenses, applicable to the branch office. The branch was not notified of these expenses.

(i) The branch office remitted $50,000 to the home office. Home office acknowledges receipt on September 29, 19X8.

(j) A branch office physical inventory of September 30, 19X8, indicated merchandise on hand of $5,500, of which $3,000 was received from the home office.

A trial balance for the home office of the O'Reilly Company, as of September 30, 19X8, is as follows:

Cash	69,000	
Accounts Receivable	75,000	
Inventory, October 1, 19X7	35,000	
Investment in Branch	46,000	
Plant and Equipment	800,000	
Accumulated Depreciation		250,000
Liabilities		70,000
Common Stock..................................		400,000
Retained Earnings.............................		227,000
Sales		405,000
Purchases	300,000	
Shipments to Branch		40,000
Unrealized Intercompany Inventory Profit.......		8,000
Selling and Administrative Expense	48,000	
Selling and Administrative Expense—Branch ...	2,000	
Depreciation Expense	20,000	
Depreciation Expense—Branch	5,000	
	1,400,000	1,400,000

The home office September 30, 19X8 inventory amounted to $30,000.

Required:

(1) Prepare the entries on the branch office books to record the transactions for the year ended September 30, 19X8. Do not close the books.

(2) Prepare a pre-closing trial balance of the branch office as of September 30, 19X8. Then prepare the closing entries.

(3) Prepare the branch's internal income statement.

(4) Calculate the branch income that would be shown on the home office non-combined statements.

(5) Prepare a work sheet necessary to prepare combined financial statements for the O'Reilly Company and branch office as of September 30, 19X8.

(6) Prepare a combined income statement and a combined balance sheet for the O'Reilly Company as of September 30, 19X8.

Problem 12-14. The general ledger trial balances at December 31, 19X8, for the West Coast Sales Company and its San Diego branch office are as follows:

	Home	Branch
Cash	36,000	8,000
Accounts Receivable	35,000	12,000
Inventory—Home Office, Jan. 1, 19X8	70,000	—
Inventory—Branch Office, Jan. 1, 19X8	—	15,000
Property, Plant, and Equipment (net)...........	90,000	—
Investment in Branch	20,000	—
Accounts Payable	(36,000)	(13,500)
Accrued Expenses.............................	(14,000)	(2,500)
Home Office Equity	—	(9,000)
Common Stock ($10 par)	(50,000)	—
Retained Earnings.............................	(45,000)	—
Home Office:		
Sales	(440,000)	
Purchases	290,000	
Expenses	44,000	
Branch Office:		
Sales		(95,000)
Purchases		24,000
Purchases from Home Office		45,000
Expenses		16,000
	0	0

An audit disclosed the following:
(a) On December 23, the branch office manager purchased $4,000 of furniture and fixtures but failed to notify the home office. The bookkeeper, knowing that all plant assets are carried on the home office books, recorded the proper entry on the branch office records. It is the company's policy not to take any depreciation on assets acquired in the last half of the year.
(b) On December 27, a branch office customer erroneously paid his account of $2,000 to the home office. The bookkeeper made the entry on the home office books but did not notify the branch office.
(c) On December 30, the branch office remitted cash of $5,000, which was received by the home office in January, 19X9.
(d) On December 31, the branch office erroneously recorded the December allocated expense from the home office as $500 instead of $1,500.
(e) On December 31, the home office shipped merchandise billed at $3,000 to the branch office. The merchandise was received in January, 19X9.
(f) The entire beginning inventory of the branch office had been purchased from the home office. Home office 19X8 shipments to the branch office were purchased by the home office in 19X8. The physical inventories at December 31, 19X8, excluding the shipment in transit, are:

Home Office .... $55,000 (at cost)
Branch Office ...... 20,000 (comprised of $18,000 from home office and $2,000 from outside vendors)

(g) The home office consistently bills shipments to the branch office at 20% above cost. The sales account is billed for the invoice price.

Required:

Prepare a work sheet showing Adjustments and Eliminations, Cost of Goods Sold, Net Income, Retained Earnings, and Combined Balance Sheet. (Disregard income taxes.)
                                                              (AICPA adapted)

Problem 12-15.   The trial balances of the home office and branch office of the LaFore Company at December 31, 19X8, are as follows:

	Home	Branch
Cash	17,000	200
Inventory, January 1, 19X8	23,000	11,550
Sundry Assets	200,000	48,450
Investment in Branch	60,000	—
Sundry Liabilities	(35,000)	(3,500)
Common Stock	(200,000)	—
Retained Earnings	(31,000)	—
Home Office Equity	—	(51,500)
Sales	(155,000)	(140,000)
Purchases	190,000	—
Shipments to Branch	(110,000)	—
Shipments from Home Office	—	105,000
Allowance for Markup in Branch Inventory	(1,000)	—
Freight-In from Home Office	—	5,250
Sundry Expenses	42,000	24,550
	0	0

The audit at December 31, 19X8, disclosed the following:

(a) The branch office deposits all cash receipts in a local bank for the account of the home office. The audit working papers for the cash cutoff revealed the following information.

Amount	Deposited by Branch	Recorded by Home Office
$1,050	December 27, 19X8	December 31, 19X8
1,100	December 30, 19X8	January 2, 19X9
600	December 31, 19X8	January 3, 19X9
300	January 2, 19X9	January 6, 19X9

(b) The branch office pays expenses incurred locally from an imprest bank account that is maintained with a balance of $2,000. Checks are drawn once a week on this imprest account, and the home office is notified of the amount needed to replenish the account. At December 31, an $1,800 reimbursement check was mailed to the branch office.

(c) The branch office receives all of its goods from the home office. The home office bills the goods at cost plus a markup of 10% of cost. At December 31, a shipment with a billing value of $5,000 was in transit to the branch. Freight costs are typically 5% of billed values. Freight costs are considered to be inventoriable costs.

(d) The trial balance beginning inventories are shown at their respective costs to the home office and to the branch office. The inventories at December 31, excluding the shipment in transit, are:

Home office, at cost	$30,000
Branch office, at billing value	10,400

Required:

Prepare a columnar work sheet for the LaFore Company and its branch, with columns for Trial Balance, Adjustments and Eliminations, Cost of Goods Sold, Net Income, Retained Earnings, and Combined Balance Sheet. (Disregard income taxes.)   (AICPA adapted)

CHAPTER 13
ACCOUNTING FOR
FOREIGN OPERATIONS

The extent of international activity by U.S. corporations has increased significantly since World War II. The number and the importance of foreign subsidiaries have been impressive and have resulted in the emergence of multinational business on a large scale. Such business investment provides opportunities for product diversification, increased profits, and enhanced corporate status. It also aids in elevating the standard of living in underdeveloped foreign countries and contributes to the balance of international payments. However, foreign investment exposes the parent corporation to a wide range of business risks and competitive disadvantages. For example, firms engaged in foreign operations may be affected by foreign cultural and political values, possible discrimination and interference by foreign host nations, and competition from established foreign firms. For U.S. corporations, these disadvantages are generally outweighed by the advantages.

Significant numbers of domestic corporations are also involved in foreign operations as a result of business transactions with foreign entities. Transactions with foreign entities frequently involve sales, purchases, and lending agreements conducted in foreign currency, and are referred to as foreign currency transactions. The accounting implications of foreign currency transactions and translation of financial statements expressed in foreign currencies are the primary concerns of this chapter.

FOREIGN CURRENCY EXCHANGE RATES

To analyze properly a domestic firm's involvement in foreign operations, results must be expressed in terms of the domestic currency, even though originally these results are expressed in terms of a foreign currency. The conversion is accomplished through the use of exchange rates, representing the amount of one currency which can be exchanged for another at a particular point in time.

In most nations, foreign currency is a commodity which is actively traded on organized exchanges, resulting in the establishment of exchange rates between various currencies. Exchange rates which vary over time as a result of supply and demand are referred to as *free market rates*. Some governments also establish *official* exchange rates and only permit the free market rate to vary within a limited range. In some cases, special rates are established for certain types of transactions, such as imports, exports, and dividend payments, to accomplish desired political and economic objectives. For example, to encourage exports and to discourage capital withdrawal, a foreign government may establish favorable official exchange rates for export sales and less favorable exchange rates governing the payment of dividends to investors in other countries. The forces of supply and demand, however, occasionally make it extremely difficult for a government to maintain an official exchange rate, and in response, the government either devalues or revalues its currency. For example, in 1967, Great Britain devalued the pound from an official rate of $2.80 to $2.40.

The exchange rate that applies to the immediate delivery of a currency is referred to as a *spot rate*. Most foreign currencies are traded at two spot rates. A buying rate is the rate used to exchange foreign currency for domestic currency (e.g., pesos for dollars). A selling rate is the rate used to exchange domestic currency for foreign currency (e.g., dollars for pesos). The difference or spread between the buying and selling rates represents the gross profit accruing to the broker in foreign currency.

In addition to exchange rates governing the immediate delivery of a currency, *forward rates* apply to the exchange of different currencies at a future point in time, such as in sixty or ninety days. The agreement to exchange currencies at a future date is contained in a *forward exchange contract*, which is designed to hedge against future changes in spot rates.

ACCOUNTING FOR FOREIGN CURRENCY TRANSACTIONS

Transactions frequently take place between domestic entities and either independent foreign entities or foreign branches or subsidiaries. The assets and liabilities arising from such transactions are said to be *denominated* in a foreign currency if their amounts are fixed in terms of the currency and do not change in response to changes in exchange rates. Although a transaction is denominated in a particular currency, it may be *measured* or quantified in terms of another currency. For example, assume that a U.S. company purchases inventory from a British vendor and that the goods must be paid for in thirty days with British pounds. The transaction is denominated in British pounds because pounds are required for settlement, but the U.S. company will measure the transaction in dollars. If the purchase by the U.S. company were payable in dollars, the transaction would be both denominated and measured in dollars by the company.

Transactions denominated in the domestic currency are accounted for in the same manner as similar domestic transactions and are not affected by changes in exchange rates because foreign currencies are not required for settlement of the transaction. Therefore, if a transaction by a domestic entity is denominated in the domestic currency, the company is not exposed to any risks due to changes in exchange rates, and exchange gains or losses will not be recognized. However, if a transaction by a domestic entity is denominated in a foreign currency, changes in exchange rates subsequent to the transaction date could result in exchange gains or losses which accrue to the domestic entity.

To illustrate, assume that a U.S. company purchases goods from a foreign firm on November 1, 19X1. The purchase in the amount of 1,000 foreign currencies (FC) is to be paid for on February 1, 19X2. To record or measure the transaction, the domestic company would make the following entry, assuming that 1 FC = $1:

Inventory	1,000	
Accounts Payable		1,000
Purchase of inventory for 1,000 FC when exchange rate is 1 FC = $1.		

If the exchange rate at the settlement date is 1 FC = $1.10, the domestic firm will discharge its liability by purchasing 1,000 FC for $1,100 rather than for $1,000, which would have been the case if settlement had taken place immediately. The $100 difference, which represents the effect of exchange rate movements, is an element of loss to the domestic firm.

Two methods have been proposed for the treatment of exchange gains or losses arising from foreign currency transactions. One method treats the transaction and subsequent settlement as *one transaction* or event. Proponents of this method view the subsequent gain or loss as an adjustment of the original transaction, and in the previous example, would value the inventory acquired at $1,100 ($1,000 + $100 loss). This method suggests that the original transaction and the effects of any subsequent exchange gains or losses should be viewed together in such a way that the final domestic cash flow associated with the event determines the dollar basis of the transaction.

The other method of accounting for foreign currency transaction gains or losses is the *two-transaction* method, which suggests that a deferred settlement of the transaction gives rise to a gain or loss. Therefore, the initial transaction is recorded independently of the settlement transaction. This method is required by the FASB and is consistent with accepted accounting techniques, which normally account for the financing of a transaction as a separate and distinct event. In the original illustration, the settlement of the liability would be recorded as follows:

```
Accounts Payable ...........................................    1,000
Exchange Loss ..............................................      100
  Cash ....................................................            1,100
      To record payment of liability for 1,000 FC when 1 FC = $1.10.
```

The exchange loss is not viewed as an extraordinary item, but should be included in determining net income from operations for the period and should be disclosed in the financial statements or in a note to the statements.[1]

Unsettled Foreign Currency Transactions

If a foreign currency transaction is unsettled at year end, a gain or loss should be recognized to reflect the change in the exchange rate occurring between the transaction date and year end. This treatment focuses on accrual accounting and the fact that exchange gains and losses occur over time rather than only at the date of settlement or payment. For example, continuing with the previous illustration, assume that at year end, December 31, 19X1, the exchange rate is 1 FC = $1.04. The following entry would be necessary at that date:

```
Exchange Loss ..............................................       40
  Accounts Payable .........................................             40
      To accrue exchange loss on unperformed portion of foreign
      currency transaction when 1 FC = $1.04.
```

Assuming that 1 FC equals $1.10 on the settlement date, the domestic entity would make the following entry to record the settlement:

```
Accounts Payable ($1,000 + $40)...........................    1,040
Exchange Loss ..............................................       60
  Cash ....................................................            1,100
      To record payment of liability for 1,000 FC when 1 FC =
      $1.10.
```

The first entry implies that if the transaction had been settled at year end, the domestic firm would have had to expend $1,040 to acquire 1,000 FC. Therefore, a loss of $40 is traceable to the unperformed portion of the transaction. Some theorists have suggested that an exchange gain or loss should not be recognized prior to settlement because the gain or loss has not been "realized" through settlement. This position fails to recognize the merits of accrual accounting and is in conflict with the position of the Financial Accounting Standards Board (FASB), which is stated as follows:

> At each balance sheet date, recorded balances that are denominated in a currency other than the functional currency of the recording entity shall be adjusted to reflect the current exchange rate.[2]

---

[1] *Statement of Financial Accounting Standards, No. 52*, "Foreign Currency Translation" (Stamford: Financial Accounting Standards Board, 1981), par. 30.

[2] *Ibid.*, par. 16.

Hedging with Forward Exchange Contracts

To avoid exposure to changes in future exchange rates when a foreign transaction is denominated in a foreign currency, it is possible to agree currently to buy or sell the foreign currency at a preestablished rather than an uncertain rate of exchange. This would be accomplished through the use of a forward exchange contract, which, as previously mentioned, is an agreement to buy or sell a foreign currency at a specified forward (future) date and at a preestablished forward rate. The forward contract allows one to hedge against the exchange losses which may arise, because the contract fixes the future rate of exchange. For example, in the previous illustration of a foreign currency transaction, the U.S. company experienced a $100 exchange loss because it had to settle a liability denominated in 1,000 FC at a settlement date rate of 1 FC = $1.10, rather than the original transaction date rate of 1 FC = $1. However, if a forward contract had provided for the delivery of the needed foreign currency at a forward rate of 1 FC = $1.04, the exchange loss would have been reduced by $60 because the transaction could have been settled at a rate of 1 FC = $1.04 rather than 1 FC = $1.10.

The forward rate specified in a contract will differ from the current spot rate. The difference between the forward rate and the spot rate at the date of inception of the contract is referred to as a *contract premium* or *discount* and is generally amortized over the life of the contract. A premium occurs when the forward rate is higher than the existing spot rate, and a discount occurs when the forward rate is lower than the existing spot rate. These differences between the forward rate and the spot rate are normally small and are due to interest differentials between the two currencies involved.

Forward contracts are purchased from foreign currency brokers, who measure the interest differentials between holding an investment in foreign currency and holding an investment in domestic currency. For example, if a broker sold a contract to deliver foreign currency in 30 days, the interest differential would be the difference between
- (a) the interest earned on investing foreign currency for the 30 days prior to delivery date and
- (b) the 30 days of interest lost on the domestic currency which was not invested but was used to acquire the foreign currency needed for delivery.

Brokers dealing in forward contracts reduce their risks by extensive trading in contracts. For example, assume that a company has a contract to sell 1,000 FC in 90 days to a broker at a forward rate of 1 FC = $1. If the spot rate in 90 days is 1 FC = $.80, the broker would experience a loss of $200. However, if the broker could have originally found a company wanting to buy 1,000 FC in 90 days at a forward rate of 1 FC = $1.10, the broker would have been able to cover the original loss and actually experience an overall gain of $100.

Forward exchange contracts are used in foreign currency transactions in one of two ways. First, a forward contract may be used to hedge against the exposed position created by a single transaction or the over-all net exposed position created by several transactions. An *exposed net asset position* exists when a transaction or series of foreign currency transactions result in assets denominated in the foreign currency exceeding liabilities denominated in the foreign currency. When such liabilities exceed assets, an *exposed net liability position* exists.

A second use of a forward contract with respect to foreign currency transactions is in response to an identifiable foreign currency commitment. In this instance, the forward contract is acquired as a hedge because there is an existing commitment that will result in a future transaction denominated in a foreign currency. This hedge is in response to an exposed position that will arise via the commitment rather than an exposed position that has already arisen via existing foreign currency transactions.

Hedge on an Exposed Position. Forward contracts are similar to purchase commitments in that both are forms of executory contracts in which future exchange rates have been established. Typically, executory contracts are not recorded until at least partial performance has taken place by one of the parties to the contract. The fact that forward contracts may be sold after inception indicates that they are economic resources, and is the basis for suggestions that unperformed forward contracts should be recorded as assets stated at market price.[3] The FASB views an unperformed forward exchange contract as an asset, for which changes in value due to exchange rate fluctuations should be recognized as a component of current operating income. The FASB states that:

> A gain or loss (whether or not deferred) on a forward contract . . . shall be computed by multiplying the foreign currency amount of the forward contract by the difference between the spot rate at the balance sheet date and the spot rate at the date of inception of the forward contract (or the spot rate last used to measure a gain or loss on that contract for an earlier period).[4]

If a forward contract represents a hedge on an exposed position resulting from an existing foreign currency transaction, the gain or loss on the contract is recognized currently rather than being deferred. To illustrate, assume the following:

1. On November 1, 19X1, a U.S. firm buys inventory from a foreign company, payable on February 1, 19X2, in the amount of 1,000 FC.
2. On November 1, 19X1, the U.S. firm purchases a 90-day forward contract to buy foreign currency at a forward rate of 1 FC = $1.012.
3. Spot rates on selected dates are as follows:

Date	Rate
November 1, 19X1	1 FC = $1.00
December 31, 19X1	1 FC = 1.04
February 1, 19X2	1 FC = 1.10

---

[3] Leonard Lorensen, *Accounting Research Study No. 12*, "Reporting Foreign Operations of U.S. Companies in U.S. Dollars" (New York: American Institute of Certified Public Accountants, 1972) p. 66.

[4] *Statement of Financial Accounting Standards, No. 52, op. cit.*, par. 18.

The following entries reflect the proper accounting for these facts:

19X1

Nov. 1

Inventory	1,000	
Accounts Payable		1,000
Purchase of inventory for 1,000 FC when 1 FC = $1.		

Foreign Currency Due from Broker	1,000	
Deferred Contract Premium	12	
Liability to Broker		1,012
Purchase of 1,000 FC to be delivered in 90 days when forward rate is 1 FC = $1.012.[5]		

Dec. 31

Exchange Loss	40	
Accounts Payable		40
To accrue exchange loss on unperformed portion of foreign currency transaction when 1 FC = $1.04.		

Contract Expense	8	
Deferred Contract Premium		8
To record 60 days of expense on forward contract.		

Foreign Currency Due from Broker	40	
Exchange Gain		40
To record gain on forward contract when year-end spot rate is FC = $1.04. At year end, the 1,000 FC is worth $1,040 versus the $1,000 initially recorded.[6]		

19X2

Feb. 1

Liability to Broker	1,012	
Investment in Foreign Currency	1,100	
Foreign Currency Due from Broker		1,040
Cash		1,012
Exchange Gain		60
To record settlement of contract when 1 FC = $1.10.		

Contract Expense	4	
Deferred Contract Premium		4
To recognize balance of interest expense on forward contract.		

Accounts Payable	1,040	
Exchange Loss	60	
Investment in Foreign Currency		1,100
To record settlement of liability when 1 FC = $1.10.		

---

[5] An alternative for this entry would be a memo entry to describe the commitment resulting from the contract. Such treatment emphasizes the executory nature of the contract.

[6] If the contract is not initially recorded, exchange gains or losses would be recognized, and an allowance for exchange gains or losses would be employed. For example, in the illustration the entry would be:

Allowance for Exchange Gains or Losses	40	
Exchange Gain		40

These entries reflect the objective of a forward contract, which is to hedge against exchange losses. Notice that if the domestic purchaser had not hedged, a net exchange loss of $100 would have been incurred. By hedging, however, the purchaser realizes a gain of $100 on the forward contract, which offsets the $100 loss on the foreign currency transaction. As a result, there is no net exchange gain or loss, although a contract expense totaling $12 is incurred.

It is important to note that forward contracts may also be used to sell foreign currencies at a more favorable rate than the spot rate existing at settlement date. To illustrate, assume that a domestic company sells goods to a foreign purchaser for 1,000 FC when the spot rate is 1 FC = $1, and that the receivable is to be paid in sixty days in foreign currency. If the spot rate at settlement date were 1 FC = $.95, the domestic company would have an exchange loss of $50 [1,000 FC × ($1 − $.95)]. A forward exchange contract to sell the 1,000 FC at a forward rate of 1 FC = $.98, or $980 (1,000 FC × $.98), would have reduced the exchange loss to a net amount of $20 [1,000 FC × ($1 − $.98)].

Hedge on Identifiable Foreign Currency Commitment. In the illustration on the preceding pages, the forward contract was acquired at the transaction date. However, it is possible to acquire a forward contract prior to the transaction date. For example, a domestic firm may enter into an uncancelable commitment with a foreign supplier to deliver goods in nine months. The purchase transaction would not be recorded until the goods are delivered. However, at the time of the commitment, the domestic firm could enter into a forward contract to receive foreign currency in nine months. During the period between the commitment date and the transaction date, rate changes may give rise to gains or losses on such forward contracts. Of concern is whether these gains or losses should be recognized prior to the transaction date or be deferred until that date.

The dollar basis of a foreign currency transaction is established at the transaction date, not at the commitment date. To recognize a gain or loss on a forward contract during the commitment period would partially result in establishing the dollar basis of the transaction prior to the transaction date. Recognizing gains or losses during the commitment period could also benefit (penalize) one period's net income, and penalize (benefit) a subsequent period's net income. After considering the views of concerned parties, the FASB concluded that gains or losses on forward contracts which met certain conditions should be deferred until the transaction date. At the transaction date, the deferred gain or loss would be considered in determining the dollar basis of the transaction. To be considered a hedge on an identifiable foreign currency commitment, a foreign currency transaction must meet both of the following conditions:

(a) The foreign currency transaction is designated as, and is effective as, a hedge of a foreign currency commitment.
(b) The foreign currency commitment is firm.[7]

It is important to note that these conditions relate to a foreign currency transaction. Although identifiable foreign currency commitments are frequently hedged through the use of forward contracts, they may be hedged with transactions which are not forward contracts. For example, if a foreign currency loan is to be repaid with the proceeds of an identifiable foreign currency sales transaction, the loan would be accounted for as a hedge on an identifiable foreign currency commitment.

Although the conditions discussed above may be satisfied, the hedging transaction may exceed the amount of the related foreign currency commitment. In this situation, the gain or loss on the transaction should be accounted for as follows: [8]

1. The gain or loss traceable to the portion of the hedging transaction in excess of the commitment should be deferred to the extent that the transaction provides an after-tax hedge. The gain or loss so deferred should be included as an offset to the related tax effects in the period such tax effects are recognized.
2. That portion of a gain or loss on a hedging transaction in excess of the amount that provides a hedge on an after-tax basis should not be deferred.
3. The gain or loss traceable to the time period after the transaction date of the commitment should not be deferred.

If a hedge on an identifiable foreign currency commitment is terminated before the transaction date of the commitment, any deferred gain or loss as of the termination date should continue to be deferred until the transaction date of the commitment.

To illustrate a hedge on an identifiable foreign currency commitment, assume the following:

1. The conditions necessary for the deferral of exchange gains or losses prior to the transaction date have been satisfied.
2. On January 1, 19X1, a domestic firm agrees to sell goods to a foreign customer, with delivery to be made on March 1, 19X1. The goods, valued at 1,000 FC and having a cost of $800, are to be paid for 60 days after delivery.
3. On January 1, 19X1, the domestic firm purchased a 120-day forward contract to sell foreign currency at a forward rate of 1 FC = $1.02.
4. Spot rates on selected dates are as follows:

Date	Rate
January 1, 19X1	1 FC = $1.00
March 1, 19X1	1 FC = 1.01
May 1, 19X1	1 FC = .99

[7] *Statement of Financial Accounting Standards, No. 52, op. cit.,* par. 21.
[8] *Ibid.*

The following entries reflect the proper accounting for these facts:

19X1

Jan. 1	Dollars Due from Broker	1,020	
	Deferred Contract Premium		20
	Liability to Broker		1,000
	Purchase of contract to sell 1,000 FC in 120 days when forward rate is 1 FC = $1.02.		

Mar. 1	Deferred Exchange Loss	10	
	Liability to Broker		10
	To record deferred loss on forward contract when spot rate is 1 FC = $1.01.		

	Accounts Receivable	1,010	
	Deferred Exchange Loss		10
	Sales		1,000
	To record sale when spot rate is 1 FC = $1.01, and to recognize deferred loss as an adjustment to sales.		

	Cost of Goods Sold	800	
	Inventory		800
	To record the cost of goods sold.		

	Deferred Contract Premium	10	
	Contract Income		10
	To recognize amortization of contract premium ($20 × 60/120 days).[9]		

May 1	Foreign Currency	990	
	Exchange Loss	20	
	Accounts Receivable		1,010
	To record collection of receivable when spot rate is 1 FC = $.99.		

	Liability to Broker	1,010	
	Exchange Gain		20
	Foreign Currency		990
	To record transfer of FC to broker when spot rate is 1 FC = $.99.		

	Cash	1,020	
	Dollars Due from Broker		1,020
	To record receipt of cash from broker at established forward rate of 1 FC = $1.02.		

	Deferred Contract Premium	10	
	Other Income		10
	To recognize remaining amortization of contract premium.		

These entries indicate that the domestic seller of goods has been able to use the hedge on the commitment to preserve gross profit on the sale

---

[9] As an alternative, the premium or discount amortization *may* be included in the determination of the dollar basis of the transaction, which would have been achieved by crediting Sales rather than Contract Income.

and offset the exchange loss experienced upon collection of the sales receivable. At the commitment date, the seller anticipated a gross profit of $200, which is the difference between the $800 inventory cost and the sales value of $1,000 (1,000 FC × spot rate of 1 FC = $1 at the commitment date). The entry on March 1, 19X1, to record the sale and adjust the sales for the previously deferred exchange loss results in establishing net sales at $1,000, which allows for the preservation of the expected gross profit of $200. Subsequent to the transaction date, the forward contract produces an exchange gain of $20, which offsets the exchange loss of $20 experienced upon collection of the sales receivable. Excluding the effect on income of the deferred contract premium, the following comparison illustrates how management was able to achieve the desired position through the use of a hedge on the identifiable foreign currency commitment:

	Desired Position	Without Hedge	With Hedge
Sales......................................	$1,000	$1,010	$1,000
Cost of goods sold	800	800	800
Gross profit	$ 200	$ 210	$ 200
Exchange loss on settlement	—	(20)	(20)
Exchange gain on forward contract	—	—	20
	$ 200	$ 190	$ 200

Although the illustration ignored the tax impact of the transactions, the FASB, as previously stated, provides for hedging on an after-tax basis. A hedge on an after-tax basis recognizes that there may be a tax impact associated with the foreign currency commitment itself and a separate tax impact associated with the gain or loss on the forward contract. In the illustration, for example, there is a tax impact associated with the sale of inventory and a tax impact associated with the gain on the forward contract to hedge the foreign currency commitment. The desired objective is for the gain (loss) on such a hedge less the net related tax impact to equal the exchange loss (gain) associated with the settlement of the foreign currency commitment.

Forward Contracts as a Means of Speculation. In addition to employing forward contracts as a means of hedging an exposed position or a foreign currency commitment, they may be employed as a means of speculating in foreign currencies. Foreign currencies are actively traded as commodities and thus provide opportunities for speculation. For example, a U.S. investor might purchase a forward contract to sell foreign currency at a given forward rate. The investor may not even possess foreign currency, but subsequently will attempt to sell the contract at a gain. Gains or losses on contracts held in speculation should be determined by:

> . . . multiplying the foreign currency amount of the forward contract by the difference between the forward rate available for the remaining maturity

of the contract and the contracted forward rate (or the forward rate last used to measure a gain or loss on that contract for an earlier period).[10]

In addition to the different basis for measuring gains or losses on speculative contracts, no separate recognition is given to the premium or discount on the contract. To illustrate the accounting for a speculative contract, assume the following:

1. On November 1, 19X2, a calendar-year investor purchased a 120-day forward contract to buy 1,000 FC at a forward rate of 1 FC = $1.01, when the spot rate was 1 FC = $1.
2. On December 31, 19X2, the forward rate for a 30-day forward contract was 1 FC = $1.02, and the spot rate was 1 FC = $1.015.
3. On February 1, 19X3, the investor paid the broker and received the foreign currency. The spot rate was 1 FC = $1.03.

The following entries reflect the proper accounting for these facts:

19X2
Nov. 1   Foreign Currency Due from Broker 1,010
        Liability to Broker 1,010
          To record purchase of contract when forward rate is
          1 FC = $1.01.

Dec. 31 Foreign Currency Due from Broker 10
        Exchange Gain 10
          To recognize speculation gain measured as the dif-
          ference between the original forward rate and the
          forward rate available for the remaining maturity
          [1,000 FC × ($1.01 − $1.02)].

19X3
Feb. 1   Liability to Broker 1,010
        Cash 1,010
          To record payment to broker at agreed rate of 1 FC
          = $1.01.

        Foreign Currency 1,030
        Foreign Currency Due from Broker 1,020
        Exchange Gain 10
          To record the receipt of 1,000 FC when the spot
          rate was 1 FC = $1.03.

Note that the investor's exchange gain prior to maturity was measured by the difference between forward rates, and that no separate recognition was given to the contract premium. The total exchange gain of $20 is the difference between the original forward rate and the spot rate at maturity of the contract [1,000 FC × ($1.01 − $1.03)].

Although the illustration assumed that the investor took delivery of the foreign currency, in a more typical situation an investor would not hold a forward contract to maturity but would sell the contract right to another party. Assuming the same facts, except that the investor sold the contract for $10 on December 31, 19X2, the following entry would

---

[10] *Statement of Financial Accounting Standards, No. 52, op. cit.,* par. 19.

have been made on December 31, in addition to the other November 1 and December 31 entries:

```
19X2
Dec. 31  Cash ...............................................       10
         Liability to Broker ..................................    1,010
              Foreign Currency Due from Broker .................           1,020
```

As mentioned previously, the special treatment given forward contracts held for speculation is also required for other forward contracts to the extent they exceed:

1. That amount required to cover a net exposed asset or liability position, and/or
2. That amount needed to hedge on an after-tax basis an identifiable foreign currency commitment.

TRANSLATION OF FOREIGN CURRENCY FINANCIAL STATEMENTS

The accounting treatment of possible relationships which may exist between a domestic entity and a foreign entity and which involve some degree of control is summarized as follows:

Domestic Entity	Foreign Entity	Accounting Treatment
Parent	Branch	Branch accounting
Parent	Subsidiary	Consolidated financial statements or separate financial statements
Investor	Investee	Investment in foreign entity at cost or equity

Objectives of Translation

The relationships indicated above suggest the need for the domestic entity to acquire the foreign entity's financial information, which is denominated in foreign (local) currency. Because it is not logical to consolidate or combine financial information which is expressed in different types of currencies, it is necessary to translate the information into a single reporting currency by a measurement conversion process. This process does not result in new principles being employed to measure attributes or relationships and should not alter the underlying significance of the results and relationships of the constituent entities. However, the translation of the constituent parts should:

(a) Provide information that is generally compatible with the expected economic effects of a rate change on an enterprise's cash flows and equity.
(b) Reflect in consolidated statements the financial results and relationships of the individual consolidated entities as measured in their functional currencies in conformity with U.S. generally accepted accounting principles.[11]

---

[11] *Ibid.*, par. 4.

The Functional Currency Approach. The financial data of an entity are expressed in the entity's functional currency prior to translation. The functional currency is normally the currency of the primary economic environment in which the entity generates cash flows. This environment is typically the country in which the entity operates. When a foreign subsidiary is a direct and integral component of a parent's operations, however, the parent's currency would be the functional currency. Also, when a foreign entity has distinct and separable operations, each of which is conducted in a different economic environment, the currency used to record activities may not be the functional currency.

If foreign financial statements are not expressed in the functional currency prior to translation, the statements must be reexpressed in the functional currency by applying procedures which are designed to measure transactions as if they were originally recorded in the functional currency. Monetary assets and liabilities should be reexpressed by using the current rate of exchange for the functional currency, nonmonetary items should be reexpressed by using historical rates, and the translation adjustment should be included in income. Examples of accounts which should be translated at historical rates are as follows: [12]

> Marketable securities carried at cost:
>   Equity securities
>   Debt securities not intended to be held until maturity
> Inventories carried at cost
> Prepaid expenses such as insurance, advertising, and rent
> Property, plant, and equipment
> Accumulated depreciation on property, plant, and equipment
> Patents, trademarks, licenses, and formulas
> Goodwill
> Other intangible assets
> Deferred charges and credits, except deferred income taxes and policy
>   acquisition costs for life insurance companies
> Deferred income
> Common stock
> Preferred stock carried at issuance price
> Examples of revenues and expenses related to nonmonetary items:
>   Cost of goods sold
>   Depreciation of property, plant, and equipment
>   Amortization of intangible items such as goodwill, patents, licenses,
>   etc.
>   Amortization of deferred charges or credits except deferred income
>   taxes and policy acquisition costs for life insurance companies

Highly Inflationary Economies. When an entity's financial statements are expressed in the functional currency, the statements are generally translated directly into the reporting currency. However, this procedure is not followed for a foreign entity in a highly inflationary economy. The FASB defines such an economy as one that has a cumulative inflation rate of approximately 100 percent or more over a 3-year period. Other

---

[12] *Ibid.*, par. 47.

factors, such as the trend of inflation, may also suggest a highly inflationary economy.[13]

If a foreign entity's currency has lost its utility as a measure of a store of value, it would probably not serve as a useful functional currency. To ignore this situation in subsequent translations might produce misleading results. Accordingly, the statements of an entity in a highly inflationary economy should be reexpressed in the reporting currency. This reexpression should follow the methodology employed when a foreign entity's currency is not the functional currency.

Differences in Generally Accepted Accounting Principles. Various factors have influenced the development of accounting principles in different countries. Among these factors are: (1) the degree of self-regulation by the accounting profession, (2) business customs, (3) tax legislation, (4) legal traditions, and (5) inflationary factors. Although it is beyond the scope of this discussion to outline the significant differences between generally accepted accounting principles in the U.S. and those in foreign countries, major differences exist with respect to tax allocation, valuation of assets, and measurement of income. For example:

1. In Belgium, where there are significant differences between accounting for financial and tax purposes, it is not the general practice to provide for the tax effect of such differences (i.e., apply tax allocation).
2. Recognition of appraised values is common in the Netherlands, South Africa, and India.
3. Lifo as an inventory valuation method cannot be used in Brazil, Denmark, Sweden, and the Philippines.

In recent years, considerable effort has been devoted to the development of international accounting standards. In 1973, the members of the Accountants' International Study Group (AISG) established the International Accounting Standards Committee (IASC), which has issued Statements of International Accounting Standards dealing with a variety of financial reporting topics. The members of the IASC are encouraging their respective countries to conform their standards to those of the IASC and to disclose any departures from established IASC standards. Similar efforts are also being undertaken by the International Federation of Accountants (IFAC), which was established in 1977.

To provide useful information, consolidated financial statements which include the results of foreign operations should employ consistent accounting principles. These principles should be understood and accepted by both internal and external users of such data. Therefore, before financial statements of a foreign operation may be analyzed and interpreted, and before the statements are translated, the foreign statements must be prepared in conformity with the generally accepted accounting principles which are followed in the U.S. This conformity of

---

[13] *Ibid.*, par. 11.

accounting principles is required by the U.S. accounting profession, the Securities and Exchange Commission, and the Internal Revenue Service.

Translation Methods

Since exchange rates fluctuate over time, a decision must be reached as to which exchange rate should be used to translate foreign accounts into the reporting currency. Several methods of translation have been proposed in the literature. Some of these methods are discussed in the following paragraphs, although a comprehensive review of these methods is beyond the scope of this chapter.

Current-Noncurrent Method. The *current-noncurrent method* was presented in Chapter 12 of Accounting Research Bulletin No. 43, and for many years was viewed as the established method of translation. According to this method, the balance sheet classification of assets and liabilities determines which exchange rate should be employed in translation. Current items would be translated at the current exchange rate, while noncurrent items would be translated at the historical rate which existed when the asset or liability was originally recorded.

Opponents of this method are quick to point out that the balance sheet classification of an item, versus the attribute of the item being measured, determines its translation rate. The treatment of inventory and long-term debt are frequently cited as examples of how the strict application of the current-noncurrent method fails to achieve the objectives of translation. For example, assume that a foreign subsidiary incurred a long-term debt, originally stated at 1,000 FC, when the exchange rate was 1 FC = $1. The current exchange rate is 1 FC = $1.10. Under the current-noncurrent method, the debt would be translated at $1,000. If the debt were settled currently, however, it would require an expenditure of 1,000 FC, or $1,100 if paid in dollars. This method thus fails to recognize the current equivalent claim on domestic currency. Furthermore, the translation of inventory, a current item stated at historical cost, produces a measure which departs from historical cost but does not reflect current replacement cost or selling price. In practice, the deficiencies of this method were reduced as a result of certain exceptions prescribed in Chapter 12 of ARB No. 43; however, such exceptions did not change the theoretical nature of the method.

Monetary-Nonmonetary Method. APB Opinion No. 6, which modified Chapter 12 of ARB No. 43, permitted the use of the *monetary-nonmonetary method*. This method views the characteristics of assets and liabilities as the basis for selecting an appropriate exchange rate. Monetary assets and liabilities are those which represent a fixed number of foreign currency units, while all other items are viewed as nonmonetary. According to this method, monetary items are translated at the current exchange rate, while other items are converted at the exchange rate which existed when the assets and liabilities were originally recorded. For example, inventory stated at replacement cost would be viewed as nonmonetary and would therefore be translated at the historical exchange rate.

Temporal Method. The *temporal method* recognizes that the accounting principles used to measure assets and liabilities should not be changed as a result of the translation process. Particular attention is paid to whether an accounting principle measures an asset or liability in terms of current values or past values. Using this method, which is compatible with the objectives of translation, the current exchange rate should be employed if the attribute measured represents the current command over foreign currency as portrayed by current values. If the attribute measured represents past foreign money prices (historical costs), however, then exchange rates which prevailed at that time should be employed. For example, money and receivables and payables presented in foreign currency statements represent the current amount of foreign money owned or promised. The attribute to be measured in terms of domestic currency is the command over domestic currency represented by these foreign monies. This temporal attribute can be measured by converting foreign monies owned or promised into domestic currency, using the current spot exchange rate which exists at the balance sheet date. Likewise, inventory stated at replacement cost would be translated at the current exchange rate.

In most instances, the use of the temporal method coincidentally produces the same results as would be achieved if the monetary-nonmonetary method were employed. However, the monetary-nonmonetary method focuses on the classification of items, while the temporal method focuses on whether current or past monetary prices are used to measure the attributes of assets and liabilities. The most obvious difference in application of the two methods is that the temporal method uses the current exchange rate to translate nonmonetary items recorded at current value.

Recognition of Exchange Gains and Losses

If exchange rates have changed over time, the sum of translated assets will not equal the sum of translated liabilities and equities, regardless of the translation method used. The difference is interpreted as an exchange gain or loss.

Numerous methods of recognizing exchange gains and losses have been employed in the past. ARB No. 43 applied a realization test for recognition of exchange gains and losses. Realized gains were recognized, while both realized and unrealized losses were charged against income. Unrealized gains were deferred, except to the extent that they offset previous unrealized losses in total.[14] Unfortunately, realization criteria were not established, and a cash transaction test was not used to distinguish between realized and unrealized items. Realization was often associated with the payment of dividends from the foreign unit to the domestic entity. The absence of sound criteria made the application of this section of ARB No. 43 impracticable.

Other methods of recognizing exchange gains and losses were developed. One of these methods deferred gains and losses to the extent that they were traceable to long-term liabilities expressed in foreign currency. The deferral would then be amortized over the remaining life of the relevant liability. Another method, in essence, deferred the gain or loss on liabilities by viewing them as adjustments to the basis of the assets acquired with such funds. Conservatism and the possible reversal of rate changes were used as arguments for justifying the deferral of exchange gains and losses. The availability of alternative translation methods and alternative methods of recognizing exchange gains and losses made it apparent that the method selected by management should be adequately disclosed.

STATEMENT OF FINANCIAL ACCOUNTING STANDARDS, NO. 52

Prior to 1973, domestic firms could employ any of the translation methods discussed previously. This situation prompted the FASB in 1973 to issue Statement of Financial Accounting Standards, No. 1, "Disclosure of Foreign Currency Translation Information." The Statement did not express a preference for any particular translation method, but required disclosure of the following information:

    (a) A statement of translation policies including identification of: (1) the balance sheet accounts that are translated at the current rate and those translated at the historical rate, (2) the rates used to translate income statement accounts (e.g., historical rates for specified accounts and a weighted average rate for all other accounts), (3) the time of recognition of gain or loss on forward exchange contracts, and (4) the method of accounting for exchange adjustments (and if any portion of the exchange adjustment is deferred, the method of disposition of the deferred amount in future years).

    (b) The aggregate amount of exchange adjustments originating in the period, the amount thereof included in the determination of income and the amount thereof deferred.

    (c) The aggregate amount of exchange adjustments included in the determination of income for the period, regardless of when the adjustments originated.

    (d) The aggregate amount of deferred exchange adjustments, regardless of when the adjustments originated, included in the balance sheet (e.g., such as in a deferral or in a "reserve" account) and how this amount is classified.

---

[14] *Accounting Research and Terminology Bulletins, No. 43.* "Restatement and Revision of Accounting Research Bulletins" (New York: American Institute of Certified Public Accountants, 1961), Ch. 12, pars. 10-11.

(e) The amount by which total long-term receivables and total long-term payables translated at historical rates would each increase or decrease at the balance sheet date if translated at current rates.
(f) The amount of gain or loss which has not been recognized on unperformed forward exchange contracts at the balance sheet date.[15]

As a result of expanding activities of U.S. firms in foreign markets, changes in the international monetary system, and the existence of alternative translation methods, the FASB began an extensive study of foreign currency translation in 1973. This effort produced Statement of Financial Accounting Standards, No. 8, "Accounting for the Translation of Foreign Currency Transactions and Foreign Currency Financial Statements," which superceded sections of previous pronouncements dealing with foreign operations and translation (ARB No. 43, APB Opinion No. 6, and FASB Statement No. 1). The Statement evaluated alternative translation methods and accepted none of them, although the temporal method appeared to be most compatible with the Statement's objectives. The FASB took the position that foreign accounts representing cash, receivables, and payables (items expressed in fixed or current amounts of foreign currency) should be translated at the current rate. Other accounts should be translated in a way that retained the accounting principles used to measure the accounts. If these accounts were measured at past exchange prices, they should be translated at historical rates. Accounts measured in current purchase or sale exchange prices should be translated at the current rate.

According to FASB Statement No. 8, exchange gains and losses that resulted from translation and foreign currency transactions should be included in the determination of net income for the period. The total exchange gain or loss should be disclosed either in the financial statements or in a related footnote. The FASB reasoned that gains and losses due to changes in the exchange rate are objectively measured historical facts and relate to the time period in which the rate change occurs.

Following its promulgation in 1975, Statement No. 8 became the subject of considerable controversy. When the Statement was applied, multinational corporations reported significant fluctuations in profits as a result of foreign currency exchange rate variations and the presentation of translation losses as a component of reported income. Statement No. 8 was criticized for its failure to reflect the underlying economic realities of foreign operations and rate changes, and for its reporting requirements which resulted in data being volatile due to rate changes rather than operating factors. In late 1981, after considering two exposure drafts in response to these criticisms, the FASB issued Statement of Financial Accounting Standards, No. 52, "Foreign Currency Translation."

---

[15] *Statement of Financial Accounting Standards, No. 1,* "Disclosure of Foreign Currency Translation Information" (Stamford: Financial Accounting Standards Board, 1973), par. 6.

The Translation Process

In studying the problems associated with foreign currency translation, the FASB concluded that the results and relationships presented in the functional currency financial statements would be retained if the translation were based exclusively on the current rate of exchange between the functional currency and the reporting currency. Therefore, all assets and liabilities should be translated at the current exchange rate at the end of the period. The income statement accounts should be translated at the current exchange rates which existed at the time of the recognition of the revenues and expenses. As a practical consideration, however, income statement amounts may be translated by using a weighted average exchange rate for the period. Stockholders' equity accounts, other than retained earnings, should be translated at historical exchange rates. The amount of retained earnings is equal to the translated retained earnings reported at the end of the prior period plus the current period's translated net income less other changes (dividends) translated at the current rate at the time of the transaction. With respect to the statement of changes in financial position, the current exchange rate is used for changes other than those that result from operations, which are translated at the rate used for the income statement.

Accounting for Translation Adjustments

Translation adjustments will result from the process of translating the balance sheet. The translation adjustment may be calculated indirectly as the amount needed to make the owners' equity equal to the translated net assets. In general, the translation adjustment may also be computed as being equal to (a) the change in exchange rates during the period, multiplied by the amount of net assets at the beginning of the period, plus (b) the difference between the average exchange rate used in translating the income statement for the period and the end-of-period exchange rate, multiplied by the increase or decrease in net assets for the period (except for increases or decreases that are attributable to capital transactions). For a capital transaction, the translation adjustment equals the increase or decrease in net assets applicable to the transaction, multiplied by the difference between the end-of-period exchange rate and the exchange rate at the time the transaction occurred.

Translation adjustments that result from exchange rate changes have an indirect effect on the net investment which may be realized upon sale or liquidation. This effect is not related to the operations of the foreign entity and is so remote and uncertain that it should not be included in computing net income. Therefore, the cumulative translation adjustments should be reported as a separate component of equity. Upon the sale or liquidation of the investment in a foreign entity, a proportionate amount of the accumulated translation adjustments should be removed from equity and included as part of the gain or loss on the liquidation transaction.

Consolidated Foreign Subsidiaries

One of the primary criteria established to determine if consolidation is appropriate deals with the extent of control the parent corporation exercises over the subsidiary. With respect to foreign subsidiaries, effective control is determined, in part, by currency restrictions and the possibility of nationalization of the operation by foreign governments. Assuming that consolidation is appropriate, the financial statements of the foreign entity must be translated into dollars according to the principles expressed in FASB Statement No. 52.

After the foreign statements have been translated, intercompany eliminations are made and the statements are consolidated according to the principles of consolidation discussed in this text. Illustration I, on page 599, provides an example of a foreign subsidiary translation, based on the following facts:

1. The Fori Corporation began operations on January 1, 19X1, as a wholly owned foreign subsidiary of the Dome Corporation.
2. Sales to Dome are billed in the foreign currency, and all receivables from Dome have been collected, except for the amount shown in the account "Due from Dome." All other sales are also billed in the foreign currency. The level of sales and purchases was constant over the year.
3. Selected exchange rates are as follows:

Date	Rate
January 1, 19X1	1 FC = $1.00
December 31, 19X1	1 FC = 1.05
19X1 average	1 FC = 1.03

Unconsolidated Foreign Subsidiaries

Unconsolidated subsidiaries are accounted for according to either the cost method or the equity method. The method used depends upon whether certain criteria established in APB Opinion No. 18 are satisfied.

Under the cost method, the investment in the subsidiary is carried at its original cost plus additional investments less the cost of securities sold. With respect to translation, this method does not present any specific difficulties, if payments in foreign currency are translated into dollars at the appropriate exchange rate. If factors existing in the environment of a foreign country suggest a permanent impairment in the value of the investment, the basis of the investment should be reduced appropriately.

Foreign statements of an investee accounted for by the equity method should first be translated into dollars and then the equity

Illustration I

Fori Corporation
Trial Balance Translation
December 31, 19X1

Account	Balance in Foreign Currency	Relevant Exchange Rate ($/FC)	Balance in Dollars
Cash	10,000 FC	1.05	$ 10,500
Accounts Receivable	20,000	1.05	21,000
Due from Dome	15,000	1.05	15,750
Inventory (at cost)	30,000	1.05	31,500
Prepaid Insurance	3,000	1.05	3,150
Land (acquired March 1, 19X1)	25,000	1.05	26,250
Depreciable Assets	120,000	1.05	126,000
Cost of Goods Sold	180,000	1.03	185,400
Depreciation Expense	13,000	1.03	13,390
Income Tax Expense	30,000	1.03	30,900
Other Expenses (including interest)	20,000	1.03	20,600
Total debits	466,000 FC		$484,440
Accounts Payable	20,000 FC	1.05	$ 21,000
Taxes Payable................................	30,000	1.05	31,500
Accrued Interest Payable	1,000	1.05	1,050
Mortgage Payable—Land	20,000	1.05	21,000
Common Stock	100,000	1.00	100,000
Retained Earnings............................	-0-	Note A	-0-
Sales—Dome.................................	80,000	1.03	82,400
Sales—Other.................................	200,000	1.03	206,000
Gain on Sale of Depreciable Assets.............	2,000	1.03	2,060
Allowance for Doubtful Accounts...............	1,000	1.05	1,050
Accumulated Depreciation	12,000	1.05	12,600
Cumulative Translation Adjustments (to balance)	-0-	—	5,780
Total credits	466,000 FC		$484,440

Note A—The translated value of zero for retained earnings represents the beginning-of-the-period translated value. The balance sheet for 19X1 would show a translated value for retained earnings equal to the translated value of net income less dividends translated at the declaration date. This value would also represent the translated value for beginning retained earnings in the 19X2 trial balance.

Recomputation of Translation Adjustment

Net assets at beginning of period, multiplied by the change in exchange rates during the period [0 × ($1.05 − $1.00)]	-0-
Increase in net assets (excluding capital transactions) multiplied by the difference between the current rate and the average rate used to translate income [39,000 FC × ($1.05 − $1.03)]....................................	$ 780
Increase in net assets due to capital transactions, multiplied by the difference between the current rate and the rate at the time of the capital transaction [100,000 FC × ($1.05 − $1.00)]	5,000
Translation adjustment	$5,780

method applied. As in the case of the cost method, if a permanent impairment in the value of the investment occurs, the basis of the investment should be reduced appropriately.

Gains and Losses Excluded from Income

The separate component of equity in which cumulative translation adjustments are reported should also include gains and losses attributable to:

> (a) Foreign currency transactions that are designated as, and are effective as, economic hedges of a net investment in a foreign entity, commencing as of the designation date.
>
> (b) Intercompany foreign currency transactions that are of a long-term-investment nature (that is, settlement is not planned or anticipated in the foreseeable future), when the entities to the transaction are consolidated, combined, or accounted for by the equity method in the reporting enterprise's financial statements.[16]

A foreign currency transaction that is a hedge of a net investment in a foreign entity should be accounted for in the same way as the effect of rate changes on the net investment. For example, a domestic corporation with an investment in a French subsidiary, in which the franc is the functional currency, might borrow francs and identify the transaction as a hedge on the net investment in the French subsidiary. Because the loan is a liability and the net investment is an asset, a rate change will have opposite effects on the loan and the translation adjustment. Therefore, the foreign currency transaction is a hedge of a net investment and will offset the translation adjustment. However, if the gain (loss) on the hedge (after tax effects) is greater than the corresponding translation loss (gain), the excess transaction gain (loss) must be included in the determination of net income.

Exchange Rates and Intercompany Profits

It is fairly common for a foreign country to have more than one exchange rate, such as a commercial rate and a financial rate. Therefore, the FASB stated that the following exchange rates should be used in the translation process:

> (a) Foreign Currency Transactions—The applicable rate at which a particular transaction could be settled at the transaction date shall be used to translate and record the transaction. At a subsequent balance sheet date, the current rate is that rate at which the related receivable or payable could be settled at that date.
>
> (b) Foreign Currency Statements—In the absence of unusual circumstances, the rate applicable to conversion of a currency for purposes of dividend remittances shall be used to translate foreign currency statements.[17]

If an exchange rate between the functional currency and the reporting currency is temporarily lacking, the first subsequently available exchange rate should be used. However, if the absence of an exchange rate is other than temporary, consolidation or equity-method accounting

---

[16] *Statement of Financial Accounting Standards, No. 52, op. cit.,* par. 20.

[17] *Ibid.,* par. 27.

may not be appropriate.

Once a foreign entity's financial statements have been translated into the reporting currency, certain eliminations due to intercompany transactions will generally be required. With regard to the exchange rate that should be used to translate such transactions, the FASB concluded that all intercompany balances, except for intercompany profits, should be translated at the rates used for all other accounts. Intercompany profits should be translated using the exchange rate which existed at the date of the sale or transfer. As a practical matter, however, average rates or approximations may be used to translate such profits.

Income Tax Allocation

Interperiod tax allocation is appropriate when gains or losses resulting from foreign currency transactions are included in income in a different period for accounting purposes than for tax purposes. The gains or losses on certain types of foreign currency transactions are presented as a component of equity rather than as a component of income. According to the principles of intraperiod tax allocation, the income taxes related to such items should also be allocated to equity. With respect to translation adjustments, the FASB decided that deferred taxes should not be provided for translation adjustments attributable to an investment in a foreign entity for which deferred taxes are not recognized on unremitted earnings. However, if deferred taxes are recognized on unremitted earnings, deferred taxes should be provided along with the translation adjustment as a separate component of stockholders' equity.

Disclosure Requirements

Statement No. 52 requires that foreign currency transaction and hedging gains and losses included in the determination of net income be disclosed in the financial statements or the accompanying notes. An analysis of the separate component of equity affected by certain foreign currency transactions and hedges and translation adjustments should be presented. The analysis may be in a separate statement, in a note to the financial statements, or as part of the statement of changes in equity. At a minimum, the analysis should disclose:

(a) Beginning and ending amount of cumulative translation adjustments.
(b) The aggregate adjustment for the period resulting from translation adjustments and gains and losses from certain hedges and intercompany balances.
(c) The amount of income taxes for the period allocated to translation adjustments.
(d) The amounts transferred from cumulative translation adjustments and included in determining net income for the period as a result of the sale or complete or substantially complete liquidation of an investment in a foreign entity.[18]

---

[18] *Ibid.*, par. 31.

Although the various effects of rate changes subsequent to the end of the period are not normally disclosed, their effect on unsettled balances arising from foreign currency transactions may be disclosed if significant.

QUESTIONS

1. Define the terms "spot rate" and "forward rate." Explain why there is normally a difference between the buying and selling spot rates. Also, explain why a positive difference usually exists between the forward and spot rates for a particular currency.

2. Explain how changes in exchange rates affect accounting for transactions with foreign entities which are denominated in the domestic currency, and transactions which are denominated in foreign currencies.

3. Discuss the two methods of accounting for gains or losses on foreign currency transactions. Identify which method is presently called for under generally accepted accounting principles.

4. Define forward exchange contracts and explain the purposes they serve in foreign currency transactions.

5. What are the criteria for a hedge on an identifiable foreign currency commitment?

6. Assuming a forward contract to buy foreign currency for purposes of settling a purchase from a foreign entity, describe how the year-end balances of the following accounts would be derived:
   (1) Foreign currency due from broker.
   (2) Liability to broker.
   (3) Deferred contract premium.

7. Explain how the gain or loss on a hedge on an identifiable foreign currency commitment should be accounted for if the amount of the hedge exceeds the amount of the commitment.

8. Explain how to measure the gain or loss on a forward contract held for speculative purposes.

9. Identify the foreign currency transaction gains or losses which should not be shown as a component of net income.

10. Specify the basic objectives in translating foreign currency financial statements.

11. Define the term "functional currency" and describe several instances in which a foreign entity's currency may not be the functional currency.

12. If a foreign entity maintains its records in a currency which is not the functional currency, explain the methodology for translating such information into the parent's reporting currency.

13. Discuss the accounting treatment of translation adjustments.

EXERCISES

Exercise 1. Milton & Associates of the United States forwarded freight to JMB International of Japan. Milton billed JMB 22,000 yen for shipping charges on March 16, 19X2, with payment due April 15, 19X2.
(1) Assume that on March 16, 19X2, 1 yen = $.44 and that on April 15, 1 yen = $.41. Prepare the journal entries on Milton's books to record the sale to and subsequent payment from JMB International.
(2) Assume the same facts as in (1), except that on March 16, Milton enters into a forward exchange contract to deliver 22,000 yen to a currency broker on April 15 at a rate of 1 yen = $.45. Prepare all journal entries on Milton's books to record the sale, collection, and forward contract.

Exercise 2. In Exercise 1, assume that Milton bills JMB 22,000 yen on March 16, 19X2, but that payment is due May 15, 19X2, 15 days after Milton's fiscal year end of April 30.
(1) Assume the following exchange rates:

Date	Rate
March 16, 19X2	1 yen = $.44
April 30, 19X2	1 yen = .40
May 15, 19X2	1 yen = .42

Prepare all journal entries on Milton's books to record the transactions with JMB International. Assume that forward exchange contracts are not employed.
(2) Assume the same facts as in (1), except that on March 16, 19X2, Milton enters into a forward exchange contract to deliver 22,000 yen to a currency broker on May 15 at a forward rate of 1 yen = $.45. Prepare all journal entries on Milton's books to record the transactions.

Exercise 3. Milwaukee Specialty Foods, Inc., is a large purveyor of sausage and other processed meat products. The majority of Milwaukee Specialty's sales and purchase transactions are with United States firms. However, in recent years the firm has made sales of its products and, to a lesser extent, purchases of supplies in West Germany. As an accommodation to German customers and suppliers, all of these transactions are denominated in deutsche marks.

To eliminate any possibility of losses due to a fall in the value of the German currency, Milwaukee Specialty always hedges its net creditor position in deutsche marks by writing forward contracts to deliver that currency to brokers. These hedges are on existing transactions rather than identifiable commitments. The most recent forward contract was entered into on December 15, 19X2, and called for the firm to deliver 400,000 deutsche marks in 90 days.

In addition to the transactions related to German activities, Milwaukee Specialty is involved in two other forward contracts. The first of these, a contract to purchase 1,000,000 Canadian dollars, was originally entered into July 1, 19X1, as a hedge against possible exchange losses on a loan from a Montreal bank, which is to be repaid in Canadian dollars on June 30, 19X3. The other forward contract which Milwaukee Specialty held was a commitment to purchase 1 million Mexican pesos on March 1, 19X3. This contract was entered into on December 1, 19X2, with the intention of earning a profit on excess funds which the firm's treasurer forecasted for early 19X3.

The following table presents relevant rates for the above forward contracts:

Date	Type of Rate	Rate in U.S. Dollars
Deutsche marks		
December 15, 19X2	Spot	1 = $.40
December 15, 19X2	Forward	1 = .42
December 31, 19X2	Spot	1 = .38
December 31, 19X2	Forward	1 = .40
Canadian Dollars		
July 1, 19X1	Spot	1 = .90
July 1, 19X1	Forward	1 = .92
December 31, 19X1	Spot	1 = .88
December 31, 19X2	Spot	1 = .90
December 31, 19X2	Forward	1 = .92
Mexican Pesos		
December 1, 19X2	Spot	1 = .04
December 1, 19X2	Forward	1 = .05
December 31, 19X2	Spot	1 = .03
December 31, 19X2	Forward	1 = .04

Compute the gain or loss on each of Milwaukee Specialty's forward contracts for the year ended December 31, 19X2. Do not attempt to compute the total foreign exchange gain or loss.

Exercise 4.   On June 1, 19X7, Marvin Foods Corporation of the U.S. contracted to purchase 60,000 pounds of coffee beans at a price of 2 FC per pound from a South American firm, Fulmar Growers. Delivery will be in three months, with payment due in foreign currency 30 days after delivery. On June 1, Marvin acquired a forward contract to purchase 305,000 FC on October 1, 19X7, at a forward rate of 1 FC = $.40. Marvin regularly acquires forward contracts to buy and sell foreign currency, both as a means of speculation and to prevent possible losses due to changes in value of the foreign currency. Exchange rates on selected dates are as follows:

Date	Spot Rate	Forward Rate for Remaining Maturity of Contract
June 1, 19X7	1 FC = $.38	1 FC = $.40
September 1, 19X7	1 FC = .41	1 FC = .42
October 1, 19X7	1 FC = .39	—

Prepare all entries associated with the transaction and the forward contract on the books of Marvin Foods Corporation.

Exercise 5.   Select the best answer for each of the following questions which relate to accounting for foreign operations and transactions.

1. The Jem Company translated foreign currency amounts at December 31, 19X5. At that time, Jem had foreign subsidiaries with 1,500,000 local currency units (LCU) in long-term receivables and 2,400,000 LCU in long-term debt. The rate of exchange in effect when the specific transactions occurred involving those foreign currency amounts was 2 LCU to $1. The rate of exchange in effect at December 31, 19X5, was 1.5 LCU to $1. The translation of the foreign currency amounts into dollars would result in long-term receivables and long-term debt, respectively, of:

a. $750,000 and $1,200,000.

b. $750,000 and $1,600,000.

c. $1,000,000 and $1,200,000.

d. $1,000,000 and $1,600,000.

2. A company is translating account balances from another currency into dollars for its December 31, 19X5 statement of financial position and its calendar year 19X5 retained earnings statement and statement of changes in financial position. The average exchange rate of the year 19X5 should be used to translate:

a. Cash at December 31, 19X5.

b. Land purchased in 19X3.

c. Retained earnings at January 1, 19X5.

d. Sales for 19X5.

3. The Dease Company owns a foreign subsidiary with 3,600,000 local currency units (LCU) of property, plant, and equipment at December 31, 19X5, before accumulated depreciation is deducted. Of this amount, 2,400,000 LCU were acquired in 19X3 when the rate of exchange was 1.6 LCU to $1, and 1,200,000 LCU were acquired in 19X4 when the rate of exchange was 1.8 LCU to $1. The rate of exchange in effect at December 31, 19X5, was 2 LCU to $1. The weighted average of exchange rates which were in effect during 19X5 was 1.92 LCU to $1. Assuming that the property, plant, and equipment are depreciated using the straight-line method over a ten-year period with no salvage value, how much depreciation expense relating to the foreign subsidiary's property, plant, and equipment should be charged in Dease's income statement for 19X5?

a. $180,000.

b. $187,500.

c. $200,000.

d. $216,667.

4. The Clark Company owns a foreign subsidiary that had net income for the year ended December 31, 19X5, of 4,800,000 local currency units (LCU), which was appropriately translated into $800,000. On October 15, 19X5, when the rate of exchange was 5.7 LCU to $1, the foreign subsidiary paid Clark a dividend of 2,400,000 LCU. The dividend represented the net income of the foreign subsidiary for the six months ended June 30, 19X5, during which time the weighted average of exchange rates was 5.8 LCU to $1. The rate of exchange in effect at December 31, 19X5, was 5.9 LCU to $1. What rate of exchange should be used to translate the dividend for the December 31, 19X5 financial statements?

a. 5.7 LCU to $1.   c. 5.9 LCU to $1.

b. 5.8 LCU to $1.   d. 6.0 LCU to $1.

5. When combined or consolidated financial statements for a domestic and a foreign company are prepared, the account balances expressed in the foreign currency must be translated into the domestic currency. The objective of the translation process is to obtain currency valuations that:

a. Are conservative.

b. Reflect current monetary equivalents.

c. Are expressed in domestic units of measure and are in conformity with domestic generally accepted accounting principles.

d. Reflect the translated account at its unexpired historical cost.

6. Lochlann Company used U.S. dollars to purchase all the outstanding common stock of Dey Company, a Canadian corporation. At the date of purchase, a portion of the investment account was appropriately allocated to goodwill. One year later, after an exchange rate decrease (U.S. dollars have become less valuable), the goodwill should be shown in the consolidated balance sheet at what amount?
   a. An increased amount, less amortization.
   b. The same amount, less amortization.
   c. A lesser amount, less amortization.
   d. An increased or lesser amount depending on management policy, less amortization. (AICPA adapted)

Exercise 6. On January 1, 19X4, Bellview, Inc., a U.S. company, incorporated Daks, Ltd., a European company, as a subsidiary by investing 1,000,000 foreign currency units to acquire all of the firm's common stock. Daks began operations immediately. Daks' December 31, 19X4 trial balance is as follows:

Cash	297,000 FC	
Accounts Receivable	625,000	
Allowance for Doubtful Accounts		50,000 FC
Due from Bellview	18,000	
Inventory (at cost)	750,000	
Prepaid Expenses	15,000	
Land	50,000	
Building and Equipment	650,000	
Accumulated Depreciation		65,000
Accounts Payable		600,000
Income Tax Payable		125,000
Accrued Liabilities		40,000
Mortgage Note Payable—Building		400,000
Common Stock		1,000,000
Sales		2,500,000
Cost of Goods Sold	2,000,000	
Depreciation Expense	65,000	
Other Expense	185,000	
Income Tax	125,000	
	4,780,000 FC	4,780,000 FC

The following information relates to Daks 19X4 transactions:
(a) Plant assets were acquired as follows:

Date	Type	Amount
January 1, 19X4	Land	50,000 FC
January 1, 19X4	Building	500,000 FC
April 1, 19X4	Machinery	100,000
October 1, 19X4	Machinery	50,000
		650,000 FC

(b) Depreciation is computed by the straight-line method over a ten-year life. Salvage value is ignored. A full year of depreciation is taken in the year of acquisition, while no depreciation is taken in the year of disposition.
(c) Inventory is acquired throughout the year and is accounted for by the fifo inventory method.

(d) Sales to Bellview are billed in the foreign currency and all receivables from Bellview have been collected, except for the amount shown in the account "Due from Bellview." All other sales are also billed in the foreign currency.

(e) Prepaid Expenses represents unexpired insurance which was purchased January 1, 19X4.

(f) Exchange rates are as follows:

Date	Exchange Rate in U.S. Dollars
January 1, 19X4	1 FC = $1.50
April 1, 19X4	1 FC = 1.60
October 1, 19X4	1 FC = 1.70
December 31, 19X4	1 FC = 1.80
19X4 average	1 FC = 1.75

Without completely translating Daks' December 31, 19X4 trial balance, calculate the translation adjustment which should appear in Bellview's stockholders' equity section of its 19X4 balance sheet.

Exercise 7. Hawkes, Inc., purchased 100% of the stock of Shaid Corporation, a foreign company, when Shaid was organized on July 1, 19X5. The Shaid Corporation's financial statements are maintained in foreign currency, but their functional currency is the U.S. dollar. Shaid's accounting records contain the following information:

(a) Inventory is accounted for by the lifo inventory method on a periodic basis. The beginning inventory is composed entirely of purchases made on July 1, 19X5. Inventory information for 19X6 is as follows:

Date	Account	Amount in Foreign Currency
January 1, 19X6	Beginning Inventory	30,000 FC
April 1, 19X6	Purchases	18,000
June 1, 19X6	Purchases	25,000
October 1, 19X6	Purchases	40,000
November 1, 19X6	Purchases	20,000
December 31, 19X6	Ending Inventory	52,000

(b) Equipment was acquired and sold as detailed in the following schedule. There were no intercompany equipment transactions.

Date	Cost Acquired (Sold)
July 1, 19X5	120,000 FC
April 1, 19X6	50,000 FC
October 1, 19X6	(16,000 FC)

The selling price of the equipment sold was 13,200 FC. This equipment was acquired on July 1, 19X5.

(c) Depreciation is computed using the straight-line method over an 8-year life. Salvage value is ignored. A half year of depreciation is taken in the years of acquisition and disposition.

(d) The November 1 inventory purchase in part (1) was acquired from Hawkes, Inc., with payment due in foreign currency in 90 days. On November 1, Hawkes purchased a 90-day forward contract to sell the 20,000 FC to a broker at a forward rate of 1 FC = $1.27.

(e) Relevant exchange rates are as follows:

Date	Rate
July 1, 19X5	1 FC = $1.19
April 1, 19X6	1 FC = 1.23
June 1, 19X6	1 FC = 1.22
October 1, 19X6	1 FC = 1.25
November 1, 19X6	1 FC = 1.26
December 31, 19X6	1 FC = 1.28
19X6 average	1 FC = 1.24

Calculate the translated value of the following accounts:
(1) Cost of goods sold for 19X6.
(2) Gain or loss on the October 1, 19X6 equipment sale.
(3) Hawkes' liability to broker associated with the forward contract, as of December 31, 19X6.

PROBLEMS

Problem 13-1. The Austin Engineering Corporation assembles small pocket calculators which it sells primarily in domestic markets. However, Austin has been developing sales markets in France and has also been purchasing subassemblies from a Japanese manufacturer. Selected transactions for 19X8 are as follows:
  (a) On March 1, Austin purchased 6,000 calculator subassemblies from the Japanese manufacturer for a total price of $9,600, to be paid in dollars on April 20, 19X8. On March 1, the exchange rate was 1 yen = $.37.
  (b) On May 5, Austin sold 22,000 calculators to a French importer for a total selling price of 1,350,000 francs. At the time of the sale, the exchange rate was 1 franc = $.18; however, when payment was received in francs on May 26, 19X8, the exchange rate was 1 franc = $.22.
  (c) On July 2, 19X8, Austin purchased more subassemblies from the Japanese manufacturer; however, due to changing economic conditions, the entire purchase price of $36,000 was to be paid in yen on September 1. The relevant exchange rates were:

  July 2 .... 1 yen = $.41
  September 1 .... 1 yen = $.44

  On July 2, to hedge against future currency devaluations, Austin purchased a 60-day forward contract to buy yen at a forward rate of 1 yen = $.43.
  (d) Another major sale for 1,000,000 francs was made to the French importer on September 8, 19X8, when the exchange rate was 1 franc = $.23. On September 25, when the exchange rate was 1 franc = $.22, Austin purchased a 30-day forward contract to sell 1,000,000 francs at a forward rate of 1 franc = $.19. When payment in francs was received from the importer on October 25, 19X8, the exchange rate was 1 franc = $.18.

     (e) A final 19X8 purchase of subassemblies took place on December 16, when the exchange rate was 1 yen = $.40. The purchase price of 200,000 yen was to be paid on January 25, 19X9. At the time of the purchase, Austin also acquired a 30-day forward contract to buy yen at a forward rate of 1 yen = $.42.

     (f) To plan properly for a noncancelable commitment to purchase subassemblies for delivery on March 25, 19X9, Austin acquired, on December 26, 19X8, a 90-day forward exchange contract to buy yen at a forward rate of 1 yen = $.45. On December 26, the exchange rate was 1 yen = $.41. The forward exchange contract was for 210,000 yen, all of which will be used to cover the noncancelable commitment.

     (g) The following exchange rates are in effect on December 31, 19X8:

$$1 \text{ yen} = \$.42$$
$$1 \text{ franc} = \$.17$$

Required:

Assuming that Austin's year end is December 31, prepare all 19X8 journal entries to account for the transactions.

Problem 13-2. On January 1, 19X7, Dudwil Corporation acquired a foreign subsidiary, Holman Company, by paying cash for all of Holman's outstanding common stock. Both companies continued to operate as separate entities. On the purchase date, the Holman Company's accounts were fairly stated in local currency units (FC).

The Holman trial balance, in functional currency units, at December 31, 19X7, follows:

Cash	58,400	
Marketable Securities	32,500	
Accounts Receivable (net)	51,370	
Inventories	108,000	
Cash Surrender Value of Life Insurance	7,200	
Intangible Assets	123,900	
Property, Plant, and Equipment	636,000	
Accumulated Depreciation		93,850
Accounts Payable		74,000
Accrued Interest Payable		7,120
Notes Payable		52,000
Bonds Payable		80,000
Capital Stock		83,000
Paid-In Capital in Excess of Par		190,300
Retained Earnings		390,400
Sales		936,300
Cost of Goods Sold	762,000	
Interest Expense	7,120	
Depreciation Expense	39,350	
Amortization Expense—Intangibles	3,100	
Other Expenses	84,230	
Gain on Sale of Equipment		2,400
Other Income		3,800
	1,913,170	1,913,170

The following additional information is available:

(a) Holman uses the lifo inventory method to account for its inventory. Purchases took place uniformly throughout 19X7. There were no intercompany sales during 19X7.

(b) During 19X7, Holman declared and paid a dividend of 7,000 FC at the end of each calendar quarter.

(c) The balances in the contributed capital accounts resulted from the following transactions:

Date	Capital Stock	Paid-In Capital in Excess of Par
January 1, 19X3	40,000 FC	80,000 FC
June 30, 19X5	40,000	104,300
January 1, 19X6	10,000	20,000
August 1, 19X6	(7,000)	(14,000)
	83,000 FC	190,300 FC

(d) The January 1, 19X7 balance in retained earnings resulted from the following:

19X3 net income	50,000 FC
19X4 net income	173,000
February 1, 19X5 dividend	(40,000)
19X5 net income	206,400
January 1, 19X6 stock dividend.........	(30,000)
February 1, 19X6 dividend	(90,000)
19X6 net income	149,000
	418,400 FC

(e) The notes payable in Holman's trial balance represents a loan from Dudwil Corporation. The loan was made on January 1, 19X7, and is to be repaid in foreign currency. However, the loan does not bear interest and is of a long-term-investment nature because settlement of the debt is not anticipated in the foreseeable future.

(f) The balance in the account Other Income represents consulting fees charged to Dudwil during 19X7. The reciprocal account on the parent company's books shows the fees at $2,300.

(g) Selected translation rates are as follows:

Date	Rates
January 1, 19X3	1 FC = $.30
19X3 average	1 FC = .32
19X4 average	1 FC = .38
February 1, 19X5	1 FC = .42
June 30, 19X5	1 FC = .45
19X5 average	1 FC = .45
January 1, 19X6	1 FC = .50
February 1, 19X6	1 FC = .52
August 1, 19X6	1 FC = .60
December 31, 19X6	1 FC = .61
19X6 average	1 FC = .56
March 31, 19X7	1 FC = .63
June 30, 19X7	1 FC = .66
September 30, 19X7	1 FC = .70
December 31, 19X7	1 FC = .75
19X7 average	1 FC = .70

Required:

    (1) Prepare a work sheet to convert the December 31, 19X7 trial balance of Holman Company from local currency units to dollars. The work sheet should show the unconverted trial balance, the conversion rate, and the converted trial balance. (Do not extend the trial balance to statement columns. Supporting schedules should be in good form.)

    (2) Prepare a schedule which details the direct computation of the 19X7 adjustment resulting from translation.

    (3) Calculate the foreign currency transaction gain or loss experienced by Dudwil with respect to the note payable. Discuss the accounting treatment of this gain or loss.

Problem 13-3. The Turppa Trading Company acquired a 30% interest in the Rico Rattan Company, a foreign manufacturer of fine rattan furniture, on January 1, 19X8. The investment in Rico is accounted for by the equity method. The initial investment cost $60,000, with any excess attributable to goodwill. Rico's December 31, 19X8 trial balance, in foreign currency, is as follows:

Cash	20,000	
Accounts Receivable	63,000	
Due from Turppa	28,000	
Inventory (at lifo cost)	120,000	
Land (acquired on 1/1/X4)	84,000	
Depreciable Assets	297,000	
Cost of Goods Sold (60% of selling price)	427,200	
Depreciation Expense	21,800	
Other Expenses	88,800	
Income Tax Expense	62,880	
Loss on Sale of Depreciable Assets	17,000	
Accounts Payable		72,000
Taxes Payable		35,000
Accrued Interest Payable		4,800
Customer Advances		12,000
Dividends Payable		6,000
Notes Payable to Turppa		30,000
Bonds Payable (issued 6/30/X5)		120,000
Capital Stock (issued 1/1/X4)		100,000
Paid-In Capital in Excess of Par		25,000
Retained Earnings		32,380
Sales—Turppa		81,500
Sales—Other		630,500
Allowance for Doubtful Accounts		4,800
Accumulated Depreciation		75,700
	1,229,680	1,229,680

The following additional information is available:

    (a) The Rico Rattan Company began operations on January 1, 19X4.

    (b) The account Due from Turppa represents a receivable for sales of merchandise purchased on December 15, 19X8. Turppa's records reflect an equivalent dollar value of $30,800 for this account. The account Notes Payable to Turppa represents the face value of a six-month, 6% note due April 1, 19X9. The note is recorded by Turppa in the amount of $32,400.

    (c) The ending balance of inventory is composed of the following cost layers:

Year of Acquisition	Cost
19X4	25,000 FC
19X6	40,000
19X7	36,000
19X8	19,000
	120,000 FC

Assume that inventory was acquired evenly throughout the given year.

(d) The balance of retained earnings reflects a reduction in the amount of 12,000 FC for dividends declared during 19X8. Dividends in the amount of 6,000 FC were declared on June 30, 19X8, and December 31, 19X8.

(e) The customer advances were received on October 1, 19X8.

(f) Of the sales to Turppa from Rico, 25 percent of the goods purchased by Turppa are unsold as of December 31, 19X8.

(g) Relevant exchange rates are as follows:

December 31, 19X7 . . . . 1 FC =	$1.06
19X7 average . . . . 1 FC =	1.05
June 30, 19X8 . . . . 1 FC =	1.06
December 15, 19X8 . . . . 1 FC =	1.10
December 31, 19X8 . . . . 1 FC =	1.11
19X8 average . . . . 1 FC =	1.07

Required:

(1) Prepare a schedule which shows the direct calculation of the 19X8 translation adjustment.

(2) Determine the December 31, 19X8 carrying value of Turppa's investment in Rico.

Problem 13-4. Reslin Corporation is a New York-based manufacturer of photographic supplies. On August 1, 19X3, Reslin expanded its network of operations by opening a branch office in Great Britain. The following information is available regarding accounts of the home office and branch for the year ended December 31, 19X5:

(a) On December 22, 19X5, the home office shipped merchandise billed at $12,600 to the branch office. The merchandise was received in January, 19X6.

(b) The branch office received all of its beginning inventory and 40% of its ending inventory from the home office. The home office bills the goods at cost plus a markup of 12% of cost. Purchases are made uniformly throughout the year, and branch inventory is accounted for by the fifo method. The 19X5 beginning inventory of the branch office is £86,000. The current cost of ending inventories at December 31, 19X5, excludes the shipment in transit.

(c) A photographer on location in Great Britain purchased film on account from the branch office. Upon returning to the U.S., however, the photographer erroneously paid the account to the New York office on December 30, 19X5. The bookkeeper recorded the $1,300 payment on the books of the home office but did not notify the branch office.

(d) On December 30, the branch office authorized a remittance of £ 4,400 to be made to the home office. Payment was received by the home office on January 2, 19X6.

(e) On December 31, the branch office recorded the December allocated general and administrative expense from the home office as £ 570 instead of £ 750.

(f) The annual insurance premium is paid by the branch office on March 31 of each year.

(g) As of May 1, 19X5, the rate of exchange is £ 1 equals $1.60. The previous rate, which had been in effect since 19X2, was £ 1 equals $1.75. The average annual rate of exchange was £ 1 equals $1.65.

Trial balances at December 31, 19X5, for the home office of Reslin Corporation and its branch are as follows. No adjustments required by home office accounting procedures have been recorded.

	Branch Office Trial Balance (In pounds)	Home Office Trial Balance (In dollars)
Cash	65,000	140,000
Accounts Receivable	100,000	205,000
Inventory, December 31	131,250	650,000
Prepaid Insurance	1,500	—
Customer Deposits (refundable)	680	2,300
Property, Plant, and Equipment	950,000	2,710,000
Investment in Branch	—	23,940
Cost of Goods sold	1,424,750	3,780,000
Selling Expenses	41,000	113,000
General and Administrative Expense	92,500	366,000
Depreciation Expense	120,000	250,000
Accounts Payable	(130,000)	(290,000)
Customer Deposits (refundable)	(680)	(2,300)
Mortgage Payable on Building	(203,000)	(512,000)
Accumulated Depreciation	(380,000)	(995,000)
Home Office Equity	(3,320)	—
Capital Stock, $2 par	—	(320,000)
Retained Earnings, January 1	—	(510,000)
Sales	(2,209,680)	(4,750,940)
Shipments to Branch (at retail)	—	(860,000)
	-0-	-0-

Required:

Prepare a columnar work sheet to present the combined income statement and combined balance sheet of Reslin Corporation and its foreign branch office, with all amounts stated in U.S. dollars. Key and explain work sheet adjustments and eliminations and show supporting computations in good form. Ignore income taxes.

Problem 13-5. Vacaro, Inc., a U.S. firm, owns a 100% interest in Spinata, a foreign firm. Spinata's December 31, 19X5 trial balance is on page 614.

The following information relates to Spinata's operations:

(a) The company was organized on July 1, 19X2, at which time 100,000 FC of common stock was issued at par value. The remaining stock was issued on August 15, 19X4, at a price in excess of par value.

Cash	80,000 FC	
Accounts Receivable (net)	210,000	
Due from Vacaro	45,000	
Inventory	414,000	
Property, Plant, and Equipment	917,000	
Accumulated Depreciation		164,000 FC
Accounts Payable		195,000
Income Tax Payable		40,000
Mortgage Payable		640,000
Common Stock		150,000
Paid-In Capital in Excess of Par		50,000
Retained Earnings		207,000
Sales		1,478,000
Cost of Goods Sold	1,057,000	
Depreciation Expense	65,000	
Interest Expense	72,000	
Tax Expense	40,000	
Miscellaneous Expenses	24,000	
	2,924,000 FC	2,924,000 FC

(b) The translated value of retained earnings at December 31, 19X4, was $525,000. During 19X5, the company paid dividends of 50,000 FC each on April 30 and October 31.

(c) During 19X5, Spinata sold inventory to Vacaro. The dates and details of the sales are as follows:

	August 15	October 31
Selling price	110,000 FC	300,000 FC
Cost of goods sold	70,000	210,000
Percent of inventory remaining in Vacaro's December 31, 19X5 inventory	10%	25%

(d) Relevant exchange rates are as follows:

Date	Rate
July 1, 19X2	1 FC = $1.20
August 15, 19X4	1 FC = 1.60
April 30, 19X5	1 FC = 2.10
August 15, 19X5	1 FC = 2.20
October 31, 19X5	1 FC = 2.60
December 31, 19X5	1 FC = 2.70
19X5 average	1 FC = 2.40

(e) On April 30, 19X5, Vacaro borrowed 400,000 FC from a bank located in Spinata's country. The loan is payable in one year and was initially designated as an economic hedge of the net investment in Spinata.

Required:

(1) Prepare a work sheet to convert the December 31, 19X5 trial balance of Spinata from the functional currency into dollars. The work sheet should show the unconverted trial balance, the conversion rate, and the converted trial balance.

(2) Compute the amount of intercompany profit which would be eliminated by Vacaro from the translated dollar amounts.

(3) Compute the effect on consolidated stockholders' equity and net income traceable to Vacaro's foreign currency transaction designed as an economic hedge.

(4) If Vacaro sells 48% of its interest in Spinata on January 1, 19X6, discuss the treatment that would be accorded the translation adjustments.

Problem 13-6. On June 30, 19X5, the Champion China Company acquired at book value the Tropo Art Studios, a foreign retailer of fine artistic figurines. The acquisition was accounted for as a purchase. The following information has been provided:

(a) Tropo's year end is December 31.

(b) Comparative trial balances for Tropo are as follows:

Account	December 31, 19X6 Debit	December 31, 19X6 Credit	June 30, 19X7 Debit	June 30, 19X7 Credit
Cash and Receivables (net).	45,000 FC		36,000 FC	
Prepaid Insurance (annual premium paid on 9/1/X6) .	8,000		2,000	
Inventory	32,000		36,000	
Deferred Contract Premium	—		20	
Depreciable Assets	40,000		46,000	
Francs Due from Broker	—		3,000	
Cost of Merchandise Sold . .	157,000		75,000	
Depreciation Expense	4,000		2,250	
Insurance Expense	12,000		6,000	
Contract Expense	—		10	
Accounts Payable		13,000 FC		10,000 FC
Liability to Broker		—		3,030
Accumulated Depreciation .		10,000		10,600
Common Stock (issued 6/30/X4)		58,000		58,000
Retained Earnings		15,000		20,000
Sales		202,000		102,650
Gain on Sale of Depreciable Assets		—		2,000
	298,000 FC	298,000 FC	206,280 FC	206,280 FC

(c) Tropo employs the lifo inventory method, and the 12/31/X6 balance of inventory represents goods acquired as follows:

June 30, 19X4 purchase	20,000 FC	
December 31, 19X5 purchase	12,000	
	32,000 FC	

Purchases of merchandise were as follows during the first six months of 19X7:

February 15, 19X7 purchase	34,000 FC	
March 1, 19X7 purchase	28,000	
May 30, 19X7 purchase	17,000	
	79,000 FC	

(d) The balance of depreciable assets on 12/31/X6 represents assets acquired on June 30, 19X4, when Tropo began operations. Additional assets in the amount of 12,000 FC were acquired on 3/1/X7, and certain assets acquired in 19X4 were disposed of on 4/1/X7. All assets are depreciated over a ten-year useful life according to the straight-line method (salvage values are ignored).

(e) On 5/30/X7, Tropo purchased a 90-day forward exchange contract to buy 10,000 francs for hedging purposes. The exchange rate between francs and Tropo's domestic currency is as follows for certain dates:

5/30/X7	1 Franc = .30 FC
6/30/X7	1 Franc = .32 FC

(f) The translated retained earnings on January 1, 19X7, was $38,300.

(g) The gain or loss on forward exchange contracts had not yet been accrued for the six-month period ending June 30, 19X7.

(h) Dividends of 24,000 FC and a dollar equivalent of $19,220 were declared and paid in April, 19X7.

(i) Relevant exchange rates are as follows:

December 31, 19X6	1 FC =	.85
19X6 average	1 FC =	.88
February 15, 19X7	1 FC =	.82
March 1, 19X7	1 FC =	.81
April 1, 19X7	1 FC =	.81
May 30, 19X7	1 FC =	.79
June 30, 19X7	1 FC =	.77
19X7 average (January-June)	1 FC =	.80

Required:

(1) Prepare (in dollars) a statement of changes in financial position (working capital basis).

(2) Explain how hedging may be employed by Champion to reduce the equity effects of fluctuating exchange rates.

Problem 13-7. The Krueger Leather Company purchased all of the outstanding stock of the El Roco Leather Company, a foreign corporation, on January 1, 19X6. El Roco began operations on January 1, 19X2. The December 31, 19X7 trial balance for El Roco, in foreign currency, is shown on page 617.

The following additional information is available:

(a) The account Due from Krueger represents a receivable for a November 1, 19X7 sale of inventory to Krueger. The amount will be collected in foreign currency. The cost of the inventory was 36,000 FC, and Krueger had 60% of the inventory on hand at year end.

(b) The account Due to Krueger represents the principal of a loan from Krueger, which is payable in dollars on June 30, 19X8. Krueger has recorded this loan at $21,000.

(c) The marketable securities are classified as noncurrent and represent investments in the stock of various customer companies. The securities were acquired in 19X6. Krueger experienced a 4,000 FC decline in value of the securities at the end of 19X6, and a further decline in value of 10,000 FC at the end of 19X7.

Cash	5,000	
Accounts Receivable	80,000	
Due from Krueger	49,029	
Inventories	230,000	
Marketable Securities	46,000	
Prepaid Insurance	4,000	
Land (acquired on January 1, 19X2)	144,000	
Buildings	253,800	
Equipment	424,000	
Cost of Goods Sold	440,000	
Selling and Administrative Expenses	110,000	
Loss Due to Decline in Value of Ending Inventory	38,000	
Depreciation Expense—Buildings	10,600	
Loss on Sale of Equipment	15,700	
Interest Expense	19,800	
Depreciation Expense—Equipment	37,530	
Income Tax Expense	99,948	
Uncollectible Accounts Expense	10,500	
Insurance Expense	12,000	
Warranty Expense	40,000	
Deferred Income Tax	1,067	
Accounts Payable		117,134
Due to Krueger		40,000
Dividends Payable		9,800
Interest Payable		3,125
Warranties Payable		26,000
Mortgage Payable—Buildings		130,000
Convertible Debt—5% (issued on January 1, 19X2)		250,000
Premium on Convertible Debt		4,500
Common Stock (issued on January 1, 19X2)		98,000
Paid-In Capital in Excess of Par		133,335
Retained Earnings		27,600
Sales		970,000
Equity—Unrealized Net Loss on Marketable Securities	14,000	
Allowance for Doubtful Accounts		7,800
Accumulated Depreciation—Buildings		58,000
Accumulated Depreciation—Equipment		157,680
Allowance for Decline in Value of Marketable Securities		14,000
Allowance for Decline in Inventory Value		38,000
	2,084,974	2,084,974

(d) The balances in the common stock and paid-in capital in excess of par accounts resulted from the following transactions:

Date of Issuance of Stock	Common Stock	Paid-In Capital in Excess of Par
January 1, 19X2	60,000 FC	30,000 FC
June 30, 19X5	10,000	23,400
June 30, 19X6	10,000	25,935
May 1, 19X7	8,000	24,000
August 15, 19X7	10,000	30,000
	98,000 FC	133,335 FC

The common stock has a par value of 10 FC per share. The May 1, 19X7 issuance of stock resulted from the declaration of a 10% stock dividend.

(e) The dividends payable account represents the fourth quarter 19X7 dividend of 1 FC per share. During 19X7, quarterly dividends of 1 FC per share were declared. The dividends were based on the number of shares outstanding at the end of each quarter.

(f) The translated balance of retained earnings on December 31, 19X6, was $34,985.

(g) Selected conversion rates are as follows:

January 1, 19X2	1 FC =	$.22
June 30, 19X5	1 FC =	.39
June 30, 19X6	1 FC =	.42
December 31, 19X6	1 FC =	.45
19X6 average	1 FC =	.43
May 1 and June 30, 19X7	1 FC =	.48
March 31 and August 15, 19X7	1 FC =	.47
September 30, 19X7	1 FC =	.52
December 31, 19X7	1 FC =	.50
19X7 average	1 FC =	.49

Required:

(1) Complete a work sheet which translates El Roco's December 31, 19X7 trial balance into dollars. The work sheet should be accompanied by all necessary supporting schedules. Round computations to the nearest whole dollar.

(2) Compute the amount of the 19X7 adjustment resulting from the translation of the 19X7 trial balance.

(3) Determine the maximum amount of the foreign currency transaction in which Krueger would have had to engage on May 1, 19X7, if the transaction were to operate as an effective economic hedge of the net investment in El Roco.

Problem 13-8. The Global Mining Corporation is a U.S. manufacturer of heavy mining equipment. The equipment is manufactured from subassemblies which are acquired from both domestic and foreign suppliers.

At the beginning of 19X8, Global arranged for 3,000,000 deutsche marks of financing in the U.S. and contributed another 2,000,000 deutsche marks to organize a wholly-owned subsidiary in Germany for manufacturing subassemblies. A condensed trial balance for the German subsidiary is as follows, in deutsche marks:

Cash	150,000	
Accounts Receivable	450,000	
Inventories	175,000	
Property, Plant, and Equipment (net)	4,525,000	
Other Assets	300,000	
Cost of Goods Sold	1,225,000	
Depreciation Expense	475,000	
Other Expenses	300,000	
Accounts Payable		100,000
Long-Term Debt		3,000,000
Common Stock		500,000
Paid-In Capital in Excess of Par		1,500,000
Sales		2,500,000
	7,600,000	7,600,000

The equipment is depreciated on a straight-line basis over ten years, and acquisitions occurred as follows:

January 1, 19X8	4,000,000	deutsche marks
April 1, 19X8	1,000,000	
Total	5,000,000	deutsche marks

The ending inventory consists of goods manufactured uniformly throughout November and December, 19X8. The cost of goods sold represents production which occurred uniformly throughout the prior ten months. Unless otherwise stated, all other elements of income occurred uniformly throughout the year. Because the German subsidiary is a direct and integral component of Global operations, its functional currency is the U.S. dollar.

Although the majority of Global's purchases of subassemblies are denominated in the U.S. dollar, the following transactions were denominated in foreign currencies:

(a) On June 1, 19X8, Global purchased inventory from a British vendor. The cost of 40,000 pounds was paid on July 15, 19X8.

(b) On September 1, 19X8, Global purchased inventory from a German vendor. The cost of 60,000 deutsche marks was paid on November 1, 19X8. At the date of purchase, Global acquired a 60-day forward contract to buy deutsche marks at the forward rate of 1 deutsche mark = $.52.

(c) On December 1, 19X8, Global entered into a firm commitment to acquire subassemblies from a French vendor. The cost of the subassemblies, which were to be delivered on February 1, 19X9, was 124,000 francs. On December 15, 19X8, Global acquired a 45-day forward contract to buy French francs at a forward rate of 1 franc = $.17. The forward contract was purchased as a hedge of the commitment to the French vendor.

On August 1, 19X8, Global sold one fourth of its 80% interest in a Mexican tin mine for $100,000. The net assets of the Mexican subsidiary were 4,200,000 pesos and 4,980,000 pesos on January 1, 19X8 and August 1, 19X8, respectively. Net income during the first seven months of 19X8 was 900,000 pesos, and the only capital transaction taking place during this period was a cash dividend of 120,000 pesos. The dividend was declared on June 30, 19X8, and paid on July 15, 19X8. On January 1, 19X8, the cumulative translation adjustment was $23,000.

Relevant exchange rates are as follows:

		Dollars per Unit of Foreign Currency
Deutsche marks:	January 1, 19X8....	$ .47
	April 1, 19X8.......	.49
	September 1, 19X8.	.50
	November 1, 19X8 .	.54
	December 31, 19X8	.55
Pounds:	June 1, 19X8	2.30
	July 15, 19X8	2.40
	December 31, 19X8	2.35
Francs:	December 1, 19X8 .	.17
	December 15, 19X8	.16
	December 31, 19X8	.18

		Dollars per Unit of Foreign Currency
Pesos:	January 1, 19X8....	.06
	June 30, 19X8	.08
	July 15, 19X8	.09
	August 1, 19X8	.10

Required:

Calculate the effect on Global's 19X8 income as a result of the above events. All average exchange rates should be calculated, using a simple average for the period involved.

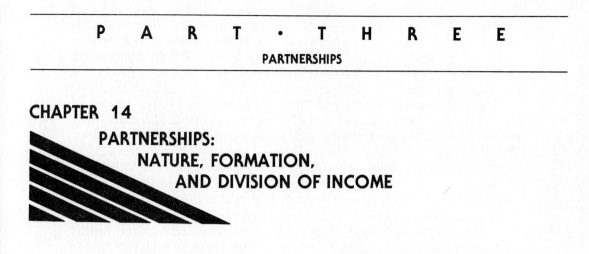

P A R T • T H R E E

CHAPTER 14
PARTNERSHIPS:
NATURE, FORMATION,
AND DIVISION OF INCOME

In a majority of states, the legal nature and functioning of partnerships is governed by the Uniform Partnership Act (UPA), which deals with the nature of a partnership, relations with persons dealing with the partnership, the rights of partners, and the dissolution and termination of a partnership. In Section 6 of this act, a partnership is defined as "an association of two or more persons to carry on as co-owners a business for profit." Such associations were dominant forms of business organization prior to the industrial revolution and still remain a popular form of organization for many small and medium-size businesses.

CHARACTERISTICS OF A PARTNERSHIP

Partnerships are normally classified as either *general* or *limited*. A *general* partnership consists of several general partners who may act publicly on behalf of the firm and who are personally liable for obligations of the partnership. A *limited* partnership consists of one or more general partners and one or more limited or special partners who contribute capital but do not participate in management of the firm. The limited partners' liability for partnership obligations is restricted to a stated amount, usually equal to their interest in the partnership.

The Relationship of Partners

A partnership represents a voluntary association of individuals to carry out a business purpose. In this association, a fiduciary relationship exists between the partners, requiring them to exercise good faith and loyalty to the firm, and to exercise sound business judgment in conducting the firm's business. An individual partner is viewed as a co-owner of partnership property, creating a *tenancy in partnership*. When specific assets are contributed by a partner, they lose their identity as to source and become the shared property of the partnership. Without the consent of all partners, such property cannot be utilized by any partner for personal purposes.

The relationship between partners is also characterized as one of *mutual agency*, which means that each partner is an agent for the other partners and the partnership when transacting partnership business. Therefore, in carrying on the business of the partnership, the acts of every partner bind the partnership itself, even when a partner commits a wrongful act or a breach of trust. However, if a partner has no authority to act for the partnership and the party with whom the partner is dealing knows this, the partnership is not bound by the partner's actions.

A general partnership is characterized by *unlimited liability*, in that all partners are liable, jointly and severally, for acts which bind the partnership. This liability is not limited to the partners' interests in the partnership, but may extend to their personal net worth. However, newly admitted partners, who are personally liable for partnership debts incurred subsequent to their admission, are liable for debts of the previous partnership only to the extent of their interest in the partnership.

Partnership Dissolution

Although a partnership is easily formed and does not need state approval, its life is limited and it may be dissolved much more easily than a corporation. A partnership is generally dissolved upon the death, withdrawal, or bankruptcy of an individual partner (owner). The admission of a new partner also results in the dissolution of the former partnership. *Dissolution* is defined in Section 29 of the UPA as "the change in the relation of the partners caused by any partner ceasing to be associated in the carrying on as distinguished from the winding up of the business." Thus, any change in the association of the individual partners is termed "dissolution."

Although dissolution occurs when there is a change in a partner's association with the original business purpose, it does not necessarily result in the termination of the basic business function. Therefore, a change in the ownership structure formally dissolves the former partnership, but often this change results in the formation of a new partnership to carry on the business purpose of the original partnership.

Tax Implications of a Partnership

The partnership is not viewed as a separate taxable entity, but rather as a conduit through which taxable items pass to the partners. Therefore, the taxable income (or loss) generated by partnership operations is allocated to the individual partners and reported by them on their personal tax returns. Elements of partnership revenue and expense maintain their special tax status on the returns of the individual partners.

Another result of viewing a partnership as a conduit for tax purposes is that assets contributed by the partners retain the same tax basis that they had prior to contribution to the partnership. For example, if assets with a tax basis of $12,000 and a fair market value of $20,000 are contributed to a partnership, the tax basis for partnership purposes will remain at $12,000. The conduit concept also results in defining the tax basis of a partner's personal interest in the partnership as the sum of:

1. The tax basis of individual assets contributed to the partnership, *plus*
2. The value of other partners' liabilities assumed by the individual partner, *less*
3. The value of the individual partner's liabilities assumed by the other partners.

To illustrate, assume that partners A and B contribute assets with tax bases of $30,000 and $15,000 respectively. Liabilities associated with these assets are $10,000 and $5,000 respectively. The partners agree to accept equal liability for the obligations associated with the contributed assets. The tax basis for each partner's interest, calculated as follows, may be used to determine the personal tax effects of a subsequent sale or liquidation of the interest.

	Partner A	Partner B
Tax basis of assets contributed	$30,000	$15,000
Tax basis of other partner's liabilities assumed (½ of $5,000 for A and ½ of $10,000 for B)	2,500	5,000
Tax basis of liabilities assumed by other partners (½ of $10,000 for A and ½ of $5,000 for B)	(5,000)	(2,500)
Tax basis of partner's interest	$27,500	$17,500

It is important to note that the sum of the tax bases of partners' interests ($27,500 plus $17,500) must equal the sum of the tax bases of assets contributed by the partners ($30,000 plus $15,000).

Partnership vs Corporation

The nature of a partnership may be better understood by comparing a partnership with a corporation. Many of the non-tax-related differences between these two forms of organization are summarized on page 624. Of these differences, one of the most significant is the partnership characteristic of unlimited liability. In a corporation, the liability of shareholders is limited to capital contributed or to legal capital, depending on the state of incorporation. Another difference is that the corporate assumption of continuing life is not as applicable to a partnership.

SIGNIFICANT NON-TAX-RELATED DIFFERENCES BETWEEN A PARTNERSHIP
AND A CORPORATION

	Partnership	Corporation
Continuity	Has a limited life and is normally dissolved when any change occurs in the ownership structure of the firm. However, the partnership need not be liquidated and may continue its original purpose.	Has a life which is theoretically defined as infinite. Changes in the ownership structure of the firm do not result in termination of the entity's life.
Formality	Little formality necessary for partnership formation. Relatively free from public supervision.	A corporation is created with the approval of the state, from which its powers are derived, and therefore it must function within limits prescribed by the state.
Liability	Unlimited liability, i.e., each individual general partner is personally liable for the debts of the partnership.	The capital contributed by a shareholder is the extent of the individual shareholder's liability for debts of the corporation. Shareholders may also be liable for the amount of any discounts that result from the original issuance of stock.
Management	General partners are active in the management of the business and exert a high degree of direct control over the business.	Corporations are characterized by absentee ownership, which means that shareholders are not normally active in management. Shareholders elect a board of directors which exercises direct control over the business. Under this arrangement, individual shareholders exercise indirect control over the business.
Ability to Attract Capital	Theoretically, a partnership may have greater borrowing power than a corporation because creditors may have access to the personal assets of partners. However, the small ownership base of a partnership makes it difficult to raise capital. The fact that ownership in a partnership is not easily transferred also restricts the firm's ability to attract capital.	The limited liability associated with a corporate investment should enhance the attractiveness of such investments. However, in smaller corporations it is common for shareholders to personally guarantee the debts of the corporation. Ease of transferability of ownership also improves the firm's ability to attract capital.

Major differences also exist between a corporation and a partnership in the area of taxation. These tax-related differences, which are summarized on page 625, are based on the concept of the corporation as a taxable entity, separate from its shareholders. The primary result of this concept is that the corporation is taxed when the income is earned, and the individual shareholders are taxed when the income is distributed as dividends. This characteristic is referred to as double taxation, and its significance depends on the extent to which dividends are distributed and the tax rates to which the owners are subject. The effect of double taxation may be minimized if employee-shareholders do not receive dividends, but are rewarded in the form of salaries, which are deductible expenses. However, the Internal Revenue Service must be satisfied that the amount of such salaries is reasonable. A corporation may also attempt to avoid double taxation by accumulating earnings or by electing to be taxed as a partnership.

SIGNIFICANT TAX-RELATED DIFFERENCES BETWEEN A PARTNERSHIP AND A CORPORATION

	Partnership	Corporation
Taxable	Not a separate taxable entity, but rather a conduit through which taxable items are passed on to the owners (partners).	Is a separate, distinct taxable entity apart from the shareholder. Therefore, income is taxed once at the corporate level and again at the shareholder level when such income is distributed, i.e., double taxation.
Tax Rates	The individual partners are taxed on their shares of partnership income, whether distributed or not, at the progressive tax rates applicable to individuals.	The corporation is taxed at the rate of 16% on the first $25,000 of taxable income, 19% on the next $25,000, 30% on the next $25,000, 40% on the next $25,000, and 46% on taxable income over $100,000. The rates that apply to the first two corporate taxable income brackets are lowered by one percentage point in 1983.
Maintaining the Identity of Various Elements of Taxable Income	Elements making up a partnership's income maintain their special tax status on the returns of the individual partners; e.g., if a partnership has tax-exempt income, it retains its identity in the preparation of the individual partners' tax returns as tax-exempt income.	Elements making up corporate income do not maintain their special status when distributed to shareholders in the form of a dividend; e.g., if corporate income includes some tax-exempt income, that income will be taxed to the shareholders when distributed in the form of a dividend.
Other Tax Items	The tax advantages associated with certain fringe benefits are much greater for employee-shareholders than they would be if the employees were partners in a firm. Such fringe benefits involve profit-sharing plans, pension plans, medical reimbursement and insurance plans, group life insurance, and death benefits.	

Accumulation of Earnings. Rather than distributing taxable dividends, the corporation may retain income, so that the shareholders are not taxed on that income. However, if the shareholders sell their stock in the corporation and the stock sells at a price which exceeds its tax basis, the gain on the sale would be taxed at the preferred rate applied to capital gains.

It should be noted, however, that the retention of income may not be practical because of the accumulated earnings tax. This tax is a penalty imposed on corporations that accumulate their earnings to avoid the income tax which would have been incurred by the shareholders if dividends had been distributed. The intent to avoid taxes may be established by demonstrating that the corporation has accumulated earnings in excess of the reasonable needs of the business. Reasonable needs of the business would include such items as plant expansion, asset replacement, debt retirement, stock retirement, customer-supplier loans, and working capital.

Subchapter S Corporations. The disadvantage associated with double taxation may be eliminated if a corporation elects to be taxed as a Subchapter S corporation. Under this election, the corporation is treated as a partnership for tax purposes. The corporate entity itself pays no tax, and the shareholders pay tax on their share of corporate income whether or not it is distributed to them. This special treatment is based on the view that certain corporations are in substance basically the same as a partnership. This analogy is appropriate for nonpublic corporations, in which major shareholders act in the same capacity as partners in a partnership.

The corporation electing to be taxed as a Subchapter S corporation must meet certain requirements. For example, the corporation may have only one class of stock owned by twenty-five or fewer stockholders. Certain technical procedures are also employed with respect to the determination and classifications of taxable income.

Underlying Equity Theories

As discussed in Chapter 1, the theoretical framework of accounting consists, in part, of various theories which explain the nature of the equities making up a particular business entity. This body of theory, known as equity theory, provides support for the accounting, reporting, and legal characteristics of a business entity. An understanding of these characteristics is aided by the identification of the supporting equity theory. Some of the characteristics of a partnership may be traced to the proprietary theory, for example, while other characteristics may be traced to the entity theory. The fact that partnerships are influenced by both the proprietary and entity theories has resulted in special accounting methods which are unique to partnerships. The following summary of various partnership characteristics relates them to the appropriate underlying equity theory.

Partnership Characteristics Traceable to the Proprietary Theory

Interest on debt is viewed as a component of the income calculation.

Salaries to partners are viewed as a distribution of income versus a component of the income calculation.

A personal relationship exists between owners and management.

The concept of unlimited liability suggests that the amount by which partnership liabilities exceed partnership assets could be satisfied by a partner's net personal assets (the amount by which personal assets exceed personal liabilities). Therefore, unsatisfied partnership liabilities could be viewed as debts of the individual owners versus the distinct partnership entity.

The partnership is not viewed as a distinct taxable entity, but rather a conduit through which income passes to the owners, at which point it is taxed.

The tax basis of assets contributed to a partnership is the same as the basis when held by the individual partners, suggesting the absence of a distinct business entity.

Unlike corporations, there is no breakdown of the sources of owners' equity on a partnership balance sheet.

The continuity of the original partnership is generally dissolved upon the admission or withdrawal of a partner.

Changes in the ownership structure of the partnership are used to suggest revaluations of partnership assets, thereby emphasizing the measurement of the partners' wealth.

Partnership Characteristics Traceable to the Entity Theory

The partnership may enter into contracts in its own name and in some states may sue and be sued in its own name.

Property contributed to the partnership becomes the property of the partnership, and the contributing partner no longer retains a claim to the specific assets contributed.

The "Marshaling of Assets" doctrine recognizes that the debts of the partnership and individual partners are separate and distinct. Upon liquidation, partnership liabilities represent claims against the assets of the partnership and the partner's personal liabilities represent claims against the partner's personal assets. (This doctrine will be discussed more fully in Chapter 15.)

If there is a change in the relation of the partners caused by the exit of any partner or the entrance of a new partner, the partnership is not necessarily liquidated and may continue its original purpose. Also, the assignment of a partner's interest to another does not dissolve the partnership.

ACCOUNTING FOR PARTNERSHIP ACTIVITIES

The remainder of this chapter discusses the accounting for a partnership's ongoing activities and the allocation of partnership profits or losses. Changes in the ownership structure of a partnership and the liquidation of a partnership are discussed in the following chapter. Accounting for a partnership's activities is influenced by both the proprietary and entity theory as discussed earlier and to a large extent by the intent of the partners.

A partnership may come into existence without having to receive formal, legal, or state approval and may even result from the actions of the parties involved. To capture properly the intent of the parties involved, it is most advisable to develop a written partnership agreement. This written agreement, referred to as the *articles of partnership*, will significantly govern the activities of the partnership. At a minimum, it should include the following provisions:

1. Partnership name and address.
2. Partners' names and addresses.
3. Effective date of partnership.
4. A description of the general business purpose and the limited duration of such purpose, if applicable.
5. Powers and duties of partners.
6. Procedures governing the valuation of assets invested.
7. Procedures governing the admission of a new partner(s).
8. Procedures governing the distribution of profits and losses.
9. Procedures governing the payment or receipt of interest on loans (versus capital contributions) with partners.
10. Salaries to be paid to partners.
11. Withdrawals of capital to be allowed each partner and the determination of what constitutes excess withdrawals.
12. Procedures governing the death of a partner and the determination of the decedent's equity in the partnership.
13. Procedures governing the retirement of a partner and the determination of the partner's equity in the partnership.
14. Matters requiring the consent of all partners.
15. The date when the profits are divided and the partnership books are closed.

As the accounting for a partnership is more fully developed in this text, it will become apparent that the articles of partnership provide crucial guidance. Even though the UPA covers certain topics found in the articles of partnership, it is important to note that many sections of the UPA are only applicable in the absence of a partnership agreement. Legal and accounting issues affecting a partnership are best resolved by evaluating the intent of the partners as set forth in a partnership agreement, rather than looking to the UPA.

Ongoing Activities of the Partnership

Except for transactions with the partners, the ongoing activities of a partnership are, for the most part, accounted for the same way as for a corporation. Activities of a partner are typically accounted for through the use of three special accounts: a drawing account, a capital account, and a partner's loan account.

A drawing account is established for each partner and is debited and credited for the following transactions:

Drawing Account

Debits	Credits
Periodic withdrawals of partnership assets	Partner's share of partnership profits
Payments made by the partnership on behalf of an individual partner	
Partner's share of partnership losses	

The debit or credit balance is closed to the capital account.

The amount and timing of a partner's withdrawal of partnership assets should be addressed in the articles of partnership. These articles may stipulate that a withdrawal in excess of a prescribed amount be considered a withdrawal of invested capital which should be debited immediately to the partner's capital account rather than to the drawing account.

After the determination of the partnership profit or loss, each partner's share is closed to the respective drawing account. The debit or credit balance in the drawing account is then closed to the respective capital account. The drawing account is a temporary account and only the balance in a partner's capital account is presented in a partnership balance sheet. It is important to note that a partnership balance sheet does not separately present initial invested capital and earnings retained in the partnership, as would be the case in a corporation balance sheet.

Each partner's interest in the net assets of the partnership is measured at book value in a capital account established for that partner. This account indicates the destination of capital (claims to net assets) upon dissolution of the partnership. In contrast, the sources of capital for a corporation are stressed by using several capital accounts, such as Capital Stock, Paid-In Capital in Excess of Par, and Retained Earnings.

A partner's capital account is debited and credited for the following transactions:

Capital Account

Debit	Credit
Withdrawals in excess of a specified amount	Initial and subsequent investments of capital
Closing of a net debit balance in the partner's drawing account	Closing of a net credit balance in the partner's drawing account

As is the case with all entities, the investment of capital in a partnership should be measured at the fair market value of all tangible and intangible assets contributed. An individual partner's liabilities which have been assumed by the partnership should also be recorded at fair market value. This valuation of the investment at fair market value contrasts with the tax basis of a partner's investment, which, as noted previously, does not reflect fair market value. The proper valuation of each partner's net investment of capital is extremely important. If an asset invested by a partner is undervalued by the partnership, for example, and is immediately sold for a gain, all the partners share in the realized gain, which properly should have accrued to the original investing partner.

The post-closing balances in the capital accounts of the various partners represent each partner's interest in the net assets of the partnership. A partner's interest in the partnership is often different from the partner's interest in the profits and losses of the partnership. To illustrate, assume that A and B have capital balances of $200 and $400 respectively. A's balance reflects a 33⅓% interest in the partnership capital. If A and B agree to divide a $400 profit equally, the capital balances of A and B will be $400 and $600 respectively. A's balance now reflects a 40% interest in the partnership.

Occasionally, partners will loan assets to the partnership, or the partnership will loan assets to partners. It is especially important from a legal standpoint to differentiate between a loan and an additional investment of capital, especially when the liquidation or "winding up" of a partnership takes place (Chapter 15). The nature of such transactions should be made clear by examining the intent of the individual partner or the partnership. If the contribution by a partner is really an additional investment of capital, it should be accounted for in the partner's capital account. However, if the transaction is truly a loan, it should be accounted for in a separate loan account for the partner, and provision for the payment of interest on the loan should be made.

The following entries reflect the nature and use of the various partnership accounts:

Event	Entry		
Partner A contributes cash to the partnership. Partner B contributes inventory and office equipment, and the partnership assumes the liability associated with the equipment.	Cash	10,000	
	Inventory	5,000	
	Office Equipment	4,000	
	Note Payable		2,000
	Partner A, Capital		10,000
	Partner B, Capital		7,000
Partner B loans the partnership $3,000 to be repaid in one year at a stated annual interest rate of 6%.	Cash	3,000	
	Partner B, Loan		3,000
A personal debt owed by Partner A is paid by the partnership.	Partner A, Drawing	500	
	Cash		500
Partners A and B withdraw cash of $500 and $1,200 respectively. Drawings in excess of $1,000 are viewed as excessive withdrawals and are charged against capital.	Partner A, Drawing	500	
	Partner B, Drawing	1,000	
	Partner B, Capital	200	
	Cash		1,700

Event	Entry

The net income of the partnership is divided equally between the partners.	Income Summary 10,000	
	Partner A, Drawing	5,000
	Partner B, Drawing	5,000
The partners' drawing accounts are closed to their respective capital accounts.	Partner A, Drawing 4,000	
	Partner B, Drawing 4,000	
	Partner A, Capital	4,000
	Partner B, Capital	4,000

Division of Profits and Losses

An important process to be outlined in the articles of partnership is the manner in which profits and losses are to be divided among the partners. There are several alternative methods of allocating profits and losses. However, if the articles of partnership are silent on this point, Section 18 of the UPA states that profits and losses are to be divided equally among the partners.

The division of partnership income should be based on an analysis of the correlation between the capital and labor committed to the firm by individual partners and the income which is subsequently generated. As a result, profits might be divided in one or more of the following ways:

1. According to a ratio,
2. According to the capital investments of the partners, and/or
3. According to the labor (or service) rendered by the partners.

Profit and Loss Ratios. Partnership agreements frequently call for the division of profits and losses according to some ratio. Normally, the ratio designed for the division of profits is also used for the division of losses, unless a specific provision to the contrary exists. This method obviously provides a simplified way of dividing profits and, if approached properly, may also provide an equitable division. Theoretically, the ratio should attempt to combine into one base the capital and service contributions made by the respective partners. Again, it is important to note that a partner's interest in profits and losses is often different from the partner's interest in total partnership capital (net assets).

To illustrate this method, assume that the articles of partnership state that partnership profits and losses should be divided between partners A and B in the ratio of 60:40. A net income of $20,000 would be divided as follows:

	Partner A	Partner B
Net income	$20,000	$20,000
Profit ratio	× 60%	× 40%
Net income to partner	$12,000	$ 8,000

Capital Investments of the Partners. The capital investments of the partners, represented by the balances in their respective capital accounts, may be employed as a basis for dividing a portion of the profits. The division is accomplished by imputing interest on the invested capital at some specified rate. This interest is not viewed as a partnership expense, but rather as a means of allocating profits and losses among the partners. Typically, the balance of profits not allocated on the basis of invested capital is allocated according to some profit and loss ratio.

When a partner's capital investment is used as the basis for allocating profits, the partnership agreement should specify:

1. Whether the respective partners' capital balances are to be determined before or after the partners' year-to-date withdrawals recorded in their drawing accounts are offset against their capital accounts.
2. Whether the amount of capital investment for allocation purposes is to be:
   a. capital at the beginning of the accounting period,
   b. capital at the end of the accounting period, or
   c. weighted average capital during the accounting period.
3. The rate of interest to be imputed on the invested capital.

With respect to the first point, it is important that the partnership agreement clearly establish how invested capital is to be determined. Since each partner's equity is a combination of capital and drawing account balances, partners' drawings may be offset against the balances in their respective capital accounts for purposes of allocating net income based on invested capital. However, a partnership agreement may state that only withdrawals above a certain limit are to be viewed as offsets against capital balances. It is also possible that a partnership agreement will call for interest to be imputed only if the amount of invested capital exceeds some prescribed limit or average amount.

To illustrate the use of invested capital as a basis for allocating partnership profits, assume that:

1. Partnership profit is $20,000.
2. Interest on invested capital is to be imputed at the rate of 10%.
3. Profits not allocated on the basis of invested capital are to be allocated equally among the partners.
4. The capital accounts of Partners A and B, prior to the closing of their drawing accounts, are as follows:

Partner A, Capital

10/1/X1	30,000	1/1/X1	100,000
		7/1/X1	10,000

Partner B, Capital

10/1/X1	10,000	1/1/X1	60,000

If interest is to be imputed on the partners' invested capital at the beginning of the period, the partnership profit of $20,000 would be allocated as follows:

	Partner A	Partner B	Total
Interest on beginning capital:			
A: 10% × $100,000	$10,000	—	$10,000
B: 10% × $ 60,000	—	$6,000	6,000
			$16,000
Balance per ratio (equally)	2,000	2,000	4,000
Allocation of profit	$12,000	$8,000	$20,000

If interest is to be imputed on the partners' invested capital at the end of the period, the partnership profit of $20,000 would be allocated as follows:

	Partner A	Partner B	Total
Interest on ending capital:			
A: 10% × $80,000	$ 8,000	—	$ 8,000
B: 10% × $50,000	—	$5,000	5,000
			$13,000
Balance per ratio (equally)	3,500	3,500	7,000
Allocation of profit	$11,500	$8,500	$20,000

If interest is to be imputed on the partners' weighted average invested capital during the period, the partnership profit of $20,000 would be allocated as follows:

	Partner A	Partner B	Total
Interest on weighted average capital:			
A: 10% × $97,500 (Schedule A)	$ 9,750	—	$ 9,750
B: 10% × $57,500 (Schedule B)	—	$5,750	5,750
			$15,500
Balance per ratio (equally)	2,250	2,250	4,500
Allocation of profit	$12,000	$8,000	$20,000

Schedule A
Weighted Average Capital of Partner A

(1) Amount Invested	(2) Number of Months Invested	(1) × (2) Weighted Dollars
$100,000	6	$ 600,000
110,000	3	330,000
80,000	3	240,000
	12	$1,170,000

Weighted average capital: $1,170,000 ÷ 12 = $ 97,500

Schedule B
Weighted Average Capital of Partner B

(1) Amount Invested	(2) Number of Months Invested	(1) × (2) Weighted Dollars
$60,000	9	$540,000
50,000	3	150,000
	12	$690,000

Weighted average capital: $690,000 ÷ 12 = $ 57,500

Services Rendered by the Partners. A partner's labor or service to the firm may be a primary force in the generation of revenue. Normally, the profit and loss agreement recognizes variations in effort by calling for a portion of net income to be allocated to partners as salary. Such salaries, like interest on capital investment, are viewed as a means of allocating income rather than as an expense. It is important to note that this treatment of partners' salaries differs from the treatment of employee/shareholder salaries in a corporation, and the difference should be considered when the performance of a partnership is compared with that of a competing corporation.

When dealing with a profit and loss agreement that employs salaries as a means of allocating income, it is important not to confuse such salaries with partners' drawings. For example, if a partner withdraws $1,000 a month from the partnership, this withdrawal may suggest that $12,000 of partnership income is being distributed to the partner as an annual salary, or this withdrawal may be ignored for purposes of dividing profits. Generally speaking, a partner's drawing is not viewed as a salary but as a withdrawal of assets that reduces the partner's equity. For clarification purposes, the partnership agreement should specifically state whether regular withdrawals of specific amounts should be viewed as salary for purposes of allocating income among the partners.

Bonuses to partners also may be used as a means of recognizing a partner's service to the firm. Such bonuses are usually figured as a percentage of income either before or after the bonus. When the bonus is to be a percentage of net income before the bonus, the calculation is straightforward. If the bonus is to be figured as a percentage of net income after the bonus, the following formula is used:

Bonus $=X\% (NI - Bonus)$
where: X% is the bonus percentage
NI is the net income before bonus

For example, if Partner A is to receive a bonus of 10% of net income after the bonus, the bonus is calculated as follows, assuming that net income before the bonus is $110,000:

(a) Bonus = 10% ($110,000 − Bonus) (c) 110% (Bonus) = $11,000
(b) Bonus = $11,000 − 10% (Bonus)   (d)   Bonus = $10,000

Multiple Bases of Allocation. In many cases, income is allocated to the respective partners by combining several allocation techniques. To illustrate, assume that a profit and loss agreement of the ABC partnership contains the following provisions:

1. Interest of 6% is to be paid on that portion of a partner's ending capital balance which exceeds $100,000.
2. Partner C is to receive a bonus equal to 10% of net income after the bonus.
3. Salaries of $10,000 and $12,000 are to be paid to partners A and C respectively.
4. The balance of net income is to be distributed in the ratio of 1:2:1 for A, B, and C respectively.

Assuming a net income of $33,000 and ending capital balances of $80,000, $150,000 and $110,000 for partners A, B, and C respectively, income is distributed to the partners as shown in Illustration I.

Illustration I—Profit Allocation: Multiple Bases

	Partner A	Partner B	Partner C	Total
Interest on excess capital balance ...	—	$3,000	$ 600	$ 3,600
Bonus................................	—	—	3,000*	3,000
Salaries	$10,000	—	12,000	22,000
Subtotal.........................	$10,000	$3,000	$15,600	$28,600
Remaining profit...................	1,100	2,200	1,100	4,400
Net income allocation	$11,100	$5,200	$16,700	$33,000

*Bonus = 10% (NI − Bonus)
  Bonus = 10% ($33,000 − Bonus)
(110%) Bonus = $3,300
  Bonus = $3.000

Allocating Profit Deficiencies and Losses. In the previous examples of profit allocations, the partnership income was sufficient in amount to satisfy all of the provisions of the profit and loss agreement. However, if the income is not sufficient or an operating loss exists, one of the two following alternatives may be employed:

1. Completely satisfy all provisions of the profit and loss agreement and use the profit and loss ratios to absorb any deficiency or additional loss caused by such action.
2. Satisfy each of the provisions to whatever extent is possible.

To illustrate these alternatives, assume the same information used in Illustration I for the ABC partnership, except that the net income is $22,000. In Illustration II, the income is divided by using the first alternative.

Illustration II—Profit Allocation: Deficiency Allocated in Profit and Loss Ratio

	Partner A	Partner B	Partner C	Total
Interest on excess capital balance ...	—	$ 3,000	$ 600	$ 3,600
Bonus	—	—	2,000*	2,000
Salaries	$10,000	—	12,000	22,000
Subtotal	$10,000	$ 3,000	$14,600	$27,600
Deficiency	(1,400)	(2,800)	(1,400)	(5,600)
Net income allocation	$ 8,600	$ 200	$13,200	$22,000

```
      *Bonus  = 10% (NI − Bonus)
       Bonus  = 10% ($22,000 − Bonus)
(110%) Bonus  = $2,200
       Bonus  = $2,000
```

Normally, the first method is also used when the partnership has an overall net loss. For example, given a net loss of $2,400, the methodology in Illustration II would be employed, except that a bonus would not be recognized. The deficiency to be allocated among the partners, in the ratio of 1:2:1, would be $28,000 (subtotal of $25,600 plus net loss of $2,400).

The second alternative, which is used less frequently, requires that the provisions of the profit and loss agreement be ranked by order of priority. Assuming that the components listed in Illustration II are already in order of priority, a net income of $22,000 would be distributed as follows:

```
$ 3,600 for interest on excess capital balances
  2,000 for bonus
 16,400 for salaries
$22,000
```

The salaries of $16,400 are allocated to partners A and C according to the ratio suggested by their normal salaries of $10,000 and $12,000 respectively. Therefore, A receives 10/22 of the $16,400, or $7,455, while C receives 12/22, or $8,945. Using this alternative, the partners' share of the $22,000 net income is $7,455, $3,000, and $11,545 respectively.

Special Allocation Procedures. A partnership profit and loss agreement may include special provisions for handling items which represent (a) corrections of prior years' net income or (b) current period nonoperating gains or losses. Even though a correction of prior years' net income may not satisfy the criteria for a prior period adjustment, as defined by the Financial Accounting Standards Board, it may be more equitable to allocate the item among the partners according to the profit and loss agreement for the relevant prior period rather than the current period. For example, assume that partners A, B, and C, who previously shared profits equally, currently share profits in the ratio of 2:2:1. Also assume that in the current year, the partnership incurs a loss of $10,000 due to the settlement of litigation involving a matter arising in a prior period. Rather than allocating the loss according to the current profit ratios, it may be more equitable to base the allocation on the prior ratios.

A similar procedure may be adopted for the current period realization of nonoperating gains or losses. Rather than allocating a gain on the sale of a plant asset according to the partners' current profit-sharing ratios, it may be more equitable to use the ratios which existed during the periods when unrealized appreciation actually took place. To illustrate, assume that land with a basis of $40,000 has been held for three years and is sold for $60,000 in the current period. Based on the assumed profit-sharing ratios of prior periods, the $20,000 gain would be allocated to partners A, B, and C as follows:

Year	Profit Ratios	Appreciation	Profit Allocation A	B	C
1	1:1:2	$ 4,000	$1,000	$1,000	$2,000
2	2:1:2	10,000	4,000	2,000	4,000
3	2:2:2	6,000	2,000	2,000	2,000
		$20,000	$7,000	$5,000	$8,000

If the partnership had not established special provisions for handling such items, the gain of $20,000 would have been allocated equally among the partners according to their current profit ratio of 2:2:2.

QUESTIONS

1. List four characteristics of a partnership which indicate that it is not a separate, distinct entity.
2. How does the liability of owners differ as to corporations and partnerships?
3. How may a corporation avoid or minimize the possibility of double taxation?
4. What factors might explain the tremendous growth in the corporate form of organization as compared to the growth of partnerships?
5. The stockholders' equity section of a corporate balance sheet is divided into several major categories. Identify these categories and indicate why they are not necessary for a partnership.
6. What purposes are served by the articles of partnership?
7. Identify the basic activities or transactions which affect a partner's capital account.
8. What are the factors which should be considered before establishing a profit and loss agreement? Which factors would be most appropriate for a partnership of CPAs?
9. How is a partner's interest in profits influenced by or related to interest in capital?
10. A partner receives $1,000 a month from the partnership. What is the significance of viewing the payment as a withdrawal versus a salary?
11. If the net income of a partnership is not sufficient to cover all elements of a profit and loss agreement, how should net income be divided?

EXERCISES

Exercise 1.   The JKL partnership was formed on January 1, 19X0. Contributions to the partnership are as follows:

		Tax Basis	Fair Market Value
Partner J:	Patent......................	$21,000	$18,000
	Machinery	9,000	5,400
	Note payable, assumed by JKL	1,800	1,800
Partner K:	Land and building.............	42,000	66,000
	Mortgage on land & building,		
	assumed by JKL	24,000	20,400
Partner L:	Cash	30,000	30,000

(1) Prepare the journal entry on the books of JKL to record the investment of capital in the partnership.
(2) Calculate the tax basis for each partner's interest if J, K, and L agree to accept equal liability for obligations associated with contributed assets.

Exercise 2.   In 19X1, a new partnership purchased land on the edge of the town of Otisville. The partners erected a building and opened a furniture and appliance store under the name of Furniture Fair. The partnership agreement specified that profits or losses should be shared equally after the allocation of partners' salary allowances and interest on average capital balances.

Otisville has grown considerably, and the store is now one of the most prominent stores in a fashionable suburban area. Good management, imaginative merchandising, and the general growth in the economy have made Furniture Fair the leading and most profitable firm of its type in the Otisville trade area.

Now the partners wish to admit another investor and incorporate the business. The original partners will purchase at par an amount of preferred stock equal to the book value of their interest in the partnership, and common stock equal to that portion of fair market value which exceeds their book value. The new investor will purchase, at a ten percent premium over par value, common and preferred stock equal to one third of the total number of shares purchased by the original partners. The corporation will then purchase the Furniture Fair partnership at its fair market value from the partners. After the consummation of the partners' plan, the corporation will acquire the partnership assets, assume the liabilities, and employ the partners to manage the corporation.

(1) List and explain the differences in terms and valuations that would be expected in comparing the assets that appear on the balance sheet of the proposed corporation and the assets which appear on the partnership balance sheet.
(2) List and explain the differences that would be expected in a comparison of an income statement prepared for the proposed corporation and an income statement prepared for the partnership.

(AICPA adapted)

Exercise 3.   Partnership agreements should specify the manner in which partnership profits and losses are to be divided among the partners. Agreements may include such profit and loss sharing features as salaries, bonuses, and interest allowances on invested capital.

(1) What is the objective of the profit and loss sharing agreement? Why may there

be a need for profit and loss features in addition to the ratio? Discuss.

(2) Discuss the arguments for and against recording salary, bonus allowance, and interest on capital to partners as expenses.

(3) In addition to other profit and loss sharing features, a partnership agreement may state that "interest is to be allowed on invested capital." List the additional provisions that should be included in the partnership agreement so that such interest can be computed.

(AICPA adapted)

Exercise 4. The partnership agreement of the Backandforth Transport Company states that interest on invested capital is to be imputed at the rate of 8% and that withdrawals in excess of $1,000 per month are to be viewed as reductions of invested capital. For the fiscal year ended October 31, 19X5, the following information is available:

	Partners		
Investments (Withdrawals) During 19X4-X5	*Back*	*And*	*Forth*
December 1, 19X4	$ 2,000	$ (500)	$(1,800)
January 1, 19X5............................	—	(1,600)	8,740
March 1, 19X5	(2,500)	6,000	—
July 1, 19X5	5,000	4,800	—
October 1, 19X5	3,000	—	(850)
Capital balance, October 31, 19X5	78,000	71,300	80,140

For each partner, determine the interest on invested capital based on (1) beginning balances, (2) ending balances, and (3) weighted average balances.

Exercise 5. Xavier, Yates, and Zale are partners in a dry cleaning business. Their partnership agreement provides that the partners shall receive interest on their respective average yearly capital balances at the rate of 8%. Any residual profits or losses shall be divided equally among the partners.

The following information is available for the second year of operations:

(a) Partners' capital balances as of January 1, 19X2:

Xavier ... $24,000

Yates $17,500

Zale $13,000

(b) Additional investments were made during the year as follows:

Xavier ...... $4,500 on April 1, 19X2

Zale .... $2,000 on July 1, 19X2, and $15,000 on September 1, 19X2

(c) Xavier, Yates, and Zales' drawing accounts have the following debit balances at the end of 19X2:

Xavier $1,000

Yates $1,000

Zale .... $ 500

(d) Net income for the year is $21,100.

(1) Discuss the advantages and disadvantages of using the weighted average capital balance as the base for determining interest on capital contributed.

(2) Determine the interest on weighted average capital balances that partners Xavier, Yates, and Zale should receive for the year 19X2. Assume that the partners' withdrawals are not to influence the capital balances for purposes of computing interest.

(3) Determine the capital account balances for Xavier, Yates, and Zale, after all closing entries have been journalized and posted at the end of 19X2.

Exercise 6. Armitage and Blake Company had net income of $31,900 for 19X7. Of this amount, $4,200 was traceable to a gain on the sale of investment securities. Profit allocation information for the partnership is as follows:

(a) Blake is to receive a bonus of 10% of net income after the bonus.

(b) Armitage and Blake are to be allocated salaries of $16,000 and $10,000, respectively. During 19X7, Blake withdrew $500 per month from the partnership; drawings are viewed as withdrawals of assets that reduce partner equity.

(c) Current period nonoperating gains and losses are allocated according to ratios in effect during relevant prior periods. Unrealized appreciation relating to the investments occurred as follows:

Year	Profit/Loss Ratios Armitage : Blake	Appreciation
19X5	3:2	$ 950
19X6	4:3	1,890
19X7	1:1	1,360
		$4,200

(d) All provisions of the partnership agreement are to be satisfied completely, and any deficiency or additional loss created is to be absorbed according to current profit and loss ratios.

Determine the allocation of 19X7 income between the partners.

Exercise 7. Burns and Egen formed a partnership on January 6, 19X1. At that time, Burns contributed capital of $25,000. Egen contributed no capital, but has a specialized expertise and manages the firm full time. There were no withdrawals by either party during the year. The partnership agreement provides for the following:

(a) Capital accounts are to be credited annually with interest at 5% of the beginning capital balance.

(b) Egen is to be paid a salary of $1,400 per month.

(c) Egen is to receive a bonus of 20% of income calculated before the partners' interest and salary are deducted.

(d) Profits are to be divided between Burns and Egen in the ratio of 9:1 respectively.

(e) Bonuses, interest, and Egen's salary are to be considered partnership expenses. The partnership 19X1 income statement is as follows:

Revenue	$101,250
Expenses (including salary, interest, and bonus)	(54,500)
Net income	$ 46,750

Assuming that Egen withdraws one half of the salary at year end, determine Egen's bonus and Burns & Egen's capital balances at year end.

(AICPA adapted)

Exercise 8. The partners Rand and Mason agree to share profits and losses as follows:

(a) Rand will receive an annual salary of $12,000.

(b) Mason will receive an annual salary of $8,000, plus a bonus equal to 12% of net income after the bonus.

(c) All remaining profits or losses will be distributed equally between the partners.

(1) Assuming a net income of $14,000, indicate how the income is allocated among the partners.
(2) Assuming a net loss of $4,000, indicate how the loss is allocated among the partners.

PROBLEMS

Problem 14-1. On January 1, 19X4, the partnership of Barber, Robly, and Tessen decided to merge with another partnership. The partners agreed that prior to the merger, the records of the partnership should be revised to put all past transactions on the accrual basis following current accounting theory.

Additional information:

(a) Barber and Tessen originally formed a law practice on January 1, 19X1, sharing profits and losses equally. Robly was admitted as a new partner on January 1, 19X2. The new partnership shared profits and losses as follows: Barber, 40%; Robly, 20%; and Tessen, 40%.

(b) Barber, Robly, and Tessen have followed accrual accounting, but the following errors have been discovered:

(1) A $5,000 advance payment on April 4, 19X1, credited to earned revenue, was unearned as of December 31, 19X1; it should have been recognized on February 15, 19X2.

(2) Law books worth $3,000 were loaned by Barber to the partnership on January 1, 19X1, and were to be returned after five years. The partnership depreciated the books evenly over five years, but they were never recorded as a partnership asset.

(3) On December 20, 19X3, the partnership received a $2,000 advance from a client, which was credited to earned revenue.

(c) The Barber, Robly, and Tessen partnership has always treated salaries as a direct reduction of capital; but as part of the new partnership agreement, the salaries are to be treated as a distribution of income, and a retroactive correction of the accounts is to be made. The following schedule indicates the salaries received and income earned by the partnership for 19X1, 19X2, and 19X3:

	Salaries Received			Income Before
Year	Barber	Robly	Tessen	Salaries
19X1	$15,000		$15,000	$25,000
19X2	20,000	$15,000	25,000	50,000
19X3	25,000	15,000	25,000	70,000

(d) A condensed balance sheet as of December 31, 19X3, for the Barber, Robly, and Tessen partnership is as follows:

Assets		Liabilities and Capital	
Cash	$ 5,000	Liabilities	$ 5,000
Receivables (net)	22,000	Barber, capital	25,000
Books (net)	14,000	Robly, capital	15,000
Other assets	24,000	Tessen, capital	20,000
Total assets	$65,000	Total liabilities and capital	$65,000

Required:

(1) Prepare schedules to compute the corrected income of the partnership on the accrual basis for each year of its existence. (Any depreciation should be computed on the straight-line basis. Ignore tax implications.)
(2) Prepare a schedule to show how the corrected income of the partnership is allocated to the individual partners.
(3) Determine the correct capital balances for each partner and prepare schedules of the changes in the partnership capital accounts by year for both the actual method used and for the corrected method. (Schedules should determine the adjustments needed among the partners due to the method of profit distribution.)

Problem 14-2. The partnership of Jaske, Goldman, and Sacks was formed on January 1, 19X1, with the partners sharing profits and losses in the ratio of 3:3:4 respectively. The partnership has always recognized revenues and expenses on a cash basis, including purchases of office equipment and law books. Specific salary allowances were stipulated in their partnership agreement: the partners were allowed $2,000 each month, which they withdrew. On January 1, 19X4, the partnership decided to admit a new partner. Prior to the admission, it was decided that the records of the partnership should be restated to adjust all past transactions in a correct manner following accrual accounting. The following information is relevant to this partnership.

(a) Billings and collections to date were as follows:

	Billings	Collections		
		19X1	*19X2*	*19X3*
19X1	$110,000	$75,000	$ 20,000	$ 5,000
19X2	100,000		80,000	15,000
19X3	120,000			90,000
	$330,000	$75,000	$100,000	$110,000

(b) No allowance for doubtful accounts was ever established. To match revenues and expenses, the partners agreed that uncollectible accounts expense should have been accrued at the rate of 2% of gross billings. An analysis of past years' collections suggests that accounts should have been written off as follows:

	Year account should have been written off		
Year of original billing	*19X1*	*19X2*	*19X3*
19X1....................	$1,500	$1,000	$ 500
19X2....................		—	2,000
19X3....................			1,000

(c) No accruals were necessary at the end of any year. On January 1, 19X1, the partnership purchased $10,000 of books with an estimated life of 10 years and $5,000 worth of furniture and equipment with an estimated 5-year life. On January 1, 19X2, the partnership purchased $15,000 worth of furniture and equipment with an estimated life of 6 years. On July 1, 19X2, $5,000 of law books, with an estimated life of 5 years, were purchased.

(d) The following schedule shows the occurrence and payment of partnership expenses, including the purchase of plant assets:

		Cash Disbursements (excluding withdrawals)		
Liability Incurred		*19X1*	*19X2*	*19X3*
19X1.............	$ 30,000	$20,000	$10,000	
19X2.............	50,000		30,000	$ 5,000
19X3.............	30,000			25,000
	$110,000	$20,000	$40,000	$30,000

(e) On December 31, 19X3, the following condensed balance sheet of the Jaske, Goldman, and Sacks partnership was obtained:

Assets		Capital	
Cash	$100,000	Jaske, capital	$ 35,000
		Goldman, capital	25,000
		Sacks, capital	40,000
Total assets	$100,000	Total capital	$100,000

Required:

(1) Prepare schedules to compute the corrected income for the partnership on an accrual basis for each year of its existence. (Any depreciation should be computed on a straight-line basis. Ignore income tax implications.)
(2) Determine the current capital balances of the partners as of December 31, 19X3, and prepare a balance sheet as of December 31, 19X3.

Problem 14-3. On January 1, 19X8, Glidding, owner of Glidding Hardware Store, and Brown, owner of Ace Hardware, agreed to form a partnership. Before combining the two proprietorships, they agreed to correct their accounts for any errors and/or discrepancies. In addition, the prospective partners agreed to value Glidding's inventory on a lifo basis and Glidding's plant assets at a value equal to book value, with depreciation calculated on a straight-line basis. Glidding had used sum-of-the-years-digits depreciation for all plant assets in the past.

Additional Information:

(a) Glidding's December 31, 19X7 fifo inventory represents 110% of its lifo value.
(b) Glidding's purchases of plant assets (assume no residual values) were as follows:

Date	Cost	Estimated Life
January 1, 19X4	$15,000	5 years
January 1, 19X6	8,400	6 years
January 1, 19X7	5,000	4 years

(c) Brown has followed acceptable accrual accounting procedures, but the following errors have been discovered:

(1) Ending inventory was understated by $2,000 on December 31, 19X6.
(2) Failed to accrue $1,000 of employees' wages on December 31, 19X7.
(3) Ending inventory was overvalued by $1,500 on December 31, 19X7.
(4) Miscellaneous supplies on hand at December 31, 19X6, totaled $500. All supply purchases were debited to Supplies Expense.

(d) Brown purchased a truck with Ace Hardware money for $7,000 on January 1, 19X5. Ace Hardware depreciated the truck using the sum-of-the-years-digits method over a 5-year life with a $1,000 residual value. Brown has used the truck almost exclusively for personal use since its purchase. Brown agrees to contribute the truck, valued at $4,000, to the partnership.

(e) The balance sheets for Ace Hardware and Glidding Hardware Store as of December 31, 19X7, are as follows:

Ace Hardware
Balance Sheet
December 31, 19X7

Assets		Liabilities and Capital	
Cash	$ 4,300	Notes payable	$ 5,000
Accounts receivable (net).....	8,500	Accounts payable	12,000
Inventory	90,000	Long-term notes payable	20,000
Other assets, net of deprecia-		Brown, capital	88,000
tion and amortization	22,200		
Total assets	$125,000	Total liabilities and capital....	$125,000

Glidding Hardware Store
Balance Sheet
December 31, 19X7

Assets		Liabilities and Capital	
Cash	$ 10,000	Notes payable	$ 8,000
Accounts receivable (net).....	1,300	Accounts payable	10,000
Inventory	88,000	Long-term notes payable	24,000
Other assets, net of deprecia-		Glidding, capital	88,000
tion and amortization	30,700		
Total assets	$130,000	Total liabilities and capital....	$130,000

Required:

(1) Prepare revised balance sheets for Glidding Hardware and Ace Hardware according to the partnership agreement.
(2) Record the entry necessary to open the books of the new partnership.

Problem 14-4. Case, Harvey, and Richards are individual practicing CPAs. However, they agree to consolidate their individual practices as of January 1, 19X7. The partnership agreement includes the following features:

(1) Each partner's capital contribution is the net amount of the assets and liabilities taken over by the partnership, which are as follows:

	Case	Harvey	Richards
Cash	$ 5,000	$ 5,000	$ 5,000
Accounts receivable	14,000	6,000	16,000
Furniture and library	4,300	2,500	6,200
Accumulated depreciation..............	(2,400)	(1,500)	(4,700)
Accounts payable	(300)	(1,400)	(700)
Capital contribution...................	$20,600	$10,600	$21,800

The partners guaranteed the collectibility of their receivables.

(2) Richards had leased office space with a monthly rental of $600 and was bound by the lease until June 30, 19X7. The partners agree to pay the rent and to occupy Richards' office space until the expiration of the lease. However, the partners expressed concern that the rent was too high and that a fair rental value would be $450 per month. The excess rent is to be charged to Richards at year end. On July 1, the partners moved to new quarters with a monthly rent of $500.

(3) No salaries are to be paid to the partners. The individual partners are to receive 20% of the gross fees billed to their respective clients during the first year of the partnership. After operating expenses are deducted, the balance of the fees billed is to be credited to the partners' capital accounts in the following ratios: Case, 40%; Harvey, 35%; Richards, 25%.

(4) On April 1, 19X7, Williams was admitted to the partnership. Williams is to receive 20% of the fees from new business obtained after April 1, after expenses applicable to that new business are deducted. Expenses are to be apportioned to the new business in the ratio of total expenses other than bad debt losses to total gross fees.

The following information pertains to the partnership's activities for the first year of operations:

(a) Fees were billed as follows:

Case's clients	$22,000
Harvey's clients	12,000
Richards' clients	11,000
New business:	
Prior to April 1	3,000
After April 1	12,000
Total	$60,000

(b) Total expenses, excluding depreciation and uncollectible accounts expense, were $19,350, including the amount actually paid for rent. Depreciation is to be computed at the rate of 10% per year of the original asset cost. Depreciable assets purchased during the year, on which one-half year's depreciation is to be taken, totaled $5,000.

(c) Individual cash drawings during the year were as follows:

Case.......................................	$ 5,200
Harvey....................................	4,400
Richards..................................	5,800
Williams	2,500
	$17,900

(d) Of Case's and Harvey's receivables, $1,200 and $450, respectively, proved to be uncollectible. A new client, billed in March for $1,600, had been adjudicated bankrupt and a settlement of fifty cents on the dollar was made.

Required:

Prepare a statement of the partners' capital accounts for the year ended December 31, 19X7. Supporting computations should be in good form. (Disregard income taxes.) (AICPA adapted)

Problem 14-5. The Bryant-Domer Company is a partnership that sells appliances to the retail trade and also sells wholesale to builders and contractors. The partnership agreement provides for a 14% imputed interest rate on invested capital, salaries of $12,000 and $16,000 for Bryant and Domer respectively, and a 10% bonus for Domer. Changes in the 19X8 capital accounts of each partner, excluding normal withdrawals, were as follows:

Bryant, Capital					Domer, Capital			
12/1/X8	5,500	1/1/X8	85,000	4/1/X8	3,000	1/1/X8	96,800
		2/1/X8	2,000			7/1/X8	6,500
		9/1/X8	1,500			10/1/X8	4,500

Required:

For each of the following independent situations, determine the profit or loss allocation schedule for Bryant-Domer Company.
  (1) Interest on invested capital is based on ending capital balances after deducting year-to-date withdrawals of $8,000 for Bryant and $6,300 for Domer. The bonus is a percentage of net income before the bonus; 19X8 net income was $39,942. The provisions of the partnership agreement are to be satisfied to whatever extent possible in the following order: interest, salaries, bonus. Any remaining partnership income is allocated 60% to Bryant and 40% to Domer.
  (2) Interest on invested capital is based on weighted average capital balances. The bonus is a percentage of net income after the bonus; 19X8 net income was $66,000. All provisions of the partnership agreement are to be satisfied completely, and any remaining income or deficiency created is to be allocated 75% to Bryant and 25% to Domer.
  (3) Interest is based on ending capital balances in excess of $62,000. Domer's bonus is a percentage of net income after the bonus; 19X8 net income after salaries and bonus was $8,000. All provisions of the partnership agreement are to be satisfied completely. The articles of partnership are silent on the matter of profit and loss division between the partners.

Problem 14-6. Conrad, Farnam, and Phillips are partners in a health food products business. Their partnership agreement includes the following features:
  (a) In 19X4, the year of partnership formation, salaries paid to Conrad, Farnam, and Phillips were $9,400, $7,600, and $8,000, respectively. Salary amounts are to increase at a rate of 10% per year unless the agreement is amended. In recognition of Farnam's effectiveness as an outside salesperson, Farnam is paid a bonus of 8% of net income after the bonus. Salaries and bonus are withdrawn in full at year end.
  (b) Interest on average invested capital is imputed at the rate of 15%.
  (c) A partner's withdrawal of assets in excess of $750 a month is considered excessive and is recorded as a debit to that partner's capital account.
  (d) All provisions of the partnership agreement are to be satisfied completely, and the balance of net income, deficiency, or additional loss is to be allocated according to the profit and loss ratios, which are: Conrad, 50%; Farnam, 20%; and Phillips, 30%. Net income after salaries and interest on invested capital was $75,350 in 19X5 and $3,887 in 19X6.
The following information relates to partnership activity for 19X5 and 19X6:

	Conrad	Farnam	Phillips
Capital balances, January 1, 19X5	$60,000	$40,800	$55,000
Investments (withdrawals):			
March 1, 19X5	2,510	—	1,600
April 1, 19X5	(860)	(1,000)	400
August 1, 19X5	1,250	(500)	—
November 1, 19X5	—	3,525	(950)
February 1, 19X6	900	700	2,150
April 1, 19X6	(320)	—	—
June 1, 19X6	—	2,200	815
October 1, 19X6	2,560	(1,350)	(2,235)
December 1, 19X6	—	(1,590)	—
Personal expenses paid by partnership:			
19X5...................................	—	2,000	5,600
19X6...................................	4,100	—	—

Required:

(1) Prepare schedules to reflect the activity in each partner's drawing and capital accounts for 19X5 and 19X6, including profit allocation schedules.

(2) Record the journal entries to close each partner's drawing account for 19X5 and 19X6.

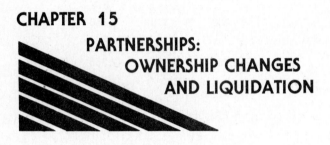

CHAPTER 15
PARTNERSHIPS:
OWNERSHIP CHANGES
AND LIQUIDATION

The Uniform Partnership Act (UPA) defines dissolution as "the change in the relation of the partners caused by any partner ceasing to be associated in the carrying on as distinguished from the winding up of the business." Sections 31 and 32 of the UPA identify the various causes of dissolution and suggest that the admission or withdrawal of a partner results in dissolution. Although dissolution ends the association of partners for their original purpose, it does not necessarily result in the termination of the partnership's basic business function. The remaining partners may continue to operate the business, or they may decide to terminate or liquidate the business. It is important that contemplated partnership changes be well planned so that either the continuation or the liquidation of the partnership may proceed smoothly and equitably.

This chapter focuses on partnership dissolution due to the ownership changes resulting from the admission and/or withdrawal of a partner and the related accounting implications. The winding up or liquidation of a partnership is also discussed.

OWNERSHIP CHANGES

Changes in the ownership structure of a corporation are everyday occurrences, as evidenced by the activity of security exchanges. These changes typically involve transactions between existing and prospective shareholders, and therefore create no special accounting problems for the corporate entity, other than updating its listings of stockholders. In the case of a partnership, however, changes in ownership structure are events that require special accounting treatment.

Accounting for changes in the ownership of a partnership is heavily influenced by the legal concept of dissolution. When there is a change in the ownership structure, the original partnership is dissolved and most often a new partnership is created. This dissolution and subsequent creation of a partnership indicates that a new legal entity has been created and that accounting should properly measure the initial contributions of capital being made to the new partnership. The proprietary theory as discussed in Chapter 1 also influences the accounting for changes in the ownership structure of a partnership. Under this theory, primary attention is focused on measuring the wealth of the individual proprietors or partners. Changes in ownership involve exchanges of consideration which reflect the current value of a partnership interest. Therefore, changes in ownership provide a basis for currently measuring partnership wealth or value.

Because of the influence of the dissolution concept and proprietary theory, ownership changes are often viewed as reliable exchanges which may indicate that:

1. The existing assets of the original partnership should be revalued,
2. Previously unrecorded intangible assets exist which are traceable to the original partnership, and/or
3. Goodwill exists which is traceable to a new incoming partner.

The extent to which such value changes are recorded should be evaluated against the information standards presented in Chapter 1 and established principles governing the recording of ownership changes.

Admission of a New Partner

The admission of a new partner requires the approval of the existing partners, although a partner's interest may be assigned to someone outside the partnership without the consent of the other partners. However, assigning an interest does not dissolve the partnership, and it does not allow the assignee to participate in the management of the partnership or to review transactions and records of the partnership. The assignee receives only the agreed portion of the assigning partner's profit or loss.

Assuming that a new partner has been approved by the existing partners, the new partner will normally experience the same general risks and rights of ownership as do the other existing partners. However, creditors presenting claims against the partnership which were incurred prior to admission of the new partner cannot attach the personal assets of the new partner for settlement of their claims. Therefore, the level of liability of a new partner is less than that of an existing partner. Section 17 of the UPA states that:

> A person admitted as a partner into an existing partnership is liable for all the obligations of the partnership arising before his admission as though he had been a partner when such obligations were incurred, except that this liability shall be satisfied only out of partnership property.

Contributing Assets to the Existing Partnership. One method of gaining admission to an existing partnership involves contributing assets directly to the partnership entity itself. In this case, the exchange represents an arm's-length transaction between the entity and the incoming partner. If the book value of the original partnership's net assets approximates their fair market value, the incoming partner's contribution would be expected to be equal to the portion of the equity which the new partner is acquiring. For example, if an incoming partner is to acquire a one-fourth interest in a partnership which has a book value and a fair market value of $60,000, the original $60,000 would now represent a three-fourths interest in the new partnership. Therefore, the total partnership capital must be $80,000, of which $60,000 is traceable to the old partners and $20,000 to the assets contributed by the new partner.

An incoming partner may also acquire an interest in the partnership for a price in excess of that indicated by the book value of the original partnership's net assets. This situation would suggest the existence of:

1. Unrecorded appreciation on identifiable net assets of the original partnership, and/or
2. Unrecorded goodwill which is also traceable to the original partnership.

However, it is also possible that an incoming partner may acquire an interest in the partnership at a price less than that indicated by the book value. This situation would suggest the existence of:

1. Unrecorded depreciation or write-downs on the identifiable net assets of the original partnership, and/or
2. A contribution by the incoming partner of some intangible asset (goodwill) in addition to a measured contribution.

When an incoming partner's contribution is different from that indicated by the book values of the original existing partnership, the admission of the partner is typically recorded by either the bonus method or the goodwill method. These two methods are mutually exclusive choices for recording the admission of a partner. Both methods permit the assumption that there is unrecorded goodwill to be recognized. However, the use of either method does not prevent the recognition of differences between the book value and fair market value of recorded net assets.

Bonus Method. The bonus method of recording the admission of a partner accounts for partnership capital at recorded book values. The proper application of this method will result in the following conditions:

1. Total capital of the new partnership will be equal to the book value of the existing partners' capital plus the recorded value of the incoming partner's investment; and
2. Upon admission, the incoming partner's capital will be determined

by multiplying the total capital of the new partnership by the acquired percentage interest in capital. The previous partners' capital balances will be reallocated to the extent of the bonus.

Bonus to Old Partners. When an incoming partner's contribution indicates the existence of unrecorded net asset appreciation and/or unrecorded goodwill, the bonus method does not record these previously unrecorded items, but rather grants a "bonus" to the old partners. The bonus, which increases the capital accounts of the old partners, is made possible by increasing the new partner's capital account for only a portion of the actual contribution to the partnership. To illustrate this method, assume the following:

Existing Partners	Capital Balance	Percentage Interest in *Capital*	Percentage Interest in *Profit*
Partner A........................	$30,000	40%	50%
Partner B	45,000	60	50

C invests $27,000 in the partnership in exchange for a 20% interest in capital and a one-third interest in profits. Since the total capital of the new partnership equals $102,000 ($30,000 + $45,000 + $27,000), and the new partner is acquiring a 20% interest in capital, it seems reasonable that the incoming partner's capital account should initially reflect 20% of the total capital, or $20,400. The $6,600 difference between C's contribution and the interest recorded for C indicates the existence of unrecorded intangibles (goodwill) or unrecorded appreciation on existing assets. Regardless of the identity of the $6,600, the value must be identified with the appropriate parties. If the unrecorded value had been realized through a sale, the resulting profit would have been divided between the old partners in accordance with their profit and loss agreement. Therefore, assuming that the $6,600 is identified as a bonus to the old partners and is divided between them according to their profit and loss ratio, the entry to record C's investment is as follows:

Assets	27,000	
A, Capital..		3,300
B, Capital..		3,300
C, Capital..		20,400

Bonus to New Partner. When the new partner invests some intangible asset, such as business acumen or an established clientele, it is possible to have a bonus credited to the new partner. For example, given the same basic facts as in the previous illustration, assume that C invests $10,000 for a 20% interest in capital and a one-third interest in profits. Total capital of the partnership would be $85,000 ($30,000 + $45,000 + $10,000), and C's share of the total capital would be 20%, or $17,000. Partner C is acquiring a $17,000 interest in capital in exchange for an investment of $10,000, and the old partners are transferring $7,000 of their capital to C in exchange for unrecorded intangible assets invested by C. Partner C's admission is recorded by the following entry:

Assets	10,000	
A, Capital...	3,500	
B, Capital...	3,500	
C, Capital		17,000

Partner C's bonus may be viewed as a cost incurred to acquire C's goodwill. Since all costs to acquire assets eventually affect income and are allocated among the partners, C's bonus is allocated to A and B according to their profit and loss ratio.

The recording of a bonus traceable to the incoming partner was based on the assumption that the new partner was contributing an intangible asset, in addition to other assets valued at $10,000. However, the substance of the transaction may indicate that no intangibles are being contributed and that the existing assets of the old partnership are overvalued. For example, in the previous illustration, C invested $10,000 in return for a 20% interest in the new partnership's total capital. Therefore, the total capital of the new partnership may be interpreted from C's investment to be $50,000 ($10,000 ÷ 20%). Of this total, $10,000 is traceable to the new partner and the balance of $40,000 represents the fair market value of the old partners' capital. Assuming that this is a proper interpretation of the substance of the transaction between the new partner and the partnership, C's admission to the partnership would be recorded as follows:

A, Capital...	17,500	
B, Capital...	17,500	
Assets		35,000
To record the write-down of the original partners' capital from a book value of $75,000 ($30,000 + $45,000) to its implied fair market value of $40,000.		
Assets	10,000	
C, Capital		10,000
To record C's contribution of assets to the partnership.		

After these entries are posted, the total capital of the new partnership is $50,000 ($30,000 + $45,000 − $35,000 + $10,000), of which C's share is $10,000 (20% × $50,000) as initially represented by the balance in C's capital account.

Goodwill Method. The goodwill method emphasizes the legal significance of a change in the ownership structure of a partnership. From a legal viewpoint, the entrance of a new partner results in the dissolution of the previous partnership and the creation of a new legal entity. Since a new entity has resulted, the assets transferred to this entity should be recorded at their current fair market value. After a complete analysis, both tangible and intangible assets acquired by the new entity, including goodwill created by the previous partnership, should be recorded.

Goodwill Traceable to Old Partners. When the bonus method is used to account for the admission of a new partner, the total capital of the entity equals the book value of the previous partners' capital plus the new partner's investment. When the goodwill method is employed, however, the total capital of the new partnership will approximate the fair market value of the entity. To illustrate the goodwill method, assume the following:

Existing Partners	Capital Balance	Percentage Interest in Capital	Percentage Interest in Profit
Partner A	$30,000	40%	50%
Partner B	45,000	60	50

C invests $27,000 in the partnership in exchange for a 20% interest in capital and a one-third interest in profit. C's investment implies that the entity has a fair market value of $135,000 ($27,000 ÷ 20%). However, the book value of the new partnership will equal only $102,000 when the former partners' capital balances of $75,000 are added to C's $27,000 investment. Thus, $33,000 must be added to the existing book value.

Another interpretation of the transaction would be that, given the $102,000 book value of the new partnership, a 20% interest should have cost $20,400 ($102,000 × 20%). The new partner paid an extra $6,600 ($27,000 − $20,400) for a 20% interest in the difference between the fair market value and the implied book value of the new entity. Therefore, the total difference must be $33,000 ($6,600 ÷ 20%).

The difference between the fair market value and the book value of the new entity may, as previously discussed, be traceable to unrecorded appreciation and/or unrecorded goodwill. Each of these possible explanations should be analyzed thoroughly to account properly for a change in the ownership structure of a partnership. If differences between the fair market value and the book value of recorded assets are identifiable, appropriate adjustments to asset balances should be considered. Since a change in the ownership structure creates a new, distinct legal entity, every attempt should be made to identify differences between fair market values and book values. However, the absence of objective and independent valuations often prevents such an analysis. For example, fair market values are not readily available for certain specialized assets, and the alternative of engaging an independent appraiser could become an expensive option. Furthermore, estimating fair market values with the use of specific price-level indexes is often difficult because of the absence of relevant indexes. Another reason for not recording changes in market values is that the resulting differences between the bases for tax purposes and the bases for book purposes would require more complex records.

Unrecorded goodwill may also be identifiable. In the previous example, assuming that there are no differences between the fair market value and book value of recorded assets, the new partner's willingness to pay more than the proportionate book value of the new entity indicates that goodwill existed prior to the new partner's admission. If this intangible asset could be sold prior to the admission of the new partner, the realized profit would be allocated to the old partners. Therefore, the goodwill is recorded and allocated to the old partners according to their profit and loss ratios. The investment by C would be recorded under the goodwill method as follows:

Assets	27,000	
Goodwill...	33,000	
A, Capital..		16,500
B, Capital..		16,500
C, Capital..		27,000

It is important to note that the new partner's capital account represents a 20% interest in the total capital of the new partnership, as verified by the following computation:

Original capital	$ 75,000
C's investment..................................	27,000
Goodwill..	33,000
	$135,000
C's interest.....................................	× 20%
C's capital balance............................	$ 27,000

The recognition of goodwill traceable to the previous partners is often criticized by some accountants. If the concept of a new legal entity is cast aside, some would argue that the goodwill is self-created and therefore should not be recognized. APB Opinion No. 17, "Intangible Assets," prohibits the recognition of goodwill unless it has been purchased from another entity. To argue that the new partnership is in substance a continuation of the previous partnership would prevent the recognition of goodwill traceable to the old partnership.

It may also be argued that the difficulties associated with the measurement of the fair market value of existing assets unjustifiably forces the recognition of goodwill for lack of a more precise analysis. However, the argument that the fair market value of a new partnership, as indicated by the new partner's investment, is not objectively or independently determined overlooks the basic nature of the transaction. Negotiations between previous partners and a new partner would be described as arm's-length, since both parties involved are independently seeking a fair price.

Goodwill Traceable to New Partner. It is also possible that goodwill may be attributable to the new partner. For example, given the same basic facts as in the previous illustrations, assume that C invests $10,000 to acquire a 20% interest in the partnership of A and B. C's investment implies a fair market value of the entity equal to $50,000 ($10,000 ÷ 20%). However, the book value of the new partnership will equal $85,000, consisting of the old partners' capital balances of $75,000 plus C's investment of $10,000. This difference between fair market value and book value indicates the existence of unrecorded write-downs and/or goodwill contributed by the incoming partner. Assuming that net assets should not be written down, the amount of the goodwill may be computed as the difference between:

1. The amount which should have been paid by the new partner, as indicated by the book value of the previous partnership (calculated by dividing the original book value of the partnership by the total percentage interest of the original partners in the new partnership, and subtracting the original book value), and
2. The amount actually paid by the new partner.

In this example, the $75,000 original book value would represent 80% of the new partnership capital, or $93,750 ($75,000 ÷ 80%). Therefore, it appears that the new partner should have paid $18,750 ($93,750 less the original $75,000 book value) for an interest in the partnership; however, the partner actually paid only $10,000. The difference between what should have been paid ($18,750) and the amount actually paid ($10,000) represents the goodwill traceable to the incoming partner. The investment by C would be recorded under the goodwill method as follows:

Assets	10,000	
Goodwill	8,750	
C, Capital		18,750

Note that the new partner's capital account represents a 20% interest in the total capital of the new partnership, as shown by the following computation:

Original capital	$75,000
C's investment	10,000
Goodwill	8,750
	$93,750
C's interest	× 20%
C's capital balance	$18,750

The fact that a new legal entity is created supports the recognition of goodwill and other contributed assets at their fair market value. If the concept of a new entity is set aside, the goodwill may be viewed as being purchased by the previous partnership in exchange for partnership equity. Accounting theory and current practice support the recording of goodwill acquired or purchased from other entities.

Methodology for Determining Goodwill. An analysis of the previous examples reveals that goodwill may be traceable to either the original partners or the incoming partner. To apply the goodwill method properly, the following methodology may be helpful in identifying the origin of the goodwill and its amount:

1. Determine the entity's fair market value, as indicated by the new partner's investment (new partner's investment divided by the percentage interest acquired in the partnership).
2. If the fair market value determined in (1) is:
   (a) Greater than the book value of the new partnership, implied goodwill is traceable to the old partners and is allocated among them according to their profit ratios. The amount of goodwill is

equal to the difference between (1) the fair market value indicated by the new partner's investment and (2) the book value of the new partnership.

    (b) Less than the book value of the new partnership, implied goodwill is traceable to the new partner. The amount of goodwill is equal to the difference between (1) the amount which should have been paid by the new partner to acquire an interest in the book value of the partnership and (2) the actual amount paid.

3. The initial capital balance of the new partner will always be equal to the new partner's interest in the total capital of the new partnership after goodwill is recognized.

Comparison of the Bonus and Goodwill Methods. The bonus method adheres to the historical cost concept and is often used in actual practice. It is objective, in that it establishes total capital of the new partnership at an amount based on actual consideration received from the new partner. The bonus method indirectly acknowledges the existence of goodwill by giving a bonus to either old or new partners.

The goodwill method results in the recognition of an asset implied by a transaction rather than recognizing an asset actually purchased. Historically, goodwill has only been recognized when purchased, so that a more objective measure of its value is established. Therefore, opponents of the goodwill method contend that goodwill is not objectively determined, and that other factors may have influenced the amount of investment required from the new partner. Also, certain recipients of partnership financial statements may question the valuation of goodwill, since increasing total assets may result in an understatement of the return on total assets or equity.

Use of the goodwill method could also produce inequitable results if either of the following conditions exist:

1. The new partner's interest in profits does not equal the new partner's initial interest in capital.
2. Former partners do not share profits and losses in the same relationship to each other as they did before the admission of a new partner.

The importance of these concepts can be illustrated using the following facts:

	Old Partners		New Partner
	A	B	C
Original capital	$30,000	$45,000	
Original profit and loss percentage	50%	50%	
New partner's capital			$27,000
New profit and loss percentage	33⅓%	33⅓%	33⅓%
New partner's interest in capital			20%

The new capital balances that result from using the goodwill method and the bonus method are as follows:

	Old Partners		New Partner
	A	B	C
Goodwill method:			
Goodwill allocation...............................	$16,500	$16,500	
New capital balances	$46,500	$61,500	$27,000
Bonus method:			
Bonus allocation................................	$ 3,300	$ 3,300	
New capital balances	$33,300	$48,300	$20,400

Assuming that the recorded goodwill proves to be worthless (or assuming that goodwill is amortized in total), the decline in asset value would reduce the partners' capital balances according to their profit and loss ratios as follows:

	Partner			
	A	B	C	Total
Capital balances if goodwill method used	$46,500	$61,500	$27,000	$135,000
Goodwill write-off (amortization)	(11,000)	(11,000)	(11,000)	(33,000)
Capital balances after write-off	$35,500	$50,500	$16,000	$102,000
Capital balances if bonus method used....................	33,300	48,300	20,400	102,000
Differences	$ 2,200	$ 2,200	$ (4,400)	-0-

The capital balances that result from using the two methods are different because the new partner's interest in profits and interest in capital are not equal. In this illustration, C acquired a 20% capital interest and a 33⅓% interest in profits. Therefore, C paid for 20% of the implied goodwill but had to absorb 33⅓% of the goodwill amortization.

To further illustrate the concepts, assume the same facts, except that the new profit and loss percentages are 50%, 30%, and 20% for partners A, B, and C respectively. If the recorded goodwill proves to be worthless, the decline in asset value would affect the partners' capital balances as follows:

	Partner			
	A	B	C	Total
Capital balances if goodwill method used	$46,500	$61,500	$27,000	$135,000
Goodwill write-off (amortization)	(16,500)	(9,900)	(6,600)	(33,000)
Capital balances after write-off	$30,000	$51,600	$20,400	$102,000
Capital balances if bonus method used....................	33,300	48,300	20,400	102,000
Differences	$ (3,300)	$ 3,300	-0-	-0-

In this case, partners A and B shared equally in the initial recording of goodwill, but unequally in the subsequent amortization of goodwill.

Now assume the same facts, except that the new profit and loss percentages are 40%, 40%, and 20% for partners A, B, and C respectively. After amortization of goodwill, the capital balances are identical to those achieved under the bonus method, as indicated in the following table:

	Partner			
	A	B	C	Total
Capital balances if goodwill method used	$46,500	$61,500	$27,000	$135,000
Goodwill write-off (amortization)	(13,200)	(13,200)	(6,600)	(33,000)
Capital balances after write-off	$33,300	$48,300	$20,400	$102,000
Capital balances if bonus method used	$33,300	$48,300	$20,400	$102,000

The equality between the capital balances is achieved because neither of the two conditions that produce inequities exist. If these conditions do exist, preference is given typically to the bonus method because of the possible inequities which may result from the write-off of goodwill.

Contributing Assets to the Existing Partners. A new partner may also be admitted to the partnership by acquiring all or part of the capital interest of one or more existing partners in exchange for some consideration (assets). In this case, the new partner deals directly with an existing partner or partners rather than with the partnership entity. Therefore, the acquisition price is paid to the selling partner(s) and not to the partnership itself. The partnership records the redistribution of capital interests by transferring all or a portion of the seller's capital to the new partner's capital account, but does not record the transfer of any assets.

To illustrate, assume the following facts:

		Percentage Interest	
Existing Partners	Capital Balance	in Capital	in Profit
Partner A....................................	$30,000	40%	50%
Partner B	45,000	60	50%

Partner C seeks to purchase 50% of A's interest in capital and 50% of B's interest in capital in exchange for $50,000. This purchase would result in C having a 50% interest in the total partnership capital.

There are several alternative ways of recording the contribution of assets by C to the existing partners. If the consideration paid by the incoming partner is *not* used to impute the fair market value of the partnership, the transaction would be recorded by the partnership entity as follows:

A, Capital (50% × $30,000)	15,000	
B, Capital (50% × $45,000)	22,500	
C, Capital		37,500

The $50,000 actually paid by C was not used as a basis for the entry because it represents consideration paid to the individual partners personally rather than to the partnership entity. This accounting treatment is frequently compared to that of a corporation when a stockholder sells shares or an interest in corporate capital to another investor in the corporation. The corporation does not record the transaction or use it as a basis for revaluing corporate assets but merely acknowledges the changing identity of its shareholders.

An alternative but less frequently used method of recording this transaction would be to impute the fair market value of the partnership entity from the consideration paid by the new partner. For example, if C paid $50,000 to acquire a 50% interest in the capital of the partnership vis-a-vis the individual partners, then the total implied current value of the partnership would be $100,000 ($50,000 ÷ 50%). The difference between the imputed value of $100,000 and the partnership's book value of $75,000 ($30,000 + $45,000) is interpreted to represent undervalued existing assets and/or goodwill traceable to the old partnership. This alternative interpretation would result in recording the transaction as follows:

Assets and/or Goodwill	25,000	
A, Capital		12,500
B, Capital		12,500
To record the previously unrecognized increase in value of the partnership.		
A, Capital [50% × ($30,000 + $12,500)]	21,250	
B, Capital [50% × ($45,000 + $12,500)]	28,750	
C, Capital		50,000
To record the transfer of the original partners' adjusted capital to incoming partner C.		

Normally this alternative method is not employed because (1) the transaction was not between the partnership and the incoming partner, but rather between individual partners, and (2) the consideration paid by the incoming partner may not provide a reliable indicator of the partnership entity's current value. However, the method may provide useful information for deciding how to allocate the acquisition price between the selling partners. The selling partners' original capital plus their share of any imputed value increments may indicate the current values for which the incoming partner was paying. For example, the purchase price of $50,000 may be allocated to partners A and B as follows:

	Partner		
	A	B	Total
Original capital	$30,000	$45,000	$ 75,000
Share of value increment........................	12,500	12,500	25,000
Total imputed value.............................	$42,500	$57,500	$100,000
Percentage acquired by new partner	50%	50%	50%
Total purchase price	$21,250	$28,750	$ 50,000

Withdrawal of a Partner

When a partner withdraws, the partnership agreement should be consulted to determine if any guidelines have been established that would influence the procedure. The withdrawal of a partner requires a determination of the fair market value of the partnership entity and a measurement of partnership income to the date of withdrawal. Also, in many cases, the equity of the retiring partner may not be equal to the partner's capital balance as a result of (1) the existence of accounting errors, (2) differences between the fair market value and the recorded book value of assets, and/or (3) unrecorded assets such as goodwill.

If accounting errors are discovered, they should be treated as prior period adjustments and corrected by adjusting the capital balances of the partners. Theoretically, an error should be allocated to partners' capital balances according to the profit and loss ratios that existed when the error was committed. Therefore, it is necessary to identify the period to which the error is traceable. This practice can become complicated, and a well-designed partnership agreement should include procedures for dealing with the correction of errors.

Recognizing differences between book value and fair market value may be as appropriate when an individual withdraws from the partnership as when an individual is admitted to the partnership. If accounting recognition of such differences is not desired, however, these differences should nevertheless influence the amount to be paid to the withdrawing partner.

Selling an Interest to Existing Partners. As is the case with the admission of a partner, the withdrawal of a partner may involve (1) a transaction with existing partners or a new partner, or (2) a transaction with the partnership entity itself. In the first case, the equity of the withdrawing partner will be purchased with the personal assets of existing or new partners rather than with the assets of the partnership. To illustrate, assume the following:

	Partner		
	A	B	C
Capital balance	$30,000	$50,000	$20,000
Profit and loss percentage	40%	40%	20%
Percentage interest in capital	30%	50%	20%

Partner A withdraws from the partnership, and C purchases A's interest at its current value of $36,000. Assuming that the price paid by C is not used to impute the value of the entity, the transaction would be recorded as follows:

A, Capital	30,000	
C, Capital		30,000

As previously discussed, an alternative treatment would be to recognize any value increment indicated by the transaction and then transfer the adjusted capital balances.

Selling an Interest to the Partnership. When a withdrawing partner sells an interest to the partnership rather than to an individual partner, the bonus or goodwill methods may be employed. The bonus method is most frequently used, but the choice between methods should be based on a thorough analysis of the transaction.

Using the same facts as in the previous illustration, and assuming the use of the bonus method, the purchase of A's equity by the partnership would be recorded as follows:

A, Capital	30,000	
B, Capital	4,000	
C, Capital	2,000	
Cash		36,000

The entry indicates that the remaining partners granted a bonus to A, measured by the difference between the recorded capital and the fair market value of A's equity. The bonus is charged to the remaining partners according to their profit and loss ratios.

The goodwill method focuses on the payment to the withdrawing partner as an indication of the fair market value of the partnership. If the imputed goodwill or undervalued assets were disposed of, the partners would divide the gain according to their profit and loss ratios. Assuming that existing assets are properly valued, the $36,000 payment to A consists of A's capital balance of $30,000 plus a $6,000 share of the unrecorded goodwill. Therefore, the $6,000 represents A's 40% interest in total goodwill of $15,000 ($6,000 ÷ 40%).

Two alternatives are now available: (1) recognize only the goodwill which is traceable to the retiring partner, or (2) recognize the amount of goodwill traceable to the entire entity. The first alternative stresses the importance of recognizing only the amount of goodwill that is actually purchased from the withdrawing partner. Using this alternative, A's withdrawal would be recorded as follows:

Goodwill	6,000	
A, Capital		6,000
A, Capital	36,000	
Cash		36,000

If the amount of goodwill traceable to the entire entity is recognized, the goodwill is allocated to the partners according to their profit and loss ratios, as reflected in the following entries to record A's withdrawal:

Goodwill	15,000	
A, Capital		6,000
B, Capital		6,000
C, Capital		3,000
A, Capital	36,000	
Cash		36,000

Whether part or all of the goodwill is recognized, opponents of this procedure contend that transactions between partners should not be viewed as arm's length; therefore, the measure of goodwill may not be determined objectively. Also, inequitable results may be produced if the remaining partners subsequently change their profit and loss ratios.

Effects of a Partner's Withdrawal. When the interest of a withdrawing partner is acquired by the remaining partners or the partnership, serious demands upon the liquidity of the partners and the partnership may result. If withdrawal is due to the death of the partner, funds may be provided from the proceeds of life insurance policies which were taken out by the partnership itself or by individual partners. For example, if Partner A takes out a life insurance policy on Partner B and B subsequently dies, the proceeds payable to A may be used to acquire B's interest.

The UPA, in Section 42, states that a retiring or deceased partner's estate may receive interest as an ordinary creditor on that portion of the withdrawing partner's capital interest which remains in the partnership (i.e., has not yet been disbursed). In lieu of interest, the UPA states that the profits attributable to the use of the withdrawing partner's capital still retained in the partnership may be received. Once again, a partnership agreement which addresses the valuation of a withdrawing partner's interest and the means of payment is a valuable aid in properly accounting for the withdrawal of a partner.

PARTNERSHIP LIQUIDATION

The process of liquidation consists of the conversion of partnership assets into a distributable form and the distribution of these assets to creditors and owners. To achieve an orderly and legally sound liquidation, some fundamental guidelines need to be identified.

Liquidation Guidelines

The underlying theme in accounting for partnership liquidation is the equitable distribution of the assets. To be equitable, a distribution should recognize the legal rights of the partnership creditors and individual partners. All liquidation expenses and gains or losses from conversion of partnership assets must also be allocated to the partners before assets are actually distributed to the individual partners. Failure to consider these factors may result in a premature or incorrect distribution of assets to a partner. If a premature or incorrect distribution of assets cannot be recovered, the partnership fiduciary who authorized the distribution may be held liable.

Ranking of Partnership Liabilities. The UPA establishes rules governing the priority in which partnership assets are distributed to creditors and partners. Subject to any agreement to the contrary, the following sequence of payments should be observed:

1. Amounts owed to creditors other than partners.
2. Amounts owed to partners other than for capital and profits, i.e., partners' loans to the partnership.
3. Amounts owed to partners as capital.
4. Amounts owed to partners as profits not currently closed to partners' capital accounts.

Although loans from partners have a higher legal priority than amounts owed as capital and profits, the doctrine of *right of offset* sets aside this ranking in favor of procedural and economic considerations which facilitate the actual liquidation process. The effect of this doctrine is that loans due to partners are used to offset actual or anticipated debit balances in partners' capital accounts. Amounts owed to partners as capital and profits are viewed typically as one element rather than two separate priority levels. Therefore, items 2, 3, and 4 may be combined without destroying the fairness of a distribution.

Liability for Debit Capital Balances. The UPA, in Section 40, states that partners should contribute assets to the partnership to the extent of their debit balances. However, if such a contribution is not possible because of special personal or legal considerations, the debit balance will be viewed as a realization loss and allocated according to the remaining partners' profit and loss ratios. For example, assume that partners A, B, and C share in profits and losses in the ratio of 1:2:1 respectively. If C is unable to contribute any asset to eliminate a debit capital balance, that balance would be allocated to A and B in the ratio of 1:2. Partners who absorb other partners' debit capital balances have a legal claim against the deficient partner. However, the collectibility of such a claim depends on the personal wealth of the deficient partner.

Marshaling of Assets. The provisions which call for the contribution of personal assets to a liquidating partnership illustrate the characteristics of unlimited liability discussed in Chapter 14. However, such personal liability depends on the legal doctrine of *marshaling of assets*. This doctrine, which is applied when either the partnership and/or one or more of the partners are insolvent, states that:

1. Partnership assets are first available for the payment of partnership debts. Any excess assets are available for payment of the individual partner's debts, but only to the extent of the partner's interest in the capital of the partnership.
2. Personal assets of a partner are applied against personal debts, ranked in order of priority as follows:
   (a) Amounts owed to personal creditors.
   (b) Amounts owed to partnership creditors.
   (c) Amounts owed to partners by way of contribution.

Amounts owed to partners by way of contribution refers to amounts owed the partnership as represented by the partner's debit capital balance. This amount is viewed by the UPA as separate from the amounts owed to personal creditors. For example, if a partner has personal assets of $12,000 and personal liabilities of $8,000, plus a debit capital balance of $16,000, personal assets would be distributed as follows:

Payable to personal creditors	$ 8,000
Payable to partnership for debit capital balance	4,000
Total personal assets	$12,000

Under common law and federal bankruptcy law, which may be applicable when the UPA has not been adopted, amounts owed to partners by way of contribution are on an equal basis (*pari passu*) with personal creditors of the partner. According to this rule, personal assets would be distributed as follows:

Payable to personal liabilities $\left(\dfrac{\$\ 8{,}000}{\$24{,}000} \times \$12{,}000\right)$	$ 4,000
Payable to partnership for debit capital balance $\left(\dfrac{\$16{,}000}{\$24{,}000} \times \$12{,}000\right)$	8,000
Total personal assets	$12,000

The legal doctrine of marshaling of assets is demonstrated by the following cases:

Case A—Insolvent Partners

The partnership is solvent, with total assets of $16,000 and total liabilities of $9,000. Information relating to the individual partners is as follows:

	Partner A	Partner B
Total personal assets	$10,000	$15,000
Total personal liabilities	13,000	18,000
Partnership capital balances	5,000	2,000

Analysis: Unsatisfied personal creditors may attach a partner's interest in the solvent partnership, but only to the extent of the partner's capital balance. Thus, unsatisfied personal creditors could seek recourse as follows:

	Partner A	Partner B
Unsatisfied personal creditors	$3,000	$3,000
Interest in partnership capital available to personal creditors	(3,000)	(2,000)
Personal liabilities not satisfied	0	$1,000

Case B—Insolvent Partnership

The partnership is insolvent, with total assets of $23,000 and total liabilities of $25,000. Information relating to individual partners is as follows:

	Partner A	Partner B
Total personal assets	$10,000	$ 8,000
Total personal liabilities	6,000	7,000
Partnership capital balances	500	(2,500)

Analysis: Unsatisfied partnership creditors may seek recourse from the individual partners in accordance with a proper marshaling of assets as reflected in Illustration I on page 665.

Illustration I—Distribution of Assets—Insolvent Partnership

	Partner A		Partner B		AB Partnership			
	Assets	Liab.	Assets	Liab.	Assets	Liab.	A, Capital	B, Capital
Beginning balances [1] ..	$10,000	$6,000	$8,000	$7,000	$23,000	$25,000	$ 500	$(2,500)
Payment of liabilities ..	(6,000)	(6,000)	(7,000)	(7,000)	(23,000)	(23,000)	—	—
	$ 4,000	0	$1,000	0	0	$ 2,000	$ 500	$(2,500)
Payment of partnership creditors [2]	(2,000)					(2,000)	2,000	
	$ 2,000	0	$1,000	0	0	0	$2,500	$(2,500)
Payment toward debit capital balance [3]			(1,000)		$ 1,000			1,000
	$ 2,000	0	0	0	$ 1,000	0	$2,500	$(1,500)
Capital distribution to A	1,000				(1,000)		(1,000)	
Balances [4]	$ 3,000	0	0	0	0	0	$1,500	$(1,500)

[1] Beginning asset balances represent realizable values.

[2] Unsatisfied partnership creditors may claim the net personal assets of a solvent partner, regardless of the amount of the partner's interest in the capital of the partnership. A's capital interest is increased by the payment of partnership liabilities.

[3] If the payment toward the debit capital balance had preceded B's payment of personal liabilities, a proper marshaling of assets would not have been achieved and B's personal creditors would not have been satisfied.

[4] If B later pays the debit capital balance, the funds would be distributed to A. However, if B cannot pay, the loss will be borne by A.

Case C—Insolvent Partner and Partnership

The partnership is insolvent, with total assets of $20,000 and total liabilities of $25,000. Information relating to individual partners is as follows:

	Partner A	Partner B
Total personal assets	$13,000	$12,000
Total personal liabilities	10,000	15,000
Partnership capital balances	(7,000)	2,000

Analysis: Partner B is insolvent also, and the recourse B's personal creditors have against the partnership depends upon A's future contribution to the partnership. Illustration II below reflects the distribution of assets in accordance with the marshaling concept.

Illustration II—Distribution of Assets—Insolvent Partner and Partnership

	Partner A		Partner B		AB Partnership			
	Assets	Liab.	Assets	Liab.	Assets	Liab.	A, Capital	B, Capital
Beginning balances[1]	$13,000	$10,000	$12,000	$15,000	$20,000	$25,000	$(7,000)	$2,000
Payment of liabilities	(10,000)	(10,000)	(12,000)	(12,000)	(20,000)	(20,000)		
	$ 3,000	0	0	$ 3,000	0	$ 5,000	$(7,000)	$2,000
Payment of partner- ship creditors ...	(3,000)					(3,000)	3,000	
Balances[2]	0	0	0	$ 3,000[3]	0	$ 2,000	$(4,000)	$2,000

[1] Beginning asset balances represent realizable values.

[2] If A later pays $4,000 to the partnership to eliminate the debit capital balance, the payment will be allocated first to the partnership liabilities and then to B. However, if A is not able to make a payment, claims against the partnership by the creditors and B will be totally uncollectible.

[3] The unsatisfied personal creditors of B are unable to seek recovery against the credit capital balance of B because the partnership itself is not solvent.

Lump Sum Liquidations

The guidelines discussed in the preceding section are important factors influencing the procedural and legal aspects of a partnership liquidation. Upon liquidation of a partnership, the amount of assets ultimately to be distributed to the individual partners is determined through the use of either a lump sum liquidation schedule or an installment liquidation schedule.

A lump sum liquidation requires that all assets be realized before a distribution is made to partners, thus avoiding the possibility of a premature distribution. To illustrate a lump sum liquidation, assume the following:

1. Asset, liability, loan, and capital balances are as shown in Illustration III, after books for the final operational period are closed.
2. Profit and loss percentages for partners A, B, and C are 40%, 40%, and 20% respectively.
3. Personal assets and debts of the partners are as follows:

	A	B	C
Total personal assets	$30,000	$40,000	$20,000
Total personal liabilities	10,000	37,200	24,000

4. Sales of assets are as follows:

Date	Book Value	Selling Price	Gain (Loss)
February 15	$50,000	$60,000	$10,000
March 2	30,000	10,000	(20,000)
March 7	40,000	20,000	(20,000)

Illustration III, on page 667, presents the lump sum distribution and demonstrates the following concepts which were previously discussed:

1. Gains and losses on realization are allocated according to the partners' profit and loss ratios.
2. Claims against the partnership are paid in the proper order.
3. The marshaling of assets doctrine is followed to determine the disposition of B's and C's debit balances in their capital accounts. That is, a partner's personal assets are first used to satisfy personal liabilities. Then, to the extent possible, remaining assets are contributed to the partnership to eliminate debit capital balances.
4. C's debit capital balance is charged against A, the only personally solvent partner.
5. Partner A will have a claim against C's personal assets for the debit balance which was absorbed.

Installment Liquidations

The complete liquidation process might easily extend over several months or longer, and it may not be possible to postpone payments to creditors and partners until all assets have been realized. Payments may therefore be made on an installment basis to creditors and partners during the liquidation process. To avoid the problem associated with premature payments, installment payments may be made to partners only after anticipating all liabilities, possible losses, and liquidation expenses. To provide a proper solution to installment liquidations, either a schedule of safe payments is prepared as amounts become available for distribution, or a predistribution plan is used to direct the distribution of any available sum.

Illustration III—Lump Sum Liquidation Statement

	Cash	Noncash Assets	Liabilities	Loan from A	Capital Balances A	B	C
Beginning balances	$10,000	$120,000	$80,000	$9,000	$25,000	$10,000	$6,000
February 15, sale of assets at a gain	60,000	(50,000)			4,000	4,000	2,000
March 2, sale of assets at a loss	10,000	(30,000)			(8,000)	(8,000)	(4,000)
Payment of liquidation expenses	(2,000)				(800)	(800)	(400)
March 7, sale of assets at a loss	20,000	(40,000)			(8,000)	(8,000)	(4,000)
Balances	$98,000	0	$80,000	$9,000	$12,200	$ (2,800)	$ (400)
Payment of liabilities	(80,000)		(80,000)				
Balances	$18,000	0	0	$9,000	$12,200	$ (2,800)	$ (400)
B's contribution	2,800					2,800	
Balances	$20,800	0	0	$9,000	$12,200	0	$ (400)
Absorption of C's balance					(400)		400
Balances	$20,800	0	0	$9,000	$11,800	0	0
Payment to A	(20,800)			(9,000)	(11,800)		
Final balances	0	0	0	0	0	0	0

Schedule of Safe Payments. The possibility of premature payments to partners is reduced by using a schedule of safe payments, which reflects a conservative approach to liquidation. The schedule indicates how available funds should be distributed to partners. It is based on the anticipation of all possible liabilities and expenses, including those expected to be incurred in the process of liquidation. The effect of these items on partnership capital is allocated among the partners according to their profit and loss agreement.

In keeping with the conservative approach, the schedule is also based on the assumption that all noncash assets will be worthless; therefore, the assumed loss is allocated among the partners according to their profit and loss ratios. The allocation of these assumed losses could produce debit balances in partners' capital accounts, and these balances are estimated to be uncollectible. Therefore, the assumed debit capital balances are allocated to those partners with credit balances according to their profit and loss ratios. When the allocation of estimated liabilities, expenses, liquidation losses, and debit balances is completed, assets may be distributed safely to the partners in amounts equal to the resulting credit capital balances.

A new schedule of safe payments is prepared each time a distribution to partners is scheduled. These schedules support an installment liquidation statement, which summarizes changes in real account balances as the liquidation proceeds. When the partners' capital balances are in the profit and loss ratio, all partners will share in a given distribution. All future distributions to partners will be allocated automatically according to their profit ratios, thus eliminating the need for another schedule of safe payments.

To illustrate the use of schedules of safe payments in conjunction with an installment liquidation, assume the following:

1. Asset, liability, loan, and capital balances are shown in Illustration IV, after books for the final operational period are closed.
2. Profit and loss percentages for partners A, B, and C are 40%, 40%, and 20% respectively.
3. Sales of assets are as follows:

Date	Book Value	Selling Price	Gain (Loss)
February 15	$60,000	$40,000	$(20,000)
March 2	30,000	15,000	(15,000)
March 17	10,000	20,000	10,000
April 1	20,000	24,000	4,000

4. Liquidation expenses are estimated to be $10,000. Cash is to be restricted in that amount until expenses are paid.
5. Installment distributions of unrestricted cash are made on February 17, March 5, March 18, and April 2.
6. Total liquidation expenses of $8,000 are paid on March 4.

Illustration IV, on page 669, is based on these facts, and demonstrates the following concepts:

1. Gains and losses on realization are allocated according to the partners' profit and loss ratios.
2. Unsold noncash assets are assumed to be worthless for purposes of determining the safe payments to partners.
3. Loan balances are combined with capital balances according to the right of offset doctrine. This offset can result in partners receiving distributions of capital before other partners' loan accounts have been paid (as in the February 17 distribution in Illustration IV). However, such distributions may be placed in escrow until it is certain that debit balances will not develop in these partners' capital accounts.
4. Typically, the doctrine of marshaling of assets is ignored until all assets have been realized, at which time debit balances in partners'

Illustration IV—Installment Liquidation Statement

	Cash	Noncash Assets	Liabilities	Loan From A	A	B	C
					Capital Balances		
Beginning balances	$10,000	$120,000	$30,000	$5,000	$25,000	$55,000	$15,000
February 15, sale of assets	40,000	(60,000)			(8,000)	(8,000)	(4,000)
Balances	$50,000	$ 60,000	$30,000	$5,000	$17,000	$47,000	$11,000
Payment of liabilities	(30,000)		(30,000)				
February 17, distribution (Schedule A)	(10,000)					(10,000)	
Balances	$10,000	$ 60,000	0	$5,000	$17,000	$37,000	$11,000
March 2, sale of assets	15,000	(30,000)			(6,000)	(6,000)	(3,000)
Payment of liquidation expenses	(8,000)				(3,200)	(3,200)	(1,600)
Balances	$17,000	$ 30,000	0	$5,000	$ 7,800	$27,800	$ 6,400
March 5, distribution (Schedule A)	(17,000)			(800)		(15,800)	(400)
Balances	0	$ 30,000	0	$4,200	$ 7,800	$12,000	$ 6,000
March 17, sale of assets ...	$20,000	(10,000)			4,000	4,000	2,000
Balances	$20,000	$ 20,000	0	$4,200	$11,800	$16,000	$ 8,000
March 18, distribution (Schedule A)	(20,000)			(4,200)	(3,800)	(8,000)	(4,000)
Balances	0	$ 20,000	0	0	$ 8,000	$ 8,000	$ 4,000
April 1, sale of assets	$24,000	(20,000)			1,600	1,600	800
Balances	$24,000	0	0	0	$ 9,600	$ 9,600	$ 4,800
Final distribution	(24,000)				(9,600)	(9,600)	(4,800)
Balances	0	0	0	0	0	0	0

Schedule A—Schedule of Safe Payments

	A	B	C	Total
Profit and loss percentage	40%	40%	20%	100%
February 17 Distribution				
Combined capital and loan balances before distribution	$22,000	$47,000	$11,000	$80,000
Estimated liquidation expenses	(4,000)	(4,000)	(2,000)	(10,000)
Balances	$18,000	$43,000	$ 9,000	$70,000
Maximum loss possible	(24,000)	(24,000)	(12,000)	(60,000)
Balances	$ (6,000)	$19,000	$ (3,000)	$10,000
Allocation of debit capital balances	6,000	(9,000)	3,000	0
Safe payment	0	$10,000	0	$10,000
March 5 Distribution				
Combined capital and loan balances before distribution	$12,800	$27,800	$ 6,400	$47,000
Maximum loss possible	(12,000)	(12,000)	(6,000)	(30,000)
Safe payments	$ 800	$15,800	$ 400	$17,000
March 18 Distribution (schedule not required)				
Combined capital and loan balances before distribution	$16,000	$16,000	$ 8,000	$40,000
Maximum loss possible	(8,000)	(8,000)	(4,000)	(20,000)
Safe payments	$ 8,000	$ 8,000	$ 4,000	$20,000

capital accounts may be satisfied through contributions of personal assets.

5. The schedule of safe payments is an iterative process which will cease when a schedule indicates that a given distribution will be shared among all partners. Further distributions will be allocated among the partners according to their profit and loss ratios. For example, when the March 5 distribution in Schedule A indicates that all partners will receive a portion of the distribution, the distribution on March 18 would be made in the profit and loss ratio, with results identical to those which would be indicated by continuing the schedule of safe payments:

Partner	(1) Total Distribution to All Partners	(2) Partner's Profit and Loss Percentage	(1) × (2) Amount To Be Distributed	Amount To Be Distributed per Schedule of Safe Payments
A	$20,000	40%	$ 8,000	$ 8,000
B	20,000	40	8,000	8,000
C	20,000	20	4,000	4,000
			$20,000	$20,000

6. The partner with the greatest ability to absorb anticipated losses (i.e., preserves a credit capital balance after allocating anticipated losses) will be the first to receive a safe payment.

Predistribution Plan. Schedules of safe payments provide a means of guaranteeing the propriety of installment distributions to partners, especially in complex situations. However, a predistribution plan provides a less tedious means of determining distributions to partners. The predistribution plan is prepared in advance of actual distributions, and provides the user with information regarding the order and amount of all future distributions. As was the case with schedules of safe payments, the predistribution plan (1) combines partners' loan balances with their capital balances; (2) anticipates all possible liabilities, losses on realization, and liquidation expenses; and (3) recognizes that the partner with the greatest ability to absorb anticipated losses will be the first partner to receive safe payments.

To prepare the predistribution plan, all anticipated but unrecorded liabilities and liquidation expenses are allocated to the various partners' capital balances according to their profit and loss ratios. The resulting capital balances are then evaluated to determine the maximum loss from realization which could be absorbed by the partners before a debit balance is created in their respective capital accounts. As suggested by the schedule of safe payments, the partner who maintains a credit capital balance after assuming that all noncash assets are worthless is the partner with the greatest ability to absorb realization losses. Therefore, that partner will be the first to receive an actual distribution of assets.

The maximum loss a partner could absorb (maximum loss absorbable), before a debit balance in the partner's capital account is created, is determined by the following calculation:

$$\text{Maximum Loss Absorbable (MLA)} \ = \ \frac{\text{Partner's Capital Balance}}{\text{Partner's Profit and Loss Percentage}}$$

Since the partner with the largest MLA will be the first to receive an actual distribution, the MLA's can be used to indicate the order in which partners will receive distributions. However, it should be noted that the MLA's do not indicate the amounts of the distributions. To illustrate, assume that a partnership consists of three partners (A, B, and C) who have capital balances, before the realization of noncash assets, of $70,000, $60,000, and $40,000 respectively, and profit and loss percentages of 35%, 25%, and 40%. The maximum losses absorbable by Partners A, B, and C are determined as follows:

Partner	(1) Capital Balance	(2) Profit and Loss Percentage	(1) ÷ (2) Maximum Loss Absorbable	Rank
A	$70,000	35%	$200,000	Second
B	60,000	25	240,000	First
C	40,000	40	100,000	Third

If all partners had identical maximum losses absorbable, then all partners would share in any given distribution. Therefore, the amount of any distribution to be paid to a particular partner can be determined by calculating the distributions needed ultimately to give all partners the same maximum loss absorbable. In the present example, if B's capital balance were reduced to $50,000 as the result of an actual distribution of $10,000, B's new maximum loss absorbable would be equal to A's original maximum loss absorbable, as follows:

Partner	(1) Capital Balance	(2) Profit and Loss Percentage	(1) ÷ (2) Maximum Loss Absorbable
A	$70,000	35%	$200,000
B	50,000	25	200,000
C	40,000	40	100,000

Therefore, the first $10,000, or any portion thereof which is available for distribution to partners, should be paid entirely to Partner B.

If A's capital balance were reduced to $35,000 and B's capital balance were reduced to $25,000 as the result of actual distributions of $35,000 and $25,000 respectively to these partners, all partners would then have equivalent maximum losses absorbable. Thus, the predistribution plan suggests that the next $60,000 available, or any portion thereof which is available for distribution to partners, should be paid to Partners A and B according to profit ratios of 35:25 respectively, and that all further distributions should be divided among all partners according to their respective profit ratios.

The process of preparing the predistribution plan is summarized as follows:

1. Calculate each partner's maximum loss absorbable.

2. Rank partners in descending order according to the amount of their maximum loss absorbable.
3. Determine what amount must be paid to the partner ranked first to achieve equality between the maximum losses absorbable of that partner and the second-ranked partner. This amount represents the safe payment that can be paid to the first-ranked partner.
4. Determine what amount must be paid in total to those partners having equivalent maximum losses absorbable so that their new maximum losses absorbable would be equal to that of the next highest-ranked partner. This amount would be divided among the partners receiving the distribution according to their profit ratios.
5. Continue Step 4 until all partners have equivalent maximum losses absorbable.
6. When all partners have equal maximum losses absorbable, distributions would be allocated according to the partners' profit ratios.

To demonstrate this entire process, the following facts are used as the basis for the predistribution plan in Illustration V on page 673:

	Partner		
	A	B	C
Profit and loss percentage	30%	50%	20%
Combined capital and loan balance	$33,000	$45,000	$14,000

Total liabilities of the partnership equal $20,000.
Total liquidation expenses are expected to be $10,000.

To relate the predistribution plan in Illustration V to an actual distribution, assume that distributions are made as follows:

Date	Amount	Purpose
February 15	$20,000	pay liabilities
March 1	5,000	pay partners
March 15............................	8,000	pay liquidation expenses
March 27............................	9,000	pay partners
April 4	30,000	pay partners

Rather than constructing numerous schedules of safe payments to determine the recipients of these distributions, the predistribution plan indicates the following distribution:

				Payable to			Level
Date	Amount	Lia-bilities	Liquidation Expenses	A	B	C	per Plan (Illus. V)
Feb. 15	$20,000	$20,000					I
Mar. 1	5,000			$ 5,000			III
Mar. 15......	8,000		$ 8,000				II
Mar. 27......	9,000			1,000			III
				3,000	$ 5,000		IV
Apr. 4	30,000			3,000	5,000		IV
				6,600	11,000	$ 4,400	V
	$72,000	$20,000	$ 8,000	$18,600	$21,000	$ 4,400	

Several aspects of this distribution need to be emphasized. First of all, notice that actual payments to partners precede the payment of the liquidation expenses. This action is acceptable because the computations in Illustration V had already allowed for liquidation expenses of $10,000. However, if liquidation expenses exceed the estimated amount of $10,000, previous payments to partners could prove to be premature and ultimately could require repayments from partners to the partnership. Another important feature is that all payments required by a specific level of the plan shown in Illustration V must be satisfied to whatever extent possible before another level of the plan is entered. Finally, when a particular distribution is divided among several partners, the amount is allocated to the sharing partners according to their respective profit ratios.

Illustration V—Predistribution Plan

Computation of Payments to Partners

	Capital Balances			Maximum Loss Absorbable		
	A	B	C	A	B	C
(1) Profit and loss percentage	30%	50%	20%			
Capital and loan balance	$33,000	$45,000	$14,000			
Allocate expected liquidation expenses .	(3,000)	(5,000)	(2,000)			
(2) Balances	$30,000	$40,000	$12,000			
Maximum loss absorbable (MLA) [(2) ÷ (1)]				$100,000	$80,000	$60,000
(3) Amount needed to reduce highest-ranked MLA to next highest-ranked MLA				(20,000)		
New MLA's				$ 80,000	$80,000	$60,000
(4) Reduction in capital (payment) needed to achieve reduction in MLA [(3) × (1)] ..	(6,000)					
(5) New capital balance [(2) − (4)]	$24,000	$40,000	$12,000			
(6) Amount needed to reduce highest-ranked MLA's to next highest-ranked MLA				(20,000)	(20,000)	
New MLA's				$ 60,000	$60,000	$60,000
(7) Reduction in capital (payment) needed to achieve reduction in MLA [(6) × (1)] ..	(6,000)	(10,000)				
(8) New capital balance [(5) − (7)]	$18,000	$30,000	$12,000			

When MLA's are equal, future distributions are allocated to all partners according to their profit and loss percentage.

				Payable to		
Level	Amount	Liabilities	Estimated Liquidation Expenses	A	B	C
I	First $20,000	$20,000				
II	Next $10,000		$10,000			
III	Next $ 6,000			100%		
IV	Next $16,000			37.5% (3/8)	62.5% (5/8)	
V	Any additional payments			30%	50%	20%

QUESTIONS

1. What is meant by dissolution and what are the causes of it?
2. What factors might be responsible for goodwill being traceable to an established partnership? to an incoming partner?
3. A student of accounting comments that: "The bonus method of accounting for changes in ownership is employed in only those cases where goodwill or unrealized appreciation is absent." Discuss the student's comment.
4. How is the amount of goodwill traceable to either old or new partners determined?
5. Why is the bonus method of accounting for ownership changes more widely used in practice?
6. If a partner's interest in the partnership is sold to a new partner, how does the partnership record this exchange? Explain.
7. In the liquidation process, what would be the possible effect of a failure to estimate liquidation expenses?
8. In what order must partnership assets be distributed? What might be the consequences of not observing this order?
9. Explain the right of offset and its significance in the liquidation process.
10. How is a partner's debit capital balance treated if the partner is personally solvent? personally insolvent?
11. What is the doctrine of marshaling of assets, and when is it applicable to a partnership?
12. If a partner's personal assets include an uncollected loan to the partnership, what constraints would affect personal creditors seeking repayment of the loan by the partnership?

EXERCISES

Exercise 1. Partners Crawford and Dinsworth share profits and losses equally and have equal capital investments of $15,000 each. On July 1, 19X1, McEnvale is admitted to the partnership with a one-third interest in profits and capital in exchange for a cash contribution of $12,000.
(1) Prepare journal entries to show three possible methods of recording in the partnership books the admission of McEnvale.
(2) State the conditions under which each method would be appropriate.

Exercise 2. Red, White, and Blue are partners in a business, and share in its profits at the respective rates of 50%, 30%, and 20%. At the beginning of the new fiscal year, they admit Green, who is to invest in the firm sufficient cash to have a one-third interest in the partnership and profits. The following trial balance is taken from the original partnership's records:

Cash	100,000	
Marketable Securities	75,000	
Accounts Receivable	225,000	
Accounts Payable......................................		50,000
Long-Term Notes Payable		30,000
Red, Capital		175,000
White, Capital		100,000
Blue, Capital		45,000
	400,000	400,000

The securities have a market value of $50,000, and an allowance of $25,000 is expected to cover collection losses on the receivables. No other adjustments of the net assets are considered necessary; however, the three partners among themselves must bring the balances in their capital accounts into agreement with their interest in profits.

(1) What amount must be invested by Green?
(2) What settlement is made between the partners?
(3) Prepare the entry to adjust the capital accounts.
(4) What are the balances in the partners' capital accounts after Green's admission?

Exercise 3. The partnership of Barker, McDonald, and Williams plans to purchase the equity of its withdrawing partner, Barker. A price of $134,550 has been agreed upon. Additional information regarding the partnership is as follows:

	Barker	McDonald	Williams
Capital balance	$114,750	$63,750	$76,500
Profit and loss percentage	55%	20%	25%
Percentage interest in capital	45%	25%	30%

(1) Prepare journal entries on the partnership books to record Barker's withdrawal under the bonus method and under both alternatives of the goodwill method. State the conditions under which each method would be appropriate.
(2) Assume that any difference between the book value and fair market value of Barker's equity is due to the undervaluation of existing assets on the partnership books. Prepare journal entries to record Barker's withdrawal and the asset appreciation traceable to (1) the entire partnership and (2) Barker's interest only.

Exercise 4. The J & L partnership has total assets of $20,000 and total liabilities of $26,000. Information relating to individual partners is as follows:

	Jacoby	Larson
Total personal assets	$21,000	$25,000
Total personal liabilities..........................	16,000	20,000
Partnership capital balance	(8,000)	2,000

(1) Prepare a schedule showing the correct distribution of assets in accordance with the marshaling of assets.
(2) Prepare a schedule showing the correct distribution of assets in accordance with the federal bankruptcy law.
(3) Discuss which distribution seems more equitable, and give reasons for its equitableness.

Exercise 5. The JKL Construction Company, a partnership, has total assets of $149,000 and total liabilities of $165,000. Assume the following information relating to the individual partners:

	Jason	Kelly	Linden
Total personal assets	$52,000	$41,500	$28,000
Total personal liabilities	47,000	33,500	34,000
Partnership capital balance	7,000	3,000	(26,000)
Profit and loss percentage	50%	30%	20%

If Linden inherits $16,000 after liquidation of the JKL partnership, what will be the priority and amount of claims existing against the $16,000? What claims (who and how much) remain unsatisfied?

Exercise 6. The following balance sheet is for the partnership of Thomas, James, and Carson, who share profits and losses in the ratio of 4:3:1 respectively:

Assets		Liabilities and Capital	
Cash	$ 45,000	Liabilities	$ 92,000
Other assets	297,000	Thomas, capital	160,000
		James, capital	65,000
		Carson, capital	25,000
Total assets	$342,000	Total liabilities and capital	$342,000

(1) Assume that the assets and liabilities are valued fairly, and that the partnership wishes to admit Rollo as a new partner with a one-fifth interest in capital. Without recording goodwill or bonus, determine what Rollo's contribution should be.
(2) If Rollo contributes $88,000, determine the new capital balances of each partner, using (1) the bonus method, and (2) the goodwill method.
(3) If the partnership decides to liquidate the business rather than admit Rollo, determine the cash distribution to each partner if the other assets are sold for $249,000.

Exercise 7. The balance sheet for the partnership of A, B, and C is as follows:

Assets		Liabilities and Capital	
Cash	$ 20,000	Liabilities	$ 50,000
Other assets	180,000	A, capital	37,000
		B, capital	65,000
		C, capital	48,000
Total assets	$200,000	Total liabilities and capital	$200,000

The partners share profits and losses in the ratio of 4:4:2 respectively.
(1) Assuming that liquidation expenses will be negligible, prepare a predistribution plan for the partnership.
(2) If the first sale of noncash assets having a book value of $90,000 realizes $50,000, and all cash available after paying creditors is distributed, determine the respective amount each partner would receive.

Exercise 8. Illustration IV, on page 669, provides the information necessary for an installment liquidation and determines the safe payments to be made at each distribution of assets as they become available.
(1) Using the information in Illustration IV, prepare a predistribution plan and

compare the results with the schedule of safe payments.

(2) Should the results be the same? Explain.

Exercise 9. The P.D.Q. Partnership is being dissolved. All liabilities have been distributed and the assets on hand are being realized gradually. The following details indicate the equity of the various partners:

	Capital Account	Loans to (from) Partnership	Profit and Loss Ratio
P	$20,500	$15,000	4
D	23,000	—	4
Q	9,000	(5,000)	2

Prepare a predistribution plan.

PROBLEMS

Problem 15-1. Richardson and George have been partners in the medical supply business since July 18, 19X3. Since the formation of the partnership, profits and losses have been shared in the ratio of 55:45 respectively. Capital balances on December 31, 19X7, were $159,000 for Richardson and $106,000 for George. They have agreed to admit Keller as a partner on January 1, 19X8. Keller will receive a 30% interest in partnership capital, and future profits and losses will be allocated equally among the partners.

Required:

Prepare journal entries in the partnership books to record Keller's admission in each of the following situations:

(1) Keller deals directly with Richardson and agrees to exchange land with a book value of $60,000 and a fair market value of $87,000 for 50% of Richardson's interest in capital. Record Keller's contribution under the two alternative methods. What assumption is made under each alternative?

(2) Keller contributes $130,000 cash and a one-year note with a value of $20,000 to the partnership entity. Record journal entries under the bonus and goodwill methods.

(3) Using the bonus method, assume that: (1) Keller contributes $84,000 and an established clientele, or (2) Keller's contribution of $84,000 is sufficient because existing partnership assets are overvalued.

(4) Keller invests $84,000 in the partnership entity. Use the goodwill method and assume that net assets should not be written down.

Problem 15-2. The partnership of Baker, Carlson, and Dill is adjusting its accounting reports to convert them uniformly to the accrual basis in anticipation of admitting Thompson as a new partner. Some accounts are on the accrual basis and others are on the cash basis. The partnership's books were closed and the trial balance at the top of page 678 was prepared as of December 31, 19X6.

Inquiries disclosed the following:

(a) The partnership was organized on January 1, 19X5, with no provision in the partnership agreement for the distribution of profits and losses. During

Cash	10,000	
Accounts Receivable	40,000	
Inventory	26,000	
Land	9,000	
Building	50,000	
Accumulated Depreciation—Building		2,000
Equipment	56,000	
Accumulated Depreciation—Equipment		6,000
Goodwill...	5,000	
Accounts Payable..		55,000
Allowance for Future Inventory Losses		3,000
Baker, Capital		40,000
Carlson, Capital...		60,000
Dill, capital		30,000
	196,000	196,000

19X5, profits were distributed equally among the partners. The partnership agreement was amended effective January 1, 19X6, to provide for the following profit and loss percentages: Baker, 50%; Carlson, 30%; and Dill, 20%. The amended partnership agreement also stated that the accounting records were to be maintained on the accrual basis and that any adjustments necessary for 19X5 should be allocated according to the 19X5 distribution of profits.

(b) The following amounts were not recorded as prepayments or accruals:

	December 31	
	19X5	*19X6*
Prepaid insurance...................	$ 650	$700
Advance from customers	1,100	200
Accrued interest expense...........	450	

The advances from customers were recorded as sales in the year cash was received.

(c) In 19X6, the partnership recorded a provision of $3,000 for an anticipated decline in inventory prices. The provision was unnecessary and inconsistent with good accounting procedure and should be reversed.

(d) The partnership expensed equipment which was purchased for $4,400 on January 7, 19X6. This equipment has an estimated life of ten years and an estimated salvage value of $400. The partnership depreciates its capitalized equipment under the declining-balance method at twice the straight-line depreciation rate.

(e) The partners agreed to establish an allowance for doubtful accounts at 2% of current accounts receivable and 5% of past due accounts. At December 31, 19X5, the partnership had $54,000 of accounts receivable, of which only $4,000 were past due. At December 31, 19X6, 15% of accounts receivable were past due, of which $4,000 represented sales made in 19X5, although they were considered collectible. The partnership had written off uncollectible accounts in the year the accounts became worthless as follows:

	Account Written Off In	
	19X6	*19X5*
19X6 account......................	$ 800	
19X5 account......................	1,000	$250

(f) Goodwill was recorded on the books in 19X6 and credited to the partners' capital accounts in the profit and loss ratio in recognition of an increase in the value of the business resulting from improved sales volume. The partners agreed to write off the goodwill before admitting the new partner.

Required:

(1) Prepare a work sheet showing the adjustments and the adjusted trial balance for the partnership on the accrual basis at December 31, 19X6. All adjustments affecting income should be made directly to the partners' capital accounts.

(2) On December 31, 19X6, Thompson invested $55,000 in the partnership. Assuming that the total capital for Baker, Carlson, and Dill is $140,000, compute the amount of goodwill to be allocated to each partner under each of the following alternative agreements:

(a) Thompson is to be granted a one-fourth interest in the partnership. The original partners will share profits and losses in the same proportion as they had before the admission of Thompson.

(b) The partnership expects to continue to earn an annual return of 15% on invested capital. The normal rate of return for a comparable partnership is 10%. The expected earnings of the new partnership in excess of the normal rate of return are to be capitalized as goodwill at the rate of 20%. The partners are to share profits and losses as follows: Baker, 40%; Carlson, 30%; Dill, 20%; Thompson, 10%.

(AICPA adapted)

Problem 15-3. Foley, Farnsworth, and Frattney have been partners in a law office for 15 years. Farnsworth has decided to retire from the partnership. To facilitate Farnsworth's withdrawal, the partnership closed its books and prepared the following balance sheet:

Assets		Liabilities and Capital	
Cash	$ 53,000	Accounts payable	$ 10,000
Accounts receivable (net)	12,000	Foley, capital	25,000
Books	20,000	Farnsworth, capital	40,000
Other assets (net).............	15,000	Frattney, capital	25,000
Total assets	$100,000	Total liabilities and capital	$100,000

Foley, Farnsworth, and Frattney share profits and losses in the ratio of 3:4:3 respectively.

Required:

Prepare the necessary journal entries on the books of the partnership to record the withdrawal of Farnsworth in each of the following situations:

(1) The partnership agrees that the books and other assets are undervalued by $6,000 and $4,000 respectively. Farnsworth is to receive a lump sum cash payment.

(2) Farnsworth is to receive $20,000 now and $16,000 in monthly installments of $2,000 each. Use the bonus method.

(3) Farnsworth is to receive $30,000 now and $3,000 at the end of each of the next 6 months.

(continued)

    (a) Use the bonus method.

    (b) Use the goodwill method and determine two possible amounts for goodwill. Discuss the advantages and disadvantages of recording the respective amounts of goodwill.

  (4) With the partners' consent, Daily purchases Farnsworth's interest in the partnership for $50,000.

Problem 15-4. V, W, and X decide to practice law together as of January 1, 19X5. They entered into an agreement by which they share profits and losses in the proportion of 50%, 25%, and 25% respectively, and agree to contribute a total of $50,000 of working capital in these same proportions. The activity of the partnership will be accounted for on a cash basis.

On January 1, 19X6, W died and the remaining partners agreed to admit Y, who would have a 20% share in the profits with a minimum guaranteed amount of $10,000 per year, whether operations are profitable or not. V and X will have profit and loss percentages of 45% and 35% respectively. On December 31, 19X6, X decides to retire. X's name is to be used in further partnerships in exchange for an annual fee of $15,000, which is to be treated as an expense of the partnership.

As of January 1, 19X7, a partnership is formed in which X's name is utilized in accordance with the proposal and to which Z is admitted. The partners' interests in profits from this partnership are as follows: V, 55%; Y, 30%; and Z, 15%.

Since there were no substantial accruals at the end of the year, disbursements for expenses made during any one period were treated as expenses of the then current partnership. These disbursements were $70,000 in 19X5, $80,000 in 19X6, and $90,000 in 19X7.

Receipts of fees were as follows:

	Earned by Partnership		
	No. 1	No. 2	No. 3
19X5	$ 80,000		
19X6	145,000	$40,000	
19X7		50,000	$70,000

All fees and expenses of the partnership are closed out through the partners' drawing accounts.

Each new partnership agreement provided for the newly created partnership to purchase from the old partnership the $50,000 capital originally paid in by V, W, and X. The agreement also provided that the partners should bear the cost of acquisition of this amount in the proportion by which they shared profits and losses. However, it was agreed that an incoming partner, or one acquiring an increased percentage, need not make a contribution in cash immediately but would have a charge made to a drawing account. All such partners availed themselves of this privilege. Partners selling all or a part of their interest or capital are credited through their drawing account and immediately withdraw the amount of such credit. In addition to drawings made under this agreement, the partners or their heirs made cash drawings as follows:

	V	W	X	Y	Z
19X5	$10,500	$27,750	$13,750		
19X6	40,000	4,750	5,000	$7,000	
19X7	10,000	5,000	15,000	2,500	$5,000

Required:

Prepare schedules or statements showing the details of transactions in the partners' drawing accounts and capital accounts for each of the years involved. These accounts should be in such form that each year-end balance, which was available for withdrawal, is shown in each partner's drawing account. The capital accounts are to reflect in total only the $50,000 original investment.

(AICPA adapted)

Problem 15-5. Financial statements are being prepared for the partnership of Bates, Smith, and Williams as of June 30, 19X7. The following information was obtained from the partnership agreement as amended and from the accounting records:

(1) The partnership was formed originally by Bates and Jefferson on July 1, 19X6. At that date:

    (a) Jefferson contributed $400,000 cash.

    (b) Bates contributed land, buildings, and equipment with fair market values of $110,000, $520,000, and $185,000 respectively. The land and buildings were subject to a mortgage securing an 8% per annum note (interest rate of similar notes at July 1, 19X6). The note is due in quarterly payments of $5,000 plus interest on January 1, April 1, July 1, and October 1 of each year. Bates made the July 1, 19X6 principal and interest payment personally. The partnership then assumed the obligation for the remaining $300,000.

    (c) The agreement further provided that Bates had contributed a certain intangible benefit to the partnership from many years of business activity in the area to be serviced by the new partnership. The assigned value of this intangible asset plus net intangible assets contributed gave Bates a 60% initial capital interest.

    (d) Bates was designated the only active partner at an annual salary of $24,000 plus an annual bonus of 4% of net income after deducting salary but before deducting interest on partners' capital investments. Both the salary and the bonus are viewed as operating expenses of the partnership.

    (e) Each partner is to receive a 6% return on average capital investment, and such interest is to be an expense of the partnership.

    (f) All remaining profits or losses are to be shared equally.

(2) On October 1, 19X6, Jefferson sold rights and partnership interest as of July 1, 19X6, to Williams for $370,000. Bates agreed to accept Williams as a partner if Williams would contribute sufficient cash to meet the October 1, 19X6 principal and interest payment on the mortgage note. Williams made the payment from personal funds.

(3) On January 1, 19X7, Bates and Williams admitted Smith as a new partner. Smith invested $150,000 cash for a 10% capital interest based on the initial investments of Bates and Jefferson at July 1, 19X6. On January 1, 19X6, the book value of the partnership's assets and liabilities approximated their fair market values. Similar to other partners, Smith is to receive a 6% return on average capital investment. Smith is also entitled to 20% of the partnership's profits or losses as defined above. However, for the year ended June 30, 19X7, Smith is to receive only one half of the pro rata share of the profits or losses. The remaining partnership profit is to be divided equally between Bates and Williams.

(4) The accounting records show that on February 1, 19X7, Other Miscellane-

ous Expenses had been charged $3,600 in payment of hospital expenses incurred by Bates' eight-year-old child.

(5) All salary payments to Bates have been charged to a drawing account. On June 1, 19X7, Williams made a $33,000 withdrawal. These are the only transactions recorded in the partners' drawing accounts.

(6) The following trial balance summarizes the partnership's general ledger balances at June 30, 19X7:

Current Assets	307,100	
Property, Plant, and Equipment (net).................	1,285,800	
Current Liabilities		157,000
8% Mortgage Note Payable		290,000
Bates, Capital		515,000
Smith, Capital		150,000
Williams, Capital		400,000
Bates, Drawing..	24,000	
Smith, Drawing	—	
Williams, Drawing	33,000	
Sales		872,600
Cost of Goods Sold	695,000	
Administrative Expenses.............................	16,900	
Other Miscellaneous Expenses	11,100	
Interest Expense	11,700	
	2,384,600	2,384,600

Required:

Prepare a work sheet to adjust the net income (loss) and partners' capital accounts for the year ended June 30, 19X7, and to close the net income (loss) to the partners' capital accounts at June 30, 19X7. Amortization of goodwill, if any, is to be over a ten-year period. Ignore all tax considerations. Use the following column headings and begin with the balances per books as shown:

		Partners' Capital			Other Accounts	
	Net Income	Bates	Smith	Williams	Amount	
Description	(Loss)	Dr. (Cr.)	Dr. (Cr.)	Dr. (Cr.)	Dr. (Cr.)	Name
Book balances at June 30, 19X7	$137,900	($515,000)	($150,000)	($400,000)		

(AICPA adapted)

Problem 15-6. Richards, Bryne, and Hughes are partners sharing profits and losses in the ratio of 4:2:4 respectively. On July 1, 19X1, prior to liquidation of the partnership, the partnership balance sheet was as shown at the top of page 683.

Personal assets and liabilities of the individual partners are as follows:

	Richards	Bryne	Hughes
Assets	$47,000	$16,000	$23,000
Liabilities	30,000	93,000	7,000

During July, noncash assets with a book value of $102,000 were sold for $38,000, and the remaining noncash assets were sold in August for $70,000.

Required:

(1) Determine how available assets would be distributed to the partners at the end of July and August. However, prior to distributing assets to the

RBH Company
Balance Sheet
July 1, 19X1

Assets		Liabilities and Capital	
Cash	$ 39,900	Liabilities	$ 73,000
Other assets.................	185,000	Richards, Loan	3,900
		Richards, Capital	16,000
		Bryne, Capital	102,000
		Hughes, Capital	30,000
Total assets	$224,900	Total liabilities and capital	$224,900

partners, the doctrine of marshaling of assets should be applied to whatever extent possible.

(2) Calculate the minimum amount which must be realized from the sale of other assets, so that Bryne will receive enough consideration from the sale of assets plus contributions from partners with capital deficits to satisfy Bryne's net personal creditors.

Problem 15-7. The profit and loss percentages of Black, Kasten, and Zerwinski are 50%, 25%, and 25% respectively. On December 31, 19X6, the trial balance of the partnership was as follows:

Cash	9,500	
Accounts Receivable	98,500	
Allowance for Doubtful Accounts		3,000
Payables		38,500
Kasten, Loan		4,500
Salary Due Black		3,000
Black, Capital		25,000
Kasten, Capital		14,000
Zerwinski, Capital......................................		20,000
	108,000	108,000

At this date, the firm decided to liquidate and a trustee was appointed to wind up its affairs. The results of the trustee's activities are as follows:

	1st Period	2d Period	3d Period
Cash collected from customers	$56,000	$18,000	$17,500
Liabilities paid in full settlement	19,300	19,000*	
Trustee's expenses and salary	2,200	1,400	2,000
Estimated future trustee expenses	4,000	2,300	

*The remaining liabilities were canceled by the creditors.

Required:

Prepare the necessary journal entries to wind up the partnership. At the end of each period, partners are to receive the amounts indicated by supporting schedules. All supporting schedules should be in good form.

Problem 15-8. On December 31, 19X4, the capital of Barns, Daley, and Rice, a partnership, was as follows:

	Partnership Interest	
	Capital	Share of Profit
Barns..................................	$80,000	40%
Daley	50,000	30
Rice	40,000	30

On January 1, 19X5, Pate paid to Barns $25,000 for one fourth of Barns' interest in capital and profit of the partnership as of that date. The new partnership continued to operate in the old firm name.

The partners are entitled to salaries as follows:

Barns.......................................	$15,000
Daley	12,000
Rice	10,000
Pate	7,500

Barns is also entitled to a bonus of 10% of the net income after treating the partners' salaries and the bonus as an expense.

The operating results for the three years ended December 31, 19X7, were:

19X5: $30,000 income after partners' salaries and bonus
19X6: $25,000 loss after partners' salaries
19X7: $11,000 income after partners' salaries but before Barns' bonus.

During the period, the partners' drawing accounts had the following year-end debit balances:

	Barns	Daley	Rice	Pate
19X5	$20,000	$15,000	$10,000	$7,500
19X6	15,000	10,000	10,000	7,500
19X7	25,000	12,000	10,000	7,500

The partnership was dissolved on December 31, 19X7, and the noncash assets were realized as follows:

19X8	Book Value	Realized	Loss
January	$175,000	$150,000	$25,000
February	30,000	10,000	20,000
March..................................	34,000	14,000	20,000
Total	$239,000	$174,000	$65,000

All of the firms' creditors were paid ($100,000 in amount) in January, 19X8, leaving a cash balance of $84,000, and cash distributions to the partners were made at the end of January and February, with a final payment at the end of March. The costs of liquidation are considered to be minimal.

Required:

(1) Prepare a schedule to determine the partners' capital balances at December 31, 19X5, 19X6, and 19X7.
(2) Prepare a schedule to determine the distribution of cash as it is realized through liquidation during January, February, and March of 19X8.

Problem 15-9. Wall, Hurd, Bemis and Lenz are considering dissolving their partnership. They plan to sell the assets gradually, so that losses will be minimized. Liquidation expenses of $12,000 are anticipated. The partners share profits and losses as follows: Wall, 40%; Hurd, 30%; Bemis, 20%; and Lenz, 10%. The partnership's trial balance as of May 1, 19X2, the date on which liquidation begins, is as follows:

Cash	500	
Receivables	18,800	
Inventory, May 1, 19X2	45,500	
Equipment (net)	32,200	
Accounts Payable		3,500
Wall, Loan		4,000
Hurd, Loan		9,000
Wall, Capital		25,000
Hurd, Capital		21,000
Bemis, Capital		23,500
Lenz, Capital		11,000
	97,000	97,000

Required:

(1) Prepare a statement as of May 1, 19X2, showing how cash may be distributed among partners by installments as it becomes available.
(2) On May 31, 19X2, if cash of $19,400 became available for creditors, liquidation expenses, and partners, how would the cash be distributed?
(3) If, instead of being dissolved, the partnership continues operations and earns a profit of $31,500, how should that profit be distributed if, in addition to the aforementioned profit-sharing arrangement, it was provided that Lenz receive a bonus of 5% of net income from operations after treating such bonus as an expense? (AICPA adapted)

Problem 15-10. *Part I:* The partnership of Aikens, Barnes, and Clinton is winding up the affairs of their partnership. The following information has been gathered:
(a) The trial balance of the partnership at June 30, 19X7, is as follows:

Cash	6,000	
Accounts Receivable	22,000	
Inventory	14,000	
Property, Plant, and Equipment (net)	99,000	
Aikens, Loan	12,000	
Clinton, Loan	7,500	
Accounts Payable		17,000
Aikens, Capital		67,000
Barnes, Capital		45,000
Clinton, Capital		31,500
	$160,500	$160,500

(b) The partners share profits and losses as follows: Aikens, 50%; Barnes, 30%; and Clinton, 20%.
(c) The partners are considering an offer of $100,000 for the accounts receivable, inventory, and plant assets as of June 30. The $100,000 would be paid to the partners in installments, but the number and amounts are to be negotiated.

Required:

Prepare a cash distribution schedule as of June 30, 19X7, showing how the

$100,000 would be distributed as it becomes available.

Part II: Assume the same facts as in Part I, except that the partners have decided to liquidate their partnership instead of accepting the offer of $100,000. Cash is distributed to the partners at the end of each month.

A summary of liquidation transactions follows:

July:

$16,500—collected on accounts receivable; balance is uncollectible
$10,000—received from sale of entire inventory
$ 1,000—liquidation expenses paid
$ 8,000—cash retained in the business at the end of month

August:

$ 1,500—liquidation expenses paid
—Clinton's capital was reduced when Clinton accepted a piece of special equipment which had a book value of $4,000. The partners agreed that a value of $10,000 should be placed on the machine for liquidation purposes.
$ 2,500—cash retained in business at end of month

September:

$75,000—received on sale of remaining plant assets
$ 1,000—liquidation expenses paid
No cash was retained in the business.

Required:

Prepare a schedule of cash payments as of September 30, 19X7, showing how the cash was actually distributed.   (AICPA adapted)

Problem 15-11. The partnership agreement of Smith, Bailey, Davis, Williams, and Perry contained a buy and sell agreement, among numerous other provisions, which would become operative in case of the death of any partner. Some provisions contained in the buy and sell agreement were as follows:

1. Purposes of the buy and sell agreement:
   (a) The partners mutually desire that the business shall be continued by the survivors without interruption or liquidation upon the death of one of the partners.
   (b) The partners also mutually desire that the deceased partner's estate shall receive the full value of the partner's interest in the partnership, and that the estate shall share in the earnings of the partnership until the deceased partner's interest shall be fully purchased by the surviving partners.
2. Purchase and sale of deceased partner's interest:
   (a) Upon the death of a partner, the partnership shall continue to operate.
   (b) Upon the partner's death, the survivors shall purchase, and the executor or administrator of the deceased partner's estate shall sell to the surviving partners, the deceased partner's interest in the partnership for the price and upon the terms and conditions hereinafter set forth.
   (c) The deceased partner's estate shall retain the deceased partner's interest until the amount specified in the next paragraph shall be paid in full by the surviving partners.

(d) The partners agree that the purchase price for the partnership interest shall be an amount equal to the deceased partner's capital account at the date of death. Said amount shall be paid to the legal representative of decedent as follows:

    (1) The first installment of 30 percent of said capital account shall be paid within 60 days from the date of death of the partner, or within 30 days from the date on which the personal representative of decedent becomes qualified by law, whichever date is later, and

    (2) The balance shall be due in four equal installments which shall be payable annually on the anniversary date of said death.

3. Deceased partner's estate's share of the earnings:

  (a) The partners mutually desire that the deceased partner's estate shall be guaranteed a share in the earnings of the partnership over the period said estate retains an interest in the partnership. Said estate shall not be deemed to have an interest in the partnership after the final installment for the deceased partner's capital account is paid, even though a portion of the guaranteed payments specified below may be unpaid and may be due and owing.

  (b) The deceased partner's estate's guaranteed share of the earnings of the partnership shall be determined from two items and shall be paid at different times as follows:

    (1) First, interest shall be paid on the unpaid balance of the deceased partner's capital account at the same date that the installment on the purchase price is paid. The amount to be paid shall be an amount equal to accrued interest at the rate of 6 percent per annum on the unpaid balance of the purchase price for the deceased partner's capital account.

    (2) Second, the partners agree that the balance of the guaranteed payment from the partnership earnings shall be an amount equal to 25 percent of the deceased partner's share of the aggregate gross receipts of the partnership for the full 36 months preceding the month of the partner's death. Said amount shall be payable in 48 equal monthly installments without interest, and the first payment shall be made within 60 days following the death of the partner or within 30 days from the date on which the personal representative of the deceased becomes qualified, whichever date is later; provided, however, that the payment so made under this provision during any twelve-month period shall not exceed the highest annual salary on a calendar year basis received by the partner for the three calendar years immediately preceding the date of the partner's death. In the event that said payment would exceed said salary, then an amount per month shall be paid which does not so exceed said highest monthly salary, and the term over which payment shall be paid to the beneficiary shall be lengthened beyond the said 48 months in order to complete said payment.

Smith and Perry were killed simultaneously in an automobile accident on January 10, 19X7. The surviving partners notified the executors of both estates that the first payment due under the buy and sell agreement would be paid on March 10, 19X7, and that subsequent payments would be paid on the tenth day of each month as due.

The following information was determined from the partnership records:

			Annual Salaries to Partners		
Partner	Profit and Loss Percentage	Capital Accounts on 1/10/X7	19X4	19X5	19X6
Smith	30%	$25,140	$16,500	$17,000	$17,400
Bailey	25	21,970	15,000	15,750	16,500
Davis	20	4,780	12,000	13,000	14,000
Williams	15	5,860	9,600	10,800	12,000
Perry	10	2,540	8,400	9,600	10,800

The partnership gross receipts for the three prior years were:

19X4	$296,470
19X5	325,310
19X6	363,220

Required:

Prepare a schedule of the amount to be paid to the Smith Estate and to the Perry Estate in March, 19X7, December, 19X7, and January, 19X8. The schedule should identify the amounts attributable to earnings, to interest in the guaranteed payments, and to capital.   (AICPA adapted)

CHAPTER 16
GOVERNMENTAL ACCOUNTING: GENERAL FUND AND THE ACCOUNT GROUPS

The federal accounting system with its myriad of agencies, each with peculiar reporting requirements, is an extensive topic. Although accounting students are not expected to demonstrate knowledge of federal governmental accounting in CPA examinations, they should have some knowledge of accounting for the smaller governmental divisions, such as states, counties, cities, and school districts. These smaller divisions are the primary area of study in this chapter and in the chapter which follows. However, since the accounting procedures for these smaller units have followed the development of accounting for the federal government, this chapter begins with a discussion of the history of federal governmental accounting.

BRIEF HISTORY OF FEDERAL GOVERNMENTAL ACCOUNTING

In a democracy, the elected members of the legislative branch have governing authority, which includes the power to levy and collect taxes and to borrow money. The Constitution of the United States assigned to Congress the control of the federal government's financial affairs, and stipulated that the Treasury could spend only money that had been appropriated by Congress. Congress soon relinquished that control by passing the Treasury Act of 1789, which created the Department of the Treasury as an agency of the executive branch, and gave the Department the authority to determine whether expenditures were legal and proper. Although the Act required the Treasury to make an annual report of public money receipts and disbursements, Congress surrendered direct control over fiscal administration to the executive branch, which, in essence, audited its own actions.

With the exceptional growth in federal expenditures resulting from World War I, Congress realized that the legislative branch should independently review expenditures. Thus, Congress passed the Budget and Accounting Act of 1921, which was the first action to return control over federal fiscal policy to the legislative branch. Among other changes, this act created the Bureau of the Budget, which is now the Office of Management and Budget, and the General Accounting Office. The director of the Office of Management and Budget is to aid the President in the creation of the annual federal budget, which must be submitted to Congress for its approval. The duties assigned to the General Accounting Office (GAO) include the establishment and review of accounting systems and procedures to be used by all agencies of the federal government.

During the next three decades, various acts and commissions attempted to respond to a general dissatisfaction with the efficiency and economy of federal operations. In the Supplemental Appropriations Act of 1956, for example, the use of accrual accounting was required for governmental operations:

> As soon as practicable after August 1, 1956, the head of each executive agency shall, in accordance with principles and standards prescribed by the Comptroller General, cause the accounts of such agency to be maintained on an accrual basis to show the resources, liabilities, and costs of operations of such agency with a view to facilitating the preparation of cost-based budgets.

Today, however, more than twenty-five years after it was required, the use of accrual accounting to report governmental operations is not universal. Both Presidents Johnson and Nixon endorsed the use of the accrual basis for the federal budget, but persons in authority have been reluctant to insist on the implementation of accrual accounting, even though it is supposedly illegal for federal agencies *not* to use the accrual system. In 1973, for example, a commission recommended to the President that there be indefinite postponement of the project to place the federal budget on an accrual basis. The commission claimed that the budget should remain on a modified cash basis, since only a minority of the agencies reported on an accrual basis.

Much of the development of governmental accounting and reporting may be attributed to the authoritative work of the National Council on Governmental Accounting (NCGA) of the Municipal Finance Officers Association. This group has attempted to establish principles within the parameters of varying statutes and enormous political pressures. In 1968, it produced the book, *Governmental Accounting, Auditing, and Financial Reporting*. In March, 1979, a revised and condensed summary was published as Statement 1, *Governmental Accounting and Financial Reporting Principles*, along with Statement 2, *Grant, Entitlement, and Shared Revenue Accounting and Reporting by State and Local Governments*. In August, 1980, the AICPA issued Statement of

Position 80-2 "Accounting and Financial Reporting by Governmental Units." It declared that financial statements presented in accordance with Statement 1 are in conformity with generally accepted accounting principles. Late in 1980, the NCGA released its revision of *Governmental Accounting, Auditing, and Financial Reporting*, an invaluable guide in this area of study.

PRINCIPLES AND PROCEDURES OF GOVERNMENTAL ACCOUNTING

The fundamental purpose of accounting is the communication of financial information to assist in the evaluation of prior performance and current financial position and in the planning of future action. Therefore, both governmental and commercial units adhere to the generally accepted accounting standards of relevance, reliability, neutrality, comparability, and full disclosure, and both use the double-entry system.

The accounting and reporting procedures for a governmental unit differ in some respects, however, from those of a commercial unit because governmental and commercial units have different purposes and operate in different environments. For example, while the primary purpose of a commercial unit is the maximization of profit within the limits of socially acceptable action, the primary purpose of a governmental unit is to provide services. Also, the freedom of conduct of governmental units is more severely limited by legal requirements and regulations. Although governmental accounting should be based on principles and techniques that promote economy and efficiency in accounting for public funds, it must also demonstrate compliance with applicable legal provisions.

Powerful pressures are being brought to bear by bond rating firms, such as Standard and Poor's Corporation, to force state and local governments to improve their accounting systems to conform to generally accepted accounting principles. Failure to do so would have a negative impact on the ratings assigned to a governmental unit's bond offering, and the unit would not be rated at all, if its reporting is inadequate or untimely. Therefore, an increasing number of state and local governmental units undergo an audit by independent accountants. If the auditors' opinions are to be unqualified, the financial statements presented must be timely and in conformity with generally accepted accounting principles.

Funds in a Governmental Unit

In a profit organization, the total business constitutes the accounting entity. For a governmental unit, accounting and reporting is designed to permit each major activity to be accounted for independently with its own self-balancing set of accounts. The activities might include constructing major assets, paying long-term debt, providing goods or services for a fee, functioning as a trustee, and conducting day-to-day operations. Each of these activities would be accounted for as a separate entity, referred to as a *fund*. The number of funds established depends on the nature and volume of activity, the degree of control desired, as well as legal requirements. However, nothing is gained, and confusion may result, if too many funds are established. In general, it is best to have the minimum number of funds necessary to meet legal and operational requirements.

There are three broad categories or types of funds:

1. *Governmental funds* account for all activities except those assigned to proprietary funds or fiduciary funds.
2. *Proprietary funds* account for sales of goods or services for which a fee is charged. An example would be a publicly owned utility.
3. *Fiduciary funds* account for resources for which the governmental unit is acting as a trustee or agent.

It is unfortunate that the term "governmental funds" was adopted, since it refers to only one of the three categories of funds used in governmental accounting.

Governmental Funds

Accounting for governmental funds concentrates on working capital—inflows and outflows of current assets. The difference between the total inflows and outflows is called *fund balance*, which represents available, spendable resources. Since governmental funds deal almost exclusively with current assets and current liabilities, the fixed assets and long-term debt must be included in some other independent accounting entity, namely the General Fixed Assets Account Group and the General Long-Term Debt Account Group. The difference in nomenclature is intentional. Account groups are not fiscal entities, in that they do not report results for a given period of time, as funds do. Account groups merely show accumulated fixed assets or unpaid long-term debt.

Operations of a state, a county, or a large city are very diverse. Trying to account for operations in one governmental fund would result in relaxation of financial control and confusing financial reports. Therefore, activities are divided into five major types or categories, each accounted for independently in its own fund. These five governmental funds are:

1. *The General Fund*, which accounts for resources with no specific restrictions and available for operational expenditures not relegated to one of the other four governmental funds. Every governmental unit has a General Fund.
2. *Special Revenue Funds*, which account for resources that are legally restricted to expenditures for specific operational purposes.
3. *Capital Projects Funds*, which account for resources to be used for

the acquisition or construction of major capital facilities that benefit the general public.
4. *Special Assessment Funds*, which account for resources to be used to finance improvements or services that primarily benefit only a limited segment of the public. Assessments are levied against the specific properties that will receive the benefit.
5. *Debt Service Funds*, which account for resources to be used for payment of general long-term debt and interest.

This chapter will discuss accounting for the General Fund, the General Fixed Assets Account Group, and the General Long-Term Debt Account Group. Chapter 17 will discuss the remaining governmental funds as well as the proprietary and fiduciary funds.

Accounting for Governmental Funds

In governmental funds, *revenues* are defined in general as inflows of resources from external parties that do not have to be repaid. These resources are available for current *expenditures*, which are outflows of resources to external parties. Note that accounting for governmental funds deals with expenditures, not expenses. The matching principle is not invoked, since income determination is not involved. Thus, the purchase of a fixed asset by the General Fund is an expenditure of that fund, because the action reduces its available resources.

Under the cash basis of accounting, revenue is recognized when cash is received, and expenses are recognized when paid. The cash basis is subject to manipulation and is inappropriate for governmental accounting. Under the pure accrual basis, revenue is recognized when it is earned, while expenses or expenditures are recognized when incurred. The accrual basis is a more accurate reflection of the substantive nature of transactions and explains why that basis was adopted for commercial entities.

Since the accounting measurement objective of the five governmental funds is the flow of resources rather than net income, the modified accrual basis of accounting is used. Under the modified accrual basis, revenue is recognized when it is both measurable and available to meet liabilities of the current period. Expenditures are generally recognized when the liability is incurred.

In essence, the modified accrual basis is a hybrid, recognizing some elements on the pure accrual basis and others on the cash basis. For example, property taxes are recognized as revenue when they are levied, since a legal claim is recognized against known property owners for a calculable amount. The property taxes are recognized as revenue at that point, because they are both measurable and will be available to meet liabilities of the current period. Other cash inflows, such as fines, permit fees, or parking fees, cannot be accrued, because it is not known from whom they will be collected or when. For recognition of such revenues, the cash basis is followed.

Use of Budgetary Accounting

A governmental unit prepares an operational budget that indicates the estimated inflows and outflows of resources. The budget of every major unit is reviewed by a legislative body. If the budget is approved and enacted, the unit has authority to generate revenues and to proceed with expenditures.

In a business, ultimate achievement and control are reflected by its net income or net loss. This control feature is missing in governmental funds, which need a method of exercising financial control over revenues and expenditures by comparing them with annual budgetary projections. The task is accomplished by introducing into the accounting system a budgetary account as a counterpart for each control account in which the actual inflow and outflow of resources is recorded. Actual inflows of resources are recorded either as revenues or as other financing sources. The latter include transfers in from other funds, proceeds from general long-term debt, and proceeds from the sale of fixed assets up to their original cost. A transfer in is not considered revenue, since it is not received from an outside source. Proceeds from general long-term debt are not considered revenue because they must be repaid. Proceeds from the sale of a fixed asset up to its original cost represent a replacement of one asset with another and would not be recorded as revenue. In the case of a sale of a fixed asset at more than its original cost, the gain would qualify as revenue. Actual outflows of resources in governmental funds are recorded either as expenditures or as other financing uses. The latter consist mainly of transfers to other funds.

The control accounts for other financing sources and for other financing uses were developed to prevent the same amount of revenue or expenditure from being recorded twice. For example, the General Fund will record taxes levied as revenue and may regularly transfer tax collections to other funds, which should not record the same item again as revenue. Instead, the recipient fund records resources received by crediting Other Financing Sources Control, while the General Fund enters the transfer by debiting Other Financing Uses Control. In this way, revenue is reported by the donor fund when it originally received the resources. The expenditure is recorded by the recipient fund when the resources are expended.

The following summary indicates the names of the budgetary accounts used to record estimates, as well as the equivalent accounts used to record actual inflows and outflows of resources:

Item Recorded	Budgetary Accounts	Equivalent Accounts for Actual Events
Inflows of resources	Estimated Revenues Control	Revenues Control
	Estimated Other Financing Sources Control	Other Financing Sources Control

Item Recorded	Budgetary Accounts	Equivalent Accounts for Actual Events
Outflows of resources	Appropriations Control Estimated Other Financing Uses Control	Expenditures Control Other Financing Uses Control

Note that the account titles are very similar, except for the budgetary estimate for expenditures, which is recorded in Appropriations Control. At any time during the fiscal year, it is possible to determine what percentage of estimated revenues and estimated other financing sources has been received and what proportion of the appropriations and estimated other financing uses has been committed. Unless the estimates are materially altered, no other entries are recorded in budgetary accounts until the end of the period, when they are closed.

ACCOUNTING FOR THE GENERAL FUND

The General Fund is the most important fund. It is used to account for unrestricted resources, mostly of a current nature, involved in the unit's operations. Even the smallest governmental unit will have a General Fund, which accounts for the major portion of revenue. Revenues result from property, income, gasoline, and sales taxes, as well as fines, penalties, permits, licenses, and grants from other governmental units.

To visualize the accounting process of the General Fund and the flow of information that produces the financial reports, the activities of Geiser City will be examined for the fiscal year ended September 30, 19X4. The General Fund trial balance on October 1, 19X3, is as follows:

Geiser City
General Fund Trial Balance
October 1, 19X3

Cash	235,000	
Taxes Receivable—Delinquent	30,000	
Allowance for Uncollectible Delinquent Taxes		20,000
Vouchers Payable		170,000
Fund Balance Reserved for Encumbrances		30,600
Unreserved Fund Balance		44,400
	265,000	265,000

Recording the Budget

The city council and the mayor have approved the budget for the following year, with estimated revenues of $1,350,000, appropriations of $1,300,000, and an estimated transfer of $30,000 to be made during the year to the Debt Service Fund. Transfers to other funds are not expenditures and in the budgetary entry are segregated from the estimated expenditures (appropriations) in a budgetary account labeled Estimated Other Financing Uses Control. The budgetary entry permits isolation of estimated amounts from actual amounts, so that the two may be compared. A convenient technique for remembering how to record the budget is to follow the logic that estimated revenues are forecasts of asset inflows and should be debited. Appropriations, as estimated authorizations to spend, and transfers to other funds will result in future asset outflows and should be credited. If the estimates of inflows and outflows are not equal in amount, the difference is recorded in the account Budgetary Fund Balance. The entry to record Geiser City's budget for its General Fund is:

Estimated Revenues Control	1,350,000	
Appropriations Control		1,300,000
Estimated Other Financing Uses Control		30,000
Budgetary Fund Balance		20,000

Almost all of the accounts in governmental accounting are control accounts, requiring the details of their composition to be maintained in subsidiary records. To support total estimated revenues of $1,350,000, a breakdown of sources should be provided in the explanation of the budget entry or in a separate schedule. In practice, there could be as many as one hundred or more revenue items. For purposes of illustration, however, the number of revenue items is condensed, as shown in the following schedule of estimated revenues:

Geiser City
General Fund Estimated Revenues
For Year Ending September 30, 19X4

General property taxes	$ **882,500**
Licenses and permits	125,500
Revenue from state grants	200,000
Other revenues	142,000
Total estimated revenues	$1,350,000

Just as the total projected income is debited to Estimated Revenues Control in the general ledger, so each of the detailed estimated sources is debited to its own account in the subsidiary revenue ledger. The following subsidiary account for general property taxes illustrates the procedure of posting to subsidiary records.

Revenue Ledger				
ACCOUNT General Property Taxes			**ACCOUNT NO.**	
DATE	ITEM	DEBIT (Estimate)	CREDIT (Actual)	BALANCE (DR.) CR.
Oct. 1	Budget estimate	882,500		(882,500)

Not only must the accounting system provide for control of revenues, but it must also accommodate expenditures. To provide a basis for comparison between expected and actual expenses, budgetary as well as actual expense accounts are an integral part of the accounting system. In the entry to record Geiser City's budget for its General Fund, the credit to Appropriations Control represents the estimate of the expenditures of $1,300,000 for the coming year. In support of the appropriations total, a summary of approved estimated expenditures by departments or activities might appear as follows:

Geiser City
Department or Activity Appropriations
For Year Ending September 30, 19X4

General government: legislative, judicial, and executive	$ 129,000
Public safety	277,300
Education	591,450
Highways and streets	94,500
Sanitation and health	97,750
Welfare	51,000
Culture and recreation	59,000
Total appropriations	$1,300,000

Each of the above departments or activities must submit detailed appropriation requests on the basis of subfunctions and object of expenditure. The Education Division, for example, might present the following estimate of expenditures:

Geiser City
Education Division
Request for Appropriation
For Year Ending September 30, 19X4

Supplies	**$160,000**
Salaries	350,000
Equipment	60,000
Professional fees	21,450
Total	$591,450

One approach to controlling expenditures is to establish subsidiary accounts by division or department. If this approach is followed by Geiser City, each of the expense items for the Education Division would have its own subsidiary account, such as the one which follows for supplies. Each expenditure account would be designed to show the

Education Division Expenditure Ledger							
ACCOUNT Supplies						**ACCOUNT NO.**	
		ENCUMBRANCES			EXPENDITURES		UNEN-CUMBERED
DATE	ITEM	DEBIT	CREDIT	BALANCE	ITEM	TOTAL	BALANCE
Oct. 1	Budget appropriation						160,000

original appropriation, the encumbrances (amounts committed), the expenditures (amounts spent), and the remaining unencumbered balance.

Recording Actual Revenues and Transfers

Property taxes are a major source of revenue for Geiser City's General Fund and are used to illustrate the recording of revenues. The property tax roll provides ownership information, legal descriptions, and amounts of tax levies, which support a debit to Taxes Receivable—Current and entries to the subsidiary revenue ledger. The following entry records the levy of the property tax and makes provision for the estimated uncollectibles:

Taxes Receivable—Current	919,000	
Revenues Control		**881,300**
Allowance for Uncollectible Current Taxes..............		37,700

Both the revenues control account in the general ledger and the general property taxes account in the subsidiary revenue ledger are credited for the actual revenue. After the above entry is posted, General Property Taxes appears as follows:

Revenue Ledger					
ACCOUNT General Property Taxes					**ACCOUNT NO.**
DATE	ITEM	DEBIT (Estimate)	CREDIT (Actual)	BALANCE (DR.) CR.	
Oct. 1	Budget estimate	882,500		(882,500)	
1	Tax levy		881,300	(1,200)	

During the fiscal period, a debit balance in a subsidiary revenue account usually represents additional revenue expected in the future. At the end of the fiscal period, a debit balance indicates a deficiency of actual revenue as compared to estimated revenue, while a credit balance shows an excess of actual over estimated revenues.

Cash inflows from property tax or income tax collections peak near the due dates for payment. Prior to their receipt, a governmental unit may have obligations that must be paid. Local banks usually provide short-term financing, using as security the taxing power of the unit, which is required to sign an instrument referred to as a *tax anticipation note*. Receipt of the cash would be recorded in the General Fund with the following entry:

Cash	xxx	
Tax Anticipation Notes Payable		xxx

Later, as cash inflows provide resources, the following entry would record the payment of the notes and the interest, with the interest recorded as an expenditure:

Tax Anticipation Notes Payable..	xxx	
Expenditures Control (for interest).................................	xxx	
Cash...		xxx

During the year, the following additional events related to revenue are recorded in the General Fund of Geiser City:

Event	Entry		
Of the total delinquent taxes of $30,000, $14,000 is collected. The balance is uncollectible.	Cash...............................	14,000	
	Allowance for Uncollectible Delinquent Taxes........................	16,000	
	Taxes Receivable—Delinquent.....		30,000
The excess allowance for uncollectible delinquent taxes is transferred to Revenues Control.	Allowance for Uncollectible Delinquent Taxes........................	4,000	
	Revenues Control.................		4,000
Of current taxes receivable, $850,000 is collected during the year and $12,700 is written off as uncollectible.	Cash...............................	850,000	
	Allowance for Uncollectible Current Taxes..............................	12,700	
	Taxes Receivable—Current........		862,700
During the year, cash was collected from the following sources: Licenses and permits ..... $320,000 Other revenues .... 150,000 Total $470,000	Cash...............................	470,000	
	Revenues Control................. (with credit posting to each subsidiary revenue account)		470,000
At year end, property taxes not collected are classified as delinquent, as are also the estimated uncollectible allowances.	Taxes Receivable—Delinquent.......	56,300	
	Taxes Receivable—Current ($919,000 − $862,700)...........		56,300
	Allowance for Uncollectible Current Taxes..............................	25,000	
	Allowance for Uncollectible Delinquent Taxes.....................		25,000

As indicated in the second entry, a revision of the estimated amount of uncollectible current and delinquent taxes and tax liens is treated as a change in accounting estimate through Revenues Control. Only adjustments of confirmed errors of prior periods are recorded directly in Unreserved Fund Balance.

Tax Liens. The law outlines the procedures to be followed in posting a lien against property when property tax payments remain delinquent after a specified time period. The following entry records the exercise of such a lien for a hypothetical county:

Tax Liens Receivable.....................................	31,000	
Allowance for Uncollectible Delinquent Taxes	12,000	
Taxes Receivable—Delinquent		31,000
Allowance for Uncollectible Tax Liens		12,000

Although the governmental unit may retain property against which foreclosure proceedings have been completed, it is customary to sell the property, in which case the entry is:

Cash	11,000	
Allowance for Uncollectible Tax Liens (for any loss on disposition)	5,000	
Tax Liens Receivable		16,000

Operating Transfers from Other Governmental Units. Resources to be received from other governmental units should be recognized as revenue in the General Fund on a modified accrual basis, i.e., when the resources are measurable and available. Such resources may be in the form of grants, entitlements, or shared revenues for operational purposes normally financed through the General Fund. For example, if a city has been notified by the federal government that it is to receive $100,000 within a short period of time to assist in the operation of its child-care program, the following entry would be made in the General Fund:

Due from Federal Government	100,000	
Revenues Control		100,000

Recording Encumbrances and Actual Expenditures

To prevent overexpenditure, the General Fund adopts an encumbrance system. Under this system, whenever a purchase order or other commitment is approved, an entry is made to record the estimated cost of the commitment. For example, an approved purchase order for school supplies, estimated to cost $10,000, is recorded as follows:

Encumbrances Control	10,000	
Fund Balance Reserved for Encumbrances		10,000

The entry is posted to the general ledger, where Encumbrances Control is a quasi-expenditure account and Fund Balance Reserved for Encumbrances is a form of restriction of the fund balance. The entry is also entered in the encumbrances section of the supplies account of the subsidiary expenditure ledger for the Education Division, reducing the unencumbered balance, as follows:

Education Division Expenditure Ledger							
ACCOUNT Supplies						ACCOUNT NO.	
		ENCUMBRANCES			EXPENDITURES		UNEN-CUMBERED
DATE	ITEM	DEBIT	CREDIT	BALANCE	ITEM	TOTAL	BALANCE
Oct. 1	Budget appropriation						160,000
4	Purchase order	10,000		10,000			150,000

When the invoice is received for the purchase of items or services, the encumbrance entry is reversed, and the encumbrance is lifted to permit the deduction of the actual amount. Note that it is always the amount of the original estimate and not the actual cost that is used in the reversing entry. Assuming that the invoice for supplies amounts to $10,200, the two entries to record the invoice are:

Fund Balance Reserved for Encumbrances	10,000	
Encumbrances Control		10,000
To reverse entry for encumbrance at estimated cost.		
Expenditures Control	10,200	
Vouchers Payable		10,200
To record invoice at actual cost.		

The supplies account in the subsidiary expenditure ledger appears as follows:

Education Division Expenditure Ledger

ACCOUNT Supplies							ACCOUNT NO.
		ENCUMBRANCES			EXPENDITURES		UNEN-CUMBERED BALANCE
DATE	ITEM	DEBIT	CREDIT	BALANCE	ITEM	TOTAL	
Oct. 1	Budget appropriation						160,000
4	Purchase order	10,000		10,000			150,000
Nov. 7	Invoice received		10,000	-0-	10,200	10,200	149,800

When the encumbrance and the actual amount are identical, the unencumbered balance is not changed. However, when the amounts are not identical, the net effect is an adjustment of the unencumbered balance to reflect the amount of the actual expenditure. Thus, at any time, the subsidiary ledgers provide a continuing record of the unencumbered balances and of how closely the actual expenditures match encumbrances. The following equation is derived from an examination of the supplies account:

Unencumbered balance = Appropriations − (Expenditures total + Encumbrances balance)

For internal expenditures, such as salaries, which are subject to little variation and to additional internal controls, it is not customary to involve the encumbrance accounts. When salaries are paid, they are recorded directly as expenditures and reduce the unencumbered balance of the salaries account in the subsidiary expenditure ledger.

Encumbrances of a Prior Period

It is not unusual to have approved purchase orders issued at the end of one year and the actual invoices received in the following year. Since the operations for each fiscal period should be segregated to validate budgetary comparisons and operational effectiveness, the account Fund Balance Reserved for Encumbrances is not closed. Most accountants prefer to reclassify the year-end amount to segregate it from the upcoming encumbrance reserve for the new fiscal period. The reserve shown in the beginning trial balance for Geiser City, on page 695, would be reclassified as follows:

```
Fund Balance Reserved for Encumbrances ................     30,600
    Fund Balance Reserved for Encumbrances—Prior Year ..                 30,600
```

Two useful procedures are now possible. First, the amount reserved acts as a reminder that commitments (encumbrances) approximating that amount have been made and should not be included in Unreserved Fund Balance. Second, when an invoice that relates to an encumbrance of the previous year is received, Fund Balance Reserved for Encumbrances—Prior Year is debited and Vouchers Payable is credited, without entering Expenditures Control of the current year, since the appropriation for the encumbrance was made last year. If there is a variation between the actual and estimated amounts, the difference should be debited or credited to Expenditures Control. To illustrate, invoices related to the previous year's encumbrances are received by Geiser City early in the next fiscal year. Assuming that a reclassification entry has been made, the following entry would record the vouchering of these invoices, which total $30,700:

```
Fund Balance Reserved for Encumbrances—Prior Year ....     30,600
Expenditures Control ...................................        100
    Vouchers Payable ......................................                30,700
```

If it is the policy of the governmental unit that all uncommitted appropriations lapse at year end, but the unit wishes to honor encumbrances, it must provide for their coverage through the subsequent year's appropriation. The accounting procedure in this case is to close both encumbrance-related accounts at year end with the following entry:

```
Fund Balance Reserved for Encumbrances ................     30,600
    Encumbrances Control ................................                 30,600
```

At the beginning of the next year, this entry is reversed, with no changes in subsequent accounting for encumbrances and expenditures. As a result, Expenditures Control will be debited for the total actual amount of invoices relating to the prior year.

A different situation results if, in error, there was a failure at year end to restrict the Unreserved Fund Balance for outstanding encumbrances not yet invoiced, and the succeeding period's appropriation was not increased to cover the amount. In that case, when the voucher is recorded, the estimated amount should be debited directly to Unreserved Fund Balance as a correction of the account's beginning balance.

Any difference between the two amounts would be cleared through Expenditures Control.

The following events relate to Geiser City's expenditures and transfers during the year. The amounts include the encumbrance and expenditure for school supplies previously discussed.

Event	Entry		
Invoices of $30,700 related to last year's encumbrances of $30,600 were received and vouchered.	Fund Balance Reserved for Encumbrances—Prior Year	30,600	
	Expenditures Control	100	
	Vouchers Payable		30,700
Throughout the year, encumbrances totaling $738,000 were recorded.	Encumbrances Control	738,000	
	Fund Balance Reserved for Encumbrances		738,000
Vouchers were approved, liquidating $700,000 of encumbrances for:	Fund Balance Reserved for Encumbrances	700,000	
Supplies $300,000	Encumbrances Control		700,000
Building 200,000			
Other expenditures 272,000	Inventory of Supplies	300,000	
Total $772,000	Expenditures Control	472,000	
	Vouchers Payable		772,000
Vouchers were approved for the following nonencumbered items:	Expenditures Control	518,000	
Salaries $490,000	Vouchers Payable		518,000
Other expenditures 28,000			
Total $518,000			
Vouchers totaling $1,400,000 were paid.	Vouchers Payable	1,400,000	
	Cash		1,400,000
Transfer of $30,000 is made to the Debt Service Fund.	Other Financing Uses Control	30,000	
	Cash		30,000
Supplies totaling $260,000 were consumed.	Expenditures Control	260,000	
	Inventory of Supplies		260,000
	Unreserved Fund Balance	40,000	
	Fund Balance Reserved for Inventory of Supplies		40,000

The amount of Unreserved Fund Balance represents net current assets available to meet future commitments. But one of those assets for Geiser City is the inventory of supplies, which will not be converted into cash and will not be available to meet future commitments. Therefore, Unreserved Fund Balance must be restricted by an amount equal to the inventory on the financial statement date. In this case, the amount of the inventory at year end is $40,000 ($300,000 − $260,000). Thereafter, the account Fund Balance Reserved for Inventory of Supplies will be kept equal to the inventory amount by periodic adjustment through Unreserved Fund Balance.

Financial Reports of the General Fund

Statement 1 declared that combined financial statements with columns for each fund type and account group constitute the basic financial statements necessary for compliance with generally accepted accounting principles. Although individual fund statements are no longer required, they may be included as supplemental data or when a more comprehensive presentation is desired. Both combined and individual fund and group reports will be illustrated when appropriate.

The trial balance of Geiser City's General Fund at the end of the fiscal year appears as follows:

Geiser City
General Fund Trial Balance
September 30, 19X4

Cash	139,000	
Taxes Receivable—Delinquent	56,300	
Allowance for Uncollectible Delinquent Taxes		25,000
Inventory of Supplies	40,000	
Vouchers Payable		90,700
Fund Balance Reserved for Encumbrances		38,000
Fund Balance Reserved for Inventory of Supplies		40,000
Unreserved Fund Balance		4,400
Revenues Control		1,355,300
Expenditures Control	1,250,100	
Other Financing Uses Control	30,000	
Encumbrances Control	38,000	
Estimated Revenues Control	1,350,000	
Appropriations Control.......................................		1,300,000
Estimated Other Financing Uses Control......................		30,000
Budgetary Fund Balance		20,000
	2,903,400	2,903,400

From this trial balance, the year-end reports of the General Fund are developed. These reports consist of a balance sheet and a statement of revenues, expenditures, and changes in fund balances. The following illustrations of these financial statements are in the form recommended by the NCGA.

Balance Sheet. The General Fund year-end balance sheet for Geiser City, shown in Illustration I on page 705, differs substantially from its private business counterpart. First, it deals almost exclusively with current assets and current liabilities, and the difference between these two amounts appears as the fund balance—either reserved (committed) or unreserved. Second, the long-term classifications of assets and liabilities are absent, since the general fixed assets are included in the General Fixed Assets Account Group, and the general long-term debt is carried in the General Long-Term Debt Account Group.

Illustration I

Geiser City
General Fund Balance Sheet
September 30, 19X4

Assets

Cash		$139,000
Taxes receivable—delinquent	$56,300	
Less allowance for uncollectible delinquent taxes	25,000	31,300
Inventory of supplies		40,000
Total assets		$210,300

Liabilities and Fund Equity

Liabilities:		
Vouchers payable		$ 90,700
Fund balances:		
Reserved for encumbrances	$38,000	
Reserved for inventory of supplies	40,000	
Unreserved	41,600	
Total fund equity		119,600
Total liabilities and fund equity		$210,300

Statement of Revenues, Expenditures, and Changes in Fund Balances.
The NCGA recommends that the statement of revenues, expenditures, and changes in fund balances be interpreted as an operating statement and be prepared on an all-inclusive basis, disclosing all elements that contributed to the change in fund balances. The statement should contain details on the major revenue sources and on expenditures by function or program. Other financing sources or uses and any corrections that altered the fund balance should also be presented. The statement is designed to show both budgeted and actual figures, along with the favorable and unfavorable variances. The statement for Geiser City, shown in Illustration II on page 706, omits the comparative figures for the preceding period, although they would normally be of assistance in a financial evaluation.

Illustration II reflects estimated and actual amounts of revenues, expenditures, and other changes that relate *to this year*. The beginning fund balances amount is available for the current period. It is the total of unreserved and reserved fund balances, excluding Fund Balance Reserved for Encumbrances—Prior Year, which is applicable to last year's operations. The fund balances amount at the end of the period is also the total of unreserved and reserved fund balances. However, it includes the Fund Balance Reserved for Encumbrances amount at the end of the year, since it is attributable to the current period. The final actual fund balances amount ($119,600) must agree with the total fund equity shown on the balance sheet.

As shown in Illustration II, the statement focuses on the total of all fund balances, both reserved and unreserved. A less frequently used

Illustration II

Geiser City
General Fund
Statement of Revenues, Expenditures, and Changes in Fund Balances—Budget and Actual
For the Fiscal Year Ended September 30, 19X4

	Budget	Actual	Variance—Favorable (Unfavorable)
Revenues:			
General property taxes	$ 882,500	$ 885,300	$ 2,800
Licenses and permits	125,500	120,000	(5,500)
Intergovernmental revenues	200,000	200,000	-0-
Miscellaneous revenues	142,000	150,000	8,000
Total revenues	$1,350,000	$1,355,300	$ 5,300
Expenditures:			
General government	$ 129,000	$ 120,305	$ 8,695
Public safety	277,300	252,795	24,505
Highways and streets	94,500	86,100	8,400
Sanitation and health	97,750	87,750	10,000
Welfare	51,000	46,000	5,000
Culture and recreation	59,000	53,400	5,600
Education	591,450	603,750	(12,300)
Total expenditures	$1,300,000	$1,250,100	$49,900
Excess of revenues over expenditures	$ 50,000	$ 105,200	$55,200
Other financing sources (uses):			
Operating transfers in (out)	(30,000)	(30,000)	-0-
Excess of revenues and other sources over expenditures and other uses	$ 20,000	$ 75,200	$55,200
Fund balances, October 1, 19X3 (available for the current period)	44,400	44,400	-0-
Fund balances, September 30, 19X4	$ 64,400	$ 119,600	$55,200

alternative would be to concentrate on the unreserved fund balance, in which case a section reporting changes in reserves during the year would appear as shown in the following partial statement:

	Budget	Actual	Variance—Favorable (Unfavorable)
Excess of revenues and other sources over expenditures and other uses (Illustration II)	$20,000	$75,200	$55,200
Unreserved fund balance, October 1, 19X3	44,400	44,400	-0-
Other changes in the unreserved balance:			
Deduct: Increase in Fund Balance Reserved for Inventory of Supplies	(45,000)	(40,000)	5,000
Balance of Fund Balance Reserved for Encumbrances	(30,000)	(38,000)	(8,000)
Unreserved fund balance, September 30, 19X4	$(10,600)	$41,600	$52,200

Closing the General Fund

The simplest closing process would first reverse the budgetary entry and then close the nominal accounts, including the other financing sources (uses) accounts, into Unreserved Fund Balance. For Geiser City, these entries would appear as follows:

Appropriations Control	1,300,000	
Estimated Other Financing Uses Control	30,000	
Budgetary Fund Balance	20,000	
Estimated Revenues Control		1,350,000
Revenues Control	1,355,300	
Expenditures Control		1,250,100
Other Financing Uses Control		30,000
Encumbrances Control		38,000
Unreserved Fund Balance		37,200

Interim Reports. Interim reports are prepared primarily for internal use and should be designed to assist in managerial control by revealing areas of strength or weakness. The reports may be prepared on a monthly or quarterly basis, comparing actual results to budgetary estimates when useful, and including data for the year to date. Interim balance sheets of governmental funds using budgetary accounts require two modifications to make them useful. First, following the total assets, a section labeled "Resources" is introduced to show the amount of estimated revenues not yet received that will become available later in the year. Second, the fund equity section is expanded to show appropriations still available. Using hypothetical amounts, an interim balance sheet would appear as shown at the top of page 708.

ACCOUNTING FOR THE GENERAL FIXED ASSETS ACCOUNT GROUP

Fixed assets of a proprietary fund or a fiduciary fund are accounted for within those funds. All other fixed assets are considered *general fixed assets* and are accounted for in the General Fixed Assets Account Group. This account group, which was created to control fixed assets that are not resources of any fund, may be thought of as an inventory record of fixed assets for the purpose of assigning responsibility for custody and proper use. The NCGA recommends five fixed asset categories: land, buildings, improvements other than buildings, machinery and equipment, and construction in progress. Each category should have a control account in the ledger and should be substantiated by supporting detailed records.

There is one class of fixed assets that many governmental units omit from their General Fixed Assets Account Group. These assets are the public domain or "infrastructure" fixed assets, such as sidewalks, streets, curbs, and bridges. Their characteristics are that they are immobile and that they are of value only to the governmental unit. The NCGA recommends but does not require their inclusion in formal

City of X
General Fund Interim Balance Sheet
July 31, 19X1

Assets and Resources

Total assets		$300,000
Resources:		
Estimated revenues	$1,350,000	
Less revenues to date	750,000	600,000
Total assets and resources.................		$900,000

Liabilities and Fund Equity

Total liabilities		$115,000
Fund equity:		
Appropriations	$1,300,000	
Less: Expenditures $670,000		
Encumbrances....................... 230,000	900,000	
Available appropriations	$ 400,000	
Reserved for encumbrances	230,000	
Reserved for inventory of supplies	55,000	
Unreserved	100,000	
Total fund equity..........................		785,000
Total liabilities and fund equity		$900,000

reports. Whatever policy is adopted, however, must be followed consistently. If they are formally included in the General Fixed Assets Account Group, they should be recorded in Improvements Other Than Buildings. Most governmental units do not record them, but maintain separate descriptive records on infrastructure fixed assets.

The acquisition of a general fixed asset is recorded in the General Fixed Assets Account Group by a debit to one of the five specific asset accounts. The credit indicates the source of the asset, selected from the following recommended titles:

Investment in General Fixed Assets from—
   Capital Project Funds:
     General Obligation Bonds
     Federal Grants
     State Grants
     Local Grants
   General Fund Revenues
   Special Revenue Fund Revenues
   Special Assessments
   Private Gifts
   Other Sources

To illustrate this procedure, a building acquired with General Fund revenues would require the following entries:

Fund or Group in Which Recorded	Entry		
General Fund	Expenditures Control	200,000	
	Vouchers Payable		200,000
	(This entry is part of the entry on page 703, which records vouchers of $772,000.)		
General Fixed Assets Account Group	Buildings	200,000	
	Investment in General Fixed Assets from General Fund Revenues		200,000

The basis of fixed assets is cost or, if the asset is donated, appraised market value. Subsequent to the acquisition of a fixed asset, capital and maintenance expenditures must be distinguished, as they are in commercial accounting, since maintenance expenditures should not increase the accountability of the General Fixed Assets Account Group.

When a governmental unit disposes of a fixed asset, the original cost of the asset is removed from the General Fixed Assets Account Group. Proceeds from the sale up to the original cost are recorded in the General Fund, with a credit to Other Financing Sources Control. In the rare case of a sale at more than the asset's original cost, the gain is credited to Revenues Control. For example, if a governmental unit sells for $110,000 equipment carried in the General Fixed Assets Account Group at $100,000, the following entries would be made:

Fund or Group in Which Recorded	Entry		
General Fund	Cash	110,000	
	Other Financing Sources Control . .		100,000
	Revenues Control		10,000
General Fixed Assets Account Group	Investment in General Fixed Assets from General Fund Revenues	100,000	
	Machinery and Equipment		100,000

Instead of selling the equipment, assume that the governmental unit traded it for a larger model costing $235,000, with an allowance of $110,000 for the smaller unit. The new fixed asset should be recorded at its total cost, $235,000, and the following entries would be made:

Fund or Group in Which Recorded	Entry		
General Fund	Expenditures Control	125,000	
	Vouchers Payable		125,000
General Fixed Assets Account Group	Investment in General Fixed Assets from General Fund Revenues	100,000	
	Machinery and Equipment		100,000
	Machinery and Equipment	235,000	
	Investment in General Fixed Assets from General Fund Revenues		235,000

Leasing affords the opportunity to acquire the service of a fixed asset with a reduced immediate outlay and without increasing bonded debt. As resources become more limited, long-term leasing by governmental units becomes more widespread.

Governmental units should adhere to the FASB statements regarding leasing. When long-term noncancelable lease arrangements resemble a purchase, the leased general fixed asset should be recorded in the General Fixed Assets Account Group. The liability for the long-term lease is recorded in the General Long-Term Debt Account Group, similar to the procedure for handling a serial bond issue, which is discussed later in this chapter and in the chapter that follows.

Notice that there is no accumulated depreciation involved in the typical recording of the sale or exchange of a general fixed asset. When net income is determined, as in proprietary funds, or when capital maintenance is important, as in some fiduciary funds, depreciation expense must be recognized. But governmental funds are not concerned with either of these elements. Emphasis is on expenditures, rather than on expenses. According to the NCGA, recording depreciation expense of general fixed assets in governmental funds would be improper:

> To record depreciation expense in governmental funds would inappropriately mix two fundamentally different measurements, expenses and expenditures. General fixed asset acquisitions require the use of governmental fund financial resources and are recorded as expenditures. General fixed asset sale proceeds provide governmental fund financial resources. Depreciation expense is neither a source nor a use of governmental fund financial resources, and thus is not properly recorded in the accounts of such funds.[1]

If it is desired to indicate asset usage or consumption to date, accumulated depreciation may be recorded in the General Fixed Assets Account Group by debiting the appropriate investment in general fixed asset account and crediting the accumulated depreciation account. Entries for the disposition of a general fixed asset would remove the related accumulated depreciation.

To illustrate the financial statements of the General Fixed Assets Account Group, a statement of general fixed assets for the City of Martinsville is shown in Illustration III on page 711. This basic statement shows the total amount for each category of fixed assets (Land, Buildings, etc.). The counter-balancing equity indicates the sources of the assets. When each of the asset categories is summarized in one amount, it is also desirable to provide a schedule which indicates the function or activity to which the fixed assets were assigned.

Governmental units generally comply with legal regulations in accounting for fixed assets. However, supporting records in a gov-

---

[1] Statement 1, *Governmental Accounting and Financial Reporting Principles* (Chicago: Municipal Finance Officers Association of the United States and Canada, March, 1979), p. 10.

Illustration III

City of Martinsville
Statement of General Fixed Assets
December 31, 19X2

General fixed assets:	
Land	$1,259,500
Buildings*	2,855,500
Improvements other than buildings	1,036,750
Machinery and equipment	452,500
Construction in progress	1,722,250
Total general fixed assets	$7,326,500
Investment in general fixed assets from:	
Capital projects funds:	
General obligation bonds	$3,954,100
Federal grants	1,000,000
State grants	300,000
County grants	625,000
General fund revenues	562,400
Special revenue fund revenues	309,500
Special assessments	400,000
Private gifts	175,500
Total investment in general fixed assets	$7,326,500

*Includes $300,000 for building under noncancelable long-term lease.

ernmental unit are often incomplete and fail to provide the data that would be the output of a properly functioning system of asset control. It is unfortunate that the law does not require adherence to the same principles and procedures which are used by commercial accounting in its treatment of plant assets. Not only would the citizenry be better informed by these procedures, but the financial management of the governmental unit would be more efficient.

ACCOUNTING FOR THE GENERAL LONG-TERM DEBT ACCOUNT GROUP

When long-term debt will be met by the resources of a specific fund, it is shown as a liability of that fund, as in the case of proprietary funds, fiduciary funds, and Special Assessment funds. All other long-term debt is labeled *general long-term debt* and is accounted for in the General Long-Term Debt Account Group. This account group, which was designed to monitor long-term debt that is not the responsibility of any particular fund, furnishes a record of the unmatured principal of all general long-term obligations of the governmental unit. Interest is not accounted for in the General Long-Term Debt Account Group. To maintain the self-balancing nature of the account group, the issuance of long-term obligations is recorded by debiting Amount To Be Provided for Payment of (properly identified) Debt and crediting a liability account.

To illustrate the entries for the General Long-Term Debt Account Group, assume that a unit incurs a general long-term obligation in the form of term bonds of $1,000,000.[2] The price at which the bonds are sold will not affect the entry to record the issuance of the bonds. As shown in the following entry, the bonds are recorded in the General Long-Term Debt Account Group at the face value to be redeemed at maturity.

Amount To Be Provided for Payment of Term Bonds	1,000,000	
Term Bonds Payable		1,000,000

Payment of both principal and interest is handled by the Debt Service Fund, where "service" is synonymous with "payment," but the General Long-Term Debt Account Group records all amounts that become available in the Debt Service Fund for retirement of general long-term debt principal. Assuming that the Debt Service Fund receives an annual appropriation of $80,000 to provide for the eventual retirement of the term bonds, the following entry is recorded in the General Long-Term Debt Account Group:

Amount Available in Debt Service Funds—Term Bonds	80,000	
Amount To Be Provided for Payment of Term Bonds		80,000

If sound actuarial practices have been employed, the Debt Service Fund will retire the obligation at the appropriate time, and the General Long-Term Debt Account Group will make the following entry:

Term Bonds Payable	1,000,000	
Amount Available in Debt Service Funds— Term Bonds.................................		1,000,000

The only statement provided by this account group is the statement of general long-term debt, which is composed of two sections. In the statement for the City of Martinsville, in Illustration IV on page 713, the first section shows the amounts available in the Debt Service Fund for term bonds, serial bonds, and long-term leases, and the amounts still to be provided for their retirement. The second section lists the total term and serial bond debt payable and the liability on capitalized leases. In this statement, the amount already available plus the amount to be provided must always equal the maturity value of the long-term debt.

REVIEW OF ENTRIES FOR THE GENERAL FUND AND ACCOUNT GROUPS

The following example will provide a comprehensive review of the General Fund and the General Fixed Assets Account Group and General Long-Term Debt Account Group. The General Fund balance sheet for Junction City, as of December 31, 19X2, is on page 713.

---

[2] A term bond is one in which the entire principal is due on one date. A serial bond issue is redeemed in periodic payments. Term bonds are rare, but better illustrate entries in the General Long-Term Debt Account Group.

Illustration IV

City of Martinsville
Statement of General Long-Term Debt
December 31, 19X2

Amount Available and To Be Provided
for the Payment of General Long-Term Debt

Term bonds:		
Amount available in debt service funds	$ 196,205	
Amount to be provided	203,795	
Total—term bonds		$ 400,000
Serial bonds:		
Amount available in debt service funds	$ 14,005	
Amount to be provided	2,385,995	
Total—serial bonds		2,400,000
Other general long-term liabilities:		
Amount to be provided for noncurrent liability on lease-purchase agreement		200,000
Total available and to be provided		$3,000,000

General Long-Term Debt

Term bonds payable	$ 400,000
Serial bonds payable	2,400,000
Liability on capitalized leases............................	200,000
Total general long-term debt payable	$3,000,000

Junction City
General Fund Balance Sheet
December 31, 19X2

Assets

Cash		$100,000
Taxes receivable—delinquent (19X2)	$50,000	
Less allowance for uncollectible delinquent taxes—19X2	20,000	30,000
Tax liens receivable—19X1	$25,000	
Less allowance for uncollectible tax liens—19X1	5,000	20,000
Inventory of supplies		20,000
Total assets		$170,000

Liabilities and Fund Equity

Liabilities:		
Vouchers payable		$ 30,000
Fund balances:		
Reserved for encumbrances—19X2	$ 40,000	
Reserved for inventory of supplies	20,000	
Unreserved	80,000	
Total fund equity		140,000
Total liabilities and fund equity		$170,000

During 19X3, the following entries were recorded in the General Fund of Junction City. If an event also requires that an entry be made in one of the account groups, the necessary entry is indicated as part of the event.

Event	Entry in the General Fund

The budget is approved. Estimated inflows are from:

Revenues	$600,000		
General long-term debt issuance	200,000		
Transfers from other funds ..	60,000		
Sales of fixed assets carried at $100,000 (amount received above carrying value is recorded as revenue) ...	114,000		

Estimated outflows are for:

Expenditures	$860,000
Transfers to other funds	50,000

Entry:

Estimated Revenues Control	614,000	
Estimated Other Financing Sources Control	360,000	
Appropriations Control		860,000
Estimated Other Financing Uses Control		50,000
Budgetary Fund Balance		64,000

Property taxes of $500,000 are levied, of which $30,000 is estimated to be uncollectible.

Taxes Receivable—Current	500,000	
Allowance for Uncollectible Current Taxes		30,000
Revenues Control		470,000

Collection of taxes and related interest for the year:

Current taxes	$450,000
Delinquent 19X2 taxes	32,000
Interest on delinquent taxes.	2,000
Tax liens—19X1	10,000
Interest on tax liens—19X1..	1,000
Total	$495,000

Entry:

Cash	495,000	
Taxes Receivable—Current		450,000
Taxes Receivable—Delinquent (19X2)		32,000
Tax Liens Receivable—19X1		10,000
Revenues Control		3,000

Property against which there are unpaid tax liens for 19X1 is sold for $7,000. (The loss is an adjustment of current revenue.)

Cash	7,000	
Allowance for Uncollectible Tax Liens—19X1	5,000	
Revenues Control	3,000	
Tax Liens Receivable—19X1		15,000

Tax liens totaling $18,000 are issued against 19X2 delinquent taxpayers.

Tax Liens Receivable—19X2	18,000	
Taxes Receivable—Delinquent (19X2)		18,000

Allowance for Uncollectible Delinquent Taxes is reclassified and is reduced, so as not to exceed the related tax liens receivable of $18,000. As a change in estimate, the credit is made to Revenues Control.

Allowance for Uncollectible Delinquent Taxes—19X2	20,000	
Allowance for Uncollectible Tax Liens—19X2		18,000
Revenues Control		2,000

Uncollected current taxes are declared delinquent and the related allowance is reclassified.

Taxes Receivable—Delinquent (19X3)	50,000	
Taxes Receivable—Current		50,000
Allowance for Uncollectible Current Taxes	30,000	
Allowance for Uncollectible Delinquent Taxes—19X3		30,000

Event	Entry in the General Fund		
Cash received for licenses, fees, and fines totals $70,000.	Cash .... Revenues Control	70,000	70,000
A general long-term $200,000 serial bond issue is sold for 102. The premium will be transferred to another fund. This event requires an entry in the General Long-Term Debt Account Group:	Cash .... Other Financing Sources Control .. Due to Other Funds	204,000	200,000 4,000

Amount To Be Provided
for Payment of Serial
Bonds 200,000
   Serial Bonds Payable   200,000

Event	Entry in the General Fund		
Other funds transfer $60,000 to the General Fund.	Cash .... Other Financing Sources Control ..	60,000	60,000
During 19X2 an entry to record a $4,500 encumbrance was omitted in error.	Unreserved Fund Balance .... Fund Balance Reserved for Encumbrances—19X2	4,500	4,500
Invoices are received totaling $46,000 and covering all 19X2 encumbrances. (The difference between the invoices and the reserve for encumbrances is treated as a change in accounting estimate.)	Fund Balance Reserved for Encumbrances—19X2 .... Expenditures Control .... Vouchers Payable	44,500 1,500	46,000
Total amount encumbered for approved 19X3 purchase orders was $600,000.	Encumbrances Control .... Fund Balance Reserved for Encumbrances—19X3	600,000	600,000

The following vouchers were approved:		Expenditures Control .... Inventory of Supplies .... Vouchers Payable	800,000 70,000	870,000
General expenditures	$760,000			
Purchase of equipment	40,000			
Purchase of supplies (a perpetual inventory system is used)	70,000			
Total	$870,000			

Event	Entry in the General Fund		
Of this total, $510,000 was encumbered. The following entry is required in the General Fixed Assets Account Group:	Fund Balance Reserved for Encumbrances—19X3 .... Encumbrances Control	510,000	510,000

Machinery and Equipment 40,000
   Investment in General Fixed Assets from General Fund Revenues 40,000

Event	Entry in the General Fund		
$50,000 was transferred from the General Fund to other funds.	Other Financing Uses Control .... Cash	50,000	50,000
Vouchers totaling $880,000 were paid.	Vouchers Payable .... Cash	880,000	880,000

Event	Entry in the General Fund		
The year-end supplies inventory amounted to $26,000.	Expenditures Control	64,000	
	Inventory of Supplies ($20,000 + $70,000 − $26,000)		64,000
Fund Balance Reserved for Inventory of Supplies is adjusted.	Unreserved Fund Balance	6,000	
	Fund Balance Reserved for Inventory of Supplies ($26,000 − $20,000)		6,000
Equipment carried at $100,000 in the General Fixed Assets Account Group is sold for $114,000. The following entry is required in the General Fixed Assets Account Group:	Cash	114,000	
	Other Financing Sources Control ..		100,000
	Revenues Control		14,000

Investment in General
Fixed Assets from Gen-
eral Fund Revenues ...   100,000
   Machinery and Equip-
   ment   100,000

Event	Entry in the General Fund		
Books are closed at year end. (a) Budgetary accounts are closed by reversing original entry.	Appropriations Control	860,000	
	Estimated Other Financing Uses Control	50,000	
	Budgetary Fund Balance	64,000	
	Estimated Revenues Control		614,000
	Estimated Other Financing Sources Control		360,000
(b) Operating accounts are closed.	Revenues Control	556,000	
	Other Financing Sources Control	360,000	
	Unreserved Fund Balance	89,500	
	Expenditures Control		865,500
	Other Financing Uses Control		50,000
	Encumbrances Control		90,000

QUESTIONS

1. Discuss the significance of creating the General Accounting Office as a legislative agency.
2. Explain the financial advantage for a governmental unit to adhere to generally accepted accounting principles.
3. Define a "fund" as the term is used in governmental accounting. How does it differ from the definition used in commercial accounting?
4. Why are fixed assets presented in a separate General Fixed Assets Account Group?
5. The NCGA has recommended the use of five governmental funds. Identify the fund described in each of the following cases:
   (a) Every governmental unit should have this fund to account for day-to-day operations.

(b) The fund that accounts for payment of principal and interest on long-term debt.

(c) The fund that accounts for revenues from a city sales tax imposed to finance construction of a new bridge.

(d) The fund that accounts for proceeds from a bond issue to be used to construct a library.

(e) The fund that accounts for charges levied against properties directly benefited by improvements.

6. Define revenues and expenditures as the terms apply to governmental funds.

7. List the advantages of introducing budgetary accounts into the accounting system.

8. Discuss the significance of the encumbrance system.

9. What is the purpose of establishing the account Fund Balance Reserved for Inventory in the General Fund?

10. What are the two major differences between the year-end balance sheet of the General Fund and the balance sheet of a commercial enterprise? What logic led to those differences?

11. How would you interpret the amount in Unreserved Fund Balance shown in a General Fund balance sheet?

12. What events would involve a debit or credit to Unreserved Fund Balance in the General Fund?

13. Explain the two principal differences between the interim and year-end balance sheets of the General Fund.

14. Contrary to general procedure, some funds do account for their own fixed assets. Why is this deviation tolerated?

15. Discuss the purpose of the General Long-Term Debt Account Group.

EXERCISES

Exercise 1. Prepare the entries to record the following General Fund transactions for the Town of Hanover for the year ended June 30, 19X4:

(a) Revenues are estimated at $500,000; appropriations are estimated at $490,000.

(b) A tax levy is set at $350,000, of which 1% will likely be uncollectible.

(c) Purchase orders amounting to $280,000 are authorized.

(d) Tax receipts total $345,000.

(e) Invoices totaling $235,000 are received and vouchered for orders originally estimated at $233,000.

(f) Salaries amounting to $140,000 are approved for payment.

(g) A federal grant-in-aid of $100,000 is received.

(h) Miscellaneous revenues of $15,000 are collected.

(i) Land is purchased for a wildlife sanctuary at a cost of $75,000. No encumbrance had been made for this item.

(j) Land adjacent to the sanctuary is donated to the town. The fair market value of the land is $40,000.

(k) Amounts of $10,000 due to other town funds are approved for payment. (Credit: Due to Other Funds)

(l) The town's share of sales tax due from the state is $35,000.

(m) All vouchers are paid.

(n) Accounts are closed at the end of the year.

Exercise 2. The following related entries were recorded in sequence in the General Fund of a municipality:

1. Encumbrances Control	12,000	
Fund Balance Reserved for Encumbrances		12,000
2. Fund Balance Reserved for Encumbrances	12,000	
Encumbrances Control		12,000
3. Expenditures Control	12,350	
Vouchers Payable		12,350

For each of the following items that relate to the series of entries, select the best answer:

1. The sequence of entries indicates that:
   a. An adverse event was foreseen and a reserve of $12,000 was created; later the reserve was canceled and a liability for the item was acknowledged.
   b. An order was placed for goods or services estimated to cost $12,000; the actual cost was $12,350, for which a liability was acknowledged upon receipt.
   c. Encumbrances were anticipated, but later failed to materialize and were reversed. A liability of $12,350 was incurred.
   d. The first entry was erroneous and was reversed; a liability of $12,350 was acknowledged.
2. Entries similar to those for the General Fund may also appear on the books of the municipality's:
   a. General Fixed Assets Account Group.
   b. General Long-Term Debt Account Group.
   c. Fiduciary Fund.
   d. Special Revenue Fund.
3. Assuming appropriate governmental accounting principles were followed, the entries:
   a. Occurred in the same fiscal period.
   b. Did not occur in the same fiscal period.
   c. Could have occurred in the same fiscal period, but it is impossible to be sure of this.
   d. Reflect the equivalent of a prior period adjustment if the entity concerned had been one that was operated for profit.
4. Immediately after entry 1 was recorded, the municipality had a balanced General Fund budget. What would be the effect of recording entries 2 and 3? The recording would:
   a. Not change the balanced condition of the budget.
   b. Cause the municipality to show a surplus.
   c. Cause the municipality to show a deficit.
   d. Not affect the current budget but would affect the budget of the following fiscal period.   (AICPA adapted)

Exercise 3. The trial balance prepared for the City of Figie for its fiscal year ended June 30, 19X5, is shown at the top of page 719.

(1) Prepare a balance sheet as of June 30, 19X5.
(2) Prepare a statement of revenues, expenditures, and changes in fund balances, using budget and actual amounts with variances for the fiscal year ended June 30, 19X5, and reflecting the total fund equity.

Cash	110,000	
Receivables (net)	40,000	
Vouchers Payable		65,000
Fund Balance Reserved for Encumbrances		60,000
Unreserved Fund Balance		18,000
Budgetary Fund Balance	5,000	
Estimated Revenues Control	600,000	
Revenues Control		610,000
Appropriations Control..............................		605,000
Expenditures Control	543,000	
Encumbrances Control	60,000	
	1,358,000	1,358,000

Exercise 4. The bookkeeper for Carson City spilled coffee on the trial balance of its General Fund, but the following balances were available as of December 31, 19X1:

Vouchers Payable		28,000
Fund Balance Reserved for Encumbrances—19X1		19,000
Fund Balance Reserved for Encumbrances—19X0		40,000
Unreserved Fund Balance		8,000
Budgetary Fund Balance		10,000
Estimated Revenues Control	430,000	
Revenues Control		437,000
Appropriations Control..............................		420,000
Expenditures Control	400,000	
Expenditures Applicable to 19X0	41,000	
Encumbrances Control	19,000	
	1,600,000	1,600,000

The bookkeeper mentioned that there was a $6,000 year-end inventory of supplies included in Expenditures Control, but did not know what to do about it.

Prepare a statement of revenues, expenditures, and changes in fund balances for the General Fund for the year ended December 31, 19X1, using the form that will result in the unreserved fund balance amount. Omit budgetary amounts and variances.

Exercise 5. Before the books were closed, the following account balances and information were extracted from the records of the General Fund of Adamsville at the end of the fiscal year, March 31, 19X6:

Unreserved Fund Balance, March 31, 19X6, $100,000.

Revenues for the year: estimated, $650,000; actual, $655,000.

Expenditures for the current fiscal year only, $600,000. Appropriations in the budget, $655,000. Balance of encumbrances on March 31, 19X6, $40,000.

Credit to Unreserved Fund Balance for a legitimate correction of an error of a prior period, $2,000.

Fund Balance Reserved for Inventory of Supplies, $3,000, created on March 31, 19X6, to make it equal to the inventory of the same amount.

(1) Sketch a T account for Unreserved Fund Balance and determine the beginning balance for that account as of April 1, 19X5.

(2) Prepare the closing entries and enter the Unreserved Fund Balance items into the T account to determine its post-closing balance.

(3) Prepare a statement of revenues, expenditures, and changes in fund balances

for the fiscal year ended March 31, 19X6, using the form that will produce the total fund equity. Incorporate the budgetary and actual amounts, as well as the favorable or unfavorable variances.

Exercise 6. For the following series of transactions, prepare the entries that would be recorded in the General Fixed Assets Account Group:

(a) The City of Gary purchased an abandoned store for $15,000 out of General Fund revenues. The store is to be used as a temporary warehouse building.

(b) A library, financed by general obligation bonds, was half completed at year end, with cost to date of $300,000.

(c) A refurbished farm house, belonging to the great-grandson of one of the city's founders, was donated to the city to be used as a historical landmark. The fair market value of the property was $200,000.

(d) A fire engine, originally purchased for $70,000, was traded for a new fire engine with a list price of $110,000. A cash difference of $80,000 was paid. Both engines were purchased from general property tax revenues.

(e) Main Street was repaved at a cost of $150,000, which is to be charged against property owners in the immediate area through special assessments.

Exercise 7. For the following series of transactions, prepare the entries that would be made in the General Long-Term Debt Account Group:

(a) To finance the construction of a library, $1,200,000 of general obligation term bonds were sold.

(b) The General Fund allocated $100,000 to a Debt Service Fund to begin to provide for retirement of the above bonds at maturity.

(c) To help finance the construction of a new school, $1,000,000 of 6%, 10-year serial bonds were sold at 101. During the year, one interest payment was made from General Fund revenues. An expenditure of $160,000 was recorded to cover the annual interest and the first serial redemption.

(d) Serial bonds of $100,000 matured and were retired through the Debt Service Fund.

(e) Special assessment bonds were sold to pay for the cost of repaving Main Street. Assessments against property owners would be sufficient to cover eventual bond retirement of $150,000 and to pay interest as it became due.

PROBLEMS

Problem 16-1. The January 1, 19X7 General Fund balance sheet for Starr Town is as follows:

Starr Town
General Fund Balance Sheet
January 1, 19X7

Assets

Cash		$ 6,500
Taxes receivable—delinquent	$12,000	
Less allowance for uncollectible delinquent taxes	5,000	7,000
Due from other funds		5,000
Inventory of supplies		3,000
Total assets		$21,500

Liabilities and Fund Equity

Vouchers payable	$ 6,000
Due to other funds..	4,000
Fund balance reserved for encumbrances—19X6	2,500
Fund balance reserved for inventory of supplies	3,000
Unreserved fund balance..	6,000
Total liabilities and fund equity	$21,500

The 19X7 General Fund transactions are summarized as follows:

(a) The town government approved a budget with estimated revenues of $200,000, appropriations of $195,000, and a planned transfer of $10,000 to the Debt Service Fund.

(b) Property taxes of $125,000 were levied, of which $4,000 is estimated to be uncollectible. Tax collections for the year totaled $125,000, of which $8,000 pertained to delinquent taxes of the previous year. The town decided that it would be fruitless to obtain tax liens on outstanding delinquent tax properties. All remaining delinquent taxes were written off as worthless. All current taxes were designated as delinquent at year end.

(c) The town received $75,000 from the state as a grant-in-aid, as was expected when the budget was prepared.

(d) A bequest of $10,000 was left to the town by A. C. Ness. The bequest, which had not been expected, is usable for current operations.

(e) Purchase orders of $175,000 were issued during the year, of which $3,000 were outstanding at year end. Total actual cost of items received was $170,000.

(f) All supplies were consumed by year end.

(g) An invoice for $3,000 was received for items purchased in 19X6. No other items applicable to 19X6 are outstanding.

(h) A total of $20,000 was paid, including $4,000 due to other funds, $10,000 transferred to the Debt Service Fund, and $6,000 for salaries.

(i) At year end, $5,000 of vouchers payable were outstanding.

Required:

(1) Prepare journal entries for the transactions. Closing entries are not required.

(2) Prepare a General Fund balance sheet as of December 31, 19X7.

(3) Prepare a statement of revenues, expenditures, and changes in fund balances for the General Fund for the year ended December 31, 19X7, producing as the final amount the total of fund balances—both reserved and unreserved. Budget and actual amounts are to be shown, along with variances.

Problem 16-2. The trial balances at the top of page 722 were taken from the accounts of the Highview School District General Fund before the books had been closed for the fiscal year ended June 30, 19X7.

Additional information:

(a) The estimated taxes receivable for the year ended June 30, 19X7, were $2,870,000, and the taxes collected during the year totaled $2,810,000.

(b) Encumbrances in the amount of $2,700,000 were recorded.

(c) During the year, the General Fund was billed $142,000 for services performed on its behalf by other city funds. (Debit Expenditures Control.)

	Trial Balance July 1, 19X6	Trial Balance June 30, 19X7
Cash	400,000	700,000
Taxes Receivable	150,000	170,000
Allowance for Uncollectible Taxes	(40,000)	(70,000)
Estimated Revenues Control...................	—	3,000,000
Expenditures Control.........................	—	2,840,000
Encumbrances Control	—	91,000
	510,000	6,731,000
Vouchers Payable	80,000	408,000
Due to Other Funds	210,000	142,000
Fund Balance Reserved for Encumbrances	60,000	91,000
Unreserved Fund Balance	160,000	160,000
Budgetary Fund Balance	—	20,000
Revenue from Taxes	—	2,800,000
Miscellaneous Revenues	—	130,000
Appropriations Control	—	2,980,000
	510,000	6,731,000

(d) An analysis of the transactions in the vouchers payable account for the year ended June 30, 19X7, follows:

Debit (Credit)

Current expenditures (liquidating all encumbrances to date)..	$(2,700,000)
Expenditures applicable to previous year	(58,000)
Vouchers for payments to other funds	(210,000)
Cash payments during year	2,640,000
Net change	$ (328,000)

(e) On May 10, 19X7, encumbrances are recorded for the purchase of next year's textbooks at an estimated cost of $91,000.

Required:

Based upon the data presented, reconstruct the original detailed journal entries that were required to record all transactions for the fiscal year ended June 30, 19X7, including the recording of the current year's budget. Do not prepare closing entries at June 30, 19X7.   (AICPA adapted)

Problem 16-3. The post-closing trial balance of the General Fund for the City of Stanley on March 31, 19X7, the end of its fiscal year, is as follows:

Cash	30,000	
Taxes Receivable—Delinquent	10,000	
Allowance for Uncollectible Delinquent Taxes		4,000
Inventory of Supplies	2,500	
Vouchers Payable		9,000
Fund Balance Reserved for Encumbrances—19X7		4,500
Fund Balance Reserved for Inventory of Supplies		2,500
Unreserved Fund Balance		22,500
	42,500	42,500

A summary of the General Fund transactions for the fiscal year ending March 31, 19X8, follows:

(a) The city authorized a budget with estimated revenues of $300,000 and

appropriations of $310,000.
- (b) Taxes of $225,000 were levied. A 2% allowance for uncollectible taxes has been justified in the past. Tax collections amounted to $225,000, of which $5,000 was applicable to delinquent taxes. Liens were obtained on outstanding delinquent taxes.
- (c) Miscellaneous fines and license fees totaling $12,500 were collected.
- (d) The city received $55,000 as its distributive portion of federal revenue sharing.
- (e) Purchase orders of $220,000 were issued. Goods received amounted to $218,000 and included $4,500 of items ordered in the previous year. The invoice price and purchase order price were identical on all items.
- (f) A gymnasium was added to the school at a cost of $85,000. Money from the General Fund was used in payment, as had been authorized.
- (g) Purchases of supplies amounted to $6,000 during the year. At year end, there were $1,500 of supplies on hand.
- (h) Unpaid vouchers at year end amounted to $3,000.

Required:

- (1) Prepare journal entries to record the transactions, indicating the fund or account group in which each entry would be made.
- (2) Prepare the General Fund balance sheet as of March 31, 19X8.
- (3) Prepare a statement of revenues, expenditures, and changes in fund balances for the General Fund for the fiscal year ended March 31, 19X8, using the alternative form that produces the unreserved fund balance.

Problem 16-4. A summary of the General Fund transactions for the City of Whitby for the year ended December 31, 19X7, is as follows:
- (a) A budget is approved, showing estimated revenues of $900,000, appropriations of $875,000, transfers in of $27,000 from other funds, and required transfers of $20,000 to other funds.
- (b) Property taxes in the amount of $550,000 were levied. In past years, 1% of property taxes levied proved uncollectible.
- (c) Encumbrances for $25,000 had not been liquidated by the end of 19X6. Invoices for all these items were received in 19X7 and totaled $24,000. An account Fund Balance Reserved for Encumbrances—19X6 existed.
- (d) Collections from property taxes totaled $544,000, of which $20,000 represented collections on delinquent taxes. Delinquent taxes of $8,000 remain uncollected, on which a $3,000 allowance is carried. Remaining taxes receivable—current and taxes receivable—delinquent were converted into taxes receivable—delinquent and tax liens receivable, respectively.
- (e) Purchase orders totaling $600,000 were issued. Subsequently, invoices were received amounting to $585,000 for items estimated to cost $580,000.
- (f) Included in the recorded expenditures are $10,000 of supplies. An ending inventory of supplies amounted to $2,000, for which the fund balance should be reserved.
- (g) A tract of land was purchased for $250,000. Payment was made from the General Fund, in whose appropriations the item had been included. The amount had not been encumbered.
- (h) Whitby received $300,000 as its part of federal revenue-sharing programs. Grants-in-aid of $60,000 due from the state government are recorded.

(i) Required transfers of $20,000 are made to other funds.
(j) An offer was received by a land developer who will pay $380,000 for the land acquired by the city in (g). The sale is approved. The developer remits $100,000 with a note due in 90 days, bearing 8% interest.
(k) Transfers received from other funds amount to $23,000.
(l) The developer in (j) remits payment for the note plus interest.

Required:

(1) Prepare journal entries to record the General Fund transactions.
(2) Prepare closing entries for the General Fund.
(3) Prepare a statement of revenues, expenditures, and changes in fund balances, using the form preferred by the NCGA and incorporating budgetary items. On January 1, 19X7, Unreserved Fund Balance showed a debit balance (deficit) of $180,000.

Problem 16-5.   The following statement of general fixed assets was obtained from the records of the City of Blade:

City of Blade
Statement of General Fixed Assets
December 31, 19X7

General fixed assets:	
Land	$1,000,000
Buildings	2,150,000
Improvements other than buildings	1,400,000
Machinery and equipment	800,000
Construction in progress	250,000
Total general fixed assets	$5,600,000
Investments in general fixed assets from:	
Capital projects funds:	
Serial bonds	$1,900,000
Federal grants	800,000
State grants	450,000
General fund revenues	1,250,000
Special assessments	1,200,000
Total investment in general fixed assets	$5,600,000

A summary of fixed asset transactions for 19X8 follows:
(a) Construction on the new school, started during 19X7, was completed at a total cost of $850,000, which was financed by a serial bond issue. No other construction was in progress at the beginning of 19X8.
(b) Jasper Lloyd donated 400 acres of land to the city to be used as a park. The land had a fair market value of $140,000 when donated.
(c) The municipal water works constructed a new pumping plant at a cost of $120,000. The plant was financed from the water utility revenues.
(d) The fire department traded in an old fire engine and $90,000 cash for a new model. The old equipment had originally cost $65,000 and $15,000 was allowed on the trade-in.
(e) The city hall was refurbished at a cost of $40,000, which was paid from General Fund revenues. The refurbishing constituted a capital improvement.
(f) Road use taxes of $30,000 were collected by a Special Assessment Fund, of which $20,000 has been used for improvements other than buildings.

Required:

(1) Prepare journal entries only for those transactions that are to be accounted for in the General Fixed Assets Account Group.
(2) Prepare a statement of general fixed assets as of December 31, 19X8.

Problem 16-6. On June 30, 19X7, the end of the fiscal year, the Longfellow School District prepared the following General Fund trial balance:

Cash	47,250	
Taxes Receivable—Current	31,800	
Allowance for Uncollectible Current Taxes		1,800
Temporary Investments	11,300	
Inventory of Supplies	11,450	
Buildings	1,300,000	
Estimated Revenues Control	1,007,000	
Appropriations Control		1,000,000
Revenue from State Grants		300,000
Bonds Payable		1,000,000
Vouchers Payable		10,200
Expenditures Control	848,200	
Debt Service from Current Funds	130,000	
Capital Outlays (equipment)	22,000	
Revenues Control		1,008,200
Unreserved Fund Balance		88,800
	3,409,000	3,409,000

An examination of the records disclosed the following information:

(a) The recorded estimate of losses for the current year taxes receivable was considered to be adequate.
(b) The local government unit gave the school district twenty acres of land to be used for a new grade school and a community playground. The unrecorded estimated value of the land was $50,000. In addition, a state grant of $300,000 was received and the full amount was used in payment of contracts pertaining to the construction of the grade school. Purchases of classroom and playground equipment costing $22,000 were paid from general funds.
(c) Five years ago, a 4%, 10-year, sinking fund bond issue in the amount of $1,000,000 for constructing school buildings was sold and is outstanding. Interest on the issue is payable at maturity. Budgetary requirements of a contribution of $130,000 to the Debt Service Fund were met. Of this amount, $100,000 represents the fifth equal contribution for principal repayment.
(d) Outstanding purchase orders not recorded in the accounts at year end totaled $2,800.
(e) A physical inventory of supplies at year end revealed $6,500 of supplies on hand.
(f) Except where indicated to the contrary, all recordings were made in the General Fund.

Required:

(1) Prepare the adjusting entries to correct the General Fund records.
(2) Prepare the adjusting entries for the General Fixed Assets Account Group and the General Long-Term Debt Account Group. (AICPA adapted)

Problem 16-7. The City of Granville has used only a General Fund in past accounting periods. An audit has revealed the following facts concerning fixed assets and long-term debt of the City of Granville as of December 31, 19X5:

(a) Albert Sperry donated 100 acres of land to the city to be used as a construction site for a school complex, recreational facility, and city park. The land had a fair market value of $90,000.

(b) To finance the school, the city issued $1,000,000 of 6%, 20-year general obligation bonds. On January 3, 19X1, immediately after the bonds were sold, a sinking fund was established to retire the bonds upon maturity. Each year, $50,000 was to be contributed to the sinking fund. The current year's contribution was made.

(c) Construction on the school was started on January 17, 19X1, with 60% of the school completed in 19X1 and the remaining 40% in 19X2. Total construction cost amounted to $1,000,000.

(d) The recreational facility was constructed in 19X3 at a cost of $250,000. Grants of $50,000 from the state government and $75,000 from the federal government were applied to the cost of the recreational facility. Robert Plate donated $20,000 in cash to be used to cover part of the cost. The remainder of the cost was paid from General Fund revenues.

(e) A summary of other asset purchases for 19X1 through 19X5 follows:

Date	Quantity	Type	Unit Cost	Total Cost
January 1, 19X1	2	Fire engines	$70,000	$140,000
February 1, 19X1	5	Trucks	17,000	85,000
March 1, 19X1	1	Machine	40,000	40,000
January 1, 19X3	2	Vans	10,000	20,000
January 1, 19X4	2	Trucks	27,500	55,000
January 1, 19X5	3	Police cars	7,000	21,000

The above purchases were financed by city property taxes.

(f) Two of the trucks purchased on February 1, 19X1, were traded in for the two trucks purchased on January 1, 19X4. The city paid a cash difference of $55,000 on the two trucks, which had a market value of $30,000 and $35,000 respectively.

(g) A municipal garage was constructed in 19X1, at a total cost of $125,000, to house the city's vehicles and equipment. A 5-year, 6% note was signed by the city and given to the contractor.

(h) Special assessments of $350,000 financed improvements to the roads and sewer system in 19X5.

(i) A court house was constructed as a capital project in 19X3 for $300,000. To cover the cost of construction, 5% serial bonds were issued. The first $50,000 would become due on January 1, 19X8.

Required:

(1) Record the transactions as they should have been entered each period in the General Fixed Assets Account Group and General Long-Term Debt Account Group.

(2) Prepare the statement of general fixed assets and the statement of general long-term debt as of December 31, 19X5.

Problem 16-8. The City of Foster was incorporated on January 1, 19X2. On December 31, 19X7, a careful study of the city's records revealed the following information regarding long-term debt:

(a) General obligation bonds in the amount of $1,500,000 were authorized and issued at face value on July 1, 19X2, to finance the construction of a school. The 6% bonds pay interest semiannually on January 1 and July 1 and mature 10 years from the issuance date.

(b) Serial bonds of $1,000,000 were sold at 99 on January 1, 19X4, to help finance a new city hall and cultural center. An additional $750,000 was received from an anonymous benefactor. The 5% serial bonds would be redeemed in annual amounts of $100,000, beginning on January 1, 19X7. A sinking fund was established on January 2, 19X4, to provide for the retirement of the serial bonds. Annual deposits of $70,000 are made on January 2 of each year, beginning in 19X4. All amounts deposited were immediately invested at a net yield of 8%.

(c) Property owners were assessed $750,000, to be paid in 5 equal annual installments to finance construction of a storm sewer system and repaving of the affected roadways. To pay for the construction, $600,000 of 5%, 5-year bonds were issued at face value.

(d) Term bonds totaling $400,000 were sold at face value on January 1, 19X5, to finance construction. The 10-year, 5% bonds pay interest semiannually on January 1 and July 1. Each year, $40,000 is to be set aside in a sinking fund to provide for retirement of the bonds at maturity. Any income earned by the sinking fund is to be applied to the semiannual interest payments.

Required:

(1) Prepare only the journal entries for the transactions that would be recorded in the General Long-Term Debt Account Group through December 31, 19X7.

(2) Prepare a statement of general long-term debt for the City of Foster as of December 31, 19X7.

Problem 16-9. You have been engaged by the Town of Ego to examine its June 30, 19X8 balance sheet. You are the first CPA to be engaged by the town, and you find that acceptable methods of municipal accounting have not been employed. The town clerk stated that the books had not been closed and presented the following trial balance of the General Fund as of June 30, 19X8:

Cash	150,000	
Taxes Receivable—Current Year	59,200	
Allowance for Estimated Losses—Current Year Taxes Receivable		18,000
Taxes Receivable—Prior Year	8,000	
Allowance for Estimated Losses—Prior Year Taxes Receivable		10,200
Estimated Revenues	310,000	
Appropriations		348,000
Donated Land	27,000	
Expenditures—Building Addition Constructed	50,000	
Expenditures—Serial Bonds Paid	16,000	
Other Expenditures	280,000	
Revenues		354,000
Accounts Payable		126,000
Unreserved Fund Balance		44,000
	900,200	900,200

Additional information:

(a) The estimated losses of $18,000 for current year taxes receivable were determined to be a reasonable estimate, but for the prior year, they should not exceed 100%.

(b) Included in the revenues account is a credit of $27,000 representing the value of land donated by the state for construction of a municipal park.

(c) The Expenditures—Building Addition Constructed balance is the cost of an addition to the Town Hall building. This addition was constructed and completed in June, 19X8. The General Fund recorded the payment as authorized.

(d) The Expenditures—Serial Bonds Paid balance reflects the transfer to the Debt Service Fund that accounts for serial bond retirement and interest payments. Transfer of interest payments of $7,000 for this bond issue is included in Other Expenditures.

(e) Operating supplies ordered in the prior fiscal year and chargeable to that year were received, recorded, and consumed in July, 19X7. The outstanding purchase orders for these supplies, which were not recorded in the accounts at June 30, 19X7, amounted to $8,800. The vendors' invoices for these supplies totaled $9,400 and were charged to Other Expenditures.

(f) Outstanding purchase orders at June 30, 19X8, for operating supplies totaled $2,100. These purchase orders were not recorded on the books.

(g) The balance in Revenues includes credits for $20,000 for a note issued to a bank to obtain cash in anticipation of tax collections and for $1,000 for the sale of scrap iron from the town's water plant. The note was still outstanding at June 30, 19X8. Operations of the water plant are accounted for in the Water Fund, which is to receive the proceeds from the scrap sale.

(h) At year end, current taxes are to be reclassified as delinquent.

Required:

(1) Prepare the adjusting entries for the General Fund for the fiscal year ended June 30, 19X8. Account titles should be respected if acceptable, even though different.

(2) Prepare formal adjusting journal entries for the General Fixed Assets Account Group and for the General Long-Term Debt Account Group.

(AICPA adapted)

Problem 16-10. You have been engaged to examine the financial statements of the town of Workville for the year ended June 30, 19X7. Your examination disclosed that due to the inexperience of the town's bookkeeper all transactions were recorded in the General Fund. The following General Fund Trial Balance as of June 30, 19X7, was furnished to you.

Cash	16,800	
Short-Term Investments	40,000	
Accounts Receivable	11,500	
Taxes Receivable—Current Year	30,000	
Tax Anticipation Notes Payable		50,000
Appropriations		400,000
Expenditures	382,000	
Estimated Revenues	320,000	
Revenues		360,000
General Property	85,400	
Bonds Payable	52,000	
Unreserved Fund Balance		127,700
	937,700	937,700

Your audit disclosed the following additional information:
  (a) The accounts receivable of $11,500 includes $1,500 due from the town's water utility for the sale of scrap sold on its behalf. Accounts for the municipal water utility operated by the town are maintained in a separate fund.
  (b) The balance in Taxes Receivable—Current Year is now considered delinquent, and the town estimates that $24,000 will be uncollectible.
  (c) On June 30, 19X7, the town retired, at face value, 6% general obligation serial bonds totaling $40,000. The bonds were issued on July 1, 19X2, at face value of $200,000. Interest paid during the year ended June 30, 19X7, was charged to Bonds Payable.
  (d) During the year, supplies totaling $128,000 were purchased and charged to Expenditures. The town conducted a physical inventory of supplies on hand at June 30, 19X7, and this physical count disclosed that supplies totaling $84,000 were used.
  (e) Expenditures for the year ended June 30, 19X7, included $11,200 applicable to purchase orders issued in the prior year. Outstanding purchase orders at June 30, 19X7, not recorded in the accounts amounted to $17,500.
  (f) On June 28, 19X7, the state informed the town that its share of a state-collected, locally-shared tax of $34,000 was remitted.
  (g) During the year, equipment with a book value of $7,900 was removed from service and sold for $4,600. In addition, new equipment costing $90,000 was purchased. The transactions were recorded in General Property.
  (h) During the year, 100 acres of land were donated to the town for use as an industrial park. The land had a value of $125,000. No recording of this donation has been made.

Required:

  (1) Prepare formal reclassification and adjusting journal entries for the General Fund as of June 30, 19X7. Account titles should be respected if acceptable, though different.
  (2) Prepare adjusting journal entries for the General Long-Term Debt Account Group and the General Fixed Assets Account Group as of June 30, 19X7.
  (AICPA adapted)

CHAPTER 17

GOVERNMENTAL ACCOUNTING: SPECIAL FUNDS

Special funds are self-balancing funds which are used to record events and to exhibit results for a specific area of responsibility. In a small town, there may not be enough activity to warrant more than a General Fund, but the larger the governmental unit and the more diverse the activities with which it is involved, the greater the necessity to introduce special funds.

SPECIAL REVENUE FUNDS

When revenue is to be devoted to a specified current operating purpose or to the acquisition of relatively minor fixed assets, and the revenues received are unrelated to the value of services rendered, its accounting is assigned to a *Special Revenue Fund*. An example of an activity that would be accounted for in a Special Revenue Fund would be the levy of a gasoline tax to finance the acquisition of snow removal equipment. In a Special Revenue Fund, the accounting must be designed to permit close scrutiny of activities. If more resources were produced than were anticipated, the project must not be permitted to expand beyond the original authorization, nor should money be permitted to accumulate beyond reasonable needs. However, sufficient resources should be generated to permit the activity to be completed successfully.

The desired control may be accomplished by using the same accounting procedures as those used by the General Fund. The budget, for example, is recorded by using the appropriate budgetary control accounts and their related subsidiary records. Commitments are recorded by using an encumbrance and expenditure system. Since both the accounting procedures and the financial statements for Special Revenue Funds parallel so closely those of the General Fund, they will not be illustrated.

A governmental unit having both a General Fund and a Special Revenue Fund would prepare a combined statement of revenues, expenditures, and changes in fund balances—budget and actual—for the two funds. The format would be similar to that illustrated on page 706. Its structure would show the following columnar amount headings, with totals as an optional feature:

General Fund			Special Revenue Funds			Total		
		Variance— Favorable			Variance— Favorable			Variance— Favorable
Budget	Actual	(Unfavorable)	Budget	Actual	(Unfavorable)	Budget	Actual	(Unfavorable)

CAPITAL PROJECTS FUNDS

Capital Projects Funds account for the construction of fixed assets benefiting the entire community. Each project should be accounted for separately in subsidiary records to demonstrate compliance with legal stipulations and contractual arrangements. The construction of fixed assets financed by proprietary funds or Special Assessment Funds, which account for their own fixed assets, should be excluded from Capital Projects Funds.

Resources for capital projects usually result from transfers received from the General Fund, proceeds of general obligation bonds, or grants from another governmental unit that has agreed to cover part of the cost. Grants from another governmental unit are recorded as revenues. Transfers from the General Fund and bond proceeds which must be repaid are not recorded as revenues but as other financing sources. When there are several nonrevenue sources, they may be accounted for in one control account, Other Financing Sources Control.

As with all governmental funds (which excludes proprietary and fiduciary funds), Capital Projects Funds concentrate on inflows and outflows of available, spendable resources. Therefore, Capital Projects Funds use the modified accrual basis of accounting. Budgetary control is advisable when capital projects are expected to take several years to complete and will involve large amounts of money. The operating budget is prepared on an *annual* basis and, therefore, includes the expected revenues, estimated other financing sources, and estimated expenditures for only the current fiscal year. In the most complicated situation, resources for a capital project are received (1) from the General Fund, (2) from the sale of general obligation bonds, and (3) from the county, state, or federal government, each sustaining part of the cost. The following entry records the annual budget:

Estimated Other Financing Sources Control (for items 1 and 2)	xxx	
Estimated Revenues Control (for item 3)	xxx	
Appropriations Control		xxx
Budgetary Fund Balance (either debited or credited)		xxx

When resources result from bond proceeds, any premium on the sale of the bonds should be transferred to the Debt Service Fund, reducing the amount to be accumulated in that fund to meet interest payments. When the bonds are sold at a discount, however, legal and practical restrictions prevent the opposite movement. The discount merely reduces the amount shown as other financing sources.

A policy should be established to provide for any difference between the estimated and actual project costs. If resources were provided by a bond issue, any final excess cash should be transferred to the Debt Service Fund. If the General Fund provided the resources, it should receive any excess cash available upon the project's completion. If actual project costs exceed the estimate, the deficiency is typically covered by a transfer from the General Fund.

Although a project may not be completed at the end of a fiscal period, typical closing entries are recorded. Annual closing permits the actual activity to be compared with the legally adopted annual operating budget. Also, in the closing process, the credit to Expenditures Control provides the amount of capitalizable expenditures to be recorded in the General Fixed Assets Account Group as Construction in Progress.

Capital Projects Funds have the authority to continue expenditures within prescribed limits until a project is completed. There is no need to assign encumbrances to specific years, as was done in the General Fund, since emphasis is on the total project, rather than on annual encumbrances. Under the encumbrance system, when actual expenditures are recorded, the encumbrance entry is reversed. To be able to continue this reversal procedure after the books have been closed for a fiscal year, but before a project is completed, Encumbrances Control must be reinstated with the following entry:

Encumbrances Control	xxx	
Unreserved Fund Balance		xxx

To illustrate accounting for Capital Projects Funds, assume that the City of Berryville plans to build a $300,000 addition to its municipal auditorium. The project will begin in 19X1 and is to be completed in 19X2. The following entries record the events that occur during construction. In these entries, payments are credited directly to Cash, although they would normally be vouchered and then paid.

Event	Entry		
The project budget is $300,000, to be financed by a general bond issue. The 19X1 operating budget is based on ⅓ of the work being completed that year. The city uses an other financing sources control account.	Estimated Other Financing Sources Control	300,000	
	Appropriations Control		100,000
	Budgetary Fund Balance		200,000
A $300,000 8% general bond issue is floated at 101. The premium is to be transferred to the Debt Service Fund.	Cash	303,000	
	Other Financing Sources Control		300,000
	Due to Other Funds		3,000
The bond premium is transferred.	Due to Other Funds	3,000	
	Cash		3,000
A contract is signed for the auditorium construction at an estimated cost of $270,000.	Encumbrances Control	270,000	
	Fund Balance Reserved for Encumbrances		270,000
The architect's bill for $10,650 is received, of which $7,650 is paid. Upon final building approval, the balance is due. The item was not encumbered.	Expenditures Control	10,650	
	Cash		7,650
	Vouchers Payable		3,000
A partial billing is received from the contractor for $60,000, equal to the amount encumbered for these items. The account Contracts Payable is credited for the liability to the principal contractors.	Expenditures Control	60,000	
	Contracts Payable		60,000
	Fund Balance Reserved for Encumbrances	60,000	
	Encumbrances Control		60,000
The contractor is paid $60,000.	Contracts Payable	60,000	
	Cash		60,000

Books for 19X1 are closed. The credit to Expenditures Control is the basis for the following entry in the General Fixed Assets Account Group:
Construction in
Progress 70,650
   Investment in General
   Fixed Assets from
   Capital Projects
   Funds 70,650
	Budgetary Fund Balance	200,000	

	Appropriations Control	100,000	
	Estimated Other Financing Sources Control		300,000
	Other Financing Sources Control	300,000	
	Encumbrances Control		210,000
	Expenditures Control		70,650
	Unreserved Fund Balance		19,350
At the beginning of 19X2, unexpended encumbrances at previous year end are reinstated.	Encumbrances Control	210,000	
	Unreserved Fund Balance		210,000
The operating budget for 19X2 is recorded; completion is estimated to cost an additional $200,000.	Budgetary Fund Balance	200,000	
	Appropriations Control		200,000
The contract is completed in 19X2. Additional cost is $227,000, of which $10,000 is withheld in a separate account, Contracts Payable—Retained Percentage, until final inspection and approval.	Expenditures Control	227,000	
	Contracts Payable		217,000
	Contracts Payable—Retained Percentage		10,000
	Fund Balance Reserved for Encumbrances	210,000	
	Encumbrances Control		210,000

Event	Entry		
Excluding the retained percentage, payment is made to the contractor.	Contracts Payable .... 217,000 Cash		217,000
Books for 19X2 are closed. The credit to Expenditures Control is the basis for the following entry in the General Fixed Assets Account Group:	Appropriations Control .... 200,000 Budgetary Fund Balance		200,000
	Unreserved Fund Balance .... 227,000 Expenditures Control		227,000

Buildings 297,650
  Construction in
  Progress 70,650
  Investment in General
  Fixed Assets from
  Capital Projects
  Funds 227,000

When a governmental unit has more than one Capital Projects Fund, *combining* financial statements are prepared. In these statements, a separate column is provided for each Capital Projects Fund. To show the structure of such statements, Illustration I is a combining balance sheet for the City of Berryville's Capital Projects Funds as of December 31, 19X1. The balance sheet presents the auditorium project for which entries were provided, plus another project for the construction of a bridge.

Illustration I

City of Berryville
Capital Projects Funds
Combining Balance Sheet
December 31, 19X1

Assets	Municipal Auditorium	Congress Avenue Bridge	Total
Cash	$232,350	$ 96,100	$328,450
Due from other funds	-0-	15,000	15,000
Total assets	$232,350	$111,100	$343,450

Liabilities and Fund Balances			
Vouchers payable	$ 3,000	$ 18,100	$ 21,100
Contracts payable	-0-	54,000	54,000
Due to other funds..	-0-	4,000	4,000
Total liabilities..	$ 3,000	$ 76,100	$ 79,100
Fund balances:			
Reserved for encumbrances	$210,000	$ 32,000	$242,000
Unreserved	19,350	3,000	22,350
Total fund balances	$229,350	$ 35,000	$264,350
Total liabilities and fund balances	$232,350	$111,100	$343,450

Unless the Capital Projects Fund has received a grant or other resources from other governmental units, the statement of revenues, expenditures, and changes in fund balances would show minimal revenues, since transfers from other funds and proceeds from sales of bonds are not considered revenue. Both are presented on the statement as other financing sources. The form presented in Illustration II is the one preferred by the NCGA, with the final amount representing the total of both reserved and unreserved fund balances.

Illustration II

City of Berryville
Capital Projects Funds
Combining Statement of Revenues, Expenditures, and Changes in Fund Balances
For the Year Ended December 31, 19X1

	Municipal Auditorium	Congress Avenue Bridge	Total
Revenues	-0-	$ 600	$ 600
Expenditures—capital projects	$ 70,650	100,600	171,250
Excess (deficiency) of revenues over expenditures	$ (70,650)	$(100,000)	$(170,650)
Other financing sources (uses):			
Proceeds of general obligation bonds	$300,000	$ 50,000	$ 350,000
Operating transfers in	-0-	61,000	61,000
Total other financing sources (uses)	$300,000	$ 111,000	$ 411,000
Excess (deficiency) of revenues and other sources over expenditures	$229,350	$ 11,000	$ 240,350
Fund balances at beginning of year	-0-	24,000	24,000
Fund balances at end of year	$229,350	$ 35,000	$ 264,350

SPECIAL ASSESSMENT FUNDS

Capital Projects Funds account for major projects that benefit the total community. Closely related are the *Special Assessment Funds* that account for public improvement projects, such as sidewalks, street lighting, or storm sewers, which primarily benefit a limited number of property owners and are paid for by assessments against those benefited. The initiative for such projects is often taken by the property owners, who request the improvement. However, authorization must be approved through appropriate governmental channels. Once the project is approved, the *annual* budget estimates, but not total project budget estimates, are recorded. An assessment is then levied against the affected property.

To promote successful collection, assessments are arranged on an installment basis. Assessments currently due are segregated from those due in future fiscal periods as the revenue is recorded:

Special Assessments Receivable—Current	100,000	
Special Assessments Receivable—Deferred	400,000	
Revenues Control		100,000
Deferred Revenues		400,000

At the end of the fiscal year, a deferred installment due within the next year is recognized as revenue, since it is measurable and will become available. Details of the assessment are entered in a subsidiary special assessment ledger, where the levy against each owner and its collection are indicated.

As a governmental fund, a Special Assessment Fund uses the modified accrual basis of accounting and follows procedures which are similar to those described for a Capital Projects Fund. Both funds account for the construction of capital facilities by using an encumbrance system; both are a function of a project rather than of an annual time period, but both use annual operating budgets. Although a special assessment project may not be completed by the end of the fiscal year, annual closing of the books is recommended. At the beginning of the next period, Encumbrances Control must be reinstated with a credit to Unreserved Fund Balance, as was the case with Capital Projects Funds.

Special assessment projects are costly, and payments cannot await the collection of installments. To meet construction costs and provide interim financing, a bond issue is floated. The proceeds are usually equal to the amount of the deferred installments, with initial costs being covered by the collection of the current installment. Redemption of the bonds and payments of the interest are the direct responsibility of the Special Assessment Fund. It must record and service the debt, making the typical entries used in financial accounting to record a bond sale, including the accrued interest, premium or discount, and amortization.

At year end, the capitalizable costs of special assessment projects are recorded in the General Fixed Assets Account Group. Interest expenditures are not capitalized, because the interest costs on special assessment bonds will be met from interest revenues on deferred special assessment installments receivable. Therefore, the net interest element will not materially affect the cost of the project. To simplify subsequent procedures, two expenditure control accounts could be established: Expenditures Control—Project (for capitalizable costs), and Expenditures Control—Interest. Accounting for the interest on deferred installment assessments receivable and on bonds payable should comply with the NCGA instruction that interest should not be accrued unless the date for payment has passed and payment has not been made.

To illustrate the journal entries for a Special Assessment Fund, assume that a street improvement project in the City of Hilton is to be financed by assessments against property owners. The series of events that occur during the first year of the project are described and recorded as follows:

Event	Entry		
The legislature approves the project, estimated to cost $250,000. Expenditures for the first year are estimated to be $170,000, including interest, and revenues are estimated to be $110,000. A bond issue will provide interim financing.	Estimated Revenues Control	110,000	
	Budgetary Fund Balance	60,000	
	Appropriations Control		170,000

Event	Entry		
Assessments of $250,000 are levied. Assessments are prorated over five years, with the first installment due this year.	Special Assessments Receivable—Current	50,000	
	Special Assessments Receivable—Deferred	200,000	
	Revenues Control		50,000
	Deferred Revenues		200,000
6% bonds with a face value of $200,000 are sold at 98 on an interest date.	Cash	196,000	
	Discount on Bonds Payable	4,000	
	Bonds Payable		200,000
A construction contract for $240,000 is signed and the amount is encumbered.	Encumbrances Control	240,000	
	Fund Balance Reserved for Encumbrances		240,000
The current assessment is collected in full.	Cash	50,000	
	Special Assessments Receivable—Current		50,000
Interest on deferred installments is received, totaling $18,000.	Cash	18,000	
	Revenues Control		18,000
Annual interest on bonds is paid. The discount is prorated over the 5-year life. Interest was not included in encumbrances.	Expenditures Control—Interest	12,800	
	Discount on Bonds Payable		800
	Cash		12,000
The next installment of $50,000 is reclassified as current. Deferred revenue is also reclassified.	Special Assessments Receivable—Current	50,000	
	Special Assessments Receivable—Deferred		50,000
	Deferred Revenues	50,000	
	Revenues Control		50,000
At year end, the street project is 60% completed. Expenditures totaling $157,000 are vouchered, liquidating encumbrances of $150,000.	Expenditures Control—Project	157,000	
	Vouchers Payable (or Contracts Payable)		157,000
	Fund Balance Reserved for Encumbrances	150,000	
	Encumbrances Control		150,000
Vouchers totaling $100,000 are paid.	Vouchers Payable	100,000	
	Cash		100,000
Additional expenditures of $5,000 not previously encumbered are approved for payment.	Expenditures Control—Project	5,000	
	Vouchers Payable		5,000
Books are closed at year end.	Appropriations Control	170,000	
	Estimated Revenues Control		110,000
	Budgetary Fund Balance		60,000
	Unreserved Fund Balance	146,800	
	Revenues Control	118,000	
	Encumbrances Control		90,000
	Expenditures Control—Project		162,000
	Expenditures Control—Interest		12,800

The following entry would also be required in the General Fixed Assets Account Group, using the amount from the closing entry for Expenditures Control—Project:

Construction in Progress	162,000	
Investment in General Fixed Assets from Special Assessments		162,000

Illustration III is a balance sheet for the Special Assessment Fund as of December 31, 19X2. The balance sheet follows a typical format, with the bonds payable and the deferred revenues appearing as liabilities of the Special Assessment Fund.

Illustration III

City of Hilton
Special Assessment Fund
Balance Sheet
December 31, 19X2

		Street Project
Assets		
Cash		$152,000
Special assessments receivable—current		50,000
Special assessments receivable—deferred		150,000
Total assets		$352,000
Liabilities and Fund Balances		
Liabilities:		
Vouchers payable		$ 62,000
Bonds payable	$ 200,000	
Less discount on bonds payable	3,200	196,800
Deferred revenues		150,000
Total liabilities		$408,800
Fund balances:		
Reserved for encumbrances	$ 90,000	
Unreserved	(146,800)	
Total fund balances		(56,800)
Total liabilities and fund balances		$352,000

The statement of revenues, expenditures, and changes in fund balances, presented in Illustration IV on page 739, has no peculiarities. If it is desired to show revenues and expenditures in detail, the information is available from the subsidiary records. If there were more than one special assessment project, combining financial statements would show one column for each project as well as a total column.

An additional statement to reveal cash movements may be provided for fiscal control and to inform property owners affected by the projects. This statement shows the beginning cash balance, receipts and disbursements, and the ending cash balance. It is merely an organized version of data in the cash account.

Illustration IV

City of Hilton
Special Assessment Fund
Statement of Revenues, Expenditures, and Changes in Fund Balances
For the Year Ended December 31, 19X2

	Street Project	
Revenues:		
Special assessments	$100,000	
Interest revenues	18,000	$118,000
Expenditures:		
Direct capital outlays.......................................	$162,000	
Interest expense on bonds	12,800	174,800
Excess (deficiency) of revenues over expenditures		$ (56,800)
Fund balances at beginning of year		-0-
Fund balances at end of year		$ (56,800)

The street improvement project for the City of Hilton is completed during the second year, with the occurrence of the following events:

Event	Entry		
Expenditures and revenues for the second year are estimated to be $105,000 and $65,000 respectively.	Estimated Revenues Control	65,000	
	Budgetary Fund Balance	40,000	
	Appropriations Control		105,000
Encumbrances closed at the end of the previous year are reestablished.	Encumbrances Control	90,000	
	Unreserved Fund Balance		90,000
The project is completed. Additional expenditures of $89,000 are vouchered, liquidating all encumbrances.	Expenditures Control—Project	89,000	
	Vouchers Payable		89,000
	Fund Balance Reserved for		
	Encumbrances	90,000	
	Encumbrances Control		90,000
With the exception of $20,000 withheld until the project is approved, the balance of vouchers is paid.	Vouchers Payable	151,000	
	Contracts Payable—		
	Retained Percentage................		20,000
	Cash		131,000
The current installment is collected in full, plus $13,500 for interest.	Cash	63,500	
	Special Assessments Receivable—		
	Current		50,000
	Revenues Control		13,500
The annual interest on bonds is paid and the discount is amortized. Neither was encumbered.	Expenditures Control—Interest	12,800	
	Discount on Bonds Payable		800
	Cash		12,000
The next installment is reclassified as current. Deferred revenue is also reclassified.	Special Assessments Receivable—		
	Current	50,000	
	Special Assessments Receivable—		
	Deferred		50,000
	Deferred Revenues	50,000	
	Revenues Control		50,000

Event	Entry		
Books are closed at year end.	Appropriations Control 105,000		
	Budgetary Fund Balance		40,000
	Estimated Revenues Control		65,000
	Revenues Control 63,500		
	Unreserved Fund Balance 38,300		
	Expenditures Control—Project		89,000
	Expenditures Control—Interest		12,800

Even though the project is completed and its costs paid for, the Special Assessment Fund continues to exist until all installments have been collected and the bond issue has been fully redeemed. The completion of the project, however, must be recorded in the General Fixed Assets Account Group, as follows:

Improvements Other Than Buildings 251,000		
Construction in Progress	162,000	
Investment in General Fixed Assets from Special		
Assessments	89,000	

DEBT SERVICE FUNDS

A governmental unit's commitment to long-term debt makes it imperative that it meet its fiscal responsibilities. If not, a unit could have problems similar to those of New York City, whose tottering financial position caused waves of financial insecurity throughout the world's money markets.

The function of the General Long-Term Debt Account Group, as discussed in Chapter 16, is to provide a record of the principal of general long-term liabilities, which are usually incurred to acquire capital facilities. Closely related to this account group are *Debt Service Funds*, whose primary function is to account for the cash accumulation to cover the payment of principal and interest on general long-term obligations. Debt Service Funds are not involved with the long-term debt of proprietary funds or Special Assessment Funds, which are responsible for redeeming their own obligations.

As in other governmental funds, revenues, other financing sources, and expenditures are recognized on the modified accrual basis in Debt Service Funds. Interest on general long-term debt is an item for which the accrual basis is modified. For example, assume that a governmental unit has a fiscal year ending June 30, with interest on long-term debt to be paid on July 31. Since expenditures are authorized by appropriations, it is essential that expenditures be recorded in the same period as the appropriations. Thus, the interest will not be accrued on June 30, because the appropriation to cover the interest will not be provided until the budget for the next period is recorded on July 1.

The most popular method of raising long-term resources is by the flotation of serial bonds, which are redeemed in a series of installments.

Term bonds, whose total face value becomes due at one time, are now extremely rare. When serial bonds are issued, there is no accumulation of cash in a sinking fund for redemption of the principal, unless the first series will not mature for several fiscal periods and contributions for retirement are to begin immediately. Instead, the budget for the year provides for interest payments and principal redemption. In Debt Service Funds, an entry to record the budget is seldom used, because expenditures for principal and interest are known, and there is no need to compare them with budgetary amounts.

Resources to cover expenditures may come from several sources. A portion of a property tax levy may be authorized to be recorded directly in a Debt Service Fund. The entries would be similar to those made in the General Fund to record a tax levy. The net amount of taxes estimated to be collected is credited to Revenues Control, since the resources are received from outsiders. Revenues Control is also credited upon the receipt of bond premium on general long-term bonds sold for a fund that transfers the premium to the Debt Service Fund. Other transfers received by the Debt Service Fund from funds that have already recorded the resources as revenues are credited to Other Financing Sources Control. As discussed in Chapter 16, this account prevents Revenues Control from being credited in two funds for the same resources—once in the originating fund (in this case, the General Fund) and again in the recipient fund (in this case, a Debt Service Fund).

Prior to redemption, no bond liability for unmatured debt is recorded in a Debt Service Fund, because it is entered in the General Long-Term Debt Account Group. However, when a serial bond matures and when payment of interest is due, the following entry is recorded in a Debt Service Fund:

```
Expenditures Control ..........................................    xxx
    Matured Bonds Payable .....................................          xxx
    Matured Interest Payable ..................................          xxx
```

An entry would then be made to record payment of these matured items. Simultaneously, an entry is made in the General Long-Term Debt Account Group to record reduction of the bond principal. Many governmental units employ the services of financial institutions to conduct actual payments for interest and serial redemptions. When cash is released to such a fiscal agent, the account debited is Cash with Fiscal Agents. Upon notification by the agent that actual payments have been made, the Debt Service Fund entry is:

```
Matured Bonds Payable ........................................    xxx
Matured Interest Payable .....................................    xxx
    Cash with Fiscal Agents ...................................          xxx
```

The following entries would be made in a Debt Service Fund for the indicated events that relate to a serial bond issue. As demonstrated by these entries, the interplay between funds and groups is especially prevalent in accounting for general bond issues.

Event	Entry		
An 8%, $300,000 general serial bond issue for bridge construction is sold at 101. The premium is transferred from the Capital Projects Fund to the Debt Service Fund. (An entry is also made in the Capital Projects Fund and the General Long-Term Debt Account Group.)	Cash .... Revenues Control	3,000	3,000

Of the property taxes, $50,000 is levied specifically to cover debt service on these bonds; 1% of the taxes levied is estimated to be uncollectible.	Taxes Receivable—Current ....
	   Allowance for Uncollectible Current
	    Taxes ....
	   Revenues Control ....
		50,000	500
			49,500

All property taxes are collected, except for $400 which is written off. The difference between estimated and actual uncollectible taxes is recorded in Revenues Control.	Cash ....
	Allowance for Uncollectible Current
	  Taxes ....
	   Taxes Receivable—Current ....
	   Revenues Control ....
		49,600
		
		500
			50,000
			100

The fund receives $7,000 of its $9,000 share of state gasoline taxes, the balance to be received late in the next period. (The modified accrual basis is used, whereby the resources recognized as revenue must be currently available.)	Cash ....
	Due from State ....
	   Revenues Control ....
	   Deferred Revenues ....
		7,000
		2,000
			7,000
			2,000

A transfer of $30,000 is received from the General Fund.	Cash .... Other Financing Sources Control	30,000	30,000
Cash is transmitted to a fiscal agent for payment of the first $60,000 of maturing bonds and $24,000 of interest due on the last day of the fiscal period.	Cash with Fiscal Agent .... Cash	84,000	84,000

The matured bonds and interest are recorded.	Expenditures Control ....
	   Matured Bonds Payable ....
	   Matured Interest Payable ....
		84,000	60,000
			24,000

The fiscal agent reports that all payments have been made, except for $1,000 of interest.	Matured Bonds Payable .... Matured Interest Payable .... Cash with Fiscal Agent	60,000 23,000	83,000

Books are closed at year end.	Revenues Control ....
	Other Financing Sources Control ......
	   Expenditures Control ....
	   Fund Balance Reserved for
	    Debt Service ....
		59,600
		30,000
			84,000
			
			5,600

Assets transferred to a Debt Service Fund must be used to redeem bonds or to pay interest. There are no unreserved assets. Any excess of assets over liabilities is reserved for debt service. Therefore, at year end, the accounts are closed to Fund Balance Reserved for Debt Service, rather than to Unreserved Fund Balance.

Debt Service Funds employ two financial statements for reporting purposes: a balance sheet and a statement of revenues, expenditures, and changes in fund balances. Illustration V is a combining balance sheet for Vernon Town. This balance sheet has a column for the Bridge Construction Debt Service Fund, for which the entries have been presented, and a Health Center Debt Service Fund.

Illustration V

Vernon Town
Debt Service Funds
Combining Balance Sheet
December 31, 19X2

Assets	Bridge Construction	Health Center	Total
Cash	$5,600	—	$ 5,600
Cash with fiscal agents	1,000	$102,000	103,000
Due from state	2,000	—	2,000
Total assets	$8,600	$102,000	$110,600
Liabilities and Fund Balance			
Liabilities:			
Matured interest payable	$1,000	$ 2,000	$ 3,000
Matured bonds payable	—	100,000	100,000
Deferred revenue	2,000	—	2,000
Fund balance:			
Reserved for debt service	5,600	—	5,600
Total liabilities and fund balance	$8,600	$102,000	$110,600

The notes to the financial statements would explain that the money to cover the final matured bonds and interest for the Health Center Debt Service Fund has been forwarded to a fiscal agent. Once word is received that these payments have been made, that fund will be closed.

The combining statement of revenues, expenditures, and changes in fund balances for Vernon Town's Debt Service Funds is shown in Illustration VI on page 744. This statement itemizes revenues by source and expenditures by nature, and summarizes the causes of changes in fund balances during the period.

PROPRIETARY FUNDS

The funds discussed to this point have been governmental funds. The second category of funds—*proprietary funds*—will now be discussed. By definition, the term ''proprietary'' means pertaining to a proprietor and implies that charges will be made for goods or services on the basis of consumption, similar to the practice in private industries.

Illustration VI

Vernon Town
Debt Service Funds
Combining Statement of Revenues, Expenditures, and Changes in Fund Balances
For the Year Ended December 31, 19X2

	Bridge Construction	Health Center	Total
Revenues:			
Taxes...	$ 49,600	—	$ 49,600
Intergovernmental................................	10,000	$ 46,000	56,000
Miscellaneous.....................................	—	3,000	3,000
Total revenues	$ 59,600	$ 49,000	$108,600
Expenditures:			
Principal retirement	$ 60,000	$100,000	$160,000
Interest charges..................................	24,000	2,000	26,000
Total expenditures	$ 84,000	$102,000	$186,000
Excess (deficiency) of revenues over expenditures	$(24,400)	$ (53,000)	$ (77,400)
Other financing sources (uses):			
Operating transfers in	30,000	—	30,000
Excess (deficiency) of revenues and other financing sources over expenditures	$ 5,600	$ (53,000)	$ (47,400)
Fund balances at beginning of year	-0-	53,000	53,000
Fund balances at end of year	$ 5,600	-0-	$ 5,600

Usually charges are set to recover as much as possible of the total cost, including depreciation. Whatever is not recovered must be subsidized.

All proprietary funds are involved with providing goods or services. If they serve the general public, their activities are accounted for in *Enterprise Funds*. If they serve other departments of the same governmental unit or a different governmental unit, their activities are accounted for in *Internal Service Funds*, formerly called Intragovernmental Service Funds.

Proprietary funds focus on the total cost of services and the amount of cost recovered by revenue. Accounting for proprietary funds is similar to that for a private enterprise, including the measurement of net income. In contrast with governmental funds, expenses rather than expenditures are emphasized. Proprietary funds account for their own assets (including fixed assets and depreciation) and liabilities (including long-term debt), and they differentiate between contributed and earned equity, just as a corporation would.

One of the rare times that amounts due from another fund are treated as revenue is in the case of proprietary funds furnishing goods or services to other funds. For example, a computer center accounted for in an Internal Service Fund may provide service to the General Fund. This transaction is quasi-external, because the item would have been treated as revenue if it had been billed to an outsider. Therefore, the billing represents revenue to the Internal Service Fund. Such treatment is necessary for the proper determination of a proprietary fund's operation and for rate setting. If the fund receiving the goods or services is proprietary, it debits an expense account; if governmental, it debits an expenditures account.

Enterprise Funds

Enterprise Funds account for goods or services provided by a governmental unit to the general public. The user is charged for these goods or services, based on consumption. For example, the operations of utilities, public housing, public parking, and airports would be covered by Enterprise Funds. These funds continue indefinitely and are self-supporting, depending upon the amounts charged to cover part or all of the costs of operation, debt service, and maintenance of capital facilities, and to yield net income that is accumulated in an account labeled Unreserved Retained Earnings. To remain self-sustaining, the fund must deduct depreciation expense in the determination of net income. Losses would eventually require either an increase in charges or a contribution from some other source.

At the inception of an Enterprise Fund, capital must be provided either by issuance of long-term debt or by transfer from some other source, such as a municipality's General Fund. In the latter case, the amount received is credited to an account labeled Contribution from Municipality. Note the similarity to the paid-in capital account of a corporation. As a measure of original asset sources, the contribution remains in the Enterprise Fund indefinitely or until the fund is terminated. If operations are profitable and arrangements specify that profits shall be shared with the General Fund, an amount analogous to a dividend is charged against Unreserved Retained Earnings.

An Enterprise Fund's operational effectiveness may be monitored in part by the net income or net loss figure. As in commercial operations, budgets are also prepared. However, budgets are not formally recorded in the accounts, perhaps because the fund's self-supporting nature requires a high degree of operational freedom, but more likely because fixed budgetary amounts would be of much less value when there is a variable demand by the public for goods and services.

Control accounts for revenues and expenses are commonly used, with details in supporting records. In accounting for revenues, two control accounts are used: Operating Revenues Control (for charges for services) and Nonoperating Revenues Control (for grants received, interest and rent earned, or other miscellaneous financial revenues). A similar breakdown is used to account for expenses: Operating Expenses Control (for expenses directly related to goods or services produced, such as salaries, depreciation, heat, light, materials, and taxes) and Nonoperating Expenses Control (for financial expenses, such as bond interest). Except for the use of these four nominal control accounts, journal entries for revenues and expenses, including adjustments, are much the same as in private enterprise accounting.

One of the unusual features of accounting for Enterprise Funds is the introduction of restricted assets and the current liabilities to be paid therewith. *Restricted assets* are current assets (cash and investments) upon which some limitation has been imposed that makes them available only for designated purposes. Examples of restricted assets are amounts of customer deposits subject to refund, and cash turned over to a fiscal agent for payment of bond interest or principal redemption.

Restricted current assets and their related current liabilities must be recorded in specially designated accounts, so that segregation of these items will be ensured. For example, if a water utility receives deposits covering meter installations for customers and these deposits are refundable, they would be recorded as follows:

```
Restricted Assets—Customers' Deposits Cash ....................    xxx
     Customers' Deposits Payable from Restricted Assets ............         xxx
```

If the deposits are invested, the entry to record the investment would be:

```
Restricted Assets—Customers' Deposits Investments .............    xxx
     Restricted Assets—Customers' Deposits Cash ..................         xxx
```

When a computer is used, it may be programmed to earmark the restricted accounts. In this case, the restriction in the account title may be omitted.

The appearance of restricted current assets and restricted current liabilities is especially common when an Enterprise Fund is accounting for a public utility. A major source of funding for utilities is the sale of revenue bonds, which are floated to permit the construction of or an addition to a facility. Since payments for these bonds depend on the existence of operating income, the bond indenture usually includes several restrictions. For example, it may require that the bond proceeds be expended only for construction, making the proceeds a restricted asset. The following entry would be required:

```
Restricted Assets—Revenue Bond Construction Cash .............    xxx
     Revenue Bonds Payable ......................................         xxx
```

As amounts are committed, the liability would be identified as payable from a restricted current asset:

```
Building .......................................................    xxx
     Construction Contracts Payable from Restricted Assets .........         xxx
```

Payment of the liability would be recorded with the following entry:

```
Construction Contracts Payable from Restricted Assets ...........    xxx
     Restricted Assets—Revenue Bond Construction Cash ...........         xxx
```

The balance sheet of a commercial utility may begin with its fixed assets, because they are extremely important. However, the combining of the balance sheet of a governmentally owned utility with the balance sheets of other governmental funds is simplified if the customary sequence is followed. The balance sheet for the Clermont County Water and Sewer Fund, in Illustration VII on pages 748 and 749, adheres to such a presentation, with restricted current assets following the regular current assets and preceding the fixed assets. Note also that current liabilities are segregated to show amounts payable from regular current assets and amounts payable from restricted current assets.

Most revenue bonds for enterprise funds are serial bonds that require the earmarking of monies for the payment of interest and for the establishment of a sinking fund for principal redemption. These resources would be restricted assets, while the current interest and serial installment payable would be recorded as current liabilities payable from restricted current assets. To further protect the bondholder, at least psychologically, many serial revenue bonds require that unreserved retained earnings be restricted in an amount equal to the excess of restricted current assets related to the bond issue over the current liability for interest and principal. If the amounts in the Water and Sewer Fund balance sheet (Illustration VII) are compared with assumed amounts at the end of the previous year, the additional amount to be reserved would be determined as follows:

	Dec. 31, 19X2	Dec. 31, 19X1 (assumed)
Restricted current assets related to revenue bonds:		
Cash with fiscal agent for bond service	$ 80,444	$ 87,200
Revenue bond debt service cash.....................	5,000	3,000
Revenue bond sinking fund	124,155	93,975
Total	$209,599	$184,175
Current liabilities related to revenue bonds:		
Accrued revenue bond interest payable	$ 32,444	$ 37,200
Matured revenue bonds payable	48,000	50,000
Total	$ 80,444	$ 87,200
Excess of bond-related restricted current assets over bond-related current liabilities......................	$129,155	$ 96,975

If the bond indenture requires that the reserves be increased to equal the bond-related restricted current assets which are not offset by bond-related current liabilities, the following entry becomes necessary:

Unreserved Retained Earnings ($129,155 − $96,975)	32,180	
Retained Earnings Reserved for Bond Debt Service ($5,000 − $3,000)		2,000
Retained Earnings Reserved for Bond Retirement ($124,155 − $93,975)		30,180

The statement of revenues, expenses (not expenditures), and changes in retained earnings for an Enterprise Fund, as shown in Statement 1, focuses on total retained earnings, both reserved and unreserved. Such a statement for the Clermont County Water and Sewer Fund is shown in Illustration VIII on page 750.

Illustration VII
Clermont
Water and
Balance
December

Assets

Current assets:

Cash	$ 257,036	
Receivables (net)	33,480	
Inventories and prepaid expenses	24,230	
Total current assets		$ 314,746

Restricted assets:

Cash with fiscal agent for bond service		$ 80,444	
Revenue bond construction cash		17,760	
Revenue bond debt service cash		5,000	
Revenue bond sinking fund:			
Cash	$ 10,355		
Investments	113,800	124,155	
Customers' deposits:			
Investments	$ 63,000		
Interest receivable on investments	650	63,650	
Total restricted assets			291,009

Property, plant, and equipment:

Land		$ 211,100	
Buildings	$ 447,700		
Less accumulated depreciation	90,718	356,982	
Improvements other than buildings	$3,887,901		
Less accumulated depreciation	348,944	3,538,957	
Machinery and equipment	$1,841,145		
Less accumulated depreciation	201,138	1,640,007	
Construction in process		22,713	
Total property, plant, and equipment			5,769,759
Total assets			$6,375,514

An alternative form of the statement emphasizes the unreserved retained earnings as the final amount. If the alternative form were used for the Water and Sewer Fund, the lower portion of the statement would appear as follows:

Net income (determined as in Illustration VIII)		$ 78,812
Retained earnings, January 1, 19X2—unreserved	$1,991,569	
Changes in unreserved retained earnings:		
Increase in reserve for bond debt service	(2,000)	
Increase in reserve for bond retirement	(30,180)	1,959,389
Retained earnings, December 31, 19X2—unreserved		$2,038,201

Since proprietary funds are nonexpendable and primarily self-supporting, a statement of changes in financial position is an aid to the financial management of these funds. This statement, which is now required for proprietary funds (but not governmental funds, which are

Enterprise Fund
County
Sewer Fund
Sheet
31, 19X2

Liabilities and Fund Equity

Liabilities:		
Current liabilities (payable from current assets):		
Vouchers payable	$ 195,071	
Accrued wages and taxes payable	2,870	
Construction contracts payable.............................	8,347	$ 206,288
Current liabilities (payable from restricted assets):		
Construction contracts payable.............................	$ 17,760	
Accrued revenue bond interest payable	32,444	
Matured revenue bonds payable	48,000	
Customer deposits	63,000	161,204
Total current liabilities		$ 367,492
Long-term liabilities:		
Revenue bonds payable		2,448,000
Total liabilities..		$2,815,492
Fund equity:		
Contributed capital:		
Contribution from municipality		$1,392,666
Retained earnings:		
Reserved for bond debt service.............................	$ 5,000	
Reserved for bond retirement	124,155	
Total reserved	$ 129,155	
Unreserved...	2,038,201	
Total retained earnings		2,167,356
Total fund equity		$3,560,022
Total liabilities and fund equity..............................		$6,375,514

expendable and depend upon budgetary appropriations), is similar to that used for private businesses, except for the handling of restricted assets and the liabilities payable therefrom. These items are treated as noncurrent, with the net increase or net decrease in each of their two totals reflected in the statement as an other source or use of working capital. The statement of changes in financial position for the Clermont County Water and Sewer Fund is shown in Illustration IX on page 751.

Internal Service Funds

Internal Service Funds are similar to Enterprise Funds in that they are self-sustaining, depend on amounts charged for services rendered, and receive start-up resources. The difference is that users of their services are other departments of the same governmental unit or

Illustration VIII—Enterprise Fund

Clermont County
Water and Sewer Fund
Statement of Revenues, Expenses, and Changes in Retained Earnings
For the Year Ended December 31, 19X2

Operating revenues:		
Charges for services		$ 727,150
Operating expenses:		
Personal services (salaries and fees)	$306,100	
Materials and supplies	106,580	
Depreciation	103,600	
Heat, light, power, and taxes	47,900	
Total operating expenses		564,180
Operating income		$ 162,970
Nonoperating revenues (expenses):		
Operating grants	$ 5,000	
Interest revenue	2,830	
Rental income	1,000	
Interest expense	(92,988)	
Total nonoperating revenues (expenses)		(84,158)
Net income		$ 78,812
Retained earnings at beginning of year (reserved and unreserved)		2,088,544
Retained earnings at end of year (reserved and unreserved)		$2,167,356

another governmental unit. A computer center, a central purchasing department, or a central garage would be accounted for in Internal Service Funds.

Since they do not deal with the general public and usually do not issue bonds that result in restrictions, Internal Service Funds do not have restricted assets. Their accounting procedures resemble those for a commercial business even more closely than do those of Enterprise Funds. Internal Service Funds must recover their costs, including depreciation, or be subsidized. Therefore, they maintain records of fixed assets and use the accrual basis of accounting. Budgetary accounts are not used, although budget forecasts facilitate the calculation of overhead rates to be applied in determining charges.

When billings to users are recorded, it is recommended that the amount be credited to Operating Revenues Control. However, some accountants prefer to credit the account Billings to Departments when such billings will be the only source of operating revenue. Providing services to other governmental units is another example of a quasi-external transaction, in which revenue recognition is permitted even though the transaction is between funds of the same governmental unit. If an Internal Service Fund also has transactions with several different governmental units, as in the case of a state providing service to other states or to its own counties and cities, the account Operating Revenues Control should be used.

Illustration IX—Enterprise Fund

Clermont County
Water and Sewer Fund
Statement of Changes in Financial Position
For the Year Ended December 31, 19X2

Sources of working capital:	
Operations:	
Net income	$ 78,812
Items not requiring (providing) working capital:	
Depreciation	103,600
Working capital provided by operations	$182,412
Other sources:	
Contribution from municipality	600,000
Total sources of working capital	$782,412
Uses of working capital:	
Acquisition of property, plant, and equipment	$700,912
Net decrease in current liabilities payable from restricted assets	7,500
Net increase in restricted assets	4,900
Total uses of working capital	$713,312
Net increase (decrease) in working capital	$ 69,100
Elements of net increase (decrease) in working capital:	
Cash	$ 96,200
Receivables (net of allowance for uncollectibles)	(3,100)
Inventories and prepaid expenses	8,400
Vouchers payable	(37,500)
Accrued wages and taxes payable	800
Construction contracts payable	4,300
Net increase (decrease) in working capital	$ 69,100

The financial statements of Internal Service Funds consist of the balance sheet, the statement of revenues, expenses, and changes in retained earnings, and the statement of changes in financial position. These statements closely resemble commercial financial statements and will not be illustrated.

FIDUCIARY FUNDS: TRUST AND AGENCY FUNDS

As mentioned in Chapter 16, *fiduciary funds* account for resources for which a governmental unit is acting as a trustee or agent. This category of funds includes Expendable Trust Funds, Nonexpendable Trust Funds, Pension Trust Funds, and Agency Funds.

Trust Funds

Assets held by a governmental unit which functions as trustee may be donated by a corporation or by an individual for the educational or cultural benefit of the community. The accounting for these assets and the operation of the Trust Fund depend on the document that created the fund. If both the assets contributed (the principal) and the earnings may be expended, the fund is an *Expendable Trust Fund*, which is accounted for in much the same manner as a General Fund, using a modified accrual basis. Budgetary accounts are essential for monitoring expenditures of the principal and income. Since they are similar to governmental funds, Expendable Trust Funds will not be reviewed.

If earnings but not principal may be expended, the fund is a *Nonexpendable Trust Fund*. Nonexpendable Trust Funds, frequently referred to as Endowment Funds, result from the acceptance of assets which are invested to produce earnings for a designated purpose. For example, a donor might contribute real property and investments, designating that earnings be used to enhance a city's art collection. Depreciation on real property included in the principal of the trust would be recognized in order to protect that principal. It would also be essential to differentiate between principal items and revenue items. The most complete segregation will result if two Endowment Funds are established—one to record principal items and another to record revenues and expenditures.

When donors establish a nonexpendable trust, the assets donated are credited to Operating Revenues Control in the Endowment Principal Fund. Revenues earned are also credited to Operating Revenues Control. A liability to the Endowment Revenues Fund for the period's net income is established by debiting Other Financing Uses Control (or Operating Transfers Out). In the closing process, that portion of Operating Revenues Control representing donated principal assets is closed into Fund Balance Reserved for Endowments, emphasizing that principal assets are to remain intact.

The only source of assets for the Endowment Revenues Fund is the net earnings transferred from the Endowment Principal Fund. These earnings are credited to Other Financing Sources Control (or Operating Transfers In). Distributions of such revenues are recorded as expenditures. In the year-end closing process for the Endowment Revenues Fund, any difference between the amounts received from the principal fund and total expenditures is closed to Fund Balance Reserved for Endowments, which indicates that the undistributed assets are restricted.

The procedures for both the Endowment Principal Fund and the Endowment Revenues Fund for Cedar City are illustrated by the events and entries shown on pages 754 and 755.

The financial statements for a Nonexpendable Trust Fund are a balance sheet, a statement of revenues, expenditures, and changes in fund balances, and a statement of changes in financial position, which is required for all Nonexpendable Trust Funds. These statements isolate principal and revenue components, which may be presented on separate statements or on one statement, with self-balancing sections or columns labeled "As to Principal" and "As to Revenue." The last two statements follow the usual format and will not be shown, but a columnar balance sheet for Cedar City's Governmental Accounting Scholarship Fund is shown in Illustration X on page 753.

Illustration X

Cedar City
Balance Sheet
Governmental Accounting Scholarship Endowment Fund
December 31, 19X2

Assets	As to Principal	As to Revenue	Total
Cash	$ 9,640	$560	$10,200
Investments	40,000	—	40,000
Unamortized premium	360	—	360
Total assets	$50,000	$560	$50,560
Liabilities and Fund Balances			
Liabilities	—	—	—
Fund balances:			
Reserved for endowments	$50,000	$560	$50,560
Total liabilities and fund balances..................	$50,000	$560	$50,560

Pension Trust Funds

Public employees retirement system funds are accounted for in *Pension Trust Funds*. In no other area of accounting is actuarial assistance so vital. Abiding by the requirements of the retirement plan and considering the employee population as to age, sex, marital status, and the myriads of other variables that affect working lives and retirement, actuaries must estimate the amount of resources necessary as of a given date to meet retirement commitments. To protect the employees' interests, Pension Trust Funds use a full accrual basis of accounting.

Contributions to a retirement plan may be from both employer and employees (a contributory plan) or from employer only (a noncontributory plan). Employees who resign usually have the option to withdraw their contributions (but not the employer's contributions) or to leave them in the plan as vested amounts, meaning that they belong to the employee, who will have access to them when prescribed retirement conditions are met.

Increases in the resources of Pension Trust Funds result from contributions and investment earnings and are recorded as operating revenues. Decreases in resources result from payments to retired employees and from refunds and are treated as operating expenses.

All assets of a pension trust belong to the employees, and these assets are reflected in either the liabilities or the restricted reserves. To indicate that there is a restriction against all resources, journal entries record reservations of all of the trust fund balance. Except for the almost nonexistent case of a trust fund being more than fully funded, there will be no credit balance in Unreserved Fund Balance.

Event

Cedar City receives an endowment of $50,000 to establish a Nonexpendable Trust Fund whose revenue is to be used to encourage students to study governmental accounting.

9% bonds with a face value of $40,000 are purchased at 101, maturing in 10 years.

Bond interest of $3,600 is received. Premium is amortized pro rata.

The liability to Endowment Revenues Fund for net revenue is recorded.

Cash due is remitted.

A grant of $3,000 is given to a student.

Books are closed at year end.

The reserved fund balances represent resources supporting the various stages of the retirement plan. There are four reserves commonly used in Pension Trust Funds:

1. **Fund Balance Reserved for Employee Contributions** represents the amount of accumulated contributions made by nonretired participating employees, plus earnings on these contributions.
2. **Fund Balance Reserved for Employer Contributions** represents the amount of accumulated contributions made by the employer pertaining to nonretired participating employees, plus earnings on these contributions. The account is increased for any unfunded liability resulting from actuarial valuation.
3. **Fund Balance Reserved for Membership Annuities** represents applicable amounts transferred from the first two reserves upon the retirement of an employee.
4. **Fund Balance Reserved for Undistributed Interest Earnings** represents amounts earned on assets attributable to the first three reserves, but not yet allocated to them.

To illustrate the accounting process for a Pension Trust Fund, the journal entries recording each event and its effect on the reserves for Desert City's Pension Trust Fund for employees' retirement are shown on pages 756 and 757. All entries illustrated are made in one trust fund and represent amounts for the entire year. The journal entries on page 756 record asset inflows and outflows and are similar to entries shown previously for other funds. The entries in the reserve accounts, shown on page 757, are made periodically, usually at year end, in order to

Entries in Endowment Principal Fund			Entries in Endowment Revenues Fund		
Cash 50,000			No entry.		
Operating Revenues Control		50,000			
Investments 40,000			No entry.		
Unamortized Premium 400					
Cash		40,400			
Cash 3,600			No entry.		
Unamortized Premium		40			
Operating Revenues Control		3,560			
Other Financing Uses Control (or			Due from Endowment Principal Fund	3,560	
Operating Transfers Out) 3,560			Other Financing Sources Control (or		
Due to Endowment Revenues Fund		3,560	Operating Transfers In)		3,560
Due to Endowment Revenues Fund 3,560			Cash	3,560	
Cash		3,560	Due from Endowment Principal Fund		3,560
No entry.			Expenditures Control	3,000	
			Cash		3,000
Operating Revenues Control 53,560			Other Financing Sources Control	3,560	
Other Financing Uses Control ..		3,560	Expenditures Control		3,000
Fund Balance Reserved for En-			Fund Balance Reserved for		
dowments		50,000	Endowments		560

update the status of the reserves that represent the assets. In this example, however, the reserve entries are recorded when the original events are recorded in order to better illustrate the flow from one reserve to another.

The fourth and fifth entries involving fund balances indicate that items recorded as operating expenses are reinstated to Unreserved Fund Balance. There would be no need for reinstatement if payments to retirees or former employees had been charged directly to the appropriate reserves, although this procedure is theoretically unsound. The reinstatement entries are necessary, however, to counteract a double reduction for an amount equal to the operating expenses. Unreserved Fund Balance had been previously reduced (debited) in order to increase Fund Balance Reserved for Employee Contributions, and some of the increase was later transferred to Fund Balance Reserved for Membership Annuities. Showing these distributions as expenses under the all-inclusive approach will reduce Unreserved Fund Balance again when the expenses are closed, unless the reinstatement entries are recorded.

The balance sheet for Desert City's Pension Trust Fund as of December 31, 19X2, is shown in Illustration XI on page 758. The retirement trust fund has been operating for several years. A feature of this balance sheet is the number of reserve accounts. Also, the Unreserved Fund Balance is typically a deficit which represents the actuarially

Event	Journal Entry for Original Event

Event	Journal Entry for Original Event
Cash contributions are received from:	Cash 150,000
Employees .... $ 60,000	Operating Revenues Control 150,000
Employer.................... 90,000	
Total $150,000	
Earnings of $84,000 on investments are received and $1,200 is accrued.	Cash .... 84,000 Interest Receivable on Investments ..... 1,200 Operating Revenues Control 85,200

Payments of $19,000 are made to retired employees and $1,500 is payable.	Operating Expenses Control 20,500
	     Cash 19,000
	     Annuities Payable 1,500

Refunds of $6,300 were made and $2,700 is due to employees who resigned and withdrew their contributions.	Operating Expenses Control 9,000
	     Cash 6,300
	     Due to Resigned Employees 2,700

Books are closed at year end.	Operating Revenues Control 235,200
	     Operating Expenses Control 29,500
	     Unreserved Fund Balance 205,700

computed additional resources needed at the balance sheet date to fund fully the future retirement benefits.

Changes in the retirement reserves of a Pension Trust Fund are so revealing that an analysis of changes in each of the reserves for the year should be prepared. It should be structured with a column for each reserve and a total, showing beginning balances, additions, deductions, and final balances.

The statement of revenues, expenses, and changes in fund balances adheres to the all-inclusive approach, whereby changes in fund balances must first appear on the operating statement. The statement of changes in financial position is required for Pension Trust Funds. These statements do not offer exceptional challenge and will not be illustrated.

Event	Journal Entry Involving Fund Balances		
Reserves are increased, based on contributions.	Unreserved Fund Balance............. 150,000		
	Fund Balance Reserved for Employee Contributions......................		60,000
	Fund Balance Reserved for Employer Contributions		90,000

Event		Journal Entry Involving Fund Balances		
Reserves are increased, based on allocated investment earnings:		Unreserved Fund Balance.............	85,200	
Employees' contributions	$23,000	Fund Balance Reserved for Employee Contributions......................		23,000
Employer's contributions.....	37,000	Fund Balance Reserved for Employer Contributions......................		37,000
Membership annuities	22,000	Fund Balance Reserved for Membership Annuities...........................		22,000
Undistributed interest earnings	3,200	Fund Balance Reserved for Undistributed Interest Earnings		3,200
Total.....................	$85,200			

Event		Journal Entry Involving Fund Balances		
For employees who are retiring, transfer to annuity reserve from contribution reserves:		Fund Balance Reserved for Employee Contributions.........................	6,000	
Of employees................	$ 6,000	Fund Balance Reserved for Employer Contributions.........................	10,000	
Of employers	10,000	Fund Balance Reserved for Membership Annuities.......................		16,000
Total.....................	$16,000			

Event	Journal Entry Involving Fund Balances		
Reinstatement of payments to Unreserved Fund Balance. (See discussion of entries on page 755.)	Fund Balance Reserved for Membership Annuities............................. 20,500		
	Unreserved Fund Balance		20,500

Event	Journal Entry Involving Fund Balances		
Refund reinstated to Unreserved Fund Balance.	Fund Balance Reserved for Employee Contributions......................... 9,000		
	Unreserved Fund Balance		9,000

Event	Journal Entry Involving Fund Balances		
Adjust balance of reserve to reflect revised unfunded accrued liability of $3,000 per periodic actuarial valuation.	Unreserved Fund Balance............. 3,000		
	Fund Balance Reserved for Employer Contributions......................		3,000

Agency Funds

An *Agency Fund* is required when money collected or withheld, such as deductions from government employees' salaries for social security or for hospitalization premiums, must be forwarded to the proper destination. Agency Funds frequently have no end-of-period balances because money is transferred prior to the end of the period. When the money has not been forwarded, a liability to the ultimate recipient is shown. There is no fund balance, and the only financial statement would be a balance sheet listing the assets held and the related liabilities. If the Agency Fund is to receive a fee for its services, the amount is usually recorded as a liability to the General Fund of the governmental unit, which records it as revenue when received. For

Illustration XI

Desert City
Balance Sheet
Employees' Retirement Trust Fund
December 31, 19X2

Assets

Cash	$ 76,152
Interest receivable on investments	1,200
Investments	1,109,549
Total assets...	$1,186,901

Liabilities and Fund Balances

Liabilities:		
Due to resigned employees...................................	$ 2,700	
Annuities payable	1,500	
Total liabilities		$ 4,200
Fund balances:		
Reserved for employee contributions	$338,564	
Reserved for employer contributions.........................	763,155	
Reserved for membership annuities	320,782	
Reserved for undistributed interest earnings	3,200	
Unreserved fund balance (deficit)	(243,000)	
Total fund balances		1,182,701
Total liabilities and fund balances		$1,186,901

example, state law may give a county the responsibility for collecting property taxes levied within its boundaries, with the county receiving a fee to cover its administration of the plan. The county, as well as each political subdivision, would record its share of taxes receivable in its General Fund. The Tax Agency Fund of Zee County would make the following series of entries for the events described:

Event	Entry in Tax Agency Fund		
Gross taxes receivable to be collected for all units are as follows:	Taxes Receivable for All Units	1,000,000	
	Due to Other Governmental Units		1,000,000
Zee County .... $ 300,000			
X City 600,000			
T Town 100,000			
$1,000,000			
Taxes are collected.	Cash	1,000,000	
	Taxes Receivable for All Units ...		1,000,000
The liability to each unit is recorded, net of 2% fee earned by the county for collection and processing for other units. (The county would not charge itself a fee.) The fee is to be remitted to the General Fund.	Due to Other Governmental Units ..	1,000,000	
	Due to Zee County General Fund .		314,000
	Due to X City		588,000
	Due to T Town		98,000

Event	Entry in Tax Agency Fund	
Cash is released to each governmental unit.	Due to Zee County General Fund ... 314,000	
	Due to X City 588,000	
	Due to T Town 98,000	
	Cash	1,000,000

The General Fund of X City records the receipt of cash from the Tax Agency Fund, net of the fee, as follows:

Cash (for net proceeds)	588,000	
Expenditures (for fee charged)	12,000	
Taxes Receivable—Current		600,000

GOVERNMENTAL ACCOUNTING—A REVIEW

In governmental accounting, each fund and group is a separate accounting entity, entrusted to record only a limited phase of an event. Complete recording, as shown in Chapters 16 and 17, often involves more than one fund or group. To serve as a reference and to review governmental accounting, Illustration XII on pages 760 and 761 is a matrix of selected events that are recorded in more than one fund or group. Used in the matrix are the five types of governmental funds (General, Special Revenue, Debt Service, Capital Projects, Special Assessment), the two types of proprietary funds (Enterprise, Internal Service), a Trust and Agency Fund, and the two account groups for general fixed assets and general long-term debt.

Statement 1 overcomes many of the inconsistencies that previously existed in governmental accounting and reporting. It requires the classification of all funds in one of the three generic categories: governmental, proprietary, or fiduciary. This requirement now permits a consistency of accounting treatment, which is summarized at the bottom of pages 760 and 761.

General purpose financial statements are those prepared for widespread distribution. To encourage citizens to review their content, separate reports for each fund and group should not be included. Instead, Statement 1 stipulates that the following five combined financial statements of the different funds and groups should constitute the basic financial statements necessary for fair presentation in accordance with generally accepted accounting principles:

1. Combined balance sheet for all fund types and account groups.
2. Combined statement of revenues, expenditures, and changes in fund balances for all governmental fund types and Expendable Trust Funds.
3. Combined statement of revenues, expenditures, and changes in fund balances—budget and actual—General and Special Revenue Funds.
4. Combined statement of revenues, expenses, and changes in retained earnings or fund balances for all proprietary funds, Nonexpendable Trust Funds, and Pension Trust Funds.
5. Combined statement of changes in financial position for all proprietary funds, Nonexpendable Trust Funds, and Pension Trust Funds.

Illustration XII—Matrix of Selected Events

<u>Events To Be Recorded</u>

Purchase of equipment with General Fund resources ....
Issuance of general obligation serial bonds for city hall construction at a premium ....
Transfer by General Fund to meet matured serial bonds and interest payments ....
Payment of bond interest and matured serial bonds ....
Completion of Special Assessment construction project...
Levy of property taxes by General Fund against city's utility...
Billing of General and Special Revenue Funds for central computer service ....
Contribution made by city to a nonexpendable endowment fund..
Remittance of city's share of pension fund costs for current period ....
Recording of depreciation ....
Redemption of final serial of ~~special assessment bonds~~, with return of excess cash to General Fund ......
Redemption of final serial of general obligation bonds, with deficiency covered by General Fund ....
Closing entry for Capital Projects Fund involving partially completed project ....

Characteristic	Governmental Funds
Method of accounting	Modified accrual
Focus of accounting	On balances of expendable assets
Formal recording of the budget: General and Special Revenue Funds	Mandatory
Other governmental funds (except Debt Service), operating on an annual budget	Discretionary (based on complexity)
Debt Service Funds	No
Other funds	
Maintains record of fixed assets used in operations	No
Maintains record of long-term debt	No (except for Special Assessment Funds)

Requiring Entry in More Than One Fund or Group

Governmental Fund Types					Proprietary Fund Types		Fiduciary Fund Type	Account Groups	
General	Special Revenue	Debt Service	Capital Projects	Special Assessment	Enterprise	Internal Service	Trust and Agency	General Fixed Assets	General Long-Term Debt
X	—	—	—	—	—	—	—	X	—
—	—	X	X	—	—	—	—	—	X
X	—	X	—	—	—	—	—	—	X
—	—	X	—	—	—	—	—	—	X
—	—	—	—	X	—	—	—	X	—
X	—	—	—	—	X	—	—	—	—
X	X	—	—	—	—	X	—	—	—
X	—	—	—	—	—	—	X	—	—
X	—	—	—	—	—	—	X	—	—
—	—	—	—	—	X	X	X	—	—
X	—	—	—	X	—	—	—	—	—
X	—	X	—	—	—	—	—	—	X
—	—	—	X	—	—	—	—	X	—

Expendable Trust Funds	Proprietary, Non-expendable Trust, and Pension Trust Funds	Agency Funds
Modified accrual	Accrual	Modified accrual
On balances of expendable assets	On net income and capital maintenance	On assets entrusted, wherein assets = liabilities
No	No	No
No	Yes	No
No	Yes	No

Portions of the first two statements, including appropriate headings, are illustrated in the format recommended by Statement 1, as follows:

ASSETS	Governmental Fund Types					Proprietary Fund Types		Fiduciary Fund Type	Account Groups		Totals (Memorandum Only)	
	General	Special Revenue	Debt Service	Capital Projects	Special Assessment	Enterprise	Internal Service	Trust and Agency	General Fixed Assets	General Long-Term Debt	December 31, 19X2	December 31, 19X1
Cash	$258,500	$101,385	$ 43,834	$ 431,600	$232,185	$ 257,036	$ 29,700	$ 216,701	$ —	$ —	$ 1,570,941	$ 1,258,909
Cash with fiscal agent	—	—	102,000	—	—	—	—	—	—	—	102,000	—
Investments, at cost or amortized cost	65,000	37,200	160,990	—	—	—	—	1,239,260	—	—	1,502,450	1,974,354

	Governmental Fund Types					Fiduciary Fund Type	Totals (Memorandum Only) Year Ended	
	General	Special Revenue	Debt Service	Capital Projects	Special Assessment	Expendable Trust	December 31, 19X2	December 31, 19X1
Revenues:								
Taxes	$ 881,300	$ 189,300	$ 79,177	$ —	$ —	$ —	$1,149,777	$1,137,900
Special assessments levied	—	—	—	—	240,000	—	240,000	250,400
Licenses and permits	103,000	—	—	—	—	—	103,000	96,500

As a matter of public record, each governmental unit should also prepare a comprehensive annual report to be available for those who need more detailed information. In addition to the general purpose financial statements, combining statements by fund type should be included. These statements display each of the funds of a given kind. For example, a report of the balance sheets of three different Special Revenue Funds and their total would be a combining balance sheet. If there is a need for greater detail, reports of the individual funds or groups could be submitted, along with their explanatory notes and supporting schedules.

QUESTIONS

1. Discuss the similarities between a Special Revenue Fund and a General Fund.
2. Why are fixed asset acquisitions from proceeds of general obligation bonds not accounted for in the General Fund?
3. If a Capital Projects Fund has authority to continue operations over several periods, why is it desirable to close its records at the end of each fiscal period?
4. What is the primary characteristic a project must have to be accounted for in a Special Assessment Fund?
5. In what way do the Debt Service Fund and General Long-Term Debt Account Group share the responsibility of accounting and reporting for long-term debt?

6. The Debt Service Fund seldom uses budgetary accounts. What is the logic for this procedure?
7. When a Debt Service Fund receives resources, it might credit Revenues Control, Operating Transfers In, or Other Financing Sources Control. Under what circumstances would each of these credits be used?
8. What is the characteristic that determines whether an activity should be accounted for in a Special Revenue Fund or in an Enterprise Fund?
9. In what ways does accounting for an Enterprise Fund closely resemble accounting for a commercial enterprise?
10. What is the purpose of contributions accounts in an Enterprise Fund?
11. In an Enterprise Fund, explain the nature of restricted assets.
12. Enterprise Funds and Internal Service Funds have similarities and one major difference. Itemize the similarities and identify the major difference.
13. Four fund balance reserve accounts are generally required in accounting for an employee Pension Trust Fund. Identify the four reserves, and briefly describe the nature of the balance in each account.
14. Explain why Agency Funds have no fund balance accounts.
15. What motives prompted the writers of Statement 1 to reduce the general purpose financial report to five combined statements and notes?

EXERCISES

Exercise 1. Prepare journal entries to record the following series of events. Identify the fund or group of accounts in which each entry is made. _capital project_
  (a) The city authorized the construction of a city hall to be financed by $100,000 from the General Fund and the proceeds of a $900,000 general obligation serial bond issue, which is sold at 99. The Capital Projects Fund uses an other financing sources control account.
  (b) The General Fund remits the $100,000 in (a) to the recipient fund.
  (c) A contract is signed with Thomas Construction Company for the construction of the city hall at an estimated cost of $1,000,000.
  (d) The project is one-half complete at the end of the year. A liability is recorded at $500,000 and encumbrances are liquidated for the same amount.

Exercise 2. In 19X3, the town of Ryan authorized the construction of concrete roadways on Mark and Marion Avenues to be financed by special assessments to property owners of the immediate area. The public works department estimates the cost of the project at $220,000. The General Fund contributed $20,000 to be used for construction. Special assessments of $200,000 are levied, to be collected equally over the next four years. The current assessment is collected. To help pay for the project, $150,000 of 4-year, 6% special assessment bonds are sold at par on July 1, 19X3. Interest payment dates are January 1 and July 1 of each year. Purchase orders totaling $40,000 are issued, and a contract is signed at an estimated additional cost for the project of $180,000. Invoices for all purchase orders total $38,000, while the actual contract cost amounts to $185,000. Liabilities for these amounts are entered. Except for $20,000 withheld on the contract until final approval, all liabilities related to the completed construction are paid. On December 31, checks are mailed to cover 6 months' interest, which had not been encumbered. The next special assessment was reclassified as current.
  Prepare all of the entries in the Special Assessment fund for the 19X3 events.

Exercise 3. Prepare the journal entries required by a Debt Service Fund for the following series of transactions:

(a) Property taxes of $80,000 are levied for the Debt Service Fund, of which $2,000 is estimated to be uncollectible.

(b) During the year, $75,000 of these property taxes are collected; $1,300 are written off; the remaining taxes and uncollectible allowance are reclassified as delinquent.

(c) General Fund transfers $25,000 to the Debt Service Fund.

(d) Bonds with a face value of $90,000 mature. The interest payment due is $6,000.

(e) The fiscal agent is sent a check for $96,000. (Credit Cash directly.)

(f) The fiscal agent reports that all principal and interest payments were made.

Exercise 4. Prepare the journal entries to record the following events for the City of Charles Metropolitan Sewage Commission, which is operated as an Enterprise Fund:

(a) The General Fund contributed $300,000 to the Sewage Commission, $100,000 of which is restricted for construction of a bacterial emulsification system.

(b) Billings for the year included $800,000 to the general public, of which 90% has been collected, and $30,000 to other funds, none of which has been received.

(c) To help finance the construction of the bacterial emulsification system, the Sewage Commission Fund issued $300,000 of 6%, 8-year, revenue bonds at face value. Proceeds are restricted for construction.

(d) The bacterial emulsification system is constructed and paid for at a cost of $385,000. The remaining $15,000 not used for construction is returned to the General Fund.

(e) Refundable deposits totaling $10,000 are received from customers.

(f) Cash of $1,800 is received, representing interest earnings from previous deposits made by customers. The earnings are to be used to increase the earmarked cash deposit balance. There is no legal obligation to compensate depositors for earnings.

Exercise 5. Select the best response for each of the following multiple-choice questions that refer to transactions of Brockton City.

1. In preparing the General Fund budget of Brockton City for the forthcoming fiscal year, the city council appropriated a sum greater than expected revenues. This action of the council will result in:
   a. A cash overdraft during that fiscal year.
   b. An increase in encumbrances by the end of that fiscal year.
   c. A decrease in Budgetary Fund Balance.
   d. A necessity for compensatory offsetting action in the Debt Service Fund.

2. Brockton City's water utility, which is an Enterprise Fund, submits a bill for $9,000 to the General Fund for water service supplied to city departments and agencies. Submission of this bill would result in:
   a. Creation of balances which will be eliminated on the city's combined balance sheet.
   b. Recognition of revenue by the Water Utility Fund and of an expenditure by the General Fund.

    c. Recognition of an encumbrance by both the Water Utility Fund and the General Fund.

    d. Creation of a balance which will be eliminated on the city's combined statement of changes in fund balances.

3. Brockton City has approved a special assessment project in accordance with applicable laws. Total assessments of $500,000, including 10% from the city, have been levied. The levy will be collected from the property owners in ten equal annual installments commencing with the current year. Recording the assessment will result in entries whose totals will be:

    a. $500,000 in the Special Assessment Fund and $50,000 in the General Fund.

    b. $450,000 in the Special Assessment Fund and $50,000 in the General Fund.

    c. $50,000 in the Special Assessment Fund and $50,000 in the General Fund.

    d. $50,000 in the Special Assessment Fund and no entry in the General Fund.

4. What would be the effect on the General Fund of recording a $15,000 purchase of a new fire truck in the current fiscal year, using General Fund resources for which a $14,600 encumbrance had been recorded in the General Fund in the previous year?

    a. Increase Expenditures Control by $15,000.

    b. Increase Expenditures Control by $14,600.

    c. Increase Expenditures Control by $400.

    d. Have no effect on the General Fund.

5. What will be the balance sheet effect of recording $50,000 of depreciation in the accounts of a utility, an Enterprise Fund, owned by Brockton City?

    a. Reduced the total assets of the Utility Fund and the General Fixed Assets Account Group by $50,000.

    b. Reduce total assets of the Utility Fund by $50,000, but have no effect on the General Fixed Assets Account Group.

    c. Reduce total assets of the General Fixed Assets Account Group by $50,000, but have no effect on assets of the Utility Fund.

    d. Have no effect on total assets of either the Utility Fund or the General Fixed Assets Account Group. (AICPA adapted)

Exercise 6. Select the best response for each of the following multiple-choice questions.

1. The liability for special assessment bonds should be recorded in:

    a. An Enterprise Fund.

    b. A Special Revenue Fund and the General Long-Term Debt Account Group.

    c. A Special Assessment Fund and the General Long-Term Debt Account Group.

    d. A Special Assessment Fund only.

    e. A Special Assessment Fund, a Debt Service Fund, and the General Long-Term Debt Account Group.

2. The proceeds of a federal grant to be used to assist in financing construction of a city's adult training center should be recorded in the city's:

    a. General Fund.

    b. Special Revenue Fund.

    c. Capital Projects Fund. *(continued)*

    d. Special Assessment Fund.

    e. General Fixed Assets Account Group.

3. The receipts from a special tax levy to pay interest on general obligation bonds and to provide for their retirement should be recorded in:

    a. A Debt Service Fund.

    b. A Capital Projects Fund.

    c. A Special Assessment Fund.

    d. A Special Revenue Fund.

    e. An Internal Service Fund.

4. The accounting for a municipal swimming pool which receives the majority of its support from charges to users should be conducted in:

    a. A Special Revenue Fund.

    b. The General Fund.

    c. An Internal Service Fund.

    d. An Enterprise Fund.

    e. The General Fixed Assets Account Group.

5. The fixed assets of a central purchasing department, which is organized to serve all municipal departments, should be recorded in:

    a. An Enterprise Fund and in the General Fixed Assets Account Group.

    b. An Enterprise Fund only.

    c. The General Fixed Assets Account Group only.

    d. The General Fund.

    e. An Internal Service Fund.

6. The monthly remittance to an insurance company of the hospital insurance premiums deducted from employees' paychecks should be recorded in:

    a. The General Fund.

    b. An Agency Fund.

    c. A Special Revenue Fund.

    d. An Internal Service Fund.

    e. The General Long-Term Debt Account Group.

7. Several years ago, a city established a sinking fund to retire an issue of general obligation bonds. This year, the city made a $50,000 contribution to the sinking fund from general revenues and realized $15,000 in revenue from securities in the sinking fund. The bonds were retired at the end of this year. Complete recording of these transactions would involve:

    a. The General Fund only.

    b. The Debt Service Fund and the General Long-Term Debt Account Group.

    c. The Debt Service Fund, the General Fund, and the General Long-Term Debt Account Group.

    d. A Capital Projects Fund, a Debt Service Fund, the General Fund, and the General Long-Term Debt Account Group.

    e. The Debt Service Fund, the Trust Fund, and the General Long-Term Debt Account Group.

8. Complete accounting for a transaction in which a municipality issues general obligation serial bonds to finance the construction of a fire station requires recognition in:

    a. The General Fund only.

    b. A Capital Projects Fund and the General Fund.

    c. A Capital Projects Fund and the General Long-Term Debt Account Group.

    d. The General Fund and the General Long-Term Debt Account Group.

    e. The General Long-Term Debt Account Group and the General Fixed Assets Account Group.

9. Expenditures of $200,000 were made during the year on the fire station mentioned in the previous item. The transaction would require accounting recognition in:

    a. The General Fund only.

    b. A Capital Projects Fund and the General Fixed Assets Account Group.

    c. A Capital Projects Fund and the General Long-Term Debt Account Group.

    d. A Capital Projects Fund, the General Fixed Assets Account Group, and the General Long-Term Debt Account Group.

    e. The General Fund and the General Fixed Assets Account Group.

10. The account Unreserved Retained Earnings:

    a. Will never be found in governmental accounting.

    b. Will be found in the General Fund if the city has more revenues than expenditures.

    c. Will be found in an Enterprise Fund only.

    d. Will be found in both Enterprise Funds and Internal Service Funds.

    e. May be found in any of the various funds.   (AICPA adapted)

Exercise 7. Select the best response for each of the following multiple-choice questions.

1. Of the items listed below, those most likely to follow similar accounting procedures and use similar accounts are:

    a. Special Revenue Funds and Special Assessment Funds.

    b. Internal Service Funds and Debt Service Funds.

    c. The General Fixed Assets Account Group and General Long-Term Debt Account Group.

    d. The General Fund and Special Revenue Funds.

2. The City of Oakley should use a Capital Projects Fund to account for:

    a. Assets constructed with the proceeds of a special assessment.

    b. Proceeds of a bond issue to be used to acquire land and develop a city park.

    c. Construction in progress on the city-owned electric utility plant financed by an issue of revenue bonds.

    d. Assets to be used to retire bonds issued to finance an addition to the city hall.

3. Bayside County collects property taxes for the benefit of the state government and the local school districts and periodically remits collections to these units. These activities should be accounted for in:

    a. An Agency Fund.

    b. The General Fund.

    c. An Internal Service Fund.

    d. A Special Assessment Fund.

4. To provide for the retirement of general obligation term bonds, the City of Clancey invests a portion of its receipts from general property taxes in marketable securities. The investment activity should be accounted for in:

    a. A Capital Projects Fund.

    b. A Debt Service Fund.

    c. An Expendable Trust Fund.

    d. The General Fund.

5. The transactions of a municipal police retirement program should be recorded in:
   a. The General Fund.
   b. A Special Revenue Fund.
   c. A Pension Trust Fund.
   d. An Internal Service Fund.
6. The activities of a municipal golf course that receives 90% of its total revenue from a special tax levy should be accounted for in:
   a. An Enterprise Fund.
   b. The General Fund.
   c. A Special Assessment Fund.
   d. A Special Revenue Fund.
7. Metro City must record depreciation as an expense in its:
   a. Enterprise and Internal Service Funds.
   b. Internal Service Fund and General Fixed Assets Account Group.
   c. Agency Fund and General Fixed Assets Account Group.
   d. Special Assessment Fund.

PROBLEMS

Problem 17-1. In a special election held on May 1, 19X7, the voters of the city of Mequon approved a $10,000,000 issue of 6% general obligation bonds maturing in 20 years. The proceeds of this sale will be used to help finance the construction of a new civic center. The total cost of the project was estimated at $15,000,000. The remaining $5,000,000 will be financed by an irrevocable state grant which has been awarded. A Capital Projects Fund was established to account for this project and was designated the Civic Center Construction Fund.

The following events occurred during the fiscal year beginning July 1, 19X7, and ending June 30, 19X8:

(a) The annual budget is recorded. It is expected that one fifth of the project will be completed in the current fiscal year.
(b) On July 1, the General Fund loaned $500,000 to the Civic Center Construction Fund for defraying engineering and other expenses.
(c) Preliminary engineering and planning costs of $320,000 were paid to Akron Engineering Company. There had been no encumbrance for this cost.
(d) The state grant receivable is recorded.
(e) On December 1, the bonds are sold at 101. The premium on the bonds was transferred to the Debt Service Fund.
(f) On March 15, a contract for $12,000,000 was entered into with Martin Construction Company for the major part of the project.
(g) Orders were placed for materials estimated to cost $55,000.
(h) On April 1, a partial payment of $2,500,000 was received from the state. The balance will be forwarded no later than July 5.
(i) The materials that were previously ordered were received at a cost of $51,000 and paid. They were immediately used on the project.
(j) On June 15, a progress billing of $2,000,000 was received from Martin Construction for work done on the project. Terms of the contract stipulate that the city will withhold 6% of any billing until the project is completed.
(k) The General Fund was repaid the $500,000 previously loaned.

Required:

(1) Prepare journal entries to record the transactions in the Civic Center Construction Fund for the period July 1, 19X7, through June 30, 19X8, and prepare the appropriate closing entries at June 30, 19X8.

(2) Prepare a balance sheet of the Civic Center Construction Fund as of June 30, 19X8. (AICPA adapted)

Problem 17-2. In May, 19X3, the city of Chestnut Hill authorizes repaving of Edgewood Avenue and the construction of concrete curbs. The project is to be financed by special assessments against the property affected. The estimate of the total cost by the Asphalt Specialty Company is $750,000. A contract is awarded for that amount early in July, 19X3. The annual project budget is based on an estimate that one third of the work will be completed during the fiscal year ending June 30, 19X4.

To finance construction, a 5-year, 6%, $600,000 serial bond issue is sold at face value on July 1, 19X3, with interest payable on December 31 and June 30. Equal serials of $120,000 mature each succeeding June 30th. Of the bond proceeds, $400,000 is invested in temporary investments. During the fiscal year ended June 30, 19X4, earnings received on the investments are $30,000. Interest and serial redemption payments are made when due. As each serial is paid, the succeeding serial is to be reclassified as current.

Special assessments are levied on July 1, 19X3, totaling $900,000, of which one fifth is due on December 31, 19X3, and one fifth will be due on each succeeding July 1. Estimated revenues for the year ending June 30, 19X4, equal the first two installments (net). It is estimated that 1% will be uncollectible.

Of the first installment assessment, $170,000 is collected during December, 19X3; the other $10,000 is delinquent, but is thought to be collectible. The delinquent assessments are recorded and the next assessment is reclassified. Interest on the deferred assessments of $17,000 is received in full by June 30, 19X4.

By June 30, 19X4, the project is on schedule, approximately one-third completed. Project expenditures total $260,000 to date, of which $200,000 is paid. Encumbrances for these expenditures equal $250,000.

Required:

(1) Prepare journal entries to record these events in the Special Assessment Fund, and prepare the closing entries as of June 30, 19X4.

(2) Prepare a balance sheet for the Special Assessment Fund as of June 30, 19X4.

Problem 17-3. A CPA has been engaged to examine the financial statements of the City of Homer for the year ended June 30, 19X9. The bookkeeper, who had recorded all transactions in the General Fund, furnished the General Fund trial balance, shown on page 770, on June 30, 19X9.

The audit discloses the following:

Years ago the City Council authorized the recording of inventories, and a physical inventory taken June 30, 19X9, shows that materials and supplies with a cost of $37,750 are on hand at that date. The inventory is recorded on a perpetual basis.

Current taxes are now considered delinquent, and it is estimated that $5,500 of such taxes will be uncollectible.

Debits:

Cash	125,180
Cash for Special Assessment Fund	174,000
Taxes Receivable—Current	8,000
Assessments Receivable—Deferred	300,000
Inventory of Materials and Supplies	38,000
Estimated Revenues	4,135,000
Interest Expense	18,000
Encumbrances	360,000
Expenditures	4,310,000
Total debits	9,468,180

Credits:

Estimated Uncollectible Current Taxes	7,000
Vouchers Payable	62,090
Interest Payable	18,000
Liability Under Street Improvement Project	10,000
Bonds Payable	300,000
Premium on Bonds Payable	3,000
Reserve for Inventory of Materials and Supplies	36,000
Reserve for Encumbrances	360,000
Appropriations	4,435,000
Fund Balance	106,090
Interest Revenue	21,000
Revenues	4,110,000
Total credits	9,468,180

Discounts of $32,000 were taken on property taxes. An appropriation is not required for discounts, but an allowance for them was not made at the time the tax levy was recorded. Discounts taken were charged to Expenditures.

On June 25, 19X9, the State Revenue Department informed the city that its share of a state-collected, locally-shared tax would be $75,000.

New equipment for the police department was acquired at a cost of $90,000 and was recorded properly in the General Fund. During the year, 100 acres of land were donated to the city for use as an industrial park. The land had a value of $250,000. No recording has been made.

The City Council authorized the paving and widening of certain streets at an estimated cost of $365,000, which included an estimated $5,000 cost for planning and engineering to be paid from the General Fund. The remaining $360,000 was to be financed by a $10,000 contribution from the city and $350,000 by assessments against property owners, payable in seven equal annual installments. Budgetary accounts will not be used in the Special Assessment Fund. The following information is also relevant to the street improvement project:

(a) Property owners paid their annual installment plus a $21,000 interest charge in full.

(b) Special assessment bonds of $300,000 were authorized and sold at a premium of $3,000. An $18,000 liability for interest due was recorded by a debit to Interest Expense. The premium should be amortized on a pro rata basis over 10 years.

(c) The city's $15,000 share of the project cost was recorded as an expenditure during the year. The $5,000 for planning and engineering fees was paid. The remaining $10,000 has not been transferred. Construction began July 5, 19X8, and the contractor has been paid $200,000 under the con-

tract, which calls for performance of the work at a total cost of $360,000. This $360,000 makes up the balance in Reserve for Encumbrances.
  (d) The account Cash for Special Assessment Fund was used for all receipts and disbursements relative to the project. It is made up of the proceeds of the bond issue and collection of assessment installments and interest, less payments to the contractor.

Required:

Prepare a work sheet to adjust the account balances at June 30, 19X9, and to distribute them to the appropriate funds or account groups. It is recommended that the work sheet be in the order of the General Fund trial balance and have the following column headings:

  Column 1 Balance per Books
         2 Adjustments—Debit
         3 Adjustments—Credit
         4 General Fund
         5 Special Assessment Fund
         6 General Fixed Assets Account Group

Number all adjusting entries. Formal journal entries or financial statements are not required. Account titles, if usable, should not be changed.
  (*Hint for solution:* Problems of this type are fairly common on the CPA examination. In the Adjustments section, only entries to correct errors or to record omissions are needed. Do not attempt to reclassify with adjusting entries. In extending the corrected amounts, first determine what balances are needed in the Special Assessment Fund and the General Fixed Assets Account Group, and allocate the remainder to the General Fund.)   (AICPA adapted)

Problem 17-4. A selected list of transactions for the City of Baylor for the fiscal year ending June 30, 19X8, follows:
  (a) The city government authorized a budget with estimated revenues of $2,500,000 and appropriations of $2,450,000.
  (b) The city's share of state gasoline taxes is estimated to be $264,500. These taxes are to be used only for highway maintenance. Appropriations are authorized in the amount of $250,000.
  (c) Property taxes of $1,400,000 are levied by the city. In the past, uncollectible taxes have averaged 2% of the gross levy.
  (d) A $1,000,000 term bond issue for construction of a school is authorized and sold at 102. The bond premium is to be transferred to the Debt Service Fund.
  (e) Contracts are signed for the construction of the school at an estimated cost of $1,000,000.
  (f) The school is constructed at a cost of $990,000.
  (g) The Debt Service Fund will need $150,000 from the General Fund for estimated interest and principal payments for the year.
  (h) A cash contribution of $100,000 is made by the General Fund to the Debt Service Fund.
  (i) Earnings of the Debt Service Fund amount to $3,050. Interest of $45,000 is paid.
  (j) Land with a fair market value of $100,000 is donated to the city.
  (k) The city received $205,000 in partial payment of its share of state gasoline

taxes, with an additional $60,000 due from the state government to be received at an unspecified future time.

(1) Vouchers totaling $210,000, which represents highway labor maintenance costs, are approved for payment by the Special Revenue Fund.

Required:

Prepare journal entries to record these events in the appropriate fund or group of accounts, using the following format:

Fund or Group: Journal Entry:

Problem 17-5. The City of Crabtree accounts for its electric utility in an Enterprise Fund. The following activity took place during 19X7 in the electric utility's cash account:

Cash Receipts		Cash Disbursements	
Accounts receivable	$350,000	Machinery and equipment......	$ 90,000
From other funds	30,000	Building addition	75,000
Customers' deposits	3,000	Salaries paid	145,000
Interest earnings	400	Vouchers paid	90,000
		Taxes paid	15,500
Total cash receipts	$383,400	Total cash disbursements	$415,500

Total billings to customers, including beginning-of-the-year unbilled receivables, amounted to $360,000. Cash receipts included $28,500 of 19X6 receivables and all of the unbilled receivables at December 31, 19X6. Accounts receivable of $1,000 were written off during the year, and the estimated uncollectibles account was adjusted to produce a balance of $1,600.

The following are correct ledger balances as of December 31, 19X7:

Vouchers Payable	$16,000	Due from Other Funds	$3,500
Accrued Wages.................	1,100	Unbilled Receivables	2,400
Accrued Taxes	4,800		

The building and the machinery and equipment had estimated future lives of 20 years and 10 years, respectively, at the beginning of 19X7. Additional fixed assets acquired are also depreciated on the basis of 20- and 10-year lives, using the straight-line method, and one-half year's depreciation is taken in the year of acquisition.

Customers' deposits are invested, but the income is available to the utility to meet current operations.

The Electric Utility Enterprise Fund balance sheet as of December 31, 19X6, is shown on page 773.

Required:

Prepare a work sheet to reflect the proper real account balances as of December 31, 19X7, using the following columnar headings:

Column 1 Balance Sheet, December 31, 19X6
       2 & 3 19X7 Transactions and Adjustments—Debit and Credit
       4 Balance Sheet, December 31, 19X7

(*Hint for solution:* Expenses and revenues should be handled directly through Unreserved Retained Earnings.)

Electric Utility Enterprise Fund
Balance Sheet
December 31, 19X6

Assets

Current assets:		
Cash		$120,000
Accounts receivable	$ 30,000	
Less allowance for estimated uncollectible accounts receivable	1,200	28,800
Due from other funds		8,500
Unbilled accounts receivable (for services provided but not yet billed)		3,200
Total current assets		$ 160,500
Restricted assets:		
Customers' deposits—cash	$ 1,400	
Customers' deposits—investments	42,600	
Total restricted assets		44,000
Property, plant, and equipment:		
Land		$150,000
Building	$600,000	
Less accumulated depreciation	150,000	450,000
Machinery and equipment	$550,000	
Less accumulated depreciation	200,000	350,000
Total property, plant, and equipment........		950,000
Total assets..................................		$1,154,500

Liabilities and Fund Equity

Liabilities:		
Current liabilities (payable from current assets):		
Vouchers payable	$ 48,000	
Accrued wages payable	1,000	
Accrued taxes payable..................................	6,500	$ 55,500
Current liabilities (payable from restricted assets):		
Customers' deposits		44,000
Total liabilities		$ 99,500
Fund equity:		
Contributions from General Fund...........................	$200,000	
Contributions from federal government	150,000	
Total contributions		350,000
Retained earnings (unreserved)		705,000
Total liabilities and fund equity		$1,154,500

Problem 17-6. The Village of Dexter was recently incorporated and began financial operations on July 1, 19X8, the beginning of its fiscal year. The following transactions occurred during this first fiscal year, July 1, 19X8, to June 30, 19X9:

   (a) The village council adopted a budget for general operations for the fiscal year ending June 30, 19X9. Revenues were estimated at $400,000. Legal authorizations for budgeted expenditures were $394,000.

   (b) Property taxes were levied in the amount of $390,000; it was estimated that 2% of this amount would prove uncollectible. These taxes are available as of the date of levy to finance current expenditures.

(c) During the year a resident of the village donated marketable securities valued at $50,000 to the village under the terms of a trust agreement. The terms of the trust agreement stipulated that the principal amount is to be kept intact. The use of revenue generated by the securities is restricted to financing college scholarships for needy students. Revenue earned and received on these marketable securities amounted to $5,500 through June 30, 19X9, and was transferred to the Endowment Revenues Fund.

(d) A General Fund transfer of $5,000 was made in order to establish an Internal Service Fund to provide for a permanent investment in inventory.

(e) The village decided to install lighting in the village park, and a special assessment project was authorized to install the lighting at a cost of $75,000. The appropriation and estimated assessment revenues of $75,000 were recorded.

(f) Assessments were levied for $72,000, with the village contributing $3,000 out of the General Fund. All assessments were collected during the year, including the village's contribution.

(g) A contract for $75,000 was let for the installation of the lighting. At June 30, 19X9, the contract was completed but not approved. The contractor was paid all but 5 percent, which was retained to insure compliance with the terms of the contract. Encumbrances and other budgetary accounts are maintained.

(h) During the year the Internal Service Fund purchased various supplies at a cost of $1,900.

(i) Cash collections recorded by the General Fund during the year were as follows:

Current property taxes $386,000
Licenses and permit fees.................. 7,000

The excessive amount of allowance for estimated uncollectible current taxes is removed.

(j) The village council decided to build a village hall at an estimated cost of $500,000 to replace space occupied in rented facilities. The village does not record project authorizations. It was decided that general obligation bonds bearing interest at 6% would be issued. On June 30, 19X9, the bonds were issued at face value of $500,000, payable in 20 years. No contracts have been signed for this project and no expenditures have been made, nor has an annual operating budget been prepared.

(k) A fire truck was purchased for $15,000 and the voucher approved and paid by the General Fund. This expenditure was previously encumbered for $15,000.

Required:

Prepare journal entries to record properly each of these transactions in the appropriate fund(s) or account groups of Dexter Village for the fiscal year ended June 30, 19X9. Use the following funds and account groups: General Fund, Capital Projects Fund, Special Assessment Fund, Internal Service Fund, Endowment Principal Fund, Endowment Revenues Fund, General Long-Term Debt Account Group, and General Fixed Assets Account Group. Each journal entry should be lettered to correspond with the transactions. Do not prepare closing entries for any fund. Your answer sheet should be organized as follows:

Transaction (a)	Fund or Account Group	Journal Entry	Amounts Debit	Credit

(AICPA adapted)

Problem 17-7. The following transactions represent practical situations frequently encountered in accounting for municipal governments. Each transaction is independent of the others.

(a) The city council of Footville adopted a general operating budget, in which revenues are estimated at $695,000 and anticipated expenditures are $650,000.

(b) Taxes of $160,000 are levied for the Special Revenue Fund of Southtown. One percent is estimated to be uncollectible.

(c) On July 25, 19X7, office supplies estimated to cost $2,390 are ordered by the Town of Puls, which operates on the calendar-year basis and does not use a perpetual inventory system. The supplies are received on August 9, 19X7, accompanied by an invoice for $2,500.

(d) On October 10, 19X7, the General Fund of Pearl Grove repaid to the Utility Fund a loan of $1,000 plus $40 interest. The loan had been made earlier in the fiscal year.

(e) A prominent citizen died and left ten acres of undeveloped land to Ridgeville for a future school site. The donor's cost of the land was $55,000. The fair market value of the land at the date of death was $90,000.

(f) On March 1, 19X4, Daleyville issued 4% special assessment bonds, payable March 1, 19X9, at face value of $90,000. Interest is payable annually. Daleyville, which operates on the calendar-year basis, will use the proceeds to finance a curbing project. On October 29, 19X4, the cost of the completed project was $84,000. The contract had not been encumbered or paid.

(g) A citizen of Cloverhill donated common stock valued at $22,000 to the city. Under the terms of an agreement, the principal amount is not to be expended. Income from the stock must be used for college scholarships. On December 14, 19X7, dividends of $1,100 are received and transferred to the Endowment Revenues Fund.

(h) On February 1, 19X3, the city of Prairiesdale, which operates on a calendar-year basis, issued 4% general obligation bonds with a face value of $300,000. Interest is payable annually on February 1. Total proceeds were $308,000; the premium was transferred to the Debt Service Fund for ultimate payment of principal. The bond issue was floated to finance the construction of an addition to the city hall, estimated to cost $300,000. On December 30, 19X3, the addition was completed at a cost of $297,000, all of which was paid.

Required:

For each of the transactions described, prepare the necessary journal entries for all of the funds and groups of accounts involved. Indicate the fund or group in which each entry would be made by using the following format:

Fund or Group: Journal Entry:

(AICPA adapted)

Problem 17-8. The City of Webster has engaged a CPA to examine the following balance sheet that was prepared by the city's bookkeeper on June 30, 19X7:

Assets

Cash	$ 177,000
Marketable securities..	500,000
Taxes receivable—current	32,000
Inventory of supplies	9,000
Land	1,000,000
Other fixed assets	7,000,000
Total assets	$8,718,000

Liabilities and Fund Balances

Vouchers payable	$ 42,000
Bonds payable	3,000,000
Reserve for inventory of supplies	8,000
Fund balance	5,668,000
Total liabilities, reserves, and fund balance	$8,718,000

The audit disclosed the following information:

(a) An analysis of Fund Balance revealed the following composition:

Fund balance, June 30, 19X6	$2,350,000
Additions:	
Donated land..	800,000
Federal grant-in-aid	2,200,000
Creation of endowment fund	250,000
Excess of actual over estimated tax revenues	24,000
Excess of appropriations over expenditures and encum-	
brances	20,000
Net income from endowment funds	10,000
Net income from other investments.......................	18,000
Total fund balance and additions	$5,672,000
Deductions:	
Cultural Center operating deficit	4,000
Fund balance, June 30, 19X7	$5,668,000

(b) In July, 19X6, land appraised at $800,000 was donated to the city for a cultural center, which was opened on April 15, 19X7. Building construction expenditures for the project were financed from a federal grant-in-aid of $2,200,000 and from an authorized 10-year $3,000,000 issue of 5% general obligation bonds sold at par on July 1, 19X6. Interest is payable on December 31 and June 30. The fair market value of the land and the cost of the building are included in the land and other fixed assets accounts respectively. Cash is to be deposited in a separate fund to pay bond interest and principal as they become due. A contribution of $400,000 was received from the General Fund, of which $250,000 was invested. Additional cash allocable to debt service was $18,000 at the end of the year. The year-end Debt Service Fund Balance is available for redemption of principal.

(c) The cultural center receives no direct state or city subsidy for current operating expenses. A Cultural Center Endowment Fund was established by a gift of marketable securities having a fair market value of $250,000 at date of receipt. The endowment principal is to be kept intact. Income is to be applied toward any operating deficit of the center.

(d) It is anticipated that $7,000 of the 19X6-19X7 tax levy is uncollectible.

(e) The physical inventory of supplies on hand at June 30, 19X7, is $12,500.

(f) Unfilled purchase orders of the General Fund on June 30, 19X7, total $5,000.

(g) On July 1, 19X6, an all-purpose building was purchased. Of the $2,000,000 purchase price, $200,000 is allotted to the land. The purchase had been authorized under the budget for the year ending June 30, 19X7.

Required:

Prepare a work sheet which shows adjustments and distributions to the proper funds or account groups. The work sheet should have the following columnar headings:

Column 1 Balance per Books
2 Adjustments—Debit
3 Adjustments—Credit
4 General Fund
5 Cultural Center Endowment Principal Fund
6 Cultural Center Endowment Revenues Fund
7 Debt Service Fund
8 General Fixed Assets Account Group
9 General Long-Term Debt Account Group

(*Hint for solution:* The approach for this solution is similar to that for Problem 17-3. Remove from Fund Balance the investments in general fixed assets and the Endowment Fund elements. Adjustments involving nominal items (revenues, expenses, or expenditures) should be recorded directly through Fund Balance. In allocating corrected balances, determine the cash balance in the Debt Service Fund in order to determine the amounts remaining for other funds.)

(AICPA adapted)

Problem 17-9. In compliance with a newly enacted state law, Hayes County assumed the responsibility of collecting all property taxes levied within its boundaries as of July 1, 19X7. The following composite property tax rate per $100 of net assessed valuation was developed for the fiscal year ending June 30, 19X8:

Hayes County General Fund	$ 6.00
Dane City General Fund	3.00
Newark Township General Fund	1.00
	$10.00

All property taxes are due in quarterly installments and, when collected, are then distributed to the governmental units represented in the composite rate. To administer the collection and distribution of such taxes, Hayes County has established a Tax Agency Fund.

Additional information:

(a) To reimburse the county for estimated administrative expenses of operating the Tax Agency Fund activities, the county is to deduct 2% from the tax collections for Dane City and Newark Township. The total amount deducted is to be remitted to the Hayes County General Fund.

(b) Current-year tax levies to be collected by the Tax Agency Fund are as follows:

	Gross Levy	Estimated Amount To Be Collected
Hayes County............................	$3,600,000	$3,500,000
Dane City	1,800,000	1,740,000
Newark Township	600,000	560,000
	$6,000,000	$5,800,000

(c) In its original computation of the gross levy, Newark Township made an error which will reduce both the gross and estimated amounts to be collected by $10,000.

(d) As of September 30, 19X7, the Tax Agency Fund has received $1,440,000 in first quarter payments. On October 1, the Agency Fund made a distribution to the three governmental units on the basis of the composite property tax rate.

Required:

For the period July 1, 19X7, through October 1, 19X7, prepare journal entries to record the transactions described above, using the following format:

	Hayes County Tax Agency Fund		Hayes County General Fund		Dane City General Fund		Newark Township General Fund	
Accounts	Debit	Credit	Debit	Credit	Debit	Credit	Debit	Credit

(AICPA adapted)

Problem 17-10. The following trial balance of the Employees' Retirement System Fund for Redford City was prepared by a clerk who used only balance sheet accounts in recording the events for the fiscal year ended December 31, 19X2:

Cash	28,000	
Investments	496,000	
Due to Resigned Employees		2,000
Annuities Payable		3,000
Surplus		519,000
	524,000	524,000

An investigation uncovered the following activity in the surplus account:

	Contributions		Retired Employees' Annuities	Total
	Employee	Employer		
Balances on January 1, 19X2	100,000	200,000	159,000	459,000
Events during 19X2:				
Amounts received (city still owes $4,000 at year end)	16,000	32,000	. . .	48,000
Payments to retired employees ...	. . .	. . .	(13,000)	(13,000)
Annuities payable at year end	. . .	. . .	(3,000)	(3,000)
Annuities established for current retirees......................	(12,000)	(17,000)	29,000	. . .
Investment earnings received (accrued earnings of $5,000 have not been recorded at year end) .	8,000	13,000	9,000	30,000
Due to resigned employees for their contributions	(2,000)	. . .	. . .	(2,000)
Balances on December 31, 19X2....	110,000	228,000	181,000	519,000

An actuarial report indicates that as of January 1, 19X2, there is an actuarially computed deficiency of $117,000 to fund plan requirements fully. As of December 31, 19X2, the deficiency is $104,000.

Required:

(1) Prepare journal entries to correct the balance sheet accounts as of January 1, 19X2, including the recording of the computed deficiency.
(2) Prepare journal entries to record the events transpiring during 19X2 as they should have been originally recorded.
(3) Prepare a balance sheet of the Employees' Retirement System Fund as of December 31, 19X2.

Problem 17-11. The Cobleskill City Council passed a resolution requiring a yearly cash budget by fund beginning with its fiscal year that ends September 30, 19X7. The city's financial director has prepared the list of expected cash receipts and disbursements shown on page 780, but is having difficulty subdividing them by fund.

The financial director has provided the following additional information:

(a) A bond issue was authorized in 19X6 for the construction of a civic center. The debt is to be paid from future civic center revenues and general property taxes.
(b) A bond issue was authorized in 19X6 for additions to the library. The debt is to be paid from general property taxes.
(c) General obligation bonds are paid from general property taxes collected by the General Fund.
(d) Ten percent (10%) of the total annual school taxes represents a tax approved by the voters for payment of bonds, the proceeds of which were used for school construction.
(e) In 19X4, a wealthy citizen donated rental property to the city. Net income from the property is to be used to assist in operating the library. The net cash increase attributable to the property is transferred to the library on September 30 of each year.
(f) All sales taxes are collected by the city; the state receives 85% of these taxes. The state's portion is remitted at the end of each month.
(g) Payment of the street construction bonds is to be made from assessments previously collected from the respective property owners. The proceeds from the assessments were invested and the principal of $312,000 will earn $15,000 interest during the coming year.
(h) In 19X6, a special assessment in the amount of $203,000 for sewer construction was made on certain property owners. During fiscal 19X7, $50,000 of this assessment is expected to be collected. The remainder of the sewer cost is to be paid from a $153,000 bond issue to be sold in fiscal 19X7. Future special assessment collections will be used to pay principal and interest on the bonds.
(i) All sewer and sanitation services are provided by a separate Enterprise Fund.
(j) The federal grant is for fiscal 19X7 school operations.
(k) The proceeds remaining at the end of the year from the sale of civic center and library bonds are to be invested.

Cash Receipts

Taxes:		
General property	$ 685,000	
School	421,000	
Franchise	223,000	$1,329,000
Licenses and permits:		
Business licenses	$ 41,000	
Auto inspection permits	24,000	
Building permits	18,000	83,000
Intergovernmental revenue:		
Sales tax	$1,012,000	
Federal grants	128,000	
State motor vehicle tax	83,500	
State gasoline tax	52,000	
State beverage licenses	16,000	1,291,500
Charges for services:		
Sanitation fees	$ 121,000	
Sewer connection fees	71,000	
Library revenues	13,000	
Park revenues	2,500	207,500
Bond issues:		
Civic center	$ 347,000	
General obligation	200,000	
Sewer	153,000	
Library	120,000	820,000
Other:		
Sale of investments	$ 312,000	
Sewer assessments	50,000	
Rental revenues	48,000	
Interest revenue	15,000	425,000
Total expected cash receipts		$4,156,000

Cash Disbursements

General government	$ 671,000	
Public safety	516,000	
Schools	458,000	
Sanitation	131,000	
Library	28,000	
Rental property	17,500	
Parks	17,000	$1,838,500
Debt service:		
General obligation bonds	$ 618,000	
Street construction bonds	327,000	
School bonds	119,000	
Sewage disposal plant bonds	37,200	1,101,200
Investments		358,000
State portion of sales tax		860,200
Capital expenditures:		
Sewer construction (assessed area)	$ 114,100	
Civic center construction	73,000	
Library construction	36,000	223,100
Total expected cash disbursements		$4,381,000

Required:

Prepare a budget of cash receipts and disbursements by fund for the year ending September 30, 19X7. The budget format should consist of three sections—receipts, disbursements, and interfund transfers—and the following headings for amount columns:

General Fund	Capital Projects Fund	Debt Service Fund	Endowment Revenues Fund	Agency Fund	Special Assessment Fund	Enterprise Fund

(AICPA adapted)

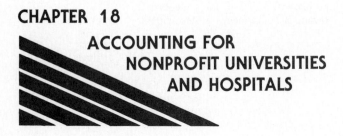

CHAPTER 18

ACCOUNTING FOR
NONPROFIT UNIVERSITIES
AND HOSPITALS

Nonprofit activities are a significant portion of the economy of the United States. This chapter discusses accounting for nonprofit colleges and universities (hereinafter referred to collectively as "universities") and nonprofit hospitals. Chapter 19 deals with voluntary health and welfare organizations. The list of nonprofit organizations also includes social clubs, philanthropic foundations, civic and religious groups, and professional organizations, but these are not dealt with in this text.

GENERAL CHARACTERISTICS

Both governmental units and nonprofit organizations have as their primary purpose the rendering of service without profit motivation. With their devotion to service rather than to profits, the success of nonprofit organizations is difficult to evaluate because of the lack of objective measures of "service". Furthermore, the lack of the profit motive is reflected in weaknesses in accounting and reporting. For example, accrual accounting might not be used and, therefore, cost procedures might not be incorporated into an organization's accounting system. With no built-in cost system, the benefits of variance analysis are not available. Recently, however, some institutions, such as hospitals and universities, have begun to analyze the cost of their services more thoroughly.

The Budget

In many nonprofit organizations, the budget is prepared perfunctorily and reviewed haphazardly, if at all. As a direct result of failing to view the budget as an essential tool for control and direction of the organization, some educational and religious groups, racquet and golf clubs, and fraternal organizations are constantly confronted with financial difficulties.

As in a commercial enterprise, the budgeting process should involve the establishment of goals, the measurement of actual performance, and the comparison of actual with projected performance to evaluate results. This process requires the input of persons who can determine what resources will become available, what the group desires to achieve with those resources, and how the resources should be applied to yield the greatest benefit. If the organization or program is well established, a useful starting point is the previous year's budget and its variances, adjusted for any changes in objectives. If the group or program is new, the preparation of an effective operating budget requires careful research to produce realistic estimates of both revenues and expenditures.

Expenditures should be planned to maximize service output without producing either a surplus or deficit. A sizable excess of revenues over expenditures implies that more or better service could be provided. A deficit may indicate the need to curtail future services, since future funds may have to be committed to cover past deficits.

In accounting for universities, it is not so common to find budgetary amounts formally entered into principal ledger accounts as it is in governmental accounting. Often, detailed budgetary amounts are entered directly in appropriate subsidiary records, and encumbrances are entered directly in an encumbrance column in the expenditures subsidiary record. Although subsidiary records are not supported by principal ledger control accounts when this procedure is followed, some degree of control is achieved by comparing the subsidiary records with actual revenues and expenditures.

If a budgetary entry is recorded, it would be similar to the one used in governmental accounting, and it would be reversed at year end. Assuming that estimated revenues exceed estimated expenditures and allocations, the budgetary entry would be:

Estimated Revenues...	XXX	
Estimated Expenditures (or Budget Allocations for Expenditures)..		XXX
Unallocated Balance		XXX

Pledges

The lifeblood of many nonprofit organizations is the promised contribution, or *pledge*. In most cases, to encourage pledges of larger amounts, donors are permitted to pay their pledges over a period of time. As a result, organizations are confronted with the accounting problem of whether to recognize revenue when the pledge commitment is made or as cash is received.

As is the case with most receivables, the longer the time interval over which payment is spread, the stronger the probability that a pledge will not be collected. Furthermore, a pledge may not be legally enforceable, and suits to collect pledges are rare because unfavorable public reaction could be disastrous for an organization. Nevertheless, when pledges due within a one-year period are a material portion of revenue, the accrual basis should be used, so that revenue is recognized when the signed pledge is received. If property other than cash is pledged, its fair market value or appraisal value is recognized as revenue. An Allowance for Uncollectible Pledges should also be created, with the amount dependent upon the organization's historical experience with collections.

If the payment period extends beyond annual limits, the technique of deferring recognition of revenue is recommended. For example, assume that a wealthy individual pledges $3,000 to an organization. Of this amount, one third is to be collected in the current year, and the remainder is collectible in equal annual installments. This pledge is recorded as follows:

Pledges Receivable	3,000	
Pledge Income		1,000
Deferred Pledge Income		2,000

Fund Accounting

Accounting processes are influenced by the nature of an organization and its goals and available resources. Since nonprofit organizations, like governmental units, must insure that resources are expended for the purposes intended, fund accounting is used.

AUDIT GUIDES

Until recently, there were no accounting opinions, standards, or guidelines that applied directly to the approximately one-half million nonprofit organizations in this country. Prior to 1972, there was no uniformity in reporting, and few rules were universally acknowledged. Since that time, however, the American Institute of Certified Public Accountants has issued four nonprofit audit guides:

Hospital Audit Guide (1972, 1978, 1980)
Audits of Colleges and Universities (1973)
Audits of Voluntary Health and Welfare Organizations (Revised, 1974)
Audits of State and Local Governmental Units (1974)

These guides give direction to accountants in their examinations of nonprofit organizations. Each guide includes appropriate accounting principles which are based on the philosophy that the reader of nonprofit financial reports needs information about the organization's service to the public and the cost of that service.

In addition to the four audit guides, the AICPA issued Statement of Position 78-10 in 1979, which provided guidance for the application of generally accepted accounting principles to nonprofit organizations not presently covered by the audit guides.

ACCOUNTING FOR COLLEGES AND UNIVERSITIES

The responsibilities of a nonprofit university may be classified as academic, financial, student services, and public relations. Academic functions include instruction, research, and public service. The financial sphere covers the management and reporting of business and financial affairs as well as auxiliary enterprises, such as housing, food service, and student union operation. Student services includes all student activities not directly classified as academic or financial, such as admissions, records, health, counseling, and publications. Public relations involves the communication and establishment of goodwill with academic and administrative staff, alumni, and the community.

The effectiveness with which a university accomplishes its objectives in these four areas depends upon the resources at its disposal. A university levies tuition fees, but these fees do not cover total operational cost. Therefore, other sources of revenue are essential. These sources include gifts, income from endowment funds, grants from governmental units or foundations, and, for public universities, appropriations from state legislatures.

The Accounting System and Financial Statements

The day-to-day activities of a university are recorded in its current funds, which consist of two self-balancing subfunds. The Unrestricted Current Fund represents amounts that are available for any current activity commensurate with the university's objectives. The Restricted Current Fund accounts for those resources available only for an externally specified purpose. The segregation of Unrestricted Current Funds from Restricted Current Funds is necessary to substantiate that the limitations placed on restricted funds by outside sources have been observed. Plant Funds account for capital assets and for resources to be used to acquire additional capital assets or to retire indebtedness related to capital assets. Plant Funds consist of several subgroups, each of which is designed to record a certain phase of activity related to fixed assets. Endowment and Similar Funds account for endowments received. In addition, a university may employ Loan Funds, Annuity Funds, and Agency Funds. Each fund may have its own accounting records, or, if the university is large, all funds may be integrated into one record system. In this situation, electronic data processing equipment would likely be used to produce reports for each fund.

Operating or current funds record revenues and expenditures in nominal accounts. In the other funds, Fund Balance may be credited directly for revenues and other additions and debited directly for expenditures and other deductions. As a result, only the current funds present a statement of revenues and expenditures. Except for depreciation, the accrual basis is used in university accounting. Revenues are recognized when due or billed, with appropriate allowances for uncollectibles. Expenditures are recognized when materials or services are received. Expenditures include debt service payments of principal and interest and the costs of acquiring capital assets.

Since service, rather than profit, is a university's objective, accounting and reporting concentrate on resources received and resources expended. Depreciation is not recognized in university accounting, because that would duplicate amounts previously recognized as expenditures when the asset was acquired. One authority points out that:

> . . . college students should not be expected to pay fees which are set to recover depreciation of educational plant inasmuch as the plant was acquired from gifts or governmental appropriations (and presumably will be replaced from similar sources.) [1]

The fact that the audit guide states that depreciation should not be recorded does not prevent its computation and use in independent determinations of the total cost of operating the university. Such cost computations are useful in establishing charges for auxiliary enterprise services, which include dormitories, bookstores, cafeterias and restaurants, medical service, and the student union. Especially for services provided to the general public, amounts charged should include depreciation considerations, even though depreciation is not formally recorded. The only university fund in which a provision for depreciation must be entered is a nonexpendable endowment fund, which must protect its principal.

As with financial statements of all nonprofit organizations, the financial statements of a university should reveal resources received and committed, rather than net income. The three principal financial statements for a university are:

1. The statement of current funds revenues, expenditures, and other changes, which provides detail on revenues, expenditures, transfers, and other changes for the period.
2. The combined balance sheet, which is a composite of the balance sheets that indicate the financial position of each fund.
3. The statement of changes in fund balances—the most important of the three financial statements—which provides a summary of activities for the period in each fund and their impact on each fund balance account.

Each of these statements is explained and illustrated at appropriate points in the discussion that follows.

---

[1] Leon E. Hay, *Accounting for Governmental and Nonprofit Entities*, 6th ed., (Homewood, Richard D. Irwin, Inc., 1980), p. 550.

University Current Funds—Unrestricted

The Unrestricted Current Fund of a university is similar to the General Fund of a governmental unit, in that it accounts for current assets available to cover current operational costs and resulting current liabilities. No outside limitations apply to its resources.

A university might establish one master control account for unrestricted revenues, with details as to major sources recorded in subsidiary records. More commonly, separate revenue accounts are established, using the following scheme for the three major groups of revenues, as suggested in the audit guide:

Educational and general revenues group, with accounts for:
Student tuition and fees
Governmental appropriations (detailed as to federal, state, and local)
Governmental grants and contracts (detailed as to federal, state, and local)
Gifts and private grants
Endowment income
Other sources
Auxiliary enterprises revenues
Expired term endowment revenues

In the interest of full disclosure, operating revenues recorded in the above accounts are closed to Fund Balance at the end of the fiscal period. Auxiliary enterprises revenues are segregated to permit the evaluation of performance and the degree of self-support. Expired term endowment income represents dollar amounts of term endowments on which the restriction has lapsed, freeing them to become unrestricted resources.

Unrestricted Current Fund expenditures are the costs incurred to conduct the university's daily operations using unrestricted resources. Expenditures may be classified in a number of ways, depending on the purpose. In financial reports, the audit guide recommends classification by function for two major groupings, which are the same as the first two used to classify revenues. The resulting expenditure accounts are as follows:

Educational and general expenditures group, with accounts for:
Instruction (expenditures for credit and noncredit courses)
Research (expenditures to produce research results)
Public support (expenditures for noninstructional services, including conferences, seminars, and consulting)
Academic support (expenditures supporting instruction and public services, such as libraries, galleries, audiovisual services, and academic deans)
Student services (expenditures for student admission and registration and cultural and athletic activities)
Institutional support (expenditures for central administration)

Operation and maintenance of plant
Student aid (expenditures for scholarships, fellowships, and outright grants)
Auxiliary enterprises expenditures

In addition to expenditures, the Unrestricted Current Fund Balance is reduced by transfers. *Discretionary* or *nonmandatory transfers*, such as transfers to a loan fund or a plant fund, are transfers of unrestricted resources to or from other funds at the discretion of the university's governing authority. *Mandatory transfers* are required transfers of resources to other funds. Some mandatory transfers, such as amounts set aside for debt retirement and interest payment, result from binding legal contracts. Other mandatory transfers arise from the acceptance of a grant or donation that requires the university to match some or all of the amounts received. Although the source of mandatory transfers may be either Unrestricted or Restricted Current Funds, it is more commonly Unrestricted Funds.

Discretionary transfers are recorded by debiting Unrestricted Current Fund Balance. Mandatory transfers, however, are recorded by debiting the account Mandatory Transfers. These transfers, which may relate to either educational and general activities or to auxiliary enterprises, are segregated on financial reports.

To illustrate the accounting process in the Unrestricted Current Fund, assume that Roger University maintains separate records for each of its funds. It uses detailed revenue and expenditure accounts recommended by the audit guide, rather than broad control accounts, and the budget is formally recorded. Encumbrance items are entered directly into subsidiary records, but no formal entries for them are made. The summarized events for Roger University are described and recorded as follows:

Event	Entry		
The following budget is approved:	Estimated Revenues	3,300,000	
Estimated revenues $3,300,000	Estimated Expenditures		3,000,000
Estimated expenditures 3,000,000	Unallocated Balance		300,000
Unallocated balance .... $ 300,000			
Educational and general revenue is earned or billed:	Accounts Receivable	3,000,000	
Student tuition and fees (of which $20,000 is considered uncollectible) $1,700,000	Revenues—Student Tuition and Fees		1,680,000
Governmental appropriations 750,000	Revenues—Governmental Appropriations		750,000
Private gifts and grants 250,000	Revenues—Private gifts and grants		250,000
Endowment income 50,000	Revenues—Endowment Income ..		50,000
Other income 250,000	Revenues—Other Income		250,000
Total $3,000,000	Allowance for Uncollectibles		20,000

Event	Entry		
Of the total revenues, $2,800,000 is collected.	Cash	2,800,000	
	Accounts Receivable		2,800,000
Revenue billed for dormitories (an auxiliary enterprise) is $400,000, of which $20,000 is not yet received.	Cash	380,000	
	Accounts Receivable	20,000	
	Revenues—Auxiliary Enterprises .		400,000
Purchases of materials and supplies total $400,000, of which $25,000 is not yet paid.	Inventory of Materials	400,000	
	Cash		375,000
	Accounts Payable		25,000

Expenditures are paid and assigned to:

Instruction	$1,050,000	Expenditures—Instruction	1,050,000	
Research	100,000	Expenditures—Research	100,000	
Academic support	150,000	Expenditures—Academic Support ..	150,000	
Student services	200,000	Expenditures—Student Services ...	200,000	
Institutional support	200,000	Expenditures—Institutional Support	200,000	
Operation and maintenance of plant	400,000	Expenditures—Operation and Maintenance of Plant	400,000	
Student aid	40,000	Expenditures—Student Aid	40,000	
Auxiliary enterprises	260,000	Expenditures—Auxiliary Enterprises	260,000	
Total	$2,400,000	Cash		2,400,000

Materials and supplies used:

Instruction	$ 268,000	Expenditures—Instruction	268,000	
Student services	22,000	Expenditures—Student Services ...	22,000	
Auxiliary enterprises	90,000	Expenditures—Auxiliary Enterprises	90,000	
Total	$ 380,000	Inventory of Materials		380,000

Cash is transferred to Plant Funds for:

Addition to plant (discretionary)	$ 147,000	Fund Balance	147,000	
		Mandatory Transfers for Principal Payment	20,000	
Payment of mortgage (mandatory)	20,000	Cash		167,000
Total	$ 167,000			

The Board of Trustees has agreed to transfer $3,000 to the Loan Fund the first day of the next fiscal year.	Fund Balance	3,000	
	Due to Other Funds		3,000

Aid is granted to students:

Remission of tuition	$ 140,000	Expenditures—Student Aid	175,000	
Cash scholarships	35,000	Accounts Receivable		140,000
Total	$ 175,000	Cash		35,000

The Board of Trustees authorizes an immediate transfer of $150,000 to the Endowment Fund.	Fund Balance	150,000	
	Cash		150,000
Term endowments expired, making $20,000 cash available. (Term endowments are discussed on page 795.)	Cash	20,000	
	Revenues—Expired Term Endowments		20,000
The budgetary entry is reversed.	Unallocated Balance	300,000	
	Estimated Expenditures	3,000,000	
	Estimated Revenues		3,300,000

Event	Entry		
The books are closed, with a separate closing entry for Auxiliary Enterprises to demonstrate the degree of success.	Revenues—Student Tuition and Fees	1,680,000	
	Revenues—Governmental Appropriations	750,000	
	Revenues—Private Gifts and Grants	250,000	
	Revenues—Endowment Income	50,000	
	Revenues—Other Income	250,000	
	Revenues—Expired Term Endowments	20,000	
	Expenditures—Instruction		1,318,000
	Expenditures—Research		100,000
	Expenditures—Academic Support		150,000
	Expenditures—Student Services		222,000
	Expenditures—Institutional Support		200,000
	Expenditures—Operation and Maintenance of Plant		400,000
	Expenditures—Student Aid		215,000
	Fund Balance		395,000
	Revenues—Auxiliary Enterprises	400,000	
	Expenditures—Auxiliary Enterprises		350,000
	Fund Balance		50,000
	Fund Balance	20,000	
	Mandatory Transfers for Principal Payment		20,000

University Current Funds—Restricted

For an activity to enter the Restricted Current Fund of a university, some limitation placed by an external entity on the resources received must exist. The same revenue and expenditure accounts used in the Unrestricted Current Fund are available, but Restricted Current Fund revenues arise primarily from governmental grants and contracts, private gifts, and endowment income. Expenditures are generally relegated to instruction, research, and student aid.

Unless the restriction placed upon contributed resources is respected, these resources may have to be returned to the donor. Until they are properly expended, they should not be considered as revenue. As a consequence, expenditures govern the recognition of revenue. This situation requires the following entries in a Restricted Current Fund:

Event	Entry		
Resources are contributed by a corporation for scholarships to minorities.	Assets Contributed	xxx	
	Fund Balance		xxx
Expenditures are made in compliance with restrictions; revenue is recognized.	Expenditures—Student Aid	xxx	
	Cash		xxx
	Fund Balance	xxx	
	Revenues—Private Gifts and Grants		xxx

Fund Balance is increased at the time of the receipt of the resources. Revenue is not recognized until resources are expended, and then in the exact amount of the expenditures. As a result, revenues will always equal expenditures in the Restricted Current Fund.

The following events affected the Restricted Current Fund of Roger University. Only one Fund Balance account is maintained. Data on sources, purposes, and applications of restricted resources are recorded in subsidiary records.

Event	Entry		
A restricted private gift of $70,000 is received to assist library operations.	Cash	70,000	
	Fund Balance		70,000
Endowment income of $8,000 is received, restricted to Student Aid activities.	Cash	8,000	
	Fund Balance		8,000
Of the following expenditures, all but $4,000 are paid: For library operations .... $67,000 For student aid .... 6,000 Total $73,000	Expenditures—Academic Support	67,000	
	Expenditures—Student Aid	6,000	
	Cash		69,000
	Accounts Payable		4,000
Revenues are recorded to the extent of expenditures.	Fund Balance	73,000	
	Revenues—Private Gifts and Grants		67,000
	Revenues—Endowment Income		6,000
The books are closed. Since revenues equal expenditures, Fund Balance is not involved.	Revenues—Private Gifts and Grants	67,000	
	Revenues—Endowment Income	6,000	
	Expenditures—Academic Support		67,000
	Expenditures—Student Aid		6,000

Statement of Revenues, Expenditures, and Other Changes. The statement of revenues, expenditures, and other changes is provided by only the Current Funds, since the other funds record changes in resources directly through their Fund Balances. This statement shows the current funds revenues by source, expenditures by function, and other changes, such as mandatory transfers. In the design recommended by the audit guide, it does not attempt to show net income or net loss, since this amount is not of primary concern to a nonprofit unit. Instead, the final amount is the net increase or decrease in the Unrestricted and Restricted Fund Balances, which is also shown in the statement of changes in fund balances. The recommended form, presented in Illustration I on page 792, shows columns for the Unrestricted Current Fund, the Restricted Current Fund, and the total.

Note that in the Restricted Current Fund column, the total revenues equal the total expenditures. Also note in this column the amount labeled "Excess of restricted receipts over transfers to revenues." As shown in the entries recorded by the Restricted Current Fund, a total of $78,000 in restricted resources was received this period, but only

Illustration I

Roger University
Statement of Current Funds Revenues, Expenditures, and Other Changes
For the Year Ended June 30, 19X0

	Unrestricted	Restricted	Total
Revenues:			
Educational and general:			
Student tuition and fees.............................	$1,680,000		$1,680,000
Governmental appropriations	750,000		750,000
Private gifts and grants.............................	250,000	$67,000	317,000
Endowment income	50,000	6,000	56,000
Other income	250,000		250,000
Total educational and general revenues	$2,980,000	$73,000	$3,053,000
Auxiliary enterprises..................................	400,000		400,000
Expired term endowments	20,000		20,000
Total revenues	$3,400,000	$73,000	$3,473,000
Expenditures and mandatory transfers:			
Educational and general:			
Instruction...	$1,318,000		$1,318,000
Research	100,000		100,000
Academic support	150,000	$67,000	217,000
Student services	222,000		222,000
Institutional support...............................	200,000		200,000
Operation and maintenance of plant	400,000		400,000
Student aid	215,000	6,000	221,000
Total educational and general expenditures........	$2,605,000	$73,000	$2,678,000
Mandatory transfers for principal payment...........	20,000		20,000
Total	$2,625,000	$73,000	$2,698,000
Auxiliary enterprises expenditures....................	350,000		350,000
Total expenditures and mandatory transfers	$2,975,000	$73,000	$3,048,000
Other transfers and additions (deductions):			
Excess of restricted receipts over transfers to revenues		$ 5,000	$ 5,000
Transfers to other funds	$ (300,000)		(300,000)
Net increase in fund balances	$ 125,000	$ 5,000	$ 130,000

$73,000 was expended, producing $5,000 of resources received and not expended. This item must be introduced on the statement of revenues and expenditures in order to produce the correct net increase in Fund Balance, which is shown in the statement of changes in fund balances.

An exceptionally high degree of accounting sophistication is required to interpret the statement of revenues, expenditures, and other changes in its present form. Its primary value is the detail it provides for revenues, expenditures, and transfers. If the primary emphasis is on resources made available (revenues) and resources applied (expenditures), however, a useful figure would be their difference, which is not furnished. The difference between total revenues and the sum of expenditures and mandatory transfers is also not provided, but it would have managerial value. The only net figure is the final amount of change in the fund balances. A superficial glance at the change of $125,000 in the Unrestricted Current Fund could lead the unwary to conclude incorrectly that the fund grew by only this amount. In reality, the increase in the fund is $425,000, which is the excess of total revenues ($3,400,000) over total expenditures and mandatory transfers ($2,975,000). The discretionary transfer of $300,000 to various other funds reduced the change to $125,000.

Balance Sheet. The audit guide presents a combined balance sheet for all funds, with separate, self-balancing totals for each fund. To facilitate the presentation and discussion of the balance sheet for Roger University, a separate balance sheet for each fund will be presented immediately after the discussion of that fund. The current funds balance sheet, subdivided as to unrestricted and restricted items, is shown in Illustration II, Part I.

Illustration II, Part 1

Roger University
Partial Balance Sheet
June 30, 19X0

Current Funds

Assets		Liabilities and Fund Balances	
Unrestricted:		Unrestricted:	
Cash	$ 260,000	Accounts payable	$ 230,000
Investments	450,000	Due to other funds	198,000
Accounts receivable (net)	306,000	Fund balance	726,000
Inventory of materials	110,000		
Prepaid expenses	28,000		
Total unrestricted	$1,154,000	Total unrestricted	$1,154,000
Restricted:		Restricted:	
Cash	$ 153,000	Accounts payable	$ 18,000
Investments	247,000	Fund balance	450,000
Accounts receivable (net)	68,000		
Total restricted	$ 468,000	Total restricted	$ 468,000
Total current funds	$1,622,000	Total current funds	$1,622,000

Loan Funds

Loan Funds are established to account for resources that are available for loans primarily to students, and possibly to faculty and staff. Loan Funds are revolving (self-perpetuating), with repayments of principal and the excess of interest collected over costs incurred becoming the base for additional loans. Both principal and earnings must be available for loan purposes. If only the income from a gift or grant may be used for loan purposes, the principal should not be in the Loan Fund but in the Endowment Fund.

The resources of Loan Funds consist mainly of gifts restricted for loan purposes and Unrestricted Current Fund resources transferred by authorization of the governing board. Although assets are not segregated by restriction, the fund balance must reveal its restricted and unrestricted portions. No revenue or expenditure accounts are used. Additions to the Loan Fund are recorded directly in the restricted or unrestricted fund balance, while expenditures and losses are deducted directly from the fund balance.

The following entries are recorded in the Loan Fund of Roger University. The balance sheet section for the Loan Fund appears in Illustration II, Part 2.

Event	Entry		
A donation of $25,000 is received from an alumnus for student loan purposes.	Cash	25,000	
	Fund Balance—Restricted		25,000
Investments costing $5,000 are sold for $5,500. Gain is restricted.	Cash	5,500	
	Investments		5,000
	Fund Balance—Restricted		500
Loans totaling $24,000 are made to students. Collections from other loans of restricted funds total $20,000 plus $1,000 of interest.	Loans Receivable	24,000	
	Cash		24,000
	Cash	21,000	
	Loans Receivable		20,000
	Fund Balance—Restricted		1,000
A $500 student loan made from restricted funds is uncollectible.	Fund Balance—Restricted	500	
	Loans Receivable		500
The board approved the transfer of $3,000 from the Unrestricted Current Fund, to be made on July 1, 19X0.	Due from Unrestricted Current Fund	3,000	
	Fund Balance—Unrestricted		3,000

Illustration II, Part 2

Roger University
Partial Balance Sheet
June 30, 19X0

Loan Fund

Assets		Fund Balance	
Cash	$29,500	Fund balance:	
Investments	5,000	Restricted	$82,500
Loans receivable	58,500	Unrestricted	13,500
Due from Unrestricted Current Fund	3,000		
Total loan fund...............	$96,000	Total loan fund................	$96,000

Endowment and Similar Funds

The following types of endowment funds, each having its own fund balance account, are included in the category of Endowment and Similar Funds for a university:

1. Regular or pure endowments are funds whose principal has been specified by the donor as nonexpendable. The resources are invested, and the earnings are available for expenditure, usually by the Unrestricted Current Fund.
2. Term endowments are funds whose principal is expendable after a specified time period or after a designated event, at which point they are added to the Unrestricted Current Fund, unless the original donor has specified some other application.
3. Quasi-endowments are funds set aside by the board or controlling body, usually from Unrestricted Current Funds. Restricted Current Funds may also be used if the donor's limitations are not violated. Since these funds are discretionary, they do not technically belong to the endowment category, hence the addition to the title of ''and Similar Funds.''

Accounting should be sufficiently detailed in subsidiary records to demonstrate compliance with the restrictions of each endowment fund. In the balance sheet, the assets are not segregated, but the fund balance section shows the endowment, term endowment, and quasi-endowment components, for which separate accounts are established.

As gifts and bequests are received, either the account Fund Balance—Endowment or Fund Balance—Term Endowment is credited. Assets received as a result of discretionary transfers are credited to Fund Balance—Quasi-Endowment. Gains or losses on the disposition of endowment assets are recorded directly in the appropriate fund balance account. Note that gains or losses are considered changes in principal and not as income or expense, unless otherwise specified by the donor.

The resources for endowment funds are often pooled for investment purposes, with the various fund balances sharing proportionately in the outcome, based on the market values of investments at the time of pooling or at specified future dates.[2] Income from restricted endowment resources should be immediately transferred to and be recorded directly in the Fund Balance of the Restricted Current Fund, the Loan Fund, the Endowment Fund, or the Plant Fund, depending upon which fund the donor has specified should reap the benefits. Income on which there is no restriction should be transferred to and recorded directly in the Unrestricted Current Fund, where it is credited to Endowment Income. If for some reason there is a delay in making the transfer, the income received should be recorded in the Endowment Fund, with a credit to a liability to the proper fund. The costs of managing endowment funds should be borne by the university's Unrestricted Current Fund, which benefits from the income from unrestricted endowment investments.

---

[2] Procedures for investment pooling are discussed in Chapter 19.

To illustrate some of the accounting techniques, the following series of events is recorded, and the portion of the balance sheet devoted to Endowment and Similar Funds is shown in Illustration II, Part 3.

Event	Entry		
The board of trustees transferred $150,000 from the Unrestricted Current Fund.	Cash	150,000	
	Fund Balance—Quasi-Endowment ...		150,000
Endowment Fund investments carried at $200,000 are sold for $260,000. Investment earnings of $40,000 are received, shared equally by the current funds.	Cash	300,000	
	Investments		200,000
	Fund Balance—Endowment		60,000
	Due to Other Funds		40,000
Common stock with a market value of $120,000 is received as a pure endowment donation.	Investments	120,000	
	Fund Balance—Endowment		120,000
Term endowments expired, resulting in $20,000 being released to the Unrestricted Current Fund.	Fund Balance—Term Endowment	20,000	
	Cash		20,000

Illustration II, Part 3

Roger University
Partial Balance Sheet
June 30, 19X0

Endowment and Similar Funds

Assets		Liabilities and Fund Balances	
Cash	$ 460,000	Liabilities:	
Investments	1,270,000	Due to other funds................	$ 40,000
		Fund balances:	
		Endowment	790,000
		Term endowment	460,000
		Quasi-endowment	440,000
Total endowment and similar funds	$1,730,000	Total endowment and similar funds	$1,730,000

Although most universities report their investments on a cost basis, the audit guide permits the use of market value, provided this basis is used for all investments of all funds. Under the market value method, unrealized gains and losses are recognized and are accounted for as if realized.

Annuity and Life Income Funds

Resources may be accepted by a university under the stipulation that periodic payments are to continue as an annuity to the donor or other designated beneficiary for an indicated time period. These resources should be accounted for in an Annuity Fund at their fair market value on the date of receipt. A liability for the actuarially computed present value of expected total annuity payments is recorded, with the excess credited to Annuity Fund Balance. As each payment is made, the difference between the actual payment and its original present value is charged directly to Annuity Fund Balance. For example, a retired professor donated $100,000 to the university. The professor is to receive annuity payments of $6,000 per year for life; thereafter, the principal is to be used for student aid. The present value of the annuity is actuarially computed to be $44,000, which is credited to Annuities Payable. At the end of the first year, the professor is mailed a check for $6,000. The present value of the first payment included in the $44,000 figure is $5,660. The entry to record the payment is:

Annuities Payable	5,660	
Annuity Fund Balance	340	
Cash—Annuity		6,000

A Life Income Fund is used if all income received on contributed assets is to be paid to the donor or other specified recipient for life. When the original contributed assets are recorded at fair market value, the corresponding credit is to Life Income Fund Balance. As income is received, a liability for its payment is immediately established.

When the annuity payments or the life income payments cease, the principal is transferred to the donor-specified fund group, or to the Unrestricted Current Fund revenue if no principal restriction exists. Also, unless otherwise specified, gains or losses on the sale of investments are treated as changes in principal and are recorded directly in the appropriate fund balance account.

Events that affected the Annuity and Life Income Funds of Roger University are described and recorded as follows. The balance sheet section for these funds appears in Illustration II, Part 4, on page 798.

Event	Entry		
Cash of $13,000 from Life Income Fund investments and $18,000 from Annuity Fund investments is received.	Cash—Life Income	13,000	
	Life Income Payable		13,000
	Cash—Annuity	18,000	
	Annuity Fund Balance		18,000
A retired professor donated $100,000. The professor is to receive $6,000 per year for life. Thereafter, the principal is to be used for student aid. The present value of an annuity is actuarially computed to be $44,000.	Cash—Annuity	100,000	
	Annuities Payable		44,000
	Annuity Fund Balance		56,000
Payments are made to:	Annuities Payable	27,000	
Annuitants (originally recorded present values, $27,000) $31,000	Annuity Fund Balance	4,000	
Life income beneficiaries....... 12,000	Cash—Annuity		31,000
Total $43,000	Life Income Payable	12,000	
	Cash—Life Income		12,000

Event	Entry		
Annuity fund investments with a book value of $50,000 are sold for $59,500.	Cash—Annuity.........................	59,500	
	Investments—Annuity................		50,000
	Annuity Fund Balance		9,500

Illustration II, Part 4

Roger University
Partial Balance Sheet
June 30, 19X0

Annuity and Life Income Funds

Assets		Liabilities and Fund Balances	
Annuity funds:		Annuity funds:	
Cash	$109,500	Annuities payable	$232,000
Investments	326,000	Fund balance	203,500
Total annuity funds	$435,500	Total annuity funds	$435,500
Life income funds:		Life income funds:	
Cash	$ 2,500	Life income payable	$ 1,500
Investments	204,500	Fund balance	205,500
Total life income funds......	$207,000	Total life income funds......	$207,000
Total annuity and life income funds	$642,500	Total annuity and life income funds	$642,500

In actual practice, the records for substantial Annuity Funds would be kept separate from those of Life Income Funds, removing the necessity to identify each component of an entry. Income, expenditures, and transfer accounts could be introduced when the Annuity or Life Income Funds are so large that more detailed data are necessary. The typical financial reports of these funds would only display the financial condition (balance sheet) and the changes in fund balances. This information could be provided by properly documenting entries without resorting to nominal accounts.

Plant Funds

Plant Funds include four separate, self-balancing subgroups:

1. *Unexpended Plant Fund* accounts for resources that are to be used to acquire properties. Such resources may be received as a gift or grant restricted to plant acquisition, in which case Fund Balance—Restricted is credited. Assets may be transferred by university authorities from the Current Funds or other funds, requiring a credit to Fund Balance—Unrestricted to record their receipt. When cash is expended to acquire existing capital assets, the appropriate fund balance account is debited as Cash is credited. The asset acquired is recorded in the Investment in Plant subgroup, discussed below, with a credit to Net Investment in Plant. For a major construction

project, a bond issue is usually floated. The proceeds and bond liability are recorded in the Unexpended Plant Fund, preferably until the construction is completed. As work is begun, costs are debited to a construction in progress account. Upon completion, the total cost is transferred to the Investment in Plant subgroup, along with the related bond liability, with any difference between the two amounts recorded in Fund Balance—Unrestricted. If financing was achieved with a mortgage, the accounting procedure would be the same, except for the designation of the liability as a mortgage payable.

2. *Plant Fund for Renewals and Replacements* accounts for resources which are available to keep the physical plant in operating condition. Such expenditures seldom lead to capitalization. Resources transferred to this subgroup as a result of discretionary action by the governing board are recorded by crediting the account Fund Balance—Unrestricted. Resources received from outside sources which specified that the amounts must be used for renewals and replacements are credited to Fund Balance—Restricted. When expenditures are made, the proper fund balance is debited, and cash or a liability is credited. The amount remaining in the two fund balance accounts represents the unexpended resources available for renewals and replacements.

3. *Plant Fund for Retirement of Indebtedness* corresponds to the Debt Service Fund of a governmental unit. This fund accounts for the resources accumulated for the payment of interest and principal of Plant Fund indebtedness. Since the liabilities are included in the Investment in Plant subgroup, payments of either interest or principal are recorded as direct reductions of the Retirement of Indebtedness Fund Balance.

4. The *Investment in Plant* subgroup controls all plant assets, except those found in the Endowment Fund. This subgroup is similar to a combination of the General Fixed Assets and General Long-Term Debt Account Groups of a governmental unit. Assets are acquired as a result of transfers from the Unexpended Plant Funds subgroup, donations, and expenditures of the Current Funds. For a university, the costs of books and other library items are considered major outlays and are classified as plant assets. Liabilities related to the Investment in Plant are also shown in this subgroup. When principal is paid by the Plant Funds for Retirement of Indebtedness subgroup, the liability is reduced in the Investment in Plant subgroup, with a corresponding increase in Net Investment in Plant. Upon completion of a construction project whose costs were accumulated in the Unexpended Plant Funds, the Investment in Plant subgroup debits the asset completed, credits any remaining related liability, such as Bonds Payable or Mortgage Payable, and credits the difference to the account Net Investment in Plant.

The entries unique to the Plant Funds of Roger University are presented on pages 800 and 801, with an indication of which of the four subgroups is recording the event. The Plant Funds section of the balance sheet is shown in Illustration II, Part 5, on page 802.

Event

Stock with a market value of $90,000 is received to finance an art gallery addition.

Cash is transferred from the Unrestricted Current Funds to cover:
Additions to plant $147,000
Payment on mortgage carried in Plant Funds   20,000

Payment of $100,000 is made on the mortgage related to completed plant.

A collection of first editions, appraised at $30,000, is donated to the university.

An $800,000 bond issue is sold at face value to finance a business school wing.

Construction of the wing is one-fourth completed.

Contract is completed at additional cost of $640,000 and is paid in full.

Completed building costs are transferred to Investment in Plant subgroup.

Land valued at $160,000 is donated by an alumnus.

Building repairs constituting a renewal of $50,000 are paid, of which $5,000 is from restricted resources.

Restricted earnings received on investments of:
Unexpended Fund... $40,000
Renewals and Replacements Fund   5,000

Plant Fund Subgroup	Entry		
Unexpended	Investments	90,000	
	Fund Balance—Restricted		90,000
Unexpended	Cash	147,000	
	Fund Balance—Unrestricted		147,000
Retirement of Indebtedness	Cash	20,000	
	Fund Balance—Unrestricted		20,000
Retirement of Indebtedness	Fund Balance—Unrestricted	100,000	
	Cash		100,000
Investment in Plant	Mortgage Payable...	100,000	
	Net Investment in Plant		100,000
Investment in Plant	Library Books...	30,000	
	Net Investment in Plant		30,000
Unexpended	Cash	800,000	
	Bonds Payable..		800,000
Unexpended	Construction in Progress	200,000	
	Contracts Payable		200,000
Unexpended	Construction in Progress	640,000	
	Contracts Payable	200,000	
	Cash		840,000
Unexpended	Bonds Payable..	800,000	
	Fund Balance—Unrestricted	40,000	
	Construction in Progress		840,000
Investment in Plant	Buildings...	840,000	
	Bonds Payable...		800,000
	Net Investment in Plant		40,000
Investment in Plant	Land	160,000	
	Net Investment in Plant		160,000
Renewals and Replacements	Fund Balance—Restricted...	5,000	
	Fund Balance—Unrestricted	45,000	
	Cash		50,000
Unexpended	Cash	40,000	
	Fund Balance—Restricted..		40,000
Renewals and Replacements	Cash	5,000	
	Fund Balance—Restricted..		5,000

Illustration II, Part 5

Roger University
Partial Balance Sheet
June 30, 19X0

Plant Funds

Assets		Liabilities and Fund Balances	
Unexpended:		Unexpended:	
Cash	$ 275,000	Accounts and notes payable	$ 110,000
Investments	1,285,000	Bonds payable	400,000
Due from other funds	150,000	Fund balances:	
		Restricted	1,000,000
		Unrestricted	200,000
Total unexpended	$ 1,710,000	Total unexpended	$ 1,710,000
Renewals and replacements:		Renewals and replacements:	
Cash	$ 10,000	Fund balances:	
Investments	150,000	Restricted	$ 25,000
Deposits	100,000	Unrestricted	235,000
Total renewals	$ 260,000	Total renewals	$ 260,000
Retirement of indebtedness:		Retirement of indebtedness:	
Cash	$ 50,000	Fund balances:	
Deposits	250,000	Restricted	$ 185,000
		Unrestricted	115,000
Total	$ 300,000	Total	$ 300,000
Investment in plant:		Investment in plant:	
Land	$ 500,000	Notes payable..................	$ 790,000
Land improvements	1,000,000	Bonds payable	1,400,000
Buildings	25,000,000	Mortgage payable	1,200,000
Equipment......................	15,000,000	Net investment in plant	38,210,000
Library books	100,000		
Total investment in plant	$41,600,000	Total investment in plant	$41,600,000
Total plant funds	$43,870,000	Total plant funds	$43,870,000

Agency Funds

Agency Funds account for resources which are not the property of the university, but which are held in the university's custody. An example of such resources is assets belonging to student organizations. The total amount of these resources represents a liability. As a result, there is no Fund Balance, and Agency Funds would not appear in the analysis of changes in fund balances. The balance sheet section for the Agency Funds of Roger University is shown on page 803.

Combined Balance Sheet

As mentioned previously, the individual balance sheets of each fund are combined to form a composite balance sheet. The Current Funds are shown first, and the other balance sheets are shown in the sequence given in this chapter. Although this form appears to be the preference of

Illustration II, Part 6

Roger University
Partial Balance Sheet
June 30, 19X0

	Agency Funds		
Assets		Liabilities	
Cash	$ 50,000	Deposits held for others	$110,000
Investments	60,000		
Total agency funds	$110,000	Total agency funds	$110,000

the audit guide, the composite balance sheet does not give the reader a conception of the university's total financial position and activities for the year. A distinct weakness in the composite balance sheet is that Roger University's cash appears in nine different places, its investments in eight, and there are fifteen various fund balances. One alternative would be to present a combined balance sheet with a column for each fund and perhaps the total. The audit guide cautions, however, that "in the balance sheet, columnar fund group figures should not be cross-footed in a total column, to reflect an overall financial position of the institution, unless all necessary disclosures are made."[3] Combining items such as cash into one total could be misleading, since all cash is not available for discretionary spending but is, in part, restricted. With sufficient and careful disclosure, however, the alternative form could be advantageous. A columnar balance sheet for Roger University is shown in Illustration III, on pages 804 and 805.

Statement of Changes in Fund Balances

The most revealing financial report for a university is the statement of changes in fund balances. It is a statement of the university's total activities for the period. In condensed form, it reveals for each fund (except Agency Funds) the revenues and other additions to fund balances, expenditures and other deductions from fund balances, and transfers between funds, both mandatory and discretionary. It concludes with the net increase or decrease in each fund balance, which is combined with the beginning balance to produce the ending fund balance as shown in the balance sheet. The Agency Funds are excluded, since they have no fund balances.

The columnar format is illustrated in the audit guide, but with the customary warning that columns should not be cross-footed unless care is taken to provide full disclosure about the restricted nature of some items. A columnar statement of changes in fund balances for Roger University is shown in Illustration IV on pages 806 and 807.

Although most items in the statement of changes in fund balances are straightforward, a few should be noted. When the Retirement of

[3] *Audits of Colleges and Universities* (New York: American Institute of Certified Public Accountants, 1973), p. 57.

Illustration III

Roger
Combined
June

| | Current Funds | | Loan Funds | Endowment and Similar Funds |
	Unrestricted	Restricted		
Assets				
Cash	$ 260,000	$153,000	$29,500	$ 460,000
Deposits				
Due from other funds			3,000	
Investments	450,000	247,000	5,000	1,270,000
Receivables (net)	306,000	68,000	58,500	
Inventories of materials	110,000			
Prepaid expenses	28,000			
Land				
Land improvements				
Buildings				
Equipment				
Library books				
Total assets	$1,154,000	$468,000	$96,000	$1,730,000
Liabilities				
Notes and accounts payable	$ 230,000	$ 18,000		
Due to other funds	198,000			$ 40,000
Deposits held for others				
Life income payable				
Annuities payable				
Bonds payable				
Mortgages payable				
Total liabilities	$ 428,000	$ 18,000		$ 40,000
Fund balances (See Illustration IV):				
Unrestricted	$ 726,000		$13,500	$ 440,000
Restricted		$450,000	82,500	1,250,000
Net investment in plant				
Total fund balances	$ 726,000	$450,000	$96,000	$1,690,000
Total liabilities and fund balances	$1,154,000	$468,000	$96,000	$1,730,000

Indebtedness subgroup is reduced by principal payments on plant obligations, the Investment in Plant subgroup is correspondingly increased. Similarly, the Unexpended Plant Fund subgroup's expenditures for plant assets also increase the Investment in Plant subgroup. As mentioned previously, most of the resources for payment come from the Unrestricted Current Fund, whose fund balance was reduced when

Alternate Form

University
Balance Sheet
30, 19X0

| Annuity and Life Income Funds | Plant Funds | | | | Agency Funds | Total |
	Unexpended	Renewals and Replacements	Retirement of Indebtedness	Investment in Plant		
$112,000	$ 275,000	$ 10,000	$ 50,000		$ 50,000	$ 1,399,500
		100,000	250,000			350,000
	150,000					153,000
530,500	1,285,000	150,000			60,000	3,997,500
						432,500
						110,000
						28,000
				$ 500,000		500,000
				1,000,000		1,000,000
				25,000,000		25,000,000
				15,000,000		15,000,000
				100,000		100,000
$642,500	$1,710,000	$260,000	$300,000	$41,600,000	$110,000	$48,070,500
	$ 110,000			$ 790,000		$ 1,148,000
						238,000
					$110,000	110,000
$ 1,500						1,500
232,000						232,000
	400,000			1,400,000		1,800,000
				1,200,000		1,200,000
$233,500	$ 510,000			$ 3,390,000	$110,000	$ 4,729,500
	$ 200,000	$235,000	$115,000			$ 1,729,500
$409,000	1,000,000	25,000	185,000			3,401,500
				$38,210,000		38,210,000
$409,000	$1,200,000	$260,000	$300,000	$38,210,000		$43,341,000
$642,500	$1,710,000	$260,000	$300,000	$41,600,000	$110,000	$48,070,500

amounts were transferred to one of the plant subgroups. When payments are actually made, there is a shifting of amounts within the subgroups, but no additional net reduction. The other noteworthy item is that the section relating to transfers between funds is self-balancing—what increases one fund balance through mandatory or discretionary transfers reduces some other fund by the same amount.

	Current Funds	
	Unrestricted	Restricted
Revenues and other additions:		
Educational and general revenues	$2,980,000	
Auxiliary enterprises revenues	400,000	
Expired term endowment revenues	20,000	
Gifts and bequests—restricted		$70,000
Investment income—restricted		8,000
Gains on investments—restricted		
Gains on investments—unrestricted		
Retirement of indebtedness		
Expended on plant facilities		
Total revenues and other additions	$3,400,000	$78,000
Expenditures and other deductions:		
Educational and general expenditures	$2,605,000	$73,000
Auxiliary enterprises expenditures	350,000	
Loan cancellations and write-offs		
Expired term endowments		
Adjustment of actuarial liability		
Retirement of indebtedness		
Expenditures for plant facilities		
Expenditures for plant maintenance		
Total expenditures and other deductions	$2,955,000	$73,000
Transfers among funds—additions (deductions):		
Mandatory principal payment	$ (20,000)	
Other transfers	(300,000)	
Total transfers	$ (320,000)	-0-
Net increase (decrease) for the year	$ 125,000	$ 5,000
Fund balance—beginning of the year	601,000	445,000
Fund balance—end of the year	$ 726,000	$450,000

The Future of Accounting for Universities

The needs of administrators and trustees to know cost per credit hour of instruction, to determine overhead charges as a part of grant requests, and to approach break-even points for auxiliary enterprise services call for inclusion of all costs, including depreciation. Although the audit guide says that depreciation expense on the physical plant should not be included in the statement of current funds revenues, expenditures, and changes in fund balances, future needs for the total

IV

University
in Fund Balances
June 30, 19X0

			Plant Funds			
Loan Funds	Endowment and Similar Funds	Annuity and Life Income Funds	Unexpended	Renewals and Replacements	Retirement of Indebtedness	Investment in Plant
$25,000	$ 120,000	$ 56,000	$ 90,000			$ 190,000
1,000		18,000	40,000	$ 5,000		
500						
	60,000	9,500				
						100,000
						40,000
$26,500	$ 180,000	$ 83,500	$ 130,000	$ 5,000	-0-	$ 330,000
$ 500						
	$ 20,000					
		$ 4,000				
					$100,000	
			$ 40,000			
				$ 50,000		
$ 500	$ 20,000	$ 4,000	$ 40,000	$ 50,000	$100,000	-0-
					$ 20,000	
$ 3,000	$ 150,000		$ 147,000			
$ 3,000	$ 150,000	-0-	$ 147,000	-0-	$ 20,000	-0-
$29,000	$ 310,000	$ 79,500	$ 237,000	$ (45,000)	$ (80,000)	$ 330,000
67,000	1,380,000	329,500	963,000	305,000	380,000	37,880,000
$96,000	$1,690,000	$409,000	$1,200,000	$260,000	$300,000	$38,210,000

costs of operation may encourage the AICPA to open the door wider for more visible acceptance of depreciation provisions. The audit guide states that:

Depreciation allowance, however, may be reported in the balance sheet and the provision for depreciation reported in the statement of changes in the balance of the investment-in-plant fund subsection of the plant funds group.[4]

---

[4] *Ibid.*, p. 10.

Financial reports for various colleges of a university and their educational programs are prepared primarily for internal planning and are seldom issued to the general public. Without data on program costs, revenues, and achievements, a citizen cannot make a valid decision about whether or not a university is operating wisely.

Some authorities believe that present financial reports would be greatly improved by structuring them with only three columns that show unrestricted, restricted, and total amounts. Their claim is that a reader is able to see the total activity without the intervention of confusing detail. The primary objective of financial reports is communication, which will only come about if readers understand what reports are saying. There is still more work to be done before that objective is reached.

ACCOUNTING FOR HOSPITALS

Hospitals may be classified in one of three categories:

1. Proprietary hospitals that are privately owned and operated for a profit.
2. Governmental hospitals (such as military or veterans hospitals) operated by a governmental unit and accounted for as an enterprise fund.
3. Voluntary nonprofit hospitals, including those with religious affiliation, that are organized and sustained by members of a community.

By far, the greatest proportion of hospitals are nonprofit governmental and voluntary institutions. Accounting guidelines for these hospitals, particularly voluntary hospitals, are set forth in the AICPA's *Hospital Audit Guide*, the third edition of which was published in 1980. The American Hospital Association also contributed to these guidelines by issuing a *Chart of Accounts for Hospitals*. These publications serve as the basis for the discussion in this chapter.

A modern hospital is a complex entity with medical, surgical, research, teaching, and public service aspects. One very unusual element about hospital operations is the manner of payment for services. In most cases, the patient does not pay the hospital directly. Instead, payment is made by a third party, such as Medicare, Medicaid, or Blue Cross. Except for some Blue Cross plans, a hospital is reimbursed not on the basis of its listed prices, but on the basis of the cost of providing services as cost is defined by the third-party payor. A cost determination must be made according to formulas agreed upon in the law (Medicare and Medicaid) or in the contract (Blue Cross). Cost determination requires allocation of overhead, including depreciation. Thus, nonprofit hospitals follow the accrual basis of accounting, permitting comparison of results with those that are profit oriented.

With the many restrictions resulting from endowments, insurance companies, and government regulations for reimbursement, a nonprofit hospital's activities lend themselves to fund accounting. The audit guide recommends the use of four types of funds: three restricted funds to account for assets contributed by a donor who has placed some restriction on their use, and an unrestricted fund to account for all other hospital activities.

Restricted Funds

Hospitals may receive bequests, gifts, or grants that are restricted as to use (1) for specific operating purposes, (2) for additions to plant, (3) for endowments, and (4) possibly for annuities or life incomes. A restricted fund is established for accumulating resources in each of these categories until they become available for expenditure by Unrestricted Funds. As restricted assets are received, they are recorded in the proper restricted fund, with a credit to the appropriate fund balance account.

The Specific Purpose Fund, which records donor-restricted resources available for current but specified operations, has only one fund balance account. The Plant Replacement and Expansion Fund, which accounts for assets that must be used for the purchase of property or equipment, segregates its fund balance between the amount restricted by third party payors and all other amounts. The Endowment Fund, which accounts for assets that are to be used to produce income, shows the fund balance of permanent endowments (for which only income may be expended) and the fund balance of term endowments (for which the principal will eventually become available for expenditure). If Annuity and Life Income Funds exist, separate fund balances are maintained for annuities and for life incomes, similar to the procedure used by a university.

Unrestricted Funds

The multitude of activities that are recorded in the Unrestricted Fund covers three distinct segments:

1. The *current* segment represents the unrestricted working capital of the hospital and includes both current assets and current liabilities.
2. *Board-designated assets* are those set aside by the governing body, but they are unrestricted because no *outside* limitation applies. For example, the board may authorize a transfer of $10,000 cash to be set aside for a project, which would be recorded as follows:

Cash—Board Designated xxx
    Cash xxx

3. The *plant* segment includes the physical properties used for hospital activities and the accumulated depreciation. Note the difference between this procedure and that followed by universities, which segregate their fixed assets in a separate Plant Fund and do not record depreciation.

The Unrestricted Fund is the operating fund, in which the hospital's revenues and expenses are recorded. With the desired detail incorporated into subsidiary support systems, three controlling revenue accounts are used in hospital accounting:

1. Patient Service Revenue, in which the *gross* revenues earned are recorded on an accrual basis at established rates for:
   a. Daily patient services (medical and surgical charges, room and board charges).
   b. Other nursing services (in operating, recovery, delivery rooms).
   c. Other professional services (lab work, pharmacy, blood bank, physical therapy).
2. Other Operating Revenue, in which revenue from patients for non-medical charges, plus revenue from nonpatients (cafeteria sales, TV rentals, vending machine and gift shop revenue) is recorded.
3. Nonoperating Revenue, in which revenue not related to patient care or service is recorded. This account is primarily financial and includes receipts of unrestricted gifts or grants, unrestricted income from endowment funds, and miscellaneous income, such as income on Unrestricted Fund or board-designated investments or gains on sales of hospital property.

Patient Service Revenues are recorded on a gross charge basis, because gross charges may be one of the factors for determining the amount reimbursable from third-party payors. For example, one of the formulas used under the Medicare programs is:

$$\text{Reimbursable amount} = \frac{\text{Gross charges to Medicare patients}}{\text{Gross charges to all patients}} \times \text{Allowable hospital costs}$$

Blue Cross may reimburse a hospital on the basis of predetermined amounts that are less than the original gross charges for described services. The difference between the gross revenue and the amount expected to be collected from the third party is referred to as the *contractual adjustment*. It is deducted from the gross patient service revenue amount on the hospital's statement of revenues and expenses. Also deducted are adjustments for charitable services to indigent patients from whom collection will not be possible, courtesy allowances granted to hospital employees, and estimated uncollectible amounts. These four deductions from patient service revenue may be grouped into one debit account, Provision for Adjustments and Uncollectibles, as the contra account for allowances is credited. The objective of grouping these items is to be able to show the net patient service revenue on the statement of revenues and expenses.

Payments made to a hospital by third parties include reimbursement for depreciation. Often this portion of the payment must be used to replace or add to hospital property, plant, or equipment. Total billings are included in revenue of the Unrestricted Fund to permit matching of total revenues and expenses. The restricted portion, however, must be transferred to the Plant Replacement and Expansion Fund, which credits the account Fund Balance—Restricted by Third-Party Payors for the amount of the assets received. Such transfers appear on the statement of changes in fund balances.

Accounting for contributions received by a hospital depends upon the limitations placed upon them by the donor. When no restrictions are placed upon the assets contributed, their use is subject to the discretion of the hospital's governing board. Their receipt is recorded in the Unrestricted Fund by crediting Nonoperating Revenue. The receipt of contributions that must be used for a designated purpose is recorded in the appropriate restricted fund with a credit to its Fund Balance. Since restricted funds usually do not use revenue or expense accounts, increases or decreases in resources are recorded directly in their Fund Balance.

Although universities have two current funds—restricted and unrestricted—in which revenues and expenditures are recorded, hospitals have only one fund—the Unrestricted—which accounts for revenues and expenses. The other funds are feeder funds, whose resources will be transferred to and expended by the Unrestricted Fund when the limitations placed on their use have been met.

When a restricted amount is to be expended for its designated purpose, it is transferred from one of the restricted funds, which debits its Fund Balance and credits the assets transferred, usually Cash. The entry for its receipt in the Unrestricted Fund debits the assets received, but the credit depends on the purposes for which the assets received may be used. Assets received from the Endowment Fund would generally be available for whatever use the governing board decides. The account credited would be Nonoperating Revenue, and the entry would be identical to that for recording the receipt of an unrestricted contribution. Resources received from the Specific Purpose Fund are usually limited to cover current operations and are, therefore, credited to Other Operating Revenue. Transfers from Plant Replacement and Expansion Fund is the account credited for resources received from that fund. The credit is not to a revenue account, because these resources will not be expensed but will be capitalized and will become a part of the capital assets.

Operating expenses of a hospital are recorded in the following accounts, with supporting details collected in subsidiary records:

1. Nursing Services Expense (for the cost of professional nursing services directly related to the patient).
2. Other Professional Services Expense (for professional services indirectly related to the patient, such as lab fees or pharmacy costs).
3. General Services Expense (for costs of the cafeteria, food service, and housekeeping).
4. Fiscal Services Expense (for admitting, cashiering, and accounting costs).
5. Administrative Services Expense (for insurance, interest, taxes, and personnel costs).
6. Provision for Depreciation.

Illustrative Entries for an Unrestricted Fund

To illustrate the recording of events for a hospital, the year's affairs of Fitale Hospital's Unrestricted Fund are summarized below and on page 813. The illustrative entries employ broad categories of control accounts, as previously discussed.

Event	Entry		
Gross charges to patients are for:	Accounts Receivable	4,200,000	
Daily patient services $2,200,000	Patient Service Revenue		4,000,000
Other nursing services 500,000	Other Operating Revenue		200,000
Other professional services.. 1,300,000			
Other nonmedical services .. 200,000			
Total $4,200,000			
Estimates are made for:	Provision for Adjustments and Un-		
Contractual adjustments .... $ 380,000	collectibles	402,000	
Uncollectibles 22,000	Allowance for Adjustments and		
Total .... $ 402,000	Uncollectibles...................		402,000
An analysis of accounts receivable shows:	Cash	4,000,000	
Cash collected.............. $4,000,000	Allowance for Adjustments and Un-		
Contractual adjustments	collectibles	290,000	
with third-party payors 200,000	Accounts Receivable		4,290,000
Uncollectible 90,000			
Total $4,290,000			
Inventory purchases amounted to $700,000; payments totaled $690,000.	Inventories	700,000	
	Cash		690,000
	Accounts Payable		10,000
Inventory is requisitioned by the following services:	Nursing Services Expense	200,000	
	Other Professional Services Expense	40,000	
Nursing services .... $ 200,000	General Services Expense	460,000	
Other professional services.. 40,000	Fiscal Services Expense	18,000	
General services 460,000	Administrative Services Expense ...	2,000	
Fiscal services 18,000	Inventories		720,000
Administrative services 2,000			
Total .... $ 720,000			
Salaries earned (ignore payroll deductions) amounted to $3,000,000, of which $2,950,000 is paid:	Nursing Services Expense	1,500,000	
	Other Professional Services Expense	1,000,000	
	General Services Expense	300,000	
Nursing services $1,500,000	Fiscal Services Expense	130,000	
Other professional services.. 1,000,000	Administrative Services Expense ...	70,000	
General services 300,000	Cash		2,950,000
Fiscal services 130,000	Accrued Liabilities		50,000
Administrative services 70,000			
Total $3,000,000			

Event	Entry

Other expenses paid are:
Nursing services . . . . $ 40,000
Other professional services . . 30,000
General services 110,000
Fiscal services 20,000
Administrative services 100,000
Total . . . . $ 300,000

Nursing Services Expense 40,000
Other Professional Services Expense 30,000
General Services Expense 110,000
Fiscal Services Expense 20,000
Administrative Services Expense . . . 100,000
Cash 300,000

Payments are made on:
Current installments of long-
term debt . . . .'. $ 80,000
Notes payable . . . . .'. 200,000
Interest for current period . . 66,000
Total . . . . $ 346,000

Current Installments of Long-Term
Debt 80,000
Notes Payable 200,000
Administrative Services Expense . . . 66,000
Cash 346,000

Received $50,000 cash from Specific Purpose Funds to cover current operations.

Cash 50,000
Other Operating Revenue 50,000

A transfer of $200,000 was made from the Plant Replacement and Expansion Fund for purchase of a coronary monitoring device.

Cash 200,000
Transfers from Plant Replacement
and Expansion Fund 200,000

Coronary monitoring device was purchased and payment was made.

Property, Plant, and Equipment 200,000
Cash 200,000

Unrestricted earnings of $540,000 are received from investments of Endowment Fund.

Cash 540,000
Unrestricted Income from Endowment Fund 540,000

Depreciation expense provision for the year is $400,000.

Provision for Depreciation 400,000
Accumulated Depreciation 400,000

Transfer of $250,000 to Plant Replacement and Expansion Fund, as required by third-party payor revenues restricted in use to plant replacement.

Transfers to Plant Replacement and
Expansion Fund 250,000
Cash 250,000

The current portion of long-term debt is reclassified from:
Bonds payable . . . . $ 50,000
Mortgage note payable 30,000
Total . . . . $ 80,000

Bonds Payable 50,000
Mortgage Note Payable 30,000
Current Installment of Long-Term
Debt 80,000

Board-designated investments receive $22,000 cash earnings, which is to remain a part of board-designated cash.

Cash—Board Designated 22,000
Income from Board-Designated
Funds 22,000

Financial Statements of a Hospital

Since the revenues and expenses of a hospital are recorded in the Unrestricted Fund, it is the only fund to present a statement of revenues and expenses. The form is straightforward, showing operating revenue minus operating expenses as the net loss or net revenue from operations. The nonoperating revenue is added to this amount. To avoid the concept of profits for a nonprofit hospital, the final line is labeled Excess of Revenue over Expenses, or vice versa, as shown in Illustration V.

Illustration V

Fitale Hospital
Statement of Revenues and Expenses
For the Year Ended December 31, 19X1

Patient service revenue	$4,000,000
Provision for contractual adjustments and uncollectibles	402,000
Net patient service revenue	$3,598,000
Other operating revenue	250,000
Total operating revenue	$3,848,000
Operating expenses:	
Nursing services	$1,740,000
Other professional services	1,070,000
General services	870,000
Fiscal services	168,000
Administrative services	238,000
Provision for depreciation	400,000
Total operating expenses	$4,486,000
Loss from operations	$ (638,000)
Nonoperating revenue:	
Unrestricted income from Endowment Fund	$ 540,000
Income from board-designated funds	22,000
Total nonoperating revenue	$ 562,000
Excess of expenses over revenues	$ (76,000)

At year end, the following closing entry would be prepared for Fitale Hospital:

Patient Service Revenue	4,000,000	
Other Operating Revenue	250,000	
Unrestricted Income from Endowment Fund	540,000	
Income from Board-Designated Funds	22,000	
Fund Balance—Unrestricted	76,000	
Provision for Adjustments and Uncollectibles		402,000
Nursing Services Expense		1,740,000
Other Professional Services Expense		1,070,000
General Services Expense		870,000
Fiscal Services Expense		168,000
Administrative Services Expense		238,000
Provision for Depreciation		400,000

In addition to the statement of revenues and expenses of the Unrestricted Fund, a voluntary hospital provides a balance sheet, a statement of changes in fund balances, and a statement of changes in financial position of the Unrestricted Funds.

The preferred balance sheet form shown in the audit guide follows the same format as for a university, wherein the individual fund balance sheets are stacked one upon the other. The sequence begins with the balance sheet of the Unrestricted Funds, whose assets are segregated according to three segments: current assets, board-designated assets, and property, plant, and equipment. Also shown are the current and long-term liabilities of the Unrestricted Funds, and a single Fund Balance amount. As shown in Illustration VI on pages 816 and 817, the restricted funds are shown in the following sequence: Specific Purpose Fund, Plant Replacement and Expansion Fund, and Endowment Fund.

In support of the fund balance amounts shown in the balance sheet at the end of the period, the statement of changes in fund balances is prepared. All items that changed fund balances, including transfers, are shown in the same sequence of funds as in the balance sheet. The form shown in the audit guide is followed in Illustration VII, on page 818. It combines the segregated fund balances of the Plant Replacement and Expansion Fund into one amount and the fund balances of the Endowment Fund into one amount.

The statement of changes in financial position of the Unrestricted Funds concentrates on changes in the current segment only. As shown in Illustration VIII on page 819, the statement is prepared following the format used for commercial enterprises. Revenues restricted by third-party payors are not available as working capital and must be deducted in arriving at working capital provided by operations. Transfers received from the Plant Replacement and Expansion Fund are added as working capital provided, because they became available for expenditure for capital acquisitions that are shown as working capital applied. If the board transfers current assets to board-designated funds during the period, they will appear as funds applied. The net increase or decrease in working capital shown on the statement is supported by a schedule in the conventional form and is not illustrated.

The Hospital Audit Guide—An Achievement

The AICPA is to be commended for its achievements in hospital accounting as displayed in its *Hospital Audit Guide*. Its foremost contribution is the decision that all unrestricted resources be accounted for in one fund that includes plant assets. As a result of this guide, the accounting for hospitals has been clarified and simplified. Further attention should be given to other nonprofit entities, so that accounting for the activities of these organizations could reach the same level of communication.

Assets

UNRESTRICTED FUNDS

Current assets:
Cash	$ 105,000	
Receivables (net)	900,000	
Due from Specific Purpose Fund	100,000	
Inventories (at lifo or market, whichever is lower)	135,000	
Prepaid expenses	60,000	
Total current assets		$1,300,000

Board-designated funds:
Cash	$ 40,000	
Investments	460,000	500,000
Property, plant, and equipment	$7,932,000	
Less accumulated depreciation	1,932,000	6,000,000
Total unrestricted funds		$7,800,000

RESTRICTED FUNDS
Specific Purpose Fund

Cash	$ 1,500
Investments	204,500
Total specific purpose fund	$ 206,000

Plant Replacement and Expansion Fund

Cash	$ 15,000
Investments	700,000
Pledges receivable (net)	35,000
Total plant replacement and expansion fund	$ 750,000

Endowment Fund

Cash	$ 80,000
Investments	5,020,000
Total endowment fund	$5,100,000

VI

Hospital
Sheet
31, 19X1

Liabilities and Fund Balances
UNRESTRICTED FUNDS

Current liabilities:

Notes and accounts payable	$ 420,000	
Current installments of long-term debt	80,000	
Advances from third-party payors	200,000	
Accrued liabilities	100,000	
Total current liabilities		$ 800,000

Long-term debt:

Bonds payable (net)	$1,090,000	
Mortgage note payable	810,000	1,900,000
Fund balance		5,100,000
Total unrestricted funds		$7,800,000

RESTRICTED FUNDS
Specific Purpose Fund

Due to Unrestricted Funds	$ 100,000
Fund balance	106,000
Total specific purpose fund	$ 206,000

Plant Replacement and Expansion Fund

Fund balances:

Restricted by third-party payors	$ 250,000
Other	500,000
Total plant replacement and expansion fund	$ 750,000

Endowment Fund

Fund balances:

Permanent endowment	$4,050,000
Term endowment	1,050,000
Total endowment fund	$5,100,000

Illustration VII

Fitale Hospital
Statement of Changes in Fund Balances
For the Year Ended December 31, 19X1

UNRESTRICTED FUNDS

Balance at beginning of the year	$5,226,000
Excess of expenses over revenues	(76,000)
Transferred from Plant Replacement and Expansion Fund to finance property, plant, or equipment expenditures	200,000
Transferred to Plant Replacement and Expansion Fund to reflect third-party payor revenue restricted to property, plant, or equipment replacement	(250,000)
Balance at the end of the year	$5,100,000

RESTRICTED FUNDS

Specific Purpose Fund:

Balance at beginning of the year	$ 109,000
Restricted gifts and bequests received...	30,000
Income from investments	15,000
Gain on sale of investments	2,000
Transferred to Unrestricted Funds for operating revenue............................	(50,000)*
Balance at the end of the year	$ 106,000

Plant Replacement and Expansion Fund:

Balance at beginning of the year	$ 610,000
Restricted gifts and bequests received...	40,000
Income from investments	50,000
Transferred to Unrestricted Funds (described above)	(200,000)
Transferred from Unrestricted Funds (described above).............................	250,000
Balance at the end of the year	$ 750,000

Endowment Fund:

Balance at beginning of the year	$3,910,000
Restricted gifts and bequests received...	800,000
Net gain on sale of investments	390,000
Balance at the end of the year	$5,100,000

* The transfer was recorded in the Unrestricted Funds as a credit to Other Operating Revenue. It is not shown above as a transfer in the Unrestricted Funds, because it is included in the item, "Excess of expenses over revenues."

QUESTIONS

1. Without the built-in monitor of a profit motive, weaknesses have developed in accounting and reporting for nonprofit organizations. Itemize these weaknesses.

Illustration VIII

Fitale Hospital
Statement of Changes in Financial Position of the Unrestricted Funds
For the Year Ended December 31, 19X1

Funds provided:	
Loss from operations..	$ (638,000)
Add items included in operations not requiring funds:	
Provision for depreciation	400,000
Revenue restricted to property, plant, and equipment, transferred to Plant Replacement and Expansion Fund	(250,000)
Funds required for operations	$ (488,000)
Nonoperating revenue..	562,000
Funds derived from operations and nonoperating revenues......................	$ 74,000
Property, plant, and equipment expenditures financed by Plant Replacement and Expansion Fund	200,000
Decrease in working capital	28,000
Total	$ 302,000
Funds applied:	
Additions to property, plant, and equipment	$ 200,000
Reduction of long-term debt..	80,000
Increase in board-designated funds...................................	22,000
Total	$ 302,000

2. Why is it unwise for a nonprofit organization to have a large excess or deficiency of revenue over expenditures?

3. Describe the function of the two subfunds of the Current Funds of a university.

4. Interpret the following closing entry for a university:

Revenues—Auxiliary Enterprises	500,000	
Expenditures—Auxiliary Enterprises		480,000
Fund Balance		20,000

5. Of the various funds used in university accounting, indicate which is probably the most complex and explain why.

6. Two of the restricted funds of a hospital have several fund balance accounts. Identify the funds, the respective fund balance accounts, and their function.

7. Explain a hospital's rigid adherence to gross revenue determination.

8. Describe the role of a third-party payor in the financial affairs of a hospital.

9. Does the contractual adjustment procedure in hospital accounting have a corresponding counterpart in commercial accounting? Explain.

10. What is the major difference in accounting for the Unrestricted Funds of a university and that of a hospital?

11. If the Unrestricted Fund of a hospital receives assets from restricted funds, Operating Revenue, Nonoperating Revenue, or a transfer account may be credited. Describe the event that would result in a credit to each of these three accounts.

12. Explain why transfers from a hospital's Endowment Fund and Specific Purpose Fund to its Unrestricted Fund do not appear in the Unrestricted Funds section of the statement of changes in fund balances.

EXERCISES

Exercise 1. Record the following events that affect the Unrestricted Current Fund of Frank University, which uses three revenue and expenditure control accounts: Educational and General, Student Aid, and Auxiliary Enterprises:

    (a) Student fees of $300,000 were assessed, of which $250,000 have been collected, and $1,000 is estimated to be uncollectible.

    (b) The book store operates in rented space and is run on a break-even basis. Revenues totaled $90,000, of which 90% was collected to date. Salaries of $20,000 and rent of $10,000 are paid. Other operating expenses amount to $55,000, of which $5,000 has not yet been paid.

    (c) The Student Aid Committee report showed:

Cash scholarships issued	$6,000
Remission of tuition	2,500

    (d) A mandatory transfer of $5,000 was made for a payment due on the gymnasium building mortgage.

    (e) A check for $7,000 is received from the local medical society to cover part of the cost of research on drug effects, a part of the university educational program.

Exercise 2. A university's controller is excessively conservative and has recognized pledges for contributions by alumni only at the time money is received. A summary of pledges follows:

Pledges uncollected on July 1, 19X1 (of which 40% are considered uncollectible)	$72,000
Cash collections from pledges during fiscal year ended June 30, 19X2	90,000
Pledges proven uncollectible during the year	18,000
Pledges uncollected on June 30, 19X2 (of which 20% are considered uncollectible)	85,000

Prepare an entry to adjust accounting for pledges from a cash basis to an accrual basis, if pledge amounts are available for current operations and books have not been closed as of June 30, 19X2.

Exercise 3. Record the following events that affect the Restricted Current Fund of Frank University:

    (a) A private grant of $100,000 was received. It is to be used exclusively for defraying tuition fees for out-of-state students during the current year.

    (b) By year end, $85,000 of the grant had been applied to the purpose stipulated.

    (c) The grant provided that amounts not awarded by year end are to be transferred to the Endowment Fund. The liability to the Endowment Fund is recorded.

    (d) The University Alumni Association contributed $5,000 to be awarded to a faculty member for excellence in teaching.

Exercise 4. Record the following events that affect the Frank University Loan Fund:

    (a) To establish a student-faculty loan fund, $40,000 is received from an estate. Students are charged a 5% annual interest rate, while faculty members are charged 7%.

(b) Loans of $20,000 are made to students and $10,000 to faculty for the academic term. Of the remainder, $5,000 is deposited in the University Credit Union.

(c) Faculty loans of $4,000 were repaid, with interest of $140.

(d) A student who had borrowed $600 was in a serious accident. The university wrote off the loan as uncollectible.

Exercise 5. Record the following events that affect Frank University's Annuity and Life Income Funds:

(a) On July 1, 19X0, J. H. March, Emeritus Professor of Accounting, moved out of the state. March donated to the university common stock with a cost basis of $50,000 and a market value of $90,000. March is to receive an annuity of $5,000 a year for life, and at death, the securities are to be sold and the remaining cash balance is to be transferred to the Student Loan Fund. At a 10% annual rate and a life expectancy of 12 years, the present value of the annuity payments is $34,000.

(b) The stock pays $5,400 in dividends each twelve-month period.

(c) One year later, a payment of $5,000 is made to Professor March. The present value of that payment included in the $34,000 figure was $4,545.

(d) A second payment was made a year later. Its present value included in the $34,000 was $4,132.

(e) A month later, Professor March died, eliminating the liability for future annuity payments.

(f) The common stock was sold for $97,000. The cash balance was transferred to the Student Loan Fund.

Exercise 6. Record the following events that affect the Unexpended Plant Fund of Frank University.

(a) A transfer of $200,000 is made from the Unrestricted Current Fund to the Unexpended Plant Fund to finance an addition to the Fine Arts Building.

(b) Work on the Fine Arts addition is in progress. At year end, costs of construction total $80,000, of which $20,000 is unpaid. The university vice-president for finance prefers that transfers to the Investment in Plant subgroup be made only upon completion of any project.

(c) The project is completed during the next year at an additional cost of $140,000. Unpaid contract costs now total $35,000.

(d) Transfer of the Fine Arts addition is made to the Investment in Plant subgroup.

Exercise 7. Record the following events that affect Frank University's Investment in Plant subgroup:

(a) A partial payment of $5,000 is made from the Unrestricted Current Fund on the gymnasium building mortgage, which is carried as a liability in the Investment in Plant subgroup.

(b) New gymnasium equipment costing $30,000 is purchased from an Unexpended Plant Fund donated by a former olympic medal winner for that purpose.

(c) The Fine Arts Building addition is completed at a total cost of $220,000, of which $35,000 in contract costs is unpaid.

(d) During a celebration after a basketball victory, $2,000 of gym equipment disappeared.

Exercise 8. Prepare journal entries to record the following events for May in the Unrestricted Fund of Restful Hospital:

(a) The following gross charges were billed:

Patient services	$200,000
Nursing services	40,000
Other professional services	90,000
Total	$330,000

(b) Charity allowances for indigent patients reduced receivables by $8,000.

(c) Contractual adjustments granted for Medicare charges totaled $7,000.

(d) Collections on account totaled $225,000. Of the remaining unpaid accounts, it is estimated that 2% will be uncollectible.

Exercise 9. Although Hospital's balance sheet showed a net increase of $620,000 in working capital of the Unrestricted Funds, the following statement of changes in financial position does not agree with that amount. Recast the statement in correct form.

Hospital
Statement of Changes in Financial Position of the Unrestricted Funds
For Year Ended December 31, 19X4

Funds provided by:			
Operations per income statement		$ 60,000	
Add: Depreciation provision	$480,000		
Less depreciation applicable to plant asset disposed of during the year	10,000	470,000	
Unrestricted contribution received from a grateful patient		50,000	
Total proceeds from sale of unrestricted fund investments at gain of $10,000		90,000	$670,000
Funds applied:			
Addition to plant financed from long-term debt			200,000
Increase in working capital			$470,000

Exercise 10. (a) Prepare journal entries for the following events that affect the Endowment Fund of a hospital:

(1) The will of a former director of the hospital bequeathed an apartment building to the hospital, valued at $600,000, on which there is an unpaid mortgage of $90,000.

(2) The will stipulates that the corpus (principal) shall remain intact, requiring that an amount of rental income equal to depreciation expense be reserved in the Endowment Fund. Depreciation for the period amounts to $20,000. The controller wishes nominal accounts to be used.

(3) Other expenses of $12,000 were paid. Rental revenues collected totaled $85,000.

(4) Under the terms of the will, the net income from the apartment building should be transferred at year end to the Unrestricted Fund. The books are closed, establishing the liability to the fund.

(b) Explain how the recording of depreciation assists in keeping the corpus intact.

PROBLEMS

Problem 18-1. The following events occur as part of the operations of State University:

(a) A gift of land and a building was received, appraised at $100,000 and $450,000 respectively. The state's leading industrialist made the gift on condition that the university would assume a $180,000 mortgage on the property.

(b) The donor's sister contributed $100,000 in cash for the acquisition of rare first editions for the library.

(c) The director of the library has located a collection of first editions that is available for $140,000. The university board transferred $40,000 from the Unrestricted Current Funds to cover the difference.

(d) The first edition collection is purchased and payment is made.

(e) To construct a new math-science complex, the university floated at par a $10,000,000, 8% serial bond issue on October 1, paying interest on June 30 and December 31. Accrued interest is to be transferred to the Retirement of Indebtedness Plant Fund when construction begins. Construction costs are to be accumulated in the Unexpended Plant Fund until the unit is completed.

(f) Since construction has begun, the accrued interest, which must be used to assist in meeting bond interest payments, is transferred. Payments for construction to date total $3,000,000.

(g) On December 31, a mandatory transfer of $200,000 is made from the Unrestricted Current Funds to cover the remainder of the interest due on December 31 on the bond issue.

(h) The bond interest due on December 31 is paid.

(i) Construction of the math-science complex is completed at an additional cost of $7,000,000. Payment is made.

(j) Cost of the completed complex is transferred.

(k) A required transfer of $1,400,000 is made from the Unrestricted Current Funds to cover redemption of the first bond serial of $1,000,000 plus interest.

(l) Payments are made for the items in (k).

Required:

Prepare journal entries to record the events, indicating in which funds the entries are made by using the following solution format:

Event	Fund	Journal Entry
(a)		

Problem 18-2. The following transactions of County College occurred during 19X2. The funds involved are the Endowment Fund, the Annuity Fund, the Plant Fund—Unexpended, the Plant Fund—Investment in Plant, Student Loan Fund, Unrestricted Current Fund, and the Restricted Current Fund.

January 1

County College, which previously held no endowment funds, received five gifts as a result of an appeal for funds. The campaign closed December 31 and all gifts received are to be recorded as of January 1. Gifts are as follows:

(a) From A. B. Smith, $10,000, the principal to be held intact and the income to be used for any purpose that the Board of Trustees of County College should indicate.

(b) From C. D. Jones, $20,000, the principal to be held intact and the income to be used to endow scholarships for worthy students.

(c) From E. F. Green, $30,000, the principal to be held intact and the interest only to be loaned to students. All income is to be reloaned; all losses from student loans are to be charged against income.

(d) From G. H. White, $200,000. During the lifetime of the donor, semiannual payments of $2,500 are to be made to the donor. After White's death, the fund is to be used to construct or purchase a residence hall for students. Since White is seriously ill, no present value of the annuity is established.

(e) From I. J. Brown, 1,000 shares of XYZ stock, which had a market value on this date of $150 per share. Such shares are to be held for not more than five years and all income received therefrom held intact. At any date designated by the Board of Trustees during this period, all assets are to be liquidated and the proceeds used to build a student hospital.

(f) The Board of Trustees consolidated the assets of the Smith and Jones funds into a pooled investments account (in the proportion of their principal accounts) and purchased $30,000 of Electric Power Company bonds at par. Interest rate, 4%. Interest dates, January 1 and July 1.

(g) The cash of the Green fund is used to purchase $30,000, 5% bonds of the Steam Company at par plus accrued interest. Interest dates, April 1 and October 1.

(h) The $200,000 cash of the White fund is used to purchase $200,000, 2% U.S. Treasury notes at par. Interest dates, January 1 and July 1.

April 1—July 1

(i) All interest has been received as stipulated on bonds and notes owned and has been transferred to the proper fund when necessary. Dividends of $4,000 are received on XYZ stock.

(j) Payment is made to G. H. White in accordance with the terms of the gift. A loan of cash is authorized from the Endowment Fund to cover the overdraft created.

(k) $20,000 par of Electric Power Company bonds are sold at 102. No commission is involved. Gain is an addition to principal.

(l) Loan made to M. N. Black, $300, from the Green student loan fund.

October 1

(m) Notice is received of the death of G. H. White. Since there is no liability to the estate, no entry need be made at this point.

(n) An award of $200 is made from the Jones scholarship fund.

(o) $200,000 par of U.S. Treasury notes held by the White fund are sold at 101 and accrued interest. The Endowment Fund loan is repaid.

(p) Interest due on bonds is received.

December 31

(q) M. N. Black paid $100 principal and $5 interest on student loan.

(r) The Board of Trustees purchased a building suitable for a residence hall for $250,000, using the available funds from the G. H. White gift as part payment therefor and giving a 20-year mortgage payable for the balance.

Required:

Prepare journal entries to record the previous events, indicating in what fund each entry would appear. Do not prepare year-end adjusting entries. Use the following format:

Event	Fund	Journal Entry
(a)		

(AICPA adapted)

Problem 18-3. The bookkeeper for the Jacob Vocational School resigned on March 1, 19X8, after preparing the following general ledger trial balance data and analysis of cash as of February 28, 19X8:

Debits

Cash for general unrestricted current operations	258,000
Cash for restricted current uses	30,900
Stock donated by D. E. Marcy	11,000
Bonds donated by E. T. Pearce	150,000
Land	22,000
Building	33,000
General current operating expenses	38,000
Faculty recruitment expenses	4,100
Total	547,000

Credits

Mortgage payable on plant assets	30,000
Income from gifts for general operations	210,000
Income from gifts for restricted uses	196,000
Student fees	31,000
Fund balance	80,000
Total	547,000

Jacob Vocational School
Analysis of Cash
For the Six Months Ended February 28, 19X8

Cash for unrestricted current operations:			
Balance, September 1, 19X7		$ 80,000	
Add: Student fees..............................	$ 31,000		
Gift from W. L. Jacob	210,000	241,000	
		$321,000	
Deduct: General current operating expenses	$ 38,000		
Payment on land and building mortgage ..	25,000	63,000	$258,000
Cash for restricted uses:			
Gift from W. L. Jacob for faculty recruitment		$ 35,000	
Less faculty recruitment expenses		4,100	30,900
Checking account balance, February 28, 19X8			$288,900

An accountant has been engaged to determine the proper balances for the school as of August 31, 19X8, the close of the school's fiscal year. An examination disclosed the following information:

(a) D. E. Marcy donated 100 shares of Trans, Inc., stock in September, 19X7, with a market value of $110 per share at the date of donation. The terms of the gift provide that the stock and any income therefrom are to be retained intact. At any date designated by the board of directors, the assets are to be liquidated and the proceeds used as a down payment to assist the school's director in acquiring a personal residence. If proceeds are not sufficient to equal the down payment, the board authorized the difference to be covered from unrestricted cash, but not to exceed $1,000. The school will not retain any financial interest in the residence.

(b) E. T. Pearce donated 6% bonds in September, 19X7, with par and market values of $150,000 at the date of donation. Annual payments of $3,500 are to be made to the donor during the donor's lifetime. Earnings in excess of these payments are to be used for current operations in the following fiscal year. Upon the donor's death, the fund is to be used to construct a school cafeteria. The actuarially determined present value of the annuity is $50,000.

(c) No transactions have been recorded on the school's books since February 28, 19X8. An employee of the school prepared the following analysis of the checking account for the period from March 1 through August 31, 19X8:

Balance, March 1, 19X8			$288,900
Deduct: General current operating expenses	$14,000		
Purchase of equipment	47,000	$61,000	
Less student fees		8,000	
Net expenses		$53,000	
Down payment for director's residence	$11,200		
Less sale of 100 shares of Trans stock	10,600	600	53,600
Total			$235,300
Add interest on 6% bonds		$ 9,000	
Less payments to E. T. Pearce (present value is $3,100)		3,500	5,500
Balance, August 31, 19X8			$240,800

The accountant feels that previous records were very poorly kept and recommends that they be closed and that new records be established for each appropriate fund. The board of education accepts the recommendation, and the old set is closed.

Required:

Prepare a journal entry to establish correct pre-closing balances as of August 31, 19X8, for the following:

(1) Annuity Fund
(2) Investment in Plant Fund
(3) Restricted Current Fund (including expenditure and revenue accounts)
(4) Unrestricted Current Fund (including expenditure and revenue accounts). Use an operating expenditures account, since detail on operational expenditures is not provided.   (AICPA adapted)

Problem 18-4. The current funds balance sheet of Burnsville University as of the end of its fiscal year ended June 30, 19X7, is shown at the top of page 827.

The following transactions occurred during the fiscal year ended June 30, 19X8:

(a) On July 7, 19X7, a gift of $100,000 was received from an alumnus. The alumnus requested that one half of the gift be used for the purchase of books for the university library and the remainder be used for the establishment of a scholarship fund. The alumnus further requested that the income generated by the scholarship fund be used annually to award a

Burnsville University
Current Funds Balance Sheet
June 30, 19X7

Assets			Liabilities and Fund Balances		
Unrestricted:			Unrestricted:		
Cash	$210,000		Accounts payable	$ 45,000	
Accounts receivable—			Deferred revenues	66,000	
student tuition and			Fund balances..........	515,000	$626,000
fees, less allowance					
for doubtful accounts					
of $9,000	341,000				
State appropriations re-					
ceivable	75,000	$626,000			
Restricted:			Restricted:		
Cash	7,000		Fund balances..........		67,000
Investments	60,000	67,000			
Total current funds		$693,000	Total current funds		$693,000

scholarship to a qualified disadvantaged student. On July 20, 19X7, the board of trustees resolved that the funds of the newly established scholarship fund would be invested in savings certificates. On July 21, 19X7, the savings certificates were purchased.

(b) Revenue from student tuition and fees applicable to the year ended June 30, 19X8, amounted to $1,900,000. Of this amount, $66,000 was collected in the prior year and $1,686,000 was collected during the year ended June 30, 19X8. In addition, at June 30, 19X8, the university had received cash of $158,000 representing fees for the session beginning July 1, 19X8.

(c) During the year ended June 30, 19X8, the university had collected $349,000 of the outstanding accounts receivable at the beginning of the year. The balance was determined to be uncollectible and was written off against the allowance account. At June 30, 19X8, the allowance account was increased by $3,000.

(d) During the year interest charges of $6,000 were earned and collected on late student fee payments.

(e) During the year the state appropriation was received. An additional unrestricted appropriation of $50,000 was made by the state, but had not been paid to the university as of June 30, 19X8.

(f) An unrestricted gift of $25,000 cash was received from alumni of the university.

(g) During the year investments of $21,000 were sold for $26,000. Investment income amounting to $1,900 was received.

(h) During the year unrestricted operating expenses of $1,777,000 were recorded. At June 30, 19X8, $59,000 of these expenses remained unpaid.

(i) Restricted current funds of $13,000 were spent for authorized purposes during the year.

(j) The accounts payable at June 30, 19X7, were paid during the year.

(k) During the year, $7,000 interest was earned and received on the savings certificates purchased in accordance with the board of trustees' resolution, as discussed in (a).

Required:

(1) Prepare journal entries to record the transactions in the Unrestricted and Restricted Current Funds and the Endowment Fund. Letter journal entries to correspond with the transactions, using the following format:

Event	Fund	Journal Entry
(a)		

(2) Prepare a statement of changes in fund balances for the year ended June 30, 19X8, using a column for each of the three funds, but no total column.

Problem 18-5. During the calendar year 19X6, the following events occurred at Marcus Hospital, a voluntary hospital:

(a) Gross charges for hospital services were debited to Accounts Receivable. The hospital controller wishes to use separate revenue accounts for:

Room and board charges	$780,000
Charges for other professional services	320,000
Other nursing services	140,000

(b) Deductions from gross billings were as follows:

Contractual adjustments	$ 50,000
Provision for uncollectible receivables	30,000
Charity services	15,000

The accounting system uses a single allowance account.

(c) Charity services accounts receivable of $15,000 were written off.

(d) During the year, the following contributions were received:

From C. Marcus for future acquisition of a new x-ray machine	$25,000
From J. Sago for an emergency fund to be used if special assistance for burn care services is required	60,000
From various sources, with no restrictions as to use	79,000

(e) In the Endowment Fund, a total of various unrestricted investment earnings of $23,000 has been collected. They are to be accumulated in the account Due to Unrestricted Fund. Periodically, transfers are made to the Unrestricted Fund, which does not accrue the amounts, since the time of transfer is unpredictable. Transfers of $21,000 of such earnings are made.

(f) A new x-ray machine costing $36,000 is acquired. A transfer of cash is made from the Plant Replacement Fund, including Marcus's contribution plus other available cash. There is a 30-day trial period before payment is due. The invoice was vouchered.

(g) The old x-ray machine is sold for $8,000. It cost $27,000 and had a book value of $6,000 when sold. The gain is unrestricted.

(h) The following data are provided regarding accounts receivable collections:

Gross billings	$980,000
Less: Contractual adjustments	(40,000)
Uncollectible accounts written off	(11,000)
Cash collected	$929,000

Cash collected includes reimbursement by third-party payors for depreciation of $63,000, which must be accumulated to update facilities.

(i) Vouchers totaling $1,190,000 were issued for the following items:

Administrative services expense	$120,000
Fiscal services expense	94,000
General services expense...................................	225,000
Nursing services expense	520,000
Other professional services expense	165,000
Supplies (perpetual inventory is used)	60,000
Expenses accrued at December 31, 19X5	6,000

(j.) Cash payments on vouchers payable during the year were $925,000.

(k) Supplies of $37,000 were issued to nursing services.

(l) Plant Replacement and Expansion Fund investments earned $7,000, of which $6,000 was received. Earnings are restricted for plant expansion.

(m) Depreciation for the year amounts to $155,000.

(n) Included in the vouchered items was a bill for burn care services of $10,000. A transfer is made to the Unrestricted Fund from Sago's contribution.

(o) A payment of $27,000 is made, covering $15,000 of mortgage bonds retired at face value and $12,000 for the annual interest.

(p) The Endowment Fund contains only permanent endowments. Investments of that fund costing $50,000 were sold for $61,000. Gains must remain in the fund.

Required:

Prepare journal entries to record events, using the following format:

Event	Fund	Journal Entry
(a)		

(Hint: Refer to Problem 18-7 for account titles to be used.)

Problem 18-6. Using the data from Problem 18-5, prepare a statement of revenues and expenses for Marcus Hospital for the year ended December 31, 19X6.

Problem 18-7. You are provided with the post-closing trial balance of Marcus Hospital as of January 1, 19X6, segregated by funds:

Marcus Hospital
Post-Closing Trial Balance by Funds
January 1, 19X6

Unrestricted Fund		
Cash	20,000	
Accounts receivable	34,000	
Allowance for adjustments and uncollectibles..................		4,000
Supplies inventory	14,000	
Property, plant, and equipment	2,830,000	
Accumulated depreciation		564,000
Vouchers payable		16,000
Accrued expenses		6,000
Mortgage bonds payable		150,000
Fund balance		2,158,000
	2,898,000	2,898,000
Plant Replacement and Expansion Fund		
Cash	53,800	
Investments	71,200	
Fund balance—other		125,000
	125,000	125,000

Endowment Fund

Cash	6,000	
Investments	260,000	
Fund balance—permanent endowments		266,000
	266,000	266,000

Required:

Using the data in Problem 18-5 and the statement prepared in Problem 18-6:
(1) Prepare a balance sheet for Marcus Hospital as of December 31, 19X6.
(2) Prepare a statement of changes in fund balances for the year ended December 31, 19X6.

Problem 18-8. Based on the data provided in Problem 18-7 and the statements prepared in Problems 18-6 and 18-7, prepare the following:
(1) A schedule to determine the net increase or decrease in working capital of the Unrestricted Fund for the year ended December 31, 19X6.
(2) A statement of changes in financial position of the Unrestricted Fund for the year ended December 31, 19X6.

Problem 18-9. When the last living relative of J. Ethington died, a new board of directors was elected for Ethington Hospital, a nonprofit organization. The accountant they employed was amazed at the violations of the principles of hospital fund accounting displayed by the records and the trial balance of January 1, 1982. As a result of the accountant's recommendations, the board decided that effective January 1, 1982:
(a) The old balances should be reversed to eliminate them. Separate funds should be established for the Unrestricted Fund, the Ethington Endowment Fund, and the Plant Replacement and Expansion Fund.
(b) The hospital had followed the policy that cash equal to the depreciation provision be invested until needed for asset replacement. The account Investment in Common Stock represents the accumulated amount to date resulting from this policy. The board wishes to continue the procedure. Because of errors previously made in recording plant assets, however, the amount that should be in the allowance for depreciation account for assets still in service should be calculated and the replacement fund should be adjusted.

The balances in the general ledger at January 1, 1982, are:

Cash	50,000	
Investment in U.S. Treasury Bills	105,000	
Investment in Common Stock	417,000	
Interest Receivable	4,000	
Accounts Receivable	40,000	
Inventory	25,000	
Land	407,000	
Building	245,000	
Equipment	283,000	
Allowance for Depreciation		376,000
Accounts Payable		70,000
Bank Loan		150,000
Endowment Fund Balance		119,500
Other Fund Balances		860,500
Total	1,576,000	1,576,000

The following additional information is available:
(a) Under the terms of the will of J. Ethington, founder of the hospital, "the principal of the bequest is to be fully invested in trust forevermore in mortgages secured by productive real estate in Central City and/or in U.S. Government securities . . . and the income therefrom is to be used to defray current expenses."
(b) The Endowment Fund consists of the following:

Cash received in 1881 by bequest from Ethington	$ 81,500
Net gains realized from 1936 through 1969 from the sale of real estate acquired in mortgage foreclosures	23,500
Income received from 1970 through 1981 from 90-day U.S. Treasury Bill investments	14,500
Balance per general ledger on January 1, 1982	$119,500

(c) The land account balance is composed of:

1890 appraisal of land at $10,000 and building at $5,000, received by donation at that time. The building was demolished in 1920	$ 15,000
Appraisal increase based on insured value in land title policies issued in 1937	380,000
Landscaping costs for trees planted	12,000
Balance per general ledger on January 1, 1982	$407,000

(d) The building balance is composed of:

Cost of present hospital building completed in January, 1941, when the hospital commenced operations	$300,000
Adjustment to record appraised value of building in 1951................	(100,000)
Cost of elevator installed in hospital building in January, 1967	45,000
Balance per general ledger on January 1, 1982	$245,000

The estimated useful lives of the hospital building and the elevator when new were 50 years and 20 years, respectively.
(e) The hospital's equipment was inventoried on January 1, 1982. The costs shown in the inventory agreed with the equipment account balance in the general ledger. The allowance for depreciation account at January 1, 1982, included $158,250 applicable to equipment, and that amount was approved by the board of directors as being accurate. All depreciation is computed on a straight-line basis.
(f) A bank loan was obtained to finance the cost of new operating room equipment purchased in 1978. Interest was paid to December 31, 1981.

Required:

Assuming that the accountant has already closed existing account balances, prepare a journal entry to establish the correct account balances as of January 1, 1982, in each of the following funds:
(1) Endowment Fund
(2) Plant Replacement and Expansion Fund
(3) Unrestricted Fund

(AICPA adapted)

Problem 18-10. The General Medical Institute is a nonprofit hospital that accounts for its activities in a single fund. The board of directors has authorized installing a multiple-fund accounting system next year. The board's immediate concern is the small increase in the cash balance. Comparative financial statements for the fiscal years 19X2 and 19X3 are as follows:

The General Medical Institute
Comparative Statement of Revenues and Expenses
For Years Ended October 31, 19X3 and 19X2

Revenue from Services Rendered	19X3	19X2	Increase (Decrease)
Services to patients	$360,000	$304,000	$ 56,000
Less free services	36,000	38,000	(2,000)
Net revenue from services rendered	$324,000	$266,000	$ 58,000

Operating Expenses

	19X3	19X2	Increase (Decrease)
Departmental expenses:			
Medical services	$ 32,700	$ 29,300	$ 3,400
Medicine and supplies	14,600	10,500	4,100
Nursing services	89,900	76,200	13,700
Therapy services	34,300	31,300	3,000
Dietary	40,700	37,100	3,600
Housekeeping and maintenance	37,300	29,500	7,800
Administration and other	33,700	23,400	10,300
General expenses:			
Rental of leased premises (net)	—	3,100	(3,100)
Depreciation—building and equipment	9,900	8,300	1,600
Provision for uncollectible accounts	5,400	3,500	1,900
Interest expense	6,500	—	6,500
Loss on sale of equipment	2,000	—	2,000
Other	16,200	6,500	9,700
Total expenses	$323,200	$258,700	$ 64,500
Excess of revenues from services rendered over expenses of patient care	$ 800	$ 7,300	$ (6,500)

Other Income (Expenses)

	19X3	19X2	Increase (Decrease)
Research	$ (13,300)	$ (13,200)	$ (100)
Gain on sale of investments	18,600	3,500	15,100
Investment income	16,500	13,300	3,200
Contributions	10,300	14,800	(4,500)
Grant from government, designated for expansion	335,000	—	335,000
Miscellaneous	2,700	1,500	1,200
Total other income	$369,800	$ 19,900	$349,900
Excess of revenues over expenses	$370,600	$ 27,200	$343,400

The General Medical Institute
Comparative Balance Sheet
October 31, 19X3 and 19X2

Assets	19X3	19X2	Increase (Decrease)
Cash	$ 28,600	$ 18,500	$ 10,100
Accounts receivable—patients (net)	75,500	55,500	20,000
Investments (cost)	413,100	463,100	(50,000)
Prepaid expenses	2,200	1,600	600
Land, building, equipment (net)	327,200	333,700	(6,500)
Construction in progress	793,800	—	793,800
Total assets	$1,640,400	$872,400	$768,000

Liabilities and Fund Balance	19X3	19X2	Increase (Decrease)
Accounts payable—construction	$ 110,800	—	$110,800
Less receivables from government agencies	80,000	—	80,000
Accounts payable—construction (net)	$ 30,800	—	$ 30,800
Accounts payable—current operations	11,800	$ 10,200	1,600
Mortgage payable	365,000	—	365,000
Total liabilities	$ 407,600	$ 10,200	$397,400
Fund balance:			
Balance, November 1	$ 862,200	$835,000	$ 27,200
Excess of revenues over expenses for year	370,600	27,200	343,400
Balance, October 31	$1,232,800	$862,200	$370,600
Total liabilities and fund balance	$1,640,400	$872,400	$768,000

The audit working papers contain the following additional information:
(a) Accounts Receivable—Patients is stated at the net of the allowance for doubtful accounts, which amounted to $10,000 at October 31, 19X2, and $14,600 at October 31, 19X3. During the year, uncollectible accounts totaling $800 were written off.
(b) The research activities are net of research grants aggregating $10,000. Included as a research expense is depreciation of $6,600 on special research equipment.
(c) During 19X3, the construction of a new building was begun. The estimated cost of the building and equipment is $1,000,000. The expansion is being financed as follows:

Grant from government	$ 335,000
Mortgage (repayment to begin upon completion of building)	500,000
Special features installed at the request of government agencies and to be paid for by the agencies	80,000
Institute funds available	85,000
Total	$1,000,000

(d) New therapy equipment costing $15,000 was purchased in 19X3. Therapy equipment with a book value of $5,000 was sold for $3,000.
(e) To obtain additional working capital, investments with a cost of $50,000 were sold during July.

Required:

Prepare a statement accounting for the increase in cash for the year ended October 31, 19X3, to be included in the annual report of The General Medical Institute. The statement should set forth information concerning cash applied to or provided by:
(1) Operations
(2) Research activities
(3) Acquisitions of assets
(4) Other sources of funds

(AICPA adapted)

CHAPTER 19

ACCOUNTING FOR VOLUNTARY HEALTH AND WELFARE ORGANIZATIONS

This chapter discusses accounting and financial reporting for voluntary health and welfare organizations. To qualify as this type of nonprofit organization, two criteria must be met. First, a primary source of revenue should be contributions from donors who do not themselves directly benefit from the organization's programs. A community symphony orchestra would not qualify, because it derives a large share of its revenue from box office receipts. Second, the programs must be in the area of health, welfare, or community service, such as care for the elderly, the indigent, or the handicapped, or projects to protect the environment.

FUNDS

Although most contributions are made with no restrictions attached, some donations specify the purpose for which they must be expended. To segregate resources and to demonstrate compliance with restrictions, fund accounting is used. The funds that are practical for most voluntary health and welfare organizations are:

> Unrestricted: Current Unrestricted Fund
> Restricted: Current Restricted Fund
> Land, Building, and Equipment Fund (or Plant Fund)
> Endowment Fund
> Custodian Fund

Although these funds are similar to the funds used in university accounting—two current funds consisting primarily of current assets and current liabilities, a separate plant fund (but without subgroups), and an endowment fund—all voluntary health and welfare organization funds (except custodian funds) record revenues and expenses. In accounting for universities, only the two current funds have revenue and expense accounts, while the other funds record changes directly through their fund balance accounts.

Current Unrestricted Fund

The *Current Unrestricted Fund* accounts for resources that have no external restrictions, and that are available for current operations at the discretion of the governing board. The board may, however, place its own restrictions on the fund balance. In the same manner that industry appropriates retained earnings, the board of directors of a health and welfare organization may designate a portion of its fund balance for a special project. To reflect such an action, the fund balance consists of two accounts. One is Fund Balance—Designated, which corresponds to an appropriated retained earnings account. The other account is Fund Balance—Undesignated, which resembles the free or unappropriated retained earnings balance. The designated fund balance may only be created from, and must ultimately be returned to, the undesignated fund balance, just as appropriated retained earnings come from and return to the free retained earnings balance.

Current Restricted Fund

The *Current Restricted Fund* accounts for assets received from outside sources for a current operating purpose specified by the donor. The distinguishing feature between unrestricted and restricted funds is whether or not an externally imposed restriction exists. A contribution received by a health agency to conduct sex education classes is an example of a restricted resource. In the Current Restricted Fund, a separate fund balance account may be established for each program. A more common procedure is to use one fund balance account as a control over supporting records that provide detailed segregation and identification. Specifically excluded from this fund are contributions of endowments or contributions restricted to the acquisition of plant assets, which are recorded in other appropriate funds.

Land, Building, and Equipment Fund (or Plant Fund)

The *Plant Fund* accounts for the activity related to fixed assets, including the accumulation of resources to acquire or replace them, the liabilities related to them, as well as their acquisition, their disposal, and their depreciation. To determine the total cost of rendering service, depreciation of assets employed in providing that service must be recorded in the Plant Fund, with the typical depreciation entry debiting Depreciation Expense and crediting Accumulated Depreciation.

Two fund balance accounts are used in the Plant Fund. The first is labeled Fund Balance—Unexpended, which represents the net assets in the fund not yet committed. The second is Fund Balance—Expended, which shows the net amount invested in plant assets, equal to the gross fixed assets minus accumulated depreciation and minus any liabilities directly related to those assets, such as a mortgage. Each time there is a change in the net amount invested in fixed assets as defined, there must be a change in the respective fund balance accounts. For example, assume that there is a payment on a mortgage liability from Plant Fund cash. In addition to the payment entry, a second entry is necessary because the reduction of the mortgage liability increases the net investment in plant and the cash payment reduces the unexpended assets. The additional entry needed is:

Fund Balance—Unexpended	xxx	
Fund Balance—Expended		xxx

This entry would also be necessary if fixed assets were purchased using Plant Fund cash.

Fixed assets may be acquired by the expenditure of Current Unrestricted Fund cash. To show the increase in the net investment in plant, the following entry is recorded in the Plant Fund:

Land, Building, and Equipment	xxx	
Fund Balance—Expended		xxx

In the Current Unrestricted Fund, the expenditure could be recorded with a debit to the account Transfer to Plant Fund, or debited directly to Fund Balance—Undesignated, as Cash is credited. As long as the records provide data for the financial statements, either method is acceptable. Since the unrestricted fund is the one most often involved in making transfers to other funds, this text will follow the procedure of using a separate account to record a transfer in the unrestricted fund, while handling transfers in other funds directly through the appropriate fund balance account.

If fixed assets are sold, the usual entry is made, with the gain or loss recorded in a miscellaneous revenue or miscellaneous expense account. A second entry is necessary to show the change in the respective fund balance accounts equal to the book value of the asset sold. At year end, the gain or loss on the sale will increase or decrease Fund Balance—Unexpended through the closing process. For example, assume that equipment costing $6,000, with $4,000 of accumulated depreciation, is sold for $3,100. The entries in the Plant Fund are:

Cash	3,100	
Accumulated Depreciation	4,000	
Land, Building, and Equipment		6,000
Miscellaneous Revenue		1,100
To record equipment sale.		
Fund Balance—Expended	2,000	
Fund Balance—Unexpended		2,000
To record decrease in net investment in plant equal to book		
value of asset sold.		

Although the unexpended net assets increased by $3,100, the portion equal to the gain of $1,100 will increase Fund Balance—Unexpended at year end, when the revenue accounts are closed.

Endowment Fund

The *Endowment Fund* accounts for gifts or bequests with the legal restriction that the principal be maintained in perpetuity or until the occurrence of a specified event. Various conditions are possible, depending upon the desires of the contributor. Unless otherwise specified, net gains or losses on the sale of Endowment Fund assets are increases or decreases of the fund principal.

Endowment Fund investment income may be restricted or unrestricted. When the investment income is identical to the cash flow, as in the case of cash dividends, the income is generally recorded directly in the fund that is to receive it. Such income not subject to any restrictions by the principal donor is recorded directly in the Current Unrestricted Fund as investment income. If the income is subject to a restriction, it is recorded directly in the appropriate restricted fund. An alternative process would be to record the cash received in the Endowment Fund, with a credit to a liability to the ultimate recipient fund. This indirect approach would require another entry to record the cash transfer between funds, at which time the liability and receivable accounts are reduced. For example, if a cash dividend on Endowment Fund investments is received and there are no restrictions on the income, the entries in the respective funds are:

Endowment Fund	Cash	xxx	
	Due to Current Unrestricted Fund		xxx
Current Unrestricted Fund	Due from Endowment Fund	xxx	
	Investment Income		xxx

Where the cash flow and the income to be recognized are not equal, as in the case of interest received on bonds purchased at a premium or discount, the indirect approach is preferable. It permits tighter control over cash flows, all of which are first recorded in the Endowment Fund. A liability is recorded for the cash to be transferred to other funds. For example, assume that $100,000 of 14%, 10-year bonds are purchased at 110 on an annual interest payment date, with interest to go to the Current Unrestricted Fund. The entry to record their purchase in the Endowment Fund is:

Investment in 14% Bonds	100,000	
Premium on Bonds Purchased	10,000	
Cash		110,000

A year later, a check for $14,000 is received. If the total $14,000 is entered as income in the Current Unrestricted Fund, eventually the principal of the Endowment Fund will be reduced by $10,000, since the Endowment Fund will receive upon bond maturity only $100,000 for its $110,000 cash outlay. To prevent such an erosion of principal, a portion of the interest equal to the premium amortization is retained as principal of the Endowment Fund and a liability for the net amount available to the Current Unrestricted Fund is established. Under pro rata amortization, the entries would be:

Endowment Fund	Cash	14,000	
	Premium on Bonds Purchased		1,000
	Due to Current Unrestricted Fund		13,000
	To retain as principal the pro rata amortization of premium on bonds purchased ($10,000 ÷ 10 years).		
Current Unrestricted Fund	Due from Endowment Fund	13,000	
	Investment Income		13,000

If bonds are purchased at a discount, the entry to record the discount accumulation in the Endowment Fund depends upon the arrangements with the donor or the decision of the controlling board. If only the immediate cash flow from the investment is available to the recipient fund, the discount accumulation is credited to Investment Income in the Endowment Fund. If total income, including discount accumulation, must be available to the fund designated as the recipient, a liability to that fund for the total is credited. To illustrate, assume that $100,000 of 10%, 10-year bonds are purchased at 95 on an annual interest payment date, with interest to go to the Current Unrestricted Fund. The entry to record the purchase in the Endowment Fund is:

Investment in 10% Bonds	100,000	
Discount on Bonds Purchased		5,000
Cash		95,000

Most endowments make only the immediate cash flow available, in which case the following entries based on pro rata accumulation are recorded one year later:

Endowment Fund	Cash	10,000	
	Discount on Bonds Purchased	500	
	Due to Current Unrestricted Fund		10,000
	Investment Income		500
Current Unrestricted Fund	Due from Endowment Fund	10,000	
	Investment Income		10,000

In the rare case in which the donor would require that total income, including discount accumulation, should be available, the entries would be:

Endowment Fund	Cash	10,000	
	Discount on Bonds Purchased	500	
	Due to Current Unrestricted Fund		10,500
Current Unrestricted Fund	Due from Endowment Fund	10,500	
	Investment Income		10,500

Custodian Fund

A *Custodian Fund* is somewhat similar to the Agency Funds of other nonprofit organizations, in that the assets do not belong to the organization holding them. There is a more technical distinction as pointed out in the audit guide, which states that "Custodian Funds are established to account for assets received by an organization to be held or disbursed only on instructions of the person or organization from whom they were received."[1]

Assets are recorded in Custodian Funds when received, along with a liability to the donor. Only when they are released by the contributor will the assets be recorded as revenue in the appropriate fund. For most organizations, Custodian Funds do not exist. If they do exist, Custodian Funds should be shown on the balance sheet, but should not be combined with amounts of other funds.

ACCOUNTING PRINCIPLES AND PROCEDURES

The full accrual basis of accounting should be used in accounting and reporting for voluntary health and welfare organizations if the reports are to be considered as prepared in accordance with generally accepted accounting principles. All funds (except Custodian Funds) use revenue and expense accounts.

A significant aspect of accounting and reporting for voluntary health and welfare organizations is that financial reports must show expenses on a program basis. As a result of this requirement, the costs of each program and supporting service can be compared, and the effectiveness with which the organization's resources have been managed can be measured.

Public Support and Revenues

The dependence upon public support for the majority of its resources influences the accounting for a voluntary health and welfare organization. Two major categories are used to record and communicate inflows of resources: public support and revenue. Public support is the inflow of resources from voluntary donors who receive no direct, personal benefit from the organization's usual programs in exchange for their contributions. Revenues are inflows of resources resulting from a charge for service or from financial activities.

The following accounts, which may be found in all funds (except Custodian Funds), are used to record receipts of assets in the public support category:

> Contributions
> Special Events Support
> Legacies and Bequests
> Received from Federated and Nonfederated Campaigns

---

[1] *Audits of Voluntary Health and Welfare Organizations* (New York: American Institute of Certified Public Accountants, 1974), p. 3.

Contributions. Cash collections that do not involve a previous pledge are credited to the account Contributions. Voluntary health and welfare organizations also receive pledges for contributions, which are recorded at the gross amount as Pledges Receivable, with a credit to Contributions. A provision and allowance for estimated uncollectible pledges is established, based on historical collection experience. The provision for uncollectible pledges is a contra account to Contributions on the operating statement, while the allowance is a contra account to Pledges Receivable on the balance sheet.

Securities and other property received should be entered in the appropriate fund at their fair market value at the time of receipt. These assets are most likely to be received as restricted contributions to the Plant Fund or to the Endowment Fund. The donor may restrict not only the purpose but also the timing of use. If the donation is not available until some future fiscal period, a deferred credit account, Contributions Designated for Future Periods, is introduced. The amount is then transferred to Contributions in the period when it becomes available.

Peculiar to voluntary health and welfare organizations is the donation of materials to be used in providing service or to be processed for subsequent sale. These materials should be recorded as inventory, with a credit to Contributions at their fair market value when received, providing they are substantial in amount and a measurable value for them can be established, either by sale shortly thereafter or by appraisal. An example would be the donation of clothing or household goods to Goodwill Industries.

Occasionally a voluntary health and welfare organization will be permitted to use building facilities rent free. In this situation, both the contribution and the rent expense should be recorded at the amount that would normally be charged for rent. Donated fixed assets for which title is received, such as equipment or land and building, should be entered as a contribution at fair market value in the Plant Fund, if the fixed asset is to be used by the organization. If the donated fixed asset is accepted with the intent to sell within the near future, it is recorded with a credit to Contributions in the Unrestricted Fund or in one of the restricted funds, depending upon the donor's stipulations.

Although the range and quantity of personal services that volunteers donate vary between organizations, these services should be recorded if they are significant and if all three of the following criteria are met:

1. Services provided would have to be performed by salaried personnel, were it not for the volunteer.
2. Duties of the volunteer are controlled by the organization.
3. The value of the volunteer's services is measurable and material. The amount paid salaried personnel for equivalent services would be a useful measure of value.

If the three tests are met, donated services are recorded with a debit to an expense account, such as Salary Expense, and a credit to Contributions. The audit guide specifically excludes from donated services the assistance of volunteers for concentrated fund drives because of the difficulty of enforcing the second criterion of control over the volunteers.

Special Events Support. Another subdivision of the public support category covers an organization's special fund-raising events, in which the participant has the opportunity to receive something of value in exchange for a contribution. Raffles, dinners, bingo games, and bake sales are examples of special events. The gross inflow of resources is credited to the account Special Events Support in the fund that is to benefit. Direct costs of the event, excluding promotional costs, are charged to the account Cost of Special Events. Comparing these two balances permits one to judge the effectiveness of the event. Promotional costs, such as advertising or the salaries of employees involved in the event, are charged against the account Fund-Raising Expense. The audit guide requires that the portion of the budget consumed by fund raising be revealed.

Legacies and Bequests. Every voluntary health and welfare organization hopes that its programs will be so deserving that they will encourage donors to make major contributions of personal property or real property through their wills. Since these items tend to be more substantial in amount, the audit guide recommends that such contributions be shown as a separate item of public support under the account Legacies and Bequests. They are entered as a credit to that account when the organization is reasonably certain of the amount to be received.

Received from Federated and Nonfederated Campaigns. The final item considered as public support is the amount received from federated (associated) and nonfederated organizations. This amount is credited to the account Received from Federated and Nonfederated Campaigns. An amount allocated by United Way to a health and welfare organization would be an example of support received from a federated organization. An amount raised by independent professional fund-raising groups would be an illustration of resources received from nonfederated campaigns.

Revenues

In addition to public support, resources may be received that are classified as revenue. These resources would include fees charged for services and investment transaction income. In the first group (fees charged for services) would be the following accounts:

1. Membership Dues Revenue for dues charged members to join and to use facilities or to receive publications.

2. Program Services Fees for amounts charged clients for services of the organization, such as consulting, testing, or advising.
3. Sales of Publications and Supplies for proceeds from the sales of these items.

The second group (investment transaction income) could include the following accounts:

1. Investment Income for interest, dividends, and other earnings.
2. Realized Gain on Investment Transactions for gains from the sale or exchange of investments.
3. Net Increase (or Decrease) in Carrying Value of Investments for the unrealized appreciation or depreciation of investments if they are carried at market value.

Each of the items of revenue would be recorded in the fund which is entitled to its use. Thus, the unrestricted income from the Endowment Fund would be recorded directly in the Current Unrestricted Fund with a credit to Investment Income. Restricted investment income is reported as revenue directly in the fund that is entitled to it in compliance with the donor's wishes.

The audit guide permits voluntary health and welfare organizations to carry their investments either at cost or at market value, but the same basis must be applied to all the investments of all of the funds. Cost includes not only the total cost of purchased investments but also the fair market value at the date of receipt of donated investments. When there is a relatively permanent reduction in market value, the impairment to cost should be recorded. If all investments are reflected at market value, the unrealized appreciation (or depreciation) is shown separately in the account Net Increase (or Decrease) in Carrying Value of Investments. Although gaining in acceptance, this alternative has been adopted by few organizations, partially as the result of the reluctance of accountants to recognize unrealized gains.

If an organization is fortunate enough to accumulate substantial investments in its various funds, pooling may be advisable. *Pooling of investments* is the process of combining the investments of various funds into one group or pool to provide greater flexibility at lower cost and to provide diversification to spread the risk. Once pooled, individual investments lose their identity as to fund. Each contributing fund merely maintains in its investment account an amount representing its portion of the pool. Before any additions or withdrawals may be made, the market value of the total portfolio must be determined. Realized gains and losses (and unrealized, if investments are carried at market value rather than cost) are allocated to each participating fund on the basis of its share of the total market value at the previous valuation date. The proportion of each fund's market value may be expressed in terms of units or in terms of percentages of the total. The latter method is more flexible and is used in Illustration I, which shows changes in pooled investments over a period of time.

Illustration I—Pooling of Investments

Fund	(1) Cash and/or FMV of Securities	(2) Original Equity Percent	(3) Total Pool December 31, 19X0 Cost	(4) Total Pool December 31, 19X0 Market	(5) Mkt. Value Including $50,000	(6) Revised Equity Percent	(7) After Withdrawal of $25,000	(8) New Equity Percent
Unrestricted ...	$ 36,000	20%	$ 40,000	$ 50,000	$ 50,000	16.67%	$ 25,000	9.09%
Plant..........	54,000	30	60,000	75,000	75,000	25.00	75,000	27.27
Endowment ...	90,000	50	100,000	125,000	175,000	58.33	175,000	63.64
Total	$180,000	100%	$200,000	$250,000	$300,000	100.00%	$275,000	100.00%

The investments of the Current Unrestricted Fund, the Plant Fund, and the Endowment Fund of a voluntary health and welfare organization were pooled as of January 2, 19X0. The investment accounts are maintained at market. Cash and/or fair market value of the securities pooled are shown in Column (1). The percentage of the total contributed by each fund is shown in Column (2). During the ensuing year, net realized gains retained by the investment pool amounted to $20,000. Based on its equity percentage, each fund records its share of the gain. Thus, the Current Unrestricted Fund's entry for 20% of the $20,000 gain would be:

Pooled Investments	4,000	
Realized Gain on Investment Transactions		4,000

The $20,000 increase in the pool results in a revised cost basis as of December 31, 19X0, shown in Column (3). On December 31, 19X0, the Endowment Fund receives a contribution of securities, which have a fair market value of $50,000 and which are to be pooled with the other investments, whose fair market value on that date must also be determined if the process is to be equitable. The total market value of the other investments is determined to be $250,000, which is allocated to each fund, as shown in Column (4), on the basis of the percentages previously computed. After acceptance of the additional $50,000 of Endowment Fund securities, the total market value is $300,000, as shown in Column (5), from which revised equity percentages are determined, shown in Column (6).

Immediately after each addition to or withdrawal from the pool, new equity percentages must be determined. To avoid numerous computations, it is common practice that changes are permitted only at the end of a calendar quarter. Assume that on December 31, 19X0, the Current Unrestricted Fund needs $25,000 to meet expenses and that amount is withdrawn from the investment pool. Since each fund has already recorded its share of the unrealized gains, the entry in the Unrestricted Fund would be:

Cash	25,000	
Pooled Investments		25,000

With this redemption, the new market value of remaining pool investments is $275,000, shown in Column (7), with the revised equity percentages listed in Column (8).

When investments are pooled, each fund involved initiates an account, Pooled Investments, that is carried at market value to reflect directly its equity in the pool. To illustrate the entries for the Endowment Fund in the previous illustration when investments are carried at market value, the following entries are presented:

Pooled Investments	90,000	
Cash		90,000
To record original investment as of January 2, 19X0.		
Pooled Investments	10,000	
Realized Gain on Investment Transactions		10,000
To record realized gain on investment transactions for 19X0 (50% × $20,000).		
Pooled Investments	25,000	
Net Increase in Carrying Value of Investments		25,000
To record increase in market value over cost at year end (50% × $50,000).		
Investments (or Securities)	50,000	
Contributions		50,000
To record securities received as a contribution.		
Pooled Investments	50,000	
Investments (or Securities)		50,000
To record transfer of contributed securities to pool at fair market value.		

After the series of entries has been posted, the balance in Pooled Investments is $175,000. This amount represents the Endowment Fund's equity in the pool at year end.

Program and Supporting Services Costs

The audit guide emphasizes that voluntary health and welfare organizations exist to render service or to conduct programs. Their operating statements will not show functional expenses, such as salaries or rent, but will show the cost of each program or service the organization provides—the costs in which the general public, the contributors, and controlling agencies are primarily interested. For example, the operating statement of an environmental protection association might show the cost of conducting a program to reduce river pollution or to provide an animal and bird sanctuary. These projects fall in an expense grouping called "Program Services." The other expense grouping shown on an operating statement is referred to as "Supporting Services," which includes fund-raising costs and management and general costs for the overall direction of the organization.

Individual expenses, such as salaries or rent, are recorded in the respective expense accounts of the appropriate funds, in much the same way that they would be recorded in the accounts of profit entities. Most of the expenses will be recorded in the unrestricted fund, since it is the principal operating fund, but some expenses may be recorded in the restricted funds. At the end of the fiscal year, the expenses recorded in each fund are allocated to the programs conducted and to the supporting services of management and fund raising. Allocation should be on some rational basis, such as assigning salaries on the basis of time expended, allotting rental charges on the basis of floor space or facilities, or apportioning supplies expense on the basis of consumption.

Closing Entries

After all expenses have been assigned, an entry is made in each fund to close the expense accounts and charge each of the expenses to the programs and supporting services. For the environmental protection association used earlier as an example, the following entry might be recorded in the Current Unrestricted Fund:

River Pollution Program	xxx	
Animal and Bird Sanctuary Program	xxx	
Management and General Services	xxx	
Fund-Raising Services	xxx	
Salary Expense, Supplies Expense, etc.		xxx

The final closing entries close each fund's support and revenue accounts as well as the program and services accounts to the appropriate fund balance. The closing entry for the Current Unrestricted Fund of the environmental protection association might be:

Contributions	xxx	
Legacies and Bequests	xxx	
Membership Dues Revenue	xxx	
Investment Income	xxx	
River Pollution Program		xxx
Animal and Bird Sanctuary Program		xxx
Management and General Services		xxx
Fund-Raising Services		xxx
Fund Balance—Undesignated		xxx

If the board of directors should decide to designate a specified sum of the Current Unrestricted Fund for a future program to reduce air pollution, the undesignated fund balance is appropriated as follows:

Fund Balance—Undesignated	xxx	
Fund Balance—Designated for Air Pollution Program		xxx

Financial Statements

The audit guide requires three financial statements for voluntary health and welfare organizations: an operating statement, which is formally referred to as a statement of support, revenue, and expenses and changes in fund balances; a statement of functional expenses; and a balance sheet. These statements are illustrated later in the chapter.

An operating statement can be prepared after the expense allocation entry has been recorded in each fund. It is structured with a column for each fund (except the Custodian Fund) to show how effectively the organization operated during the period.

Since program costs and not functional expenses are shown in an operating statement, a summary of expenses by function is provided in a separate statement. This statement of functional expenses, as required by the audit guide, supplements the operating statement. It disregards individual funds and presents the total of each expense for all funds combined and the allocation of each expense to the various programs and services.

A balance sheet is prepared either in columnar form for each fund or with individual fund balance sheets layered one upon the other. The latter form is followed in the audit guide.

ILLUSTRATION OF ACCOUNTING FOR A VOLUNTARY HEALTH AND WELFARE ORGANIZATION

To illustrate the recording of events and the preparation of financial reports for a voluntary health and welfare organization, assume that the People's Environmental Protection (PEP) Association, a voluntary community organization, has three programs: Valley Air Pollution, Keep Fish in the Lakes, and Flood Control. The trial balances of the various funds of PEP on January 1, 19X5, are as follows:

People's Environmental Protection Association
Fund Trial Balances
January 1, 19X5

| | Current Funds | | Plant Fund | Endowment Fund |
	Unrestricted	Restricted		
Cash	40,000	12,500	2,000	9,000
Pledges Receivable	24,000	600	—	—
Allowance for Uncollectible Pledges	(3,000)	(100)	—	—
Investments	61,000	—		244,000
Land, Building, and Equipment	—	—	92,700	—
Accumulated Depreciation	—	—	(16,700)	—
Totals	122,000	13,000	78,000	253,000
Accounts Payable	33,000	4,000	—	—
Fund Balances:				
Designated	25,000	—	—	—
Undesignated	64,000	—	—	—
Restricted	—	9,000	—	253,000
Expended	—	—	76,000	—
Unexpended	—	—	2,000	—
Totals	122,000	13,000	78,000	253,000

The following events occur during the calendar year 19X5. They are summarized to conserve space and minimize duplication. The entries are shown following each transaction, with the designation of the fund in which the entry is recorded appearing above the amounts for that entry.

1. As a result of its fund-raising program, cash contributions and pledges were received.

	Unrestricted		Restricted	
Cash	235,000		90,000	
Pledges Receivable	80,000		20,000	
Contributions		315,000		110,000

2. Based on past experience, 5% of the pledges are estimated to be uncollectible.

	Unrestricted		Restricted	
Provision for Uncollectible Pledges.................	4,000		1,000	
Allowance for Uncollectible Pledges..............		4,000		1,000

3. During the year, cash was collected from some pledges, while others were written off as uncollectible.

	Unrestricted		Restricted	
Cash	78,000		17,500	
Allowance for Uncollectible Pledges................	5,000		600	
Pledges Receivable		83,000		18,100

4. A cash donation of $40,000 was received, on condition that it be used to acquire equipment that will assist in water quality improvement.

	Plant	
Cash	40,000	
Contributions		40,000

5. With the donor's approval, the $40,000 served as a partial payment on the purchase of a weed cutter costing $50,000. A note was signed for the unpaid balance.

	Plant	
Land, Building, and Equipment	50,000	
Cash		40,000
Notes Payable on Equipment		10,000
Fund Balance—Unexpended	40,000	
Fund Balance—Expended		40,000

6. The following bequests were received: $100,000 unrestricted, and $20,000 as a permanent endowment fund whose earnings were unrestricted.

	Unrestricted		Endowment	
Cash	100,000		20,000	
Legacies and Bequests		100,000		20,000

7. PEP held a special summer event to promote its activities, the net proceeds of which were unrestricted. Gross revenues totaled $9,000, with direct costs for the event amounting to $2,000.

	Unrestricted	
Cash	9,000	
Special Events Support		9,000
Cost of Special Events	2,000	
Cash		2,000

8. An annual membership to PEP is $100, permitting members and their families to use lake facilities for swimming, sailing (no motors allowed), or fishing. The proceeds are not restricted.

	Unrestricted	
Cash	118,000	
Membership Dues Revenue...		118,000

9. The local PEP unit receives unrestricted cash of $16,000 as its share of a campaign run by its national affiliate.

	Unrestricted	
Cash	16,000	
Received from Federated and Nonfederated Campaigns		16,000

10. The Endowment Fund reports investment income of $28,000, of which $21,000 is not restricted and $7,000 is restricted to publication of pamphlets on flood control. Earnings of the Endowment Fund are recorded directly in the fund that is entitled to them.

	Unrestricted	Restricted
Cash	21,000	7,000
Investment Income	21,000	7,000

11. PEP carries its investments in all funds at market value. The Endowment Fund sold investments for $27,000. They had a cost of $20,000 and a carrying value of $25,000 in the investment account.

	Endowment	
Cash	27,000	
Investments (at market)		25,000
Gain on Sale of Investments		2,000

12. The Endowment Fund purchased additional investments costing $46,000.

	Endowment	
Investments	46,000	
Cash		46,000

13. The investments of the Current Unrestricted Fund have shown no material change in market value over the year. At year end, the market value of investments in the Endowment Fund has increased from $265,000 to $294,000.

	Endowment	
Investments	29,000	
Net Increase in Carrying Value of Investments		29,000

14. A special recreational building and dock costing $96,000 was purchased with Unrestricted Fund cash.

	Unrestricted	
Transfer to Plant Fund (or Fund Balance—Undesignated)	96,000	
Cash		96,000

	Plant	
Land, Building, and Equipment..	96,000	
Fund Balance—Expended		96,000

15. Accounts payable and expenses were paid or established.

	Unrestricted		Restricted	
Accounts Payable (January 1)	33,000		4,000	
Salaries Expense	180,000		20,000	
Payroll Taxes	24,000		6,000	
Mailing and Postage Expense	40,000		10,000	
Rent Expense	23,000		5,000	
Telephone Expense	5,000		1,000	
Research Expense	165,000		50,000	
Professional Services: Legal and Audit	27,000		7,000	
Supplies Expense	10,000		3,000	
Miscellaneous Expenses	4,000		1,000	
Accounts Payable		31,000		1,000
Cash		480,000		106,000

16. Depreciation for the year amounted to $22,000.

	Plant	
Depreciation Expense	22,000	
Accumulated Depreciation		22,000

17. Early in the year, cash contributions for current operations were received, but they cannot be used until late in the following year.

	Unrestricted		Restricted	
Cash	2,000		3,000	
Contributions Designated for Future Periods		2,000		3,000

18. At year end, the expenses of each fund were allocated to the various programs and supporting services. The Endowment Fund has no expenses to allocate. For the two current funds, the following entry closed the expenses and recorded the allocation:

	Unrestricted		Restricted	
Valley Air Project	117,000		13,000	
Fish in the Lakes Program	131,000		49,000	
Flood Control Program	204,000		31,000	
Management and General Services	22,000		8,000	
Fund-Raising Services	4,000		2,000	
Salaries Expense		180,000		20,000
Payroll Taxes		24,000		6,000
Mailing and Postage Expense		40,000		10,000
Rent Expense		23,000		5,000
Telephone Expense		5,000		1,000
Research Expense		165,000		50,000
Professional Services: Legal and Audit		27,000		7,000
Supplies Expense		10,000		3,000
Miscellaneous Expenses		4,000		1,000

The Plant Fund has only one expense to allocate—depreciation.

	Plant	
Valley Air Project	2,000	
Fish in the Lakes Program	3,000	
Flood Control Program	16,000	
Management and General Services	1,000	
Depreciation Expense		22,000

In the allocation process and in the closing entries, two expense items were not included because they are shown on the operating statement as direct deductions from public support resources. One is the provision for estimated uncollectible pledges, which is subtracted from the gross contributions amount. The other is the direct cost of a special event, which is subtracted from the gross proceeds of that event. These two items would be closed when the accounts to which they relate are closed.

With expenses allocated to programs and supporting services, it is now possible to prepare the statement of support, revenue, and expenses and changes in fund balances, as shown in Illustration II on page 851. The sequence of items is suggested by the title. Inflows of resources from public support and revenues are listed first, followed by the expense totals for each program and supporting service, taken directly from the closing and allocation entries. The next items shown are changes in fund balances other than those resulting from operational revenue and expenses, such as corrections for prior periods or transfers to or from other funds. The beginning balance for each fund is added, resulting in the fund balance at the end of the period.

The final entry at year end for each fund closes the support and revenue accounts as well as the program and supporting services expenses into the appropriate fund balance accounts. Using the statement of support in Illustration II, the following entry closes the current funds accounts, including the provision for uncollectible pledges and cost of special events accounts and their related resource inflow accounts:

	Unrestricted	Restricted
Contributions	315,000	110,000
Special Events Support	9,000	
Legacies and Bequests	100,000	
Received from Federated and Nonfederated Campaigns	16,000	
Membership Dues Revenue	118,000	
Investment Income	21,000	7,000
Fund Balance—Undesignated	1,000	
Provision for Uncollectible Pledges	4,000	1,000
Cost of Special Events	2,000	
Valley Air Project	117,000	13,000
Keep Fish in the Lakes Program	131,000	49,000
Flood Control Program	204,000	31,000
Management and General Services	22,000	8,000
Fund-Raising Services	4,000	2,000
Transfer to Plant Fund	96,000	
Fund Balance		13,000

For the Plant Fund, one item that deserves special attention in the closing process is depreciation. The balance in the account Fund Balance—Expended, representing the net investment in plant, should equal gross fixed assets minus accumulated depreciation minus related liabilities. In the entry that recorded depreciation, the credit to Accumulated Depreciation decreases the amount that should be in Fund

Illustration II

People's Environmental Protection (PEP) Association
Statement of Support, Revenue, and Expenses and Changes in Fund Balances
For the Year Ended December 31, 19X5

	Current Funds Unre- stricted	Current Funds Re- stricted	Plant Fund	Endow- ment Fund	Total All Funds
Public support and revenue:					
Public support:					
Contributions (net of provision for uncollectible pledges for current funds of $4,000 and $1,000, respectively)	$311,000	$109,000	$ 40,000	—	$460,000
Special events (net of direct costs of $2,000)	7,000	—	—	—	7,000
Legacies and bequests	100,000	—	—	$ 20,000	120,000
Received from federated and non-federated campaigns	16,000	—	—	—	16,000
Total public support	$434,000	$109,000	$ 40,000	$ 20,000	$603,000
Revenue:					
Membership dues	$118,000	—	—	—	$118,000
Investment income	21,000	$ 7,000	—	—	28,000
Net increase in carrying value of investments *	—	—	—	$ 29,000	29,000
Realized gain on investments	—	—	—	2,000	2,000
Total revenue	$139,000	$ 7,000		$ 31,000	$177,000
Total support and revenue	$573,000	$116,000	$ 40,000	$ 51,000	$780,000
Expenses:					
Program services:					
Valley air project	$117,000	$ 13,000	$ 2,000	—	$132,000
Keep fish in the lakes	131,000	49,000	3,000	—	183,000
Flood control	204,000	31,000	16,000	—	251,000
Total program services	$452,000	$ 93,000	$ 21,000	—	$566,000
Supporting services:					
Management and general	$ 22,000	$ 8,000	$ 1,000	—	$ 31,000
Fund raising	4,000	2,000		—	6,000
Total supporting services	$ 26,000	$ 10,000	$ 1,000	—	$ 37,000
Total expenses	$478,000	$103,000	$ 22,000	—	$603,000
Excess of public support and revenue over expenses	$ 95,000	$ 13,000	$ 18,000	$ 51,000	$177,000
Other changes in fund balances:					
Plant acquired from unrestricted funds	(96,000)	—	96,000	—	—
Fund balances, January 1, 19X5	89,000	9,000	78,000	253,000	429,000
Fund balances, December 31, 19X5	$ 88,000	$ 22,000	$192,000	$304,000	$606,000

* PEP has adopted the market value method for carrying its investments. The method requires that unrealized appreciation of investments be recognized.

Balance—Expended. Since the depreciation expense account was eliminated when it was assigned to specific programs and services, Fund Balance—Expended must be reduced by the depreciation amount assigned. The reduction is formally accomplished in the following closing entry:

	Plant Fund	
Contributions	40,000	
Fund Balance—Expended (for depreciation assigned)	22,000	
Valley Air Project		2,000
Keep Fish in the Lakes Program		3,000
Flood Control Program		16,000
Management and General Services		1,000
Fund Balance—Unexpended		40,000

The final closing entry for the Endowment Fund consists of debiting accounts that show resource inflows, crediting loss or expense accounts, and clearing the difference through Fund Balance. The entry is as follows:

	Endowment	
Legacies and Bequests	20,000	
Net Increase in Carrying Value of Investments	29,000	
Gain on Sale of Investments	2,000	
Fund Balance		51,000

Since the investments account of the Endowment Fund is carried at market value, it is entirely possible that the carrying value may decrease. If this situation occurs, the account Net Decrease in Carrying Value of Investments is debited and the investments account is credited. The closing entry would credit Net Decrease in Carrying Value of Investments.

The operating statement of a voluntary health and welfare organization provides valuable data on the total cost per period of each program and of supporting services. To provide the reader of its financial statements with additional information, the audit guide states that a statement of functional expenses should be included in the reports. This statement shows the allocation of each expense (salaries, rent, etc.) to respective programs and supporting services in order to reveal the cost by function of carrying on the organization's activities. The statement of functional expenses for PEP is shown in Illustration III on page 853.

The balance sheet for PEP on December 31, 19X5, is shown in Illustration IV on page 854. It follows the form shown in the audit guide by stacking the individual balance sheets of the various funds.

As is true in reporting for profit enterprises, financial statements of voluntary health and welfare organizations would be prepared with comparative figures for the preceding year. The statements should also be accompanied by notes that would summarize significant accounting policies.

AICPA SOP 78-10

In December, 1978, the AICPA issued Statement of Position (SOP) 78-10, "Accounting and Reporting for Certain Nonprofit Organiza-

Illustration III

People's Environmental Protection (PEP) Association
Statement of Functional Expenses
For the Year Ended December 31, 19X5

	Total All Funds	Program Services				Supporting Services		
		Valley Air Project	Fish in the Lakes	Flood Control	Total Programs	Management and General	Fund Raising	Total Supporting
Salaries	$200,000	$ 36,000	$ 60,000	$ 80,000	$176,000	$20,000	$4,000	$24,000
Payroll taxes	30,000	5,400	9,000	12,000	26,400	3,000	600	3,600
Mailing and postage	50,000	10,000	20,000	19,700	49,700	—	300	300
Rent	28,000	8,000	5,000	11,600	24,600	3,000	400	3,400
Telephone	6,000	1,500	1,300	2,500	5,300	—	700	700
Research	215,000	35,000	80,000	100,000	215,000	—	—	—
Professional: legal and audit	34,000	24,000	2,000	4,000	30,000	4,000	—	4,000
Supplies	13,000	10,100	—	2,900	13,000	—	—	—
Miscellaneous	5,000	—	2,700	2,300	5,000	—	—	—
Total expenses before depreciation	$581,000	$130,000	$180,000	$235,000	$545,000	$30,000	$6,000	$36,000
Depreciation of buildings and equipment	22,000	2,000	3,000	16,000	21,000	1,000	—	1,000
Total expenses	$603,000	$132,000	$183,000	$251,000	$566,000	$31,000	$6,000	$37,000

tions." It provides guidance on the application of generally accepted accounting principles to nonprofit organizations that are not presently covered by AICPA audit guides. Among the nonprofit entities that are affected are:

Cemetery organizations
Civic and fraternal organizations
Labor unions
Libraries and museums
Performing arts and other
cultural organizations
Political parties
Private and community foundations

Private elementary and secondary schools
Professional associations
Public broadcasting stations
Religious organizations
Research and scientific organizations
Social and country clubs
Trade associations
Zoological and botanical
societies

Specifically excluded from SOP 78-10 are those covered by audit guides: hospitals, colleges and universities, voluntary health and welfare organizations, and state and local governmental units.

Nonprofit organizations not covered by audit guides had been issuing financial reports supposedly in conformity with generally accepted accounting principles, but there was no official position on what those principles were. SOP 78-10 was released to fill the gap and to offer badly needed guidance. It declares that to be in conformity with generally accepted accounting principles, financial reports require the use of the

Illustration IV

People's Environmental Protection (PEP) Association
Balance Sheets
December 31, 19X5

Assets		Liabilities and Fund Balances	

CURRENT FUNDS

Unrestricted

Cash	$ 41,000	Accounts payable	$ 31,000
Investments (at market, which approximates cost)	61,000	Contributions designated for future periods	2,000
Pledges receivable (less allowance for uncollectibles of $2,000)	19,000	Total liabilities and deferred revenues	$ 33,000
		Fund balances:	
		Designated for long-term investments	$ 25,000
		Undesignated	63,000
		Total fund balances	$ 88,000
Total	$121,000	Total	$121,000

Restricted

Cash	$ 24,000	Accounts payable	$ 1,000
Pledges receivable (less allowance for uncollectibles of $500)	2,000	Contributions designated for future periods	3,000
		Total liabilities and deferred revenues	$ 4,000
		Fund balance (restricted)	22,000
Total	$ 26,000	Total	$ 26,000

PLANT FUND (OR LAND, BUILDING, AND EQUIPMENT FUND)

Cash	$ 2,000	Notes payable on equipment	$ 10,000
Land, building, and equipment (less accumulated depreciation of $38,700)	200,000	Fund balances:	
		Expended	$190,000
		Unexpended	2,000
		Total fund balances	$192,000
Total	$202,000	Total	$202,000

ENDOWMENT FUND

Cash	$ 10,000	Fund balance	$304,000
Investments at market (cost, $210,000)	294,000		
Total	$304,000	Total	$304,000

accrual basis of accounting. However, the organization's books may be maintained on some other basis and adjusted at year end, since a cash basis is more practical for maintaining the records of many of these organizations. Entities that have restricted resources should use fund accounting for reporting purposes to demonstrate compliance with externally imposed restrictions. Financial statements to be provided are a balance sheet, a statement of operations and changes in fund balances, and a statement of changes in financial position, along with notes for appropriate disclosures of policy. More than half of SOP 78-10 consists of representative financial statements for the major groups listed previously.

At the present time, the FASB's agenda includes a project labeled "Objectives of Financial Reporting by Nonbusiness Organizations." Its purpose is to determine whether or not nonbusiness organizations require a separate conceptual framework of accounting from the one developed for profit entities. The outcome of this project may affect financial reporting by organizations covered by SOP 78-10. In deference to that project, SOP 78-10 was issued without an effective date. Nevertheless, an organization to which it applies should adopt its principles and procedures voluntarily in order to communicate the nature of its programs and their cost and to enable the reader of its financial reports to evaluate performance.

QUESTIONS

1. Name the two criteria that must be met for an entity to qualify as a voluntary health and welfare organization.
2. Differentiate between the accounts Fund Balance—Designated and Fund Balance—Undesignated in the Current Unrestricted Fund of a voluntary health and welfare organization.
3. Defend the statement that accounting for voluntary health and welfare organizations closely resembles accounting for universities. What are two major differences in accounting for these types of nonprofit entities?
4. Indicate in which fund the following entry would appear, and identify an event that would require the entry:

   Fund Balance—Expended xxx
       Fund Balance—Unexpended xxx

5. Differentiate between public support and revenue as sources of assets.
6. A volunteer participates in a house-to-house canvass during a one-week fund drive for United Way. Explain why that organization should or should not record the value of the volunteer's service.
7. Explain the logic (not the process) of pooling of investments.
8. Why does the operating statement of a voluntary health and welfare organization not show expenses by their natural classification, such as salary expense?
9. Given the following events, list by letter the sequence in which the events should normally occur:

   (a) Journal entries to allocate expenses to programs and services are made.
   (b) Journal entries to transfer public support and revenue account balances as well as program and service costs to fund balances are made.

(continued)

    (c) Journal entries to record functional expenses, public support, and revenue are made.

    (d) A statement of functional expenses is prepared.

    (e) A statement of support, revenue, and expenses and changes in fund balances is prepared.

    (f) A balance sheet is prepared.

10. To what nonprofit organizations does SOP 78-10 *not* apply?

EXERCISES

Exercise 1. Select the best answer for each of the following items:

1. A reason for a voluntary health and welfare organization to adopt fund accounting is that:
   a. Restrictions have been placed on certain of its assets by donors.
   b. It provides more than one type of program service.
   c. Fixed assets are significant.
   d. Donated services are significant.

2. Depreciation should be recognized in the financial statements of:
   a. Hospitals, universities, health and welfare organizations, and governmental units.
   b. Hospitals, universities, health and welfare organizations, but not in those of governmental units.
   c. Hospitals and health and welfare organizations, but not in those of universities and governmental units.
   d. Universities and health and welfare organizations, but not in those of hospitals and governmental units.

3. Which of the following funds of a voluntary health and welfare organization does not have a counterpart fund in governmental accounting?
   a. Current Unrestricted.
   b. Land, Building, and Equipment.
   c. Custodian.
   d. Endowment.

4. Why do voluntary health and welfare organizations, unlike some nonprofit organizations, record and recognize depreciation of fixed assets?
   a. Fixed assets are more likely to be material in amount in a voluntary health and welfare organization than in other nonprofit organizations.
   b. Voluntary health and welfare organizations purchase their fixed assets and therefore have a historical cost basis from which to determine amounts to be depreciated.
   c. A fixed asset used by a voluntary health and welfare organization has alternative uses in private industry and this opportunity cost should be reflected in the organization's financial statements.
   d. Contributors look for the most efficient use of funds, and since depreciation represents a cost of employing fixed assets, it is appropriate that a voluntary health and welfare organization reflect it as a cost of providing services.

(AICPA adapted)

Exercise 2. Indicate the fund in which each of the following fund balance accounts would be found, and describe the nature of its balance:

    (a) Fund Balance—Expended

    (b) Fund Balance Designated for Purchase of Equipment

    (c) Fund Balance Restricted for Professional Education

Exercise 3. On January 2, 19X1, the available cash in the following funds was placed into an investment pool:

Fund	Original Cash Pooled
Unrestricted.....................	$40,000
Restricted	30,000
Plant...........................	10,000
Total	$80,000

During the next year, no additional cash was placed into the pool nor was any amount withdrawn. At the end of the year, the pooled investments had a cost basis of $100,000, representing original contributions plus $20,000 of realized gains that remained in the investment pool. At year end, the market value of the pooled investments amounted to $104,000.

Prepare the journal entry to record the Restricted Fund's share of the realized gains. If the Plant Fund wished to withdraw its holdings in the pool, how much would it receive at year end?

Exercise 4. By placing a check mark in the appropriate column, indicate in which fund of a voluntary health and welfare organization the following events would normally be recorded. (*Hint:* An event may require entries in more than one fund.)

| | Current Funds | | Plant Fund | Endowment Fund |
	Unrestricted	Restricted		
(a) Payment of salaries	___	___	___	___
(b) Transfer of unrestricted resources to a fund for fixed asset acquisition	___	___	___	___
(c) Endowment Fund income designated for a special program and recorded using the direct method	___	___	___	___
(d) Sale of endowment investments at a loss	___	___	___	___
(e) Allocation of natural expenses to programs and services	___	___	___	___
(f) Recording of depreciation ...	___	___	___	___

Exercise 5. Record the following events that involved the Current Unrestricted Fund of the Mental Health Clinic, a voluntary health and welfare organization:
- (a) Cash contributions of $18,000 and pledges for $32,000 were received.
- (b) It is estimated that 10% of the pledges will prove uncollectible.
- (c) A fund-raising dinner grossed $6,300 from the sale of 420 tickets. The catered dinner cost $7 per plate for the 360 people who attended, plus $180 for rental of the dining room. Payment for costs was made.
- (d) To expand the services of the clinic, a professional fund-raising group was hired to undertake a 9-month campaign. At the end of that time, it submitted the following report:

Cash collected	$ 70,000
Pledges (should be 95% collectible)	30,000
Total proceeds.........................	$100,000
Less 20% fund-raising fee	20,000
Net proceeds from drive	$ 80,000

Exercise 6. Record the following events that involved the Land, Building, and Equipment (Plant) Fund of the Mental Health Clinic, a voluntary health and welfare organization:
- (a) A contribution of $4,000 was received to be used for the purchase of equipment, but not until there would be an addition to the building. This event is not likely to occur during the next two years.
- (b) Equipment costing $7,000, with a book value of $2,000, was sold for $3,000. The proceeds are to remain in the Land, Building, and Equipment Fund.
- (c) Depreciation of $6,000 is recorded on various plant items.
- (d) Equipment was purchased for $9,000, with payment due in 30 days.
- (e) Liability for the equipment purchased in (d) was paid.

Exercise 7. Record the following events that involved the Endowment Fund of the Mental Health Clinic, a voluntary health and welfare organization:
- (a) Viola Collins, the town's leading citizen, died. She left $50,000 to the Mental Health Clinic, with the stipulation that the income only could be used for an alcohol abuse educational program. The attorney forwarded a check for the full amount, which was invested in 8% municipal bonds, purchased at face value.
- (b) Endowment Fund income of $2,000 was received. The amount is not subject to any limitations and is recorded directly in the recipient fund.
- (c) The bequest of Viola Collins earned $4,000. The money was received.
- (d) Investments are carried at cost. Half of the 8% municipal bonds were sold at 103. No specifications relative to gains or losses appeared in the will.

Exercise 8. Using the balance sheets of the individual funds shown in Illustration IV on page 854:
- (1) Prepare a columnar balance sheet, with a column for each fund and a total column.
- (2) Indicate what difficulties in physical construction are encountered in the process of preparing the columnar balance sheet.
- (3) Discuss the advantages and disadvantages for the reader of the columnar form versus the layered form followed by the AICPA and illustrated in the chapter.

Exercise 9. The characteristics of voluntary health and welfare organizations differ in certain respects from the characteristics of state or local governmental units. As an example, voluntary health and welfare organizations derive their revenues primarily from voluntary contributions from the general public, while governmental units derive their revenues from taxes and services provided to their jurisdictions.
- (1) Describe fund accounting and discuss whether its use is consistent with the concept that an accounting entity is an economic unit which has control over resources, accepts responsibilities for making and carrying out commitments, and conducts economic activity.
- (2) Distinguish between accrual accounting and modified accrual accounting and indicate which method would be used for a voluntary health and welfare organization.
- (3) Discuss how methods used to account for fixed assets differ between voluntary health and welfare organizations and governmental units.   (AICPA adapted)

PROBLEMS

Problem 19-1. The Senior Citizens Agency is a voluntary health and welfare organization. The following events occur in its current funds:

(a) This year's fund drive resulted in unrestricted pledges totaling $130,000. Pledges of $25,000 were received for a special hot meal program.

(b) Cash collected from pledges: unrestricted, $100,000; restricted, $18,000.

(c) A philanthropist, who is an attorney, contributed a painting valued at $4,000, which is to be auctioned off at a Thanksgiving supper organized to raise funds for a legal assistance program for the elderly. The event was an unexpected success. The painting was sold for $7,800. Additional gross cash revenues were $4,900. Direct costs paid were $1,700.

(d) The agency received $11,000 from the local division of United Way for general support.

(e) Salaries amounted to $70,000, payroll taxes were $6,000, and other employee benefits amounted to $10,000. Of these items, $5,000 is unpaid, with the balance paid from unrestricted cash.

(f) Arrangements have been made to have a local catering firm bring in a hot lunch. Senior citizens are charged seventy-five cents per meal. To date, payments to the catering service are $2,300. Cash collections from the meal program service totaled $900.

(g) It is estimated that 10% of the remaining unrestricted pledges and 5% of the remaining restricted pledges will prove uncollectible.

(h) At the end of the previous year, $10,000 of the fund balance of the Unrestricted Current Fund had been designated for a special program for handicapped elderly persons, to be conducted during the current year if sufficient support could be generated. The idea was abandoned this year for lack of interest. The governing board authorizes the reclassification of the amount as undesignated.

(i) The Senior Citizens Agency had budgeted $500 per month for rent of space to conduct its general activities. A generous citizen permits it to occupy equivalent space at a nominal fee of $100 per year. The annual fee is paid, and the appropriate expense for the year is recorded.

Required:

Prepare journal entries to record the events in the current funds. Identify in which current funds the entry would be made by placing the amounts in the proper columns, using the following format:

		Amounts	
		Unrestricted	Restricted
Event	Entry	Fund	Fund
(a)			

Problem 19-2. The Senior Citizens Agency is a voluntary health and welfare organization. The following events affect its Land, Building, and Equipment Fund (Plant Fund). The agency uses one control account for all of its fixed assets, with supporting subsidiary records.

(a) Property was purchased for $200,000, of which $50,000 is allocable to land and the remainder to the building. A down payment of $40,000 was made, and a 14% mortgage was signed for the remainder.

(b) Office furniture was purchased for $9,000 on open account.

(c) A local corporation donated and installed room partitions. The value of the donated items and services was $4,000.

(d) At year end, a payment is made covering mortgage interest for one year plus a $10,000 payment on the principal.

(e) Office equipment costing $3,000, with a book value of $1,000, is sold for $1,800 cash.

(f) Fully depreciated equipment costing $7,000 is written off. There was no scrap value.

(g) A depreciation schedule was prepared, showing annual depreciation expense of $46,000 to be recorded.

Required:

Prepare journal entries to record the events in the Land, Building, and Equipment Fund (Plant Fund). (*Hint:* Pay particular attention to entries that change the net investment in plant assets. These will also require an entry to change the respective fund balance accounts.)

Problem 19-3. The Child Welfare Organization is a voluntary health and welfare organization. The following trial balances of its current funds as of December 31, 19X2, were prepared. Allocations of natural expenses have already been made to its programs and supporting services.

Child Welfare Organization
Current Funds Trial Balances
December 31, 19X2

	Unrestricted		Restricted	
Cash	102,800		22,600	
Investments (market)	76,000			
Pledges Receivable	4,500		1,000	
Accounts Receivable	3,000			
Accounts Payable		48,000		900
Deferred Revenue		2,600		4,500
Allowance for Uncollectible Pledges		2,500		100
Fund Balances, January 1, 19X2:				
Designated		50,000		
Undesignated		83,700		
Restricted				14,600
Transfers of Endowment Fund Income		19,000		
Contributions		260,000		10,000
Membership Dues Revenue		20,500		3,000
Child Care Fees Revenue		33,000		
Investment Income Earned		6,000		
Appreciation of Investments		8,000		
Toddlers' Program	106,000			
Pre-Kindergarten Program	124,000			
Day School Program	67,000		4,000	
Management and General Services	28,000		3,000	
Fund-Raising Services	19,000		2,000	
Provision for Uncollectible Pledges	3,000		500	
	533,300	533,300	33,100	33,100

Required:

(1) In a columnar form that incorporates a total column, prepare the statement of support, revenues, and expenses and changes in fund balances for the current funds for the year ended December 31, 19X2.
(2) Prepare a separate balance sheet for each of the current funds as of December 31, 19X2.
(3) Prepare the closing entry for each current fund.

Problem 19-4. The bookkeeper for Forest Conservation, a voluntary health and welfare organization, knew how to make routine cash receipts and cash payment entries, but was having difficulty in making entries for the following events:

(a) At the end of the previous fiscal period, the auditor established in the unrestricted fund an amount of $7,000 as "Contributions Designated for Future Periods." The amount is now available, but no entry has been made.
(b) An automobile was purchased at a cost of $8,000, for which a note was signed. The car is to be awarded in a raffle, as part of a general operating fund-raising drive that will start next month. The bookkeeper made one entry in the Land, Building, and Equipment Fund, debiting Land, Building, and Equipment and crediting Notes Payable.
(c) Cash of $1,900 has been received from the sale of tickets for the raffle mentioned in (b). In the restricted fund, the bookkeeper credited Sales for the cash received.
(d) Annual depreciation of $11,400 was recorded in the Land, Building, and Equipment Fund, with a single entry debiting the expense and crediting Fund Balance—Expended.
(e) A $10,000 payment against a mortgage on a building was recorded in the Land, Building, and Equipment Fund, with a debit to Mortgage Payable and a credit to Cash. No other entry was made.
(f) The directors of the organization have long-range plans for developing a reforestation program that will require accumulating resources. To inform the readers of its financial statements of these plans, they request that $20,000 of the fund balance of the unrestricted fund be so earmarked. No entry has been made by the bookkeeper.
(g) Investments are carried at market value. A year-end analysis revealed that their market value in the Endowment Fund had decreased by $16,000. No entry was made.

Required:

Using the following format, provide the journal entries needed to correct the records:

Event	Fund	Journal Entry
(a)		

Problem 19-5. The Abuse Clinic, a voluntary health and welfare organization, conducts two programs: Alcohol and Drug Abuse, and Outreach to Teens. It has the typical supporting services of management and fund raising. The trial balances of its various funds as of January 1, 19X2, are as follows:

Abuse Clinic
Trial Balances
January 1, 19X2

Debits	Current Funds Unrestricted	Current Funds Restricted	Plant Fund	Endowment Fund
Cash	53,000	5,000	12,000	1,000
Investments (at cost)	120,000	7,000	45,000	200,000
Accrued Investment Income	6,000	—	—	—
Pledges Receivable	45,000	—	—	—
Grants Receivable	—	16,000	—	—
Inventories of Educational Materials	11,000	—	—	—
Inventories of Medical Supplies	12,000	—	—	—
Land, Building, and Equipment..................	—	—	173,000	—
Total	247,000	28,000	230,000	201,000

Credits				
Allowance for Uncollectible Pledges	9,000	—	—	—
Accumulated Depreciation	—	—	22,000	—
Accounts Payable..............................	14,000	—	—	—
Contributions Designated for Future Periods	22,000	—	—	—
10% Mortgage Payable	—	—	40,000	—
Fund Balances:				
Designated for Research	50,000	—	—	—
Designated for Long-Term Investments	40,000	—	—	—
Undesignated	112,000	—	—	—
Restricted....................................	—	28,000	—	201,000
Expended	—	—	111,000	—
Unexpended..................................	—	—	57,000	—
Total	247,000	28,000	230,000	201,000

During 19X2, the following events related to the clinic occurred. To minimize repetition, similar events for the year are combined.

	Unrestricted	Restricted
(a) Contribution pledges received	$396,000	$162,000
(b) Estimated uncollectible pledges	20,000	6,000
(c) Cash collected on pledges	380,000	148,000
Pledges written off as uncollectible	18,000	5,000
(d) Investment income received (including accrued)	9,000	1,000
(e) The following items were paid:		
Accounts payable as of January 1, 19X2 ...	14,000	
Salaries and payroll taxes	60,000	23,000
Rent expense		10,000
Telephone and miscellaneous expenses	10,000	2,000
Nursing and medical fees	70,000	50,000
Educational seminars expenses...........	38,000	20,000
Research expenses	137,000	16,000
Medical supplies (perpetual inventory is used)	71,000	29,000
Total	$400,000	$150,000

(f) In his will, Carlos Lopez bequeathed his residence to the clinic. After his death, it was found that the building was not suitable for clinical use, and it would be sold as soon as possible. The residence was appraised at $92,000. The will stipulated that the proceeds must be used to expand the clinical building. The will also provided $30,000 in cash to create a fund, the income from which must be devoted to an alcohol abuse program.

(g) During the year, a dinner was held to raise additional funds for the clinical building. Gross cash proceeds were $48,000, of which $18,000 was paid for direct costs.

(h) Bids for construction of a wing for the clinical building were sought. The contract was let at a cost of $250,000. The residence received from Lopez was sold for $100,000, which was used as a partial payment on the contract, along with the net proceeds from the dinner mentioned in (g). The wing was completed. A 12%, 20-year mortgage was signed for the remaining $120,000.

(i) A grant of $16,000 from the state government, awarded last year for a special drug abuse program, was received. The item was originally recorded as a grant receivable.

(j) At year end, a physical inventory shows $3,000 of educational materials in the Unrestricted Fund, $18,000 of medical supplies in the Unrestricted Fund, and $7,000 of medical supplies in the Restricted Fund.

(k) Annual depreciation amounts to $20,000.

(l) A payment of $5,000 was made against the 10% mortgage payable, plus payment of $4,000 for interest.

(m) Plant Fund investment income was $4,000, of which $3,000 was received. Income must be used for plant purposes.

(n) Endowment Fund investment income received amounted to $16,000. There is no restriction on $10,000 of the income. The remaining $6,000 must be devoted to alcohol abuse programs. Items are entered directly in recipient funds.

(o) Half of the contributions designated for future periods in the unrestricted fund became available.

(p) The board of directors has decided to increase the Fund Balance Designated for Research from $50,000 to $90,000.

(q) Unpaid items in the unrestricted fund on December 31, 19X2, consist of $3,000 accrued salaries and $10,000 for educational materials that are maintained on a perpetual inventory basis.

(r) Endowment Fund investments costing $40,000 were sold for $65,000. Gain remains a part of the fund principal.

Required:

(1) Prepare journal entries to record the events, using the following format:

Event	Fund	Journal Entry
(a)		

(2) Prepare pre-allocation trial balances, reflecting balances immediately after the above entries are posted, in the same format as the trial balance at the beginning of the problem.

Problem 19-6. The Abuse Clinic, a voluntary health and welfare organization, conducts two programs: Alcohol and Drug Abuse, and Outreach to Teens. It has the typical supporting services of management and fund raising. The condensed pre-allocation trial balances of its four funds as of December 31, 19X2, are as follows:

Abuse Clinic
Condensed Pre-Allocation Trial Balances
December 31, 19X2

| | Current | | Plant Fund | Endowment Fund |
Debits	Unrestricted	Restricted		
Assets (net)	235,000	48,000	433,000	256,000
Salaries and Payroll Taxes.......................	63,000	23,000	—	—
Telephone and Miscellaneous Expenses..........	10,000	2,000	—	—
Nursing and Medical Fees.......................	70,000	50,000	—	—
Educational Seminars Expenses	46,000	20,000	—	—
Research Expense	137,000	16,000	—	—
Medical Supplies Expense.......................	65,000	22,000	—	—
Rent Expense	—	10,000	—	—
Interest Expense	—	—	4,000	—
Depreciation Expense...........................	—	—	20,000	—
Provision for Uncollectible Pledges	20,000	6,000	—	—
Cost of Special Events	—	—	18,000	—
Total......................................	646,000	197,000	475,000	256,000

Credits				
Liabilities	24,000	—	155,000	—
Fund Balances:				
Designated	130,000	—	—	—
Undesignated	72,000	—	—	—
Restricted..................................	—	28,000	—	201,000
Expended	—	—	226,000	—
Unexpended................................	—	—	(58,000)	—
Contributions..................................	407,000	162,000	92,000	—
Legacies and Bequests	—	—	—	30,000
Special Events Support	—	—	48,000	—
Investment Income	13,000	7,000	4,000	—
Gain on Sale of Investments.....................	—	—	8,000	25,000
Total......................................	646,000	197,000	475,000	256,000

In preparation for the allocation of expenses to programs and supporting services, a study was conducted to determine an equitable manner for assigning each expense. The study resulted in the following table for percentage allocations:

Percentage of Allocations

| | Programs | | Supporting Services | |
| | Alcohol and Drug Abuse | Outreach to Teens | Management | Fund Raising |
Expenses to Be Allocated				
All expenses of the restricted fund	60%	40%	—	—
Expenses of the unrestricted fund:				
Salaries and payroll taxes	30	20	30%	20%
Telephone and miscellaneous	20	20	15	45
Nursing and medical fees	70	30	—	—
Educational seminars	30	60	—	10
Research...................................	60	40	—	—
Medical supplies...........................	90	10	—	—
Expenses of the Plant Fund:				
Interest expense...........................	50	10	30	10
Depreciation expense	50	10	30	10

Required:

(1) Using a total of allocable expenses of the Current Restricted Fund, prepare a journal entry to assign those expenses to the programs.

(2) In the following format, prepare a schedule to show the assignment of the Current Unrestricted Fund's allocable expenses to the various programs and supporting services, using the percentages provided by the problem:

Abuse Clinic
Allocation of Expenses of Current Unrestricted Funds
For the Year Ended December 31, 19X2

		Programs		Supporting Services	
Expense Allocated	Total Amount	*Alcohol and Drug Abuse*	*Outreach to Teens*	*Management*	*Fund Raising*

(3) Using the schedule from requirement (2), prepare a journal entry to record the allocation and closing of expenses of the Current Unrestricted Fund.

(4) Prepare a journal entry to record the allocation and closing of the expenses of the Plant Fund.

Problem 19-7. The Abuse Clinic, a voluntary health and welfare organization, conducts two programs: Alcohol and Drug Abuse, and Outreach to Teens. It has the typical supporting services of management and fund raising. The condensed trial balances of its four funds after allocable expenses have been assigned is as follows:

Abuse Clinic
Condensed Post-Allocation Trial Balances
December 31, 19X2

Debits	Current Fund Unrestricted	Current Fund Restricted	Plant Fund	Endowment Fund
Assets (net)	235,000	48,000	433,000	256,000
Alcohol and Drug Abuse Program	224,400	85,800	12,000	—
Outreach to Teens Program	124,500	57,200	2,400	—
Management and General Services	20,400	—	7,200	—
Fund-Raising Services	21,700	—	2,400	—
Provision for Uncollectible Pledges	20,000	6,000	—	—
Cost of Special Events	—	—	18,000	—
Totals	646,000	197,000	475,000	256,000

Credits				
Liabilities	24,000	—	155,000	—
Fund Balances:				
Designated	130,000	—	—	—
Undesignated	72,000	—	—	—
Restricted	—	28,000	—	201,000
Expended	—	—	246,000	—
Unexpended	—	—	(78,000)	—
Contributions	407,000	162,000	92,000	—
Special Events Support	—	—	48,000	—
Legacies and Bequests	—	—	—	30,000
Investment Income	13,000	7,000	4,000	—
Gain on Sale of Investments....................	—	—	8,000	25,000
Totals	646,000	197,000	475,000	256,000

Required:

(1) Prepare a statement of support, revenue, and expenses and changes in fund balances in the format shown in Illustration II on page 851. Fund balance amounts as of January 1, 19X2, are shown in Problem 19-5.

(2) Prepare closing entries for each fund.

Problem 19-8. From the condensed pre-allocation trial balance and allocation schedule shown in Problem 19-6, prepare a statement of functional expenses for the Abuse Clinic for the year ended December 31, 19X2.

Problem 19-9. From the pre-allocation trial balance prepared as a solution for Problem 19-5, prepare a balance sheet in the format recommended by the audit guide and illustrated in the chapter. Verify that totals of the fund balances for each fund agree with the final amounts shown in the statement of support prepared as part of the solution of Problem 19-7.

CHAPTER 20

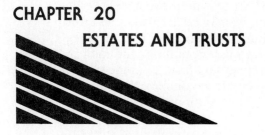

ESTATES AND TRUSTS

An estate consists of the net assets owned by a person at the time of death, and may include both real property and personal property. Historically, the distinction between these two kinds of property developed through legal processes. For example, redress for trespass or dispossession of immovable and indestructible property, such as land, was sought by taking action to recover the property. The action was labeled a "real action," and property involved in such action became known as real property. If movable or destructible property were damaged, action to recover for the damage was taken against the person responsible, and such property was referred to as personal property. The distinction between real and personal property is pertinent to an estate, since title or right to real property passes directly to the recipient, while the right to personal property passes to the estate administrator or executor until it is distributed.

An estate ceases to exist when all the property has been distributed according to the terms of a valid will or the terms of law. This distribution may include a transfer of property to a trust, which holds the property for the benefit of others. Since both an estate and a trust consist of property which may be under the control of someone other than the owner, the accounting procedures for the two entities are quite similar. These procedures and related legal aspects are discussed in this chapter.

ESTATE PLANNING—TAX REFORM ACT OF 1976, REVENUE ACT OF 1978, AND ECONOMIC RECOVERY TAX ACT OF 1981

Tax planning may be defined as an effort to reduce the cost of living by minimizing income taxes. Estate planning may be defined as an effort to reduce the cost of dying by minimizing estate and inheritance taxes. Estate planning is complex, since the circumstances differ for each individual. As with all tax planning, estate planning must be done well in advance of death. The larger the estate, the more complex the planning and the greater the necessity for involving an estate planning specialist, a lawyer, and an accountant, one of whom should be a tax expert. Therefore, this chapter is only an introduction to a complicated subject.

Significant changes regarding gratuitous transfers of property resulted from the Tax Reform Act of 1976. Prior to its enactment, transfers of property during the owner's lifetime were subject to the federal gift tax, while property passing as a result of death was subject to the federal estate tax. The rules and rates for these taxes were different. Most of the distinction was removed by the Tax Reform Act, which substituted a unified transfer tax for life and death transfers made after 1976.

The starting point for the computation of the unified transfer tax at death is the determination of the gross estate, which includes the fair market value of property owned by the decedent at date of death, regardless of the nature of the property. Whether real or personal, tangible or intangible, business or nonbusiness, the property is includible. The adjusted gross estate is then determined by deducting the total of:

1. Allowable expenses, such as funeral and administrative expenses;
2. Indebtedness against property included in the gross estate, such as a mortgage;
3. Unpaid property and income taxes of the decedent to date of death; and
4. Losses from casualty or theft of estate assets during the period of settlement.

From the adjusted gross estate, transfers to qualifying charities and a marital deduction may be deducted. The Economic Recovery Tax (ERT) Act of 1981 specifies that, for decedents dying on or after January 1, 1982, transfers of property by gift to a spouse are completely deductible in computing taxable gifts, and transfers of property at death to a surviving spouse are also completely deductible in computing the taxable estate.

The Revenue Act of 1978 required that the taxable estate be increased by any taxable gifts made after 1976. Gifts would be taxable to the donor if their fair market value for the tax year exceeded $3,000

($6,000 for consenting spouse gifts) per donee through 1981. For gifts made after 1981, the ERT Act increases the exclusion to $10,000 ($20,000 for consenting spouse gifts). After taxable gifts are added to the taxable estate, the tax rates found in the Unified Rate Schedule are applied to the total transfers during life and at death. The resulting tentative tax is then reduced by a unified death tax credit, which is $62,800 for 1982 and which increases annually until 1987, when it will reach $192,800. At that point, there will be no estate or gift tax on taxable transfers aggregating $600,000 or less. The tentative tax is also reduced by state death taxes and possible other taxes to produce the unified transfer tax due, if any.

The computation of the unified transfer tax at death is summarized as follows:

Gross estate		xx
Less:		
Allowable expenses	xx	
Indebtedness related to gross estate	xx	
Taxes of decedent	xx	
Losses on estate assets	xx	xx
Adjusted gross estate		xx
Less:		
Charitable bequests	xx	
Marital deduction	xx	xx
Taxable estate		xx
Add taxable gifts made after 1976 in excess of limits		xx
Total taxable transfers during life and at death		xx
Tenative tax on taxable transfers		xx
Less credits:		
Unified death tax credit	xx	
State death taxes paid	xx	
Taxes paid on taxable gifts after 1976	xx	xx
Unified transfer tax at death		xx

Changes produced by the ERT Act are intended to reduce the tax burden on smaller estates and to alleviate some of the burden resulting from inflation. Under the ERT Act, the tax rate on transfers over $2,500,000 is reduced during a four-year transitional period beginning in 1982. In 1985 when the change is completely implemented, the maximum rate on transfers of $2,500,000 or more will be 50%. Even though this rate is a significant reduction from the 70% maximum of prior law, tax planning is essential to achieve maximum benefit provided in the law, especially when the impact of continued inflation is considered. For example, consenting spouses who participate for ten years, beginning in 1982, in an annual gift program involving six family members would be able to transfer $1,200,000 ($20,000 × 6 × 10) without incurring any gift tax liability. This amount would also escape the unified transfer tax at death.

Valuation of Estate Assets

Fair market value must be established for assets included in an estate. Some valuations, such as the values for stocks and bonds traded on recognized exchanges, pose no problems. For other assets, such as property, jewelry, art objects, or antiques, a competent appraisal in writing is necessary. Assets are included in the estate at their value on the date of death or on an alternate valuation date, if the executor or administrator so elects. If the alternate valuation date is elected, all estate property must be valued as of six months after the decedent's death, except for property sold, distributed, or otherwise disposed of during the six-month period. Such property is valued as of the date of disposition. The alternate valuation date provides an opportunity to select a more advantageous time for establishing value.

Establishing valuation is critical. To the recipient, the basis of property acquired from a decedent is fair market value on the date of death or on the alternate valuation date. For example, at the time of her death, Mary Bower held stock with an adjusted basis (cost, in her case), of $100,000. At the date of death, it was worth $500,000 and was included in the gross estate at that amount. The stock was willed to Mary's nephew, whose basis now becomes $500,000. A subsequent sale by him for $500,000 would result in no taxable gain. Although the value of the stock must be included in the inventory of estate assets, which might be subject to the unified transfer tax if the estate is large enough, the $400,000 gain has escaped federal income taxation because of the step-up in basis. If Mary had sold the stock before her death, the gain would have been subject to income tax. Tax planning would suggest that, if possible, property that has appreciated substantially in value should be held as part of an estate, because of the advantage of the step-up in basis. The opposite is true if there is a substantial decline in value. If Mary's stock had a value of $5,000 on the valuation date, that would become the basis to her nephew. Neither he nor the estate will derive any benefit from the $95,000 loss in value. If Mary had sold the stock prior to death, benefits resulting from the deductibility of the loss for income tax purposes would have materialized.

There are times when it is beneficial to increase death tax valuations. In the case of small estates that have little or no death taxes to pay, the increased basis could be a definite advantage to the heirs, with no penalty to the estate. In the case of large estates, the alternate valuation date protects the estate if there should be a significant decrease in property values during the six-month interval.

Perhaps the single most important step in tax planning is to have a valid will prepared. Only then may the wishes of the decedent be known and fulfilled. With no valid will, assets will be distributed in accordance with the fairly impersonal provisions of the law. Among other considerations, family tax planning would involve:

1. Making gifts during one's lifetime.
2. Taking actions to benefit from a loss in property values.

3. Protecting increases in property values by use of the stepped-up basis.
4. Maximizing the benefits of the marital deduction.
5. Maneuvering with charitable deductions.
6. Planning estate liquidity.

To be protected, an estate must have a certain amount of liquid assets to pay death taxes and the probate costs of establishing the validity of the will; otherwise, a forced sale of estate assets might result. Some form of insurance is often purchased prior to death to provide liquidity and flexibility.

Income Taxation of Estates and Trusts

Under the tax code, estates and trusts are separate tax entities. The code requires the filing of an estate tax return, in which the unified transfer tax is computed, within nine months after the death of the decedent. In addition, income tax returns for the estate or trust must be filed. Generally, income from estate or trust assets will be taxed either to the estate or trust or to the beneficiary, but not to both. Income from property is normally taxed to the holder of its title. Since title to real property passes directly to the heir at the date of death, income from such property is taxed to the heir and not to the estate.

An estate or trust may function merely as a conduit, as in the case of receiving income designated for a specific beneficiary. Such income retains its identity when it passes to the beneficiary. If the income received is taxable to the estate or trust, it is taxable to the beneficiary. If the income received is not taxable to the estate or trust, such as tax-free interest on municipal bonds, it is not taxable to the beneficiary. In contrast, if a corporation receives tax-free interest on an investment in municipal bonds, and later makes a dividend distribution, the dividend received by the stockholder is taxable.

Although there are some exceptions and special provisions, the taxable income of an estate or trust is computed on Form 1041 (U.S. Fiduciary Income Tax Return), in a manner similar to that of an individual. No gain or loss is generally recognized when property is distributed to a beneficiary in accordance with the will or trust agreement, unless an obligation is met with property that has a basis different from the amount of the obligation. For example, if a will decrees that $25,000 in cash be paid, and a settlement is reached to accept property with an equal fair market value on the date of distribution but with a basis of $18,000 to the estate, a gain of $7,000 is taxable to the estate.

SETTLING AN ESTATE

When a person dies *intestate* (leaving no valid will), the probate court appoints an administrator to handle the settling of the estate according to applicable state laws. These laws vary between states. Although a Uniform Probate Code was drafted in 1969 and approved by the American Bar Association, it has been adopted with revisions by less than half of the states. Nevertheless, the provisions of the Code are treated as the majority position in this text.

In an intestate situation, real property is distributed according to the laws of descent of the state where the property is located, while personal property is distributed according to the laws of distribution of the decedent's home state, called the *state of domicile*. In general, only a spouse or blood relative may receive an intestate distribution. As shown in the following diagram, the spouse or blood relative may be described as an heir or as next of kin, depending on the kind of property distributed.

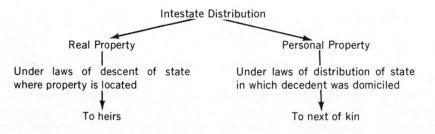

If a person dies *testate* (leaving a valid will), the probate court must establish the validity of the will. Property may then be distributed according to the terms of the will by an executor who is nominated in the will, subject to approval of the court. The executor may be one or more persons or an institution, such as a bank, but if the named executor is unable or has no desire to function in that capacity, the court will appoint an administrator.

In a testate situation, a distribution of real property is a *devise* and the recipient of the property is the *devisee*. Distributions of personal property are called bequests or *legacies*, and the recipient of personal property is called the *legatee*. The following diagram identifies the recipients of a testate distribution:

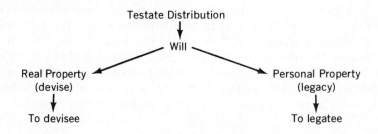

A devise is usually a gift of a specific piece of property. In contrast, legacies may include one or more of the following types:

1. A *general* legacy is a gift of an indicated amount or quantity of something: five thousand dollars, or 20 bottles of wine.
2. A *specific* legacy is a gift of a particular, specified thing, distinguishable from others: my three-carat diamond ring, or the 20 bottles of Romanee Conti Burgundy 1961 on the north wall of the wine cellar.
3. A *demonstrative* legacy is a gift of an amount from a specific source, with the will stipulating that if the amount cannot be satisfied from that source, it shall be satisfied from the general estate: $50,000 from several identified insurance policies, but if proceeds are inadequate to meet the amount, the difference shall constitute a general legacy.
4. A *residuary* legacy is composed of all estate property remaining after assigning the general, specific, and demonstrative legacies.
5. A *pecuniary* legacy is any legacy of money. Therefore, it could be a general, specific, or demonstrative legacy, but it must be money.

Administrators and executors are referred to as personal representatives or *fiduciaries* because they function as stewards of the estate. Their duty is to safeguard property, which includes the interim management of any business in which the decedent functioned in a managerial capacity.

One of the first responsibilities of the fiduciary is to determine the *homestead allowance* and the *family allowance*, which are exempt from claims against the estate. Most states provide for these rights, which are described in the Uniform Probate Code as follows:

> A surviving spouse of a decedent . . . is entitled to a homestead allowance of $5,000. If there is no surviving spouse, each minor child and each dependent child of the decedent is entitled to a homestead allowance amounting to $5,000 divided by the number of minor and dependent children of the decedent.[1]

> . . . the surviving spouse and minor children whom the decedent was obligated to support . . . are entitled to a reasonable allowance in money out of the estate for their maintenance during the period of administration.[2]

The family allowance consists of intimate objects of the deceased and an amount of cash or productive property to provide funds for the surviving family until matters are settled. What constitutes a "reasonable allowance" depends upon the circumstances in each case, but the fiduciary may not grant more than $500 per month for one year. If a greater allowance is deemed necessary, a special court order must be obtained.

After the immediate needs of the family are satisfied, the fiduciary takes a complete inventory of the estate and files a report with the court. The fiduciary also publishes a notice to creditors, requesting that all

---

[1] *Uniform Probate Code (U.L.A.)* (St. Paul: West Publishing Company, 1972), Sec. 2-401.
[2] *Ibid.*, Sec. 2-403.

claims against the estate be filed. These claims are reviewed as to amount and authenticity. Accepted claims are paid, a schedule of planned distribution of estate property is prepared and filed, and the distribution is accomplished. The settlement process is completed when the fiduciary accounts to the court for the period of stewardship.

If funds are not adequate to satisfy all accepted claims, state laws provide a priority for settlement. Although the sequence may differ from state to state, the most common order is:

1. Claims having a special lien against property, but not to exceed the value of the property.
2. Funeral and administrative expenses.
3. Taxes: income, estate, and inheritance.
4. Debts due the United States and various states.
5. Judgments of any court of competent jurisdiction.
6. Wages due domestic servants for a period of not more than one year prior to date of death and medical claims for the same period.
7. All other claims.

Within a class, each claim is satisfied on a pro rata basis, if funds are inadequate to accomplish total payment for that class.

ACCOUNTING FOR ESTATES

Estate accounting is designed to facilitate reporting to the court for the term of the fiduciary's accountability. This accountability is increased by an inflow of assets and reduced by an outflow of assets. Therefore, accounting procedures for an estate should accommodate these inflows and outflows.

Accounting for an estate is also based on a distinction between principal and income. This distinction is essential because a will usually provides for the spouse and/or other beneficiaries to share in income earned subsequent to the date of death. Furthermore, income may be assigned to an income beneficiary for a stipulated period, after which time the assets may be distributed to a party called the *remainderman*. For example, income from a group of assets may be granted to the spouse for life (a *life tenant*) and upon the spouse's death, the assets are distributed to the children (the remaindermen). The distinction between principal and income must also be respected because certain expenses and claims may be paid only from principal, while others may be paid only from income.

To account for the distinction between principal and income, two control accounts are used: Estate Principal and Estate Income. The balances of these accounts must be equal to the total of the assets which belong to each group after closing entries are posted. In addition to the two control accounts, two cash accounts are used: Cash—Principal and Cash—Income.

The inventory of property owned by the decedent on the date of death constitutes the initial *principal* or *corpus* (body) of the estate.

Included in principal would be accruals of income to the date of death, providing that the accruals were available on that date. Thus, interest on bond investments accrued to the date of death would be included, since it was available and could have been received by sale of the bonds. Interest on a money market certificate that is available only upon maturity of the certificate would not be accrued. Interest that is not accrued as a part of principal is treated as income when received. Cash dividends are generally accrued as of the date of death, if the dividends were declared prior to death. Stock dividends remain a part of principal. Rents receivable at the date of death become a part of principal in most states, with rents earned after death considered income.

When the initial inventory of estate assets has been completed, a copy is filed with the probate court. The fiduciary records the inventory by debiting each asset for its fair market value at the date of death or the alternate valuation date and crediting the account Estate Principal. Although the title to real property goes directly to the devisee, many fiduciaries prefer to include it to make the listing of assets complete and in agreement with the amount of the gross estate. Subsequently, an entry showing the transfer of such property to the devisee is made. If principal assets are discovered subsequent to the filing of the inventory, the court must be notified. An entry is made by the fiduciary, debiting the assets discovered at their fair market value on the date of death or on the alternate valuation date and crediting the account Assets Subsequently Discovered. Gains on the sale or other disposition of principal assets increase principal, while losses on disposition reduce principal.

Liabilities are not recorded until paid, since the accountability of the fiduciary is reduced only by payment. After claims have been proved and accepted, the source of payment, whether principal or income, must be determined. The payment of expenses such as interest, rent, and other payables accrued to the date of death is charged against principal. The payment of expenses incurred after death is charged against income. In most states, whether property taxes are charged against principal or income depends on the date the taxes become a lien against the property. If they become a lien prior to the date of death, they are charged totally against principal. If they become a lien after death, they are charged against income. A few states allow proration.

The elements of the estate or trust relating to principal are self-balancing, as are also the income elements. It would be possible to set up two sets of books—one for principal and one for income—but this procedure is seldom followed. Instead, journal entries are designed to have equal debits and credits that affect principal accounts or equal debits and credits that affect income accounts. Even in a compound entry affecting both principal and income, the entry must not destroy the self-balancing nature of the two categories of elements in an estate or trust.

The items which are usually chargeable against principal and the account debited when each item is recorded are as follows:

Item	Account Debited
Debts of the decedent incurred prior to death	Debts of Decedent Paid
Funeral and administrative expenses	Funeral and Administrative Expenses
Costs incurred in probating the will	Funeral and Administrative Expenses
Final income taxes of decedent	Debts of Decedent Paid
Federal estate tax[3] and any state inheritance tax	Funeral and Administrative Expenses
Legal and other professional fees to preserve estate principal	Funeral and Administrative Expenses
Charges applicable to principal property which produces no income	Expenses Chargeable Against Principal
Distributions of legacies or devises in a testate distribution	Legacies Distributed ⎫ often combined or ⎬ in the first Devises Distributed ⎭ account
Distributions to heirs or next of kin in an intestate distribution	Distributions to Heirs ⎫ often combined or ⎬ in the first Distributions to Next ⎭ account of Kin
Disposition of estate assets at a loss	Loss on Realization of Principal Assets (a gain would be credited to Gain on Realization of Principal Assets, with total proceeds on any sale of a principal asset debited to Principal Cash)

When income cash is received, Estate Income is credited and, if the estate is large, a subsidiary ledger is maintained, which details the types of income. The items for which income cash is usually disbursed are as follows, and the amount debited when each item is recorded is also shown:

Item	Account Debited
Expenses incurred to protect income flow	Expenses Chargeable Against Income
Ordinary repairs to income-producing property	Expenses Chargeable Against Income
Distributions of income cash to beneficiaries	Distributions to Income Beneficiaries

Illustrative Entries and Reports

To illustrate the accounting for an estate, assume that Todd Shortlife, a bachelor, died on June 30, 19X1. In his will, Shortlife named Mary Doyle as the executrix of his estate. The events which occurred after the death of Shortlife are described and recorded as follows:

---

[3] The Uniform Probate Code provides that where the will does not stipulate treatment of estate taxes, they are to be prorated to the recipients of estate assets on the basis of the value of the asset received relative to the aggregate value of all estate assets subject to tax.

Event	Entry		
June 30, 19X1: An inventory of estate assets is taken: Cash in bank .... $ 70,000 9% X Co. bonds, $100,000 face value; interest dates of May 1 and November 1; fair market value (FMV) .... 97,000 Q Corporation stock (FMV) .... 100,000 Dividend on Q Corp. stock, declared June 10, payable July 10 4,000	Cash—Principal .... 9% X Co. Bonds .... Accrued Interest on X Co. Bonds .... Q Corp. Stock .... Dividends Receivable .... Estate Principal	70,000 97,000 1,500 100,000 4,000	 272,500
July 10: The dividend is received.	Cash—Principal .... Dividends Receivable	4,000	 4,000

July 15 to November 30: The following items are paid:
Funeral expenses .... $ 3,800
Administrative fees, $100 of which are chargeable against income 5,100
Income tax to date of death .. 30,000
Debts incurred prior to death . 11,200
	Funeral and Administrative Expenses ($3,800 + $5,000) ....
	Debts of Decedent Paid ....
	   Cash—Principal ....
	
	Expenses Chargeable Against Income ...
	   Cash—Income ....
		8,800
		41,200
		
		100
			
			50,000
			
			100

Nov. 1: Bond interest is received.	Cash—Principal ....
	Cash—Income ....
	   Estate Income ....
	   Accrued Interest on X Co. Bonds .....
		1,500
		3,000
			
			3,000
			1,500

Nov. 1: X Co. Bonds are sold for $101,000.	Cash—Principal ....
	   9% X Co. Bonds ....
	   Gain on Realization of Principal Assets ....
		101,000	
			97,000
			
			4,000

Nov. 8: Fiduciary discovers a safety deposit box with $8,000 cash.	Cash—Principal .... Assets Subsequently Discovered	8,000	 8,000

Dec. 1: The following legacies are distributed:
To Todd's brother, one half of Q Corp. stock
To Todd's church, $10,000
	Legacies Distributed ....
	   Q Corp. Stock ....
	   Cash—Principal ....
		60,000	
			50,000
			10,000

Dec. 10: A dividend of $1,500 is received on Q Corp. stock.	Cash—Income .... Estate Income	1,500	 1,500
Dec. 15: Todd's nephew is to receive ¾ of any income cash available on December 31 of each year until a trust becomes operative. The money is paid.	Distributions to Income Beneficiaries ... Cash—Income (¾ × $4,400)	3,300	 3,300

A review of the journal entries in the example substantiates the self-balancing nature of the entries involving principal, and those related to income. Thus, a double trial balance may be prepared for the estate—one as to principal and one as to income—as follows:

Estate of Todd Shortlife
Mary Doyle, Executrix
Trial Balance
December 31, 19X1

	As to Principal		As to Income	
Cash—Principal	124,500			
Cash—Income			1,100	
Q Corp. Stock	50,000			
Assets Subsequently Discovered		8,000		
Gain on Realization of Principal Assets		4,000		
Funeral and Administrative Expenses	8,800			
Debts of Decedent Paid	41,200			
Legacies Distributed	60,000			
Estate Principal		272,500		
Expenses Chargeable Against Income			100	
Distributions to Income Beneficiaries			3,300	
Estate Income				4,500
	284,500	284,500	4,500	4,500

Periodically, the fiduciary will prepare a report to the court, summarizing the results during the period of stewardship. This report is called a *charge and discharge statement*. The preparation of the report is simplified if a double trial balance has been prepared, since the charge and discharge statement is divided into two parts—one as to principal and one as to income. The statement for the estate of Todd Shortlife, on December 31, 19X1, is shown at the top of page 879.

In a more complex estate, each of the items in the charge and discharge statement would be supported by a schedule providing detail. For example, a supporting schedule for gains and losses on realization of principal assets might appear as follows:

Schedule of Gains and Losses on Realization
of Principal Assets

Asset	Inventory Value	Proceeds on Realization	Loss	Gain
Geiser Corp. stock	$ 80,000	$ 60,000	$(20,000)	
Glory bonds	90,000	120,000		$30,000
Land	10,000	50,000		40,000
Totals	$180,000	$230,000	$(20,000)	$70,000

The final clause of Shortlife's will involves the establishment of a trust for his nephew. The will indicates that, when the trust becomes operative, the nephew shall receive all income from the trust until he is 25 years of age, at which time the principal of the trust will be released to him. To account for the fulfillment of this clause, the fiduciary would prepare entries to transfer all of the assets to the trust. However, adjustment to a pure accrual basis would be necessary only if it would alter the amounts to be distributed to different parties.

Estate of Todd Shortlife
Mary Doyle, Executrix
Charge and Discharge Statement
For the Period June 30, 19X1, to December 31, 19X1

As to Principal

I charge myself with:

Assets per original inventory	$272,500	
Assets subsequently discovered	8,000	
Gain on realization of principal assets	4,000	
Total charges		$284,500

I credit myself with:

Funeral and administrative expenses	$ 8,800	
Debts of decedent paid	41,200	
Legacies distributed	60,000	
Total credits		110,000

Balances as to estate principal, consisting of:

Cash—principal	$124,500	
Q Corp. stock	50,000	$174,500

As to Income

I charge myself with:

Estate income		$ 4,500

I credit myself with:

Expenses chargeable against income	$ 100	
Distributions to income beneficiaries	3,300	
Total credits		3,400

Balance as to estate income, consisting of:

Cash—income		$ 1,100

The entries to transfer the Shortlife assets to the trust as of December 31, 19X1, are as follows:

Principal Assets Transferred to First National Trust		
Company	174,500	
Cash—Principal		124,500
Q Corp. Stock		50,000
Income Assets Transferred to First National Trust		
Company	1,100	
Cash—Income		1,100

When the duties of the fiduciary cease, the estate records are closed. Estate Principal and Estate Income are the clearing accounts, as shown in the following entries:

Estate Principal	98,000	
Assets Subsequently Discovered	8,000	
Gain on Realization of Principal Assets	4,000	
Funeral and Administrative Expenses		8,800
Debts of Decedent Paid		41,200
Legacies Distributed		60,000

Estate Principal	174,500	
Principal Assets Transferred to First National Trust Company		174,500
Estate Income	3,400	
Expenses Chargeable Against Income		100
Distributions to Income Beneficiaries..................		3,300
Estate Income	1,100	
Income Assets Transferred to First National Trust Company		1,100

Bond Premium and Discount

When bonds are a part of the estate at the time of death, the premium or discount for bonds acquired by the decedent before death is usually not amortized. If the bonds are held to maturity and face value is received, the excess or deficiency is treated as a gain or loss on realization of principal assets.

The same procedure is followed if the bonds are sold prior to maturity. For example, the $100,000 bonds in the Shortlife estate were recorded at $97,000, which was their fair market value at the date of death. When the bonds were sold for $101,000 on November 1, the gain on the sale was the $4,000 difference between the selling price and the fair market value at the date of death, with no adjustment for discount accumulation.

A different approach must be used if bonds are purchased by the fiduciary for either an estate or a trust. Generally, premium should be amortized, but discount should not be accumulated. To illustrate the logic in this rule, assume that a $1,000, 9% bond is purchased by a fiduciary for $1,100 on an interest payment date. The bond matures in five years. The following entry records the purchase:

Bond Investment	1,000	
Premium on Bond Purchased	100	
Cash—Principal		1,100

If the premium were *not* amortized when the first six-months' interest check is received, the interest would be recorded as follows:

Cash—Income	45	
Estate Income		45

When the bond matures, there would be a return to principal of only the $1,000 face value. Principal would be reduced, while income would benefit. Since the 9% contract interest was received only because of the premium paid when the bond was purchased, income should be entitled to market interest, while principal is granted an amount equal to the premium amortization. Therefore, the correct entry to record the interest received and the straight-line amortization of premium should be:

Cash—Income	35	
Cash—Principal [½ × ($100 ÷ 5)].......................	10	
Estate Income		35
Premium on Bond Purchased		10

As another example, assume that a 7% bond is purchased by a fiduciary at 95 on an interest date, five years before maturity. The following entry records the purchase:

Bond Investment	1,000	
Cash—Principal		950
Discount on Bond Purchased		50

If a pro rata portion of the discount is accumulated when the six-months' interest check is received, the following entry would result:

Cash—Income	35	
Discount on Bond Purchased	5	
Estate Income		40

The credit to Estate Income exceeds the cash received, which suggests that more income is available for distribution than actually exists. Thus, accumulation of discount on purchased bonds is improper. At maturity, the discount is recognized as a gain on realization of a principal asset. These procedures are necessary if estate principal is to be protected and excessive distributions to income beneficiaries are to be prevented.

Taxes

Unless the will contains instructions to the contrary, the decedent's final income tax and the estate tax are chargeable against principal. The federal government offers an unusual opportunity to pay federal estate taxes at a discount through the purchase of certain U.S. Treasury bonds, referred to as "flower" bonds. The name is derived from the association of flowers and death. Flower bonds have an effective yield that is considerably below market interest rates. They are sold at a discount, but the government will accept them at par value to pay federal estate taxes, if the bonds were owned by the decedent at the date of death. The bonds should be purchased as late as possible because of their low effective yield. The Internal Revenue Service is amazingly cooperative, since it accepts the trade date, rather than the later settlement date, as the acquisition date of the bonds. When death is near, a purchase of flower bonds in the name of the dying individual may be made by a party having a power of attorney. For example, Martha Jensen is seriously ill. Upon the advice of her tax counselor, she purchases flower bonds with a face value of $200,000 at 73, or $146,000. A week later, she dies. The executor of her estate may redeem the bonds at $200,000 to pay federal estate taxes. Although the $200,000 is includible in her estate, the beneficiaries will receive an additional $54,000, reduced by any estate tax due on that amount.

For the period subsequent to the date of death, the estate is also subject to income taxes, which must be allocated between principal and income. Estate income tax on gains on principal assets realized is charged against principal, while income taxes on interest earned and dividends declared and received after the date of death are a reduction of income. Property taxes are generally not accrued, but are recorded as of the date they become a lien against the property.

Depreciation and Depletion

If the will does not mention plant asset write-offs, the common procedure is not to make any charge against income for depreciation. If the decedent wishes to protect principal for the depreciation factor, there should be a statement in the will that depreciation should be charged against income, and an amount equal to the depreciation should be transferred from income to principal. For depletion on wasting assets, the general rule is that income should be charged for depletion because of the possibility of total consumption of principal.

TRUSTS

The primary reason for the creation of a trust is that the owner does not wish the property to be released to the heirs, at least not for a period of time. The need for trusts has been described as follows:

> A trust is designed to supply one or more elements lacking in a given person's character or ability or taste which are essential to the proper care, management, and use of property. These elements are physical capacity, mental competence, thrift, interest, maturity, experience, and prudence. If a testator decides that any individual to whom he would make a gift under his will lacks any one of these elements, he should consider putting that gift in trust instead of making it outright.[4]

A trust is particularly significant when the heir is a minor or a spouse who is not knowledgeable about money matters or who has no experience in financial affairs. Too often, a spouse has received large amounts of insurance settlements, for example, that are channeled into unwise investments or distributed too generously, with the result that the spouse experiences financial hardship. To prevent this situation, a life insurance trust could be created, under which a trust is made the beneficiary of the insurance proceeds, with the trustee investing and protecting the assets, while distributing income to the designated beneficiaries.

There is no limit to the number and variations of trust arrangements, but all trusts have the basic advantage that legal title and responsibilities of ownership and management are granted to one party, while the benefits flow to another, who need do nothing but enjoy them. Trusts may become operative while the grantor is still alive (an *inter vivos,* or *living trust*), or may be created through a will to become effective upon death (a *testamentary trust*). If a will creates a testamen-

---

4 Gilbert Thomas Stephenson, *Estates and Trusts* (New York: Appleton-Century-Crofts, Inc., 1965), p. 81.

tary trust, the will must still be probated before property may be released by the fiduciary to the trustee.

The *trustee* may be an individual, or the trustee may be a bank, since every major bank has a trust department whose services are available for a fee. The primary duties of a trustee are to carry out the terms of the trust, to protect the property, and to be fair and impartial on matters affecting the income beneficiaries and remaindermen. Care should be exercised in the choice of a trustee, for once title to the property is transferred, the trustee cannot be removed except for proven illegal or unwise actions.

Accounting for Trusts

The accounting procedures for a trust and an estate are very similar. For both, there must be separation of principal and income. For both, charge and discharge statements are used as the medium for reporting. The following entries briefly illustrate the accounting for a trust and the similarity to estate entries. These entries would be recorded by the trustee for the Shortlife trust (page 878) when the assets from the fiduciary of the Shortlife estate are accepted. Thereafter, the journal entries for a trust are patterned closely after those of an estate.

Cash—Principal	124,500	
Q Corp. Stock	50,000	
Trust Principal		174,500
Cash—Income	1,100	
Trust Income		1,100

To demonstrate adherence to the terms of the trust, the trustee must provide annual, confidential reports to income beneficiaries and remaindermen. For a testamentary trust, a report must also be rendered to the probate court of the county in which the will was admitted to probate. The nature of the report is dependent upon the statutory requirement of the relevant state. Generally within 30 days after the end of each year, a report must be filed that shows:

1. The trust principal on hand at the beginning of the period.
2. Changes in the trust principal during the period, such as asset acquisitions or dispositions.
3. The trust principal on hand at the end of the period, its composition, and the estimated market values of all investments.

As to trust income, the report shows:

1. The trust income on hand at the beginning of the period.
2. Trust income received during the period, detailing the sources and amounts.
3. Distributions of trust income made during the period to income beneficiaries.
4. The trust income on hand at the end of the period and how it is invested.

These requirements may be met by the periodic filing of a charge and discharge statement, provided sufficient detail as to principal and as to income is incorporated into the report. At the time of submitting the statement to the court, many trustees prefer to close trust books to have them correspond to the annual time frame used in filing reports. Trust Principal and Trust Income are the clearing accounts used in the closing process, paralleling the procedures for closing an estate.

A procedure followed by trustees is to accrue income or expense only when it is necessary to protect the rights of the parties involved. If a trust is established in which the income beneficiary is also the remainderman, generally nothing is achieved by making accrual adjustments at year end prior to preparing necessary reports. An occasion when it would be appropriate to accrue is a situation in which the trust agreement states that income beneficiaries are entitled to income until their death. Upon the demise of one of the income beneficiaries, accrual basis adjustments would be made to the date of death in order to compute the amount of income entitlement.

The trust will terminate when all trust property is distributed in accordance with the trust arrangement. For example, a trust may have been created to provide a beneficiary with income until a certain age is reached, at which time trust principal is released. The trustee's final report will take the same form as the periodic reports, but in addition, will itemize total distribution of trust principal and income to indicate termination of stewardship.

Tax Planning with Trusts

A trust may be established to remove income that would normally be taxed to the grantor and to pass it on to one or more beneficiaries who are in a lower tax bracket or who have no tax liability at all. One of the requirements is that the grantor relinquish control over the property producing the income for a minimum of ten years. For example, a parent may establish a trust for a child by transferring to a trustee bonds having a face value of $30,000 and paying 11% annually. All rights to the bonds are relinquished for ten years, when the bonds will revert back to the grantor. The annual interest of $3,300 is no longer taxable to the grantor. The trust itself would not be subject to tax because it distributes all of its income currently. The beneficiary must report the interest. Assuming it is the only income received by the beneficiary, there would be no income tax to pay, because the amount is below the minimum subject to tax (as of this writing). Over the ten-year period, this one effort in tax planning permits $33,000 to escape taxation, based on a trust of only $30,000. An additional appealing feature is that the procedure may be adopted for any number of beneficiaries.

Another tax-saving device is a charitable remainder trust, which pays its income to one or more beneficiaries for life. With the death of the last income beneficiary, the assets of the trust go to the remainderman, which must be a charitable organization. Under such an arrangement, a charitable contribution deduction is available to the grantor when the trust is created. The income from trust assets is allocated to the beneficiaries, who may be in a lower tax bracket or have no tax to pay. Upon death, the property is excluded from the grantor's estate, thus escaping estate taxes.

Many opportunities for tax planning are available for individuals, businesses, and fiduciaries. The rules are complex and require careful study, but the effort to reduce income taxes can be exciting and rewarding.

QUESTIONS

1. What is the legal distinction between real and personal property? What relevancy does the distinction have for estate planning?
2. Enumerate three far-reaching changes involving estate and gift taxation that resulted from the ERT Act of 1981.
3. State the maximum gratuitous transfer of property (gift) for years after 1981, so as not to incur any federal gift tax (a) for a married couple; (b) for a single taxpayer.
4. Explain why family tax planning would generally attempt to shift items subject to income taxes to items subject to the unified death tax.
5. State the rule that establishes the alternative valuation date for estate tax purposes. Should the date that results in the lower amount subject to the tentative tax always be selected?
6. In general, what procedure should be followed in the selective retention of certain assets as part of the estate and the disposition of other assets before death?
7. After providing for the special reservation of assets because of the state's family allowance and homestead allowance, the estate does not have sufficient assets to settle all accepted claims. The fiduciary informs the funeral director who handled final arrangements that the funeral expenses will have to be paid on a pro rata basis with all other claims. Is the statement of the fiduciary correct?
8. In accounting for estates or trusts, why is there no account titled Cash?
9. In estate accounting, when is accrual accounting used?
10. What is the double trial balance found in estate accounting and what is its purpose?
11. Outline the steps that are followed to settle the estate of a decedent who left a valid will.
12. On an essay examination on estate accounting, a student submitted the following statement: "On bonds that constitute a part of the estate principal, premium should not be amortized but discount should." Identify the errors in the statement and submit a corrected statement.

13. What purpose would be served by recognizing depreciation on estate plant assets?

14. Someone once said, "A trust is established because people have weaknesses or are ignorant." Do you agree?

EXERCISES

Exercise 1. Answer the following questions related to maximizing the advantage of lifetime giving for years after 1981:

(a) Mr. and Mrs. Ben Gehrig have two sons, who are married, an unmarried daughter, and three grandchildren. Before they retire in seven years, they would like to make the maximum total gifts to their descendants (and their spouses) without incurring any federal gift tax. What would this total amount be?

(b) Joan Center, who is single, has three nieces and one nephew. What is the maximum total gifts she can make to them over the next five years without incurring any federal gift tax?

Exercise 2. Barney Toven owned an insurance policy on the life of his wife, with their daughter named as beneficiary. On the date of Mr. Toven's death, the cash surrender value of the policy was $50,000. Its face value was $600,000. As a result of the strain of her husband's death, Mrs. Toven died within three months of her husband. The insurance company paid $600,000 to the daughter. Discuss the importance of the proper choice of valuation dates for estate assets under these circumstances.

Exercise 3. On October 1, 1982, Billie Baird died. She owned stock in two corporations—Zen Corporation and Bud Corporation—which declared cash dividends on September 1, 1982, with the following dates of record:

Zen Corporation date of record—September 29, 1982

Bud Corporation date of record—October 2, 1982

Which of these assets would be included in Billie Baird's gross estate, if state law specifies that the date of record is the governing date?

Exercise 4. Assuming that no stipulation is made in the will, indicate by placing an "x" in the appropriate column whether the typical accounting treatment of each of the following estate items would affect principal only, income only, or both:

	Would Affect Only Principal	Would Affect Only Income	Would Affect Both
(a) Payment of funeral expenses	___	___	___
(b) Payment of executor's fee to conserve both principal and income assets	___	___	___
(c) Distribution of a specific legacy	___	___	___
(d) Distribution of a residuary legacy	___	___	___
(e) Distribution to an income beneficiary	___	___	___
(f) Payment of final income tax of decedent	___	___	___
(g) Payment of ordinary repairs to income-producing property	___	___	___
(h) Gain on sale of assets in original inventory of the estate	___	___	___
(i) Depletion charge on a producing wasting asset	___	___	___

	Would Affect Only		Would
	Principal	Income	Affect Both
(j) First interest received on bonds in estate inventory when date of death does not coincide with interest payment date	_____	_____	_____
(k) Next interest payment received	_____	_____	_____

Exercise 5. Casey Jones died testate on May 1, 19X0. As the approved executor, prepare journal entries to record the following activities related to the estate:

(a) The assets are inventoried, and the following listing is filed with the probate court:

Cash	$ 60,000
Stock of Trains, Inc.	40,000
Zip Railroad 10% bonds, interest payable March 1 and September 1, at face value (also market value)	120,000
Accrued interest on Zip bonds	2,000
Personal and household effects	30,000
Total	$252,000

(b) Funeral expenses paid, $2,800.

(c) Dividends were declared on May 10 by Trains, Inc., and the check for $800 was received on June 1.

(d) Interest on Zip Railroad bonds was collected on September 1.

(e) Half of the Zip Railroad bonds were sold on October 1 at 103 plus accrued interest.

(f) Casey was a bachelor. The will stipulates that his personal and household effects be given to his housekeeper, Karen Kay. The executor released the items to her.

(g) On December 1, the executor's fee of $3,000 was approved by the court and paid. Of the total amount, $200 is to be charged against income of the estate.

Exercise 6. After giving effect to the data in Exercise 5, prepare a charge and discharge statement.

Exercise 7. The will of Casey Jones, detailed in Exercise 5, stipulated that, when feasible, all remaining assets should be used to establish a trust at State National Bank, the income from which is to be given to charity.

(1) Prepare journal entries to transfer estate principal and income assets to the trust.

(2) Prepare journal entries to close the executor's records.

Exercise 8. On February 1, a duly appointed administrator of an estate purchased twelve (12) $1,000, 12% bonds at 103 plus accrued interest. The bonds pay interest on April 1 and October 1. The following entry to record the purchase was made:

Feb. 1	Bond Investment................................	12,840	
	Cash—Principal		12,840
	To record bond investment.		

On April 1, when the interest was received, the following entry was made:

Apr. 1	Cash—Income	720	
	Estate Income		720

The administrator is not certain that the entries are correct. Assuming that amortization of premium is $10 per month, prepare an entry to correct the records on April 2.

PROBLEMS

Problem 20-1. The will of Marlene Black, deceased, directed that the executor, Kenneth Lawson, liquidate the entire estate within two years of the date of Black's death and pay the net proceeds and income, if any, to the Sunnydale Orphanage. Black, who was unmarried, died on February 1, 1984.

An inventory of the decedent's property was prepared, and the fair market value of all items was determined. The preliminary inventory, before the computation of any appropriate income accruals on inventory items, follows:

	Fair Market Value
First National Bank checking account	$ 6,000
$60,000 City of Laguna school bonds, interest rate 6%, payable January 1 and July 1, maturity date July 1, 1988	59,000
2,000 shares of Jones Corporation capital stock	220,000
Term life insurance. Beneficiary is the estate of Marlene Black	20,000
Personal residence ($45,000) and furnishings ($5,000)	50,000

During 1984, the following transactions occurred:

(a) The interest on the City of Laguna school bonds was collected. The bonds were sold on July 1 for $62,000. Proceeds and interest were transferred to Sunnydale Orphanage.

(b) The Jones Corporation paid cash dividends of $1 per share on March 1 and December 1, as well as a 10% stock dividend on July 1. All dividends were declared 45 days before each payment date and were payable to holders of record as of 40 days before each payment date. On September 1, 1,000 shares were sold at $105 per share, and the proceeds were paid to the Orphanage.

(c) Because of a depressed real estate market, the personal residence was rented furnished at $300 per month, commencing April 1. The rent is paid monthly, in advance. Real estate taxes of $900 were paid for the calendar year of 1984. The house and furnishings have estimated lives of 45 years and 10 years, respectively. On April 30, the part-time gardener-handyman was paid four months' wages totaling $500 for services performed, and was released. Applicable law requires proration of both property taxes and wages.

(d) The First National Bank checking account was closed, and the balance of $6,000 was transferred to an estate bank account.

(e) The term life insurance payment was received on March 1 and deposited in the estate bank account.

(f) The following disbursements were made:

Funeral expenses, $2,000
Final illness expenses, $1,500
April 15 income tax of decedent, $700
Attorney's and accountant's fees, $12,000

(g) On December 31, the balance of the undistributed income, except for $1,000, was paid to the beneficiary. The balance of the cash on hand derived from the corpus of the estate was also paid to the beneficiary on December 31.

As of December 31, 1984, the executor was asked to file, with the probate court, records of activities to date.

Required:

Prepare journal entries for all events through December 31, 1984. Closing entries are not required.   (AICPA adapted)

Problem 20-2. After the journal entries have been prepared for the events detailed in Problem 20-1, relating to the estate of Marlene Black, the executor decides to resign effective December 31, 1984, because of his inadequate knowledge of estate accounting.

Required:

Prepare a charge and discharge statement for the period from February 1 through December 31, 1984. The following supporting schedules should also be included:
    (1) Original principal of the estate
    (2) Gain on realization of principal assets
    (3) Funeral and administrative expenses
    (4) Debts of decedent paid
    (5) Legacies distributed
    (6) Assets (corpus) on hand, December 31, 1984
    (7) Estate income
    (8) Expenses chargeable to income
    (9) Distributions to income beneficiary   (AICPA adapted)

Problem 20-3. On February 1, 1983, Larry Lauret died. He is survived by his wife and their 17-year-old daughter. His will was admitted to probate and named Judy Gaul as executrix. During the first six months of her fiduciary responsibility, the following events occurred:
    (a) An inventory of assets shows:

Cash in bank accounts	$ 40,000
A six-month money market certificate that has not matured. Interest is available only at maturity. Accrued interest to date is $900	30,000
State of California 10% highway bonds, with interest payment dates of January 1 and July 1:	
Face value	$120,000
Fair market value at date of death	106,000
Cost to decedent	98,000
Apartment building:	
Cost	$400,000
Accumulated depreciation to date of death	130,000
Fair market value at date of death	570,000
Mortgage payable on apartment	120,000

(b) The will stipulates that upon settlement of the estate, remaining assets are to be put in trust. Income from the assets, net of related expenses, is to be paid periodically to the widow. Upon her death, the net income will be paid to the daughter. The will indicates that title to the apartment building shall be vested in the daughter upon her 25th birthday or upon the death of her mother, whichever occurs later. To protect the principal, an amount equal to the depreciation expense shall be transferred from income cash to principal cash, to be put in trust along with the building. The executor decided to debit a special account Cash—Principal (Restricted), to accumulate these cash transfers from income and to credit Accumulated Depreciation. The procedure was approved by the court. The will also specifies that payment of the apartment mortgage shall be charged against principal, but mortgage interest payments and depreciation expense shall be charged against income. The events related to the apartment building were as follows:

Apartment rentals received to date	$78,000
Apartment maintenance expenses paid	8,000
Property taxes paid	11,000
Property taxes become a lien against property on April 1. State law does not allow proration of property taxes.	
Income released to Mrs. Lauret	42,000
Depreciation expense recorded and cash transfer made in accordance with the terms of the will	6,000

(c) The following additional payments were made:

Decedent's final income tax	$13,000
For purchases charged by Mr. Lauret on bank credit cards	2,000
Burial costs	4,800
Legal services for probating of will and services of the executor	3,200
Interest on apartment building mortgage	4,000

(d) A month after filing an inventory of the estate assets with the probate court, the executor was talking with Mrs. Lauret. She casually mentioned that her husband had traveled to Europe many years ago and had brought back some paintings that were stored in the garage. The executor took the six paintings to an art dealer, who stated that five had negligible value, but the sixth appeared to be a small Picasso painting. An expert corroborated the statement and offered $300,000 for the painting. The executor postponed a decision, but filed an amendment to the estate inventory with the probate court.

(e) In again reviewing the will, the executor found a clause that stated that all objects of art were to be given to the Guggenheim Museum of Modern Art. The Picasso painting was delivered to the museum.

(f) The money market certificate matured. A check for $34,000 was received.

(g) Interest for six months was received on the State of California bonds.

Required:

(1) Prepare journal entries to record the events.

(2) Prepare a double trial balance, as illustrated in the text, resulting from posting the entries.

(3) Prepare a charge and discharge statement for the six-month period ending July 31, 1983.

Problem 20-4. The probate court is dissatisfied with the procedures followed by the executor of the estate of Jean O'Brien and demands the records. The executor submits the following:

Journal Entries for the Estate of Jean O'Brien—Died, May 1, 1982

May 8	Bank Checking Account	14,100	
	Insurance Policy at Cash Surrender Value (face of policy is $100,000 and is payable to the estate)	18,000	
	Shannon Corporation 12% Bonds (interest is payable April 1 and October 1; face value, $100,000; fair market value at date of death, $106,000; recorded at Jean's cost)	124,000	
	O'Brien Corporation Common Stock (10,000 shares of $10 par. Stock was quoted at $18 when Jean died. These shares were a gift from her father, the founder of the corporation, so I've entered them at $1, just to make a record.)	1	
	Condominium (Her condo is just like mine, which cost me $96,000 a week before she died. Her cost was $73,000.)	73,000	
	Paintings (I don't understand these, but a dealer says they are worth $25,000. They cost Jean $9,000.)	25,000	
	Gain on Paintings		16,000
	Total Estate		238,101

        This is a list of the assets I found so far. I made a copy of this entry and filed it with the court. I omitted a Silver Cloud Rolls-Royce, worth about $30,000. I'll keep the car instead of asking for a fee. Jean always said she wanted me to have it. She must have forgotten it when she made out her will.

9	Cash	2,000	
	O'Brien Corporation Dividend		2,000

        Received a check for a dividend declared April 2 to holders of record on April 25.

June 1	Cash	100,000	
	Insurance Policy at Cash Surrender Value		18,000
	Gain on Loss of Jean O'Brien		82,000

        This is the check from the insurance company.

5	Expenses	44,000	
	Cash		44,000

        I issued checks to cover:

Funeral expenses	$ 5,100
Jean's medical bills	300
Final income tax payments	17,900
Jean's charges on American Express	700
Partial payment on estate tax. The will says it should be charged against principal, whatever that means	20,000
Total	$44,000

30	Expenses	25,000	
	Paintings		25,000

        Turned paintings over to Art Institute, as the will said I should do.

Sept. 1	Cash	6,000	
	Interest Received		6,000

        To record check received from Shannon Corporation.

Sept. 10	Loss on O'Brien Corporation Common Stock............................	1	
	O'Brien Corporation Common Stock...............................		1
	The will stated that the stock should be returned to the corporation, so I did it.		
Oct. 1	Cash..	90,000	
	Condominium...		73,000
	Gain on Sale of Condominium		17,000
	To record sale of condo. The will says the proceeds should be used to establish a Jean O'Brien Scholarship Endowment Fund at State University, her alma mater.		
3	Cash Turned over to State University	90,000	
	Cash		90,000
	I sent a check to the university for the scholarship endowment fund.		
31	Expenses..	3,000	
	Cash		3,000
	The court relieved me as executor and said I could not have the Rolls-Royce. This payment to me is to be charged to principal. I don't think what they did is fair to me.		

Required:

(1) The probate judge is disgusted with the records, terminates the executor's responsibilities, and appoints you as the replacement. Prepare a correct set of entries to date.

(2) Prepare a charge and discharge statement. No supporting schedules are necessary.

Problem 20-5. Arthur Taine died in an accident on May 31, 1982. His will, dated February 28, 1980, provided that all just debts and expenses be paid and that his property be disposed of as follows:

Personal residence is devised to Bertha Taine, widow.

U.S. Treasury bonds and Puritan Company stock are to be placed in trust. All income is to go to Bertha Taine during her lifetime, with right of appointment upon her death.

Seneca Company mortgage notes are bequeathed to Elaine Taine Langer, daughter.

A cash bequest of $10,000 is to be made to David Taine, son.

The remainder of the estate is to be divided equally between the two children, Elaine Taine Langer and David Taine.

The will further provided that during the administration period, Bertha Taine was to be paid $300 a month out of estate income. Estate and inheritance taxes are to be borne by the principal of the estate. David Taine was named as executor and trustee.

An inventory of the decedent's property was prepared. The fair market value of all items as of the date of death was determined. The preliminary inventory, before the computation of any appropriate income accruals on inventory items, follows:

Personal residence...	$ 45,000
Jewelry—diamond ring	9,600
York Life Insurance Company—term life insurance policy on life of Arthur Taine, with Bertha Taine designated as beneficiary...............................	120,000
Granite Trust Co.—5% savings bank account, in trust for Philip Langer (grandchild), interest credited January 1 and July 1; balance May 31	400
Fidelity National Bank checking account balance	143,000

$100,000 U.S. Treasury bonds, 3%, 1999, interest payable March 1 and September 1 .... $100,000
$9,700 Seneca Co. first mortgage notes, 6%, 1985, interest payable May 31 and November 30 9,900
800 shares Puritan Company common stock 64,000
700 shares Meta Manufacturing common stock 70,000

The executor opened an estate bank account, to which he transferred the decedent's checking account balance. Other deposits, through July 1, 1983, were as follows:

Interest collected on U.S. Treasury bonds:
September 1, 1982 .... $ 1,500
March 1, 1983 1,500
Dividends received on Puritan Company stock:
June 15, 1982, declared May 7, 1982, payable to holders of record May 27, 1982 800
September 15, 1982 800
December 15, 1982 1,200
March 15, 1983 800
June 15, 1983 800
Net proceeds of June 19, 1982, sale of 700 shares of Meta Manufacturing common stock 68,810

Payments were made from the estate's checking account through July 1, 1983, for the following:

Funeral expenses .... $ 2,000
Assessments for additional 1980 federal and state income taxes ($1,700) plus interest ($110) to May 31, 1982 1,810
1982 income taxes of Arthur Taine for the period January 1 through May 31, 1982, in excess of amounts paid by the decedent on Declaration of Estimated Tax 9,100
Federal and state fiduciary income taxes, fiscal year ending June 30, 1982 ($75), and June 30, 1983 ($1,400) 1,475
Federal and state estate taxes 58,000
Monthly payments to Bertha Taine: 13 payments of $300 each 3,900
Attorney's and accountant's fees 25,000

The executor waived his commission. However, he desired to receive his father's diamond ring in lieu of the $10,000 specific legacy. All parties agreed to this in writing, and the court's approval was secured. All other specific legacies were delivered by July 15, 1982. On July 2, 1983, final distributions of the residuary legacies were made to Elaine and David, the latter continuing to function as trustee, establishing separate records for the trust.

Required:

Prepare journal entries to record all events related to the estate of Arthur Taine, including transfer to the trust and final closing entries for the estate.

(AICPA adapted)

Problem 20-6. Using the information detailed in Problem 20-5, prepare a charge and discharge statement and supporting schedules to accompany the attorney's formal court accounting on behalf of the executor of the estate of Arthur Taine for the period May 31, 1982, through July 1, 1983. The following supporting schedules should be included:

Schedule 1—Original principal of the estate
        2—Gains and losses on realization of principal assets
        3—Funeral and administrative expenses
        4—Debts of decedent paid
        5—Legacies distributed
        6—Principal assets on hand, July 1, 1983
        7—Proposed plan of distribution of estate assets as of July 1, 1983
        8—Income collected
        9—Expenses chargeable to income
        10—Distributions to income beneficiary   (AICPA adapted)

Problem 20-7. Bruce Locke, Jr., died on January 15, 1983. Records disclose the following estate:

Cash in the bank	$ 3,750
6% note receivable, including $50 accrued interest	5,050
Stocks	50,000
Dividends declared on stocks	600
9% mortgage receivable, including $150 accrued interest	20,150
Real estate—apartment house	135,000
Household effects	18,450
Dividends receivable from Bruce Locke, Sr., Trust Fund	250,000
Total	$483,000

Twenty years earlier, Bruce Locke, Sr., created a trust fund, with his son, Bruce Locke, Jr., as life tenant, and his grandson, Paul Locke, as remainderman. The assets in the trust fund consist solely of the outstanding capital stock of Locke, Inc., namely, 2,000 shares of $100 par stock. At the creation of the trust, the book value as well as the market value of these shares was $400,000, and at January 1, 1983, the market value of these shares was $500,000. On January 2, 1983, Locke, Inc., declared a 125% cash dividend payable February 2, 1983, to shareholders of record January 12, 1983.

The executor's transactions from January 15 through January 31, 1983, were:

Cash receipts:		
Jan. 20	Dividends	$ 1,500
25	6% note receivable	5,000
	Interest on 6% note receivable	58
	Stocks sold, inventoried at $22,500	20,000
	9% mortgage sold	21,000
	Interest accrued on mortgage	200
28	Sale of assets not inventoried	250
29	Sale of apartment house	130,000
	Total cash receipts	$178,008

Cash disbursements:		
Jan. 20	Funeral expenses	$ 2,750
23	Decedent's debts	8,000
25	Decedent's bequests	10,000
31	Payment to widow, including all estate income	20,000
	Total cash disbursements	$ 40,750

Required:

Prepare journal entries to record the events and a charge and discharge statement for the period January 15 through January 31, 1983. Design the statement in such a manner that no supporting schedules are necessary.   (AICPA adapted)

Problem 20-8. The will of William Kraus, deceased, provided that as soon as possible a trust be established to assist his daughter, Sandy, to continue voice lessons in New York City in preparation for a career in opera. Providing her progress is satisfactory, she shall receive $1,000 on the first day of each month. An additional $5,000 shall be made available during the summer, if she is accepted at a recognized school for opera singers. Payments to Sandy shall be charged against trust income during the year. If income for the year is inadequate to cover expenses chargeable against income and income distributions, the deficiency shall be covered by principal, with no need for reimbursement from later income. If within six years Sandy has made a successful debut, the remaining assets shall be released to her. If she has not made her debut within that period, the payments shall cease, with any remaining assets turned over to UWM University for music scholarships.

The following events occurred that involved the trust:

(a) The will specified that principal and income assets of the estate retain their identity when transferred to the trust. The following assets were accepted by the trustee on January 2, 1983:

As to principal:	Cash	$40,000	
	AMD common stock	15,000	
	Parrot 6% preferred stock	30,000	
	Rental property	80,000	$165,000
As to income:	Cash		4,000

(b) A $20,000 six-month money market certificate was purchased with principal cash on February 10, when the annual rate was 14%.

(c) On March 15, a dividend of $1,200 was received on the AMD Common Stock. By year end, the value of the stock increased from $15,000 to $18,000.

(d) Rental income of $4,200 for the first six months of 1983 was received. Ordinary property expenses of $1,200 were paid. The trustee believed that the net return was not adequate to justify retaining the property in the trust. It was sold for $73,000 on July 1, 1983.

(e) On July 1, principal cash was invested in 15% industrial bonds with a face value of $80,000, purchased at 105 plus accrued interest from May 1, the last semiannual interest payment date. Bonds mature on November 1, 1986.

(f) Sandy was notified that she was accepted for the summer session master classes in voice at the La Scala School for Voice in Italy. On July 3, a payment of $5,000 was made to her in accordance with the will.

(g) On August 12, a check for the interest on the money market certificate was received. The trustee renewed the certificate for another six months.

(h) The annual dividend of $1,800 on the Parrot 6% preferred was received on September 2. The trustee believed the return was minimal. When a takeover bidder offered $42,000 for the stock, the trustee sold. Most of the proceeds were invested in $36,000 face value of City of Madison 10% bonds, purchased at 96 and accrued interest on October 1. Semiannual interest payment dates are June 1 and December 1. The bonds mature December 1, 1989.

(i) Interest was received on the industrial bonds on November 1. When necessary, the trustee uses pro rata amortization techniques on interest collection dates only. Since Sandy is the only income beneficiary, the trustee does not accrue at calendar year end, an acceptable procedure under the circumstances.

(j) On December 1, interest on the City of Madison 10% bonds was received.

(k) During the year, twelve monthly payments of $1,000 were made to Sandy. (Make one entry for the twelve payments.)

(l) The trustee's fee of $4,000, which is to be charged against principal, was withdrawn.

(m) Since trust income was inadequate to meet expenses chargeable against income and income distributions, an entry was to be made to cover the deficiency.

Required:

(1) Prepare journal entries to record the events for the year.

(2) Prepare a charge and discharge statement for the trust for the year ended December 31, 1983.

Problem 20-9. Clyde Rivers died January 1, 1983, and left his property in trust for his daughter, Bonnie. Income from the trust was to be paid to her as she requested it, and at her death the trust principal was to go to his nephew, Billy Rivers. Any income, including accrued interest, not withdrawn by Bonnie at the time of her death would be paid to her estate. Clyde appointed Sharon Wynn as trustee at a fixed fee of $4,800 per year. All expenses of settling Clyde's estate were paid and accounted for by the executor before the trustee took over.

Bonnie died on September 30, 1986, and left her property in trust to her cousin, Kathy Hyatt. Sharon Wynn was also appointed executor and trustee of this estate, and she agreed not to make any additional charges for these services. All income subsequent to September 30, 1986, was to be paid to Kathy. The estate of Bonnie Rivers consisted solely of Bonnie's unexpended income from the Clyde Rivers Trust, which was invested on October 1, 1986, to yield 9%, payable on the last day of March, June, September, and December.

Until legal papers could be prepared and the property officially transferred to Billy on December 31, 1987, he received payments from the trustee totaling $30,000. The property received by Sharon Wynn under the will of Clyde Rivers, as of January 1, 1983, was:

> 10,000 shares of Farnham Corporation, valued at $100 each.
>
> $200,000 of Farnham Corporation 9% bonds, paying interest semiannually on June 30 and December 31. Their market value and face value were identical at the date of death.

On February 1, 1983, 1984, and 1985, the trustee received $40,000 of annual dividends from the Farnham stock. Dividends increased to $60,000 on February 1, 1986 and 1987.

Payments made by the trustee were as follows:

> Expenses averaged $100 per month.
>
> Trustee's fee was $400 per month.

To the beneficiaries:	Bonnie Rivers	— 1983	$27,000	
		1984	35,000	
		1985	30,000	
		1986	25,000	$117,000
	Billy Rivers	— 1986	$10,000	
		1987	20,000	$ 30,000
	Kathy Hyatt	— 1986 and 1987—All income received during the respective periods.		

Required:

(1) Prepare a statement of income for the Clyde Rivers Trust during the period Bonnie Rivers was the life tenant, showing the undistributed income that became the principal of the Bonnie Rivers Trust.
(2) Prepare a schedule showing the computation of the total assets released to Billy Rivers on December 31, 1987.
(3) Prepare a schedule showing the amount of income received by Kathy Hyatt in 1986 and 1987.   (AICPA adapted)

CHAPTER 21

INSOLVENCY

Dun and Bradstreet reports that almost ninety percent of all business failures are attributable to incapable management. If individuals or business management have not learned to plan effectively, to organize efficiently, and to recognize problems, they may be confronted with a situation of insolvency—being unable to meet financial obligations as they become due. This chapter will discuss various relief procedures that do not involve court actions, as well as the legal procedures available under the Bankruptcy Reform Act of 1978.

RELIEF PROCEDURES NOT REQUIRING COURT ACTION

When a business becomes insolvent, the simplest procedure is to arrange an *agreement with creditors*, which grants an extension of time for meeting obligations. This approach could be useful when the debtor has suffered only a temporary financial setback and has previously demonstrated successful operational capabilities. Another approach is the composition agreement, by which creditors agree to a scaling down of the amounts owed by the debtor. For example, each creditor might be willing to accept $.80 per dollar of debt, if resorting to other processes would result in receiving less. These two procedures are possible without involving court action.

A corporation may not be insolvent, but may have accumulated a relatively large deficit as a result of such problems as an excessive investment in plant assets or inventory, or management's inability to recognize and influence market demands. If management is replaced, and if profits result from new policies, most state laws will still not permit declaration of dividends until the deficit is eliminated. The turnabout period and deficit elimination may take so long that the investors' interest in the company vanishes, and capital acquisition becomes difficult. To overcome such a handicap, the corporation might seek a *quasi-reorganization*.

Quasi-reorganization does not require court action, nor does it require the consent of creditors, since creditor interests are not altered. However, the procedure is described in state laws, many of which require approval by two thirds of the stockholders.

The primary purpose of a quasi-reorganization is to eliminate a large deficit and to take such action as will permit successful operations in the future. Excessive plant capacity and equipment may be sold. Plant assets that are retained may be revalued to reflect a lower but fair value, thereby reducing depreciation charges allocated to future periods. For example, as part of the quasi-reorganization process, a corporation's board of directors reduces plant assets from a cost of $1,000,000 to a more realistic fair value of $400,000 and accumulated depreciation from $200,000 to $80,000. Future annual depreciation charges will be reduced from $50,000 to $20,000. The entry to record the revaluation would be:

Accumulated Depreciation	120,000	
Retained Earnings	480,000	
Property, Plant, and Equipment		600,000

It should be noted that the write-down of the assets increases the deficit, which will then be eliminated by subsequent changes in the capital structure.

The deficit is eliminated by charges against the existing paid-in capital in excess of par or stated values. If no such paid-in capital exists, it may be created by altering the capital structure and substituting a lower par value or no-par value stock for units of a higher stated value. To illustrate the manner in which the owners' equity section in the balance sheet is revised by a quasi-reorganization, assume the following stockholders' equity:

Common stock ($10 par, 12,000 shares outstanding)	$120,000
Retained earnings (deficit)	(45,000)
Total stockholders' equity	$ 75,000

On March 1, 19X0, the stockholders approve a reduction in par value to $1. Note that such a maneuver has absolutely no effect on the proportionate interests of each stockholder.

The entries to record the quasi-reorganization are as follows:

Common Stock ($10 par)	120,000	
Common Stock ($1 par)		12,000
Paid-In Capital from Reduction in Stock Par Value (or Reorganization Capital)		108,000
To record the reduction in par value.		
Paid-In Capital from Reduction in Stock Par Value	45,000	
Retained Earnings		45,000
To eliminate the deficit.		

Immediately following the quasi-reorganization, the owners' equity section would show:

Common stock ($1 par, 12,000 shares outstanding)...............	$12,000
Paid-in capital from reduction in stock par value...................	63,000
Retained earnings (subsequent to March 1, 19X0)	-0-
Total stockholders' equity	$75,000

In future financial statements, retained earnings must be dated to indicate the starting point of new accumulations. The process of dating retained earnings should be continued for as long a period of time as is deemed advisable, but rarely does it exceed ten years.

INSOLVENCY AND THE BANKRUPTCY REFORM ACT OF 1978

If a satisfactory solution cannot be reached under the procedures described in the previous paragraphs, the legal proceedings for bankruptcy may be initiated. Attitudes toward bankruptcy have changed considerably from the time of the Romans, when unpaid creditors were permitted to kill the debtor and divide the body among them. Modern bankruptcy procedures attempt to give a debtor a fresh start, unburdened by former obligations, while simultaneously accomplishing an equitable distribution of the debtor's property among creditors.

In an attempt to modernize an antiquated system existing under the Bankruptcy Act of 1898, as amended by the Chandler Act of 1938, Congress passed the Bankruptcy Reform Act of 1978 (Title 11 of the U.S. Code), which became effective on October 1, 1979. Under the former acts, U.S. District Courts were given the responsibility of functioning as courts of bankruptcy. The office of *referee* was created, granting it jurisdiction over bankruptcy proceedings. Later, referees were assigned the title of *bankruptcy judge*. As cases became more complicated, it was sometimes difficult to determine whether an issue should be settled under the Rules of Bankruptcy Procedure governing the courts of bankruptcy or under the Rules of Civil Procedure used by the District Courts.

The Bankruptcy Reform Act of 1978 (hereafter referred to as the Act) initiated an interesting experiment whose objective was to expedite the formulation and handling of administrative procedures for bankruptcy cases. It established a five-year pilot program that relieves bankruptcy judges of most administrative duties and permits them to concentrate on the resolution of substantive matters. In each of the eighteen experimental judicial districts created by the Act, a U.S. trustee is appointed under the supervision of the U.S. Assistant Attorney General. The U.S. trustees are responsible for: (1) monitoring the performance of the private trustees that they appoint to bankruptcy cases, (2) functioning as trustees when private trustees are unable or unwilling to serve, and (3) overseeing the general administration of bankruptcy cases. Results of the pilot program will influence Congress in its decisions regarding the final structure of the bankruptcy courts which are to be created, effective April 1, 1984. Until that time, the present bankruptcy courts which are not in the experimental program have broadened powers to carry out duties outlined by the new law. They function as separate departments of the District Court, with exclusive jurisdiction over bankruptcy cases.

The Act provides that a bankruptcy case may be filed under one of the following operative chapters:

Chapter 7   Liquidation
Any business or nonbusiness debtor, except a railroad, governmental unit, bank, insurance company, or savings and loan association, may file a petition under this chapter. Filing of a joint case by debtor and spouse is permissible.

Chapter 9   Adjustments of Debts of a Municipality
This topic is not covered in this text.

Chapter 11   Reorganization
The purpose of this chapter is to permit the debtor to remain in business by restructuring debt in accordance with an approved plan. Primarily partnerships and corporations will be involved. Although the chapter may be used by an individual proprietor, the proceedings are more cumbersome than are those of Chapter 13, which is designed specifically for individuals.

Chapter 13   Adjustment of Debts of an Individual with Regular Income
This chapter is limited exclusively to individuals, including sole proprietors, with less than $100,000 in unsecured debt and less than $350,000 in secured debt. A joint case of debtor and spouse is permissible, if their combined debt does not exceed the two limitations.

There are provisions for the movement or conversion of a case from one chapter to another, such as converting an unsuccessful reorganization (Chapter 11) to a liquidation (Chapter 7).

Commencement of a Bankruptcy Case

The Act defines a debtor as a person (individual, partnership, or corporation) residing in or having a domicile, business, or property in the United States, or a municipality. If a debtor initiates the action of filing a petition with the court of bankruptcy under the appropriate chapter of the Act, it is a *voluntary* case. Filing constitutes an *order for relief*, which represents a stay of action by prohibiting commencement or continuation of legal action against the debtor to recover a claim.

If the petition is filed by someone other than the debtor, an *involuntary* proceeding results. Such proceedings may be filed under Chapter 7

(Liquidation) or Chapter 11 (Reorganization), but not under Chapter 13, where the individual debtor is willing to make payments to creditors. Involuntary proceedings may not be initiated against a farmer or a charitable organization. Under Chapters 7 and 11, if a debtor has twelve or more creditors, three or more of them may file an involuntary petition, providing the total of their noncontingent, unsecured claims is $5,000 or more. If there are less than twelve creditors, one or more of them may initiate an involuntary case, but the same limit of $5,000 applies. In an involuntary case, the claims must have arisen before the order for relief was issued. The court will issue such an order if the debtor files no answer to the involuntary petition. If an answer is filed by the debtor, the court will hold a trial, following which it will either dismiss the case or issue an order for relief, if the debtor is not paying debts as they become due.

Chapter 7—Liquidation

The commencement of a voluntary or involuntary case under Chapter 7 (Liquidation) creates an estate that consists of the assets of the debtor, who must file an inventory of debts and property on a form called the Statement of Assets and Liabilities. This form consists of the following schedules:

Schedule A—Statement of All Liabilities of Debtor
   Schedule A-1—Creditors Having Priority (with amount of claims)
   Schedule A-2—Creditors Holding Security (with market value of security and amount of claim)
   Schedule A-3—Creditors Having Unsecured Claims Without Priority (with amount of claim)
Schedule B—Statement of All Property of Debtor
   Schedule B-1—Real Property (with market values)
   Schedule B-2—Personal Property (with market values)
   Schedule B-3—Property Not Otherwise Scheduled (includes property transferred for benefit of creditors within four months prior to filing of the petition)
   Schedule B-4—Property Claimed as Exempt (with reference to the statute creating the exemption and value claimed as exempt)

A debtor who is an individual files a list of property claimed as exempt. Such property is to be retained by the debtor in order to achieve financial survival without becoming a public charge. Exempt property normally may not be attached to satisfy claims. To determine what property is exempt, the debtor may follow either the applicable state law or the itemization under the Act, which exempts the following:

1. A homestead equity, not to exceed $7,500 in value.
2. An equity in one motor vehicle, not to exceed $1,200.
3. Household furnishings, wearing apparel, appliances, books, animals, crops, or musical instruments held primarily for use of the

    debtor or dependents, not to exceed $200 in value in any particular item.

4. An equity in family jewelry, not to exceed $500 in value.
5. An equity in any property up to $400, plus any unused amount of the $7,500 household exemption in (1). This provision offers additional protection for the debtor who does not own a home.
6. An equity in implements, professional books, or tools used in the trade of the debtor or dependents, not to exceed $750 in value.
7. Any unmatured life insurance contract owned by the debtor.
8. Debtor's right to receive social security benefits, unemployment benefits, veterans benefits, or disability benefits.

If a case is properly structured, the debtor may retain a substantial portion of property because of the exemptions. Since a debtor may use either the state or federal exemptions, a couple filing jointly may enjoy the better features of each, if one spouse uses the federal list, which is more generous in regard to personal property, while the other selects the state list, which may be more liberal in regard to real property. For example, Wisconsin law permits a debtor to retain a $25,000 equity in a homestead, in contrast to the $7,500 equity permitted by the federal law. If the debtor has a homestead worth $100,000, with a $75,000 mortgage, Wisconsin law allows retention of the $25,000 equity and, therefore, of the home. The retainable equity interest may be increased to $32,500 under a joint filing, if advantage of the federal law is retained by one spouse, who selects the $7,500 federal household equity exemption. These features have caused some to comment that the Act is unduly generous to the debtor at the expense of creditors.

As soon as possible after issuing the order for relief, the court appoints an interim trustee to take charge until a permanent trustee is selected, and a meeting of creditors is called. Creditors may either elect a permanent trustee or have the interim trustee serve in that capacity. If desired, creditors may elect a creditors' committee of 3 to 11 creditors to assist and advise the trustee in the administration of the estate. Only creditors who have filed a written proof of claim at or before the meeting are entitled to vote. Proofs of claim are examined by the trustee, who may accept them or, if they are improper, disallow them. To be considered, a claim must normally be filed within six months after the date set for the first meeting of creditors.

The debtor is required to be present at the meeting of creditors to be subject to examination by the creditors or the trustee, and must cooperate with the trustee in the preparation of an inventory of property, the examination of proofs of claim, and the general administration of the estate. To assist the trustee, a debtor files a *statement of affairs*, consisting of answers to a series of stated questions about the identity of the debtor's records and books, transactions, and events affecting the financial condition of the debtor, including any prior bankruptcy proceedings. This legal statement of affairs is not to be confused with the accounting statement of affairs discussed later in the chapter.

Duties of the Trustee. The trustee shall:

1. Collect and reduce to money the nonexempt property of the estate.
2. Account for all money and property received, maintaining a record of cash receipts and disbursements.
3. Investigate the financial affairs of the debtor, including a review of the forms filed by the debtor.
4. Examine proofs of claim and disallow any improper claim.
5. Furnish information reasonably requested by a party of interest.
6. Operate the business of the debtor, if any, when so authorized by the court, if such operation is in the best interest of the estate and consistent with its orderly liquidation.
7. Pay dividends to creditors as promptly as practicable, with regard for priorities. (The law applies the term "dividend" to any payment made to a creditor.)
8. File reports of progress, with the final report accompanied by a detailed statement of receipts and disbursements.

Disposition of Property. One duty of the trustee is to dispose of property, even if another entity has an allowed claim secured by a lien on the property. The claim is secured to the amount of the value of the property. For example, if a creditor has an allowed claim of $20,000, with a sole lien against real property whose market value is $30,000, the claim is fully secured. Upon realization of the property, the excess of $10,000 would be available to meet unsecured claims in the order of priority. However, if the creditor has an allowed claim of $35,000, there is a secured claim of $30,000 and an unsecured claim of $5,000.

Priorities for Unsecured Claims. An order of priority to receive distributions from amounts available to meet unsecured claims has been established by the Act. Each rank must be paid in full or provided for before any amount is paid to the next lower rank. When the amount is inadequate to pay all claims of a given rank, the amount is distributed on a pro rata basis within that rank. When the amount is sufficient to pay the claims of all ranks, which is highly unlikely, the excess amount is returned to the debtor. The order of priority for allowed unsecured claims is as follows:

1. Expenses to administer the estate. Those who administer the estate should be assured of payment; otherwise, competent attorneys and accountants would not be willing to participate.
2. Debts incurred after the commencement of a case of involuntary bankruptcy, but before the order for relief or appointment of a trustee. These items are granted priority in order to permit the business to carry on its operations during the period of legal proceedings.
3. Wages up to $2,000 per individual, earned within 90 days before the filing of the petition or the cessation of the debtor's business, whichever occurs first.
4. Unpaid contributions to employee benefit plans to the extent of $2,000 per employee covered by the plan, less any amount paid to participating employees under priority 3.

5. Deposits up to $900 each for goods or services never received from the debtor.
6. Tax claims of a governmental unit. Since these taxes are nondischargeable (i.e., they must still be met by the debtor after the termination of the case), the arrangement favors the debtor. Whatever funds are available for this priority will reduce the amount the debtor will have to pay later. For this reason, if a governmental unit fails to file a claim for taxes, the Act permits the debtor to do so.
7. Claims of general creditors not granted priority. All remaining unsecured claims fall into this category.

For a successful case under Chapter 11 (Reorganization) or Chapter 13 (Individual), the sequence of priority also has significance. In a Chapter 11 case, the plan of reorganization will not be confirmed unless the court has determined that creditors will receive at least as much as they would under Chapter 7. The same idea is used for Chapter 13 cases, for which the code states that the court will approve the plan only if the value of the property to be distributed on account of each allowed unsecured claim is not less than the amount that would be paid under Chapter 7.

Discharge of the Debtor. After the trustee has issued the final report, the court will grant a discharge of indebtedness, provided that the debtor is an individual and has not committed any act that would deny discharge, such as fraud, lack of cooperation, or having been granted a discharge within the past six years. The discharge absolves the debtor from debts that arose before the order for relief and voids any action to recover on such debts. Certain debts survive discharge and continue to be the responsibility of the debtor. These debts are referred to as *nondischargeable debts* and include the following:

1. Tax claims of a governmental unit.
2. Debts resulting from obtaining property or services under false pretenses.
3. Claims known by the debtor but not listed, unless the creditor had ample notice to file.
4. A claim against the debtor for larceny, embezzlement, or fraud.
5. Alimony and child support payments.
6. Debts for willful and malicious injury by the debtor to another entity or to property.
7. Fines and penalties payable to a governmental unit.
8. Most debts for educational loans, unless they first became due more than five years before the date of the petition.
9. Debts declared nondischargeable in an earlier bankruptcy proceeding.

Except for the claims listed, the discharge accomplishes the primary purpose of bankruptcy proceedings—granting the debtor a fresh start by providing relief from indebtedness.

Chapter 11—Reorganization

The ultimate purpose of an action under Chapter 11, either voluntary or involuntary, is to formulate and have confirmed a plan of reorganization that will permit continued operation of the business. Generally the debtor remains in charge, although a trustee may be appointed, but only for just cause, such as proven fraud or the debtor's inability to manage. Whether the debtor remains in possession or a trustee is appointed, the same legal statement of affairs must be filed, as in the case of a liquidation. A decision must be made on the wisdom of continuing the business operation, and a plan of reorganization must be designed and approved, or a recommendation to convert to a liquidation under Chapter 7 or a debt adjustment plan under Chapter 13 must be made.

After the filing of the petition, the law provides that the debtor shall not be harassed by creditors or stockholders, in order to afford the debtor the opportunity to devote full energy to the reorganization. For the first 120 days, the debtor has the exclusive right to file a plan of reorganization. Thereafter, a plan may be filed by any party of interest. The court appoints a committee of the creditors holding the seven largest claims against the debtor. A committee of equity security holders may also be appointed. Their primary functions are to consult with the debtor in possession (or the trustee) about the administration of the case and to assist in the formulation of a plan of reorganization.

The Plan of Reorganization. The plan of reorganization must detail the methods and means by which it will achieve its objectives. Possible arrangements will involve eliminating some debt, reducing debt principal and/or interest, reducing interest rates, postponing payment, and exchanging an equity interest for creditor claims or exchanging a lower ranking for a higher equity interest, such as substitution of common stock for preferred stock. The plan identifies the various classes of claims (secured versus unsecured) and classes of interests (stockholders or limited partners). It indicates the claims or interests that are not impaired, as well as the treatment to be accorded those that are impaired. A class is impaired if the plan alters its legal or contractual rights.

If a class is not impaired, it is considered to have accepted the plan. The holder of a claim or interest impaired by the plan may accept or reject it. If at least two thirds in amount and more than one half in number of a class of claims and at least two thirds in amount of a class of interests accept a plan, it may be confirmed by the court. Before confirmation, the court verifies that each holder of a claim or interest will receive or retain under the plan property of a value that is not less than the amount such holder would receive under a Chapter 7 liquidation.

Once a plan is confirmed by the court, its provisions are binding on the debtor and on all creditors and equity security holders, whether or not they accepted the plan. Confirmation vests property of the estate in the debtor in possession or trustee. Such property is free of all claims of creditors and interests of equity holders, except as stipulated in the provisions of the plan. If the reorganization is not accomplishing its intended objectives during the period outlined in the plan, a request for modification may be submitted to the court for approval, or a request may be filed to convert to a Chapter 7 liquidation or to a Chapter 13 adjustment of debts, whichever will be in the best interest of the parties involved. Subsequent procedures must follow those applicable to the appropriate chapter.

Accounting for a Reorganization. In accounting for a reorganization, it is useful to introduce the account Reorganization Capital, in which to collect the results of changes in the interests of various parties. To illustrate, various portions of an approved plan of reorganization are described and recorded as follows:

Reorganization Plan	Entry

100,000 shares of $50 par common are replaced by 100,000 shares of $10 par common.	Common Stock ($50 par) 5,000,000
	  Common Stock ($10 par) 1,000,000
	  Reorganization Capital 4,000,000

Preferred stockholders relinquish undeclared dividends in arrears of $160,000.	No entry is made, since dividends are undeclared and would appear only in the notes to the financial statements.
Bondholders will not collect $100,000 of unpaid interest.	Accrued Interest Payable .... 100,000 Reorganization Capital 100,000
Plant and equipment is to be reduced by $2,000,000, decreasing future depreciation charges and reflecting fair, but not unduly conservative, amounts.	Reorganization Capital .... 2,000,000 Plant and Equipment (or Accumulated Depreciation) 2,000,000
Unsecured creditors reflected in Vouchers Payable will receive 40¢ on the dollar for the $1,000,000 owed.	Vouchers Payable .... 600,000 Reorganization Capital 600,000
The deficit of $2,100,000 is to be eliminated.	Reorganization Capital .... 2,100,000 Retained Earnings 2,100,000

At this point, Retained Earnings shows no balance, and the account should be dated, as in the case of quasi-reorganizations. If the plan has been fully accomplished, the balance of $600,000 in Reorganization Capital would be shown on future balance sheets as a part of paid-in capital, rather than retained earnings.

Chapter 13—Adjustment of Debts of an Individual with Regular Income

Cases under Chapter 13 will become more numerous under the new law. Formerly, the individual had to be a wage earner, which excluded single proprietors. The Act now permits any individual whose income is sufficiently stable to meet payments under a proposed plan to request financial comfort under Chapter 13, provided that unsecured claims against the debtor do not exceed $100,000 and secured claims do not exceed $350,000. Only the debtor may file a plan to meet obligations under Chapter 13. There is no involuntary approach; debtors cannot be forced into a plan under this chapter. Upon the voluntary filing of a plan by the debtor, a trustee is appointed, whose primary responsibilities are to be present at any hearings and to advise and assist the debtor in carrying out the plan. If a business is involved, the debtor remains in charge, with the trustee reviewing its operation.

To be confirmed, the debtor's plan must provide for the transmission of all or such part of the future earnings as will permit its successful execution. The plan may modify the rights of secured claim holders or of unsecured claims, with the following restrictions:

1. That each secured claim holder has accepted the plan, or provision is made for transfer of the property securing such claim to its holder.
2. That unsecured claims entitled to priority (page 904) will be paid in full under a deferred payment arrangement.
3. That other unsecured claims shall be treated equitably and shall receive not less than they would under a Chapter 7 liquidation. No approval by unsecured claim holders is required.

After due notice, the court will hold a hearing and issue a confirmation of the plan, if there is no unresolved objection and no violation of the chapter. The plan should not normally extend beyond three years, except by specific approval of the court, in which case it may be extended, but not to exceed two additional years. Once confirmed, the plan binds the debtor and claimants. The debtor remains in possession of all property of the estate, including earnings from the debtor's services from the inception of the case until discharge. At any time, a debtor may voluntarily request a conversion from this chapter to another chapter under the Act. If the debtor fails to comply with the plan or displays unusual delay prejudicial to carrying out its requirements, any party in interest may request the court for a conversion to Chapters 7 or 11, if such action is in the best interest of the parties concerned.

When conditions of the plan have been met and payments have been completed, the court will issue a discharge, relieving the debtor of obligations provided for by the plan. A discharge may be granted by the court after a hearing, even if plan payments have not been completed, if failure to make payments is the result of circumstances over which the debtor did not have control, as in the case of a natural catastrophe that destroys the debtor's assets.

THE ACCOUNTING STATEMENT OF AFFAIRS

Earlier in this chapter a reference was made to the legal statement of affairs, which consists of responses to questions regarding a debtor's financial condition. The other report with the same name is the accounting statement of affairs, which is discussed in the remainder of this chapter. Under both a reorganization and an adjustment of the debts of an individual, the plans will not be confirmed by the court unless creditors will receive at least as much as they would under a liquidation. It is mandatory, therefore, that the estimated amounts to be received by all parties be determined. The primary purpose of the accounting statement of affairs is to approximate the dividend to each class of claims and party of interest. It thereby assists all parties concerned in reaching a decision as to what insolvency action is preferable. It is a balance sheet of a potentially liquidating concern, rather than a going concern. Thus, it shifts the emphasis for assets from historical cost to estimated realizable values and the allocation of proceeds to creditors and stockholders.

In the past, the preparation and the format of the statement of affairs have been cumbersome and confusing. Thus, a revised form is recommended, in which the statement of affairs is split into two sections, one dealing with the assets and the other with the liabilities and the owners' equity. Before the statement of affairs is prepared, however, the account balances should be fully adjusted, an income statement should be prepared, and owners' equity should be adjusted to include the net profit or net loss to date.

The asset portion of the statement of affairs in revised form would have the following columnar headings:

Assets	Book Values	Shrinkage or (Excess)	Estimated Realizable Value	Assignable to	
				Secured	Unsecured

The asset account titles and their adjusted book values are entered in the first two columns. Working with net balances is helpful, since the elimination of contra accounts, such as Allowance for Doubtful Accounts or Accumulated Depreciation, permits the direct calculation of the shrinkage or excess on realization.

The equity section is designed with the following columnar headings:

Liabilities and Owners' Equity	Book Values		Claims of		
	Owners' Equity	Liabilities	Secured	Unsecured	
				Class 1-6	Class 7

Equity accounts are listed and their adjusted balances are entered in either the Owners' Equity or the Liabilities column. Since the last three columns represent the reclassification of liabilities into legal categories, the process is easier if all liabilities appear in the adjacent column. After the amounts are entered in the book value columns, the combined sum of the Owners' Equity and Liabilities columns should equal the total of the asset Book Values column.

For each asset, the net realizable value must be estimated, using whatever information is available. For example, receivables would exclude unrealizable amounts; marketable securities would be based on current market reports; and real estate would reflect current market appraisals. Some assets, such as goodwill, may have no realizable value. The estimated realizable values are entered in the third amount column to facilitate assignment to the two categories that follow. For each asset, the difference between realizable value and book value is entered as a shrinkage or an excess. Total shrinkage or excess and total amount realizable are determined. These totals are verifiable, since total book values plus net excess or minus net shrinkage must equal total realizable values.

Estimated realizable amounts are extended, so that the amounts can be identified with the appropriate type of claim. When the amount realizable from pledged assets exceeds the claim, an amount equal to the claim is entered in the Secured column of the asset section, and any excess is entered in the Unsecured column. At the same time, in the equity section, the corresponding liability is classified as Secured. If the estimated realizable value of pledged assets is less than the claim, the entire amount expected to be realized is entered in the Secured column of the asset section, the same amount is entered in the equity section in the Secured column, and the unsecured portion of the liability is extended as a Class 7 unsecured claim, as described on page 905.

The simultaneous completion of the asset and equity sections of the statement of affairs is limited to secured portions of claims. The estimated proceeds from assets on which there is no lien are entered in the Unsecured column of the asset section, and no related entry is made in the equity section. When all estimated asset proceeds have been extended, the accuracy of the assignment of the assets should be checked by verifying that the combined totals of the amounts assigned to the Secured and Unsecured columns equal the Estimated Realizable Value column total.

In the equity section, any remaining liabilities that have not been classified must be unsecured. The six classes having a priority are grouped to determine if their total claims can be met. Class 7 claims are shown separately. The combined totals of the three columns of claims must equal the total of the Liabilities column.

The total of unsecured claims which have priority (Classes 1 through 6) is subtracted from the total realizable amount available for unsecured creditors in the asset section. The resulting difference represents the amount available to Class 7 general creditors. If the amount available for these creditors is less than their claims, there is a deficiency. If the amount available is greater than their claims, the general creditors may expect payment in full, and the excess would become available for the owners. The estimated amount available for the unsecured creditors may be inadequate to cover unsecured claims with priority in Classes 1 through 6. In this situation, the sequence of priority stipulated in the Act must be followed.

To illustrate the preparation of a statement of affairs, assume the following data for Troubled Corporation:

Cash includes $300 of uncollectible IOU memos.
Receivables are estimated to produce $14,000.
Marketable securities have a market value of $9,000.
Sale of inventories should yield $11,000.
Land and buildings can be sold for $12,000 cash, with the buyer assuming the mortgage and its unpaid interest.
The machinery will realize $4,000, of which $3,000 must be assigned to a creditor (account payable) who is owed $3,800.
All salaries qualify for priority.

The following fully adjusted balance sheet for Troubled Corporation is the basis for the statement of affairs on page 912.

Troubled Corporation
Balance Sheet
February 28, 19X0

Assets

Current assets:

Cash		$ 4,000	
Accounts receivable	$20,000		
Less allowance for doubtful accounts	2,000	18,000	
Marketable securities...		8,000	
Inventories...		40,000	$ 70,000

Property, plant, and equipment:

	Cost	Accumulated Depreciation	Book Value		
Land	$ 10,000	—	$10,000		
Buildings	70,000	$20,000	50,000		
Machinery ...	30,000	16,000	14,000		
Total	$110,000	$36,000		74,000	
Goodwill				6,000	
Total assets				$150,000	

Liabilities and Stockholders' Equity

Current liabilities:

Accounts payable...	$ 45,000	
Accrued income taxes.......................................	4,000	
Accrued interest on mortgage payable	2,000	
Accrued salaries	13,000	$ 64,000

Long-term liability:

Mortgage payable		50,000
Total liabilities...		$114,000

Stockholders' equity:

Common stock..	$ 54,000	
Additional paid-in capital....................................	6,000	
Deficit	(24,000)	36,000
Total liabilities and stockholders' equity.........................		$150,000

Troubled Corporation
Statement of Affairs
February 28, 19X0

Assets	Book Values	Shrinkage or (Excess)	Estimated Realizable Value	Assignable to Secured	Assignable to Unsecured
Cash	$ 4,000	$ 300	$ 3,700		$ 3,700
Accounts receivable (net) .	18,000	4,000	14,000		14,000
Marketable securities.....	8,000	(1,000)	9,000		9,000
Inventories..............	40,000	29,000	11,000		11,000
Land	10,000				
Buildings (net)	50,000	(4,000)	64,000	$52,000	12,000
Machinery (net)	14,000	10,000	4,000	3,000	1,000
Goodwill	6,000	6,000	-0-		
Total	$150,000	$44,300	$105,700	$55,000	$50,700
Less unsecured claims with priority (Class 1 through 6)					17,000
Available for Class 7 unsecured claims					$33,700
Class 7 unsecured claims					(42,000)
Deficiency to unsecured creditors in Class 7					$ (8,300)

Liabilities and Owners' Equity	Book Values Owners' Equity	Book Values Liabilities	Claims of Secured	Claims of Unsecured Class 1-6	Claims of Unsecured Class 7
Accounts payable		$ 45,000	$ 3,000		$42,000
Accrued items:					
Income taxes		4,000		$ 4,000	
Interest on mortgage					
payable		2,000	2,000		
Salaries................		13,000		13,000	
Mortgage payable		50,000	50,000		
Common stock	$54,000				
Additional paid-in capital .	6,000				
Deficit	(24,000)				
Total	$36,000	$114,000	$55,000	$17,000	$42,000

Since the amount of owners' equity functions as a financial cushion for creditors, the deficiency of $8,300 for Troubled Corporation is verified as follows:

Net shrinkage of assets per statement of affairs $44,300
Less stockholders' equity 36,000
Deficiency .... $ 8,300

Of interest to the unsecured creditors in Class 7 and the bankruptcy court is a ratio which is referred to as the *dividend* to general unsecured creditors. This ratio is computed as follows:

$$\text{Dividend} = \frac{\text{Net proceeds available to unsecured creditors in Class 7}}{\text{Total claims of unsecured creditors in Class 7}}$$

The dividend is an estimate of how much will be received by the unsecured creditors for each dollar owed to them, and it is expressed either in absolute amount or in percentage form.

The approximate dividend to Class 7 unsecured creditors of Troubled Corporation will be:

$$\frac{\$33,700}{\$42,000} = \$.80 \text{ on } \$1, \text{ or } 80\%$$

The secured portion of claims receives 100 cents on the dollar. Since some claims are in part fully secured and in part unsecured, they may receive different percentages of their claim, depending upon the proportion that is secured. For example, one of the accounts payable of $3,800 had a lien on machinery that is expected to realize $3,000. For the remaining $800, the amount realizable is 80%, or $640. Thus, the creditor may expect to receive $3,640, or approximately 96% of the $3,800 claim.

In a manufacturing organization, where inventories are in various stages of completion, the preparation of the statement of affairs is simplified if inventories are entered at estimated book values based on projected actions. For example, assume that the following inventory amounts appear in the trial balance of a manufacturing company:

Finished goods $110,000
Work in process 200,000
Raw materials 77,000

The plant manager estimates that the work in process in its present stages of completion would realize only $30,000 as scrap. However, if the work in process is completed by adding $27,000 of raw materials now on hand and by incurring $40,000 of additional labor, an estimated $180,000 can be realized. Thus, by investing $67,000 of additional material and labor, $150,000 may be gained.

If the book value of raw materials is realized, if $120,000 is realized for goods already completed, and if the decision is made to complete work in process, one method to show the inventories in the statement of affairs would be based on the estimated cash inflow, reduced by any required cash outlay, as follows:

Assets	Book Values	Shrinkage or (Excess)	Estimated Realizable Value
Finished goods	$110,000	$(10,000)	$120,000
Work in process	200,000	60,000	140,000*
Raw materials	77,000	27,000	50,000

*Realizable value of $180,000, less $40,000 additional labor cost.

This portrayal is inaccurate, however, since the total book value of raw materials would be realized, either by requisition to complete the work in process or by sale. The labor cost would probably not be met from the proceeds of the sale of inventory, but from whatever cash is available. Furthermore, it is not the work in process inventory that will be realized, but that inventory converted to its finished state. Therefore, a better procedure would be to adjust the inventory balances to reflect the amounts that would result if suggested actions were consummated. The amounts are determined as shown in the following T accounts, using a cost completion approach:

	Raw Materials		Work in Process		Finished Goods	
Beginning balances	77,000		200,000		110,000	
Transfer of raw materials		27,000	27,000			
Additional labor			40,000			
Transfer to finished goods				267,000	267,000	
Balances for statement of affairs	50,000		0		377,000	

The revised inventories would appear in the statement of affairs as follows:

Assets	Book Values	Shrinkage or (Excess)	Estimated Realizable Value
Finished goods	$377,000	$77,000	$300,000
Work in process	-0-		-0-
Raw materials	50,000	-0-	50,000

With this procedure, it is apparent that no shrinkage resulted from raw material realization, that work in process inventory was completed, and that finished goods would yield $300,000. The additional labor of $40,000 must appear in the equity section as accrued wages.

In addition to its use in an insolvency situation, the statement of affairs would also be useful when a company is seeking additional capital and wishes to demonstrate the strength of its financial position. The statement would be especially helpful when a company's assets have appreciated substantially. Another potential user of the statement is a company that anticipates the sale of a bond issue. If such a company prepared a pro forma statement of affairs, potential buyers of the bonds could be shown what conditions might be if the bonds were sold and the proceeds were applied to the intended project.

FIDUCIARY ACCOUNTING AND REPORTING

A fiduciary relationship is established whenever one person is entrusted with the property of another and must account for and report on its stewardship to the interested parties. In Chapter 7 liquidation cases, a fiduciary (the trustee) is responsible for specified assets, including those involved in the operation of the debtor's business until it is sold. Although the debtor usually remains in possession of the business in Chapter 11 reorganizations, a trustee may be appointed if there is evidence of mismanagement, fraud, or incompetence.

Accounting Records and Procedures

To illustrate fiduciary accounting resulting from the Act, assume that a trustee has been appointed under a Chapter 11 corporate reorganization, requiring partial liquidation of a mismanaged segment of operations, after which control is returned to a new group of officers. The fiduciary may continue with the accounting records formerly in existence or may initiate a new set, the latter procedure being more common, because it isolates results more clearly. If new accounting records are to be established, the assets accepted by the fiduciary are debited at their book values, with a credit to an account called X Corporation in Trusteeship. On the corporate books, the transfer of assets is recorded by debiting an account to charge the fiduciary, such as E. Schenker, Trustee. These new accounts are reciprocal and represent the accountability of the trustee.

The fiduciary is not responsible for commitments made by the corporation prior to the period of stewardship. Therefore, those liabilities remain on the corporate books. However, the courts may direct payment of such liabilities. In this case, the trustee may either debit X Corporation in Trusteeship directly, or create a temporary account, such as Accounts Payable—X Corporation, which is periodically closed into the major reciprocal account. The corporation would reflect payment with a debit to Accounts Payable and a credit to the account E. Schenker, Trustee.

The usual accounting procedures are followed by the trustee to record revenues and expenses. At the end of the year or at termination of the period of stewardship, the profit or loss on the trustee's books is closed into the accountability account, X Corporation in Trusteeship. On the corporate books, net income is recorded with a debit to the trustee account and a credit to Retained Earnings, while a net loss is recorded by the reverse procedure. When control is returned to the owners, the trustee eliminates all account balances, including the X Corporation in Trusteeship balance. The corporation records these accounts and eliminates the trustee account.

While the trustee is in control, the corporation's financial story is contained partly in the records of the trustee and partly in those of the corporation. The two records must be combined in order to prepare financial statements. The following skeleton work sheet is designed to accomplish the objective of reuniting the two sets of financial information:

X Corporation in Trusteeship
E. Schenker, Trustee
Work Sheet for Combined Trial Balance
For Year Ended June 30, 19X1

Account Title	Trial Balance		Adjustments and Eliminations	Combined Trial Balance
	Trustee	Corporation		
Debits:				
E. Schenker, Trustee		90,000	(a)90,000	
Total debits	500,000	420,000		
Credits:				
X Corp. in Trusteeship	90,000		(a)90,000	
Total credits	500,000	420,000		

The work sheet begins with the trial balances of the trustee's records and the corporation's records. These trial balances should be fully adjusted before they are entered on the work sheet. Any additional adjustments discovered subsequently are entered, and the two reciprocal account balances are eliminated. The items are then combined to produce a trial balance from which financial statements may be prepared.

Realization and Liquidation Account

After a trustee is appointed, the court expects to receive periodic reports on the status of the fiduciary's activities. The special report for this purpose is a legal form, called the *realization and liquidation account*. The conventional realization and liquidation account derives the title "account" from its structure, which resembles a T account. The statement consists of three main sections: assets, liabilities, and revenues and expenses. The asset section is divided into four parts, as shown on page 917.

In the Assets To Be Realized section, assets accepted by the fiduciary are itemized at book value amounts. Cash is excluded from the asset section, since it is already "realized." As an adjunct to the report, however, the court is provided with a duplication of the cash account,

Realization and Liquidation Account	
Assets	
Assets to be realized: (Itemized assets originally accepted by fiduciary) Assets acquired (or discovered): (Itemized assets subsequently acquired by fiduciary)	Assets realized: (Itemized proceeds of assets realized by fiduciary) Assets not realized: (Itemized)

which shows the beginning balance of cash as well as all receipts and disbursements. Supplementary detail is also furnished for the owners' equity. Neither the supplementary cash schedule nor the owners' equity detail is considered a part of the formal realization and liquidation account.

Additional noncash assets acquired by the fiduciary through normal activities, such as receivables resulting from sales on open account, are presented under Assets Acquired. Also included in this section are assets discovered by the fiduciary, such as additional inventory. The combination of assets to be realized and assets acquired represents the total noncash asset responsibility of the fiduciary.

Under the usual procedure, the proceeds from any asset realized are shown in the Assets Realized section. The book values of assets still unrealized at the end of the period are listed in the final section. This procedure, however, has some weaknesses, among which is the treatment of the gain or loss on realization of an asset. For example, if land which is carried in Assets To Be Realized at $10,000 is sold for $15,000, the entire $15,000 proceeds would usually be shown in Assets Realized, without specifically identifying the gain. If book values, rather than proceeds, are listed in Assets Realized, and if the gain is presented in the revenues and expenses section, tighter control is possible, since the following relationship will result:

$$\left.\begin{array}{c} \text{Total assets to be realized} \\ \text{plus} \\ \text{Total assets acquired} \end{array}\right\} \text{equals} \left\{\begin{array}{c} \text{Total assets realized} \\ \text{plus} \\ \text{Total assets not realized} \end{array}\right.$$

Another example of the weakness of the gross proceeds approach is the treatment of the sale of merchandise. The proceeds of the sale would appear in the Assets Realized section and would also appear either as an increase in cash in the supplementary cash schedule, or as an Asset Acquired in the form of receivables. Nowhere would the gross profit or loss appear. If the typical accounting approach were followed, however, the sales revenue and cost of sales would be shown in the revenues and expenses section.

Although the same net income or net loss will result from either procedure, the recommended approach is seldom found. To date, courts have been reluctant to adopt the book value approach for reflecting dispositions of assets, as is normally done in accounting. Most of the discussion that follows will, therefore, adhere to the conventional legal format in spite of its limitations.

The conventional report is also peculiar in its treatment of depreciation. Equipment accepted by the fiduciary at a net book value of $6,000, which is not yet realized and which has depreciated $1,000 at the time of the report, is typically shown in the respective sections of the realization and liquidation account as follows:

Partial Realization and Liquidation Account
Assets

Assets to be realized:	
Equipment (net) $6,000	
	Assets not realized:
	Equipment (net) $5,000

The $1,000 of depreciation is not explicitly shown. If it is desired to maintain the equality of the four divisions of the assets category, the depreciation could be shown as an expense and as an asset realized, as follows:

Partial Realization and Liquidation Account
Assets

Assets to be realized:	Assets realized:
Equipment (net) $6,000	Equipment depreciation $1,000
	Assets not realized:
	Equipment (net) $5,000

The liabilities section of the realization and liquidation account is also segmented into four parts, as follows:

Realization and Liquidation Account (continued)
Liabilities

Liabilities liquidated:	Liabilities to be liquidated:
(Itemized)	(Itemized)
Liabilities not liquidated:	Liabilities incurred:
(Itemized)	(Itemized)

The Liabilities To Be Liquidated section includes the liabilities which existed when the fiduciary was appointed. Additional liabilities arising after that time are listed under Liabilities Incurred. At the end of the period, either the liabilities will be paid or they remain to be liquidated.

Book values are more commonly used in the liabilities section than in the assets section. Thus, the following relationship exists:

$$\left.\begin{array}{c}\text{Liabilities liquidated}\\ \text{plus}\\ \text{Liabilities not liquidated}\end{array}\right\}\quad\text{equals}\quad\left\{\begin{array}{c}\text{Liabilities to be liquidated}\\ \text{plus}\\ \text{Liabilities incurred}\end{array}\right.$$

When settlement of a liability is made at less than its book value, it is recommended that the gain on the settlement be shown in the Supplementary Revenues, so that the above relationship is maintained.

The revenues and expenses section of the realization and liquidation account lists the expenses incurred by the fiduciary and the revenues earned during the period of stewardship, as follows:

Realization and Liquidation Account (continued)	
Revenues and Expenses	
Supplementary expenses: (Itemized)	Supplementary revenues: (Itemized)

The quantity and nature of the supplementary expenses and revenues included will depend on the manner in which asset and liability movements are portrayed. If book values are used, the gains and losses on these movements are listed with the expenses or the revenues, and the net income or net loss is produced within the Revenues and Expenses section itself. If presentation is based on gross proceeds, there are fewer items in this section, and the section is less revealing, because none of the gains or losses are shown. To determine the net income or net loss under the conventional gross proceeds method, it is necessary to add all debits and all credits for the three sections involved—Assets, Liabilities, and Revenues and Expenses. The difference between the two totals equals the net income or net loss for the reporting period.

To illustrate the preparation of a realization and liquidation account, assume that the Troubled Corporation on pages 911-913 is insolvent. Under Chapter 7, a trustee is appointed. All liabilities are liquidated, except the Class 7 claims and the $2,000 fee of the trustee. Assets realized the following amounts:

Assets	Book Value	Amount Realized	
Accounts receivable	$ 9,000	$ 7,000	
Marketable securities	4,000	5,000	
Inventories	40,000	11,000	sold on account
Land and buildings	60,000	12,000	cash plus assumption of mortgage and interest
Machinery	14,000	4,000	
Goodwill	6,000	-0-	

The realization and liquidation account under the conventional form of presentation appears in Illustration I on page 920. The supplementary schedules of cash and owners' equity appear on page 921.

Illustration I—Conventional Approach

Troubled Corporation
Realization and Liquidation Account
For the Ten Months Ended December 31, 19X0
Submitted by J. Hart, Trustee

Assets

Assets to be realized:			Assets realized:		
Accounts receivable (net)—			Accounts receivable—old....	$ 7,000	
old	$18,000		Marketable securities	5,000	
Marketable securities	8,000		Inventories	11,000	
Inventories	40,000		Land }	64,000	
Land	10,000		Buildings }		
Buildings (net).............	50,000		Machinery..................	4,000	$ 91,000
Machinery (net)............	14,000				
Goodwill...................	6,000	$146,000	Assets not realized:		
Assets acquired:			Accounts receivable—old....	$ 9,000	
Accounts receivable—new			—new ...	11,000	
(from sale of inventory) ...		11,000	Marketable securities	4,000	24,000

Liabilities

Liabilities liquidated:			Liabilities to be liquidated:		
Accounts payable	$ 3,000		Accounts payable ....$	45,000	
Accrued income taxes.......	4,000		Accrued income taxes.......	4,000	
Accrued interest on mortgage			Accrued interest on mortgage		
payable	2,000		payable	2,000	
Accrued salaries	13,000		Accrued salaries	13,000	
Mortgage payable	50,000	72,000	Mortgage payable	50,000	114,000
Liabilities not liquidated:			Liabilities incurred:		
Accounts payable	$42,000		Trustee's fee payable		2,000
Trustee's fee payable	2,000	44,000			

Revenues and Expenses

Supplementary expenses:			Supplementary revenues:	
Trustee's fee		2,000	(none)	
Subtotal		$275,000	Subtotal	$231,000
			Net loss	44,000
		$275,000		$275,000

Supplementary Schedules

Cash

Beginning balance	$ 4,000	Cash IOU's written off	$ 300
Proceeds from: Accounts receivable....	7,000	Payment of: Accounts payable	3,000
Marketable securities ..	5,000	Accrued income taxes.....	4,000
Land and buildings	12,000	Accrued salaries	13,000
Machinery	4,000		
Subtotal	$32,000	Subtotal	$20,300
		Balance	11,700
	$32,000		$32,000
Ending balance	$11,700		

Owners' Equity

		Common stock	$54,000
		Additional paid-in capital..............	6,000
		Deficit	(24,000)
Write-off of cash IOU's	$ 300	Beginning balance	$36,000
Net loss per realization and liquidation account	44,000		
Subtotal	$44,300		$36,000
		Balance	8,300
	$44,300		$44,300
Ending balance	$ 8,300		

Before the realization and liquidation account is submitted to the court, a condensed balance sheet should be prepared in order to verify that the major elements are still in balance. The condensed balance sheet for the Troubled Corporation is shown below.

Troubled Corporation
Condensed Balance Sheet
December 31, 19X0

Cash	$11,700	Liabilities not liquidated	$44,000
Assets not realized...........	24,000	Owners' equity...............	(8,300)
	$35,700		$35,700

A verification of net loss or net gain statement has been promoted as a substitution for the realization and liquidation account, because the verification statement is less awkward and is a more effective medium for communicating results, especially to nonaccountants. In this statement, the net loss of $44,000 is verified by comparing the book values of assets realized with their proceeds, and adding the trustee's fee to the resulting loss, as follows:

Verification of Net Loss
As Presented in Realization and Liquidation Account

	Book Value	Proceeds	Loss (Gain)
Accounts receivable—old....................	$ 9,000	$ 7,000	$ 2,000
Marketable securities	4,000	5,000	(1,000)
Inventories	40,000	11,000	29,000
Land and buildings	60,000	64,000	(4,000)
Machinery...................................	14,000	4,000	10,000
Goodwill.....................................	6,000	-0-	6,000
Subtotal.................................	$133,000	$91,000	$42,000
Trustee's fee			2,000
Net loss...................................			$44,000

The necessity for a verification of net loss or net gain statement supports the position that the conventional approach is not informative. Illustration II presents a realization and liquidation account resulting from the adoption of the book value technique. Three points in particular should be noted: (1) use of book values in the Assets Realized section, (2) the self-balancing nature of the Assets and Liabilities sections, and (3) production of the $44,000 net loss exclusively in the Revenues and Expenses section. The supplementary schedules of cash and owners' equity would remain the same.

In the realization and liquidation account, several items have possible alternative treatments. For example, the write-off of the worthless IOU's in the cash balance could have been shown as a supplementary expense, rather than as a direct debit to owners' equity. The sale of

Illustration II—Alternate Book Value Approach

Realization and Liquidation Account
For the Ten Months Ended December 31, 19X0
Submitted by J. Hart, Trustee

Assets

Assets to be realized:			Assets realized:		
Accounts receivable (net)—			Accounts receivable—old....	$ 9,000	
old......................	$18,000		Marketable securities	4,000	
Marketable securities	8,000		Inventories	40,000	
Inventories	40,000		Land and buildings	60,000	
Land.......................	10,000		Machinery..................	14,000	
Buildings (net).............	50,000		Goodwill...................	6,000	$133,000
Machinery (net).............	14,000				
Goodwill...................	6,000	$146,000			
Assets acquired:			Assets not realized:		
Accounts receivable—new			Accounts receivable—old....	$ 9,000	
(from sale of inventory) ...	11,000		—new ...	11,000	
			Marketable securities	4,000	24,000
		$157,000			$157,000

Liabilities

Liabilities liquidated:			Liabilities to be liquidated:		
Accounts payable	$ 3,000		Accounts payable	$45,000	
Accrued income taxes	4,000		Accrued income taxes	4,000	
Accrued interest on mortgage			Accrued interest on mortgage		
payable	2,000		payable	2,000	
Accrued salaries	13,000		Accrued salaries	13,000	
Mortgage payable	50,000	$ 72,000	Mortgage payable	50,000	$114,000
Liabilities not liquidated:			Liabilities incurred:		
Accounts payable	$42,000		Trustee's fee payable		2,000
Trustee's fee payable	2,000	44,000			
		$116,000			$116,000

Revenues and Expenses

Supplementary expenses:			Supplementary revenues:		
Loss on realization of:			Sales of inventory	$11,000	
Accounts receivable—old ..	$ 2,000		Gain on sale of marketable		
Machinery	10,000		securities	1,000	
Goodwill	6,000		Gain on sale of land and build-		
Cost of inventory sold	40,000		ings	4,000	$ 16,000
Trustee's fee	2,000	$ 60,000	Net loss		44,000
		$ 60,000			$ 60,000

inventory on account could be shown as a supplementary revenue, rather than as an asset realized. If book values are maintained in the Assets Realized section, the write-off of goodwill could be shown as a supplementary expense and as an asset realized.

Variations in treatment are more significant in the preparation of a realization and liquidation account for a fiduciary who continues to operate a company while attempting to resolve its problems. Since the fiduciary prepares periodic statements of income in which nominal elements of revenue and expense are presented in their customary form, it would seem advisable to manipulate the realization and liquidation account so that these elements can simply be transferred to the revenues and expenses section. Thus, depreciation and other write-offs, as well as gains and losses on realizations, would be entered as supplementary expenses or revenues. This process would be logical for accountants, since they would be basing their report on standard accounting procedures and entries. For example, the purchase of inventory and the sale of goods under a perpetual inventory system would require the following normal entries and would be reported in the realization and liquidation account, as follows:

Event	Entry
Purchase of inventory	Inventory (Assets acquired) Accounts Payable (Liabilities incurred)
Cost of sales	Cost of Goods Sold (Supplementary expenses) Inventory (Assets realized)

Although the courts generally require reports to be based on the perpetual system, a periodic system could be used. Under such a system, the same events would be presented as follows:

Event	Entry
Purchase of inventory	Purchases (Supplementary expenses) Accounts Payable (Liabilities incurred)
Cost of sales	No entry for cost of sales

The totals of the realization and liquidation account will be influenced automatically by the cost of goods sold, as a result of reporting the following items:

Debits	Credits
Beginning inventory (Assets to be realized) Purchases (Supplementary expenses)	Ending inventory (Assets not realized)

In reports of stewardship, the fiduciary must follow the wishes of the court. However, communication and reporting techniques could be improved by a cooperative effort between the legal and accounting professions.

QUESTIONS

1. Of the various procedures available to an insolvent debtor, which is the simplest? Under what conditions would the procedure be accepted by creditors?
2. What are the four operative chapters of the Bankruptcy Reform Act of 1978, and what area does each one cover?
3. Distinguish between a voluntary and an involuntary case under the Bankruptcy Reform Act.
4. Under a Chapter 7 liquidation, what procedure should a debtor follow to maximize the amount of property claimed as exempt?
5. What are the responsibilities of a debtor under a Chapter 7 liquidation, once a trustee has been appointed?
6. Explain under what condition a creditor's claim could be in part secured and in part unsecured.
7. Under the Bankruptcy Reform Act, do all unsecured creditors share pro rata in funds as they become available? Explain.
8. Define *nondischargeable debts* and give several illustrations.
9. What is the primary difference between a full and a quasi-reorganization?
10. What purpose is served by the account Reorganization Capital?

11. Explain the requirement for dating retained earnings after a reorganization.
12. Differentiate between the legal statement of affairs and the accounting statement of affairs.
13. When an accounting statement of affairs is prepared by the method illustrated in the chapter, five checkpoints are available to monitor whether equalities are being maintained. List the five equality checkpoints.
14. What is the nature of the dividend as typically computed from the accounting statement of affairs? Will all creditors receive this percentage of their claims?
15. Describe the preferred procedure for dealing with work in process inventory in the accounting statement of affairs, when the intention is to complete the inventory to maximize the amount to be realized.
16. Describe the nature of a fiduciary relationship.
17. Explain the relationship between the accounts Carter Corporation in Trustee-ship and J. Haertel, Trustee.
18. Explain why it is often necessary to use a work sheet to produce a combined trial balance for a company in trusteeship.
19. What function does the realization and liquidation account serve? Explain the nature of its three principal segments.
20. Discuss variations in the treatment of items that might be included in a realization and liquidation account.

EXERCISES

Exercise 1. The stockholders of the Walt Company have authorized the company to go through a quasi-reorganization to revise asset valuations and eliminate its deficit. A condensed balance sheet at October 1, 19X3, just prior to the quasi-reorganization, is as follows:

Current assets	$100,000	Liabilities	$150,000
Property, plant, and equip-		Capital stock ($10 par)	550,000
ment (net)	500,000	Deficit	(100,000)
	$600,000		$600,000

Additional data:
  (a) Inventories have been determined to be overvalued by $40,000.
  (b) Plant assets have been currently appraised at $400,000.
  (c) Stockholders have approved a reduction in par value of the capital stock to $5 per share.
(1) Prepare the journal entries necessary to record the quasi-reorganization.
(2) Prepare a balance sheet immediately after the above reorganization.

Exercise 2. The Kline Corporation received the necessary approval of two thirds of its stockholders to undergo a quasi-reorganization. A condensed current balance sheet at June 1, 19X8, and the plan to implement the quasi-reorganization are as follows:
  The plan of quasi-reorganization calls for the following procedures:
  (a) Plant and equipment is to be reduced to a book value of $300,000 through an adjustment to the accumulated depreciation account.
  (b) For each share of 6%, $100 par, cumulative preferred stock, holders are to receive 2 shares of 8%, $40 par, noncumulative preferred stock. Dividends in arrears are to be sacrificed.
  (c) The par value of common stock is to be reduced to $5 per share.

Assets

Current assets:
Cash	$ 40,000	
Accounts receivable (net)	120,000	
Inventories	100,000	
Total current assets.............................		$260,000

Property, plant, and equipment:
Land		$200,000	
Plant and equipment...........................	$500,000		
Less accumulated depreciation	150,000	350,000	550,000
Total assets			$810,000

Liabilities and Stockholders' Equity

Current liabilities	$150,000	
8% Bonds payable	300,000	
Total liabilities.....................................		$450,000
Preferred stock (cumulative 6%, $100 par; dividends are three years in arrears)	$200,000	
Common stock ($20 par)	400,000	
Deficit	(240,000)	360,000
Total liabilities and stockholders' equity.............		$810,000

(1) Prepare the journal entries to reflect the quasi-reorganization.
(2) Prepare a balance sheet, after giving effect to the reorganization.

Exercise 3. J. Wachs, CPA, has prepared a statement of affairs. Assets against which there are no claims or liens are expected to produce $70,000, which must be allocated to unsecured claims of all classes totaling $105,000. The following are some of the claims outstanding:
  (a) Accounting fees for Wachs, $1,500.
  (b) An unsecured note for $1,000, on which $60 of interest has accrued, held by S. Bart.
  (c) A note for $3,000, secured by $4,000 of receivables, estimated to be 60% collectible, held by J. Gamble.
  (d) A $1,500 note, on which $30 of interest has accrued, held by B. Land. Property with a book value of $1,000 and a market value of $1,800 is pledged to guarantee payment of principal and interest.
  (e) Unpaid income taxes of $3,500.

From the information above, determine:
(1) The total amount allocable to unsecured claims with priority.
(2) The dividend per each dollar of Class 7 unsecured claims.
(3) The amount each of the claimants may expect to realize.

Exercise 4. Starr Manufacturing Company is in financial trouble. The following information relative to its inventories has been gathered:
  Before completion, work in process and finished goods have cost bases of $30,000 and $28,000, respectively. To complete the processing, it is estimated that $13,000 of the $24,000 of raw materials now in stock will be used, and $16,000 of other expenses will be incurred. Unused raw materials will realize $.50 on the dollar. All finished goods are expected to realize 120% of cost. No liens exist on any inventories.

Using the cost completion approach and supporting T accounts for the three inventories, show how the inventories would appear in the asset section of the accounting statement of affairs.

Exercise 5. The book values and estimated realizable values of the assets of Lamp Company are as follows:

	Book Value	Realizable Value
Cash	$ 5,000	$ 5,000
Receivables	50,000	30,000
Inventory	70,000	52,000
Land and Building	300,000	220,000
Equipment	200,000	50,000
Total	$625,000	$357,000

Liabilities of the Lamp Company are as follows:

Accounts payable	$ 80,000
Wages payable (eligible for priority)	5,000
Taxes payable	10,000
Interest on notes payable	2,000
Interest on mortgage payable	4,000
Notes payable (secured by receivables and inventory)	200,000
Mortgage payable (secured by land and building)	200,000
Total	$501,000

(1) Prepare a schedule to determine the amount available for Class 7 unsecured claims.
(2) Determine the dividend to Class 7 unsecured claims.
(3) Prepare a schedule showing the amount to be paid each of the creditor groups upon distribution of the $357,000 estimated proceeds.

Exercise 6. Under Chapter 7 of the Bankruptcy Reform Act, Martin Company is to proceed with liquidation. A trustee has been appointed, and the following transactions occurred:

    a. Receivables collected amount to $9,000. Uncollectible accounts of $1,500 are written off.
    b. Accrued wages of $1,200 are paid.
    c. Bonds payable of $100,000 face value, originally sold at face value, are retired at 85, plus accrued interest of $3,000.
    d. Securities costing $8,000 are sold for $7,500, less brokerage fee of $210.
    e. Depreciation on machinery is $600.
    f. Payments on accounts payable total $6,500.
    g. A machine that originally cost $15,000 and has a book value of $5,000 is sold for $6,000.

Using the preferred accounting approach, indicate how each of the transactions would be shown on the realization and liquidation account and on the supplementary schedules.

    Example:
        Inventory with a book value of $9,000 was sold for $10,000, of which $2,500 was collected in cash.
    Solution:

Cash (in Cash Schedule)	2,500	
Assets Acquired—Receivables	7,500	
Supplementary Revenues—Sales		10,000
Supplementary Expenses—Cost of Goods Sold	9,000	
Assets Realized—Inventory		9,000

Exercise 7. The partially completed asset section of a realization and liquidation account is as follows:

Rainbow Company
Realization and Liquidation Account
For the Six Months Ended June 30, 19X2
Submitted by M. Mares, Trustee

Assets

Assets to be realized:		Assets realized:	
Receivables (net)—old	$20,000		
Marketable securities	8,000		
Inventory	?	Inventory	$15,000
Land	30,000		
Building (net)	20,000		
Equipment (net)	20,000		
Assets acquired:		Assets not realized:	
		Receivables (net)—old	$ 8,000

Additional information:
(a) All of the inventory was sold on account at 20% above cost.
(b) Of the old receivables, $3,000 were written off as uncollectible. Of the new receivables, 50% were collected.
(c) The marketable securities consisted of 100 shares of Day Industries stock. These shares were sold at 60. Brokerage commissions and fees were $180.
(d) The land and building were sold for $30,000, subject to a $25,000 mortgage.
(e) The equipment was sold for $15,000 on terms of ⅓ down and a six-month, 8% note accepted for the remainder.

Complete the asset section of the realization and liquidation account, using net proceeds for assets realized, rather than book values.

PROBLEMS

Problem 21-1. Current conditions warrant that the Peters Company have a quasi-reorganization (corporate readjustment) at December 31, 19X1. Selected balance sheet items prior to the quasi-reorganization are as follows:
(a) Inventory was recorded in the accounting records at December 31, 19X1, at its market value of $3,000,000.
(b) Property, plant, and equipment was recorded in the accounting records at December 31, 19X1, at $6,000,000 net of accumulated depreciation.
(c) Stockholders' equity consisted of:

Common stock, $10 par; 350,000 shares authorized, issued, and outstanding	$3,500,000
Additional paid-in capital	800,000
Retained earnings (deficit)	(450,000)
Total stockholders' equity	$3,850,000

Additional information is as follows:
(d) Inventory cost at December 31, 19X1, was $3,250,000.
(e) Property, plant, and equipment had a fair value of $4,000,000 on

December 31, 19X1.

(f) The par value of the common stock is to be reduced from $10 per share to $5 per share.

Required:

(1) Prepare the journal entries to record the quasi-reorganization.

(2) Prepare the stockholders' equity section of the Peters Company's balance sheet at December 31, 19X1, as it should appear after the quasi-reorganization has been accomplished. Ignore income tax and deferred tax considerations.   (AICPA adapted)

Problem 21-2.   The audit of Shaky Company has just begun for the year ended December 31, 19X6. The president indicates that the company is insolvent and may require liquidation, unless a large loan can be obtained immediately. A lender who is willing to advance $450,000 to the company has been located, but the loan will be subject to the following conditions:

(a) A $600,000, 9% mortgage payable on the company's land and buildings held by a major stockholder will be canceled, with four months' accrued interest. The mortgage will be replaced by 5,000 shares of $100 par, 6% cumulative (if earned) nonparticipating preferred stock.

(b) The $450,000 loan will require that a 10% mortgage be placed on the land and buildings as security. The 10% mortgage principal is payable in equal installments over 15 years.

(c) On May 1, 19X5, the company's trade creditors accepted $360,000 in notes payable on demand at 6% interest in settlement of all past due accounts. No payment has been made to date. The company will offer to settle these liabilities at $.75 per $1 owed or to replace the notes payable on demand with new notes payable for the full amount of the indebtedness, including accrued interest. The new notes pay interest at 8% and mature in five years. It is estimated that $200,000 of the demand notes will be exchanged for the longer-term notes and that the other creditors will accept the offer of a reduced cash settlement.

(d) A new issue of 500 shares of $100 par, 5% noncumulative, nonparticipating preferred stock will replace 500 outstanding shares of $100 par, 7% cumulative, participating preferred stock. Preferred stockholders will repudiate all claims to $21,000 of dividends in arrears. The company has never formally declared the dividends.

(e) A new issue of 600 shares of $50 par, class A common stock will replace 600 outstanding shares of $100 par, class A common stock.

(f) A new issue of 650 shares of $40 par, class B common stock will replace 650 outstanding shares of $100 par, class B common stock.

The president of the Shaky Company requests that the auditor determine the effect of the foregoing on the company and furnishes the following condensed account balances, which the auditor believes are fairly presented:

Bank overdraft	$ 15,000
Other current assets	410,000
Property, plant, and equipment	840,000
Trade accounts payable	235,000
Other current liabilities	85,000
Paid-in capital in excess of par on 7% cumulative preferred	125,000
Retained earnings (deficit)	345,000

Required:

    (1) Prepare pro forma journal entries to give effect to the foregoing as of January 1, 19X7. Key entries to lettered information.

    (2) Prepare a pro forma balance sheet as of January 1, 19X7, as if the reorganization had been consummated.   (AICPA adapted)

Problem 21-3. A proposal for the reorganization of Duke Corporation has been presented to the court. To aid the court in deciding on the efficacy of the proposal, an accountant has been asked to examine it and to prepare comparative balance sheets before and after the proposed reorganization. The following balance sheet and summary of the proposed reorganization are provided:

Duke Corporation
Balance Sheet
October 31, 19X1

Assets

Cash	$ 287,500
Other current assets	1,437,500
Bond sinking fund	625,000
Land	1,350,000
Plant and equipment	9,000,000
Accumulated depreciation	(5,000,000)
Total assets	$7,700,000

Liabilities and Stockholders' Equity

Preferred dividends payable	$ 45,000
Bond interest payable	424,760
Other current liabilities	44,400
Mortgage bonds payable—11%	2,500,000
Mortgage bonds payable—8%	1,872,000
Discount on 8% bonds payable	(212,500)
Preferred stock, $6 cumulative, no par, 7,500 shares issued	843,750
Preferred stock, $7.50 noncumulative, no par, 20,000 shares issued	2,125,000
Common stock, no par, 50,000 shares issued	781,250
Deficit	(723,660)
Total liabilities and stockholders' equity	$7,700,000

Details of the reorganization proposal are as follows:

    (a) The preferred dividends payable constitute an illegal dividend declaration because of the deficit. The dividends are to be eliminated.

    (b) Consolidated first mortgage 10% bonds of $3,750,000, dated November 1, 19X1, and redeemable on November 1 ten years hence, are to be sold on December 1, 19X1, at 95 plus accrued interest.

    (c) Outstanding 8% and 11% bonds are to be redeemed on December 1, 19X1, at their November 1, 19X1 book values plus accrued interest for 6 months only.

    (d) The $6 preferred stock is to be replaced by 6%, $100 par preferred stock.

    (e) New $5 par common stock is to be exchanged on the following basis: 20 shares of new common for each share of $7.50 preferred stock; 2 shares of new common for each share of old, no-par common stock.

Required:

On 4-column journal paper, indicate the revisions in the present balance sheet and produce a pro forma balance sheet resulting from the plan of reorganization. Suggested headings for the amount columns are:

Column 1—Balance Sheet before Reorganization

2 and 3—Reorganization Entries

4—Balance Sheet after Reorganization

Problem 21-4. Creditors of Lap Company are concerned because payments are not being met. On March 15, 19X4, the following balance sheet was prepared:

Assets

Cash		$ 10,000
Notes receivable (net of discounted notes)		15,000
Accounts receivable (net of allowance for uncollectibles)......		24,000
Inventory		20,000
Prepaid expenses		1,000
Land		16,000
Buildings	$50,000	
Less accumulated depreciation	20,000	30,000
Machinery	$30,000	
Less accumulated depreciation	18,000	12,000
Goodwill		4,000
Total assets		$132,000

Liabilities and Stockholders' Equity

Notes payable		$ 15,000
Accounts payable		20,000
Accrued interest on notes payable		450
Accrued interest on mortgage payable		700
Accrued wages payable		6,100
Taxes payable		2,200
Mortgage payable		25,000
Total liabilities		$ 69,450
Capital stock	$80,000	
Deficit	(17,450)	62,550
Total liabilities and stockholders' equity....................		$132,000

Additional information:

(a) Customers' notes receivable of $5,000 were discounted at the bank with recourse. These notes were due March 10, 19X4. No payments have been made to the bank, nor is the liability reflected in the balance sheet. Accrued interest and protest fees on the dishonored notes will amount to $250. In addition, $10,000 of notes receivable have been pledged to one of the creditors for an account payable of $12,000. All nondiscounted notes are collectible.

(b) Accounts receivable are classified as follows:

	Book Value	Estimated Realization
Good accounts	$ 8,000	$ 8,000
Doubtful accounts ...	10,000	6,000
Bad accounts........	6,000	-0-
Total	$24,000	$14,000

Good accounts receivable of $4,000 have been pledged to the holder of a $3,000 note payable on which there is $100 of accrued interest.

(c) The mortgage payable held by the bank is secured by a lien upon the land and buildings. Lap Company has received an offer to purchase the land and buildings for $38,000.

(d) Machinery will realize about $9,000. Inventory can be sold at 80% of cost. Nothing is realizable from prepaid expenses.

(e) Liquidation expenses are expected to be $1,000, plus a trustee's fee of $2,000.

(f) Wages payable include $2,400 of unpaid salary to the company president. All wages are earned within the preceding 90-day period.

Required:

(1) Prepare a statement of affairs. (*Suggestion:* Adjust or create any real accounts necessary, based on the data provided, before entering book values in the statement of affairs.)

(2) Determine the dividend to Class 7 unsecured claims.

Problem 21-5. The balance sheet of the Warren Manufacturing Company as of August 31, 19X7, is shown on page 933.

Carbo Corporation, a subsidiary of Warren, is undergoing liquidation, with the prospect of paying its creditors at the rate of $.40 on the dollar. The Warren Manufacturing Company is thereby in financial difficulty, and its creditors call for a statement of affairs and a deficiency statement.

The following additional information is available:

(a) Estimated realizable values of:

Land	$11,000
Buildings	16,500
Machinery and equipment	17,600
Finished goods	4,400
Work in process	2,200
Raw materials	8,800

(b) In the cash drawer are found $55 of collectible IOU's, not included in the cash account balance.

(c) Notes receivable and interest are collectible.

(d) Accounts receivable are expected to realize the following amounts:

	Book Value	Realizable Value
Good accounts	$13,200	$13,200
Doubtful accounts	11,000	5,610
Bad accounts....................	9,240	-0-
Total	$33,440	$18,810

(e) Prepaid expenses have no realizable value.

(f) Notes payable consist of:

A note for $9,900, secured by notes receivable of $1,100 and by warehouse receipts for raw materials having a book value of $3,850 and an estimated realizable value of $3,300.

A note for $7,150, which is unsecured.

A note for $2,750, on which $33 interest has accrued, secured by notes receivable of $3,300.

A note for $29,700, with accrued interest of $187. The holder of the note also holds the Carbo Corporation stock as collateral.

(g) All wages payable qualify as priority items.

Assets

Current assets:

Cash		$ 660	
Notes receivable		5,500	
Accrued interest on notes receivable		44	
Accounts receivable	$33,440		
Less allowance for doubtful accounts	275	33,165	
Inventories: Finished goods	$ 6,050		
Work in process	7,150		
Raw materials	14,300	27,500	
Prepaid expenses		540	$ 67,409

Investments:

Carbo Corporation stock		$52,800	
Advance to Carbo Corporation		22,000	74,800

Property, plant, equipment, and intangibles:

Land		$ 9,900	
Buildings	$38,500		
Less accumulated depreciation	6,600	31,900	
Machinery and equipment	$30,000		
Less accumulated depreciation	4,590	25,410	
Goodwill		13,200	80,410
Total assets			$222,619

Liabilities and Stockholders' Equity

Current liabilities:

Notes payable		$49,500	
Accounts payable		44,000	
Wages payable		880	
Taxes payable		825	
Mortgage interest payable		440	
Note interest payable		220	$ 95,865

Long-term liabilities:

8% Mortgage payable on land and buildings			11,000
Total liabilities			$106,865

Stockholders' equity:

Common stock ($10 par)		$66,000	
Retained earnings:			
Appropriated for expansion	$16,500		
Unappropriated balance	33,254	49,754	115,754
Total liabilities and stockholders' equity			$222,619

Required:

(1) Prepare a statement of affairs.

(2) Prepare a deficiency statement.

Problem 21-6. The Scott Furniture Company has been finding it increasingly difficult to meet its obligations. Although its sales volume appeared to be satisfactory and it was showing a profit, the requirements for capital for inventory and time contracts were greater than the company could provide. Finally, after pledging all of its installment accounts, it found itself unable to meet the bills falling due on October 10, 19X4. It is the opinion of management that if it could obtain an extension of time in which to pay its obligations, it could meet its liabilities in full. The corporation has arranged for a meeting of creditors to determine if the company should be granted an extension or file for liquidation under Chapter 7.

The company's trial balance for the current calendar year on September 30, 19X4, is as follows:

Cash	2,120	
Installment Contracts (pledged)	215,000	
Allowance for Bad Contracts		13,440
Accounts Receivable (30 day)	20,830	
Allowance for Doubtful Accounts		1,050
Inventories—January 1, 19X4	151,150	
Prepaid Insurance	1,490	
Land	10,240	
Buildings	89,760	
Accumulated Depreciation—Buildings		7,530
Furniture and Equipment	12,500	
Accumulated Depreciation—Furniture and Equipment		2,140
Autos and Trucks	22,380	
Accumulated Depreciation—Autos and Trucks		14,960
Organization Expense	880	
Customer Deposit		2,000
Trade Accounts Payable		100,100
Contract Payable (on furniture and equipment)		5,800
Chattel Mortgage (on auto and trucks)		10,000
Bank Loan (secured by installment contracts)		161,250
Taxes Payable		14,220
Accrued Salaries and Retirement Plan Contributions		34,680
Accrued Interest		10,990
Notes Payable (stockholder)		100,000
First Mortgage Payable		49,000
Capital Stock		100,000
Deficit	65,290	
Sales		708,900
Purchases	527,630	
Expenses and Miscellaneous Income (net)	216,790	
	1,336,060	1,336,060

The following additional data are obtained from further investigation:
(a) Depreciation, doubtful accounts, and prepaid and accrued items had all been adjusted as of September 30, 19X4.
(b) All installment contracts had been pledged with the bank on September 30, 19X4. The bank had deducted its interest to date and had increased the company loan to equal 75% of the face amount of the contracts in accordance with a loan agreement. It was estimated that a forced liquidation would result in a loss of $40,000 from the face amount of the contracts.
(c) Thirty-day accounts receivable were not pledged, and it was estimated that they would provide $16,500 on a liquidation basis.
(d) It was estimated that since January 1, 19X4, the company had made a gross profit of 33⅓%, but that the inventory on hand would provide only $100,000 on a forced liquidation.
(e) Cancellation of the insurance would provide $990.

(f) All autos and trucks were covered by a chattel mortgage, and their total market value was $8,000. State law permits attempt of full recovery on a chattel mortgage.

(g) The store had been remodeled in 19X3, and the furniture and equipment had been acquired on contract. Because of its special utility, it was estimated that on a forced sale, no more than $5,000 could be expected. The contractor has a lien against the furniture and equipment.

(h) The land and buildings were subject to a 6% first mortgage on which interest had been paid to July 30, 19X4. It was estimated that the property could be sold for $75,000.

(i) The notes payable to stockholders had not been subordinated to general creditors. The notes carried a 6% rate of interest, but no interest had been paid since December 31, 19X2.

(j) Since prior income tax returns disclosed a large available net operating loss carryover, no current income tax need be considered.

(k) The cost of liquidation proceedings was estimated to be $5,000.

(l) Unpaid salaries were earned within the past three months. Payroll and retirement fund records reveal the following:

Employee	Unpaid Salary	Retirement Contributions Payable	Total
V. Gehrig	$ 1,000	$1,100	$ 2,100
J. Pascale	2,400	-0-	2,400
A. Knapp	-0-	2,800	2,800
R. Elder	1,700	600	2,300
P. Tellier	1,400	300	1,700
M. Taylor	2,600	900	3,500
Subtotal.....	$ 9,100	$5,700	$14,800
Other employees whose salaries qualify for priority	19,880	-0-	19,880
Total	$28,980	$5,700	$34,680

(m) The customer deposit was received for a leather sofa. It was learned that the style has been discontinued by the manufacturer.

(n) There appeared to be no other values upon liquidation and no unrecorded liabilities.

Required:

(1) Prepare a statement of affairs as of September 30, 19X4.

(2) Compute the percentage of recovery for Class 7 unsecured claims.

(AICPA adapted)

Problem 21-7. A creditors' committee of the Carole Company has obtained the March 31, 19X5 balance sheet shown on page 936.

An analysis of the company's accounts disclosed the following:

(a) Carole Company started business on April 1, 19X0, with authorized stock of $100 par. Of the 1,000 authorized shares, 750 were paid for in full at par, and 250 were subscribed at par, with a required 20% down payment and the balance payable upon call. The Subscriptions Receivable is all due from Wesley Krueger, president of the company, and is fully collectible.

(b) Marketable securities include the $25,000 cost of U.S. Treasury bonds and 25 shares of common stock of Groves Company, costing $2,750, with a

Assets

Current assets:

Cash		$ 11,250	
Marketable securities		28,750	
Notes receivable	$ 10,000		
Less notes receivable discounted	10,000	-0-	
Accounts receivable	$ 15,000		
Less allowance for doubtful accounts	1,000	14,000	
Subscriptions receivable		20,000	
Inventories:			
Finished goods...............................	$ 27,500		
Work in process	11,250		
Raw materials	15,000	53,750	
Total current assets			$127,750
Property, plant, and equipment:			
Land and building.............................	$112,500		
Equipment	60,000	$172,500	
Less accumulated depreciation		50,000	
Total property, plant, and equipment			122,500
Total assets			$250,250

Liabilities and Stockholders' Equity

Current liabilities:			
Notes payable		$ 87,500	
Accounts payable		60,000	
Salaries payable		2,650	
Property tax payable		1,150	
Total current liabilities		$151,300	
Long-term liabilities:			
First mortgage payable	$ 37,500		
Second mortgage payable	50,000	87,500	
Total liabilities			$238,800
Stockholders' equity:			
Common stock, $100 par (1,000 shares authorized)			
750 shares issued		$ 75,000	
250 shares subscribed		25,000	
Total		$100,000	
Retained earnings (deficit)		(88,550)	
Total stockholders' equity			11,450
Total liabilities and stockholders' equity			$250,250

market value of $3,300. Treasury stock was also included in the marketable securities at a cost of $1,000 for the 40 shares.

(c) The land originally cost $10,000, and the building was erected at a cost of $102,500. Of the accumulated depreciation, $30,000 is applicable to the building. The realizable value of the real estate is $75,000.

(d) Notes receivable were endorsed with recourse when discounted and are expected to be dishonored. Of the accounts receivable, $3,000 are considered collectible.

(e) Inventories are shown at cost. Any finished goods are expected to yield 110% of cost. If scrapped, goods in process have a realizable value of only

$2,200. It is estimated, however, that the work in process can be completed by the addition of $3,000 of present raw materials and an expenditure of $3,500 for labor. The raw materials deteriorate rapidly and will realize only 20% of cost. (Use the cost completion method illustrated in the text.)

(f) Equipment is estimated to have a realizable value of $12,000.

(g) Notes payable include a $25,000 note to Aerotex Company and a $62,500 note to B. Williams. Aerotex holds $15,000 of U.S. Treasury bonds as security for its loans. It also holds the first mortgage of $37,500 on the company's real estate, interest on which is paid through March 31, 19X5. The note payable to Williams is secured by a chattel mortgage on factory equipment. Interest on the note has been paid through March 31, 19X5. Williams also holds the second mortgage on the real estate.

(h) Any expenses not specifically mentioned need not be considered. All salaries qualify for priority, including labor to complete the work in process.

Required:

(1) Prepare a statement of affairs for the Carole Company.

(2) Prepare a schedule indicating the percentage of recovery by each creditor.

Problem 21-8. In an attempt to save the Sammer Company, a fiduciary was appointed by the court to conduct the company's operations. An examination showed that the balance sheet as of June 1, 19X5, was as follows:

Assets		Liabilities and Capital	
Marketable securities	$ 12,000	Cash overdraft	$ 6,000
Accounts receivable	60,000	Notes payable	24,000
Allowance for doubtful accounts	(4,000)	Accrued interest on notes	400
		Accounts payable	56,000
Inventory	42,000	Mortgage payable	50,000
Plant and equipment	206,000	R. Sammer, Capital	39,600
Accumulated depreciation	(140,000)		
Total assets	$176,000	Total liabilities and capital	$176,000

During the five months that the fiduciary was guiding the company's activities, the cash account showed the following events:

CASH

Cash receipts:		June 1, 19X5 overdraft	6,000
New accounts receivable	54,000	Cash disbursements:	
Old accounts receivable	44,000	Mortgage payable	8,000
		Notes payable	20,000
Sale of all securities	8,000	Accrued interest on notes	400
		Accounts payable—old	40,000
		Operating expenses	18,000
		Fiduciary's fee	2,000
			94,400
		October 31 balance	11,600
	106,000		106,000
October 31 balance	11,600		

Additional data:

Sales on account for the five months	$70,000
Purchases of inventory on account for the five months	16,000
Inventory as of October 31	9,000
Old accounts receivable written off as uncollectible .	12,000
Depreciation on plant and equipment for five months	3,600
Accrued expenses on October 31	1,100

Required:

Prepare a realization and liquidation account in conventional form for the five months ended October 31, 19X5. Use proceeds rather than book values, and include a supplementary schedule for owner's equity.

Problem 21-9. The following balance sheet was prepared for Hamilton Industries on July 1, 19X9, the date a trustee was appointed to take over control because of serious disagreement among major stockholders:

Assets

Current assets:		
Cash	$ 6,000	
Receivables (net)	14,000	
Inventory	22,000	$42,000
Property, plant, and equipment:		
Land	$20,000	
Building (net)	18,000	
Equipment (net)	24,000	62,000
Total assets		$104,000

Liabilities and Stockholders' Equity

Current liabilities:		
Notes payable	$12,000	
Accounts payable	18,000	
Taxes payable	4,000	
Accrued mortgage interest	500	$ 34,500
Long-term liabilities:		
Mortgage payable		25,000
Total liabilities		$ 59,500
Stockholders' equity:		
Common stock ($100 par)	$60,000	
Retained earnings (deficit)	(15,500)	44,500
Total liabilities and stockholders' equity		$104,000

Transactions for July are summarized as follows:

Cash receipts:	
Sales for cash	$18,000
Collection of receivables	8,000
Sale of equipment	4,000
	$30,000

Cash disbursed for payment of:

Accounts payable	$ 6,000
Mortgage interest	500
Taxes	4,000
Salaries	1,000
	$11,500

Inventory sold for cash during July cost $14,000.
Receivables of $1,500 were written off during July.
Equipment sold had a book value of $5,000.
Depreciation on the building and equipment for July was $150 and $320, respectively.

Required:

Prepare a realization and liquidation account for July, using the conventional gross proceeds approach. Include proper supplementary schedules.

Problem 21-10. Using the information in Problem 21-9, prepare a realization and liquidation account for July, following the approach that uses book values, as recommended in the chapter. The supplementary schedules for cash and for owners' equity need not be prepared, since they would be identical to the schedules prepared for Problem 21-9.

Problem 21-11. On petition of creditors, CB Radio Corporation was placed in trusteeship by order of a district court in an attempt to reinstate it on a sound financial base. As of January 1, 19X1, the trustee took over all of the corporate assets shown in the balance sheet on page 941, but would record only payments of liabilities previously incurred by the corporation. Gains and losses on the disposition of assets acquired by the corporation are to be attributed to the corporation rather than to the trustee.

Additional data to be considered:

(a) Old accounts receivable amounting to $13,000 were written off. On the new accounts receivable, a provision to cover estimated uncollectible accounts of $2,000 is made.

(b) Depreciation expense for the year was 12% on machinery and equipment, 4% on buildings (80% to factory and 10% each to selling and administrative), and 10% on office equipment.

(c) Prepaid insurance as of January 1, 19X1, should be charged as follows: $2,000 to manufacturing, $600 to selling, and $400 to administrative expenses.

(d) The following summary of transactions occurring during the next calendar year was prepared:

Sales on account, $500,000
Purchases of raw materials on account, $150,000
Cash receipts include:

Collection on old accounts receivable	$197,000
Collection on old notes receivable	30,000
Collection on new accounts receivable	400,000
Net proceeds from sale of all securities	80,000
Proceeds from sale of additional 1,500 shares of no-par common stock	90,000
	$797,000

Cash disbursements include:
  Payments of the following old corporate liabilities approved
    by the court:

Accounts payable	$250,000
Mortgage interest payable	2,500
Wages payable..	20,000
Taxes payable	10,000
Notes payable	200,000
	$482,500

  Payments of items incurred during the period of trusteeship:

Accounts payable	$ 90,000
Mortgage interest	2,500
Direct labor	80,000
Manufacturing expenses	39,000
Selling expenses	58,000
Administrative expenses	36,000
Insurance premium	4,000
	$309,500

(e) Ending inventories as of December 31, 19X1, are:

Finished goods	$40,000
Work in process	20,000
Raw materials	30,000
Prepaid insurance	4,000

(f) All discounted notes receivable were paid to the bank by the makers.

(g) The books of the trustee were closed as of December 31, 19X1, since a
     court order had been received to return the CB Radio Corporation opera-
     tions to its former management. The trustee's fee of $15,000 was approved
     for payment by the court on January 3, 19X2.

Required:

(1) Prepare journal entries to record the events on the books of the trustee and
     on the books of the corporation.
(2) Prepare an income statement in accordance with the wishes of the court.
(3) Prepare a realization and liquidation account, using book values, as rec-
     ommended in the chapter.

CB Radio Corporation
Balance Sheet
December 31, 19X0

Assets

Current assets:

Cash		$ 24,000	
Accounts receivable	$210,000		
Less allowance for doubtful accounts	10,000	200,000	
Notes receivable	$ 80,000		
Less notes receivable discounted	50,000	30,000	
Marketable securities		60,000	
Finished goods		110,000	
Work in process		10,000	
Raw materials		40,000	
Prepaid insurance		3,000	$477,000

	Cost	Accumulated Depreciation	Book Value
Property, plant, and equipment:			
Land	$ 30,000	—	$30,000
Building	100,000	$12,000	88,000
Machinery and equipment ...	120,000	40,000	80,000
Office equipment	20,000	4,000	16,000
Total	$270,000	$56,000	

		214,000
Other assets:		
Goodwill		100,000
Total assets		$791,000

Liabilities and Stockholders' Equity

Current liabilities:		
Accounts payable	$250,000	
Notes payable	200,000	
Wages payable.................................	20,000	
Taxes payable	10,000	
Mortgage interest payable	2,500	$482,500
Long-term liability:		
10% Mortgage payable..........................		25,000
Total liabilities....................................		$507,500
Stockholders' equity:		
Common stock, no par, 4,000 shares authorized, 1,500 shares outstanding	$300,000	
Deficit	(16,500)	283,500
Total liabilities and stockholders' equity............		$791,000

Present Value of $1 Due in n Periods

$$PV = A\left[\frac{1}{(1+i)^n}\right] = A(PVF_{\overline{n}|i})$$

n	2%	3%	4%	5%	6%	8%	10%	12%	16%	20%
1	0.9804	0.9709	0.9615	0.9524	0.9434	0.9259	0.9091	0.8929	0.8621	0.8333
2	0.9612	0.9426	0.9246	0.9070	0.8900	0.8573	0.8264	0.7972	0.7432	0.6944
3	0.9423	0.9151	0.8890	0.8638	0.8396	0.7938	0.7513	0.7118	0.6407	0.5787
4	0.9238	0.8885	0.8548	0.8227	0.7921	0.7350	0.6830	0.6355	0.5523	0.4823
5	0.9057	0.8626	0.8219	0.7835	0.7473	0.6806	0.6209	0.5674	0.4761	0.4019
6	0.8880	0.8375	0.7903	0.7462	0.7050	0.6302	0.5645	0.5066	0.4104	0.3349
7	0.8706	0.8131	0.7599	0.7107	0.6651	0.5835	0.5132	0.4523	0.3538	0.2791
8	0.8535	0.7894	0.7307	0.6768	0.6274	0.5403	0.4665	0.4039	0.3050	0.2326
9	0.8368	0.7664	0.7026	0.6446	0.5919	0.5002	0.4241	0.3606	0.2630	0.1938
10	0.8203	0.7441	0.6756	0.6139	0.5584	0.4632	0.3855	0.3220	0.2267	0.1615
11	0.8043	0.7224	0.6496	0.5847	0.5268	0.4289	0.3505	0.2875	0.1954	0.1346
12	0.7885	0.7014	0.6246	0.5568	0.4970	0.3971	0.3186	0.2567	0.1685	0.1122
13	0.7730	0.6810	0.6006	0.5303	0.4688	0.3677	0.2897	0.2292	0.1452	0.0935
14	0.7579	0.6611	0.5775	0.5051	0.4423	0.3405	0.2633	0.2046	0.1252	0.0779
15	0.7430	0.6419	0.5553	0.4810	0.4173	0.3152	0.2394	0.1827	0.1079	0.0649
16	0.7284	0.6232	0.5339	0.4581	0.3936	0.2919	0.2176	0.1631	0.0930	0.0541
17	0.7142	0.6050	0.5134	0.4363	0.3714	0.2703	0.1978	0.1456	0.0802	0.0451
18	0.7002	0.5874	0.4936	0.4155	0.3503	0.2502	0.1799	0.1300	0.0691	0.0376
19	0.6864	0.5703	0.4746	0.3957	0.3305	0.2317	0.1635	0.1161	0.0596	0.0313
20	0.6730	0.5537	0.4564	0.3769	0.3118	0.2145	0.1486	0.1037	0.0514	0.0261
25	0.6095	0.4776	0.3751	0.2953	0.2330	0.1460	0.0923	0.0588	0.0245	0.0105
30	0.5521	0.4120	0.3083	0.2314	0.1741	0.0994	0.0573	0.0334	0.0116	0.0042
40	0.4529	0.3066	0.2083	0.1420	0.0972	0.0460	0.0221	0.0107	0.0026	0.0007
50	0.3715	0.2281	0.1407	0.0872	0.0543	0.0213	0.0085	0.0035	0.0006	0.0001

Present Value of an Annuity of $1 per Period

$$PV_n = R\left[\frac{1 - \frac{1}{(1+i)^n}}{i}\right] = R(PVAF_{\overline{n}|i})$$

n	2%	3%	4%	5%	6%	8%	10%	12%	16%	20%
1	0.9804	0.9709	0.9615	0.9524	0.9434	0.9259	0.9091	0.8929	0.8621	0.8333
2	1.9416	1.9135	1.8861	1.8594	1.8334	1.7833	1.7355	1.6901	1.6052	1.5278
3	2.8839	2.8286	2.7751	2.7232	2.6730	2.5771	2.4869	2.4018	2.2459	2.1065
4	3.8077	3.7171	3.6299	3.5460	3.4651	3.3121	3.1699	3.0373	2.7982	2.5887
5	4.7135	4.5797	4.4518	4.3295	4.2124	3.9927	3.7908	3.6048	3.2743	2.9906
6	5.6014	5.4172	5.2421	5.0757	4.9173	4.6229	4.3553	4.1114	3.6847	3.3255
7	6.4720	6.2303	6.0021	5.7864	5.5824	5.2064	4.8684	4.5638	4.0386	3.6016
8	7.3255	7.0197	6.7327	6.4632	6.2098	5.7466	5.3349	4.9676	4.3436	3.8372
9	8.1622	7.7861	7.4353	7.1078	6.8017	6.2469	5.7590	5.3282	4.6065	4.0310
10	8.9826	8.5302	8.1109	7.7217	7.3601	6.7101	6.1446	5.6502	4.8332	4.1925
11	9.7868	9.2526	8.7605	8.3064	7.8869	7.1390	6.4951	5.9377	5.0286	4.3271
12	10.5753	9.9540	9.3851	8.8633	8.3838	7.5361	6.8137	6.1944	5.1971	4.4392
13	11.3484	10.6350	9.9856	9.3936	8.8527	7.9038	7.1034	6.4235	5.3423	4.5327
14	12.1062	11.2961	10.5631	9.8986	9.2950	8.2442	7.3667	6.6282	5.4675	4.6106
15	12.8493	11.9379	11.1184	10.3797	9.7122	8.5595	7.6061	6.8109	5.5755	4.6755
16	13.5777	12.5611	11.6523	10.8378	10.1059	8.8514	7.8237	6.9740	5.6685	4.7296
17	14.2919	13.1661	12.1657	11.2741	10.4773	9.1216	8.0216	7.1196	5.7487	4.7746
18	14.9920	13.7535	12.6593	11.6896	10.8276	9.3719	8.2014	7.2497	5.8178	4.8122
19	15.6785	14.3238	13.1339	12.0853	11.1581	9.6036	8.3649	7.3658	5.8775	4.8435
20	16.3514	14.8775	13.5903	12.4622	11.4699	9.8181	8.5136	7.4694	5.9288	4.8696
25	19.5235	17.4131	15.6221	14.0939	12.7834	10.6748	9.0770	7.8431	6.0971	4.9476
30	22.3965	19.6004	17.2920	15.3725	13.7648	11.2578	9.4269	8.0552	6.1772	4.9789
40	27.3555	23.1148	19.7928	17.1591	15.0463	11.9246	9.7791	8.2438	6.2335	4.9966
50	31.4236	25.7298	21.4822	18.2559	15.7619	12.2335	9.9148	8.3045	6.2463	4.9995

INDEX